Switzerland

written and researched by

Matthew Teller

with additional contributions by

Lucy Ratcliffe and Kev Reynolds

ROUGH
GUIDES

www.roughguides.com

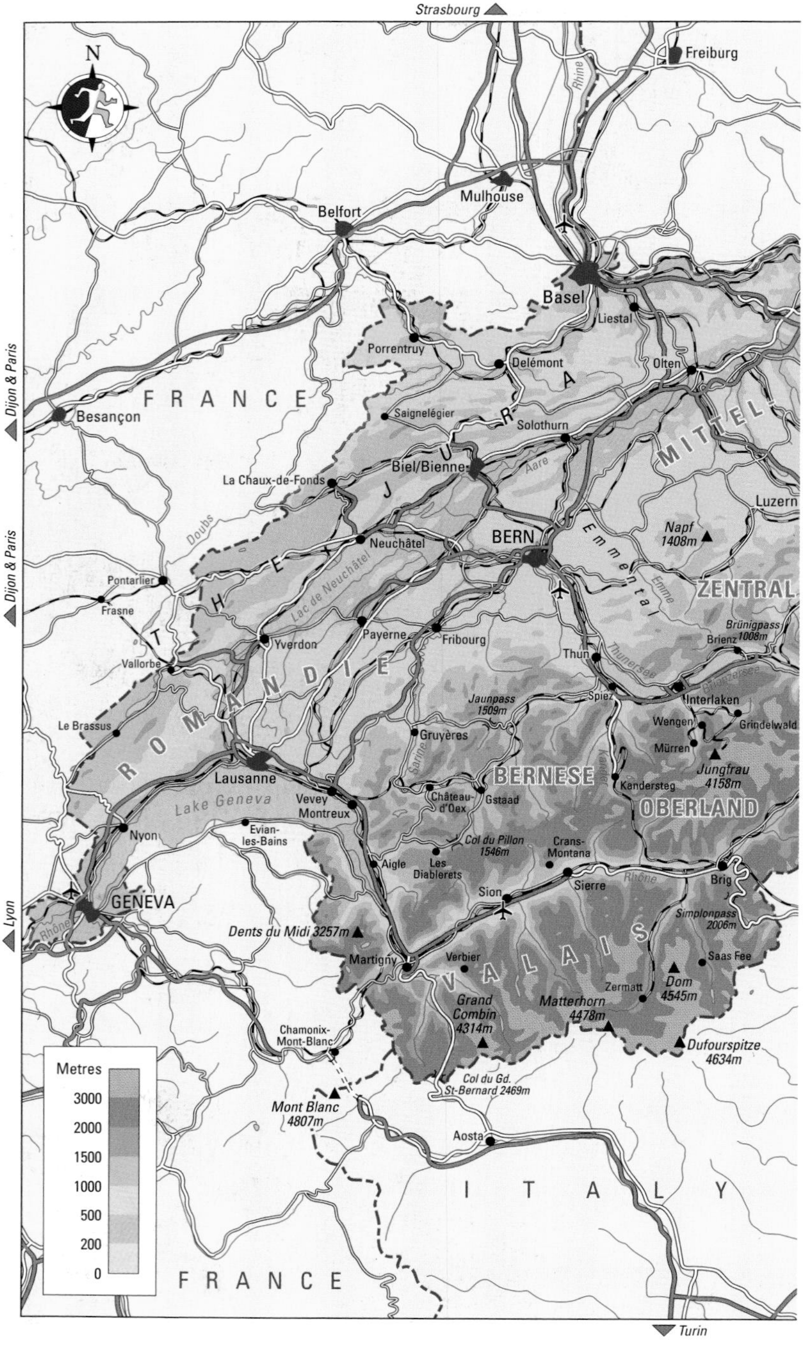
Strasbourg
Dijon & Paris
Dijon & Paris
Lyon
Turin
N
Freiburg
Rhine
Mulhouse
Belfort
Basel
Liestal
Porrentruy
Delémont
Olten
FRANCE
Besançon
Saignelégier
Solothurn
MITTEL
THE JURA
Biel/Bienne
Aare
La Chaux-de-Fonds
Luzern
Doubs
Neuchâtel
BERN
Emmental
Napf
1408m
Pontarlier
Frasne
Lac de Neuchâtel
Emme
ZENTRAL
Brünigpass
1008m
Brienz
Payerne
Fribourg
Yverdon
Thun
Thunersee
Vallorbe
ROMANDIE
Brienzersee
Interlaken
Spiez
Jaunpass
1509m
Le Brassus
Wengen
Grindelwald
Gruyères
Mürren
Jungfrau
4158m
Sarine
Kander
BERNESE
Lausanne
Kandersteg
Vevey
Montreux
Château-d'Oex
Gstaad
OBERLAND
Lake Geneva
Nyon
Evian-les-Bains
Col du Pillon
1546m
Crans-Montana
Aigle
Les Diablerets
Brig
Sierre
Rhône
Sion
GENEVA
Rhône
Simplonpass
2006m
Dents du Midi 3257m
VALAIS
Martigny
Verbier
Saas Fee
Zermatt
Dom
4545m
Grand Combin
4314m
Matterhorn
4478m
Chamonix-Mont-Blanc
Dufourspitze
4634m
Metres
3000
2000
1500
1000
500
200
0
Col du Gd. St-Bernard 2469m
Mont Blanc
4807m
Aosta
ITALY
FRANCE

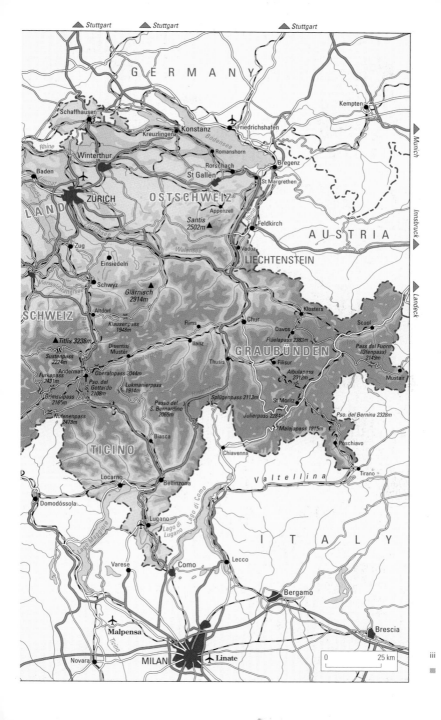

Introduction to

Switzerland

"In Italy for thirty years under the Borgias they had warfare, terror, murder, bloodshed, but they produced Michelangelo, Leonardo da Vinci and the Renaissance. In Switzerland they had brotherly love; they had 500 years of democracy and peace. And what did that produce? The cuckoo clock."

Orson Welles as Harry Lime, in *The Third Man* (1949)

Never has one throwaway movie line done so much to damage the reputation of a whole country. Even now, despite being one of the most visited countries in Europe, Switzerland remains one of the least understood. The facts are that until national reconciliation in 1848, Switzerland was the most consistently turbulent, war-torn area of Europe (so much for brotherly love), and yet, both before and after it found stability, it brought forth such literary and artistic pioneers as Hans Holbein, Jean-Jacques Rousseau, Paul Klee, Hermann Hesse and Alberto Giacometti (so much for the cuckoo clock – a Bavarian invention, anyway).

But two centuries of tourism have left their mark: faced by an ever-increasing onslaught of visitors, these days the Swiss are content to abide by a quaint stereotype of Switzerland that's easily packaged and sold – the familiar Alpine idyll of cheese and chocolate, Heidi and the Matterhorn – while keeping the best bits for themselves. Come for a "Lakes and Mountains" package, or a week of skiing, or a short city-break, and you'll get all the pristine beauty, genteel calm and well-oiled efficiency of the Switzerland that the locals deem suitable for public consumption. The other Switzerland – the one the Swiss inhabit – needs time and patience to

Fact file

• Switzerland covers an area of 41,285 square kilometres – roughly the size of Wales or West Virginia. At the most it is 220km from north to south, and 348km from west to east. The highest point is the Dufourspitze peak at 4634m above sea level, the lowest is Lago Maggiore at 193m. The total population is around 7.3 million, of whom 5.8 million are Swiss citizens.

• The Swiss Confederation is ruled by a seven-member government called the Federal Council, with the presidency rotating annually between all seven members. Both this and the Supreme Court are elected by the bicameral Parliament. Constitutional amendments can be proposed either by Parliament or by popular initiative, the latter requiring 100,000 signatures; in either case a referendum ensues, and a double majority – of votes cast both nationally and canton-by-canton – sees the proposal becoming law. 50,000 signatures can also put any existing law to a referendum.

• Each of the 26 cantons has its own constitution, parliament, government and courts, and there is also a considerable degree of autonomy vested in the 2942 communes, which vary in size from small, crowded city districts to thinly populated tracts of mountain terrain.

winkle out of its shell, but can be an infinitely more rewarding place to explore.

Within this rugged environment, **community spirit** is perhaps stronger than anywhere else in Europe. Since the country is not an ethnic, linguistic or religious unity, it has survived – so the Swiss are fond of saying – simply through the will of its people to resolve their differences. Today, a unique style of "bottom-up" democracy ensures real power still rests with the people, who seem to vote almost monthly on a series of referenda affecting all aspects of life from local recycling projects to national economic policy. The constitution devolves power upwards from the people to municipal governments and up again to the regions (known as **cantons**), only as a last resort granting certain powers to the federal government.

This kind of decentralized structure means that the cantons – which are, in essence, tiny self-governing republics who have volunteered to join together – have mostly held onto their own, unique flavours. Although Swiss people value their shared Swissness above

all, they also cherish their own home-town identity and their differences from their neighbours. Tensions exist between the four **language** communities, as they do between Catholic and Protestant, or between urban and rural areas, while **regional characteristics** remain sharply defined and diverse. Local pride is fuelled by a range of traditional **folkloric customs**, most of which stem from pagan or medieval Christian festivals. Most prominent of these is **carnival**, held around the country on or around Mardi Gras, the last day before Lent. The most exuberant celebrations, held in Luzern, Bern and Basel, feature bands, masked parades, street dancing and spontaneous partying that belie the stereotype of a placid, unadventurous Switzerland. A host of smaller events fills out the calendar and it's still easily possible to stumble on village festivals that have been staged by local people for centuries past.

This sense of cultural continuity sits oddly with the fact that Switzerland has grown into one of the world's **richest** countries. Its economy is small-scale but thoroughly modern: traditional industries such as watchmaking and textiles now thrive by focusing closely on the luxury end of the market and have ceded prime position to engineering, pharmaceuticals and service industries galore. **Tourism** has been a high earner since the mid-nineteenth century, when the Alps became both a fashionable destination for wealthy

Schweiz, Suisse, Svizzera, Svizra

For such a tiny country, Switzerland is remarkably polyglot. There are four official languages: about two-thirds of the population have German as their first language; about a fifth French; six percent Italian; while Romansh, a direct descendant of Latin, has clung on in pockets of the mountainous southeast. Around one in ten people use English every day, and many are comfortably tri- or quadrilingual.

These language divisions are reflected in divisions of culture and identity. In the centre and the east, the old isolation of tight-knit mountain communities lingers on in Swiss German *Kantönligeist* ("little cantonal spirit"), a stubborn parochialism leavened by down-to-earth rumbustiousness. To the west lies the Röstigraben, a comical but slightly discomfiting name given to the invisible language border – a *Graben* is a military trench – between French-speaking Switzerland where they don't eat the traditional potato dish *Rösti*, and German-speaking Switzerland where they do. The gentler landscape of Suisse Romande has long encouraged cultural interchange with neighbouring France, which expresses itself these days in widespread enthusiasm for joining the EU. On the south side of the Alpine chain, Swiss Italian-speakers have tended to feel cut off, both from the rest of Switzerland by the lack of shared language and culture, and from the economic powerhouse of northern Italy by the implacable presence of the international border.

travellers and a prescribed retreat for sufferers from respiratory diseases needing curative sunshine and fresh mountain air. And yet the country, seized by an increasingly anachronistic national *Kantönligeist*, still stands alone. In the 1940s, Switzerland was surrounded by hostile Axis powers; these days, it's encircled by the "friendly" EU. With the end of the Cold War, recent damaging revelations of Swiss collaboration with the Nazi Third Reich, and increasingly close ties amongst Western European nations, Swiss **neutrality** rings ever more hollow – and yet, far from embracing a wider perspective, the country has collectively taken a step into conservatism. Commentators are noting sadly that Switzerland is only now embarking on the kind of multiethnic social integration that its neighbours began in the 1950s.

Having taken centuries to bolt their country together from diverse elements, the Swiss seem instinctively to return to their sense of community spirit, expressed most tangibly in the order and cleanliness you'll see on show everywhere. Yet the sterility so decried by Graham Greene (who wrote Harry Lime's jibe about brotherly love), if it characterizes any part of the country, applies only to the glossy, neatly packaged tourist idyll of lakes and mountains. The three great Swiss cities of Geneva, Zürich and Basel are crammed with world-class **museums** and galleries. In Zürich and Lausanne, there's a humming arts scene and underground club culture

The Swiss are content to abide by a quaint stereotype of Switzerland that's easily packaged and sold. The other Switzerland – the one the Swiss inhabit – needs time and patience to winkle out of its shell.

that feeds **nightlife** as vibrant as anything you'll find in much larger European cities. The **landscapes** are dominated by the Alps and their foothills, but mountains aren't the only story. In the north and centre are lush, rolling grasslands epitomized by the velvety green hills of the Emmental, traditional dairy-farming country. Vineyards rise tiered above Lake Geneva, the Rhône valley and the Rhine. The fairytale southeast is cut through by wild, high-sided valleys, lonely, dark and thickly forested. Most surprisingly of all, bordering Italy in the south you'll find subtropical Mediterranean-style flower gardens, sugarloaf hills and sunny, palm-fringed lakes. For a small, little-regarded mid-continental country with a profound image problem, Switzerland has plenty more to offer than most visitors suspect.

◁ Château d'Oex balloon festival (see p.320)

Where to go – and when

Although Switzerland is best known for its mountain scenery, there are any number of hooks on which to hang a visit, whether you choose to stay in one city or resort, take in the hiking or cycling possibilities of a region, or make a tour of exploration around the whole country. Getting about is easy, with an unrivalled network of trains, buses and boats cutting journey times between the regions to an hour or two in most cases. You'll find places to stay and get a hearty meal wherever you end up, even in the wildest of mountain valleys.

Thankfully, Switzerland has no big metropolises on the scale of Paris or London. Swiss towns and cities were preserved from bombing in World War II, and all of them have at their core explorable networks of medi-

◁ View from Gornergrat, above Zermatt (see p.363)

▽ Schloss Thun (see p.307)

eval alleys and old houses and churches. **Geneva** is positioned at the tip of the idyllic **Lake Geneva** in the southwest, a short distance from the graceful lakeside city of **Lausanne**. In the northeast, **Zürich** too is set on its own lake, within striking distance of the peaceful **Bodensee** (Lake Constance). The diminutive Swiss capital **Bern** has a fine cobbled Old Town, while equally attractive **Luzern** (Lucerne) lies in the cen-

◁ The Matterhorn (see p.359)

tre of the country on its own, famously beautiful lake. **Basel** is located on the Rhine at the point where France, Germany and Switzerland meet, while at the opposite end of the country, **Lugano** basks on the shores of an azure lake a few kilometres from the Italian border. Any of these – or smaller but no less characterful regional towns such as St Gallen, Schaffhausen, Neuchâtel, Chur, Fribourg, Sion or Bellinzona – could serve as a base for a relaxing short break, especially during the temperate summer months (June–Sept). At other times they can get distinctly chilly, although most receive generous dumps of snow in the winter, which, combined with glittering sunshine and frozen lakes and rivers, paints the most romantic of urban pictures.

There are almost limitless possibilities for exploring the great outdoors. The Alps run in a band across the centre and south of the country, with resorts big and small plus stunning scenery guaranteed wherever you head for. The two main **seasons** run from late May to October, and from mid-December to mid-April; between these times, most mountain resorts close down altogether (see p.436 for more). The best-known Alpine region is the

△ Zürich's Grossmünster (see p.436)

FASHION

Bernese Oberland, focused around the tourist hub of **Interlaken** and boasting such famous names as **Wengen** and **Grindelwald**; to the south, in Valais, sit **Verbier**, **Crans Montana** and, at the foot of the iconic Matterhorn, **Zermatt**. In Graubünden in the southeast are **Davos**, **Klosters** and **St Moritz**. Justifiably popular, all these places boast some of the best skiing and hiking in Europe. It's relatively easy in even the busiest centres (which are still nothing like the mega-resorts of the French and Italian Alps) to head off the beaten path and explore alone, or to aim for smaller, more manageable satellite resorts in adjacent side-valleys. However, you may prefer to shun the big names altogether and seek peace and quiet in the less frenetic hinterlands. Two regions stand out: in the northwest, the scrubby **Jura** mountains are an ideal landscape for long lonely walks and bike rides; while in the south, the wild valleys of **Alto Ticino** lace the southern foothills of the Alps with little-known hiking trails, a world away from the chic lakeside resort of **Locarno** nearby.

▽ Funicular from Lauterbrunnen to Grütschalp (see p.291)

Switzerland's climate

The table shows average monthly minimum and maximum temperatures (in °C), and average monthly precipitation (in mm). Precipitation patterns vary widely, with the northern cities (Bern, Zürich) experiencing more overcast skies than, for instance, Lugano, which tends to have long periods of sunshine occasionally punctuated by sudden summer downpours.

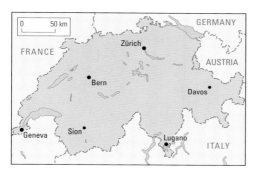

	Jan	Feb	Mar	Apr	May	Jun	Jul	Aug	Sep	Oct	Nov	Dec
Bern												
Av min °C	-5	-3	-1	3	8	10	11	11	8	4	-2	-5
Av max °C	0	4	9	13	18	20	21	20	17	11	5	0
Precipitation, mm	56	49	62	77	97	120	118	114	96	71	68	65
Davos												
Av min °C	-11	-11	-8	-4	1	4	8	7	4	0	-4	-8
Av max °C	-1	-1	3	8	10	14	18	18	14	10	7	1
Precipitation, mm	71	60	57	60	66	121	140	135	90	69	63	70
Geneva												
Av min °C	-2	-1	0	4	8	10	12	13	11	7	3	0
Av max °C	3	5	10	14	19	20	22	22	21	15	9	5
Precipitation, mm	63	57	55	50	67	92	64	98	102	77	84	59
Lugano												
Av min °C	-2	-1	2	6	9	11	14	14	11	9	5	0
Av max °C	6	8	11	17	20	23	28	29	25	19	13	8
Precipitation, mm	61	64	96	148	217	199	183	196	160	172	158	95
Sion												
Av min °C	-6	-3	1	3	8	10	11	10	9	4	0	-3
Av max °C	3	6	9	14	20	21	25	24	21	15	9	5
Precipitation, mm	51	45	40	37	39	46	50	64	45	50	53	62
Zürich												
Av min °C	-5	-2	0	3	9	11	13	13	11	8	2	-2
Av max °C	0	4	9	15	20	22	25	23	20	14	9	3
Precipitation, mm	75	70	64	81	108	137	144	135	110	80	76	64

28

things not to miss

It's not possible to see everything that Switzerland has to offer in one trip – and we don't suggest you try. What follows is a selective and subjective taste of the country's highlights: beautiful cities and lakes, top mountain resorts, spectacular train journeys and secluded Alpine getaways. They're arranged in five colour-coded categories to help you find the very best things to see, do and experience. All entries have a page reference to take you straight into the guide, where you can find out more.

01 **Winter sports** Page **66** • The glacial bowl above the village of Saas-Fee offers some of the most scenic snowboarding anywhere in the Alps.

02 Lake Geneva Page **142** • From the vineyards of St-Saphorin on the Swiss shore of Lake Geneva, stunning views look westwards up the valley of the Rhône.

03 Luzerner Fasnacht Page **383** • Switzerland has a long tradition of carnival and this is the best of the bunch, a hedonistic weekend when thousands pack into Luzern's old town for parades, music and raucous merry-making.

04 Adventure sports Page **394** • The area around Engelberg in Central Switzerland is one of the top destinations for canyoning, bungee-jumping and paragliding.

06 **Basel** Page **207** • Ancient Rhine-side city straddling the French and German borders, enhanced by fine medieval architecture and one of Switzerland's best art museums.

05 **Wine** Page **52** • Switzerland's wine industry is modest but Swiss wines – some of the best of which come from near Sion – can compete on equal terms with better-known labels from around the world.

07 **Château de Chillon** Page **161** • Grand medieval castle, majestically located on the Lake Geneva shore.

08 **Bern** Page **235** • Switzerland's uniquely attractive federal capital, loomed over by a giant cathedral tower, has a medieval street-plan that has survived unchanged for five centuries.

09 **Lake Luzern** Page **379** • The most dramatically sited of all Switzerland's lakes, ringed by mist-wreathed cliffs.

10 **Igloo-building** Page **394** • Classic low-impact adventure excursion, where you build your own igloo out in the icy wilderness, then spend the night in it.

11 **Lugano** Page **568** • A taste of the Italian Mediterranean at the Piazza della Riforma, just a stone's throw from the glittering Lago di Lugano.

12 **Rhätische Bahn** Page **502** • The southeastern corner of Switzerland is the setting for some of Europe's most spectacular train rides aboard the RhB.

13 **Appenzell** Page **485** • Endearingly old-fashioned dairy village, tucked away amidst hilly countryside that is ideal for long walks.

14 **Lausanne** Page **119** • Tiered above Lake Geneva and crowned by a stunning Gothic cathedral, Lausanne is Switzerland's most visually dramatic city.

16 Cheese Page **47** • There's nothing more warming on a winter's night than a plate of raclette – a half-round of Alpine cheese melted in front of a fire and scraped onto a plate.

15 Schaffhausen Page **468** • This quiet, little-visited market town, replete with medieval frescoed mansions, stands just upstream from the mighty Rhine falls.

17 The Matterhorn Page **359** • No mountain in the world is so immediately recognizable, dominating the horizon above the world-class skiing, snowboarding and hiking resort of Zermatt.

18 Geneva Page **93** • At the centre of this most discreet, hard-working of cities stands a monument to Calvin and the Reformers, who proclaimed Geneva a "Protestant Rome" in the sixteenth century.

19 Zürich Page **417** • Beneath a medieval cityscape of spires and steeples, Zürich's old town is filled with cobbled lanes and courtyards to explore.

21 Montreux Jazz Festival Page **158** • Stellar annual music event in this ritzy lakeside resort; Isaac Hayes is just one of the top-drawer names in soul, dance, rock, world music, jazz and blues to have played in recent years.

20 Bernese Oberland Page **296** • You can enjoy classic Swiss Alpine scenery from Wengen village, one of a trio of beautifully sited resorts in the mighty Bernese Oberland that includes Mürren and Grindelwald.

22 Jungfrau Railways Page **290** • Of the host of Alpine rack-railway routes in the Bernese Oberland, the line up to the superb panoramic viewpoint of Schynige Platte gives amazing vistas over the triple-peaked ridge of the Eiger, Mönch and Jungfrau.

23 **Davos** Page **518** • Boarders and freeriders will find that there are few better destinations in the world than Davos.

24 **Alto Ticino** Page **554** • Giornico, with its picturesque bridge, is one of a string of attractive villages in the lush, high valleys of this Italian-speaking region that offer long, lonesome countryside rambles.

25 **Riders Palace, Laax** Page **516** • The hippest hotel in the Swiss Alps, set amidst the up-and-coming resort of Flims-Laax-Falera.

26 **Walking** Page **63** • The high-level route from Schynige Platte past the Bachalpsee and down to Grindelwald is just one of many memorably scenic walks throughout the Swiss Alps.

28 **St Gallen** Page **483** • The library of St Gallen's ancient abbey has one of the most impressive secular Rococo interiors in Europe.

27 **St Moritz** Page **532** • Switzerland's sunniest mountain resort, boasting outstanding skiing and snowboarding as well as the infamous Cresta Run luge course.

Contents

Using the Rough Guide

We've tried to make this Rough Guide a good read and easy to use. The book is divided into six main sections, and you should be able to find whatever you want in one of them.

Colour section

The front colour section offers a quick tour of Switzerland. The **introduction** aims to give you a feel for the country, with suggestions on where to go. We also tell you what the weather is like and include a basic fact file. Next, our author rounds up his favourite aspects of Switzerland in the **things not to miss** section – whether it's great food, amazing sights or a special journey.

Basics

The Basics section covers all the **pre-departure** nitty-gritty to help you plan your trip. This is where to find out which airlines fly to your destination, what paperwork you'll need, what to do about money and insurance, about Internet access, food, public transport, car rental – in fact just about every piece of **general practical information** you might need.

Guide

This is the heart of the Rough Guide, divided into user-friendly chapters, each of which covers a specific area. Every chapter starts with a list of **highlights** and an **introduction** that helps you to decide where to go, depending on your time and budget. Likewise, introductions to the various towns and smaller regions within each chapter should help you plan your itinerary. We start most town accounts with information on arrival and accommodation, followed by a tour of the sights, and finally reviews of places to eat and drink, and details of nightlife. Longer accounts also have a directory of practical listings. Each chapter concludes with **public transport details** for that region.

Contexts

Read Contexts to get a deeper understanding of what makes Switzerland tick. We include a brief **history** of the country, articles about **architecture** and **Alpine flora and fauna**, and a detailed further reading section that reviews dozens of **books**.

Language

The **language** section gives useful guidance for speaking Swiss German, French, Italian and Romansh and pulls together all the vocabulary you might need on your trip, including a comprehensive **menu reader**. Here you'll also find a **glossary** of terms.

Index & small print

Apart from a **full index**, which includes maps as well as places, this section covers publishing information, credits and acknowledgements, and also has our contact details in case you want to send in updates and corrections to the book – or suggestions as to how we might improve it.

Chapter list and map

- Colour section
- Contents
- **B** Basics
- **1** Geneva
- **2** Lausanne and Lake Geneva
- **3** The Arc Jurassien

- **4** Basel and around
- **5** Bern and around
- **6** The Bernese Oberland
- **7** Valais
- **8** Luzern and Zentralschweiz
- **9** Zürich

- **10** Ostschweiz and Liechtenstein
- **11** Graubünden
- **12** Ticino
- **C** Contexts
- **L** Language
- **I** Index and small print

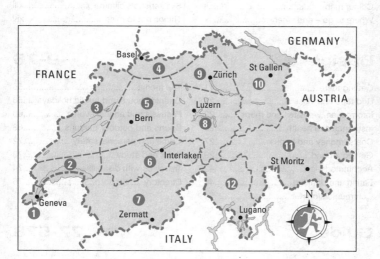

Contents

Colour section

i–xxiv

Colour map ii
Where to go – and when ix

Switzerland's climate xiii
Things not to miss xiv

Basics

9–76

Getting there 11
Red tape and visas 21
Information, websites and maps..........22
Insurance and health 25
Costs, money and banks 27
Getting around 29
Accommodation 42
Eating and drinking.............................46
Communications..................................54

The media 56
Opening hours and public holidays 58
Festivals and annual events 60
Sports and outdoor pursuits................63
Crime and personal safety 72
Work and study....................................73
Travellers with disabilities 74
Directory 76

Guide

77–578

❶ **Geneva** 79–114
Highlights 80
Some history...82
Arrival and information 83
City transport and tours 85
Accommodation 88
The Rive Gauche...................................91
Carouge 99
The Rive Droite 100
The international area 101
Eating and drinking............................106
Nightlife and entertainment...............110
Listings 112

Around Geneva 112
Travel details 114

❷ **Lausanne and Lake Geneva**
....115–165
Highlights 116
Lausanne 119
Gruyères 139
Romont and the Gros de Vaud 141
Coppet 144
Nyon 145
Rolle and Morges 148
The Lavaux wine villages 150

Vevey 151
Montreux 157
Château de Chillon 161
Travel details 164

❸ The Arc Jurassien 167–204
Highlights 168
Neuchâtel 172
La Chaux-de-Fonds 179
Le Locle 181
Yverdon-les-Bains 182
Grandson 185
Sainte-Croix 188
Vallorbe 188
The Vallée de Joux 190
Estavayer-le-Lac 191
Payerne 191
Avenches 191
Murten/Morat 193
Biel/Bienne 195
Delémont.............................199
Saignelégier 200
Porrentruy 202
Travel details 204

❹ Basel and around 205–231
Highlights 206
Some history.......................207
Arrival and information 209
Accommodation 213
The City...............................215
Eating and drinking 222
Nightlife and entertainment...224
Listings 225
Augusta Raurica 225
Baden 227
Travel details 231

❺ Bern and around 233–276
Highlights 234
Some history.......................238
Arrival and information 240
City transport and tours 241
Accommodation 242
The City...............................244
Eating and drinking 255
Nightlife and entertainment...257

Listings 258
The Emmental 259
Solothurn 265
Fribourg..............................267
Travel details 276

**❻ The Bernese
Oberland** 277–322
Highlights 278
Interlaken 283
Lauterbrunnen.....................291
Mürren 295
Wengen 296
Grindelwald 298
Kleine Scheidegg 303
The Jungfraujoch 305
Thun 307
Spiez 310
Brienz 311
Meiringen 312
Kandersteg 315
Gstaad 317
Rougemont 320
Château d'Oex....................320
Travel details 321

❼ Valais 323–370
Highlights 324
Aigle 328
Villars-Gryon 331
Les Diablerets 332
Leysin 333
Portes du Soleil...................334
St-Maurice 334
Martigny 335
Grand-St-Bernard...............339
Verbier.................................341
Sion.....................................345
Sierre 351
Crans Montana 353
Leuk and Leukerbad 355
The Lötschental 357
Brig 357
The Simplon Pass 358
Zermatt 359
Saas-Fee.............................366
The Goms 368
Travel details 370

❽ Luzern and Zentralschweiz 371–416
Highlights 372
Luzern 375
Stans...................................395
Hergiswil 395
Engelberg 398
The Rigi 401
Weggis 402
Vitznau 402
Zug 403
Brunnen 406
Schwyz 407
Einsiedeln 408
Flüelen.................................410
Andermatt 411
The Gotthard Pass 414
Travel details 416

❾ Zürich 417–457
Highlights 418
Some history.........................420
Arrival and information 422
City transport 426
Accommodation 429
The City 433
Niederdorf 433
Bahnhofstrasse....................441
Zürich West 445
Eating and drinking 447
Nightlife and entertainment....452
Listings 455
Rapperswil 457
Travel details 457

❿ Ostschweiz and Liechtenstein 459–496
Highlights 460
Winterthur 464
Schaffhausen 468
The Rhine falls 472
Stein-am-Rhein....................474
The Bodensee......................476
St Gallen 480
Appenzell 485
Glarus 489

Liechtenstein................................490
Travel details 496

⓫ Graubünden 497–542
Highlights 498
Chur 500
Arosa...................................508
Heidiland 510
Thusis and Tiefencastel 511
The Albula Pass 512
The Julier Pass 513
The San Bernardino Pass 514
Flims-Laax-Falera.................515
Ilanz....................................517
Davos 518
Klosters................................523
Scuol 526
Parc Naziunal Svizzer 529
Val Müstair 530
St Moritz 532
Celerina 538
Pontresina 538
Val Poschiavo 539
Silvaplana 540
Sils and Maloja 540
Val Bregaglia 541
Travel details 542

⓬ Ticino 543–578
Highlights 544
Bellinzona 549
Alto Ticino 554
Biasca 556
Val Blenio 557
Valle Leventina 558
Locarno................................559
Ascona 565
Valle Maggia 566
Val Verzasca 567
Centovalli 567
Lugano 568
The Ceresio peninsula 575
Mendrisio 577
Monte Generoso 578
Travel details 578

Contexts

579–612

The historical framework...................581
Contemporary architecture...............597
Alpine flora and fauna.......................601
Books 605

Language

613–632

German 616
French 618
Italian..619
Words and phrases............................619
Menu reader 625
Glossary 630

Index & small print

633–645

Full index...634
Rough Guide credits..........................643
Publishing information 643
Help us update 643
Acknowledgements 644
Readers' letters and emails 644
Photo credits.....................................644

Map symbols

maps are listed in the full index using coloured text

▬▬▬	Motorway	☽	Viewpoint
═══	Major road	✈	Airport
═══	Minor road	♦	Point of interest
┄┄┄┄	Tunnel	⋈	Bridge
- - - - -	Footpath	⋈	Viaduct
▥▥▥▥	Steps	⚠	Campsite
▪▪▪▪▪	Wall	✿	Vineyard
═══	Railway	⊞	Hospital
────	Metro line	⊙	Statue
⋯⋯⋯	Funicular railway	ⓘ	Tourist information
●┄┄●	Cable car	⊠	Post office
─ ─ ─	Ferry route	Ⓜ	Metro station
────	River	ℙ	Parking
▬▬▬	National boundary	▬	Building
▬▬ ··	Canton boundary	⬭	Stadium
─ ─ ─ ·	Chapter boundary	─✛─	Church/cathedral
▲	Mountain peak	▨	Park
⋈	Mountain pass	▨	Forest
𝕸	Cliffs	⊞	Cemetery
/⎮\	Hill shading	▨	Glacier
𝕵	Waterfall		

Basics

Basics

Getting there 11

Red tape and visas 21

Information, websites and maps 22

Insurance and health 25

Costs, money and banks..27

Getting around 29

Accommodation..42

Eating and drinking..46

Communications...54

The media 56

Opening hours and public holidays...58

Festivals and annual events...60

Sports and outdoor pursuits..63

Crime and personal safety...72

Work and study..73

Travellers with disabilities 74

Directory...76

Getting there

The easiest way to get to Switzerland is, of course, to fly. Zürich and Geneva are both major international hubs, served by short- and long-haul airlines, while the slick, modern airport at Basel handles dozens of European flights a day.

Aside from **Zürich** (ZRH), **Geneva** (GVA) and **Basel** (EAP), smaller Swiss airports such as **Lugano** (LUG) in the south, **Sion** (SIR) in the Alps and **Bern** (BRN) are useful entry points to specific regions. In addition, Milan's second airport, **Milan Malpensa** (MXP) – which handles a good deal of intercontinental traffic – is only 25km south of the Swiss border:

High and low seasons

The main thing to take into account when planning your trip is the **high and low seasons**, since hotel prices, pressure on rooms and periods of opening of hotels, shops and restaurants – especially in mountain resorts – can fluctuate dramatically. Problems come in trying to pin down the seasons, since they vary according to the town.

At all locations across the country, July and August are **high season** (*Hochsaison, haute saison, alta stagione*), when everything is open but prices are highest. The major lowland cities and lakeside resorts have a **summer season** which extends from at the earliest mid-May until at the latest mid-October. However, the higher in altitude you go, the more the season is truncated: the Alpine pass roads may not be cleared until mid-June, and snow may fall again in mid-September, limiting the opening times of the highest huts and mountain refuges to ten or twelve crowded weeks. You may find that some cable-cars and mountain railways don't start operation, and trails may not be open for walkers, until well into June, even if hotels and services take bookings for several weeks earlier. If you're travelling specifically for a walking or activity holiday in late May or early September, you should check in advance – online and with the tourist office – exactly what the conditions are likely to be, to avoid disappointment.

Countrywide, the **low season** (*Vorsaison, Nachsaison* or *Zwischensaison, basse saison, bassa stagione*) comprises April, May, and mid-October to early December: cities and lowland towns still welcome tourists at these times (and, indeed, often have cut-price deals on accommodation), but many mountain resorts – including hotels and shops within them – close down altogether and use the time for renovations.

The **winter high season** matches the ski season, which traditionally opens in the week before Christmas and lasts until the week after Easter (but in practice depends on snow cover); this is when prices in Alpine resorts climb to their peak again, and mountain transport, accommodation and services are all open for business. Prices in the mountains are highest around Christmas and New Year, and again in mid-February, whereas the months of January and March are less crowded and so less expensive: plenty of resorts offer cut-price skiing packages at the beginning and end of the season in mid-December and early April. Resorts with access to slopes above about 2500m tend to extend the season: there may be good snow at these places from mid-November through to early May. Cities and lowland towns are bitterly cold for general street wanderings in the winter, and – unless they offer direct access to the mountains – tend to flog accommodation at rock-bottom prices.

it's quite feasible to fly there and catch a bus straight from the airport to Lugano without spending any time or money in Italy. Similarly, **Friedrichshafen** (FDH) in Germany, with budget flights from London, lies just across the Bodensee lake from the Swiss railhead of Romanshorn, access point for a sizeable part of eastern Switzerland.

In this section, we cover independent travel first – details of package deals and organized tours follow on p.17.

Flights from the UK

The principal **full-service** carriers flying **from the UK** to Switzerland are British Airways and Swiss, the renamed and revamped national airline, which has built upon the global reputation of the old Swissair for offering a quietly memorable flying experience. The perception that they're stratospherically expensive does them down – you'd do better to judge them on value for money: for fares that can compete across the board

you get padded leather seats in all classes, comfortable leg-room, light, appetizing food (including fresh-baked crusty bread and free chocolate) and smooth, careful personal service.

A clutch of **no-frills** airlines flies to Switzerland, led by easyJet, but also including Buzz (bought by Ryanair in 2003), bmi baby (part of BMI British Midland) and MyTravelLite (a budget airline set up in 2002 by the group that owns the Airtours charter firm). Bear in mind that competition in the no-frills sector is hotting up: new routings often open up and existing ones are abandoned, as these tightly run operations struggle to secure a market share.

What **charter flights** exist are usually block-booked by package holiday firms, but even at high season spare seats are often sold off at a discount; their major disadvantage is the fixed return date. For an idea of current prices, contact any high-street travel agent or some of the larger package operators on p.18.

"Fly Rail Baggage"

The Swiss have come up with one of the greatest, and simplest, ideas around for easing the stress of air travel. For a relatively small fee, you can send your bags direct from the **check-in desk** at your home airport through to pretty much any train station in Switzerland for collection at your convenience, entirely eliminating the hassle of reclaiming your bags at the airport carousel and then lugging them around while you find your hotel. Whoever you're flying with – it doesn't have to be Swiss, and it can be from any airport in the world – all you need to do is to fill out a special green **customs label** and attach one to each item of baggage. Each label costs the equivalent of around £10/US$15; they're obtainable from Swiss Air Lines offices and most Rail Europe outlets worldwide. The service extends to all flights into Zürich and Geneva (easyJet and British Airways e-tickets excluded); if you're flying into Basel, check in advance whether your flight is served. Flights into smaller Swiss airports aren't covered.

Baggage is normally available for pick-up four to eight hours after you land, depending on how far away you end up from the airport you flew into. **Baggage counters** at larger Swiss train stations are open long hours for collection, often 7am to 11pm or so daily, but note that counters at smaller stations quite often close at 7 or 8pm. You don't have to pick up your bags in person, since the station staff only need to see ID and your label-stub: check with your hotel whether or not they'll charge for sending a porter to collect your bags for you.

For full **information**, check ⓦ www.rail.ch/pv/fly_e.htm, which has complete lists of processing times at all Swiss stations served; SBB produces a multilingual pamphlet with the same information, available at main European rail offices around the world. The homeward-bound version of "Fly Rail Baggage" – by which you can check-in at the train station for your flight home – is covered on p.35.

Flight time from London is around an hour and a half, from the north of England or Scotland two to three hours.

Routings and fares

From **Heathrow**, BA and Swiss compete on routes into Geneva, Zürich and Basel, while Swiss also has winter flights nonstop to Sion. If you prefer to fly from **Gatwick**, the options are BA into Geneva or easyJet into Geneva or Zürich. From **Stansted**, you can fly Buzz to Geneva (winter only), or Ryanair to the German city of Friedrichshafen, a short ferry ride from eastern Switzerland. easyJet flies from **Luton** to Geneva and Zürich, while from **London City**, Swiss has plenty of flights to Geneva, Zürich and Basel.

From **Birmingham**, BA fly to Geneva, as do MyTravelLite (winter only), and Swiss fly to Zürich and Basel. From **East Midlands**, easyJet and bmibaby fly to Geneva; bmibaby also has winter flights to Geneva from **Cardiff**. From **Manchester**, there's a choice between BA and Swiss to Zürich, BA to Geneva, and Swiss to Basel. easyJet flies from **Liverpool** to Geneva. From Scotland, the only nonstop flights are from **Edinburgh** to Zürich on Swiss; and Swiss also fly from **Guernsey** and **Jersey** to Zürich.

If you prefer the convenience of a more local departure point, and don't mind changing planes midway, you might do better to plump for KLM; they fly from smaller UK airports such as Aberdeen, Bristol, Cardiff, Humberside, Leeds-Bradford, Newcastle, Norwich and Teesside to Amsterdam, with easy connections there on to Geneva and Zürich.

Fare structures are fiendishly complex, and often involve arbitrarily large chunks of tax, levied by both UK and Swiss authorities; the sample quotes here are including tax. The cheapest fares are invariably to be found online, rather than by phone enquiry. On any of the **no-frills airlines**, if you book far enough in advance – several weeks at least – you should be able to find tickets for £50–70 return, but these often apply only to midweek early morning or late evening flights, and are either non- or partially refundable and non-exchangeable. For more reasonable flight times and/or a more flexible fare from these budget airlines, you're looking at £120–140 return, a price that the **full-service airlines** can often compete with. The cheapest fares with BA and Swiss –

which need to be booked months ahead – are around £110–130 return, but once these are gone, you're looking at £180–200 return from anywhere in the UK. Last-minute fares can touch £500.

Airlines in the UK

bmibaby ☎0870/264 2229, ⊛www.bmibaby. com.
British Airways ☎0845/773 3377, ⊛www.ba. com.
Buzz ☎0870/240 7070, ⊛www.buzz.co.uk.
easyJet ☎0870/600 0000, ⊛www.easyjet.com.
KLM ☎0870/507 4074, ⊛www.klmuk.com.
MyTravelLite ☎0870/156 4564, ⊛www. mytravellite.com.
Ryanair ☎0871/246 0000, ⊛www.ryanair.com.
Swiss ☎0845/601 0956, ⊛www.swiss.com.

Flight agents in the UK

Bridge the World ☎0870/444 7474, ⊛www. bridgetheworld.com. Good deals aimed at the backpacker market.
Cheapflights.com ⊛www.cheapflights.com. Flight deals.
Co-op Travel Care ☎0870/902 0033, ⊛www. travelcareonline.com. Flights and holidays around the world.
Destination Group ☎020/7400 7045, ⊛www. destination-group.com. Good discount airfares.
Expedia ⊛www.expedia.co.uk. Discount airfares, all-airline search engine and daily deals.
Flightbookers ☎0870/010 7000, ⊛www. ebookers.com. Low fares on an extensive selection of scheduled flights.
Flynow ☎0870/444 0045, ⊛www.flynow.com. Large range of discounted tickets.
Lastminute.com ⊛www.lastminute.com. Good last-minute holiday package and flight-only deals.
North South Travel ☎01245/608 291, ⊛www.northsouthtravel.co.uk. Friendly, competitive travel agency, offering discounted fares worldwide. Profits are used to support projects in the developing world, especially the promotion of sustainable tourism.
Premier Travel ☎028/7126 3333, ⊛www.premiertravel.uk.com. Discount flight specialists.
Priceline ⊛www.priceline.co.uk. Name-your-own-price website that has deals at around forty percent off standard fares. You cannot specify flight times (although you do specify dates).
STA Travel ☎0870/160 0599, ⊛www.statravel .co.uk. Specialists in low-cost flights and tours.

Top Deck ☎ 020/7244 8000, ⓦ www.topdecktravel.co.uk. Long-established agent dealing in discount flights.

Trailfinders ☎ 020/7628 7628, ⓦ www.trailfinders.com. One of the best-informed and most efficient agents for independent travellers.

Travel Cuts ☎ 020/7255 2082, ⓦ www.travelcuts.co.uk. Specialists in budget, student and youth travel.

Travelocity ⓦ www.travelocity.co.uk. Destination guides, hot Web fares and best deals for car rental and accommodation.

By train from the UK

Travelling by **train** still has much of its old leisurely romance and can be a pleasant, scenic and relaxing way to get to Switzerland – although rarely as cheap as flying. Time is also a factor: the fastest route (which still involves changing trains in Paris), takes about eight hours London–Geneva.

Eurostar trains depart more or less hourly from London Waterloo through the Channel Tunnel direct to **Paris Gare du Nord** (journey time 3hr). From Paris, many trains serve Switzerland, but unfortunately not from the Gare du Nord, and also not from one single station, meaning you have to plan your route in advance and be prepared to lug your bags through the Paris metro. From the **Gare de Lyon**, high-speed TGV trains (for which you must pay a small supplement) depart throughout the day on three different routes: to Geneva (3hr 40min); under the Lyria brand (ⓦ www.lyria.biz) to Lausanne (3hr 50min), continuing on summer weekends direct to Sion, Sierre, Visp and Brig (6hr); or on a separate line to Neuchâtel (4hr), Bern (4hr 30min) and Zürich (6hr). The **Gare de l'Est**, handily situated beside the Gare du Nord, has non-TGV trains departing frequently to Bâle/Basel (5hr 30min), as well as daily overnight sleeper services delivering you to Zürich or Chur for breakfast.

There's complete **timetable information** on all trains from Paris and Brussels to all points in Switzerland at ⓦ www.rail.ch. The red-covered *Thomas Cook European Timetables* (ⓦ www.thomascookpublishing. com) details schedules of over 50,000 trains in Europe, as well as timings of over 200 ferry routes and rail-connecting bus services. It's updated and issued every month.

To book, your best bet is the Swiss Federal Railways office in London. Their top **fare** offer is £95 for a second-class return between London and Basel (via Paris), which must be booked 14 days in advance. Add £22 for a couchette on the night sleeper. The least expensive fare on the TGV route, from London to Geneva or Lausanne (via Paris), is £170 return, with no restrictions.

Eurostar ☎ 0870/160 6600, ⓦ www.eurostar. com. Gives the latest fares and offers for trains to Paris, but no bookings to Switzerland. Through-ticketing to Paris from stations around Britain is available from Eurostar, most travel agents and mainline train stations.

Rail Europe ☎ 0870/584 8848, ⓦ www. raileurope.co.uk. Information and bookings for point-to-point tickets, Eurostar and all European and Swiss passes.

Swiss Federal Railways Freephone ☎ 00800/ 100 200 30, ⓦ www.rail.ch. Complete timetable information and fares for trains to, from and within Switzerland, plus the full array of Swiss travel passes.

Driving from the UK

Switzerland is just about within reach of the UK on a day's **drive**: the Swiss border is very roughly 850km from the Channel coast and, given an early start and clear *autoroutes*, you could be in Basel, or even Bern or Lausanne, for dinner. It's fifty-fifty whether to aim for Calais or a ferry to Oostende. The Oostende route suffers from traffic around Brussels and Luxembourg, but then has better motorway access to eastern Switzerland. The Calais route – benefiting also from rapid Eurotunnel service – is shorter as the crow flies, and avoids large cities, but the *autoroute* runs out as you approach the Jura mountains, forcing you onto main roads instead.

Eurotunnel runs shuttle trains for vehicles between Folkestone and Coquelles, near Calais, via the **Channel Tunnel**. You can just turn up and go, though booking is advisable. Boarding is quick and easy – there are up to four departures per hour (one per hour midnight–6am) – and the journey takes a smooth, hassle-free 35–45 minutes. **Fares** vary a lot; travelling between 10pm and 6am can cut costs, while travelling at weekends, or in July and August, adds a premium. A two-week return in the summer peak can be £160–180 per car, though last-minute fares are likely to be much higher.

Frequent **ferries** and **catamarans** between Dover and Calais are operated by Hoverspeed, P&O Stena and Sea France. Booking months in advance could turn up a return fare of £140–170 for a car plus passengers; leaving it until nearer your date of travel could mean paying £270–300. Boats in summer can get very crowded and booking ahead is strongly advised. A car plus four people on Hoverspeed's rapid SeaCat between Dover and Oostende costs upwards of £300 return.

From the north of England, P&O North Sea Ferries have daily services **from Hull** to both Rotterdam and Zeebrugge; both take fourteen hours or so, giving you a full night's sleep on board. Booking well in advance, a car plus four people, with a basic cabin and meals included, costs around £600 on either route. **From Newcastle** (North Shields), DFDS sails to IJmuiden near Amsterdam (14hr); booking 21 days ahead nets a Seapex fare from £64 per person return.
DFDS Seaways ℡0870/533 3000, ⓦwww.dfdsseaways.co.uk.
Eurotunnel ℡0870/535 3535, ⓦwww.eurotunnel.com.
Hoverspeed ℡0870/240 8070, ⓦwww.hoverspeed.co.uk.
P&O North Sea Ferries ℡0870/129 6002, ⓦwww.ponsf.com.
P&O Stena Line ℡0870/600 0600, ⓦwww.posl.com.
Sea France ℡0870/571 1711, ⓦwww.seafrance.com.

From Ireland

From Ireland, the daily nonstop **flights** from Dublin to Zürich on Swiss (codesharing with Aer Lingus) are €250–300 return, a bit less if you book ahead. Aer Lingus's less regular flights nonstop Dublin–Geneva can save money (costing around €150–180) as can their routings into London City for onward connections. On Swiss, transfers which fly you to Zürich and then double back to Geneva or Basel might seem counterproductive, but connection times at Zürich are so well coordinated that they can save time on other airlines' routings, such as BA via London. A budget alternative – about €120–140 if you book well ahead – is on Ryanair from Dublin or Shannon into London Stansted then on to Friedrichshafen in Germany,

from where eastern Switzerland is a ferry ride away.

By **car**, you can either cross to Britain and then drive to the Channel ports for another ferry or the Eurotunnel shuttle train; or you might prefer to put your feet up for the extra-long crossings to France direct from Cork or Rosslare: the seventeen-hour voyage to Cherbourg leaves you within a (very long) day's drive of the Alps. Prices vary tremendously according to the day of travel; as an example, booking well ahead for a car plus two adults and two kids, with a cabin, costs in the order of €1000–1300 in the summer peak.

Airlines in Ireland

Aer Lingus ℡0818/365 000, ⓦwww.aerlingus.ie.
British Airways ℡1800/626 747, ⓦwww.ba.com.
Ryanair ℡0818/303 030, ⓦwww.ryanair.com.
Swiss ℡1890/200 515, ⓦwww.swiss.com.

Flight agents in Ireland

Aran Travel International ℡091/562 595, ⓦhomepages.iol.ie/~arantvl/aranmain.htm. Good-value flights.
CIE Tours ℡01/703 1888, ⓦwww.cietours.ie. General flight and tour agent.
Go Holidays ℡01/874 4126, ⓦwww.goholidays.ie. Package tour specialists.
Joe Walsh Tours ℡01/676 0991, ⓦwww.joewalshtours.ie. General budget fares agent.
Lee Travel ℡021/427 7111, ⓦwww.leetravel.ie. Flights and holidays worldwide.
McCarthy's Travel ℡021/427 0127, ⓦwww.mccarthystravel.ie. General flight agent.
Neenan Travel ℡01/607 9900, ⓦwww.neenantrav.ie. Specialists in European city breaks.
Student & Group Travel ℡01/677 7834. Student and group specialists.
Trailfinders ℡01/677 7888, ⓦwww.trailfinders.ie. One of the best-informed and most efficient agents for independent travellers.

Ferry companies in Ireland

Brittany Ferries ℡021/427 7801, ⓦwww.brittanyferries.co.uk. Cork to Roscoff (March–Oct only).
Irish Ferries ℡1890/313 131, ⓦwww.irishferries.com. Dublin to Holyhead; Rosslare to Pembroke; Rosslare to Cherbourg or Roscoff (March–Sept only).
Norse Merchant Ferries ℡01/819 2999, ⓦwww.norsemerchant.com. Dublin or Belfast to Liverpool.

P&O Irish Sea ☎1800/409 049, ⓦwww. poirishsea.com. Larne to Fleetwood; Dublin to Liverpool.

Stena Line ☎01/204 7777, ⓦwww.stenaline.co.uk. Dun Laoghaire and Dublin to Holyhead; Rosslare to Fishguard.

Swansea Cork Ferries ☎021/427 1166, ⓦwww.swansea-cork.ie. Cork to Swansea (March–Oct only).

From North America

Several airlines fly **from North America** nonstop to Zürich, and many other airlines have flights via other European hubs. Swiss is the obvious first choice, flying into **Zürich** daily nonstop from **New York JFK**, **Newark**, **Boston**, **Montréal**, **Washington Dulles**, **Miami**, **Chicago** and **LA**, and daily nonstop into **Geneva** from JFK. Swiss are busy forging partnership links with American Airlines, which gives them code-sharing rights on many domestic routings into all these hub cities from around the US. Other nonstop routings into Zürich are from Newark on Continental, from JFK and **Dallas** on American, and from **Atlanta** on Delta.

The lowest **fares** are invariably to be found online, rather than by phone inquiry. It shouldn't be difficult to find round-trip fares for nonstop routings of US$500–700 from the East Coast, perhaps $250–450 more from the West Coast; flying in the height of peak season is liable to add $350–550. Fares for weekday travel can be $60–70 lower than those for weekend flights. Swiss, despite its reputation for expense, can often compete with its homegrown rivals on price – and it's worth bearing in mind that you may find it beating them hollow on seat comfort, personal service and the quality of onboard meals.

Better deals than these may exist on routings via other European hubs – Air France via Paris, British Airways via London, or Iberia via Madrid, for example, which occasionally have special fares of around $350 from New York, $550 from LA – but there's something to be said for paying a little more to avoid an airport stopover after a tiring transatlantic flight.

Airlines in North America

Aer Lingus ☎1-800/223-6537, ⓦwww.aerlingus.ie.

Air Canada ☎1-888/247-2262, ⓦwww.aircanada.ca.

Air France US ☎1-800/237-2747, Canada ☎1-800/667-2747, ⓦwww.airfrance.com.

American Airlines ☎1-800/433-7300, ⓦwww.aa.com.

British Airways ☎1-800/247-9297, ⓦwww.ba.com.

Continental ☎1-800/231-0856, ⓦwww.continental.com.

Delta ☎1-800/241-4141, ⓦwww.delta.com.

Iberia ☎1-800/772-4642, ⓦwww.iberia.com.

Lufthansa US ☎1-800/645-3880, Canada ☎1-800/563-5954, ⓦwww.lufthansa.com.

Northwest/KLM ☎1-800/447-4747, ⓦwww.nwa.com, ⓦwww.klm.com.

Swiss ☎1-877/359-7947, ⓦwww.swiss.com.

Flight agents in North America

Air Brokers International ☎1-800/883-3273, ⓦwww.airbrokers.com. Consolidator.

Airtech ☎212/219-7000, ⓦwww.airtech.com. Standby seat broker and consolidator.

Cheapflight.com ⓦwww.cheapflight.com & ⓦwww.cheapflights.ca. Flight deals, travel agents, plus links to other travel sites.

Cheaptickets.com ⓦwww.cheaptickets.com. Discount flight specialists.

Council Travel ☎1-800/2COUNCIL, ⓦwww.counciltravel.com. Specialists in student/budget travel.

Expedia ⓦwww.expedia.com & ⓦwww.expedia.ca. Discount airfares, all-airline search engine and daily deals.

Hotwire ⓦwww.hotwire.com. Last-minute savings of up to forty percent on regular published fares.

New Frontiers ☎1-800/677-0720 or 310/670-7318, ⓦwww.newfrontiers.com. Discount-travel firm.

Priceline ⓦwww.priceline.com. Name-your-own-price website that has deals at around forty percent off standard fares. You cannot specify flight times (although you do specify dates).

Skylink US ☎1-800/247-6659 or 212/573-8980, Canada ☎1-800/759-5465, ⓦwww.skylinkus.com. Consolidator.

STA Travel ☎1-800/781-4040, ⓦwww.statravel.com. Worldwide specialists in independent travel; also student IDs, travel insurance, car rental, rail passes, and more.

TFI Tours ☎1-800/745-8000 or 212/736-1140, ⓦwww.lowestairprice.com. Consolidator.

Travel Avenue ☎1-800/333-3335, ⓦwww.travelavenue.com. Full-service agent.

Travel Cuts US ☎1-866/246-9762, Canada

☎ 1-800/667-2887, ⓦ www.travelcuts.com.
Student travel organization.

Travelers Advantage ☎ 1-877/259-2691,
ⓦwww.travelersadvantage.com. Discount travel
club; membership fee currently $1 for 3 months' trial.

Travelocity ⓦwww.travelocity.com &
ⓦwww.travelocity.ca. Destination guides, hot Web
fares and best deals for car hire, accommodation
and lodging as well as fares.

From Australia and New Zealand

There are no direct flights **from Australia or New Zealand** to Switzerland, although there's plenty of choice to Zürich via major Asian hubs. The most convenient routings going west are with Thai (who codeshare with Swiss), Malaysian or Singapore Airlines; they all fly from major Australian cities and Auckland to their hubs (**Bangkok**, **Kuala Lumpur** and **Singapore** respectively) and on directly to Zürich. Alternatively, you could find an inexpensive shuttle flight to Singapore or Bangkok on any of a fistful of carriers – including all the above, Qantas, BA, Air New Zealand and others – and switch to Swiss for the nonstop leg to Zürich. Emirates fly a handy route Perth–Dubai–Zürich. Perhaps the most useful direct routings on European carriers are with Austrian Airlines from Melbourne to **Vienna** or Alitalia from Melbourne to **Rome**, from either of which the short hop to Zürich or Geneva is a piece of cake; going via London may be cheaper, but adds several hours onto your journey time. Flying to **Tokyo**, say with Qantas, and from there nonstop to Zürich with Swiss is another viable option. However, it doesn't take any longer to head east with – depending on the origin city – Qantas, Air New Zealand, United or American to **Los Angeles**, from where Swiss again fly nonstop to Zürich.

Fares vary tremendously – the lowest invariably to be found online – but as a broad outline, expect A$1800–2800 from major Australian cities (roughly NZ$2000–3000 from Auckland); Thai, Malaysian and Austrian fall at the lower end of this bracket, Qantas, BA, Singapore, Emirates and US carriers at the higher end.

Airlines in Australia & NZ

Air New Zealand Australia ☎ 13 24 76, NZ
☎ 0800/737 000, ⓦ www.airnz.com.

Alitalia Australia ☎ 02/9244 2445, NZ ☎ 09/308 3357, ⓦ www.alitalia.com.
American Airlines Australia ☎ 1300/650 747, NZ ☎ 09/309 9159, ⓦ www.aa.com.
British Airways Australia ☎ 02/8904 8800, NZ ☎ 0800/274 847, ⓦ www.ba.com.
Emirates Australia ☎ 1300/303 777, NZ ☎ 09/377 6004, ⓦ www.emirates.com.
Japan Airlines Australia ☎ 02/9272 1111, NZ ☎ 09/379 9906, ⓦ www.japanair.com.
Malaysia Airlines Australia ☎ 13 26 27, NZ ☎ 0800/777 747, ⓦ www.mas.com.my.
Qantas Australia ☎ 13 13 13, NZ ☎ 09/357 8900, ⓦ www.qantas.com.
Singapore Australia ☎ 13 10 11, NZ ☎ 09/303 2129, ⓦ www.singaporeair.com.
Swiss Australia ☎ 1300/724 666, ⓦ www.swiss.com.
Thai Airways Australia ☎ 1300/651 960, NZ ☎ 09/377 0268, ⓦ www.thaiair.com.
United Airlines Australia ☎ 13 17 77, NZ ☎ 0800/508 648, ⓦ www.unitedairlines.com.

Flight agents in Australia & NZ

Budget Travel NZ ☎ 0800/808 480, ⓦ www.budgettravel.co.nz.
Cheapflights.com ⓦwww.cheapflights.com.au.
Flight deals, travel agents, plus links to other travel sites.
CIT Australia ☎ 02/9267 1255,
ⓦ www.cittravel.com.au. One of the main agents for Eurail and Swiss passes.
Destinations Unlimited NZ ☎ 09/373 4033.
Flight Centre Australia ☎ 13 31 33 or 02/9235 3522, ⓦ www.flightcentre.com.au, NZ ☎ 0800 243 544 or 09/358 4310, ⓦ www.flightcentre.co.nz.
Lastminute.com ⓦwww.lastminute.com.au. Good last-minute holiday package and flight-only deals.
Northern Gateway Australia ☎ 1800/174 800, ⓦ www.northerngateway.com.au.
STA Travel Australia ☎ 1300/733 035, ⓦ www.statravel.com.au, NZ ☎ 0508/782 872, ⓦ www.statravel.co.nz.
Student Uni Travel Australia ☎ 02/9232 8444, NZ ☎ 09/300 8266, ⓦ www.sut.com.au.
Trailfinders Australia ☎ 02/9247 7666, ⓦ www.trailfinders.com.au.
Travelshop.com.au ⓦ www.travelshop.com.au.
Discounted flights, packages and insurance.

Packages and organized tours

Package tours may not sound like your kind of travel, but don't dismiss the idea out of hand. In addition to the fully escorted variety, many agents can put together very flexible deals, sometimes amounting to no more than a flight plus car or rail pass and accommodation; if you're planning to travel in moderate or luxury style, and especially if your trip is geared around special interests, such packages can work out cheaper than the same arrangements made on arrival.

Ski packages

The main focus of packages to Switzerland is of course **skiing**, and most agents offering winter holidays in the Alps include at least one or two Swiss destinations. Skiing packages tend to include flights, transfers and half-board accommodation (breakfast and an evening meal), but exclude lift passes. Prices vary tremendously depending on the operator, the resort, the style of accommodation and the time of the season. For more, see p.66.

Accommodation is almost always of high quality, if not exactly inventive: standard two- and three-star resort hotels abound, although deals in Verbier, for instance (which doesn't have a great range of hotels), or Zermatt, tend to include a choice of **catered chalets**, which can sleep anything from two people to a group of fifteen or more; obviously, the more people sharing a chalet, the less expensive it works out for everyone. Free or discounted **extras** to look out for, which can turn a mediocre-value deal into a bargain, include lift passes, rental of skis or snowboards and other gear, lessons, train passes to allow you to get around from resort to resort, and reductions for children. Most UK operators also offer self-drive car-rental that can cut well over £100 per person off a package price if you choose to drive to and from Switzerland rather than fly.

"Lakes and Mountains" and other packages

Most travel agents in Britain, and plenty further afield, stock brochures for packages to Swiss destinations, but you may find that the standard "Lakes and Mountains" umbrella title used by dozens of companies includes only one or two Swiss resorts. The most famous are Interlaken and Luzern, which offer a wide choice of budget, midrange or luxury hotels; prices drop if you choose self-catering accommodation, or stay in less

famous lakeside resorts such as, perhaps, Thun or Vevey.

Specialist companies worldwide offer summer **walking holidays**, mostly following the high Alpine routes around and between Mont Blanc and the Matterhorn, and also in the Bernese Oberland (see p.63). These can be a great way for experienced hikers and novices alike to get well off the beaten path and out into nature, without having to worry about the practicalities of bed and board or getting lost in the snows. Some put you up in campsites, others use mountain huts and refuges, and a few may include vehicle support and/or porterage. All stick to small groups of around 10–15 people. In the same vein, **cycling holidays** are becoming more popular, taking advantage not only of the scenery but also of Switzerland's extensive cycle-path network (see p.69) and high degree of trail support. A handful of operators make use of the outstanding Swiss public transport system to offer holidays that link together series of **rail journeys** on classic Alpine routes (see p.30) over one or two weeks.

A few UK operators offer short **city-breaks** in summer or winter. For a quick getaway and guaranteed accommodation with minimum hassle, these can represent excellent value (especially in the low seasons), not least because they often include flights, transfers, accommodation, breakfasts and – handily – a discount travel card. Favoured destinations are Geneva, Lausanne, Bern, Luzern and Zürich, but some specialist operators can come up with deals to Lugano or Basel, as well as resorts such as Zermatt, Wengen or Mürren, and even all-in weekends in St Moritz, Davos or Klosters.

Tour operators in the UK

Airtours ☎ 0870/238 7777, ⍟ www.mytravel.co .uk. Standard summer packages to Interlaken and Luzern, winter packages to Verbier, plus short breaks.
British Airways Holidays ☎ 0870/442 3872, ⍟ www.baholidays.co.uk. Year-round city-break packages to Geneva, Luzern and Zürich.
Crystal Holidays ☎ 0870/848 7000, ⍟ www.crystalholidays.co.uk. Well-respected winter sports specialists, with a range of Swiss destinations including all the top names plus less well-known resorts such as Engelberg and Villars/Les Diablerets. Also standard summer city-breaks and "Lakes and Mountains" deals.

Exodus ⓣ 020/8675 5550, ⓦ www.exodustravels. co.uk. Experienced adventure tour operator running excellent small-group walking tours in the Swiss Alps at all levels of difficulty, plus novelty expeditions such as snowshoe trekking.

Field Studies Council Overseas ⓣ 01743/852 150, ⓦ www.fscoverseas.org.uk. Respected educational charity that organizes specialized small-group botanical/zoological holidays to Switzerland.

Great Rail Journeys ⓣ 01904/521 900, ⓦ www.greatrail.com. Specialists in train tours worldwide, with a full range of some classic Alpine journeys. Travel from Britain is by train, with a Swiss train pass thrown in.

Inghams ⓣ 020/8780 4433, ⓦ www.inghams. co.uk. Major operator with summer and winter packages of all kinds, competitive prices and plenty of experience. Especially strong on ski deals.

Interhome ⓣ 020/8891 1294, ⓦ www.interhome.co.uk. Swiss company with a massive, easily searchable database of self-catering holiday homes and apartments in towns and villages all over Switzerland.

Keycamp ⓣ 0870/700 0123, ⓦ www.keycamp.co.uk. Specialists in summer camping and mobile-home holidays at Alpine sites, with good deals for families.

Kuoni ⓣ 01306/747002, ⓦ www.kuoni.co.uk. A wealth of flexible summer and winter package holidays around Switzerland, taking in all the major resorts and most of the minor ones, with good family offers.

Naturetrek ⓣ 01962/733051, ⓦ www.naturetrek. co.uk. Acknowledged leaders in birdwatching and botanical holidays worldwide, offering sympathetic, expert guidance for small-group summer tours to Wengen and the Bernese Alps.

Martin Randall Travel ⓣ 020/8742 3355, ⓦ www.martinrandall.com. Small group cultural tours: experts on art or music lead travellers on week-long summer packages taking in galleries throughout Switzerland.

Plus Travel ⓣ 020/7734 0383, ⓦ www. plustravel.co.uk. Dedicated Switzerland specialists, Swiss-owned and Swiss-run, with winter and summer brochures, including city-breaks, fly-drives, tailor-mades and combination possibilities around the country. Options include train itineraries, bike or adventure holidays and gourmet tours, as well as plenty of more orthodox packages and skiing at resorts big and small.

Powder Byrne ⓣ 020/8246 5300, ⓦ www. powderbyrne.com. Slick, upmarket ski and summer operator, with a Swiss office and plenty of choice at major hotels in top resorts.

Skiers Travel ⓣ 0870/010 0032, ⓦ www.skiers-travel.co.uk. Major ski operator, with a good, diverse range of options.

Swiss Travel Service ⓣ 0870/191 7275, ⓦ www.swisstravel.co.uk. Specialist tour operators with a wealth of experience and local knowledge. Almost limitless choices around the country, covering one-centre and two-centre packages, city-breaks, train tours, walking weeks, golf holidays, adventure excursions and biking, farmhouse stays, health and beauty holidays, even open-air painting tuition for budding Alpine artists. Winter skiing possibilities are equally comprehensive.

Switzerland Travel Centre Freephone ⓣ 00800/100 200 30, ⓦ www.myswitzerland.com. From the horse's mouth: the travel and holiday arm of Switzerland Tourism has a vast range of tours and breaks of all kinds, from art and culture to inline skating to spa and wellbeing retreats.

Travel Renaissance ⓣ 01372/744 455, ⓦ www.travelrenaissance.co.uk. Week-long stays at classic grand hotels in Luzern or Interlaken, followed by a stately train journey back to Britain aboard the Venice-Simplon Orient Express.

Waymark ⓣ 01753/516 477, ⓦ www. waymarkholidays.co.uk. Small operator specializing in walking and cross-country skiing packages to lesser-known resorts around Switzerland.

Tour operators in North America

Abercrombie & Kent ⓣ 1-800/323-7308 or 630/954-2944, ⓦ www.abercrombiekent.com. Five-star guided sightseeing tours and customized tours with a heavy accent on resort towns like St Moritz and the scenery of the Alpine rail routes.

Above the Clouds Trekking ⓣ 1-800/233-4499 or 802/482-4848, ⓦ www.aboveclouds.com. Summer trekking tours in the Swiss Alps.

Adventure Center ⓣ 1-800/228-8747 or 510/654-1879, ⓦ www.adventure-center.com. Lots of different trekking trips in the Swiss, French and Italian Alps; be prepared to camp the whole way.

Adventures Abroad ⓣ 1-800/665-3998 or 360/775-9926, ⓦ www.adventures-abroad.com. Adventure specialists, with plenty of Swiss options.

Adventures on Skis ⓣ 1-800/628-9655 or 413/568-2855, ⓦ www.advonskis.com. Full range of packages to a fistful of Swiss resorts.

Alphorn Tours ⓣ 215/794-5653 or 775/832-2577. Quality summer hiking trips and winter ski packages to all the major resorts.

CBT Tours ⓣ 1-800/736-2453 or 312/475-0625, ⓦ www.cbttours.com. A variety of mountain biking tours, some including hiking.

Ciao Travel ⓣ 1-800/942-2426, ⓦ www.ciaotravel.com. Jazz festival specialists, with tours to the Montreux Jazz Festival and others.

Collette Tours ☎401/728-3805,
Ⓦwww.collettetours.com. Luxury, leisurely paced
sightseeing tours of Switzerland and the Alpine
countries.
Cross-Culture ☎1-800/491-1148, Ⓦwww.
crosscultureinc.com. Small-group cultural tours,
including some to Switzerland.
Euro-Bike & Walking Tours ☎1-800/321-6060,
Ⓦwww.eurobike.com. A good selection of cycling
and hiking holidays around the country.
Europe Train Tours ☎1-800/551-2085 or
845/758-1777, Ⓦwww.etttours.com. Plenty of
options for seeing Switzerland from the rails.
European Journeys ☎1-800/337-3057,
Ⓦhome.att.net/~europeanjourneys. Ski packages
to all the major Swiss resorts, plus golf vacations and
sightseeing tours.
Himalayan Travel ☎1-800/225-2380 or
203/743-2349, Ⓦwww.himalayantravelinc.com.
Independent and guided hiking trips on various
routes in the Swiss Alps.
Holidaze Ski Tours ☎1-800/526-2827 or
732/280-1120, Ⓦwww.holidaze.com. Well-crafted
ski packages to half-a-dozen major resorts.
Maupintour ☎1-800/255-4266,
Ⓦwww.maupintour.com. Luxury tours by train
through Switzerland and Austria.
Mountain Travel Sobek ☎1-888/MTSOBEK or
510/527-8100, Ⓦwww.mtsobek.com. A broad
selection of mountain hiking tours, including,
unusually, in the Ticino.
Rail Europe US ☎1-877/257-2887, Canada ☎1-
800/361-RAIL, Ⓦwww.raileurope.com. Rail, air,
hotel and car reservations.
Switzerland Tourism
Ⓦwww.myswitzerland.com. From the horse's
mouth: a vast range of tours and breaks of all kinds,
from art and culture to inline skating to spa and
wellbeing retreats.
Wilderness Travel ☎1-800/368-2794 or
510/558-2488, Ⓦwww.wildernesstravel.com.
Supported hikes in the Swiss mountains.

Tour operators in Australia & NZ

Adventure World Australia ☎02/8913 0755,
Ⓦwww.adventureworld.com.au, New Zealand
☎09/524 5118, Ⓦwww.adventureworld.co.nz.
Agents for a vast array of international adventure
travel companies.
CIT Australia ☎02/9267 1255, Ⓦwww.
cittravel.com.au. Tours of the Swiss and Italian
lakes.
Explore Holidays Australia ☎02/9857 6200 or
1300/731 000, Ⓦwww.exploreholidays.com.au.
Accommodation and package tours to Switzerland.
Ski and Snowboard Travel Co. Australia
☎02/9955 5201, Ⓦwww.skiandsnowboard.
com.au. Customised skiing holidays.
Snow Bookings Only Ⓦwww.snowbookingsonly.
com.au. Skiing trips in glitzy Swiss resorts.
Swiss Travel Centre ☎1800 251 911,
Ⓦwww.sydneytravel.com.au/swiss. Far and away
the widest choice and sharpest knowledge. Specialist
operator for escorted tours and ski packages, and
can book car rental, train passes and inexpensive
accommodation.
Switzerland Tourism Ⓦwww.myswitzerland.
com. From the horse's mouth: a vast range of tours
and breaks of all kinds, from art and culture to inline
skating to spa and wellbeing retreats.
Travel Australia ☎1300/130 482, Ⓦwww.travel.
com.au, NZ ☎0800/468 332, Ⓦwww.travel.co.nz.
Comprehensive online travel company.
Travel Plan Australia ☎02/9958 1888 or
1300/130 754, Ⓦwww.travelplan.com.au. Top
choice ski operator, with a wide choice of packages
to Swiss resorts.
Walkabout Gourmet Adventures Australia
☎03/5159 6556, Ⓦwww.walkaboutgourmet.com.
Classy food, wine and walking tours.

Red tape and visas

All EU nationals and citizens of the US, Canada, Australia and New Zealand need only a valid passport to visit Switzerland and Liechtenstein. In theory, stays are limited to a three-month maximum per trip, and six months total per year, but in practice border officials rarely stamp passports unless asked.

Duty-free allowances for visitors arriving from Europe are 200 cigarettes or 50 cigars or 250g of tobacco, 2 litres of wine under 15 percent and 1 litre of alcohol over 15 percent. There are no restrictions on the import of currency. ⓦ www.zoll.admin.ch has full information.

Work permits and residency

Short-term employment in Switzerland can bring rich rewards: serving in a fast-food restaurant could net you £9/$14 per hour; working as a manual labourer half as much again. The problem is getting the right **permits**. An agreement on the free movement of labour between Switzerland and the EU is now in force, with a timetable for increased relaxation of the rules and abandonment of quotas until complete liberalization in 2014. The complicated system of permits has been eased, although without the backing of a zero-rich bank account and/or some unique work skills, if you try for work – especially if you're not an EU national – you'll still have a sticky time of it in the dense web woven by Swiss bureaucrats. The official line is that only those foreigners who have skills not shared by any Swiss people will be considered for a work permit, and that applications for permits will only be considered from people outside the country at the time (ie you can't enter as a tourist and then take up work). This also applies to au pairs. However, even in Switzerland, rigid rules tend to flex in the face of real life, and if you go out looking for seasonal work in a ski resort or on a building site (see p.73), you may find employers willing and able to get you issued with permits within a few weeks.

The **short-term residence permit** (*Kurzaufenthaltsbewilligung, Autorisation de séjour de courte durée, Permesso per dimoranti temporanei*), valid for between three months and a year, is the best you can

hope for – but you'll need a valid work contract to get one. A **residence permit** (*Aufenthaltsbewilligung, Autorisation de séjour, Permesso per dimora*), valid for five years, is generally issued only to salaried permanent employees. You can only get a **settlement permit** (*Niederlassungsbewilligung, Autorisation d'établissement, Permesso di domicilio*) after five years' residency. Without any of these, you can't stay in the country for more than six months per year. All foreigners living in Switzerland for more than three months must also register with the authorities of the commune (not the canton) in which they reside.

For complete information, contact the nearest Swiss embassy or ⓦ www.bfa.admin.ch, or – for plainer answers – get *Living and Working in Switzerland* by David Hampshire (Survival Books).

Swiss embassies and consulates abroad

Full listing at ⓦ www.eda.admin.ch.
Australia Embassy: 7 Melbourne Ave, Forrest, ACT 2603 ⓣ 02/6273 3977. Consulates in Adelaide ⓣ 08/8271 8854, Brisbane ⓣ 07/3621 8099, Darwin ⓣ 08/8945 9760, Hobart ⓣ 03/6229 1289, Melbourne ⓣ 03/9825 4000, Perth ⓣ 08/9389 7097 and Sydney ⓣ 02/8383 4000.
Canada ⓦ www.eda.admin.ch/canada. Embassy: 5 Marlborough Ave, Ottawa, ON, K1N 8E6 ⓣ 613/235-1837. Consulates in Edmonton ⓣ 780/462-9221, Halifax ⓣ 902/420-6500, Montréal ⓣ 514/932-7181, Québec ⓣ 418/527-3787, Toronto ⓣ 416/593-5371, Vancouver ⓣ 604/684-2231 and Winnipeg ⓣ 204/338-4242.
Ireland ⓦ www.swissembassy.ie. Embassy: 6 Ailesbury Rd, Ballsbridge, Dublin 4 ⓣ 01/218 6382.
New Zealand Embassy: 22 Panama St, Wellington ⓣ 04/472 1593. Consulate in Auckland ⓣ 09/366 0403.

UK ⓦwww.swissembassy.org.uk. Embassy: 16–18 Montagu Place, London W1H 2BQ ☎020/7616 6000. Consulate in Manchester ☎0161/236 2933.
USA ⓦwww.swissemb.org. Embassy: 2900 Cathedral Ave NW, Washington DC 20008

☎202/745-7900. Consulates in Atlanta ☎404/870-2000, Chicago ☎312/915-0061, Houston ☎713/650-0000, Los Angeles ☎310/575-1145, New York ☎212/599-5700 and San Francisco ☎415/788-2272.

Information, websites and maps

Information on Switzerland is not hard to come by: the Swiss tourist industry has had 150 years or so to refine its approach to visitors, and the efficient, super-helpful tourist offices in Switzerland, abroad and online are only too happy to regale you with exhaustive detail on any city, region or the whole country.

All cities, virtually all towns, and a sizeable number of villages have a **tourist office** (*Verkehrsverein*, *Verkehrsbüro* or *Tourismus*, *Office du Tourisme*, *Ente Turistico*), pretty much always located next to, opposite, or within five minutes' walk of, the train station, and invariably signposted on approach roads. Most staff nationwide speak at least some English and are scrupulously helpful. They can provide you with city or town maps (free, or costing a franc or two), lists of hotels, restaurants, campsites and apart-ment rentals, and information on local sights and events, as well as detailed hiking maps and guides to the surrounding area and transport information. Some sell transport tickets and parking permits. Most offices will

phone around local hotels to book a room for you for free, and some extend the serv-ice nationwide (for which a fee – Fr.10 or so – is usually charged).

Beware of **seasonal opening hours**: in the low season (in the mountains this means mid-Oct to mid-Dec plus April & May; elsewhere Sept–June), most tourist offices outside major cities and resorts operate on limited hours, perhaps only Mon–Fri 9am–noon and 2–5pm, plus two or three hours on Saturday morning. Outside these times, it's still worth going to the office: many keep racks of leaflets outside for passers-by to take and almost all post lists of hotels, restaurants and forthcoming events in the window. Alternatively, you could find an

Swiss Museum Passport (SMP)

If you're planning to visit even a handful of museums in Switzerland, you'll save money with a **Swiss Museum Passport** (*Schweizer Museumspass*, *Passeport musées suisses*, *Passaporto musei svizzeri*), which gives free entry to almost 300 museums, galleries and castles around the country; full details are at ⓦwww.museums.ch/pass. The pass, plus a little booklet giving addresses and opening days of all the places included, costs Fr.30 for a month (students Fr.25); you can pay Fr.5 extra to have up to five children included on the same pass. Covering virtually every significant attraction in the country, it can easily pay for itself in a weekend of gallery-hopping; there are just a few unmissable institutions which aren't part of the scheme (Zürich's Kunsthaus and Basel's Fondation Beyeler stick out like a sore thumb by their absence). You can only buy the pass in Switzerland – from larger tourist offices, branches of Ticket Corner, or at the ticket desk of any of the museums in the scheme (all of which display a sticker).

In the guide, we've indicated those museums and attractions that offer free admission to Museum Passport holders with **"SMP"**.

Internet café and check the local tourist office website for information, or ask at the train station, where staff generally keep a small stock of maps and pamphlets behind the counter.

Switzerland Tourism

Worldwide ⓦwww.myswitzerland.com.
UK & Ireland Swiss Centre, 10 Wardour St, London W1D 6QF. Freephone ☎00800/100 200 30.
US & Canada 608 5th Ave, New York, NY 10020. Toll-free from US ☎1-877/SWITZERLAND, toll-free from Canada ☎011800/100 200 30.
Other countries PO Box 695, CH-8027 Zürich. International toll-free number ☎+800/100 200 30 (add your international prefix: 0011 from Australia, 00 from New Zealand, etc).

The Internet

There's a vast quantity of useful information on the **Internet**. Switzerland Tourism, the national tourist organization, has a superb, encyclopedic homepage at ⓦwww.myswitzerland.com, with virtual tours around every resort, weather and snow forecasts, live pictures, stacks of background information, booking details, special offers and tons more. "Hôtellerie Suisse", the Swiss Hotel Association, has a full listing at ⓦwww.swisshotels.ch of their thousands of quality-controlled hotels nationwide, and plenty of last-minute offers for cut-price multi-night deals. Most individual cities and resorts run efficient and informative sites geared towards tourists, which we've flagged in the guide text where relevant (often they're just the town name prefixed by "www" and suffixed by "ch"). There's loads of other online information devoted to Switzerland, official and unofficial; what follows is a personal selection.

Useful websites

Tourism and transport

ⓦ**www.myswitzerland.com** Official tourist office site, with a vast amount of useful information.
ⓦ**www.rail.ch** Comprehensive English-language homepage of Swiss Federal Railways, with massively detailed information on train routes (down to platform numbers of arrivals and departures), including fares and exact connection times. Book tickets and passes online.

ⓦ**www.rail-info.ch** Lovingly detailed site for narrow-gauge train buffs.
ⓦ**mikeaz.free.fr** Exhaustive database of Swiss funiculars.
ⓦ**www.alptransit.ch** Progress report on the new subalpine high-speed-train tunnels.
ⓦ**www.post.ch** Full details of postbus excursions and fares.
ⓦ**www.tcs.ch** Homepage of the Swiss Touring Club, with information for drivers.
ⓦ**www.museums.ch** Catalogue and description of all museums nationwide.
ⓦ**www.swisscastles.ch** Private fan-site devoted to Switzerland's 495 castles.
ⓦ**www.swiss-ski.ch** Swiss Ski Federation.
ⓦ**www.ssba.ch** Swiss Snowboard Association.
ⓦ**www.topevents.ch** Tourist-office rundown of the glitziest and chic-est of Switzerland's annual festivals and events.

Current affairs and culture

ⓦ**www.swissinfo.org** Daily updated news and features from Swiss Radio International, with an extensive archive and plenty of excellent links.
ⓦ**www.nzz.ch/english** Daily stories and weekly digest of news and comment from the respected Neue Zürcher Zeitung newspaper.
ⓦ**www.culturelinks.ch** Searchable database of links to culture websites.
ⓦ**www.swissart.net** News and events on the Swiss art scene.
ⓦ**www.ticketcorner.ch** Book tickets for just about any forthcoming show, gig, club or happening.
ⓦ**www.liarumantscha.ch** The Lia Rumantscha, devoted to promoting Romansh, Switzerland's fourth language.
ⓦ**www.hugo.ch** Underground club culture.
ⓦ**www.dancefloor.ch** Loads of club news and events.
ⓦ**www.findagrave.com** Locate the Swiss resting place of notable people.

General information

ⓦ**www.meteoswiss.ch** Detailed forecasts from the national weather service.
ⓦ**www.slf.ch** Continuously updated avalanche warnings and snow forecasts.
ⓦ**www.topin.ch** Live pictures from around the country.
ⓦ**www.swisswine.ch** Umbrella site puffing the merits of Swiss wine. Local sites include ⓦwww.vins-vaudois.com and ⓦwww.walliswine.ch.
ⓦ**www.wine.ch** Useful directory of wine shops and other wine information.

ⓦ www.swisshelpdesk.org Ask anything, and Swiss Radio International will reply.

ⓦ www.switzerland-in-sight.ch Huge amount of easily surfable social, political and geographical information.

ⓦ www.directories.ch Search the Swiss phonebook and Yellow Pages.

ⓦ www.admin.ch Official site of the Federal Government, with detailed reports, statistical analyses and other highbrow bits and bobs. You'll find better and more engaging information in English about the country and its politics at the Swiss embassy sites for London ⓦ www.swissembassy.org.uk and Washington ⓦ www.swissemb.org. All 26 cantons maintain local-info sites, accessed with the relevant two-letter abbreviation (eg the homepage of Vaud is ⓦ www.vd.ch).

ⓦ www.liechtenstein.li Everything to do with the principality.

Maps

Our **maps** of town centres and regions should be fine for most purposes; otherwise tourist offices always have town maps to give out, either free or for a franc or two. The best-respected commercial series – which depicts Switzerland's varied terrain superbly well – is that published by the Federal Office of Topography (**ⓦ www.swisstopo.ch**); they do a full range starting at 1:1 million, including an excellent full-country two-sheet set (1:200,000) updated annually, detailed 1:100,000 regional maps and 1:50,000 and 1:25,000 hikers' maps, as well as specialist maps on different scales detailing cycling and inline-skating routes, ski runs, historic sites, vineyards, cultural attractions and more. All can be ordered online; major map bookshops worldwide (such as Stanfords in London) stock most sheets, and many general bookshops in Swiss towns and cities sell a wide selection. **Hallwag** and **Kümmerly & Frey** are two major Swiss cartographic publishers with worldwide distribution and a host of products on many different scales; the latter's 1:301,000 full-country

sheet, published with the Touring Club Schweiz, comes with a 68-page booklet including an index, lists of service areas, main urban car parks, railway car shuttles, and more. Many Migrol service stations give out a perfectly usable fold-out road map of the country for free, pinpointing locations of their outlets along with some advertising.

Map outlets

UK & Ireland

Blackwell's UK ☎01865/793 550, ⓦ www.blackwell.co.uk.
Easons Dublin ☎01/858 3881, ⓦ www.eason.ie.
Hodges Figgis Dublin ☎01/677 4754, ⓦ www.hodgesfiggis.com.
Map Shop UK ☎0116/247 1400, ⓦ www.mapshopleicester.co.uk.
Stanfords UK ☎020/7836 1321, ⓦ www.stanfords.co.uk.

US & Canada

Adventurous Traveler US ☎1-800/282-3963, ⓦ www.adventuroustraveler.com.
Elliot Bay Book Co US ☎1-800/962-5311, ⓦ www.elliotbaybook.com.
Globe Corner US ☎1-800/358-6013, ⓦ www.globecorner.com.
Rand McNally US ☎1-800/333-0136, ⓦ www.randmcnally.com.
World of Maps Canada ☎1-800/214-8524, ⓦ www.worldofmaps.com.

Australia & NZ

Map Shop Australia ☎08/8231 2033, ⓦ www.mapshop.net.au.
Mapland Australia ☎03/9670 4383, ⓦ www.mapland.com.au.
Perth Map Centre Australia ☎08/9322 5733, ⓦ www.perthmap.com.au.
Specialty Maps NZ ☎09/307 2217, ⓦ www.ubdonline.co.nz/maps.

Insurance and health

Even for travel in a supposedly "safe" country such as Switzerland, it's advisable to have good travel insurance. Aside from absorbing the horrendous costs of medical emergencies and treatment (break an ankle on a mountain path and you might need a Fr.50,000 helicopter rescue), insurance also covers the loss or theft of your property, flight tickets and money. Many companies will tailor policies for you if you plan on going skiing, or if you want to take part in other "dangerous" sports or adventure activities.

Before paying for a new policy, it's worth checking whether you're already covered: some all-risks home insurance policies may cover your possessions when overseas, and many private medical schemes include cover when abroad. In Canada, provincial health plans usually provide partial cover for medical mishaps overseas, while holders of official student/teacher/youth cards in Canada and the US are entitled to meagre accident coverage and hospital in-patient benefits. Students will often find that their student health coverage extends during the vacations and for one term beyond the date of last enrollment.

After exhausting these possibilities, you might want to contact a specialist travel insurance company, or consider the travel insurance deal offered by Rough Guides (see box). A typical policy usually provides cover for the loss of baggage, tickets and – up to a certain limit – cash or cheques, as well as cancellation or curtailment of your journey. Many policies can be chopped and changed to exclude coverage you don't need: sickness and accident benefits can often be excluded or included at will. If you do take medical coverage, ascertain whether benefits will be paid as treatment proceeds or only after your return home, and whether there's a 24-hour medical emergency number. When securing baggage cover, make sure that the per-article limit – typically under £500/$750 – will cover your most valuable possession. If you need to make a claim, you should keep all receipts, and in the event you have anything stolen, you must obtain an official statement from the police.

Health

If you're arriving from Europe, North America or Australasia, you don't need any jabs. Virtually all travellers' afflictions arise from a lack of awareness of the impact of the high Alpine environment on those used to lowland life.

EU citizens are entitled to discounted emergency medical care in Switzerland and Liechtenstein on production of a stamped **Form E111** ("one-eleven"), available in Britain from post offices and online at ⓦwww.doh.gov.uk/traveladvice. It's a good idea to always keep your original E111 and several photocopies to hand, to show to doctors or ambulance crews in case of emergency. You normally have to pay the full cost of treatment upfront – which never comes cheap – and claim it back when you get home (minus a small excess); make very sure you hang onto full doctors' reports, signed prescription details and ALL receipts to back up your claim.

Every village and town district has a rota system whereby one local **pharmacy** (*Apotheke, pharmacie, farmacia*) stays open outside shopping hours: each pharmacy will have a sign in the window telling you where the nearest open one is, or you could ask your hotel reception to phone the operator on ☎111 to get an address. Local newspapers also have details. Virtually every Swiss **hospital** (*Spital, hôpital, ospedale*) has some kind of 24-hour emergency service. Wherever possible, seek advice from your embassy in Bern as well as your insurer at home before getting hospital treatment.

Ambulance emergency ☎144

Health issues

You can get **sunburnt** very quickly in the mountains, due to the combination of a thin atmosphere and reflection off snow, ice and/or water. High-factor sunscreen, a hat, and total sunblock for sensitive areas such as lips, nose and ears are essential. Reflection of the sun's glare can also damage your eyes, so always wear UV-protective sunglasses or a ski visor.

There are no rules about judging weather in the mountains. Conditions can change from calm to stormy in minutes, and if you're heading into the snows you should be prepared for the worst at all times. **Layered all-weather gear** is essential equipment for Alpine hikers at any time of year, and you'd do well to consult a travel clinic and/or a

specialist Alpine tour operator in advance for advice both on what to take for your particular trip and on how to keep yourself and others alive in emergency situations. **Hypothermia**, when the body loses heat faster than it can conserve it, is most often brought on by a combination of cold, wind and driving rain, with hunger and fatigue also playing their part. Symptoms include exhaustion, lethargy or dizziness, shivering, numbness in the extremities and slurring of speech. In these initial stages, you must get the sufferer out of the elements and under cover, replace any of their clothing that is wet (with your own dry garments if necessary), give them hot liquids and high-calorie sugary foods such as chocolate, and encourage and reassure them by talking. Despite the Alpine heroics of brandy-laden St Bernard dogs in the past, alcohol is a bad idea at such a critical time. Prompt action will head off acute hypothermia which, if allowed to develop, can be fatal.

Virtually all high-altitude walks in Switzerland stay below 3000m, the rough cut-off point above which **altitude sickness** can kick in. Headaches, dizziness and breathlessness are the main symptoms, all of which should pass after a day or two at altitude. If they don't, the only treatment is to head down.

If you're hiking in woodland below 1200m, there's a slight risk of receiving attention from **ticks**. These can occasionally carry nasty diseases such as encephalitis; proper hiking boots and socks significantly cut down your chances of a bite. The medically favoured way of extracting them, contrary to tales of dabbing with alcohol or heating with a match-flame, is to pull them out carefully with small tweezers. Switzerland also has a couple of species of non-fatal **snakes**, but to find them you'll have to creep around stealthily; tread heavily, and any present will slither away.

Medical resources for travellers

ⓦ**www.cdc.gov** First-choice source for travel health information.
ⓦ**health.yahoo.com** Information on specific diseases and conditions, drugs and herbal remedies.
ⓦ**www.fitfortravel.scot.nhs.uk** Information about travel-related diseases.
ⓦ**www.istm.org** International Society of Travel Medicine, with a full list of clinics worldwide.

Ⓦ www.tmvc.com.au Contains a list of all
Travellers Medical and Vaccination Centres
throughout Australia and New Zealand, plus general

information on travel health.
Ⓦ www.tripprep.com Destination and medical
service-provider information.

Costs, money and banks

Contrary to the stereotype, it's no more expensive to travel in Switzerland than in parts of Germany, Italy or England – and Swiss standards of service and facilities across all budgets far outstrip those elsewhere. The country's reputation for priciness is misleading: value for money is the national motto, and in most situations you get what you pay for.

Switzerland is the wealthiest country in the world, nursing an average per-capita income of around £28,000 a year – and that's *after* paying taxes of some thirty percent. The country is infamous as one of the safest places to stash a fortune, hard-earned or otherwise, and it's been estimated that there's about £1,000,000,000,000 squirrelled away in the anonymous numbered accounts of the various Swiss banks. The Swiss franc (CHF) is renowned for its stability and is one of the benchmarks against which international standards are set, while Zürich is one of the world's main financial centres.

Currency

Prices in both Switzerland and Liechtenstein are in **Swiss francs** (*Schweizer Franken, francs suisses, franchi svizzeri*). The most common abbreviation is "Fr." – but you may also see "fr", "sFr", "Sfr", "SF", "FS", or the official bank abbreviation "**CHF**". Each franc is divided into 100; these are called *Rappen* (Rp.) in German-speaking areas, *centimes* (c) in francophone areas, and *centisimi* (also c) in Italian-speaking areas. There are coins of 5c, 10c, 20c, 50c, Fr.1, Fr.2 and Fr.5, and notes of Fr.10, Fr.20, Fr.50, Fr.100, Fr.200 and Fr.1000.

The currency in all the neighbouring countries – France, Germany, Austria and Italy – as well as elsewhere across Europe is the **euro** (€), divided into 100 cents. Design of the coins may vary, but all euro currency is legal tender in all eurozone countries. Across Switzerland, and especially in areas close to

the borders (notably Geneva and Basel), you'll find vending machines, ticket dispensers and phone booths which may accept euro coins as well as Swiss coins, or which may accept only one or the other; they'll be clearly marked either way. Tourist brochures and hotel lists often quote prices in CHF and €, generally side-by-side: check which column you're reading. Approximate **exchange rates** at the time of writing were £1=Fr.2.30, US$1=Fr.1.50, and €1=Fr.1.45.

Carrying and changing money

Switzerland has a healthy mix of small rural communities where cash is the sole method of payment, and international cities dedicated to the art of high finance, where (almost) anything will do nicely. The best advice, since places still exist where you can't use debit/credit cards, is to carry your money in a mixture of **cash** and **plastic**. Fees on plastic transactions can often work out less than commissions on purchases of **travellers' cheques**. Most banks in the West keep Swiss francs on hand for over-the-counter **exchange**, and it's a good idea to bring a small supply with you to cover first-night expenses in case of difficulties.

Debit and credit cards

Every corner of Switzerland is plastered with banks, almost all of which – notably UBS and Crédit Suisse, which are present in every town – have English-language **ATMs** (cash machines) which accept foreign **debit and credit cards** in a panoply of brands including Visa, MasterCard, EC, Maestro, Cirrus and Plus. You can pay for most goods and services around the country using a foreign debit/credit card, although there may be a lower limit of Fr.20 or Fr.30, and some shops (most irritatingly certain supermarkets) don't accept foreign cards at all. As usual, **charge cards** such as Amex or Diners Club are less widely accepted. There's a growing push nationwide to reduce the reliance on cash: you'll see stickers at supermarket checkouts and on lots of vending machines (such as transport ticket machines, which increasingly often don't accept banknotes) for a domestic Swiss cashless smart-card, known – rather confusingly – as **"CASH"**. This often has wider acceptance than international brands of plastic. Before relying on being able to pay for goods or services with your own card, it's always a good idea to check with staff. Comfortingly, in the last resort most places still accept notes and coins for most transactions.

Visa TravelMoney (🌐 www.visa.com) combines the security of travellers' cheques with the convenience of plastic. It's a disposable debit card, charged up before you leave home with whatever amount you like, separate from your normal banking or credit accounts. You can then access these dedicated travel funds from any ATM that accepts Visa worldwide, with a PIN that you select yourself. Travelex/Interpayment outlets sell the card worldwide (see 🌐 www.travelex.com for locations). When your money runs out, you just throw the card away. Since you can buy up to nine cards to access the same funds – useful for families travelling together – it's recommended that you buy at least one extra card as a back-up in case your first is lost or stolen. The 24-hour Visa customer service line from Switzerland is ☎ 0800 896 046.

Cash and cheques

Invariably, the best place to change foreign **cash** or **travellers' cheques** is the desk to be found next to the ticket counters at virtually all train stations around the country: rates are identical with the banks, no commission is charged (except at some airport locations), and they're usually open seven days a week for long hours.

Some basic costs

It'll come as no surprise to learn that Switzerland is **expensive**. If you're prepared to cut all corners by walking or cycling your own bike around the country, staying in hostels or campsites, and never eating out, you could scrape by on Fr.40–50 (£18/$30) a day; add in one cheap meal and a beer, and Fr.55–65 (£26/$42) is more realistic, while budgeting something for visiting a few sights or museums (average Fr.5–7 per place, or £2.50/$4) would mean you might actually enjoy your trip too. If you don't have a bike, you'd have to factor in transport costs on top of this (see p.32 for more).

Staying at simple inns or guesthouses in one or two rural areas, avoiding cities altogether, and spending your days hiking or just relaxing in reasonable comfort is unlikely to set you back more than Fr.100/day each (£42/$67), but going up a mountain – which may be the whole point of your visiting Switzerland in the first place – can wipe out a day's budget. A journey to the Jungfraujoch, for instance, costs roughly Fr.120 (£50/$81): hiking part or all of the way up or down can bring big savings. If you're planning a skiing holiday, you should definitely book an all-in package from home, which costs a fraction of the equivalent over-the-counter rates.

A comfortable double room in a two- or three-star city hotel is on average Fr.130–160 (£62/$100), depending on the season and the city. Two people using this kind of accommodation, eating lunch and dinner in modest restaurants, taking in a scattering of sights, the odd boat trip or train ride, and a luxury or two, are likely to shell out, on average, roughly Fr.320 (£140/$215) a day between them.

If you're planning to visit more than a couple of museums, the **Swiss Museum Passport** (see box p.22) will save you plenty on admission tickets.

Youth/student ID cards soon pay for themselves in savings, principally on international air, rail and bus fares, admission to larger museums and attractions and on some resorts' lift passes; crucially, however, not on Swiss public transport. Full-time students are eligible for the International Student ID Card (**ISIC**); anybody aged 26 or less qualifies for the International Youth Travel Card; and teachers qualify for the

International Teacher Card – all carrying the same benefits. Check ⓦ www.isic.org for details of outlets selling the cards. **Children** get in half-price or less to many museums in Switzerland, and can travel free with their parents on a Family Card, issued free alongside any kind of Swiss travel pass (see p.32).

Getting around

The efficiency of the massively comprehensive Swiss public transport system remains one of the wonders of the modern world. It's hard to overstate just how good it is: you can get anywhere you want quickly, easily and relatively cheaply; everybody relies on it as a matter of course; and it's clean, safe and pleasant.

Services always depart on the dot, and **train** timetables are well integrated with those of the **postbuses**, which operate on routes not covered by rail, including the more remote villages and valleys, as well as **ferry** services on Switzerland's many lakes (and some of its rivers). **Cyclists** are well served by the Swiss instinct for encouraging green thinking in all things; see p.69 for details of cycling routes and bike rental. **Domestic flights** can't compete economically or environmentally with the trains, and ongoing expansion of the rail network will render most air routes redundant: Zürich–Basel is already equally fast by train or plane.

Tickets and ticket machines

One point can't be stressed enough. Millions of Swiss people virtually never pay full fare on their own public transport systems, and you should follow suit: unless you're planning to drive or cycle everywhere, you will definitely save money by travelling on a **Swiss travel pass** (see box p.33). All give free or discounted travel on trains, buses, boats, cable-cars and funiculars nationwide, and some are also valid on urban tram, bus and metro networks in nearly all Swiss cities. Pan-European rail passes such as **Inter-Rail** or **Eurail** are never as good, since they're not valid on buses or trams and give only partial discounts – or no discount at all – on boats and mountain transport. If you're based in one resort, investigate the terms of the local **guest card** (*Gästekarte*,

carte des visiteurs, *tessera di soggiorno*), issued for free when you check in at your hotel; these often give free transport on local buses and trains and – sometimes – cable-cars and funiculars. Lift passes at ski resorts invariably give free valley-floor transport to and from outlying cable-car stations.

Unless you're holding the Swiss Pass (which is almost universally valid; all you have to do is show it on demand), you're likely to find yourself tangling with **automated ticket machines** at some point, even if only to buy a ticket for a cross-town tram. Most urban transport networks are divided up into **zones**. Note that these never follow the system – familiar from, say, London – of concentric rings with consecutive numbering: in Zürich, for instance, the most central area is Zone 10, bordered on various sides by zones 21, 40 and 54. Fares are calculated by how many zones you travel in, and you nearly always have to buy your ticket before you board from the machines located at every stop. These generally follow a pattern, but are rarely marked in English and can be frustratingly difficult to fathom. First, press a button for your **journey** – either a destination code or an option to let you travel across, say, one, two or three zones. This choice often incorporates a **time validity** (a short-hop ticket may be valid for unlimited changes within an hour), or you could instead select a full day pass. You may then need to choose either **one-way** (a single arrow) or **round-trip** (a double arrow). Then,

29

press a button for yourself – adult or child. Some machines (in Zürich, for instance, where tickets are also valid on class-segregated trains and boats) give you the option to choose **1st class**. You'll also see an option for "**1/1**" or "**1/2**"; press the latter if you hold a pass that permits you to travel half-price. The readout will then show the fare. With the rise of the smart-card payment system "CASH" (see p.28), you may not

Excursions by train, bus and boat

Although few Swiss journeys are short on scenery, there are a handful of exceptionally beautiful routes around the country which are marketed as unified single journeys. On most – after having **reserved** a seat the day before for a few francs – you just sit back, flash your travel pass and drink in the views. Some require you to change from train to boat, or bus to train, but you never have to walk more than the length of a station platform, and timetables always allow enough leeway that you're never in a hurry. Plus, of course, you can always send your heavy bags ahead. Some of the more spectacular routings run special **panoramic** train carriages, either with partial or total glass roofs, or (in first class) with some raised seating inside a transparent bubble in the roof giving 360° views, but for these – and for extras such as onboard lunches – you always pay a **supplement**. For information, timings and routings, check well in advance at train stations, online or at larger tourist offices. Note, too, that it's easy to follow the same routes on ordinary trains and pay no extras, or to get on or off at intermediate points: the Centovalli line, for instance, is worth exploring regardless of its marketed Lötschberg add-on. And, it should be added, these are only the trips in the spotlight: equally spectacular shorter rides such as Chur to Arosa or the tiny Lauterbrunnen to Mürren line, are just as deserving of your attention. We've described the journeys in one direction, but you could just as easily travel in the other direction instead. Most need advance reservation, and some cross international borders (in which case, you'll need your passport). Note that some tour operators will let you add these excursions to a package holiday at the time of booking for bargain rates.

• **Bernina Express** and **Heidi Express** ⓦwww.rhb.ch. Various routes from Chur, St Moritz or Davos over the high Bernina Pass and through the stunning Val Poschiavo to Tirano (Italy), where – in summer only – you switch onto a postbus and skirt Lake Como to Lugano. Total, including a couple of hours in Tirano, 8hr. Daily. Panoramic carriages. Reserve at any station (train Fr.7, bus Fr.12).

• **Glacier Express** ⓦwww.glacierexpress.ch. A spectacular and understandably popular route, and – given its ups and downs – the slowest express in the world (average speed 30kph). From St Moritz (1775m) or Davos down to Chur (585m), then up the Rhine valley to the high Alps, crossing the Oberalp Pass (2033m) to Andermatt, through the tunnel beneath the Furka Pass and down the Rhône valley to Brig (671m), before climbing to Zermatt (1604m). Total 8hr, 291 bridges and 91 tunnels. Daily. Panoramic carriages on most trains. Reserve seats at any station (from Fr.9). Dining-car reservations taken at any station or at ⓔrail.sales.chur@passaggio.ch.

• **Golden Pass** ⓦwww.goldenpass.ch. Flagship panorama route from Luzern, running over the Brünig Pass to Interlaken and the glorious countryside around Gstaad, then a spectacular descent through vineyards to the lakeshore at Montreux, with a variety of different panoramic carriages on various legs of the journey. Total 7hr. Daily. Reservations needed for some stretches; ask at any station.

• **Lötschberg–Centovalli** ⓦwww.bls.ch & ⓦwww.centovalli.ch. South from Bern beneath both great Alpine ranges, courtesy of the Lötschberg tunnel into Canton

have the option to pay with a banknote; coins are always acceptable – either Swiss francs or, in some areas, euro coins. Some machines selling long-distance train tickets let you pay by **debit/credit card.**

Trains

The Swiss are the most frequent **train** users in Europe – not surprising, given the quality of the network. Travelling through

Valais, and the Simplon tunnel from Brig to Domodossola (Italy), where you switch to the tiny, rackety trains which ply the wild and gorgeous Centovalli east to Locarno. Daily. Total 4hr. No reservations needed.

• **Mont Blanc Express** Ⓦwww.momc.ch. Dramatic narrow-gauge route climbing from Martigny to the French border and then on into the high Alps to the resort of Chamonix (France), on the slopes of Mont Blanc. Swiss tickets are valid only to the border station of Châtelard; you can buy add-ons to Chamonix on the train. Daily. Total 1hr 30min. No reservations possible.

• **Palm Express** Ⓦwww.post.ch/route-express-lines. Postbus from St Moritz over the Maloja Pass into the dreamy Val Bregaglia, crossing the border to Chiavenna (Italy) and the shores of Lake Como, then crossing back into Switzerland to end at Lugano. No train-track exists on this route. Total 4hr 15min. June–Oct daily; rest of year Fri–Sun only. Reservations mandatory (Fr.10): at St Moritz bus station ⓣ081 837 67 64, Lugano bus station ⓣ091 807 85 20, or Ⓔpadtourismus@post.ch.

• **Rhône Express** Ⓦwww.rhoneexpress.ch. Memorably diverse scenery, with a boat ride from Geneva to Montreux, and a train running the length of the Rhône valley up to Brig, changing again for the rack railway to Zermatt. If you take the whole package (with a hefty supplement), you get a ride on an old-time paddle steamer with three-course lunch, and first-class train transport; otherwise, it's easy to link ordinary boat and train services together to form the same ride without supplements. The website lists a range of ways to tie the journey in with other routes. Total 9hr. Mid-May to mid-Sept daily. Reservations needed for some stretches; ask at any station.

• **Romantic Route Express** Ⓦwww.post.ch/route-express-lines. Linked series of postbus journeys on some of the highest roads in Europe – from Andermatt over the Furka Pass and past the Rhône glacier to Gletsch, then the tortuous route up and over the wild Grimsel Pass to Meiringen, from where the final leg takes you through some lovely scenery to the Grosse Scheidegg Pass and down to Grindelwald at the foot of the Eiger. Reservations mandatory (Fr.20): Ⓔpadtourismus@post.ch.

• **St Bernard Express** Ⓦwww.momc.ch. Narrow-gauge trains from Martigny climb south to the terminus station of Orsières, from where buses (summer only) continue up to the high Grand-St-Bernard Pass. Daily. Total 1hr 30min. No reservations possible.

• **Voralpen Express** Ⓦwww.voralpen-express.ch. Route between Romanshorn on the Bodensee (Lake Constance) and Luzern, scheduled trains speeding through the pretty countryside of the Prealps around St Gallen, the Zürichsee and the Rigi. Hourly. Total 2hr 45min. No reservations possible.

• **William Tell Express** Ⓦwww.lakelucerne.ch. Another incredibly beautiful journey, from Luzern by boat across the whole of Lake Luzern to Flüelen, then a train south, corkscrewing its way up into the Gotthard Tunnel beneath the Alps and then down again through the Ticino to Lugano. If you go for the whole package, you get a three-course lunch in a lake paddle steamer, plus first-class panoramic seating on the train (total supplement Fr.45 on top of a 1st-class ticket or pass). Avoid the supplement by making your own way on scheduled trains and boats. First-class package available on north–south travel only. Total 6hr. May–Oct daily. Reserve at any station.

Switzerland by train is invariably comfortable, hassle-free and extremely scenic, with many mountain routes an attraction in their own right. Swiss Federal Railways, or **SBB CFF FFS** (*Schweizerische Bundesbahnen, Chemins de fer fédéraux suisses, Ferrovie federali svizzere*), long heavily subsidized by the state, was opened up to competition in 1999 but retains a monopoly on most of the network. Maintaining a modern, integrated, ecologically sound transport system remains a top priority of Swiss governments and today fares are affordable, equipment and rolling stock are state-of-the-art, and staff motivation is high.

SBB covers virtually the whole country, but there are some routes, especially Alpine lines, which are operated by the individual rail companies which constructed them often a century or more ago. Two of the largest of these are **BLS**, which runs the pivotal Bern–Lötschberg–Simplon route between the Swiss capital and Milan; and **RhB**, the Rhätische Bahn, which operates trains within Canton Graubünden. There are dozens more of these private lines, often tiny concerns used by local people to get to and from their nearest town, sometimes (such as the Bernese Oberland's **Jungfraubahnen**) massive enterprises ferrying thousands of tourists from valley to summit and back again. However, ticketing systems are well integrated, and you don't really need to know which company is which, since each route has only one company providing services: you never have to shop around between competing train companies.

All trains, apart from local stopping services and mountain lines, have **first-class** and **second-class** sections, with at least part of one carriage in each class always set aside for **smokers**.

Fares and passes

The wide range of Swiss **passes** offer the most economical way to get around the country on public transport; the pan-European passes have limited coverage by comparison.

One-way **fares**, if you're rash enough to buy ordinary tickets for each journey, work out at a reasonable Fr.31 per 100km in second class. However, there's a plethora of ways to save money using passes and season tickets (see opposite). With no barriers on the platforms, inspectors on the trains are the sole method of **fare-enforcement**, and they'll move through the whole train more or less between every station: get caught without a valid ticket or pass for your journey and they'll slap a Fr.60 **fine** on you, to which a surcharge is added if you can't pay on the spot. Most regional and local trains are marked with a prominent **swirly eye pictogram**: this means that there's no conductor and that you're trusted to buy a ticket, either from the station staff or from a platform ticket machine. Roving bands of inspectors may board at any point to check tickets. If you intend using any kind of multi-day pass or undated ticket, you must stamp it before you board in the little boxes marked with the same swirly eye pictogram on platforms or near escalators.

Swiss travel passes

There's a confusing array of different **Swiss travel passes**. All are good value, also bringing a discount on bike rental from train stations (see p.69): it just takes some untangling to see which is best suited for your trip.

Top of the pile is the **Swiss Pass**. This gives free unlimited travel on 4, 8, 15, 22 or 30 *consecutive* days on all SBB and most other trains, as well as on all boats and post-buses and most city tram-and-bus networks. Where travel isn't free (eg on cable-cars and mountain railways), discounts of at least 25 percent apply. The **Swiss Youth Pass** is the same thing, reduced in price for those under 26 on the first date of travel. The **Swiss Flexi Pass** gives the same privileges as the Swiss Pass on any 3, 4, 5, 6 or 8 days within a month. Two or more people travelling together (up to a maximum of five) all get 15 percent off the cost of a Swiss Pass or Flexi Pass under the "Saver" scheme. These three are available from Swiss tourist offices at home (see p.23) and, in francs only, from major stations within Switzerland on production of a foreign passport. The **Swiss Transfer Ticket**, only available outside Switzerland, gives one free journey from the airport or border to anywhere in the country, and back again within a month – ideal for skiers. The **Swiss Card**, buyable abroad and at airport or border stations within Switzerland, extends the terms of the Transfer Ticket: as well as a free journey at the start and end of your holiday, it gives a month's travel by train, postbus and boat at fifty percent discount (plus partially reduced fares on most mountain railways). The **Family Card** is a free add-on to any of the above: kids up to 16 accompanied by their parents travel free, while kids without their parents go for half price.

Note that although the convenience and universal validity of the Swiss Pass or Flexi Pass is alluring, it pays to do some sums before you splash out on one: depending on the kind of journeys you're liable to take (all of which are fully researchable online), you may well find that you can save substantial amounts by getting a humble Swiss Card and shelling out for half-price travel tickets each time, rather than buying an expensive Swiss Pass and travelling for free.

If you're planning to concentrate on one area of the country, but still want the flexibility to visit local sights, it might be more economical to get a **regional pass** for your particular region. These vary across the country in both price and validity, but normally give 5 days' free travel in 15 within a limited region,

often including discounts for the other 10 days. Regional passes are most popular in the Berner Oberland, the Gstaad–Château d'Oex region, Central Switzerland around Lake Luzern, and the Lake Geneva shoreline, but are also offered by many other regional tourist offices. It would be pointless to list every one, and you'd do best to contact the Swiss tourist office in your home country for details.

The passes above are targeted at foreigners staying less than 30 days. If you intend being in Switzerland for longer, you'd do well to investigate the outstandingly good-value domestic **half-fare travel card** (*Halbtax-Abo, Abonnement demi-tarif, Abbonamento metà prezzo*), which costs Fr.150 for a year and lets you buy unlimited first- or second-class tickets at a fifty percent discount across virtually the entire network. This is such a popular deal for the locals that most published offers, and nearly all automatic ticket machines, are marked for full price (1/1) and half price (1/2): the card is certain

Swiss passes – some sample prices

The handful of sample prices given here for Swiss, Youth and Flexi passes are for **second class** travel. Add about 50 percent to travel first class. "Individual" means the price per person travelling alone; "saver" means the price for each person when there are two or more travelling together (maximum of five). Full price-lists are at ⓦwww.myswitzerland.com.

	£	US$	Fr.
Swiss Pass			
– 4 consecutive days, individual	107	160	240
– 4 consecutive days, saver	91	136	204
– 8 consecutive days, saver	128	192	289
– 15 consecutive days, individual	182	270	410
– 15 consecutive days, saver	155	230	349
Swiss Youth Pass			
– 4 consecutive days	80	120	180
– 8 consecutive days	113	169	255
Swiss Flexi Pass			
– 3 days/month, individual	102	156	230
– 3 days/month, saver	87	132	196
– 5 days/month, individual	142	212	320
– 8 days/month, saver	159	240	357
Swiss Transfer Ticket	51	76	114
Swiss Card	73	110	165

to repay itself. You need a passport-sized photo to buy it. Once you have one, you can then buy day-card add-ons for Fr.52 to give free unlimited second-class travel nationwide for that day; multi-day add-ons, valid for any six days, cost Fr.260. Full details are at ⓦwww.rail.ch.

Inter-Rail and Eurail

An **Inter-Rail pass** (ⓦwww.inter-rail.co.uk) is only available to European residents, and comes in under-26 and over-26 versions. The pass covers 28 countries (including Turkey and Morocco) grouped together in zones; Switzerland falls in Zone C, along with Austria, Germany and Denmark. It's available for 12 or 22 days (one zone only) or a month (one or more zones). A 12-day pass for one zone costs £119/169 for under/over-26s. Online purchase is discounted, as are trains within the UK (including London–Paris by Eurostar) and cross-Channel ferries.

A **Eurailpass** (ⓦwww.eurail.com) – for non-EU residents only – allows first-class train travel in 17 countries, including Switzerland (on SBB main routes only; some smaller lines give discounts, detailed on the website). The pass, only buyable outside Europe, is available for 15 days (US$588), 21 days (US$762), or 1, 2 or 3 months. A **Eurailpass Youth** is valid for second-class travel for under-26s; 2–5 people travelling together can get a joint **Eurailpass Saver**. A **Eurailpass Flexi** is good for 10 days' (US$694) or 15 days' (US$914) first-class travel within a two-month period, and has under-26 (**Eurailpass Youth Flexi**) and group (**Eurailpass Saver Flexi**) versions. Finally, the **Eurail Selectpass** lets you travel in 3, 4 or 5 adjoining countries for either 5, 6, 8, 10 or 15 days within a two-month period; a 5-day pass over 3 countries costs US$356. It also comes in under-26 (**Eurail Selectpass Youth**) and group (**Eurail Selectpass Saver**) versions.

A **Euro-Domino** pass (ⓦwww.raileurope.co.uk) – for those who've lived in the EU for at least six months – is valid on major Swiss lines for between 3 and 8 days' travel within a one-month period; for a 5-day pass, under/over-26s pay £64/84.

Timetables and information

The national **timetable** (*Kursbuch* or *Fahrplan*, *indicateur* or *horaire*, *orario*) costs

Fr.16, covering all rail, boat and cable-car services in one book (blue) and all bus services in another book (yellow); most main stations keep a public copy to consult. You can buy it at just about all stations, where you'll also find piles of leaflets and free pocket timetables covering the local region. Check times carefully if you're travelling in December, when the timetable is revamped each year. The complete timetable, including fare details, precise connection timings and full information down to platform numbers and the kind of onboard refreshments available on each train is in English at ⓦwww.rail.ch. You can ask ticket-office staff how to get from any station to any other and they'll print out an itinerary for you showing exact connection times. The national train enquiry number is ☏0900 300 300.

Train and bus timetables posted on station hoardings are always colour coded: the yellow timetable always shows departures (*Abfahrt*, *départ*, *partenza*), while the white one always indicates arrivals (*Ankunft*, *arrivée*, *arrivo*). It's easy, though, to mix up train and bus timetables, which look alike: check in the top corner for the relevant pictogram.

Trains are identified on the timetable by an alphabet soup of initials, which denote where, when and how fast they go. **CIS** are tilting express "Pendolino" trains run by Cisalpino between Switzerland and Italy; **ICE** are Inter-City Express services between Switzerland and Germany; **TGV** are high-speed trains between Switzerland and France. Sleeper services are either **CNL** (CityNightLine) or **EN** (EuroNight). Day trains between major European cities – that may stop at only two or three places in Switzerland – are denoted **EC** (EuroCity). If you're holding an ordinary ticket or train pass, all of these are free of any surcharges within Swiss borders; you must pay supplements only if you cross an international frontier, or if the train is marked in the timetable with an R in a square box. In these cases, a seat reservation costs a few francs.

Within Switzerland, **IC** InterCity expresses cross the country stopping at larger cities only; those marked **ICN** tilt round corners for extra speed. **IR** InterRegio trains ply between regions, stopping at a few more places in between. **RX** RegioExpress services are one step slower. Something misleadingly described as a *Schnellzug*, train direct or *treno diretto* goes from village to village; while a *Regionalzug*, *train regional* or *treno regionale* stops at every haystack on the way.

Platforms are marked out in **sectors**, from A to D: beware of truncated one- or two-carriage local trains departing from Platform 3 Sector A while you're standing 150m away at Platform 3 Sector D tapping your watch. For mainline services, the PA announcement (and a detailed plan in blue posted next to the timetable boards) tells you which sectors the first- and second-class carriages will arrive at, saving you running up and down the train. Sometimes two short trains will depart in opposite directions from different sectors of the same platform.

Stations and services

It takes something of a leap of faith to realize, but in Switzerland a **train station** (*Bahnhof*, *gare*, *stazione*) isn't the dregs-of-the-earth place it might be in another coun-

try. Many Swiss stations harbour genuinely good restaurants alongside their formica-table buffets – going out for a nice meal at the station is a new experience for most visitors – and many also shelter the only shops and supermarkets in their town open after 6pm. Where supermarkets and kiosks stop, large 24-hour vending machines take over, quite often dispensing loaves of bread, salami and cartons of milk in addition to Coke and chocolate.

Just about the only people you'll see lugging suitcases or rucksacks through train compartments are foreigners. Most Swiss register their heavy bags at the station **baggage counter** before boarding (for around Fr.10 per item per journey): SBB's team of baggage-handlers take the strain, and the bags are ready for collection at your destination station later that day. This is a great service to take advantage of if you want to see a lot of things in a day but don't fancy carting your gear from locker to locker.

Airport check-in at the train station

This is the outward-bound flipside of the "Fly Rail Baggage" incoming service (see box p.12), and is just as useful, letting you check your bags in ahead of time for Fr.20 per item at any one of 126 Swiss train stations, from where they're transported independently to your departure airport and loaded onto your flight; you don't have to lay a finger on them until the baggage-reclaim carousel in your home airport.

You'll need to show the station staff your flight ticket (with an "OK" reservation), and – most importantly – a train ticket or pass to prove that you'll be travelling to the airport by train; otherwise, you pay a surcharge of Fr.30 extra per item. Virtually all flights out of Zürich and Geneva are served, but all US carriers and all easyJet flights are **excluded**, as are all flights out of Bern, Lugano and Sion. If you're flying out of Basel, check with the station staff in advance or call ☏0900 300 300 to see if your flight is served. Bulky items such as bicycles are excluded.

At the same time, and for no extra cost, you can (at certain stations) make a seat reservation and receive a **boarding card**, cutting out all hassle at the airport and letting you proceed directly to your departure gate. This service is available – on production of your passport – at fifty major stations, including Arosa, Basel SBB, Bern, Biel/Bienne, Chur, Davos Dorf and Platz, Fribourg, Geneva, Interlaken Ost and West, Klosters, Konstanz, Lausanne, Locarno, Lugano, Luzern, Montreux, Neuchâtel, Schaffhausen, Sierre, Sion, St Gallen, St Moritz, Vevey and Zürich HB.

You can do a station check-in at the **earliest** 24 hours before your flight departure. A multilingual pamphlet "Check-in and Fly Rail Baggage", available from most train stations, has a list showing the **latest** possible check-in times for all 126 stations, which vary depending on which airport you're flying out of and what your scheduled take-off time is: for a morning or lunchtime take-off, you may need to check your bags in at the station the day before to ensure they reach the airport in time. Full information is at ☏0900 300 300, 🌐www.rail.ch.

You can find many convenient facilities at just about all train stations. **Luggage lockers** are universal, found at all but the tiniest country halts, and normally come in two or three sizes: average prices are Fr.3 for a small one (into which you can just about stuff a full rucksack), Fr.5 for a large and – only at main stations – Fr.8 for an extra-large. Once they're locked, you can open them only once. Your gear is safe in them for several days without a problem, but – especially at the large city stations – after a week or two staff may open the locker, impound your property at the left-luggage office, and require you to pay through the nose to get it back. Ask at the information counters beforehand what the time limit is. Access to lockers may also be prohibited between midnight and 5am.

Virtually every station also has a staffed **left-luggage office** (Fr.5 per item per day), invariably open daily for long hours, and often combined with a **lost-property office**, a **bike-rental counter** (see p.69), and the **airport check-in** service (see box p.35).

Train-station **lost property** offices are linked by computer, so they can all run a nationwide check for you; it costs Fr.5 to retrieve a small item, Fr.20 for a large or heavy piece. Other services you'll find in all stations are **bureaux de change** and money-wiring facilities, invariably spotless toilets (free or Fr.1–1.50) and, in city stations, equally spotless shower cubicles (Fr.10) – the last two often run by the oddly named **McClean** company.

Buses

Backing up the train network is a yet more comprehensive system of **buses**, which get to every single village and hamlet in the country, covering ground – such as in the high mountains or deep countryside – left untouched by the trains. Many travellers don't even consider using the buses, imagining them to be too slow or too much hassle to figure out; this is a shame, since buses are not there to compete with the trains but to complement them, and they can get you to all kinds of out-of-the-way places – and some essential ones – quickly and easily. In addition, all Swiss travel passes are valid for travel on buses as well as trains (a plus-point over the limited-validity European train passes).

Bus stations are nearly always located in the forecourt of train stations. Even more handily, the bus and train **timetables** are co-ordinated together, ensuring watertight connections from one to the other. Perhaps uniquely in Europe, Swiss buses stick to their schedules with utter reliability.

Most long-distance bus-lines are operated, in an endearing remnant of pioneer times, as yellow **postbuses**, with *Die Post*, *La Poste* or *La Posta* on the side. Various regions have their own local bus companies, either instead of or as well as postbuses, but all are equally reliable. Switzerland's largest postbus stations are at Sion and Chur, both set amidst mountainous but well-populated landscapes too difficult for trains to access. Note that some longer, more difficult or direct bus-routes – such as over the Alpine passes – require either advance **seat reservation** and/or a small supplement of Fr.5–10 to be paid: check in the timetables or with bus-station staff ahead of time.

For a flat fee of Fr.12 you can send **unaccompanied baggage** ahead by postbus to a post office for picking up later – a particularly handy service for hikers using buses to reach remote countryside trails and wanting to walk unencumbered.

Boats

All of Switzerland's bigger lakes, and many of its smaller ones, are crossed by regular **ferry services**. Most run only during the summer season – which can vary, but at its broadest covers the period from April to October – and are primarily pleasure-oriented, duplicating routes which can be covered more cheaply and quickly by rail. However, if you have the time, a leisurely cruise through the Alpine foothills to Interlaken, for example, or between the three lakes of Neuchâtel, Morat and Biel/Bienne, or from shore to shore along the length of Lake Geneva, beats the equivalent train journeys hands down. Apart from on Lago Maggiore (which is mostly in Italy), travel by boat is covered by all Swiss travel passes (see p.32). The **Swiss Boat Pass** (Fr.35), valid for a year, knocks fifty percent off fares on fourteen of Switzerland's bigger lakes; the **Swiss Family Boat Pass** (Fr.50) has the same benefits and also lets the kids travel free.

Most of Switzerland's **rivers** are too young and fast-flowing to be navigable. However, boats ply a scenic, wooded section of the **Rhône** west of Geneva before the French border. Northeast of Biel/Bienne, there's a lovely stretch of the **Aare** – which runs past an island stork colony – navigable until Solothurn. Best of all, and one of Europe's great river journeys, is the uniquely peaceful part of the **Rhine** between Konstanz (or its neighbour Kreuzlingen) and the falls at Schaffhausen, the sole stretch of that river that is free from any kind of bankside industry. The falls merit a journey in themselves.

Mountain transport

It's inevitable that at some point during your stay you'll use transport to get to the top of a **mountain**. There are few areas or ranges that have no means of getting to the top of at least one local peak, and even relatively unsung Swiss summits can be breathtakingly beautiful. Most peaks that can be accessed by public transport also feature at least one mountain-top restaurant or terrace café for refreshment and relaxation; if you need solitude and tranquillity you generally have to hike away from the summit station.

The train/boat/cable-car timetable lists every funicular, cable-car, gondola and chairlift in the country, all of which are operated by small local transport companies, not the SBB. Fares – except on the flagship tourist routes such as to the Jungfraujoch or the Titlis – aren't excessive, and are usually discounted a little (25 percent is common) if you hold a Swiss travel pass. Where timetables don't show exact timings (often because departures may be continuous), they at least note the first **ascent** (*Bergfahrt, montée, salita*) of the day, the frequency of service, and the final **descent** (*Talfahrt, descente, discesa*) from the mountain in the evening. On the high peaks you may have to leave the top station in mid-afternoon, say 3–4pm, if you want to reach the valley without hiking or skiing part or all of the way down.

Cable-car *Luftseilbahn, téléphérique, funivia.*
Chairlift *Sesselbahn, télésiège, seggiovia.*
Draglift *Schlepplift, téléski, sciovia.*
Funicular *Standseilbahn, funiculaire, funicolare.*
Gondola *Gondelbahn, télécabine, cabinovia.*
Rack railway *Zahnradbahn, train à crémaillère, ferrovia à cremagliera.*

Best mountain excursions

Arosa p.508. A stunning journey up by road or rail from Chur.

Cardada p.563. Within minutes, you can leave the lakeside bustle of Locarno behind for the cool pine forest on the slopes above.

Gornergrat p.363. Rack railway from Zermatt that crawls way up to view the Alpine giants close-to.

Jungfraujoch p.302. Flagship route from Interlaken up to Europe's highest train station, at 3454m.

Pilatus p.387. The steepest rack-railway in the world climbs high above Luzern.

Rigi p.401. Alpine giant looming above Lake Luzern, notable for its ease of access at, among other points, Arth-Goldau, a rail junction on the Zürich–Luzern–Lugano main line.

Rochers de Naye p.164. Prominent rocky summit perched high above Montreux and Lake Geneva.

Schilthorn p.295. Superbly scenic cable-car trip above Interlaken – quicker, cheaper and more spectacular than the Jungfraujoch.

Schynige Platte p.290. Another outstanding route from Interlaken, by rack railway up to all-round panoramic views over lakes, towns and mountains.

Titlis p.400. Snowbound giant south of Luzern, with a rotating cable-car up to the summit.

Trümmelbach falls p.291. Take a detour from the Schilthorn route to this stunning set of waterfalls that have carved their way through the rockface.

City transport

The most common form of transport within cities is **buses**, whether the ordinary petrol-driven kind or electric-powered **trolley buses**. Many cities also have **trams**, and a few hillside ones have a **funicular** or two, but the only true **metro** system is in and around Lausanne. Larger cities have dense networks of suburban commuter trains (**S-Bahn** in German, **RER** in

French), which may extend to neighbouring towns.

Within each city or local area, all transport is integrated under one **ticketing system**, with no limitations on changing from buses to trams or even some boats within the time validity of your ticket. The Swiss Pass and Swiss Flexi Pass cover free travel within 35 cities across the country (listed on the card); tourist-oriented regional passes give free travel within their allotted area; and city tourist offices sell various **day passes** of their own giving free or discounted travel, which can be excellent value. You must always hold a valid ticket before boarding; see p.29 for more. Ticket inspections are common within cities.

There are plenty of metered **taxis** sharking around every town and city in the country, but given the density of public transport they're pretty much unnecessary, and besides you need to be on a Swiss salary to afford them: flagfalls of Fr.6, plus per-kilometre rates of up to Fr.3, are normal.

Driving

Driving obviously gives you extra freedom to explore nooks and crannies that others zip past without stopping. Switzerland's road network is comprehensive and well-planned, and although the mountainous terrain can make for some circuitous routes there is, of course, the compensation of impressively scenic – if sometimes hair-raising – mountain drives. However, Swiss transport policy means that cars are slowly being given the squeeze, with tough city parking regulations and strict law enforcement.

Driving your own vehicle

Minimum driving age is 18, international licences are recognized for one year's driving in Switzerland and, as across Europe, **third-party insurance** is compulsory. It's obligatory to carry both a red warning triangle and the registration documents of the vehicle. If you intend driving on Swiss motorways, you have to stick a **vignette** inside your windscreen. These cost Fr.40 for any vehicle up to 3.5 tonnes, are bought most easily from the customs officials when you first cross the border (also at post offices and petrol stations), and remain valid until January 31 of the following year. Trailers or caravans must

have their own, additional vignette. Getting caught without one lays you open to a Fr.100 fine. However, it's quite easy to avoid motorways altogether and stick to ordinary main roads, which are free and – outside urban centres at least – reasonably fast.

Motoring organizations

Australia AAA ☏02/6247 7311, ⓦwww.aaa.asn.au.

Canada CAA ☏613/247-0117, ⓦwww.caa.ca.

Ireland AA ☏01/617 9988, ⓦwww.aaireland.ie.

New Zealand AA ☏09/377 4660, ⓦwww.nzaa.co.nz.

Switzerland TCS ☏022 417 27 27, ⓦwww.tcs.ch.

UK AA ☏0800/444 500, ⓦwww.theaa.co.uk; RAC ☏0800/550 055, ⓦwww.rac.co.uk.

US AAA ☏1-800/222-4357, ⓦwww.aaa.com.

Renting a car

Car rental in Switzerland can be nastily expensive. You can significantly cut costs by renting in advance from the big international agencies; they all cover Switzerland, with offices in all major towns, most minor ones, and at all airports. **One-way rentals** are simple to arrange, although they may attract a handling fee. Hertz has a deal with SBB whereby you can reserve, pick up or drop off cars at any of 700 train stations across the country for a small surcharge. There are dozens of local rental companies in most towns, usually operating out of ordinary petrol stations or garages, with mostly trustworthy cars at prices that undercut the big agencies' walk-in rates: find them in the phonebook under *Autovermietungen* or *Mietwagen*, *location des voitures*, *noleggio di automobili*.

To rent a car, you need a valid, clean UK, EU or international **driving licence** that you've held for more than a year. Minimum driver's age is 20 or 21, occasionally 25, depending on the rental company. All rental cars have the annual motorway vignette pre-paid and, in winter, are fitted with snow tyres, and supplied with snow-chains (and even a ski rack) for free.

Although it's usually no problem to drive **across borders** in most Swiss rental cars – for a jaunt from Montreux to Evian, say, or a day-trip from Lugano around Lake Como – you should always check the rules with your

Principal Swiss Alpine passes

There are 72 **Alpine passes** in Switzerland that are open to motor traffic, and hundreds more that are for hikers or cyclists only. We've given the names (in alternative languages where necessary) of the most important ones; their altitude above sea level; the approximate period during which the pass road (and any tunnel road) is open to traffic, barring significant weather disruption; and the main towns/regions on either side of the pass. Approach roads to all passes have large signboards displaying whether the pass, and the high-altitude towns or resorts on the way, are **open** (*offen, ouvert, aperto*) or **closed** (*geschlossen, fermé, chiuso*).

Albula/Alvra 2312m; June–Oct; Tiefencastel GR, La Punt GR
Bernina 2328m; all year; St Moritz GR, Poschiavo GR
Brünig 1008m; all year; Sarnen OW, Brienz BE
Croix 1778m; all year; Villars VD, Les Diablerets VD
Flüela 2383m; June–Oct; Davos GR, Zernez GR
Forclaz 1526m; all year; Martigny VS, Chamonix (France)
Fuorn/Ofen 2149m; all year; Zernez GR, Val Müstair GR
Furka 2431m; June–Oct; Gletsch VS, Andermatt UR
Grand-St-Bernard 2469m; pass June–Oct, tunnel all year; Martigny VS, Aosta (Italy)
Grimsel 2165m; June–Oct; Gletsch VS, Meiringen BE
Jaun 1509m; all year; Bulle FR, Simmental BE
Julier/Güglia 2284m; all year; Tiefencastel GR, St Moritz GR
Klausen 1948m; June–Oct; Altdorf UR, Linthal GL
Lukmanier/Lucomagno 1914m; May–Nov; Disentis/Mustér GR, Biasca TI
Maloja 1815m; all year; St Moritz GR, Val Bregaglia GR
Mosses 1445m; all year; Aigle VD, Château d'Oex VD
Nufenen/Novena 2478m; June–Sept; Ulrichen VS, Airolo TI
Oberalp 2044m; June–Oct; Andermatt UR, Disentis/Mustér GR
Pillon 1546m; all year; Les Diablerets VD, Gstaad BE
San Bernadino 2065m; pass June–Oct, tunnel all year; Thusis GR, Bellinzona TI
St Gotthard/San Gottardo 2109m; pass May–Oct, tunnel all year; Göschenen UR, Airolo TI
Simplon/Sempione 2005m; all year; Brig VS, Domodossola (Italy)
Splügen 2113m; May–Oct; Thusis GR, Chiavenna (Italy)
Susten 2224m; June–Oct; Meiringen BE, Andermatt UR

rental company in advance: Switzerland is not in the EU, although it's surrounded by EU countries. Border controls can be stringent, especially at heavily used crossing points; you'd do well to be certain, before you depart Switzerland, that you're not going to inadvertently break customs regulations or passport/visa requirements on your way back in.

Car rental agencies

Avis UK ☎0870/606 0100, ⓦwww.avis.co.uk; Ireland ☎01/605 7500, ⓦwww.avis.ie; US ☎1-800/331-1084, Canada ☎1-800/272-5871, ⓦwww.avis.com; Australia ☎13 63 33, ⓦwww.avis.com.au; NZ ☎09/526 2847, ⓦwww.avis.co.nz; Switzerland ☎0848 811 818, ⓦwww.avis.ch.
Budget UK ☎0800/181 181, ⓦwww.budget.co.uk; Ireland ☎0903/27711, ⓦwww.budget.ie; US ☎1-800/527-0700, ⓦwww.budget.com; Australia ☎1300/362 848, ⓦwww.budget.com.au; NZ ☎09/976 2222, ⓦwww.budget.co.nz.
Europcar UK ☎0870/607 5000, ⓦwww.europcar.co.uk; Ireland ☎01/614 2800, ⓦwww.europcar.ie; US & Canada ☎1-877/940 6900, ⓦwww.europcar.com; Switzerland ☎0848 808 099, ⓦwww.europcar.ch.
Hertz UK ☎0870/848 4848, ⓦwww.hertz.co.uk; Ireland ☎01/676 7476, ⓦwww.hertz.ie; US ☎1-800/654-3001, Canada ☎1-800/263-0600, ⓦwww.hertz.com; Australia ☎13 30 39; NZ

⊤0800/654 321; Switzerland ⊤0848 822 020,
ⓦwww.hertz.ch.
Holiday Autos UK ⊤0870/400 0099, Ireland
⊤01/872 9366, US ⊤1-800/422-7737, Australia
⊤1300/554 432, New Zealand ⊤0800/144 040,
Switzerland ⊤056 675 75 85,
ⓦwww.holidayautos.com.
National UK ⊤0870/536 5365, ⓦwww.
nationalcar.co.uk; US ⊤1-800/227-7368,
ⓦwww.nationalcar.com; Australia ⊤13 10 45,
ⓦwww.nationalcar.com.au; NZ ⊤0800/800 115,
ⓦwww.nationalcar.co.nz.
Thrifty UK ⊤01494/751 600, ⓦwww.thrifty.
co.uk; Ireland ⊤1800/515 800, ⓦwww.thrifty.ie;
US ⊤1-800/367-2277, ⓦwww.thrifty.com;
Australia ⊤1300/367 227, ⓦwww.thrifty.com.au,
NZ ⊤09/309 0111, ⓦwww.thrifty.co.nz.

On the road

Switzerland and Liechtenstein drive on the
right, **seatbelts** are compulsory for all, and
penalties for **drink driving** are tough (one
glass of beer has you on the limit). For safety
reasons, always drive with **dipped head-
lights**, day and night. Beware of driving with
sunglasses on, since there are hundreds of
road tunnels, plenty of them single-bore
with one lane in each direction and no central divider: you can be plunged from sunshine into scary blackness with little warning.
Usefully, all tunnels have a small plaque at
their entrance stating their length. If you're in
a traffic jam in a tunnel, waiting for temporary
traffic lights at roadworks or at level-crossing
barriers, copy the locals and **switch your
engine off**.

Swiss motorways/freeways are **signed in
green**, while main roads are signed in blue;
it's common to see a green sign and a blue
sign to the same place pointing in opposite
directions. A motorway (*Autobahn,
autoroute, autostrada*) has two sets of identi-
fiers, the national system (N) and the pan-
European system (E): the main route through
the Gotthard tunnel, for example, doubles as
the N2/E35. **Speed limits** are 120kph
(75mph) on motorways, 80kph (50mph) on
main roads, 50kph (30mph) in urban areas,
and 30kph (18mph) on speed-bumped residential streets. There are dozens of cameras,
radars and laser traps around the country to
catch speeders: if you're caught doing 5kph
above, expect a **spot fine** of Fr.40; if you
were 20kph above, expect Fr.200; any more
and you'll be taken to court.

At junctions, yellow diamonds painted on
the road show who has **priority**; if in doubt,
always let trams and buses go first, and give
way to traffic coming from your right. On
gradients, vehicles heading **uphill** have priority over those coming down; some narrow
mountain tracks have controlled times for
ascent and descent. If you hear an outrageously loud horn or klaxon sounding on
country lanes or twisting mountain roads, it
means that a **postbus** is approaching: it
always has priority, up or down, so get out
of the way. In cities, it's forbidden to overtake
trams when they're at their stops. In the
winter, signs indicate where **snow chains**
are necessary (it's a good idea to practise fitting and removing them beforehand).

You can find **fuel** in just about every village
in the country. **Unleaded** fuel (*Bleifrei, sans
plomb, senza piombo*; green pumps) is the
standard. Filling stations in more remote
places, such as mountain resorts, charge
much more than those on lowland routes
easily accessible by tankers. Unstaffed 24-
hour automatic filling stations – where you
feed cash or a credit card into a machine –
are cheapest of all. Super-plus unleaded is
widely available (also green pumps), as is
diesel (black pumps). Leaded fuel (red
pumps) is less common.

You might have unexpected problems with
navigation, since motorway signs often
show the names of distant Alpine passes as
general indicators of direction, rather than
naming the next major town: if you want to
drive on the *autoroute* from Geneva to
Montreux, for instance, you'll have to follow
signs to "Simplon" and "Grand-St-Bernard",
since these are the passes that lie at the end
of the road, hundreds of kilometres beyond
Montreux (there are no signs to Montreux
until you're almost upon it). Similarly, as far
away as Zürich and Luzern, the main motorway heading south is simply signed
"Gotthard", rather than naming wayside
towns like Schwyz or regions such as Uri.
However, signs to specific towns are always
in the language of that town: Geneva is
always "Genève", never "Genf" or "Ginevra".
As for crossing the language border, there'll
just come a point speeding between
Fribourg and Bern when you'll notice that
the exits, previously marked "Sortie", suddenly become "Ausfahrt".

For **breakdown assistance**, call ⊤140.

Parking

Parking in Switzerland is hellish, and can be very limited and prohibitively expensive. In cities across the country, full car parks will quite often harbour queues of cars, their engines off, drivers waiting – sometimes for over an hour – for the next person to finish their shopping and so liberate a space.

Unlimited-stay covered **parking garages** are signposted in all cities. Prices can be outrageous: Fr.30/day or more in central Geneva and Zürich, an average Fr.15/day around the country, and rarely less than Fr.1/hour anywhere. Out-of-town car parks, often located near motorway exits and tagged **P+R** (Park and Ride), are sometimes free or discounted; they're always served by a bus or tram heading into the town centre, for which you must pay.

Onstreet parking and open **car parks** are colour-coded, as in much of the rest of Europe. Spaces delineated with white lines – the **White Zone** – are most common, controlled either by individual meters or, more usually, a prominently marked central pay-point or *Zentrale Parkuhr, Parcomètre collectif, Parchimetro collettivo*. These take coins only; costs can vary from Fr.0.50/hour in small towns to Fr.4/hour in cities. In most cases, White Zone spaces are time-limited. If your space is numbered, press the corresponding button on the machine (or key the

number in), then pay. Sometimes that's enough; other times, you must press another button to get a ticket to display in your car. If your space isn't numbered, then just pay and display your ticket. Outside the hours posted on the pay-point, and where there isn't a machine at all (in a small village, say), White Zone spaces are free, unless there's a sign reserving them – as in *nur für Kunden*, "only for customers" of a particular shop nearby.

You can park in **Blue Zone** spaces if you have a special parking disc (available for free from tourist offices, car rental agencies, police stations and banks). Spin the wheel round to show your time of arrival and leave it on your dashboard: this gives you 90 minutes' free parking if you arrive between 8am and 11.30am or between 1.30pm and 6pm. If you arrive between 11.30am and 1.30pm, you're safe until 2.30pm; if you arrive after 6pm, you're OK until 9am next day. Rarer **Red Zone** spaces are free for up to 15 hours, as long as you display the disc. Spaces marked in **yellow** indicate private parking for, say, staff of a nearby company or perhaps guests of a local hotel; the only way to know is to ask.

Illegal parking of any kind is much less tolerated in Switzerland than in its neighbours, and fines of Fr.50–100 for minor transgressions are common.

Accommodation

As a general rule, it's no problem to turn up in any Swiss town at any time of the year and find a room. With the popularity of the bigger cities and resorts, though, booking ahead – especially in the summer and winter high seasons – is strongly advised. This saves you the effort of searching once you arrive, and means you won't be forced into spending over budget. Despite the fact that Geneva and Zürich suffer from high hotel prices, Fr.90–120 will buy you some kind of double room in any town in the country.

Compared with other European countries, Swiss accommodation is expensive but nearly always excellent, conscientiously run and hospitable. Tourist offices always have lists of hotels, hostels, campsites and apartments in their area, and outside office hours they normally have a display board on the street with details of the local hotels, often with a courtesy phone. In many cases you'll find these boards at train stations as well. All towns and cities, and many villages, display distinctive **yellow-and-brown signposts** directing drivers to named hotels; you're allowed to drive to the door to load and unload, even in a pedestrian-only zone.

Swiss hoteliers, campsite managers and hostel staff almost always speak English, but in the unlikely event that you can't make yourself understood, the local tourist office will make a booking for you, either for free or for a small fee. It's rare to be able to negotiate **multi-night bargain rates** over the counter, but many tourist offices run deals throughout the year that can save plenty if you book three or seven nights in a row. Wherever you check in, you should always

ask for a free **guest card** (*Gästekarte, carte des visiteurs, tessera di soggiorno*), as this perk for overnight visitors can give substantial discounts for local attractions and transport.

Bear in mind the fluctuating **high and low seasons** between lowland and highland resorts, described in detail on p.11.

Some towns quote accommodation prices **per person**, while others quote prices **per room**. Our code system (see box) standardizes them across the board, but you'd do well to ascertain what the terms are if you ask for prices direct from a hotel or tourist office.

Hotels

Swiss **hotels** are among the best in the world, with renowned high standards of service. Value-for-money is the motive force behind the hotel industry, rather than cost-cutting, so you'll find that even the cheapest hotels offer rooms that are perfectly comfortable, clean and respectable, if a little pricey compared to dingier bottom-end establishments in other countries.

Accommodation price codes

All the hostels and hotels in this book have been graded according to the following **price codes**, which indicate the price for the cheapest double room available during high season. For dormitories in hostels or mountain inns, the price per bed in Swiss francs has been quoted. Single rooms generally cost between sixty and eighty percent of the double-room rate. Bear in mind that an establishment graded, for example, as a ❸ may also have more comfortable rooms at ❹ prices, and/or may have different rates for the summer and winter peak seasons, reflected by a range (eg ❸–❺).

❶ under Fr.100	❹ Fr.200–250	❼ Fr.350–400
❷ Fr.100–150	❺ Fr.250–300	❽ Fr.400–500
❸ Fr.150–200	❻ Fr.300–350	❾ over Fr.500

At the least expensive level, what makes a difference in price is whether a room contains a shower or an **ensuite bathroom**, since these can add Fr.20 or more to the rate as compared with rooms where the shared shower and toilet are down the corridor.

Breakfast is included in the room price at virtually all hotels apart from the very cheapest and the most expensive; what you get varies with the hotel's classification. One thing to watch out for is that in many mountain resorts, hotel prices quoted for the summer season are **bed and breakfast**, while those quoted for the winter season tend to be **half board** (ie bed plus two meals – normally breakfast and an evening meal après-ski); we've marked this differentiation clearly in the guide text where relevant, but to be certain you should check what you're paying for at the time of reservation. Note that a hotel advertising itself as "**garni**" has no restaurant, and serves only breakfast to its overnight guests.

In the accommodation listings throughout the guide, rooms in every hotel reviewed are ensuite unless mentioned otherwise.

Hotel groups

Aside from international brands such as Best Western or The Leading Hotels Of The World, there are a number of Swiss **hotel groups** which, if you can fight your way through their marketing blurb, can be useful for seeking out establishments with particular features that appeal to you, whether they be top-notch five-star quality (Swiss Deluxe), historic buildings and locations (Romantik), complete quiet (Silence), or just plain, good-value inexpensive accommodation (E&G).

E&G Swiss Budget Hotels Ⓦ www.rooms.ch. Zero- to three-star places (180 of them) off the beaten track, most with character, ranging from small city hotels to dorms and mountain lodges. E&G stands for *einfach und gemütlich*, roughly "simple and cosy".

Idyll Hotels Ⓦ www.idyll.ch. Peaceful country hotels, two- and three-star, run on ecologically sound lines.

Kidshotels Ⓦ www.kidshotels.ch. Small group of family-friendly hotels, most in mountain resorts, featuring babysitting and childminding, children's menus, entertainment and more.

Minotel Suisse Ⓦ www.minotel.ch. Wide-ranging group of 115 small, family-run, two- to four-star hotels in locations from city centres to rural villages. Useful central booking facility online.

Romantik Ⓦ www.romantikhotels.com. High-quality grouping of 23 personally run and managed three- and four-star hotels (none of them chain- or corporate-owned). All are historic properties in their own right, often architecturally unique, placing a focus squarely on pamperment amidst characterful surroundings.

Silence Hotels Ⓦ www.silence.ch. Local arm of the international Relais du Silence chain (Ⓦwww.relais-du-silence.com), concentrating on providing tranquillity, leisure and relaxation in its 32 hotels, all in countryside locations far from traffic and towns.

Swiss Deluxe Hotels Ⓦ www.swissdeluxehotels.com. Exclusive group of 35 uncompromisingly luxurious hotels, all of them five-star and most of them internationally famous names.

Hostels and "backpackers"

If you're travelling on a budget, a **hostel** or a "**backpacker**" is likely to be your accommodation of choice, whether you're youthful or not. They can often be extremely good value, and offer clean and comfortable dorms as well as a choice of rooms (doubles and sometimes singles) that can often undercut normal hotel prices. Both city and country locations can get very full between June and September, when you should book in advance.

There are two main hostel associations in Switzerland. The 70-odd properties of **Swiss Youth Hostels** (Ⓦ www.youthhostel.ch) are the only ones to use the specific term "youth hostel" (*Jugendherberge, auberge de jeunesse, albergo/ostello della gioventù*), and are listed in the fold-out map and brochure entitled "Know-How", widely available at tourist offices. They're all affiliated to the Hostelling International network (aka IYHF, International Youth Hostel Federation) and are referred to throughout this guide as "**HI hostels**". They're of a universally high standard, although they tend to be better choices in countryside and mountain locations than in cities, where they are quite often located awkwardly far from town centres and can suffer from an atmosphere of institutionality. Most are closed for cleaning between roughly 10am and 6pm, and lock their doors sometime between 10pm and midnight (although checked-in guests can use entry systems to get in later at many hostels). Almost all close down in the low seasons: spring and autumn in the mountains, winter in the cities. Prices vary, covering the range Fr.20–34 (average Fr.28) for a dorm bed including breakfast and bedding. Extras such as kitchens for guest use and TV rooms are common, and evening meals, where available, cost a bargain Fr.12.50 or so. If you're not already an HI member (see below for contacts), you pay Fr.6 extra per night, or you can get annual membership while in Switzerland at any affiliated hostel for Fr.33, or Fr.22 for under-18s (membership is also automatic after any six nights of paying the supplement). All accept Internet reservations, and many take online bookings.

A rival grouping of independent hostels goes under the name **Swiss Backpackers** (ⓦwww.backpacker.ch). These lively places – referred to throughout this guide as "**SB hostels**" – are less institutional than HI hostels, often in prime locations in the centres of cities and resorts, and priced competitively (average about Fr.27). Most are busy, sociable, resourceful, laid-back places in the mould of backpacker joints everywhere, with kitchen and/or cheap restaurant attached, Internet access and no curfew. No membership is required. They're all listed – along with a load of spot-on practical information for getting around Switzerland on the cheap – in the detailed and very useful *Swiss Backpacker* newspaper, published two or three times a year and available for free in all SB hostels, most tourist offices and other prominent touristed places around the country.

Otherwise, pretty much all ski resorts have places offering **dormitory** accommodation, quite often hotels putting a converted annexe to good use. Such a dorm (*Touristenlager*, *Massenlager* or *Matratzenlager*, *dortoir*, *dormitorio*) may simply comprise one room with as many mattresses as possible squeezed into it side-by-side, each "bed" sold at bargain-basement prices. This is also the style of dorm accommodation in the 150 or so **Alpine huts** (see p.65) dotted around higher altitudes on or close to hiking trails (some of the more isolated ones may only be accessible to full-blown mountaineers), although bed prices tend to rise according to how remote the place is.

Hostel organizations

HI worldwide

Australia ☎02/9261 1111, ⓦwww.yha.org.au.
Canada ☎800/663-5777, ⓦwww.hihostels.ca.
England & Wales ☎0870/770 8868, ⓦwww.yha.org.uk.
New Zealand ☎03/379 9970, ⓦwww.yha.org.nz.
Northern Ireland ☎028/9032 4733, ⓦwww.hini.org.uk.
Republic of Ireland ☎01/830 4555, ⓦwww.anoige.ie.
Scotland ☎0870/155 3255, ⓦwww.syha.org.uk.
USA ☎202/783-6161, ⓦwww.hiayh.org.

Swiss groups

Swiss Backpackers (SB) ☎01 251 90 15, ⓦwww.backpacker.ch.
Swiss Youth Hostels (HI) ☎01 360 14 14, ⓦwww.youthhostel.ch.

Mountain inns

Whole books have been written about the joys of staying in a Swiss **mountain inn** (*Berghaus*, *Berggasthaus*, *Berggasthof* or *Berghotel*, *auberge de montagne*). The term is a tricky one to pin down, since it can refer to varying styles of simple rustic accommodation in a mountain setting. All, though, possess unique character, by dint both of their often spectacular isolated location (generally accessible only by foot, and then often involving long, hard hikes) and of their history – many are old Alpine farmhouses converted more than a century ago to meet the needs of the first holidaying British gentlemen and ladies on their summer tours of the Swiss Alps. Most have undergone some renovation over the intervening decades, but often not much: in general, you can expect an all-wood building in the local architectural style, with rustic decor throughout (window boxes, antiques on the sideboard, ticking grandfather clocks) and a uniquely relaxed, informal atmosphere of cosy communality. Hikers are the main clientele, and Swiss families may return season after season to hike their favourite paths, stay at their favourite *Berghaus*, and catch up on news from the family who owns and runs the place.

Nature, not amenities, is the focus: most *Berghäuser* maintain charmingly old-style bedrooms, with chunky old beds smothered under plump duvets, but very few offer private bathrooms, some may not have showers, and a handful have no hot water, or must generate their own electricity. Most have plenty of **dorm** places (*Massenlager* or *Matratzenlager*). Food is universally good: a *Berghaus* that skimps on sustenance is a contradiction in terms. Prices are not that much higher than elsewhere – an average Fr.130 for a double, or Fr.45 for a dorm place, both including dinner and breakfast – but you invariably have to pay in cash. It's customary to settle your bill the night before you depart.

Peaceful **Naturfreunde** hotels, run by the Swiss Federation of the Friends of Nature, fall midway between mountain inns and countryside hostels. Often not as remote as *Berghäuser*, they are mostly nonetheless historic buildings well away from beaten tracks, lovingly restored and maintained, and run by individuals with a passion for nature and the environment. About a hundred are scattered around the country; see ⓦwww.naturfreunde.ch for details.

Farm-stays, B&Bs and private rooms

Schlaf im Stroh, *Aventure sur la paille* or **Sleeping in the Hay** is a great way to get a feel for countryside life while guaranteeing accommodation at a fixed price wherever you are. Hundreds of farming families from all over the country have collaborated in the scheme, which runs from May to October only, each offering 10–15 places to sleep on straw in a barn (but as fresh and pristine a barn as you could wish for), sometimes also offering a handful of bed spaces within the farmhouse, and occasionally a place to pitch a tent or two. An overnight stay costs a flat Fr.20 including breakfast at all farms (less for children). You must bring your own sleeping bag if you want to sleep on straw. Your host family can also offer a range of services for modest fees, including putting together a picnic, serving a home-cooked dinner, providing horses, renting bikes and offering guided tours of the countryside around and about. There's full information, and the chance to order a booklet, at ⓦwww. abenteuer-stroh.ch.

A slightly less raw option for farm-stays are the 250 **Swiss Holiday Farms**, which offer full-blown apartments and rooms for daily or weekly rent on the farm, year-round. Full details are at ⓦwww.bauernhof-ferien.ch.

Bed and breakfasts, where you normally lodge in a room in someone's private house or farmhouse, are something of an innovation in Switzerland, but are becoming steadily more popular. Many tourist offices can give you details of B&Bs in their area, or you can consult the excellent, fully detailed lists online at ⓦwww.bnb.ch. Prices can vary quite a bit, depending on the house and the location, but a rough average is a bargain Fr.30–40 per person. You may also come across signs in rural and Alpine resort areas offering **rooms** in private houses (*Zimmer frei*, *chambres à louer*, *affitasi camere*). Again, these aren't as widespread as in other parts of Europe, but still can be less expensive, and much more welcoming, than hostel accommodation.

Chalets and apartments

Self-catering accommodation in holiday **chalets**, bungalows and apartments tends to be booked solid for entire summer and winter seasons. For chalets in places like Zermatt, Verbier, Gstaad and so on, you may have to book six months or more ahead. Most are let only for a week at a time. Interhome (ⓦwww.interhome.ch) is one of the largest and most efficient **international agencies**, dealing with more than 5000 chalets and apartments all over Switzerland, sleeping from two to twelve people. Prices vary tremendously depending on the property and the season, but start from a bargain Fr.16–18 per person per night. High-season bookings are for a minimum of seven nights, Saturday to Saturday, but in the low season you may be able to find properties available for three or four nights only. Booking months in advance ensures you get a full choice of places to stay, but if you leave things to a week before departure, some chalet owners will knock up to a third off their usual prices.

Camping

The typical Swiss **campsite** is clean, well equipped and well maintained. The higher the altitude the more limited the opening times: many close altogether outside the summer season (May or June until Sept or Oct). Just about every town and village in the country has a site or two, classified according to facilities from one to five stars. Average **charges** are Fr.6–8 per person, plus Fr.5–8 for a tent, and Fr.4–5 for a car. Booking ahead is recommended at all times of the year. The motoring organization **TCS** (Swiss Touring Club; ⓦ www.tcs.ch) runs a network of sites and is a particularly useful source of information, publishing a national map stocked by larger tourist offices that locates every campsite in the country (theirs and others), with contact details and opening months, as well as an intricately detailed Camping Guidebook (*Campingführer*, *Guide Camping*, *Guida dei Campeggi*), available in Swiss bookshops or from ⓔcpg@tcs.ch.

An inexpensive **international camping carnet** gives discounts at member sites, serves as identification and covers you for third-party insurance when camping. It's available in the UK from the AA, RAC and Camping & Caravanning Club (☏024/7669 4995, ⓦ www.campingandcaravanning-club.co.uk), and in North America from Family Campers and RVers (☏1-800/245-9755, ⓦ www.fcrv.org).

Camping rough, outside authorized sites, is formally prohibited by Swiss law, and you may well find yourself with a fine or worse if you try it in populated or cultivated areas, but in the mountain wilds – as long as you take care to clean up properly after yourself – it's hard to envisage how anyone could complain. Discretion and environmental respect are everything.

Eating and drinking

Switzerland is overshadowed by its near neighbours when it comes to food and drink, and yet the country nurtures a wide range of local cuisines, absorbing influences and styles from the diversity of French, German and Italian cooking while sticking close to its rural and Alpine roots. Extreme cultural decentralization means that if you dig below the surface of the national staples, you'll consistently come across delicious regional dishes relying on local ingredients and idiosyncratic styles of preparation that are unknown in the next canton, let alone elsewhere in Europe.

The Swiss take the joy of communal eating to heart, and many eateries rely on old-style rustic decor, wood beams, plenty of Swiss kitsch (cow-bells, alphorns and the like) and a cosy, hearty, family-like atmosphere – and that may just be for a lunchtime diner in Zürich's financial district. For the Swiss, much as for the Italians or the French, eating is an expression of local culture, and many people have no time or patience for **foreign cuisines**. High levels of immigration over the 1980s and 1990s have resulted in a host of Turkish, Arabic and, to a lesser extent, East Asian eateries opening up in towns and cities across the country, but they tend to be fast-food joints for wolfing down kebabs or

chow mein on the hoof rather than musing on the subtle flavours of the orient: you'll only find quality international cooking in Geneva, Zürich and possibly Bern.

Every town and village market groans with top-quality farm produce, much of it organically produced, and you're very likely to stumble on unpretentious family-run restaurants around the country that serve up inexpensive village fare to the locals. That's not to say that you can't eat like a gourmet in Switzerland – you can, and very easily – but your most memorable meals may well come from the simplest of kitchens and the most ordinary-looking of restaurants. See p.76 for advice on **tipping**.

Unsurprisingly, Swiss cooking is firmly rooted in **dairy products**: cheese, milk, cream, butter and/or yoghurt find their way into most dishes. It's not hard to find good-quality, interesting and varied **vegetarian** options – all but a handful of places offer vegetarian set menus alongside the standard meaty ones – but veggies should be aware that most restaurants default onto **meat-based** dishes: innocent-looking tomato soup may have bits of bacon added, and fresh salads may come layered with ham or salami. **Vegans** will no doubt come prepared to cook their own food at least some of the time but, with careful choices, you should be able to pick your way through a menu with the help of restaurant staff. Alternative-style cooperative-run diners, many in squats in the major cities, offer budget vegetarian and vegan meals as standard.

Cheese

Cheese (*Käse*, *fromage*, *formaggio*) is an institution in Switzerland: locally produced cheeses are savoured much as local beers are in Britain or local wines in France. Delis, local markets and supermarket chill-cabinets nationwide are crammed with dozens of cheeses, and everyone eats the stuff, morning noon and night. Some cheese is still made in the traditional way by hand on summer mountain pastures (and so represents the very core of Swissness to the Swiss themselves), and plenty is exported to serve as an ambassador for Switzerland to the world. Check out @www.switzerland-cheese.com for the full, mouthwatering story.

Cheese has been around in Switzerland at least since the Romans. For centuries, cheesemaking was a skill confined to mountain farmers, sequestered for months with their herds in summer pastures, but these days, some 1200 village dairies are in daily operation, processing fresh, mostly raw, milk from local cows. (Pasteurization is frowned upon by most cheesemakers, who claim it undermines the full body and aroma of the cheese; helpfully, Swiss hygiene regulations on the matter are much less stringent than those of the EU. All Swiss cheese is made from **raw milk** unless otherwise stated – and is thus not a good idea for pregnant women.) Unlike in France, Switzerland has no system of control over use of the names

of its cheeses, and nowadays only 2.5 percent of world Emmental production is Swiss. Nonetheless, aficionados – and your own taste buds – will confirm that the best Emmental comes from Emmental.

Most cheese is now produced in the valleys, but the tradition of making **Alpine cheese** (*Bergkäse* or *Alpkäse*, *fromage des alpes*, *formaggio alpe*) over the short summers on high pastures is very much alive. The ceremonies driving cattle up to the lush alps in June, and down again in October, are festive celebrations in rural areas such as Appenzell or Gruyères. Only cheese which has been made on the alp from raw milk processed from cows fed on fresh grass, wildflowers and clover can qualify for the *Bergkäse* name. Such cheeses are produced by hand, allowed to ripen for a few months, and then at the end of the summer are handed out to the farmers proportionately, according to how many head of cattle they own. Many are sold on to specialist cheese shops and market stalls around the country, where they are much in demand for their richness and individual nuances of flavour.

Appenzeller @www.appenzeller.ch. Family name for some of the world's smelliest cheeses. The most pungent, known as Räss, gains its odour from being brushed with a herb-and-brine marinade throughout the ripening process; it's hugely popular within Switzerland but virtually unknown outside.

Emmental @www.emmentaler.ch. The holey mousetrap classic, known simply as "swiss" in the US. King of Swiss cheeses, with a massive 55,000 tonnes produced annually, in Emmental and across the German-speaking lowlands. Although coming in various grades, it tends to be mild, and has a subtle, nutty flavour.

Gruyère @www.gruyere.com. Smooth, rich and creamy-tasting hard cheese, with a distinctive salty-dry sharpness that makes it the favourite of the Swiss themselves; it's a prime ingredient in fondue, and is one of the best-known exported Swiss cheeses.

Sbrinz @www.sbrinz.ch. Originating in Brienz, but now produced in and around Luzern, this is Switzerland's Parmesan, matured over three years – crumbly, grainy and powerful.

Schabziger aka Sapsago @www.schabziger.ch. Distinctive green conical cheese made in Glarus for centuries according to the same recipe, using an intensely strong herb known as melilot that was originally imported from the Middle East by returning Crusaders.

Tête de Moine aka Bellelay Ⓦwww.
tetedemoine.ch. First made at Bellelay monastery in
the Jura in the twelfth century, but gleefully renamed
"Monk's Head" following widespread guillotining
during the French Revolution. Only made in Canton
Jura and the Jura Bernois. The small cylinders of
aromatic, spicy cheese are spiked and then shaved
by hand into tissuey rosettes at the table with a
special revolving blade.

Tilsiter Ⓦwww.tilsiter.ch. Creamy, full-flavoured
semi-hard cheese developed by Swiss emigrés in
Tilsit in eastern Prussia in the late nineteenth
century, and brought back to Switzerland shortly
after. Produced in the eastern cantons bordering the
Bodensee.

Vacherin Fribourgeois Ⓦwww.vacherin.ch. A
recipe reputed to have been brought back from
Catalonia by a Swiss monk in the thirteenth century,
and produced only in Canton Fribourg since then to
serve primarily as the fondue cheese par
excellence.

Vacherin Mont d'Or Ⓦwww.vacherin.ch. A
delectably smooth, creamy soft cheese made only in
winter in the Jura Vaudois.

Valais cheese and Raclette Ⓦwww.
raclette-suisse.ch. Spicy, easily meltable cheese in
high demand, now produced throughout Switzerland
for the winter speciality raclette.

Chocolate

Chocolate (*Schokolade, chocolat, cioccolata*) is a way of life in Switzerland: the Swiss
eat a world record 12.3kg of the stuff per
person per annum (compared to 8.4kg in
England and 5.3kg in the US). Conscripts in
the Swiss army get free chocolate, wrapped
in special foil bearing the Swiss flag, adults
bring each other chocolate as a dinner-party
gift, and, like cheese, chocolate stands as
one of the iconic Swiss exports, defining
Swissness to the world.

Swiss chocolate is held by many aficionados to be the best in the world, rich with
scrupulously high levels of expensive cocoa
butter, super-smooth, and above all creamy:
the industry imports most ingredients except
milk, which comes in fresh from the clover-
munching Alpine herds. Switzerland has had
since 1819 to perfect its chocolate-making,

Chocolate factory visits

Alprose (Caslano) p.574.
Lindt (Kilchberg) p.456.
Nestlé/Cailler (Broc) p.138.

and these days there are three big names.
Nestlé is the biggest, with its ubiquitous
Cailler marque; Philip Morris controls brands
such as **Toblerone, Suchard** and **Milka**;
while **Lindt & Sprüngli** remains an independent concern.

Aside from daily consumption – the chocolate aisle in Swiss supermarkets is quite a
sight – Switzerland has a long tradition of
small local confectioners producing handmade filled gourmet chocolates for special
occasions. Chocolate is **seasonal**, with the
usual bunnies at Easter accompanied during
the year by chocolate chestnuts and chocolate mushrooms in autumn and chocolate
flowers in spring. Chocolate is **regional**, too,
with *chocolatiers* in the Jura making presentation boxes of chocolate watches, those in
Bern producing elaborate chocolate bears,
Geneva turning out stacks of little chocolate
marmites (cauldrons full of marzipan "vegetables") for the Escalade festival each
December, and Zürich making miniature
chocolate *Bööggs* for the Sechseläuten
spring festival.

For plenty of earnest detail, check out the
Association of Swiss Chocolate Manu-
facturers website Ⓦwww.chocosuisse.ch.

Breakfast and snacks

Most Swiss eat their **breakfast** at home,
and it's not that much different in essence
from the kind of fare served up in hotels
(above the very cheapest establishments
anyway). Hotel breakfasts tend to take the
form of substantial **buffets** of juices, butter
croissants, fresh-baked crusty bread, a
choice of hard and soft cheeses, boiled
eggs, an array of cold meats and salamis,
and tea or coffee. At more expensive places
you'll also find a range of **muesli** and cereals with lashings of fresh milk, but despite
global marketing extolling the Alpine virtues
of Swiss muesli – Dr Bircher-Benner of
Zürich invented the stuff at the end of the
nineteenth century to serve to patients at his
health clinic – the Swiss themselves seem to
steer clear of it at breakfast. You'll see
Birchermuesli (a lumpy, stomach-lining concoction of muesli with plenty of fruit and
yoghurt already mixed in) available at big-
hotel buffets, but rarely anywhere else; a few
older mountain folk keep tradition alive by
indulging in a bowl in the afternoon or even
at night with bread and milk.

Bread is different from canton to canton, but as a rule you'll find light, white breads in the French- and Italian-speaking regions, and more substantial loaves in the German-speaking cantons: Basel's double loaf is thick and doughy, Zürich's drier and oval shaped, and so on. Rye bread abounds in Graubünden (Poschiavo's is flavoured with aniseed) and in the Valais, where nuts are often added. The Emmental has its own delectable *Züpfe*, a plaited white loaf rich with milk.

In the towns and larger resorts, you'll have no trouble finding chances to **snack** on the universal standbys of burgers, pizza slices, kebabs and falafels. You'll also find various different kinds of sausage (*Wurst, saucisse, salsiccia*) around the country served as chargrilled fast food in a warmed bread roll with mustard. The most popular are pork *Bratwürste*, but you may also find smoked *Frankfurterli* and *Wienerli, Blutwurst* (blood sausage) made from black pudding, and *Leberwurst* (liver sausage). One seasonal treat, in late autumn and winter, is delicious and filling roast chestnuts (*Marroni, marrons, marroni*) sold by street vendors countrywide.

Main meals

The line between a **café** and a **restaurant** is blurred: either can normally do you a meal, although generally only at set times (mostly noon–2pm & 6–10pm), with only snacks available in between. A *Restaurant, restaurant* or *ristorante* is more or less the same as an **inn** (*Beiz, Gasthof, Gaststätte* or *Gasthaus, auberge, grotto* or *osteria*), although somewhere with the latter name probably serves more traditional local cuisine. Both generally take at least one day a week off as a holiday (*Ruhetag, jour de repos, giorno di chiusura*), posted prominently on the door. Also watch out for *alkohol-frei* or *sinalco* establishments, as well as the noticeably tiny number of places with restrictions on **smoking**.

Eating out can knock a big hole in your budget. The key to avoiding excessive

---

Eating on the cheap

Budget travellers should head for the often surprisingly good, and always packed, **self-service restaurants** in chain department stores in town-centres nationwide: **Manora** (⊛www.manor.ch) is almost always best, but Migros, EPA, and Co-op are all worth checking out. The best of these places offer a wide variety of fresh-cooked generic dishes – soups, casseroles, pasta and the like – with by far the best bargains coming on the large buffets of fresh salads and chicken-and-rice staples, plus a choice of fresh-squeezed juices and fruit smoothies. Veggie and vegan ranges help non-carnivores to gorge. With pricing generally going by the size of the plate rather than by the amount you actually pile onto it, you can easily get a full meal for Fr.11–13 at these places, and with all-day opening they're ideal mid-afternoon stand-bys for when most other eateries are closed. Watch out for the places which allow you to pile the food on, but then charge you by weight (say Fr.2.30 per 100g), which can work out quite a bit more expensive. Another option is a **student dining hall**, or *mensa*, attached to a university, often open to everyone and serving cut-price meals at limited lunch- and (early) dinner-times.

Migros is also the largest national chain of **supermarkets**, with outlets in almost all towns which are marked by a big orange initial: a single M indicates a small shop, while a triple MMM is a giant hypermarket. **Denner** is another Swiss chain, while the French conglomerate **Carrefour** is establishing its presence. **Aperto** are small deli-style outlets with usefully long opening hours found at main train stations. Range of products is normally excellent, but prices – if you do the comparison to equivalents at home – can be high. The tradition of individually owned specialist food shops survives in most places, with a baker (*Bäckerei, boulangerie, panetteria*), a grocer (*Lebensmittelgeschäft, épicerie, negozio alimentari*), a cheese shop (*Käserei, fromagerie, bottega del formaggio*) and a health-food shop (*Reformhaus, magasin diététique, erboristeria*) offering high-quality **picnic supplies** in most town centres.

expense is to make lunch your main meal, and always to plump for the dish of the day or *menu* (*Tagesmenu*, *Tagesteller* or *Tageshit*, *plat/assiette du jour*, *piatto del giorno*) – often comprising two or even three courses of substantial, quality nosh, whether in a café or a proper restaurant, for around Fr.15. The English term can be confusing: note that in all eating-places the **menu** is the particular dish or dishes on offer that day, while the house list from which you select individual courses is called the *Karte* or *Speisekarte*, *carte*, *carta*. Lunch *menus* are by far the least expensive way to sample the best of Swiss cuisine, and even Michelin-starred gourmet restaurants will offer exquisite multi-course lunches for Fr.30–45 (not including wine). The same meal in the evening, or choosing à la carte anytime, can easily cost double, although beerhalls in the German-speaking cities often serve hearty inexpensive evening meals, and – depending on where you are – pizza-pasta joints and simple informal eateries can fill your stomach for Fr.15–20.

Fondue

These days, you'll find **cheese fondue** all over the country, but it's really a speciality of Suisse-Romande. The word "fondue" refers to the broad, shallow earthenware or cast-iron pot used to heat the cheese… but that's where agreement runs out, and you'll find myriad varieties served across the country. The classic style, mainstay of eateries in the fondue heartland of Fribourg and the Vaud countryside, is a *moitié-moitié*, or half-and-half, using either Gruyère and Vacherin Fribourgeois, or Gruyère and Emmental. Others may use several grades of Gruyère, or mix in some local Alpine cheese, Valaisian raclette cheese or Appenzeller. Whichever, it's a winter dish designed to be sampled with friends: a restaurant offering it in the summer is a restaurant to be avoided. Also, since they're never eaten alone, fondues are generally priced as a two-person (or more) deal, or as "fondue à discrétion" or "fondue à gogo" (both of which mean "all you can eat").

There's a whole ritual surrounding fondue consumption, which most Swiss take seriously. The cheeses are melted together behind the scenes, generally with a shot of

Fuming

Switzerland suffers from a widespread lack of restrictions on **smoking** in restaurants. Most establishments, in all classes and styles, in all areas of the country, permit smoking throughout: very few have designated no-smoking areas, and those that do rarely create a physical barrier, meaning that non-smoking diners must put up with drifting fumes. There's little or nothing you can do about this, apart from make a personal stand; after a few days in the country, the sound of lighters clicking at half-a-dozen nearby tables just as your starter arrives will get to be a familiar one. Ⓦ www.eat-smokefree.ch has more.

some kind of alcohol (cider in the orchard-rich east, Kirsch in the cherry-growing central regions, white wine in Neuchâtel and Vaud), after which the aromatic pot is brought steaming to your table and set over a small paraffin burner. You use a special long fork to spear a small cube of bread (some places also serve little chunks of boiled potato and/or vegetables), swirl it through the cheese, twirl off the trailing ends, and pop it in. Don't be shy to give it a good vigorous swirl through the pot, since this helps stop the cheese mixture from separating; lose your bread in the fondue, though, and traditionally the drinks are on you. The trick, as the pot gets emptier, is to regularly adjust the heat: have it high enough to keep the cheese from solidifying, but not so high that the mixture boils or burns to the base of the pot.

With roughly 250g of molten cheese consumed per person, a fondue can be quite a heavy load on your system: the Swiss-German remedy is to gulp plenty of hot herbal tea throughout, thus making sure the cheese doesn't solidify in your innards, but the fearless Romands go the other way and favour plenty of chilled white wine. Their *coup de milieu* of a shot of Kirsch (or some other spirit) halfway through supposedly helps things settle – or at least helps mask the stomachache.

On menus nationwide, you'll also see **fondue chinoise**, an entirely different thing where you dip slivers of meat into spicy bouillon; **fondue bourguignonne**, only for the stoutest of constitutions since it involves dousing lumps of red meat in hot spitting oil; **fish** fondues; Valaisan **fondue Bacchus** using mulled wine; and even novelty **chocolate** fondues.

Regional specialities

Fondue is the prime speciality of **French Switzerland**, but there's a host of other cheesy dishes claiming their roots in the region, including **raclette**, known countrywide but born and best savoured in the Valais. A large half-round of special raclette cheese is held in front of a fire, and as it melts it's scraped (*raclé*) onto a plate, and served with boiled potatoes, pearl onions and pickles, often "à gogo". The **saucisson vaudois**, or mixed pork and beef Vaud sausage, is famous for its delicately smoked flavour, served boiled or steamed, and accompanied by *papet vaudois*, a delicious purée of potatoes and leeks. Lakeside resorts prepare fresh fish in a hundred different ways, most deliciously as **truite meunière**, fresh trout floured and sautéed in butter. Autumn across Romandie (and across Ticino too) sees **wild mushrooms** (*Pilzen*, *champignons*, *funghi*) making an appearance on the menu, from simple *croûtes aux champignons* (creamy mushrooms on toast) up to flavourful game and mushroom casseroles. In high summer, Valais overflows with golden apricots and peaches, while apples and plums thrive in the lowlands from Lake Geneva to Basel and across to the Bodensee.

All across **German Switzerland** you'll find plentiful variations of **Rösti** or *Röschti*, grated potato formed into a large patty and fried golden-brown on both sides. This can either be an accompaniment to a main course, or, with the embellishment of ham, melted cheese, a fried egg and/or bacon bits, be a comfortably affordable main course itself. An Alpine stomach-liner that has made its way into the lowlands is **Älpler Magrone**, essentially macaroni cheese with extra onion, bacon, potatoes and cream, often served with puréed apples with cinnamon. *Käseschnitten*, in different forms, is Welsh rarebit (toasted cheese), while *Spätzli* and *Knöpfli* are tiny buttons of boiled dough served drizzled with butter. In and around Bern, you'll find **Bernerteller** or *Bernerplatte*,

a hefty pile of cold and hot meats including pork sausage, bacon, various hams, smoked pork, knuckles and beef tongue served with beans and plenty of *Sauerkraut*. Zürich has **Züri Gschnetzlets**, diced veal in a creamy mushroom sauce, served with *Rösti*, while St Gallen is known for its own pale, milky veal sausages. In Basel, winter menus offer **Basler Mehlsuppe**, a heavy brown brew of onions, pork lard and cream, thickened with flour and topped with grated Sbrinz cheese. Graubünden is best known for **Bündnerfleisch**, prime beef air-dried in an attic and served paper-thin as part of an aromatic plate of mixed meats known as a *Bündnerteller*, or as prime ingredient in **Bündner Gerstensuppe** (barley cream soup with vegetables). With hunting still very popular in Graubünden, you'll also see plenty of **game** on autumn menus, such as stews (*Pfeffer*, *fratem*) of chamois (*Gemse*, *chamutsch*) or deer (*Hirsch*, *tschierv*). Zug and Luzern are famous for their black **cherries**, while Basel has its own dark red variety. **Meringue** was invented in or near Meiringen, and most Emmental and Bernese Oberland villages offer their own spectacular super-rich, cream-laden meringue creations.

Italian Switzerland has its own cuisine, entirely different from what's on offer in the rest of the country and more akin to the flavours and methods of neighbouring Piedmont and Lombardy. **Polenta** (cornmeal) and **risotto** are staples; leafy salads abound, dressed lightly with olive oil instead of the mayonnaise-based concoctions favoured further north; and fresh homemade pastas and **gnocchi** (bite-sized potato dumplings), with the familiar tomato- or pesto-based sauces, are delectable. **Pollo alla cacciatora** is a spicy chicken-and-tomato stew with mushrooms and white wine, served with polenta or boiled potatoes. The Ticinesi also love their sausages, with Mardi Gras in Lugano serving as an excuse for a public pig-out on risotto with **luganiga**, an extra-rich pork sausage. Spicy *mortadella* is unlike the Italian version, and can either be cooked or air-dried for eating raw.

Drink

Swiss **cafés**, open from breakfast onwards, often sell alcohol and might also be called **bars**, although the latter tend to open their doors for late-afternoon and evening business only. Most people just pop in and pop out – a coffee in the morning, a quick beer – and tend not to while away the daytime hours. In the early evening, bars and terraces fill up with folk enjoying an **apéro**, a universally recognized term derived from the French *apéritif*, meaning a drink before dinner.

Around the country, daytime places for tea and cakes are dubbed **tearooms**, or left as nameless nooks attached to a *Konditorei*, *pâtisserie* or *confiserie*, *pasticceria*. Other than ordinary **pubs**, drinking venues vary according to region. A cosy *Bierstube* or *Stübli* – replete with wood beams and Swiss kitsch – is the evening meeting place of choice in both city and village in German-speaking Switzerland, while in Romandie and Ticino pavement cafés are more common.

Coffee, tea and water

As well as espresso, cappuccino and the rest, **coffee** has some local variations: in German-speaking areas *Kaffee creme*, coffee with sugar and cream, is popular, as is *Milchkaffee*, with fresh milk. Ask for *Kaffee fertig* and you'll get coffee with Schnapps. In Romandie, *café renversée* is the local name for a frothy French-style *café au lait*. **Tea** (*Tee*, *thé*, *tè*) has its usual variety of styles, with or without milk, or, most refreshingly, as iced tea (*Eistee*, *thé froid*, *tè freddo*) in summer. A herbal tea is a *Krautentee*, *tisane* or *infusion*, *tisana*. **Soft drinks** comprise all the familiar brands, aside from a hugely popular flavoured fizzy soda called Rivella that tastes quite pleasant until you discover that it's made from milk serum.

Water is safe to drink all over Switzerland, whether from taps or from the public street-fountains that you'll see dotted throughout cities, towns and villages. These fountains, even though they (or the horse-trough beneath them) may look manky, almost always gush with pure spring water. It's only ever worth paying for **mineral water** (*Mineralwasser*, *eau minérale*, *acqua minerale*) in restaurants if you fancy it sparkling (*mit Kohlensäure*, *gazeuse*, *gassata*).

There are a few exceptions to the fountain rule, always marked "kein Trinkwasser", "eau non potable" or "acqua non potabile", often also with a pictogram of a crossed-out drinking glass. Also take care with mountain streams, which look crystal-clear but which may be hosting a herd of happily splashing cows just upstream.

Beer and spirits

Beer (*Bier*, *bière*, *birra*) varies from region to region, with breweries such as Feldschlösschen in Basel and Cardinal in Fribourg supplying their local area. Most local beers on draught (*vom Fass*, *à la pression*, *alla pressione*) are flavourful if unremarkable lager-type brews, always served with a sizeable head of foam. The standard measure (*e'Schtange*, *une pression*, *una birra*) is three decilitres (3dl, just under a third of a litre), which costs about Fr.3–4, or you can ask for a *Grosses Bier*, *demi*, *birra grande*, which will either turn up a half-litre of the same, or possibly a 0.58-litre bottle. There's also a 2dl chaser measure universally known, for some reason, as a *Herrgöttli*. A *panaché* is a mixed beer-lemonade shandy. Most bars also have a choice of familiar bottled beers from around Europe. Alcoholic **cider** is *suure Most*, *cidre*, *sidro* – but if you leave the "*suure*" off in Swiss-German you may end up with non-alcoholic apple juice, or *Süssmost*, instead.

With extensive fruit cultivation, Switzerland has plenty of **distilled spirits** or liquor (*Schnapps*, *eau de vie*, *aquavite*) to choose from, king of which is powerful *Kirsch* (cherry spirit) from Zug and around Lake Luzern. Plums and quetsches go to make *Zwetschgenwasser* or *eau de vie de quetsche*. A kind of mini-plum known as a damassine, which was reputedly brought back from Damascus by a crusading knight and which now grows only in the Ajoie region of Canton Jura, is distilled into a delectably fragrant *eau de vie* also called Damassine. Apple-spirits turn up as *Träsch*, *Gravensteiner* and many more, while Valaisian pears go to make aromatic *Williamine*. The Ticino nurtures its own, unique range of *grappa*, a heady Italian fire-water made from grape-skins, stalks and pips left over after the vine harvest.

Wine

Wine is often referred to as Switzerland's best-kept secret, since viticulture is flourishing, quality and standards are high, annual production regularly hits 200 million bottles, but – in the usual Swiss way – many wines don't get beyond the borders of their canton. Just one percent is exported.

Even the simplest restaurants and bars will have wine, both on a wine list (*Weinkarte*, *carte des vins*, *carta dei vini*) and – much more affordably – as *Offene Wein*, *vin ouvert*, *vino aperto*, a handful of house reds and whites chalked up on a board and sold by the decilitre. Standard measures are 1dl and 2dl, which come to you in glasses; and 3dl and 5dl, which come in a small carafe. Paying around Fr.3–6 per decilitre is normal.

Switzerland's best-known wines come from the steeply terraced vineyards of the **Valais**. Of the whites, bright and floral *Fendant* is king, named for the ripeness of its golden Chasselas grapes, which, when pressed, *se fendre*, or split, rather than squish. Other Valais whites include fruity and alcoholic *Johannisberg*, sweeter *Ermitage*, and *Malvoisie* from the Pinot Gris grape (the late harvests, marked *flétrie*, or shrivelled, are particularly sought-after). Valais's reds, led by *Dôle*, a blend of Pinot Noir and Gamay grapes, are equally respected. Bottles of 100 percent Pinot Noir have recently begun to make an appearance, but the connoisseur's Valais red is a *Humagne Rouge*. *Dôle blanche* is one of Switzerland's few rosé wines.

Until the mid-twentieth century, **Vaud** was Switzerland's leading wine-growing canton, and the vineyards lining the **Côte** and **Lavaux** shores of Lake Geneva hold some of the most picturesque walks in the whole country. Chasselas is ubiquitous, and with their concentration on this one white grape to the exclusion of all others, Vaudois *vignerons*, particularly those at Dézaley, St-Saphorin and Epesses, produce some of the best of all Swiss wines. In the **Chablais** region southeast of Montreux are the vineyards of Château d'Aigle, home to a wine museum, and Yvorne. Canton **Geneva** also has extensive Chasselas vines – the Genevois *Perlan* is more affordable than its Vaudois competitors – and low-priced Gamays have recently taken on imported French Beaujolais with some success.

Around **Neuchâtel** and Biel/Bienne, the combination of a plate of fresh lake fish and a bottle of local white is unbeatable; there are dozens of local producers, and each estate brings forth something different from the Chasselas grapes that still dominate. In the German-speaking north and east, though, Chasselas gives way to the Riesling-Sylvaner grape, perhaps best known on the **"Gold Coast"** of Lake Zürich's eastern shore, so named for its glow in the afternoon sunshine. The Rhine shores at **Schaffhausen** are mostly given over to Pinot Noir, while only the warm southern *Föhn* wind allows Pinot Noir grapes to flourish in an area known as the **Bündner Herrschaft**, around Maienfeld in Graubünden, Fläsch in St Gallen, and Liechtenstein. **Ticino**'s vine growing is dominated by Merlot, and almost every village has its own brand of *Merlot del Ticino*. The Sopraceneri region, north of Bellinzona, is less successful than the Sottoceneri, around Lugano and especially Mendrisio, but you'd have to struggle to find a truly bad specimen anywhere.

Communications

Communications to, from and within Switzerland are as efficient as you'd expect: new-generation public phones have a touch screen from which you can send an email, a text message or a fax, surf the Web, search the complete Swiss phone directory, book a train journey, find somewhere to eat... or even make a call, with everything onscreen in English.

Post

Post offices (☎0800 888 777, ⊛www.post.ch) – identified by a yellow logo and *Die Post*, *La Poste* or *La Posta* – generally open Monday to Friday 7.30am–noon and 1.30–6.30pm, and Saturday 8–11am, although watch out for slight regional variations and restricted hours in smaller branches. Some main offices stay open over the lunch break.

For both domestic and international post, there's a two-tier system. **A–Priority post** is delivered next day in Switzerland, within five days to Europe, and within ten days worldwide; **B–Economy post** takes three days domestic, up to ten days to Europe, and up to eight weeks by surface delivery worldwide. Sending a postcard or a 20g letter by A/B post costs Fr.1.30/1.20 to Europe, Fr.1.80/1.40 worldwide. Liechtenstein has stamps which look different but cost the same. For all Priority post, you should write a prominent "A" with a box around it above the address, or ask for one of the blue stickers.

Poste restante is available at any post office: all you need to know is that town or city's four-figure postal code (plus any suffixed digits identifying a particular office in a large city district). They're displayed outside each post office, and Swiss phonebooks and ⊛www.post.ch list the lot. The correct format is, for example: Your Name, Poste Restante, CH-3920 Zermatt ("CH" is the standard postal designation for Switzerland). Liechtenstein shares the Swiss postal system, but uses its own prefix: Your Name, Poste Restante, FL-9490 Vaduz. To minimize confusion at pickup, you should ask anyone writing to you to print your surname in underlined capitals, and include only one initial. If you want to receive mail at a smaller countryside office in the German-speaking part of the country, where the term "Poste Restante" may be less understood, you should get your correspondents to add the German equivalent – *Postlagernde Briefe*. You need your passport to pick up your mail, and the service is always free. Uncollected mail is returned to sender after 30 days.

Phones

Another first for Switzerland: the country has more public **phones** per square kilometre than anywhere else in the world. There are always at least one or two phones (sometimes ranks of them) outside post offices and at train stations, and invariably you'll find that the most remote mountain refuge or country cottage has a phone or two. The former public utility **Swisscom** (☎0800 800 800, ⊛www.swisscom.com) was privatized in 1998, and although it currently retains its monopoly over land-lines and local calls, and still owns and operates all the public phones, there is competition in the long-distance and international call markets, and prices are dropping.

A few **public phones** still accept coins (both Swiss francs and euros, which you can put in together), but the majority take cards only. The easiest, if priciest, option is to insert a Swisscom phonecard (known as a **"taxcard"**), available from post offices, many hotels, newsagents, kiosks, train station ticket counters, and some vending machines in Fr.5, Fr.10 and Fr.20 denominations. You can also swipe a credit/charge card (Visa, MasterCard, Diners, Amex and others); unusually, this doesn't attract any supplementary charges above the cost of the call itself. Pressing button L on the phone switches the display to English. Most phones have a keyboard and **"Teleguide"** screen attached, from which you can send

Useful numbers

Emergencies

Police ☎117
Fire, accidents and life-threatening situations ☎118
Ambulance ☎144
Helicopter rescue
– Rega ☎1414
– Air Glaciers ☎1415
Poisoning centre ☎01 251 51 51

Information

Domestic operator ☎111
Directory enquiries
– for Switzerland ☎111
– for Austria ☎1151
– for Germany ☎1152
– for France ☎1153
– for Italy ☎1154
– for all other countries ☎1159
International operator ☎1141

Public services

Breakdown service ☎140
Traffic information ☎163
Alarm call ☎0900 77 24
The Samaritans (crisis line) ☎143
*Weather forecast** ☎162
*Speaking clock** ☎161
*Avalanche bulletin** ☎187
in local languages only

an email, a fax or a text message (the charge is deducted from your taxcard or credit/charge card as normal), or you can search the complete Swiss business and residential phone directory for free. Full onscreen instructions are given in English. In and around Zürich you'll also spot the new breed of Webpayphones, featuring a touch screen, keyboard and built-in printer, from which you can – in addition to all the above – also surf the Web, all using a taxcard or a credit/charge card to pay.

For calls **within Switzerland**, you must **dial all ten digits** (nine or ten digits for Zürich numbers), even if you're in the same area. Over the next few years, Zürich's ☎01 code will be replaced, to bring the city's numbers up to the full ten digits; all ☎01 numbers will remain valid until 2007, although you may notice some new numbers prefixed ☎043 and ☎044 appearing before then. Note that numbers beginning

☎0800 are free; ☎0900 are more expensive than normal; ☎0842 and ☎0848 are charged as local calls. Domestic rates are highest on weekdays between 8am and 5pm.

Liechtenstein has its own phone company – Telecom FL – although the public phones look and work the same as those in Switzerland, and they accept Swisscom taxcards. Local calls are straightforward (dial all seven digits), but calling between Liechtenstein and Switzerland counts as international (see "Calling from abroad" p.56). Some pre-paid discount taxcards may not work from Liechtenstein.

Phoning home

To call **internationally**, there's a wide choice of carriers. It's no problem to use a Swisscom taxcard to dial internationally direct from public phones, but this ties you to Swisscom's prices, which are some of the highest in Europe. You'd do better to go for one of Swisscom's many competitors, who can give you equal service for a fraction of the cost; printed on the back of their taxcards is a toll-free number to access their lines and, beneath a scratch-off layer, a password. One of the better known is **ProfiTel** (formerly Teleline; ☎0842 800 842, ⓦwww.profitel.ch) – but you have to ask vendors for their taxcards (in Fr.20, Fr.50 and Fr.100 denominations) by name, and even then they may take some sniffing out. Staff at some kiosks may have them but not know what they're for: beware of being sold cards intended for use in Swiss mobile phones, which look the same, but which are useless for public phones. Other kiosks may not stock anything other than Swisscom taxcards. You can also use **credit cards** in public phones (Visa, MasterCard, Amex, etc), with no surcharges – you're charged only for the call cost.

Alternatively, you might consider a **phone charge card** from your phone company back home; most providers in Europe, North America, Australia and New Zealand have their own versions. Using a PIN number, they let you make calls from most hotel, public and private phones – via a toll-free Swiss number – that are charged to your home account. Most are free to obtain.
To the UK ☎0044 + area code without zero + number.

To Ireland ☎00353 + area code without zero + number.
To the US or Canada ☎001 + area code + number.
To Australia ☎0061 + area code without zero + number.
To New Zealand ☎0064 + area code without zero + number.

Calling from abroad

First dial your **international access code** (00 from the UK, Ireland and New Zealand; 011 from the US and Canada; 0011 from Australia), followed by **41** for Switzerland, followed by the local number **excluding the initial zero**.

To call Liechtenstein, dial your international access code (from Switzerland it's 00), followed by 423, followed by the seven-digit local number.

Mobile phones

To use your **mobile phone**, check with your provider whether it will work in Switzerland and what the charges will be; technology is GSM (🖰www.gsmworld.com), and coverage – even in the mountains – is generally good. Unless you have a triband phone, it's unlikely that a mobile bought for use in North America will work elsewhere. Most mobiles in Australia and New Zealand are GSM, but it pays to check before you leave home. Alternatively, you can **rent** a Swiss mobile

from Rentaphone (🖰www.rentaphone.ch), over the counter or by advance booking from desks at Zürich Airport Terminal B arrivals (☎01 816 50 63; Mon–Fri 7am–7pm, Sat & Sun 8am–7pm) or Geneva Airport arrivals (☎022 717 82 63; same hours); current rates are Fr.45 for the first day, Fr.10/day thereafter, or Fr.100/week, with discounted airtime. You can reserve a Rentaphone mobile when booking a flight with Swiss or renting a car with Hertz.

Email

Access to the **Internet** is everywhere, with cybercafés or public-access terminals either free or costing a few francs. Many tourist offices and hotel receptions have a PC or two available for public access at nominal rates. You can type in and send a short email from the Teleguide screens in phone-booths for Fr.1.50 (Swisscom taxcard needed), although you can't pick up any email this way. If you're travelling with a **laptop** or palmtop and just need a phoneline, some Swiss phones use the US-style RJ-11, but most of them – and the majority in non-luxury hotel rooms – use either a non-standard chunky square jack or (rarely) an ancient four-pin plug. None uses the British-style design. Many business hotels keep a supply of adaptors and leads for lending to guests; otherwise, you may have to seek advice from an electronics store. Check out 🖰**www.kropla.com** for invaluable advice.

The media

In general, the Swiss have a healthy disregard for the mass media, and watch much less TV than the European average: the German Swiss have the distinction of watching the least TV in Europe. To make up for it they read more, and more locally oriented, newspapers than anyone else on the continent.

Swiss TV and radio

Switzerland has at least six terrestrial **TV stations** available everywhere, two channels each from Schweizer Fernsehen (SF), Télévision Suisse Romande (TSR) and Televisione Svizzera Italiana (TSI), plus a

handful of national channels from mostly German-speaking private operators, and plenty of local stations for each area. None is what you might call glittering, offering an undemanding diet of chat shows, game shows, made-for-TV movies (dubbed) and lots of local news and local interest programming. Full details at ⓦwww.srg.ch.

Each language area of the country has three broad-coverage regional **radio stations**, one channel devoted to each of news, classical music and popular music (see ⓦwww.srg.ch), as well as a fistful of local city or community stations and networks from neighbouring countries leaking across the border. The Swiss-German **DRS-1** quite often broadcasts concerts of traditional Alpine music and alphorn recitals, but that aside, the French-language station **Couleur-Trois** is the most entertaining station by miles, playing consistently good cutting-edge rock, pop, world and dance music from France, the US and the UK with tolerable bursts of chat in between. The German-language national equivalent, **DRS-3**, is much less adventurous, sticking with blander chart and mainstream club sounds. Both are on varying frequencies around 104–107FM. Italian-language music stations are eurobland in the extreme. English-language **World Radio Geneva** (88.4FM in Geneva only; ⓦwww.wrgfm.com) broadcasts BBC world news, analysis and music shows in amongst its own curiously parochial programming. **Swiss Radio International** has a daily news service, with audio and video options, at ⓦwww.swissinfo.org.

The Swiss press

Switzerland has a ton of **newspapers** – more than 200 nationwide – but almost without exception they're parochial local news-sheets, reporting cantonal and municipal affairs in some detail, but relegating the rest of Switzerland, let alone the world, to a few inside columns. It's a mark of differing attitudes within the country that whereas French-speaking Swiss regularly turn to Paris's *Le Monde* or *Libération* for opinion from beyond their own borders, and the Ticinesi are happy to jump on the coat-tails of Milan's *Corriere della Sera*, newspapers from Germany have barely any readers at all amongst the proudly Swiss folk south of the border.

Zürich's **Neue Zürcher Zeitung**, or *NZZ* (ⓦwww.nzz.ch), is the best known of Swiss newspapers. Conservative and highbrow in the extreme – you'll rarely see a photo on its close-printed front page – it nonetheless has

gained its reputation by reporting Swiss and world events with scrupulously high journalistic standards. Its francophone equivalent is the much more dynamic **Le Temps** (ⓦwww.letemps.ch), published in Geneva, fiercely pro-EU and with consistently progressive stances on social and political issues; it's the only Swiss newspaper that makes it onto Paris newsstands each morning. Otherwise, the field is thin, though Zürich's quality *Tages Anzeiger* offers a lively alternative to the NZZ's ponderousness. Switzerland's biggest-selling paper is *Blick*, a blaring, reactionary rag that regularly espouses anti-immigration and anti-asylum causes. Of the **weeklies**, *Die Weltwoche* offers quality, left-leaning world news analysis, while the *Wochen Zeitung*, or *WOZ*, has a radical alternative agenda, pushing green issues particularly strongly and packaging once a month the German translation of the highly respected journal of world affairs *Le Monde Diplomatique*. Lausanne's *L'Hebdo* leads the field of francophone weeklies, but lacks any kind of newsy bite.

The Arts Council of Switzerland *Pro Helvetia* (ⓦwww.prohelvetia.ch) twice a year – on paper and online – publishes *Passages*, a heavily intellectual magazine in English of musings on Swiss culture and society, interviews with Swiss artists and short fiction. Subscriptions are free if you live outside Switzerland.

Foreign media

You'll find most British **newspapers** on sale the same day in main train stations and some city kiosks in Geneva, Lausanne, Zürich, Basel and Bern, as well as in well-touristed resorts such as Zermatt, Saas-Fee, Gstaad and Interlaken, and a day late in some other towns. Prices for the normal papers are extraordinary – Fr.5.50 or more for the broadsheets – but most outlets stock *The Guardian*'s condensed European edition, the *Financial Times*, *International Herald Tribune* and *USA Today* for less.

If a hotel room has a **TV** it's very likely to be hooked up to cable or satellite, giving you the dubious pleasure of 30 or 40 channels covering the panoply of European languages, plus a few more exotic offerings such as Turkish or Arabic. CNN news is the only English-language dead cert wherever you are, although many places have BBC

Prime, showing British soaps, drama and comedy, and some also have BBC World, with rolling news and features.

As for **radio**, the BBC World Service is on 648kHz medium wave more or less all day and most of the night, but in practice it seems that the mountains can quite often block reception, forcing you onto short wave instead (12.095, 9.760, 9.410, 7.325, 6.195, 5.975 or 3.955MHz). World Radio Geneva (88.4FM in Geneva) takes the BBC news on the hour. Thousands of stations, including all BBC output (🌐 www.bbc.co.uk), Voice of America (🌐 www.voa.gov), Radio Canada (🌐 www.rcinet.ca) and Radio Australia (🌐 www.abc.net.au), broadcast online.

Opening hours and public holidays

Switzerland's reputation for calmness and domesticity is borne out by its down-to-earth attitude to the consumer revolution: in contrast to most of the rest of the Western world, Swiss laws on strictly limited opening times reflect universal public concern to uphold the rights of serving staff at the expense of consumers.

You'll find that banks, post offices, shops, supermarkets, tourist offices – just about everything – in most Swiss towns and villages still shut between noon and 2pm, to allow staff to go home for lunch. This is slowly being eroded in favour of consumer-friendly all-day opening, especially in the big towns and cities, but old habits are dying hard.

Shop opening hours are customarily Monday to Friday 9am–noon and 2–6.30pm, Saturday 8.30am–noon, although it's becoming more common to stay open over the lunch break and also stay open on Saturdays until 5pm; the flipside is that some places then take Monday morning off. Quiet Sundays are sacrosanct. Most towns operate universal late opening until 9pm for one day a week, generally Thursday (Friday in Graubünden). The main exceptions to all this are shops and cafés within the subterranean malls at train stations, where everything stays open daily, and also closes later in the evening.

Bank opening hours vary, but in the cities are generally Mon–Fri 8.30am–4.30pm, sometimes with a break for lunch; town and village branches have shorter hours. Some city and tourist-resort banks also open on Saturday, often 9am–4pm.

Cafés fall into two broad categories. Those that open in the morning for coffee and breakfasts might then close when the shops shut, at about 6 or 6.30pm. Some, though, open at noon for lunch or in mid-afternoon (say 4 or 5pm), and then metamorphose into **bars** until midnight or so. Those that serve full meals (which is most of them) will only do so at the customary mealtimes: roughly noon to 2pm and 6 to 10pm. Outside those hours, you'll generally be able to find only snacks. Formal **restaurants** keep to the same mealtimes, closing altogether in-between times. Closing times of all establishments are regulated by each individual municipality: Lausanne, for instance, carouses until 1am, Lugano insists on midnight, while Bern plumps for 12.30am. All places can stay open an hour later than normal on Friday and Saturday nights.

Very many **museums** and public attractions are open on Sundays and **closed on Mondays**; a few also take Tuesdays off.

Fairytale castles

Château d'Aigle p.329.
Castelgrande, Bellinzona p.552.
Schloss Burgdorf p.261.
Château de Chillon p.161.
Château de Grandson p.185.
Château de Gruyères p.139.
Schloss Thun p.307.
Schloss Vaduz p.493.

Top art galleries

Major museums

Fondation Beyeler, Basel p.221. Twentieth-century.
Kunstmuseum, Basel p.219. Holbein, moderns.
Kunstmuseum, Bern p.251. Klee and Kandinsky.
Musée d'Art et d'Histoire, Geneva p.97. Rodin, Rembrandt, Hodler.
Sammlung Rosengart, Luzern p.386. Picasso, Klee.
Fondation Pierre Gianadda, Martigny p.337. Temporary shows.
Oskar Reinhart, Winterthur p.466. Holbein, Delacroix, Impressionists.
Kunsthaus, Zürich p.438. Dutch, Flemish, Baroque, Surrealists, Giacometti, Picasso, Munch...

Outstanding smaller museums

Collections Baur, Geneva p.98. East Asian ceramics.
Collection de l'Art Brut, Lausanne p.129. Outsider art.
Sammlung Im Obersteg, Oberhofen p.309. Chagall, Soutine.
Musée Jenisch, Vevey p.154. Modernists, Rembrandt, Dürer.
Villa Flora, Winterthur p.467. Impressionists.
Museum Rietberg, Zürich p.445. Asian art.

Contemporary art and photography

Kunsthalle, Basel p.219. Contemporary art.
Museum Jean Tinguely, Basel p.221. Tinguely.
MAMCO, Geneva p.98. Contemporary art.
Musée de l'Elysée, Lausanne p.133. Photography.
Hallen für Neue Kunst, Schaffhausen p.472. Contemporary art.
Fotomuseum, Winterthur p.467. Photography.
Kunsthalle, Zürich p.447. Contemporary art.
Museum für Gestaltung, Zürich p.446. Contemporary design.

Public holidays

National **public holidays** – when almost everything is closed – are listed below, but they're only part of the story. Most cantons supplement these with a handful of often religious holidays of their own, which can tie in with local festivals: various Catholic cantons, for instance, observe various saints' days (Ticino manages to authorize 17 annual holidays for itself). Common **cantonal holidays** include January 2 (St Bertold's Day, *Berchtoldstag*), January 6 (Epiphany, *Dreikönigstag, Epiphanie, Epifania*), May 1 (Labour Day, *Tag der Arbeit, Fête du Travail, Festa del Lavoro*), late May's Corpus Christi, August 15 (Assumption, *Mariä Himmelsfahrt, Assomption, Assunzione*) and November 1 (All Saints' Day, *Allerheiligen, Toussaint, Ognissanti*). Look out also for the seasonal pageants centred in various cities, and the often tumultuous celebrations of **carnival** on and around Mardi Gras in mid-February, which – amidst raucous partying in Luzern

and Basel in particular – can often affect shop opening hours.

Liechtenstein has all the same Swiss public holidays except August 1: the national holiday is on August 15 instead. It also celebrates May 1 (*Tag der Arbeit*).

January 1 New Year's Day, *Neujahr, Nouvel An, Capodanno*

March/April Good Friday, *Karfreitag, Vendredi saint, Venerdì Santo*

March/April Easter Monday, *Ostermontag, lundi de Pâques, Lunedì di Pasqua*

May Ascension Day, *Auffahrt/Christi Himmelfahrt, Ascension, Ascensione*

May/June Whit Monday, *Pfingstmontag, lundi de Pentecôte, Lunedì di Pentecoste*

August 1 Swiss National Day, *Nationalfeiertag, Fête nationale, Festa nazionale* (public institutions, and some shops and banks, closed)

December 25 Christmas Day, *Weihnachten, Noël, Natale*

December 26 Boxing Day, *Stefanstag, St-Etienne, Santo Stefano*

Festivals and annual events

Running counter to the dour national stereotype, Switzerland has masses of festivals (*Feiertage, jours féries, festività*), held in towns and villages all over the country for the slightest excuse, from celebrating the joys of carrots up to St Moritz's inimitable horseracing-on-ice extravaganza.

Listing them all would be impossible, and anyway would ruin the experience – well within the bounds of possibility – of stumbling by chance onto some small Swiss village's unadvertised annual knees-up of folk-dancing, street-barbecuing and general merriment. Switzerland Tourism maintains an encyclopedic events calendar at ⓦ www.myswitzerland.com, detailing hundreds of pageants big and small.

In **music**, the biggest show is July's **Montreux Jazz Festival**, televised around the world and these days featuring as much rock, dance and world music as jazz and blues. Massive open-air weekends in July at Bern, Nyon and St Gallen are regular stopoffs on the European festival circuit, and Bern's own orthodox jazz festival pulls in top artists year after year. Zürich's August **Street Parade** attracts a million techno revellers from all over Europe. In classical music, the **Lucerne Festival** – comprising separate events in March, August and November – is one of the premier events of its kind, with opera at Avenches and summer performance cycles at Verbier, Gstaad and Sion no less stellar. The **Locarno International Film Festival** is one of the top five in the world.

Of the more **traditional festivals**, carnival, in mid-February, features huge street parties in Luzern, Basel and Bern in particular, with Zürich, Lugano and smaller towns also mounting parades. Spring festivals in Zürich and Lausanne, and autumn harvest festivals all round the country, keep alive traditions of costume and cuisine stretching back to the Middle Ages. Some of the moveable events worth looking out for include **Schwingen**, traditional Swiss wrestling that's hugely popular in rural areas and is generally accompanied by traditional markets, beer-quaffing and hearty sausage-feasting. Weekends devoted to *Schwingen* championships take place all over the centre and east of the country at various dates between April and

September; ask at tourist offices or keep your eyes peeled for posters. There are also many **yodelling** events through the springtime, culminating in the annual Swiss Alpine Yodelling Championships, held in early July in a different town each year.

Aside from the large international events, which are primarily moneyspinners, you'll find the dozens of local festivals celebrating **food** or **wine** to be heartfelt community experiences, staged for pleasure. Similarly, in Catholic areas – French-, German-, Italian- and Romansh-speaking – each town or region keeps one day a year to honour the local **patron saint**; these are jovial local events, by, with and for the townspeople, with not a thought of tourism in mind.

Events calendar

January

early Basel – Vogel Gryff: traditional costumed dance and drum festival ⓦ www.vogel-gryff.ch.
mid Wengen – World Cup downhill ski-racing on the Lauberhorn ⓦ www.lauberhorn.ch.
late Mürren – Inferno giant-slalom ski race ⓦ www.inferno-muerren.ch.
late Château d'Oex – international hot-air ballooning week ⓦ www.chateau-doex.ch.

February

early Lötschental VS – Roitschäggättä: elaborate masked parades ⓦ www.loetschental.ch.
early St Moritz – horse-racing on the frozen lake ⓦ www.stmoritz.ch.
mid St Moritz – toboggan competitions on the Cresta Run ⓦ www.cresta-run.com.
mid Around Switzerland – Carnival: the biggest events, which run contiguously, are in Luzern (six days, from the Thursday before Mardi Gras up to Mardi Gras night; ⓦ www.luzerner-fasnacht.ch), Bern (two days, beginning on the Thursday evening

after Mardi Gras; ⊛www.baernerfasnacht.ch), and Basel (three days, beginning at 4am on the Monday after Mardi Gras; ⊛www.fasnacht.ch). Many towns and villages celebrate Carnival at various times from mid-February until early March.

March

early Geneva – International Motor Show ⊛www.palexpo.ch.
mid Lucerne Festival – Easter programme of classical music ⊛www.lucernefestival.ch.
mid St Moritz and around – Engadin Ski Marathon ⊛www.engadin-skimarathon.ch.
mid St Moritz – Snow and Symphony classical music festival ⊛www.snowandsymphony.ch.
late Verbier – Xtreme snowboarding championship ⊛www.xtremeverbier.com.
late Davos – world snowboard finals ⊛www.snowboarddavos.ch.

April

mid Visp – traditional Valaisian cow fights ⊛www.valaistourism.ch.
mid Zürich – Sechseläuten: traditional spring festival, with parades and fireworks ⊛www.sechselaeuten.ch.
late Appenzell – Landsgemeinde: annual session of public voting on local issues ⊛www.ai.ch.
late Lausanne – Fête du Soleil: live bands, open-air restaurants and markets ⊛www.carnavalausanne.ch.

May

early Glarus – Landsgemeinde: annual session of public voting on local issues ⊛www.gl.ch.
early Bern International Jazz Festival ⊛www.jazzfestivalbern.ch.
mid Aproz, near Sion – the cantonal cow-fighting champions' meeting ⊛www.valaistourism.ch.

June

early Appenzell, Gruyères and many villages in central and eastern Switzerland – celebration of the cattle's ascent to Alpine pastures
until Sept Interlaken – open-air performances of Schiller's play *William Tell* ⊛www.tellspiele.ch.
until July Zürich Festival: theatre, opera, music and art ⊛www.zuercher-festspiele.ch.
mid Tour de Suisse cycle race ⊛www.cycling.ch.
mid Basel – Art Basel, international contemporary art fair ⊛www.artbasel.com.
late Zürich – inline skating marathon ⊛www.swiss-inline-cup.ch.
late St Moritz – inline skating marathon ⊛www.swiss-inline-cup.ch.
late Bellinzona – Piazza Blues festival ⊛www.piazzablues.ch.
late Winterthur – Albanifäscht: music festival ⊛www.stadtfest.ch.
late St Gallen – open-air rock festival ⊛www.openairsg.ch.
late Ascona Jazz Festival – New Orleans-style ⊛www.jazzascona.ch.

July

4 Geneva – US Independence Day celebrations: the biggest outside the US ⊛www.genevatourism.ch.
all month Avenches Opera Festival: open-air performances in the Roman amphitheatre ⊛www.avenches.ch.
early Montreux Jazz Festival: everyone from Alannis Morrisette to Femi Kuti ⊛www.montreuxjazz.com.
early Lausanne – Festival de la Cité: free open-air performances and music ⊛www.lausanne.ch.
early Gstaad – Swiss Open international tennis tournament ⊛www.swissopengstaad.com.
mid Lugano – Estival Jazz open-air event ⊛www.estivaljazz.ch.
mid St Ursanne – Medieval Festival: medieval costumes, music and food ⊛www.jura.ch.
mid Bern – Gurten Festival: mass hilltop rock festival ⊛www.gurtenfestival.ch.
late Nyon – Paléo Festival: huge rock and dance happening ⊛www.paleo.ch.
late Bellinzona – open-air opera at Castelgrande ⊛www.bellinzona.ch.
late Verbier Festival and Academy: world-renowned classical soloists and conductors ⊛www.verbierfestival.com.
until Sept Gstaad – Menuhin Festival: top classical performances ⊛www.menuhinfestivalgstaad.com.
until Sept Sion – Tibor Varga Music Festival: classical, focused on the violin ⊛www.tiborvarga.org.

August

1st Swiss National Day: fireworks, folkloric shows, parades and more, in every corner of the country.
early Geneva – Fêtes de Genève: fireworks, parades and concerts ⊛www.fetes-de-geneve.ch.
early Locarno International Film Festival ⊛www.pardo.ch.
early Saignelégier – Marché Concours: national horse festival ⊛www.marcheconcours.ch.
early Winterthur – Kyburgiade chamber music festival ⊛www.kyburgiade.ch.

mid St Gallen – One-Eleven 111km inline skating race ⓦ www.one-eleven.ch.

mid Zürich – Street Parade: immense techno/dance gathering ⓦ www.streetparade.ch.

mid Zürich – Weltklasse: international athletics meeting ⓦ www.weltklasse.ch.

mid Lausanne – International Roller and Inline Contest ⓦ www.roller-contest.ch.

15 Liechtenstein National Day ⓦ www.tourismus.li.

late Chur – City Festival ⓦ www.chur.ch.

late Willisau Jazz Festival: experimental and modern jazz groups from around the world, performing in the Luzern countryside ⓦ www.jazzwillisau.ch.

late Montreux & Vevey – classical music and lyric poetry ⓦ www.montreux-festival.com.

until mid-Sept Lucerne Festival: one of Europe's leading classical music events, with soloists and orchestras of world renown ⓦ www.lucernefestival .ch.

September

early Zürich – Theater Spektakel: international open-air drama festival ⓦ www.theaterspektakel.ch.

early Bern – Old Town Festival ⓦ www.bern.ch.

early Fribourg – La Bénichon: traditional Thanksgiving festival ⓦ www.fribourgtourism.ch.

mid/late Around Switzerland – winegrowers' festivals: dozens of local village and town celebrations of the grape harvest, especially in cantons Vaud, Valais, Neuchâtel, Bern, Schaffhausen and Ticino

October

early Charmey, Appenzell and many villages in central and eastern Switzerland – celebration of the cattle's descent from Alpine pastures, often tied in with cheese markets.

late Basel Autumn Fair: traditional food fair held since 1470 ⓦ www.basel.ch.

November

early Vevey and Porrentruy – St Martin's market: festivals devoted to sausages, ham and pork.

early Aarau – Rüeblimärt: festival devoted to carrots ⓦ www.aarau.ch.

late Bern – Zibelemärit: festival devoted to onions ⓦ www.markt-bern.ch.

late Lucerne International Piano Festival ⓦ www.lucernefestival.ch.

December

early Around Switzerland – celebrations either side of Dec 6 for the arrival of St Nicholas (Santa Claus).

10–12 Geneva – Fête de l'Escalade: celebrating Geneva's independence ⓦ www.compagniede1602 .ch.

mid Zürich – Lichterschwimmen: candles floated down the River Limmat ⓦ www.zurichtourism.ch.

late Davos – Spengler Cup international ice-hockey tournament ⓦ www.spenglercup.ch.

31 Urnäsch and other Appenzell villages – masked parades for St Sylvester ⓦ www.appenzell.ch.

Sports and outdoor pursuits

Switzerland is heaven for indulging in sports and outdoorsiness of all kinds. Facilities abound in all areas of sport and exercise for literally all ages and abilities: kids start skiing as young as 2 or 3, while plenty of Swiss grandparents spend their retirement years hiking or cycling around the Alps. Safety is taken very seriously and standards are very high.

Walking

Swiss mountains are among the most dramatic and challenging of all the Alpine ranges, but you don't have to be a skilled mountaineer or climber to enjoy an active holiday among them, for Switzerland contains some of Europe's finest **walking** terrain, with enough variety to suit every taste. In the northwest of the country, for example, the rolling Jura hills are heavily wooded, but with open meadows that provide long views across the lowlands to Alpine giants. The Bernese Alps, with notoriously savage peaks such as the Eiger, Schreckhorn and Finsteraarhorn, harbour a glacial heartland but they also feature gentle valleys, pastoral ridges and charming alp hamlets with well-marked trails weaving through. On the south side of the Rhône Valley the Pennine Alps are burdened with snow and glaciers, yet walkers' paths lead along their moraines to give a taste of adventure without overtly courting danger. By contrast the mountains of Canton Ticino projecting south into Italy are almost completely snow- and ice-free in summer, and you'll find a wonderland of trails among their modest, lake-jewelled peaks.

In major tourist areas walkers can use chairlifts, gondolas and cable-cars in summer and autumn to reach high and otherwise remote trails, while rustic inns and a network of **Alpine or mountain huts** (*Hütte, refuge, rifugio* or *cabane* or *capanna*) provide rudimentary dormitory accommodation, and often meals too, for those who plan to make multi-day walking tours.

For more information, and general guidance about walking, contact the **Swiss Hiking Federation** (ⓦ www.swisshiking.ch). Switzerland Tourism publishes a brochure "Ways to Switzerland", introducing and mapping six major long-distance hiking routes of

particular cultural interest, including the network of Roman roads in Switzerland, the "Chemins de St Jacques", followed for centuries by pilgrims heading from Germany to Santiago de Compostela in Spain, and trans-Alpine mule-tracks used by traders in former ages.

Paths and signposts

Paths are well maintained, and always clearly marked with regular yellow signposts displaying the names of major landmark destinations, often with an estimate of the time it takes to walk to them. Most signposts also have a white plate giving the name and altitude of the spot you're standing on. There are three major types of path.

A *Wanderweg, chemin de randonnée pédestre* or *sentiero escursionistico* remains either in the valley or travels the hillsides at a modest altitude, is sometimes surfaced and will be graded at a relatively gentle angle. **Yellow** diamonds or pointers show the continuation of the route. (You may also spot some cultural trails – old pilgrims' roads and the like – signposted in **brown**.)

A *Bergweg, chemin de montagne* or *sentiero di montagna* is a mountain path which runs higher or steeper and can be quite demanding, often rough, narrow and sometimes fading if not in regular use. They're marked with the same yellow signposts, but with a **red and white** pointer instead of yellow. Waymarks along a mountain path are marked with similar white-red-white bars, and you may occasionally come across cairns directing the way across boulder slopes, or where poor visibility could create difficulties.

Higher, extremely hard-going Alpine trails, marked in **blue**, are only for those accompanied by a mountain guide and carrying specialist equipment.

Best hikes

Best half- or full-day walks

Davos Testing, little-used trail from the Weissfluh over to Arosa. p.519.

Grindelwald Of dozens of possibilities, the walk up through rolling pastures from Grund to Männlichen is stunning. p.301.

Kleine Scheidegg A classic high-country strolling path along the ridge to Männlichen. p.303.

Lake Geneva Plenty of paths weave in and around the Lavaux vineyards above the lake. p.150.

St Moritz Among many superb full-day trails is a panoramic route from Murtèl to Fuorcla Surlej, then over the pass to Pontresina. p.537.

Val Bavona One of the most beautiful valleys of Alto Ticino, with easy routes down to Bignasco. p.566.

Zermatt Routes around the Schwarzsee offer photogenic views of the Matterhorn. p.365.

Best multi-day walks

Interlaken Schynige Platte–Faulhorn–First–Grindelwald; one of the most scenic high-level walks in the Bernese Oberland, best done over two easy days. p.297.

Jura Höhenweg Long, often isolated trail along the length of the Swiss Jura from Zürich to Geneva. p.226.

Kandersteg Outstanding back-country trail into the Gasterntal, over the Lötschen Pass and down into the tranquil Lötschental. p.317.

Parc Naziunal Svizzer Superb walk from Zernez through the pristine park countryside, overnighting at Cluozza. p.529.

Swiss Path Easy route around the romantic, cliff-girt Urnersee, walkable in two days or dividable into sections. p.397.

Walker's Haute Route Demanding two-week trek from Chamonix, traversing a series of craggy valleys to Zermatt. p.342.

Planning your walk

No one should venture among the mountains, whatever level of walking is proposed, without consulting a good **map** (see p.24). Local shops and tourist offices usually have a selection on offer, and the latter sometimes also publish their own walkers' maps with suggested routes and times given on the reverse. On occasion **guided walks** are arranged by tourist offices in mountain areas, which may be free of charge for guests staying in local hotels. A series of excellent English-language **guidebooks** for walkers covering the Bernese Alps, Central Switzerland, Engadine, Ticino, and the Valais, plus several long-distance Alpine walks, are published by Cicerone Press in the UK, most written by Kev Reynolds.

Always check the **weather** forecast before setting out. The local tourist office or mountain guides' bureau invariably displays a two- or three-day forecast. Needless to say, do not venture to high altitudes if bad weather is expected. In any case, though, it's sensible to take a pullover or fleece and a waterproof jacket as minimum protection even if you simply plan to take a cable-car ride followed by a short stroll. On more ambitious outings it is essential to be properly equipped with wind- and waterproof clothing and good footwear. Trainers may be adequate for short valley walks, but for tackling steep hillsides and mountain paths, walking boots with ankle support and hard-wearing soles are indispensable.

Avalanche warnings, published morning and evening 365 days a year by the Federal Institute for Snow and Avalanche Research (@www.slf.ch), are posted online and publicized widely in mountain areas.

One-day walks

Never embark on a walk that under normal conditions cannot be completed **well before**

dark. Reasonably fit walkers carrying a light rucksack should be able to manage 4.5kph (2mph) on the flat, plus an additional hour for every 350m of ascent. Carry food for the day, including emergency rations, and at least one litre of water per person. Take extra care when crossing snow patches, exposed rocks and mountain streams. On some *Bergweg* routes, fixed ropes are provided as safeguards. Elsewhere there may be sections of metal ladder fitted to enable walkers to overcome a short stretch of rock. Always check these first before committing your weight to them. Do not stray onto glaciers and snowfields unless accompanied by a mountaineer experienced in glacier travel and with the necessary equipment to deal with crevasse rescue. Perhaps the best advice of all is don't be too proud to turn back should the weather deteriorate or the route become difficult or dangerous.

Multi-day walks

When tackling **hut-to-hut walks** the list of what to take with you increases. It is prudent to carry a map and compass – and to know how to use them. You should also take a first-aid kit. Don't rely on a mobile phone, since mountain coverage may be patchy; always carry a whistle and torch/flashlight in case of emergencies. Leave a note of your planned itinerary and expected time of return with a responsible person who's staying behind in a fixed location, and when staying in mountain huts enter your route details in the book provided. If for some reason you can't reach the destination where you're expected, try to send a message ahead to prevent the mountain rescue team being called out. In an emergency, give the **International Distress Signal**: six short blasts on a whistle (or flashes with a torch), followed by a minute's pause. Repeat until

you receive an answer; the response is three signals followed by a minute's silence.

Switzerland has no free mountain rescue service, and the cost of an accident can be extremely high. Standard travel **insurance** policies do not cover such emergencies, so if you are devoting all or most of your holiday to serious walking in the mountains, it's sensible to choose a policy which specifically covers mountain activity and includes emergency rescue.

Mountain huts

Mountain huts provide simple accommodation for climbers and walkers, are invariably situated in remote and scenically spectacular locations and are owned either by local groups of the **Swiss Alpine Club** (ⓦwww.sac-cas.ch), other clubs, or private companies or individuals. Many are staffed by a guardian during the summer months – usually from mid-June to mid-September – who will prepare simple meals and drinks. Mixed-sex dormitories with large, side-by-side sleeping platforms are the norm. Blankets and pillows, but not sheets, are supplied, so it's a good idea to take a sleeping bag liner (sheet sleeping bag) with you if you plan to use huts. Prices vary, but hover around Fr.25–30 for a bed, plus about the same again if you include dinner and breakfast.

Most huts have a phone and as a matter of courtesy you should phone ahead to book a place; we've listed numbers of the more popular and accessible huts throughout the book, but local tourist offices will have details of all of them, and they're also listed in a very useful book, *Schweizer Hüttenverzeichnis*, available throughout bookshops in Switzerland, as well as at ⓦwww.bergtourismus.ch.

Membership of an Alpine club in your home country may entitle you to reduced

---

Favourite views

Cardada p.563. Panoramas over Ascona and Lago Maggiore.
Monte Brè p.573. Eyrie above Lugano and its sugarloaf mountains.
Muottas Muragl p.538. The glittering Engadine lakes.
Schynige Platte p.290. Classic Berner Oberland panoramas.

Vue des Alpes p.179. Jura belvedere with an uninterrupted 100km view.
Wengen p.296. Perched between the Lauterbrunnen valley and the mighty Jungfrau.
Zermatt p.359. Jaw-dropping views up to the Matterhorn.

Top mountain resorts

Resort	Elevation	Lift pass (1/6 days)	No. of lifts	Piste difficulty (% beg/int/adv)
Alpenarena (Flims, Laax, Falera)	1160–3292m	Fr.59/301	29	28/53/19
Arosa	1750–2653m	Fr.54/251	13	26/60/14
Crans Montana	1500–3000m	Fr.54/262	30	38/50/12
Davos/Klosters	810–2817m	Fr.61/279	54	20/60/20
Engelberg	1050–3020m	Fr.49/240	25	20/60/20
Gstaad region	1000–3000m	Fr.51/251	66	30/60/10
Jungfrau region (Wengen, Mürren, Grindelwald)	1050–3454m	Fr.52/254	41	30/50/20
Upper Engadine (St Moritz, Pontresina)	1750–3303m	Fr.66/314	56	35/25/40
Saas-Fee	1800–3600m	Fr.59/278	22	37/40/23
Verbier	1500–3330m	Fr.51/303	37	33/42/25
Zermatt	1620–3820m	Fr.64/320	30	9/55/36

overnight charges in SAC huts, or you can join the SAC itself (Fr.75–125 for a year). Members of the British Mountaineering Council (@www.thebmc.co.uk), the New Zealand Alpine Club (@www.nzalpine. org.nz), the Australian Sport Climbing Federation (@www.climbing.com.au) and the Alpine Club of Canada (@www. alpineclubofcanada.ca) can purchase a Reciprocal Rights Pass (about Fr.40) from the Swiss Alpine Club on arrival in the country. The US has no national Alpine club.

Skiing and winter sports

It goes without saying that Switzerland is one of the best **winter sports** destinations in the world. The country managed to escape the worst of the 1960s boom in resort construction which afflicted many parts of the Alps, and benefits today from resorts which are generally small in scale and retain a good deal of character compared to the concrete monstrosities just

Snowboarding	No. halfpipes & boardparks	Cross-country pistes	Summer skiing	Page
2200–3000m	7	56km	Yes	515
2016–2052m	1	32km	No	508
2200–2500m	2	40km	Yes	353
2000–2600m	8	110km	Yes	518
2200–3020m	4	39km	Yes	398
1500–3000m	6	50km	Yes	317
2000–2501m	5	15km	Yes	282
2312–2659m	3	180km	Yes	531
3300–3400m	4	6km	Yes	366
2260m	3	8km	Yes	341
2571–2939m	10	9km	Yes	359

over the western and southern borders. These days you can often get better value for money skiing in Switzerland than in France or Italy, and the general tenor of Swiss ski resorts is much more cosy and village-based than elsewhere. Although Switzerland is only now starting to catch up on investment in cable-cars and gondolas to ease peak-time queues, its resorts benefit from peaceful, mostly entirely natural Alpine runs – many of them starting well above the treeline and set against some of the greatest mountain vistas to be seen anywhere.

The **winter season** runs from mid-December to mid-April – though at altitudes above about 2500m the season extends from November to May. The busiest times, when you'll pay most for ski passes and accommodation, are clustered together in early January and mid-February. The last week of March and first week of April are when you can take advantage of late snow and snap up deals on resort accommodation.

Skiing, snowboarding and beyond

Skiing, controlled by the Swiss Ski Federation (🌐www.swiss-ski.ch), is generally split into two varieties. Alpine or **downhill skiing** (*Skifahren, ski alpin, sci*) is the more popular, and involves swooshing down the mountain on **blue** (easy), **red** (intermediate) or **black** (difficult) runs, according to your ability, or – if you're entirely confident of your skills and take all necessary precautions – venturing off-piste. Downhill gets all the glamour and attention, while Nordic or **cross-country skiing** (*Ski Langlauf* or *Ski Wandern, ski de fond* or *ski nordique, sci di fondo*) is seen as much harder work for much less thrill. However, cross-country eliminates all the queues for lifts up the mountain, most of the expensive equipment associated with downhill and all the hassle. It allows you to get way out into the tranquil countryside, is much less punishing for your body and, in fact, gives a much better workout: not for nothing do enthusiasts claim that *Langläufer leben länger* ("Cross-country skiers live longer"). Prepared cross-country trails, known as *Loipen* or *loipes*, are laid on signposted routes fanning out from most resorts, the cream of the crop being in the Engadine Valley around St Moritz.

Snowboarding is massively popular throughout the country, with all major resorts – and plenty of minor ones too – encouraging the sport with well-maintained half pipes, lessons for all abilities and boarding tournaments all winter long. Check out the Swiss Snowboard Association (🌐www.ssba.ch) and its Liechtenstein equivalent (🌐www.lsba.li) for more.

There's any number of more or less crazed minor sports which tag along on the heels of skiing and snowboarding. **Mono-skiing**, like head-on snowboarding, uses a single extra-wide ski into which both feet are strapped side by side. **Ski-joring**, where you're pulled along by galloping horses, is one of the more exhilarating thrills in the snow, as is **snow-biking** or **snow-bobbing** – essentially cycling on snow. **Tobogganing** or sledding is hugely popular, and many places have pistes reserved for it; **bobsleighing** (for instance at St Moritz's death-defying Cresta Run), is the pro's version, while **luge** is a one-person tea-tray, on which you shoot feet-first down a bob-run. If you're getting bored with all those simple black runs, try **heli-skiing**, where you pay a helicopter pilot to dump you in an inaccessible spot at 4000m amidst virgin powder, or **ski hang-gliding**, where you float to earth out of an aeroplane, and then ski back to the pub. **Zorbing**, which counts as a winter or summer "sport", has gained new devotees in the classier thrill-seeking resorts of the Valais in particular; it involves being strapped immobile inside a giant plastic sphere, arms and legs spread, and then rolled down a mountainside.

Destinations

The **classic destinations**, a selection (or all) of which are offered by most package operators, include Davos, Klosters, Saas-Fee, Zermatt, St Moritz, Verbier, Crans Montana, Wengen, Mürren and Grindelwald. Flims is also rapidly making a name for itself. However, it's quite possible that slightly less famous resorts will turn out to be more rewarding, especially for first-timers or relative novices; they'll be cheaper and less crowded to start with, but also with a greater emphasis on the personal touch, and with less of a daunting competitive edge on the slopes. A sample of these might include Arosa, Engelberg, Kandersteg, Villars/Les Diablerets, Leysin, Champéry/Portes du Soleil, Lenzerheide, Savognin, Adelboden/Lenk, the Aletsch region, or Airolo and Alto Ticino. **Beginners** are perhaps best served at Arosa, Kandersteg, Saas-Fee or Mürren; dedicated **family** resorts – major names like Villars or Meiringen, and smaller, tucked-away places such as Malbun or Braunwald – are great for **kids** finding their feet; sporty thrills and spills on the slopes followed by buzzing après-ski **nightlife** is best sampled at Davos, Verbier or St Moritz; while Zermatt, Wengen and Klosters offer top-notch skiing amidst relatively quiet village-style surroundings. Some big-name resorts – most notably Gstaad – tend to deliver more designer-label shopping than on-piste satisfaction.

Year-round **summer skiing** is possible in a few resorts with access to glacier pistes above 3000m; these include Verbier, Zermatt, Les Diablerets (also with access from Gstaad), Engelberg, Crans Montana and Saas-Fee.

Passes and equipment

Passes for the ski lifts and cable-cars in and around each resort vary hugely in price: a rough average is Fr.40–50 per day, decreasing for longer periods; the big names charge upwards of Fr.60, smaller or harder-to-reach places as little as Fr.20. You can always get half-day passes, and most resorts offer an array of multi-day passes, non-consecutive day passes, weekday discounts, early- and late-season offers, and more. Many places offer discounted online booking, and you can often get a bargain if you buy your pass before the season starts (by, say, November). Use of buses and other valley transport in and around resorts is invariably included.

You can always **rent** any amount of equipment after you arrive: one day's downhill gear is approximately Fr.45–50, cross-country gear around Fr.20–25. InterSport (ⓦwww.intersport.ch/rent) and SwissRent (ⓦwww.swissrent.com) have outlets in virtually every resort in the country, and both also allow you to reserve equipment online. All Swiss resorts have **ski schools** attached, where you can, in most cases, just turn up and pay for a day's or a week's tuition in a group or one-to-one. Prices vary dramatically, roughly Fr.150–200 for five mornings' tuition; for more information, check with Swiss Ski & Snowboard Schools (ⓦwww.snowsports.ch).

Joining a **ski club** at home gives you access to plenty of information and impartial recommendations for resorts around Switzerland. Most can also provide details of tour operators which concentrate on ski- or winter-packages (or occasionally may offer such packages themselves). The Ski Club of Great Britain (ⓦwww.skiclub.co.uk) has particularly good information.

Cycling and mountain-biking

Given the nature of the landscape, **cycling** is not the easiest way of exploring the country, but the scenery more than compensates for the extra effort required. It's a very popular Swiss pursuit, and the locals don't restrict themselves to flat lakeside or valley-floor routes: summer weekends see plenty of sinewy, lycra-clad characters pumping their way slowly up the long 12 or 14 percent gradients of the high Alpine passes. Cycle routes – in the cities too – are plentiful. If you're arriving in Switzerland with **your own bike**, you have to buy a **vignette** from post offices for around Fr.5, which covers road tax and third-party insurance for a year. The Swiss Cycling Federation is at ⓦwww. cycling.ch.

Under the banner of *Veloland Schweiz*, *La Suisse à vélo*, *La Svizzera in bici* (ⓦwww.cycling-in-switzerland.ch), nine long-distance **cycle routes** crisscross the country on 3300km of dedicated signposted paths, mostly well away from traffic. These vary between, say, the Rhône Route (Andermatt to Geneva, 324km), the Alpine Panorama Route (Rorschach to Aigle, 483km) and the North–South Route (Basel to Chiasso, 363km). Tourist offices can give you a map of all nine routes, and information in English on each one, as well as maps showing other cycle routes within their region or city. The website has full details. **Mountain biking** is very popular at loads of Swiss resorts, many of which produce their own local guides to bike routes in their area. Move (ⓦwww.move.ch) is the top Swiss mountain bike magazine and ⓦwww. ig-mtb.ch is an enthusiasts' site. Check out the maps at ⓦwww.singletrailmap.ch.

A day-pass to let you **transport a bike** by train anywhere in Switzerland costs Fr.15; you have to load and unload it yourself using the special carriage marked with a big bicycle pictogram, and you must have a ticket or pass for the same destination. Some EC trains and the Bern and Zürich S-Bahn are prohibited during rush hours: yellow train timetables mark those trains on which bikes cannot be transported with a crossed-out pictogram. Alternatively, you can let SBB train staff load and unload it for you; this costs Fr.12 if you have a ticket for the same destination, or Fr.48 if you don't. Station staff have full details, as do ⓦwww.rail.ch and ☎0900 300 300.

Bike rental

You can **rent** a new seven-gear country bike or a quality 21-gear mountain bike from Rent-A-Bike (ⓦwww.rentabike.ch), located at most Swiss train stations (look for *Mietvelos*, *location de vélos*, *bici da noleggiare*). If there's no dedicated bike office, you normally rent from left-luggage counters. **Prices** are Fr.23 for a half-day (the cutoff time is

12.30pm) or Fr.30 for a full day. The popular option of one-way rental (for a full day or more) attracts a Fr.6 surcharge; you must let staff know where and when you intend to drop the bike off when you rent. Note that if you hold any kind of Swiss travel pass, all these prices are discounted by about 20 percent. Kids' bikes and seats for children which you can attach to an adult's bike are also available. Station bike rental is massively popular, especially throughout the summer months, and if you're planning to rent you should always **reserve** as far as possible in advance (normally, a day or two is OK). Look for the bike-train leaflet at stations, which has a list of stations, phone numbers and the number of rental bikes at each one. Even so, on summer weekends, stations like Bern and Zürich that hold dozens of bikes for rent can be completely cleaned out: in these cases, you may have to take a train (or call ahead) to a smaller town and try there.

As a way to teach local unemployed people new skills and get them back to work, Zürich, Bern, Geneva and a handful of other cities run **free bike-rental** schemes year-round, invariably from depots beside or opposite the train station. All you do is pay a Fr.20 deposit and leave some ID, and you're free to cycle off for as long as you like.

Another option is to take advantage of a cut-price offer whereby you can rent a brand-new 24-gear mountain bike from certain **HI hostels** for just Fr.15 a day (or Fr.10 for a four-hour half-day) – you don't have to be staying overnight to be able to rent. Check ⓦ www.youthhostel.ch for full details; you need to reserve ahead. To rent, you must show ID, leave a Fr.100 deposit (cash or credit-card slip) and return the bike to the same hostel you rented from.

Other sports and activities

The tourist office site ⓦ www.myswitzerland.com has plenty of information on the range of sports and activites on offer.

To complement the country's many cycle routes, there are currently three long-distance **inline skating** routes of around 200km each, from Geneva to Brig, Zürich to Yverdon, and Bad Ragaz to Schaffhausen. Inline skating and roller-skating are popular all round the country, from the lakeside

promenade at Lausanne to the runway of Samedan airfield, in the mountains near St Moritz. ⓦ www.swiss-skate-map.ch shows skating routes nationwide, and ⓦ www.skate.ch has a good set of links.

Swimming and **watersports** have big followings at all the lakeside resorts, and almost everywhere is clean enough (signs are posted otherwise). Boats and equipment for windsurfing are available for rent on almost all lakes, and wakeboarding and kitesurfing are also attracting attention, not least at Silvaplana, near St Moritz. **Rowing** and **canoeing** are also popular, especially on the Rotsee near Luzern, which regularly stages the rowing world championships.

The boom in **adventure sports** has arrived in Switzerland with a vengeance, and places like Interlaken and the Ticino have dozens of companies offering canyoning and bungee-jumping, as well as **aerial sports** such as paragliding, hang-gliding and a host of others; we've outlined the options throughout the guide. **Hot-air ballooning** is headquartered in Château d'Oex, nerve centre of the 1998 record-breaking balloon flight around the world. Holly Ballon (ⓦ www.holly.ch) is one company offering hot-air balloon rides short and long from a number of starting points in northern Switzerland, including sunrise excursions and trips over the mountains; prices start from around Fr.350 per person.

Swiss sports

On a more pedestrian level, the Swiss have a number of sports of their own, most of them rooted in celebrations of Alpine brawn. They tend to be indulged in by local communities – often in traditional dress – on open field sites during spring and summer months, along with much festivity and carousing. **Schwingen** (ⓦ www.esv.ch) is an idiosyncratic kind of sumo-wrestling, in which both participants wear leather or canvas over-shorts; you've got to keep at least one hand on your opponent's shorts at all times, and still manage to heave him onto his back within a laid-out circle of sawdust. It's taken very seriously, and champs become rural folk heroes. **Steintossen**, a much less refined activity, involves flinging a massive rock as far as possible.

The classic Swiss sport – completely unlike anything else, and so loved and

Spectator sports

Switzerland hosts a fair spread of world-class annual sporting events. In **tennis**, the leading events are the Swiss Open, held at Gstaad in early July (ⓦ www.swissopengstaad.com), and the Swiss Indoors, at Basel in October (ⓦ www.swissindoors.ch). Zürich's Weltklasse **athletics** meeting every August (ⓦ www.weltklasse.ch) is a highlight of the IAAF Golden League. The European Masters **golf** tournament takes place in early September at the stunning Alpine course at Crans Montana (ⓦ golf.european-masters.com). The **cycling** Tour de Suisse (ⓦ www.cycling.ch) happens in June. **Football** has never been Switzerland's strong point (ⓦ www.football.ch), but it does boast the oldest club in continental Europe, FC St Gallen, founded in 1879. Geneva's Servette, Grasshoppers of Zürich and FC Basel are the current big fish. The most prestigious of dozens of winter sports events is the World Cup **downhill skiing** at Wengen in January (ⓦ www.lauberhorn.ch), although the Spengler Cup **ice hockey** tournament (ⓦ www.spenglercup.ch) in Davos in late December can match it for thrills and spills.

cherished as an expression of true Swissness – is **Hornussen** (ⓦ www. hornussen.ch): one person launches the *hornuss*, a puck, into the air by hitting it along a curved track with a long cane; the other players, standing well back, try to knock it aside with large wooden bats before it falls to the ground. Tournaments last for some time, with much discussion of the finer points of skill; foreign onlookers rarely make any sense of it all.

Crime and personal safety

Compared to most Europeans, the Swiss are law-abiding to a fault, rendering even the minimal police presence superfluous. There's only a small force of plain-clothes federal police (*Polizei, police, polizia*), since most police duties are managed by the cantonal authorities, all of which maintain uniformed, armed police. Towns and cities also have their own armed police, operating in conjunction with the cantonal force.

It's very rare you'll even see a police officer in Switzerland, although you may come across one or two directing the traffic. Nonetheless, Swiss police are nothing of a soft touch, and draw continuing approbation from Amnesty International for their heavy-handed approach to foreigners, asylum seekers and Swiss citizens of non-European descent in particular, with random street searches and "unjustified use of violence" cited.

If you do come into contact with the police, they'll want to see your **passport**, which you're obliged to carry at all times. Ordinary traffic offences will be dealt with swiftly and courteously – as long as you pay the fine – although police officers, especially outside the cities, may not speak any English; should there be any disputes, they may insist you accompany them to the nearest police station to have all the necessaries explained. As across Europe, urban Switzerland has a serious **hard-drug** problem. All drugs are illegal, but curiously, drug laws are enforced less rigorously in the German-speaking cities than elsewhere: limited personal cannabis-smoking in Bern and Zürich is usually ignored (except when there's a blitz on), but anywhere else you can expect fines and major hassle. Possession of more than a joint or two's worth of cannabis, or of any other drug at all, will land you in serious trouble, involving either prison or deportation plus a criminal record. Expect no sympathy from your embassy.

If you're unfortunate enough to be **robbed**, you should always go to the nearest police station to get a report filled out (you'll need it for your insurance if nothing else). It may take hours to complete all the paperwork required.

Police emergency ☎117

Work and study

Switzerland is notoriously difficult for outsiders trying to find casual work. Getting any kind of permit is your first headache (see p.21); being expected to work like the Swiss – hard, and for long hours – is your second; and being able to show at least a smattering of the local lingo is your third. The rewards are salaries and per-hour wages way above anything you'll be able to get at home.

The following are some pointers for casual, seasonal jobs; getting longer-term work or securing permanent contracts are a whole other book.

Key hunting grounds are **ski resorts**, although you should note that you don't qualify for unemployment insurance: if the snow is bad and tourist levels are down, you may be summarily fired. Chalet-rental companies need staff to cook in and clean their hundreds of chalets. Qualified ski/snowboard instructors and unqualified guides for foreign tour operators are always in demand, as are technicians for maintaining ski equipment and fitting skis and boots in resort shops, large hotels and for tour companies. In addition, of course, people are needed all summer and winter at big hotels as kitchen assistants, porters, messengers, dishwashers, cleaners and so on. All of these jobs can, if you're lucky, result in a permit being organized by your employer within a few weeks, allowing you to start work on the spot. It's more prudent, but not necessarily any more guaranteed, to write to potential employers months ahead of the season: in August for winter jobs, March for summer ones. Resorts seeing a lot of English and American tourists (and so more likely to hire an English speaker) include Arosa, Crans-Montana, Davos, Grindelwald, Klosters, Saas-Fee, St Moritz, Verbier, Wengen and Zermatt, but smaller resorts than these have the advantage of less competition from jobseekers.

The publisher Vacation Work (www. vacationwork.co.uk) has books on summer jobs abroad and how to work your way around the world, including the very useful *Working in Ski Resorts – Europe* by Victoria Pybus and Charles James.

The main other form of casual employment in Switzerland is **voluntary work**, or work for nominal pay, mostly on farms. The Swiss Farm Work Association can place unskilled French- or German-speakers between 18 and 25 on farms around the country over a summer; up to 48 long, hard hours a week pays you at most Fr.20 a day, plus board and lodging. Consult www.landdienst.ch well ahead of time. Otherwise, the Swiss branch of WWOOF (Willing Workers on Organic Farms; www.welcome.to/wwoof) can organize placements at 45 farms around the country, for which you get the experience but no wages.

For **study**, there's a range of international organizations that run programs in Switzerland, and students may also be able to take an accredited semester, or even year, at a Swiss university as part of their degree.

Work and study contacts

UK & Ireland

British Council ☎020/7930 8466, www.britishcouncil.org. Produces a free leaflet on study abroad, and a book *Year Between* aimed at gap-year students.

Earthwatch Institute ☎01865/311 600, www.earthwatch.org. Long-established international charity with environmental and archeological research projects worldwide.

Erasmus europa.eu.int/comm/education /erasmus.html. EU-run student exchange programme. Grants available.

Field Studies Council Overseas t01743/852 150, www.fscoverseas.org.uk. Respected educational charity that organizes specialized small-group botanical/zoological holidays.

US

AFS Intercultural Programs ☎1-800/876-2377 or 212/299 9000, www.afs.org/usa. Summer experiential programs aimed at fostering international understanding.

Association for International Practical Training ☎410/997-2200, ⓦwww.aipt.org. Summer internships for students who have completed at least two years of college in certain fields.

Bernan Associates ☎1-800/274-4888, ⓦwww.bernan.com. Distributes UNESCO's encyclopedic Study Abroad.

Council on International Educational Exchange ☎1-800/2-COUNCIL, ⓦwww.ciee.org/study. Non-profit organization running summer, semester and year programs, as well as volunteer projects.

Earthwatch Institute ☎1-800/776-0188 or 978/461-0081, ⓦwww.earthwatch.org. International non-profit organization with ongoing field research projects.

Experiment in International Living ☎1-800/345-2929, ⓦwww.usexperiment.org. Summer program to Switzerland for high-school students.

World Learning ☎802/257-7751, ⓦwww.worldlearning.org. Its School for International Training runs accredited college semesters abroad.

Australia

Australians Studying Abroad ☎1800/645 755 or 03/9509 1955, ⓦwww.asatravinfo.com.au. Study tours focusing on art and culture.

Council on International Educational Exchange ☎1300/135 331 or 02/8235 7000, ⓦwww.councilexchanges.org.au. International student exchange programmes.

Travellers with disabilities

Switzerland is one of the most enlightened European countries with regard to travellers with disabilities. There's a wealth of information available in advance to help in planning your trip, and once you arrive you'll find most tourist facilities have been designed with everybody, not just the able-bodied, in mind.

There are many organized **tours** and **holidays** specifically put together for people with disabilities; the contacts below will be able to put you in touch with specialists. Switzerland Tourism (see p.23 for worldwide contacts) publishes a very useful **hotel guide** specifically for visitors with disabilities, listing and assessing hotels around the country according to their access for people with limited mobility or in wheelchairs. Mobility International Switzerland has its own list, and also publishes **city guides** for 26 localities around the country for around Fr.5 each, written for tourists with disabilities. Procap also sells a **map** and **brochure** in four languages covering travel in Switzerland.

Swiss Federal Railways posts good information online at ⓦwww.rail.ch and also publishes a brochure covering **train travel** around the country, which includes a table of stations detailing accessible facilities, such as ramps or lifts, waiting rooms and toilets, and a full table of all bus and taxi companies able to accommodate wheelchairs. If you contact their "**Call Center Handicap**" team

(see opposite) at least two hours before you want to travel, giving them your full name, phone number, date of travel, desired departure and arrival times, and the nature of your disability, they can arrange for people to help you on and off the train and access the "Mobilifts" at most stations; this is a free service. All fast trains (single- and double-decker), and most regional trains have spaces within second-class carriages to park wheelchairs, identified by a wheelchair pictogram. Facilities are being upgraded nationwide: stations such as Kreuzlingen and Stein-am-Rhein have newly replaced steps with ramps; city **trams** and **buses** around the country are increasingly wheelchair-accessible; **boats** are generally easy to board and often have facilities such as disabled toilets; and private narrow-gauge train companies including MOB (between Montreux, Gstaad and the Bernese Oberland) and FART (the Centovalli line from Locarno) are converting carriages for passengers with disabilities. The Call Center Handicap office has full details.

Contacts for travellers with disabilities

UK & Ireland

Access Travel ☎01942/888 844,
ⓦ www.access-travel.co.uk. Small, personal-
service tour operator that can arrange flights,
transfers and accommodation.
Holiday Care ☎01293/774 535, Minicom
☎01293/776 943, ⓦ www.holidaycare.org.uk.
Provides a free list of accessible accommodation in
Switzerland, and gives information on financial help
for holidays.
Irish Wheelchair Association ☎01/833 8241,
ⓦ www.iwa.ie. Useful travel information.
**RADAR (Royal Association for Disability and
Rehabilitation)** ☎020/7250 3222, Minicom
☎020/7250 4119, ⓦ www.radar.org.uk. A good
source of advice, with a useful website.
Tripscope ☎0845/758 5641,
ⓦwww.justmobility.co.uk/tripscope. Registered
charity providing free advice on international transport.

US & Canada

Access-Able ⓦwww.access-able.com. Online
resource for travellers with disabilities.
Directions Unlimited ☎1-800/533-5343 or
914/241-1700. Tour operator.
Mobility International USA ☎541/343-1284,
ⓦ www.miusa.org. Information and referral
services, guides, tours and exchange programmes.
**Society for the Advancement of Travelers
with Handicaps (SATH)** ☎212/447-7284,
ⓦ www.sath.org. Non-profit educational
organization.
Travel Information Service ☎215/456-9600.
Information and referral service.
Twin Peaks Press ☎1-800/637-2256 or
360/694-2462, ⓦ disabilitybookshop.
virtualave.net. Disability-oriented publisher.
Wheels Up! ☎1-888/389-4335,
ⓦ www.wheelsup.com. Provides discounted airfare
and tour prices and a free monthly newsletter.
Comprehensive website.

Australia & NZ

**ACROD (Australian Council for Rehabilitation
of the Disabled)** ☎02/6282 4333. Provides lists
of travel agencies and tour operators.
Disabled Persons Assembly (NZ) ☎04/801
9100. Resource centre with lists of travel agencies
and tour operators.

Switzerland

Active Motion Mühleholzstrasse 13, CH-3800
Unterseen/Interlaken ☎033 823 59 74,
ⓦwww.activemotion.ch. Snow sports school for
disabled people.
**BöV/HTP (Swiss Office for People with
Disabilities and Public Transport)**
Froburgstrasse 4, CH-4601 Olten ☎062 206 88
40, ⓔ boev@bluewin.ch.
Call Center Handicap Mobil Services Handicap,
Bahnhofplatz 1, CH-3900 Brig ☎0800 007 102,
ⓔ mobil@sbb.ch. Part of the Passenger Division of
SBB. Gives full details of accessibility on all forms of
public transport, and makes arrangements for travel
anywhere in Switzerland.
Car rental The following organizations rent cars
that have been adapted for people with disabilities:
Garage Zgraggen, Altdorf ☎041 872 11 72; Verein
Behindertenbus, Brugg ☎056 444 06 60; Transport-
Handicap, Lausanne ☎021 648 53 53; Mietauto,
Winterthur ☎052 202 33 33, ⓦwww.mietauto.ch;
Amt für baulichen Zivilschutz Stadt, Zürich ☎01 411
21 12; Behindertentransport LZU, Zürich ☎01 781
49 49. The Schweizerische Paraplegiker-Vereinigung,
in Nottwil LU ☎041 939 54 00, can rent you a car
with hand controls.
Mobility International Switzerland (MIS)
☎062 206 88 35, ⓦwww.mis-ch.ch. Loads of
useful information and links.
Nautilus Reisen ☎062 206 88 30,
ⓦwww.nautilus.ch. Fully bonded travel agency.
Procap ☎062 206 88 88, ⓦwww.siv.ch.
Switzerland's largest self-help association for people
with disabilities.

Directory

Contraceptives You can buy condoms (Kondoms or präservatives, préservatifs, preservativi) over the counter at all pharmacies and most supermarkets. If you use other forms of contraception, you should bring enough supplies to last the duration of your trip.

Electricity 220v, 50Hz (the same as in the rest of continental Europe). Plug sockets are generally of the round or flat two-pin type. British appliances will need a plug adaptor, while North American appliances will also need a 220-to-110v transformer.

Gay and lesbian travellers You'll find Switzerland to be generally very tolerant towards gay (schwul, gai, gay) and lesbian (lesbisch, lesbien, lesbico) lifestyles. The age of consent has been unified at 16 and equality of treatment under the law is guaranteed. All major urban areas have organizations lobbying local and cantonal governments on gay issues which serve as a focus for the local scene, while the national mouthpieces are the Pink Cross (Ⓦwww.pinkcross.ch) for men, and the Swiss Lesbian Organization (Ⓦwww.los.ch). Nightlife is varied and welcoming, with Zürich and Geneva enjoying the lion's share of the action; we've listed some bars and contacts in the major town accounts. There's tons of information online, starting with Ⓦwww.myswitzerland.com/gay, Ⓦwww.gay.ch and Ⓦwww.swissgay.ch.

Laundry Public coin-op laundries aren't a very common sight, since all Swiss apartment blocks have their own washing machines for residents' use in the cellar. University towns such as Geneva, Lausanne and Zürich have a few coin-ops for students living without such facilities, or otherwise you may have to resort to the many places offering specialist service washes, which are hideously expensive.

Racism Racism is perhaps the biggest current social issue in Switzerland, with ongoing, none-too-civil debates raging about the absorption of foreigners into Swiss society, and the high levels of asylum seekers arriving from conflict-torn parts of Europe and the world. Small-town Switzerland is hopping from foot to foot, forced to address the issue but unable to reconcile traditional Swiss hospitality and respect for others with the equally traditional mistrust and rejection of outsiders. While society is in flux, the fact remains that outside certain parts of Geneva, Lausanne, Basel, Bern and Zürich, non-white faces are a rare sight on the street. Across the country there's some antagonism directed towards both refugees from the former Yugoslavia, who are commonly perceived as gangsters, and tourists from East Asia, who are often seen as an irritant. Luzern is infamous as the major recruiting ground for Switzerland's expanding extreme right-wing political parties. Despite all this, you're very unlikely actually to encounter any trouble, but some neanderthal attitudes – stares or condescension – may persist in out-of-the-way corners.

Time Switzerland is on Central European Time (CET), 1hr ahead of London, 6hr ahead of New York, and 8hr behind Sydney.

Tipping All bar, restaurant and hotel bills are calculated with fifteen percent service included: tipping is officially abolished. Nonetheless, unless service was truly diabolical, everyone rounds things up at least to the nearest franc; in restaurants, it's common to add a few francs.

Guide

Guide

1 Geneva 79–114

2 Lausanne and Lake Geneva 115–165

3 The Arc Jurassien..167–204

4 Basel and around 205–231

5 Bern and around..233–276

6 The Bernese Oberland 277–322

7 Valais 323–370

8 Luzern and Zentralschweiz 371–416

9 Zürich..417–457

10 Ostschweiz and Liechtenstein 459–496

11 Graubünden..497–542

12 Ticino 543–578

Geneva

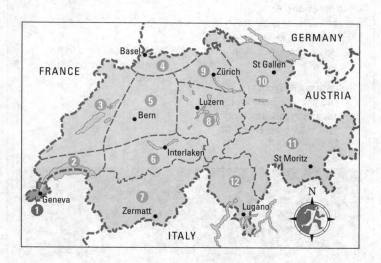

CHAPTER 1

Highlights

✳ **Jet d'Eau** Giant fountain, symbol of the city. **See p.93**

✳ **Cathédrale St-Pierre** The seat of Calvin's Reformation, at the heart of Geneva's Old Town. **See p.94**

✳ **Collections Baur** Museum of exquisite Chinese and Japanese art and ceramics. **See p.98**

✳ **Carouge** Easygoing sub-urb with Italianate architecture, good shopping and lively bars. **See p.99**

✳ **Les Pâquis** Gritty, multi-ethnic district with diverse restaurants and engaging streetlife. **See p.100**

✳ **Musée de la Croix-Rouge** Superb museum-with-a-conscience, devoted to the history of the Red Cross. **See p.103**

✳ **The UN tour** Stand in the footsteps of history. **See p.104**

Geneva

ENEVA is an anomaly, the nearest thing the world has to a truly international city, and yet with nothing of the pizzazz such a description might suggest. From its profile in world events, you'd imagine a megalopolis on the scale of London or New York, but Geneva is little more than town-sized. From its demographic diversity – 38 percent of the population are non-Swiss – you'd imagine its streets to be thronged with the nationalities of the world, but across most of the city centre (bar the cosmopolitan Pâquis district) you'd be hard pushed to spot a non-white face or eavesdrop on a conversation that wasn't in French or US-accented English. It's in the most beautiful of locations, centred around the point where the River Rhône flows out of **Lake Geneva** (Lac Léman in French), flanked on one side by the Jura ridges and on the other by the first peaks of the Savoy Alps, but for all that, it's a curiously unsatisfying place to spend more than a few days.

The spiritual father of the city is the Reformer **Jean Calvin**, the inspiration behind Puritanism and Scottish Presbyterianism, who turned Geneva into what was dubbed a "Protestant Rome" in the sixteenth century. His parsimonious spirit remains the motive force behind this wealthiest and least exuberant of city-states. What's officially still known as "the Republic and Canton of Geneva" is only nominally within Switzerland's borders, squeezed into a bulge of land that shares just 4km of internal border with the neighbouring Swiss canton but 108km with France all around. Some thirty thousand French *frontaliers* commute daily to their workplaces in Geneva from dormitory towns just over the border, benefiting from a high Swiss salary and relatively low French living expenses, and equally large numbers of Genevois save money by doing their shopping in France. The Gallic influence is what defines the city, and yet this is tempered by a streak of Calvinism so ingrained that the conservative Genevois – surrounded as they are by some of the world's most expensive shops and most exquisite restaurants – can't quite bring themselves to indulge, and leave most of the high living to the international jetset glitterati who've taken up residence on the lakeside hills.

Instead, Geneva has become the businessperson's city *par excellence*, unruffable, efficient and packed with hotels. The cobbled **Old Town**, high on its central hill, is atmospheric but strangely austere, with abiding impressions of high, grey walls and the stern tap-tap of passing footsteps. At the heart of the city is the huge **Cathédrale St-Pierre**, and packed in all around is an array of top-class **museums**, including the giant Musée d'Art et d'Histoire and an impressive gallery of East Asian art, the Collections Baur. Livelier residential neighbourhoods on both banks of the Rhône, such as **Les Pâquis** and **Plainpalais**, offer more appealing wandering, while a short way south of the centre is **Carouge**, an attractive eighteenth-century suburb built in Sardinian style to be a place of decadence and freedom beyond Geneva's control; its reputation lives on in its population of artists and designers.

Last but not least, Geneva is home to dozens of international organizations. Two of them – the **United Nations**' European headquarters and the International Committee of the **Red Cross**, the latter with an award-winning museum – allow visitors a glimpse of the unseen lifeblood of the city, the diplomatic and administrative instinct that has made Geneva world capital of bureaucracy.

Some history

Pile dwellings have been unearthed on the lakeshore dating back to 3000 BC, but Geneva's high ground wasn't inhabited until 500 BC, when the Celtic Allobroges tribe settled. By 58 BC, **Rome** had taken over: the first recorded use of the name *Genua* was by Julius Caesar. The town grew rapidly, and was a bishopric by 400 AD but, located on the turbulent mid-line of Europe, Geneva was continually conquered and reconquered, by Burgundians, Franks, Merovingians, Carolingians and more, until the fifteenth century, when the famous **Geneva Fairs** gave the city a reputation as a trading capital. The dukes of **Savoy** retained their grip on the town's affairs up until 1530, when citizens took matters into their own hands and formed a pact with Bern and Fribourg. The Savoyards granted Geneva independence shortly after.

In 1535, the Genevois accepted the **Reformation**; the following year, the preacher **Jean Calvin** visited the city for the first time. Born in Picardy in 1509, Calvin was expelled from the University of Paris in 1533 for his heterodox views, and arrived by chance in Geneva three years later, where he was called upon by the leader of the religious community in the city, Guillaume Farel, to help consolidate the Reformation. After two years of opposition from city politicians, both were expelled, only to return in 1541 with Calvin at the helm. From a position of authority, Calvin was able to institute sweeping social and political reforms within a strict, uncompromising Protestant theocracy.

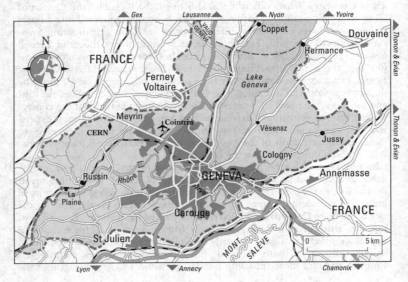

Geneva became a beacon of **refuge** for the persecuted of Europe, and French Huguenots and Italian Protestants in particular flooded to the city, which also rapidly became a centre of academic excellence. The Geneva Bible of 1560 was the first English translation to be organized methodically, with numbered verses, and the city's printing presses turned out hundreds of radical texts, unprintable elsewhere.

In 1602, forces of the Duke of Savoy tried to retake Geneva, but were repulsed in an event that is still commemorated today, in a celebration of the city's independent, patriotic spirit, as **L'Escalade** (see p.86). Wave after wave of refugees flowed into the city, shaping a cosmopolitanism and religious liberality which continue today. Commerce, banking and watchmaking all flourished, and in 1792 the aristocratic rulers of the city were overthrown and a **Republic** was declared with political equality for all. Geneva was annexed by France in 1798, and following the defeat of Napoleon in 1813, threw in its lot with the Swiss Confederation in 1815. A Genevan businessman, Henri Dunant, shaped the **Geneva Convention** of 1864, setting down for the first time rules for soldiers' conduct in war. This led to the creation of the International Red Cross, designed to help soldiers or civilians caught up in war or natural disasters (see p.104).

After World War I, Geneva was chosen as seat of the League of Nations and in 1945 as the European headquarters of the **United Nations**. Since then, the city has looked outwards for inspiration, away from the rest of Switzerland and towards the international community, many of whose conflicts have been negotiated away in the halls and chambers of Geneva's Palais des Nations.

Arrival and information

Geneva's **airport** (Ⓦ www.gva.ch), 5km northwest at Cointrin, is one of the best-designed in the world. With just 200m walking distance from plane to train, it needn't take more than half-an-hour from touchdown for you to be done with all the formalities and heading into the city. There's only one terminal, replete with English-language signing. The **tourist information** desk (daily 6am–midnight) is in plain view, offering free maps and advice and hotel reservations boards (with complimentary phone). To the left is a revolving door giving access into the adjacent train station ("Gare CFF").

The simplest onward transport is city **bus** #10, which departs from the top of the escalators just inside the train station's revolving door, and can drop you fifteen minutes later in the centre of town on the Rue du Mont-Blanc (for the Rive Droite) or Place Bel-Air (for the Rive Gauche). If you don't have a transport pass, you'll need coins to buy a ticket from the machine before you board, valid for unlimited changes in either one hour (button B; Fr.2.20) or a day (button E; Fr.6). The airport **train** station is the beginning of the line, and all trains from here stop at Geneva's main station (Fr.5; 6min; last 12.02am) before going on direct to places all over the country, including Lausanne, Vevey, Montreux, Sion, Brig, Neuchâtel, Biel/Bienne, Basel, Fribourg, Bern, Luzern, Zürich and St Gallen, cutting out the need to change in Geneva. The train station is the best place to **change money** (daily 6.20am–8pm), and the concourse also has luggage lockers (Fr.3/5) and a staffed left-luggage office (daily 6.40am–8.40pm; Fr.5/day). **Taxis** charge a steep Fr.30–35 into the city.

By train

Geneva's main **train** station – the **Gare de Cornavin** – couldn't be more central, barely 300m north of the lake. It's also a terminus of the French SNCF rail network: if you're arriving on an intercity train (TGV or not) from Paris, Lyon or Grenoble – which come in on platforms 7 and 8, separate from the rest – you'll pass through customs and passport control before joining the throng within the station proper. The station has the usual array of facilities, including a change bureau (daily 6.45am–9.30pm; Oct–April closes 8pm) and bike rental (Mon–Fri 6.50am–6.45pm, Sat & Sun 7am–12.30pm & 1.30–5.45pm). There's also a TPG (*Transports publics genevois*) office (Mon–Sat 7am–7pm, Sun 10am–6pm), giving out city tram and bus maps and selling tickets. Sporadic French SNCF local trains from Evian, Chamonix and Annecy, connecting at Annemasse and La Roche, arrive at the tiny **Gare des Eaux-Vives**, well to the east of the centre; opposite is a terrace of houses, to the right of which is the Rue de Savoie heading 50m up to the main road, from where trams #12 and #16 head right into the centre.

By car, bus and boat

Geneva is surrounded on all sides by France: the only Swiss *autoroute* into the city is the N1 from Lausanne. **Parking** is a nightmare: you'd do well to arrange matters with your hotel or get rid of your vehicle on the city limits. Parking garages citywide

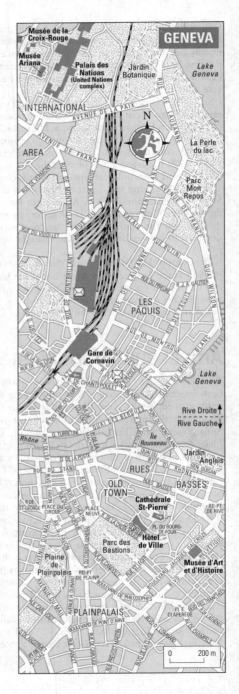

are listed at ⓦ www.geneve.ch/parkings/parkings.html. At the airport, long-term car parks P51, 300m from the terminal beside World Trade Centre-2 (bus #10 stops outside the adjacent WTC-1), and P26 beneath Palexpo Hall 7 are both around Fr.15–20 for the first 24 hours, plus about half that thereafter; the more convenient car park at the airport train station (signposted "Aérogare") costs more, but is discounted to similar levels for train users only. On-street parking in the centre (see p.41 for details) is very hard to find; garages are fine for short periods (roughly Fr.2/hr), but tend to charge a stiff Fr.35/day. The biggest is beneath the Pont du Mont-Blanc (☎022 310 01 30). Note that the one under Place Cornavin (☎022 827 44 90) in front of the train station is cheaper the lower down you go, and is also discounted for train users (Fr.19/day).

All international **buses** arrive at the Gare Routière, on Place Dorcière (☎022 732 02 30, ⓦwww.coach-station.com), just off Rue du Mont-Blanc in the city centre. Most are massive hauls from the far corners of Europe (including a 16hr journey from London via Dijon), although there are also plenty of arrivals from nearby points in France, such as Chamonix, Grenoble, Lyon, Annecy and Evian.

The most romantic way to arrive is by **boat**, on one of the many CGN services (☎0848 811 848, ⓦwww.cgn.ch) that village-hop their way along both shores of the lake from Lausanne, Evian and Nyon. Boats drop off at one or more of the four CGN jetties within Geneva: **Eaux-Vives**, east of the Jet d'Eau; **Les Pâquis**, near the Casino; and **Jardin Anglais** and **Mont-Blanc**, at either end of the Pont du Mont-Blanc.

Information

Geneva's **tourist office** is a mine of information on everything to do with the city and canton. The main branch is in the central post office at 18 Rue du Mont-Blanc (Mon–Sat 9am–6pm, July & Aug also Sun 9am–6pm; ☎022 909 70 00, ⓦwww.genevatourism.ch), and there's also a desk within the information office of the Municipality of Geneva, situated on the Pont de la Machine (Mon noon–6pm, Tues–Fri 9am–6pm, Sat 10am–5pm; ☎022 311 99 70, ⓦwww.ville-ge.ch). Both have stacks of material in English, including a handbook of 101 "visits and discoveries", the encyclopedic *Geneva At Hand* and the useful *Young People* brochure listing budget hotels and ideas, and both maintain detailed and useful websites. During the summer, a bus parked at the station end of the Rue du Mont-Blanc houses the "CAR" info-centre; they can help with accommodation and transport information (mid-June to early Sept daily 9am–11pm; ☎022 731 46 47).

The weekly *Genève Agenda*, available free from the tourist office and most hotels, is a useful source of information on sightseeing, the latest exhibitions and other bits and bobs. The municipality counters with the monthly *Genève: Le Guide* (ⓦwww.le-guide.ch), which costs a few francs; its maps are good and its information trustworthy.

City transport and tours

Walking is feasible enough for the heart of Geneva, and even getting to further-flung attractions such as Carouge or the UN takes only twenty or thirty minutes on foot, but you'll probably want to use **city transport** at least once or twice. Trams and buses form the core of the transport network, with a few boats linking the two lakefronts; renting a bike (see p.112) can make sense.

Geneva's festivals

Geneva's biggest celebration is **L'Escalade** (ⓦwww.compagniede1602.ch), commemorating the failed attempt by the Duke of Savoy to seize the town by surprise on the night of December 11–12, 1602. Locals dress up in costume and parade by torchlight around the streets with drums and fifes, groups of kids sing in city-centre cafés, and confectioners sell the *Marmite d'Escalade*, a small pot made of chocolate and filled with marzipan "vegetables" to commemorate a Genevan housewife who dispatched a Savoyard soldier by tipping her boiling soup over his head from a high window. A few days before is the Course d'Escalade, a fun-run through town. Geneva's **Fourth-of-July** celebrations for US Independence Day are the biggest in the world outside the States, and its **Swiss National Day** festivities, every August 1, are equally spectacular. The **Fêtes de Genève** (Geneva Festival; ⓦwww. fetes-de-geneve.ch) is the city's premier annual pageant, held in early August on the waterfront, with music of all kinds, lovemobiles and techno floats on the lake, theatre, funfairs, street entertainers, stalls selling food from around the world, and an enormous lakeside musical fireworks display. During the last week of August and early September, **La Bâtie Festival de Genève** features live music and theatrical performances. Finally, Geneva's famous **Motor Show** (ⓦwww.palexpo.ch), held every March in the Palexpo arena, is the largest and most prestigious in Europe.

Taxis are only for the rich and famous. You can hail them in the street, take them from ranks at the station and elsewhere, or call ☎022 331 41 33 – but with a Fr.6.30 flagfall, Fr.2.90 per kilometre (more on Sunday and at night), plus Fr.1.50 per piece of luggage, they're only a ski-mask short of daylight robbery.

Trams, buses and boats

Geneva's **trams and buses** (ⓦwww.tpg.ch) are fast, efficient, clean, safe, affordable and they go everywhere. Those running within the city are identified with numbers; those running into the suburbs, or across into France, are marked with letters. The only problem comes if you don't hold a Swiss Pass (which lets you travel free): Eurail and InterRail bring no discounts, and the "unireso" ticket machines, located at every stop, are absurdly complicated to figure out.

Tickets are valid on all trains, boats and buses within the relevant zones, and you must buy them before you board – but the machines accept **coins only** (Swiss francs and euros). The central Zone 11 covers the city, from Place des Nations in the north to the borders of Carouge in the south and from Jonction east to Eaux-Vives; the outer Zone 12 includes Carouge and the airport; and there are further numbered zones beyond (Hermance, for instance, is in Zone 31). Instructions are far from clear. Press button A for travel in one zone only (valid 30min; Fr.1.80), button B for travel across two zones (valid 60min; Fr.2.20), button C for three zones (valid 90min; Fr.4), or button D for all zones (valid 90min; Fr.5.60), or – more likely – choose a **day-pass** (button E two zones Fr.6; button F all zones Fr.12). A sticker on the side of the machine has guidance in English, or you could ask TPG customer service (☎022 308 34 34) during office hours. TPG transport information offices (within the train station and at the large Rive interchange below the old town; both Mon–Sat 7am–7pm, Sun 10am–6pm) can help, and also give out a map of the network and sell weekly and monthly passes.

Tiny **mouettes** run by SMGN (March–Oct only; ⓦwww.swissboat.com) ferry passengers across the mouth of the lake on three routes, all covered by normal city transport tickets. Route M1 shuttles between the Pâquis jetty ("Port des Mouettes" on Quai du Mont-Blanc) and Place du Molard; M2 between Pâquis and Eaux-Vives (both Mon–Fri every 10min 7.30am–7pm, Sat & Sun 10am–6pm). The longer route M3 runs from Pâquis to the Perle du Lac park, then across to Parc des Eaux-Vives and return (daily every 50min 10am–6.20pm, shorter hours in winter).

City tours

There are literally dozens of **tours** around the city and its environs. The most popular by far – only worth attempting if seething crowds don't put you off – is the expensive bus trip to Chamonix in France, departing from the Gare Routière (daily 8.30am; Fr.95; passport needed; return 6pm), with the option of adding lunch (Fr.32) and/or a cable-car ride from Chamonix up the 3842m Aiguille du Midi (Fr.55).

For **self-guided walks**, simplest is to pick up a Walkman and headphones from the tourist office for an informative 26-point walk in the Old Town at your own pace (free; Fr.50 deposit; max. 4hr). Alternatively, you could choose one of half-a-dozen excellent "Geneva On Foot" brochure-led walks through the various parks and neighbourhoods; tourist offices stock the range of brochures, which include proper route-maps and detailed notes in English.

Official **guided walks** through the Old Town depart from the tourist office on the Pont de la Machine and cost Fr.12; there's a general introductory stroll (mid-June to Sept Mon–Sat 10am, rest of year Sat only 10am; 2hr; glass of wine included), and a more lively historical walk (mid-June to Sept Tues & Thurs 6.30pm; 1hr 30min). Guided walks through Carouge start from the Mairie de Carouge, Place du Marché 14 (Sat 11am; 1hr 15min; Fr.10). The Patek Philippe Museum runs a guided walk through the Old Town focused on Geneva's history of watchmaking, starting from the Pont de la Machine (mid-June to Sept Sat 2pm; Fr.15; Ⓦ www.patekmuseum.com) and ending up at the museum itself (see p.98; admission included).

There are dozens of **boat tours**. The CGN (Ⓦ www.cgn.ch) has plenty of cruises, starting from the Mont-Blanc jetty, including *Les Belles Rives Genevoises* – a circular tour of both lakeshores (April–Oct daily 11am & hourly 1–4pm; mid-May to mid-Sept also 5pm & 6pm; 55min; Fr.12) – and dozens of eat-

---

Easy day-trips from Geneva by train

Château de Chillon p.161. Fairytale lakeside castle. Change at Vevey onto bus #1. 1hr 30min.

Château d'Oex p.320. Stunning scenery on the panoramic Golden Pass line (p.164) to this quiet Alpine resort. Train continues to Gstaad. Change at Montreux. 2hr.

Fribourg p.267. Wander the medieval lanes of this relaxed, bilingual university town. Direct. 1hr 20min.

Lausanne p.119. Lively, colourful city with outstanding galleries and a hip waterfront promenade. Direct. 35min.

Les Diablerets p.332. Tiny mountain village on a scenic train line, offering year-round glacier skiing at 3000m. Change at Aigle. 2hr 10min.

Mont Salève p.113. Cable-car ride up Geneva's home mountain for views and walks. Passport needed. City bus #8 to Veyrier-Douane. 50min.

St-Cergue p.147. Away from the city and the lowlands, refresh yourself with mountain air and tranquil views from 1047m. Change at Nyon. 50min.

St-Saphorin p.151. Beautiful old wine village set amidst the Lavaux vineyards. Change at Lausanne. 1hr.

aboard brunch, lunch and evening cruises for Fr.20–30. Smaller companies ranged along both lakefronts, including Swissboat and SMGN, tend to offer more regular departures; just wander along until you see a trip you fancy. Top choice is the excellent *Croisière Les Rives du Rhône*, starting from the Quai des Moulins on the Pont de l'Ile in the city centre, which heads downriver, past cliffs, hamlets and densely wooded shores to Verbois dam near the French border, and back (June to mid-Sept Tues & Fri 2.15pm, Wed, Thurs, Sat & Sun 10am & 2.15pm; May & late Sept Wed & Thurs 2.15pm, Sat & Sun 10am & 2.15pm; April & Oct Wed, Sat & Sun 2.15pm; Fr.22; 2hr 45min). Reservations are essential (☏022 732 29 44).

Accommodation

Geneva has a good selection of budget and mid-range **accommodation**, adding to the swathe of palace hotels catering to diplomats and the international glitterati. Booking ahead is essential, since all affordable rooms can easily get snapped up by delegates to the continuous round of congresses, conferences and international events that are the lifeblood of the city. The tourist office's dedicated **hotel reservation service** (☏022 909 70 20, ✉reservation @geneve-tourisme.ch, or over the counter) can book a room in the hotel of your choice for an unnecessarily high Fr.5, but it's worth asking them about any weekend or off-season deals the city happens to be running, which can often slash walk-in rates to bargain levels.

Hotels

Contrary to the stereotype, Geneva has plenty of **inexpensive** hotels, many in the centre of town – although bear in mind that parts of the Pâquis district in particular can get sleazy. There's a wealth of choice in **mid-range** rooms, with some bargains available from hotels which haven't yet updated to the slick, generic style that tends to prevail. Many of these renovated places are poor value: often you'll find that characterful old buildings and/or swish reception areas prelude boxy, impersonal little rooms. The Geneva-only chain Manotel is an exception, with six classy hotels (3 three-star, 3 four-star) located within five minutes of each other in the Pâquis offering unusually good value for money.

As you might expect from a city which plays regular host to top-level suits on unlimited expense accounts, Geneva has no shortage of stratospherically **expensive** hotels: the Quai des Bergues and Quai du Mont-Blanc in particular are shoulder-to-shoulder with them, offering a total of 4000 five-star beds – not bad for a city of just 200,000.

Inexpensive hotels
Station area and Les Pâquis

At Home 16 Rue de Fribourg ☏022 906 19 00, ⓦwww.kis.ch/at-home. Clean, modern Pâquis rooms, convenient for the location, but small, soulless and, despite the name, thoroughly unhomely. Discounts for students. ❷

Balzac 14 Rue de l'Ancien-Port ☏022 731 01 60, ⓦwww.hotel-balzac.ch. Quiet and very spacious rooms – unrenovated but still comfortable – just

off the Place de la Navigation. Good value. Parking Fr.10/day. ❸

De la Cloche 6 Rue de la Cloche ☏022 732 94 81, ⓦwww.tbh-ge.ch/cloche. Eight spotless, characterful, high-ceilinged rooms in what was formerly a private apartment in a quiet area of the Pâquis 50m from the lake. The pleasant atmosphere is enhanced by the ministerings of the *patronne*. Regularly full. ❶–❷

Ibis 10 Rue Voltaire ☏022 338 20 20,

www.accor-hotels.com. Generic, functional chain hotel in the city centre, characterless but low-priced. ②–③

International & Terminus 20 Rue des Alpes ☎022 732 80 95, www.international-terminus. ch. Clean and comfortable, a stone's throw from the station but off the main traffic street. Ask for an upper floor. ③

Luserna 12 Avenue de Luserna ☎022 345 45 45, www.hotel-luserna.ch. Very quiet and friendly family-run place with its own garden north of the centre, with pleasantly renovated wood-floor chalet-style rooms, most ensuite (ask for the attic), and great breakfasts. Super-attentive management lifts it well out of the ordinary. Bus #3, #9 or #10 to Servette, then walk via Avenue Wendt. ①–②

Des Quatre-Nations 43 Rue de Zurich ☎022 732 02 24. Divey little Pâquis den above a lowlife Portuguese bar, with blithely unhelpful staff (if you can find them) and dead cheap shower-free rooms. ①

Rivoli 6 Rue des Pâquis ☎022 731 85 50, www.tbh-ge.ch/rivoli. Good, quiet central location, but a little gloomy inside: rooms are nothing

to write home about, studios are slightly better value. ③

Windsor 31 Rue de Berne ☎022 731 71 30, www.hotel-windsor.ch. Simple, unadorned rooms, adequate and not without character – higher floors avoid the Pâquis street-noise. Formal, friendly staff. ③

Old Town and Plainpalais

Bel'Espérance 1 Rue de la Vallée ☎022 818 37 37, www.hotel.bel-esperance.ch. Formerly Salvation Army, now completely renovated into an excellent, modern, family-run hotel on a steep Old Town alley. Exceptionally quiet rooms are bright and simple, with free use of kitchen and great views. A renowned dentist nearby attracts toothache sufferers from all over Europe, making for quirky, cosmopolitan breakfast-times. One no-smoking floor. ②–③

Central 2 Rue de la Rôtisserie ☎022 818 81 00, www.hotelcentral.ch. Quiet, comfortable, renovated top-floor rooms just below the Old Town, all with balcony. Prices depend on the room size, but are all good value. ②

Mid-range hotels

Auberge d'Hermance 12 Rue du Midi, Hermance ☎022 751 13 68, www.hotel-hermance.ch. Charming inn set amidst the medieval lakeshore village of Hermance 15km northeast of Geneva, with five cosy and attractive rooms. The restaurant is celebrated for its excellent French cuisine. ④

Edelweiss Manotel 2 Place de la Navigation ☎022 544 51 51, www.manotel.com. Comfortable three-star, entirely done-up with Swiss kitsch – carved light pine, images of St Bernard dogs and Alpine flowers and, to top it all, folkloric dinner-shows nightly in the basement restaurant. Ignore it all: beneath the veneer, this remains an excellent city-centre small hotel, with courteous, switched-on staff and good facilities (all rooms have air con). Ask for a top-floor room, facing back over a quiet rooftop panorama. ④–⑤

Epsom Manotel 18 Rue Richemont ☎022 544 66 66, www.manotel.com. Completely renovated in 2002, with hundreds of affordable, spacious and well-appointed business rooms off the Rue de Lausanne, less expensive ones on lower floors. Parking available. ⑤–⑥

Montbrillant 2 Rue du Montbrillant ☎022 733 77 84, www.montbrillant.ch. Award-winning hotel overlooking the station, with some style, plus quiet

and atmospheric modern rooms – those under the sloping roof are particularly good. Sound-proofing throughout. ④–⑤

Royal Manotel 41 Rue de Lausanne ☎022 906 14 14, www.manotel.com. Flagship Manotel property on eight floors (one non-smoking), renovated throughout and offering outstanding value. Rooms are large and comfortable, with air con; superb top-floor suites feature effortless, modern luxury styling – canopied bed, parquet floor, Jacuzzi – at four-star prices. All guests have access to the sauna, hammam and small gym, and there's secure underground parking. ⑤–⑥

Strasbourg 10 Rue Pradier ☎022 906 58 00, www.strasbourg-geneva.ch. Best Western chain hotel on a quiet backstreet very near the station, renovated in classic style, with good service and cosy, if generic, rooms. ④

Tiffany 1 Rue des Marbriers ☎022 708 16 16, www.hotel-tiffany.ch. Highly successful, attractive and charming Belle Epoque hotel near Plainpalais, with efficient, helpful staff and classic Art Deco styling throughout – from stained glass to swirly bathroom tiles and a stunning painted ceiling. ⑥

Expensive hotels

Les Armures 1 Rue du Puits St-Pierre ☎ 022 310 91 72, 🌐 www.hotel-les-armures.ch. Quiet seventeenth-century building in the heart of the cobbled Old Town, with uniquely characterful rooms featuring wood beams and frescoed decor. The height of tasteful, understated luxury. **❽**

Beau Rivage 13 Quai du Mont-Blanc ☎ 022 716 66 66, 🌐 www.beau-rivage.ch. Dreamy classical-style palace, centred on a huge atrium with tinkling fountain and characterized by luxury redolent of its 1865 foundation. The same family tends to the hotel's guests now as then, and a farther cry from international business-class anonymity you couldn't find. Its tragic claim to fame is that Empress Elisabeth ("Sissi") of Austria died in one of the drawing rooms in 1898, stabbed out on the street by an Italian anarchist. **❾**

Des Bergues 33 Quai des Bergues ☎ 022 908 70 00, 🌐 www.hoteldesbergues.com. Oldest of Geneva's palace-style hotels, this much-loved 1834 landmark was recently renovated to glittering international standards, yet retains its atmosphere of discreet and unassailable opulence. Its history takes in – quite literally – the crowned heads of Europe. **❾**

Bristol 10 Rue du Mont-Blanc ☎ 022 716 57 00, 🌐 www.bristol.ch. A venerable city-centre institution, dating from 1896, with subtle modern decor and calm, efficient service. **❽**

Intercontinental 7 Chemin du Petit-Saconnex ☎ 022 919 39 39, 🌐 www.interconti.com. A vast Sixties high-rise out near the UN, some rooms boasting spectacular lake views, that is the favoured choice of politicos and visiting international delegations. Cosy decor softens the generic interior, but sombre, world-affairs formality is the tone. The visitors' book reads like a roll call of history, running through the last half-dozen US presidents, King Hussein, Fidel Castro and Nelson Mandela, to name a few. **❼–❾**

President Wilson 47 Quai Wilson ☎ 022 906 66 66, 🌐 www.hotelpwilson.com. Outstanding five-star palace on the Rive Droite, with a vast lobby and public areas accented by mock-Classical stonework and original antiques and tapestries. Rooms are spacious, airy, light and modern, and – with the hotel's location, facing away from the city centre – benefit from uncluttered lake views. **❾**

Camping and hostels

There are two easily accessible **campsites**, both northeast on the Rive Gauche lakefront and both on the route of bus #E in Zone 31 (Fr.4). *Pointe-à-la-Bise* is 7km out on Chemin de la Bise in Vésanaz (☎ 022 752 12 96, 🄔 camping.geneve@tcs.ch; April–Oct), and *Camping d'Hermance* is another 7km on by the French border, at 44 Rue du Nord (☎ 022 751 14 83; April–Sept); it has free access to the lake.

Geneva has plenty of **hostel** beds, partly because many student dorms open their doors to visitors out of term-time: the tourist office brochure *Young People* lists 21 places (including seven that are women-only).

Auberge de Jeunesse (HI hostel) 30 Rue Rothschild ☎ 022 732 62 60, 🌐 www.youthhostel .ch & 🌐 www.yh-geneva.ch. 330 beds in a good, central location in the Pâquis, open year-round. Big, bustling and well maintained, with cheap meals and good services. Dorm beds Fr.25. Bus #1 to Wilson. **❶**

Centre Masaryk 11 Avenue de la Paix ☎ 022 733 07 72. Some 2km north of town and a little institutional, with Fr.27 dorms and inexpensive rooms. **❶**

Cité Universitaire 46 Avenue Miremont ☎ 022 839 22 22, 🌐 www.unige.ch/cite-uni. 550-bed behemoth nearly 3km south of the centre. Dorm beds for individuals are Fr.20 in July & August (Sept–June groups only), but there are plenty of cut-price singles, doubles and studios year-round. Breakfast is extra. Bus #3. **❶**

City Hostel (SB hostel) 2 Rue Ferrier ☎ 022 901 15 00, 🌐 www.cityhostel.ch. Excellent, recently opened backpacker place a short walk from the HI hostel in the Pâquis, with plenty of services (including laundry facilities), inexpensive rooms and dorm beds from Fr.24. Bus #4 to Prieuré. **❶**

Home St-Pierre 4 Cour St-Pierre ☎ 022 310 37 07, 🌐 www.homestpierre.ch. In the heart of the Old Town next to the cathedral, with two dorms (one of them women-only) plus single and double rooms (all women-only); dorm beds Fr.23 excluding breakfast. **❶**

The City

Genevans orient the city centre around the Rhône, which flows west into France from the **Rade**, the narrow lake harbour flanked by grand facades. The **Rive Gauche**, on the south bank, takes in a grid of waterfront streets which comprise the main shopping district (Les Rues-Basses) and the adjacent high ground of the Old Town. Just south is the university, spilling over into the Plainpalais district, and a little northeast is the populous working neighbourhood of Eaux-Vives. South, just beyond the city limits, lies the community of **Carouge**, characterized by artisans' shops, picturesque Italianate architecture and a lively, independent spirit.

Six bridges, including the main Pont du Mont-Blanc, link the Rive Gauche to the **Rive Droite** waterfront, where most of Geneva's grand hotels sit. Behind them lies the main train station, alongside the cosmopolitan and occasionally rough Les Pâquis district. The **international area**, centred on Place des Nations 1.5km north, is home to the European headquarters of the UN, set amidst the grand offices of a clutch of major world organizations – not least the International Committee of the Red Cross, which has, as a sideline, one of Switzerland's best museums.

The Rive Gauche

Characteristically, Geneva's **Rive Gauche** (Left Bank, or southern bank) is lined with the tall, blank facades of dozens of bank buildings. Behind the banks, the arrow-straight **Rue du Rhône** – principal thoroughfare of Les Rues-Basses, once a dockside slum and now Geneva's fanciest shopping district – stretches a kilometre or more east, crammed with jewellers, department stores and designer boutiques of all kinds. A throng of traffic streams over the **Pont du Mont-Blanc** beneath the spectacular view of Europe's highest mountain (4807m), which stands some 80km distant amidst the Savoy Alps, seemingly just beside the shimmering blue lake. At the foot of the bridge is the charming lakeside **Jardin Anglais**, focused around a double statue celebrating Geneva's joining the Confederation in 1815, a fountain, bandstand and famous Flower Clock. The **Jet d'Eau** spouts 400m along the lakeshore (see box p.93), while **Parc La Grange**, 1km further east along the lakeshore, is a landscaped expanse of some forty thousand rose bushes which drench the air with scent for most of the year.

West of the Pont du Mont-Blanc, past the bustling Place du Molard with its medieval tower, is the pedestrianized **Pont des Bergues**, with a footpath midway along it linking to a tiny island, the **Île Rousseau**, formerly a bastion and now a minuscule public garden graced with a statue of the Genevan philosopher. With such controversy surrounding Rousseau, even half a century after his death the city authorities were grudging in honouring him, and the statue, behind its sheltering camouflage of trees, originally faced the empty lake – to all intents and purposes cut off from view until the Pont du Mont-Blanc was built alongside in 1861.

Place Neuve and around

At its western end, the Rue du Rhône feeds into hectic Place Bel-Air, sliced across by tramlines and bus-wires. The Pont de l'Île spans the river here across an island, which boasts the diminutive **Tour de l'Île**, last remaining tower of a thirteenth-century château. Grandiose Rue de la Corraterie heads south to yet more grandiose **Place Neuve**, dominated by the high retaining wall of the

GENEVA: RIVE GAUCHE

EATING & DRINKING

Le Béarn	E
Café des Forces Motrices	C
Café Gallay	J
Café Mozart	B
Café de l'Usine	B
Cave Valaisanne/	
Chalet Suisse	L
L'Esquisse	G
Hang Zhou	A
Kantine	D
L'Opera de Huissoud	I
Le Pain Quotidien	F
Le Thé	K
Vesuvio	H

ACCOMMODATION

Cité Universitaire	2
Tiffany	1

Cologny & Hermance

Parc La Grange

Gare des Eaux-Vives

ROUTE DE CHÊNE

Jet d'Eau

Lake Geneva

Train Station

Russian Church

Baur Collections

Petit Palais

Musée d'Art et d'Histoire

Cathédrale St-Pierre

Jardin Anglais

Île Rousseau

Hôtel de Ville

Mur de la Réformation

Parc des Bastions

See Geneva Old Town map

Musée Rath

Grand Théâtre

Bâtiments des Forces-Motrices

Cimitière de Plainpalais

Plaine de Plainpalais

MAMCO

Patek Philippe Museum

Musée Jean Tua

Musée d'Ethnographie

Parc Gourgas

Arve

Rhône

Jonction

Carouge

0   200 m

Liquid asset

The **Jet d'Eau** fountain (May to mid-Sept daily 9.30am–11.15pm; late March, April & mid-Sept to Oct Mon–Fri 10am–sunset, Sat & Sun 10am–10.30pm; also during the Motor Show in early March), the icon of Geneva, is inescapable: it's the logo of the tourist office and Geneva's prime photo-op, emblazoned on every piece of tourist literature and every book about the city; it's also illuminated after dark. Even if you happen to visit off season when it's switched off, you'll be in no doubt what you're missing.

Its predecessor dated from 1886, when the new hydraulic turbines on the Rhône built up excessive water pressure every evening after the city's craftsmen had closed the valves in their workshops and gone home. While a reservoir system was being developed to get around the problem, an engineer created a temporary outlet which spurted a 30m fountain to release the pressure – but by the time the reservoir was in operation and the fountain had become unnecessary, a few wily Genevois had caught on to its power as a tourist attraction. By then purely decorative, it was moved from the river to an exposed lakeside location, and furnished with more and more powerful pumps. Today, the height of the jet is an incredible 140m, with 500 litres of water forced out of the nozzle every second at about 200kph. Each drop takes sixteen seconds to complete the round-trip from nozzle to lake and, on windy days, the plume can rapidly drench the surroundings (they tend to turn it off if the wind picks up). It's worth risking a dousing by walking out onto the jetty to appreciate the force and noise of the thing close up.

Old Town and a host of Neoclassical buildings. The street joins the square beside the **Musée Rath**, Geneva's first art museum, opened in 1826, and still holding a changing series of world-class art shows (Tues & Thurs–Sun 10am–5pm, Wed noon–9pm; admission varies; Ⓦmah.ville-ge.ch). Adjacent is the **Grand-Théâtre**, Geneva's opera house and principal theatre stage, which only just clung onto its facade after the devastating fire of 1951, when a rehearsal of the last act of Wagner's *Walkyrie*, in which Brunhilde is encircled by flames, got out of hand. Further round the square is the equally ornate Conservatoire de Musique.

Heading south from Place Neuve through the enormous gates brings you into the **Parc des Bastions**, a tranquil patch of green below the Old Town ramparts that's much beloved of students (the university buildings are all around) and oldtimers playing giant chess under the trees. At the east edge of the park, in a dramatic location propping up the Old Town, is the gigantic **Mur de la Réformation**, a 100m-long wall erected in 1917 and dominated by forbidding, 5m-high statues of the four major Genevan reformers: Guillaume Farel, first to preach the Reformation in Geneva; Jean Calvin, leader of the Reform movement and spiritual father of the city; Théodore de Bèze, successor to Calvin; and John Knox, friend of Calvin and founder of Scottish Presbyterianism. Behind runs the motto of the city and the Reformation, *Post Tenebras Lux* ("After the Darkness, Light"). Various figures and bas-reliefs show scenes from Protestant history: just to the right of the main statues is Roger Williams, a Calvinist Puritan who sailed on the *Mayflower* and founded the city of Providence, Rhode Island. The English Parliament's 1689 Bill of Rights – which established a constitutional monarchy under the Protestant king William of Orange, and barred Catholics from the throne – is also depicted, but Luther and Zwingli (see p.437), with whom Calvin came to disagree, are relegated to plain blocks flanking the wall, carved only with their surnames.

The Old Town

A gate at the back of the Parc des Bastions brings you up to a small junction and Rue St-Léger, which winds further up into the atmospheric **Old Town**, characterized by quiet, cobbled streets and tall, shuttered, grey-stone houses that give nothing away. Rue St-Léger curls up into the oddly split-level **Place du Bourg-de-Four**, a marketplace since medieval times that was probably built over the Roman forum, these days adorned with a fountain and lined with relaxed terrace cafés. From here, Rue Fontaine descends to the north to Temple de la Madeleine, a picturesque Gothic church that has clung on to its Romanesque tower, but if you head up the other way on Rue de l'Hôtel-de-Ville, you'll come to **Place de la Taconnerie**, dominated by the cathedral. Tucked on your right is the **Auditoire de Calvin**, a small thirteenth-century chapel built over a fifth-century predecessor. Following Geneva's acceptance of the Reformation, refugees flooded into the city from all over Europe and, in the knowledge that most of them spoke no French, Calvin gave this chapel over for the refugees to worship in their own languages – Geneva's first international building. John Knox preached here in the 1550s (there's still a Church of Scotland service every Sunday, slotted between Dutch and Italian), and the austere building also doubled as Calvin's lecture hall.

Cathédrale St-Pierre

Geneva's **Cathédrale St-Pierre** (June–Sept Mon–Sat 9am–7pm, Sun 11am–7pm; Oct–May Mon–Sat 10am–noon & 2–5pm, Sun 11am–12.30pm & 1.30–5pm) is a rather odd mishmash of architectural elements. Begun in 1160, the original building took some 72 years to complete and has had a multitude of bits and pieces stuck on over the centuries. A small side-chapel, the Chapelle des Macchabées, was added in 1397; an incongruous Neoclassical portico – more reminiscent of a museum than a church – was tacked onto the main west front of the building in 1752, facing onto Cour St-Pierre; the two square towers above the east end are totally dissimilar; and between them rises a curious greenish steeple added in the late nineteenth century.

As you enter, though, all confusion is stripped away and you're left with the clean lines of dour, severely austere stonework. In 1535, spurred on by Bern, the people of Geneva accepted the Reformation and embarked on an iconoclastic rampage: all the altars in the cathedral, as well as every statue and icon, were destroyed, the organs were smashed and the painted decoration on the interior walls was whitewashed. Only the great **pulpit** and, by chance, the stained glass of the chancel, survived. As you wander through the soaring interior, the architecture, and the austerity, draw your gaze upwards; almost the only decoration to survive is on the capitals of the nave's clustered pillars, grotesque monsters and a bare-breasted double-tailed mermaid. What is purportedly **Calvin's chair** sits at the back of the church on the left, near the door to the North Tower, climbable for spectacular views over the city (Fr.3). You shouldn't leave without spending time in the delightful **Chapelle des Macchabées**, last on the left before you leave. Used as a warehouse and later as a lecture hall, it was rededicated as a place of worship in 1878 and is filled with lavish and beautiful decoration dating from then. Copies of the only fifteenth-century frescoes to survive the Reformation – angels playing musical instruments – are on the ornamented vaults of the chancel within the chapel.

The cathedral is built on the remains of occupation going back to the Romans: the first church, just north of the present cathedral, has been dated to around 350 AD. From then on, the hill on which the cathedral stands was the site of almost continuous building and rebuilding. Since 1976, archeologists

1

GENEVA: OLD TOWN

▲ Pont du Mont-Blanc

▲ Pont des Bergues

▲ Plaine de Plainpalais

Jardin Anglais

QUAI DU GENERAL GUISAN

QUAI DU MONT-BLANC

PLACE DU PORT

PL DES FLORENTINS

QUAI GUSTAVE ADOR

R DE LA SCIE

R DE LA BLANDERIE

SQ. DE LA BLANDERIE

RUE L. DUCOSSAL

RUE L. DUCOSSAL

HELVETIQUE

RUE DE RIVE

R DE GLACIS DE RIVE

RUE DU PRINCE

RUE DU PORT

PL LONGEMALLE

RUE DE RIVE

RUE DU RHÔNE

RUE DU MARCHÉ

RUE DE LA CROIX D'OR

RUE DU VIEUX-COLLÈGE

ROND POINT DE RIVE

RUE AMI-LULLIN

COURS D'ITALIE

RUE FERD HODLER

RUE P. FATIO

RUE D'AOSTE

RUE DE LA TOUR MAÎTRESSE

RUE ÉTIENNE

R DE LA FAUCONNERIE

RUE DE LA VALLÉE

Temple de la Madeleine

Palais de Justice

RUE VERDAINE

RUE DE LA FONTAINE

RUE DES CHAUDRONNIERS

RUE E. DUMONT

RUE ÉTIENNE DUMONT

JAQUES-DALCROZE

PROM. ST-ANTOINE

Prom. l'Observatoire

Musée d'Art et d'Histoire

Russian Church

HELVETIQUE

RUE CH. GALLAND

BLVD

RUE TOEPFFER

SQ. R. TOEPFFER

RUE TH. DE BÈZE

RUE DES GRANGES

Cathédrale St Pierre

Auditoire Calvin

PL DU BOURG-DE-FOUR

Hôtel de Ville

RUE DU SOLEIL LEVANT

RUE DE L'HÔTEL DE VILLE

RUE DE LA TACONNERIE

RUE FAREL

COUR ST-PIERRE

Maison Tavel

Musée Barbier-Müller

RUE J. CALVIN

PL DE MONET

GRAND RUE

RUE DU PERRON

RUE DE LA PÉLISSERIE

RUE DE LA ROTISSERIE

RUE DE LA MADELEINE

PURGAT

R. MADELEINE

R. DE LA CROIX D'OR

Tour Molard

Place du Molard

PLACE DE LA FUSTERIE

PLACE DE LA CONFÉDÉRATION

RUE DE LA CITÉ

RUE DE LA CORRATERIE

3-PERDRIX

PL. BÉMONT

R BÉMONT

BÉMONT

PL DU GD. MÉZEL

RAMPE DE LA TREILLE

Musée Rath

Mur de la Reformation

Parc des Bastions

Université Bastions

RUE DE LA CROIX - ROUGE

RUE H. FAZY

RUE DE LA TERRASSE

RUE DE CANDOLLE

RUE DE SAINT-LÉGER

R TABAZAN

R BEAUREGARD

R CHAUSSE COQ

R PIACHAUD

BLVD E.

BLVD JAQUES-DALCROZE

Conservatoire de Musique

PLACE DE NEUVE

Grand Théâtre

RUE F. DIDAY

RUE A. CALAME

RUE DU THÉÂTRE

RUE BOVY-LYSBERG

R D'HO'LLANDE

R. D. GRÜTLI

RUE DU GÉN DUFOUR

RUE BARTHOLONI

RUE DU CONSEIL GÉNÉRAL

Université Dufour

RUE BELMAT

R DE SAUSSURE

BLVD GEORGE-FAVON

R.J. PETITOT

ACCOMMODATION	
Les Armures	3
Bel Espérance	2
Central	1
Home St-Pierre	4

EATING & DRINKING	
Alhambar	C
Chocolaterie du Rhône	A
Flanagan's	F
Café du Centre	B
La Favola	E
Le Pied de Cochon	G
Taverne de la Madeleine	D

0   100 m

N

have been working to expose walls, rooms and mosaic floors beneath the cathedral, and the huge **archeological site** is open to the public (June–Sept Tues–Sat 11am–5pm, Sun 10am–5pm; Oct–May Tues–Sat 2–5pm, Sun 10am–noon & 2–5pm; Fr.5), pretty rarefied stuff but exceptionally well presented and labelled, subterranean catwalks weaving around and over the crumbling remains. With more than 200 levels of building work so far discovered in eleven zones, it's necessarily difficult to tweeze out exactly what's going on, but the free audioguide helps.

Maison Tavel

From the cathedral portico, an alley leads you on to the Rue du Puits-St-Pierre. A few metres left, at no. 6, is the distinctive grey-blue sandstone facade – etched with *trompe l'oeil* mortar-lines – of Geneva's oldest house, now the **Maison Tavel** museum (Tues–Sun 10am–5pm; free; temporary exhibits Fr.3; ⓦmah.ville-ge.ch). Built by the Tavel family in the twelfth century, the house was renovated after a fire in 1334, but in the sixteenth century the Tavel line died out. The house was maintained by various noble families until it was bought by the city in 1963 to display items from the history and urban life of Geneva. The vast cellars, which survived the fire intact, are the oldest part of the house, and they and the three upper floors are filled with moderately diverting items – massive carved doors, painted inn-signs and a complete twelve-room apartment showing everyday life in the seventeenth century. The highlight of the museum is in the attic, a giant **relief map of Geneva** dating from 1850, showing the city complete with its fortifications, before the Pont du Mont-Blanc or the railway had been built. There's a sound-and-light show talking you through points of interest on the map; ask the staff to play the English version for you.

Around the Old Town

It's a few steps west from the Maison Tavel to a cobbled crossroads. To the right is Grand-Rue, birthplace of Rousseau, and parallel to it **Rue des Granges**, named "Street of Barns" in response to the huge mansions built in the eighteenth century in French style to house Geneva's wealthiest residents. Looming over the junction is the **Hôtel-de-Ville**, ranged around an atmospheric internal arcaded courtyard from where it's easy to spot the different styles of the building – going counterclockwise, the sixteenth, seventeenth and eighteenth centuries. Ahead is the Alabama Room, where the Geneva Convention on the humanitarian rules of war was signed by sixteen countries in 1864, and where, in 1872, conflict between two states was solved in a neutral state for the first time, when Britain and the US settled their differences over British support for the Confederacy during the Civil War. The League of Nations also assembled here for the first time in 1920. This is one of only three buildings in Europe to have a sloping ramp inside instead of stairs (the others are on the Loire and at Schaffhausen), to facilitate cannons being pulled up to the ramparts and, so it's said, to enable councillors to arrive at meetings on horseback or in their sedan chair. You can work your way up to the top – feeling like an Escher drawing come to life – but all the doors are firmly locked. Behind the building is the lovely **Promenade de la Treille**, with a view over the city framed by chestnut trees and the longest wooden bench in the world, at 126m. The last tree on the left, bent forward, is the official tree of Geneva: tradition has it that the chief city councillor must record the day its first bud blossoms as being the first day of spring. A board of dates has been kept in the Town Hall since 1818 and is added to annually.

Back along the Rue du Puits-St-Pierre, you'll come to a set of stairs leading down towards the Rues-Basses. Off to the left is Rue Calvin, with, at no. 10, the **Musée Barbier-Müller** (daily 11am–5pm; Fr.5; SMP; ⓦwww.barbier-mueller.ch), housing a beautifully displayed collection of non-European sculpture and artwork. Notes are copious, guiding you from a room filled with antique African gold to huge carved masks from Oceania, and more.

Musée d'Art et d'Histoire

A few metres east of the Old Town is the **Musée d'Art et d'Histoire**, 2 Rue Charles-Galland (Tues–Sun 10am–5pm; free; ⓦmah.ville-ge.ch), Geneva's biggest and most important museum and Switzerland's unofficial national collection. It's a gigantic place, that covers in encyclopedic fashion the whole sweep of Western culture from antiquity to the present; to do it justice would take days, but you could spend a worthwhile few hours absorbing the different areas.

For the marvellous **fine-art** collection, head up the grand staircase. What confronts you at the top is perhaps the highlight of the museum, a graceful and heart-stoppingly romantic sculpture in marble of Venus and Adonis, standing alone and lit by a skylight. Antonio Canova, the pre-eminent Neoclassical sculptor, has given Venus the fingers of a pianist. Also at the head of the stairs are two Rodins, *The Thinker* and *The Tragic Muse*. The collection begins in Hall 401 to the right of *Venus and Adonis* and, although it more or less keeps a chronological thread, don't be surprised if you come across photography, concrete installations or even video art scattered in amongst the painting. In room 402 you'll find Konrad Witz's famous altarpiece, made for the cathedral in 1444, which shows Christ and the fisherman transposed onto Lake Geneva. As you work your way around the perimeter rooms, Rembrandt and other Dutch and Flemish artists are in room 406, nineteenth-century Swiss in 408–9, while the inner ring of smaller rooms features work by the eighteenth-century Genevois painter Liotard in 419–20. Perimeter rooms 412–14 are devoted to Vallotton, Pissaro, Cézanne, Renoir and Modigliani, with some striking Hodlers on the inner ring, including a mystical *Lac de Thoune* (1909) in room 425.

Back downstairs, the **applied arts** collection is on the mezzanine gallery and the ground floor, a wealth of silverware, pewter, armour and costume. The Cartigny room, with 1805 wood panelling by the Genevois craftsman Jean Jaquet, shows exquisitely elegant Louis XV and XVI furniture. The ground floor also often features temporary exhibits (admission charged).

The lower floor is given over to the massive **archeological** collection. Turn right for the breathtaking Egyptian rooms, including sections from the Book of the Dead, a complete ninth-century BC mummy, and a beautiful granite statue of the goddess Sekhmet, with the body of a woman and the head of a lioness, from the fourteenth century BC. There's also an excellent display on hieroglyphics. The halls devoted to Ancient Greece and Rome are no less impressive, filled with statuary, glassware and good historical notes. Also down here are a **gift shop** and small **café**.

South and west of the Old Town

Within sight of the Musée d'Art, on the high ground opposite, rise the gilded onion domes of the **Russian Church** (open sporadically), built in 1863 on the remains of a sixteenth-century Benedictine priory – at that time isolated on an empty hilltop – with money donated by Grand Duchess Anna Feodorovna Constancia, aunt of Queen Victoria and a longtime Geneva resident. A gridlike neighbourhood of long, straight boulevards lined with solid town houses rapidly grew up around the church at the end of the nineteenth century, and the area, known as Les Tranchées, is still grand and quiet today. Five minutes from the church, at 8 Rue Munier-Romilly, is the **Collections Baur** (Tues–Sun 2–6pm; Fr.5; ⓦ www.collections-baur.ch), the country's premier collection of East Asian art. Start at the top floor, with a bright-lit display of nineteenth-century Japanese ceramics. One floor down is the Chinese collection: aim for room 8, featuring some delicately luminescent yellow Yongzhang ceramics. The ground floor has some older Chinese work, including beautifully simple white bowls from the ninth century, a little interior garden and fountain in room 3 surrounded by Ming porcelain, and other rooms with brilliant cobalt-blue ceramics and spectacular Qing jade, almost translucent.

Barely five minutes' walk northwest, at 2 Terrasse St-Victor, is a grand mansion, its doorway flanked by torch-holding figures. This is the **Petit Palais** (Mon–Fri 10am–6pm, Sat & Sun 10am–5pm; Fr.10), housing yet another art museum, this time devoted solely to French modernism 1870–1930. A wide selection of works traces the period's evolution of style but, despite the presence of a few big names, there are no major works and it's probably more for buffs than general passers-by.

Plainpalais

The broad Boulevard des Philosophes traces a path around the Parc des Bastions and the university district to the Rond-Point de Plainpalais, on the eastern tip of a diamond of open space known as the **Plaine de Plainpalais**. If Geneva still has a village green or a marketplace, this is it – a little oasis of humanity ringed around by buzzing traffic. Most days see a market of one kind or another, whether fruit and veg or the famous Wednesday and Saturday flea markets, and the space is always bustling with people walking their dogs, students reading on the benches or kids testing their skills on the skateboarding ramps.

Just off the western angle of the diamond is **MAMCO**, the Musée d'Art Moderne et Contemporain, housed in an old industrial space at 10 Rue des Vieux-Grenadiers (Tues–Sun noon–6pm; mid-June to mid-Sept Tues until 9pm; Fr.8). The museum has kept the former factory's concrete floors and overhead strip lighting to display its often stark but high-quality collection, covering installations, video art, photographs, sculptures and painting produced since the 1960s, both permanent acquisitions and a running series of temporary exhibits. Next door, the **Centre d'Art Contemporain** (Tues–Sun 11am–6pm; Fr.4; ⓦ www.centre.ch) also holds many temporary shows of young Genevois and Swiss artists in all fields, while down the road at no. 7 is the **Patek Philippe Museum** (Tues–Fri 2–5pm, Sat 10am–5pm; Fr.10; ⓦ www. patekmuseum.com), a fine horological collection encompassing works dating from the sixteenth century to the present. Two other museums nearby are the **Musée Jean Tua**, 28 Rue des Bains (Wed–Sun 2–6pm; Fr.8), showcasing vintage cars; and the **Musée d'Ethnographie**, 65 Bd Carl-Vogt (Tues–Sun 10am–5pm; free), with a vast collection especially strong on weapons and art from Edo-period Japan, traditional objects from central America and western Africa, and pieces illustrating aboriginal Australian culture.

From the Place du Cirque at Plainpalais' northern tip, Boulevard de St Georges heads due west through one of Geneva's funkiest and most engaging young neighbourhoods. A short way along, a brick wall conceals the beautiful **Cimitière de Plainpalais**, permanent home to, among others, Sir Humphry Davy, who invented the miners' lamp. Gravestone #707, close to the wall and the object of much recent care, is marked only with a faint "J.C.": this is presumed to be the last resting place of Calvin. Adjacent to the cemetery's western wall is an area of what look like derelict, graffitied warehouses, but which are in fact the studios and workshops of Artamis (as in *art-amis*, "friends of art"), an artists' collective. Behind, Rue de la Coulouvrenière feeds into the atmospheric **Place des Volontaires**, with a scattering of cafés and the L'Usine squat, Geneva's biggest alternative arts venue, with galleries, a theatre space, music venue, café and more (see p.111). The riverfront Quai des Forces Motrices, also with cafés and clubs, is dominated by the arched windows of the **Bâtiments des Forces Motrices**, which once housed gigantic hydraulic turbines supplying the city with water and which has now been converted into a massive space for opera and drama (see p.111). Further along Boulevard de St-Georges is the rundown district of **Jonction**, at the point where the Arve meets the Rhône; residents have a tradition, in the torrid days of summer, of flinging themselves off the Pont de Sous-Terre for a refreshing float downstream in the cool water.

Carouge

Some 2km south of the city centre, the suburb of **Carouge** is a quite different experience from Geneva proper. Practically deserted until 1754, the township, then – as now – beyond the city limits, was granted to Victor Amideus, King of Sardinia (ruling from Turin). The king envisioned Carouge as a trading competitor to Geneva and turned it into a refuge for Catholics, Protestants unable to stomach Geneva's puritanical ways and, uniquely in Europe for the time, even Jews. Turinese architects developed a chessboard design of crisscrossing streets planted with trees, and low houses with wooden, Mediterranean-style galleries looking into internal gardens. From 1774 to 1792, this hamlet of a hundred people grew to a bustling town of four thousand and, although Carouge never overtook Geneva, it's still something of a refuge from the city, its quiet, attractive streets packed with artists' workshops, old-style cafés and some of the city's best small-scale nightlife.

Trams #12 or #13 from the city centre can drop you at the **Place du Marché** in the heart of Carouge, still used as a marketplace and starting point for ran-

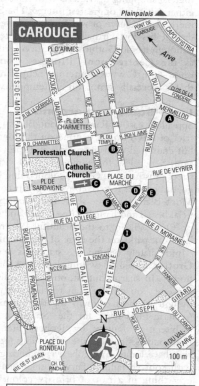

CAROUGE

CAFÉS & RESTAURANTS			
L'Ange du Dix Vins	H	Le Chat Noir	E
Bar du Nord	K	La Cuccagna	B
La Bourse	C	La Marchand de Sable	G
Café des Amis	J	Martel Tea Room	F
Café de la Plage	D	Sawasdee	A
Cave a Bière	I		

dom exploration of the quarter. **Rue St-Joseph** is shoulder-to-shoulder artisans, from carpenters to milliners – check out the elegant exposed-mechanism clocks of Jean Kazes at no. 21, Anne-Claude Virchaux's linen-cotton clothes at no. 13, and the delicate artworks of the florist Les Cinq Sens round the corner on **Place du Temple**. A major feature of Carouge are the delightful internal galleried gardens which lurk behind almost every gate: most are open, so feel free to explore. The **Musée de Carouge**, 2 Place de Sardaigne (SMP), is only open during the four temporary exhibits staged there each year.

The Rive Droite

Geneva's **Rive Droite** (Right Bank), on the north side of the Rhône, features only a couple of moderately interesting neighbourhoods – the Pâquis for café life, and Les Grottes for architecture. **Rue du Mont-Blanc** is Geneva's landmark street, a broad boulevard lined with airline offices and souvenir shops that slopes up the hill towards the train station and stands at the heart of the commercial shopping district. As with most such streets, though, it's what happens either side that's of greatest interest. The **St Gervais** quarter, just west, was formerly the preserve of watchmakers, jewellers, engravers and goldsmiths. These days it has lost virtually all its character to traffic and modern commerce, although its old Gothic church survives on Rue du Temple, on the same street as the **Centre pour l'Image Contemporaine**, at no. 5 (Tues–Sun noon–6pm; ⓦ www.centreimage.ch), a mediatheque and permanent collection that is especially strong on contemporary video art.

Les Pâquis and around

Spreading east of Rue du Mont-Blanc is the cosmopolitan, rough-edged district of **Les Pâquis**, centred on the long Rue de Berne – not a pretty place but crammed with restaurants and cafés devoted to every conceivable cuisine from Senegalese to Filipino. Equally visible are the numerous sex shops and street prostitutes of Geneva's flourishing red-light trade. The further north you go, the quieter it gets; conversely, you could head out to the lakeside Quai du Mont-Blanc for a tree-shaded stroll north, past the fine **Bains des Pâquis** artificial beach and hangout (see p.106) and the marina and ranks of luxury hotels on Quai Wilson, to the beautiful Parc Mon-Repos, first of several adjoining lakefront parks on the edge of the international area.

Immediately behind the station is a small residential area known as **Les Grottes**, a web of twisting lanes and mostly unrenovated nineteenth-century houses. In sharp contrast, on Rue Louis-Favre, just off the main Rue de la Servette, you couldn't fail to spot the public-housing estate which looks as though it's been thrown together from plasticine. This is the **Schtrumpfs** (generic Euro-speak for the "Smurfs"), a whimsical exercise in Gaudi-esque architectural fantasy by Robert Frei, Christian Hunziker and Georges Berthoud, designed in the early 1980s for the municipality. All the estate's highrises have lumps and blobs everywhere, giant mushrooms holding up balconies with cobweb railings, fairytale spiral staircases and twisted-liquorice columns, everything in a riot of primary colours. By all accounts the residents, who inevitably have come to be called Smurfs themselves, love it.

Just west of the city centre is the **Musée Voltaire**, 25 Rue des Délices (Mon–Fri 2–5pm; free), occupying the eighteenth-century villa and estate where Voltaire lived before his exile to France; a library of books and manuscripts is filled out with paintings and objects associated with the writer and philosopher.

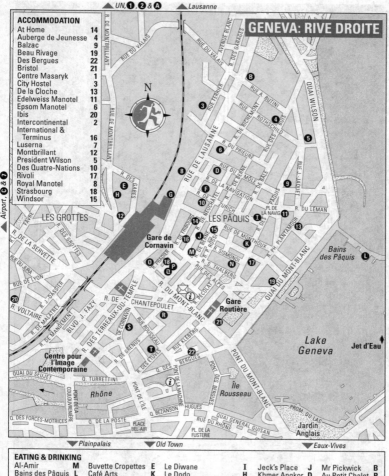

▲ *UN,* **❶** *,* **❷** *&* **Ⓐ**   ▲ *Lausanne*

GENEVA: RIVE DROITE

ACCOMMODATION

At Home	14
Auberge de Jeunesse	4
Balzac	9
Beau Rivage	19
Des Bergues	22
Bristol	21
Centre Masaryk	1
City Hostel	3
De la Cloche	13
Edelweiss Manotel	11
Epsom Manotel	6
Ibis	20
Intercontinental	2
International &	
Terminus	16
Luserna	7
Montbrillant	12
President Wilson	5
Des Quatre-Nations	10
Rivoli	17
Royal Manotel	8
Strasbourg	18
Windsor	15

◀ *Airport,* **Ⓒ** *&* **❼**

LES GROTTES

Gare de Cornavin

LES PÂQUIS

Bains des Pâquis

Gare Routière

Centre pour l'Image Contemporaine

Rhône

Île Rousseau

Lake Geneva

Jet d'Eau

Jardin Anglais

▼ *Plainpalais*   ▼ *Old Town*   ▼ *Eaux-Vives*

EATING & DRINKING

Al-Amir	**M**	Buvette Cropettes	**E**	Le Diwane	**I**	Jeck's Place	**J**	Mr Pickwick	**B**
Bains des Pâquis	**L**	Café Arts	**K**	Le Dodo	**H**	Khmer Angkor	**D**	Au Petit Chalet	**P**
Bookworm	**N**	Café de Paris	**O**	Domaine Châteauvieux	**C**	Manora	**S**	Teranga	**F**
La Bretelle	**T**	Café Zara	**G**	El Mektoub	**Q**	Miyako	**R**	Vieux-Bois	**A**

The international area

A little over 1km north of the station, at the heart of the so-called **international area**, is the open square of the **Place des Nations**, surrounded by offices of the dozens of international organizations headquartered in Geneva – everything from the World Council of Churches to Eurovision. Gates on the square open to the **Palais des Nations**, now occupied by UNOG, the United Nations Office at Geneva; the huge monolith just off the square to the west (like a bent playing card on its edge) is WIPO, the World Intellectual Property Organization; the high-rise to the south is ITU, the International Telecommunications Union; just to the east is UNHCR, United Nations High

GENEVA | The City

1

△ Geneva's grand Russian Church (see p.97)

Commissioner for Refugees... and so the alphabet soup continues. Most of these are just ordinary office buildings filled with working people; only the ICRC (International Committee of the Red Cross) and the UN are open to visitors.

The square itself is an obvious gathering place for those who wish to make a point, and the little patch of grass in the middle is consistently trampled flat by the many demonstrators who march here. The giant **Broken Chair** which looms over it was installed in 1997 for the international conference at Ottawa banning the use of land mines, a graphic symbol of the victims of such weapons. The Place des Nations is an easy walk from the station, or you can take any of an array of buses – #8, #18, #F, #V or #Z – all of which go past the square to Appia, the best stop for the museums.

Musée International de la Croix-Rouge

Housed within the headquarters of the International Committee of the Red Cross (ICRC), the **Musée International de la Croix-Rouge et du Croissant-Rouge**, 17 Avenue de la Paix (Mon & Wed–Sun 10am–5pm; Fr.10; SMP; Ⓦwww.micr.org) is acclaimed as one of the best museums in Europe. Using highly effective video displays, slide-shows and interactive technology (always with an English-language option), it chronicles in detail the history of conflict in the twentieth century, and the role the Red Cross has played in providing aid to combatants and civilians caught up in both war and natural disasters. The displays are strikingly affecting, always using clear single images to tell a story instead of swamping you with facts and figures, and always avoiding judgement or ideological point-scoring.

You enter through a trench in the hillside opposite the UN, emerging into an enclosed glass courtyard, surrounded by reflected images of yourself beside a group of stone figures, bound and blindfolded, representing the continual worldwide violation of human rights. Inside, above the ticket desk, is a quotation in French from Dostoevsky: "Everyone is responsible to everyone else for everything." The museum's very useful audioguide (Fr.5) takes you through the eleven undemarcated sections, all packed into a small floor area, which piece together in chronological order the history of kindness, from the Good Samaritan and Saladin to the experiences of nineteenth-century Genevan businessman **Henri Dunant** which prompted him to found the Red Cross (see box p.104). In one area of the museum are ranged aisle after aisle of **record cards** from World War I – an astonishing seven million of them – detailing prisoners' particulars in order that they could be traced and reunited with their families. In another is a **reconstructed cell**, 3m by 2m, which an ICRC delegate reported housed seventeen prisoners: 34 footprints on the cell floor only go some way towards helping imagine the conditions. Also memorable is the eye-opening **Wall of Time**, an ingenious representation of those wars and natural disasters which have killed more than 100,000 people, year by year since the Red Cross's foundation: as you reach the second half of the last century, the dizzyingly long lists of wars around the world tell their own, sombre story.

A final note of achievement: despite its skill and artistry, the museum's construction didn't use a penny of Red Cross funds, relying solely on outside donors.

Palais des Nations

The **Palais des Nations** was built from 1929 to 1936 to serve as the world headquarters of the League of Nations, an organization set up to prevent a recurrence of war on the scale of World War I but stymied soon after its birth

The creation of modern humanitarian law, as expressed in the 1949 Geneva Conventions, is closely tied to the history of the **International Committee of the Red Cross** (ⓦ www.icrc.org).

On a single day – June 24, 1859 – during the war of Italian Unification, over 40,000 people were killed or wounded at a battle near the northern Italian town of **Solferino**. Genevan businessman **Henri Dunant**, who happened to be travelling in the area, was shocked at the sight of thousands of wounded soldiers left to fend for themselves with little or no medical provision. Thousands perished where they fell, despite Dunant's efforts to rally local people to give aid. On his return to Geneva, Dunant wrote *A Memory of Solferino*, an eyewitness account of the horror, which ended with appeals for the formation of internationally protected nursing corps, ready to care for the wounded during times of war. The book was a runaway success, read in translation all over Europe. The Geneva Public Welfare Society, a local charity, set up a committee in 1863 to look at Dunant's proposals; this committee, which took a reversed red-on-white Swiss flag as the emblem to identify its workers in the field, later became known as the **International Committee of the Red Cross**.

In 1864, a conference of sixteen states – chaired by Dunant – signed the "Geneva Convention for the Amelioration of the Condition of the Wounded in Armies in the Field", the first instrument of international humanitarian law. As the ICRC expanded its work during a succession of conflicts, more treaties were agreed by states around the world – banning poison gas and bacteriological warfare, defining combatants and non-combatants, and more. These culminated in the four **1949 Geneva Conventions**, which still provide the legal foundation for humanitarian law and are among the most widely ratified of all treaties. The first and second cover protection of members of armed forces in the field and at sea, the third is concerned solely with the rights of prisoners of war, and the fourth concentrates on protection of civilians in wartime. **Protocols** adopted in 1977 extend the conventions to cover victims of civil wars.

These Geneva Conventions laid down rules of war which are taken for granted

by the outbreak of World War II. When the organization was re-founded in 1945 as the **United Nations** (*l'Organisation des Nations Unies* in French, abbreviated to ONU), with its headquarters at New York, this complex became European HQ and was retitled UNOG ("the UN office at Geneva"). Since then it has burgeoned, and now encompasses' offices administering a vast array of economic and social development work, as well as bodies dealing with the negotiation and signing of treaties and conventions of all kinds. It's also the hub of UN operations to deliver humanitarian aid and uphold human rights around the world.

The UN tour

Some areas of the Palais des Nations are open to the public for **guided tours** (July & Aug daily 10am–5pm; April–June, Sept & Oct daily 10am–noon & 2–4pm; rest of year Mon–Fri 10am–noon & 2–4pm; Fr.8.50; takes 1hr; ⓦ www.unog.ch). The tours – in any of the UN's fifteen official languages – are only moderately interesting in themselves, but are packed with star quality for those who want to hobnob with history. This is the world's single largest conference centre for multilateral diplomacy and top-level international politicking: when the news has reports of "negotiations taking place in Geneva", they mean here. If this impresses, then you'll enjoy the visit; if it signals only the dreary prospect of traipsing along corridors and standing in empty conference halls, you should probably take your francs elsewhere.

today – for instance, that **prisoners of war** are entitled to withhold all information from their captors except their name, rank, serial number and birth date. Certain definitions have also changed: under the 1949 conventions, **journalists** – who, at the time, often covered conflicts while armed and uniformed – were regarded as combatants, but, with the developing independence of the media, the 1977 Protocols explicitly recognized them to be non-combatant civilians as long as they identify themselves as such, which is why war correspondents now emblazon their flak-jackets with the word "PRESS".

Governments are responsible for enforcing the Geneva Conventions, but the ICRC remains the only organization recognized to carry out relief activities for the victims of armed conflicts; it publicizes the rules of war to all sides involved in hostilities and, through national Red Cross and Red Crescent societies around the world, serves as a global network to help trace prisoners of war and civilians displaced by conflict and provide aid to civilians during and after wars, as well as monitoring conflict conditions. Four-fifths of its budget of about **Fr.1 billion** (US$700m) is spent on field operations, covering relief work on the ground in Afghanistan, the Middle East, central Africa and elsewhere. Its **red cross** emblem is now one of the world's best-known symbols, almost universally recognizable – along with the red crescent and red star-of-David in the Muslim and Jewish worlds respectively – as indicating an impartial source of medical care.

Controversy surrounding interpretation of the Geneva Conventions arose in 2001, after the US defined prisoners from the Afghan war that it was holding in Cuba as "combatants"; many onlookers challenged this, claiming that the US was breaking the conventions by imprisoning "non-combatants". To address the dispute, and other issues of international law arising from the 9/11 attacks, Switzerland and the ICRC convened a **multinational conference** in early 2003 to reaffirm and re-evaluate the Geneva Conventions. As war changes, the need to define and enforce its rules is gaining increased urgency.

The main entrance of the Palais des Nations, facing onto Place des Nations, is for UN staff only; the **public entrance** is up Avenue de la Paix opposite the Red Cross Museum. To enter, you'll have to hand in your **passport** and go through airport-style security procedures (you're effectively leaving Switzerland and entering international territory). You should then walk down the hill to the left, towards *Porte 39* in the new wing, from where tours depart. Note that you may have to wait twenty minutes for the next tour in English (there's a bookshop for browsing) and you have to carry your bags with you.

Once you get going, you're regaled with a potted history of the UN and its philosophy, and odd factoids such as when the US denied Yasser Arafat a visa to address the UN in New York in 1988, the entire General Assembly had to fly to Geneva to hear him speak in the great **Assembly Hall**, visitable today in more or less the same condition as when it was inaugurated in 1937. The **Council Chamber**, which hosted the negotiations to end the 1991 Gulf War, is decorated with gold-and-sepia murals painted in 1934 by the Catalan artist José Maria Sert, depicting the progress of humankind through health, technology, freedom and peace; all very heroic. Indeed, the whole style of the main wing – granted to a consortium after Le Corbusier's visionary modernist design had been rejected – is, rather ironically, a prime example of 1930s Fascist architecture, complete with cold marble floors, gigantic bronze doors and the hard lines of Neoclassicist Art Deco. That the building's rear extension, built in the late 1960s, today resembles the worst of London or Paris's inner-city office blocks, merely adds insult to injury.

Musée Ariana

Just down the hill from the Palais des Nations, in a distinctive 1880s Neo-Baroque mansion set in the same park, is the **Musée Ariana** (Mon & Wed–Sun 10am–5pm; free; ⓦmah.ville-ge.ch), devoted to seven centuries of glass and ceramics from Europe and the East. Unless you're a fan, though, the building – semicircular galleries overlooking an internal atrium – is likely to be at least as inspiring as its contents. Highlights of the lavish collection include beautiful and intricately decorated European faience and porcelain from the sixteenth to eighteenth centuries, the earth tones of Spanish ware contrasting with deep creamy French colours and light Italian pastels. There are plenty of English notes to mug up on as you go around.

Eating and drinking

With more than a thousand restaurants in the city, you could **eat and drink** your way around the world in Geneva – at a price. The most visible establishments might give you the impression that you could afford nothing more adventurous than a filled baguette, but Genevois café culture is alive and well, and inexpensive diners do exist. If you're prepared to splash, you could dine as grandly as in Paris, London or New York.

Cafés and café-bars

Almost every corner has its **café**, and the following list is highly selective, serving as much to give pointers as to what to expect in each neighbourhood as to recommend these particular establishments over others. The Old Town's Place du Bourg-de-Four, for instance, is lined with busy terrace cafés offering coffees, *apéros* and snacks to fuel hours of reading and people-watching, and there's little point picking one out to recommend. Wherever you end up, you'll have no trouble finding somewhere congenial to rest your feet and sample a little something.

Station area and Les Pâquis

Bains des Pâquis 30 Quai du Mont-Blanc. Excellent and very popular café-bar attached to the lakefront swimming areas, renowned for some of the best people-watching in the city – atmospheric, colourful and cool. Summer only.

Bookworm 5 Rue Sismondi. Mini teashop within a crammed secondhand English bookshop, with tootling Thirties music and a faultless "pot of tea for two with biscuits". Closed Mon & Tues.

La Bretelle 15 Rue des Etuves. Tiny kitsch tavern just off the Rive Droite, a glitz-drenched haven from the mean streets outside, that pulls in plenty of camp, alternative young-at-hearts, especially for the live accordion and/or drag cabaret (Thurs–Sat nights).

Buvette des Cropettes Place Gruet, off Rue de Montbrillant. Tiny atmospheric six-table wood-floor café-bar tucked behind the station, opposite the sunny Cropettes park. Closed Sun & Mon.

Café Arts 17 Rue des Pâquis. Bright café-bar with a young, excited clientele. A pleasant slice of sleaze-free Pâquis. Daily 5pm–midnight.

Café de Paris 26 Rue du Mont-Blanc. Very central café that does one meal only, but does it spectacularly well – entrecôte steak in a herb-and-butter sauce with golden chips and salad, for Fr.37. Otherwise, it's a perfect place for down-time, seconds from the station.

Mr Pickwick 80 Rue de Lausanne. One of a chain of English pubs present in most Swiss towns. Generic, rather down-at-heel and a bit expensive, but nonetheless with the right kind of atmosphere and live football on the telly.

Old Town area and Plainpalais

Alhambar 10 Rue Rôtisserie. Relaxed glittery bar behind a Rues-Basses cinema, with a yuppyish tone, plenty of tapas and evening DJs. Sunday's laidback piano-brunch is worth checking out.

Café des Forces Motrices Place des Volontaires. Directly opposite the *L'Usine* (see below), this is one of the best options in a buzzing area, not grand or trendy, but just calm, friendly, attractive and welcoming.

Café Gallay 42 Boulevard St Georges. Friendly neighbourhood café-bar opposite Plainpalais cemetery, attracting an arty young crowd of students and theatre people. Good, inexpensive food and shared tables add to the appeal. Closed Sun.

Café Mozart 4 Quai des Forces Motrices. Cool split-level designer wine bar on the riverfront, regularly featuring live classical and jazz quartets (Thurs–Sat). An expensive menu promotes quaffing over scoffing. Closed Sun & Mon.

Café de l'Usine In L'Usine squat, Place des Volontaires. Graffitied upstairs bar-café that once sported a rough-edged clientele puffing clouds of sweet smoke to a background of heavy noise. These days, it's been cleaned up a bit, but is still a good place to access the city's underground. Solid meals for Fr.10 or so. Closed Sun & Mon.

Chocolaterie du Rhône 3 Rue de la Confédération. Outlet for fine handmade chocolates, with a small tea room in the back serving heavenly cakes and confections to accompany tea and coffee. Closed Sun.

Le 2e (Deuxième) Bureau 9 Rue du Stand. Sleek postmodern bar, with sleek postmodern people draped over the sofas as deep beats rattle the glasses. Occasionally features live music or readings.

Flanagan's Rue du Cheval-Blanc. Top-rated Irish pub, hidden on an Old Town alley and generally packed with expats and Genevois alike.

L'Opera de Huissoud 51 Rue du Stand. Charming little nook dedicated to the delights of French pop music over five decades, with photos and record sleeves adorning the walls and Charles Aznavour crackling over the speakers.

Le Pain Quotidien 21 Boulevard Helvétique. No-nonsense café ("Daily Bread") with a well-deserved reputation for superb breakfasts (Fr.7 or Fr.12) and, especially, weekend brunches of smoked salmon, salads, pastries, eggs, warm bread and fresh-squeezed juices (Fr.28). Seating is on benches at long wooden tables. Closed Tues eve.

Carouge

Bar du Nord 66 Rue Ancienne. Dark, plasticky and filled with young designerish Carougeois carousing beneath murals by a local cartoonist.

Café des Amis 23 Rue Ancienne. Oldest of the traditional cafés on Ancienne, full of atmosphere from an age now past. Join the locals for a trip down memory lane.

Café de la Plage 10 Rue Vautier. Trendy alternative hangout, with long carved wooden benches and a pleasant, talkative ambience, regularly spilling drinkers out onto the street. It's a long way from any kind of *plage*, though.

Cave à Bière 19 Rue Ancienne. Bar with almost 400 beers from around the world that attracts connoisseurs and serious drinkers in equal measure. Closed Sun & Mon.

La Marchand de Sable 4 Rue Vautier. Loud, graffitied little nook with a rough edge and student clientele, packed most nights.

Martel Tea Room 4 Rue du Marché. Perfect spot to punctuate an afternoon walk around Carouge, founded in 1818 and still offering exquisite chocolates and pastries as well as good, inexpensive meals. Closed Mon.

Restaurants

Geneva's excellent Swiss **restaurants** are somewhat overshadowed by a plethora of French places, drawing on influences from *haute-cuisine* Lyon to the west. The **Old Town** in particular (around the Place du Bourg-de-Four) has a host of atmospheric Swiss eateries. **Carouge** is a foodie's paradise, with plenty of sometimes pricey choices. **Eaux-Vives** is much more down-to-earth, with some quality inexpensive Italian joints. Cosmopolitan – and occasionally sleazy – **Les Pâquis** has dozens of low-priced, authentic Arabic, East Asian, South American and African cafés and restaurants.

There's almost limitless choice in **inexpensive and mid-range** dining, with good-value, characterful places just off the main streets in all corners of the city. As you might expect, Geneva has dozens of top-drawer **expensive** restaurants, where you can find cuisine to match the best in the world.

Station area and Les Pâquis

Al-Amir 12 Rue des Alpes. Excellent Lebanese place, its stool-and-counter area favoured by falafel-munching locals over the sit-down table section. Quality range of *mezze* (Fr.8–14 each), plus chicken or lamb *shwarmas* (Fr.10) as good as they should be. Top choice of the many Pâquis kebab dens.

Le Diwane 6 Rue de Zurich ☏022 732 73 91. Excellent, authentically prepared Arabic cuisine. A meal of classy *mezze* is about Fr.25, or you can blowout and order the entire menu for Fr.160 – either way, don't miss the delicious *maamoul* rose-scented cookies afterwards. Closed Sat lunch & Sun.

Le Dodo 20 Rue de Montbrillant ☏022 734 39 57. Much-loved Mauritian restaurant, with a dodo on the bar and an intriguing menu full of dishes that blend seafood and Indian-style spicing to perfection. Under Fr.20 for lunch; double that in the evenings. Closed Sun.

El Mektoub 5 Rue Chaponnière ☏022 738 70 31. Discreet central hideaway for quality North African cooking in a pleasant ambience. Excellent cous-cous and a wealth of *tajines* are Fr.30–35, with a handful of veggie options too. Closed Sun.

Jeck's Place 14 Rue de Neuchâtel ☏022 731 33 03. Excellent Thai restaurant, with nice wood-and-rattan decor and superb, authentic food that is surprisingly affordable (around Fr.30, or half that at lunch). House speciality is a range of Singaporean dishes, mixing influences from Malaysia, China and India. Closed Sat lunch.

Khmer Angkor 31 Rue du Môle ☏022 732 38 43. Tiny, easygoing family-run Cambodian restaurant in the heart of the Pâquis, serving such specialities as fried dorada with pineapple and grilled shrimps with mint leaves. Expect to spend up to Fr.50. Closed Sat lunch & Sun.

Manora 4 Rue de Cornavin. Excellent, down-to-earth self-service nosh at this huge outlet of the Swiss chain (see p.49). With such a fast customer turnover, its food is very fresh as well as rock-bottom cheap: you can easily stuff yourself for Fr.12.

Au Petit Chalet 6 Rue Chaponnière. Unpretentious city-centre Swiss place for fondues, *rösti* and pizza (Fr.20–25) in a refreshingly untouristic dark-wood setting. Closed Mon.

Teranga 38bis Rue de Zurich ☏022 731 15 22. Tiny backstreet Senegalese place, attractively decorated, with good service and great food, including plantains, yassa (braised chicken in onion sauce) and fresh ginger juice. Around Fr.25. Closed Sat lunch & Sun.

Café Zara 25 Rue de Lausanne. Simple little Eritrean/Ethiopian café-restaurant near the station, with uncomplicated menus (meat and vegetarian) for Fr.20–25 and, unusually, weekend breakfasts from 5am.

Old Town area and Plainpalais

Les Armures 1 Rue du Puits-St-Pierre ☏022 310 34 42. Traditional stone-floored Old Town institution on three storeys, refreshingly kitsch-free and once graced by Bill Clinton and family (with a plaque by the door to prove it). A full range of perfectly prepared Swiss dishes cost from Fr.30.

Café du Centre 5 Place du Molard ☏022 311 85 86, ⊛www.cafeducentre.ch. A very handy Rues-Basses pitstop with terrace seating in summer. The smell of the sea hits you as you push the door and that's really what this plain, very popular café-restaurant is all about, offering everything from 100g of periwinkles up to a dozen fresh oysters, aided by a huge wine list. Not cheap for dining, at Fr.30–50, but worth a coffee just to sample the old-style atmosphere.

Cave Valaisanne/Chalet Suisse Place du Cirque. Touristically minded place for those seeking that authentic fondue experience. The chalet side is all dim lights, dark wood-beamed interior and endless Swiss kitsch; the *cave* side less contrived and so slightly less grating. The food is fine at both, and affordable (Fr.20 or so), but neither is what you might call heart-warming.

La Favola 15 Rue Jean Calvin ☏022 311 74 37, ⊛www.lafavola.com. Charming little family-run restaurant on a cobbled Old Town alley, with a small menu of choice Ticinese specialities to dally over in an atmospheric setting. A romantic evening tête-à-tête could touch Fr.45 each; lunches much less. Closed Sat & Sun.

Hang Zhou 19 Rue de la Coulouvrenière ☏022 781 41 47. Excellent inexpensive Chinese, with a full vegetarian menu and *dim sum* galore (Fr.13–23). Closed Sun.

Kantine In Artamis squat community, off Boulevard de St-Georges. On the far left side, tucked among the graffitied warehouses and studios of Artamis, divey *Kantine* offers one of the cheapest meals in Geneva, home-made food in big portions for Fr.10. Roughly Mon–Fri 11am–4pm, maybe later, maybe earlier.

Le Pied de Cochon 4 Place du Bourg-de-Four ☏022 310 47 97, ⊛www.pieddecochon.ch. Bow-tied waiters bustle their way between the tinkling cutlery of one of Geneva's best-loved bistros, serving meaty Genevois and Lyonnais gutliners (Fr.35), including the namesake grilled pigs' trotters, to a clientele not short of a *centime* or two.

Taverne de la Madeleine 20 Rue Toutes-Âmes. Quite possibly the oldest restaurant in the city, now an alcohol-free café-bistro, serving only lunches – unreconstructed home-made fare (Fr.15) – in a tiny old dining room below the Old Town. Closed Sun.

Le Thé 65 Rue des Bains ☎ 079 436 77 18. Tiny place decorated with teapots and handleless sipping cups serving outstanding, inexpensive Chinese food – especially steamed dishes. Only has a handful of tables, so you either need to book or turn up outside standard mealtimes.

Eaux-Vives

Vesuvio 7 Rue Cherbuliez ☎ 022 736 30 40. Eaux-Vives has many Italian restaurants, but this is one of the best, boasting fresh-made pasta, a wood-fired pizza oven, relaxed open decor and friendly service. Meals are not expensive, mostly

under Fr.20. Closed Sat lunch, Sun & Mon.

Carouge

La Bourse 7 Place du Marché, Carouge ☎ 022 342 04 66. Celebrated nineteenth-century café-brasserie in the heart of Carouge, with a wide, heavily fishy menu, taking in *moules* and *huitres* as well as a protein-packed *marmite du pêcheur* (Fisherman's Pot). Fondue, salads and steak help out less briny diners, and a quality lunch *menu* can be had for Fr.15. The cellar doubles as a pizzeria. Closed Sun & Mon.

La Cuccagna Place du Temple. Quality among Carouge's high-class cuisine that won't break the bank, with simple, delicious pizza and pasta dishes for Fr.25 or so.

Sawasdee 24 Avenue Cardinal Mermillod ☎ 022 300 08 42. Best Thai in Geneva, with calm, attentive service, simply exquisite food and a bill at the end of it to lighten your spirits: a mere Fr.15–18 for lunch, twice that in the evening. Definitely worth the tram ride.

Expensive restaurants

L'Ange du Dix Vins 31 Rue Jacques Dalphin, Carouge ☎ 022 342 03 18. Much-loved little place, with warm Provençale ochre-and-sky-blue decor and cuisine to match. A convivial atmosphere in both the restaurant and less formal bistro adjacent fits precisely the relaxed appreciation of good food and wine, overseen by a chef "qui oppose au snobisme de la gastro les magies chaleureuses du restau". Daily specials around Fr.23, full menu Fr.60, truffle menu Fr.110. Closed Sat & Sun.

Le Béarn 4 Quai de la Poste ☎ 022 321 00 28. Geneva's premier establishment, supremely elegant and with lavish and inventive cuisine earning plaudits from those in the know and a star from Michelin. *Menus* are from Fr.50, but most meals probably won't remain in mere double figures. Closed Sat & Sun (winter open Sat eve) and mid-July to Aug.

Le Chat Botté In *Hôtel Beau-Rivage*, 13 Quai du Mont-Blanc ☎ 022 716 66 66. Classic French fine dining – with fish dishes celebrated above all – in this most traditional of hotels, with a choice between the somewhat stuffy formal dining room and, in summer, the lighter, easier-going terrace overlooking the lake. Expect Fr.130 at least. Open daily.

Domaine de Châteauvieux 16 Rue Châteauvieux, Peney-Dessus, Satigny ☎ 022 753 15 11. An atmospheric château a short drive west of the city, in the heart of Geneva's wine region, complete with a cobbled approach, ancient beams, old stones and a giant open fireplace dominating

the dining room (or, in summer, views from the terrace over the vineyards). The fine, traditional cuisine with some innovative modern touches, emphasizing simplicity and seasonal, local ingredients, is highly acclaimed – not least by Michelin, who give the place two stars. Closed Sun & Mon.

L'Esquisse 7 Rue du Lac ☎ 022 786 50 44. Gourmet French cuisine – priced lower than elsewhere – in the unlikely surroundings of an Eaux-Vives backstreet. The place is also a gallery for local artists, and pleasant decor and respectful service aids peaceful digestion of the *foie gras* and *filet mignon de veau*. Lunch is Fr.40, evening *menus* around Fr.85. Closed Sat lunch & Sun.

Miyako 11 Rue de Chantepoulet ☎ 022 738 01 20, ⓦ www.miyako.ch. Superb Japanese restaurant, calm, modern and attractive, with three separate areas. The sushi and sashimi bar is first as you walk in, downstairs is a quiet dining room, with low tables and traditional seating, but the best location is the lively main *teppan yaki* area in the rear, ranged at counters around several open hotplates, where chefs expertly slice, dice, toss and sauté your meal in front of you. Quality is outstanding, with everything melt-in-the-mouth fresh. Servers will talk you through the long menu, which includes several options of set meals ("Menu Sushi", "Menu Sashimi" etc) for around Fr.50. Leave space for the exquisite *glace au thé vert* (green-tea ice cream). Expect around Fr.75 a head. Closed Sun.

Vieux-Bois 12 Avenue de la Paix ☎ 022 919 24 26. High-quality showcase of the world-famous catering school *L'École Hôtelière de Genève*: all the chefs and waiting staff are students, which means you'll get sharp, attentive service and an *haute cuisine* lunch – French, with light, inventive touches and veggie options – for a fraction of prices elsewhere. Scoff a four-course *menu* for as little as Fr.45, or choose from the daily specials for half that, and then retire to the garden for coffee. Mon–Sat noon–2.30pm; garden May–Sept Mon–Sat noon–6pm. Closed Easter, mid-July to mid-Aug, Christmas & New Year.

Nightlife and entertainment

Geneva's **nightlife** is unlikely to set your pulse racing. Endless venues cater to visiting businesspeople and wealthy locals – formal dinner-dance, yawnworthy cabaret, and vast quantities of strip-shows and hostess bars – but aside from checking out the handful of alternative arts venues, it's not easy to find what young Genevois get up to… often because they've vanished up the road to the cutting-edge **clubs** in and around Lausanne instead. That said, you can find top-notch **classical music** and **opera**, with a world-famous orchestra dividing its time between Geneva and Lausanne, as well as major international performers. **Dance** and **drama** are also well accounted for. The **Fêtes de Genève** is the city's premier annual arts festival, held in early August on the waterfront, with music of all kinds, theatre, funfairs and street entertainers.

What's on **listings** are published weekly in *Genève-Agenda*, the free city guide available from the tourist office and hotels. You can get **tickets** for almost any event from Ticket Corner (☎ 0848 800 800), or Manor on Rue Cornavin (Mon–Fri 8.30am–6.45pm, Thurs until 8pm, Sat 8am–5pm): about Fr.10–20 for ordinary live bands and clubs, Fr.25–30 for special events, Fr.15–60 for classical concerts, and Fr.24–200 for the opera.

Note that bars stay open all night during March's Motor Show weekend, August's Fêtes de Genève, and L'Escalade in December.

Clubs and live music

Geneva has a handful of worthwhile dance **clubs**, but nothing to compete with Lausanne or Zürich. The city suffers from too many places catering to jaded businessmen: often you'll find that places billing themselves as *discothèques* turn out to enforce a smart-casual door policy for entry to a deeply depressing floorshow (occasionally nude dancing girls) and/or a Top 40 disco. There are a few venues around town for **live music**; Friday and Saturday nights are when the bars and clubs lining Rue Vautier in Carouge come into their own. There's a festival of rock, jazz and folk in July and August at Parc La Grange in Eaux-Vives, but if you're around in the summer you should aim for the big Paléo festival at Nyon just around the lake (see p.146).

Le Chat Noir 13 Rue Vautier, Carouge ⓦ www. chatnoir.ch. Bar and cellar venue dedicated to live performance, with three or four concerts a week, everything from *chansons* to drum'n'bass, acid jazz and acoustic blues. DJs follow on. Mon–Thurs 6pm–4am, Fri 6pm–5am, Sat & Sun 9pm–5am.
L'Interdit 18 Quai de Seujet. Pumping and hugely popular disco cavern, sharing its clientele and energy with the *New Loft* next door (see "Gay and Lesbian" box).

Liquid Club 4 Quai des Forces-Motrices ⓦ www.liquidclub.ch. Exposed-metal interior of an old riverfront warehouse vibrates nightly to house and jungle, with forays into drum'n'bass and triphop.
La Pirogue 4 Ruelle des Templiers. Reggae and African beats.
Sud des Alpes 10 Rue des Alpes. Jazz buffs' mecca, with live music that sometimes pushes the boat out a fraction. Generally Thurs–Sat at 9.30pm.

Gay and lesbian Geneva

Geneva's **gay** scene is centred around Dialogai, 11 Rue de la Navigation (Tues–Fri 3–6pm, Wed until 10pm; ☎022 906 40 40, ⓦwww.dialogai.ch), which, as well as being a library and resource centre for the whole of Romandie, has news about one-offs around the city as well as a regular programme of events; their magazine *Dialogai* (in French) is packed with information and ads, and the adjacent café always has something going on. Every week, they put on a mass candlelit dinner in a back room, guys crowding at long tables for the home-made food (Wed 7–10pm; Fr.14; maximum 80 – arrive early). *Le New Loft*, 20 Quai de Seujet, is a big, glitzy campy disco, with top-quality drag shows during the week. *La Bretelle* (see p.106), *Nathan*, 6 Rue Baudit, and *L'Evidence*, 13 Rue des Grottes, are gay- or gay-friendly café-bars. You'll find no shortage of cruising possibilities among the Pâquis sex-shops. The Gay International Group (ⓔcontact@forhum.org) meets every fortnight and welcomes newcomers.

Dialogai can help out with **lesbian**-oriented information, or you can call the Centre Femmes Natalie Barney (☎022 797 27 14, ⓦwww.club-association.ch/cfnb), or La Clef, 3bis Rue du Stand (☎022 781 71 30), both of which have bars; La Clef also runs lesbian dance nights (Fri & Sat 10pm–3am). L'Inédite is a bookshop and resource centre for women – lesbian and not – at 15 Rue St Joseph, Carouge.

L'Usine Place des Volontaires. Alternative arts squat venue, featuring live bands at the Salle PTR ("Post Tenebras Rock"), experimental dance and drama at the Théâtre de l'Usine and non-commercial movies at the Cinéma Spoutnik.

Weetamix 114 Route de Vernier ⓦwww. weetamix.com. House and techno weekend all-nighters, with international DJs.
XS 21 Grand-Rue. Easy dancing to reggae, disco and popular tunes. Tues–Sat 10pm–5am.

Classical music, theatre and film

There's plenty of **classical music** in Geneva. The Orchestre de la Suisse Romande (ⓦwww.osr.ch), which shuttles between Geneva and Lausanne, is one of Europe's best, and often performs – in amongst big-name visiting orchestras and soloists – at the glittering Victoria Hall, 14 Rue Général-Dufour. The Grand Théâtre (ⓦwww.geneveopera.ch), on Place Neuve, has a continuous programme of classical concerts, chamber music and **opera**, and the Conservatoire de Musique, also on Place Neuve, hosts a prestigious annual international competition for young soloists in late September as well as recitals all year round. Many of the most innovative opera productions, as well as concerts and some dance events, take place at the lofty Bâtiments des Forces-Motrices (ⓦwww.bfm.ch), 2 Place des Volontaires, formerly home to hydro-electric turbines on the Rhône. There are also free classical concerts in many of Geneva's churches year-round, and open-air concerts at the Hôtel-de-Ville in July and August.

The Comédie de Genève, 6 Boulevard des Philosophes, is the main stage for classic **drama**, and there are dozens of smaller experimental stages, including the celebrated Théâtre du Grütli, 16 Rue Général-Dufour. Theatre in English (ⓦwww.theatreinenglish.ch) has details of high-quality amateur productions by the Geneva English Drama Society and Geneva Amateur Operatic Society.

As for **film**, you'll find dozens of city-centre cinemas showing Hollywood releases (often ahead of London), but you should check in the listings for "v.o." (*version originale*), which indicates original dialogue with French subtitles – many prime-time showings are dubbed. Every summer there are big *Cinélac* open-air screenings on the waterfront at Port Noir. The **Geneva Film Festival**, every October, is devoted to airing the work of unknowns from around Europe.

Listings

Bike rental The station has the usual bike-rental facilities (Mon–Fri 6.50am–6.45pm, Sat & Sun 7am–12.30pm & 1.30–5.45pm) or you could take advantage of the *Genèv'Roule* scheme, 17 Place de Montbrillant (May–Oct daily 7.30am–9.30pm), with rental bikes for free and to rent at Fr.5/day (deposit Fr.50). Horizon Motos, 22 Rue des Pâquis, rents mopeds and scooters.

Boat rental You can rent boats from a handful of quayside operators, including Les Corsaires, 33 Quai Gustave-Ador (ⓦwww.lescorsaires.ch), and Marti Marine, 31 Quai du Mont-Blanc: roughly, a pedalo is Fr.18/hr, a small motorboat Fr.40–50/hr.

Books The best place for English-language media is Elm Books, 5 Rue Versonnex, near Rive (ⓦwww.elmworld.ch), with the largest selection in French Switzerland. L'Inédite, 15 Rue St-Joseph in Carouge, has a quirky selection of English and French books by, for and about women. Bookworm (see p.106) is piled high with secondhand English books of all kinds.

Changing money In the station (April–Oct daily 6.45am–9.30pm; Nov–March daily 6.45am–8pm).

Consulates Australia, 2 Chemin des Fins ⓣ022 799 91 00, ⓦwww.australia.ch; Canada, 5 Ave de l'Ariana ⓣ022 919 92 00; New Zealand, 2 Chemin des Fins ⓣ022 929 03 50; UK, 37 Rue de Vermont ⓣ022 918 24 00; USA, 7 Rue Versonnex ⓣ022 840 51 60. Embassies are listed on p.258.

Flights Flight enquiries from Geneva-Cointrin ⓣ0900 57 15 00, ⓦwww.gva.ch. Leopair (ⓣ022 798 21 10) is one of nine firms at the airport offering sightseeing flights.

Laundry Lavseul, 29 Rue de Monthoux (daily 7am–midnight).

Lost property If you lost something on a plane, call ⓣ022 799 33 35; if you lost it in the airport, call ⓣ022 427 92 31; if you lost it in a train station or on a train, call ⓣ051 225 14 33. The main CFF lost property office is on platform 1B of Gare Cornavin (Mon–Fri 6am–9pm, Sat & Sun 9am–7.45pm), and the city's lost property office is at 7 Glacis-de-Rive (Mon–Fri 7.30am–4pm; ⓣ022 327 41 11).

Markets The best markets in the city are the venerable old flea market on the Plaine de Plainpalais (Wed & Sat 8am–5pm); the general market on Place de la Madeleine (Mon–Sat 8am–6pm); and crafts (Thurs 8am–6pm) and books (April–Oct Fri 8am–5pm), both on Place de la Fusterie. Plainpalais also has big fruit & veg markets (Tues, Fri & Sun).

Medical facilities The Cantonal Hospital, 24 Rue Micheli-du-Crest (ⓣ022 372 33 11), has a 24-hour emergency room, as does the central Permanance medical centre, 1 Rue Chantepoulet ⓣ022 731 21 20. ASMDI, 2 Rue Georges-Leschot (Mon–Fri 6.15am–7pm; ⓣ022 320 31 22), can do emergency dental work.

Post Geneva's most convenient large post office is at 18 Rue du Mont-Blanc (Mon–Fri 7.30am–6pm, Sat 8am–noon). You can collect mail sent to you at Poste Restante, Mont-Blanc, CH-1211 Geneva 1, from windows 3–7 with your passport.

Radio World Radio Geneva, 88.4FM (ⓦwww.wrgfm.com), is an oddly parochial English-language expat station, with BBC news plus music and phone-ins – as is Family Radio 74, at 88.8FM.

Swimming Two large outdoor swimming complexes have pools and access to the lake waters: Genève Plage is on the Rive Gauche at Port-Noir (daily: June–Aug 9am–8pm, May & Sept 9am–7pm; Fr.5; bus #2), with a heated pool and waterslide, basketball, volleyball, waterskiing and windsurfing; the Bains des Pâquis at 30 Quai du Mont-Blanc (daily: June–Aug 9am–8pm, May & Sept 10am–6pm; Fr.1), dating from the 1930s, is more popular but has fewer facilities.

Around Geneva

If you're on an unhurried visit, there's plenty of opportunity to get out into the beautiful countryside of **Canton Geneva**, Switzerland's smallest. The tourist office brochure *Sites naturels et cours d'eau de la campagne genevoise* features eight two- or three-hour **countryside walks** that are easily manageable from the city itself, but it's also simple to strike out alone and discover bucolic villages, châteaux, views of the mountains or the lake for yourself. In general, the slopes of the Rive Droite (north bank) are winegrowing territory, those of the Rive Gauche (south bank) devoted to farmland. Public transport of all kinds – from boats to buses – extends to every corner, but you'd do just as well

Rafting and paragliding

Rafting Genève (℡079 213 41 40, Ⓦwww.rafting.ch) runs canoeing, rafting and kayaking trips daily on the Arve's 7km of rapids, as well as whitewater trips on the Dranse and elsewhere, from about Fr.60 per person. They also rent canoes and kayaks and make tandem paragliding jumps off Mont Salève (Fr.150). Their info-shack is on Quai des Vernets south of Plainpalais (May–Oct only).

renting a bike or on foot. Many vineyards offer **free wine-tastings** on Saturday mornings; the tourist office brochure *Viticulteurs genevois* lists them all, with opening hours and what's on offer.

Spots to aim for include **Mont Salève**, the nearest high mountain to Geneva – a perfect place for sunshine when the lake is foggy – as well as the atmospheric and easy-to-reach Rive Gauche village of **Cologny**. In an entirely different vein, **CERN**, Europe's leading particle physics laboratory and the place where the World Wide Web was born, straddles the French border at Meyrin to the northwest.

Mont Salève

First ridge of the Alps rising southeast of Geneva is **Mont Salève** (1380m), the city-dwellers' principal retreat into nature, with wide-open countryside for walking or skiing, and views over the city, the whole canton and the Jura hills opposite. There are footpaths galore on top (which become cross-country skiing trails in winter), both through woodland and, higher up, across expansive green meadows dotted with wildflowers in season. In contrast to the sheer face presented to Geneva, the other, southern side of the mountain is a gentle slope, looking out onto Mont Blanc and the Savoy Alps.

Bear in mind that Salève is across the French border, so if you're going to need a visa (either to get into France, or to get back into Switzerland), you should give it a miss. Bus #8 terminates on the border at Veyrier, from where it's a short walk through customs to the **cable-car**, which rises to a crest of the ridge (May–Sept daily; April & Oct closed Mon; check at other times). TPG offices at Gare de Cornavin and Rive, and the Place Dorcière coach station, sell a day pass that includes the cable-car round-trip for Fr.19. There's a panoramic restaurant on top. You can do the trip to the summit and back in a couple of easy hours. Randonnées au Salève organizes **guided hikes** up to the ridge and around on the top, meeting at the bus #8 terminus (1st & 3rd Sun of month 10am; free; no booking necessary; information ℡022 796 41 33).

Cologny and Hermance

The Rive Gauche lakeside slopes are dotted with peaceful, attractive villages that can offer beautiful walks. **COLOGNY**, 6km northeast of the city (bus A), has long been known as an exclusive and somewhat refined suburb, and the difference from Geneva is striking, with country lanes weaving between fields and open woods, and many large detached houses set back behind walls. **Byron** wrote the third canto of *Childe Harold* in 1816 while staying at the Villa Deodati, at 9 Chemin de Ruth in Cologny, and waxed lyrical about the rarity of seeing Mont Blanc reflected in the lake from up here. **Milton**, too, came visiting in 1639. If you follow Chemin de Ruth north, you'll come to the district of Montalègre, and the Maison Chapuis, where **Shelley** and Clairmont stayed in 1816 with **Mary Godwin**, who began writing *Frankenstein* here. The association with fame has stayed rock solid over the centuries, and Cologny still has its fair share of resident big-names, including Isabelle Adjani, Charles Aznavour, various sheikhs and Petula Clark. True to form, the tourist office has obligingly dubbed the place the "Beverly Hills of Geneva". Cologny also has an esoteric museum attraction, the **Bibliotheca Bodmeriana**, 19 Route de Guignard next to the bus stop (closed at time of writing; formerly Thurs 2–6pm, also first Tues in month 6–8pm; Fr.5). One of the greatest private libraries ever assembled, it takes in 160,000 works of literature, including illuminated medieval manuscripts, one of the few copies of the Gutenberg Bible and the oldest surviving text of the Gospel of St John.

Some 10km further along the lakeshore on a minor road, the tiny village of **HERMANCE**, last before you cross into France and reachable on bus E (or summertime boats), is even more tranquil, with a gorgeous lakeside location, remnants of its thirteenth-century walls and many medieval houses.

CERN

Northwest of Geneva, the suburbs dribble on either side of the *autoroute* to the French border at **Meyrin**. The only reason to come out here is to visit the European Laboratory for Particle Physics, known as **CERN** (℡022 767 84 84, Ⓦwww.cern.ch; bus #9), one of the world's largest scientific laboratories. A joint venture by a welter of European countries, which between them provide the near-Fr.1 billion annual budget, it's truly international, with scientists from eighty countries conducting mammoth months- or years-long experiments. CERN's – and the world's – largest particle accelerator, a 27km circular tunnel around which electrons are fired at just under the speed of light to see what happens when they hit their antimatter counterparts, is buried 100m below the French-Swiss border here. CERN has another unique claim to fame: Tim Berners-Lee, a scientist working there in 1989 but constrained by the limitations of the data-only Internet of the day, created the **World Wide Web** in order to facilitate the transmission of text and images. CERN's website is suitably encyclopedic on this and other matters. The public visits office is exceptionally well-organized, and runs regular **tours** of the entire site (Mon–Sat 9am & 2pm; 3hr; free), for which you must book ahead; if you visit between October and March, you'll also get to stand inside the accelerator tunnel (it's switched off in winter). There's also a less engaging schools-oriented exhibition, **Microcosm** (Mon–Sat 9am–5pm; free).

Travel details

Trains

Geneva to: Aigle (hourly; 1hr 20min); Basel (hourly; 2hr 50min); Bern (hourly; 1hr 45min); Bex (every 2hr; 1hr 35min); Biel/Bienne (hourly; 1hr 40min); Brig (twice hourly; 2hr 20min); Delémont (hourly; 2hr 15min); Fribourg (twice hourly; 1hr 20min); Geneva airport (5 times hourly; 10min); Lausanne (3 times hourly; 35min); Martigny (hourly; 1hr 35min); Montreux (hourly; 1hr 5min); Neuchâtel (hourly; 1hr 20min); Nyon (3 times hourly; 15min); St Gallen (hourly; 4hr 20min); Sierre (hourly; 2hr); Sion (twice hourly; 1hr 50min); Solothurn (hourly; 2hr); Vevey (hourly; 1hr); Yverdon (hourly; 55min); Zürich (hourly; 3hr).

Boats

(Following is a summary of May–Sept summer services; fewer boats run in other months, generally Sat & Sun only, if at all.)
Geneva (Quai du Mont-Blanc or Jardin Anglais) to: Evian, France (2 daily; 2hr 45min); Hermance (1 or 2 daily; 45min); Lausanne (3 daily; 3hr 30min); Montreux (3 daily; 5hr); Nyon (4–7 daily; 1hr–1hr 30min); Vevey (3 daily; 4hr 30min).

2

Lausanne and Lake Geneva

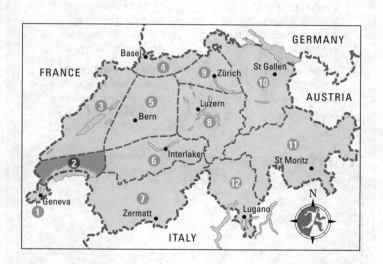

CHAPTER 2   # Highlights

* **Collection de l'Art Brut** Moving and highly memorable gallery of "outsider" art. **See p.129**

* **Cathédrale Notre-Dame** Lausanne's elegant Gothic centrepiece. **See p.130**

* **Ouchy waterfront** Lakeside catwalk for hip bladers and old-fashioned promenaders taking the air. **See p.132**

* **Gruyères** Medieval hilltop castle-village in the heart of cheese country. **See p.139**

* **Vevey** The most refined and alluring of lakeside towns. **See p.151**

* **Montreux** Lake Geneva's most upmarket destination – beautiful, expensive and exclusive. **See p.157**

* **Château de Chillon** One of the best preserved medieval castles in Europe, perched over deep water. **See p.161**

* **Golden Pass** Superbly scenic train journey from Montreux into the mountains. **See p.164**

Lausanne and Lake Geneva

Y ou can find the whole of Switzerland on the shores of **Lake Geneva**: snowy mountains, bucolic wine-villages, city nightlife, the sound of cow-bells in rolling pastureland, castles, cathedrals and the dreamily beautiful, cerulean blue lake itself (Lac Léman in French). The southern shore of the lake is in France, taking in the mighty Savoy Alps as well as Mont Blanc a little further south. The northern shore forms the economic and cultural focus of

Exploring Vaud

Mainline CFF **trains** describe an arc around the northern lakeshore, from Geneva to Nyon, Lausanne, Vevey, Montreux and on into the Valais. Smaller lines branch off at various points into the hills which cup the lake on both sides – the Jura foothills in the west and the Prealps in the east. However, you shouldn't miss the chance to take a **boat trip** on the lake. The CGN (✆www.cgn.ch) links all the towns and villages on both the Swiss and French shores in a web of routings, some of which run year-round. Tourist offices in all towns stock their timetable brochures, which are also posted at every *débarcadère* (landing-stage). The lake is divided into three: the **Petit-Lac** in the southwest, between Geneva and Nyon; the **Grand-Lac** between Nyon and Lausanne; and the **Haut-Lac** in the east around Vevey and Montreux. Boats run on short and long tours within and between all three areas, as well as hopping along the shoreline villages. Some also cross the lake, from Nyon and Rolle to Yvoire (France); from Lausanne to Evian (France); and from Vevey to St-Gingolph (a divided village on the French–Swiss border) – for all of which you need your passport. Eurail and Swiss Pass holders travel free on CGN boats, but InterRailers get no discounts.

The Office du Tourisme du Canton de Vaud (✆www.lake-geneva-region.ch) offers an excellent **regional pass**, sold at local tourist offices and train stations. Coverage is wide, taking in buses, trains and cable-cars in a core sector – the entire eastern half of the lake (Lausanne, Vevey, Montreux, Evian, Chillon and intermediate villages), mountain lines from Vevey to Mont-Pèlerin and Les Pléiades, and from Montreux to Rochers-de-Naye and Gstaad, plus routes to Gruyères via Bulle or via Montbovon. For Fr.83 (less if you hold a Swiss Pass, Swiss Card or Half-Fare Card), you get seven consecutive days of validity: any three days of free travel in the core sector, plus travel on all seven days at a discount of 25 to 50 percent on an extended network taking in routes to Geneva, Aigle, Les Diablerets and as far as Interlaken.

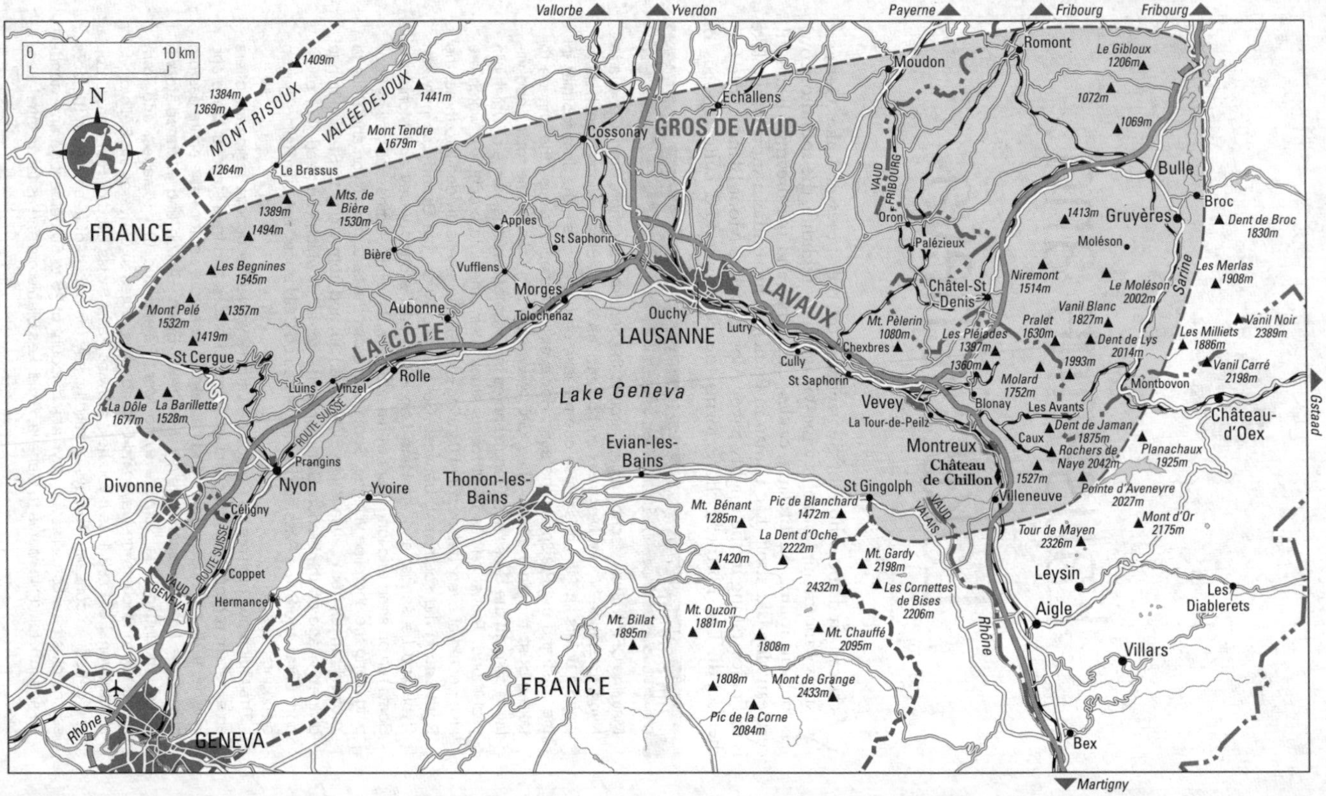
Vallorbe
Yverdon
Payerne
Fribourg
Fribourg
Gstaad
Martigny
0
10 km
N
FRANCE
FRANCE
1409m
1384m
1369m
MONT RISOUX
VALLÉE DE JOUX
1441m
Mont Tendre
1679m
1264m
Le Brassus
1389m
Mts. de
Bière
1530m
1494m
Les Begnines
1545m
Mont Pelé
1532m
1357m
1419m
St Cergue
La Dôle
1677m
La Barillette
1528m
Divonne
Céligny
ROUTE SUISSE
VAUD
GENEVA
Coppet
Hermance
Rhône
GENEVA
Nyon
Prangins
ROUTE SUISSE
Luins
Vinzel
Rolle
LA CÔTE
Aubonne
Bière
Apples
Vufflens
Morges
Tolochenaz
St Saphorin
Cossonay
GROS DE VAUD
Echallens
Moudon
Romont
Le Gibloux
1206m
1072m
1069m
Bulle
Broc
Gruyères
Dent de Broc
1830m
1413m
Moléson
VAUD
FRIBOURG
Oron
Palézieux
Sarine
Les Merlas
1908m
Niremont
1514m
Le Moléson
2002m
Châtel-St
Denis
Vanil Noir
2389m
Les Milliets
1886m
Vanil Blanc
1827m
Pralet
1630m
Dent de Lys
2014m
Mt. Pèlerin
1080m
Les Pléiades
1397m
1993m
Vanil Carré
2198m
1360m
Molard
1752m
Montbovon
Château-
d'Oex
Blonay
Les Avants
Dent de Jaman
1875m
Caux
Rochers de
Naye 2042m
Planachaux
1925m
1527m
Pointe d'Aveneyre
2027m
Ouchy
LAUSANNE
Lutry
LAVAUX
Chexbres
Cully
St Saphorin
Vevey
La Tour-de-Peilz
Montreux
Château
de Chillon
Villeneuve
Lake Geneva
Evian-les-
Bains
Thonon-les-
Bains
Yvoire
St Gingolph
VAUD
VALAIS
Mt. Bénant
1285m
Pic de Blanchard
1472m
La Dent d'Oche
2222m
1420m
Mt. Gardy
2198m
2432m
Les Cornettes
de Bises
2206m
Mt. Ouzon
1881m
Mt. Billat
1895m
1808m
Mt. Chauffé
2095m
1808m
Mont de Grange
2433m
Pic de la Corne
2084m
Tour de Mayen
2326m
Mont d'Or
2175m
Leysin
Les
Diablerets
Aigle
Rhône
Villars
Bex

French Switzerland, centred around **Lausanne**, an energetic, endearing city that's too often skimmed over in favour of Geneva's more restricted pleasures.

Aside from Geneva in the southwest and fragments of Valais in the southeast and Fribourg in the northeast, this is all **Canton Vaud** (pronounced *voh*), economically and politically the strongest of the French-speaking cantons, with a turbulent past. A 1798 revolution backed by France returned control to the Vaudois after two centuries of rule by Bernese bailiffs, a struggle commemorated by Napoleon, who formally created a new canton out of the territory. Vaud duly joined the Swiss Confederation in 1803 under a green-and-white flag which still flies in towns and villages to this day bearing the words "Liberté et Patrie". The ambience of the region is thoroughly Gallic: historical animosity towards Catholic France has given way to a yearning on the part of most urban francophone Swiss to abandon their heel-dragging compatriots in the more stolid east and embrace the EU. The short train ride from the Swiss-German cities of the *Mittelland* crosses more than just a linguistic boundary: it seems to span a whole continent of attitude.

Lausanne

[From] the terrace of the cathedral, I saw the lake above the roofs, the mountains above the lake, the clouds above the mountains, and the stars above the clouds. It was like a staircase where my thoughts climbed up step by step and broadened at each new height.

Victor Hugo

LAUSANNE tends to inspire hyperbole. In a country of spectacular natural beauty it is the most beautiful of cities, Switzerland's San Francisco, a city of incredibly steep hills that has developed tiered above the lake on a succession of compact, south-facing terraces. Vistas of blue water, glittering sunlight and the purple and grey of the looming, white-capped Savoy Alps peep through between gaps in buildings or at the ends of steeply dropping alleys. Much of the city is still wooded, there are plenty of parks, and the tree-lined lakefront promenades spill over with beds of vibrantly colourful flowers. Attractive, interesting, worldly, and well aware of how to have a good time, it's simply Switzerland's sexiest city.

The comparisons with San Francisco don't stop at the gorgeous setting. If Switzerland has a counterculture, it lives in the clubs and cafés of Lausanne, a fact which – odd though it seems – lies broadly within the city's long tradition of fostering intellectual and cultural innovation. From medieval times, Lausanne has stood at the Swiss cultural avant-garde. Back then, the **cathedral** crowned the city the most influential of the region; it still sits resplendent on an Old Town hill, the country's most impressive Gothic monument. After the Reformation, students flocked to Lausanne's pioneering university, and in the eighteenth and nineteenth centuries, restless Romantics sought and found inspiration in the setting and the life of Lausanne. It remains a grand-looking city (population 300,000), full of shuttered foursquare mansions and ritzy shopping streets, and with its own glamorous lakeside resort of **Ouchy**; there are also few cities in Europe that so actively value and support the pleasure principle. For decades, the municipality has generously subsidized art and culture of all shades, resulting in a range of festivals, live music, clubs, theatre, opera and dance to rival a more sluggish metropolis ten times bigger.

Aiding the dynamism, a defining feature of the city is its international population of **students**, attracted to the prestigious University of Lausanne, Switzerland's biggest, and the French-language arm of the Federal Institute of Technology. Hundreds of language schools and private academies enhance the city's reputation for learning, along with the world-famous École Hotelière, training ground for top chefs and hotel staff. An array of international study programmes helps to feed Lausanne's uniquely diverse multi-ethnic make-up. This youthful spirit, and the city's hilly aspect, have also given Lausanne a new role as European **blading and skateboarding** capital: when the sun shines, every public space hisses with the spinning of tiny wheels, and the Ouchy waterfront in summer echoes to the clack of skateboards. Bladers have been clocked doing 90kph on the city's hills.

Lausanne is the home of the highest Swiss federal court of appeal, and has also attracted many multinational companies, not least Philip Morris, who chose the city as a base from which to sell their Marlboro, Chesterfield, Suchard and Toblerone brands to Europe and Africa. However, the feature which the tourist office has lit upon is that the International Olympic Committee has been headquartered in Lausanne since 1915, and has attracted to the city an array of world governing bodies in sports ranging from chess to volleyball; they tout the city as "**Olympic Capital**" and endlessly plug the rather vapid Olympic Museum. It's a mark of Lausannois spirit that given the chance to host the 1994 winter games, the locals dismayed the municipality and the IOC by voting the idea down and embracing the annual International Roller Contest instead.

Some history

Vidy, on the waterfront immediately west of Ouchy, was the focus of settlement in the Lausanne area from **Neolithic** times onwards, and was where the **Romans** founded the small town of Lousonna in 15 BC. Lousonna flourished as a trading town, but during increasingly troubled times in the fourth century, the lakefront site was abandoned for a better-defended spot on the heights overlooking the lake, today the site of the Old Town. In 590, Bishop Marius transferred his bishopric from Avenches to Lausanne, confirming the city's rising influence. Succeeding bishops gathered power, even becoming imperial princes in 1125, until by the thirteenth century they were overseeing one of the largest cities in the region, with some nine thousand inhabitants. Both Pope Gregory X and Emperor Rudolf of Habsburg considered the consecration of Lausanne's fabulous **cathedral** in 1275 important enough to grace the ceremony with their presence.

During the fourteenth and fifteenth centuries, Lausanne was buffeted by a series of devastating fires and plague epidemics, as well as increasing social disorder stemming from the division of the city between the opulent lifestyle of the bishops in their lofty palace and the poverty of the people in the *Ville Basse*, or lower town. (Meanwhile, far below, the last remaining stragglers and fisherfolk had finally abandoned the lakeside ruins at Vidy, and decamped eastwards to the area around the Château d'Ouchy, protecting a small port.) In 1525, in an attempt to lift the yoke of the bishops from their neck, the Lausannois made a pact of mutual military assistance with Bern and Fribourg; eleven years later when the **Bernese** army, fired with the zeal of the **Reformation**, swept down towards Lake Geneva, the Lausannois were finally able to eject the bishops. Their independence was short-lived, though, since no sooner had the bishops departed (founding a new see in Catholic Fribourg) than the Bernese installed bailiffs of their own and reduced Lausanne to the status of a subject city.

Lausanne's university was founded in 1540 as the first French-language centre of Protestant theology, but the city remained a Bernese-run backwater until, in 1803, **Napoleon** hived Canton Vaud away from Bern and granted Lausanne the status of Vaudois capital. Shortly after, the modernizing municipality filled in the rivers Flon and Louve, which wound between the city's summits, and threw grand arching bridges over the ditches to link disparate neighbourhoods for the first time. Foreigners had already spotted Lausanne, and artists, romantics and adventurers soon flocked to both the city and the adjacent *commune libre et indépendante* of Ouchy, turning the place into a rather genteel stop on the Grand Tour of Europe (see box p.142). By the turn of the century, Lausanne was hosting a thriving community of expats – including forty retired British colonels – and boasted four English churches, a hundred English boarding schools, a cricket pitch, a football field and an English library serving afternoon tea. Lausanne had a quiet twentieth century, flourishing commercially, socially and culturally while happy to remain in the shadow of its over-illustrious, sober and considerably less desirable neighbour, Geneva.

Orientation, arrival and information

Lausanne's topography looks confusing on a map (see over), but isn't too hard to grasp. At the top is the Old Town, in the middle are the train station and commercial districts, and at the bottom is the one-time fishing village of **Ouchy**, now prime territory for waterfront strolling and café-lounging. But the gradients between them all are no joke: the peak of Mont Jorat, only 10km northeast of the city, rises to 927m; just north of the Old Town is a viewpoint at 643m; the central districts are ranged around 475m; while residential neighbourhoods slide on down for another kilometre to the lakeshore at 372m.

Focus of the city centre is the grand **Place St-François**, hub of bus routes and heart of the shopping district. Gilt-edged **Rue de Bourg** entices shoppers uphill from St-François, while beside it Rue St-François drops down north into the valley and up the other side to the cobbled **Place de la Palud**, an ancient, fountained square plum in the heart of the Old Town and flanked by the arcades of the Renaissance town hall. The elegant Gothic turrets of the **cathedral** rise loftily above, while the foursquare **château** stands even further up, at the highest and most northerly tip of the Old Town. Beyond rise the Jorat forests and open parkland.

Northwest of St-François, the giant Grand-Pont soars over the warehouse district of **Le Flon**, hotbed of Lausanne's burgeoning club culture, to **Place Bel-Air** and on to Place Chauderon at the head of the Pont Chauderon, which also rises above Le Flon. The steep slope south of St-François ends at the main **train station**, south of which a succession of opulent and elegant residential districts trickle down to **Place de la Navigation** on the Ouchy waterfront. Lakeside promenades lead in both directions from Ouchy, east to the gentle villages of **Pully** and **Lutry**, west to the parkland of **Vidy** and the lakeside campuses of the **university** and adjacent Federal Institute of Technology at Dorigny.

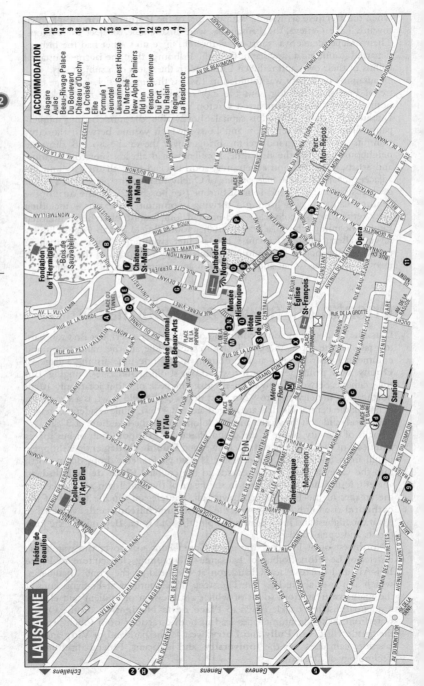

LAUSANNE

ACCOMMODATION

Alagare	10
Aulac	15
Beau-Rivage Palace	14
Du Boulevard	9
Château d'Ouchy	18
La Croisée	5
Elite	7
Formule 1	2
Jeunotel	13
Lausanne Guest House	8
Du Marché	1
New Alpha Palmiers	6
Old Inn	11
Pension Bienvenue	12
Du Port	16
Du Raisin	3
Regina	4
La Residence	17

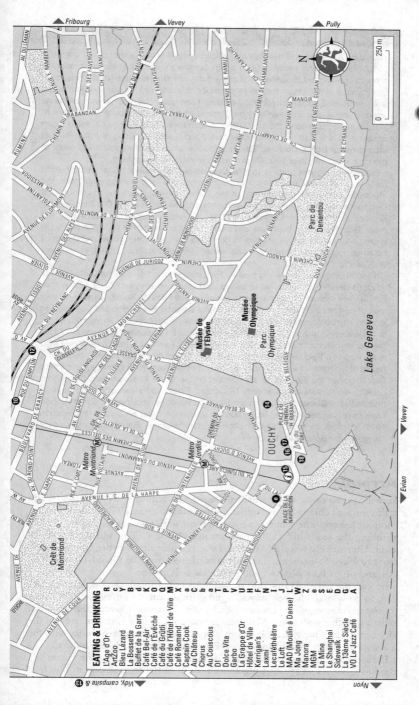

250 m

0

N

▲ Fribourg   ▲ Vevey   ▲ Pully

Lake Geneva

Musée de
l'Elysée

Musée
Olympique

Parc
Olympique

Parc du
Denantou

OUCHY

▲ Vidy, campsite & 13

Nyon ▼

◀ Evian   ◀ Vevey

123

EATING & DRINKING

L'Age d'Or	R
ArtZoo	c
Bleu Lézard	Y
La Bossette	B
Buffet de la Gare	d
Café Bel-Air	K
Café de l'Évéché	O
Café du Grütli	Q
Café de l'Hôtel de Ville	X
Café Romand	a
Captain Cook	C
Au Château	b
Chorus	a
Au Couscous	T
D!	P
Dolce Vita	V
Garbo	U
La Grappe d'Or	H
Hôtel de Ville	F
Kerrigan's	N
Laxmi	I
Lecaféthéâtre	J
Le Loft	L
MAD (Moulin à Danse)	W
Ma Jong	Z
Manora	e
MGM	S
La Mine	E
Le Shanghai	D
Sidewalk	G
La 13ème Siècle	A
VO Le Jazz Café	

Lausanne's festivals

With such a vibrant and healthily subsidized cultural scene, aided by an energetic population of young people, it can seem like there's always some celebration or other happening in Lausanne. All summer long, the **Ouchy waterfront** hosts informal music events – from techno to chamber music to African dance – just about every weekend, and always free. **Entrée libre pour un été** (@www.lausanne .ch/pourunete) is a summer-long programme of free music, dance and culture at various locations around the city, taking in such diversities as Friday evening organ concerts in the cathedral and hip-hop/DJ acts staged during the late-August **International Roller Contest**, Europe's premier skateboarding and inline event of the year, attracting over 100,000 skaters (@www.roller-contest.ch).

Lausanne's biggest party is the **Festival de la Cité** (@www.lausanne.ch) held in early July, in many ways much more spontaneous and cutting-edge than the Montreux Jazz Festival happening at the same time just down the road, not least because everything is free and out in the streets: the whole of the Old Town (*la cité*) is given over to live performance of all kinds – music, dance, drama, mime, and more. Both the best in their field and student novices vie for the promenading audiences, with performances starting at dusk and running continuously until the small hours on more than half-a-dozen open-air stages, with stalls all around selling beer and food to the crowds.

If you're in town at the wrong time for that, try and coincide with the **Cully-Lavaux Jazz Festival**, held in the wine cellars and medieval alleys of Cully village (see p.150), 8km east of Lausanne, in late March; or the **Fête du Soleil**, Lausanne's version of carnival held each April; or the Flon's **Atlantis Festival** in May, devoted to leading electronic music and dance; or the **Fête de la Musique**, impromptu music in the streets and bars in mid-June; or the **Fête à Lausanne**, a weekend of fairground attractions in late June; or the **Paleo Rock Festival**, a mammoth event held every July in a field outside Nyon (see p.146), which draws top-name artists and a crowd of a quarter of a million; or the **Festival of Contemporary Dance**, held in late September at the Sévelin 36 arts centre; or the **Bach Festival**, held throughout Lausanne over two weeks in early November. Finally, chilly January hosts both an **International Circus Festival** on the Place de Bellerive, and the acclaimed **Prix de Lausanne** competition and workshop for young dancers, an annual fixture since 1970, inspired by world-famous choreographer Maurice Béjart and his resident company, the Béjart Ballet Lausanne.

Arrival

Lausanne's imposing **train station** is served by regular TGVs from Paris and trains from all corners of Switzerland. **Boats** dock at the CGN jetty in Ouchy, more or less opposite which is a metro station, with regular shuttles on line M2 climbing the steep hill to the train station ("Gare CFF"), and further up to Flon. Alternatively, bus #2 (direction Désert) snakes up from the Ouchy waterfront to Place St-François, then heads northwest over the Grand-Pont to Bel-Air, and on to Rue Neuve beside Place de la Riponne.

By **car**, the *autoroutes* describe an awkward jink through the outskirts, and it's easy to go wrong. The best way to avoid getting snarled in suburban traffic is to follow *autoroute* signs for "Lausanne-Sud", not "Lausanne-Centre"; this leads you onto a spur that ends at the Maladière roundabout, a scant kilometre west of the city centre and Ouchy. Coming from Vevey or Montreux, don't bother with the *autoroute* at all, but follow blue signs for Lausanne along the lakeshore road.

Parking is expensive or awkward, or both. Street parking in the centre is a dead loss, but it's worth cruising around south of the train station in search of a blue-zone space. The largest car park is under Place du Riponne (Ⓦ www.parking-riponne.ch), but it's more expensive than the easy-to-find one on the Ouchy lakefront, which has buses and metro nearby. Otherwise, aim for the signed **P+R** (Park and Ride) car parks (in Ouchy and on several more approach roads), where you pay Fr.7 or so, depending on the number of people, for a Carte Journalière, which includes your parking space for the day and free public transport for the driver and all passengers.

Information

Lausanne has two **tourist offices**, one in the train station (daily 9am–7pm; ☎021 613 73 73, Ⓦ www.lausanne-tourisme.ch), and the other beside Ouchy metro station (daily 9am–8pm; Oct–March closes 6pm). Both have stacks of information on the whole lake region, including free maps, a handy *Welcome* booklet crammed with useful background material, a museum guide, timetables for the boats, and so on. Their best buy is the **Lausanne Card** (Fr.15), which gives free city transport as well as discounts at loads of shops and attractions around town, including twenty percent off museums, opera tickets and meals at *Manora* on Place St-François (see p.135), plus reduced entry to the huge indoor skate park on Rue Sévelin and free entry to municipal swimming pools.

For more focused information on cultural happenings and the life of the city, or to buy tickets for local shows, drop into the municipality's **information office**, in the Old Town at 2 Escaliers du Marché (Mon–Fri 7.45am–noon & 1.15–5pm; ☎021 315 25 55, Ⓦ www.lausanne.ch).

"Tempo", the Saturday supplement of Geneva's *Le Temps* newspaper, is the best source of **listings** and reviews of film openings, performances and cultural events throughout Romandie (although all in French). Lausanne's own *24 Heures* tabloid has cinema reviews but only a handful of other events listed. The tourist office puts out its own bimonthly offering.

City transport and tours

Although the Old Town is compact, and flying-crow distances don't look too bad, maps can only give half the story: you'll soon find that negotiating Lausanne's mountainous gradients and cat's cradle of valleys and bridges can get wearying. The excellent **public transport** is run by TL (☎0900 564 900, Ⓦ www.t-l.ch); zone 10 covers the whole city. A short journey of up to three stops costs Fr.1.50, while a journey across Zone 10 costs Fr.2.40 (valid 1hr); tickets bought after 7.30pm can be used until the end of the day. A *Carte 24 Heures*, valid for 24 hours from the time of issue, costs Fr.7.20.

You'll mostly be using the **buses**, many of them electric. Most lines skirt the Old Town from St-François to Bel-Air to Riponne: only bus #16 winds through it. There's also a **metro**: the steep M2 line (known fondly as *la Ficelle*, the String) links the Ouchy waterfront with Flon in the city centre, via the train station (Gare CFF); the Métro-Gare shuttles continuously to and fro between Flon and the train station; and M1 runs from Flon west to the university. LEB commuter **trains** serve Echallens (see p.141) from Flon. For details of the commercial **boat** services on the lake, see p.117.

The station has **bikes** for rent as normal (daily 6.40am–7.40pm), but even the locals have to get off and wheel them up and down the city's hills. Where bikes score is if you fancy a leisurely day cycling through the lakeshore vineyards either side of Lausanne, dropping your bike off in Nyon or Vevey and getting the train back to the city in the evening. You could also take a bike up into the hilly forests above Lausanne and then freewheel down again. To blend in imperceptibly with the locals, rent some **blades** or a **skateboard** from the kiosk at 6 Place de la Navigation in Ouchy (June–Sept daily 11am–10pm, April, May & Oct Sat & Sun 11am–7pm; ⓦ www.delacombaz.ch); they also rent good bikes, including 21-speed tandems.

If you can afford them, **taxis** are a good standby for conquering those hills. Most of Lausanne's cabs come under the umbrella of the Taxi Services' central computerized network; call ⓣ 0800 810 810.

Walking tours

The tourist office sponsors two-hour multilingual **walking tours** of the Old Town, which start from the Place de la Palud (May–Sept Mon–Sat 10am & 3pm; Fr.10). You can request tours at other times, and during the low season, from ⓣ 021 321 77 66. During the *Entrée libre pour un été* season of summer cultural activities, there are a handful of literary and historical walking tours of Lausanne guided in English; check with the tourist office or the municipality information office for dates and details. Otherwise, the tourist office's *Lausanne Promenade* booklet details excellent self-guided walks with maps and notes on subjects such as "The Old Town", "Gracious Houses", "Parks and Gardens" and "The Modern City".

Accommodation

Lausanne has plenty of **accommodation** to suit all budgets and aspirations, from simple hostels and pensions up to luxury palaces no less opulent than those in Geneva or Zürich. There's only a couple of hotels within the Old Town, plus a few more in the heart of the city centre; you're unlikely to be troubled by street noise anywhere. Hotels on the Ouchy lakefront have an entirely different, graceful ambience, although the lakefront road sees plenty of traffic. Between the two are a handful of places around the train station that are something of a bargain.

Hotels

There's a fair spread of inexpensive **hotels** across the centre, but unfortunately few remain in the old port area of Ouchy, which is increasingly aiming for a better class of guest. Any number of luxury palace hotels capitalize on Lausanne's unique topography to offer romantic lake views along with a more or less tasteful line in opulence, but the best-value deals come at the array of upmarket central business hotels, where you'll find cut-price rates at weekends and some special offers to draw in holidaymakers.

Inexpensive

Formule 1 67 Rue de l'Industrie, Bussigny ⓣ 021 701 02 02, ⓦ www.hotelformule1.com. Chain motel, offering 73 generic, functional rooms priced at an unbeatable Fr.59 for single, twin or triple occupancy. Located about 6km northwest of the centre, close to the Crissier/Bussigny *autoroute* exit, with free parking. Bus #MMM (not Sun) stops 200m away on a route between the Migros hypermarket at Crissier and Renens station (which has trains, buses and metro into Lausanne). Alternatively, Bussigny train station is a 500m walk away. ❶

Du Marché 42 Rue Pré-du-Marché ⓣ 021 647 99 00, ⓦ www.hotel-du-marche.com. Plain and comfortable small hotel, with spacious and very clean rooms, both with and without ensuite bathrooms. Usefully placed near Place de la Riponne, with some parking spaces. ❷

Old Inn 11 Avenue de la Gare ☎021 323 62 21, ⓔold_inn@bluewin.ch. Quiet, spartan and lived-in little pension, with a friendly *patronne* and three large doubles. ❶

Pension Bienvenue 2 Rue du Simplon ☎021 616 29 86, ⓦwww.pension-bienvenue.ch. Clean, decent and respectable women-only guesthouse a few yards behind the station, with 25 rooms. Breakfast included. ❶

Du Raisin 19 Place de la Palud ☎ & ⓕ021 312 27 56. A handful of rooms above an old café in the heart of the Old Town, with character and atmosphere but not much else. ❷

Mid-range

AlaGare 14 Rue du Simplon ☎021 617 92 52, ⓦwww.alagare.com. Decent, serviceable, mid-sized hotel in a quiet pedestrian zone just below the station, part of the Minotel group. ❸–❹

Aulac 4 Place de la Navigation, Ouchy ☎021 613 15 00, ⓦwww.aulac.ch. Large Belle-Epoque building looming over the Ouchy waterfront beside the metro station. Rooms are comfortable, balconied ones at the front with lake views (but more expensive, and exposed to street noise), those at the back cheaper and perfectly quiet. ❸–❹

Du Boulevard 51 Boulevard de Grancy ☎021 617 28 11, ⓦwww.hotelboulevard.ch. Respectable little city hotel that has managed to retain and nurture a hint of a weekend romantic getaway. All doubles with kitchenette, pleasantly done up (many with bathtub). ❸

Elite 1 Avenue St-Luce ☎021 320 23 61, ⓦwww.elite-lausanne.ch. Extremely pleasant, very quiet and well-run hotel, surrounded by greenery and centrally located between the train station and St-François. Top-floor balconied rooms perch you above the roofs for views over the lake. Best value in this bracket. ❸–❹

Du Port 5 Place du Port, Ouchy ☎021 612 04 44, ⓦwww.hotel-du-port.ch. Quality little three-star lakefront hotel, in the same family for forty years and fully upgraded in 2001, with excellent facilities and no-smoking rooms. Road noise can be a problem, though: ask for a room on an upper floor. Closed Jan. ❸–❹

Regina 18 Rue Grand St-Jean ☎021 320 24 41,

ⓦwww.hotel-regina.ch. Friendly little place owned by an English-speaking couple, steps from the central Place de la Palud, offering quality renovated rooms in modern style, with marvellous top-floor views. ❸–❹

Expensive

Beau-Rivage Palace 17 Place du Port, Ouchy ☎021 613 33 33, ⓦwww.brp.ch. Lausanne's top hotel and one of Switzerland's finest, set in its own 10-acre waterside garden estate and sparklingly restored to its original 1861 grandeur. Sumptuous decor and fittings, huge, balconied rooms and stylish, contemporary touches in every room raise it well above the standards of the many Swiss five-star palace hotels, while sharp service adds to the allure. ❾

Château d'Ouchy 2 Place du Port, Ouchy ☎021 616 74 51, ⓦwww.chateau-d-ouchy.com. Grandiose Neo-Gothic pile put up in the 1890s on the ruins of a twelfth-century bishop's palace (of which the tower survives). This is the only hotel situated on the lake side of the main road, separated from the water only by lush gardens. Stout, woody decor, open fireplaces and some surprisingly affordable rooms add to the charm; the slightly faded grandeur suits the four (not five) star rating. Romantics will relish the lofty tower room, its Romanesque windows framing dreamy lake views. ❺–❻

New Alpha Palmiers 34 Rue du Petit-Chêne ☎021 323 01 31, ⓦwww.fhotels.ch. Recently upgraded from two stars to four-star superior, after Fr.40 million of investment. This is now a swanky business hotel, very well located on a busy, central pedestrian street just up from the station, boasting interior palm gardens and ultra-modern rooms – the antithesis of the grand palace hotels that prevail in Lausanne. ❺–❻

La Residence 15 Place du Port, Ouchy ☎021 613 34 34, ⓦwww.laresidence.ch. Classy hotel occupying four eighteenth-century mansions on the Ouchy waterfront, including the stately former *Hôtel d'Angleterre*, where Lord Byron is reputed to have written *The Prisoner of Chillon*. Historic features remain, and the tone is one of refined, tasteful comforts, with a range of rooms in various wings and superb personal service. Guests can use all facilities of the *Beau-Rivage Palace* alongside. ❻–❽

Camping and hostels

The closest **campsite** to town is lakeside *Vidy* (☎021 622 50 00, ⓦwww.campinglausannevidy.ch), sandwiched between the Roman ruins and the International Olympic Committee's château; it's a five-star site, with plenty of facilities. From St-François take bus #2 (direction Bourdonette) to Bois de Vaux, or from the station take bus #1 to Maladière and walk five minutes.

The City

Lausanne's **city centre** spans several hilltops, linked by bridges spanning deep, riverless gorges. **Place St-François** dominates the hilltop district known as the **Bourg**, formerly the wealthiest part of the city and still known for its upmarket shops and boutiques. To the north, the hill of the **Old Town**, crowned by the **cathedral**, dominates the city, while more heights to the west and east were roped in during expansion in the nineteenth century. The whole of Lausanne's explorable centre lies north of and above the train station, with Place St-François at the edge of a pedestrian-only zone covering virtually the entire Old Town. Walking is the best, and often the only, way to explore.

St-François and the Bourg

The train station looks over the unprepossessing Place de la Gare, continuously hectic with human and motorized traffic. A gap between buildings directly ahead marks the steep **Rue du Petit-Chêne** which winds up to **Place St-François** on the terrace above. Bedecked with bus-wires, buskers and shoppers, with traffic surging through, St-François – given the adenoidal nickname *Sainf* by the locals – is the heart of Lausanne's modern commercial centre, dominated by the giant bulk of the post office and, opposite, the considerably more attractive **Église St-François**, one of the city's landmarks. Bishop Jean de Cossonay invited the Franciscans to found a community in Lausanne in 1258; by 1272, they had completed their new church, which then stood at the centre of a monastic complex hard up against the southern city walls. However, various medieval fires took their toll, and in 1536 the Reformation arrived, the monastery was dissolved, and the building was cleared of religious imagery to become the parish church of Lausanne's *Ville Basse* (lower town). Further renovations, not all in especially good taste, disfigured the interior during later centuries, and although the church remains an atmospheric retreat from the bustle outside, today not a great deal is left of its illustrious past.

The quarter in which St-François stands, the **Bourg**, spreads over a narrow ridge between two gorges, and before the nineteenth century stood alone as a separate community, rather wealthier than those all around: the **Rue de Bourg**, today a fashionable shopping street rising steeply from behind the church, had much the same style in the past too, lined then with restaurants, inns and luxury shops. In the 1780s, the English historian Edward Gibbon lived in a house on the site of the St-François post office, right at the heart of the high society of the day.

A massive expansion of the city in the early nineteenth century included the razing of many of the old slums, the filling in of the Flon river – which followed the course of the present Rue Centrale – and the construction of grand bridges unifying the disparate neighbourhoods of the city. Most dramatic of these is the **Pont Bessières**, spanning the yawning Flon gorge from the eastern top end of the Rue de Bourg over to the Old Town. In recent years this has become the favoured spot for suicidal Lausannois to shake off this mortal coil, so much so that every New Year's Eve the city posts guardians halfway along the bridge to make sure no melodramatic revellers decide to test out their theories of flight; it's a tradition for locals to stop by sometime during the evening, warm their hands over the fire, share a tot or two and wish each one *"Bonne Année!"* A walk over the **Grand-Pont**, first of the bridges to be built (in 1844), from Place St-François northwest to **Place Bel-Air**, can highlight Lausanne's extraordinary topography – stairs and alleys running off at odd angles, traffic surging along the valley road way beneath, the lake glittering below on one side and the cathedral crowning the hill above on the other. Below the Grand-Pont, and also accessed by stairs leading down from beside the distinctive Bel-Air tower (Switzerland's modest first skyscraper, dating from the 1930s), is the **Flon** district; once full of merchants and traders, today its warehouses have been converted into dance clubs, alternative cafés, galleries and theatre spaces.

Collection de l'Art Brut

A fifteen-minute walk northwest of Bel-Air (or bus #2 from St-François or Bel-Air to Beaulieu) brings you to one of the most original art galleries in the country, the **Collection de l'Art Brut**, 11 Avenue des Bergières (Tues–Sun 11am–6pm; Fr.6; SMP; Ⓦwww.artbrut.ch). This quite unique collection, founded by Jean Dubuffet, is devoted to what's been called "outsider art", the creative output of ordinary people with no artistic training at all – often loners, psychotics or the criminally insane – who for some reason suddenly began making their own art, on many occasions in middle or old age. What results is art entirely free from any conception of formal artistic rules or conventions, which challenges both how we tend to view such "outsiders" in our own communities, and our expectations of what art should be about.

Without really doing or saying anything, the gallery and its collection forces you to be open-minded about the artists and their lives, even though short biographies alongside each piece tell some heart-rendingly sad or disturbing stories. One highlight is the work of Henry Darger, a hospital porter in Chicago, who died alone, an old man unknown by his neighbours; it was only after his death that his 19,000-page novel, illustrated with dozens of detailed watercolours up to three metres long, came to light. Scottie Wilson, an illiterate Glaswegian junk dealer, began at the age of 40 to produce whimsical and incredibly intricate Escheresque drawings; while a London art gallery was selling his drawings for hundreds of pounds, Wilson was found outside in the street hawking others to passers-by for a pound or two. There's art on show from a factory worker whose talent was only discovered because he pinned his drawings up in his workshop, from a medium imprisoned in the 1930s for her interest in spirituality, from a postman who believed his hand was being directed by an external force, and so on.

As well as its permanent collection, the gallery has regular temporary exhibitions of *art brut* from artists around the world. Whatever is showing, it's worth going some distance out of your way to see.

The Old Town

Located in the tranquil core of Lausanne's **Old Town**, the cobbled **Place de la Palud** is a perfect spot for people-watching: with shopping streets cascading through the square from all sides, plenty of pavement cafés and the handy **Fontaine de la Justice** usually ringed with promenaders perching on its wide rim, it's a tempting place to take a break for a reviving *café renversée*, especially if the Wednesday and Saturday morning markets are in full swing. Every hour on the hour, mechanical figures emerge on the wall behind the fountain for a little chiming display. Dominating the south side of the square is the arcaded **Hôtel de Ville** (Town Hall), built in 1675 on the site of a covered marketplace dating back to the fourteenth century.

Place de la Riponne and around

From the Place de la Palud, Rue Madeleine leads up to the huge **Place de la Riponne**, a plain of concrete usually dotted with students hanging out or sitting on the steps of the overbearing **Palais de Rumine** on the far side – an absurdly grandiose late nineteenth-century neo-Renaissance structure adorned with lions, angels and pink marble, named after a local philanthropist and designed by a Parisian architect who hadn't actually bothered to visit Lausanne beforehand. The palace is now home to a clutch of museums, most interesting of which is the **Musée cantonal des Beaux-Arts** (Tues & Wed 11am–6pm, Thurs 11am–8pm, Fri & Sat 11am–5pm; Fr.6; SMP). A huge percentage of its works, including those from the medieval and Baroque periods, and all its Renoirs, are currently in storage in the basement; instead it displays three rooms of Swiss art from the eighteenth to twentieth centuries (including many Vaudois artists), and devotes most of its time and energy to high-quality exhibitions of contemporary art hung in the brighter, less fussy rooms at the back.

From Riponne, Rue Haldimand heads down to the church of **St Laurent**, in the heart of the old quarter also known as St-Laurent. The Rue de l'Ale and Rue de la Tour bring you further west – past the crooked *Pinte Besson*, the city's oldest tavern, to the stout, circular **Tour de l'Ale** atop the hill, built in 1340 during a reorganization of the city's defences. The traffic hub of Place Chauderon is a few metres south and downhill, at the head of the **Pont Chauderon**, third of the major bridges spanning the Flon valley. On the south side of the bridge is the Montbenon park with, tucked into the trees, the Swiss film archives, housed in the *fin-de-siècle* casino building now transformed into the Cinématheque Suisse (see p.136).

Cathédrale Notre-Dame

Stairs lead up from both Place de la Palud and Place de la Riponne to the higher points of the Old Town. The atmospheric **Escaliers du Marché**, covered wooden stairs heading up from Palud, deliver you to Rue Viret, circling around the pinnacle of the hill, from where more stairs bring you up to the **Cathédrale Notre-Dame** (daily 8am–7pm), generally acclaimed as Switzerland's finest Gothic building, on a par with the greatest of French Gothic architecture. Elegant and proportioned towers, turrets and spires claw their way up stage by stage into the sky; the south facade is studded with a spectacular giant Gothic rose window of stained glass, and flying buttresses encircle the exterior of the choir and ambulatory. The foundations of the current building were probably laid in the mid-twelfth century, with construction continuing from 1190 through to the cathedral's consecration in 1275. Despite extensive renovations and alterations just before the Reformation, and the loss of the altars, screens, and most of the statuary, paintings and glass during and after it, the cathedral has lost none of its grace and poise.

You enter through the west portal, bedecked with figures and dubbed the **Montfalcon portal** after a sixteenth-century bishop. The interior **Great Porch**, an unusual lofty open arcade with its recessed doorway and two tiers of columns, echoes similar setups in English cathedrals such as Lincoln and Canterbury, and it's been suggested that Notre-Dame's main architect, Jean de Cotereel, may have been Norman or part English himself. Just beyond, a squarish vestibule gives into the vast, broad **Great Bay** which, prior to 1504, was actually an open thoroughfare which connected the Rue Cité-Devant (to your left) with the Rue St-Étienne (to your right) under a vaulted gallery and beneath arches which seem extra-large now that they have been enclosed within the building.

The interior of the cathedral is stunning, every line and detail drawing your eye dizzily up to the lofty vaulted heights. On the south side of the nave is the impressive **Painted Portal**, dating from 1215–30; its exterior is still encrusted with original statues, but has suffered badly from weathering in recent years, and may still be covered for protection. The crossing and transept, a few steps up from the nave and filled with light, are endowed on the south side with the glowing thirteenth-century **rose window**. Opposite is the doorway to the former cloister, above which columns in front of the rectangular windows have been snapped off to allow more light to enter the building. A few steps up again is the **choir**, housing some exceptionally beautiful thirteenth-century carved choir stalls; on the left is the tomb of Otto of Grandson, a rather diminutive figure for such a celebrated medieval knight (see p.185). You'll find more, extremely worn tombs ranged around the **ambulatory** running under the walls, and also in the **crypt** beneath the choir. With a truly spectacular view over the whole of the city and most of Lake Geneva too, climbing the southwest **tower** (Mon–Sat 8.30–11.30am & 1.30–5.30pm, Sun 2–5.30pm; Fr.2) is one of the highlights of visiting Lausanne.

Right next to the cathedral building is the Ancien Évêché, the old Bishop's Palace, which has been converted into the **Musée Historique** (Tues–Thurs 11am–6pm, Fri–Sun 11am–5pm; Fr.4; SMP; Ⓦ www.lausanne.ch/mhl). Crammed with all kinds of displays illustrating the history of Lausanne, its highlight is the giant scale model of the city in the basement, with an excellent accompanying commentary (in English) detailing the history of the various neighbourhoods since medieval times; the least of it is that you can finally get a clear, bird's-eye view of how the city's hills and valleys lie in relation to each other.

The nightwatch

Lausanne suffered from many devastating medieval fires, and is the last city in Europe to keep alive the tradition of the **nightwatch** (*le guet*). If you install yourself on the cathedral terrace, every night between 10pm and 2am, after the bells have struck the hour, you'll hear – and possibly spot – a sonorous-voiced civil servant calling out from all sides of the cathedral's 75-metre tower *"C'est le guet; il a sonné l'heure"* ("This is the nightwatch; the hour has struck"), assuring the lovers and assorted drunks sprawled under the trees that all is well. Having fulfilled his civic duty, he then retreats to a comfortable little room within the tower for the next 59 minutes. For ten years up to 2002, this post was filled by Philippe Becquelin, a cartoonist on Lausanne's weekly *L'Hebdo*, who spent the four hours nightly drawing his strips. He's now handed over the job – which involves much traipsing up and down the tower's 160 steps – to his former deputy, sports teacher Renato Häusler.

North of the cathedral

Two parallel streets, Rue Cité-Devant and Rue Cité-Derrière, lead up from the cathedral to the top of the Old Town. Oldtimers bemoan the fact that the **Ancienne Académie** at 7 Rue Cité-Devant, built in the 1580s as Lausanne's first university, formerly lay at the heart of a bustling student quarter, but that the students have all departed since the new out-of-town campus opened. It's true that the alleyways are now tranquil, but they're also uniquely atmospheric, the blank old facades giving away little of their long history. A number of tiny cellar theatres, as well as mouthwatering smells wafting from the dark interiors of small bistros, hint that the quarter is far from dead. At the very top of the Old Town sits the unshakeable **Château St-Maire**, begun in the fourteenth-century and completed in brick by northern Italian masons a century later. The structure symbolizes political power: in former times it was the residence of the Bernese bailiffs, and today it is the seat of the cantonal government of Vaud.

Rue de la Barre continues north, rising over the workaday district known as **Tunnel**, busy with traffic and home to many students, accessed by stairs down to the left (west) of the street. Place du Tunnel is ringed by bars, cafés and music venues, while the eponymous tunnel itself – a major traffic route – cuts beneath Rue de la Barre and the whole Old Town hill through to the eastern districts of the city, which hold another of the city's ground-breaking museums, the **Fondation Claude Verdan** (Tues–Fri 1–6pm, Sat & Sun 11am–5pm; Fr.6; SMP; ⓦwww.verdan.ch), 21 Rue du Bugnon, accessed also by bus #5 and #6 (to Montagibert). Otherwise known as the Musée de la Main (Museum of the Hand), it's dedicated to Professor Verdan, a specialist in reconstructive hand surgery, and is a surprisingly engaging tour through how we use our hands – to communicate, to shape our environment, and to kill – mostly avoiding the preachy and the overly scientific.

The open **Bois de Sauvabelin**, the beginnings of the Jorat forests, flanks Rue de la Barre northwards. Set into the park some way up (and this is no mean hill; take bus #16) is an expansive, beautifully preserved nineteenth-century villa housing the **Fondation de l'Hermitage** art gallery, 2 Route du Signal (Tues–Sun 10am–6pm, Thurs until 9pm; Fr.13; SMP; ⓦwww.fondation-hermitage.ch). The foundation owns a permanent collection taking in Degas, Sisley and Magritte, but displays only portions of it to complement the two or three world-class shows it mounts each year. The park, and bus #16, continue further up the hill to the Signal viewpoint (643m), and on past lawns and copses to the pretty Lac de Sauvabelin, encircled by pines and oaks.

Ouchy and the lakefront

As if Lausanne weren't relaxed enough already, it has **Ouchy** as a lakeside terrace on which to stroll, chill out, and enjoy the mountain views and fresh breezes. Officially – and proudly – a separate commune from Lausanne, Ouchy for years survived as a fishing port, but these days, although some fishing continues, it's become one of the more chic of the Swiss lakeside resorts, with palace hotels and waterfront cafés abounding.

Musée Olympique

Some 500m west of Ouchy's neo-Gothic château – now a hotel – and beyond the majestically opulent *Beau-Rivage Palace*, set in its own grounds, you'll come to the Parc Olympique, home of Lausanne's much-touted flagship **Musée Olympique** (daily 9am–6pm, Thurs until 8pm; Oct–April closed Mon; Fr.14;

Across the lake to Evian

One of the best excursions from Lausanne is the short but scenic voyage across the lake to the venerable French spa town of **EVIAN**, almost directly opposite Ouchy. The best of the trip is on the water: little Evian (population 7500) has been gentrified almost to stupefaction, and there's not much to do other than stroll the boulevards, poke around the backstreets, and gawp at the modern spa complex that exploits the famous mineral springs. One of the grand nineteenth-century edifices, the **Hall d'Exposition** on Rue Nationale, has an exhibition on the town's watery past (May–Sept daily; free), and can take bookings for a visit to Evian's giant bottling plant, 5km out of town (mid-June to mid-Sept; €1.60, includes transport). The **tourist office** is on Place d'Allinges (W www.eviantourism.com). Take your pick of the cafés and restaurants that line every street: all of them are shameless about flogging the local product.

In high summer, **boats** shuttle across from Ouchy almost hourly, the last one heading back at 9.30pm (Fri & Sat 1am, for late-night casino-goers); service is reduced in other seasons, but this is one of the few Lake Geneva routes that runs daily, all year round. You can **change money** at the customs desk on arrival, or withdraw some euros from any of the plentiful bank ATMs. Don't forget your passport.

SMP; W www.olympic.org). It's a very grand affair, with formal gardens and fountains preluding the sweeping pomp of the interior design, but rather unsatisfying, a showcase more for the IOC (International Olympic Committee, headquartered in Lausanne) than for the achievements of the athletes.

Displays on the Olympics of ancient Greece and the restoration of the games in modern times are moderately engaging, but the main focus of the museum – banks of video screens replaying events from past summer and winter games, to the accompaniment of suitably stirring music – ends up as little more than glorified TV. Rows of medals, sheets of Olympic postage stamps, and cases of objects from athletes past (signed swimming trunks, basketballs and Carl Lewis's old running shoes) do nothing to help tell any special stories, flung together here in a rather self-congratulatory manner.

In the basement, the computerized **video library**, which lets you select and view any of several hundred past events from the Olympics, the soccer World Cup, European championships, the NBA, Wimbledon or the Tour de France, *would* make the museum unmissable but for the fact that you're only allowed to choose two events, and they tend to comprise, for instance, three or four minutes of goal action, or one single track event. Even for sports fans, it's a washout.

Musée de l'Elysée

On an upper level in the same park, set back from the Olympic Museum, you'll find the much more worthwhile **Musée de l'Elysée** (daily 11am–6pm; Fr.8; SMP; free on 1st Sat of month; W www.elysee.ch), dedicated to photography from the earliest daguerrotypes up to contemporary photojournalism. Its continuous cycle of exhibitions are generally outstanding, and there are often a range of shows on different subject matter running concurrently, so even if Czech avant-garde photography from the 1920s isn't your thing, a retrospective of David Hockney's photos might be.

Vidy

A kilometre or so west of Ouchy is the district of **VIDY**; one of the first indications that you're approaching the place is a boxy building on stilts in a lakeside park: this is the Théâtre de Vidy (see p.137), home of Switzerland's leading contemporary drama company. The parkland just beyond the theatre was the location of the first settlements in the Lausanne area, in Neolithic times, and then later under the Romans. Approaching through the park, you'll discover remnants and ruins of the Roman town of Lousonna, an assembly of low walls and tumbled stones with an explanatory board nearby. A short distance beyond, at 24 Chemin du Bois-de-Vaux, is the modern and well laid out **Musée Romain** (Tues–Sun 11am–6pm, Thurs until 8pm; Fr.4; SMP; Ⓦ www.lausanne.ch/mrv). Finds are displayed with explanatory boards mostly in French (although they do have a leaflet in English), with particularly impressive glassware, some mosaic work and interesting displays of artefacts and other bits and bobs.

Eating and drinking

If all you want is a reviving drink and somewhere to take the weight off your feet, the city centre and the Old Town can offer dozens of **cafés and café-bars**: almost every corner of every quarter has its local haunt, most of which offer food as well. Ouchy is a little less straightforward, since the cafés lining the waterfront are universally overpriced and under-quality, and although there's no shortage of port-side **restaurants** offering fresh lake fish, none stands out as particularly noteworthy.

Aside from the city's reasonable choice of ethnic eateries, there are plenty of places offering Vaudois specialities. A *tomme* is a round soft cheese baked to melting point within its white Brie-like rind, and often served on a bed of leafy salad. A local speciality of the La Côte region just west of Lausanne is a *malakoff*, a hot, rich fried round of cheese served on a bread or pastry base; the nearby villages of Vinzel and Luins (see p.148) compete for whose *malakoff* is the best, but you can also easily find Lausannois versions in the city's more traditional diners. The mighty *saucisson vaudois*, a smoked pork and beef sausage, is served hot, accompanied by *papet vaudois*, a purée of leek and potato, and graded according to quality, with the best labelled reverentially with the green cantonal flag.

Cafés and café-bars

ArtZoo 27 Rue du Petit-Chêne. Bright, modern café attached to a cinema, popular with turtleneck urbanites.

Bleu Lézard 10 Rue Enning. Fashionable and lively café-bar on a busy corner, with a windowful of gnomes and a comfy colourful interior. The mood mutates into restaurant territory in the evenings, when food (including veggie options) is pricey – but you don't have to eat and the atmosphere is free.

La Bossette 4 Place du Nord, east of Tunnel. Comfortable and uniquely friendly local café on a patch of green beneath the château, serving a range of speciality beers along with excellent food.

Buffet de la Gare In the train station. Deeply atmospheric station buffet, with high ceilings,

wood-panelled walls, white-aproned waiters and more than a hint of the age of steam. If your eye's on the minute hand, ask for the *assiette express*.

Café Bel-Air Place Bel-Air. The place to be seen, with the gentle tinkle of teaspoons accompanying the most discreet of gossip behind plate-glass windows.

Café de l'Évêché 4 Rue Curtat. Atmospheric little haunt of talkative students and local old-timers just below the cathedral – perfect for morning coffee, authentic fondue, or beer and dominoes.

Café de l'Hôtel de Ville 10 Place de la Palud. Wonderful little intimate wood-floor café, with excellent Vaudois specialities – including hot and cold goats' cheeses with salad – quality service and especially fancy desserts. The cellar features small-scale shows of *chansons*, jazz and comedians.

Café Romand Place St-François (under *Pizza Hut*). Unmissable and much-loved city-centre retreat, a bustling, heartwarming place with parquet floor and cosy alcoves for beer, coffee or heavy Swiss fare.

Lecaféthéâtre 10 Rue de Genève. Appealing café-bar in the Flon, with a cellar atmosphere, fantasy art on the walls and nightly live sessions of piano, guitar or French *chansons* for entertainment. Food is excellent, home-cooked style, and not expensive. Closed Sun & Mon.

MGM 14 Rue du Lac. Café-bar in Ouchy, the best of the bunch, with tunes and rather tacky decor which aim for Miami Beach and miss.

Du Raisin 19 Place de la Palud. Prime people-watching terrace café in the Old Town.

Sidewalk 7 Place du Tunnel. Popular local joint in a little-visited area.

Restaurants

Inexpensive and mid-range

L'Age d'Or 3 Pont Bessières ☎ 021 323 73 14. The city's top vegetarian restaurant (and one of its best in any category), with a spectacular terrace tucked beneath the bridge. *Menus* range from Fr.28 to Fr.100 or more, with mains on their own hovering around Fr.21. Exquisite fresh fish is a highlight. Closed Mon eve & Sun.

Café du Grütli 4 Rue de la Mercerie. Venerable old tile-and-darkwood brasserie in the heart of the Old Town, with very affordable *menus* (Fr.16 or so), or idiosyncratic options like a dozen snails. Head past the pavement tables and make for the hum of conversation within. Closed Sun.

Au Couscous 2 Rue Enning ☎ 021 321 38 40. Long-standing Arabic restaurant in a lively part of town, lacking some atmosphere but making up for it with excellent couscous and tajine (Fr.22+) and mezze (Fr.25), with veggie and macrobiotic dishes too. *Menus* from Fr.15. Closed Sat & Sun lunchtimes.

Da Geppetto In *Hôtel Boulevard*, 51 Boulevard de Grancy ☎ 021 617 28 11. *Menus* for Fr.16, or fresh pasta dishes for Fr.25–30, in a lively, pleasant ambience away from the city-centre hubbub. Closed Sun.

Laxmi 5 Escaliers du Marché. Excellent authentic Indian/veggie food, well prepared and cooked. Budget all-you-can-eat buffet lunches are Fr.15, or Fr.11 for veggies, or Fr.10 for cold dishes; evening *menus* cost no more. Students get a ten percent discount. Closed Mon lunch & Sun.

Ma Jong 3 Escaliers du Grand-Pont. Just down from *Manora*, with excellent-value freshly wok-fried meals, piled high for Fr.14. Sushi too. Closed Sun.

Manora 17 Place St-François. Self-service place with a wide range of excellent cheap food. Daily 9am–10.30pm.

Le Shanghai 6 Place du Tunnel. Rock-bottom cheap Chinese, plain and serviceable. Lunches for less than Fr.15. Closed Sun.

Expensive

La Grappe d'Or 3 Cheneau-de-Bourg ☎ 021 323 07 60. Top gourmet temple for classic and modern French cuisine, benefiting from attentive service and a warm ambience. Expect no change from Fr.100. Closed Sat lunch & Sun.

Hôtel de Ville 1 Rue d'Yverdon, Crissier ☎ 021 634 05 05. Formerly the domain of the legendary Frédy Girardet, said to be the greatest chef in the world in his day, and now taken over by Philippe Rochat, an underling for some seventeen years. Many consider this Switzerland's best restaurant – Michelin give it three stars. The style is classic, the presentation and service are impeccable. Reserve two months ahead for dinner, two weeks ahead for lunch. Located 7km west of the city. Closed Sun & Mon, and early Aug.

Nightlife and entertainment

Lausanne's **nightlife** and cultural offerings are second to none in Switzerland, with a vast range of music and performance to check out aside from the swathe of festivals listed in the box on p.124.

Bars, clubs and live music

Bars and clubby nightlife abound. First place to look is Le Flon, a low-lying warehouse district bounded by Bel-Air, Grand-Pont and the metro station, where following your ears after dark will bring you to the happening joints of the moment. Otherwise, good areas for concentrations of bars and night-people are Rue Enning; Le Tunnel, around Place du Tunnel; and, on a more sedate note, the streets immediately behind the château. The bars listed here all close at 1–2am, the clubs at 4–5am.

(see p.134)

Bleu Lézard 10 Rue Enning ⓦwww.carte-blanche.ch. Hip and exciting cellar venue, beneath a lively bar/restaurant (see p.134), staging DJ nights, live music, jam sessions, dance nights and more.

Café Freeport Train station. Quite a pleasant, if tackily neon, bar, with an intriguingly random clientele and the longest opening hours in town (Sun–Thurs 5am–1am, Fri & Sat 5am–2am).

Café de l'Hôtel de Ville 10 Place de la Palud. Wonderful little wood-floor café with *chansons* and jazz quartets in the cellar.

Captain Cook 2 Rue Enning. Crammed and smoky pub in the heart of the action, offering English TV football.

Au Château 1 Place du Tunnel. Funky music bar serving flavourful home-brewed beers – pale, dark and red – to an excited, talkative crowd.

Chorus 3 Avenue Mon-Repos. Prime basement spot for live jazz. Closed Mon & Tues.

D! Place Centrale ⓦwww.dclub.ch. Highly respected Flon basement club, close and sweaty, playing house some nights, jungle other nights, and able to pull in some international DJs. Entry Fri & Sat Fr.15. Closed Mon–Wed.

Dolce Vita 30 Rue César-Roux. Excellent live venue and club, a Swiss institution since 1985, with a regular programme covering all musical genres. Admission varies. Closed Mon & Tues.

Garbo 3 Rue Caroline. One of the better Caroline bars, split between a hectic downstairs and quieter upstairs. Open nightly.

Kerrigan's 8 Rue de la Barre. Hilltop Irish pub in a peaceful spot behind the château. Closed Sun.

Lecaféthéâtre 10 Rue de Genève. Flon café-bar with live entertainments most nights. Closed Sun & Mon.

Le Loft 1 Escaliers Bel-Air ⓦwww.loftclub.ch. A techno club on the stairs up from the Flon, which has a rather tougher reputation than its near neighbours, but has free Friday night admission (Sat Fr.15). Occasional live acts. Closed Mon & Tues.

MAD (Moulin à Danse) 23 Rue de Genève. Infamous and hugely popular Flon dance club with adjoining theatre, galleries and alternative-style café. The club is open from 11pm, and comprises a basement "parlour", dancefloor, bar and chillout room. Entry Fri & Sat Fr.20. Gay night Sun. Closed Mon & Tues.

La Mine 2 Place Pépinet. All-day techno bar. Closed Sun.

Le 13ème Siècle Rue Cité-Devant. Atmospheric cellar DJ-bar in an Old Town street above the cathedral.

VO Le Jazz Café 11 Place du Tunnel. Café-bar plus live venue, also with regular DJ nights featuring British and European big names. Open nightly.

Classical music, dance, opera, film and theatre

Contemporary and classical dance, theatre and music are all represented in Lausanne by some of Switzerland's best performers. The Théâtre de Beaulieu, 10 Avenue des Bergières, is the main venue for full-scale **classical music** productions – the Orchestre de la Suisse Romande (ⓦwww.osr.ch) performs here regularly when not in Geneva – and is also famous as the place where the highly acclaimed **Béjart Ballet** (ⓦwww.bejart.ch) presents new material every June and November. The **Opéra de Lausanne** performs at Beaulieu too, as well as at its home at 12 Avenue du Théâtre (ⓦwww.opera-lausanne.ch), while the **Orchestre de Chambre de Lausanne** stages concerts at the Salle Métropole (ⓦwww.regart.ch/ocl), also the venue for many Béjart productions. The arts centre at Rue Sevelin 36 is the home of **contemporary dance**, with continuous seasons of productions year-round. Don't miss the cycle of free Friday evening concerts in the **cathedral** (June–Oct, plus Easter, Whitsun and Christmas) – mostly, but not exclusively, organ recitals. Some 3km west of Lausanne in the ancient lakefront village of **St-Sulpice** (ⓦwww.st-sulpice.ch), an impressive triple-apsed Romanesque church built by Cluniac monks in the eleventh century also stages a cycle of year-round classical concerts.

Plenty of **cinemas** around town show latest releases, often with afternoon shows in the original language (v.o., or *version originale*) and evening shows dubbed into French. The Cinématheque Suisse, housed in the casino in

Montbenon park (Ⓦ www.cinematheque.ch), has a continually changing programme of non-commercial movies from Europe and around the world, sometimes (but rarely) with English subtitles.

The Théâtre de Vidy, 5 Avenue É-Jacques-Dalcroze (Ⓦ www.vidy.ch), is one of Europe's premier **theatres**, with innovative productions and extremely high standards – but universally in French. The city also has dozens of smaller spaces for classical and contemporary drama, and cabaret: L'Atelier Volant, 12 Rue des Côtes-de-Montbenon (Ⓣ 021 311 52 80), and Le Lapin Vert, 2 Ruelle du Lapin-Vert (Ⓣ 021 320 09 94), are renowned, while Théâtre de l'Arsenic, 57 Rue de Genève (Ⓣ 021 625 11 36), is a Flon-based alternative theatre venue.

Tickets can be had direct from the venue; from the centralized Service Culturel Migros-Vaud, 12 Passage St-François (Ⓣ 021 318 71 71); or from tourist offices or the city information office.

Listings

Boat rental Rowing boats and pedalos are available to rent from opposite the *Hôtel d'Angleterre* for around Fr.19/hr, motorboats for about Fr.45/hr.

Books Librairie Payot, 4 Place Pépinet, has a sizeable selection.

Changing money The best place to change money is in the station (daily 6.20am–7.30pm).

Flights La Blécherette, 123 Avenue du Grey (Ⓣ 021 646 15 51 Ⓦ www.gvm.ch/arlb), operates sightseeing flights from Lausanne's tiny airfield over the Alps.

Gay and lesbian life VoGay, 10 Chemin des Epinettes (Ⓣ 021 601 46 15, Ⓦ www.vogay.ch), is the gay association for Canton Vaud, with get-togethers and a phone helpline. *Le Saxo*, Rue de la Grotte 3 (Ⓦ www.lesaxo.com), is a central bar-restaurant; *Tramway*, 6b Rue de la Pontaise (closed Sun & Mon), is a bit further out. There's an array of gay club nights, including at *D!*, Place Centrale (Fri & Sat), *Trixx*, Route de Genève 23 (Sun) and *Cult*, Place Chauderon 18 (Wed). Lilith, 60 Route Aloys-Fauquez (Ⓣ 021 646 26 18, Ⓦ www.lilith-vd.ch), is a lesbian organization which hosts parties and events.

Laundry At the top of town, 24 Rue de l'Université (Mon & Wed–Sun 9am–9pm, Tues noon–9pm); and behind the station, 15 Rue Simplon (daily 8am–9pm).

Lost property The city office is at 7 Place Chauderon (Mon–Fri 8am–noon & 1.45–5.45pm, Sat 8–11.30am; Ⓣ 021 315 33 85), or try in the train station (Mon–Fri 8am–noon & 2–6pm; Ⓣ 051 224 27 07).

Markets The Place de la Palud and the town centre host a regular lively food market (Wed & Sat 6am–2.30pm) as does the Petit-Chêne (Fri 6am–1pm). Palud also has a crafts market (March–Dec 1st Fri of month 6am–7pm), and Place Chauderon's weekly flea market is renowned (Thurs 6am–7pm). Riponne is the focus for Lausanne's Christmas celebrations, with a market of mulled wine, candles and roasted chestnuts from mid-December.

Medical facilities The Centre hospitalier universitaire vaudois (CHUV) is at 46 Rue du Bugnon Ⓣ 021 314 11 11. The Centre médical d'urgences, 32 Avenue Ruchonnet (Mon–Sat 7am–9pm, Sun 9am–9pm; Ⓣ 021 320 19 61), is more central. If you need a doctor, call Ⓣ 021 213 77 77 (24hr). The train station has a pharmacy (daily 6am–9pm).

Post Main office is beside the station (Mon–Fri 7.30am–noon & 1.30–6.30pm, Sat 8am–noon), but the most convenient large office is at Place St-François (Mon–Fri 7.30am–6.30pm, Sat 8am–noon).

Sport Prime arena for Lausanne's passion, blading and skateboarding, is the giant indoor La Fièvre skatepark, also called HS36 (36 Avenue Sévelin; Ⓦ www.fievre.ch), open daily – you'll also find dance companies, artists' ateliers and music rehearsal rooms in the same complex. For summer swimming, pricey Plage de Bellerive, 23 Avenue de Rhodanie, offers an Olympic-sized pool as well as access to the lake, but the beach is free at Vidy. The open-air ice rink Patinoire de la Pontaise (11 Route des Plaines-du-Loup) is one of five in the city open from October to March. Waterskiing on the lake happens only in fine summer weather.

Around Lausanne

Past the hills **northeast of Lausanne**, beyond the Bois de Sauvabelin, you leave the tourist trails behind and enter the classic scenery of Switzerland's rural heartland – rolling emerald-green hills backed by distant peaks and tinkling with the neck-bells of cows happily munching their way across the slopes. Vaud's cantonal boundary is only about 20km northeast of Lausanne, and most of the sights in this region fall inside Canton Fribourg; however, unless you have your own transport, Fribourg's famous cheese-making centre of **Gruyères** is most easily accessible by train from Lausanne. **Romont**'s Gothic church and thirteenth-century town centre make a beautiful detour on the journey to or from Fribourg itself (see p.267), while the untouristed **Gros de Vaud** region north of Lausanne is perfect for countryside cycling tours. The northern stretches of Canton Vaud – Yverdon, Payerne and Avenches, as well as the Vallée de Joux – are covered in Chapter 3.

La Gruyère region

The walls and turrets of **Gruyères**'s fairytale castle, 50km northeast of Lausanne, bristle atop a single crag rising above the rolling lowlands of Canton Fribourg. The whole region – of which Gruyères village is the best-known attraction – is known as **LA GRUYÈRE** (ⓦ www.la-gruyere.ch), taking in the long Lac de la Gruyère and the Sarine valley south of Fribourg, the market town and regional transport hub of **Bulle**, and a handful of resorts clinging to the slopes of the Prealpine peaks which prelude the Pays d'Enhaut (see p.320) further south. Dominating the landscape is the great towering wedge of the **Moléson**, a jutting chunk of mountain rising to 2000m with plenty of hiking possibilities and some gentle skiing in winter. This is dairy country, the most famous product by far being Gruyère cheese, run a close second by the local butterfat-rich double cream, served with forest fruits in Gruyères's heavenly, artery-clogging version of afternoon tea.

Bulle and Broc

Some 30km northeast of Lausanne, **BULLE** isn't lacking in charm, but there's little reason to visit other than to switch transport. Its medieval town centre features a solid castle, housing the **Musée Gruérien** (Tues–Sat 10am–noon & 2–5pm, Sun 2–5pm; Fr.4; SMP) with a collection devoted to traditional costumes and farm implements. On the road to Gruyères, you'll pass through **La Tour de Trême**, its eponymous thirteenth-century tower plum in the middle of the village.

On the edge of the village of **BROC**, which lies 4km east of La Trême astride the route leading up through the tiny resort of Charmey to the Jaun Pass, you'll detect luscious scents emanating from the Nestlé **chocolate factory** (June–Oct Mon 1.30–4pm, Tues–Fri 9–11am & 1.30–4pm; free; reservations essential on ☎026 921 51 51). This factory, founded in 1898, is the sole production facility for Nestlé's Cailler brand, named after one of the nineteenth-century pioneers of chocolate-making. On arrival, you're led through to watch a super-schmaltzy costume-drama movie about life, love and chocolate in a small Swiss town, after which a guide leads you on an explanatory tour of part of the factory. The climax comes in the Tasting Room, where you're let loose on tables piled with bite-sized chunks of every Cailler product, in unlimited quantities; placards outline how a professional chocolate taster measures quality, but most people are far too busy scoffing to notice. Just beyond lies a shop where you can buy discounted Nestlé chocolate.

The Swiss Chocolate Train

One of the region's top excursions is a full-day package on the **Swiss Chocolate Train**. Classic old-fashioned 1st-class Pullman carriages and modern panoramic carriages run **from Montreux** (June–Oct Wed; July & Aug also Mon) on the spectacular climb above Lake Geneva to **Gruyères**, where there's a stop to visit a cheese factory and the château, and have lunch. In the afternoon, you move on to **Broc** for a visit to the Nestlé-Cailler chocolate factory, and then, around 4pm, settle back for the scenic return journey from Broc to Montreux. There's a compulsory supplement of around Fr.20 on top of a 1st-class ticket or pass, covering seat reservation, coffee and croissants on the train, bus transfers and all admission fees; lunch is excluded. You can reserve at any station in Switzerland, or with the MOB train company (℡021 963 65 31, ⊛www.mob.ch).

The factory, signposted on all approach roads, is a short walk from Broc-Fabrique **train station**, which is served by local scheduled trains from Bulle and La Tour and also by the **Swiss Chocolate Train**, a packaged excursion from Montreux (see box).

Gruyères

A perfectly preserved old castle-village, isolated on its crag but within easy reach of Lake Geneva, **GRUYÈRES** is one of Switzerland's most photogenic sights and attracts hordes of daytrippers throughout the summer season, come to stroll on the village's only street and explore the impressive château. By 10am in season, the village can get uncomfortably crowded, and can stay so until late afternoon. Cars are banned, but you'll find several large parking areas on the hillside just below.

At the foot of Gruyères village in **Pringy** (the location of Gruyères train station) is the **Maison du Gruyère**, a working dairy (daily 9am–7pm; Oct–May closes 6pm; Fr.5; ⊛www.lamaisondugruyere.ch) where you can watch the cheesemaking process close up (production stops at 3pm), plus restaurant (daily 7.30am–11pm) and shop (daily 7.30am–7pm), both concentrating on local produce.

Up on the hill, the **Château de Gruyères** (daily: April–Oct 9am–6pm; Nov–March 10am–4.30pm; last entry 30min before closing; Fr.6; joint ticket with H.R. Giger Museum Fr.12; SMP) was formerly the regional seat of power, occupied from 1080 to 1554 by the nineteen counts of Gruyères, but was decimated by a fire in 1493 which destroyed virtually everything but the dungeons. The last occupants reconstructed the living quarters in a lavish Savoyard style; Michael, the final Count of Gruyères, ran up huge debts doing this and then fled, leaving his creditors – the governments of Fribourg and Bern – to divide up his lands between them. A rich Geneva dynasty, the Bovy and Balland families, bought the castle in 1848 and supported a number of artists in residence, including the French landscape painter Corot, before the cantonal government of Fribourg took over maintenance of the castle in 1938. To approach it, you must walk the length of Gruyères's dipping, picturesque main street with its central fountain and quaint old houses on either side bedecked with hanging signs. A huge **gate** at the end affords entry to the castle grounds. Highlights include Flemish **tapestries** decorating the count's bedchamber, Corot's room with landscapes painted by him, and other rooms throughout the castle with grand fireplaces, heraldic stained glass, often featuring the dynastic symbol of a crane (*grue* in French), and booty from the Battle of Murten (see p.193) where Louis II, Count of Gruyère, fought on the Swiss side. The wood-panelled Knights' Hall is impressive, as is the small formal garden at the very back, on the tip of the hill. Beside the castle, Gruyères's **church** is in an exceptionally beautiful location, backed by valley vistas.

In a couple of extremely odd counterpoints to the grandeur of the castle, you'll find at the gate of the castle (and covered by the same entrance fee and opening hours), the **Centre International de l'Art Fantastique**, a small gallery devoted to modern fantasy art – which is fine if you like that kind of thing but has no connection with the cobbled quaintness all around. This, though, is as nothing compared with the truly nasty **H.R. Giger Museum** adjacent (April–Oct daily 10am–6pm; Nov–March Tues–Fri 11am–5pm, Sat & Sun 10am–6pm; Fr.10; joint ticket with château Fr.12; SMP; ⓦ www.hrgiger.com). Giger is a graphic artist, born in Chur, who is most famous for designing the special effects for the movie *Alien* – for which he won an Oscar – as well as *Poltergeist II*, *Alien 3* and others. Flushed with success, he took a shine to Gruyères, bought one of the old houses, and has turned it into a showcase for his unique brand of grotesque art, sexualized surrealist visions of machine-like humanoids, nightmarish cityscapes and fantasy-porn gynaecological obsessions crowding over three dark and unpleasant floors. "Giger," enthused Timothy Leary, 1960s acid guru, "you razor-shave sections of my brain and plaster them still pulsing across your canvas; [you] give us courage to say hello to our insectoid selves." The latest innovation is an *Alien*-style bar in the castle grounds, due to open in 2003. Heaven help Gruyères.

Practicalities

Trains from Lausanne to Fribourg pass through **Palézieux**, where you must change for the local GFM trains that wind slowly through the countryside to Bulle, and then further on to **Gruyères-gare** at the foot of the village; it's a short but stiff walk from the station up the hill to Gruyères, or you could time your arrival to coincide with one of the half-dozen buses a day shuttling between Gruyères-gare and Gruyères-ville. The Palézieux–Gruyères trains trundle on to terminate at **Montbovon**, on the MOB line between Montreux and Gstaad. If you're approaching from Fribourg, take a GFM express bus to Bulle and switch onto a train there. One lunchtime bus a day goes direct to Gruyères-ville from Bulle station.

Everything in Gruyères is on the village's single street. The **tourist office** is at the car park end (mid-May to mid-Oct daily 9am–noon & 1.30–5.45pm; mid-Oct to mid-May Mon–Fri 10am–noon & 1.30–5pm; ☎026 921 10 30, ⓦ www.gruyeres.ch). There are only a few **hotels**, most of which take one or two days a week off in the winter; turning up without a booking is a risky business. Whichever side of the street you're on, getting a room at the back gives you a view over the valley. The pinewood *Fleur de Lys* (☎026 921 21 08, ⓦ www.hotelfleurdelys.ch; ❸) is a sound choice; the grand *Hôtel de Ville* (☎026 921 24 24, ⓦ www.hoteldeville.ch; ❸–❹) is a step up in comfort and cuisine; and best of the bunch is the idyllic *Hostellerie des Chevaliers* (☎026 921 19 33, ⓦ www.gruyeres-hotels.ch/chevaliers; ❸–❹), just outside the village.

Finding a place to **eat** is a case of strolling until you spot something that takes your fancy. Everywhere offers terraces on both the village-side and the valley-side at which to partake of a substantial range of cheesy delights, as well as bowls of berries slathered in the village's silky *crème-double*. The *Auberge de la Halle* is one of the least pretentious places to get a proper meal, with Fr.17 *menus* incorporating the house speciality: thick cheesy vegetable soup. Otherwise, all the hotels offer quality traditional Gruyères and French cuisine, with the *Hostellerie St-Georges* (☎026 921 83 00) top choice within the village.

Moléson

Ten minutes on the bus past Gruyères-gare is **MOLÉSON** village, a small, bucolic resort giving access to the heights of **Le Moléson** mountain, via a funicular and gondola. The village square has as its focus the **Fromagerie d'Alpage**, dating from 1686 (May–Oct daily 9.30am–7pm; Fr.3), where cheese is made according to the old mountain ways (9.45am & 2.45pm). Panoramic views from the summit of the Moléson, at 2002m, take in Lake Geneva, the Prealps and even Mont Blanc, and there are plenty of ridge-top walks and, in winter, easy-to-medium ski runs; the Moléson tourist office (☎026 921 85 00, ⓦwww.moleson.ch) has details.

Romont and the Gros de Vaud

Train-tracks and the minor roads between Lausanne and Fribourg pass by **ROMONT**, a small medieval town perched atop an isolated round hill, with lofty 360-degree views over the surroundings. From the train station, below the hill, the town's wall and two distinctive round towers stand out against the sky. It's a steep ten-minute walk up from the train station.

Thirteenth-century ramparts surround the town, which consists of little more than two broad streets with a round tower at each end. The **castle** dominates, with one tower converted into the **Musée du Vitrail** (Museum of Stained Glass; April–Oct Tues–Sun 10am–1pm & 2–6pm; Nov–March Thurs–Sun 10am–1pm & 2–5pm; Fr.7; SMP), holding mostly modern examples along with an informative slide-show. Nearby is the town's beautiful Gothic *Collégiale* **church** of Our Lady of the Assumption, also dating from the thirteenth century, replete with original woodcarving from a rebuilding in 1434 and some wonderfully detailed stonework. The **tourist office** is at 112 Rue du Château (Mon–Fri 10am–noon & 2–4pm, April–Oct also Sat 10am–noon; ☎026 652 31 52, ⓦwww.romont.ch).

The Gros de Vaud

The peaceful country between Lausanne and Yverdon is known as the **Gros de Vaud** (ⓦwww.gros-de-vaud.ch), rural heart of the canton and breadbasket for the region. **ECHALLENS**, 15km north of Lausanne, is the main centre, formerly an important market town which earned the right to be called a city in the fourteenth century but has now metamorphosed into a popular retreat for young families looking to escape big-city life. Despite its sometimes twee touches of renovation, it's still a picturesque place, with a thirteenth-century château and many eighteenth-century buildings testifying to past grandeur. Arrive on a Thursday in high summer and you might run into one of the regular crafts markets held in the town centre. The **tourist office**, 5 Place de la Gare (☎021 881 11 15, ⓦwww.echallens.ch), has details of the dozens of especially good walking and cycling routes through the fields round about.

The ancient LEB narrow-gauge **railway** – Switzerland's oldest, opened in 1873 (ⓦwww.leb.ch) – runs from Lausanne's Flon station north to Echallens and, in summer especially, is one of the more scenic rides in the country. One or two steam trains a day make the run, for no supplement above the ordinary fare.

Lake Geneva

The croissant-shaped **LAKE GENEVA** (Lac Léman in French), bluest of the Swiss lakes, is ringed with villages, castles and gorgeous walks that demand attention. This is wine country, with vineyards spread around the full sweep of the lakeshore and carpeting the first slopes of the hills which rise behind. Genteel small towns such as **Nyon** and **Vevey**, either side of Lausanne, have made a living recharging the batteries of frazzled urbanites for generations. Over the decades, the lake has also attracted the world's wealthiest people, and

The Lake Geneva hall of fame

Hundreds of notable writers, artists, musicians and poets have visited Lake Geneva over the centuries. For cultured nineteenth-century sophisticates, the lakeside was as important a stop on the Grand Tour of Europe as Paris, Florence or Vienna, and where one artist settled others inevitably followed, drawn – depending on individual circumstance – by the fresh air, the romance of the Château de Chillon, political neutrality, or the numbered bank accounts.

Edward Gibbon spent long periods in Lausanne, meeting **Voltaire** there in the 1750s, and completing his monumental *Decline and Fall of the Roman Empire* during an eleven-year stay between 1783 and 1793. Jean-Jacques **Rousseau**, a native of Geneva, set his *La Nouvelle Héloïse*, completed in 1761, in Clarens near Montreux. **Wordsworth** came through Lausanne in 1790 and 1820. The English artist **Turner** first visited the area in 1802, painting watercolours of the landscape around Chillon. In 1816, while **Mary Shelley** stayed in Geneva to write *Frankenstein*, **Lord Byron** and **Percy Bysshe Shelley** set off on an eight-day boat tour of the lake; they both almost drowned off St Gingolph, then toured the Château de Chillon, which inspired Byron to dash off *The Prisoner of Chillon* in his Ouchy hotel room. **Robert Southey** waxed lyrical about Lausanne following a visit in 1817, as did **Victor Hugo** in 1839. The famous English actor **John Kemble** died and was buried in Lausanne in 1823. **Alexandre Dumas**, on one of his many Swiss journeys, wrote of a visit to Chillon in 1832. **Tennyson**, **Thackeray** and others dropped in to visit **Charles Dickens**, who began *Dombey and Son* while staying in Lausanne in 1846; Thackeray himself worked on *The Newcomes* in Vevey in 1853. **George Eliot** spent nine months writing in Geneva over the winter of 1849–50. In 1861, **Hans Christian Andersen** wrote *The Ice Maiden* in Montreux. **Tolstoy** and **Dostoevsky** both passed through Lausanne, the latter spending two years in Geneva writing *The Idiot*, followed by a summer writing *The Gambler* in Vevey; **Gogol** began *Dead Souls* in Vevey, which was the setting for **Henry James**'s *Daisy Miller* and which was also where **Arnold Bennett** spent 1908–09 writing *The Card*. **Tchaikovsky** composed his Violin Concerto in F major (Op.35), and also began *Eugène Onegin* while in Clarens in 1877–78. **Stravinsky** spent 1911–14 in the same town, where he composed his revolutionary *The Rite of Spring*; he spent the World War I years working in Lausanne. **T.S. Eliot** convalesced in Lausanne in 1921 and 1922 while writing his equally revolutionary *The Waste Land*. In 1952, at the age of 63, **Charlie Chaplin** moved to Vevey to escape Hollywood's McCarthyism, and died there 25 years later. **Noël Coward** lived in Les Avants, above Montreux, from 1958, while **Audrey Hepburn** lived in Tolochenaz, near Morges, from 1963. **Vladimir Nabokov** spent the last sixteen years of his life in Montreux (after 1961); and **Graham Greene** died in Vevey in 1991. Of the dozens of pop musicians who've dabbled with second, third or fourth houses on the lake, **Freddie Mercury** had a particularly soft spot for Montreux, and returned many times during the last ten years of his life.

the shores around the jetset playground of **Montreux** in particular are lined with opulent villas – although a lakeside stroll can still let you taste the unspoilt beauty which drew Byron and the Romantic poets in a former age. Relaxing on one of the boats which crisscross the lake beneath the looming presence of the Savoy Alps and the Dents-du-Midi mountains on the French side helps bring home the full grandeur of the setting.

Aside from the people working on the lake's ferries, some 150 French and Swiss families currently earn their living on the water by fishing for perch, pike, trout and more, selling the majority of their catch directly to restaurants and supermarkets in the shoreside towns. A new trend for whitefish smoked over beechwood has given them a much-needed shot in the arm of late.

La Côte

The gently curving northwestern shore of the lake from Geneva to Lausanne (some 65km) is known as **La Côte** (Ⓦ www.lacote.ch), characterized by a succession of hamlets and small villages, almost without exception pretty, well kept and pristinely picturesque. Those along the minor shoreline road, the *Route Suisse*, are less numerous and more visited than those placed back behind the main *autoroute* on the first slopes of the Jura foothills, amongst vineyards tilted towards the sun which produce some of the highest-prized wine in Vaud. Things are much less developed here for **wine-tasting tours** than in the Lavaux region east of Lausanne. However, if you rent a bike from larger train stations for a day's gentle exploration along the narrow *Route des Vignerons*, which winds from vineyard to vineyard along the gentle slope, you'll find plenty of *caveaux* (wine cellars) offering *dégustations* (tastings) of local products. You have to pay for the tasting – which generally comprises two, three or four choices of wine, in 1dl glasses – but can then turn up a bargain if you choose to buy a bottle or two. Countless *auberges* and *pintes* (country taverns) along the way offer local home-cooked specialities.

Whether down by the lake or up among the vineyards, you'll pass dozens of **châteaux**, evidence both of the region's key strategic significance in medieval times, and its attraction to Europe's nobility in more recent centuries. Some are now museums, but most remain in private hands. Major stopoffs include the historic **Château de Coppet**, close to Geneva, the attractive little harbour-town of **Nyon** with its own château and Roman museum, and the nearby **Château de Prangins**, housing an excellent museum devoted to Swiss history.

Facts and figures

Lake Geneva is the largest freshwater lake in Western Europe, holding some 89 trillion litres. It's really just a big bulge in the course of the River Rhône, which rises at the Furkapass and flows westwards between the mountains of Canton Valais to enter the lake near Villeneuve. Its water takes an estimated seventeen years to cover the 73km to Geneva before flowing on through France to an outlet into the Mediterranean near Marseille. Although the lake is only 14km wide at its broadest point, it plunges to 310m maximum depth and is subject to heavy winds which rip across the surface, causing stormy conditions not unlike an inland sea.

Coppet and Céligny

From the landing-stage at **COPPET**, 2km inside Vaud, it's easy to make out Geneva's huge Jet d'Eau fountain (see p.93), only 12km away; opposite, the bulge of low hills is French territory, culminating in the thickly wooded head-land of Yvoire. Coppet sits plum astride the lakeshore *Route Suisse* and has an attractive arcaded main street but is unremarkable but for the lavish **Château de Coppet** (ⓦwww.swisscastles.ch), which in the turbulent years around the French Revolution was dubbed "the Parliament of European Opinion" for the glittering and controversial *salon* hosted by Madame de Staël (see box) and attended by the leading figures of the day. Entry is only on the multilingual, 35-minute **guided tours** (daily: Easter–Oct 2–6pm, July & Aug also 10am–noon; Fr.10) given by the extremely knowledgeable staff: these run every half-hour or so, according to demand.

The approach to the château – grand, but no Versailles – is beneath a vault-ed arch into a peaceful interior courtyard, open on one side to the gardens behind a wrought-iron gate surmounted with the elaborate initials "N.C.", demonstrating the partnership between Jacques Necker and his wife Suzanne

Château de Coppet

The Château de Coppet was built by **Jacques Necker**, a Genevois banker and Minister of Finance to the French king Louis XVI from 1776 until the Revolution in 1789. He seems to have been more liberal than his masters, and was rather dis-gusted by the ostentatious excesses of the regime he was publicly responsible for: from his uniquely privileged position, he built up a dossier carefully documenting the full extent of the financial corruption of the regime, eventually publishing the accounts in full. The revelations, it's said, helped to initiate the Revolution.

In 1784, perhaps sensing the upheavals to come in France, Necker had bought the barony of Coppet to serve as a safe haven. His only daughter **Germaine**, then 18, was already gaining a reputation in the Paris *salons* for her intellect and vivacity, and had an array of suitors from whom she picked the man she "least disliked", the stol-id and self-important Baron de Staël Holstein, chamberlain to the Queen of Sweden. The marriage seems to have proved unsatisfactory for both of them, and the Baron took very much the back seat, overshadowed by his wife's high profile and her pas-sionate *joie de vivre*.

Necker retired to Coppet in 1790 after the Revolution, from when Germaine's (now **Madame de Staël**'s) literary and philosophical *salon* began to attract the leading intellects of the day. The Swiss author Benjamin Constant (with whom de Staël may have conducted a long-lasting affair) was a regular visitor, as were the philosopher Schlegel, Chateaubriand, Lord Byron, and others. Madame de Staël organized life at the château around her constant flow of guests: lunch, it is said, was served at 5pm, dinner at 11pm, with musical *soirées* and lavishly staged playlets presented in the library in between, and debates and discussions afterwards which continued late into the night.

In 1804 Necker died, and the château passed into the hands of Madame de Staël, who was forced to remain there in permanent exile after 1806 following her persist-ent public denunciation of Napoleon. She died a celebrated writer and commenta-tor in 1817, at the age of 51, and the château is still in her family to this day. The renowned portraitist Ingres painted Madame de Staël's granddaughter Louise de Broglie, Countess of Haussonville, and proceeds from the recent sale of this mas-terpiece to a gallery in New York enabled the current Count to retain ownership of the château. The Haussonvilles stay in Coppet for just a couple of weeks each sum-mer, but still maintain the house in its original eighteenth-century grandeur.

Curchod. Some nine rooms are open to the public, including the grand library, formerly the main reception room, filled with Empire and Directoire furniture; Madame de Staël's bedroom, with her Louis XVI bed draped in Lyon silk; Juliette Récamier's bedroom next door, hung with exquisite eighteenth-century Chinese wallpaper; and, upstairs, a drawing-room and a gallery of family portraits.

In addition to a scattering of plain **eating** places along the main street, Coppet boasts the glorious **hotel** *Du Lac*, 51 Grand'Rue (T022 776 15 21, Wwww.hoteldulac.ch; ❹–❺). This wood-beamed inn was classified as a *grand logis* in 1628, granting it "the exclusive right to receive and lodge people arriving by coach or on horseback"; the atmosphere hasn't changed much, and after ducking in off the busy road, you trail through grand dining-rooms and antique-laden drawing rooms until you reach the shady, perfectly calm lakeside terrace at the back. Common foot travellers in days of yore presumably stayed at simpler places like the *Hôtel d'Orange* (T022 776 10 37, F022 776 25 40; ❷), a few doors down at no. 61.

Céligny

Tucked in a tiny enclave of Canton Geneva, surrounded by Vaud, gentle **CÉLIGNY** is about as endearing a rural gem as you could hope to find, enjoying waterside lawns, vineyards all around and, through the village, an atmospheric church and château (not open to the public). The air of undisturbed tranquillity hanging over the fountained village square proved particularly balming for the actor Richard Burton, who spent the last few years of his life here. If you walk up into the village from the train station, across the square and then head left, cutting around a parking area, you'll eventually stumble on the Vieux Cimitière, a damp and mossy grove on the bank of a little stream (the other bank is Vaudois territory) that is Burton's final resting place.

Céligny's real treasure is the *Hôtel du Soleil* on the village square (T022 960 96 33, F022 776 08 00; closed Mon eve & Tues), a characterful country *auberge* with friendly staff that has a wide choice of light, imaginatively prepared food, including delicious fresh perch; *menus* are Fr.25 or so. You'd do well to reserve a table to **eat**, especially in summer – the place is well known to the locals and to La Côte's many expat families – although you might just as well savour the atmosphere over a glass or two of wine on the terrace. A handful of comfortable **rooms** on the upper floor (❷) add to the appeal.

Nyon

NYON – a major town under the Romans which has mellowed into a laconic and attractive little port, 9km north of Coppet – is a perfect stopover on a leisurely tour of the area. The town, on a flattish plain sandwiched between the Jura and the lake, is spread out among verdant fields and lawns which reach down to the water, and is backed by acres of vineyards on the gentle slopes behind. There's a château and an excellent Roman museum, and the nearby **Château de Prangins** houses the regional branch of the National Museum. And if museums aren't your thing, there's the option of riding a mountain railway up to the little Jura resort of **St-Cergue**.

After Julius Caesar conquered Gallia Comata (Long-Haired Gaul) in 52 BC, he retired his cavalry veterans to the **Colonia Julia Equestris**, founded on the shores of the lake over the Helvetian settlement of Noviodunum which had stood there previously. For two centuries, the town flourished, becoming an urban centre of 3000 people (the population didn't reach such heights again

Paleo Rock Festival

Nyon's biggest party is also one of Europe's biggest – the giant **Paleo Rock Festival** (ⓦwww.paleo.ch), which takes place over a week in late July in a field outside town, with a consistently excellent line-up of musicians attracting hundreds of thousands of revellers. Acts in past years have been as diverse as Bryan Adams and Ruben Gonzalez, the Fun Lovin' Criminals and Cesaria Evora, MC Solaar and Supertramp. If you buy early, you can snap up a day ticket for as little as Fr.40, or a full six-day pass for around Fr.200; transport from Nyon to the site and back is free. The tourist office has festival-plus-hotel packages, which rise in price the later you book.

until the mid-nineteenth century).The late third century saw increasing attacks from Alemans and Franks, and by the mid-fifth century the colony was virtually deserted. Only its Roman name survived, the Latin "Colonia" compressed into the single nasal syllable "Nyon".The region was integrated into the kingdom of **Burgundy** after 443, then was passed from lord to lord until the Bernese conquered Vaud in 1536. In 1781 a French entrepreneur Jacques Dortu opened a **porcelain** workshop in the town, staffed by local artisans who produced work of exceptionally high quality, rapidly establishing Nyon as a centre of the craft: museums around Europe now display Nyon porcelain alongside the best of Limoges china as some of the highest-prized ceramic art of the period.

The Town

Heading southeast from the train station towards the lake will bring you in a couple of minutes into the compact Old Town, centred on **Place du Château**, a shady, charmingly laid-back square with terrace cafés that is backed by the **château** itself, a mighty twelfth-century turreted fortress looking out over the lake. Closed for renovations, it's due to reopen in 2005 with the town's **Musée Historique** occupying all six floors, displaying silver, fine art, photographs and a comprehensive collection of Nyon porcelain. Opposite, at 4 Place du Château, is the headquarters of Focale, one of the most important associations of Swiss photographers; their cramped **bookshop** is excellent, as is the gallery downstairs showing contemporary photography. Rue du Vieux Marché leading west off the square brings you past a statue of Julius Caesar to the impressive **Musée Romain** on Rue Maupertuis (July & Aug Mon–Sat 10am–noon & 2–6pm; April–June, Sept & Oct closed Mon; Nov–March Tues–Sat 2–6pm; joint ticket with Musée du Leman Fr.6; SMP; ⓦwww.mrn.ch).The museum is housed in a Roman basilica, originally part of Nyon's forum; a giant trompe l'oeil fresco of the original basilica's interior on the wall outside, as well as a model in the museum, give an idea of the size of Nyon's public buildings in its Roman heyday.The museum's extensive collection is well laid out; you pass first into the central area (the nave of the basilica) which houses inscriptions, statues and architectural details, and from there move around the walls of the room through zones devoted to daily life, crafts and religion.

The street ends at the small **Église Notre-Dame**, dating from 1110 and of unusual asymmetrical design, endowed with new stained glass. The arched Porte Ste-Marie round the corner gives onto the **Esplanade des Marronniers** (Chestnut Trees), exposed to fresh lake breezes and dominated by two and a half Roman columns, sited impressively against the blue. Walking along the city walls east and down some steps to the lakefront delivers you to the small, diverting **Musée du Léman**, 8 Quai Louis-Bonnard (same hours and ticket as Musée Romain; SMP; Ⓦ www.museeduleman.ch). The ground floor has informative displays on the lake fauna, with large aquariums, while upstairs are paintings, models of ships and disquisitions (in French) on how to protect the lake's natural resources. From the **Place de Savoie**, 150m to the east, with its jetty from which you can make out the plume of Geneva's Jet d'Eau some 20km away, atmospheric Rue de Rive heads slightly uphill, lined with antique shops and some very odd murals on sidewalls of cartoonish figures peeping out of painted windows. At the end, Rue de la Colombière continues uphill, and where it meets Rue de la Porcelaine you should spot Nyon's **Roman amphitheatre** half hidden in the grass a little east, virtually the same size as the one at Avenches (see p.192) but much more ruined and unfortunately now hemmed in by modern housing developments.

Practicalities

Plenty of **trains** serve Nyon from both directions, although note that not all those heading east go to Lausanne: some branch off at Morges on their way to Yverdon. Regular **boats** serve Nyon from both Geneva and Lausanne. The **tourist office** is one minute's walk from the station, at 7 Avenue Viollier (June–Sept daily 8.30am–noon & 1.30–5.30pm; Oct–May Mon–Fri same times; ☏022 361 62 61, Ⓦ www.nyon.ch), and offers a **guided walk** around the town, starting from the Place du Château (May–Sept Thurs & Fri 10am, Sat 2pm; Fr.10).

Nyon's best **hotel** is the *Beau-Rivage*, 49 Rue de Rive (☏022 365 41 41, Ⓦ www.hotel-beau-rivage-nyon.ch; ➎–➏), a fabulous pile below the castle that's been in business since 1481 and boasts large, traditionally furnished rooms, most looking lakewards. The charming *Hostellerie du XVIe Siècle*, 2 Place du Marché (☏022 994 88 00, Ⓕ022 994 88 09; ➋), is an atmospheric arcaded building in the cobbled Old Town, renovated throughout; some rooms are ensuite, others not. Rue de Rive has any number of places to **eat** fresh fish, but the fillet of perch (Fr.30) served at *Du Cheval Blanc* at no. 62 must rank with the best. More affordable pizzas and pasta *menus* (Fr.16–18) can be munched at *Le Léman*, 28 Rue de Rive.

Château de Prangins

A kilometre or two east of Nyon is the idyllic village of **PRANGINS**, in the midst of which, set in its own formal English gardens, is the **Château de**

Above Nyon – St-Cergue

Rising above Nyon are the final stretches of the Jura range within Switzerland, known as the **Pied du Jura**, sliced across by the international border which separates the French Pays de Gex above Geneva from the Swiss mountain resort of **ST-CERGUE**. This quiet, unassuming town is set in some wild countryside with hiking trails that see few ramblers; the tourist office on Place Sy-Vieuxville (closed Mon; ☏022 360 13 14, Ⓦ www.st-cergue.ch) has details. In winter, the town concentrates on providing safe, quality downhill **skiing** for families, and plenty of excellent cross-country routes. The *desalpe*, or annual descent of cattle from the high pastures to winter quarters in the valley, accompanied by much floral decoration and folkloric celebrations, is a highlight of St-Cergue's calendar, taking place on a Saturday in late September. Riding on the little red NStCM **trains** (InterRail not valid) which depart from the forecourt of Nyon station on a winding narrow-gauge route up into the green hills is worth an afternoon in itself, whether you get off at St-Cergue or shuttle on over the **Col de la Givrine** (1228m) to the hamlet of **La Cure** on the border.

Prangins (Tues–Sun 10am–5pm; Fr.5; SMP; ⓦwww.musee-suisse.com), built in the 1730s in the French style and now an arm of the Swiss National Museum devoted to the history of Switzerland in the eighteenth and nineteenth centuries. It's a huge place holding an imaginative and engaging collection that's well worth a couple of hours; all the rooms are numbered sequentially, but the layout can be very confusing and you may find yourself backtracking more than once.

Exhibits on the ground floor, outlining the ideals of aristocrats and the bourgeoisie around 1800, and in the cellars, detailing Switzerland's pre-industrial rural economy, are less engaging than those on the two upper floors, which are devoted to Swiss cultural history from 1750 into the twentieth century. Each room ("From Birth to Death", "The Display of Power", "Travellers and Tourists") has good English notes, with items from everyday life displayed next to historically significant objects. The multimedia stations that are dotted around enhance wanderings by letting you play period music while you're examining the cases; for instance, as well as selecting readings from contemporary accounts of history, you can listen to original songs from the Swiss Revolution. Reconstructed interiors, such as that of a late-nineteenth century schoolroom, display uncanny attention to detail. Outside, an extensive kitchen garden has been planted with fruit and vegetables according to eighteenth-century literary accounts of horticulture.

Bus #5 runs hourly from Nyon's train station on a circular route through Prangins, stopping either at the village post office three minutes from the château (Mon–Sat) or at the château itself (Sun).

Luins and Vinzel

Some 10km northeast of Nyon on the *Route des Vignerons* are the neighbouring wine villages of **LUINS** and **VINZEL**, both famous for their *malakoffs*. These little gastronomic heartwarmers – a rich, fried cheese-and-egg mixture served hot on a round bread base – are a local speciality, renamed to celebrate the triumphant return of a band of Vaudois mercenaries under the Russian general Malakoff from the 1855 siege of Sebastopol; the two villages, which are no more than ten minutes' walk apart, have competed since then for whose *malakoff* is better. Take the taste test at the *Auberge Communale* in Luins (☎021 824 11 59), then wander down the road past the vineyards to *Au Coeur de la Côte* in Vinzel (☎021 824 11 41) – both are open daily, serving *malakoffs* for around Fr.6 each; while you're at it, take the chance to compare and contrast the excellent village wines. A good hike reaches above Luins to a tiny church-with-a-view, dating from 1393, and on up past the vineyards into thick woodland – beech, chestnut and oak – eventually emerging into the open pasture and cultivated fields of the plateau above.

Rolle, Morges and around

ROLLE is a little-visited town roughly midway between Nyon and Lausanne, at the heart of the La Côte wine country. Its huge lakeside château dates from 1270 but is not open to the public. Just offshore is the tiny **Île de la Harpe**, built up in 1835 from earth dumped during construction of the town's harbour; unfortunately for posterity, the harbour works destroyed many pre-hewn oak posts which had stood in the lake for as long as anyone could remember – remnants, no doubt, of prehistoric stilt dwellings. It's a tragic irony that shortly afterwards the railway arrived, negating the whole point of building a harbour in the first place. The island, named after local revolutionary and statesman

A shaggy dog story

The château of **St-Saphorin-sur-Morges** (not to be confused with St-Saphorin near Vevey) was built in the eighteenth century. Elisabeth Upton-Eichenberger, in her excellent book on Vaud (see "Books", p.607), tells the story of a twentieth-century occupant, one **Georges de Mestral**, who had studied engineering in Lausanne and returned to live in the château. Mestral was on a shooting trip one day in 1948 in the Jura foothills when, as usual, he found himself spending ages extracting burrs that had got caught in his dog's soft furry ears. The legend goes that it was here, on his knees in the forest, that de Mestral had the idea to copy nature and invent a fabric using sharp little burr-like hooks to stick to soft furry material. Thus, he thought, could rackety unreliable zips be consigned to history. He patented his idea and started production in nearby Aubonne; although zips have survived, his **Velcro** – a conflation of the words "velour" and "crochet" (®www.velcro.com) – is now a household name, manufactured under licence around the world. St-Saphorin-sur-Morges, though, has largely forgotten its most famous son.

Frédéric-César de la Harpe, is now the focus for Rolle's active community of yachties, who regularly organize sailing festivals and races around it.

Some 5km east stands the massive **Château d'Allaman** (Wed–Sun 2–6pm) built in the twelfth century, torched in 1530, rebuilt in 1723 and now serving as one of the most impressive furniture showrooms you're likely to see: twenty antique dealers rent space within the castle to display their wares, which suit the grand halls and corridors perfectly, although the price tags might give you indigestion. The annexe, La Grange, has more reasonably priced art and collectibles, and the vaulted cellar has wine-tastings and sales.

The lakeside road winds on to Lausanne through **MORGES**, another peaceful little harbour town famed for its kilometre-long Quais du Dahlia and the Fête de la Tulipe held during April and May in the lakefront Parc de l'Indépendance. Its huge château holds a military museum. Until very recently, the main reason to come was to take the bus from the train station 1km west to the village of **TOLOCHENAZ**, home of the actress Audrey Hepburn from 1963 until her death in 1993, where the commune and local volunteers had set up the **Pavillon Audrey Hepburn** (formerly Tues–Sun: March–Oct 10am–6pm, rest of year 1.30–5.30pm; Fr.10; bus-stop La Plantaz; ®www. geocities.com/audreyhepburnunicef). This small, well-presented exhibition offered a chronological tour through Hepburn's career, including her first contract, dated 1948 (paying £9 a week as a chorus girl), both her Oscars, a fan letter from Samuel Goldwyn, the black dress worn for *Breakfast at Tiffany's* and dozens of photos and film posters. However, in November 2002, after six years, Hepburn's two sons effectively closed the museum by taking back all the exhibits, claiming over-commercialization of their mother's memory. At the time of writing, it's unclear what the future holds; local people are said to be dismayed, while the significant proceeds from the pavilion – some Fr.400,000, all of which went to the Audrey Hepburn Foundation for Children, supporting UNICEF – have been cut off. Before heading out here, it's worth checking the latest situation with Morges tourist office, opposite the château (Mon–Fri 9am–12.30pm & 1.30–5.30pm, Sat 9am–12.30pm; ☎021 801 32 33, ®www.morges.ch).

The Lavaux wine villages

The compact stretch of Lake Geneva shore east from Lausanne to Vevey – known as the **Lavaux** (W www.lavaux.com) – is one of the most alluring regions of the country, its lush floral waterside promenades flanked on one side by wide expanses of vines and on the other by vistas across to the Savoy Alps rising behind the Dents-du-Midi on the far shore. Trains heading to Montreux and beyond hug the shoreline, the tracks passing within a few metres of the water, seeming to whisk you along inches above the glittering lake itself. Some of the country's best **wines** come from the dozens of vineyards clustered cheek by jowl along the steep Lavaux slopes: this is perfect country for gentle walks and bike rides punctuated by samplings of the local nectar. Cafés and *pintes* abound, set in the cobbled streets of the region's gloriously picturesque villages.

Tourist offices offer plenty of information guiding you through the Lavaux's **wine villages**, a line of hamlets strung along the slopes between Lausanne and Vevey devoted for centuries past to the art of viticulture. Pick up the pamphlet entitled *À la decouverte des terrasses de Lavaux*, which has a good map of routes throughout the area. Between May and October, most reliably on weekends (Thurs–Sun), you'll find *caveaux* (cellars) and *carnotzets* (cellars with rough benches and tables for extended wine- and food-sampling sessions) open in every village, some of them belonging to that commune's *vignerons* association, others attached to private châteaux or independent *vignobles*. The Lavaux website and Vevey tourist office have full lists of phone numbers to make reservations.

Cully and Rivaz

The shuttered village of **CULLY** (pronounced "kwee"), 8km east of Lausanne, is crammed full of *caveaux* and *carnotzets* offering the rich, forest-fruity wines of nearby Epesses, Calamin, Riex, Villette and Lutry. The village also boasts the extraordinary **Auberge du Raisin**, 1 Place de l'Hôtel de Ville (T 021 799 21 31, W www.relaischateaux.ch/raisin; ⑥–⑧), the old thirteenth-century town hall, which has been converted into a uniquely characterful hotel, filled with period furniture, original Old Masters and ten individually decorated rooms which vary tremendously in price. Its creative cuisine is outstanding, acclaimed by Michelin, Gault & Millau and others, but not cheap (*menus* from Fr.50). If you're around on the last Friday in November, stop in Cully for the *Nuit du vin cuit* ("Night of Cooked Wine") – a festive all-night masked musical parade

---

Exploring the Lavaux

The best path to follow through the Lavaux is termed the **Corniche**, winding scenically through the vineyards between the main lakefront traffic road and the *autoroute* and Lausanne–Bern train tracks on a terrace higher up. The **Grande Traversée** route, marked with a "GT" signpost, starts in Ouchy, follows the lakefront to Lutry, then snakes up to the Corniche, ending 32km away at Chillon. You can follow any number of shorter trails on and around the Corniche, marked with **Parcours Viticole** (Vineyard Trail) signposts. Local **trains** along the lakefront line are plentiful, meaning you can hop on and off at will; alternatively, the narrow-gauge **"Train des Vignes"** shuttles hourly from Puidoux-Chexbres station (on the line between Lausanne and Fribourg) on a short but steep track down through the vineyards to Vevey (takes 12min). Another option is to rent a **bike** in Lausanne, dropping it off in the evening in Vevey or Montreux, or taking it back to Lausanne on the train. **Boats** stop at Lutry, Cully and Rivaz.

accompanied by quaffing of must (new unfermented wine) mulled on open fires.

Some 3km east are the open vineyards of **Dézaley**, producing some of the highest-rated *grand cru* wines in Switzerland; the lakeside *Auberge* in next-door **RIVAZ** (☎021 946 10 55, 🖷021 946 38 82; ❷) has a dozen or so clean, comfortable rooms.

St-Saphorin and beyond

A kilometre east of Rivaz is **ST-SAPHORIN**, about as romantic and photogenic a waterside hamlet as you could ever hope for, piled up on steep slopes above the lake, with an old church, skinny cobbled alleys that crook their way up between crumbling old cottages, and superb flinty, smoke-perfumed wines best sampled at the village's central *Auberge de l'Onde*. This atmospheric old inn, once a major halt for stagecoaches plying between Geneva and Italy, is simply bewitching: you could easily find its languorous combination of wood-beamed quaintness, day-fresh perch sautéed delectably in herb-butter and a heady carafe or three of the village wine charming you into abandoning whatever plans you had for the rest of the day. The seven comfortable rooms at *Le Castel* (☎021 921 47 51; ❸) are on hand for just such a turn of events.

If your legs haven't already turned to spaghetti, you could try strolling 2km up the hill from St-Saphorin to picturesque **Chexbres**, a minor resort clinging to a terrace with views over the lake and mountains and a choice of hotels and restaurants, and then 4km further east to **Chardonne** on the slopes of towering Mont Pèlerin, home of the consistently excellent *Cure d'Attalens* wine. An amble under the funicular tracks and through uninspiring **Jongny** brings you down to Corsier, on the western edges of Vevey.

Vevey

At the little town of Vevey, there is a particularly comfortable hotel...
The entertainment of tourists is the business of the place, which, as many travellers will remember, is seated upon the edge of a remarkably blue lake – a lake that it behoves every tourist to visit.

Henry James, from *Daisy Miller* (1878)

Whereas brassy Montreux, a few kilometres down the road, has over the years freely embraced all that glisters – gold, paper or otherwise – its old-fashioned neighbour **VEVEY** is more discriminating. Vevey quietly cleans its streets, tends its flowerbeds, makes sure it has enough, but not too many, hotels and then waits for visitors of a certain style to find the town for themselves, become enchanted, and stay. It's a hard place to quantify, neither prim, nor stuffy, nor sophisticated, nor especially graceful... yet it somehow manages to incorporate strands of all of them in an ambience of tasteful, restrained gentility. It *is* enchanting, a world apart (or a remnant of a world now past), and you may well find yourself lulled into staying.

Henry James set his *Daisy Miller* – the story of a headstrong young woman on the Grand Tour who broke the rules of propriety by visiting the Château de Chillon unchaperoned, and so got her comeuppance – in Vevey, specifically at the *Hôtel des Trois Couronnes*, which is much the same now as it seems it must have been in James's day. And, in a similar vein, **Anita Brookner** set her

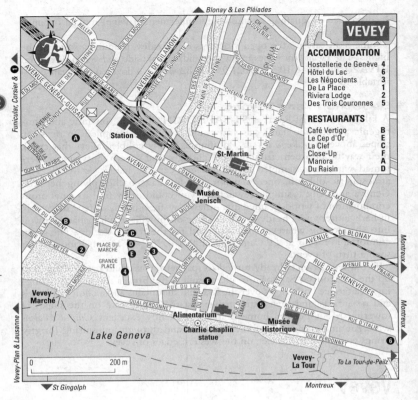

Map labels:

VEVEY

ACCOMMODATION

Hostellerie de Genève	4
Hôtel du Lac	6
Les Négociants	3
De La Place	1
Riviera Lodge	2
Des Trois Couronnes	5

RESTAURANTS

Café Vertigo	B
Le Cep d'Or	E
La Clef	C
Close-Up	F
Manora	A
Du Raisin	D

Blonay & Les Pléiades

Station
St-Martin
Musée Jenisch
Place du Marché
Grande Place
Vevey-Marché
Alimentarium
Charlie Chaplin statue
Musée Historique
Lake Geneva
Vevey-La Tour
To La Tour-de-Peilz
St Gingolph
Montreux

0 — 200 m

Funicular, Corsier &
Vevey-Plan & Lausanne

Booker Prize-winning novel *Hotel du Lac* in a reserved, taciturn but anonymous lakeside town opposite the Dent d'Oche (the huge 2222m mountain on the French shore facing Vevey). Generations of tourists return to Vevey to stroll the flowered promenades, muse on the Dent d'Oche, venture across the water on the Belle-Epoque ships of the Lake Geneva fleet, and take high tea in grand hotels. Yet there's plenty more to do than this suggests: the shops, museums and local life are far more engaging than in Montreux, and if big cities such as Lausanne or Geneva don't appeal, you could easily use smalltown Vevey as a comfortable base for a couple of days or weeks from which to explore the whole lake and surrounding region.

Arrival, information and accommodation

Vevey's **train station**, on the main line between Lausanne and Montreux, is 300m north of the lakeshore on a busy east–west main road: cross over and head towards the lake on the Rue de Lausanne, and within a minute or two you'll come to the gigantic central square of Grande-Place, also known as Place du Marché, which fronts directly onto the lake. The Old Town alleys are clustered to the east. The town has three **ferry stops**: Vevey-Plan is to the west, behind the Nestlé building; Vevey-Marché is metres from Place du Marché in the town centre; and Vevey-La Tour is east, close to La Tour-de-Peilz.

Vevey–Montreux transport

If you're shuttling between Vevey and Montreux, it's worth abandoning the trains in favour of the much more useful electric **city bus #1** (Ⓦwww.vmcv.ch). This runs on a straight lakeside route from Vevey's funicular station (west of the centre), past Vevey train station, on through La Tour-de-Peilz and Clarens into Montreux town centre, on through Territet (stopping outside the Château de Chillon), and terminating in Villeneuve. Buses run to and fro every ten minutes, and journey time between Vevey and Montreux is twenty minutes. Vevey and La Tour are in Zone 1; Montreux is in Zone 2; Chillon and Villeneuve are in Zone 3. A journey across two zones is Fr.2.40, across three is Fr.3, a day pass is Fr.8, but all Swiss passes are valid for free travel. Ticket machines in buses dispense one-way fares only.

The **tourist offices** of Vevey and Montreux have joined forces: you can get exactly the same information from both. Vevey's office is in the pillared Grenette building on Grande-Place (mid-June to mid-Sept Mon–Fri 9am–6pm, Sat 9am–4pm; rest of year Mon–Fri 8.30am–12.30pm & 1.30–6pm, Sat 8.30am–noon; Ⓣ0848 868 484, Ⓦwww.montreux-vevey.com). The local **museum passport** covers entry to ten museums in Vevey and Montreux (including the Château de Chillon) for Fr.15. If you're staying around Vevey or Montreux for any length of time, you should splash out on the 80-page **magazine** *Tourist Info Pass* (Fr.8), which is crammed with useful information about the whole region and discount offers.

If you happen to be around in July, you might want to check out the **International Festival of Comedy Films**, held annually in memory of the town's adopted son Charlie Chaplin.

Accommodation

Vevey has a limited, but high-quality, range of accommodation options. The pristine *Riviera Lodge* **SB hostel**, 5 Place du Marché (Ⓣ021 923 80 40, Ⓦwww.rivieralodge.ch; ❶), has excellent dorms in the centre of town for Fr.26, while you can **camp** on the lakeside 2km west at *La Pichette* (Ⓣ021 921 09 97, Ⓕ021 925 53 35).

Of the **hotels**, *Les Négociants*, 27 Rue du Conseil (Ⓣ021 922 70 11, Ⓦwww.hotelnegociants.ch; ❷–❸), and *Hostellerie de Genève*, 11 Place du Marché (Ⓣ021 921 45 77, Ⓦwww.hotelgeneve.ch; ❸), are both simple, family-run places in the centre; while rustic *De La Place*, 5 Place du Temple in Corsier (Ⓣ021 921 12 87, Ⓦwww.swissnew.ch/hoteldelaplace; ❷) is a building dating from 1692 overlooking an ancient church on the slopes above Vevey, with spartan but atmospheric rooms. At the top end of the scale, lapping up the lakeside panoramas, the heavenly *Hôtel du Lac*, 1 Rue d'Italie (Ⓣ021 921 10 41, Ⓦwww.montreux.ch; ❺), offers small-scale, understated grandeur, with inevitable associations with Anita Brookner; while *Des Trois Couronnes*, 49 Rue d'Italie (Ⓣ021 923 32 00, Ⓦwww.hotel3couronnes.com; ❽) – the original setting for Henry James's *Daisy Miller* – retains all its period style, stuffy but utterly charming. It was named as Swiss Historic Hotel of the Year for 2002, in honour of its superb restoration work and minute attention to original detailing.

The Town

The best way to get the flavour of Vevey is simply to wander: its narrow Old Town alleys, enclosing the huge **Grande-Place** – or **Place du Marché** – in a cat's cradle of arcades and shuttered facades, are alive with people, shops and activity. Arrive on a Tuesday or Saturday and you'll find the marketplace packed with stalls: food, crafts, wine or all three. The huge pillared building dominating the square is the Grenette, or town granary, dating from 1808 and now housing the tourist office.

Vevey's excellent fine-art museum is the **Musée Jenisch**, 2 Rue de la Gare (Tues–Sun 11am–5.30pm; Fr.12; SMP; ⓦ www.museejenisch.ch), an impressive Neoclassical-style temple built in 1897 with a donation from a Hamburg émigré family named Jenisch; despite the tide of Swiss who apparently make the long journey from Graubünden expecting exhibits on the Jenisch gypsy people (see p.506), there's no connection. The museum, now about ten times too small for its massive collection, stages changing exhibitions of Swiss art on various themes, while its Cabinet cantonal des Estampes (Cantonal Museum of Prints) holds the largest collection of Rembrandt lithographs in Europe, as well as hundreds of graphic works by Dürer, Corot, Le Corbusier and others. Not least, the museum is also the repository of the Oskar Kokoschka Foundation, owning and displaying examples of work from this expressionist Austrian painter and graphic artist who spent the last 26 years of his life in Villeneuve.

Some 500m west of the centre you can't miss the giant green building on the waterfront, Nestlé's world HQ (see box). A little uphill on the Chemin de Meruz is the atmospheric village of **CORSIER**; on the right of the road you'll find a small cemetery, location of the graves of Oona and Charlie Chaplin, who moved to Corsier in the 1950s as an escape from McCarthyite America and never left. Further up the hill is Corsier's tiny church (also accessible on bus #11), watched over by graceful angels and holding inside some frescoes dating from 1420–30 which were plastered over during the Reformation and rediscovered in the nineteenth century. Back on the main lakefront Route de Lavaux some 200m west of the Nestlé building you'll find **Villa Le Lac**, an elegant low white bungalow designed by modernist architect Le Corbusier for his parents in 1924 (guided tours March–Oct Wed 1.30–5pm; free), which also features much original Corbusier-designed furniture.

To the east, Vevey merges imperceptibly with its neighbour, the colourful port village of La Tour-de-Peilz. Along the way, you'll pass a photogenic statue of a bowler-hatted Chaplin twirling his cane amidst the roses on the Quai

Walks around Vevey

The tourist office runs a two-hour **guided walk** around the town (May–Sept Wed–Fri 10am; Fr.10), starting from the train station, but you should check in advance about the availability of an English-speaking guide. Otherwise, their excellent brochure *On The Trail of Hemingway* pinpoints a welter of sites in the area with famous-name associations.

One of the most pleasant long walks in the area is the three-hour **Chemin Fleuri** (Flowered Path), covering the sumptuous 9km lakefront promenade between Vevey and Villeneuve (aside from a short stretch east of La Tour-de-Peilz, where private lakefront properties force you back into the town). The tourist office has a brochure describing the walk and its various highlights.

Alternatively, the tourist office has a **"Poets' Ramble"** brochure (Fr.2), which outlines a long route from bench to bench through Vevey and the surrounding hillside villages; each bench is dedicated to a particular writer or philosopher with some connection either to Vevey or to that particular location, and at each one, you can press a button to hear a short extract of their writings while enjoying the view. It's a great idea that works very well; the map is good enough to follow easily and the walk could take anything from 2 to 4 hours.

Perdonnet just east of Place du Marché, followed shortly after by the **Alimentarium** (Tues–Sun 10am–6pm; Fr.10; SMP; ⓦwww.alimentarium .ch), a rather dull Nestlé-sponsored exhibition on food and nutrition. Another 200m brings you to the **Musée Historique**, 2 Rue du Château (Tues–Sun: March–Oct 10.30am–noon & 2–5.30pm; Nov–Feb 2–5.30pm; Fr.5; SMP; ⓦwww.vevey.ch/museehistorique), with a large section devoted to Vevey's mammoth Fête des Vignerons (Wine-Growers' Festival), a Bacchic celebration in music, costume and dance of the region's viticulture that's traditionally held about every 25 years – most recently in 1999. The Quai d'Entre Deux Villes leads you on into **LA TOUR-DE-PEILZ**, 1km east of Vevey and dominated by its white château (the towers of which were apparently once roofed with animal pelts – hence the odd name). Inside is the **Musée Suisse du Jeu** (Museum of Games; same hours as Musée Historique; Fr.6; SMP; ⓦwww.msj.ch), an absorbing run-through of diversions and entertainments down the millennia, from 2500-year-old ancient Egyptian dice to the latest video games; you're encouraged to play and tinker as much as you like.

Eating and drinking

There are plenty of pavement **cafés and restaurants** throughout the centre. Excitable *Café Vertigo*, 6 Rue du Torrent, is spacious and friendly, with quality nosh for under Fr.15; *Close-Up*, 8 Rue du Lac, is smaller, peaceful and jazzy; *La Clef*, 1 Rue du Théâtre, is an atmospheric little corner bistro serving up steaming Vaudois specialities; while the cafés all around Place du Marché, including *Du Raisin* and *Le Cep d'Or* on the east side of the square, offer terraces for people-watching and simple *menus* for under Fr.20. The boss of *Hôtel Les Négociants* rolls up his sleeves

> ### Nestlé
>
> **Henri Nestlé** was born in Frankfurt in 1814, and moved to Vevey in his 20s, a merchant and small-scale inventor. He gravitated towards foodstuffs, experimenting with various recipes for baby-food to help mothers who were unable to breastfeed. In 1867, he fed his *"farine lactée"* to a premature baby boy whose mother was dangerously ill; the boy survived, and Nestlé's reputation skyrocketed. The following year he opened an office in London to cope with the quantity of orders, and within five years was exporting to South America and Australia. In 1874 he sold his company for a million francs. In 1929, Nestlé bought out Peter, Cailler and Kohler – pioneers in making milk chocolate – and started to diversify, launching the world's first instant coffee, Nescafé, in 1938. More takeovers followed, and by the 1960s, Nestlé was Switzerland's biggest company, a huge multinational still based in Vevey.
>
> Today, having swallowed up cosmetic company L'Oréal in 1974 and British confectioner Rowntree's in 1991, Nestlé employs almost a quarter of a million people, and buys up more than ten percent of the world's entire crop of coffee and cacao beans. However, its most controversial product is, strangely, its original one: baby formula. With a marketing policy in developing-world countries that many see as aggressively profit-driven, Nestlé has been riding a storm of anger in recent years from children's organizations and health watchdogs. Many of these groups continue to lobby for boycotts of Nestlé products unless the company takes a role in helping educate mothers in the developing world to breastfeed whenever possible, and to buy formula only as a last resort. The company maintains its ads don't dissuade mothers from breastfeeding, and are merely offering them a choice. The dispute shows few signs of resolution and, frankly, little chance of toppling such a mighty global industrial entity as Nestlé.

of an evening and cooks solid, unpretentious fare in the hotel brasserie. There's also a self-service *Manora* in the St Antoine mall opposite the station.

Above Vevey

Aside from the titchy Train des Vignes (see box p.150), there are two routes for excursions by train into the hills above Vevey.

From Vevey-Funi station opposite the Nestlé building (at the terminus of bus #1), a **funicular** rises every twenty minutes through the wine village of Chardonne to a terrace on the slope of **Mont–Pèlerin** at 800m, where you'll find two luxury hotels and plenty of places to appreciate the views over a little something to whet the whistle. A stiff hike (or a four-times-daily bus) up to the summit brings you to the TV tower, with its high-speed **Plein–Ciel** glass lift whisking you up to the even better views at 1100m (April–Oct daily 9am–6pm, July & Aug until 8pm; lift Fr.5; funicular, bus & lift Fr.16).

More dramatic is the curving train line from Vevey station up to the vantage point of **Les Pléiades**, perched in the hills way above the lake at 1364m. The section beyond **Blonay** village – a junction for the line down to Montreux as well as the old steam railway to **Chamby** (see p.164) – is rack-and-pinion to cope with the gradient, but the ride still takes an hour to the top. The penultimate station, **Lally**, is situated next to the cosy old-world *Hôtel Les Sapins* (☎021 943 1395, Ⓦwww.les-sapins.ch; ❷–❸), a peaceful little place set amongst hiking trails with great food and a few simple rooms. From here, it's

---

Taking to the water

The section of Lake Geneva around Vevey and Montreux – the **Haut-Lac Supérieur** – dominated by the Dent d'Oche on one side, the heights above Montreux on the other, and glimpses of the snowy Pennine Alps above the Rhône valley further south, is utterly spectacular, and the best way to take it all in is **by boat**. Daily in summer (mid-May to mid-Sept), CGN (Ⓦwww.cgn.ch) operates a ferry continuously from 10am to 7pm on a circuit between Vevey, Montreux, Château de Chillon, Le Bouveret, St-Gingolph and Vevey: you can get on anywhere and be taken round for two hours back to your starting-point (Fr.27; free to Swiss Pass and Eurail holders, full price to InterRailers). Boats follow similar, direct routings between the same points all year round.

A few kilometres round the lakeshore from the Château de Chillon, across the Rhône (which marks the Vaud–Valais cantonal border), **LE BOUVERET** is a holiday village heavily touted for its family-friendly attractions. First up is the **Swiss Vapeur Parc** (May–Sept daily 10am–6pm; March, April, Sept & Oct Mon–Fri 1.30–6pm, Sat & Sun 10am–6pm; Fr.12; Ⓦwww.swissvapeur.ch), a miniature railway complex featuring replica locos pulling passengers around 1.5km of track. A stroll away is the giant, all-year **Aquaparc** (Mon–Thurs & Sun 10am–10pm, Fri & Sat 10am–midnight; office closes 8pm; Ⓦwww.aquaparc.ch), a heated, indoor waterpark complete with multiple flumes, slides, rides and a *McDonalds*; a half/full day adult ticket costs Fr.35/44, more at weekends; kids and families get discounts.

About 5km west is the divided village of **ST-GINGOLPH** (Ⓦwww.st-gingolph.ch), half in Switzerland and half in France. Apart from the busy border crossing, it's a soporific place that lets you draw breath away from the crowds, although its location directly opposite Vevey means that it misses out on the best lake vistas. It lives a quite different life from its lake neighbours, connected more to the Valais villages south along the Rhône: trains run not to Montreux but to St-Maurice (see p.334). Down by the water on the Swiss side are a clutch of pleasant cafés and restaurants; on the French side is a supervised beach, with pedalos for rent. **Evian** (see p.133) is about 20km west.

a quarter-hour climb (or the last six minutes of the train ride) to the summit, face to face with the mighty Dent de Jaman peak, only 1875m but prominent and pyramidal enough to earn the nickname of the Vaudois Matterhorn. Views yawn out in all directions, as do hiking trails – a long, leg-stretching one leads east across the exposed hilltops above the lake to Les Avants (see p.164).

Montreux and around

If you want your soul to find peace, go to Montreux.

Freddie Mercury

MONTREUX can be a snooty place, full of money and not particularly exciting. It's spectacularly located, bathed in afternoon sunshine streaming across the lake and protected from chill northerlies by a wall of giant mountains, but once you've had your fill of window-shopping and strolling beneath the palm trees, it's really rather dull.

From the early nineteenth century, Montreux was one of the centres for pan-European – and particularly British – tourism to Switzerland, following on from the importance of the impressive medieval **Château de Chillon** 3km away as a controlling presence on the transalpine road: an edict dated 1689 authorized the building of inns in the area to accommodate travellers making their way to and from the Grand-St-Bernard pass, and since then travel and tourism have been mainstays of the local economy. Up until the 1960s, the name Montreux referred to just one village in a loose affiliation of some 24 vineyard-communes spread around the neighbouring hills, including picturesque **Clarens** to the west, and **Territet** to the east. Both of these are now super-plush suburbs, their long and venerable visitors' books taking in the great

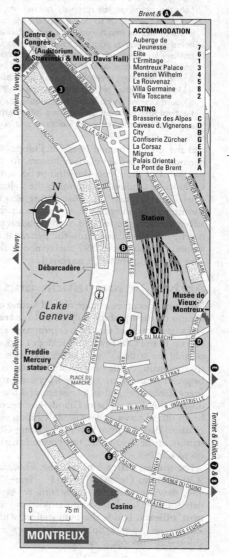

ACCOMMODATION

Auberge de Jeunesse	7
Elite	6
L'Ermitage	1
Montreux Palace	3
Pension Wilhelm	4
La Rouvenaz	5
Villa Germaine	8
Villa Toscane	2

EATING

Brasserie des Alpes	C
Caveau d. Vignerons	D
City	B
Confiserie Zürcher	G
La Corsaz	E
Migros	H
Palais Oriental	F
Le Pont de Brent	A

Montreux's festivals

The star-studded **Montreux Jazz Festival** (Ⓦwww.montreuxjazz.com) – featuring world-famous artists from REM to B.B. King – takes place over two weeks in early July, mainly at the two stages (Auditorium Stravinski and Miles Davis Hall) within the Congress Centre, plus at the Casino; it covers the gamut of music from around the world, these day's only very loosely committed to formal jazz. Check online for tickets (Fr.40–120); otherwise, just join the street parties and free entertainment which spring up on the lakefront. Montreux is turned upside down during festival-time, with only the mornings left relatively normal: from mid-afternoon onwards, the main roads are blocked off by police checkpoints, with huge car parks set up on the outskirts served by free buses. Bars and restaurants do a roaring trade until the early hours as thousands pour into town, and there's a constant thrumming of music from buskers and live stages on the lakefront promenades. All accommodation is booked solid, although special post-event trains and buses run every night from about 1am onwards, returning revellers to towns as far afield as Sion and Bern.

Montreux's other big jamboree is late April's **Golden Rose Television Festival** (Rose d'Or), for which swarms of media folk descend on the town. The classical **Festival International de Musique** (Ⓦwww.montreux-festival.com) runs in August and September at venues in Montreux and Vevey.

and the good, crowned heads of Europe and Russia, and literary and artistic personages galore. The main reasons to visit are to absorb the spectacular panorama of the Dents-du-Midi peaks across the lake, to visit the unmissable Château de Chillon, and to catch the stellar annual **Montreux Jazz Festival**.

In a gleeful case of truth being stranger than fiction, a century ago Montreux's hoteliers were casting about for a logo they could attach to the advertisements they placed in the English press each season. On a walk in the nearby hills they came across the perfect answer, growing in lush abundance all around; and so since 1897 the symbolic flower of Montreux has been, with ever-increasing aptness, a **narcissus**.

Arrival, information and accommodation

Montreux occupies a bulge of land jutting out into the lake, with the landmark Casino on the tip of the bulge. The large **train station** is set on a terrace above and slightly west of the town centre; stairs and escalators within the station raise you up to the Old Town on the slopes above, while Avenue des Alpes, the street outside the station's ticket office, has stairs and a lift which shuttle you down to the main central boulevard, Grand-Rue. A patch of park sandwiched between Grand-Rue and the lakefront promenade has at its western end the **ferry** *débarcadère*, and at its eastern end the town's huge covered market, Place du Marché. East of here, Grand-Rue becomes the Avenue du Casino which heads out of town as Avenue de Chillon on its way along the lakefront to the château. **Bus #1** from Vevey runs along Grand-Rue, stopping below the train station, at the *débarcadère*, the covered market and the Casino, before heading on to Chillon.

The **tourist office** is next to the *débarcadère* on the lakefront (June–Sept daily 9.30am–6pm; Oct–May Mon–Fri 9am–12.30pm & 1.30–6pm; ☎0848 868 484, Ⓦwww.montreux-vevey.com & Ⓦwww.montreux.ch). See p.153 for details of the local museum passport and *Tourist Info Pass* magazine. The main **post office** is beside the train station, with a smaller office next to *Confiserie Zürcher* on Avenue du Casino. There's a **laundry** at 30 Rue Industrielle (Mon–Fri 9am–6pm, Sat 10am–5pm).

As you might expect, when it comes to **accommodation** Montreux favours its high-rollers more than its backpackers – and prices rise across the board in summer. If you're arriving in late April (during the Golden Rose TV festival) or in early July (the Jazz Festival) you're likely to find the town booked solid.

Hotels

Elite 25 Avenue du Casino ☎021 966 03 03, ℻021 966 03 10. Small, generic place – well located slap in the heart of town. ❷

L'Ermitage 75 Rue du Lac, Clarens ☎021 964 44 11, ⓦwww.forum.ch/ermitage-clarens. A waterside villa set in its own grounds, with only seven rooms, all fresh and attractive, accompanied by spectacular gastronomic delights from the resident chef. ❺ –❻

Le Montreux Palace 100 Grand-Rue ☎021 962 12 12, ⓦwww.montreux-palace.com. Legendary luxury palace hotel, dominating the Montreux lakefront. This giant Belle-Epoque folly, one of the most famous hotels in the world, was opened in 1906 and later expanded both along the main street and across the road to the *Petit Palais* restaurant and teahouse, set in its own gardens on the lake. Newer wing or original wing, rooms are spacious, superbly well equipped and retain a good deal of character; plump for one of the lakeside balconies with sweeping panoramic views over the water. The public areas are effortlessly grand, and the associations with Vladimir Nabokov (he occupied the older wing's penthouse apartment for his last sixteen years) still resonate. ❾

Pension Wilhelm 13 Rue du Marché ☎021 963

14 31, ℻021 963 32 85. Welcoming place, best of the few small *pensions* within Montreux. ❶

La Rouvenaz 1 Rue du Marché ☎021 963 27 36, ℻021 963 43 94. Six comfy enough rooms in a central but quiet family-run place with Italian restaurant. ❷

Villa Germaine 3 Avenue Collonge, Territet ☎021 963 15 28, ℰcecileparisi@gve.ch. Attractive, fin-de-siècle villa, considerably more characterful than in-town options, and well out of the hubbub to boot. ❷

Villa Toscane 2 Rue du Lac ☎021 963 84 21, ⓦwww.montreux.ch/villa-toscane. A fabulous white, Art Nouveau creation on the Montreux waterfront, with balconies, meticulous service and a good deal of style; it's a "garni" place (without restaurant), so prices are lower than they might otherwise be. ❺ –❻

Hostel

Auberge de Jeunesse (HI hostel) Passage de l'Auberge 8, Territet ☎021 963 49 34, ⓦwww.youthhostel.ch. Good hostel located 1500m east of Montreux centre, beside Territet train station (slow trains only) and near the L'Eaudine stop on bus #1. Dorm bed Fr.30. Mid-Feb to mid-Nov. ❶

The Town

Aside from rubbing shoulders with the hoi polloi of international tourism amidst the thronging honky-tonk of Grand-Rue and Avenue de Casino – everyone looking at everyone else wondering where all the rich people are – there's actually precious little to do in Montreux; it's worth taking time for the lakeside stroll along the flowered promenades. Backing onto the Place du Marché, with impressive views across the water to the Dents-du-Midi, stands the town's most popular photo-op: a flamboyant statue in bronze of long-time local resident **Freddie Mercury**. His group Queen first recorded an album in Montreux in 1978 and returned many times afterwards, Freddie eventually buying an apartment on the Territet waterfront (now private property), where he spent his last few months in 1991.

Associations with rock music continue when you reach the **Casino**, on Rue du Théâtre: this grating modern building replaced the grand original, which opened in 1883 and was burned to the ground on December 4, 1971, during a concert by Frank Zappa and the Mothers of Invention. During the show, someone in the audience let off a rocket-flare, which immediately set the ceiling on fire; everyone got out without injury, but the building continued to burn all night. Ian Gillan, lead singer of the band Deep Purple, who were holed up in a hotel nearby, watched the flames leaping into the sky and was thus inspired to write his seminal rock classic "Smoke On The Water".

△ The Château de Chillon

Walks around Montreux

There's a two-hour **walking tour** of the town, which leaves from beside the *débar-cadère* (April–Sept Wed–Sat 10am; Fr.10); check in advance about the availability of an English-speaking guide, and beware too that the walk will take you up the mountainous slopes into the Old Town and down again.

Alternatively, the other side of the tourist office's **"Poets' Ramble"** brochure on Vevey (see p.154; Fr.2) has a similar map outlining a long route from bench to bench all across hilly Montreux; each bench is dedicated to a particular writer or philosopher with some connection either to Montreux or to that particular location, and at each one, you can press a button to hear a short extract of their writings while enjoying the view. The walk can take anything from 3 to 5 hours.

The zigzagging streets and hillside terraces of the steep Old Town above the train station provide marginally more interest. A group of eighteenth-century buildings houses the modest **Musée de Vieux-Montreux**, 40 Rue de la Gare (April–Oct daily 10am–noon & 2–5pm; Fr.6; SMP; Ⓦ www.museemontreux.ch), illustrating the town's history.

Eating and drinking

There are plenty of inexpensive places to **eat and drink** around the station on Avenue des Alpes offering meals for Fr.13–15, including some with lake-view terraces: *Brasserie des Alpes*, at no. 23, has pasta staples, while *Restaurant City*, at no. 37, and *Migros*, 49 Avenue du Casino, are both self-service. In the Old Town, check out the fondue and Swiss dishes at *Caveau des Vignerons*, 30 Rue Industrielle; or take a chance with the home-style fare – tripe, sauerkraut and all – at the local diner variously entitled *La Corsaz*, *La Petite Brasserie Alsacienne* or *Le Flamm's* at Rue de la Corsaz 24. *Confiserie Zürcher*, 45 Avenue du Casino (☎021 963 59 63), is Montreux's most venerable old tearoom (since 1894), perfectly situated with plate-glass windows for crowd-watching, a patisserie for exquisite cakey creations and a restaurant section with mid-priced *menus*. The most appealing place to eat is the fantasy *Palais Oriental*, 14 Quai du Casino (☎021 963 12 71); Arabic/Persian meals start from Fr.25, with plenty for veggies, or you could just savour the lakeside views over a Moroccan mint tea. If you've got a spare Fr.150, take a taxi to the unassuming *Le Pont de Brent*, in the nearby suburb of Brent (☎021 964 52 30), which has three Michelin stars for the excellence of its cuisine and its service (closed Sun & Mon, late July, Christmas and New Year).

Château de Chillon

There are seven pillars of Gothic mould,
In Chillon's dungeons deep and old,
There are seven columns massy and grey,
Dim with a dull imprison'd ray,
A sunbeam which hath lost its way...

Lord Byron, *The Prisoner of Chillon*

The climax of a journey around Lake Geneva is the stunning thirteenth-century **CHÂTEAU DE CHILLON** (daily: April–Sept 9am–6pm; March & Oct 9.30am–5pm; Nov–Feb 10am–4pm; Fr.7; SMP; Ⓦ www.chillon.ch). This impressive specimen, among the best-preserved medieval castles in Europe, is in Veytaux, only about 3km south of Montreux; whether you opt for the

45-minute shoreline walk, bus #1 from Vevey or Montreux, a bike, or best of all a boat (which run year-round), your first glimpse of the castle is unforgettable – an elegant, turreted pile jutting out into the water, framed by trees and the craggy mountains. You could easily spend a half-day soaking up the atmosphere.

Some history

Although the scenery all around the castle is impressive enough, the **location** of the building is more impressive still – and is the key to its history. The mountains in front of the castle fall directly into the lake, with only the narrowest of through-routes between the sheer rock wall and the water. Directly opposite the defile, a razor-edge, sheer-sided islet rises from the water, of which only the very top is visible. This is where Chillon sits: if you were to drain the lake, the castle would teeter above an incredible drop of over 300m, as high as the Eiffel Tower. Such depths are cold and the lake's weather is capricious, making attack from open water extremely unlikely. Equally, the road is narrow, the heights are virtually unscaleable, and there's no other way to pass, making it impossible to avoid the castle. Whoever controlled the castle could control the traffic, and exact tolls from a position of unassailable security.

In **Bronze Age** times, there was no path around the lake: travellers had to climb the steep, 200m slopes at Chillon to a village on the heights above, then drop back down to rejoin the path. The **Romans** cut a narrow ledge along the lakeshore, and also opened up the Grand-St-Bernard pass over the Alps further south, turning the road past the unfortified islet just offshore into the only route connecting northern and southern Europe through the mountains. By the **Middle Ages**, the quantity of traffic meant the road had to be widened and also that a form of toll could be set up. The village above was abandoned in favour of a new town (*ville neuve*, today's Villeneuve) built on open, accessible land a little way south on the valley floor. First surviving mention of a "guardian of the stronghold of Chillun" dates from 1150.

The Counts of **Savoy**, particularly Pierre (1203–68), made Chillon a princely residence, also developing Villeneuve into a major trading centre which poured tolls and customs duties into Chillon's coffers; in 1283, on average, one horse rider and perhaps a dozen foot travellers were crossing the Grand-St-Bernard pass every hour of daylight, on every day of the year. Pierre's architects and engineers transformed Chillon, rebuilding the half facing the shore as a fortress with three strong towers and a keep, and filling the half facing the water with grand halls and royal apartments.

As the Savoyards began to threaten the Habsburgs, Chillon became their military and naval headquarters. The castle was both the centre of court life and a much-feared prison: when **plague** broke out in Villeneuve in 1348, the town's Jews were accused of plotting with Christian accomplices to poison the water supply, and large numbers of both were tortured in Chillon's dungeons. By this time, the Gotthard Pass further east was in use, and the transfer of traffic away from Chillon and the Grand-St-Bernard led to the castle's terminal decline as a military fortress, although it remained handy as a secure jail. In 1530, the Savoyards imprisoned a scholar, **François Bonivard**, at Chillon for inciting the Genevois people to form an alliance with the Swiss against Savoy. They left him shackled to a pillar in the dungeons for six years, until his release in 1536, when the **Bernese** army took control.

Fortunately for posterity, Chillon became a quiet backwater. In 1816, after Vaud had won independence from Bern, **Byron** (aged 28) and **Shelley** (24) visited the castle on their tour of the lake. A guide took them into the dungeons where Bonivard had been shackled and wove enough of a tale around him, and around the castle's history, to catch the poets' imagination. In his Ouchy hotel, Byron scribbled out his *Prisoner of Chillon*, a long narrative poem supposedly spoken by Bonivard (but entirely fictitious throughout), which celebrates the cause of individual liberty, and which brought Chillon to the attention of the wealthy tourists who were starting to explore the Alps. Archeologists and historians launched renovations of the crumbling infrastructure in the late nineteenth century, which restored a great deal of the castle's original grandeur. Work to maintain the castle continues today.

The château

As throughout history, the **road** passes outside the castle walls – these days, it's the Montreux–Villeneuve highway, served by bus #1 (the *autoroute* clings to the hillside high above). The eighteenth-century **gatehouse** is supported on stilts, replacing the original drawbridge. At the ticket window you'll get a follow-the-numbers pamphlet, which plunges you straight down into the vaulted and atmospheric **dungeons** (rooms 4–7) where the dukes of Savoy imprisoned François Bonivard: he was manacled to the fifth pillar along, which still bears a ring and a length of chain. Bonivard wrote that the dungeon was excavated to below the water-line, and Byron also wrote about the damp, but the room is in fact above the water and quite airy. The Irish novelist Maria Edgeworth, visiting in 1820, perhaps missed the point when she brightly chipped in: "If I were to take lodgings in a dungeon I should prefer this to any I have ever seen because it is high and dry with beautiful groined arches and no bad smells." She also noted that Byron's name was cut into the third pillar of the dungeon, as it still is, and that the guide remembered his visit four years previously. A grille in the external wall gives onto the lake, facilitating a rapid exit by rowing boat should things have ever got nasty up above.

The real wonder of the castle lies in the rooms upstairs, gloriously grand knights' halls, secret twisting passages between lavish bedchambers, gothic windows with dreamy views, a frescoed chapel, and more. The **Grand Kitchen** (room 8) still has its original wooden ceiling and two massive oak pillars, installed around 1260. The **Bernese Bedchamber** (room 10) has original bird and ribbon decorations dating from the 1580s, while the expansive **Hall of Arms** (room 12), complete with fireplace and windows over the lake, is covered with escutcheons of the Bernese bailiffs. The **Lord's Chamber** adjacent (room 13) retains its original thirteenth- and fourteenth-century wall paintings, rustic scenes of animals in an orchard with St George slaying the dragon on the chimneypiece. The **chapel** (room 18) features an impression of the full glory of the fourteenth-century decoration, with slides projected onto the partly decorated walls. Next door, the breathtaking **Great Hall of the Count** (room 19) has slender black marble pillars, shimmering chequered wall decoration, a coffered ceiling dating from the fifteenth century, and four windows over the lake topped by a beautiful four-leafed clover design.

Above Montreux

Montreux's train station is served by three different gauges of track. As well as the mainline CFF trains running west along the lake and south into the Valais, there are two different narrow-gauge lines operated by **MOB** (Montreux–Oberland-Bernois; Ⓦwww.mob.ch) climbing up into the hills above Montreux that offer spectacular viewpoints, excellent hill walking, and panoramic rides through the countryside towards the high Alps of the Bernese Oberland.

The smaller line has creaking trains winding their laborious way northeast up to the giant Rochers-de-Naye summit (Eurail not valid, InterRail gets half-price, and the Swiss Pass is free to Caux, with a 25 percent discount from there to Rochers). Emerging from a series of corkscrew tunnels you come to **GLION**, an eyrie of a village perched amidst fields of narcissi directly above Montreux, with jaw-dropping views over the lake and the Rhône. There are a couple of luxury old-world hotels up here, but the more affordable *Hôtel des Alpes Vaudoises*, on Rue du Bugnon and with its own train station (☏021 963 20 76, Ⓦ www.montreux-mountain.ch; ❸; closed Nov–March), is just as characterful and tranquil a place to unwind. A steep **funicular** also serves Glion from Territet on the lakeside below.

Further up on the train line is **CAUX**, home to the Conference Centre for Moral Re-Armament, the dramatically sited and turreted headquarters of a rather odd collective which seeks to ease global political and economic strife through personal religious reconciliation. After another half-hour, trains reach the rugged vantage point of **ROCHERS-DE-NAYE** (2045m), with suitably incredible views over the lake, plenty of hiking trails over the grassy hilltops and the basic *Plein-Roc* restaurant.

The Golden Pass line

The more important MOB narrow-gauge line above Montreux climbs northwest through the steep hills into Canton Bern (Eurail, InterRail and Swiss Pass all qualify for free travel). This is the route of the **Golden Pass**, one of the showcase journeys of Swiss railways (see p.30) – you must pay a small supplement on the special panoramic trains, but not on the ordinary ones. A little above Montreux is **CHAMBY**, one end of the Chemin de Fer-Musée (Museum Railway; May–Oct Sat & Sun 10am–6pm; Fr.14; SMP; Ⓦ www.blonay-chamby.ch), which has steam trains running on a 3km stretch of track to and from **Blonay**, on the Vevey–Les Pléiades line (see p.156), as well as a depot full of old rolling stock.

The trains from Montreux continue up on a spectacular route, coiling through the village of **LES AVANTS** – starting point of a number of beautiful walks – to **Montbovon**, junction point for trains north into the countryside around **Gruyères** (see p.139). The Golden Pass line continues east to **Château d'Oex** and **Gstaad** (see p.317), but runs out at **Zweisimmen**, where you must change for connections to Interlaken and Bern.

Travel details

Trains

Bulle to: Gruyères (hourly; 10min); Montbovon (for Montreux or Gstaad; hourly; 30min); Palézieux (for Lausanne; hourly; 40min).

Coppet to: Céligny (hourly; 5min); Geneva (hourly; 20min); Nyon (hourly; 10min).

Gruyères to: Bulle (for Fribourg; hourly; 10min); Montbovon (for Montreux or Gstaad; hourly; 20min); Palézieux (for Lausanne; hourly; 50min).

Lausanne to: Aigle (every 30min; 30min); Basel (twice hourly; 2hr 35min); Bern (hourly; 1hr 10min); Biel/Bienne (hourly; 1hr 10min); Brig (twice hourly; 1hr 40min); La Chaux-de-Fonds (hourly; 1hr 30min); Delémont (hourly; 1hr 50min); Echallens (every 30min; 20min); Fribourg (twice hourly; 45min); Geneva (4 hourly; 35min); Interlaken Ost (hourly; 2hr 10min); Martigny (every 30min; 50min); Montreux (twice hourly; 20min); Neuchâtel (hourly; 50min); Nyon (every 30min; 25min); Palézieux (for Gruyères; hourly; 15min); Sierre (twice hourly; 1hr 15min); Sion (twice hourly; 1hr 5min); Vallorbe (hourly; 45min); Vevey (twice hourly; 15min); Yverdon (hourly; 25min);

Zürich (hourly; 2hr 25min).

Montreux to: Caux (hourly; 25min); Geneva (every 30min; 1hr 10min); Gstaad (hourly; 1hr 20min); Lausanne (4 hourly; 20min); Martigny (every 30min; 30min); Montbovon (for Gruyères; hourly; 45min); Vevey (4 hourly; 7min); Zürich (hourly; 2hr 45min).

Nyon to: Céligny (hourly; 7min); Coppet (hourly; 10min); Geneva (3 hourly; 25min); Lausanne (every 30min; 25min); Neuchâtel (hourly; 1hr); St Cergue (every 30min; 35min); Yverdon (hourly; 25min).

Palézieux to: Bulle (hourly; 40min); Gruyères (hourly; 50min); Lausanne (hourly; 15min).

Vevey to: Geneva (every 30min; 1hr 5min); Lausanne (4 hourly; 10min); Martigny (every 30min; 25min); Montreux (4 hourly; 7min); Zürich (hourly; 2hr 40min).

Buses

Bulle to: Fribourg (hourly; 30min); Gruyères (3 daily; 20min).

Gruyères to: Bulle (3 daily; 20min); Moléson (every 2hr; 15min).

Montreux to: Chillon (every 10min; 10min); Vevey (every 10min; 20min).

Vevey to: Chillon (every 10min; 30min); Montreux (every 10min; 20min).

Boats

(Following is a summary of May–Sept summer services; fewer boats run in other months, generally Sat & Sun only, if at all.)

Chillon (Château) to: Lausanne (3 daily; 1hr 45min); Montreux (4–5 daily; 20min); Vevey (3 daily; 35min).

Coppet to: Geneva (2–3 daily; 45min); Lausanne (2–3 daily; 2hr 45min).

Lausanne (Ouchy) to: Céligny (1 daily; 2hr 30min); Chillon (3 daily; 1hr 45min); Coppet (2–3 daily; 2hr 45min); Evian, France (10–15 daily; 40min); Geneva (3 daily; 3hr 30min); Montreux (5–6 daily; 1hr 20min); Nyon (3–4 daily; 2hr 10min); Vevey (5–6 daily; 1hr).

Montreux to: Chillon (4–5 daily; 20min); Geneva (3 daily; 5hr); Lausanne (5–6 daily; 1hr 20min); St-Gingolph (3–4 daily; 50min); Vevey (5–6 daily; 20min).

Nyon to: Geneva (4–7 daily; 1hr–1hr 30min); Lausanne (3–4 daily; 2hr 10min); Yvoire, France (6 daily; 20min).

Vevey to: Chillon (3 daily; 35min); Geneva (3 daily; 4hr 30min); Lausanne (5–6 daily; 1hr); Montreux (5–6 daily; 20min); St-Gingolph (6–7 daily; 1hr 20min).

The Arc Jurassien

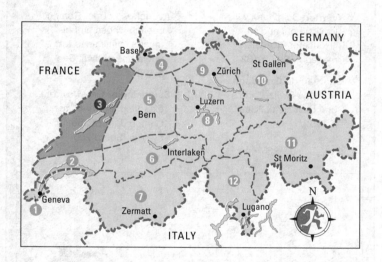

CHAPTER 3

Highlights

✳ **The three lakes** Ferries crisscross their way between the scenic lakes of Neuchâtel, Murten and Biel/Bienne. See p.172

✳ **Neuchâtel** Attractive, graceful city with a fine old quarter. See p.172

✳ **Yverdon** Sci-fi fans will love the outlandish "House of Elsewhere" museum. See p.182

✳ **Château de Grandson** Perhaps Switzerland's grandest castle. See p.185

✳ **Vallée de Joux** High, remote Jura valley, perfect for lonely hikes and cross-country skiing. See p.190

✳ **Payerne** A superb Romanesque abbey dominates this quiet country town. See p.192

✳ **Avenches** Former Roman capital, whose amphi-theatre is still used for opera and shows. See p.192

✳ **Saignelégier** Gateway to exploring the far-flung Canton Jura on foot or by bike. See p.200

The Arc Jurassien

The northwest frontier dividing Switzerland from France is the **Jura** mountain range – line after line of long, northeast-southwest ridges that trap between them a succession of sausage-shaped lakes. The Jura are nothing like the Alps: much lower to start with (rarely more than 1500m), with none of the majesty but all of the ruggedness. Scrubby rounded hilltops and deep, parallel valleys are dotted by windswept, privately minded villages nursing a weatherbeaten Gallic culture cut off for centuries from both France and Switzerland. The whole **Arc Jurassien**, which takes in the highlands of the Jura Vaudois, the region's three largest lakes – the Lac de Neuchâtel, Murtensee and Bielersee/Lac de Bienne, which lie clustered together at the foot of the Jura range – Canton Neuchâtel, and Canton Jura in the far northwest, is well off the beaten track of most visitors to Switzerland. Guidebooks and brochures tend to skimp on detail, since it doesn't easily fit into the usual Swiss pigeonholes. If you choose to venture out here, you'll find a minimum of tourist hype and few actual sights other than the main towns of **Neuchâtel** and **Biel/Bienne**, but what exists in abundance is virtually untouched nature – and this is why the Swiss know and love the place.

Once you leave the lakes and the lowlands, **public transport** isn't easy, and even main roads are a relatively recent innovation. If you don't have a car, the best way to get around is by bike, or, if your legs can take it, on foot. Tourist offices in the area know their clientele and can direct you onto any number of cycling trails or footpaths that reach all scenic spots. On p.226, we've outlined a long, multi-day **walk** through the area, which starts near Zürich, winds through the whole Jura region and ends up at Lake Geneva.

The majority of the area covered by this chapter is francophone, and yet it straddles the **linguistic divide**, the *Röstigraben*, between French- and German-speaking Switzerland (see p.630). As many places or regions have two names, travelling to and fro across the language border can get confusing; glossy publicity material may use the German word *Seeland* ("Lake District") or *Drei-Seen-Region* alongside *La Région des Trois-Lacs* and the recent marketing brainwave "Watch Valley" to refer to the whole area, but since local tourist offices and bus and boat timetables tend to stick to either French or German, it's useful to be aware of dual naming.

Neuchâtel, the main town of the region, is entirely French-speaking, but German speakers call it **Neuenburg** and expect you to understand; the Lac de Neuchâtel is one and the same as the Neuenburgersee. Nearby is the small majority-German-speaking lake resort of **Murten**, known to French speakers as **Morat**, sitting alongside the Murtensee/Lac de Morat. Just south of here the language border weaves between communities, and you'll find, for instance, the

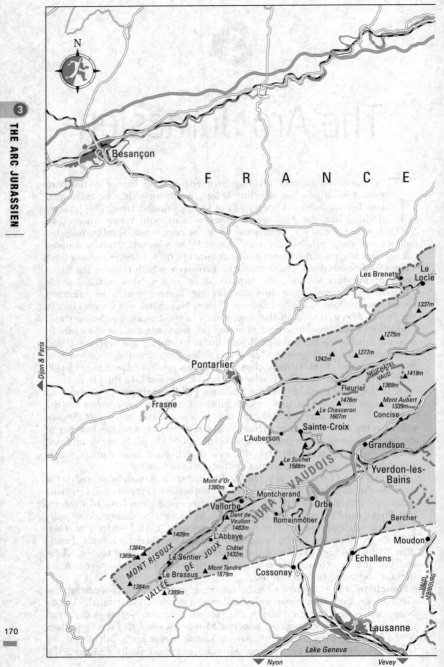

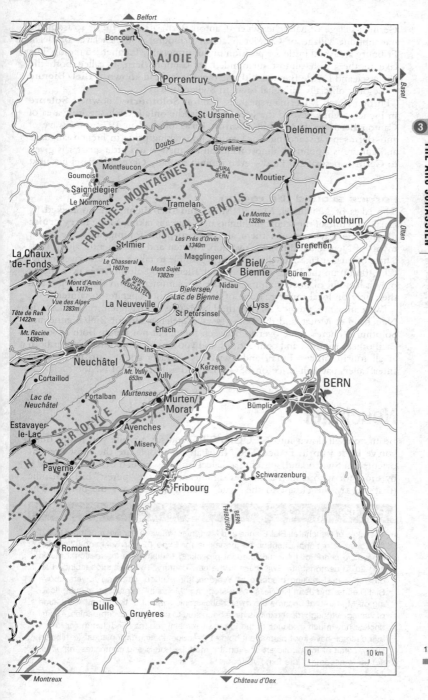

▲ *Belfort*

Boncourt

AJOIE

▶ *Basel*

Porrentruy

St Ursanne

Delémont

Doubs

Glovelier

JURA BERN

Moutier

Montfaucon

Goumois

FRANCHES-MONTAGNES

Saignelégier

Le Noirmont

Tramelan

JURA BERNOIS

▲ *Le Montoz 1328m*

Solothurn

▶ *Olten*

St-Imier

Les Prés d'Orvin 1340m

Grenchen

La Chaux-de-Fonds

▲ *Le Chasseral 1607m*

Magglingen

Biel/Bienne

Büren

▲ *Mont Sujet 1382m*

BERN NEUCHÂTEL

Nidau

▲ *Mont d'Amin 1417m*

Bielersee/ Lac de Bienne

▲ *Vue des Alpes 1283m*

La Neuveville

Lyss

Tête de Ran 1422m ▲

St Petersinsel

▲ *Mt. Racine 1439m*

Erlach

Ins

Kerzers

Neuchâtel

▲ *Mt. Vully 653m*

Vully

BERN

Cortaillod

Bümpliz

Lac de Neuchâtel

Portalban

Murtensee

Murten/Morat

Estavayer-le-Lac

THE BROŸE

Avenches

Misery

Schwarzenburg

Payerne

BERN FRIBOURG

Fribourg

Romont

Bulle

Gruyères

0		10 km

▼ *Montreux*

▼ *Château d'Oex*

German village of Münchenwiler (Canton Bern) a kilometre or so from the francophone village of Cressier (Canton Fribourg). Tiny enclaves of Bern, Fribourg and Vaud jostle for position in this impossibly fragmented region. The lake to the north, almost surrounded by Canton Bern, is called both the Bielersee and Lac de Bienne, with the town at its head known as **Biel/Bienne** – the only officially bilingual town in Switzerland.

Further north is German-speaking Canton **Solothurn** (known as **Soleure** in French), while beyond the **Jura Bernois**, the only French-speaking area of Canton Bern, lies francophile **Canton Jura**, founded in 1979 on a wave of anti-Bern separatist feeling. For Canton Jura, taking pride in French language and culture is a political, almost nationalistic, matter, and little quarter is given to German-ness of any kind – even though strongly Germanic Basel lies next door.

Ferries around the region

The lakes of Neuchâtel, Murten/Morat and Biel/Bienne are connected by canals, and one of the scenic highlights of the area is taking a long **ferry cruise** (3–4hr one-way) between them all. Point-to-point routings link the major towns of Neuchâtel, Estavayer, Yverdon, Murten and Biel/Bienne, along with a host of smaller lakeside villages. It's also possible to take a peaceful river-cruise (2hr 40min) up the River Aare from Biel/Bienne to Solothurn. As ever, there's only a handful of boats running outside the summer season (June–Sept), and then only on local routings: none of the long cruises operates in winter.

Two companies provide service: the LNM (⬤www.navig.ch) on the Lacs de Neuchâtel et Morat, and the BSG (⬤www.bielersee.ch) for Biel/Bienne and Solothurn. There's some overlap between them, but not much. Both advertise each other's routings and connections, and you can pick up timetables for both at all tourist offices. Eurail and Swiss Pass holders go free on both, while InterRailers pay half-price on BSG boats and full price on LNM.

Neuchâtel

Beam yourself down into **NEUCHÂTEL**, and for a while you might think you've landed up in France. The Neuchâtelois people are the most French-oriented in Switzerland, speaking a dialect of Swiss-French that is celebrated – by those for whom such a thing is significant – as the "purest" in Romandie (that's to say, the closest to the "true" French spoken over the border). The

---

Expo 02

The lakes of Neuchâtel, Biel/Bienne and Murten/Morat were, for five months in 2002, the focus of national attention as the venue for **Expo 02** (⬤www.expo.02.ch), an innovative series of futuristic, thought-provoking exhibits and international music and art to demonstrate Swissness in the new century. The best sites included an ethereal cloud-making machine at Yverdon, three huge, glittering towers above Biel/Bienne, and Jean Nouvel's show-stopping "Monolith", a giant steel cube floating off Murten that became the mysterious, iconic symbol of the Expo. At the time of writing, although most exhibits have been sold to collectors or companies, it's still unclear how much evidence of the Expo will remain; you may find that major towns in the region have kept permanent hold of the huge floating "arteplages" (exhibition sites), some of the public art or even the modular hotels and campsites that were set up to accommodate Expo visitors.

town's air of dignity and easy grace is fuelled by a profusion of French-influenced architecture: many of the seventeenth- and eighteenth-century buildings are made from local yellow sandstone, a fact which led Alexandre Dumas to describe Neuchâtel as looking "like a toytown carved out of butter". And the modern and disarmingly Gallic street life of pavement cafés and studenty night bars, upscale street markets and hip designer boutiques, has the slightly unreal flavour of a town actively seeking influences from beyond its own borders – a rare thing indeed in Switzerland.

The Neuchâtelois, for whom the issue of joining the EU is a matter of the plainest common sense, are perhaps the epitome of the Swiss mystery; they are about as far removed in attitude, values, style and language from the people of Luzern – with whom their future is inextricably linked – to the east, as they are closely related to the people of Dijon – the supposed foreigners – to the west. You get the feeling while in Neuchâtel that the locals have thrown up their hands in disbelief at such injustice, and, ensconced between their broad lake and the mountain border, have sought solace in a life of fine wines, rich foods and French TV while waiting for their compatriots to see sense.

The town's main attractions are its café-lounging Gallic atmosphere and its location, with **boats** weaving to and fro across the lake and the first ridges of the high **Jura** range standing poised over the town. However, the **Musée d'Art** is worth going out of your way to experience, both for its innovative fine-art collection, and for its set of charming eighteenth-century mechanical figurines which demonstrate in understated style the exceptional skills of the Neuchâtel watchmakers of the era.

You may find some leftovers of Neuchâtel's leading role in Expo 02 dotted around town in the form of public exhibits or infrastructure; at the time of writing, it was uncertain what might stay and what would be sold off.

Some history

In 1011, Rudolf III of Burgundy presented a new castle (*neu-châtel*) on the lakeshore to his wife Irmengarde. The first Counts of Neuchâtel were named shortly afterwards, and in 1214 their domain was officially dubbed a city. For three centuries, the **Earldom of Neuchâtel** flourished, and in 1530, the people of Neuchâtel accepted the **Reformation**; their city and territory were proclaimed to be indivisible from then on. Future rulers were required to seek investiture from the citizens.

With increasing power and prestige, Neuchâtel was raised to the level of a **principality** in the seventeenth century. On the death in 1707 of Mary of Orléans, Duchess of Nemours and Princess of Neuchâtel, the people had to choose her successor from among fifteen claimants. They wanted their new prince to be a Protestant, and also to be strong enough to protect their territory but based far enough away to leave them in peace. Louis XIV actively promoted the many French pretenders to the title, but the Neuchâtelois people passed them over in favour of Frederick I, King of Prussia. With the requisite stability assured, Neuchâtel entered its golden age, with commerce, banking and industry (including watchmaking and lace) undergoing steady expansion.

At the turn of the nineteenth century, the Prussian king was defeated by Napoleon and forced to surrender Neuchâtel in order to keep Hanover. Napoleon's marshal, Berthier, became Prince of Neuchâtel, building roads and restoring infrastructure, but never actually setting foot in his domain. After the fall of Napoleon, Frederick III of Prussia reasserted his rights by proposing that Neuchâtel be linked with the other **Swiss** cantons (the better to exert influence over the lot of them). On September 12, 1814, Neuchâtel became the

NEUCHÂTEL

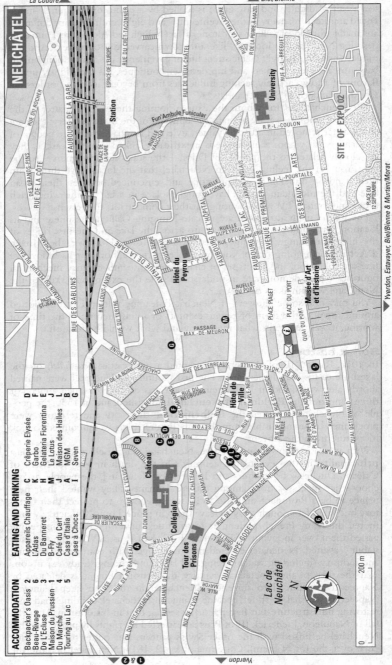

ACCOMMODATION
Backpacker's Oasis 2
Beau-Rivage 6
De L'Ecluse 3
Maison du Prussien 1
Du Marché 4
Touring au Lac 5

EATING AND DRINKING
Appareils Chauffage C Crêperie Elysée D
L'Atlas   F Garbo   K
Du Banneret   E Gelateria Fiorentina H
B-Fly   J Le Lotus   M
Casa d'Italia   A Maison des Halles L
Café du Cerf   I MGM   B
Casa à Chocs   G Seven

21st canton, but confusingly also remained a Prussian principality. It took a bloodless revolution for the region to shake off its princely past and declare itself, in 1848, a **republic** within the Swiss Confederation.

Arrival, information and accommodation

Neuchâtel's **train station** – with bike rental (Mon–Sat 6am–9pm, Sun 6.30am–9pm) and an exchange counter – is perched above the town; it's a walk of about ten minutes, or a short hop by bus, down to the compact lakefront town centre focused around Place Pury, at the foot of the Old Town on a slender stretch of flat ground. The Fun'Ambule **funicular** runs from the station down to the university on Avenue du Premier-Mars. Pury is 100m west of Place du Port, which backs onto the harbour and the *débarcadère*: **boats** arrive at Neuchâtel from all points around the three lakes, including Yverdon, Estavayer, Murten/Morat and Biel/Bienne. The main **post office** is at Place du Port; another is up opposite the train station. There's a **laundry**, Salon Lavoir, at 27 Rue des Moulins (Mon–Fri 7am–8pm, Sat & Sun 8am–8pm).

The **tourist office**, which has information on the city and the canton, is in the Hôtel des Postes building (main post office) on Place du Port (July & Aug Mon–Fri 9am–6.30pm, Sat 9am–4pm, Sun 10am–4pm; rest of year Mon–Fri 9am–noon & 1.30–5.30pm, Sat 9am–noon; ℡032 889 68 90, ⓦwww.ne.ch). Unless you fancy shelling out for your own guide, the only **tours** of town are by tourist mini-train (May–Oct daily; Fr.6).

Neuchâtel is not a grandiose city, and the **accommodation** on offer is serviceable but not spectacular. In addition to a range of hotels, **campsites** either side of Neuchâtel are pretty good: 7km west is *Paradis Plage* in Colombier (℡032 841 24 46; March–Oct), while 5km east at the head of the lake in Marin-Epagnier is *La Tène* (℡032 753 73 40; April–Sept).

Hotels

Beau-Rivage 1 Esplanade du Mont-Blanc ℡032 723 15 15, ⓦwww.beau-rivage-hotel.ch. Top of the range lakefront palace, with double-swanky rooms and views to match. ❽

De L'Ecluse 24 Rue de l'Ecluse ℡032 729 93 10, ⓦwww.hoteldelecluse.ch. Simple, beautiful rooms, characterized by ochre tones, tasteful wrought-iron furniture and stone floors, in this fine small hotel above the town centre. ❸

Maison du Prussien Gor du Vauseyon ℡032 730 54 54, ⓦwww.hotel-prussien.ch. One of Neuchâtel's most characterful choices: a restored sixteenth-century mill beside a stream 2km west of town, with six comfortable, well-appointed wood-beamed rooms and four expensive suites. ❸–❹

Du Marché 4 Place des Halles ℡032 723 23 30,

℡032 723 23 33. The only hotel in the Old Town, with ten pleasant and spacious rooms (none ensuite) overlooking a bustling café-lined square. ❷

Touring au Lac Place Numa-Droz 1 ℡032 725 55 01, ⓦwww.touring-au-lac.ch. Not a tranquil location beside both the harbour and the main road, but with some nice views. Its boxy rooms (some ensuite) are nothing to write home about. ❸–❹

Hostel

Backpacker's Oasis 35 Rue du Suchiez ℡032 731 31 90, ⓦwww.backpacker.ch. Pleasant, well-maintained hostel over 2km west of town at the mouth of the Gorges du Seyon, signposted from the Vauseyon stop on bus #1. Dorms Fr.27. Closed Nov–April. ❶

The Town

Neuchâtel's atmospheric **Old Town** is extremely attractive, and random wanderings through its steep alleys are as good a way as any to appreciate the golden beauty of the architecture, as well as the 140-odd street fountains, a handful of which date from the sixteenth century. From the rather anonymous **Place Pury** – hub of buses and shoppers alike – with the main artery of Rue

From the suburb of **La Coudre**, some 4km east of the town centre and reached on bus #7, a panoramic funicular (ⓦwww.tnneuchatel.ch) rises through thick forests to the village of **CHAUMONT** (1087m). Set on a balcony above Neuchâtel, on the first of the Jura ridges, the viewpoint of Le Signal (1171m), a short walk from the funicular station, offers a vista over the three lakes of Neuchâtel, Murten and Biel/Bienne, with the plateau of Mont Vully rising opposite Murten and a patchwork of fields and forests stretching clear across the Swiss flatlands to the distant snowy fringe of the Bernese Alps. On the clearest of days, with such an unobstructed view across the whole country, it's claimed that you can even make out Mont Blanc and the Matterhorn.

Beside the top station is the *Hôtel Chaumont* (ⓣ032 754 21 75, ⓦwww. hotel-chaumont.ch; ❹), a seminar and golfing hotel with very comfortable, if bland, rooms, great views and plenty of hilltop hiking routes fanning out on all sides.

du Seyon leading northwards, alleys to the west bring you to **Place des Halles**, perpetually filled with talkers and drinkers spilling out of a handful of cafés. The square itself is overlooked by fine Louis XIV architecture: shuttered facades and the turreted orioles of the sixteenth-century **Maison des Halles**. You'll find informal lunchtime *boules* sessions on the nearby Rue du Coq d'Inde, a broad, tranquil courtyard away from the bustle. A two-minute walk east, on Rue de l'Hôpital, is the grand 1790 **Hôtel de Ville** (Town Hall), designed by Louis XVI's chief architect Pierre-Adrien Paris.

The highlights of the Old Town are poised on the very top of the hill, accessed by the steeply winding Rue du Château. The **Collégiale** church (daily 8am–6pm), begun in 1185 and consecrated in 1276, is a graceful example of early Gothic. Stairs from Rue du Château bring you up to the east end of the church, with its three Norman apses. The main entrance, to the west, is crowned by a giant rose window of stained glass. Within the vaulted interior, the nave draws you along to the glowing transept, lit by a lantern tower, and the unique **Cenotaph of the Counts of Neuchâtel** on the north wall of the choir. Begun in 1372, and the only artwork of its kind to survive north of the Alps, the monument comprises fifteen near-life-size painted statues of various knights and ladies from Neuchâtel's past, framed by fifteenth-century arches and gables.

Beside the church is the imposing **château**, begun in the twelfth century and still in use as the offices of the cantonal government: entry is only on 45-minute guided tours, which start from the signposted Door no. 1 (on the hour: April–Sept Mon–Fri 10am–noon & 2–4pm, Sat 10am, 11am & 2–4pm, Sun 2–4pm; free). The nearby turreted **Tour des Prisons** (April–Sept daily 8am–6pm; Fr.1), remains of a medieval bastion, has panoramic views over the town, along with interesting models of Neuchâtel in different eras.

Musée d'Art et d'Histoire
The flagship **Musée d'Art et d'Histoire**, Esplanade Léopold-Robert (Tues–Sun 10am–6pm; Fr.7, free on Wed; SMP; ⓦwww.ne.ch/neuchatel /mahn), and its star attractions, the astonishing Automates Jaquet-Droz (Jaquet-Droz Mechanical Figurines), is unmissable.

The ground floor is devoted to the **historical** collections, with absorbing rooms on the history of Neuchâtel aided by an excellent self-start slide show (in English). Upstairs are the rooms devoted to **fine art**; instead of displaying works by period, or artist, or genre, the collection is grouped by theme, with

The celebrated Monsieur Jaquet-Droz

Pierre Jaquet-Droz (1721–90) was born in La Chaux-de-Fonds into a wealthy local family. After studying theology at university, he returned to Neuchâtel – by then already a centre for clock and watchmaking – and worked to combine his interest in mathematics with the skills of applied mechanics used by the artisans of the watch industry. By the age of 26, he had gained a reputation for technical brilliance, and in 1758 Jaquet-Droz and his father-in-law, a craftsman named Abram Sandoz, travelled to Madrid to show off the skill of Neuchâtelois clockmakers at the Spanish court (Jaquet-Droz's so-called "Shepherd's Clock" is still on display in one of the king of Spain's palace museums).

Jaquet-Droz was by now wealthy enough to retreat from business life and concentrate on problems of applied mathematics, exemplified in his construction of incredibly complex mechanical figurines – the earliest of computers – designed to do particular tasks. He trained his son, Henri-Louis, and a colleague, Jean-Frédéric Leschot, to work with him; together, they produced **the Writer, the Draughtsman** and **the Musician**, and presented all three for the first time to the public in La Chaux-de-Fonds in 1774. Writers of the day reported that people flocked from all over the country to see such extraordinary works of whimsy and technical skill. The same year, the three craftsmen showed their figurines in drawing rooms and royal palaces all across Europe, from London to Russia and Paris to Madrid, receiving high acclaim wherever they went.

Perhaps aware of impending revolutionary violence in France and Switzerland, Jaquet-Droz sold the figurines to a collector in Spain in 1778. After the conflicts, in 1812, they reappeared in Paris and began touring again. Some twenty years later, they became the centrepiece of Martin and Bourquin's "Museum of Illusions", which toured Central Europe until the turn of the century. In 1906, helped by a grant from the Swiss federal government, Neuchâtel bought the figurines back, and they have been on display in the town's museum ever since, in virtually the same condition as when they were first made, 230 years ago.

the various rooms labelled Nature, Civilization, The Sacred, and so on. In an inspired piece of creative design harking back to earlier centuries, the curators have crammed each room with art from floor to ceiling, with medieval still lifes, contemporary abstractions, Impressionistic indulgences and more all mounted higgledy-piggledy, inducing you to make dynamic connections between diverse works. In each room you can climb podia – each one hung all round with paintings – in order to get a better view of the works hung high on the four walls.

But the most extraordinary exhibits are kept in a room at the rear of the ground floor: the **Automates Jaquet-Droz**, three mechanical figurines built to the most exacting technical standards by a Neuchâtelois watchmaker in the 1770s (see box) and still in perfect working order today. The three – the Draughtsman, the Writer and the Musician – are displayed static behind glass, with a fascinating accompanying slide-show in English by way of explanation, but if you can you should really time your visit for the first Sunday of the month, when they are brought to life for a demonstration (2pm, 3pm & 4pm only). The **Draughtsman** is a child sitting at a mahogany desk and holding a piece of paper with his left hand; his right hand, holding a pencil, performs extraordinarily complex motions to produce intricate little pictures of a dog, the god Eros in a chariot pulled by a butterfly, or a noble profile of Louis XV. The **Writer**, a chubby-cheeked little boy, also sits at a mahogany desk, with a goose quill in his right hand and a tiny pot of ink nearby for dipping. He writes in a florid and chunky style, and staggeringly enough, can be programmed to produce any text of up to forty characters. While he writes, his eyes follow the words across the page. But perhaps the most charming of the three is the **Musician**, a gracious young girl with slender and dexterous fingers who plays a small organ – a real instrument, not a disguised musical-box. As her fingers strike the keys to produce the notes and her eyes, head and body move subtly from side to side in time, her chest rises and falls delicately in an imitation of rhythmic breathing. Her melodies were composed in the early 1770s by Henri-Louis Jaquet-Drozén, a fleeting and unique auditory time capsule from pre-Revolutionary Europe.

Eating and drinking

With such a heavy French influence, Neuchâtel takes **eating and drinking** seriously, with dozens of pavement cafés and relaxed bistros all over the centre. Local specialities, best sampled at places like the *Hôtel du Marché* (see below) include tripe in wine, *tomme panée* (baked cheese) and fresh lake fish; a *fondue neuchâteloise* takes full advantage of the nearby vineyards, with local whites splashed liberally into the bubbling pot for an especially heady cheese-dipping experience. In a quiet Old Town courtyard off the main street is *Gelateria Fiorentina*, 31 Rue des Moulins, a perfect place to relax with an ice cream.

Restaurants

L'Atlas 14 Rue Fleury ☎ 032 724 11 98. Tiny Moroccan restaurant tucked away on an Old Town alley, with Fr.13–15 *menus*, authentic couscous and *tajine*, Moroccan wine, and sweet mint tea as it should be.

Du Banneret 1 Rue Fleury ☎ 032 725 28 61. Peaceful little spot in a crook of the Old Town's steep alleys, opposite a fountain at the foot of Rue du Château. The food is consistently good – regional specialities, lightly prepared, with fresh fish a staple. *Menus* around Fr.23. Closed Sun.

Crêperie Elysée 26 Rue des Moulins. Old Town joint for crêpes with dozens of fillings to choose from, from a Fr.4 snack up to a Fr.13 meal. Closed Sun.

Hôtel du Marché Place des Halles ☎ 032 723 23 30. Central Old Town landmark, serving hearty Swiss and French cuisine for Fr.20 or so. Closed Sun & Mon lunch.

Hôtel Touring au Lac Place Numa-Droz. Overlooking the harbour and the open lake, one of the best terraces for croissant-and-*renversée* breakfasts, mellow salad lunches and long sundowner *apéros*. Excellent fresh fish is an added attraction.

Le Lotus 4 Rue de l'Ancien Hôtel-de-Ville ☎ 032 724 27 44. Upper-floor Cambodian restaurant, with high-quality Asian cuisine for Fr.20-odd (*menus*) or Fr.30 (à la carte). Closed Sun.

Maison des Halles Place des Halles ☎ 032 724 31 41. Not to be confused with the *Hôtel du Marché*, this is in the fairy-tale turreted building

next door – an excellent wood-fired pizzeria down below (from Fr.13), and perhaps the town's most refined *haute cuisine* restaurant (closed Mon, Sat lunch & Sun) up above.

Maison du Prussien Gor du Vauseyon ☎ 032 730 54 54; see p.175. One of Neuchâtel's gourmet highlights, with characterful French-oriented *menus* for as little as Fr.30 or so. Closed Sun.

Bars and clubs

Appareils de Chauffage et de Cuisine 37 Rue des Moulins. Wonderful old place converted from a shop ("Heaters and Cookers") into a friendly, sociable Old Town bar.

B-Fly 16 Faubourg de l'Hôpital. Very popular techno and house club. Thurs–Sun only.

Café du Cerf 4 Rue de l'Ancien Hôtel-de-Ville. Lively central watering hole, serving beers from around the world.

Casa d'Italia 1 Rue Prébarreau. Night café behind the château – avoid the *Cobra* cabaret in the same building. Closed Mon.

Case à Chocs 16 Quai Godet. Top club in town, with innovative DJ nights of everything from ska to acid jazz and drum'n'bass, plus occasional live bands. Thurs–Sat only.

Garbo 7 Rue des Chavannes. Classy night café in the Old Town, with dancefloor. Closed Mon.

MGM 45 Rue des Moulins. Posey night-bar. Closed Mon.

Seven 15 Avenue de la Gare. Minor glitz at this disco/live-band venue. Fri & Sat only.

Around Canton Neuchâtel

Above Neuchâtel, roads and train tracks rise steeply into the folds and ridges of the Jura range – known within the canton as the **Montagnes Neuchâteloises**. Like the continuation of the mountains to either side, this is wild and hilly country, not exactly mountainous compared with the high Alps further south but still characterized by remote, windswept settlements and deep, rugged valleys. It is also the heartland of the celebrated Swiss watchmaking industry, centred on the once-famous towns of **La Chaux-de-Fonds** and **Le Locle**, which both rely heavily on their horological past to draw in visitors. The Doubs river marks the border with France, set down in a gorge and forming along its path an impressive waterfall, the **Saut du Doubs**, and lake, the **Lac des Brenets**, both of them together making a pleasant day out.

La Chaux-de-Fonds

LA CHAUX-DE-FONDS is an oddity. To start with, more people live there than in Neuchâtel, although you'd never guess it from the sparsity of street life. Then it touts itself as Switzerland's highest city, though at 1000m that's no great shakes, and with just 37,000 people it would barely qualify as a town in most countries. Strangest of all, however, is the fact that this rather unprepossessing place was once a household name across Europe and the world, the humming centre of the Swiss **watchmaking** industry, which in its heyday of the late eighteenth and nineteenth centuries was largely responsible for establishing Switzerland's reputation – which survives today – for producing refined luxury goods of the highest quality. The town was burned to the ground in 1794, and was rebuilt shortly after on a strict grid system, characterized by enormously long, very broad parallel boulevards. Over the decades, the authorities have placed a high value on modern and postmodern architecture, with glass-built towers featuring prominently. This combination has given La Chaux-de-Fonds today the rather unfortunate air – very odd for Switzerland, and frankly bizarre for such an historic place – of a new town transported from somewhere in anonymous Middle America. It's rather an exhausting place to walk around, even though its museums definitely merit a visit.

If you have your own transport and are approaching from Neuchâtel (whether on the winding minor road or through the climbing motorway tunnels), make sure you stop for a while at the **Vue des Alpes** (1283m), a magnificent viewpoint just short of La Chaux-de-Fonds, giving a broad panorama of the Swiss plateau backed by the snowy Bernese Alps.

Arrival, information and accommodation

The **train station** (with change counter daily 5.45am–8.30pm, and bike rental) is reasonably central, set back 100m from the main Avenue Robert, which cuts a perfectly straight northeast–southwest groove through the centre of town. In the tall Espacité cylindrical glass tower on the north side of Avenue Robert some 500m east of the station you'll find the **tourist office** (July & Aug Mon–Fri 9am–6.30pm, Sat 10am–4pm; rest of year Mon–Fri 9am–noon & 1.30–5.30pm, Sat 9am–noon; ☎032 919 68 95, ⓦwww.ne.ch). In front of the tower is a monumental nineteenth-century fountain, central landmark of the town.

The town's **buses** (ⓦwww.trn.ch) run on circular routes, and all pass in front of the train station. A day ticket is Fr.5. After 7pm on weekdays, and all day at weekends, some route numbers don't operate and others combine in a very un-Swiss way to make completely new route numbers. Alternatively, you could book at the tourist office for a two-hour tour of town by **horse-drawn carriage** (May–Oct daily; Fr.15 per person).

The *Bois du Couvent* four-star **campsite** (T032 913 25 55) is in a nice forest setting about 1500m southeast of the station, but no buses stop nearby. The *France* **hotel** is next to the station (T032 913 11 16, F032 913 18 49; ❶–❷), a "garni" place with slightly shabby rooms both ensuite and not; almost 1km east off Rue de la Balance is *Maharajah* (T032 968 03 40; ❶–❷), with a few rooms above an Indian/Pakistani restaurant. The pleasant *Fleur-de-Lys*, 13 Avenue Robert by the fountain (T032 913 37 31, Wwww.fleur-de-lys.ch; ❹), has been recently upgraded, as has the stylish *Premier Mars*, Rue du 1er Mars 7a (T032 968 28 32, F032 968 90 22; ❸). On the approach to town is *Motel du Jura*, 50 Rue de l'Hôtel de Ville (T032 968 28 22, F032 968 92 15; ❷), with free parking.

The Town

La Chaux-de-Fonds' main draw is the impressive **Musée international d'horlogerie**, 29 Rue des Musées (Tues–Sun: June–Sept 10am–6pm; Oct–May 10am–noon & 2–5pm; Fr.8; SMP; Wwww.mih.ch), about 500m east of the station, set back 150m from Avenue Robert. Even if you don't find clocks and watches the height of inspiration, there'll be something in this award-winning subterranean museum to divert you for an hour or two. There are hundreds of items on display, tracing the art of keeping time from the very beginnings up to the most recent models, with a concentration of exceptionally beautiful pieces from La Chaux's heyday in the eighteenth and nineteenth centuries. Upstairs you'll find various atomic and electronic clocks, including one that keeps time to within 0.000,000,000,0001 of a second per year. There are also various videos which show the history and technical side of horology, as well as a few diversions such as a machine which tests reaction times in fractions of a second. In one corner local watchmaking firms (which are also the world market leaders) put their latest bejewelled creations on display – but without price tags. In the park outside is a giant tubular-steel **carillon** with digital readout – all the rage when it was built in 1980 – that chimes every quarter-hour.

Immediately adjacent is the **Musée des Beaux-Arts**, 33 Rue des Musées (Tues–Sun 10am–5pm; Fr.6; SMP), housed in an impressive Neoclassical building with an annexe for temporary exhibits that's refreshingly light, open and airy. The permanent collection takes in a Modigliani, a couple of Van Goghs, Delacroix and Renoir among a selection of mostly little-known early modern works. The troubled face of local artist Léopold Robert, in a portrait by his son Aurèle, hints at his disturbing fate: he cut his own throat in 1835 at the age of 41 after the failure of an unhappy relationship with Charlotte Bonaparte. Plenty of Robert's own romantic images of Venetian sailors, exotic peasant women and rogueish mountain bandits – as well as mawkish works on death and impending mortality – cover the walls.

Perhaps La Chaux's most famous son was the modernist architect Charles-Edouard Jeanneret, known as **Le Corbusier** (his face adorns the ten-franc note). He was born in 1887 at 38 Rue de la Serre; dotted around the town are several examples of his work, including the Villa Jeanneret, 12 Chemin de Pouillerel (not open to the public), built in white following a journey aged 25 to Eastern and Southern Europe. The Mediterranean-style Villa Schwob, also known as **Villa Turque**, 167 Rue du Doubs, now houses the public relations arm of the Ebel watchmaking firm; it's open for visits twice monthly (1st &

last Sat 11am–4pm; free), or by appointment (☎032 912 31 23). The tourist office has a brochure outlining an eleven-point Le Corbusier itinerary through the town.

Eating, drinking and nightlife

For **eating and drinking**, a few pavement cafés are dotted along Avenue Robert offering standard brasserie fare – the *Trattoria Toscana* at no. 13 is typical. Tiny *Café du Musée*, 7 Rue Daniel Jeanrichard, has a couscous *menu* for Fr.10, while the *Croix d'Or*, 15 Rue de la Balance, has pizzas for Fr.14 and quality fish for under Fr.20. There's a reliably good *Manora* at 20 Boulevard des Eplatures, and traditional fare such as fondue, and tripe at the *Pinte Neuchâteloise*, 8 Rue Grenier. The best view in town is from the *Citérama* café, on the 14th floor of the Espacité tower; aside from ice cream, coffee and light snacks, they have a spectacular outside terrace with bird's-eye views over the whole town and, most dramatically, along the full, arrow-straight length of Avenue Robert – best after dark, when with a beer or two inside you, you might just imagine yourself in LA for a brief second.

The town's best **live music** and arts venue is the *Bikini Test*, 3 Rue Joux-Perret (ⓦwww.bikinitest.ch), hosting everything from death metal to dance-hall to world jazz. The vaulted *P'tit Paris*, in the centre at 4 Rue du Progrès, as well as serving good inexpensive food, stages live music sessions in the cellar on weekend nights.

Le Locle and around

About 8km west of La Chaux is the small town of **LE LOCLE**, where Swiss watchmaking was born. Daniel Jeanrichard, a native of Neuchâtel (where he made his first watch in 1681, aged 16) settled in Le Locle in 1705 and taught the trade to his family and a small group of apprentices, who then took the skill on to La Chaux and elsewhere in the Jura. Today, there's not an awful lot to see in the town, although if the watch bug has bitten you, you'll enjoy the **Musée d'horlogerie** in the grand Château de Monts above the town (Tues–Sun: May–Oct 10am–5pm; Nov–April 2–5pm; Fr.7), its rooms furnished in eighteenth-century style crammed with ticking timepieces of all kinds, including a roomful of whimsical and intricate mechanical figures by Maurice Sandoz. From La Chaux, it's easiest to get the regular **buses** #60 or #61 to Le Locle, which stop at the central Place du Marché.

Hourly postbuses from Le Locle to La Brévine stop at the **Col-des-Roches underground mills** (May–Oct daily 10am–5.30pm; Nov–April Tues–Sun 2–5pm; Fr.9; SMP; ⓦwww.lesmoulins.ch), 2km west of Le Locle on the French border. These vast, dank chambers were chiselled out of the rock little by little in the seventeenth century in order to take advantage of the flow of water heading down to the Doubs basin: there are two mills for grinding flour, a sawmill, and various other bits of heavy machinery down there, perhaps memorable for kids but otherwise not gripping. The guided tour is in spoken French and German, with English notes.

A sideroad branches 3km north from the Col-des-Roches down to the small riverside village of **LES BRENETS**, where the Doubs broadens slightly into the **Lac des Brenets** (known to the French on the other bank as the Lac de Chaillexon), which freezes over in winter to form the largest natural ice rink in Europe. Narrow-gauge trains from Le Locle pull into Les Brenets train station; walk left down through the village for twenty minutes to the river bank to reach the landing stage, which is also served by direct buses from Le Locle.

From here, you can take a fine **boat** trip (takes 20min; ⓦwww.nlb.ch) east along the lake, through an impressively high, sheer craggy gorge to the 27m-high **Saut du Doubs** waterfall.

Yverdon-les-Bains and around

A busy, attractive market town on the southern tip of Lac de Neuchâtel, **YVERDON-LES-BAINS** is best known for its thermal springs – celebrated at least since Roman times – and is handy as a jumping-off point both for the terrific old castle at nearby **Grandson**, and for trips into the Vaudois hinterland around **Vallorbe** (see p.188) and into the little-visited **Vallée de Joux** (see p.190).

The town was founded in 1260 when Pierre of Savoy, who worked on the Château de Chillon (see p.161), built a castle on what was then the lakefront to defend against attack from the east (the lake has since silted up so that the fortress is now the best part of a kilometre inland). However, the presence of prehistoric standing stones, and also of Roman remains scattered throughout the area, indicates that the Savoyards were not the first to see the strategic importance of Yverdon's location on one of Europe's most significant ancient crossroads. The shortest routes from central France to Italy, and from southern France to Middle Europe and Germany, not to mention the vital water route linking the Rhône and the Rhine, all passed through Yverdon, which was known as Eburodunum (the Fortress of the Yew Tree) in Gallo-Roman times.

These days, Yverdon lies second in Vaud to Lausanne, and is a gentle place, with its solid castle, a pleasant and compact Old Town with many Baroque and Neoclassical facades, 5km of sandy beaches, and a marshland nature reserve stretching along the lakeshore northeast of town. In 2002, it was the location of one of the prime sites of the Swiss national Expo: just offshore, a giant walk-through machine sucked up lake water and gently spat it out in a fine mist to, literally, create a cloud. This – and Yverdon's excellent programme of music, dance and gastronomic events – was one of the most successful draws of the Expo, and it was hoped that some of the good publicity would help subsequently to regenerate Yverdon's lakefront, which was under-used before then. At the time of writing, immediately post-Expo, plans for the area remain uncertain, but it may be worth venturing down to the lakefront to see what's new when you visit.

Arrival, information and accommodation

Yverdon's **train station** (with change counter Mon–Sat 5.20am–8.40pm, Sun 5.50am–8.40pm, and bike rental) is 100m northeast of the Old Town, and about 600m southwest of the lakeshore; the **post office** is next door. **Boats** dock at the *débarcadère* on Quai de Nogent near the racecourse; it's a fifteen-minute walk south along the River Thièle and under the train tracks (or take bus #2) to reach the Old Town. The focus of the Old Town is Place Pestalozzi, in front of the castle walls. The **tourist office** is left of the station, 1 Avenue de la Gare (Mon–Fri 8.30am–noon & 1.30–6pm, Sat 9am–noon; Nov–March Mon–Fri closes 5.30pm, closed Sat; ☎024 423 61 01, ⓦwww.yverdon-les-bains.ch).

Accommodation is thin on the ground. The only **hotel** within the town proper is *L'Ecusson Vaudois*, 29 Rue de la Plaine (☎024 425 40 15, ⓦwww.

ecussonvaudois.ch; ❷), a pretty good option featuring rooms ensuite and not, and pleasant staff. Fifteen minutes east of town is the rather charming *Hôtel de l'Ange*, 25 Rue de Clendy (☏024 425 25 85, ℻024 426 31 20; ❶), on a busy traffic street but also with a mix of rooms and a wisp of character too. Clustering around the Centre Thermal on Avenue des Bains, you'll find the generic *Motel des Bains* (☏024 426 92 81, ℻024 426 14 94; ❸), *Hôtel La Prairie* (☏024 425 19 19, ℻024 425 00 79; ❹) and, cream of the crop boasting its own thermal pools, *Grand Hôtel des Bains* (☏024 424 64 64, ⓦwww.thermes-yverdon.ch; ❻). *Des Iris* **campsite** is on the lakefront northeast of the station (☏024 425 10 89; April–Sept).

The Town

The central **Place Pestalozzi** is dominated by the broad-fronted Louis XV-style Hôtel de Ville and, next to it, the foursquare turreted **château**, built after 1260 by Pierre II of Savoy, occupied by the Bernese in 1536, and taken by force during the Vaudois revolution in 1798. From 1805 to 1825 the château housed an educational institute set up by the visionary reformer Heinrich Pestalozzi (see box); Yverdon's schoolchildren continued to be taught within the castle walls right up until 1974. Today it's the home of the moderately interesting town **museum** (Tues–Sun: June–Sept 10am–noon & 2–5pm; Oct–May 2–5pm; Fr.8; joint ticket with Maison d'Ailleurs Fr.10; SMP), for which you can get extensive English notes when you enter. Highlights include the castle

Johann Heinrich Pestalozzi

Johann Heinrich (Henri) Pestalozzi, born in Zürich in 1746, was a visionary educationalist, who devoted his life's work – twenty years of it in Yverdon – to giving poor and underprivileged children from around Europe the chance to have a decent education. Pestalozzi married at 23, and first lived with his wife Anna Schulthess in Birr (Canton Aargau), where they tried to organize help for local abandoned children and from where Pestalozzi wrote books and newspaper articles to bring the problem of children in poverty to wider attention.

After four years as a schoolteacher in Bern, Pestalozzi was invited in 1804 by the Yverdon municipality to come and set up in the château an educational institute for underprivileged children. Pestalozzi took in up to 150 boys aged 7 to 15 who would otherwise have been begging on the streets, fed and clothed them, and organized a flexible school curriculum suited to each child's abilities, covering mathematics, languages, music, gymnastics, biology, astronomy and more, thus gaining worldwide attention from social scientists of the day. Two years later, he set up a similar school for girls, followed in 1813 by Switzerland's – and one of the world's – first schools for children with hearing and/or speech disabilities.

His wife died in 1815, but Pestalozzi continued his work in Yverdon for another ten years, eventually returning to Birr where he died in 1827. To this day there remains a great deal of interest in his methodology, documented in sheaves of letters and articles written during his lifetime. His vision of education for all was seized upon by Victorian reformers in Britain and elsewhere as a cornerstone of the development of welfare policy through the nineteenth century and into the twentieth. If anything, Pestalozzi's legacy is only beginning to be fully realized today, with the UN acknowledging education to be a human right and recognizing that children have a right to be treated with the same respect as adults. When Pestalozzi wrote, "Development of a child's mind should be made continuously relevant to that child's personality and everyday life," such an idea was laughable; today it seems obvious, largely due to his inspiration.

chapel (room 2), modernized and now used for marriage services; a couple of impressive Gallo-Roman dugout canoes, on display in a high-tech setting below the doughty keep (room 4); a rather homesick Egyptian mummy in the Jew's Tower (room 6); and a costume collection in room 7. Room 10 beside the exit is filled with Pestalozzi memorabilia.

Far more engaging is the **Maison d'Ailleurs** opposite the château ("House of Elsewhere"; Wed–Sun 2–6pm; Fr.6; joint ticket with château Fr.10; SMP; ⓦ www.ailleurs.ch). This self-billed "museum of science-fiction, utopia and extraordinary journeys", housed in the old prison, holds a massive collection of some 80,000 items, with several hundred antiquarian books from as early as the fifteenth century (notably a 1631 Amsterdam edition of Thomas More's *Utopia* in Latin), and several thousand paperbacks including an array of Asimovs in what seems like all the languages of the world. Changing exhibits cover various futuristic themes, including fantasy art, posters, old sci-fi magazines, videos, sketches and unpublished drawings from Hollywood movie designers, and samples from its amazing collection of toys (1950s ray-guns, original Superman dolls, Star Trek and Star Wars figures, and more). You're welcome to browse through their huge English library, and kick back in their "Giger Cell" – a room kitted out by *Alien* designer H.R. Giger (see p.140) – for a spot of solo literary journeying during the afternoon.

Yverdon is suffixed "-les-Bains" for its **spa waters**, 14,000-year-old mineral springs bubbling up from 500m below ground and rich with all kinds of curative properties, most notably easing joint pain and helping with respiratory problems. The water emerges at between 28 and 34°C, and is these days corralled into various indoor and outdoor pools about 1km southeast of the Old Town at the **Centre Thermal**, a state-of-the-art complex off Avenue des Bains (Mon–Fri 8am–10pm, Sat & Sun 9am–8pm; Fr.15; ⓦ www.thermes-yverdon .ch). Over a thousand people come here every day to take the waters. Extras include a sauna to yourself (Fr.33), or use of the collective sauna and hammam (Fr.12), as well as massages (from Fr.58) and any amount of physiotherapy and inhalation courses. You can even drink the stuff, which is bottled and sold around Switzerland as "Arkina".

Eating and drinking

There's a good range of **eating and drinking** options in Yverdon, including the self-service diner at *Manora* on Rue de l'Ancienne Poste (Mon–Thurs &

The Clendy stones

About 1500m northeast of Yverdon, in a wood between the suburb of **Clendy** and the lakeshore, is a set of **standing stones**, or menhirs, some five thousand years old. Take bus #1 to Clendy, walk left (north) under the railway bridge, and then head straight along a footpath beside a wood for about 50m. Cut right on paths through the trees, and you'll emerge into a neatly mown clearing set with the stones.

The Clendy stones were reset in their original positions in 1986, just one of many significant clusters of **Neolithic** stone circles and dolmens on the north shore of Lac de Neuchâtel, the greatest concentration of them in Switzerland (more are on Lake Geneva and around Sion). The pitted and blotchy Clendy stones – big, but no Stonehenge – form a rough rhomboid shape, with a line extending out from one corner; their purpose is unknown, but may have been connected with worship and/or ley-lines, since Yverdon sits at a conjunction of ancient roads. The atmosphere of the place is tangible, but unfortunately today the stones lie beside a main road, shielded by trees from all but the sound of modern traffic.

Sat 8am–7pm, Fri 8am–8pm, Sun 11.30am–7pm). Tunisian *Orient Express*, 22 Rue de la Plaine, has quality falafel and kebabs, while *Crêperie l'Ange Bleu*, 11 Rue du Collège (closed Mon), has salads, crêpes and light *menus* for around Fr.10. *Don Camillo*, 10 Rue du Pré (closed Sun), has excellent pizza/pasta dishes; and *La Fourchette*, 8 Rue du Casino, offers simple but well-prepared French and Italian favourites. *Intemporel*, 8 Rue du Lac, is an upstairs **café-bar** popular with young people and open late nightly, with ten kinds of coffees and teas, plus salad meals. *Restaurant de Champ-Pittet* (T024 425 65 14; March–Oct Wed–Sun only; W www.pronatura.ch/champ-pittet) is part of the Champ-Pittet marshland nature reserve 2km northeast of Yverdon on the lakeshore, and uses wild plants and herbs in its delectable organic creations that are beautiful as well as healthy.

Grandson

A village on the lakeshore some 4km north of Yverdon, **GRANDSON** resonates in the mind of every Swiss schoolchild as the location of one of the three greatest victories ever won by a Swiss army. Its castle – focus of the battle (against Charles of Burgundy in 1476) – now houses one of the best **castle museums** in the country.

Although a tower was built by Adalbert of Grandson as early as 1050, the main buildings date from 1281, when **Otto I of Grandson** returned from the Eighth Crusade wealthy enough to build a new castle, a Franciscan cloister in the village and a Carthusian monastery further along the lake near Concise. Otto's tomb is prominent within Lausanne cathedral (see p.131).

In 1475, during clashes throughout western Switzerland and eastern France as **Charles the Bold**, duke of Burgundy, expanded his territory and influence, the Swiss confederate army besieged the fortress at Grandson for the first time; after less than a month, the Burgundian garrison surrendered and was allowed to escape. Early the following year, on February 26, the Burgundian army under Charles retook the town of Grandson and, on the 28th, the castle. Treacherously, the Swiss garrison of 412 men were hanged from the apple trees in the castle orchard. Two days later, on March 2, the Swiss army marched against Charles, and met him in **battle** north of Grandson, lining up rank after rank of their feared fusiliers, pikemen and halberdiers. "The sun was opposite them," reports an eyewitness, "and their weapons sparkled like mirrors. At the same time, the raised bugles and battle-trumpets of Uri and the Luzerner battalion were bellowing, and the din was such that the Duke's men took fright and began to retreat." The Swiss had no cavalry to give chase, and so they let most of the Burgundians run away unscathed, only to discover that the Bold Duke had abandoned his vast riches on the battlefield: 400 decorated tents and precious tapestries, countless items of gold and silver, 400 cannon, 10,000 horses, 600 flags, 300 tons of powder… booty totalling several hundred million pounds at today's value, much of which remains on display in Grandson and other Swiss museums.

Soon afterwards, the Swiss defeated Charles twice more, at Murten and conclusively at Nancy, thus in short order eliminating the principal threat to the French throne and, in at least a small way, permitting France instead of Burgundy to grow as a united imperial force in the centuries following. The château at Grandson, meanwhile, faded from central importance, passing between the governments of Bern, Fribourg and Canton Vaud until its rejuvenation as a museum in the 1980s.

The castle and village

Grandson's **train station**, 700m west of the castle along Rue Basse, is served only by occasional *trains regionaux* between Yverdon and Neuchâtel. It's better to get the regular **postbus** from Yverdon to Gorgier-St-Aubin, which can drop you directly in Grandson's Place du Château (takes 10min).

At the castle **ticket desk** (April–Oct daily 9am–6pm; Feb & March Mon–Sat 8.30–11.30am & 1.30–5pm, Sun 9am–5pm; Nov–Jan Sat 1–5pm, Sun 9am–5pm; Fr.10; SMP) – which doubles as the **tourist office** (same hours; ☎024 445 29 26, ⓦwww.grandson.ch) – you're given a follow-the-numbers leaflet. It's worth pausing awhile at the foot of the walls to look out over the lake and up at the massively strong turreted fortress above; Grandson sees a fraction of the visitors who cram into the Château de Chillon (see p.161), and its past lingers more tangibly in the old stones. (Bear in mind, though, that Wednesday tends to be school-trip day.)

Highlights inside include the Torture Chamber (room 3), with original wheel and executioners' axe; an exceptionally informative and watchable English-language **slide-show** on the history of Grandson and the Burgundian Wars in room 7; vast quantities of booty from 1476, as well as a life-size mock-up of Charles the Bold's war tent (room 12); the claustrophobic Prison (room 16); and a ramparts walk leading through the various towers and watch-rooms. Accessed by stairs leading down from a corner of the Banqueting Hall (room 15) is an incongruous **Vintage Car Museum** (rooms 17–19), displaying a whole wealth of dream machines, including Greta Garbo's immaculate 1927 white Rolls-Royce Phantom, Winston Churchill's 1938 Austin Cambridge, a 1913 Bugatti, and various others.

Five minutes' walk southwest from Place du Château up ancient Rue Haute brings you to **St-Jean-Baptiste**, a beautiful and atmospheric Romanesque church renovated by the Crusader Otto I in the thirteenth century as part of an ecclesiastical complex in the village.

The Jura Vaudois

To the west of Yverdon is a stretch of hilly countryside known as the **Jura Vaudois**, characterized by rushing streams (and the remnants of iron-working industries which exploited their power), hidden valleys and ancient cobbled villages. The area lies wholly within Canton Vaud hard up against the French frontier – one of Europe's oldest borders, unchanged since 1186. Main town of the region is **Vallorbe**, of only passing interest in itself, but positioned at the southern end of a pass through the Jura mountains that has been used since antiquity as a route from France southeast to the Grand-St-Bernard pass, and thus into Italy. Railway engineers followed the old roads when they carved a tunnel from Vallorbe beneath the Jura early in the twentieth century, forming the last link in a chain that allowed the launch of the classic Orient-Express train journey from Paris to Venice and on to Istanbul. The Jura Vaudois was also a stopoff for medieval pilgrims following the Chemin de St-Jacques from Germany southwest to Santiago de Compostela in Spain: Romanesque and Gothic churches at **Orbe** and **Montcherand** and the huge priory at **Romainmôtier** fulfilled both spiritual and material needs on the mammoth journey. Behind parallel bands of hills, and guarded by high peaks at either end, the secluded **Vallée de Joux** has only a couple of roads, a handful of villages, and some great walking and cross-country skiing routes.

△ The Ring in Biel/Bienne (see p.197)

Sainte-Croix

A small village up in the Jura near the French border, 19km northwest of Yverdon on a steep and tortuous road, **SAINTE-CROIX**'s claim to fame is its 200-year history of making musical boxes, on show at the surprisingly diverting **Musée du CIMA** (Centre International de la Méchanique d'Art), 2 Rue de l'Industrie (guided tours June–Aug Mon 3pm, Tues–Sun 10.30am & 2–5pm; rest of year Tues–Sun 2–5pm; Fr.9; SMP). The tours, which are in French with English notes available, last an hour and a quarter, and take in the full history, design and development of the art. As you go around, the guide starts up loads of intriguing musical figures, including an acrobat balancing on a chair-back, a whimsical Pierrot writing with a long quill, pianos, orchestras and fairground musicians. Some 6km west of Sainte-Croix is the village of **L'AUBERSON**, with – on much the same lines – the **Musée Baud**, 23 Grand-Rue (July to mid-Sept daily 2–5pm; rest of year Sat 2–4pm, Sun 10am–noon & 2–6pm; Fr.7; SMP), displaying a grand Parisian fair-organ from 1900 and various musical figurines.

Northeast of Sainte-Croix, a sharp-edged ridge culminates in **Mont Chasseron** (1607m), one of the highest of Jura peaks, commanding a majestic panorama across the whole sweep of the distant Alps. There's plenty of moderately taxing downhill skiing in winter, focused on the village of **Les Rasses** below the slopes at 1200m.

Hourly narrow-gauge trains climb from Yverdon to Sainte-Croix, terminating at the lower end of Rue de l'Industrie, 200m from the Musée du CIMA, which also houses the **tourist office** (Mon–Sat 8am–noon & 2–6pm; ☎024 454 27 02, ⓦwww.ste-croix.ch). Buses shuttle between Sainte-Croix and L'Auberson, and Sainte-Croix and Les Rasses. Within Sainte-Croix, there's a good HI **hostel**, 18 Rue Centrale (☎024 454 18 10, ⓦwww.youthhostel.ch; ❶; May–Oct), with small dorms from Fr.31 and bikes for rent. Of the **hotels**, *Les Fleurettes*, 3 Chemin des Fleurettes (☎ & ⒡024 454 22 94; ❶) has plain rooms and some dorm beds, while the pine-shaded *Grand Hôtel Résidence* in Les Rasses (☎024 454 19 61, ⒡024 454 19 42; ❸–❹) lives up to its name, with spacious balconied rooms facing south to drink in the sunshiny views.

Vallorbe and around

VALLORBE, right on the Franco-Swiss frontier, is known – if at all these days – simply as a stop on the TGV line between Paris and Lausanne, but in times past this small, rather austere town, loomed over from the southwest by the 700m-high Dent de Vaulion, was the centre of a thriving iron industry. This is commemorated in the riverside Grandes-Forges building, dating from 1495 and now housing the **Musée du Fer et du Chemin de Fer** (Iron and Railway Museum; April–Oct daily 9.30am–noon & 1.30–6pm; rest of year Mon–Fri same hours; Fr.9; SMP). The main draw is the working smithy, powered by waterwheels on the River Orbe outside and still turning out iron tools and implements much as the whole town did throughout the Middle Ages. Upstairs is the romantic railway section, where loads of memorabilia and old signboards from the Venice-Simplon Orient Express do well to resurrect the exoticism of early twentieth-century train travel. There's also a lengthy – and rather good – slide-show (in French only, but you can still enjoy the pictures) detailing the construction of the tunnel from Vallorbe through the Jura, and the expansion of rail travel.

Several fast **buses** a day link Vallorbe with Yverdon, beating the tortuous train ride by more than an hour. Vallorbe's **train station** is perched on a terrace high above the town and offers bike rental; it's a ten-minute walk down to the **tourist office** (☎021 843 25 83, ⓦwww.vallorbe.ch), in the same building as the museum. Their Fr.30 Carte Trèfle covers entry to the Musée du Fer, the Grottes and the Prè-Giroud fort (see below). Aside from the switched-on *Auberge Pour Tous* hostel, 11 Rue du Simplon (☎021 843 13 49, ⓦwww. geocities.com/aubergepourtous), with good dorms from Fr.21, the only **accommodation** in town is *Hôtel de l'Orbe*, 41 Rue de Lausanne (☎021 843 04 34; ❶), with five serviceable rooms. The main street, Grand-Rue, has plenty of inexpensive **eating and drinking** options, including the pleasant *Le France* brasserie/pizzeria at no. 20, and cosy *Café de la Poste* on parallel Rue de l'Ancienne Poste.

Around Vallorbe

Much more rewarding than Vallorbe itself is the wild and largely unvisited countryside around and about. Local trains and buses go everywhere but, with hourly schedules at best, they're rather less convenient than your own transport.

Just over 2km southwest of Vallorbe are some caves, **Les Grottes de Vallorbe** (daily: June–Aug 9.30am–5.30pm; April & May 9.30am–4.30pm; Fr.13), forming a tunnel over the River Orbe and replete with impressive stalactites and stalagmites, along with an exhibition of minerals dubbed Le Trésor des Fées (Fairy Treasure). Some forty minutes' walk from Le Day train station just outside Vallorbe is the **Fort de Pré-Giroud** (July & Aug daily noon–5.30pm; May, June, Sept & Oct Sat & Sun same times; Fr.10; SMP), an extensive military complex dug into a hillside in 1937 to defend against possible incursion by enemy forces over the nearby Col de Jougne from France. An innocuous chalet on the surface hides vertical shafts giving access to chilly labyrinthine tunnels and a whole subterranean bunker, complete with kitchen, dorms and a hospital, capable of supporting 130 people.

ROMAINMÔTIER, a small village in a secluded valley about 14km east of Vallorbe near Croy, has managed to preserve in near-mint condition its extraordinarily grand Romanesque **priory church**. Switzerland's oldest monastery was founded on the same site in about 450, and the current building was constructed by Cluniac monks in 990–1028. The church (daily 7am–6pm) is approached from the picturesque village street beneath an even more picturesque fourteenth-century clock-tower. As you enter, you pass into the impressive and harmonious nave, with its massive piers and a vividly painted thirteenth-century vault overhead. On the left of the choir and chancel, with fourteenth-century frescoes, is the separate Chapel of the Holy Virgin, with a beautiful medieval statue of Mary. The remains of the cloister run along the outside of the south wall.

Continuing the ecclesiastical theme, **MONTCHERAND**, a tranquil village 8km northeast of Romainmôtier with a view over the Orbe valley, shelters a small but notable tenth-century **church** (daily 8.30am–8.30pm; Oct–April closes 6.30pm). Its most striking feature is a set of twelfth-century frescoes in the apse, depicting the saints Paulus, Ithos, Andreas, Jacobus, Matias and Filipus standing shoulder to shoulder in brilliantly restored colours.

ORBE, halfway between Vallorbe and Yverdon on the bus or train, is a picturesque old town up on a rock, with steep cobbled streets and another atmospheric church, a five-naved effort dating from the fifteenth century. Orbe was known to the Romans as *Urba*, and 2km north of the town, in a muddy field at the hamlet of **Boscéaz** near the junction of the *autoroute* and highway, are some of the best **Roman mosaics** to be seen in Switzerland (Easter–Oct

Mon–Fri 9am–noon & 1.30–5pm, Sat & Sun 1.30–5.30pm; Fr.3; ⓦwww.orbe.ch). Nearest to the ticket hut is Pavillon IV, sheltering hexagonal mosaics of gods and goddesses, with the central medallions showing the deities of the seven days of the week. Further on, Pavillon III has a countryside procession, led by a trumpeter; and Pavillon II displays an intriguingly complex mosaic maze. Excavations are ongoing.

The Vallée de Joux

About 5km southwest of Vallorbe, the sharp Dent de Vaulion rises to 1483m, standing guard over the secluded **Vallée de Joux**, a long thin valley sandwiched at 1000m between the Grand Risoud pine forest, which conceals it from France, and the parallel Mont Tendre range, which cuts it off from Lake Geneva. It's perfect summer walking country, with many routes along the valley floor beside the **Lac de Joux**, while the thickly wooded valley sides turn into cross-country skiing heaven in winter. The valley has its own, bracing microclimate, reminiscent of Alpine areas 400m higher in altitude: temperatures of -20°C on the valley floor are not unknown in winter, and precipitation tops 1800mm a year. High winds can also rip their way along the valley. It's no surprise that the first people to consider settling in the valley were ascetic monks: even by 1700 there were still just 173 inhabitants, plus 22 bears.

Between the small **Lac Brenet** and Lac de Joux is **LE PONT** village. In front of the train station is what's left of a colossal hangar, used between 1880 and 1936 (before the age of fridges) to store ice which was hacked from the lakes and then transported by fast train to Paris, Lyon and Geneva. (In April 1927, the hangar was somehow gutted by fire.) Roads run west from Le Pont along both shores of the Lac de Joux: the south road passes through **L'ABBAYE** with ruins of a medieval abbey, meeting up at the end of the lake with the northern road and **LE SENTIER**, chief town of the valley and a one-time watchmaking centre to rival those in the Neuchâtel mountains (such prestigious names as Audemars Piguet, Blancpain and Breguet still make watches in this valley). **LE BRASSUS**, 4km southwest, is being developed as a resort, although you'd barely notice much actual development going on: the place is pretty, quiet and boasts nothing at all to divert you from the wilds of nature all around. From here all the way southwest to the Col de la Givrine above Nyon is the huge **Parc Jurassien Vaudois** – Switzerland's second-largest protected natural environment.

Practicalities

Hourly **trains** from Vallorbe (connecting with services from Lausanne at Le Day) run along the north shore of the Lac de Joux, terminating at Le Brassus. One **boat** a day in summer does a circular cruise of the lake, to and from Le Pont. A summer **road** from Le Brassus surfs over the mountains at Marchairuz before dropping down to Lake Geneva.

The **tourist office** for the valley is in the giant sports centre at the southern end of Le Sentier (daily 9am–noon & 1–6pm; ☏021 845 17 77, ⓦwww.myvalleedejoux.ch). They have plenty of leaflets and brochures, as well as a useful 1:25,000 map and *guide touristique* (in French; Fr.15) detailing walks. You can rent ice skates here (Fr.6) for either the indoor ice stadium (admission Fr.7) or, when everyone is skating on it, the lake itself. They also have mountain bikes (Fr.40/day), cross-country skis (Fr.22), a climbing wall, tennis courts, and even plain dorms (Fr.17). Most amenable **hotels** are in Le Brassus: *La Lande* (☏021 845 44 41, ⓕ021 845 45 40, ⓦwww.hotellalande.com; ❷–❸) is fresh and pleasant, as is the *France* nearby (☎021 845 44 33, 📠021 845 44 31; ②–③) – but the former is family-owned, whereas the latter is a generic chain. *Hôtel du Cygne* in Les Charbonnières on the south side of the lake (☎021 841 12 81, 📠021 841 12 82; ①) wins no prizes for charm, but has plenty of dorm beds. **Camp** year-round at *Le Rocheray* in Le Sentier (☎021 845 51 74). **Eating and drinking** is a hotel experience, but for one or two small brasseries in Le Pont and Le Brassus.

The Broye

The mellow countryside between Yverdon and Bern is known as the **Broye**, after the River Broye which flows gently through the area. Not a great deal happens here, and it's perfect cycling country: reasonably flat, with plenty of small villages, a dearth of even middling-sized towns, and the shores of both the Lac de Neuchâtel and the Murtensee (Lac de Morat) to explore. **Estavayer-le-Lac** is a lakeside resort town with peace and quiet as its main attributes; nearby **Payerne** is home to a spectacular Romanesque abbey, while **Avenches** was once the capital of Roman Switzerland and has plenty for ruin-hunters to enjoy. **Murten/Morat**, on the line where French-speaking Western Europe meets German-speaking Central Europe, is a variation on the theme of attractive but staid lakeside resorts with well-preserved medieval centres.

Estavayer-le-Lac

ESTAVAYER-LE-LAC is a picturesque little yachties' town on the lakeside 19km northeast of Yverdon, with plenty of medieval architecture scattered throughout a centre which has remained largely unchanged since 1599. Today it occupies a little enclave of Canton Fribourg, surrounded on three sides by Vaud. It trades on two features: the town museum, which has a collection of stuffed frogs, and the climbing roses which cover its ancient stones throughout the summer, giving the place its nickname of the City of the Rose.

It's a ten-minute walk from the station northwest along Route de la Gare to **Place du Midi** on the edge of the Old Town. Heading east from here takes you past the Hôtel de Ville to the Gothic **Église St-Laurent**. Left (north) from here brings you to the open Place de Moudon, the medieval marketplace which formerly looked over the lakeshore. Over to the east is the solid **Château de Chenaux**, built and added to over 450 years, with towers and turrets sprouting all over. It's the seat of the local government, but you can wander around and through its courtyards. South of the church, Grand-Rue heads out of town via the mighty **Porte des Religieuses**. Partway down, Rue du Musée branches off to the medieval Maison de la Dîme, housing a diverting **museum** (July & Aug daily 10am–noon & 2–5pm; March–June, Sept & Oct Tues–Sun same times; Nov–Feb Sat & Sun 2–5pm; Fr.4; SMP). A random collection of bits and bobs – ivory Chinese chesspieces from the eighteenth century, some old playing cards, assorted railway memorabilia – is overshadowed by 108 small frogs, stuffed in the 1860s by François Perrier, a retired captain of the Vatican's Swiss Guard, and arranged in glass cases in various poses to mimic the social life of the period. It's all utterly pointless, and more than a bit macabre; the frogs don't look impressed in the least.

The **train station** – on the slow Yverdon–Fribourg line – has bikes for rent and is 600m southwest of Place du Midi, where the **tourist office** is situated

(Mon–Fri 8.30am–noon & 1.30–6pm; June–Sept also Sat 10am–4pm; ☎026 663 12 37, ⓦwww.estavayer-le-lac.ch). Plenty of **boats** serve Estavayer from both Yverdon and Neuchâtel. **Campsite** *Nouvelle Plage* (☎026 663 16 93; April–Sept) is on the lakeshore east of the harbour, about 1km north of the Old Town. The most appealing **hotel** is *My Lady's Manor*, Route St-Pierre 7 (☎026 663 23 16, Ⓕ026 663 19 93; ❶), a romantic manor house set in its own fragrant gardens, with very large, characterful rooms (none ensuite); prices drop if you stay more than three nights. Otherwise, you're looking at the pleasant and quiet *Fleur-de-Lys* in town (☎026 663 42 63, Ⓕ026 663 48 78; ❷) or the similar *Hôtel de Ville* next door (☎026 663 12 62; ❷), the latter with a posh Chinese **restaurant** upstairs and a plainer brasserie downstairs (closed Tues eve).

Payerne

Some 8km inland from Estavayer is the small market town of **PAYERNE**, highlight of which is the breathtaking **Abbatiale** (Tues–Sat 10am–noon & 2–6pm, Sun 10.30am–noon & 2–6pm; winter closes 5pm; Fr.3 or more, depending on exhibition; SMP), one of the most impressive examples of Romanesque architecture in the country. There's a wealth of detail in the five-naved church, which dates from the eleventh and twelfth centuries and which stands amidst the buildings of an abbey; its square, turreted **tower**, with a slender **twisted spire**, dominates the town. The lofty barrel-vaulted interior is impressive, with natural light reflecting off the variegated sandstone pillars of the nave to set the whole space glowing. Carved **capitals** in the transept and detailed **frescoes** from around 1200 on the vaultings of the porch and in the narthex are gorgeous. However, the church has not been used as a house of worship since 1562, and it's unfortunate that you may well find modern art exhibitions filling the nave and aisles with distractions and the hum of conversation.

Avenches

About 10km northeast of Payerne, **AVENCHES** was the capital of Roman Switzerland, at one time supporting a population of 20,000. These days, life in the town is more smugly suburban, but it's well worth visiting, both for the medieval town centre and the extensive Roman remains.

After a defeat at the hands of Julius Caesar, the **Helvetians** founded their new capital of Aventicum in the early first century BC (Aventia was the name of the local Celtic goddess of water). Emperor Vespasian granted it the status of colony in 72 AD, whereupon Aventicum entered its golden age. During the second and third centuries, the huge city wall boasted 73 watchtowers, and many of the public buildings of that period – a baths, temples, the amphitheatre, and more – have been excavated. The Aleman tribes raided the town around 277 AD, and sacked large parts of it; by 450, Aventicum's glory days were over.

Climbing the hill from the train station, the first thing you come to is the large oval **amphitheatre** crowning the eastern edge of the Old Town, well restored and now the scene of an annual summer opera festival (see box). The tower at the rear of the arena houses the excellent **Musée Romain** (Tues–Sun: April–Sept 10am–noon & 1–5pm; Oct–March 2–5pm; Fr.3; SMP). The ground floor is filled with statuary and mosaics, while upstairs are very impressive collections of Roman bits and bobs, sensibly organized and with English notes available. Fascinating details of ordinary life – such as the fact that

Avenches' festivals

Every July, little Avenches hosts a prestigious **opera festival** (ⓦwww.avenches.ch), with atmospheric open-air productions in the 8000-seat amphitheatre that draw world-class artists and thousands of promenading spectators. Performances start around 9pm and last until after midnight – many people stay overnight, booking the town's few hotels out months ahead of time. Tickets are Fr.70–150, discounted if you book before January; limited-view tickets are sold on the day for Fr.40.

Every August, the same amphitheatre sees the **Rock oz'Arènes** festival (ⓦwww.rockozarenes.ch), running since 1992 with headliners like P.J. Harvey, the Wailers and Neneh Cherry, plus smaller stages with jugglers, acoustic sets and more.

a glass of wine cost a quarter of a sesterce, while commissioning a statue of the goddess Aventia with an inscription would set you back 5200 sesterces – are filled out with maps and figurines, including a copy of a spectacular gold bust of Emperor Marcus Aurelius (the original is in Lausanne). Dotted around the town are seven other Roman sites – the tourist office has a brochure – all of which are well signposted and free. One of the most impressive is the **Tour de la Cigogne**, a gnarled old column almost swamped by suburbia but still standing tall in a field: it once formed part of a giant temple sanctuary.

Avenches' **tourist office**, 3 Place de l'Église (Mon–Fri 8am–noon & 1.30–5pm, Sat 9am–noon; ☎026 676 99 22, ⓦwww.avenches.ch), has plenty of books and brochures on the Roman and medieval town. An HI **hostel** is five minutes' walk south, at 5 Rue du Lavoir (☎026 675 26 66, ⓦwww .youthhostel.ch; ❶; mid-April to mid-Oct), with dorms from Fr.29. The nicest **hotel** is the grand *Couronne*, 20 Rue Centrale (☎026 675 54 14, ⓦwww.lacouronne.ch; ❹; closed Jan), which also has the poshest **brasserie** around (*menus* Fr.25). There are plenty more pavement cafés along Rue Centrale, or you could try inexpensive pizza/pasta in *Tearoom du Musée*, opposite the amphitheatre.

Avenches' **train station**, with bike rental, is on the Murten–Payerne line. There are also plenty of **buses**: the ride from Fribourg is especially picturesque and, as a bonus, passes through the intriguingly named village of Misery – which actually looks rather self-satisfied.

Murten/Morat

Belying its deep historical resonance for the Swiss, **MURTEN**, 6km northeast of Avenches, has the air of a holiday town, its neat suburban streets and low-key waterfront promenade reminiscent of the English south coast. It's bang on the *Röstigraben* (linguistic divide), though among its 5000 inhabitants, German speakers far outnumber French (who call the place **MORAT**). It's also one of the best preserved of Switzerland's medieval towns, and is still encircled by its fifteenth-century walls. These days, offering nothing much to do other than strolling on cobbled lanes, sipping drinks at lakeview terrace cafés and boating around the lakes, it's the perfect place for a lazy, romantic getaway. The Old Town's hotels oblige with a range of "honeymoon" suites.

The town's name is derived from the Celtic word *moriduno*, meaning "lakeside fortress". Fire in 1416 led to rebuilding in stone, a useful move since in 1476, Murten allied itself with Bern and Fribourg against the Burgundians and found itself facing down a concerted siege from **Charles the Bold**. The town hung on for thirteen days, whereupon a Bernese force arrived from over the hills, weighed into the Burgundian army and massacred the lot: some 10,000 were slaughtered, and local legend tells of bones being washed up on the lakeshore even eighteen years later. A runner took news of the victory 17km to Fribourg, but expired after recounting his tale; his exploit is commemorated today by thousands who take part in a fun run between the two towns on the first Sunday in October.

Murten's **Old Town** is a simple three-street affair, full of picturesque medieval vaulted arcades and facades. You're most likely to enter at the **castle**, which, although closed to the public, has a peaceful internal courtyard with lake views. Rathausgasse leads east, packed with hotels whose rear terraces afford prime views across the lake to the Vully vineyards. Parallel to the south are Hauptgasse, crammed with bars and eateries; and tranquil Schulgasse/Deutsche Kirchgasse, providing some relief from the hubbub. One of the best ways to see Murten is from the **ramparts**, accessible at a number of points along Deutsche Kirchgasse. The main eastern gate is the **Berntor**, or Porte de Berne, with a distinctive clock face; paths lead from here downhill to the tiny **harbour**. Five minutes west along the lakefront promenade, just below the castle, is an old mill, now the town's **museum** (May–Sept Tues–Sun 10am–noon & 2–5pm; Oct–Dec & March–April Tues–Sun 2–5pm; Jan & Feb Sat & Sun 2–5pm; Fr.4), housing a diverting collection of archeological bits and pieces exposed when dredging of the marshes to the east lowered the water level in the lake to reveal evidence of Neolithic settlement.

Practicalities

The **station** – with trains from Fribourg and Payerne, as well as connections from Neuchâtel (via Ins) and Bern (via Kerzers) – is a five-minute walk west of the Old Town and has bikes for rent. **Boats** (Ⓦwww.navig.ch & Ⓦwww.bielersee.ch) cruise in summer to and from Neuchâtel and Biel/Bienne. The **tourist office** is within the Old Town, at Französische Kirchgasse 6 (April–Oct Mon–Fri 9am–noon & 2–6pm; May–Oct also Sat 10am–2pm; July & Aug also Sun 10am–2pm; Nov–March Mon–Fri closes 5pm; ℡026 670 51 12, Ⓦwww.murten.ch).

Top **hotel** is the stunning *Vieux Manoir au Lac*, 1km west of town at 18 Rue de Lausanne (℡026 678 61 61, Ⓦwww.vieuxmanoir.ch; ❼–❽), a romantic manor house set in its own gardens, with a private beach and harbour. In town, *Murtenhof*, Rathausgasse 1 (℡026 672 90 30, Ⓦwww.murtenhof.ch; ❷–❹), is prime choice, a medieval house renovated throughout: there are some plain but attractive inexpensive rooms as well as spectacular boudoirs boasting original beams, a round king-size bed, or a semicircular bedside bathtub-for-two. A more refined option is *Weisses Kreuz*, Rathausgasse 31 (℡026 670 26 41, Ⓦwww.weisses-kreuz.ch; ❸), in the same family for eighty years; the modern rooms in its seaview wing are outdone by the jaw-dropping ones in the town-view annexe opposite, boasting antique beds and furnishings in broad, wood-panelled splendour (ask for room 33). *Ringmauer*, Deutsche Kirchgasse 2 (℡026 670 11 01, Ⓕ026 672 20 83; ❷), is a comfortable budget alternative.

Eating and drinking are well taken care of at the Hauptgasse cafés and hotel restaurants, although many cater for day-trippers and so can be over-priced; the *Murtenhof* menu is long and inexpensive, with veggie options, and *Anatolia*, on Hauptgasse, can do pizza or kebabs for under Fr.20. The restaurant at *Weisses Kreuz* is one of the many gourmet options, with its excellent fish specialities starting at Fr.25, but for formal dining you won't get much better than *Le Vieux Manoir au Lac* (see above): their top-rated French cuisine (*menus* around Fr.80) is served in a delightful waterside dining room.

Biel/Bienne and around

The double-barrelled town 32km northeast of Murten, and almost exactly halfway between Geneva and Zürich, can get a little confusing. German-speakers call it **BIEL**, French speakers know it as **BIENNE**, but it's Switzerland's only officially **bilingual** town and so all road signs, documents and public information must be produced in both languages. Train timetables, maps and books always call the place "Biel/Bienne", and the locals cheerfully straddle the *Röstigraben* without a second thought – perhaps chatting with a friend in German whilst ordering lunch in French. In addition, some forty per-cent of the town's inhabitants originate from outside Switzerland, with promi-nent numbers of Italian and Spanish residents as well as Turks, Slavs, Arabs and more. Eavesdropping can be an entertaining pastime.

It's a lively, modern town, utterly different in both style and mood from its near-neighbours Neuchâtel and Bern. The main attractions are strolling in the

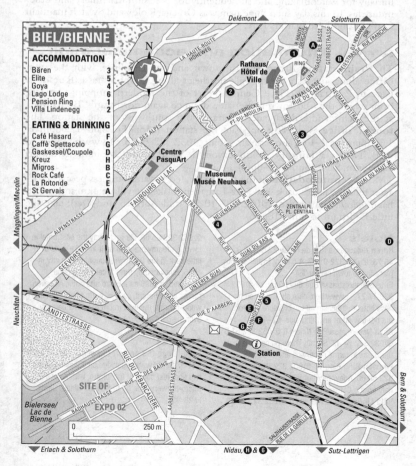

BIEL/BIENNE

ACCOMMODATION

Bären 3
Elite 5
Goya 4
Lago Lodge 6
Pension Ring 1
Villa Lindenegg 2

EATING & DRINKING

Café Hasard F
Caffè Spettacolo G
Gaskessel/Coupole D
Kreuz H
Migros B
Rock Café C
La Rotonde E
St Gervais A

Old Town, dropping in on a couple of small museums and taking a boat ride on the lake or the river. Nonetheless, it takes a certain shift in attitude in order to find your way around smoothly. Unless you're a linguist, there's no reason why you should know that the street called Seevorstadt, for instance, is one and the same as Faubourg du Lac, or even that the body of water stretching south-west from the town is either the **Bielersee** or the **Lac de Bienne** depending on who you're talking to.

Aside from the town's continuous shifting between German- and French-speaking control, Biel/Bienne's **history** isn't particularly distinguished, and it was only when the railway arrived in the latter half of the nineteenth century that it began to expand beyond its old walls. Watchmaking had been a main-stay of the regional economy for a century or more, but had been suffering from the inefficiency of tiny cottage industries: there were some 350 enterprises throughout the Jura at one point, each employing a few artisans working by hand. Mechanization meant that production could be expanded and made more competitive, and Biel/Bienne took on the role of factory centre, initially for watchmaking and subsequently for precision machinery and other industries. To this day, such huge names as Omega, Rolex and Swatch maintain factories and headquarters here.

Arrival, information and accommodation

The **train station** is between the town and the lakeshore, with the **post office** alongside: it's a 500m walk northeast along Bahnhofstrasse/Rue de la Gare to Zentralplatz/Place Central, heart of the modern shopping districts, from where the Old Town is the same distance again northwards. **Boats** dock at the Schiffländte/débarcadère, some 500m southwest of the station. The **tourist office** is directly opposite the station (Mon–Fri 8am–12.30pm & 1.30–6pm; May–Oct also Sat 9am–3pm; ☎032 322 75 75, ⓦwww.biel-seeland .net). There's a **laundry**, Salon Lavoir, at 27 Rue des Moulins (Mon–Fri 7am–8pm, Sat & Sun 8am–8pm).

Most **accommodation** in the town is geared towards business people: character tends to take a back seat. Sutz-Lattrigen, a lakeside village 4km southwest, has *Lindenhof* **campsite** (☎032 397 10 77; mid-April to mid-Oct); take the little BTI train to Sutz (10min).

Hotels

Bären Nidaugasse/Rue de Nidau 22 ☎032 322 45 73, ⓕ032 322 91 57. A creaky, rather shabby place in the town centre. ❸

Elite Bahnhofstrasse/Rue de la Gare 14 ☎032 328 77 77, ⓦwww.hotelelite.ch. Top-rated business hotel that boasts all the creature comforts but not a whiff of anything else. ❹–❺

Goya Neuengasse/Rue Neuve 6 ☎032 322 61 61, ⓕ032 322 74 42. Slightly more going for it than the *Bären* in terms of service and decor. ❸

Pension Ring Ring 16 ☎032 322 81 08, ⓕ032 323 69 60. A few airy but frill-free rooms above a café on the Old Town's central square. ❶

Villa Lindenegg Lindenegg 5 ☎032 322 94 66, ⓕ032 322 95 66. Far and away the best hotel in town, a dreamy mansion built in 1831 in its own little park in the Old Town, bought by the city in 1985, renovated by three local women and reopened in 1996 as a bistro and hotel. All seven rooms are different, each of them fresh, light and wood-floored, the best (room 4) with a balcony over the garden. ❸

Hostel

Lago Lodge (SB hostel) Uferweg 5, Nidau ☎032 331 37 32, ⓦwww.lagolodge.ch. Pleasant, attractive spot just south of the centre, with its own micro-brewery; bus #4 to Schloss Nidau. Dorms Fr.28. ❶

The Town

Heading from the station along the main shopping streets of Bahnhofstrasse/Rue de la Gare, and on along Nidaugasse/Rue de Nidau, the bustle and high-street brand names suddenly fade painlessly away as you cross the line into the cobbled **Old Town**. Burggasse climbs past the old Zeughaus (arsenal), rejuvenated as the city's theatre, and the impressive 1676 step-gabled Rathaus (Town Hall), now police headquarters, into the open **Burgplatz/Place de Bourg**. Quaint shuttered old houses line the square, which centres on the Fountain of Justice, dating from 1714. Continue uphill, and head right to the **Ring**, core of the Old Town and named for the circle of head shakers who would sit here to deliberate on the fate of criminals brought for trial. Head east along arcaded Obergasse/Rue Haute, and then double back onto Untergasse/Rue Basse to stroll past the town's oldest houses.

A couple of the town's museums are worth a look. **Museum Neuhaus**, Schüsspromenade/Promenade de la Suze 26 (Tues–Sun 11am–5pm, Wed until 7pm; Fr.4; SMP; ⓦ www.mn-biel.ch), covers local art and history in a jumble of paintings, costumes, cinema posters and cameras, and also stages temporary exhibitions. The **Centre PasquArt**, Seevorstadt/Faubourg du Lac 71 (Wed–Fri 2–6pm, Sat & Sun 11am–6pm; admission varies), is devoted to contemporary art and photography, with a range of often interesting shows.

Eating and drinking

There are inexpensive places to **eat** all through the centre, including self-service meals at the huge Migros supermarket at Freiestrasse 3. The best place for restaurants, though, is in the Old Town. Biel/Bienne's sizeable student population ensures plenty of **bars** around the centre, including the grungy *Rock Café* on Zentralstrasse/Rue Centrale and the trendy bar of the *La Rotonde* brasserie, Bahnhofstrasse/Rue de la Gare 11. Also check out the impromptu happenings and weekend dance nights at the *Gaskessel/Coupole*, a youth centre under a dome in a car park off Zentralstrasse.

Cafés and restaurants

L'Amphitryon In *Hôtel Elite* ☎ 032 328 77 77. Takes the biscuit as one of the highest star-rated restaurants in the country (*menus* from Fr.80) – although there are frankly more characterful choices around. Closed Sun.

Café Hasard Bahnhofstrasse/Rue de la Gare 4. A small and attractive little daytime nook just round the corner from the *Spettacolo*.

Kreuz Hauptstrasse/Rue Principale 23 in Nidau ☎ 032 331 93 03. Wonderfully relaxed co-opera-tive-run café and restaurant in this pleasant little

---

Above Biel/Bienne

A favourite getaway for locals is to ride the **funicular** from Seevorstadt/Faubourg du Lac, west of the station, up through the forested slopes overlooking the town to the village of **MAGGLINGEN/MACOLIN** on the ridge 400m above. Even when the town is swathed in fog (not such an unusual occurrence in autumn), the funicular can lift you above the clouds into sunshine. Once you're up there, there's not an awful lot to do, other than to head further up for some refreshing hikes around and about: you'll be in fit company, since Magglingen is known across the country as home of the Federal Institute of Sport. With strong legs, you can get 16km west to **Le Chasseral** (1607m), one of the highest summits in the Jura, where you'll find a simple hotel and mountain restaurant, *Chasseral* (☎ 032 751 24 51), along with spectacular views yawning out over the whole Swiss plateau towards the high Alps. Buses run between the hotel and St-Imier on the other side of the ridge.

town contiguous with Biel/Bienne to the south. Old wood floors inside, and a garden terrace out back – the food is excellent, organic and veggie (*menus* from Fr.15).

St Gervais Untergasse/Rue Basse 21. Lively, friendly, alternative-style joint in the Old Town with quality nosh; not the only choice on this street.

Caffè Spettacolo Opposite the station, with coffees and focaccia-style snacks.

Villa Lindenegg Lindenegg 5 ☏ 032 322 94 66. This hotel restaurant has gourmet evening *menus* (Fr.20) with or without meat, using market-fresh produce inventively and attractively.

Around Biel/Bienne

The northern shore of the Bielersee/Lac de Bienne is carpeted with **vineyards**, and wandering or cycling through the wine villages on the lakeshore can be a peaceful way to spend an afternoon. The tourist office in Biel/Bienne can give you a booklet detailing paths in and around the vineyards and places for sampling and buying the local wine.

From **Erlach/Cerlier**, opposite Biel/Bienne at the southwestern end of the lake and served by plenty of boats, a footpath leads out for an hour-and-a-half's pleasant walk along a causeway to the wonderful **St Petersinsel/Île de St-Pierre**. No longer an island (the level of the lake dropped in the late nineteenth century during engineering work to control water flow throughout the Jura), this little dot of car-free, sun-dappled forest amidst the lake is well worth an afternoon. Cluniac monks were the first inhabitants, building a monastery here in 1127, but its most famous resident was the Genevois philosopher Jean-Jacques Rousseau, who spent two months here in 1765, later calling it the happiest time of his life. The renovated monastery buildings, idyllically set amidst vineyards, now house a gourmet **restaurant** (*menus* from Fr.20) and **hotel** (☏ 032 338 11 14, ⓦ www.st-petersinsel.ch; ❸; April–Oct), with eleven characterful and perfectly quiet rooms.

Northeast of Biel/Bienne is the **Taubenloch Gorge**, accessible on regular bus #1 or #3N (10min) or on foot from Magglingen (see p.197) above. Legend has it that a local young man fell in love with a young woman named Dove (Taube in German), and they agreed to marry. But the evil Lord of Rondchâtel wanted her for himself, and tried to force her to marry him instead. Rather than submit to his desires, she flung herself into the deep-set and fast-flowing **River Schüss/Suze**, and the gorge has been named after her ever since. There's a well-engineered path running through the dark and craggy defile for about 2km, and entry is free (although there's a donations box near the entrance). Check with the Biel tourist office for details of local adventure operators running canyoning trips in the gorge.

One of the best boat trips in the region is the river trip up the Aare from Biel/Bienne to Solothurn, which takes about two and a half hours and passes the stork colony at **Altreu** on the way.

Canton Jura

Ignored by most travellers, but well loved by the Swiss themselves, **Canton Jura**, in the far northwest corner of the country, is a rural gem, perfect if all you want from your holiday is to walk or cycle your way through gentle, rolling countryside and dark, fragrant forests, with only the smallest of villages and simplest of hotels (or campsites) to provide material comforts. This little bulge of land has over the centuries been shunted from pillar to post:

Chemins de fer du Jura (⑩www.cj-transports.ch) run some of the local trains and buses in the region; their website has full details. The *Carte journalière Region CJ* (Fr.17) gives a day's travel on CJ's network; the *Railevasion* pass (Fr.44) is valid for any three days' travel in 14. The *Carte journalière Arc jurassien* (Fr.25) has a wider validity, including some mainline CFF trains, extending to La Chaux-de-Fonds and Les Brenets. Train stations in the region have brochures showing the different ranges, and sell both cards.

from the dukes of Burgundy to the bishops of Basel, seized by the Swiss, ruled by the French, handed to the Bernese, and finally in the 1970s – after decades of political turmoil that briefly threatened to ignite violent conflict (see box on p.200) – granted independence to form its own government. Graffiti throughout the region showing the cantonal flag and the pro-separatist slogan "Jura libre" speak of a turbulent and politically active recent past. There's only a handful of towns, but most, including the cantonal capital **Delémont**, have spent the last centuries sidelined, well away from heavy industry and the major currents of European history, and so have retained a graceful, historic, Gallic air.

More than forty churches and chapels around the canton are decorated with **stained glass** by an array of modern and contemporary artists, including Fernand Léger; the tourist office has put together an itinerary, with notes, at ⑩www.vitrauxjurassiens.ch.

Delémont

An ancient town first mentioned in 737, **DELÉMONT** retains much of its medieval centre, and is an atmospheric place to stop over for an afternoon or a day. Its main historical claim to fame was as the summer residence of the prince-bishops of nearby Basel from the Middle Ages through to the Revolution. Last century, the stirrings for Jurassien independence (see box) led to Delémont being named in 1976 as capital of the new canton, but it retains a small-town charm – only around 12,000 people live here – and has good access into the rolling Jura countryside for walks and rides.

It takes five minutes to cross the river and stroll northwest from the station into the Old Town. The main street is Rue du 23-Juin, longer and more impressive than you might expect for a little town, and home to the eighteenth-century **Hôtel de Ville**, set skewed to the road and shaded by a huge tree. This ornate building was the scene, in 1947, of a historic demonstration which sparked the subsequent liberation movement. A few steps west is the **Église St-Marcel**, built in the 1770s in a mixture of the lavish decoration of Rococo and the formal lines of Neoclassical, and with some lovely dark oakwood stalls. Beside the church is the **château**, built in 1721.

At the western end of the road is the Porte de Porrentruy, one of the old city gates, with the Fontaine du Sauvage topped with a statue of a wild man of the woods and, adjacent, the **Musée Jurassien d'Art et d'Histoire** (Tues–Sun 2–5pm; Fr.6; SMP; ⑩www.jura.ch/musees). This modest but interesting museum houses in the basement the treasures from the St-Marcel church. Prime exhibit, prominent and proudly spotlit, is the beautiful golden mitre of St Germain, first abbot of Moutier in the seventh century. It's a shame that his twisted old leather sandals, which are far more evocative, get rather shorter shrift.

Discontent and secession

From the 1940s to the 1970s, Switzerland underwent serious political crisis, as a group of disaffected, historically marginalized people from the Jura pushed the flexibility of Swiss democracy to its limits. The origins of the conflict can be dated back to the 1815 Congress of Vienna which handed the area to Canton Bern. Bern welcomed the **Protestants** who lived in Biel/Bienne and the southern districts of the Jura around Moutier, while being powerful enough to ignore the destitute French-speaking **Catholic** peasants of the northern districts around Delémont and Porrentruy. Bernese moved into the region, bringing a new language and culture with them. Economic boom in the nineteenth century brought prosperity to Biel/Bienne, and largely passed Porrentruy by – but any rumblings of discontent in the north were quelled by the extreme hardship suffered by the whole region in the depression of the 1930s.

On September 20, 1947, a Jurassien member of Bern's parliament was refused election to the cantonal government because he spoke French. The outrage that followed led to the formation of a hardline anti-Bern grouping, which commanded popular support throughout the northern districts, and which got enough backing to force an extremely controversial **cantonal referendum** on splitting the Jura away from Bern. The voters of Canton Bern unsurprisingly rejected the proposal. However, it surprised the separatists that Jura too had voted against it: Porrentruy, Delémont and Saignelégier had supported separation two-to-one, but Moutier and its neighbours rejected it by three-to-one. The francophone, separatist Catholics of the north, a minority both within Protestant, German-speaking Bern as a whole but also within the Jura itself, decided to resort to direct action.

The late 1960s were taken up with obscure and complex attempts by Canton Bern to solve the problem, none of which garnered any support in the Jura. Hardliners became more entrenched in their demands for out-and-out secession, and **paramilitaries** – with their slogan "Jura libre" – stepped up their campaigns, seizing a police station in Delémont, the Swiss Embassy in Paris, sabotaging Bern's trams,

A couple of kilometres northeast of Delémont is the atmospheric **Chapelle de Vorbourg**, a pilgrimage site tended by monks that's dramatically located up on a forested crag below the ruins of a medieval castle.

Practicalities

Delémont's tiny **tourist office**, 12 Place de la Gare (Mon–Fri 9am–noon & 2–6pm, Sat 10am–4pm; ☏0901 123 401, ⊛www.delemont.ch), can help with local odds and ends, but the main cantonal office is in Saignelégier (see below). The train station has a **change counter** (Mon–Sat 5.45am–9.15pm, Sun 6.30am–9.15pm) and bike rental, with a **post office** opposite.

A kilometre east of the centre is an excellent HI **hostel**, 185 Route de Bâle (☏032 422 20 54, ⊛www.youthhostel.ch; ❶; April–Oct), with good facilities for families and quality food; dorms are Fr.25. *Hôtel du Boeuf*, 17 Rue de la Préfecture (☏032 422 16 91, ⓕ032 422 20 91; ❷), is a clean, well-run **hotel** within the Old Town. On the same street you'll find places to **eat**, including *La Cigogne* at no. 7 (closed Tues) serving home-made pasta and wood-fired pizzas. Place Roland-Béguelin, one street west, has plenty of shaded pavement cafés, and is also the scene of the town **market** (Wed & Sat morning).

Saignelégier and Franches-Montagnes

The stretch of the Jura range within Canton Jura itself is called **Franches-Montagnes**. Following wars between local lords in the twelfth and thirteenth

and, in a show of support for Walloon separatists, simultaneously storming the Belgian Embassy in Bern and the Swiss Embassy in Brussels. In 1973, Bern's cantonal government accepted terms for a **referendum on separation**, and on June 23, 1974, over ninety percent of eligible voters turned out, with a majority backing separation.

This shocked the Protestant southern districts of the Jura to the core, and immediately afterwards a pro-Bern, **anti-separatist bloc** formed, threatening violence against the Catholics of the north and demanding another referendum to allow the south to detach itself from the Jurassien independence movement and remain part of Bern. On March 16, 1975, this proposal was carried, but with a majority in Moutier of just 286 votes. Amidst the accusations of manipulation that followed, a pro-Jura demonstration turned into a full-scale riot, with 800 militants involved in an all-night running battle with police. Discontent simmered throughout the year, bursting into violence again in September.

Nonetheless, after a series of commune-by-commune referenda, popular opinion was shown to favour both the formation of a new canton in the north, and the adherence of the south to Bern. The split was inevitable. Moutier remained in Bern, and a new **Canton Jura** came into existence on January 1, 1979. Individual communes continued to shift over the next two decades: in 1989, the residents of Laufenthal voted to leave Bern and join Canton Basel-Land, and in 1995, Vellerat (population 70) voted to leave Bern and join Canton Jura.

As Jonathan Steinberg notes in his excellent book *Why Switzerland?* (see "Books", p.608), it was this minute concentration on opinion within the tiniest linguistic, cultural or ethnic units, as well as a political structure able to take such micro-referenda into account, that meant that the Swiss could address Jurassien discontent, allow it to be expressed (with a minimum of violence and no casualties) and then have the flexibility to incorporate it into a new national order. Most countries facing similar discontent have neither the political structures nor the flexibility to effect similar solutions.

centuries, Bishop Imier de Ramstein granted tax exemptions (*franchises* in French) to the whole area as a way to encourage repopulation, thus giving the area its name. It's a gorgeous landscape of rolling green hills and wide meadows flanked by fir trees, and is fiercely loved by the locals: one writer commented, "A Franc-Montagnard who sells off the land for profit is considered a traitor." In the 1960s, when the Swiss army proposed creating military installations and storehouses in the beloved hills, the locals got together and ensured (by voting) that such philistinism didn't get off the drawing board.

SAIGNELÉGIER is the main – indeed only – town in the region, just a shop or two larger than a village. Opposite the train station, which has bike rental, is the cantonal **tourist office** (Mon–Fri 9am–noon & 2–6pm, Sat 10am–4pm; May–Oct also Sun 10am–4pm; ℡0901 123 400, ⓦwww.juratourisme.ch), with an array of information, as well as local crafts and bottles of the delectable local firewater – a plum-based *eau-de-vie* called Damassine – for sale. On the second weekend in August, the **Marché-Concours National de Chevaux** rolls into town (ⓦwww.marcheconcours.ch), a giant horse market and show occupying an arena south of town with parades, races and celebrations.

There are limitless possibilities for hikes and cycle routes through the countryside around and about: aim southeast to the idyllic **Étang de la Gruère** lake, or southwest along the ridge to the ancient village of **LE NOIRMONT**, or north, down into the Doubs valley for plenty of riverside forest trails around the border hamlet of **GOUMOIS**; the Saignelégier–Goumois bus runs four times daily.

You can **camp** at *Sous La Neuvevie* (☎032 951 10 82; May–Oct), 2km south beyond the arena, or at the municipal site in Goumois (☎032 951 27 07; April–Sept). **Hotels** and pensions abound, in every hamlet and scenic spot. The friendly *Café-Hôtel du Soleil*, two minutes south of the station in Saignelégier (☎032 951 16 88, ⓦwww.cafe-du-soleil.ch; ❶), has seven rooms and a dorm (Fr.23), and doubles as a local arts centre, with some concerts and exhibitions, as well as good veggie food in their restaurant (closed Mon). *Hôtel du Doubs*, just by the riverside border crossing in Goumois (☎032 951 13 23, Ⓕ032 951 14 89; ❷; closed Feb), offers comfortable, rustic rooms as well as excellent cuisine.

With your own transport, you can get to a couple of excellent **restaurants**. *Le Theusseret* (☎032 951 14 51; closed Wed & Dec–Jan), just uphill from Goumois, is an outstanding place in an idyllic old mill beside a weir, specializing in fresh local produce and melt-in-the-mouth fish (*menus* from Fr.20). The pricier *Hôtel-Restaurant de la Gare* in Le Noirmont (☎032 953 11 10, ⓦwww.georges-wenger.ch; ❺; closed Jan; restaurant closed Mon & Tues) has won national acclaim; the fresh, locally inspired cuisine has a Michelin star, while the hotel embraces a handful of classic, individually styled guest rooms.

Porrentruy

In the heart of the **Ajoie** region – the bulge of Canton Jura that sticks out into France – is the rather attractive town of **PORRENTRUY**. Its graceful old centre is filled with eighteenth-century buildings, while a total of nine schools and colleges lend the cobbled streets a vivacity lacking in towns twice the size. Walking 500m west from the train station brings you onto the main Grand-Rue, dotted with medieval fountains and lined with ornate facades, including the **tourist office** housed in the old hospital at no. 5 (Mon–Fri 9am–noon & 2–6pm, Sat 10am–4pm; ☎0901 123 402). Following the street down to the river leaves you a few metres west of the fourteenth-century **Porte de France** and at the foot of the impressive **château** towering above. Its mighty Tour Refouss (daily 9–11.45am & 1.30–6pm; free) gives an expansive view.

Hôtel De La Poste, 15 Rue Malvoisins (☎032 466 18 27, ⓦwww.porrentruy .com/hoteldelaposte; ❶–❷), is a tidy little **hotel** in the Old Town with pleasant, quiet rooms. The same street has many pavement **cafés**, including jolly *Aux Deux Clefs* at no. 7 and the *Monkey Bar* opposite, which serves inexpensive crêpes (Fr.5–10). *Au Faucon*, 15 Rue des Annonciades, is a lively student bar, with DJs and bands in the cellar. Don't miss *Guillaume Tell*, 36 Grand-Rue, a combination bistro (with terrific fondues) and patisserie: they make fresh cheesecake every Friday morning, which is as good a reason as any for spending Thursday night in Porrentruy. In November, the huge **Marché de St-Martin** is an excuse for scoffing vast quantities of the local pork *saucisse d'Ajoie* at stand-up stalls, along with plenty of local Tête-de-Moine cheese and Damassine to wash it down.

St-Ursanne

South of Porrentruy, the River Doubs loops into Swiss territory for the only time, enclosing a neck of land known as the **Clos de Doubs**: the scenic road from Saignelégier running alongside the valley is dubbed, romantically, the Corniche du Jura. **ST-URSANNE** is a picturesque old walled village on the river, 10km from Porrentruy, blessed with both a twelfth-century church and five small hotels. The 1km walk down from the station is lovely, and you approach the village through its eastern, sixteenth-century Porte de St-Pierre.

The same road passes through to the Porte de St-Paul at the village's western end, while midway along, an alley branches south past the **tourist office**, 18 Rue du Quartier (Mon–Fri 9am–noon & 2–6pm, Sat 10am–4pm; ☎0901 123 403), through the Porte de St-Jean to an ancient, narrow bridge over the river. The beautiful **collégiale** church in the heart of the village, with its sculptured and painted south doorway, is airy and impressive inside, its Romanesque choir filled with lavish Baroque ornament. Above the nave, which has fifteenth-century frescoes, the vaulting is crowned with carved keystones giving the date 1301, and you'll find fewer more peaceful corners to spend a sunny hour or two than the Gothic cloister to the north.

Of the **places to stay**, the *Demi-Lune* (☎032 461 35 31, Ⓦwww. demi-lune.ch; ❷) and *Hotel du Boeuf* (☎032 461 31 49, Ⓕ032 461 38 92; ❷) are both clean and serviceable. If you're in the area at the right time, don't miss St-Ursanne's **Fête Médiévale**, on a weekend in early July, with everyone in costume, medieval foods and beers on offer, minstrels and musicians, dancers, acrobats, jugglers and fire-eaters, and, to top it all, a grand Gregorian mass on Sunday morning.

Travel details

Trains

Avenches to: Kerzers (for Bern; hourly; 30min); Murten (hourly; 5min); Payerne (hourly; 15min).
Biel/Bienne to: Basel (hourly; 1hr 10min); Bern (3 hourly; 30min); La Chaux-de-Fonds (hourly; 40min); Delémont (hourly; 30min); Lausanne (hourly; 1hr 10min); Neuchâtel (twice hourly; 20min); Solothurn (hourly; 20min); Yverdon (twice hourly; 45min).
La Chaux-de-Fonds to: Basel (hourly; 2hr); Bern (twice hourly; 1hr 20min); Biel/Bienne (hourly; 40min); Delémont (hourly; 1hr 20min); Lausanne (hourly; 1hr 30min); Le Locle (twice hourly; 7min); Neuchâtel (hourly; 30min); Saignelégier (hourly; 40min); Solothurn (hourly; 1hr 5min); Yverdon (hourly; 1hr).
Delémont to: Basel (hourly; 35min); Bern (hourly; 1hr); Biel/Bienne (hourly; 30min); Neuchâtel (hourly; 55min); Porrentruy (hourly; 30min); St-Ursanne (hourly; 20min); Solothurn (hourly; 40min).
Estavayer-le-Lac to: Fribourg (hourly; 35min); Payerne (hourly; 10min); Yverdon (hourly; 15min).
Murten/Morat to: Avenches (hourly; 5min); Fribourg (hourly; 25min); Ins (for Neuchâtel; hourly; 40min); Kerzers (for Bern; hourly; 15min); Payerne (hourly; 20min).
Neuchâtel to: Basel (hourly; 1hr 35min); Bern (hourly; 35min); Biel/Bienne (twice hourly; 20min); La Chaux-de-Fonds (hourly; 35min); Delémont (hourly; 1hr); Geneva (hourly; 1hr 20min); Lausanne (hourly; 50min); Le Locle (hourly;

45min); Porrentruy (hourly; 1hr 35min); Solothurn (hourly; 40min); Yverdon (twice hourly; 25min); Zürich (hourly; 1hr 55min).
Saignelégier to: La Chaux-de-Fonds (hourly; 40min).
Vallorbe to: Le Brassus (hourly; 45min); Croy-Romainmôtier (hourly; 15min); Lausanne (hourly; 45min).
Yverdon to: Basel (hourly; 2hr); Bern (hourly; 1hr 10min); Biel/Bienne (hourly; 45min); La Chaux-de-Fonds (hourly; 1hr); Delémont (hourly; 1hr 20min); Estavayer (hourly; 15min); Fribourg (hourly; 50min); Geneva (hourly; 55min); Lausanne (hourly; 25min); Neuchâtel (twice hourly; 25min); Payerne (hourly; 25min); Sainte-Croix (hourly; 40min); Solothurn (hourly; 1hr 5min).

Buses

Avenches to: Estavayer (4 daily; 45min); Fribourg (8 daily; 25min).
La Chaux-de-Fonds to: Le Locle (every 30min; 25min).
Orbe to: Croy-Romainmôtier (3 daily; 10min).
Yverdon to: Orbe (hourly; 25min); Vallorbe (11 daily; 30min).

Boats

(Following is a summary of June–Sept summer services; fewer boats run in other months, generally Sat & Sun only, if at all.)
Biel/Bienne to: Erlach & St Petersinsel (at least 3

daily; 45min–1hr); Neuchâtel (2 daily except Mon; 2hr 20min); Murten/Morat (1 daily; 2hr 50min); Solothurn (Soleure; at least 4 daily except Mon; 2hr 30min).

Estavayer-le-Lac to: Neuchâtel (at least 3 daily except Mon; 1hr 30min); Yverdon (at least 3 daily except Mon; 1hr 25min).

Murten/Morat to: Biel/Bienne (1 daily; 3hr 45min); Neuchâtel (at least 4 daily; 1hr 40min);

Môtier/Vully (at least 3 daily year-round; 40min).

Neuchâtel to: Biel/Bienne (at least 1 daily; 2hr 20min); Estavayer (at least 3 daily except Mon; 1hr 35min); Erlach & St Petersinsel (at least 1 daily; 1hr–1hr 30min); Murten/Morat at least 4 daily; 1hr 45min).

Yverdon to: Estavayer (at least 3 daily except Mon; 1hr 25min).

Basel and around

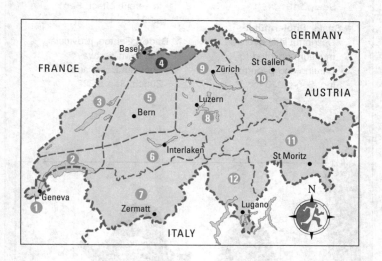

CHAPTER 4

Highlights

✳ **Fasnacht** Basel's carnival, an exultant three days of music, parades and merry-making. See p.216

✳ **The Münster** Highlight of a cathedral visit is a peaceful stroll around the adjoining cloisters. See p.218

✳ **Basler Papiermühle** Delightful little riverside museum devoted to printing and papermaking. See p.220

✳ **Museum Jean Tinguely** A stunning home for the mechanical sculptures of Switzerland's best-loved artist. See p.221

✳ **Fondation Beyeler** The city's best gallery, where the architecture sets off the modernist art within to serene effect. See p.221

✳ **Baden** Genteel provincial spa town partway between Basel and Zürich. See p.227

Basel and around

You might expect **BASEL** (Bâle in French, and often anglicized to Basle), situated on the Rhine exactly where Switzerland, Germany and France touch noses, to be the focal point of the continent, humming with pan-European energy. It's true that Basel's voters are the most fervently pro-European of all Switzerland's German speakers but, somehow, the close proximity of foreign languages and cultures has introverted the city rather than energized it: Basel's a curiously measured place, where equilibrium is everything. You won't find anyone shouting about the new Europe here; in fact, you're unlikely to find anyone shouting about anything at all. Even the city's massive carnival is a rigorously organized set piece.

With both a gigantic river port – Switzerland's only outlet to the sea – and the research headquarters of several pharmaceutical multinationals (including Novartis, one of the principal players in global development of GM crops and foods), Basel nurtures its reputation as Switzerland's wealthiest and most discreet city. Its historic centre, dominated by the awe-inspiring **Münster**, is definitely worth seeing, and the city's long-standing patronage of the arts has resulted in a panoply of first-rate museums and galleries – 35 in all, including the stunning **Fondation Beyeler**. And yet, bequeathed a glittering medieval past endowed with some of the greatest minds of European history (Erasmus, Holbein and Nietzsche, to name just three) and centuries-long access to the best of three neighbouring worlds, it's almost as if Baslers lost the plot when it came to defining their city for today. Most people seem to back the standard Swiss default option of gathering wealth in a discreet and orderly fashion, saving money shopping in France and having a better time partying in Germany. Which is all very well, but it tends to leave their own city rather bereft in the process; no town in Switzerland is harder for outsiders to penetrate.

Another fly in the ointment has been the recent Nazi gold controversy (see Contexts, p.593), in which it was indicated that venerable Basel – and, more specifically, the little-known but extremely powerful Bank for International Settlements headquartered in the city – spent the 1930s and 1940s quietly laundering the Nazis' ill-gotten gains under a cloak of neutrality. Evidence of such murky banking practice was received with shock, anger and disbelief in Basel and around the country, and has yet to be fully accepted. Unaccustomed to being faced with pointing fingers, Baslers may take some decades to assess and absorb the accusations.

Some history

A **Celtic** town stood on the hill now occupied by Basel's cathedral in the first century BC, but the city is traditionally dated to 44 BC, when the nearby

Roman city of Augusta Raurica (see p.225) was also founded. By 374 AD, **Basilia** was a fort, and seat of a bishopric following the Alemans' destruction of Augusta Raurica in the fifth century. In 917, the **Huns** swept through, sacking the town and destroying the Carolingian cathedral, but nonetheless by the thirteenth century, Basel had become a prominent town in the region. In 1225, Bishop Heinrich II of Thun built the first **bridge** across the Rhine – ancestor

Dr Hofmann's problem child

It was a Friday afternoon, April 16, 1943, in the laboratories of one of Basel's major pharmaceutical companies, Sandoz. The 37-year-old **Dr Albert Hofmann**, who had worked for Sandoz for fourteen years, was doing research into the various properties of rye fungus, in a search for a cure for migraine. During the afternoon he began to feel peculiar, and went home to lie down. "With eyes closed," he wrote, "I perceived an uninterrupted stream of fantastic pictures, extraordinary shapes with intense, kaleidoscopic play of colours." Unwittingly, Dr Hofmann had taken the first-ever acid trip: he had synthesized lysergic acid diethylamide, or **LSD**, from the fungus and had absorbed the drug through his fingertips.

After the weekend, he decided to experiment on himself with more scientific precision, and so dosed himself with some more LSD. This time, though, his apprehension at exploring an untested area of pharmacology led to unforeseen paranoias. While cycling home, "a demon had invaded me," he later wrote. Thinking that milk would act as an antidote to the drug, he knocked on his neighbour's door to ask for some, only to discover that "she was no longer Mrs R., but rather a malevolent, insidious witch with a coloured mask." He took to his bed. Next morning, he wrote, "breakfast tasted delicious and gave me extraordinary pleasure. When I later walked out into the garden, in which the sun shone after a spring rain, everything glistened and sparkled in a fresh light."

Dr Hofmann continued his quiet work into the psychoactive properties of both LSD and other **hallucinogens**, such as magic mushrooms, in Basel, while the drug itself – his so-called "problem child" – escaped the confines of the laboratory. A small band of writers were attracted to LSD as a way of unlocking the secrets of the mind: Aldous Huxley's *Doors of Perception* (1954) is probably the most famous creative work to stem from experiments with mescalin, an LSD derivative. Underground tests on volunteers by the British and American military were so dramatic that subsequent top-secret reports suggested that if LSD could be deployed in a missile fired at the Soviet Union, it could at a stroke put the entire Red Army out of action. The drug hit the headlines through its role at the core of the 1960s hippy counterculture: the turmoil it appeared to be causing to US society, with teenagers dropping out of college and discovering alternative lifestyles, unnerved the establishment to such an extent that the US Congress passed a bill criminalizing LSD in 1966. Worldwide governments followed suit shortly afterwards. In the late 1980s and 1990s, illegality notwithstanding, a whole new generation of partygoers rediscovered LSD, on a wave which popularized a variant hallucinogen, Ecstasy, and gave rise to "club culture".

Massive controversy persists as to the medical uses of LSD and hallucinogens in general (such as cannabis) – but any meaningful research is hampered by the drug's continuing outlawed status. Dr Hofmann himself, in an interview given in 1993 at the age of 87 to the British *Independent* newspaper, said: "LSD is not addictive, it is not toxic. The danger with LSD is this very deep change in consciousness: it can be beautiful, it can be terrifying. We have integrated alcohol and tobacco, but we've not integrated the hallucinogens. The next step is that it should be put into the hands of the psychiatrists. Fifty years' experience is nothing. For a substance which exhibits such new and extraordinary properties you must have much longer. It should be possible to study this substance properly."

of today's Mittlere Brücke – which coincided with the opening of a road over the Gotthard Pass into Italy, thus ensuring Basel's continuing growth as a natural focus for trade. Plague ravaged the population in 1349, killing some 14,000, and just seven years later a major earthquake and subsequent fire razed much of the city. Shortly after, the two communities on either side of the Rhine – Grossbasel and Kleinbasel – united as a single city. For almost twenty years (1431–49), the ecumenical **Council of Basel** pushed the city into the European limelight as the church set about reforming itself; Pope Felix V was crowned in Basel during the council's deliberations in 1440, and merchants, philosophers, emperors, princes and bishops flocked to the city, spurring the growth of papermaking, printing, and the development of ideas and trade in the region.

Responding to the impetus of the Renaissance, in 1460 Pope Pius II founded Basel's **university**, Switzerland's oldest and a major centre for humanism which was home to the philosopher **Erasmus of Rotterdam** throughout the 1520s and 1530s. During the sixteenth and seventeenth centuries, Protestant refugees from France, Flanders and Italy expanded Basel's industries but, since the city remained under the thumb of both noble families and the church, most were not accepted as citizens. In 1831, disaffected residents in the rural communities around Basel launched a **rebellion** against the city oligarchs and after a brief civil war managed to secede, forming their own half-canton of Basel-Land (countryside), separate to this day from Basel-Stadt (city).

Throughout the nineteenth century, a massive growth in industry led to the construction of the gigantic **port** facilities on the Rhine at the turn of the twentieth century, which still handle a large proportion of Swiss import/export trade a century later. But Basel is best known these days as a centre of both banking and chemical industry: the companies which started out dyeing silk ribbons woven by Huguenot refugees centuries ago are now the world's largest **pharmaceutical** companies, with their headquarters and laboratory facilities still in Basel.

Arrival, information and city transport

Basel has two **train stations** straddling three countries. **Basel SBB** is the main one; most of it is in Switzerland, although platforms 30–36 at the far end, used by trains to and from France, form an area known as **Bâle SNCF** which is in French territory, divided from the main concourse by passport control. Lots of trams pass through Centralbahnplatz outside the main doors; trams #1 and #8 run to Barfüsserplatz and the city centre. Many fast trains from Germany serve Basel SBB, but plenty – including local trains from Freiburg-im-Breisgau – stop short at Basel Badischer Bahnhof (**Basel Bad.** for short), run by Deutsche Bahn (DB) and located in an enclave of German territory within Kleinbasel; passport control separates the platforms from the ticket hall. Tram #6 from outside runs to Barfüsserplatz.

The **airport** (ⓦ www.euroairport.com) is 5km north in France, shared between Basel (Switzerland), Mulhouse (France) and Freiburg (Germany). A special customs-free fenced road links the Swiss terminal with Switzerland proper, along which express postbus #50 runs to and from Basel SBB station (daily every 15min 5am–11.30pm; Fr.6.60; takes 15min); slower city bus #30 also does this run (daily every 15–30min 6am–8pm; Fr.3.60; takes 20min). Swiss passes are valid on both. A taxi into the centre costs about Fr.35.

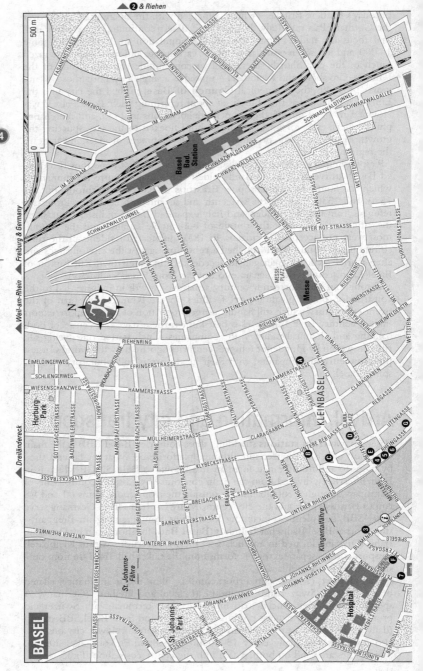

▲ ❷ & Riehen

◀ Dreiländereck   ◀ Weil-am-Rhein   ▲ Freiburg & Germany

500 m

0

BASEL

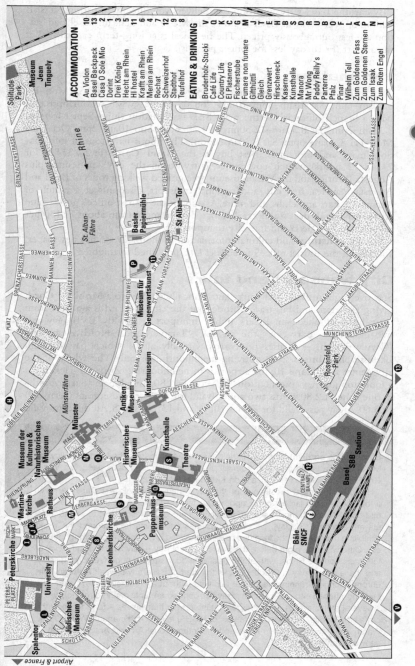

By **car**, the Basel-City autobahn exit delivers you directly to parking at SBB station, but car parks in Basel-Nord at the Messe and beneath Basel Bad. station are less outrageously priced. The best deal is at long-term car park S3 at the airport (Fr.18/day, less for longer periods).

Information

The main **tourist office** is in the city centre, Schifflände 5 (Mon–Fri 8.30am–6pm, Sat 10am–4pm; ☎061 268 68 68, ⓦwww.baseltourismus.ch), with a branch office inside the main SBB train station (June–Sept Mon–Fri 8.30am–7pm, Sat 8.30am–12.30pm & 1.30–6pm, Sun 10am–2pm; Oct–May Mon–Fri 8.30am–6pm, Sat 8.30am–noon). They both have tons of information, maps and brochures. Best buy is the **Basel Card** (Fr.25/33/45 for 24/48/72 hours), which covers free entry to all the city's museums, plus Augusta Raurica and the Vitra museum, free guided walking tours of Basel and Augusta Raurica, free city and regional transport, discounts at a clutch of restaurants, bars and clubs, and more. Ask about the tourist office's good-value **weekend-break** deal (valid Fri–Mon): a double room from about Fr.130 per night, including B&B and free city transport.

You'll find **listings** and cultural information in the *Basler Zeitung* newspaper, and also in the tourist office's free *Basel Live*, published fortnightly.

City transport and tours

Stay overnight in Basel and you're automatically entitled to a **Mobility Card**, giving free tram and bus travel throughout the city; the card is available from your hotel at check-in. Basel's public transport – run by BVB (ⓦwww.bvb-basel.ch), part of the TNW Tarifverbund Nordwestschweiz (ⓦwww.tnw.ch) – focuses on **trams**, virtually all of which pass through Barfüsserplatz; **buses** serve outlying neighbourhoods only. The whole of the city centre is in Zone 10; the airport is in neighbouring Zone 13. Tickets for a four-stop journey (press button "K") cost Fr.1.80, for a longer journey within one zone Fr.2.80, across two zones (valid for the Vitra museum in Germany) Fr.3.60. A day pass, valid for Zones 10, 11 and 13, costs Fr.8. All these are valid

---

Basel's festivals

Basel's huge **carnival** (see p.216), held over three days from the Monday following Mardi Gras, attracts attention from all over Switzerland, as does January's **Vogel Gryff** festival, centred specifically on Kleinbasel (see p.220).

However, the most prestigious of the city's many events is **Art Basel** (ⓦwww.artbasel.com), the largest contemporary art fair in the world, held at the Messe in mid-June. Although more trade- than public-oriented, it's fascinating to attend (tickets are around Fr.30/day), with major galleries and artists from around the world exhibiting a range of work, inspiring many associated arty happenings throughout the city. Otherwise, the night before the Swiss National Day – **July 31** – sees a festival of folk music on the Rhine, with stalls, traditional foods and a huge fireworks display, and the last Saturday in October marks the start of Basel's two-week **Autumn Fair**, Europe's longest-running traditional fair, held without a break since 1471 and now metamorphosed into sub-carnival festivities centred on funfairs and street jollity.

Several major events – of little general interest in themselves – tend to book the city's hotels solid: the Swiss Trade Fair, or MUBA, in March; the annual World Clock, Watch and Jewellery Fair in April; and the International Art and Antiques Show in early autumn.

for unlimited changes between trams, buses and local trains within the zonal boundaries. Ticket machines take Swiss coins and euros, but rarely notes. Swiss Pass holders travel free, but Eurailers and InterRailers pay full price. Transport offices in the station (daily 5.30am–10pm) and on Barfüsserplatz (Mon–Fri 8am–6pm, Thurs until 7pm, Sat 9am–5pm) provide information and sell tickets.

There are three bridges linking the city centre with Kleinbasel, but a more fun way to cross the Rhine – and a method used by many locals – is on one of the **cable-ferries** (ⓦ www.faehri.ch) that have plied to and fro for centuries (although the boats themselves are newer than that). The most useful, from north to south, are the *Vogel Gryff*, or **Klingentalfähre** (March–Oct Mon–Fri 7am–7pm, Sat & Sun 9am–7pm; Feb & Nov daily 9am–7pm); the *Leu*, or **Münsterfähre** (March–Oct daily 9am–noon & 1–7pm, except Fri morning); and the *Wild Maa*, or **St Alban-Fähre** (April–Sept Mon–Fri 7am–7pm, Sat & Sun 10am–7pm; March, Oct & Nov Mon–Fri 7–8am & 11.30am–6pm, Sat & Sun 10am–6pm). Fares are in the order of Fr.1.

As well as a host of eat-aboard cruises, the **ferry** company Basler Personenschifffahrt (☎061 639 95 00, ⓦwww.bpg.ch) runs a couple of scheduled boats to nearby points on the Rhine (May–Oct only), including a round trip to the German border at Dreiländereck (Fr.13), and longer journeys east to Kaiseraugst (Fr.40) and Rheinfelden (Fr.45). Boats depart from Schifflände beside the tourist office in the city centre, where there's a BPG ticket booth (Mon–Fri 9am–noon & 1–6pm; April–Oct also Sat 10am–4pm & Sun 8am–3pm).

Taxis, such as those from 33er (☎061 633 33 33), are a great way to get around if you think a Fr.5.60 flagfall plus Fr.2.85/km is a fair and reasonable price.

Tours

Guided **walking tours** of the Old Town start from the tourist office (May to mid-Oct Mon–Sat 2.30pm; rest of year Sat 2.30pm; Fr.15; takes 2hr). Otherwise, you can follow any of five **self-guided** historical wanders, all starting from Marktplatz (corner of Sattelgasse) and marked by small blue information signs: the Erasmus Walk (red on blue; 30min); Burckhardt Walk (light blue on blue; 45min); Platter Walk (yellow on blue; 45min); Paracelsus Walk (grey on blue; 1hr); or Holbein Walk (green on blue; 1hr 30min). All of them are described in a free leaflet available from the tourist office. The tourist office also has a brochure showing two self-guided **bike tours** of the city.

Accommodation

Basel thrives on the conference and convention trade: the vast Messe in Kleinbasel is Switzerland's largest exhibition centre, and attendees to major events often fill all **accommodation** in the city (and most in neighbouring cities too). Reserving ahead is strongly advised. As a way to service the tide of expense-account travellers, Basel's hoteliers tend to focus more on providing comforting extras, such as minibars and big-screen cable TV, than on character. You'll also find prices hiked during the week and/or while a big trade fair is on. Modest, inexpensive hotels are rarer than sharks in the Rhine, although the **B&B Agency Basel** (☎061 702 21 51, ⓦwww.bbbasel.ch) controls 150 inexpensive private rooms and furnished apartments in and around the city.

The tourist office has a dedicated **accommodation service**, targeted at visiting business people (☎061 271 36 84, ⓔhotel@messebasel.ch): bookings cost a stiff Fr.10 within Basel, Fr.15 elsewhere.

Hotels

Although staying in the Old Town has obvious attractions – and there are a couple of **inexpensive hotels** to oblige – Kleinbasel, with its easygoing, everyday atmosphere, is by no means a second best. Atmospheric Rheingasse, one street back from the river, is lined with hotels and bars. As you might expect, there are plenty of outrageously **expensive hotels** in Basel, filled most weekday nights with happily pampered businesspeople; plump instead for a night inside a work of art at the *Teufelhof*.

Inexpensive

Au Violon Im Lohnhof 4 ☎061 269 87 11, ⓦwww.au-violon.com. Once a convent, then a women's prison, now beautifully renovated to offer comfortable, stylish rooms above a quiet Old Town courtyard. Service is faultless, and they offer discounts for entry to the nearby *Bird's Eye Jazz Club*. ❸

Casa O Sole Mio Gatternweg 41, Riehen ☎061 641 54 16, ⓦwww.basel-bed-breakfast.ch. Fine B&B on the outskirts (tram #6 to Pfaffenloh), decorated in Laura Ashley style, with three separate two-room apartments and a studio, all demonstrating the kind of personal touch no hotel can manage. Keen prices, large breakfasts and free use of bikes make this an excellent choice. ❷

Hecht am Rhein Rheingasse 8 ☎061 691 22 20, ⓕ061 681 07 88. Plain, unfussy "garni" place, with some pricier rooms overlooking the river and both ensuite and shared-bath options. ❸

Rochat Petersgraben 23 ☎061 261 81 40, ⓦwww.hotelrochat.ch. Centrally placed two-star option beside the Peterskirche, with pleasant, if generic, rooms and a modestly cosy atmosphere. ❸–❹

Stadthof Gerbergasse 84 ☎061 261 87 11, ⓦwww.stadthof.ch. Plain and simple little hotel, bang on the main shopping drag. No ensuite rooms. ❷

Mid-range and expensive

Dorint Schönaustrasse 10 ☎061 695 70 00, ⓦwww.dorint.de. Excellent new business hotel in the heart of Kleinbasel's Messe district: the surrounding streets are dull, but the comfortable rooms compensate with superb facilities, such as multi-channel TV and hi-tech bathrooms. Onsite parking is an added bonus. ❺–❻

Drei Könige/Trois Rois Blumenrain 8 ☎061 260 50 50, ⓦwww.drei-koenige-basel.ch. Venerable Basel institution which began life as a small inn in 1026; that year it hosted Emperor Conrad II, his son Heinrich (later Heinrich III) and Rudolf III of Burgundy – the three kings of the title – who met to thrash out the details of Switzerland's absorption into the German Empire. These days, having received most of the crowned heads of Europe over the past millennium, it's still the haunt of presidents and royalty – who of course occupy the more expensive Rhineside rooms. ❾

Krafft am Rhein Rheingasse 12 ☎061 690 91 30, ⓦwww.krafftamrhein.ch. Atmospheric old pile on the Kleinbasel waterfront, with ornate and elegant rooms – shared-bath and ensuite – plus friendly service to go with them. Riverside rooms are pricier. ❸–❹

Merian am Rhein Rheingasse 2 ☎061 685 11 11, ⓦwww.merian-hotel.ch. Affordable quality above the renowned waterfront *Café Spitz*, with spacious rooms furnished in a pleasant, non-traditional style. ❺–❻

Schweizerhof Centralbahnplatz 1 ☎061 271 28 33, ⓕ061 271 29 19. Faded grandeur near the SBB station, once the absolute bee's knees but these days merely calm, cosy, tasteful and welcoming – expertly run by the same family for more than a century. ❹–❻

Teufelhof Leonhardsgraben 47 ☎061 261 10 10, ⓦwww.teufelhof.com. Outstanding and highly acclaimed boutique hotel in the heart of the city centre. The prestigious "Kunsthotel" section has eight rooms, redecorated every two or three years by a different artist; if you're prepared to do without minibars or TVs, you get the opportunity to live inside a work of art. The "Galeriehotel" bit, with 25 rooms, is less lavishly done up, and so less expensive, but still reworked annually by a local artist. A breath of fresh air compared with Basel's standard business hotels. ❺–❼

Camping and hostels

The nearest **campsite** is *Waldhort*, Heideweg 16 in Reinach (☎061 711 64 29, ⓕ061 711 48 33; March–Oct), about 10km south (tram #11 to Landhof).

Basel's pleasant riverside HI **hostel**, St Alban–Kirchrain 10 (☎061 272 05 72, ⓦwww.youthhostel.ch; ❶; closed late Dec), is quiet, spotless and well-run;

dorms are Fr.30. Tough competition comes from *Basel Backpack*, Dornacherstrasse 192 (℡061 333 00 37, ⓦwww.baselbackpack.ch; ❶; dorms Fr.29), a friendly independent hostel opened in 2002, a short walk behind the SBB station.

The City

The River **Rhine** describes an elegant right-angled curve through the centre of Basel, flowing from east to north and dividing the city in two. On the south/west bank is **Grossbasel** (Greater Basel), focused on the historic Old Town. Glitzy shopping streets connect **Barfüsserplatz** and **Marktplatz**, the two main Old Town squares, while medieval charm is retained in the steep lanes leading off to either side, where you'll find peaceful leafy courtyards surrounded by sixteenth-century town houses, a host of medieval churches, and the majestic steepled **Münster** dominating the skyline from its lofty Rhineside terrace. The Old Town and surrounding districts comprise the main business, shopping and nightlife areas of the city. The university, off Petersgraben, overlooks the Old Town from the west, while the main Swiss and French train stations are about a kilometre south. On the north/east bank of the Rhine is down-to-earth **Kleinbasel** (Lesser Basel), more residential and less weightily historical than its neighbour, with some laid-back nightlife and the German train station near the giant Messe conference centre some 500m east of Kleinbasel's central Claraplatz.

The **international border** with France is on the west bank of the Rhine, about 2km north of the city centre; that with Germany is on the east bank, about 3km north.

Barfüsserplatz and around

The focus of the Old Town is hectic **Barfüsserplatz**, crisscrossed by trams and surrounded by terrace cafés. Rubbing shoulders with the fast food joints and raucous pubs, on the corner with Steinenvorstadt, is the **Yellow House**, designed by Roger Diener, a yellowish concrete building adored by architects but ignored by the general public. Across the way is the **Puppenhausmuseum** (Doll's House Museum; daily 11am–5pm, Thurs until 8pm; Fr.7; ⓦwww. puppenhausmuseum.ch), with rather fun displays telling the story of the teddy – including plenty of venerable old bears – as well as glass-case displays of some gigantic doll's houses.

Historisches Museum

Overlooking the square are the soaring, pointed-arch windows of the **Barfüsserkirche**. This elegant white church, built by and named after the bare-footed Franciscans, dates from the fourteenth century, was deconsecrated in the eighteenth, and is now home to the impressive **Historisches Museum** (Mon & Wed–Sun 10am–5pm; Fr.7; ⓦwww.historischesmuseumbasel .ch), devoted to documenting Basel's cultural pre-eminence during the Middle Ages. Once you've absorbed the stunning detail of the monumental **choir stall** (1598) facing into the church, the highlight of the ground floor is the collection of sumptuous fifteenth-century **tapestries** (press the button to raise the protective blind shielding each one); these vivid, wall-sized pieces were woven to decorate private houses and churches, specifically in Basel and Strasbourg, and are exceptionally rare, both for their artistic quality and their excellent condition. Their imagery frequently concentrates on woodsmen, fabulous animals and courtly lovers – only three of the sixteen pieces show religious imagery – and one of the best is no. 235 (from 1490), the allegorical *Garden of Love*, showing two lovers playing cards inside a summer pavilion. The man has just slapped down a card with the words, "That last play of yours was a good one," while the woman nods in anticipatory triumph: "And it's won me the game!"

Downstairs you'll find an excellent detailed survey of Basel's history, including a board locating ancient buildings, maps and globes galore, the original 1640 **Lällekeenig** (see p.218), and bedchambers and elaborate wood-panelled rooms from the seventeenth century. Head to the back, and you'll come across a side room displaying the **treasury** of Basel cathedral, including two stunning silver-and-copper busts dating from 1270–1325, of St Pantalus (no. 251) and, with an even, almond-eyed gaze, a Buddhic St Ursula (no. 253). Another

Basel Fasnacht

Basel is famous around Switzerland and Europe for its ancient masked carnival, or **Fasnacht** (www.fasnacht.ch), a three-day affair starting on the Monday after Mardi Gras.

Some history
The earliest documented record of carnival is from 1376, although celebrations undoubtedly date back to well before that (earlier city records were destroyed in a fire in 1356): it's said that *Fasnacht* is related to an old word *faseln*, meaning fruitfulness. In the fourteenth century, carnival took the form of **knightly tournaments** held on Münsterplatz, events which may have had an origin in pagan ancestor worship since noble families had been buried in and around the Münster for generations. Through the **Middle Ages**, theologians railed against both excessive drinking at carnival time and the use of devilish masks and disguises: it's no coincidence that the iconoclasm which marked the beginning of Basel's Reformation broke out on Mardi Gras, 1529. For some unexplained reason, over time celebrations were shifted one week later to after the beginning of Lent (Basel still celebrated carnival despite its embrace of Protestantism after the Reformation), and were transformed into a series of **processions** organized by the city's guilds and associations. Drum-and-pipe bands accompanied the display of weaponry, dancing and fancy-dress revelry. Greater organization throughout the nineteenth and early twentieth century resulted in the carnival of today, where some 12,000 people take part under the auspices of several hundred **Cliques**, groups or musical bands, all of which must apply in advance to the Fasnachts-Comité for permission to march.

The night before
On the Sunday after Mardi Gras, thousands of *Fasnächtler* kick off their celebrations at the town of **Liestal**, 17km south of Basel, where, after dark, the **Chienbesen** parade begins, giant bonfires dragged through the medieval town on floats with onlookers brandishing flaming torches of pine branches above their heads in a dramatic, ancient spectacle. The tradition is a long-standing one, described as far back as the sixteenth century, but it's been dogged by controversy, at one time from the Church, which regarded it (with some justification) as diabolic in origin, and in more recent times from the fire service which regards it (with equal justification) as being dangerous to life and property. Despite the raging inferno dragged through Liestal's narrow streets each year, flames as high as the houses and people crammed shoulder to shoulder throughout the Old Town amidst the flying cinders and scorching heat, no harm has yet been done. Neighbouring **Sissach** has similar fiery revels, with

high-light is a series of paintings showing the **Dance of Death**. The sequence originally formed part of a sixty-metre-long mural, which covered the inside of the cemetery wall of Basel's Dominican convent until its demolition in 1805. The mural depicts, in a graphic reminder of human mortality, an array of people of all different ages and professions on a macabre procession, which leads, eventually, to the cemetery's charnel house.

Marktplatz and around

Shop-lined Gerbergasse and Freiestrasse, as well as a dense network of narrow, sloping medieval alleys such as Schneidergasse (Tailor Street), Sattelgasse (Saddle Street) and Imbergässlein (Ginger Alley), run north from Barfüsserplatz to **Marktplatz**, the Old Town's other main square, crowded every morning with fruit-and-veg stalls. Lighting up the broad rectangular space with a splash

the torching of a 10m-high effigy, the Chluris, while in **Biel-Benken** to the west, locals fling burning wooden discs into the night sky in an equally mesmeric fire-orgy termed the Reedlischigge.

Morgestraich, Schnitzelbängg and Guggemuusige

Well after midnight, everyone decamps back to Basel in preparation for the **Morgestraich**, a magical and unmissable parade of huge illuminated lanterns through the city centre which begins in invariably freezing darkness at 4am on the Monday morning. From lunch time, the various masked *Cliques* parade through the city in a **Cortège**, with much music, dancing and jollity, followed in the evening by masked bands and small groups with fifes and drums roving through the Old Town. The ornately decorated Morgestraich lanterns are left on display in Münsterplatz from Monday evening through to Wednesday morning.

Baslers take their costumes seriously (half-masks and face paint are taboo), and many people spend weeks in advance making huge, cartoonish papier-mâché heads and sewing lavish jester-like costumes. However, it's a feature of Basel's carnival that unless you're part of a performing *Clique*, you have to stay as an **observer** – unlike, for instance, in Luzern, where carnival is an all-in street party. You're encouraged to contribute to the *Cliques*' expenses by buying a **Blaggedde**, a metal badge produced by the Fasnachts-Comité each year in copper (Fr.7), silver (Fr.14) and gold (Fr.45) versions; get them on the street, from kiosks and hotels, or the tourist office.

During the Monday and Wednesday evenings, it's a tradition for locals to recite **Schnitzelbängg**, satirical verses directed at local bigwigs, in the city's taverns and restaurants. Tuesday night sees **Guggemuusige** concerts of comical oompah, played on old and dented brass instruments by bands gathered in Barfüsser-, Clara- and Marktplatz, and musical groups and masked *Cliques* continue to prowl through the Old Town during Wednesday afternoon until nightfall – whereupon everybody turns in for some restorative sleep. Throughout the celebrations, you'll come across places selling *Fasnachtsküchli*, a light, thin round cake covered in icing sugar, and *Fastenwähe*, a kind of caraway-seed pretzel.

If you're serious about attending Basel *Fasnacht*, you'd do well to read Peter Habicht's excellent book *Lifting The Mask* (see p.606), the most evocative description in English of the topsy-turvy few days, replete with personal anecdotes, explanations of otherwise incomprehensible carnival behaviour and, most importantly, plenty of dos and don'ts.

of eye-catching colour is the elaborate scarlet facade of the **Rathaus** (Town Hall), the central arcaded section sixteenth-century, the tower and side annexe both late nineteenth-century. Feel free to wander into the frescoed interior courtyard.

At the northern end of Marktplatz is the small Fischmarkt, with its central fountain, just beyond which is the tourist office at the southern end of the **Mittlere Brücke**, a modern construction at the site of what was for centuries the only bridge over the Rhine between the Bodensee and the North Sea. On a facade looking along the bridge, you'll spot an odd little bust of a bearded man: this is the **Lällekeenig**, or Tongue King. The original Lällekeenig adorned the gate of the bridge from the mid-seventeenth century, greeting all arrivals to the city until the gate's demolition in 1839, and had a clockwork motor so that he rolled his eyes and stuck out his tongue in time with the ticking. He was probably made to demonstrate what Grossbaslers thought of their down-at-heel Kleinbasel neighbours, but these days the city is united, the clockwork original is in the Historisches Museum, and the Lällekeenig still staring along the bridge is a static copy.

From Marktplatz and Fischmarkt, quiet old lanes climb steeply west towards the former city walls; up here are the Gothic **Peterskirche** (Tues–Sun 10am–5pm) on Petersgraben, the plain exterior of which harbours late-medieval frescoes, and more or less opposite, Basel's **university** campus. Among many famous names connected with the university, Nietzsche taught classical philosophy here from 1869 to 1879. The narrow Spalenvorstadt leads west to the **Spalentor**, most elaborate of the surviving city gates, with massive wooden doors and a huge portcullis. Nietzsche lived round the corner, at Schützengraben 47. The small **Jüdisches Museum der Schweiz**, Kornhausgasse 8 (Jewish Museum; Mon & Wed 2–5pm, Sun 11am–5pm; free; Ⓦ www.igb.ch), displays gravestone fragments with Hebrew inscriptions which date back to 1222, as well as plenty of interesting historical items from religious and everyday Jewish life. Their short video (in English) on the history of the Jews in Basel is excellent.

Both Leonhardsgraben and the lovely Heuberg trickle on through a delightful old residential quarter to the beautiful **Leonhardskirche**, a Gothic construction built after the great 1356 earthquake with attractive portholed windows and an elaborate cat's cradle of vaulting within. The gallery is accessible, but only up the tightest, narrowest spiral staircase imaginable. Barfüsserplatz is just down the hill.

The Münster

Sixteenth-century lanes lead up behind Barfüsserplatz to Basel's cathedral, the impressive **Münster** (Easter–Oct Mon–Fri 10am–5pm, Sat 10am–4pm, Sun 1–5pm; rest of year Mon–Sat 11am–4pm, Sun 2–4pm), built in the thirteenth century of red sandstone with a patterned roof and rebuilt following an earthquake in 1356. The tower of St George, on the left of the main frontage, has some white stonework dating from the original church (consecrated in 1019), as well as a thirteenth-century statue of the saint impaling a dragon. Stone carving from 1280 above the main portal shows the cathedral's founder, Emperor Heinrich II, holding a model of the church, with his wife Kunigunde to the left. To the right is a Foolish Virgin, with her Satanic seducer.

Inside, in the north aisle, is the tomb of the Renaissance humanist Erasmus. Close by is the **St Vincent panel**, a Romanesque relief from around 1100 telling the story of the martyr who was killed in 312 AD: on the top left,

Vincent speaks up for his bishop and is flogged for it; to the right he is tortured and led into a furnace; below, angels carry his soul to heaven while ravens protect his body before it is dumped at sea, retrieved and buried in a proper tomb. The lacy **pulpit** was carved – incredibly – from a single block of stone in 1486. On the north side of the choir, which has some intricate capitals, is the **tomb of Queen Anna**, wife of Rudolf of Habsburg, who chose to be buried in Basel, alongside her three-year-old son Karl, in an attempt to make up for her husband's cruelty whilst ruling the town during the 1270s. In the **crypt** you'll find ninth-century remains of an earlier cathedral along with some late-Romanesque frescoes.

One of the highlights of Basel is a wander through the memorably atmospheric **cloisters** adjoining the cathedral to the south, filled to bursting point with timeworn tombs and memorial stones. You emerge onto the **Pfalz**, an open, tree-lined terraced bastion behind the cathedral choir which overlooks the Rhine and gives views as far as the Black Forest. Carved elephants and grotesque creatures support the arches of the choir, and round the corner, on the north side of the church, is the spectacular **St Gallus Doorway**, a rich piece of Romanesque carving, with Christ at top centre, Wise and Foolish Virgins below him, and John the Baptist on the extreme left below a kneeling angel sounding a trumpet to wake the dead. Above is a round window depicting the wheel of fortune.

Tranquil alleys run northwest from Münsterplatz, amongst them Augustinergasse, with, at no. 2, the **Museum der Kulturen** (Tues–Sun 10am–5pm; Fr.7; SMP; ⓦwww.mkb.ch) housing an overwhelmingly massive anthropological collection, and, separately in the same building, the equally daunting **Naturhistorisches Museum** (same hours and ticket; SMP; ⓦwww.nmb.ch).

The narrow Rheinsprung lane leads on to the **St Martinskirche** with, beside it, the little Elftausendjungfern-Gasse, or Alley of the Eleven Thousand Virgins; its curious name commemorates the martyrdom in Cologne of St Ursula (who refused to marry a pagan prince) and her legendary company of female supporters. The tiny lane feeds down to the Mittlere Brücke.

East of Barfüsserplatz

From Barfüsserplatz, Steinenberg climbs east. A short way up, past the sputtering Tinguely fountain in the grounds of the theatre, is the **Kunsthalle** (Tues–Sun 11am–5pm, Wed until 8.30pm; Fr.9, ⓦwww.kunsthallebasel.ch), its big white rooms staging a continual flow of cutting-edge contemporary art shows.

At the top of the hill, St Alban-Graben heads northeast to the river. The venerable **Antikenmuseum** is at no. 5 (Tues–Sun 10am–5pm; Fr.7; SMP; ⓦwww.antikenmuseumbasel.ch). Chronological displays begin on the top floor and work downwards, with superb Greek and Etruscan pottery, decorated in beautiful detail, standing out on every floor. The upper-floor vestibule of House B has a set of fourth-century BC floor-standing funerary vases from Apulia in southern Italy, one of which is painted with an entertaining scene of three men stealing honey and being chased by a swarm of bees. The basement of the museum holds temporary exhibitions, often of Egyptian or Middle Eastern antiquities.

The Kunstmuseum

Basel's world-famous **Kunstmuseum** is at St Alban-Graben 16 (Tues–Sun 10am–5pm; Fr.10, also gives entry to Museum für Gegenwartskunst; free on

Dating back to the thirteenth century or so, Kleinbasel's strange **Vogel Gryff** festival (⊛www.vogel-gryff.ch) incorporates pagan rituals and customs in the guise of fêting the head of one of the three guild associations of Kleinbasel. It takes place on January 13, 20 or 27, depending on which association holds the baton that year. At 11am, a raft carries the **Wild Maa** (a hairy figure symbolizing fertility) down the Rhine to the Mittlere Brücke, where he holds an uprooted pine sapling and dances – with his back always turned to Grossbasel – to an ancient drum march. The **Leu** (lion) and **Vogel Gryff** (griffon) meet him on the bank to the accompaniment of booming cannon, and at noon the three of them stand at the midpoint of the Mittlere Brücke and dance a traditional, highly ritualized dance to the sound of a drum, every precise step documented from the origins of the festival in the Middle Ages. This is as close as the party gets to Grossbasel, since everyone then heads back to Kleinbasel for the **Gryffemähli**, a luncheon for the members of the three guilds (where the symbolic dance is repeated), and a procession through the streets accompanied by four jingling jesters who collect money for Kleinbasel's poor. During the evening, the party enters full swing, with much drinking and merrymaking, while the three figures continue to dance their odd and mysterious dance in the older Kleinbasel restaurants.

1st Sun of month; SMP; ⊛www.kunstmuseumbasel.ch). It's a rather stern Neoclassical building – all marble floors, high ceilings and grand staircases – which tends to do its absorbing collection down a bit, but don't let yourself be put off. There's a dazzling array of **twentieth-century art**, including Dali's nightmarish *Perspectives*, roomfuls of paintings by Arp, Klee, Léger, Munch, Braque and the Impressionists, a fantastically attenuated cat by Giacometti, and fluid sculptures in wood by Kirchner and Scherer. In 1967, the Basel electorate voted to use Fr.6 million of public funds to buy two Picassos for the museum, *Arlequin assis* and *Les deux frères* – and then stumped up another Fr.2.4 million to guarantee the purchase. The artist was so impressed by this popular enthusiasm that he personally donated four more works.

The gallery's modern art, and its large collection of nineteenth-century German, French and Swiss painting, is however completely overshadowed by its vast and absorbing **medieval** collection. Dozens of rooms are devoted to works by the prolific Holbein family in particular, including the extraordinary two-metre long *Body of the Dead Christ in the Tomb* (1521), a painting which obsessed Dostoevsky when he visited the museum on August 23, 1867. He climbed on a chair to get a better view of it, and then started to shout "Holbein was a great painter and a poet!" His wife, who thought he was about to have a fit, had to usher him from the room. The work subsequently popped up in Dostoevsky's novel *The Idiot*, when a character's recollections of it lead him to question the existence of God.

Down to the river

St Alban-Vorstadt continues east to the **St Alban-Tor**, one of the city's thirteenth-century gates. Close by, down by the river, is the **Museum für Gegenwartskunst**, St Alban-Rheinweg 60 (Contemporary Art; Tues–Sun 11am–5pm; joint admission with Kunstmuseum; SMP), its installations by Frank Stella, Joseph Beuys and others sharing space with recent German painting.

A stroll away, in a restored medieval waterfront mill at St Alban-Tal 37, is the **Basler Papiermühle** (Basel Papermill), housing the wonderful Schweizerisches Papiermuseum und Museum für Schrift und Druck (Swiss

Museum of Paper, Writing and Printing; Tues–Sun 2–5pm; Fr.9; SMP; Ⓦ www.papiermuseum.ch). The waterwheel alongside, remnant of the growth of the industry in the fifteenth century, still functions, and, in amongst exhibits of paper and typography, the museum stages demonstrations of typecasting, typesetting, bookbinding and – most engagingly – papermaking, where you can work through the whole process yourself, from pulp to final product.

A landing-stage across from the mill marks the St Alban **ferry** *Wild Maa* (see p.213), which can scoot you across the Rhine to the north bank for the leisurely stroll east along Solitude Promenade to the Tinguely Museum.

Museum Jean Tinguely

On the north bank of the Rhine, in Solitude Park under the Wettsteinbrücke, in a building designed by the celebrated Swiss architect Mario Botta that is a work of art on its own terms, is the outstanding **Museum Jean Tinguely** (Wed–Sun 11am–7pm; Fr.7; Ⓦ www.tinguely.ch). Tinguely, who was born in Fribourg in 1925 and died in Bern in 1991, is perhaps Switzerland's best-loved artist, a maverick postmodernist who broadened the confines of static sculpture to incorporate mechanical motion. Living for years on a farm in the Swiss countryside with his long-time partner and fellow artist Niki de St-Phalle, Tinguely used scrap metal, plastic and bits of everyday junk to create room-sized Monty-Pythonesque machines that – with the touch of a foot-button – judder into life, squeaking, clanking and scraping in entertaining parody of the slickness of our modern performance-driven world. Most are imbued with an irreverent sense of humour (*Klamauk*, or Din, is a moving tractor complete with banging bells and cymbals, smoke, smells and fireworks), but some, such as *Mengele Dance of Death*, are darkly apocalyptic. Elsewhere in the city, a Tinguely fountain spits and burbles outside the Kunsthalle.

Fondation Beyeler

If you had to pick just one of Basel's many top-rated museums to visit, go for the gallery run by **Fondation Beyeler**, at Baselstrasse 101 in the northeastern suburb of Riehen (daily 10am–6pm, Wed until 8pm; Fr.12; tram #6 to Riehen Dorf; Ⓦ www.beyeler.com). A masterfully elegant building, designed by Renzo Piano, houses a small but exceptionally high-quality art collection featuring some of the best works by some of the twentieth century's best artists – Picasso,

---

Three Countries' Corner

One of Basel's curiosities is its location at the meeting point of France, Germany and Switzerland: there are few places in the world where you can stand at the exact point where three countries meet. If you take tram #8 to its terminus amongst the massive warehouses and shipping cranes at Kleinhüningen, cross to the north bank of the River Wiese, head left 200m to the Rhine, then right (north) along a spit of land beside more warehouses and train sidings for 300m, you'll come to **Dreiländereck** (Three Countries' Corner), marked by a futuristic rounded steel-and-glass building. This is the *Restaurant Dreiländereck* (☎ 061 639 95 40, Ⓦ www.dreilaendereck.ch), a pricey and rather soulless place for eating, but not bad for a riverside coffee and bun. Just beyond, on the very nose of the spit of land, is a tall, slender sculpture pointing the way west to the French bank of the Rhine, north to the German customs shed 50m away, and south into Switzerland. Unfortunately, as you might have predicted, everything looks more or less the same on all shores. Boats depart from beside the restaurant to take you back to Basel Schifflände.

Giacometti, Warhol, Rothko, Rodin, Klee, Kandinsky, Bacon, Miró and more. Both Matisse's paper cutouts (*Nu bleu* and others) and Mondrian's geometric abstractions – familiar from innumerable posters and T-shirts – still have the power to startle as full-size originals, as do Mark Tobey's crazed *White Journey* and *Oncoming White*.

For some gentle relief, sink into a huge white sofa opposite a giant Monet to indulge in dreamy contemplation both of the waterlilies in front of you and, through the floor-to-ceiling window, the watery gardens outside.

Vitra Design Museum

Across the border in Germany, 10km north of Basel, is the small town of **WEIL-AM-RHEIN**, unremarkable but for being the location of Vitra, a famous design company which collaborates with top international designers to produce office and home furniture, and whose premises – on an out-of-town green-field site – are the work of some of the world's leading contemporary architects. If you're halfway interested in design, you'll love the **Vitra Design Museum** (Charles Eames Strasse 2; Tues–Sun 11am–6pm; €5.50; Ⓦwww.design-museum.de). Bus #55 from the forecourt of Basel Bad. station takes twenty minutes to drop you outside the museum (passport needed); a Fr.3.60 two-zone transport ticket is valid, but the free mobility ticket you get from your hotel and all Swiss passes are not.

The building itself is engaging enough to start with, a teetering, almost Cubist concoction by American architect Frank O. Gehry, while inside you'll find a changing series of exhibitions on various themes of design, anything from furniture – with original chairs by Frank Lloyd Wright, Charles and Ray Eames, Philippe Starck and others – to lighting or industrial design. It's also possible to join a guided tour of the array of avant-garde architecture comprising the Vitra site (check times and price with museum in advance), which includes two factory buildings by Nicholas Grimshaw, a supremely elegant, award-winning fire station by Zaha Hadid (now used as an extension to the museum), Tadao Ando's serene conference centre and Alvaro Siza's assembly hall.

Eating and drinking

Drawing influences from the cuisines of France and Germany into its native Swiss culinary tradition, Basel manages deftly to sit on the fence as far as **eating and drinking** go. Beer and sausages is the snack of choice, but it's equally possible to find venues to savour classic French cuisine and, if the city could be said to have a local speciality, it's salmon (originally plucked from the Rhine but these days more likely to be imported) marinated in the fruity local white wine and topped with fried onions.

Cafés and café-bars

There are plenty of **cafés** and *Bierstuben* around Marktplatz and Barfüsserplatz, with nearby Steinenvorstadt also core snacking territory. Perfect accompaniment to a Basel teatime is the local speciality *Leckerli*, a melt-in-the-mouth ginger biscuit made with honey, spices, almonds and candied orange- and lemon-peel: buy over-the-counter at the Läckerli-huus patisserie at Gerbergasse 57 or in *Café Spitz* (see "Restaurants", p.224).

Grossbasel

Fumare non fumare Gerbergasse 38. Cool, high-ceilinged espresso bar on a people-watching junction, also with its own beer – one side is smoking, one non-smoking (hence the name). Open late.

Paddy Reilly's Steinentorstrasse 45. Standard Irish pub, Guinness and all, also serving up fish and chips and shepherd's pie for around Fr.16.

Pfalz Münsterberg 11. Tiny, bright nook, with excellent fresh juices, sandwiches, quiches and a salad buffet. Closed Sat & Sun.

Teufelhof Leonhardsgraben 47. Supremely trendy wine bar attached to the art-hotel of the same name, with a wide range of bottles to sample and a clientele that knows it's living at the city's artistic cutting edge.

Zum Isaak Münsterplatz 16. A tranquil, much-loved tea-drinkers' café and cellar-theatre that knows its Darjeeling from its Lapsang Souchong, and also offers lovingly prepared snacks and full meals. Also with a courtyard terrace. Closed Mon.

Zum Roten Engel Andreasplatz. Cosy den on a secluded Old Town courtyard, with trestle tables outside and amiable, alternatively minded regulars scoffing veggie snacks, fresh juices and full meals (Fr.16).

Kleinbasel

El Platanero Webergasse 21. Incongruously exuberant little corner deli-café, with two or three tables for *chorizo picante con arroz* and fried bananas, with red-hot salsa bottled on the tables and playing on the stereo.

Fischerstube Rheingasse 45. Excellent backstreet beerhall, full of atmosphere, that brews its own beers as a snub to the big-name breweries and so attracts dedicated, single-minded drinkers. Salted pretzels hanging from wooden stands on every table, a dark, smoky interior, rich, powerful beer plus a uniquely hearty clientele make for a memorably convivial evening.

Grenzwert Rheingasse 3. Cool, jazzy, spotlit little bar, attracting black-clad Kleinbaslers by the score.

Hirscheneck Lindenberg 23 ⓦ www.hirscheneck .ch. Graffitied budget café-bar-restaurant, co-op owned and popular with a rough-edged crowd, with loud music and simple food in generous portions (Fr.15).

Kaserne Klybeckstrasse 1 ⓦ www. restaurantkaserne.ch. An alternative-style hangout, with shady outdoor trestle tables and benches, offering veggie *menus* from Fr.16 and a very popular weekend brunch buffet that exemplifies the difference between laid-back Kleinbaslers and their more traditional neighbours across the river. The evening bar section retains much the same atmosphere, on Tuesdays becoming Basel's premier gay and lesbian meeting place. Closed Mon.

Parterre Klybeckstrasse 1 ⓦ www.parterre.net. A friendly, atmospheric café-bar next to *Kaserne* with Tom Waits on the stereo and light bulbs hanging on strings. Excellent food from Fr.10. Closed Sun.

Zum Goldenen Fass Hammerstrasse 108. Small but very popular bar attached to a restaurant (see p.224), regularly packed.

Restaurants

The host of international visitors to Basel with access to high-end expense accounts pushes up **restaurant** costs, but it's also not hard to uncover cosy local eateries for home-cooked fare in all corners of the city centre. Aside from these listed, you'll find straightforward places to nosh on all the main squares, including a *Mövenpick* brasserie on Marktplatz, although we've bypassed the clutch of rather stiff restaurants within all the big business hotels around the Messe.

Inexpensive

Café Damas Steinenberg. Small Arabic eatery beside the Puppenhausmuseum, steps from Barfüsserplatz, offering takeaway falafel and kebabs, as well as sit-down dishes like *magloubah* (chicken with rice).

Country Life Sattelgasse 3. Small veggie and wholefood diner off Marktplatz (*menus* Fr.17–20).

Manora Greifengasse. Self-service restaurant in this department store chain (see p.49).

Mr Wong Steinenvorstadt 3. Popular fast-food joint just off Barfüsserplatz that piles your dish high with fresh-cooked Asian fare for Fr.12 or so.

Pinar Herbergsgasse 1. Plain Turkish neighbourhood diner, with inexpensive *pide* (Turkish pizza).

Mid-priced and expensive

Au Violon Im Lohnhof 4 ☎061 269 87 11. Very pleasant brasserie in a renovated old building near the Leonhardskirche, offering seasonal specialities prepared with care. *Menus* from Fr.20. Closed Sun & Mon.

Bruderholz-Stucki Bruderholzallee 42 ☎061 361 82 22, ⓦ www.stucki-bruderholz.ch. One of Switzerland's best restaurants, awarded two

Michelin stars for its classic style and inventive touches. Expect *menus* starting from Fr.85 – if you can book far enough ahead to secure a table. Closed Sun & Mon.

Café Spitz In *Hotel Merian*, Rheingasse 2 ☎061 685 11 11. Historic building in the Kleinbasel district, with a fine riverside terrace and the best fish in Basel, if not Switzerland. Fr.30 upwards.

Gifthüttli Schneidergasse 11 ☎061 261 16 56. The best place for traditional local cooking (even the menu is in Basel dialect), whether in the standard *Stube* downstairs or the more formal restaurant upstairs. They specialize in *cordon bleus* – slabs of cheese-slathered meat – with thirteen choices (around Fr.33), as well as plenty of other Swiss belt-bulgers.

Gleich Steinenvorstadt 23. Upscale, very genteel vegetarian restaurant, with nothing but the tinkling of cutlery to disturb the low hum of discreet chat. Closed Sat & Sun.

Kunsthalle Steinenberg 7. Contemporary-art gallery with a leafy terrace-café favoured by Basel's sizeable crowd of arty literati. The restaurant section is a reliable city-centre choice, open daily with 600 covers and a range of *menus* from Fr.20 upwards.

Teufelhof Leonhardsgraben 47. Gourmet restaurant attached to a super-trendy design hotel. The food is of impeccable quality, although the cuisine is like the art: avant-garde. No classics here, with a constantly changing menu marrying diverse flavours and styles with panache. A broad array of wines by the glass and bottle complete the picture. Expect to pay well over Fr.100 a head.

Wilhelm Tell Spalenvorstadt 38. Cosy, quiet den for solid Swiss fare, *rösti*, sausages and all, from Fr.15. Closed Sun.

Zum Goldenen Fass Hammerstrasse 108 ☎061 693 11 11. Quality formal restaurant with an informal air in a Kleinbasel residential neighbourhood. Excellent, top-quality organic food, lightly prepared (plus veggie options), with lunchtime *menus* around Fr.20, evening ones double that.

Zum Goldenen Sternen St Alban-Rheinweg 70 ☎061 272 16 66, ⓦwww.sternen-basel.ch. Gracious old riverside wood-beamed inn, restored perfectly, serving upmarket, old-fashioned French cuisine in the banqueting room and the waterfront garden terrace, with a number of highly regarded fish dishes. Expect to pay Fr.25 and up.

Nightlife and entertainment

You wouldn't really come to Basel for the **nightlife**, and even the locals tend quite often to prefer skipping across the border to nearby towns in Germany or France to let their hair down. Even the presence of university students doesn't lighten the tone tremendously. You can get **tickets** for almost any event from TicketCorner (☎0848 800 800) or Musik Hug, Freiestrasse 70 (☎061 272 33 95).

The Basel Symphony (ⓦwww.sinfonieorchesterbasel.ch) and Chamber (ⓦwww.kammerorchesterbasel.ch) **orchestras** both perform at the central Stadtcasino, along with a host of guest performers. The Musik–Akademie, Leonhardsstrasse 6 (ⓦwww.unibas.ch/mab), has an international reputation, often presenting concerts and recitals from students and visiting soloists. Basel's main draw is its burgeoning **theatre** scene (universally in German), with the Stadttheater, Theaterstrasse 7, and the Komödie, Steinenvorstadt 63, leading the field; book for both on ☎061 295 11 33. Of the dozens of smaller theatres, Baseldytschi Bihni, Im Lohnhof 4 (☎061 261 33 12), offers a truly incomprehensible evening of drama in the local dialect. The Stadtkino, Klostergasse 5, is an arthouse **cinema**.

Clubs and music venues

Atlantis Klosterberg 13 ⓦwww.atlan-tis.ch. Universally known as "Tis", and the most popular venue in Basel, hosting live bands and dance nights, generally with a Fr.15 entrance.

Babalabar Gerbergasse 4. City-centre club, with

plenty of variation in dance styles (nightly), and famed all-nighters (Sat). Fr.10–15.

Bird's Eye Kohlenberg 20 ⓦwww.jsb.ch. Live jazz every weekend (Thurs–Sun), jazz DJ-ing the rest of the week – very popular, very lively. Around Fr.15.

Hirscheneck Lindenberg 23. Grungy hardcore, metal and ska acts in this café-bar venue, generally on weekends.
Kaserne Klybeckstrasse 1b ⓦwww.kaserne-basel .ch. Focus of Kleinbasel nightlife, a café-bar with adjacent venue for live bands, DJs, readings and happenings. Fr.10–15.
Kuppel Binningerstrasse 14. Lively meeting place with Friday salsa nights.
Parterre Klybeckstrasse 1b ⓦwww.parterre.net. Folky, jazz-trio music nights, often midweek.

Listings

Bike rental At the station (daily 7am–9pm).
Books Bergli Bookshop, Rümelinsplatz 19, right near Marktplatz, is the hub of Basel's sizeable English-speaking community, with a broad range of books in English plus community information and regular events. Bider & Tanner, Aeschenvorstadt 2, is the city's top bookshop, a multi-department outlet with a diverse English-language section.
Changing money In the SBB train station (daily 6am–9pm).
Flights Flight enquiries from Basel-Mulhouse ☎061 325 31 11, ⓦwww.euroairport.com. MFG ☎061 921 36 75 offers pricey sightseeing flights, as does Airport Helicopter ☎061 325 48 88.
Gay and lesbian life You'll generally find livelier scenes in nearby Freiburg and Mulhouse. The local support group HABS (ⓦwww.habs.ch) has information and links, but Kaserne, Klybeckstrasse 1, is the place to start, with its popular Tuesday evening gathering named Zisch.
Lost property SBB station ☎051 229 24 67; Bad. station ☎061 690 12 51; on a tram, bus or on the street ☎061 267 70 34.
Markets Basel's main fruit and veg market is in Marktplatz (Mon–Sat mornings; also Mon, Wed & Fri afternoons); otherwise, check out the flea markets in Barfüsserplatz (2nd & 4th Wed in month) and Petersplatz near the university (Sat).
Medical facilities 24-hour emergency room at Kantonsspital Basel Universitätsklinik, Hebelstrasse 30 ☎061 265 25 25.
Post The most central office is on Rüdengasse, with another near the station.
Train information Swiss: Basel SBB ☎0900 300 300, ⓦwww.rail.ch. French: Bâle SNCF ☎0900 571 056, ⓦwww.sncf.com. German: Basel Bad. ☎061 690 11 11, ⓦwww.bahn.de.

Around Basel

There's little to stop for in the countryside around Basel, known as the Baselbiet, although on a journey south you may find yourself having to change trains at **Olten**, beyond the Hauenstein range in Canton Solothurn, which has a quiet, attractive old quarter but not much else to recommend it. More deserving of special attention is an impressive set of Roman ruins on the Rhine a short boat-ride east of Basel at **Augusta Raurica**, while further east, just fifteen minutes from the outskirts of Zürich, is the comfortable spa town of **Baden**.

Augusta Raurica

In its heyday, **AUGUSTA RAURICA** – a Roman Rhineside provincial capital 20km east of Basel near the modern village of **Kaiseraugst** – was home to some twenty thousand people. These days it comprises the largest set of Roman ruins in Switzerland, and is an easy day-trip from Basel.

Augusta was founded at the same time as Basel, 44 BC, in the territory of the Gallic Raurici tribe. During the first and second centuries AD it was a prosperous city, but was virtually destroyed by an invasion of the Alemanni tribes around 260 AD. Many of its stones were pilfered during the Middle Ages. Exploration of the site has been continuous for more than a century, and has uncovered the best-preserved classical theatre north of the Alps, temples, a forum, taverns, many public buildings and more.

Focus of the site, well signposted from all over the village, is the **Römermuseum** (Roman Museum; Glebenacherstrasse 17; Mon 1–5pm, Tues–Sun 10am–5pm; Nov–Feb closed noon–1.30pm; Fr.5; SMP; ⓦwww .augusta-raurica.ch). If you can fight your way through the stream of school parties, you'll find a well-laid-out display of finds from the site, including a full reconstruction of a Roman house. The ticket desk can give you a leaflet showing a map of the whole site and recommended walks through the ruins (which are open and free), spreading out across a wide area all around the museum and down to the river. The impressive 10,000-seat **theatre** is directly opposite the museum, still under excavation and renovation, with a small sculpture garden to one side. Schönbuhl Hill in front of the theatre is topped by a **temple**. Some 200m south of the theatre is a large **amphitheatre**, with to the east of the theatre the **forum** and an exhibition of mosaics in the basement of the **curia** (Town Hall). Further east are taverns, potteries and houses in varying states of crumble. Down on the riverbank beside the boat jetty, 500m north, is an enclosed **fortress**, housing an extensive baths complex. Excellent signboards and displays all over the site ensure that you're never short of information.

There are two or three slow **boats** a day (May–Oct only) from Basel to Rheinfelden, stopping at the jetty at Kaiseraugst, about fifteen minutes' walk below the Roman Museum. Otherwise, regular local **trains** take about ten

Walking the Jura Höhenweg

The **Jura Höhenweg** (or High Route) makes for a multi-day hiking tour through a region unlike any other in Switzerland, stretching 199km along the length of the Swiss Jura from Dielsdorf, 12km east of Baden, to Borex near Geneva. End to end it takes about fourteen days to complete. Small villages and isolated farms indicate a scant population throughout the region, and you can often find yourself walking for long distances without signs of habitation. In this limestone country there's a rich flora in summer, and long views across the *Mittelland* from open ridge crests show either the abrupt wall of the Bernese Alps or the snowy Mont Blanc range.

The notes below are meant as a guideline only: you shouldn't set off without a good **map** (those covering the route are LS 5005, 5019, 5016, 241, 242, 5020 and 260 – all at 1:50,000). The essential accompaniment to any part of the walk is *The Jura* by Kev Reynolds and R. Brian Evans (see p.607), which gives details of accommodation to be had along the route in modest inns or mountain farms with outhouse dormitories, and also includes winter ski traverses. Local tourist offices can also supply information on hiking short stretches. See p.63 for the basics.

Reached by S-Bahn train from Zürich, **Dielsdorf** slumbers in a countryside of farms and market gardens, but within an hour of setting out the way goes through **Regensburg** which, with its thirteenth-century castle turret, stone-walled houses and cobbled square, is the finest village of the whole route. You'll also pass through **Baden** and **Brugg** on the first day, but thereafter the true nature of the Jura becomes evident, with the well-marked trail undulating to the horizon through steep green hills and charming farmland basins. From Brugg the route takes to high ground north of the River Aare, and beyond **Staffelegg** it almost reaches 1000m on the wooded summit of the Geissflue with views between the trees to the Black Forest. Edging above **Olten**, on day four the route joins a track engineered by Swiss soldiers during World War I across the flank of the 1098m Belchenflue, adorned with large regimental insignia carved and painted on the steep rock walls. Later the same

minutes to Kaiseraugst, or **bus** #70 (every 20min) from Basel's Aeschenplatz goes to August village, ten minutes' walk from the museum.

Baden

A pleasant, relaxing spa town on the River Limmat, 24km downstream from Zürich in Canton Aargau, **BADEN** makes for a good stopover on a journey across the north of the country. There's not an awful lot to do, other than enjoy the ancient Old Town, take in a fine collection of Impressionist art, and enjoy a soothing dip in the warm, sulphurous spring waters… but that's the point. People have been coming to Baden for centuries to sit around doing absolutely nothing, and there are few more genteel and stately towns in the country in which to follow suit.

Arrival, information and accommodation

The town is divided into two, with the **station** in the middle. South of the station is the centre, focused around the **Old Town** with the ruined Stein castle above. North of the station, in a bend of the Limmat, is the low-lying **spa area** (signed as *ThermalBaden*), with the thermal baths and a handful of venerable old buildings clustered around Kurplatz. The main Badstrasse, which becomes Bäderstrasse, connects the two neighbourhoods, running along a terrace above the Limmat valley. The friendly and helpful **tourist office** is opposite the station (platform 1 exit), at Bahnhofplatz 1 (Mon noon–7pm, Tues–Fri 9.30am–7pm, Sat 9.30am–4pm; ☎056 200 83 83,

day hundreds of reinforced timber steps take the path up towards the Roggenflue to emerge on a prominent limestone cliff with more expansive views before descending to **Balsthal**. Day five ends on the Weissenstein (1284m), whose panorama was immortalized in *The Path to Rome* by Hilaire Belloc: "One saw the sky beyond the edge of the world getting purer as the vault rose. But right up… ran peak and field and needle of intense ice, remote from the world."

On reaching **Frinvillier** on day six the Höhenweg passes suddenly from German to French Switzerland, to become known as the **Chemin des Crêtes**. Architectural styles change too, as though you've crossed an international frontier. Above Frinvillier you'll gain the 1607m **Chasseral** (see p.197); ribs of limestone project through the turf, and a hotel just below (☎032 751 24 51) gazes out to Lac de Neuchâtel with the Eiger, Mönch and Jungfrau floating on the horizon. On day nine the trail edges a huge limestone cauldron, the Creux du Van, the most dramatic feature on the long walk. A farm nearby offers a mattress in an outhouse for the simplest of overnight lodgings, and next day the path leads down to **Sainte-Croix**, home of the Swiss musical-box industry (see p.188). A steady climb then gains an open plateau close to the French border with military defences in evidence, before a sharp pull culminates on the summit of Le Suchet at 1588m. Passing through **Vallorbe** on day twelve (see p.188), the route investigates the Source de l'Orbe in a woodland whose glades are soggy with newborn streams. Mont Tendre, crossed on the same day, marks the highest point of the Jura at 1679m. From it, you can absorb a panorama of Lake Geneva and the snowcapped Alps. The last two days are spent mostly along the ridge among flowers – from the final high point of La Dôle, walkers can share Rousseau's pleasure: "The moment when from the very top of the Jura mountains I discovered Lake Geneva, was a moment of ecstasy and delight." From there, 1200m of descent through woodland, meadows and an open plain of wheatfields, brings the wanderer at last to **Borex** above Lake Geneva itself.

△ Relaxing at the Tinguely fountain in Basel, near the Kunsthalle (see p.219)

@www.baden.ch), with excellent guided **walking tours** of the town (Mon 2pm).

On the east side of the Limmat, about 200m south of the wooden bridge, is the clean and safe HI **hostel** *Jugendherberge*, Kanalstrasse 7 (☎056 221 67 36, @www.youthhostel.ch; ❶; mid-March to Christmas; dorms Fr.28), and on the busy riverside street in Ennetbaden, directly opposite the spa district, is *Hirschen*, Badstrasse 22 (☎056 222 69 66; ❶), with dead-simple rooms. Baden's **hotels** are good value, but they're geared towards monied long-stayers and you'll need deepish pockets. Top choice is the *Blume*, Kurplatz 4 (☎056 222 55 69, @www.blume-baden.ch; ❸–❹), a fine Belle Epoque building in the spa district, built around an amazing interior atrium space, with classically grand public areas and a range of elegant rooms; it's been on this site since 1421. The modern *Du Parc*, nearby at Römerstrasse 24 (☎056 203 15 15, @www.duparc.ch; ❺), is a fallback option, part of the Best Western chain and with little charm.

The Town

At Schlossbergplatz at the southern end of Badstrasse is the turreted fifteenth-century **Stadtturm**, gateway into the Old Town. On a hill above to the west, and visible from all over town, is the **Stein castle**, partially destroyed in 1712 by the Protestant forces of Bern, Basel and Zürich during a battle against the Catholic cantons. Rathausgasse runs east from the Stadtturm just inside the walls, and partway along you'll find the **Stadthaus** (Town Hall): take a look inside at the whimsical modern ceiling murals of clouds and sky, and then head two floors up to the old **Tagsatzungssaal** (Meeting Hall), for three centuries the meeting place of the Confederate Diet (Switzerland's parliament of the day), with a gorgeously restored interior dating from 1497, complete with full wood panelling and original stained glass showing the Swiss cantonal flags. You'll have to ask in one of the offices on the same floor for the key, since the anonymous modern door to the hall is kept locked. An alley from Rathausgasse leads through to Kirchplatz, with its atmospheric **church**, built in 1420 (and retaining its Gothic arches) but later renovated in a surprisingly frill-free Baroque style. Stairways and steep alleys head down to a picturesque covered **wooden bridge** of 1813, leading to the stout bailiff's castle on the other bank. If the rock nearby looks oddly flat, it's because after the rainy night of June 25, 1899, the whole top of the crag sheared off and crashed into the river – such a momentous event that it's still talked about today.

It's a short, pleasant walk north along the banks of the Limmat, on a footpath fragrant with wild garlic, to the tranquil **spa area**. Kurplatz, a peaceful little square, is surrounded on all sides by Belle Epoque hotel architecture that is the height of dignified elegance. Baden's nineteen **springs** were well known to the Romans, who called the place *Aquae Helveticae* and built a lavish baths complex to exploit the hot water, a million litres of which emerges every day at a toasty 47°C, having spent the last 30,000 years rising from 3km down. All through the Middle Ages, and well into the nineteenth century, Baden was infamous for the high jinks that took place in its pools, but these days your flesh is more likely to receive attention from a no-nonsense white-coated masseur than from an amorous wooer. In the Baden tradition, all the Kurhotels are built over their own **springs** which serve their own thermal pools; the **public pools**, dubbed *ThermalBaden* (Mon–Fri 7.30am–9pm, Sat & Sun 7.30am–8pm; Fr.16; @www.thermalbaden.ch), are on Kurplatz, with a drinking fountain outside – although you may have trouble keeping the warm, smelly water down long enough for it to do any internal good. As an extra, you can enjoy an hour and three-quarters in your own private tub (one/two person Fr.18/36), a sauna (Fr.16.50), massage (limited hours only; Fr.46 for 25min) or a host of other treatments.

The Langmatt Foundation
At Römerstrasse 30, 150m west of the spa area, is the **Langmatt Foundation** (April–Oct Tues–Fri 2–5pm, Sat & Sun 11am–5pm; Fr.10; SMP), housing a small but excellent collection of French Impressionist art. The charming house, dating from 1900–05 and resplendent in its own gardens, belonged to one Sidney Brown, a founder of the engineering multinational ABB, still headquartered in Baden. Off the reception area, the **Venetian salon** (room 3), with Louis XV and XVI furniture, is hung with views of the city painted by an unknown artist around 1745; next door you'll find work by Cézanne, Renoir and Pissarro. A wonderful Degas nude, and several small Renoir portraits, are curiously hung in a corridor (room 7) opposite the toilets. The atmospheric **library** (room 8) has several shining landscapes by Corot and Degas, while the purpose-built **gallery** (room 9) is hung with several Cézannes, works by Van Gogh, Monet, Gauguin and the beautiful *Portrait of Suzanne Valadon plaiting her hair* by Renoir. Upstairs rooms are mostly devoted to the history of the family.

Eating and drinking
For **eating**, there are plenty of pavement cafés and restaurants along Badstrasse and in the Old Town. The *Schwyzerhüsli*, Badstrasse 38 (T056 222 62 63; closed Sun), is a popular place to sit and watch the world go by, and has plenty of healthy salads as well as substantial Swiss fare, with *menus* from Fr.17. *Rose*, Weitegasse 23, is a bright, modern, friendly little place with good food (Fri & Sat until 1.30am). Round the corner, *Bar Spuntino*, Vordere Metzggasse 4, is a *paninoteca* with a huge range of hot and cold *paninis* for Fr.5–8, as well as pasta dishes for Fr.12. Up on the east bank of the Limmat is the *Schloss Schartenfels* (T056 426 19 27; closed Tues), an 1894 folly now housing a gourmet restaurant with terrace overlooking the town. Below the station is a handy late-opening *Migros* with takeaway. For **drinking**, check out *Stadttor* on Schlossbergplatz, a cosy local watering hole. *Gasthof zum Wilden Mann*, Oberegasse 33, has a super-hip bar replete with candles, sofas and more than its fair share of floppy haircuts.

Lengnau and Endingen
The gentle Aargauer countryside around Baden holds a succession of quiet farming villages with little to mark them out as special, other than **LENGNAU**, 8km north of Baden, and **ENDINGEN**, 3km further on. These two villages, for centuries up to about 100 years ago, were almost exclusively Jewish. Since the early thirteenth century Jews had lived in Basel and Zürich: Jewish financing, for instance, made it possible for Basel's bishops to buy Kleinbasel outright in the 1220s and to build the first Rhine bridge shortly afterwards. On January 16, 1349, the Basel government decided to pack the town's Jews into a wooden house on an island in the Rhine and burn it to the ground; those who escaped were expelled six months later when plague arrived, accused of poisoning the city's water supply. Jews were allowed back to the city after the 1356 earthquake in order to finance rebuilding work, but in 1397 they were again expelled, this time for good. They took refuge in the Baden countryside, settling at Lengnau and Endingen, where Jewish life in Switzerland was concentrated for more than four centuries. In 1805, a Jewish

community was refounded in Basel, but it was only in 1874, after extreme pressure was brought to bear by the US and France, that Switzerland finally guaranteed full religious and civil rights to all religious denominations in its constitution, one of the last European states to do so.

Today, Lengnau and Endingen – despite being largely depopulated of their Jews – still bear many traces of the past. Lengnau's little village square is overlooked not by a church, but by a large **synagogue**, and the village has many characteristic old double-doored houses, not seen elsewhere in the country. The great **domed synagogue** in the middle of Endingen has been extensively renovated. Between the two villages, in a quiet location off the road, is an overgrown **Israelitischer Friedhof** (Jewish Cemetery), with graves dating back to 1750. All these sites are kept locked, but staff at the Jüdisches Museum in Basel (see p.218), or at the Lengnau municipality (T056 266 50 10), can – with some notice – put you in touch with a guide from the local Jewish community, who will take you round and explain more.

Travel details

Trains

Baden to: Basel (hourly; 50min); Bern (hourly; 1hr 20min); Zürich (every 30min; 15min).
Basel SBB to: Baden (hourly; 50min); Bellinzona (hourly; 3hr 35min); Bern (twice hourly; 1hr 10min); Biel/Bienne (hourly; 1hr 10min); Brig (hourly; 3hr); Chur (hourly; 2hr 40min); Geneva (hourly; 2hr 50min); Interlaken Ost (hourly; 2hr 10min); Kaiseraugst (twice hourly; 10min); Lausanne (hourly; 2hr 30min); Lugano (hourly; 3hr 45min); Luzern (hourly; 1hr 10min); Neuchâtel (hourly; 1hr 30min); Olten (3 hourly; 25min); Zürich (3 hourly; 1hr 5min).

Buses

Baden to: Endingen (hourly; 25min); Lengnau AG (hourly; 18min).

Boats

Basel (Schifflände) to: Kaiseraugst (May–Oct 1–3 daily; 2hr 10min); Dreiländereck (May–Oct Mon–Sat 1 daily; 1hr 45min).

Bern and around

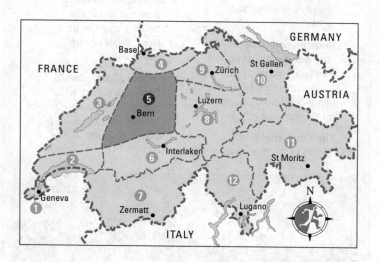

CHAPTER 5

Highlights

* **Old Town, Bern** Wander the atmospheric cobbled streets, dipping in and out of the arcades on a street plan unchanged since medieval times. See p.244

* **Münster, Bern** Switzerland's tallest steeple adorns this mighty cathedral. See p.248

* **Kunstmuseum, Bern** The world's largest collection of works by Paul Klee, supported by an array of art from Duccio to Rothko. See p.251

* **The Emmental** Home region of the best-known Swiss cheese, featuring classic scenery of velvety green hills. See p.259

* **Kemmeriboden** Tiny trailhead village in the upper Emmental that makes meringues to die for. See p.262

* **Solothurn** The finest Baroque city in the country, day-trip from Bern, Basel or Zürich. See p.265

* **Fribourg** Switzerland's best-kept secret, a genial, bilingual university town with a fine tradition of fondues. See p.267

5

Bern and around

The giant Canton Bern is one of the country's largest, taking in a swathe of diverse countryside from snowy Alpine peaks to gently rolling farmland. The north of the canton is focused around the small city of **Bern** itself, Switzerland's low-key and attractive federal capital. With a grand and glorious history at the fulcrum of Swiss history, Bern has often dominated the economic and political fortunes of the populated west-central heartland – or **Mittelland** – of the country. This arc of territory stretching from Lake Geneva to Zürich holds, and has always held, the most fertile country, the densest population, and the greatest wealth of all the diverse areas of Switzerland. The Reformation may have begun in Zürich, and flourished in Geneva, but it was the Bernese army that seized hearts and minds in the countryside between the two. For centuries after the Burgundian wars, the patrician nobility of Bern controlled a wealthy city-state covering the entire Mittelland; it was only a French-backed revolution in 1798 that saw Bern stripped both of its Lake Geneva breadbasket (carved out to form Canton Vaud) and the rolling farmland of the north (Canton Aargau). Nonetheless, Bern was a natural choice for Swiss federal capital under the 1848 constitution, and with overwhelming economic and political clout, Bern can still to this day call the shots in its home region.

Every Swiss values his or her home canton above all the others, but the Bernese seem to be able to draw on a particularly deep wellspring of nationalistic pride in celebrating their own identity, culture and language. They're famous around the country for their slow, deliberate manner, and you'll pick up a sing-song tone in the lethargic Bernese dialect of Swiss German that sparks inevitable associations with Welsh or Texan accents of English. Parallels with Wales and Texas don't stop at language: like them, Bern – once an independent state – is now bound into a larger polity but has a relatively static, self-assured population who tend to feel little affinity with the people over the border. Luzerners and Fribourgeois are strangers, with whom the Bernese share a nationality but neither a cultural nor a religious identity. The slow-talking Bernese traditionally decry Zürchers for being big-city hotheads, and Baslers and Genfers for being snobs – and the compliment is returned, with the Bernese dismissed as hair-splitting dullards.

Around Bern, the lush hills and tidy, picturesque farming communities of the **Berner Mittelland** hold plenty of rustic charm, not least in the **Emmental** region to the east. (The Berner Oberland, or Bernese Alps, in the south of the canton, has its own chapter, beginning on p.277.) Two cities near Bern well worth making time for are **Solothurn** to the north, and the much-overlooked town of **Fribourg** to the southwest.

Bern

Of all Swiss cities, **BERN** (Berne in French) is perhaps the most immediately charming. Crammed onto a steep-sided peninsula in a crook of the fast-flowing River Aare, its quiet, cobbled lanes, lined with sandstone arcaded buildings straddling the pavement, have changed barely at all in over five hundred years but for the adornment of modern shop signs and the odd car or tram rattling past. The hills all around, and the steep banks of the river, are still liberally wooded. Views, both of the Old Town's clustered roofs and of the majestic Alps

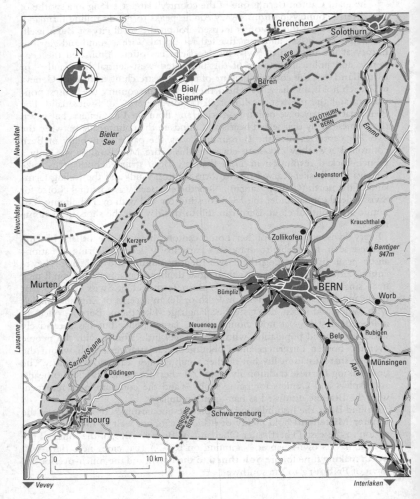

on the horizon, are breathtaking. Coming from Zürich or Geneva, it's hard to remember that Bern – once voted Europe's most floral city – is the nation's capital, home of the Swiss parliament and wielder of final federal authority.

For all its political status, Bern is a tiny city of barely 130,000 people and retains a small town's easy approach to life. The attraction of the place is its ambience; traffic is kept out of the Old Town and you could spend days just wandering the streets and alleys, café-hopping and – if it's warm – joining the locals for a plunge into the river. The perfectly preserved medieval street plan, with its arcades, street fountains and doughty towers, persuaded UNESCO to deem Bern a World Heritage Site, placing it in the company of such legendary sites as Florence, Petra and the Taj Mahal. In a competition for the world's most beautiful and relaxing capital city, it's hard to think what could knock Bern into second place.

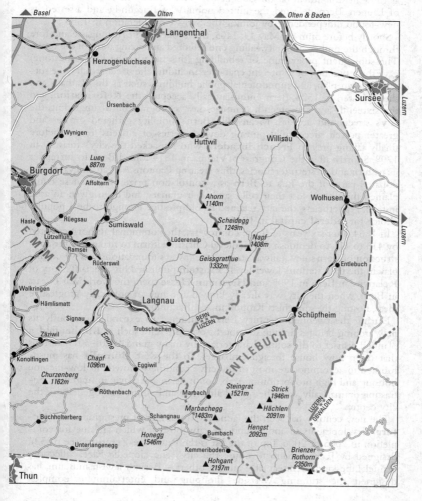

Some history

A castle probably stood at **Nydegg**, on the eastern tip of Bern's peninsula, from the eleventh century, before Berchtold V, Duke of Zähringen, chose the strategically ideal spot to found a new city in 1191. He had the oak forests covering the peninsula felled, using the timber for the first houses, and then – legend has it – went hunting nearby and named the new city after his first kill, a **bear** (*Bär* in German). Bern's coat of arms, sporting a bear, first appeared in 1224, and to this day bears remain indelibly associated with the city.

The Aare encircles Bern's Old Town on three sides; Berchtold's fourth defence was a wall, which initially ran through the Zytglogge tower. Under the Zähringens, and by virtue too of being in close proximity to the wealthy and powerful kingdom of **Burgundy**, Bern expanded rapidly. By 1256 it had a new wall at the present Käfigturm, and a century later the city reached as far as the Christoffelturm (at the present-day train station). In 1339, at the battle of Laupen, Bern defeated the united nobility of Burgundy, and asserted its new-found independence by joining the Swiss Confederation in 1353.

Shortly before 5pm on May 14, 1405, **fire** broke out in Brunngasse and tore through the timber-built city, killing one hundred and razing most of the town. The subsequent programme of rebuilding (this time in the local sandstone) gave the city much of its present character, including the street arcades, the surviving town plan, and monumental public buildings such as the Rathaus and the Münster. In 1528, Bern enthusiastically accepted the **Reformation**, and the sixteenth and seventeenth centuries saw a programme of upgrading the city's streets and arcades. Meanwhile Bern's nobility gathered greater and greater power, successfully putting down a series of citizens' revolts before finally falling prey to **French invaders**, who ransacked the city's treasury in 1798. Shortly after, the Congress of Vienna in 1814 forced Bern to surrender its eastern and western territories, thus creating Cantons Aargau and Vaud, and donated parts of the Jura to Bern as a consolation prize; the Bernese complained that they'd lost their cellar and their granary, and been given an attic instead. Nonetheless, the city retained its old prestige enough to be a popular choice for **federal capital** in 1848.

In 1864, after six years of fierce controversy, the communal authorities voted by 415 to 411 to demolish the medieval Christoffelturm to make way for construction of Bern's new railway station (the tower's foundations survive on display in the train station's lower level). **Einstein** published his Special Theory of Relativity in Bern in 1905, and **Hermann Hesse** spent the World War I years in Bern, when the city was already known as a hub of politically progressive ideas, hosting the anarchists Kropotkin and Bakunin.

During the twentieth century Bern continued to expand enormously, its new, arching bridges linking to suburbs over the Aare such as **Kirchenfeld**, a planned district to the south characterized by many grand 1920s–30s mansions that often now house foreign embassies. To the west, **Bümpliz** has mushroomed to accommodate most of the city's rapid new growth, its low-income housing and high proportion of Arab, South Asian and Slavic immigrants contrasting dramatically with the settled affluence and ethnic homogeneity of the city centre.

The new century has seen the launch of a number of prestigious **architectural** developments in and around the city, most of which are due for completion in 2005 or 2006. Top of the list is the Paul Klee-Zentrum (see p.252), designed by Renzo Piano to house the city's encyclopedic Klee collection. Daniel Libeskind, architect of – among others – Berlin's Jewish museum, has designed the stunning Westside shopping and entertainment complex

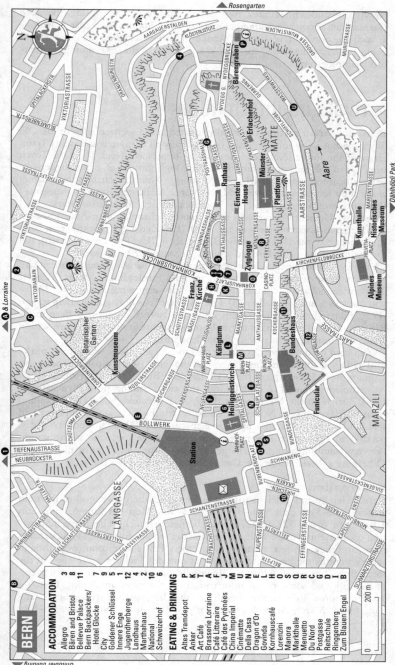

▼ Dählhölzli Park

◀ A & Lorraine

B

▲ Unitobler building

BERN

ACCOMMODATION

Allegro	3
Bären and Bristol	8
Bellevue Palace	11
Bern Backpackers/ Hotel Glocke	7
City	9
Goldener Schlüssel	5
Innere Enge	1
Jugendherberge	12
Landhaus	4
Marthahaus	2
National	10
Schweizerhof	6

EATING & DRINKING

Altes Tramdepot	P
Anker	K
Art Café	T
Brasserie Lorraine	A
Café Litteraire	F
Café des Pyrénées	J
China Imperial	M
Cinématte	N
Della Casa	U
Dragon d'Or	E
Govinda	L
Kornhauscafé	H
Lorenzini	O
Manora	S
Markthalle	Q
Menuetto	R
Du Nord	C
Postgasse	G
Reitschule	D
Ringgenberg	I
Zum Blauen Engel	B

0   200 m

239

(⓪www.westside.ch), located west of the city to act as a bridge between German- and French-speaking communities. In addition, Switzerland's national stadium, northeast of Bern at Wankdorf (⓪www.stadion-wankdorf.ch), is being entirely redeveloped for its role as a venue in the 2008 European football championships.

Arrival and information

Bern's huge **train station** is centrally situated at the western edge of the Old Town, within a few minutes' walk of practically all the hotels and sights. Trains arrive at the lower level, postbuses on the uppermost level. The **Old Town** stretches to the east, occupying the central high ground of a thin, finger-like peninsula: three long, parallel cobbled streets (which all change their names along their length) define the Old Town area: Aarbergergasse-Zeughausgasse-Rathausgasse-Postgasse is the northernmost; Spitalgasse-Marktgasse-Kramgasse-Gerechtigkeitsgasse is in the centre; Schauplatzgasse-Amthausgasse-Münstergasse-Junkerngasse is to the south. The Zytglogge clocktower is bang in the centre of the Old Town; the Bärengraben (Bear Pits) are to the east; and the main museums are clustered around Helvetiaplatz to the south.

Very few **flights** operate into Bern's tiny airport (⓪www.flughafenbern.ch), 9km southeast of the city in Belp. A minibus (misleadingly named "Airport Taxi") meets all arrivals, shuttling to Bern's city-centre train station (Fr.14), or you can take a taxi (around Fr.35). The "Airliner" bus only goes to Belp station (Fr.3), from where ordinary trains cover the twenty minutes to Bern every half-hour. Flying out, a minibus heads to the airport from outside Bern station about fifty minutes before every flight departure.

With your own transport, you'd do well to take advantage of the free "**park-and-ride**" facilities on the fringes of the city (⓪www.parking-bern.ch). Coming from Fribourg on the N12, take the Bümpliz exit for the P+R at Ausserholligen (bus #12 or #13 into the city); coming from Neuchâtel or Basel/Zürich on the N1, head for the P+R at Neufeld (bus #11); or coming from Interlaken on the N6, exit at Wankdorf for the P+R at Guisanplatz (tram #9). Unless you can find a blue-zone space (see p.41), at around Fr.8 a day, parking in the centre is very expensive; the huge car park at the station (⓪www.bahnhofparking.ch) charges Fr.4 per hour, and Fr.30 or more a day. Others are at Waisenhausplatz, Casinoplatz and behind the Rathaus.

Information

Bern's friendly and efficient **tourist office** is on the upper level of the train station (June–Sept daily 9am–8.30pm; Oct–May Mon–Sat 9am–6.30pm, Sun 10am–5pm; ☎031 328 12 12, ⓪www.bernetourism.ch). They have information on everything to do with the city and the whole region, including detailed maps, and they can reserve hotel rooms for a Fr.3 commission (even though there's a complimentary hotel-phone just outside). Pick up a free copy of the fortnightly *Bern aktuell*, which has English listings of mainstream cultural events in the city and some useful information on the city's attractions. There's a smaller tourist information booth at the Bärengraben (June–Sept daily 9am–6pm; March–May & Oct daily 10am–4pm; Nov–Feb Fri–Sun 11am–4pm).

City transport and tours

Bern's city centre is small enough that you can easily **walk** everywhere: the stroll from the train station to the Bärengraben is only around fifteen minutes and takes in the length of the Old Town on the way. Walking is the only way you're going to be able to get a sense of the atmosphere of the arcades – and it's the principal delight of Bern – but a close second-best comes in the form of **horse-drawn carriages**, which ply for trade in the central squares during the summer months.

Bern's network of **buses and trams** (ⓦwww.bernmobil.ch) is comprehensive and efficient. Pretty much all lines run through Bahnhofplatz, which is bedecked with directional signs. The most useful routes are tram #9 (direction Wabern) for the Gurtenbahn station, bus #12 (direction Länggasse) for the university, and bus #20 (direction Wyler) for Lorraine, although the last two destinations are no more than ten minutes' walk from the train station anyway. Bus #12 (direction Schosshalde) goes to the Bärengraben – less necessary going down than it is coming back up (this is also the only bus that follows the scenic route through the heart of the Old Town).

Bern's festivals

The famous **Zibelemärit** (Onion Market) – held on the fourth Monday in November, preceded by a very chilly mass swim in the Aare on the day before – is Bern's major annual festival, an excuse, despite the food stalls and the rustic-sounding name, for people to run around Spitalgasse throwing confetti, spraying silly-string and brandishing blow-up bananas. It is claimed that the spectacle originated after the fire of 1405, when people from nearby Fribourg helped Bern clean up the mess and, in gratitude, the Bernese granted the Fribourgeois the right to sell their onions every autumn in the city (down the centuries, the onions developing into blow-up bananas). In fact, Bern's Zibelemärit began – much more mundanely – in the mid-nineteenth century, when rural women, selling onions and other vegetables, began to turn up in Bern on the first day of the city's Martinmas Fairs, which had been celebrated since the Middle Ages to mark the transition to winter. The quality of the produce, and the engaging demeanour of the vendors, meant that news of the women's market spread rapidly, until the newspapers got hold of the story in 1860 and proclaimed the Onion Market to be the "traditional" start of Martinmas. The tale quickly wove its way into popular thinking, somehow getting muddled with the 1405 fire and the Fribourgeois along the way. Linkage to a defining event in Bern's history guaranteed the event's survival into the modern age, even though today the Martinmas Fairs, the transition into winter and the farmers' wives themselves are long forgotten.

Zibelemärit aside, Bern's biggest party is probably its **Fasnacht/carnival** (ⓦwww.baernerfasnacht.ch), spread over a weekend conveniently slotted in between the massive celebrations in Luzern (before) and Basel (after). From mid-May onwards, following a fragrant **Geranium Market** on Bundesplatz, the city is bedecked with flowers. Spring and summer see a host of cultural events, including an international **jazz festival** in May (ⓦwww.jazzfestivalbern.ch) – Bern is home to one of Switzerland's best jazz schools – a **modern dance festival** (ⓦwww.tanztage.ch) in June, and the hilltop **Gurten festival** (ⓦwww.gurtenfestival.ch) of rock, dance and folk in July. Various athletic events include the **Grand Prix**, a 16,000-strong fun-run through the city in May (ⓦwww.gpbern.ch), the 5km **Women's Run** in June (ⓦwww.frauenlauf.ch), a 750m **swimming** race in the Aare through the city centre in August (ⓦwww.aareschwuemme.ch), and a prestigious international **curling** tournament in October.

A **fare** for up to six stops is Fr.1.70 (valid 45min), for seven or more stops Fr.2.60 (valid 1hr 30min). Within the city, the Visitors' Card, buyable from the tourist office and hotels, gives unlimited travel for Fr.7 (24hr), Fr.11 (48hr) or Fr.15 (72hr). A Bäre-Abi Tageskarte (Fr.9) is valid all day on the broader city and suburban network, including the Gurtenbahn (but excluding night buses, which cost a flat Fr.5). A multiple ticket (Mehrfahrtenkarte) and Bäre-Abi passes for a week and more are available. Make sure you have a ticket before you start your journey, since you can't get one on board and the fine for travelling without one is Fr.60. Eurailers and InterRailers get no reductions, but Swiss Pass holders travel free; see p.32 for more. For **information** and tickets, head for the Bernmobil office (Mon–Fri 6.30am–7.30pm, Thurs until 9pm, Sat & Sun 7.30am–6.30pm), just off Bahnhofplatz by UBS bank.

The station has the usual paid **bike-rental** facilities (daily 7am–9pm), but during the summer months (May–Oct), the municipality runs *Bern rollt* (ⓦwww.bernrollt.ch), a free bike-rental scheme to help unemployed people get back to work. There are pickup points on Bahnhofplatz and Casinoplatz (both daily 7.30am–9.30pm), with new city bikes, electric bikes, skateboards, kickboards, scooters and more; for a Fr.20 deposit plus your passport, you can ride away for free. If you don't return your transport the same day, you're charged Fr.20/day.

With a Fr.6.90 flagfall, plus Fr.3.20 per kilometre (more at nights and Sundays), Bern's **taxis** are vying to be the most expensive in Europe: they're about twice as pricey as London's. There are public ranks at the train station, Casinoplatz and Waisenhausplatz; two companies are Bären (☎031 371 11 11) and Nova (☎031 331 33 13).

Tours

The tourist office has a wide range of organized **tours** of Bern and the surrounding area, including a two-hour **guided walk** through the Old Town, starting from the station tourist office (June–Sept daily 11am; Fr.14). One of the more interesting ways to see the city is from a **river raft** (you're likely to get at least a bit wet, so sports gear is advisable) – ask at the tourist office for details of where to meet (June–Sept daily 5pm; Fr.35). Otherwise, there are plenty of **bus tours** of the city and various **boat trips** on the river (Fr.23–30), as well as day-trips to the Thunersee and into the Bernese Oberland mountains. Beware that most of the tours run in the summer season only.

Accommodation

Bern's **accommodation** is good value: it's easy to choose an inexpensive hotel and still find yourself in a tasteful, tranquil room overlooking historic cobbled streets, with only voices and church bells as background. Standards, even within historic buildings, are as high as ever – the only drawback is the need always to book ahead. The tourist office has a hotel booking service (☎031 328 12 10, ⓔinfo-res@bernetourism.ch), and plenty of good-value multi-night packages. Many hoteliers have got together to form the Bern Hotels Association (ⓦwww.bernhotels.ch), offering central booking online.

Hotels

With **hotels**, location is only an issue around the train station, which can get a little noisy in the morning rush hour. Bern has a couple of truly grand and characterful luxury hotels, but unless money is no object you'd probably do better to hang on to your francs until you get to one of the mountain resorts, where you'll probably get more for your card-swipe. None of these places is more than ten minutes' walk from the train station, or a few stops on a tram or bus.

Inexpensive

Bern Backpackers/Hotel Glocke Rathausgasse 75 ☏031 311 37 71, ⓦwww.chilisbackpackers.ch. Old Town fixture benefiting – like the *Goldener Schlüssel* nearby – from a perfect location. Newly renovated into a hostel (see p.244), but with fresh, pleasant, bargain-priced singles and doubles on the top two floors. ②

City Bubenbergplatz 7 ☏031 311 53 77, ⓦwww.fhotels.ch. Geared towards an anonymous business clientele, with slick, futuristic designer interiors. Seconds from the train station and not at all bad; a sound choice for facilities and location. Street-side rooms are marginally noisier. ③

Goldener Schlüssel Rathausgasse 72 ☏031 311 02 16, ⓦwww.goldener-schluessel.ch. Comfortable place on a quiet Old Town street, with efficient, pleasant service. Simple, spacious rooms are very clean, mostly ensuite but with some good-value shared-bath rooms up under the eaves. ②

Landhaus Altenbergstrasse 4 ☏031 331 41 66, Ⓔlandhaus@spectraweb.ch. The most attractive budget rooms in town, in an historic, renovated building (with spiralling wooden stairs but no lift) overlooking a curve in the river. Spacious, modern design prevails throughout, with ensuite or shared facilities, and some rooms have floor-to-ceiling windows and balcony. Also with hostel dorms (see p.244). Bus #12 to Bärengraben (direction Schosshalde). ②

Marthahaus Wyttenbachstrasse 22a ☏031 332 41 35, ⓦwww.marthahaus.ch. Best all-round value. A characterful building on a quiet cul-de-sac a few minutes out of the Old Town, friendly, well run and cosy. The few shared-bath rooms have sinks, and both the ensuite and hallway bathrooms are spotless. Free kitchen and Internet, plus winter and long-stay discounts. Bus #20 to Gewerbeschule (direction Wyler). ①–②

National Hirschengraben 24 ☏031 381 19 88, ⓦwww.nationalbern.ch. Something of an institution, with a restaurant, theatre and – up above – a hotel occupying a lovely old building on an atmospheric tree- and tram-lined street. The ancient wooden lift rattles you up to characterful, renovated rooms with big windows and wood floors; some are ensuite, all have modern facilities. ②

Mid-range and expensive

Allegro In the Kursaal, Kornhausstrasse 3 ☏031 339 55 00, ⓦwww.allegro-hotel.ch. Innovative business hotel set in the ultra-modern renovated Kursaal building (which also boasts a large casino). Super-slick postmodern design swishes you into stylish rooms – go for the Warhol ones – featuring widescreen TVs, video games, Internet and more. Top-floor balconies with Alpine vistas cost more. Weekend discounts can make this the best value, and least traditional, top-end accommodation anywhere in the country. Tram #9 (direction Guisanplatz). ⑤

Bären and **Bristol** Within 50m of each other at Schauplatzgasse 4 & 10 ☏031 311 33 67, ⓦwww.baerenbern.ch & ⓦwww.bristolbern.ch. Two identical hotels seconds from the Bundeshaus, with different owners but shared Best Western management. Following recent renovation, rooms are very modern, well designed and comfortable, though rather soulless. ⑤–⑥

Bellevue Palace Kochergasse 3 ☏031 320 45 45, ⓦwww.bellevue-palace.ch. Top hotel in the city, right next to the Bundeshaus and the haunt of presidents, diplomats and billionaires, with as much palatial grandeur as you'd expect plus the added bonus of views of the river winding far below the hotel walls and, in the distance, the snow-capped Alps. Rooms are spacious, sumptuous, traditionally styled and horribly expensive. Completely renovated in 2002. ⑧–⑨

Innere Enge Engestrasse 54 ☏031 309 61 11, ⓦwww.zghotels.ch. Lovely choice, well out of the city on the edge of open parkland but only five minutes from the centre. This fine old building, which hosted Empress Josephine in 1810, features superb Art Nouveau styling throughout; rooms are characterful and quiet, many with expansive views of the Alps. Breakfast – which is optional – is served in the marvellous octagonal Park Pavilion, while the intimate Marian's Jazzroom in the basement (closed July & Aug) hosts top international jazz performers. Free parking. Bus #21 (direction Bremgarten). ⑤

Schweizerhof Bahnhofplatz 11 ☏031 326 80 80, ⓦwww.schweizerhof-bern.ch. Opposite the train station, this is one of Bern's grandest piles, 140 years old and still family-run with a personal touch. Traditional rooms are individually decorated and uniquely characterful, with some ordinary doubles boasting wood panelling, deep sofas and marble bathrooms. Gourmet dining completes the picture. ⑧

Camping and hostels

There are two **campsites** near Bern. *Eichholz* is the nicer, at Strandweg 49 (☎031 961 26 02, ⓦwww.campingeichholz.ch; mid-April to Sept), on the riverbank in Wabern a few minutes south of the city by tram #9 (to Gurten). *Kappelenbrücke* (☎031 901 10 07, ⓕ031 901 25 91; closed mid-Nov & mid-Jan) is on the river 5km northwest of town on the edge of the huge Bremgarten forest; take a postbus to Eymatt in Hinterkappelen village (20min).

Hostels

Bern Backpackers/Hotel Glocke (SB hostel) Rathausgasse 75 ☎031 311 37 71, ⓦwww.chilisbackpackers.ch. Well located in the Old Town, and newly renovated into a good, high-quality hostel. Dorm beds are Fr.27, plus a rather unnecessary Fr.5 surcharge if you stay only one night. ❷

Jugendherberge (HI hostel) Weihergasse 4 ☎031 311 63 16, ⓦwww.youthhostel.ch & ⓦwww.jugibern.ch. Well-run place, with good facilities and a nice riverside location in Marzili – it's regularly chock-full. Dorm beds are Fr.29, and they do good solid lunches and evening meals for around Fr.12. Walk down from the Bundesterrace, or take the funicular and then the lowest of three left-hand streets when you emerge. Closed mid-Jan. ❶

Landhaus (SB hostel) Altenbergstrasse 4 ☎031 331 41 66, ⓔlandhaus@spectraweb.ch. Attractive building in an old part of town by the river, with beds in quiet, super-clean partitioned dorms for Fr.30; you can use the kitchen for free, and there's a café downstairs. Bus #12 to Bärengraben (direction Schosshalde). ❷

The City

Wandering through Bern's UNESCO-protected **Old Town** can be a magical experience: few cities in the world are so visibly wedded to their distant past, with architecture and a street plan essentially unchanged since medieval times. The most hectic shopping goes on in the **western half** of the Old Town, on Marktgasse and Spitalgasse in particular; the older, **eastern half** is slow-paced and tranquil. However, not for nothing does the tourist office tout the famous arcades, lining both sides of every street in the Old Town, as being "the longest covered shopping promenade in the world". In a strange turnaround of expectations, it's when you walk under the crowded arcades that you get a full-on blast of modern consumerism, with music, shop windows and advertising vying for your attention. Step a few metres to the side to walk in the open air and – with a little imagination – it's easy to picture yourself in the Bern of the sixteenth century.

The Zytglogge

An imposing presence at the centre of the Old Town, the **Zytglogge** (*tseet-klok-uh*), Zeitglockenturm or Clock Tower, is as much the symbol of Bern as the bear. The focal point of public transport and walking routes within the Old Town – and both the benchmark of official Bern time and the point from which all distances in the canton are measured – its squat shape, oversized spired roof and giant, gilded clock face will imprint themselves on your memory of the city.

The tower was originally constructed partly in wood as the westernmost city gate in 1218–20, but by 1256 the city walls had moved west to the Käfigturm; the stranded tower was then converted into a prison for those prostitutes who made a living servicing the clergy. The devastating fire of 1405 razed the tower and it was rebuilt in stone with a new, squat design, a turreted staircase to one side (still used today) and a clock mechanism. The clock soon broke and stayed broken for 122 years until one Caspar Brunner designed an intricate and elegant new mechanism which has functioned since he installed it in 1530, and which is still complete with nearly all its original parts. Below the main east face of the clock is an intricate astronomical and astrological device, which, in one small diameter, displays a 24-hour clock, the twelve hours of daylight, the position of the sun in the zodiac, the day of the week, the date and the month, the phases of the moon and the elevation of the sun above the horizon throughout the year, everything kept accurate by linkage to the main clock mechanism. The external appearance of the Zytglogge as it is today dates from Baroque embellishments of 1770–71.

The main draw of the thing is generally touted to be a rather underwhelming little **display** of mechanical figures – a crowing cock, a parade of bears, Chronos with his hourglass and a dancing jester – which is set into motion four minutes before every hour on the clock's east face. What's far more interesting is to see close-up (and have explained) the actual inner workings of the mechanism as the pendulum swings and linked cogs turn gracefully: the tourist office runs an exemplary and fascinating one-hour **guided tour** (May–Oct daily 4.30pm; July & Aug also 11.30am; Fr.8) inside the tower, which also lets you explore the rooms inside the spire and take in the romantic rooftop view.

The eastern Old Town

From the Zytglogge, the atmospheric lanes of the Old Town branch out in all directions. The meandering walking tour outlined below covers notable sights, but what's just as appealing is to follow your nose and explore unremarkable alleys and passageways that cut through and around the main routes.

The impressively wide main cobbled thoroughfare of the Old Town stretches away on both sides of the Zytglogge: Marktgasse (the heart of Bern's shopping district) is to the west, while elegant **Kramgasse** runs east, also with its fair share of commerce, and featuring many Baroque facades stuck on to the medieval arcaded buildings early in the eighteenth century. At no. 49 is the **Einstein-Haus** (Tues–Fri 10am–5pm, Sat 10am–4pm; closed Dec & Jan; Fr.3; ⓦ www.einstein-bern.ch), the apartment and workplace of the famous scientist, who developed his Theory of Relativity in 1905 while working in the Bern Patent Office, having graduated from the Zürich Institute of Technology a few years before. It's also on Kramgasse that you'll come across the first of Bern's many ornamented **fountains**, an armoured bear holding the standard of the city's founder, Berchtold von Zähringen (dating from 1535). Halfway along the street is another, with a copy of a 1545 statue of Samson, and just before the Kreuzgasse junction is a statue-less fountain dating from 1779. At this eastern end of Kramgasse, and above head height, you'll also spot several eighteenth-century oversized figures mounted on pedestals, which indicated the location of Bern's various craft guilds: the Moor represented the clothworkers, the ape stonemasons and bricklayers, and the axe-wielding carpenter graphically demonstrates his own trade.

While the main street continues ahead, changing its name to **Gerechtigkeitsgasse**, the small Kreuzgasse heads left (north), past a quaint little shop which has been a pharmacy since 1571, to **Rathausplatz**, dominated by the double-staircased **Rathaus**. Although the building dates from 1406–17, it's been much altered over the centuries – not least in 1939–42, when the ground floor was entirely rebuilt. Opposite is a 1542 fountain sporting a Bernese standard-bearer in full armour. Next to the Rathaus is the **St Peter**

In 1870, the **First Vatican Council** confirmed the rule of the Pope over the whole of the Catholic Church and asserted the doctrine of papal infallibility. At the same time, political unification in Italy, and Bismarck's *Kulturkampf*, or Culture Struggle, in Germany – a thinly veiled assault on church authority – drew Switzerland inexorably into the broader conflicts between church and state that were beginning to rage across Europe. Swiss liberals in particular saw the Vatican's dogmatism as challenging the basic principles of the church and the right to individual freedoms in decision making. In a meeting in Olten in 1872, they were troubled enough to form a separate church hierarchy. When the Bishop of Basel began to excommunicate priests who refused to accept the notion of papal infallibility, cantonal authorities in the north of Switzerland deposed him, and the dissenting priests formed their new church.

Known in Germany, Austria and the Netherlands as "Old Catholic" but generally in Switzerland as **"Christ Catholic"**, the church flourishes today in the areas of the north of the country influenced by political liberalism, principally cantons Bern, Basel, Aargau and Solothurn, with scattered communities as far apart as Geneva and St Gallen. About 140,000 Swiss consider themselves Christ Catholics, as opposed to Roman Catholics (of which there are 3.2m); they follow a church which holds that there is a priesthood of all believers, that priests are allowed to marry, that women can be ordained as deacons, and that services should always be performed in the language of the congregation. This has brought it closer in spirit to Anglicanism than to Roman Catholicism, with which relations have often been bitter and strained.

und St Paul-Kirche, built in 1858 as the first Catholic parish church to go up in the city since the Reformation. It's a cool, musty place in a mock-Gothic style which since 1875 has belonged to the heterodox Christ Catholic church (see box). This is one of the most peaceful and atmospheric corners in the Old Town. **Rathausgasse** to the west retains its facades, but has seen much cautious interior redevelopment in recent years for conversion of the old upper floors into luxury apartments, while to the east, tiny **Postgasse**, with a handful of endearing little cafés and antiquarian booksellers, trickles its way down the slope towards the oldest part of the city around Nydegg.

An alternative route heads the other way on Kreuzgasse, right (south) onto tranquil **Junkerngasse**; the apse of the Münster (see p.248) is opposite, but if you head east (left), down the street, you'll pass a succession of fine town houses on the route to Nydegg. First, set back from the street on the right at no. 59, is the Beatrice von Wattenwyl-Haus, its frontage and arcades dating from the 1440s, the south wing and upper floors from a major expansion in 1705. At no. 51 is the sixteenth-century Zeerlederhaus, with neo-Gothic heraldic exterior murals done in 1897. The main draw, at no. 47, is the mighty **Erlacherhof**, the grandest patrician mansion in the city, designed in 1746 around its own courtyard; it's been the seat of the municipal government since 1832 and for a decade after 1848 housed the federal government. A short stroll past the Louis-XVI Lerberhaus at no. 43 and Morlothaus at no. 32 leads on down to Nydegg.

Nydegg

The three quietest and most characterful streets in the Old Town – Postgasse, Gerechtigkeitsgasse and Junkerngasse – all meet at the **Nydeggbrücke** (*nee-dek*), the easternmost point of Bern's peninsula and the location of Nydegg

Castle, built probably before the 1191 founding of Bern and the spur to the city's construction. It was destroyed in the mid-thirteenth century and its location is now marked by the **Nydeggkirche**, although parts of its massive stone foundations survive here and there. The church is a mishmash of elements added to an original 1341 building, and it's worth stopping to savour the tranquil atmosphere of the courtyard outside, with a well which originally stood within the precincts of the twelfth-century castle and a picturesque view of the medieval houses clustering on the slopes all around. The covered Burgtreppe steps lead down from the courtyard to **Gerberngasse**; at the bottom, if you cross the street and walk 20m or so left, you'll find more steps leading down to the riverside, through a thirteenth-century arch which originally belonged to the **Ländtetor**, landing stage for the first ferry across the river. The wall fresco beneath the arch depicts the neighbourhood in the early nineteenth century.

Matte

Emerging back onto Gerberngasse, to the right (northeast) is **Läuferplatz**, its fountain-statue of the city herald standing at the head of the low **Untertorbrücke**, one of the oldest bridges in Switzerland (1468). To the left (southwest), Gerberngasse follows the bend of the river down into one of the most appealing districts of the Old Town, **Matte**. For many centuries this was a self-contained district of craftspeople and dockworkers which long retained its own dialect, related to the Jenisch language of the Swiss gypsies (see p.506) and dubbed *Mattenenglisch* by the other Bernese, to whom it was an incomprehensible language (as obscure as *Englisch*) spoken in a meadow (*Matte*). Gentrification of the neighbourhood in the 1970s brought sweeping social changes. The river is still channelled into an open canal along the main street, and there are plenty of crooked half-timbered houses all around, but a look at wall plaques will turn up more software companies, Internet consultancies and design partnerships than you could shake a stick at. The fact that the district now has its own website (ⓦ www.matte.ch) speaks volumes. You'll find a great deal of graffiti down here too, a legacy no doubt of the presence of the *Wasserwerk*, Bern's premier techno club (see p.257). During the disastrous floods of 1999, Matte spent several weeks underwater, and you may still see evidence of high-water marks here and there.

From Matte, the least energetic way to get back to the Old Town is to continue southwest along the riverside Schifflaube until Badgasse, where there is a **lift** (Mon–Sat 6am–8.30pm, Sun 7am–8.30pm; Fr.1) to whisk you up to the Münsterplattform overhead. Many flights of steps wend their way up the hillside all around too. Otherwise, you could continue a riverside stroll under the Kirchenfeldbrücke into **Marzili**, a peaceful residential district with a handful of old industrial buildings on the riverbank now converted into music venues and arts centres. The Aare is particularly fast at Bern, and the locals have come up with a novel idea to go with the flow. Summer sees hordes crowding the riverbank lawns, and many people leave their possessions at the pool complexes at Marzili or Lorraine and walk or take public transport south to a convenient jumping-in point to let the strong current float them back north again. Cheapskates wrap their clothes up in a plastic bag and tie it to their wrist as they float along.

Across the Nydeggbrücke

There are few attractions on the eastern bank of the Aare. At the bridgehead across the river is the rather sad **Bärengraben** (Bear Pits; daily: summer 8am–5.30pm; winter 9am–4pm; free), two large, open, sunken dens which have housed a collection of shaggy brown bears – the symbol of Bern – since the early sixteenth century, although the current occupants look as if they're struggling to find a reason to go on with life. The tourist complex adjacent, housed in a century-old converted tram depot, has a restaurant-bar and tourist information desk, as well as the much-touted **Bern Show** (every 20min: June–Sept daily 9am–6pm; March–May & Oct daily 10am–4pm; Nov–Feb Fri–Sun 11am–4pm; free), where – having waited for the English version to come round – you sit on benches to watch a potted history of Bern, evoked by a large model of the city and clever use of lights, automated scenery and a slideshow. It's a valiant attempt to bring history to life, but is just too cheesy for its own good.

Heading left up the steep hill next to the Bärengraben will bring you to the **Rosengarten** (Rose Garden), which has a lovely collection of flora (220 varieties of rose, 200 of iris, and more) and spectacular morning views over the Old Town.

The Münster

Bern's late-Gothic **Münster** (Easter–Oct Tues–Sat 10am–5pm, Sun 11.30am–5pm; Nov–Easter Tues–Fri 10am–noon & 2–4pm, Sat until 5pm, Sun 11.30am–2pm) is unmistakeable, its feathery spire – the highest in Switzerland – towering over the Old Town and its sonorous bells dominating the quiet city. It's a reverential and quite awe-inspiring place, both for its lofty, gloomy interior and the terrific views from its tower.

The first chapel on the site – recorded in 1224 – probably dated from the founding of the city. On March 11, 1421, when just five thousand people lived in Bern, Matthäus Ensinger, a master builder from Strasbourg who already had three cathedrals under his belt, started construction on the new minster using the greenish local sandstone. Work continued according to his original plans until the mid-sixteenth century and, after a gap of three centuries or so, was finally completed in 1893 with the addition of the spire. Bern was a rapid convert to the Reformation and most of the church's treasures were destroyed in or soon after 1528, although some notable pieces such as the portal sculpture, choir stalls and stained-glass windows survived.

Outside the cathedral, cobbled **Münsterplatz** features the imposing Baroque facades of, among other buildings, the chapterhouse, and a 1790 fountain showing Moses, fired with the zeal of the Reformation, pointing to the Second Commandment (the one forbidding idolatry). It's worth stopping at the **central portal** of the cathedral before heading inside – this spectacular depiction of the **Last Judgement** is one of the only remaining unified examples of such late-Gothic sculpture in Europe. The 170 smaller figures are the fifteenth-century originals (the 47 larger freestanding pieces were replaced by copies in 1964, the originals now sitting in the Bernisches Historisches Museum; see p.252). The left half of the portal depicts the saved, the right half the damned: you can imagine that the graphic, didactic counterpoint between the beatific smiles of one side and the naked, screaming torment of the other would have appealed even to the iconoclastic Reformers, who chose to spare it from destruction. In the very centre is Justice, flanked by angels, the Wise and Foolish Virgins and, above, the Archangel Michael wielding a sword and scales.

Entry is through the right-hand gate, and the hushed **interior** is immediately impressive. The immense roof span is laced around with vaulting (1572–3), the aisles are flanked by rows of porches and small chapels, and the nave, with

Nasty, brutish and short?

There was much social unrest in Switzerland in 1980, most noticeably among radical leftists. Zürich's Autonomous Youth Centre (AJZ) – intended as a police-no-go building where young people could run their own entertainment free from mainstream commercial and social pressures – was violently suppressed, and a similar AJZ movement in Bern which took over the **Reitschule** (an abandoned city-owned former riding school near the train station, also known as the **Reithalle**; ⓦwww .reithalle.ch) was also evicted by the police. The situation simmered until late 1987 when, following the eviction of the riverside Zaffaraya community, thousands demonstrated in the city centre, a large group re-squatted the Reitschule and, perhaps most significantly, retailers reported a ten-percent loss in profits over the Christmas shopping season. In the face of such a groundswell of discontent, the police and city council adopted a damage-limitation policy, and left the Reitschule squatters to their own devices.

Despite problems with violent anarchist gangs in the early 1990s, the Reitschule – now an arts centre and activist collective – has come to be highly valued by alternatively minded Bernese, and has even gained a certain official legitimacy while remaining in a curious legal grey area. Its cinema, for instance, is licensed with the council but the bar next to it is illegal; the concert venue pays its taxes, while the adjacent café is packed with dope-smokers. Unlike the similar *Rote Fabrik* movement in Zürich (see p.421), the Reitschule cooperative has consistently rejected proposals to accept funding from the city council, sticking tight to its counter-cultural principles ("No violence, no sexism, no commercial exploitation") by raising its own money through ticket sales, bar profits and an extremely popular annual fundraising party. Through effective word-of-mouth networking, it's been able to stage gigs by British, European and American bands and DJs, raising its profile still further, yet to this day, the police don't venture into the complex, turning a deliberate blind eye to such a self-contained concentration of – mostly very innocuous – lawbreaking. It's a rundown, heavily lived-in place and an obvious honeypot for drug dealers (who are barred from entry, but nonetheless gather outside), yet these days is quite safe. More to the point, it's become an icon of opposition to the city council, which has been trying for years to turn it into a multistorey car park and supermarket. A huge graffito as you approach reads *Reitschule bleibt autonom* ("Reitschule still rules itself"). In a remarkably effective and purposeful demonstration of communal self-government, virtually unknown in other European countries and running entirely counter to the Swiss stereotype, it's true.

square pillars placed diagonally and the original 1470 pulpit, channels attention towards the stained glass of the choir. Keystone busts of saints, Mary, Christ and others were left untouched by the Reformers, possibly because they were too high to reach. The 1520s **choir stalls** are marvellous, carved with faces of the prophets and much intricate detail of ordinary life. The gorgeous **stained-glass windows** of the choir date from 1441–50, although a hailstorm in 1520 damaged the right-hand windows (two replacements were installed in 1868).

If you have even a dram of energy, you shouldn't spurn the chance to climb the **tower**, the tallest in Switzerland. The way up is just inside the church door (closes 30min early; Fr.4), but be warned: this is a 100m climb up a steep and narrow spiral of 254 stone stairs. (You might want to ask in the church when the bells will be rung and make your ascent to coincide, since the experience of standing literally right next to a gigantic, tolling ten-and-a-half tonne bell – the largest in the country, cast in 1611 – is one you and your ribcage will remember.) The 360-degree vistas over the whole city, most of the surrounding countryside, and out towards the Alps, are dreamy.

On the south side of the church is the **Münsterplattform**, a buttressed terrace above the Aare which took about a hundred years from 1334 to build. Abandoned icons were dumped here during the Reformation, but later it was planted with lime and chestnut trees and given elegant Baroque corner pavilions in order to serve as an open promenade, which is how it has remained. The views of the Aare and of silhouetted trams creeping along the soaring Kirchenfeldbrücke are spectacular. The net below the parapet was added a few years ago as a disincentive to desperate Bernese who chose this rather dramatic and beautiful spot to end it all.

The western Old Town

Some 100m west of the Münster is Casinoplatz – the actual Casino sees more concertgoers than gamblers – from where trams head south to the Helvetiaplatz museums (see p.252). The Zytglogge is a few steps north, and just beyond it is the nightmarish **Kindlifresserbrunnen**, or Ogre Fountain (1544), which shows a man devouring a struggling baby. The Bernese authorities would have you believe it's a light-hearted carnival scene, but the statue was once painted yellow (the colour used to stigmatize Jews) and may possibly be an unusually graphic representation of the suspicion held throughout medieval Europe that Jewish religious ritual involved the murder of children. Whichever, Bern's happy shoppers of today seem unfazed by images of cannibalistic infanticide in their midst.

A little north is the large **Kornhaus** (Granary; Tues–Fri 10am–7pm, Sat & Sun 10am–5pm; admission varies; ⓦwww.kornhaus.org), now occupied by offices, a chic bar and an attractive exhibition space used for shows of design, photography, multimedia and architecture. Just behind is the **Französische Kirche** (French Church), the city's oldest, which originally formed part of a thirteenth-century Dominican monastery. The compact but beautiful interior (Mon–Sat 9–11am & 2–5pm) has been much renovated, but retains its stalls (1302) and a rare frescoed rood screen (1495).

From the main **Kornhausplatz**, trams weave their way west along Marktgasse, heart of the city-centre shopping district, neatly avoiding the fountain statues of a musketeer in full armour and Anna Seiler, founder of Bern's first hospital, who's been set up to serve as an allegory of moderation. Just beyond the Seilerbrunnen is the **Käfigturm**, an early city gate (1256–1344) which was used as a prison from 1642 until 1897. The broad, sunny marketplace of **Bärenplatz** opens beyond, and a little further west along hectic Spitalgasse, with its bagpiper fountain, lies the late-1720s **Heiliggeistkirche** (Holy Spirit Church; Tues–Fri 11am–7pm), acclaimed as Switzerland's finest example of Protestant church building, boasting a gorgeous Baroque pillared-and-galleried interior. It stands alone, trams, buses and people weaving a cat's cradle all around it. The train station – metres away – marks the limit of the medieval city: several sections of excavated city wall are exposed on the lower shopping concourse.

The Bundeshaus

Immediately south of Bärenplatz is Bundesplatz, dominated by the **Bundeshaus**, or Federal Assembly building, built in Renaissance style in 1902 and inscribed *Curia Confoederationis Helveticae* (Assembly Building of the Swiss Confederation). When the parliamentarians are not in session, you can join a free 45-minute guided tour (on the hour Mon–Fri 9–11am & 2–4pm; ☏031 322 85 22), which takes you through the various chambers, decorated with coats of arms, statues and paintings commemorating events in Swiss history.

When the assembly is sitting (the flag overhead will be flying), you can watch proceedings from the public gallery. The building sits on a cliff-edge above the Aare, and the **Bundesterrasse** behind rests on a massive retaining wall; this promenade has rather ironically become the heart of Bern's flourishing drug market, and is often scattered with glazed-eyed characters shooting up literally under the noses of the lawmakers. On one side, a quirky little **funicular** runs down to the riverside district of Marzili (daily 6.30am–9pm; Fr.1).

The Kunstmuseum

Bern's marvellous **Kunstmuseum** is five minutes' walk northeast of the train station, in an impressive building at Hodlerstrasse 8–12 (Tues 10am–9pm; Wed–Sun 10am–5pm; Fr.7; temporary shows Fr.8–18; SMP; ⓦwww .kunstmuseumbern.ch). Aside from often excellent changing exhibits, the main draw, and reason enough to stump up the admission fee, is the **Paul Klee** collection,

Paul Klee

Born in Münchenbuchsee, just north of Bern, on December 18, 1879, **Paul Klee** is perhaps the best known of all Swiss artists, his attractive, dream-like works filled with allusions to music and poetry and suffused with an endearing humour and humanity. Art historians have a great deal of difficulty classifying his work, since his unique style takes in elements of primitive art, cubism, surrealism, naïve art and expressionism. Klee was a major influence on the abstract expressionist movement and on non-figurative painting of all kinds in the second half of the century.

His family was very musical, and it was only after a great deal of hesitation that Klee gave up developing his early proficiency on the violin to enrol in the Munich Academy of Art in 1900. There he met the pianist Lily Stumpf, playing duets on violin and piano with her. Shortly afterwards Klee toured Italy, finding particular pleasure and inspiration in Byzantine and early Christian art. He made many sketches, ink drawings and etchings during this period, two of the most famous of which, from 1903, are *Virgin in a Tree* and *Two Men Meet, Each Believing the Other to Be of Higher Rank*, both currently on display in Bern's Kunstmuseum.

In 1906 Klee and Stumpf married and settled in Munich, at that time a dynamic centre for avant-garde art. There, Klee met the painter Wassily Kandinsky, starting a lasting friendship; on Kandinsky's urging, Klee joined the expressionist circle Der Blaue Reiter (The Blue Rider), and in 1914 journeyed to Tunisia on a trip which was to change his life. "Colour has taken possession of me," he wrote. "No longer do I have to chase after it, I know that it has hold of me forever. Colour and I are one. I am a painter." The same year, the Sturm gallery in Berlin staged a joint exhibition of Klee and Chagall.

After the Great War, Klee taught at the famous Bauhaus school in Germany, alongside Kandinsky and the architect Walter Gropius. In 1931 he moved to the Düsseldorf Academy, but after Hitler's rise to power, the Nazis condemned Klee's art – which by now was using delicate, ethereal colour harmonies in subtle, semi-abstract figurative compositions – as "degenerate". Klee fled back to Bern just before Christmas 1933, continuing both his painting and his elaborate ink drawings based on fantasy imagery. He soon, however, developed a crippling disease of the skin and muscles, which affected his ability to work and would eventually kill him. After 1935, his style changed to incorporate thick, crayonish lines and blocks of muted colour in a set of increasingly gloomy musings on war and death. Picasso visited the sick artist late in 1937, as did Braque. Following a giant retrospective of 213 later works at the Zürich Kunsthaus early in 1940, Klee died on June 29, in hospital in Locarno.

the largest in the world with over two thousand works. They represent every stage of Klee's artistic development, from well before his evocative *Before the Gates of Kairouan* (1914) to *Ad Parnassum* (1932) and the delightfully abstract *Park bei Lu* (1938). Aside from Klee, the permanent collection comprises large numbers of works by **Kandinsky**, Modigliani, Giacometti, Rothko, Miró, Pollock and more. Cézanne's *Self-portrait with Black Felt Hat* (1879) stands out, as does a depressing, dark Picasso drinker from 1902 and the accomplished, late *Blue Blouse* by Matisse (1936). The finest work in a small group of Old Masters is a luminous gold *Maesta* by Duccio (1290) – rather out of place amidst the rest. Elsewhere, you'll find a range of works by contemporary artists, a wide selection from **Swiss artists** such as Anker and Hodler, as well as the curious naïve art of Adolf Wölfli (1864–1930), a paedophile farmworker who spent most of his life confined to a Bernese asylum creating thousands of pages of writing, musical scores and drawings (his work is also displayed at the Collection de l'Art Brut in Lausanne; see p.129).

Over the next few years there'll be a lot of changes at the Kunstmuseum, which is now far too small to display its holdings. In 2005, the entire Klee collection will move to the new **Paul Klee-Zentrum** (Ⓦ www.paulkleezentrum .ch), designed by Renzo Piano in the eastern district of Schöngrün (tram #5 to Ostring). In addition, in the city centre on Waisenhausplatz, an old school building is being converted into the new **Museum für Kunst der Gegenwart** (Contemporary Art; Ⓦ www.gegenwart.com), scheduled for opening in 2005.

The Helvetiaplatz museums

Most of Bern's museums are clustered together around **Helvetiaplatz**, on the south side of the Kirchenfeldbrücke. Some, like the Bernisches Historisches Museum, shouldn't really be missed; others have less going for them. Trams #3 (direction Saali) and #5 (direction Ostring) shuttle from the train station and the Zytglogge to Helvetiaplatz.

Bernisches Historisches Museum

You could spend a long time exploring the fascinating **Bernisches Historisches Museum** (Tues–Sun 10am–5pm, Wed until 8pm; Fr.8; SMP; Ⓦ www.bhm.ch), a grandiose turreted castle purpose-built in 1894. With seven floors of diverse bits and pieces, it's a good idea to pick up a floor plan before you start. Information is generally very good, with the scholarly German labelling nearly always given in English and French translation in leaflets kept in wall racks.

The ground floor is given over to temporary exhibitions, which tend not to have English explanations, and it's worth heading straight down to the basement (taking in, if you've time, the extensive porcelain and silver collection on the lower mezzanine on the way). At the bottom, to the left side of the staircase, is perhaps the highlight of the whole museum, a collection of extraordinary and macabre paintings showing "**The Dance of Death**"; these are 1649 copies of originals painted in 1516–17 on the wall of Bern's Dominican monastery and now lost. The sequence of 24 vivid images, showing a hideously grinning and fooling skeleton leading kings, prostitutes, nuns and lawyers alike to their inevitable fate, is enough to send a chill down your spine – as, no doubt, it was intended to. Equally impressive is the pillared room directly opposite, filled with the original sandstone figures from the **Last Judgement** portal of the Münster and fascinating for the chance to view their details up close. Through in another part of the basement are several rooms featuring rural and urban interiors from the seventeenth and eighteenth centuries, reconstructed down to the chamber pots and creaky floors.

From the ground floor all the way up the main staircase is a series of rather unflattering **portraits** of 280 Swiss peasants and craftspeople in traditional dress, made late in the eighteenth century as a kind of ethnographic record. The mezzanine is devoted to a spectacular **Islamic collection**, with daggers galore, a mounted Turkestan warrior in full armour, jewellery, ceramics and a reconstructed Persian sitting room. Stairs to the first upper floor bring you to an intricate **scale model of Bern** in 1800 (made in 1850). Nearby in the same room, for some unknown reason, sits a bust of Brigitte Bardot. Halls left and right display extremely impressive wall-sized medieval **Flemish tapestries**; the Burgundian Hall holds the Caesar Tapestries, telling the story of Caesar's life in Burgundian-style dress, and, highlight of the collection, the **Thousand Flowers Tapestry**, the only one surviving of a set of eight made in Brussels in 1466, which was looted by Bern during the Burgundian wars of 1474–77. Rooms further on with coins and medals include a mesmerizing 1828 three-way portrait of Calvin, Luther and Zwingli. On the other side of the stairs is the **Trajan Hall**, with suits of armour, weapons, cavalry standards and heraldic tapestries galore.

The second upper floor features more military uniforms from different periods, and a series of overwhelmingly meticulous rooms devoted to "**Changes in Daily Life**", covering everything from reconstructed shops and schoolrooms from different periods to ephemera, old vending machines and musical instruments. The top floor has a small **archeological collection**, and above is a belvedere offering bird's-eye views of the Bundeshaus and the Alps.

Schweizerisches Alpines Museum

Beside the Historical Museum, the **Schweizerisches Alpines Museum** (Mon 2–5pm, Tues–Sun 10am–5pm; Fr.7; SMP; Ⓦ www.alpinesmuseum.ch) is surprisingly good, taking an intelligent, sensitive look at all aspects of life in the mountains, from tourism, the history of mountaineering and the social identity of mountain dwellers to surveys of Alpine flora and fauna and the impact of industry on the mountain environment. There's plenty to play with and read up on (in English). Crowded all over the museum are dozens of examples of relief mapmaking gone berserk, with mountains, whole valley systems and complete Swiss ranges rendered in perfect scale detail, almost rock by rock, by enthusiasts whose energy and patience can only be imagined.

Other museums

There are plenty of other museums on or very close to Helvetiaplatz. The porticoed **Kunsthalle**, Helvetiaplatz 1 (Tues 10am–9pm, Wed–Sun 10am–5pm; Fr.6; Ⓦ www.kunsthallebern.ch) has changing exhibits of contemporary art, usually of very high quality. Behind the Historical Museum, the **Naturhistorisches Museum**, Bernastrasse 15 (Mon 2–5pm, Tues–Fri 9am–5pm, Wed until 8pm, Sat & Sun 10am–5pm; Fr.5; SMP; Ⓦ www.nmbe.ch), has the largest diorama exhibit in Europe – a somewhat fancy way to describe an array of stuffed animals behind glass, including a rather threadbare "Barry", the famous St Bernard mountain-rescue dog. Its mineralogical displays are more engaging, with meteorites and cut diamonds, but they're scant recompense for fighting the tide of schoolkids. The **Museum für Kommunikation**, Helvetiastrasse 16 (Tues–Sun 10am–5pm; Fr.6; SMP; Ⓦ www.mfk.ch), surveys media and communication from postage stamps and early telephones to the Internet and beyond. Just nearby are the Swiss national library and federal archives.

Outer districts

If you're on an extended visit to Bern, or if you just fancy something a bit different from medieval history at every turn, more modern districts slightly out from the Old Town can provide a little urban realism. Easiest to reach – just a short walk north of the train station across the river – is **Lorraine** (Ⓦwww.lorraine.ch). Late in the nineteenth century a dyed-in-the-wool working-class district, in the last decades Lorraine has attracted a growing population of students and young people who have created a funky, relaxed community atmosphere which nonetheless doesn't exclude the many old-timers still in the neighbourhood. Developers caught on to the appeal of the place in the 1990s, and more and more glass-and-steel architecture is appearing in amongst the old houses, but Lorrainestrasse and the streets around still retain much charm. On the way there, you could pass by Bern's wonderful **Botanischer Garten**, just across the river from the Kunstmuseum, at Altenbergrain 21 (daily 8am–5pm; free; Ⓦwww.botanischergarten.ch). It's been in existence since 1858, and has a host of Alpine flora in open-air cultivation, as well as hothouses to explore.

If you follow Schanzenstrasse up behind the train station, a short climb will bring you to Länggassstrasse, heart of the bustling university district of **Länggasse**. The **Unitobler** building, at no. 49a, 300m along on the left (bus #12 stops outside), was formerly the factory where, for most of the twentieth century, the famous Toblerone chocolate was produced. In the 1980s, production moved to a more modern site outside Bern, and the building was renovated for use by the university (hence the Unitobler name), subsequently receiving numerous architectural awards for sensitivity of renovation. You're basically free to explore: the student café spills onto a sunny plaza behind the building, and the library occupies an extraordinary below-ground site between two wings of the building that has been converted into an impressive three-storey atrium space. Just behind Unitobler, on Freiestrasse, is the elegant **Pauluskirche**, dating from 1905 and one of the best examples of Art Nouveau in the country.

Above Bern – Gurten

A favourite Bernese getaway – if one were needed from such a gentle, slow-paced capital – is to the hill of **Gurten** (Ⓦwww.gurtenpark.ch), which towers over the city from the south. Take tram #9 to Gurtenbahn, in the neat suburb of Wabern, and walk 100m along Dorfstrasse to the **funicular** (every 10–20min Mon–Sat 7am–11.30pm, Sun 7.40am–10pm; Fr.8 return; Bäre-Abi – see p.242 – and Swiss passes valid; Ⓦwww.gurtenbahn.ch). The whole journey from the train station to the summit only takes about half an hour. On top you'll find a kids' play area, a lavish folly of a castle (housing the gourmet restaurant *Bel Etage* and the more down-to-earth eatery *Tapis Rouge*, plus a bar, exhibition space and, separately, the *UPtown* club and music venue) and wide expanses of countryside laced with hiking trails that give views over Bern, out towards the Jura, and across the peaks of the Bernese Oberland. In winter the hill and snowy slopes are crowded with sledding families; in summer, you might have difficulty escaping the hikers and picnickers. Every year, for a weekend in mid-July, Gurten plays host to a very popular **rock festival** (Ⓦwww.gurtenfestival.ch); ask for details at the tourist office.

Well south of the centre beyond Helvetiaplatz, **Tierpark Dählhölzli**, Tierparkweg 1 (daily: summer 8am–6.30pm; winter 9am–5pm; Fr.7; Ⓦ www.tierpark-bern.ch), is in the midst of open-access riverside woods, with a zoo section devoted to local fauna such as wolves, chamois and bears and a vivarium housing reptiles and fish.

Eating and drinking

Bern's compact Old Town groans with **eating and drinking** possibilities, and you'll have no trouble finding something to suit your palate and your budget. The broad Bärenplatz, always busy with people, performers and market stalls, is shoulder to shoulder with cafés – *Gfeller* is a Bernese institution – and is top choice for cappuccinos in the sunshine, but there's a host of places all through the cobbled lanes offering *al fresco* consumption during the summer and firelit warmth in winter.

Cafés and café-bars

Altes Tramdepot Beside the Bärengraben Ⓦ www.altestramdepot.ch. Weave your way past the tourist crowds and into this fine old high-ceilinged place, formerly a tram depot and now a microbrewery, offering three house beers and a speciality monthly brew. The food is solid Bernese, Viennese and Bavarian fare, heavy on game, sausages and rich desserts. It's a sociable place, with good panoramic views from the garden terrace.

Art Café Gurtengasse 3 Ⓦ www.artcafe.ch. Bright, trendy café just off the main shopping streets that discovers a new line in studied urban dissipation after the shops shut.

Brasserie Lorraine Quartiergasse 17. Just about the last café in Bern still owned by a cooperative, with excellent, inexpensive food, wood floors and a summer terrace. Games galore fill the cupboards for free use, and the Sunday brunch is the best in Bern. A cosy, calm meeting place for alternative types and politicos. Take bus #20 to Lorraine (direction Wyler); Quartiergasse is a little ahead on the left. Closed Mon.

Café Litteraire In Stauffacher bookshop, Neuengasse 25. Cosy espresso bar in Bern's largest bookshop, with snacks and newspapers. Closed Sun.

Café des Pyrénées Kornhausplatz 17. Jovial and unpretentious meeting place for artists, alcoholics and others with loud voices. Equal quantities of twenty- and forty-somethings crowd the place out nightly, with the *Ringgenberg* next door catching the overflow. Closed Sun.

Kornhauscafé In the Kornhaus. The vaulted and renovated interior of the city's former granary is now home to a starkly postmodern-style café, with coiffed customers and pricey desserts and sand-

wiches. A cool contrast to the raucous *Pyrénées* opposite.

Du Nord Lorrainestrasse 2 ☎ 031 332 23 38. A quality Lorraine café-bar and eatery, offering a nice mixture of heavy meat-and-potatoes dishes and lighter veggie options. A meal might only come to Fr.23 in the evening, or as little as Fr.13 at lunchtime. All the food is organic and comes from small local producers ensuring freshness, and monthly dance events and occasional concerts add to the allure. Bus #20 to Gewerbeschule (direction Wyler). Closed Wed.

Reitschule (aka Reithalle), graffitied buildings next to the railway bridge 5min north of the station Ⓦ www.reithalle.ch. See also box p.249. Cooperative-run bastion of Bernese counterculture. The hash-smoky café-bar (named *Sous Le Pont*) is uniquely amiable; however, if sharing a scratched-up table with a green-haired character in a holey sweater rolling a joint isn't your idea of fun, you should head elsewhere. A red traffic light means table service, green means bar service. Open Tues–Thurs 11.30am–12.30am, Fri 11.30am–2.30am, Sat 5.30pm–2.30am, Sun 8pm–12.30am, with food generally noon–2pm & 6–11pm, during which dope-smoking is generally forbidden.

Zum Blauen Engel Seidenweg 9b. Cosy student café near the university, with *objets trouvés*, worn gilt mirrors, hosts of candles and a crowd of young, arty regulars creating a pleasantly seductive atmosphere in which to while away the evening. Eat before you come, though, since the food is disappointing. Bus #12 to Mittelstrasse (direction Länggasse) – Seidenweg is first right. Closed Mon.

Cheap eats

It's not hard to find good, filling food in Bern for Fr.10–15, and the best way to cut costs is to take advantage of lunchtime specials and daily *menus* – *Brasserie Lorraine* and *Cinématte* stand out as places where you can get great food for bargain prices. *Sous Le Pont* in the Reitschule has consistently appealing fare, and a feature of their social policy is to offer one square meal a day for a rock-bottom Fr.5. Bern's branch of the **self-service** *Manora* chain (see p.49), opposite the station at Bubenbergplatz 5a (Mon–Sat 7am–10.30pm, Sun 9am–10.30pm), is a good one, while the station itself has the usual array of low-priced diners in the underground shopping level. Another good option is to head for the **university**: the *Unitobler* café at Länggassstrasse 49a (side entrance on Lerchenweg; Mon–Fri 8.30am–4pm; food 11.30am–1.45pm) is a self-service student dining hall, with the added attraction of a sunny terrace for lounging or playing *boules*. Opposite at no. 44 is *Mappamondo*, a self-service Italian with an echoing exam hall for a dining area; or check out the Fr.11 lunch *menu* at the cosy *Länggassträff* café at nearby Lerchenweg 33.

Restaurants

Anker Kornhausplatz 16. Cosy, smoky pub, with a restaurant section in the back where you can scoff Swiss stomach-liners such as fondue, *Röschti* and a meat-laden Berner-Teller (around Fr.20) without embarrassment, since the place is invariably full of hearty locals tucking in too.

China Imperial Bärenplatz 21. Moderately good Chinese, worth mentioning only for its unique "Tellerservice": for under Fr.20, choose from a large buffet of uncooked ingredients and marinades, and present the lot to the chef who will wok-fry it all on the spot for piling over rice. They also have à-la-carte options, but at a premium. Tellerservice Mon–Fri 11am–2.30pm & 10–11.30pm only.

Cinématte Wasserwerkgasse 7 ☎031 312 45 46. Pleasant riverside nook attached to Bern's premier arthouse cinema. *Menus* (meat or veggie) and the à-la-carte choice are varied and not expensive. It's a small place, though, so booking is advised. Closed at lunch, and all day Tues.

Della Casa Schauplatzgasse 16 ☎031 311 21 42. An unprepossessing exterior preludes a fine old Bernese institution serving high-quality Swiss fare. The Bernerplatte – a plateful of half-a-dozen varieties of meats with potatoes and sauerkraut – is a house speciality, but doesn't come cheap: you'd be lucky to walk out with change from Fr.50. Closed Sat eve & Sun.

Dragon d'Or Bollwerk 41. Small, high-quality Thai/Chinese restaurant, on an unromantic, trafficky corner by the Lorrainebrücke, but nonetheless with a long and inventive menu and well-prepared fare.

Govinda Marktgasse 7, 3rd floor. Tiny Krishna-run diner, serving pristinely healthy vegetarian food in an unlikely location above a menswear store.

Lunch (Mon–Fri only) is a reasonable Fr.18 or so, and the weekly dinner (Thurs) is Fr.29. Closed Sat & Sun.

Kornhauskeller Below the Kornhaus ☎031 327 72 72, ⊛www.kornhaus.org. An atmospheric subterranean restaurant in the vaulted cellars of the former town granary, once a hearty folksy beerhall and now morphed into a classic formal restaurant, serving international and Mediterranean-style cuisine to the accompaniment of live cocktail jazz nightly.

Lorenzini Theaterplatz 5 ☎031 311 78 50. High-flying young professionals flock here both for the café-bar and the top-drawer Tuscan cuisine, although you'll be looking at over Fr.30 for a meal. Closed Sun.

Markthalle Bubenbergplatz 9. A slick indoor mall devoted to food from around the world – espressos, tapas, cheese, wine, bread, chocolates, and more. There's a host of different ways to satisfy munchies, at counters and small eateries serving sushi, pizzas, Thai food, Indian, Indonesian, Turkish and more, as well as the less adventurous *Markthalle* restaurant in the back. Despite the contrivance, the whole thing works rather well. Closed Sun.

Menuetto Herrengasse 22 / Münstergasse 47 ☎031 311 14 48. Chic veggie place with entrances from both streets, offering delectable, imaginative dishes and lots of choice (Fr.25 and up). Daily specials can drop as low as Fr.13. Closed Sun.

Postgasse Postgasse 48. Tiny old den on the quietest of alleys, with wood tables and an intimate, cosy atmosphere. The *menu* is good and not expensive (Fr.19), but the joy of the place is its dark, convivial ambience. Closed Mon & Tues.

Ringgenberg Kornhausplatz 19 ☏ 031 311 25 40. Warm and comfortable place that styles itself a *Brasserie Bernoise*; it's as much a bar as an eatery – although, unlike the *Pyrénées* next door, it's actually worth coming here for the food (around Fr.30). Closed Sun eve.

Nightlife and entertainment

Bern's **nightlife** is surprisingly vibrant, with live music (contemporary and classical), dance nights, theatre, opera and film all getting a substantial look-in. Posters all over town advertise events, or otherwise you can find complete city nightlife **listings** in *Agenda*, the Thursday supplement of *Berner Zeitung* newspaper, available free from many cinemas. For cutting-edge news about clubs and music events (in German), pick up the free *Bewegungsmelder* from the tourist office and elsewhere (ⓦ www.bewegungsmelder.ch). The free fortnightly *Bern aktuell* has English listings of major cultural events, but nothing out of the mainstream. You can buy **tickets** for most big events from the tourist office.

Bars, clubs and live music

Aside from its **bars**, Bern's nightlife tends to be concentrated in a handful of large, multipurpose venues which offer a changing diet of live bands, DJs and other bits and pieces, mostly for Fr.15–20 entry. There's also a fair smattering of decent **clubs**, which charge more or less the same.

Babalu Gurtengasse 3. Brash, city-centre club booming glitzy techno and house.

Dampfzentrale Marzilistrasse 47 ⓦ www.dampfzentrale.ch. An old steam factory down on the riverbank, now hosting hugely popular nights featuring jazz, drum'n'bass, dance, theatre and film, as well as a daytime café-bar. Either walk, or take evening bus #30 (8.45–11.55pm only).

Drei Eidgenossen Rathausgasse 69. A small, noisy bar in the Old Town, its wooden benches very popular with a loquacious, alternative young crowd.

ISC Neubrückstrasse 10 ⓦ www.hugo.ch/isc. Premier student venue and club.

Marians Jazzroom At *Hotel Innere Enge* (see p.243), ⓦ www.mariansjazzroom.ch. Major basement jazz venue in a genteel out-of-town hotel.

Mühle Hunziken 13km south of town near Rubigen ⓦ www.muehlehunziken.ch. An old wooden mill out in the countryside that has, over the years, hosted a jaw-dropping array of top-flight international jazz, blues and soul performers in an intimate, raucous setting more reminiscent of a delta juke-joint than the Swiss capital. If you see a gig advertised here, it's worth the taxi ride. Make friends quickly in order to nab a lift back to town after the show.

Reitschule (aka Reithalle ⓦ www.reitschule.ch; see also box p.249). Heart of the city's underground. Facilities include a cinema, concert venue, disco, women-only area and the *Sous Le Pont* café-bar.

Schwarz & Trionfini's Cocktail Club Brunngasshalde 63. An unmarked wooden facade gives into an atmospheric bar, with a bare-rock cellar chiselled out of the hillside furnished with sagging red sofas and candelabra. The chic clientele are rather less dramatic than the space, sipping sidecars at each other like it was coming back into fashion, but the late-night blend of Jack Daniels and Miles Davis is a heady (if expensive) one nonetheless. Closed Sun.

Shakira Hirschengraben 24. Mainstream Latino DJ-bar with salsa and regular Cuban nights.

Tübeli Rathausgasse 50. A barfly's dream tucked away on a cobbled street in the Old Town, with lino on the floor, a long greasy counter and sad songs playing into the small hours.

U1 Junkerngasse 1. Atmospheric subterranean DJ-bar near Nydegg.

Wasserwerk Wasserwerkgasse 5, below Nydeggbrücke ⓦ www.wasserwerk.ch. Bern's big techno joint, also hosting regular live bands.

Classical music, opera, theatre and film

Classical music is well served by the Bern Symphony Orchestra (ⓦ www.bernorchester.ch), which performs regularly at the Casino (Herrengasse 25) and the Stadttheater (Kornhausplatz 20), the latter also staging occasional **opera**.

Aside from major **theatre** productions at the Stadttheater, most nights of the week see a host of fringe shows in the many Old Town cellar studios. The Käfigturm theatre (Marktgasse 67) is the best known, with experimental drama, cabaret, pantos and comedy, and the Puppentheater (Gerechtigkeitsgasse 31) has striking and funny puppet shows, but there are literally dozens more – drop into the Stadttheater ticket office at Kornhausplatz 18 (Mon–Sat 10am–6.30pm, Sun 10am–12.30pm) for details.

All **cinemas** in the city (ⓦ www.bernerkino.ch) cut their prices on Mondays. There's plenty of mainstream choice, and both the Cinématte (Wasserwerkgasse 7; ⓦ www.cinematte.ch) and the Kunstmuseum (see p.251) run non-commercial programmes.

Listings

Books Bern's biggest bookstore, and the only one with a sizeable quality range in English, is Stauffacher, Neuengasse 25 (Mon–Sat 8am–6.30pm, Thurs until 9pm). You'll find travel accessories and books – including Rough Guides – at Atlas, Schauplatzgasse 21.

Changing money The best place is the change bureau on the lower level of the train station (June to mid-Oct daily 6.15am–9.45pm; mid-Oct to May daily 6.15am–8.45pm).

Embassies Australia: embassy in Berlin ☎ 004930/880 0880, consulate in Geneva (see p.112). Canada, Kirchenfeldstrasse 88 ☎ 031 357 32 00. Ireland, Kirchenfeldstrasse 68 ☎ 031 352 14 42. New Zealand: embassy in Berlin ☎ 004930/20 6210, consulate in Geneva (see p.112). UK, Thunstrasse 50 ☎ 031 359 77 70, ⓦ www.britain-in-switzerland.ch. USA, Jubiläumstrasse 93 ☎ 031 357 70 11, ⓦ www.usembassy.ch.

Flights Flight enquiries from Bern-Belp ☎ 031 960 21 11, ⓦ www.flughafenbern.ch. Alp-Air ☎ 031 960 22 22, ⓦ www.alp-air.ch) flies light aircraft on nine sightseeing routes, ranging from a short overfly of Bern to flights as far afield as Mont Blanc.

Gay and lesbian life *Anderland*, Mühleplatz 11, is the most popular gay café-bar, also home to HAB, the Homosexuelle Arbeitsgruppen Bern (☎ 031 311 63 53, ⓦ www.gay-bern.ch). *Anderland*, the Reithalle (see p.255) and the ISC (see p.257) have reasonably regular gay and lesbian club nights, the Reithalle café is gay- and lesbian-friendly at all times, and within the Reithalle complex is a club

and bar for women only.

Laundry Jet Wash, Dammweg 43 in Lorraine (Mon–Sat 7am–9pm, Sun 9am–6pm). Alongside is the sociable *Café Kairo*, handy for a beer or a light meal while waiting.

Lost property If you've lost something in town, head for the city Fundbüro, Predigergasse 5 (Mon–Fri 10am–4pm, Thurs until 6pm; ☎ 031 321 50 50). For enquiries about tracking property lost on the trains, head for the train station's Fundbüro (Mon–Fri 8am–noon & 2–6pm; ☎ 0512 202 337).

Markets Bern has a wealth of markets (ⓦ www.markt-bern.ch), both year-round and annual one-off events. There are general markets on Tuesdays and Saturdays all year on Waisenhausplatz, Bundesplatz and Bärenplatz, with Bärenplatz in particular turned into a daily open-air jumble of stalls throughout the summer. Münsterplatz has a handicrafts market on the first Saturday of every month, and there's a wonderful riverside flea market on Mühlerplatz in Matte on the third Saturday of the month (May–Oct only). In December Münsterplatz and Waisenhausplatz both have Christmas markets (ⓦ www.weihnachtsmarktbern.ch), featuring scented candles and mulled wine. Bern's famous Onion Market (see p.241) is more of an excuse for a street party than anything else.

Medical facilities The Inselspital university hospital on Freiburgstrasse (☎ 031 632 21 11) has a 24-hour emergency room. Bahnhof Apotheke Hörning, on the upper level of the train station, is open daily 6.30am to 10pm.

Police Headquarters is at Waisenhausplatz 32 (☏031 321 21 21), but a more convenient office is in the change bureau in the train station lower level (daily 7am–9.15pm).

Post Main office is the Schanzenpost (full service Mon–Fri 7.30am–6.30pm, Thurs until 8pm, Sat 8am–noon; limited service Mon–Fri 6am–8pm, Sat 7am–6pm, Sun 3.30–10pm), on Schanzenstrasse just behind the train station. You can collect poste restante mail from counter 16 with your passport.

Radio One of Switzerland's more engaging radio stations is Radio Bern (known as RaBe; ⓦwww.rabe.ch), at 91.1FM, with diverse, multi-cultural programming by everyone from Brazilian expats spinning salsa to Reithalle activists con-demning the city council to a soundtrack of deep ambient beats.

Around Bern

To the east of Bern, a blissfully bucolic region of farmhouses and dairies, undu-lating hills and peaceful villages, spreads through and around the **Emmental**, the valley (*tal*) of the River Emme. Somehow or other, despite the presence of a show dairy and the region's prominent place in the hearts of the rurally minded, cheese-loving Swiss, the Emmental has managed to escape heavy tourist development. It's a wonderful place for long country walks or bike rides. To the north, generic suburban prosperity quietly covers the land as far as the dignified old city of **Solothurn**, capital of its own canton – a fact which rather awkwardly forced tourist offices to rename the Berner Mittelland as the "Schweizer Mittelland", in deference to non-Bernese sensibilities.

To the west and south, the Mittelland merges into the lakeside country of Canton Fribourg and the Broye (see p.191), with the extremely attractive and much overlooked city of **Fribourg** set in gorgeous countryside southwest of Bern on the French–German language border.

The Emmental

Just outside the eastern city limits of Bern rises the Bantiger mountain (947m); behind it stretches the **EMMENTAL**, a quintessentially Swiss landscape of peaceful, vibrantly green hills dotted with happily munching brown cows,

Exploring the Mittelland

You can get information on the whole Mittelland region from the **Schweizer Mittelland tourist office** (☏031 328 12 28, ⓦwww.smit.ch), which is based in the same offices as Bern tourist office, in Bern's main train station. They have plenty of contacts with companies running multi-day adventure packages in the area, and can put together any kind of itinerary covering hikes or long-distance cycling or inline skating on the hundreds of trails through the Mittelland, often throwing in extras to tempt you, such as canoeing on the Aare and – a particular local attraction – panning for gold in the rolling Emmental hills. A two-day package including riding, hiking and a night in a farmhouse costs from Fr.252. Pro Emmental (ⓦwww .emmental.ch) also has details of many package deals in the area; see p.264.

sleepy rustic hamlets and isolated timber-built dairies. This is where Emmental cheese (the one with the holes) originates. A local nineteenth-century clergyman-writer celebrated the sturdiness and moral rectitude of Emmentaler dairy farmers in a series of famous novels under the pseudonym Jeremias Gotthelf; since then the place has gathered to itself an atmosphere of earnest rural stability and honesty. The salt-of-the-earth locals have the reputation of being the most reliable, the most sensible, the most Swiss of all the Swiss – a reputation which, in a distasteful modern turnaround, has been exploited by politicians: the extreme right-wing SVP (Swiss People's Party) has recently begun to expand out of its traditional base in Luzern to make significant gains in the Emmental countryside on a tide of anti-immigration, anti-foreigner, anti-EU rhetoric.

Emmentaler **architecture** is distinctive, the local timber-built inns and dairies crowned by huge roofs with overarching eaves, ringed by wooden balconies, and encrusted with rows of tiny windows, each with its window box and neatly tied-back set of net curtains. Emmentaler **cooking**, featuring cheese or cream with everything, is renowned around the country (this is where you can find some of Switzerland's finest meringue creations), and in 1999, a couple of dozen local inns and restaurants got together to regulate the quality of

Customs and festivals in the Mittelland

The Mittelland is one of the more traditional areas of the country, and has hundreds of **folk customs and festivals** surviving in various forms, many of them dating back to the pre-Christian pagan religions of the Celts. "Chilbi" is the generic name given to the summer highland festivals of the Emmental, raucous events taking in folk singers and dancers, yodellers, flag-throwers, alphorn blowers and more. The **Lüderenchilbi** is one of the most famous, held on the Lüderenalp meadow every second Sunday in August and centred on a Schwingfest, a traditional Swiss wrestling contest held in a sawdust ring. The winner gets to take home a heifer decked out in garlands. The **Schafsheid**, or sheep-sorting, held in Riffenmatt, 20km south of Bern, on the first Thursday in September, is a colourful event, when the sheep, after spending the summer on the alp, are sorted out by owner, amidst market stalls and celebrations. The **Sichlete** is a communal autumn meal, where in years gone by everyone who'd worked to bring in the harvest would sit down to gorge on stew, sausages, hams and fresh garden produce, helped down by huge meringues and local apple Schnapps; these days, with increasing farm mechanization (and so fewer seasonal farmhands taken on), the Sichlete has become merely an excuse for two or three villages to get together for a feast and a knees-up. In Burgdorf, the last Monday in June sees the **Solennität**, a 250-year-old festival for children, featuring contests, games and traditional costumes.

Many pagan New Year's Eve rituals survive in the villages of the Mittelland. Laupen's **Achetringele** stems from a Celtic exorcising of evil spirits and demons on the winter solstice; now shifted to December 31, it involves all the boys in the village chasing away the old year either as one of the masked Bäsemänner (broom-sweepers) or as a noisy, cowbell-swinging Tringeler (bell-ringer). One of the most bizarre customs, however, survives in Schwarzenburg, 8km north of Riffenmatt, where the **Altjahrsesel** (Old-Year Donkey) – these days a man dressed in a donkey suit – is whipped and beaten before being led away by a grim figure representing death. As well as the group of exorcists, various other characters take part in the ritual, including a bride and groom, representing joy in the year to come, the devil, a priest, and, most chillingly of all, a two-faced woman, the Hinnefürfraueli, whose beautiful front face looks forward to the new year, while her hideous rear face despatches the old year to memory.

cuisine on offer in the region. All of these now offer – among other dishes – the **Ämmitaler Ruschtig** *menu*, a gut-busting four-course blowout for around Fr.50: from *Beeri Schämpis* (sparkling berry wine), and a cheese salad served with the local *Züpfe* plaited bread, it takes in soup with whipped cream and *Chlepfer Ännis Schwynsschnitzu* (pork escalope in cream sauce, with creamy mashed potatoes and vegetables), then moves on to *Meielis Merängge Gschlaber* (fresh meringue with whipped cream, ice cream and caramelized cream), before rounding it (and you) off with Schnapps-laced coffee. Local tourist offices and ⓦwww.aemmitaler-ruschtig.ch have the full list of *Ämmitaler Ruschtig* establishments.

Burgdorf and the northern Emmental

On a pleasant road 19km northeast of Bern through Krauchthal village, the picturesque old town of **BURGDORF** is built on a prominence above the Emme. From the train station, follow Bahnhofstrasse south and then head east on Oberstadtweg to meander up into the Old Town, an atmospheric quarter characterized by steep cobbled streets. At the top is the mighty **Schloss Burgdorf**, the Zähringens' largest castle, begun in the seventh century and expanded in the twelfth. Several rooms grouped around an attractive courtyard comprise the **Schlossmuseum** (April–Oct Mon–Sat 2–5pm, Sun 11am–5pm; Nov–March Sun 11am–5pm; Fr.5; ⓦwww.schloss-burgdorf.ch), outlining local history; the ticket also lets you into the adjacent **Goldmuseum** (same hours), tribute to the history of gold-panning in these hills. Below, the late-Gothic **Stadtkirche** features an elaborate choir screen that looks rather too big and grand for the church housing it. Every Thursday, the Old Town hosts Burgdorf's weekly **market**.

Roads climb northeast from Burgdorf to a viewpoint at **Lueg** (887m), offering classic panoramas over the rolling countryside. Nearby is **AFFOLTERN**, a pleasant village that's home to the Emmental's flagship **Schaukäserei** (Show Dairy; daily 8.30am–6.30pm; free; ⓦwww.showdairy.ch), a rather hectic place that seems always to be full of busloads of excitable Swiss-German old ladies. As well as being able to watch the various cheesemaking processes – the dairy gets through some seven billion litres of milk a year – you can take in plenty of English-language videos on the cheese industry. A noisy and rather pricey café-restaurant adjacent serves the *Ämmitaler Ruschtig Menü*. Plus, of course, you can buy any amount of cheese, ranging from a bag of "Schnouserli" (bite-sized cubes of different strengths of Emmental, for Fr.2) up to a full 9kg round of Emmental shipped direct to your door (Fr.240). A booth also has tourist information on the area.

Hasle-Rüegsau and Lützelflüh

Roads drop back down from Affoltern into the Emme valley at **HASLE-RÜEGSAU**, two small villages which, over the years, have grown to hate each other like only next-door neighbours can. Pressured by economic hardship a century or so ago, the farmers of Rüegsau were forced to move down from their original hillside village (tiny Rüegsbach) through an intermediate settlement (Rüegsau itself) to a village down on the Emme (Rüegsauschachen), alongside the settled folk of Hasle; spurred on by displacement, they've since developed a strong community and prosperous commercial base. Static, conservative Hasle has been left behind, and is now struggling with old-fashioned, unrenovated buildings and a stagnating economy. To this day, the two merely tolerate each other: Rüegsauschachen has carefully kept gardens, modern houses and an air of suburban pride, and tends to regard its neighbour as back-ward, while in Hasle resentment and bitterness run high. Attempts to link social services failed in 2002, and this stretch of the river has become known locally as the Jordan, symbolizing the depth of feeling on both sides.

The two were formerly linked across the river by the largest arched wooden bridge in Europe, **Holzbrücke**, a mightily impressive 69m-long construction built in 1839. Unfortunately, it was damaged by cars in 1955 and – another nail in the coffin of neighbourly relations – was shifted 800m downstream to its current position, a five-minute walk west in a hard-to-spot woodsy location behind the train tracks. Hasle and Rüegsau now have an undistinguished modern bridge that seems to divide them as much as join them.

Along the valley floor 8km is a turning for **LÜTZELFLÜH**, a captivatingly charming village at the heart of the Emmental that was home to the local novelist Gotthelf from 1831 to 1854. On the outskirts of the village you'll pass the **Kulturmühle**, an old mill from 1821 that has been turned into a cultural centre (Ⓦ www.luetzelflueh.ch/kulturmuehle), staging everything from the Emmentaler Cock-Crowing Contest to monthly classical music concerts which attract the Bern cognoscenti out into the sticks. The oddly formal small Baroque garden nearby, laid out in classic French style, isn't out of place: you can find similar examples outside farmhouses throughout the Emmental – a legacy of French influence over Bern following the 1798 revolution – though today the formal squares and circle patterns are just as likely to be planted with carrots and lettuces. From Lützelflüh, back roads climb to Affoltern, while the main valley road runs on south beside the Emme.

Langnau and the southern Emmental

Some 17km southeast of Bern, the tranquil town of **Konolfingen** marks the start of a scenic road along the Kiese valley through Zäziwil to **LANGNAU**, the main town of the Emmental, but a singularly sleepy place nonetheless, with not much traffic and less than 10,000 people. A small **tourist office** in a travel agent off the main square, Dorfmühle 22 (Mon–Fri 8am–noon & 1–6pm, Fri until 9pm, Sat 9am–4pm), has information on the region, including details of the dozens of local walking routes. Look out for the Friday morning **market** on Viehmarktplatz.

East of Langnau, the main road passes through the extremely picturesque village of **TRUBSCHACHEN**, with big old wooden Emmentaler houses lining the street and a demonstration **pottery** turning out examples of the pretty local ornamental ware. To the north rises the **Napf** (1408m), the most famous of the Emmental's hills and a mecca for hikers and Sunday hill walkers. East of Trubschachen, the road crosses briefly into Canton Luzern and an area known as the **ENTLEBUCH** (Ⓦ www.entlebuch.ch), with its small countryside resort of **Marbach** boasting a couple of ski lifts serving the Marbachegg (1483m); in 2001, the Entlebuch became a UNESCO-affiliated Biosphere Reserve (Ⓦ www.unesco.org/mab), in a move to protect this rural area and kickstart sustainable development.

Less than 5km southwest, and back in Canton Bern again, is **Schangnau** village, at the upper end of the Emme valley. A minor road southeast from here winds dramatically between the cliffs, which rise to 2000m on both sides, through tiny **Bumbach** (with lifts up to the giant wedge-shaped Hohgant, towering overhead at 2197m) and on to **KEMMERIBODEN** (976m). This end-of-the-road hamlet, sliced through by the rushing, tumbling Emme – a mountain torrent at this stage – is the place to get the single best **meringue**

△ The Zytglogge, Bern (see p.244)

in Switzerland (see below), and is also the trailhead for many wilderness hikes, principally the tough path through the mountains to the 2350m Brienzer Rothorn (7hr), from where a rack railway can take you down to Brienz (see p.311).

From Schangnau, the main road crosses the Emme and heads north through **Eggiwil** to Langnau, crossing nine picturesque wooden covered bridges that are typical of the area. From Eggiwil, you can also reach Langnau by a parallel road further west over the crest of **Chuderhüsi** (1103m), which offers spectacular views over the Emmental hills and valleys backed by the snowy Alps.

Emmental practicalities

The best way to get around in the Emmental is **by bike** or **on foot**, both of which allow you to set your own itinerary and pace, and explore as much or as little as you want; stations at Bern, Langnau and Burgdorf have bikes for rent. A scenic **train** line between Bern and Luzern passes through Konolfingen and Langnau, while a branch line runs north from Langnau through Hasle to Burgdorf, shadowing the Emme through verdant countryside. Hourly **post-buses** from Marbach run through Schangnau to Kemmeriboden.

The umbrella **tourist organization** Pro Emmental is at Schlossstrasse 3 in Langnau (☎034 402 42 52, ⓦwww.emmental.ch); they, and tourist offices in Bern and Langnau, heavily tout the **hiking** possibilities of the area, with maps and route suggestions galore. Walking through hillside pastureland from Burgdorf to Affoltern, for instance, takes about three hours; from Burgdorf along the riverbank to Hasle, or Walkringen (above Konolfingen) to Lützelflüh, a little less. For a ramble down the Emme from Langnau to Burgdorf, or a stiffer hike from Langnau up to the Napf, reckon on a leisurely six hours or more. Pro Emmental also has details of companies that can inexpensively transport your bags around the region, enabling you to spend the day walking unencumbered.

One of the more unusual ways to see the Emmental is from the back of a **llama**: Pro Emmental can set up a minimum of four people with a two-day llama trek for around Fr.190 each, and can also put you in touch with companies running multi-day cycling or hiking adventure holidays in the area.

Accommodation and restaurants

There are **campsites** around the area: modest *Mettlen* at Gohl, 2km north of Langnau (☎034 402 36 58), and *Sternen* at Marbach (☎041 493 41 05); a wilder option at Bumbach (☎034 493 47 00); and high-quality *Waldegg* at Burgdorf (☎034 422 79 43; April–Sept). The spartan HI **hostel** *Jugendherberge*, Mooseggstrasse 32 in Langnau (☎034 402 45 26, ⓦwww.youthhostel.ch; closed Feb & Oct), has dorm beds for Fr.14 excluding breakfast, while the Berghotels on the summits of the Napf (☎034 495 54 08, ⓕ034 495 60 02; ❶; closed Mon in winter) and the Marbachegg (☎034 493 32 66, ⓕ034 493 47 94) have dorm places for Fr.30–35.

Otherwise, every hamlet has its choice of small-scale country inns which double as **hotel** and **restaurant**, virtually all of which, big and small, use farm-fresh produce and ingredients brought straight into the kitchen from that morning's market – bad Emmentaler cooking is a contradiction in terms. Affoltern, for instance, has the impressive *Sonne* (☎034 435 80 00, ⓕ034 435 80 19; ❷), with a few pleasantly renovated rooms above a good local restaurant; while dominating the centre of Langnau is the *Hirschen* (☎034 402 15 17, ⓦwww.hirschen-langnau.ch; ❷), a huge inn in typical Emmentaler style. In far-flung Kemmeriboden is one of the region's best hotels, the wonderful

Kemmeriboden-Bad (☎034 493 77 77, ⓦwww.kemmeriboden.ch; ❸), with comfortable rooms, dorm places (Fr.32), superb local cooking and simply dreamy homemade meringues.

Solothurn

SOLOTHURN (Soleure in French), some 35km north of Bern at the confluence of the Emme and the Aare, is touted as the most beautiful Baroque city in Switzerland – with justification. Its compact but very characterful Old Town is crammed with an odd architectural mix of Swiss-German sturdiness and lavish Italianate excess dating from the town's heyday in the seventeenth and eighteenth centuries. It's an easy day-trip from points all over the Mittelland, with a couple of spectacular Baroque churches, a very worthwhile art gallery, and a high viewpoint nearby for breezy walks.

In Celtic times, Salodurum was a fortified town; after Roman domination and Alemannic invasion, it was only in the tenth century that Solothurn rediscovered some stability. With the demise of the Zähringen dynasty in 1218, the city expanded its territory to form a buffer zone between Bern and Basel, and joined the Swiss Confederation in 1481. In the decades following, despite the turmoil of the Reformation all around, Solothurn remained Catholic and so, in 1530, was chosen by the Catholic ambassadors of the king of France as their place of residence. For more than 250 years, these **French ambassadors** lived in Solothurn, overseeing the town's redevelopment in the contemporary **Baroque** style. Some destruction followed the 1798 revolution, but a great deal of Solothurn's graceful Old Town has survived. These days it's a lively, cosmopolitan place, with thriving industry (watchmaking and precision manufacturing figure large) and a curiously varied mixture of ethnicities on its streets.

Arrival, information and accommodation

Solothurn is on the main SBB **train** line between Biel/Bienne and the big rail junction at Olten. It's also served by regular mini-trains from Bern operated by RBS (ⓦwww.rbs.ch); these don't appear on the big departures board in Bern station – aim instead for platforms U1–4. Solothurn's oddly huge **train station** is a few minutes' walk south of the river, with a **change** bureau and bike rental (both daily 5am–8.50pm) and, just to one side, the main **post office**.

Rötistrasse is the highway heading north from in front of the station, but quieter Hauptbahnhofstrasse, one street to the left, will deliver you to the pedestrian-only Kreuzackerbrücke, leading into the heart of the Old Town. **River boats** on the fine *Aarefahrt* route to and from Biel/Bienne (May–Oct; see p.195; ⓦwww.bielersee.ch) dock at the Romandie jetty beside the railway bridge, two west (upstream) of the Kreuzackerbrücke. The **tourist office** is at the foot of the cathedral steps, Hauptgasse 69 (Mon–Fri 8.30am–noon & 1.30–6pm, Sat 9am–noon; ☎032 626 46 46, ⓦwww.solothurn–city.ch & ⓦwww.mysolothurn.com), and runs excellent ninety-minute **walking tours** of the town beginning from the Baseltor (May–Sept Sat 2.30pm; Fr.5).

Hotels

Baseltor Hauptgasse 79 ☎032 622 34 22, ⓦwww.baseltor.ch. Popular and friendly brasserie with just six ensuite rooms, all appealingly simple and fresh, and so generally snapped up well in advance. Worth booking for. ❸

Kreuz Kreuzgasse 4 ☎032 622 20 20, Ⓔkreuz@solnet.ch, ⓦwww.kreuzkultur.ch. Rough-and-ready cooperative, offering shared-bath rooms – spartan and wood-floor creaky (newer rooms are upstairs) – plus discounts for stays beyond one night and free kitchen use. ❶

Krone Hauptgasse 64 ☏ 032 626 44 44,
ⓦ www.hotelkrone-solothurn.ch. Top choice in
town, its Baroque decor preluding solidly comfortable old-style rooms, with stout, tasteful furnishings and rooms at the back looking over the
cathedral steps. ❺
Zunfthaus zur Wirthen Hauptgasse 41 ☏ 032
626 28 48, ⓦ www.wirthen.ch. An all-wood guildhouse with plasticky but spacious rooms, some
ensuite, some not. ❷

Hostel

Jugendherberge (HI hostel) Landhausquai 23
☏ 032 623 17 06, ⓦ www.youthhostel.ch. One of
the country's best hostels, modern steel-and-glass
decor insinuated into a seventeenth-century building on the Old Town riverbank just west of the
Kreuzackerbrücke. There's a wide choice of dorms
(from Fr.27) and rooms with and without river
views, and as well as all the usual services,
including bike rental, they'll put together an inexpensive packed lunch for you. ❶

The Town

Centrepiece of the town is the massive **St-Ursen-Kathedrale** (daily
8am–noon & 2–7pm; Oct–Easter closes 6pm), an Italianate vision in local
grey-white stone that seems to float above the main Hauptgasse. It's crowned
by a greenish tower which rises to 62m. (Incongruously, the steps leading up
to the entrance are a favourite smoking spot for the local kids; not all the fragrant odours drifting about are ecclesiastical incense.) Overhead, the Latin
inscription in gold running around the building refers to Solothurn's patron
saints, Ursus and Victor, who refused to worship Roman gods and were martyred. The bright, soaring wedding-cake interior has a riot of intricate stucco
covering the white stone walls that is typical of the lavish late-Baroque era in
which the church was built (1762–73).

Sandwiched between shop fronts barely 100m along Hauptgasse is the atmospheric **Jesuit church**: push the unremarkable door to gain entry to the
extremely remarkable interior, dating from the 1680s and encrusted with a
dizzying amount of lacy stuccowork. Halfway along Hauptgasse, overlooking
the central Marktplatz, is the **Zytglogge**, Solothurn's oldest building, the lower
part dating from the twelfth century, the upper part from 1467, and the astronomical device in the centre from 1545. The hour hand on the giant clock face
is longer than the minute hand.

A few steps north of the cathedral is the doughty **Altes Zeughaus** (Old
Arsenal), housing a moderately interesting museum of militaria (May–Oct
Tues–Sun 10am–noon & 2–5pm; Nov–April Tues–Fri 2–5pm, Sat & Sun
10am–noon & 2–5pm; Fr.6; SMP). This massive collection documents
Solothurn's history of battles and booty, most impressively with a gigantic hall
full of swords and suits of armour. Some 50m east is the **Baseltor**, an old city
gate dating from 1508. Hug the walls north to the corner bastion of the Old
Town and you'll come to the circular **Riedholz** tower, now the location of a
summer cycle of prestigious classical concerts.

Across the lawns to the north lies the impressive **Kunstmuseum** (Tues–Fri
10am–noon & 2–5pm, Sat & Sun 10am–5pm; free; ⓦ www.kunstmuseum-so
.ch). Highlights of this surprisingly good collection are Holbein's *Solothurner
Madonna* (1522), on a panel backed by the delightful *Madonna in the Strawberries*
(1425), painted by the anonymous Master of the Garden of Paradise. Some
spectacular Alpine canvases are led by Ferdinand Hodler's much-reproduced
portrait of a Herculean William Tell emerging from a break in the clouds. One
of Hodler's famous sequences of larger-than-life moving bodies decorates the
stairs, while Klimt's luscious *Goldfish* is another highlight.

Last but not least, way on the other side of town, on the southern bank near
the river-boat landing stage, is the highly odd **Krummer Turm**, or Twisted
Tower, a fortification of the town dating from the 1460s. Looked at from any

Above Solothurn – the Weissenstein

One of the best viewpoints in the Swiss Jura is the **Weissenstein**, a ridge rising to 1284m with a breathtaking panorama over the entire Mittelland and out to the Bernese Alps. Local **trains** from Solothurn to Moutier stop at Oberdorf, from where you can either hike up or take the **chairlift** – which is closed on Mondays – to the summit (Fr.19 return; Ⓦwww.seilbahnweissenstein.ch). On top is the super-slick *Weissenstein Hotel* (☎032 628 61 61, Ⓦwww.hotel-weissenstein.ch; ❷–❸), complete with gourmet restaurant, modern conference facilities and, alongside, a lovely garden planted with Jura flowers and plants, best in June and July. Plenty of walks branch out from the hotel, mostly along the crest of the ridge; you could also do a chunk of the long-distance Jura Höhenweg walk from here (see box p.226; Ⓦwww.jura-hoehenwege.ch).

point other than its axis of symmetry, it appears to be hopelessly lopsided; in fact, though, its base is an irregular pentagon (due to the tower's original location at the sharp corner of a bastion of entrenchments). The spire on its scalene-pentagonal roof, although it seems about to topple off any minute, has been safe and secure these past five centuries. From the tower, you can cross to the northern bank and hike the riverside road for two hours west to the stork colony at **Altreu**.

Eating and drinking

Of all the many Old Town terrace **cafés**, *Rust* on Marktplatz has the edge, overlooked by the Zytglogge and facing the cathedral along the length of Hauptgasse. Look out for the local delicacy *Solothurner Kuchen*, a tart of nut fondant and whipped cream piled on a biscuit base, supplied by the slice in cafés and whole – in many sizes – by any of the *confiseries* in the centre.

Manora, the self-service **restaurant** in the Manor department store just off Marktplatz, has a rooftop terrace and a range of fresh-cooked dishes at rock-bottom prices (Mon–Fri 9am–6.30pm, Thurs until 9pm, Sat 8am–5pm). Both *Kreuz* and *Baseltor* hotels have cooperative café-bar-restaurants serving up delectable organic food in gargantuan portions; *Kreuz* is less expensive (*menus* from Fr.12, day and night), while *Baseltor* has the slight edge on quality (both closed Sun lunch). Otherwise, reflecting Solothurn's cultural mix, *Taverna Amphora*, Hauptgasse 51, offers Greek specialities for well under Fr.20; *Trattoria Alfredo*, Goldgasse 15, the same with an Italian bent; and tiny *Pittaria*, Kreuzgasse 12, has cut-price, but authentic, Arabic snacks – wash down your falafel (Fr.8) with delicious cardamom-spiced coffee.

Fribourg

Some 34km southwest of Bern, **FRIBOURG** (Freiburg in German) is one of Switzerland's best-kept secrets. Its winningly attractive medieval Old Town, almost perfectly preserved, is set on a forested peninsula in a meander of the River Sarine. Steep, cobbled streets, bedecked with wrought-iron lamp standards and ornate inn signs, are picturesque and characterful. Six bridges, from medieval wooden fords to lofty modern valley spans, provide woodcut-pretty views back across the town of the old houses piled up together on the slopes.

But the views only scratch the surface of Fribourg. For, behind its visual

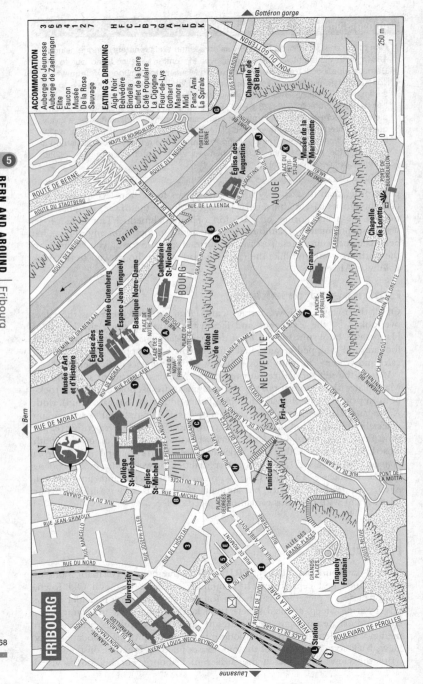

▲ Gottéron gorge

ACCOMMODATION
Auberge de Jeunesse 3
Auberge de Zaehringen 6
Elite 5
Faucon 4
Musée 1
De la Rose 2
Sauvage 7

EATING & DRINKING
Aigle Noir H
Belvédère F
Bindella C
Buffet de la Gare L
Café Populaire B
La Cigogne J
Fleur-de-Lys G
Gothard A
Manora I
Midi E
Pans Ami D
La Spirale K

FRIBOURG

0   250 m

charm, Fribourg is perhaps Switzerland's most amiable and easygoing town, thoroughly modern at heart despite the medieval appearance of some quarters. It's small enough to have kept most of its city centre residential, but large enough to have attracted a lively, cosmopolitan mix of people to fuel the community atmosphere. One of the country's most prestigious universities – and its sole Catholic one – attracts a massive student body to Fribourg from all over the country, and especially from Italian-speaking Ticino, thereby generating a social dynamism that is tangible on the streets. In addition, the Sarine (Saane in German), which carves a path through the town, is the local defining line of the *Röstigraben*: Fribourg is split roughly 70:30 between French Swiss, who call their town *free-boor* and are a majority on the western bank, and German Swiss, to whom the place is *fry-berg* and who form a majority on the eastern bank. The town's radio station has two separate channels, many streets have two names, and almost everyone is instinctively bilingual. Some of Fribourg's older folk even cling on to the ancient Bolze dialect, a mixture, unsurprisingly, of French and German which you might be able to catch in the taverns and public squares of the Basse-Ville (Lower Town): in Bolze, the town is *Fryburg*, and you'll hear people calling each other *Ggopäingj* ("pal").

Within easy reach of both Bern and Lausanne, Fribourg is an understated town. For the time-pressed must-see visitor, it merits barely an hour or two – which is all the better for those on a long, slow journey of familiarity around Switzerland, who could spend a week in the place and not see it all.

Some history

Bertold IV of Zähringen founded Fribourg in 1157 as part of his consolidation of regional power, which also saw the establishment of Bern, Burgdorf, Thun and Murten, as well as Freiburg-im-Breisgau in Germany. After 1218, the Zähringens were succeeded by the Counts of Kyburg, who were themselves bought out by the Austrian Habsburgs in 1277, Fribourg passing from hand to hand with each succession. In 1452, Savoy took over, although in the Burgundian Wars shortly afterwards Fribourg backed the victorious Swiss against Savoy, and so became a free city. In 1481, it joined the Swiss Confederation.

For reasons which haven't been fully explained, Fribourg remained Catholic throughout the Reformation (and is still determinedly Catholic today): virtually surrounded by Protestant Bern, it became a place of refuge for the exiled bishops of Geneva and Lausanne. The oligarchic ruling families retained their grip on power even throughout the 1798 upheavals, and in 1846 Fribourg joined the reactionary Sonderbund, fighting against Protestant liberalism all around. It lost, and suffered expulsion of its Jesuits as revenge. Intolerance was short-lived, though: Jews were allowed to return to Fribourg in 1866 after almost 400 years of banishment from the city, and a local entrepreneur, Georges Python, founded the Catholic university in 1889. Fribourg stagnated for much of the twentieth century, stymied by economic depression, but the boom of the last few decades has brought new wealth and energy to the city.

Arrival, information and city transport

Fribourg's **train station** is high on the hill overlooking the Old Town from the northwest, with the **bus** terminal beneath (with fast buses to and from Bulle; see p.138) and the main **post office** alongside. As you emerge from the station, Avenue de la Gare heads at an angled left down to the central Place Python (pronounced *pee-tohh*). From here, the various districts of the Old Town

Fribourg's festivals

In February, Fribourg's **carnival** is focused on the ritual mass torching of the Grand Rababou effigy, bearer of the winter and of all evil. However, the event to watch out for is **Bénichon** (Kilbi in German), a kind of harvest feast held in the first half of September similar to the Emmental's Sichlete (see p.260). In former years, this would take the form of huge communal meals: lamb stews and hams and meringues and all kinds of seasonal specialities, such as a special mild mustard spread on oven-hot bread, *poires à botzi* (a sweet pear compote not found anywhere else), and paper-thin *beignets de Bénichon* (pastry leaves sprinkled with icing sugar, served elsewhere in the country only at carnival time). These days, the celebrations have lost their communal, seasonal edge, and tend to be more public affairs, with food stalls and tastings in the street.

Every July, Fribourg stages the prestigious **Festival de Musiques Sacrées** (⊛www.fms-fribourg.ch), featuring concerts of ancient and modern sacred music by performers from around the world. In early September, the Auge district hosts a **Semaine Médiévale**, featuring markets, events, costumed processions, concerts and food stalls designed to evoke the fifteenth century. In the first week of October, there's a **fun run** over the 17km between Murten/Morat and Fribourg, to commemorate the messenger who brought news to the town of victory at the Battle of Murten in 1476 (see p.193). **St Nicholas Day**, in the first week of December, sees an evening parade headed by a jolly old man with a long white beard, who rides in on a donkey distributing *biscômes* (spicy cake squares) to the children of the town amid much revelry.

cover the hill in front of you. Rue de Lausanne is the main thoroughfare, heading east and down to the **Bourg** district, centred on Place Notre-Dame (aka Place Tilleul) and the cathedral. From the Bourg, steep lanes cascade south down the hillside into **Neuveville**, while Grand'Rue heads east down to **Auge**, the oldest part of the Old Town at the tip of Fribourg's peninsula. It's a walk of about 1.5km – downhill all the way – from the station to Auge.

The **tourist office** is beside the station – turn right as you come out (Mon–Fri 9am–6pm, Sat 9am–3pm; winter Sat closes 12.30pm; ☎026 321 31 75, ⊛www.fribourgtourism.ch & ⊛www.pays-de-fribourg.ch). Cheery and efficient staff can book rooms and provide a wealth of information on the city and the whole canton, which extends as far south as Gruyères (covered in Chapter 2) and also takes in Murten/Morat and Estavayer-le-Lac (in Chapter 3). Ask for details on the many easy **countryside walks** which start from the city centre. You'd do well to book ahead to ensure an English-speaking guide for a two-hour **walking tour** of the town (April–Sept Mon & Sat 10am; Fr.10).

Vegetable and flower **markets** occupy Place Python (Wed morning) and the area around the Hôtel de Ville (Sat morning) all year round. The Place du Petit-St-Jean features a traditional flea market on the first Saturday of the month (April–Nov), while there's a crafts market on Rue de Lausanne on the last Saturday of the month (March–Dec).

City transport

Fribourg is definitely a **walking** city, but the hills are steep enough that you may want to take advantage of at least one **bus** line: bus #4 runs every fifteen minutes on a handy route between Auge and the station, running via Place du Petit-St-Jean, Planche-Supérieure and Neuveville. This is the only bus to serve the lowest reaches of the peninsula; others (#2 and #6) run through the Bourg but then cross the Pont de Zaehringen. Individual **tickets** are Fr.2.20 (or Fr.12 for six); or you can buy a general **city pass** for one day (Fr.6) or three days (Fr.11) – less if you're under 25. **Bike rental** is available from the station (Mon–Sat 6am–8.45pm, Sun 7am–8.45pm).

For more information, and to buy these passes, head for the TPF public transport office at the train station (Mon–Sat 5.45am–7.45pm, Sun 7am–7.45pm; Ⓦwww.tpf.ch).

Accommodation

Business **hotels** aside, Fribourg has some characterful accommodation options, all well located in or next to the Old Town, and covering a range of budgets.

5

BERN AND AROUND | Fribourg

Hotels

Auberge de Zaehringen 13 Rue de Zaehringen ☏026 322 42 36, Ⓦwww.auberge-de-zaehringen .ch. Fribourg's oldest patrician mansion is now a venerable and beautiful gourmet restaurant with just five guest rooms – spacious, luxurious and characterful like five-star hotels can never be. For once, you can splash out on a hotel and be quite certain that it will be a room to remember. ❹

Elite 7 Rue du Criblet ☏026 350 22 60, ℻026 350 22 61. Plain, unremarkable, but perfectly adequate rooms within a couple of minutes of the station. Discounts apply for weekend stays. Cheaper attic rooms. ❷–❸

Faucon 76 Rue de Lausanne ☏026 347 16 70, ℻026 347 16 75. Lino on the floor and primary colours on the walls, but don't be put off – this is excellent value for money, simple, friendly and clean, with a choice of ensuite or shared-bath rooms. Prices drop for stays over three nights. ❶

Musée 11 Rue Pierre-Aeby ☏ & ℻026 322 32 09. Large-ish, spartan rooms seconds from the cathedral and the Musée d'Art, with both ensuite

and shared-bath options. Reception closed Sun. ❷

De la Rose 1 Rue de Morat ☏026 351 01 01, Ⓦwww.hotelrose.com. Cosy and very central Minotel hotel, with efficient and friendly staff. Good value, but can be a little gloomy inside. ❸

Sauvage 12 Planche-Supérieure ☏026 347 30 60, Ⓦwww.hotel-sauvage.ch. Stylish renovated rooms in an old Neuveville house, spacious and individually decorated. Free parking, and bus #4 stops outside. ❹–❺

Hostel

Auberge de Jeunesse (HI hostel) 2 Rue de l'Hôpital ☏026 323 19 16, Ⓦwww.youthhostel.ch. Good-quality hostel occupying part of the old city hospital a few minutes' walk north of the station, with clean dorms (Fr.29) that are a tad institutional. Closed Dec & Jan. ❶

Campsite

La Follaz ☏026 436 24 95. Basic riverside site in Marly, 5km south. April–Sept.

The Town

Just south of the train station, the grassy, open **Grands-Places** marks an entry into the commercial heart of the city, overlooked both by department stores galore and the intensely ugly *Golden Tulip* hotel skyscraper – shown to be even uglier by its proximity to a beautiful shuttered medieval house on the square, now a café. The ensemble is mocked by one of Jean Tinguely's famous **fountains**, a spouting, spitting affair installed in 1984 and described by one critic as "a firework in iron and water".

Shopping streets lead east to the busy **Place Python**, at the centre of the modern city. From here, three routes lead you into the Old Town. To the south, the trafficky **Route des Alpes** is supported on pillars above Neuveville; its valley-side railings offer wonderful views of the river and of Fribourg's rustic location. The central **Rue de Lausanne**, a picturesque cobbled thoroughfare of pavement cafés and bookshops, heads directly downhill from Place Python. It's worth, though, cutting north from Python on the narrow, steeply rising **Ruelle de Lycée** up to the atmospheric medieval **Collège St-Michel**, for most of its history a Jesuit seminary and now part of Fribourg University; the shaded grounds of the academy are very peaceful, and there's a terrace from where you can look out over the city. Ancient covered steps, the **Escaliers du Collège**, lead down from the terrace to join the lower end of Rue de Lausanne.

The Bourg

All routes from the new town converge in the Old Town's most historically important and prestigious district, known as the **Bourg**, home to churches, the cathedral, the town hall and an array of mansions and patrician town houses. The Bourg's central square is a small space actually comprising four separate areas. At the foot of Rue de Lausanne is **Place de Nova-Friburgo** with, opposite it, **Place de l'Hôtel de Ville**; next to it is a tree-lined square known either as Place des Ormeaux (Elm Trees) or **Place de Tilleul** (Lime Tree); and next to that is **Place de Notre-Dame**. Just to confuse matters, the indeterminate, 50m-long Rue du Pont-Muré connects them all.

An impressive presence to one side is the late-Gothic **Hôtel de Ville** (Town Hall), a highly photogenic building dating from 1501–22, whose double exterior staircase was added in 1663. St George spears the dragon on a fountain statue dating from 1525 in the square in front of the building. A regular Saturday morning market spills over into the streets around, one of which, Rue des Épouses (Street of Spouses), is spanned by a decorative old sign attesting to the fidelity of the couples who once lived there. The dourly impressive **Grand'Rue** heads off down the hill, a virtually intact example of a seventeenth- to eighteenth-century street, complete with Baroque, Regency, Rococo and Louis-XVI facades jostling for position all the way down.

Fribourg's highlight is the towering, High Gothic **Cathédrale St-Nicolas** (Mon–Sat 7.30am–7pm, Sun 8.30am–9.30pm), just off Place Notre-Dame. Take a moment to absorb the breathtaking, soaring, buttressed **tower**, exposed to view for its entire 73m height clear to the ring of feathery spires on top. Built over a church dating from the city's foundation in 1157, the present building was begun in 1283, and took two centuries to complete. Traffic swishes past the elaborate main portal, featuring a tympanum with the Last Judgement. The vast interior is immediately impressive, its mustiness and gloominess redolent with old incense. The **pulpit** (1516) and, opposite it, the octagonal **font** (1499) are both particularly ornate, and the tracery **choir screen** (1466) is dazzlingly intricate. Virtually all the stained glass in the cathedral is modern Art Nouveau. Don't miss the tiny **Chapel of the Holy Sepulchre**, to the left of the door as you head out, beside a plaque commemorating the mass celebrated here by Pope John Paul II in 1984: inside you'll find a group of 10 figures, sculpted from sandstone in about 1430. Christ is being laid in the tomb by Nicodemus and Joseph of Arimathea; behind, Mary is supported by John the Baptist, Mary Magdalene, two other women and two angels. Three sleeping soldiers are placed nearby. The life-sized ensemble, drenched in a blueish submarine light from modern stained-glass windows, is extraordinarily moving, every stony figure conveying an intense emotion that effortlessly spans the six centuries it has stood here.

About 50m north of the cathedral is the porticoed **Basilique Notre-Dame**, with white-and-gold stucco work dating from the late eighteenth century adorning the spacious, airy interior. Samson prises apart the lion's jaws on a fountain statue in front (1547), copied from a design by Dürer. Adjacent on Rue de Morat is the Espace Jean Tinguely museum (see below), with beside it the Franciscan **Église des Cordeliers**. Originally part of a friary founded in 1256, the church was renovated in the eighteenth and nineteenth centuries, but retains its impressive medieval decor, including a vast altar painting (1480) showing the crucifixion and, on the opened wings, the adoration. High Gothic oak choir stalls (1300), the oldest in Switzerland, and a larger-than-life 1438 statue of Christ at the whipping post also stand out. Between the two is the **Musée Gutenberg**, Place Notre-Dame 16 (Wed–Sun 11am–6pm, Thurs until 8pm; Fr.9; ⓦ www.gutenbergmuseum.ch), with engaging displays of printing, graphics and bookbinding.

Espace Jean Tinguely and Musée d'Art et d'Histoire

In front of the Musée Gutenberg is the highly recommended **Espace Jean Tinguely–Niki de St-Phalle**, 2 Rue de Morat (Wed–Sun 11am–6pm, Thurs until 8pm; Fr.5; ⓦ www.fr.ch/mahf), devoted to the twentieth-century Swiss kinetic artist, who was born in Fribourg, and his wife. Housed in an old transport depot, this museum complements the more famous one in Basel (see p.221), documenting Tinguely's whimsical but trenchantly purposeful sculptural machines. Old rusty wheels, bits of iron and *objets trouvés* are all recycled in extraordinary constructions which use a lot of energy and demonstrate great skill and ingenuity – but which go absolutely nowhere. One of the most spectacular on display is the grand *Retable de l'Abondance occidentale et du Mercantilisme totalitaire*; press the foot button to set things in eccentric but somehow poetic motion. Also on display, in addition to several pieces by St-Phalle, is *La Mythologie blessée*, one of the last works on which the couple collaborated.

About 150m north, within sight of the medieval Porte de Morat, is the **Musée d'Art et d'Histoire**, 12 Rue de Morat (Tues–Sun 11am–6pm, Thurs until 8pm; Fr.6; ⓦ www.fr.ch/mahf). This broad collection is housed in an elegant sixteenth-century patrician mansion and, bizarrely, an adjacent slaughterhouse. Begin on the left in the Ratzé mansion, filled with medieval art and reliquaries with, upstairs, a particularly striking series of fourteen intricate biblical scenes carved in relief from panels of lime wood (1600). Upstairs again is the especially revolting jewel-bedecked skeleton of St Felix, dating from 1755, with glitter for lips and a phial of dried blood resting beside the bones. From the ticket desk, a subterranean tunnel runs through to the old abattoir, whose sombre stones now shelter a line of fourteen saints taken from the cathedral portal alongside a particularly mournful Tinguely sculpture. Upstairs is a collection of Swiss art from the nineteenth and twentieth centuries.

Neuveville and Planche-Supérieure

From the Hôtel de Ville, the ancient cobbled Rue de la Grand-Fontaine heads sharply downhill into **Neuveville** – men walking here, may find themselves whistled and clicked at by women hanging from the top windows of the old buildings, since this street amounts to Fribourg's red-light district. Neuveville is, nonetheless, perhaps the most peaceful and picturesque area of the city, exemplified by the Escaliers du Court-Chemin (Short-Cut Stairs), which clatter down the hill through a triangular open square adorned with the tinkling Fountain of Strength (1550) onto **Rue de la Neuveville**, which boasts whole rows of original Gothic buildings overlooked by the Hôtel de Ville on high. A quirky **funicular** runs down from St-Pierre, beside Place Python, to Place du Pertuis at the western end of Rue de la Neuveville (daily 9.30am–7pm; Fr.1, city passes valid): it works by tapping the city's sewers and diverting raw sewage into a chamber beneath the car at the top to make it heavy enough to be able to haul its partner up the slope. It's the smelliest ride in Switzerland.

A back street off Rue de la Neuveville is home to the **Fri-Art** centre for contemporary art, Petites-Rames 22 (Tues–Fri 2–6pm, Sat & Sun 2–5pm; Thurs also 8–10pm; Fr.4; ⓦ www.fri-art.ch), hosting a challenging array of shows of anything from painting to video art and multimedia.

From Neuveville, the triple-arched Pont de St-Jean crosses the river and leads past a tiny church up into the huge, open **Planche-Supérieure**, overlooked by a fountain statue of John the Baptist (1547) and these days used as a car park. Dominating the square is the old **granary** (1708), in shimmering white with dizzily zigzagging step gables and equally dizzy chevron-design shutters. At some point, the building is due to open as a museum of archeology. Cafés on the square offer incredible afternoon panoramas across the valley to the backs of the Grand'Rue mansions, all of which are supported on foundations that plunge as far down to the bedrock as the house is built above: they may show seven or more storeys of windows to the valley, but only the uppermost three or four are above the level of the street.

Stepped paths from the square climb south up to the ridgeside **Porte de Bourguillon** and, beside it on a lofty terrace, the **Chapelle de Lorette**, an ornate little building dating from 1648 that offers spectacular vistas out over the whole city.

Auge

From the cathedral, Grand'Rue and its parallel neighbours channel traffic down to cross the lofty Pont de Zaehringen, leaving the lower quarter of the Basse-Ville (Lower Town) – known as **Auge** – mostly to pedestrians. This district, absorbed into the city as early as the 1160s, is the oldest in Fribourg outside the Zähringens' original fortress (which stood on the site of the current Hôtel de Ville). It's full of atmosphere, with its cobbled streets and crumbling old Gothic houses and inns still very much lived-in; the sense of community surviving in such ancient surroundings is what really marks Fribourg out as being special. The **Place du Petit-St-Jean** is the local hub, ringed by cafés overlooked from the fountain by St Anne, the patron saint of the tanners who used to live here. A little northwest is the **Église des Augustins**, part of a monastery founded in the mid-thirteenth century, with impressive later Baroque decoration. The **Pont de Milieu** beetles southwest from the square to Planche-Supérieure, below the mighty precipices cut by the Sarine; to one side of the bridge is the titchy **Musée Suisse de la Marionnette** (Mon–Fri 10am–noon, Sat & Sun 2–6pm; Fr.5), with a lovely collection of puppets, face masks and other theatrical paraphernalia.

Northeast from the Place du Petit-St-Jean is the covered wooden **Pont de Berne**, leading to the ancient Rue des Forgerons (Street of the Blacksmiths) on the east bank of the river. The little bridgehead square, one of Fribourg's prettiest, holds the celebrated Loyalty Fountain (1553), decorated with angels. To the left (northwest) is the **Porte de Berne**, a city gate dating from 1270 that has somehow clung on to its original doors. Rue des Forgerons itself – a narrow, medieval track – heads east into the **Gottéron gorge**, beneath the immensely graceful modern Pont de Gottéron some 60m up. On the south side of the stream, a footpath leads up to the minuscule Chapel de St-Beat hugging the rocky walls of the gorge, but the road itself follows the northern bank of the stream into the forest, past old mills and cottages. The romantic riverside trail is well marked and maintained, drawing you into the cool, mossy gorge for an hour or so east to a crossing point at **Ameismühle**; from here, high-level routes to both left and right bring you back to the Pont de Berne in a bit over an hour.

Eating and drinking

Fribourg has plenty of quality places for **eating and drinking**. Fondue is a local speciality, and you can find some of the best in the country in Fribourg's cafés and brasseries. The giant Cardinal brewery, which sends its highly palatable beers out across Switzerland, is located in the town.

Cafés and café-bars

Belvédère 36 Grand'Rue. Uniquely amiable and atmospheric old student café, tucked away virtually out of sight at the head of the precipitous street Stalden. The mood is warm, the service friendly, but the appeal of the place is its comfy old armchairs, saggy sofas and bookcase-lined walls. An outside terrace is true to the café's name, giving eagle-eye views over the river. Also serves good, inexpensive food. Closes around midnight (Fri & Sat 3am). Closed Mon.

Café Populaire 9 Rue St-Michel. A popular student café-bar, also offering simple stomach-fillers like bagels, baked potatoes, and fish and chips. Closed Sun.

Maison du Peuple 76 Rue de Lausanne.

Cheapest of cheap bars, big, rough and loud, with cut-price beer and plenty of student life. Also has simple veggie food – often Indian – for Fr.13 or less.

Midi 25 Rue de Romont. One of the best pavement cafés along this central street, in prime Fribourgeois-watching territory.

Pans'Ami 5 Rue du Temple. Smoky, friendly café-bar near the station open until 3am Friday and Saturday. Closed Sun.

La Spirale 39 Place du Petit-St-Jean ⓦ www.laspirale.ch. Cellar bar and major venue for live music, with small-scale gigs, very cool DJ-ing and a range of jazzy, folky, worldish performers (Fr.15–25). Wed–Sun 8.30pm–2am.

Restaurants

Aigle Noir 10 Rue des Alpes ⓣ 026 322 49 77. Quality French cuisine (from Fr.30) in the heart of the Old Town, with an attractive modern interior and warmly efficient service. Closed Sun & Mon.

Auberge de Zaehringen 13 Rue de Zaehringen ⓣ 026 322 42 36. Fribourg's finest establishment, housed in an old patrician mansion, with a cosy brasserie that serves up fresh and interesting gourmet *menus* from Fr.20 or so at lunch time, a little more in the evenings, and an adjacent formal restaurant where prices – and *haute-cuisine* quality – rise dramatically. Closed Sun & Mon.

Bindella 38 Rue de Lausanne ⓣ 026 322 49 05. Classy Italian in the city centre, with cosy, warm decor and excellent fresh pastas (*menus* around Fr.23). Closed Sun.

Buffet de la Gare In the station. Three different areas – a shabby café-bar, a slightly more upmarket brasserie section, and, upstairs, one of the city's better restaurants (ⓣ 026 323 27 45), specializing in exquisite fish dishes – although it's not cheap (*menus* from Fr.50).

La Cigogne 24 Rue d'Or ⓣ 026 322 68 34. Beautiful little bistro in a medieval house opposite the Pont de Berne, using market-fresh produce to produce subtle, inventive dishes. Perfect for a romantic tête-à-tête. *Menus* around Fr.25. Closed Sun & Mon and Sept.

Fleur-de-Lys 18 Rue Forgerons ⓣ 026 322 79 61. A gastronome's delight on a medieval lane by the river. A tumbledown exterior preludes a cosy, atmospheric interior and fresh seasonal dishes of the highest quality (*menus* from Fr.30). Locals love the place, which is a high recommendation. Closed Sun & Mon, Feb and mid-July to mid-Aug.

Gothard 18 Rue du Pont-Muré. A Fribourg institution, beloved of Jean Tinguely, that is just about the last old-fashioned café in town, opened in 1861 and in the hands of the same *patronne* for knocking on a quarter of a century. You'll find it equally full of old-timers at their regular seats sipping at their beer and excitable students downing an espresso before heading off to a party. Posters, ephemera and intriguing bits and pieces cover the walls under a riot of fairy-light decoration, but the food is solid quality – excellent fondues, and daily *menus* for Fr.15 or so. Unmissable.

Manora Grands-Places. The Manor department store houses an excellent, low-priced self-service restaurant (see p.49), with fifth-floor views. Closed Sun.

Travel details

Trains

Bern to: Baden (hourly; 1hr 25min); Basel (every 30min; 1hr); Biel/Bienne (hourly; 25min); Brig (hourly; 1hr 40min); Burgdorf (3 hourly; 15min); Fribourg (every 30min; 20min); Geneva (every 30min; 1hr 45min); Interlaken West & Ost (hourly; 45min); Langnau (every 30min; 40min); Lausanne (every 30min; 1hr 10min); Luzern (hourly; 1hr 15min); Neuchâtel (hourly; 35min); Solothurn (every 30min; 35min); Thun (twice hourly; 20min); Zürich (every 30min; 1hr 10min).

Burgdorf to: Bern (3 hourly; 15min); Fribourg (every 30min; 45min); Hasle-Rüegsau (3 hourly; 10min); Lützelflüh (twice hourly; 10min); Konolfingen (every 30min; 30min); Langnau (hourly; 25min); Luzern (every 30min; 1hr 25min).

Fribourg to: Bern (every 30min; 20min); Estavayer (hourly; 40min); Lausanne (twice hourly; 45min); Murten/Morat (hourly; 25min); Payerne (hourly; 25min); Yverdon (hourly; 1hr).

Langnau to: Bern (every 30min; 40min); Burgdorf (hourly; 25min); Hasle-Rüegsau (hourly; 15min); Lützelflüh (hourly; 10min); Luzern (every 30min; 1hr).

Solothurn to: Bern (every 30min; 35min); Biel/Bienne (twice hourly; 20min); Neuchâtel (hourly; 40min); Yverdon (hourly; 1hr 10min); Zürich (hourly; 1hr 10min).

Buses

Fribourg to: Avenches (8 daily; 25min); Bulle (for Gruyères; hourly; 30min).

Kemmeriboden to: Schangnau (hourly; 15min).

Boats

Solothurn to: Biel/Bienne (May–Sept 3 daily; 2hr 30min).

The Bernese
Oberland

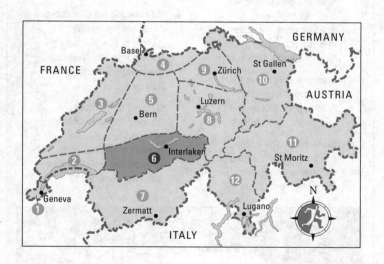

CHAPTER 6

Highlights

✳ **Interlaken** Bustling resort town at the hub of the region's excellent mountain railway network. See p.283

✳ **Schynige Platte** One of the finest Alpine viewpoints. See p.290

✳ **Lauterbrunnen valley** Breathtaking U-shaped cleft, its high, craggy walls doused by waterfalls such as the Trümmelbach. See p.291

✳ **Wengen & Mürren** Car-free mountain resorts with superb skiing and fine hiking. See p.295

✳ **Schilthorn** The cable-car ride up to this lofty summit is unforgettably dramatic. See p.295

✳ **Grindelwald** Long-acclaimed ski and sports resort at the foot of the mighty Eiger. See p.298

✳ **Jungfraujoch** The train ride up to Europe's highest station is expensive, but easily done in a day from Interlaken. See p.302

✳ **Sammlung Im Obersteg** Outstanding small gallery of Chagall and Picasso on the shores of the beautiful Thunersee. See p.309

✳ **Gstaad** Legendary Alpine hideaway of the rich and famous, set amidst lovely countryside on the Golden Pass train line. See p.317

The Bernese Oberland

S outh of Bern and Luzern lies the grand Alpine heart of Switzerland, a massively impressive region of classic Swiss scenery – high peaks, sheer valleys and cool lakes – that makes for great hiking and gentle walking, not to mention world-class winter sports. The **BERNESE OBERLAND** is the most accessible and touristed area, and also the most spectacular, best known for a grand triple-peaked ridge of Alpine giants at its core: the Eiger, Mönch and Jungfrau, cresting 4000m. However, the Oberland takes in a

Exploring the Bernese Oberland

Train stations and tourist offices throughout the region sell the **Bernese Oberland Regional Pass** (@www.regiopass-berneroberland.ch), which has a vast area of validity well beyond the borders of Canton Bern, from Montreux in the west to Andermatt in the east, and from Bern and Luzern as far south as Zermatt. It's pricey but eminently worthwhile if you're based in the Oberland for a week or two's holiday. There are two passes, both available in the summer season only (May–Oct). The **seven-day pass** (Fr.195) covers any three days of free travel in the core region (see below), plus the remaining four days' travel throughout the area at half-price. The **fifteen-day pass** (Fr.240) covers any five days' core-region travel for free, plus the remaining ten days at half-price across the area.

The **core region** extends from Gstaad to Meiringen, and includes boats and trains between Thun, Interlaken and Brienz, as well as trains, buses, funiculars and cable-cars serving Schynige Platte, Lauterbrunnen, Mürren, Stechelberg, Wengen, Grindelwald, First and Kleine Scheidegg, and trains to Kandersteg and through the Lötschberg Tunnel as far as Brig. Core-region transport is free on the days you choose, and half-price the rest of the time. **All other transport** in the region is half-price throughout the pass's validity (aside from a few cable-cars which offer only a 25 percent discount): this includes the rides up to the Jungfraujoch and the Schilthorn; trains from Bern to Thun, Luzern to Brienz, and Montreux to Gstaad; buses over the high passes of the Grimsel, Furka and Susten; and a network of connections outside Canton Bern, including those from Luzern to Engelberg, from Brig to Andermatt or Zermatt, and even the mountain climb from Zermatt to the Gornergrat.

For more information on the region, check @**www.berneroberland.com**, and for details of hotel deals and bookings, consult @**www.berneroberland-hotels.ch**.

vast tract of territory, and the approaches to the high mountains have their own, less daunting pleasures: the twin lakes of the **Thunersee** (with the atmospheric old town of **Thun** at its head) and the **Brienzersee** (with **Brienz**) offer Alpine horizons and beauty enough to merit a stop of their own. Between the two, the bustling town of **Interlaken** is the main transport hub for the region, but the sheer volume of tourist traffic passing through can make it a less-than-restful place to stay. Coming from the big cities, many people aim for Interlaken as a supposed necessary stop, but it truthfully has little to offer beyond dozens of hotels and a handful of souvenir shops, and you'd do better to head straight for the mountains.

On a visit to the region, and stunned by the natural drama all around, the composer Felix Mendelssohn wrote: "Anyone who has not seen the scenery which surrounds Interlaken does not know Switzerland." Once you've seen it, you'll know what he means. Arguably the single most captivating place in the entire Alps lies just a short way south of Interlaken – the gorgeous **Lauterbrunnen valley**, with the resorts of **Wengen** and **Mürren** perched on plateaux above providing excellent winter skiing and summer hiking. **Grindelwald** is another bustling resort in its own valley slightly to the east.

Both offer access to one of Switzerland's top excursions, the amazing rack-railway journey winding up through spectacular mountain scenery to the ice-bound **Jungfraujoch**, a windswept col nestling at 3454m just below the peak of the Jungfrau itself, and the site of the highest train station in Europe. Further west, the Oberland rolls on and on through less-visited wooded valleys and pastureland, out to the borders of the German-speaking area, where sits probably the most famous name in the region: **Gstaad**.

Tourist offices, scattered in virtually every town, control the Oberland's thousands of **chalets and private rooms**, most of which, at higher altitudes anyway, close in the quiet off-season. Tourist offices can also provide details of the region's numerous **mountain huts** (generally open June–Sept), which offer hikers or ski trekkers a bed and simple comforts in the wilds of nature.

Beware that almost everything in the high resorts – shops, hotels, attractions, walking routes, mountain railways and cable-cars – may be **closed during off-season** (mid-April to early June & mid-Oct to mid-Dec), or possibly operate with limited service only. We've specified months of opening only when they differ from this pattern.

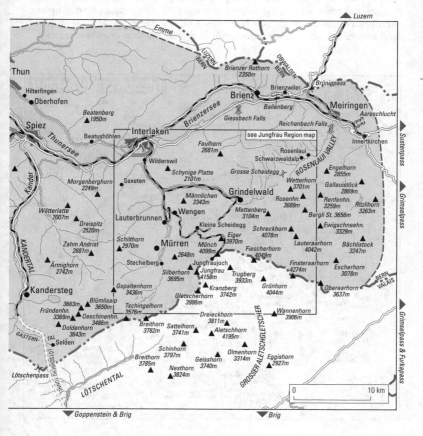

The Jungfrau region

The **JUNGFRAU REGION** (Ⓦ www.jungfrau.ch) lying south of the major gateway resort of **Interlaken** is the rather uninspiring title foisted on what is perhaps the most dramatic, certainly the most memorable, mountain scenery in the whole of Switzerland. The Matterhorn may be more recognizable, Davos and St Moritz may be flashier, but the quantity and sheer scale of the awesome giants on offer here at close quarters takes your breath away.

Sightlines throughout the area are dominated by the mighty triple crest of the **Eiger**, **Mönch and Jungfrau** (Ogre, Monk and Virgin) – three giant peaks rising side-by-side to 4000m and seemingly always mentioned in the same breath. The Jungfrau is the focus, partly because it's the highest (at 4158m), and partly because the network of mountain trains from Interlaken Ost culminates at the **Jungfraujoch**, a saddle below the peak that claims the honour of hosting the highest train station in Europe. The ride up – dubbed the "Top of Europe" – is touted endlessly in Interlaken and beyond as being the highlight of your holiday; despite the hype, it's not far wrong, although the competing journey up the **Schilthorn**, also accessed from Interlaken Ost, is cheaper, quicker, less crowded and uses cable-cars – always more scenic and dramatic than cogwheel trains.

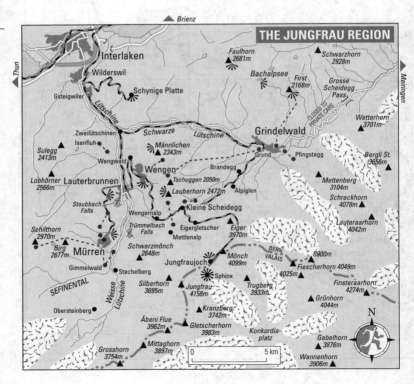

Exploring the Jungfrau region

Mountain transport throughout the region comes under the umbrella of the **Jungfraubahnen** (ⓦwww.jungfraubahn.ch), which takes in BOB trains from Interlaken Ost to Lauterbrunnen and Grindelwald; WAB trains from Lauterbrunnen, Wengen and Grindelwald up to Kleine Scheidegg; JB trains from Kleine Scheidegg to the Jungfraujoch; the SPB line to Schynige Platte; the BLM route from Lauterbrunnen to Mürren; the HB funicular from Interlaken to Harderkulm; a load of cable-car routes (including GGM Grindelwald–Männlichen, LWM Wengen–Männlichen, BGF Grindelwald–First and LGP Grindelwald–Pfingstegg); and Grindelwald's buses as far as the Grosse Scheidegg pass.

Swiss Pass holders get free travel on all transport as far up as Mürren, Wengen and Grindelwald, and a 25 percent discount on journeys higher than this. Eurailers get a 25 percent discount on all Jungfraubahnen routes, except where mentioned in the guide text. InterRail brings no discount at all, apart from on the few occasions mentioned in the guide text.

The **Jungfraubahnen Pass** (May–Oct only; Fr.165) is valid for five days of free travel on the entire network – apart from the Eigergletscher–Jungfraujoch section, on which passholders pay half-fare (Fr.48).

There's plenty of equally stunning scenery to be enjoyed at lower altitudes. The region is centred on two valleys, which divide a few kilometres south of Interlaken. To the west is the famous **Lauterbrunnen valley**, celebrated with justification as the loveliest mountain valley in Europe, with its alluring car-free resorts of Wengen and Mürren. To the east, the narrow Lütschental widens out on its way to the bustling town of **Grindelwald**, perfectly placed for its many visitors to take advantage of the hiking and skiing possibilities all around. Excellent transport around all these places – mostly trains, but also taking in cable-cars, funiculars and the odd bus – means that you can roam to your heart's content, which, with the quality of natural scenery on offer, may take a while.

Interlaken

Don't be ashamed of being a tourist in **INTERLAKEN** – that's what the place exists for. Interlaken is all that many visitors ever see of Switzerland, whisked through the country on a rapid lakes-and-mountains tour. The town is perfectly positioned as the gateway into the Oberland, linked into main train routes to and from Bern and Zürich, with branch lines feeding out in all directions into the high Alps nearby. It's a pleasant enough place, even if bustling and commercial and packed with Swiss-kitsch souvenir shops, and it's useful for its proximity to the mountains.

The town is situated on the Bödeli, a small alluvial neck of land between the twin **lakes** (see p.305) of the Thunersee and Brienzersee. It's one of the oldest resorts in the country, famed for its superb **views** towards the Jungfrau massif, which lies perfectly framed between two hills to the south of town. And that's pretty much the whole story: history, character and tradition take a back seat to the necessities of providing for the millions of trippers who pass through on their way to more dramatic backdrops. One thing you can't fail to notice is that many of the shops which cram the centre of town have prominent signs in Japanese; of Interlaken's tourists, fully a quarter are from Japan, as many as from around Switzerland.

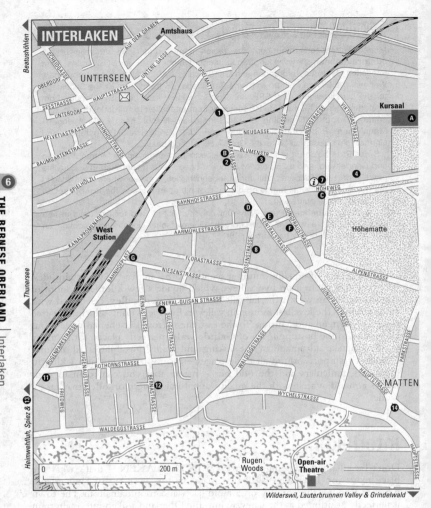

Wilderswil, Lauterbrunnen Valley & Grindelwald ▼

Arrival and information

The town hasn't much more to offer than its long main street, **Höheweg**, with a train station at each end. Mainline trains terminate at **Interlaken Ost** station, 1km east of the centre, but those coming from the Bern/Thun direction pass first through **Interlaken West** station, a more useful place to get off since it's right beside the centre. (Be aware that branch-line trains into the mountains depart only from Ost station.) Both stations are linked by trains and city buses, which run roughly every ten minutes from one to the other.

See the box on p.306 for details of the **boats** which run on the lakes flanking Interlaken; those from the Brienzersee dock directly behind Ost station, those from the Thunersee behind West station.

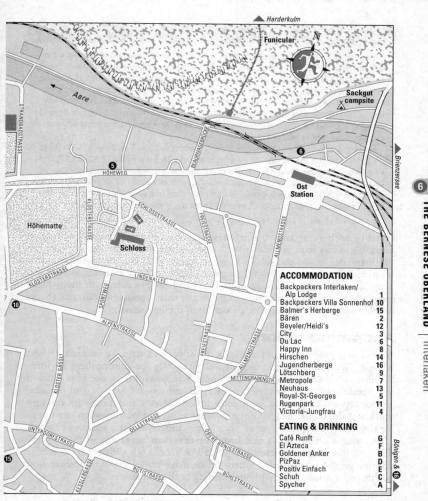

ACCOMMODATION

Backpackers Interlaken/ Alp Lodge	1
Backpackers Villa Sonnenhof	10
Balmer's Herberge	15
Bären	2
Beyeler/Heidi's	12
City	3
Du Lac	6
Happy Inn	8
Hirschen	14
Jugendherberge	16
Lötschberg	9
Metropole	7
Neuhaus	13
Royal-St-Georges	5
Rugenpark	11
Victoria-Jungfrau	4

EATING & DRINKING

Café Runft	G
El Azteca	F
Goldener Anker	B
PizPaz	D
Positiv Einfach	E
Schuh	C
Spycher	A

Strictly speaking, Interlaken is only one of five communities on the neck of land between the two lakes: to the west is **Unterseen**; to the south are **Matten** and, a little further out, **Wilderswil**; to the east is **Bönigen**. Although the built-up area is contiguous from one to another, all five retain their individual identity and postal codes: if you go looking for something on Hauptstrasse, you should know that Unterseen's Hauptstrasse is a long way from Matten's Hauptstrasse.

The **tourist office** is in the town centre, on the ground floor of the *Hotel Metropole*, Interlaken's only skyscraper, at Höheweg 37 (July–Sept Mon–Fri 8am–6.30pm, Sat 8am–5pm, Sun 10am–noon & 4–6pm; May, June & Oct Mon–Fri 8am–6pm, Sat 8am–noon; Nov–April Mon–Fri 8am–noon & 1.30–6pm, Sat 9am–noon; ☎033 826 53 00, ⓦwww.interlakentourism.ch).

Open-air Tell

Interlaken is famous throughout Switzerland for its annual staging of Schiller's play **William Tell**, performed every summer since 1912 in an open-air theatre (with covered seating) in the Rugen woods near Matten. The stage is framed by old wooden houses in thirteenth-century style, and backed by the forest – the perfect backdrop for the cast of 250, all sporting Swiss national dress and authentic medieval uniforms, and the several dozen horses, cattle and farm animals which wander around bringing a festive air to the show. The dialogue is in German only, but it's pretty obvious what the plot is (see p.412).

Evening performances run twice weekly throughout July and August. **Tickets** (Fr.25–40) are available online (ⓦ www.tellspiele.ch), by phone (☎ 033 822 37 22) and in person from the West station ticket office, several hotels around town, most tourist offices in the region and from the Tellbüro at Höheweg 37 in Interlaken (July & Aug daily 8–11.30am & 2–5pm). The tourist office has packages comprising one or two nights' accommodation, plus tickets for the show, from around Fr.170.

Faced by such an onslaught of business, they remain surprisingly cheerful and helpful, and can load you down with more maps, brochures and information about Interlaken and the whole Jungfrau region than you could ever possibly want, including the very useful *Jungfrau Magazine*, with ideas for excursions. They also have details of a host of packages and cut-price deals for multi-night stays at hotels; if you're planning to stay more than a couple of days, it's always worth asking for any discounts, especially in the low seasons.

Accommodation

Almost everyone who ventures into the Oberland stays for at least a short while in Interlaken, and the town is well geared up for visitors: there are literally dozens of **accommodation** options. The downside of the popularity is that breakfasts can be skimpier, corners dusted less assiduously, and personal service less expansive than in quieter towns. Beware that hotels fill up very quickly at the frantic height of the summer season; in winter, when most people stay in the mountains, many places close altogether for a month or two.

The tourist office runs a free **hotel reservation service**: call ☎ 0800 558 555 (toll-free within Switzerland) or ☎ 033 826 53 01. Otherwise, to relieve pressure on the overcrowded tourist office, make use of the hotel information boards and complimentary phones outside both train stations.

Inexpensive hotels

Bären Marktgasse 19 ☎ 033 822 76 76, ℱ 033 822 28 55. Huge, unrenovated old dive with low prices, especially on the shared-bath rooms. ①–②

Beyeler/Heidi's Bernastrasse 37 ☎ & ℱ 033 822 90 30. Comfortable enough garni stopgap, with some OK rooms (and some not-OK ones). ①

City Marktgasse 6 ☎ 033 822 10 22, ⓦ www. city-hotel.ch. Generic modern place in the heart of town, a little characterless but efficient enough on providing the creature comforts. ③

Lötschberg General-Guisanstrasse 31 ☎ 033 822 25 45, ⓦ www.lotschberg.ch. Characterful family-run hotel in a residential quarter, with excellent-value attic rooms in particular and a good-value

B&B guesthouse attached. Keenly priced apartments also available. Discounts for stays over six nights. Closed Jan. ②–③

Rugenpark Rugenparkstrasse 19 ☎ 033 822 36 61, Ⓔ rugenpark@tcnet.ch. Quiet, very friendly family-run little place close to West station, with modest, attractive rooms that are cosily unrenovated – only some are ensuite. Also with a non-smoking floor. ①–②

Mid-range and expensive hotels

Du Lac Höheweg 225 ☎ 033 822 29 22, ⓦ www.bestwestern.ch. Comfortable, stylish old house in a perfectly quiet riverside location beside

Ost station. In the same family since 1888 (and at one time hosting Field Marshal Montgomery during World War II), it now offers bright, light rooms that are far and away the best mid-range bargains in town. Closed Dec–Feb. **④–⑤**

Hirschen Hauptstrasse 11, Matten ℡ 033 822 15 45, ⓦ www.hirschen-interlaken.ch. Atmospheric old inn on a crossroads south of the centre, in the same family for some 300 years, with freshly redone pinewood rooms – comfortable and pleasant – boosted by the wonderful dark-beamed *Stübli* and restaurant. Also with plenty of parking. Closed Nov. **③–④**

Metropole Höheweg 37 ℡ 033 828 66 66, ⓦ www.metropole-interlaken.ch. The town's major landmark, and its sole high-rise, soaring above the tourist office. Utterly generic business-class facilities inside, memorable only for the stunning upper-floor views (the fourteenth is top), which are worth paying for. **⑤–⑦**

Neuhaus Seestrasse 121, Neuhaus/Thunersee ℡ 033 822 82 82, ⓦ www.hotel-neuhaus.ch. Far and away the most relaxing spot in and around Interlaken, a lone old inn guarding this end of the Thunersee, 4km west of the centre. It styles itself a golf and beach hotel – stretching the definition

on both scores – and, with sailing and watersports on offer, is a popular weekend draw for locals, but you can always find a quiet spot on the lakeside lawns to take in the stunning views over to the Niesen. Reception is in the modern annexe to one side, but ask for a room in the main house (which doubles as a fine restaurant): they're neither big nor modern, but retain some character and are wonderfully quiet. The welcome is warm – this is a corner few tourists find – and boosts the feeling of being well out of the Interlaken hubbub. Free parking. **③–④**

Royal-St-Georges Höheweg 139 ℡ 033 822 75 75, ⓦ www.royal-stgeorges.ch. Gorgeously stuffy town-centre palace hotel, renovated to prime Victorian-era condition throughout. Closed Nov–Jan. **④–⑤**

Victoria-Jungfrau Höheweg 41 ℡ 033 828 28 28, ⓦ www.victoria-jungfrau.ch. One of the grandest hotels in the country, dating from 1864–65, which hosted Mark Twain on his journey around Switzerland. Located perfectly in the town centre. These days it's been entirely restored, with its pricier front rooms overlooking the Höhematte for views of the Jungfrau between the hills. **⑨**

Camping and hostels

There are thirteen **campsites** within 4km of town. The closest is the simple *Sackgut* (℡ 033 822 44 34, ⓦ www.campinginterlaken.ch; May–Oct) behind Ost station. Less than 1km south of the centre is *Jungfraublick* (℡ 033 822 44 14, ⓦ www.jungfrablick.ch; May–Sept), a more comfortable family choice. Of the five sites in Unterseen, the inland *Lazy Rancho* (℡ 033 822 87 16, ⓦ www.lazyrancho.ch; April to mid-Oct) offers best value, and lakeside *Manor Farm* (℡ 033 822 22 64, ⓦ www.manorfarm.ch) is open all year, but *Alpenblick* (℡ 033 822 77 57, ⓦ www.campinginterlaken.ch) is most convenient, on the Thunersee right by the *Neuhaus* hotel and restaurant.

Hostels

Backpackers Interlaken/Alp Lodge Marktgasse 59 ℡ 033 822 47 48, ⓦ www.backpackers-interlaken.com. Modest place, with dorms from Fr.20 and rock-bottom room prices. **①**

Backpackers Villa Sonnenhof (SB hostel) Alpenstrasse 16 ℡ 033 826 71 71, ⓦ www.villa.ch. Quality hostel – an attractive chalet with comfortable, spotless rooms, a good shared kitchen, and dorm beds from Fr.29; rooms at the back, with stunning views of the Jungfrau, command a small surcharge. **①**

Balmer's Herberge (SB hostel) Hauptstrasse 23, Matten ℡ 033 822 19 61, ⓦ www.balmers.com. Best in town, fifteen minutes south of the centre. This is the oldest privately run hostel in the country, with fifty years' experience of catering to back-

packers, offering kitchen access, laundry, and spartan comforts in well-tended pinewood dorms (from Fr.22, plus Fr.1 for a shower), quads, triples and doubles. The atmosphere is brash and convivial, a perfect place to hook up with other travellers for trips into the mountains; you can get discounts on extreme sports and activity excursions if you book direct through the hostel. In summer, when the frat-party atmosphere and queues for the shower and for breakfast get too much, they set up a giant tent in a field 800m south, with bunks sleeping over a hundred at Fr.19. **①**

Happy Inn (SB hostel) Rosenstrasse 17 ℡ 033 822 32 25, ⓦ www.happy-inn.com. A backup dorm option, clean and centrally located but uninspiring. Fr.27. Partying downstairs in the bar can go on until after midnight. **①**

Jugendherberge (HI hostel) Aareweg 21,
Bönigen ☎ 033 822 43 53, ⓦ www.youthhostel.ch.
Quiet, pleasant place in this Brienzersee village

2km east of Interlaken town centre, with dorms
from Fr.28 and bike rental. Closed mid-Nov to mid-
Dec. ❶

In and above the town

The town itself is only of passing interest, with precious little to see or do other
than a couple of hours of exploratory wanderings, either on foot or from the
back of one of the horse-drawn carriages which ply for business outside West
station (Fr.35 for 30min for one or two people). The large grassy parkland of
the **Höhematte** in the centre of town was where the monks of Interlaken's
ancient Augustinian monastery pastured their cattle; on the east side of the park
is the **Schloss**, dating from 1747 but incorporating some of the fifteenth-century monastical buildings. Parts of the Gothic church survive in the renovated
Schlosskirche adjacent, which has also clung onto its old cloister, each window of which, curiously, is of a different design.

Otherwise, you're just as well served by strolling along the Aare beneath the
looming cliffs west into pretty **Unterseen**, north of West station. This atmospheric village houses some of the area's oldest buildings: the square in front of
the Amtshaus off Untere Gasse is particularly picturesque.

Interlaken starts to reveal its secrets when you explore further afield. Before
you even venture into the mountains, there are a couple of viewpoints above
the town to enjoy, both laced around with hiking trails galore. A funicular
(May–Oct) rises from behind Ost station through the woods to the
Harderkulm (1310m), offering vistas over the town, both lakes and a panorama of snowy peaks close enough to touch. Friday evening sees folk music and
dancing at the summit restaurant, with special late trains laid on; book through
the tourist office. On the other side of town, some 500m south of West station,

Touring the Alpine passes

The configuration of roads over the high Alps means that it's straightforward to put
together a looping day-long driving tour of the highest roads in Europe, bringing with
it spectacular scenery from every angle. Every one of the passes mentioned below
has at least a restaurant on top, and most have some form of inn accommodation
as well, making it easy to break your journey.

The easiest way to go is with the excellent **Three-Passes tour** by postbus, which
runs once or twice a week in summer (late June to mid-Oct generally Tues & Fri;
Fr.49; ⓦ www.post.ch); you must reserve a seat in advance at any bus station. You
can board from any of the resorts in the area, with morning pickups (8–9.30am) from
– among others – Grindelwald, Lauterbrunnen, Interlaken, Brienz and Meiringen.
After Meiringen, the bus stops at the summit of the **Susten Pass** (2224m), before
going on for lunch at Andermatt (another possible starting point; see p.411); then,
after breathtaking drives up to the **Furka Pass** (2431m; see p.415) and the nearby
Grimsel Pass (2165m; see p.369), you're returned to Meiringen and the other
boarding points in the late afternoon (5–7pm).

You can add a fourth pass – the **Grosse Scheidegg Pass** (1962m) – if you start
from Grindelwald and opt to take a bus direct to Meiringen to join the tour there (private cars are not permitted to cross the Grosse Scheidegg). With your own transport you can also add a long midway loop, cutting south from Andermatt over the
celebrated **Gotthard Pass** (2108m; see p.414), then to the relatively little-used
Nufenen Pass (2478m; see p.369), then back north over the Grimsel to Meiringen
again – this way, though, you miss the Furka pass.

is a station for the vintage red funicular (May–Oct) serving the **Heimwehfluh** (669m), a more touristic venture, with the summit often crowded with parents taking the kids round the model–train exhibition and the miniature bob–run.

Near the local airfield just east of the centre is the **Mystery Park** (Ⓦwww.mysterypark.ch), a glittering theme park devoted to unexplained phenomena, due for opening by summer 2003. A central tower is to be surrounded by seven pavilions dedicated to the Pyramids of Giza, ancient Indian mysticism, the earth patterns of Nazca in Peru, Stonehenge, and so on. There's no telling how it will turn out, although there'll most likely be plenty of slick multimedia gadgetry, flight simulators and pop–science experiments, as well as shops, cafés and restaurants. Good for a rainy day.

Eating and drinking

Food is not an especially high priority in Interlaken, and much of what's on offer is fairly basic, unadventurous fare. *Migros* restaurant opposite West station has self-service staples (closed Sun).

Cafés and café-bars

Balmer's Herberge See "Hostels". The sociable travellers' bar attached to this busy hostel serves up cheap beer nightly to its backpacking clientele.

Brasserie 17 Rosenstrasse 17. Loud central bar beneath the *Happy Inn* hostel, with cheap food (sandwiches, snacks and veggie fare) and big beers.

Café Runft Opposite West station. A cosy tearoom, snackery and bar open daily until 3am.

Goldener Anker Marktgasse 57. Local pub crammed most nights with young people hanging out and shooting pool. The food is cheap and simple (*menus* around Fr.14), and occasional live bands fill out the atmosphere a bit.

Panoramic Café Top floor of *Hotel Metropole*, Höheweg 37. Fifteenth-floor views out over the town and lakes, with an outdoor terrace.

Positiv Einfach Centralstrasse 11. Popular crowded little DJ-bar in the centre of town.

Schuh Höheweg 56. A tearoom-cum-restaurant on the corner of the Höhematte – refinement in the midst of kitsch-souvenir hell. The supremely elegant interior preludes equally elegant tea-and-cakes, or Swiss cuisine (plus veggie options), helped down by the cocktail pianist tinkling away in the corner.

Restaurants

El Azteca Jungfraustrasse 30 ☎033 822 71 31. Attractive little Mexican place on a side street, with *menus* from Fr.14 and live mariachi (Fri & Sat).

Closed Wed in winter.

Hirschen Hauptstrasse 11, Matten ☎033 822 15 45. Traditional, rustic old wood-beamed inn serving up huge portions of steaming Swiss fare, with *menus* from Fr.25 or so. Closed Tues & Nov.

Matahari In *Hotel Lötschberg*, General-Guisanstrasse 31 ☎033 823 80 01. Quality Indonesian cuisine, including *rijsttafel*, a sampler of many Indonesian dishes, plus a range of Indian dishes with plenty for vegetarians. *Menus* around Fr.22. Closed Tues & lunch Wed.

Neuhaus See "Accommodation". Comfortable old inn situated right on the Thunersee shore, with views across the water from the large waterside terrace. Quality of both the cooking and the service is high. The speciality is, of course, freshly caught fish (around Fr.30), and there are some excellent vegetarian dishes (Fr.23 or so).

PizPaz Centralplatz ☎033 822 25 33. Pleasant but generic pasta, pizza and fish dishes for Fr.16 upwards, on a central crossroads. Closed Mon in off-season.

Spycher In Casino Kursaal, Strandbadstrasse 44 ☎033 827 61 00. Just one part of this entertainment complex, housing a casino, bars, cafés and a formal garden, this restaurant is dedicated to touristic dinner-plus-folklore shows. They run three to six nights a week (May–Oct), and you can just watch the dancing and alphorn blowing for around Fr.16, or choose from five *menus* of typical Swiss fare for Fr.40–60, which include the show.

Listings

Bike and skate rental More than half-a-dozen operators in town have mountain and city bikes for rent, including both train stations, the HI hostel, the

Action Sport rental centre in Matten, Hang Loose surfshop at Neuhaus and Eiger-Sport, Bahnhofstrasse 2, Unterseen. Many also offer guided mountain-bike tours of the countryside around Interlaken, for around Fr.70/day, and have inline skates for rent.

Changing money In Ost station (daily 6am–8pm) and in West station (daily 7am–7.30pm).

Flights Several operators run sightseeing flights over the high mountains. Scenic Air (☎033 826 77 17, ⓦwww.scenicair.ch) can do a landing on a glacier for Fr.220 (plus a champagne picnic on request) or a sightseeing flight for Fr.120 in a light aircraft; Bohag (☎033 828 90 00, ⓦwww.bohag.ch) does the same thing in a heli-copter, from near Interlaken or a spectacular take-off point at Männlichen. Air Glaciers (☎033 856 05 60) operates from a base at Lauterbrunnen.

Laundry Beatenbergstrasse 5, Unterseen (open 24hr daily for self-service washes).

Post office Junction of Bahnhofstrasse and Marktgasse (Mon–Fri 8am–noon & 1.45–6pm, Sat 8.30–11am).

Radio Radio Berner Oberland broadcasts tourist information and weather reports in English (Mon–Fri 8–8.30am, Sat 9–10am; Interlaken 96.8FM, Lauterbrunnen & Grindelwald 95.9FM).

Schynige Platte

The best easy trip from Interlaken – and one of the finest mountain excursions in the country – is the ride up to the breathtaking **SCHYNIGE PLATTE** at 2000m, from where you can survey some of the best panoramic views in the entire Alps.

The rack-railway (June–Oct only) up to Schynige Platte starts from the peaceful village of **Wilderswil**, a few kilometres south of Interlaken, reachable from Ost station by train or from West station by bus #5. It's an attractive little place in its own right, full of traditional wooden houses; the main road bypasses the village centre. From Wilderswil, trains coil their way up for almost an hour through some spectacular scenery to the top station, from where perfect views of the Eiger, Mönch and Jungfrau, ranged high above the valley opposite, open up. A short walk away is the busy restaurant and *Kulm* **hotel** (☎033 822 34 31, ⓦwww.schynigeplatte.ch; ❷), within which is **Teddyland** (ⓦwww.teddyland.ch), an excessively over-marketed exhibition of 1600 soft toys.

One of the kiosks at the top station is a test centre for Lowa hiking boots: you can select any pair you like and try them out for free all day, with no obligation to buy – handy, since marked trails lead out in all directions from here. The **Panoramaweg** is really unmissable: an easy trail, it leads you on a two-hour circuit of the summit ridge above the station, with, at the halfway point, an unforgettable panoramic view taking in the full sweep of the Thunersee, Interlaken and the Brienzersee. The return leg continues in a wide arc through meadows to the **Botanischer Alpengarten** (Fr.3), filled with the local flora, and one of the few places where you can be guaranteed to see a genuine living edelweiss.

As a longer alternative, one of the most attractive walks in the whole Oberland region leads from Schynige Platte along the crest up to the Faulhorn (2681m), and then down past the tranquil Bachalpsee to First and Grindelwald (roughly 6hr). This is worth doing at any time, but if you're around in July and August, grab the unique opportunity to walk the route **by moonlight**: on the two Saturday nights with the fullest moon, trains leave Interlaken Ost at 10.30pm and Wilderswil at 11pm, bringing you to Schynige Platte by midnight, from where a local guide leads you along the six-hour trail. Ask the Interlaken tourist office for more details.

The standard **fare** is Fr.50 return (Eurail and Swiss Pass 25 percent discount, InterRail not valid), or Fr.30 after 2pm; two kids can travel free with a fare-paying adult. Buying a cheaper ticket to the midway station of Breitlauenen and enjoying the views on the walk to the top (1hr 30min) is no hardship. Every Wednesday in July and August, trains depart Wilderswil at 5.40am to catch the summit **sunrise**, with the optional extra of breakfast (Fr.15) at the *Kulm* hotel.

The Lauterbrunnen valley

It's hard to overstate just how stunning the **LAUTERBRUNNEN VALLEY** is – even hardened Alpinists shrug their shoulders and call it the most beautiful example in Europe, bar none. An immense U-shaped valley (the world's deepest) with bluffs on either side rising 1000m sheer, doused by some 72 waterfalls, it is utterly spectacular. Staying in Interlaken or Grindelwald comes a poor second to basing yourself in or above Lauterbrunnen for your time in the Oberland: whether you stay two hours or two weeks, you won't want to leave.

Lauterbrunnen village stands on the valley floor, while the slopes above nurture two of Switzerland's most appealing little resorts. **Mürren** to the west is the transfer point for the dramatic cable-car ride up to the **Schilthorn** peak, while **Wengen** to the east is a stop on the train line up to Kleine Scheidegg and the **Jungfraujoch**. Both of them are car-free, perched on narrow shelves of pasture way above the world below, and both offer some of the best hiking and skiing to be had in the Alps.

Lauterbrunnen

The road south from Interlaken shadows the train tracks and the Lütschine river through Wilderswil and on into the deep countryside. Cliffs close in either side as you reach **Zweilütschinen**: the Schwarze Lütschine tumbles in from Grindelwald further east, while the road and railway continue south alongside the rushing Weisse Lütschine (named "white" for its foaminess) through a charming wooded gorge. At the point where the valley opens up, airily broad, sunlit and impossibly picturesque, you enter the busy little village of **LAUTERBRUNNEN** (796m). The train station here is the junction point for journeys up to Wengen and on up to the Jungfraujoch.

Opportunities for sightseeing and exploring around and about are virtually limitless. At the entrance to the village, opposite the train station, a funicular run by BLM ("Mürrenbahn") crests the west wall of the valley to **Grütschalp**, from where a train – one of the most scenic rides in Switzerland – trundles its way along the cliff-edge, in full view of the snowy giants across the way, to Mürren (see p.295). You might, instead, fancy the steep path up to Grütschalp (rising 690m in 2hr), in order to take advantage of the panoramic stroll alongside the tracks to Mürren (1hr 10min).

Just before Lauterbrunnen, precipitous roads and footpaths wind up west to **Isenfluh**, an isolated little hamlet on a tiny patch of green alp, from where little-trod hiking trails fan out and a cable-car rises to the Sulwald alp, at the foot of the distinctively jagged Lobhörner crag (2566m).

Just beyond the southern end of Lauterbrunnen village, the delicate **Staubbach falls** – at nearly 300m, the highest in Switzerland – gush out of a sheer cliff, like a lacy decoration on the rugged precipice. It's a scenic half-hour walk, or an hourly postbus, 3km up the valley to the hugely enjoyable **Trümmelbach falls** (daily: July & Aug 8.30am–6pm; April–June & Sept–Nov 9am–5pm; Fr.10; ⓦwww.truemmelbach.ch). These impressively thunderous

The Jungfrau region offers a vast array of **sports and activities**. We've outlined the best summer walks throughout the guide text, and highlighted a linked, week-long trail in the box on p.297. You'll also find a fistful of operators offering adventure sports all summer long (and some year-round). In winter, resorts like Wengen, Mürren and Grindelwald can offer some of the finest skiing and snowboarding in the Alps: ⓦ**www.jungfrauwinter.ch** has the full rundown.

Winter sports

The Jungfrau region is divided into three ski sectors: **Grindelwald-First** (ⓦwww.gofirst.ch), **Kleine Scheidegg-Männlichen** (which includes lifts from both the Grindelwald and Wengen sides; ⓦwww.maennlichen.ch) and **Mürren-Schilthorn** (ⓦwww.schilthorn.ch). There's skiing and snowboarding for all levels and, with access to very high altitudes, the season is unusually long: from mid-November right through to the end of April. Beginners are best served at **Wengen** and **Grindelwald**, both of which have nursery slopes and plenty of blue runs very close to the village centres. Red pistes run beneath the long Männlichen–Grindelwald gondola line, while there are long blue runs from **Kleine Scheidegg** down to Brandegg and Grindelwald-Grund. **First** (2168m), above Grindelwald, also has a host of leg-stretching blue and red runs. **Mürren** offers some wonderfully scenic skiing, with a chairlift accessing more than half-a-dozen routes down from the Schiltgrat (2145m), and the Allmendhubel funicular linking with a draglift to access lots more pistes-with-a-view.

There are thrilling red and black runs from the **Lauberhorn** down to Wengen, following the course of the famous World Cup downhills and slaloms: at 4km, this is the world's longest competition piste (the downhill record is currently held by Kristian Ghedina at an amazing 2min 24.23sec) and, aside from skiing it yourself, if you're around in mid-January you should try and catch a glimpse of the professionals. Black runs around the region are satisfyingly testing, most notably those down to Wengen from the **Eigergletscher** (2320m). The incredibly steep "Inferno" piste from the Schilthorn summit (2970m), through difficult mogul fields and the infamous "Gun Barrel" down to Mürren, covers 11km.

The best location for **snowboarding** is the Snowpark at Oberjoch (2501m), above First, where there's an array of rails, bank jumps, waves and kickers, plus a giant superpipe at Schreckfeld. Kleine Scheidegg also has a popular boarder park. Plenty of options for **sledging** include from Alpiglen to Brandegg in the shadow of the Eiger's North Wall, and a huge 15km run from First round to Bussalp and down to Grindelwald.

Passes are good value. For the Mürren-Schilthorn sector, 1/6 days cost Fr.55/239, for the joint First-Kleine Scheidegg-Männlichen sectors, 1/6 days cost Fr.55/254. The Jungfrau Region Sportpass, valid in all sectors, costs Fr.118 for 2 days, Fr.282 for 6 days, or Fr.800 for the whole season. (Note that all these are not valid for lifts descending from the Schilthorn, only those ascending.) Among the various discount deals for early/late season skiing, the best is **Happy Birthday**: if your birthday

waterfalls – the runoff from the high mountains – have carved corkscrew channels through the valley walls: a stepped catwalk leads you over and around the enclosed, boiling cauldrons of rushing water (up to 20,000 litres a second), which throw up plenty of spray and have gradually eroded the rock into weird and wonderful shapes.

From the top, above the falls, trails from Mettlenalp connect to paths leading to Wengen and Wengernalp.

coincides with your stay of at least 6 nights with at least one (other) adult at a participating hotel, then your entire B&B arrangement is free of charge; if your partner (or accompanying adult) has bought a six-day ski pass, then you also get the same pass for free. Check the details with local tourist offices. All the resorts have **schools** offering both daily classes and private lessons in skiing, snowboarding and other, wackier techniques for all proficiencies; class lessons tend to cost from around Fr.45 for three hours. All of them also lay on various diversions for skiers taking a break, including curling, ice-skating, sledging and adventure activities such as tandem paragliding; there's even a dedicated hiking/sledging lift pass for non-skiers (6 days Fr.212).

Adventure sports

Loads of companies in and around Interlaken run all kinds of adventure sports, many of them year-round. A popular choice is **tandem paragliding** (from about Fr.150), with tandem hang-gliding not far behind: top takeoff spots are the Beatenberg, Schynige Platte, the Niederhorn and even the Schilthorn. **Tandem skydiving** from 4000m or 4600m (around Fr.400) gives you up to a minute of freefall at 125mph. **Bungee jumping** is also hugely popular, from various vantage points around the region (Fr.125 or more), and plenty of operators offer **canyoning** on any of several whitewater rivers above the Thunersee, Brienzersee and further afield (half-day about Fr.110, full day Fr.170). **Rafting** on the Lütschine, the Simme, the Saane and elsewhere costs around Fr.100. Summer **ice-climbing** – no experience necessary, and all equipment provided – is about Fr.150 for the day, **rock-climbing** Fr.90 for half a day. More extreme options including **zorbing** (Fr.100), where you're pinned immobile inside a giant plastic sphere and rolled down a mountainside. Calmer **horse-trekking** is Fr.75 for 2hr.

The biggest operators include **Alpin Raft**, beside *Balmer's Herberge* (℡033 823 41 00, ⓦwww.alpinraft.ch), **Alpin Center**, opposite *Balmer's* and at Wilderswil station (℡033 823 55 23, ⓦwww.alpincenter.ch), and **Swissraft**, Jungfraustrasse 72 (℡033 823 02 10, ⓦwww.swissraft.ch), but also check out Outdoor Interlaken (ⓦwww.outdoor-interlaken.ch), Paragliding Grindelwald (ⓦwww.paragliding-grindelwald.ch), Paragliding Interlaken (ⓦwww.paragliding-interlaken.ch), Skydive Interlaken (ⓦwww.skydiveinterlaken.ch) and Basecamp (ⓦwww.basecamp.ch). You can generally book at your hotel too.

Otherwise, Gunten on the Thunersee is a centre for **windsurfing, waterskiing** and **wakeboarding** (ⓦwww.aquasport.ch & ⓦwww.wasserskischule.ch), and there are tons of options all around the region for **mountain-biking** solo (tourist offices stock maps and route details) or on guided trips (ⓦwww.mtbeer.ch).

On a different level altogether, Swiss Alpine Guides (ⓦwww.swissalpineguides.ch), the Bergsteigerzentrum Grindelwald (ⓦwww.gomountain.ch) and Bergsteigen für Jedermann (ⓦwww.bergsteigen-jedermann.ch), among others, run full- or multi-day **guided treks** in the high mountains; these are serious excursions with full equipment on tough terrain – often glaciers – and cost, accordingly, hundreds of francs.

Practicalities

Lauterbrunnen's **train station** is at the northernmost end of the village, directly opposite both the funicular station for Mürren and the **tourist office** (July & Aug Mon–Fri 8am–7pm, Sat 9am–12.30pm & 1.30–5pm, Sun 9am–12.30pm & 1.30–4pm; June & Sept Mon–Fri 8am–12.30pm & 1.30–6pm, Sat & Sun 9am–12.30pm & 1.30–4pm; Oct–May Mon–Fri 8am–12.30pm & 1.30–5pm; ℡033 856 85 68, ⓦwww.lauterbrunnen.ch).

Lots of places offer dorm **accommodation**. Down by the tracks is the cosy

Long-term parking

Since both Wengen and Mürren are car-free, Lauterbrunnen has built for itself a huge multistorey **car park** directly behind the train station at the northernmost edge of the village. Horrendous though that sounds, the community knows the value of its views, and has ensured both that the car park doesn't disturb the eye, and that it filters most of the traffic away from the village centre. Parking for a 24-hour day costs Fr.12 (July to mid-Sept), Fr.12/16 (mid-Dec to mid-April weekdays/weekends) and Fr.8 at other times; eight-day equivalents are Fr.59, Fr.80 and Fr.57. You should always try and reserve in advance – at least two weeks ahead if you intend to park for seven days (☎033 828 74 00, @parkhaus@jungfrau.ch). Two other small open-air parking areas within the village cost Fr.6–8 per day. Stechelberg has another large parking area at the foot of the Schilthornbahn cable-car (Fr.6/day, Fr.23/week).

SB *Valley Hostel* (☎033 855 20 08, ⓦwww.valleyhostel.ch; Fr.22), most of its rooms with balconies. There are two **campsites**, both at the southern end of the village: *Jungfrau* (☎033 856 20 10, ⓦwww.camping-jungfrau.ch) is on the west bank, while quieter *Schützenbach* (☎033 855 12 68, ⓦwww.schutzenbach-retreat.ch) is on the other side, alongside the road to Stechelberg – both also have dorms (Fr.15–20) and rooms (❶). Among the **hotels** are jovial, backpacker-ish *Horner* (☎033 855 16 73, ⓦwww.hornerpub.ch; ❶), just beyond the tourist office, whose staff have been known to slash rates for post-9pm check-in. Beside the station is the *Bahnhof* (☎033 855 17 23, ⓦwww.bahnhof-hotel.ch; ❷), with cosy, uncomplicated rooms and cooking to match. *Silberhorn* (☎033 856 22 10, ⓦwww.silberhorn.com; ❸) is up off the main drag but only a minute from the station, with pristinely quiet rooms – slightly pricier ones with a view. **Eating and drinking** are best done in the various hotels along the main street: the *Horner* has bargain pizza/pasta meals for under Fr.13, while the *Oberland* and *Schützen*, either side of the tourist office, are solid places for solid fare, both also specializing in afternoon tea with fresh apple strudel.

Stechelberg and beyond

The bus from Lauterbrunnen to the Trümmelbach falls continues on to **STECHELBERG** (900m), a peaceful hamlet at the end of the road. It has a minuscule **tourist office** (☎033 855 10 32, ⓦwww.stechelberg.ch), open limited hours. Stechelberg is famous for being the starting point for the **cable-car ride** (see opposite) up to Gimmelwald and Mürren, and on to the Schilthorn; the huge base station complex is 1km before the hamlet. This is where some of Interlaken's thrill merchants do their bungee-jumping – a quality spectator sport in itself. Buses terminate at the end of the road in front of the *Hotel Stechelberg* (☎033 855 29 21, @hotel@stechelberg.ch; ❶), a fine old hikers' inn with creaky rooms upstairs. Round the corner are dorm beds in the friendly *Naturfreundehaus Alpenhof* (☎033 855 12 02, ⓦwww.naturfreunde.ch; Fr.19; bring your own sleeping bag), also with some spartan rooms (❶).

Beyond Stechelberg, trails continue into the undeveloped and unpopulated upper part of the valley, which forms part of the hiking circuit described in the box on p.297. Only the hardiest outdoorsy types venture here, but the trails aren't difficult and can offer some of the most rewarding hikes in the region, both for the spectacular views and for the isolation. There are no roads, and a short distance beyond Stechelberg begins a large area of land protected as a **nature reserve**. Three comfortable old **inns** along the main trail, all open May to October only and all requiring advance reservation, might persuade you to stay a night or two.

An hour beyond Stechelberg is the *Berghaus Trachsellauenen* (☎033 855 12 35, ℗033 855 23 65; ❶), a pretty half-timbered house set in the woods; an hour and a quarter further is the atmospheric and characterful *Hotel Tschingelhorn* (☎033 855 13 43; ❶), while twenty minutes on up the trail is the *Obersteinberg* (☎033 855 20 33, ℗033 855 15 85; ❶), a working farm that relies on candlelight after dark and has no showers. Both the *Tschingelhorn* and the *Obersteinberg* also have dorm places, and both are above the treeline, giving spectacular views.

Mürren

The Schilthorn cable-car from Stechelberg leaps the valley's west wall to reach the idyllically quiet hamlet of **GIMMELWALD** (1400m; ⓦwww.gimmel-wald-news.ch), a little-visited spot set among meadows ablaze with spring and summer wildflowers. Walking is lovely and peaceful here, and there's a fine hostel (see p.296).

You have to switch cable-cars at Gimmelwald, rising further to car-free **MÜRREN** (1650m), an eyrie of a village set on an elevated shelf of pasture which has managed to retain its endearing desert-island atmosphere (in the off season at least). It's worth the journey for the **views**. From Mürren, the valley floor is 800m straight down, and the panorama of snowy peaks filling the sky is dazzling: you gaze across at the blank wall of the Schwarzmönch, with the great Trümmelbach gorge slicing a wedge of light into the dark rock, while the awesome trio of the Eiger, Mönch and Jungfrau are ranged above and behind in picture-perfect formation.

Mürren itself was "discovered" by the British in the 1840s, and has a long tra-dition both of winter sports (see p.292) and of hospitable gentility: some of the first competition **skiing** in Switzerland was done on the slopes around Mürren. An Englishman, Arnold Lunn, claims to have invented the slalom here in 1922, while the famous "Inferno" amateur downhill race from the

Above Mürren – the Schilthorn

One of the most dramatic mountain excursions in the region is by a series of cable-cars from the valley floor at Stechelberg, via Mürren, on a breathtaking ride up to Birg and then the **Schilthorn** summit (2970m; ⓦwww.schilthorn.ch). The trip's less expensive than that to the Jungfraujoch, and also less of a tourist merry-go-round, but just as memorable. The exposed terrace on the top is, if anything, even more dramatic than the Jungfraujoch, with a wraparound vista of icy peaks, from the Eiger to the Matterhorn to Mont Blanc, plus a clear view down to Thun and Bern. You can enjoy the exceptional views and sip cocktails in the revolving *Piz Gloria* summit restaurant, featured in the James Bond film *On Her Majesty's Secret Service*; the Bond-centred audiovisual show in the basement is less kitschy than plain touristy.

As with the Jungfraujoch, it's easy – if you're based in Interlaken, say – to go up one way and down another. The train from Interlaken Ost to Lauterbrunnen connects well with the link to Mürren (by funicular to Grütschalp and then clifftop train), from where the cable-car rises to the summit. On the way down, you can stay with the cable-car to Stechelberg, and then make your way by bus back down the valley floor to Lauterbrunnen (perhaps via the Trümmelbach falls), from where trains return to Interlaken. This whole trip, with an hour on top to enjoy the views, takes four hours, compared with six for the equivalent ride from Interlaken up the Jungfraujoch (the last 40min of which is climbing inside a dark tunnel).

Fares on the Schilthornbahn are steep, but not outrageous. From Stechelberg to the top is Fr.94 round trip, from Mürren Fr.63. Eurailers pay 75 percent; Swiss Pass holders travel free to Mürren and pay 75 percent from there upwards.

Schilthorn peak to Mürren (a descent of 2170m) was held for the first time in 1928, and is still an annual fixture in February.

The Schilthorn cable-car station is at the southern end of the village; at the opposite, northern, end is the Mürrenbahn BLM train station, starting point for the cliff-edge train (see p.291) to Grütschalp. Between the two a vintage funicular rises from between the chalets up to the **Allmendhubel** meadow (1907m), from where hiking trails connect to the Blumental (see opposite) and another trail (3hr 15min) leads up to Marchegg, then down into the rugged Saustal and through the Sprissenwald forest to Grütschalp.

Practicalities

Mürren's sports centre houses the **tourist office** (Mon–Fri 9am–noon & 1–6.30pm, Thurs until 8.30pm; July–Sept & Dec–April also Sat & Sun 1–5.30pm; ☎033 856 86 86, ⓦwww.wengen-muerren.ch), with plenty of information on hiking and skiing routes around the area and listings of the many chalets and apartments.

Accommodation in the village is excellent, and service is unreservedly good wherever you go. Almost all places close for April and November. Most hotels will arrange to pick you and your bags up from either the cable-car or the train station, if you've reserved in advance. *Eiger* (☎033 856 54 54, ⓦwww.hoteleiger.com; ❺–❻) is opposite the train station, an excellent four-star hotel, with a modern, well-equipped guesthouse annexe, run by a Swiss-Scottish couple (☎033 856 54 60, ⓦwww.muerren.ch/eigerguesthouse; ❷). The *Regina* (☎033 855 42 42, ⓦwww.regina-muerren.ch; ❷–❸; closed May, June & Sept) has well-appointed, Art-Deco-style rooms; the *Alpenblick* (☎033 855 13 27, ⓦwww.muerren.ch/alpenblick; ❸) is comfortable with large balconies; while the *Alpenruh*, beside the Schilthorn cable-car (☎033 856 88 00, ⓦwww.muerren.ch/alpenruh; ❹), is tops: simply one of the most appealing little hotels in the whole region – cosy, attractive, friendly and with dreamy views.

For cut-price sleeping head for the popular self-catering *Mountain Hostel* down the slope in Gimmelwald (☎033 855 17 04, ⓦwww.mountainhostel .com; Fr.20).

Eating, as ever, is a hotel affair, with top billing going to the *Alpenruh*'s excellent fare. *Snacks and Drinks*, on the main street, has – incongruously enough – authentic Japanese and Thai food done to order for around Fr.16. For an early-morning excursion, a few hotels (notably the *Alpenruh*) allow you to defer your breakfast until you reach the Schilthorn summit restaurant – and the food (the cost of which is covered by your hotel deal) is actually not that bad once you get there.

Above Mürren, a short half-hour hike east brings you up to the *Sonnenberg* (☎033 855 11 27, ⓦwww.muerren.ch/sonnenberg; dorms Fr.42), a cosy and atmospheric modern inn in the **Blumental** (so-called for its carpet of wild-flowers). A little further on is the *Suppenalp* (☎033 855 17 26; dorms Fr.42), a much older building with simple comforts and simpler rooms.

Wengen

On the opposite side of the valley from Mürren, trains bound for Kleine Scheidegg (see p.303) grind up from Lauterbrunnen to **WENGEN** (1274m), another gorgeous, car-free haven perched on a shelf of tranquil southwest-facing meadow. Wengen is one of Switzerland's best-known ski resorts (see p.292 for winter sports information), most famous for hosting World Cup downhill and slalom races on the Lauberhorn every January. It's slightly bigger and livelier than Mürren but still no more than a chalet-style village, with as long a tradition of hospitality as its competitor. The resort stays bustling with skiers well into April. Once the snows have receded, Wengen sits amidst ideal hiking country, overlooked by the Jungfrau and the distinctive creamy cone of the Silberhorn. Its lofty outlook means it enjoys unrivalled valley sunsets.

Walks of varying degrees of toughness from simple strolls to taxing hikes thread through the countryside around and above Wengen. Even simple little excursions such as down to **Wengwald** below the village can reveal flower-strewn meadows, romantic footpaths and stunning views out over the great chasm of the Lauterbrunnen valley. Opposite, the horse's tail of the Staubbach

Walking in the Bernese Alps

Making a loop around the Lauterbrunnen valley, the week-long **Grindelwald Circuit** enjoys magnificent big-mountain scenery without treading glaciers or major screes, and is ideally suited to keen walkers. The paths are mostly good, but with some very long and steep slopes to negotiate – both in ascent and descent – and you'll need to be fit. With an abundance of accommodation along the route, each stage could be shortened or lengthened to suit personal preference, and there's the option of staying either in major resorts or in more peaceful lodgings in idyllic surroundings. The map LS 5004 (1:50,000), and the paperback *The Bernese Alps, a Walking Guide* by Kev Reynolds (see "Books", p.607), are both essential companions.

Start by riding the rack railway from **Wilderswil** outside Interlaken to the tremendous viewpoint of **Schynige Platte** (see p.290) and set out on what many consider to be *the* classic walk of the area, the high route to Grindelwald by way of the Faulhorn and Bachsee. Instead of going all the way to Grindelwald though, it's better to spend the first night at the hotel on the summit of the **Faulhorn** (see p.301) in order to enjoy sunset and sunrise over the mountains. On day two descend past the tranquil Bachsee lake before the crowds gather – there are stunning views directly ahead to the Wetterhorn, Schreckhorn and witch's-peak Finsteraarhorn (4274m) – and from there continue down to **Grindelwald**.

Below Grindelwald head southwest up steep meadows at the foot of the notorious North Face of the Eiger to **Kleine Scheidegg** and one of the nearby inns (see p.303). Crossing the saddle on day three, a track leads down to Wengernalp and Mettlenalp from whose meadows you can safely watch avalanches pour down the face of the Mönch and Jungfrau. Either take the easy way to **Wengen**, and steeply down from there to **Lauterbrunnen**, or for preference tackle a knee-testingly steep path via the little alp of Preech which descends through the **Trümmelbach Gorge** into the Lauterbrunnen valley. Wherever you reach the valley, wander upstream to **Stechelberg** and continue on into the secluded upper valley where several rustic mountain inns provide peaceful lodging with romantic views from every window (see p.294).

On day four take the path which climbs steeply above the *Berghotel Obersteinberg* to gain the crown of the **Busengrat** at an astonishing little meadow known as the Tanzbödeli (the dance floor). The pasture plunges dizzyingly to great depths on two sides, but a 360° panorama will hold you in its spell. On the north side of the Busengrat the path descends to the wild Sefinen valley (also with accommodation), then climbs to **Gimmelwald** and **Mürren**. Next day go up into the Blumen valley and follow a gentle trail across pastures to Grütschalp, and then through forest to the Soustal before tackling a final climb that leads to the **Lobhorn Hut** (☎033 855 30 85). The hut enjoys a privileged view of the Jungfrau – unforgettable at sunset. Day six is spent climbing to the Ballehochst viewpoint, then descending to **Saxeten** and finally all the way down to **Wilderswil** to complete the circuit.

falls is clearly visible, while the jagged Lobhörner peak stands out, silhouetted against the sky. The cliff-edge **Mönchblick** viewpoint beyond Wengwald is less than an hour's stroll (120m down) from Wengen. Longer walks lead up to **Wengernalp** (also with a useful train station) and on up to the rail junction at Kleine Scheidegg (3hr total). The LWM cable-car from Wengen crests the bluff overlooking the village to the beautiful plateau of **Männlichen** (see p.303); you can, as an alternative, hike the steep three-hour trail, which rises a testing 1070m.

Practicalities

Heading out of the **train station** and up onto Wengen's main street brings you to the **tourist office** (Mon–Fri 8am–noon & 2–6pm, Sat 8.30–11.30am; July–Sept & Dec–April also Sat & Sun 4–6pm; ℡033 855 14 14, Ⓦwww .wengen-muerren.ch & Ⓦwww.wengen.com). Trains from Lauterbrunnen to Wengen are free to Swiss Pass holders, a quarter off to Eurailers and full price for InterRailers, but beware that they can be crowded even in the between-seasons; during the summer and winter peak periods, you'll be unlikely to get a seat.

Accommodation is plentiful, but watch out for between-season closures (as at Mürren) and also for the international skiing in January, which is great to watch but which can book the village, and the valley, out. Several hotels offer dorm beds: best is the Christian-run *Bergheim* (℡033 855 27 55, Ⓦwww.jungfraublick.com; dorms Fr.22), part of *Hotel Jungfraublick* at the top of the village, which is itself not a bad budget choice (②). Lower down the street, *Eddy's Hostel* (℡033 855 16 34, Ⓕ033 855 39 50; Fr.27) has comfortable clean dorms. Smoke-free *Edelweiss* (℡033 855 23 88, Ⓕ033 855 42 88; ②–③) is a cosy choice overlooking the valley. The *Belvédère* (℡033 856 68 68, Ⓕ033 856 68 69; ③–④) is a beautiful old Jugendstil house from 1912 in a quiet location above the village centre. A handful of grand old palaces, including the stunning *Regina* (℡033 856 58 58, Ⓦwww.wengen.com/hotel/regina; ⑤–⑥), of 1894 vintage, have got the room-with-a-view-plus-all-the-luxury-trimmings service down to perfection.

There's not much to **eat** outside the hotel restaurants – the popular *Hot Chili Peppers Café* on the main street does plenty of budget food (*menus* from Fr.14), while *Da Sina's* is a pleasant and similarly priced pizzeria and pasta joint at the end of the main street, also with a pub attached.

Grindelwald and around

At Zweilütschinen south of Wilderswil, the road and the train tracks divide: one branch heads south to Lauterbrunnen, while the other follows the course of the Schwarze Lütschine torrent east through the Lütschental into broad, open uplands and the hugely popular resort of **GRINDELWALD** (1034m). Unlike Wengen and Mürren over the ridge, Grindelwald *is* accessible by car and bus, and thus sees a great deal more tourist traffic than the Lauterbrunnen resorts. Although there are many ways to escape the crush, the village's main drag can come as a jarring blast of commercial reality.

Rural character is to be found out of the village. Nestling under the craggy trio of the Wetterhorn, Mettenberg and Eiger, Grindelwald offers easy access to explore some large glaciers close-to, and has a network of cable-cars leading up to numerous short- and long-distance trails throughout the region and beyond. Skiing is excellent (see p.292), but there are also plenty of hiking trails which stay as such all winter, making this a top choice for non-skiers on a winter holiday.

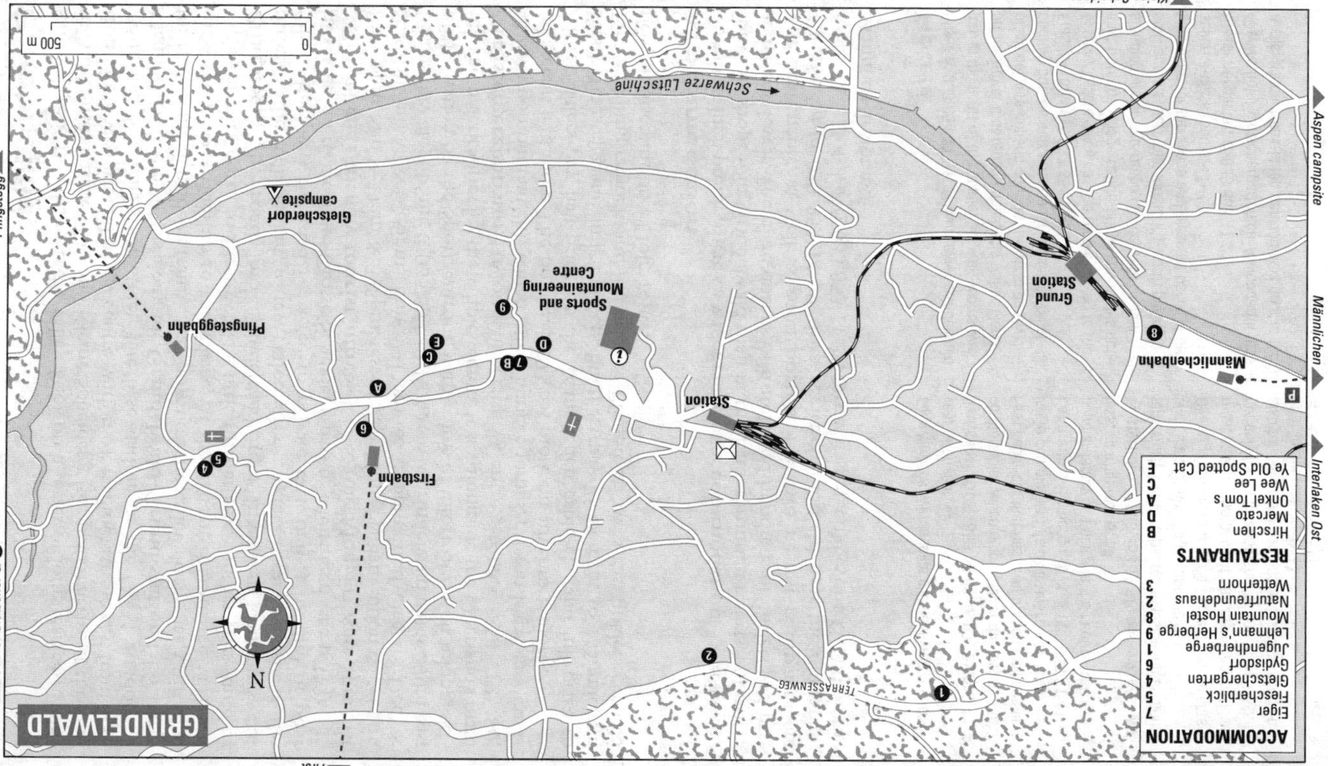

6

299

GRINDELWALD

N

ACCOMMODATION
Eiger	7
Fiescherblick	5
Gletschergarten	4
Gydisdorf	6
Jugendherberge	1
Lehmann's Herberge	9
Mountain Hostel	8
Naturfreundehaus	2
Wetterhorn	3

RESTAURANTS
Hirschen	B
Mercato	D
Onkel Tom's	A
Wee Lee	C
Ye Old Spotted Cat	E

Oberer Gletscher & **3**

Pfingstegg

First

Firstbahn **6**

Pfingsteggbahn

Gletscherdorf campsite

A

C

E

5 4

7 B

9

D

Sports and Mountaineering Centre

Schwarze Lütschine

2

TERRASSENWEG

Station

1

Interlaken

Grund Station

Männlichenbahn **8**

Kleine Scheidegg

Interlaken Ost

Männlichen

Aspen campsite

500 m

0

Practicalities

The village is tiered above the valley floor on a series of long terraces. Trains to and from Interlaken Ost and Kleine Scheidegg (see p.303) arrive at the **station**, at the western end of the centre, with most facilities strung east from here along the 1km-long main street. The base-station for the GGM gondola to Männlichen (see p.303) is alongside **Grindelwald-Grund station** (also a stop for the Kleine Scheidegg trains), way down on the valley floor – it's a stiff hike (or a shuttle-bus ride) up to the village. At the eastern edge of the village, a cable-car rises north to **First**; while a little further east, another rises south to **Pfingstegg**. The **road** into Grindelwald from Interlaken continues east through the village, but a few kilometres on (at a car park near the Oberergletscher) the road is barred to private cars; only a handful of **post buses** go on to cross the Grosse Scheidegg pass to Meiringen (see p.312).

Grindelwald's friendly **tourist office** (July & Aug Mon–Fri 8am–7pm, Sat 8am–6pm, Sun 9–11am & 3–5pm; rest of year Mon–Fri 8am–noon & 2–6pm, Sat 8am–noon & 2–5pm, Sun 9–11am & 3–5pm; mid-Oct to Dec & Easter–July closed Sun; ☎033 854 12 12, ⓦwww.grindelwald.ch) is 200m east of the station by the Sportzentrum, with reams of information on hiking, skiing and practicalities for the whole region. It sits alongside the Oberland's main **Bergsteigerzentrum** (Mountaineering Centre; ☎033 854 12 80, ⓦwww.gomountain.ch), which offers bungee jumps, canyon leaps, easy guided ascents and more. The box on p.293 has more on adventure sports.

InterRailers pay half-price on the Männlichen cable-car, and full price to First, Pfingstegg and Jungfraujoch. Eurailers pay 75 percent to Männlichen, First and Jungfraujoch, and full price to Pfingstegg. Swiss Pass holders get a 25 percent discount on all four routes.

Accommodation

To suit its high profile, there's a wider range of **accommodation** – and kitschy souvenir shops – in Grindelwald than in the Lauterbrunnen resorts, but prices aren't any lower. There are dozens of **hotels** and hundreds of chalets and private apartments, as well as good **hostels**. The two nearest **campsites** are *Gletscherdorf* (☎033 853 14 29, ⓦwww.gletscherdorf.ch) near the Pfingstegg cable-car and *Aspen* (☎033 853 11 24, ⓦwww.aspen.ch) beyond Grund on the Männlichen slopes.

Hotels

Eiger ☎033 854 31 31, ⓦwww.eiger-grindelwald .ch. In the heart of the bustle, but with rooms well off the street that remain quiet, this rather bland place delivers generic comforts – warm and welcoming but reminiscent of a city business hotel. ❻
Fiescherblick ☎033 854 53 53, ⓦwww.fiescherblick.ch. The road climbing to the east from the village centre brings you to this outstanding upper/mid-range choice, with friendly staff and a superb restaurant. It's worth paying a little extra for the space and pleasant decor of the superior-class rooms. ❹–❺
Gletschergarten ☎033 853 17 21, ⓦwww.hotel-gletschergarten.ch. A wonderful old, rustic, window-box-laden pension next door to the

Fiescherblick, with a loyal clientele who return year after year. ❹
Gydisdorf ☎033 853 13 03, ⓕ033 853 13 11. A comfortable, welcoming hotel at the foot of the First cable-car that has a reputation for fine service to complement its pleasant rooms. ❸
Lehmann's Herberge ☎ & ⓕ033 853 31 41. A popular family-run place in the centre, with spotless, spartan rooms. ❶
Wetterhorn ☎033 853 12 18, ⓦwww.hotel-wetterhorn.ch. Comfortable old roadside inn an hour's walk east of the village opposite the Oberergletscher, at the point where private cars must park or turn back. It attracts plenty of hikers, not only for its location and its dorms (Fr.35) but also for the hearty portions of Swiss cooking on offer in the restaurant. ❷

Hostels

Jugendherberge (HI hostel) ☎033 853 10 09, Ⓦ www.youthhostel.ch. A bus from opposite *Hotel Bernerhof* outside the station, or a steep fifteen-minute walk north, will get you to Terrassenweg, a quiet lane running on a terrace 100m above the village proper. Up here is this excellent hostel, with a cosy atmosphere, spotless dorms (Fr.30), good facilities and amazing views; they also rent out bikes and, in winter, *Velogemel*, or snow bikes – wooden bikes with runners instead of wheels (Fr.15/day). ❶

Mountain Hostel (SB hostel) ☎033 853 39 00, Ⓦ www.mountainhostel.ch. Good alternative option, a lively and well-run hostel on the valley floor beside Grindelwald-Grund station. Dorms are either basic (Fr.34) or standard (Fr.39) – deluxe (Fr.44) is only if you stay more than 3 nights. ❶

Naturfreundehaus ☎033 853 13 33, Ⓦ www.naturfreunde.ch. Spartan, less studenty dorms (Fr.38) not far from the HI hostel on the same street, Terrassenweg. ❶

Eating and drinking

Eating and drinking, again, can be limited to your hotel, but there are a few places to sniff out. On the main street, *Mercato* has reasonably good pizzas and pasta for Fr.16, or a little more in the evenings, while the fish at *Hirschen* is rightly celebrated (Fr.20–25). The latter also has good veggie dishes for Fr.14 or so. *Onkel Tom's* is a tiny chalet at the east of town (closed Mon) serving up excellent (and enormous) wood-fired pizzas in a cosy ambience. For authentic, quality Chinese cuisine, try *Wee Lee*, on the main drag beneath *Hotel Spinne* (closed Mon), though it's not cheap (Fr.35 and up); they do equally good Japanese specialities, with veggie options.

There are a couple of obvious **bars** up and down the main street – including the misleadingly titled *Espresso Bar* – but the back terrace of *Ye Old Spotted Cat* in the *Hotel Bellevue* (closed Sun) is the quietest and most atmospheric place to enjoy a tipple as the sunset fades on the Eiger.

First, Pfingstegg and the glaciers

The possibilities for exploring the area are endless. The area around **First** (2168m; Ⓦ www.gofirst.ch) has some particularly lovely hiking trails (for skiing, see p.292): the gondola rises in three stages, and from the hotel/restaurant on top relatively easy routes lead off in all directions – to the Schwarzhorn summit (3hr) passing through Schilt, renowned for its population of marmots; on a high-level route over the Grosse Scheidegg pass (2hr or so); back down to Grindelwald (2hr 30min); or, best of all, on a breathtakingly expansive ridge-top walk to the gorgeous Bachalpsee lake and on to the **Faulhorn** summit (2hr 30min) with its atmospheric *Berghaus* (☎033 853 27 13, ℻033 853 07 50; Fr.35); the stunning sunset and sunrise views from here are one of the high points of a walking tour of Switzerland. Schynige Platte (see p.290) is about the same distance again further on.

The cable-car (May–Oct) up to **Pfingstegg** (1391m) and the little café at the top station with its giant views, make for a pleasant excursion for non-athletic types; an interesting trail leads for a little over an hour from Pfingstegg through varying geological formations on the slopes of the Mettenberg (the Breitlouwina terrace is celebrated for its evidence of glacial action), to the Oberergletscher (see p.302), from where an easy valley-floor hour's stroll brings you back into Grindelwald.

Grund station is the start for several fine walks, including a two-hour ramble up the sloping pastureland through Brandegg to the *Berghaus des Alpes* at **Alpiglen** (☎033 853 11 30, Ⓦ www.alpiglen.ch; ❷; dorms Fr.35; June–Oct), a stop at 1616m on the Kleine Scheidegg train line. Starting from here cuts the cost of the ride up to the Jungfraujoch (see p.302), as would carrying on up the Eiger-Trail from Alpiglen to the hut alongside Eigergletscher station (see opposite), a spectacular, but steep, route that passes directly beneath the awesome North Face (3hr).

The five-hour trail from Grund beneath the gondola line to Männlichen (see opposite) brings you up through meadows and rolling open countryside, also with the towering Eiger a constant presence. From Grund, if you cross the river and head southeast for a few minutes, you'll come to the **Gletscherschlucht** (Glacier gorge; May–Oct daily 9am–6pm; Fr.5), catwalks leading you for 1km or more into a narrow defile above the Lütschine river, with evidence of glacial erosion everywhere, including polished valley walls, corkscrew potholes and lumps of green and pinkish marble in the river bed.

An hourly bus from Grindelwald station (or an hour's walk east) leads you close to the icy caverns of the **Oberergletscher** – from the *Hotel Wetterhorn* bus stop, follow the leafy trail down to the river and, on the other side, climb the 890 stairs to the nose of the glacier. There's a missable ice-grotto up there (May–Oct daily 9am–6pm; Fr.5), and, a ten-minute walk further up, a much more dramatic path which runs alongside the glacier itself, giving spectacular views.

To the Jungfraujoch

Switzerland's most popular (and expensive) mountain railway excursion is touted endlessly throughout the Oberland under the shoutline "Top of Europe": for once, though, the reality justifies the hype. Trains trundle through lush countryside south from Interlaken before coiling spectacularly up across the high pastures above either Wengen or Grindelwald, breaking the treeline at Kleine Scheidegg and tunnelling clean through the Eiger to emerge at the **JUNGFRAUJOCH**, an icy, windswept col at 3454m, just below the Jungfrau summit. This is – it's true – the highest train station in Europe, and offers an unforgettable experience of the mountains; you'd be missing out if you decided against shelling out the exorbitant sums necessary to get there.

Trains run all year round, come rain, fog, snow or shine. However, **good weather** is essential for the views: if there's a hint of cloud you'd be wasting your time heading up. Check the pictures from the summit, broadcast live on Ⓦ www.jungfrau.ch and on cable TV throughout the region, for an idea of the weather conditions, or ask your hotel or nearest tourist office for the latest forecasts. Remember, too, that it takes two and a half hours to reach the summit from Interlaken, and weather conditions can change rapidly on the journey. You should also bring **sunglasses** with you, even if you plan nothing more adventurous than looking out of the windows: the snows never melt up here, and if the sky is blue, the sun's glare and glitter can be painful.

There are two **routes** to the top. BOB trains head southwest from Interlaken Ost along the valley floor to Lauterbrunnen, from where you pick up the WAB mountain line which climbs through Wengen to Kleine Scheidegg. Alternatively, different BOB trains head southeast from Interlaken Ost to Grindelwald, where you change for the climb, arriving at Kleine Scheidegg from the other direction. All trains terminate at Kleine Scheidegg, where you must change for the final pull to Jungfraujoch; the popular practice is to go up one way and down the other.

Currently, the adult round-trip **fare** to Jungfraujoch from Interlaken is a budget-crunching Fr.163. One way to cut costs is to take advantage of the discounted **Good Morning ticket** (Fr.126), valid if you travel up on the first train of the day (6.35am from Interlaken), and leave the summit by noon (Nov–April: first or second train plus later departure permitted).

Walking some sections of the journey, up or down, is perfectly feasible in summer, and can also save plenty, with fares from intermediate points along the route considerably lower. The Good Morning ticket from Lauterbrunnen is Fr.109 (7.05am train), from Grindelwald Fr.108 (7.20am), from Wengen Fr.97 (7.25am), from Kleine Scheidegg Fr.62 (8.02am) and from Eigergletscher Fr.60 (8.12am). Excellent transport networks and vista-rich footpaths linking all stations mean that with judicious use of a hiking map and timetable you can see and do a great deal in a day and still get back to Interlaken, or even Bern or Zürich, by bedtime.

Kleine Scheidegg

Trains heading up from Wengen and Grindelwald meet at **KLEINE SCHEIDEGG** (2061m) – four buildings huddled in the most dramatic of locations directly below the soaring Eiger Nordwand, or **North Face of the Eiger**, a sheer wall of rock 2300m high. The settlement (it doesn't even count as a hamlet) throngs with daytime crowds switching trains on their way to or from the Jungfraujoch, but sees virtually nobody staying overnight.

The station building, which doubles as *Mountain Lodge* (☎033 828 78 28, ⓦwww.bahnhof-scheidegg.ch; ❷), has spartan, comfortable **dorms** (Fr.46) and rooms, while the grand old *Bellevue des Alpes* (☎033 855 12 12, ⓦwww .scheidegg-hotels.ch; ❺–❻, including half board; closed Easter–June & Oct–Dec) – the two large chalets beside the station, focus of the Clint Eastwood film *The Eiger Sanction* – has historically been the base station for worried relatives scanning the Eiger wall to track the progress of loved ones engaged in what's become known as one of the most difficult mountaineering ascents in the world. The hotel decor, all chintzy pelmets, wood panelling and armchairs by the fire, is from another world – an odd counterpoint to the muddy-boot hiking fraternity who tramp the area. Within view behind the hotel is the *Grindelwaldblick* (☎033 855 13 74, ⓦwww.grindelwaldblick.ch; Fr.38), a serviceable restaurant with dorms.

Kleine Scheidegg is the trailhead for a wealth of **high-country walks**. Hikes down to Wengen (roughly 2hr) or Grindelwald (roughly 4hr), or up the "back" of the nearby Lauberhorn (1hr), are relatively easy-going. There's a tougher one-hour trail up to the **EIGERGLETSCHER** train station (2320m), overlooking the massive sheet of ice sliding down from the high peaks; the station has well-maintained double and triple rooms (☎033 828 78 66, Ⓔguesthouse @jungfrau.ch; ❷) alongside husky kennels. A superb two-hour walking trail from here arcs around directly beneath the looming North Face down to Alpiglen (see p.301).

Männlichen

North from Kleine Scheidegg, away from the Eiger, a picturesque ninety-minute trail to **MÄNNLICHEN**, perched on a ridge and with one of the best mountain refuges in the region (☎033 853 10 68, ⓦwww.maennlichen.ch; ❷; dorms Fr.35), is particularly lovely and virtually flat the whole way. From Männlichen, the LWM cable-car drops down to Wengen in one direction, while in the other, the GGM gondola glides for an amazing half-hour – the longest gondola line in the world – across the pastures to Grindelwald-Grund (both closed May & Nov).

△ Kleine Scheidegg (see p.303), overlooked by the Eiger

The Jungfraujoch

Most people at Kleine Scheidegg don't leave the area of the station buildings, only stopping to switch trains for the final leg up to the "Top of Europe". After the short run to the Eigergletscher station (see p.303), the train enters a long tunnel carved out of the heart of the Eiger. There are five-minute stops at Eigerwand and Eismeer stations, both with viewing galleries out over the frozen landscape, and after forty minutes in the dark, you pull into the **Jungfraujoch** summit station (3454m).

Inevitably, the place is a tourist circus of ice sculptures, husky sleigh rides, glacier walks, a short ski run, dismal restaurants and a post office, all invariably overflowing with tour groups. Nonetheless, panoramic views from the open-air **Sphinx Terrace**, at 3571m, to Germany's Black Forest, the Vosges in France and across a gleaming wasteland to the Italian Alps are heart-thumping – as is the thin atmosphere up here. Yawning away below the silver-domed weather station on top is the mighty Jungfraufirn glacier, which joins up with several others (including the Aletschgletscher, largest in the Alps) at the resonantly named Konkordiaplatz ice plain 3km southeast.

The best way to avoid being smothered by snap-happy crowds is to travel up on the first train of the day, and on arrival follow the signs quickly straight to the high-speed lift for the Sphinx Terrace – that way, you can snatch five or ten minutes of crisp, undisturbed silence at the loftiest point of all, and be the first of the day to sweep the snow off the railings. At other times, you may have to queue for an hour or more just to get your nose into the fresh air. Once you've finished at the terrace, it's easy to leave the bustling summit station behind and head out across the snows into solitude and silence, although you must stick to the marked trails (crevasses give no warning).

If you've had experience of snow hiking in the mountains, and you have good boots, a map, sunglasses and proper clothing, let the tourist office in Interlaken know that you want to head out on the simple one-hour trail from the Jungfraujoch around the base of the Mönch to the **Mönchsjochhütte** at 3629m (☎033 971 34 72, ⓦwww.moenchsjoch.ch; April–May & July–Sept; dorms Fr.26, half board Fr.56) – you don't need a guide, and the isolation of the hut offers a night to remember. You should walk at half pace, or you may find yourself dizzy and labouring to catch your breath. A handful of other glacier-bound huts are dotted around the area, but you need a mountain guide and all the professional gear to reach them.

The lakes

Flanking Interlaken in the heart of the Bernese Oberland, the two lakes of the **Thunersee** and the **Brienzersee** form the gateway to the region. They are often overlooked by visitors in a hurry to get into the mountains, or returning to the lowlands, but there's something very peaceful about them, poised between the big cities of the north and the high Alps further south. Even the most hurried of Oberland tours should leave a day or two for enjoying the

The **BLS** company (named for its main rail route "Bern-Lötschberg-Simplon", between the Swiss capital and Milan; Ⓦwww.bls.ch) runs boats on both lakes, which are free to Eurail and Swiss Pass holders, and half-price to InterRailers.

The Thunersee is the more picturesque of the two, overlooked by the pyramidal Niesen and the Stockhorn on the west, the wooded slopes of the Beatenberg on the east, and with the snowy peaks of the Eiger, Mönch and Jungfrau always in view to the south. There are at least half-a-dozen boats a day in summer (June–Sept) between **Thun and Interlaken West** (2hr), stopping at – among other places – Hilterfingen, Oberhofen, Spiez and the Beatushöhlen; one of the boats, the Drachenschiff, is done up to look like the giant green dragon vanquished by St Beatus (see p.309) – quite a sight on the water, huffing smoke from between its huge teeth. Service is just as regular on the bleaker, cliff-girt Brienzersee between **Brienz and Interlaken Ost** (1hr 15min). If you're visiting out of season, note that boats run on both lakes at least once daily from April to October, although in winter, service is drastically reduced and may be cut altogether.

There's also a host of eat-aboard **cruises**, some on vintage steamships, generally running three times a day throughout the summer. Special evening cruises run on Friday and Saturday evenings all summer long departing from Thun, and once a month departing from Interlaken Ost (around Fr.24). The paddle steamer *Blümlisalp* makes a six-hour meander from Thun to Interlaken West, while its sister ship the *Lötschberg* does a similar three-hour round trip from Interlaken Ost (both daily mid-June to mid-Sept; ordinary tickets valid).

beauty of the lakes, set amidst cliffs and forested hillsides, dotted with quiet villages, and backed by a long chain of dramatic snowy heights.

Both lakes are well served by transport, with mainline **trains** running between Thun, Spiez, Interlaken West & Ost, Brienz and on to Luzern, quite often swishing along within metres of the water, plunging in and out of tunnels cut beneath the mountains which ring the shoreline. Unless speed is of the essence, though, you'd do well to take at least one trip by **boat** (see box).

Around the Thunersee

The **Thunersee** (Lake Thun) is one of the prettiest in the country, a tranquil patch of misty blue loomed over by high shoreline mountains. The presence of the snowy Bernese Alps to the south, ranged above the water in a breathtaking panorama, constantly beckons you on. **Thun**, at the northernmost tip of the lake where the Aare flows out towards Bern, is an attractive overnight stop on the way into or out of the mountains – much more relaxing than Interlaken – and small, rather twee little lakeside resorts such as **Spiez** can pleasantly break a slow journey south. The **Sammlung Im Obersteg**, one of Switzerland's finest small art galleries, adds a cultural dimension, located in a pleasant lakeside park alongside the castle of **Oberhofen**.

The Thunersee tourist office (☎033 251 00 00, Ⓦwww.thunersee.ch) has devised an easy five-day walking tour around the lake (May–Oct) for Fr.550 per person, including four nights' half-board, luggage transport and documentation.

Thun

Set astride the River Aare on the lake which bears its name, **THUN** (pronounced *toon*) is much overlooked by visitors pressing on to Interlaken. This is a shame, since with its picturesque castle and quaint medieval centre it's well worth a visit; views of the Eiger, Mönch and Jungfrau and, closer at hand, the giant pyramidal Niesen (2362m) and flat-topped Stockhorn (2190m) are a gentle prelude to the Alpine vistas further south.

The town has an odd secret, however. After World War II, the authorities decided that in the event of a future invasion, the whole of Switzerland south to Thun was to be abandoned, and the entire population was to assemble here for dispersal into mountain retreats. Switzerland's largest hospital was hollowed out of the Niesen, but despite constant upkeep, has never been used; it remains pristine and fully equipped, and there are probably dozens of other major military and civil emergency installations hidden in the mountains nearby.

Across the river from the station, Thun's low-lying Old Town – disastrously flooded in 1999 – is renowned for the arcading both of the main street, split-level **Obere Hauptgasse**, and the tranquil, cobbled **Rathausplatz** at its northwestern end. Steps lead up from various points along the picturesque street to the fairy-tale turreted **castle** which looms above, built in 1190 and

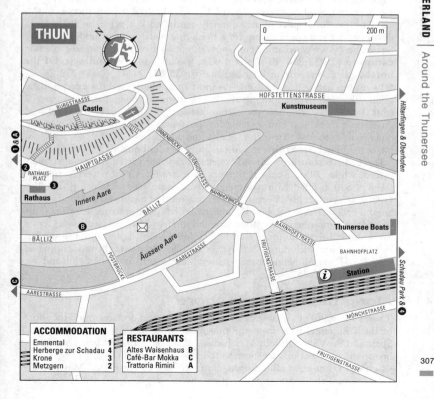

ACCOMMODATION	
Emmental	1
Herberge zur Schadau	4
Krone	3
Metzgern	2

RESTAURANTS	
Altes Waisenhaus	B
Café-Bar Mokka	C
Trattoria Rimini	A

occupied by the Bernese in 1386. Its lofty halls now contain a historical **museum** (April–Oct daily 10am–5pm; Feb & March daily 1–4pm; Nov–Jan Sun 1–4pm; Fr.6; SMP; Ⓦwww.schlossthun.ch), with the usual period furniture and militaria. A short walk east is a grand Belle-Epoque lakeside building housing the **Kunstmuseum** (Tues–Sun 10am–5pm, Wed until 9pm; Fr.6.50; SMP; Ⓦwww.kunstmuseumthun.ch), which stages worthwhile exhibitions of modern Swiss and international art.

At the lakeshore but on the station side of the river is the lush **Schadau Park**, home to perfectly tended flowerbeds, stunning views across the water to the mountains, and a lavish nineteenth-century folly planted majestically on the waterside. Beside it is an odd cylindrical building housing the **Wocher Panorama** (May–Oct Tues–Sun 10am–5pm, July & Aug until 6pm; free), a giant painting – the oldest of its kind in the world – running all the way around the interior wall, which depicts the daily life of Thun circa 1810.

Practicalities

The **train station** is five minutes southwest of the centre, with bikes for rent; adjacent is the **tourist office** (July & Aug Mon–Fri 9am–7pm, Sat 9am–4pm; rest of year Mon–Fri 9am–noon & 1–6pm, Sat 9am–noon; ℡033 222 23 40, Ⓦwww.thuntourismus.ch), with information on the town and the whole region. **Boats** around the lake, and to Interlaken, depart from outside the station.

For **accommodation**, walk right from the station for the spotless *Herberge zur Schadau* **hostel**, Seestrasse 22 (℡033 222 52 22, Ⓦwww.herberge.ch; ❶), an old house in a quiet location, newly renovated but pricey at Fr.39 for a dorm bed; or you could plump for a bunk in a metal tubular module built by Swisstube (Ⓦwww.swisstube.ch) at *Younotent*, part of the *Bettlereiche* lakeside **campsite** (℡033 336 40 67) at Gwatt, a 3km bus-ride southwest. Of the **hotels**, quiet *Metzgern* on Rathausplatz (℡033 222 21 41, Ⓕ033 222 21 82; ❷) – an inn dating back to 1361 – is most atmospheric, and has exceptionally good-value rooms overlooking the cobbled square. *Emmental*, Bernstrasse 2 (℡033 222 01 20, Ⓦwww.essenundtrinken.ch; ❷), is a colourful old guesthouse that's now also a venue for live music, with a handful of pleasant, comfortable rooms. *Krone* on Rathausplatz (℡033 227 88 88, Ⓦwww. hauensteinhotels.ch; ❸) is a step up in ambience and quality.

The many **restaurants** around Scheibenstrasse are varied and competitively priced, while Bälliz, a central shopping street with a twice-weekly **market** (Wed & Sat), is lined with pavement cafés, most relaxed of which is the *Altes Waisenhaus*, perfect for a beer in the sun or a meal of quality Italian food (*menus* around Fr.25). *Trattoria Rimini*, Bernstrasse 26, has good, inexpensive pasta dishes, and the atmospheric restaurant attached to *Hotel Metzgern* (see above) serves Swiss and Italian *menus* for around Fr.20 (closed Mon). Scheibenstrasse also has numerous **bars**, including *Nachtwerk* at no. 29 (Ⓦwww.nachtwerk.ch), while *Café-Bar Mokka*, Allmendstrasse 14 (Ⓦwww.mokka.ch), is the best club and live music venue (closed Mon).

Along the northern shore

There's a handful of visitable castles and stately homes dotted around the shore of the Thunersee, aside from the fine medieval specimens within Thun and Spiez and the Victorian folly at Schadau. All are served – and best visited – by boats which stop at or very close to the castles themselves.

Schloss Hünegg at Hilterfingen, 2km southeast of Thun (mid-May to mid-Oct Mon–Sat 2–5pm, Sun 10am–noon & 2–5pm; Fr.5; Ⓦwww

.schlosshuenegg.ch), is worth a visit. Built in the 1860s in the style of a Loire château, Hünegg houses an interior unchanged since 1900, extraordinarily lavish bedchambers, boudoirs and halls displaying the wealthiest of lifestyles (the owner was a former officer in the Prussian army).

A couple of kilometres further along the lakeshore is the mighty **Schloss Oberhofen** (mid-May to mid-Oct Mon 2–5pm, Tues–Sun 11am–5pm; Fr.5; SMP), set in its own lush gardens. It dates from the thirteenth century, and houses collections of furnishings from the Bernisches Historisches Museum (see p.252): a range of restored interiors, a stone-flagged knights' hall, salons furnished in Empire style and even a Turkish *selamlik*, or smoking room, way up under the eaves. The formal waterside **park** (March–Nov daily 9am–dusk; free) is delightful, shaded by trees and planted with all kinds of flowers. The lakeside road continues south of Oberhofen to the St Beatus-Höhlen (see below) and Interlaken.

Sammlung Im Obersteg

A short walk east of Schloss Oberhofen, in the same park, is a house that once belonged to local tycoon Karl Im Obersteg, and now holds the **Sammlung Im Obersteg** (mid-May to mid-Oct Tues–Sat 10am–noon & 2–5pm, Sun 10am–5pm; Fr.8; SMP), one of Switzerland's finest small art collections. It is signed on the lakeside road, and there's covered parking opposite.

On the ground floor, room 2 features an impressive double-sided canvas painted by **Picasso** at the age of 20 in his Blue Period – the superbly observed, melancholic *Absinthe Drinker* backed by *Woman in the Theatre Box* – as well as a small Cézanne nude. The highlight of Room 3 is Maillol's bronze *Springtime*, an eerily lifelike female nude that has been placed in front of a mirror, allowing intimate scrutiny from all angles. On the walls of the same room hang a moving series of five Expressionist portraits by **Chaim Soutine** (1893–1944), a Lithuanian-born Jewish artist who worked in Paris between the world wars; all of them feature dark backgrounds, thickly applied paint and tragic eyes. A portrait alongside by **Modigliani** – whom Soutine befriended in Paris – serves as a counterpoint: it is more graceful and insightful, yet lacks the passion and skill of Soutine's works.

Upstairs, room 4 – the "hunting room", with a polychrome ceiling – features a typically muscular Rodin bronze as well as a fine 1920s Parisian street scene by Utrillo. Room 5 holds the main draw of the collection, three monumental works by **Chagall**, painted in his hometown of Vitebsk in 1914: *Jew in Red*, *Jew in Black and White* and *Jew in Green*, the last the most potent of all. An extraordinary Chagall self-portrait, aged 27, delicate and effeminate, hangs in the same room. Two more rooms on this floor hold temporary exhibits.

St-Beatus-Höhlen

On the same shore of the Thunersee, beyond the funicular at Beatenbucht, are the **ST-BEATUS-HÖHLEN** (St Beatus Caves; ⓦ www.beatushoehlen.ch), an impressive set of drippy subterranean chambers filled with stalactites and stalagmites that were formerly the residence of the early Christian ascetic St Beatus. The caves are tucked into the cliffs just 3km northwest of Interlaken; it's a **walk** of about 2hr from Interlaken, or you can take hourly **bus** #21, which runs both ways along the shoreside road between Thun and Ost and West stations. In the summer, about half-a-dozen **boats** a day between Thun and Interlaken West stop at Beatushöhlen-Sundlauenen, ten minutes' walk south of the cave entrance.

Beatus himself reputedly came from Britain. The story goes that having given all his wealth to the poor to follow Christ, he was baptized in Rome by

St Peter and sent with a companion, Justus, into the Alps as the first apostle to the heathen Helvetians. (In all probability, though, Beatus was one of the Irish followers of St Columba who brought Christianity to Switzerland in the sixth century.) When Beatus and Justus came to the lake, local people told them of a terrible **dragon** who occupied a cave overlooking the water. Beatus climbed up to the cave alone, and when the dragon emerged, raised his cross and spoke the name of the Holy Trinity, thereby sending the monster over the cliff edge into the water below. Beatus took over its cave, praying and working miracles until his death at the age of 90. A cult of pilgrimage rapidly grew up around him and the cave, which, after being walled up during the Reformation, was restored for public visits in the nineteenth century.

Today, you can visit only on **guided tours**, which depart every half-hour (April–Oct daily 10.30am–5pm; Fr.16; duration 50min) from the ticket office a short climb above the lakeside road. Note that a visit involves a full 2km walk through the caves (1km each way), which are chilly year-round. You can leave bags at the ticket desk for Fr.1. The guides lead you past the grotto where Beatus reputedly passed his days, and then on into the cool gloom of the cave interior, filled with the noise of rushing underground streams – the best time to visit is springtime, when a wet winter and snowmelt conspire to shoot torrents of water through the corkscrewing channels.

Spiez

On the opposite, southern shore, huddled above and around a small bay 11km south of Thun, **SPIEZ** is a gentle little resort village, dominated by its medieval waterside castle and stunning views over the lake to the high mountains all around. It lies at a major **rail junction**, where the main line from Bern splits: one branch continues to Interlaken, another climbs south into the Kander valley (see p.315) to the Lötschberg Tunnel under the Alps and on to Brig. In addition, trains from Spiez head west to Zweisimmen, Gstaad and Montreux on the celebrated Golden Pass panoramic route (see p.164).

The **train station** is in a modern shopping area high above the Old Town, or Städtli; find your way down on stairs and the descending main Seestrasse. Boats from Thun and Interlaken dock right beside the Old Town. The castle, **Schloss Spiez** (April–Oct Mon 2–5pm, Tues–Sun 10am–5pm; July–Sept closes 6pm; Fr.4; SMP), dating from the fifteenth and sixteenth centuries but with earlier foundations, was the residence of the Stretlingen family before passing to the Bernese noble dynasties of Von Bubenberg and, from 1516 to 1875, Von Erlach. You can visit several of the grand halls within, including the Baroque Banqueting Hall of 1614. The Romanesque **church** adjacent, with its seventeenth-century spire, has original frescoes in the apse and the crypt. Wandering through the tiny lanes around the castle, and around the bay filled with yachts (Spiez is home to a renowned sailing school), is a good way to get a feel for the town.

Spiez's friendly **tourist office** is on platform 1 of the station (May–Sept Mon–Fri 8am–6pm, Sat 9am–noon; July & Aug Sat also 2–4pm; Oct–April Mon–Fri 8am–noon & 2–6pm; ☎033 654 20 20, Ⓦwww.thunersee.ch). The town's popularity with holidaying German and Swiss-German families means that there are plenty of **hotels**, but most are rather conservative. *Krone*, Oberlandstrasse 28 (☎033 654 41 31, Ⓕ033 654 94 31; ❶), is an old, lived-in place near the station with shared bathrooms and parking. Down a bit further is *Bellevue*, Seestrasse 36 (☎033 654 84 64, Ⓦwww.bellevue-spiez.ch; ❷), a cosier place with more modern rooms. Beside the lake, *Aqua Welle* (☎033 654 40 44,

ⒻⒻ033 654 76 75; ❸) has better views but less character. A few kilometres south
of town at Leissingen is the HI **hostel** *La Nichée* (☎033 847 12 14,
Ⓦwww.youthhostel.ch; ❶; May–Oct), a peaceful place with only a few dorm
beds (Fr.31). Next to Spiez station is a self-service *Migros* **restaurant**, with views
over the castle and the lake, while Seestrasse holds a clutch of inexpensive tearooms and pizzerias, including the popular *Brasserie 66* up near the station.

The Brienzersee and beyond

Stretching east of Interlaken, the **Brienzersee** (Lake Brienz) is much vaunted
as the cleanest lake in Switzerland, beautifully set in an enclosed bowl amidst
forested slopes, streams tumbling down from on high, overlooked to the south
by the Faulhorn (2681m) and to the northeast by the Brienzer Rothorn
(2350m), the latter served by a nostalgic old rack railway from the main town
of the lake, **Brienz**. East of Brienz, a tortuous road crosses the Brünig Pass into
Canton Obwalden, heading for Luzern, while the main road scoots along the
floor of the Haslital, beside the youthful Aare, to **Meiringen**, scene of the
"death" of Sherlock Holmes and final staging-post before the major trans-
Alpine routes over the Grimsel and Susten passes.

Brienz

At the easternmost tip of the lake, **BRIENZ** has a quiet, community feel; not
many people come visiting, and those that do mostly stop for just an hour or
two before catching the boat back to Interlaken. The town is known as the
most accomplished centre for **woodcarving** in Switzerland, and has many
low-key workshops and souvenir shops hawking everything from mass-
produced tat to quality hand-tooled busts, figurines and nativity scenes in lime-
wood. Brienz also boasts the last steam-driven rack railway in Switzerland, with
a fine old beast puffing its way up the flower-strewn slopes for an hour, from
the lake at 566m to the **Brienz Rothorn** summit station at 2244m (daily
June–Oct; Eurail and InterRail not valid, Swiss Pass 25 percent discount;
Ⓦwww.brienz-rothorn-bahn.ch). There are plenty of strolls around and about
on the top, as well as a tough trail heading northwest through the mountains
to Kemmeriboden (see p.262).

Brienz **tourist office**, Hauptstrasse 143 (July & Aug Mon–Fri 8am–6.30pm,
Sat 8am–noon & 4–6pm; Sept–June Mon–Fri 8am–noon & 2–6pm;
April–June & Sept also Sat 8am–noon; ☎033 952 80 80, Ⓦwww.alpenregion
.ch) is metres from the jetty where **boats** dock from Interlaken Ost and directly opposite the **train station**. A stone's throw away is the Rothornbahn station, departure point of the vintage locos. **Hotels** within Brienz take in some
generic options in the ❷ range along the lakefront, but a better choice is up
on a slope above the town: the *Schönegg*, Talstrasse 6 (☎033 951 11 13, Ⓕ033
951 38 13; ❷), is a rustic chalet, carefully managed by an attentive owner, and
providing neat, pretty rooms, ensuite and not. On the Rothorn summit is the
Rothorn Kulm hotel (☎033 951 12 21, Ⓦwww.brienz-rothorn-bahn.ch; ❷)
with plain, unremarkable rooms. Brienz's comfortable HI **hostel** is at
Strandweg 10, a fifteen-minute walk east around the head of the lake (☎033
951 11 52, Ⓦwww.youthhostel.ch; ❶; April–Oct), with dorms (Fr.28) and bike
rental. A little further east is the *Aaregg* **campsite** (☎033 951 18 43,
Ⓦwww.aaregg.ch; April–Oct).

All along the waterfront Hauptstrasse are any number of **restaurants**, all offering fresh lake fish: the best by a long streak is the *Steinbock* chalet, at no. 123 (℡033 951 40 55; closed Tues), a rather fussy place but with the best fish in town (*menus* from Fr.20).

Just opposite Brienz, reachable by boat or on a scenic lakeside trail from the hamlet of Iseltwald, are the **Giessbach falls**, which tumble over a series of terraces down the cliffside. Above stands the *Grandhotel Giessbach* (℡033 952 25 25, Ⓦwww.giessbach.com; ➎–➑; April–Oct), saved from redevelopment and now restored to its turn-of-the-century elegance.

Freilichtmuseum Ballenberg

The major draw of Brienz is its proximity to the **Freilichtmuseum Ballenberg** (Open-Air Museum; April–Oct daily 10am–5pm; Ⓦwww. ballenberg.ch; Fr.16; SMP), 3km or so east of the town, a huge area of rolling parkland which serves as a living showcase for traditional Swiss architecture and crafts. There are two entrances, the West nearest Brienz and, some 4km away, the East entrance near Brienzwiler; regular postbuses from outside Brienz station serve both. In-between are thirteen separate areas, each containing several examples of traditional houses from different parts of Switzerland, transported here piece by piece from their original settings, reassembled and restored. Within each building are held daily demonstrations of traditional crafts, everything from needlework to faggot binding. The whole place is fascinating, but it's really too big to absorb in one go; you'd do well to select a few areas from the museum map (Fr.2) and aim for them alone – or, alternatively, ask for a discounted two-day pass and spread your visit. There are three restaurants on site, as well as groceries where you can buy provisions for a barbecue (free firewood provided).

Meiringen and around

The creation of meringue and the death of Sherlock Holmes are the two claims to fame of the old town of **MEIRINGEN**. From the way visitors approach the place, though, it seems that many have difficulty deciding which story is real and which invented.

Set at the heart of the Hasliberg hiking region, the town has long been a favourite mountain-walking resort of the English. Sir Arthur Conan Doyle, creator of Sherlock Holmes, stayed in genteel Meiringen many times, and the town's sole attraction is the **Sherlock Holmes Museum** in Conan Doyle Place (May–Sept daily 10am–6pm; Oct–April Wed–Sun 3–6pm; Fr.3.80; joint ticket with Reichenbach falls funicular Fr.8.50; SMP). This interesting little den is in the cellar of the English Church, and includes a life-size replica of the detective's study at 221b Baker Street, complete with taped commentary. The town **church**, north of the centre on Kirchgasse, has a free-standing Romanesque tower with a wooden spire, some fourteenth-century interior frescoes, and interesting archeological investigations below the crypt of the eleventh-century predecessor. Meiringen was popular enough with English visitors of a bygone age to attract not only Conan Doyle, but also semi-official trinket hunters: ancient bits and pieces from Meiringen's old church now sit in the vaults of the British Museum in London.

Meiringen's **train station** is in the town centre, with the **tourist office** opposite (July & Aug Mon–Fri 8am–6pm, Sat 8am–noon & 4–6pm; Sept–June Mon–Fri 8am–noon & 2–6pm, Sat 8am–noon; ℡033 972 50 50, Ⓦwww.alpenregion.ch). Innertkirchen, 1km beyond the Aare gorge and served

The novelist **Sir Arthur Conan Doyle** chose the Reichenbach falls as the setting for the death of his character Sherlock Holmes. In *The Final Problem* (1891), Conan Doyle wrote of Reichenbach:

It is, indeed, a fearful place. The torrent, swollen by the melting snow, plunges into a tremendous abyss, from which the spray rolls up like the smoke from a burning house. The shaft into which the river hurls itself is an immense chasm, lined by glistening coal-black rock, and narrowing into a creaming, boiling pit of incalculable depth, which brims over and shoots the stream onward over its jagged lip.

The story goes on to tell of the death of Holmes. On May 4, 1891, the detective met his archenemy Professor Moriarty on a ledge above the falls. The two became locked in a titanic hand-to-hand struggle before both tumbled over the precipice, presumably to their deaths. This neat device was Conan Doyle's way to free himself of the burden of constantly churning out pulpy detective stories and was intended to give himself the freedom to write more elevated literature instead. But he didn't reckon on public opinion. The outcry against the death of such a popular character as Holmes was so great that in 1903 Conan Doyle was forced to give in to the pressure of his fan mail. He resurrected his nemesis by claiming that Holmes had managed to grab a tuft of grass during the fall into the "dreadful cauldron" and so had lived to solve another mystery. Conan Doyle – much to his chagrin – was far more celebrated during his lifetime for his detective stories than for his various expeditions and good works; these days his numerous elevated writings have largely been forgotten, while his 45 Holmes tales are world-famous.

Every year on May 4, members of the international Sherlock Holmes Society make a pilgrimage to the falls to commemorate the "death" of their beloved hero.

by regular buses, has four **campsites**, best of which is the year-round *Aareschlucht* (☏033 971 53 32, ⓦwww.swisscamps.ch). **Hotels** within Meiringen include the *Victoria* on Bahnhofplatz (☏033 972 10 40, ⓦwww .victoria-meiringen.ch; ❸–❹), entirely renovated and excellent value, although undercut in price by the appealing old *Hirschen*, 300m east on Rudenz (☏033 971 18 12, ⓕ033 971 47 12; ❷), with shared-bath old-style rooms. Conan Doyle's old haunt, the *Parkhotel du Sauvage* (☏033 971 41 41, ⓦwww.sauvage.ch; ❸–❺), is still around: the management undoubtedly benefits by a few francs from associations with fame, but can still come up with the appropriate atmosphere and comforts. **Eating and drinking** is a case of follow-your-nose: the *Victoria* has a decent-ish restaurant, with some veggie options, as does the *Alpin Sherpa* hotel opposite. The best **meringue** in Meiringen, by all accounts, is served at the low-key *Café Brunner*, Bahnhofstrasse 8 – but on careful analysis you may feel that the ones whipped up over the mountains at Kemmeriboden (see p.262) steal a march.

Around Meiringen

Meiringen itself is much less appealing than the countryside all around. The tourist office can supply details of the many hikes in and around the Hasli valley and Hasliberg region, but the most accessible excursion is to the dramatic **Reichenbach falls**. A wonderful old funicular (May–Oct; Fr.7; joint ticket with Sherlock Holmes Museum Fr.8.50; ⓦwww.reichenbachfall.ch) runs from the south of town up to a vantage point below the roaring falls, best visited in spring laden with snowmelt from the glaciers further upstream.

A sticky end

Odd though it seems for such a delicate creation, **meringue** originated in the rural Bernese Oberland. At some unknown time in the pre-Revolutionary eighteenth century, an Italian baker by the name of Gasparini invented a baked concoction of egg whites, sugar and cream, and named it after Meiringen, the scene of his inspiration. Documented names of the rich dessert include *meiring* (plural *meiringe*) and *meirinken* – until Louis XV took a liking to Gasparini's creation, whereupon the French name "meringue" took over.

Unfortunately, the documentary evidence for Meiringen's noble patrimony went up in smoke long ago during two disastrous town fires. Undaunted, researchers in Frankfurt's Culinary Museum early in the twentieth century turned up further solid evidence. Meiringen's bigwigs thought their claim to fame was secure… but Allied fighter pilots during World War II had other ideas, and bombed Frankfurt – and the museum – into dust. Nonetheless, the locals are sticking to their story, and patisseries in Meiringen still churn out 1500 top-quality meringues a day to fuel the legend.

Stepped paths lead up beside the falls through the mossy forests to **Zwirgi** village, at the foot of the deep and dramatic Reichenbach valley. Trails lead on southwest up the valley past the hamlet of Kaltenbrunnen to **ROSENLAUI**, where a grand four-storey pile, the atmospheric *Rosenlaui Hotel* (☎033 971 29 12, ⓦwww.rosenlaui.ch; ❷; dorms Fr.35; May–Oct), sits overlooking a stream. The hotel was built a hundred years ago to service tourists coming to explore the Rosenlaui valley and its mighty glacier, and to bathe in the valley's mineral springs, and its public rooms are a breath of elegance from a former age. From Rosenlaui, trails head on up to Schwarzwaldalp (beyond which private cars are forbidden) and over the **Grosse Scheidegg** pass to Grindelwald. This route through the Reichenbach valley to Grindelwald is also served by hourly postbuses from Meiringen (June–Sept).

A couple of kilometres east of Meiringen, served by buses to Innertkirchen, is the **Aareschlucht** (Aare gorge; daily: July & Aug 8am–6pm; April–June, Sept & Oct 9am–5pm; Fr.6; ⓦwww.aareschlucht.ch), with a path snaking for 1.4km through the deep and dramatic sheer-sided gorge, which is floodlit on summer nights (July & Aug Wed & Fri 9–11pm).

The western valleys

The section of the Bernese Oberland west of the Thunersee, which holds the only route through the mountains towards Lake Geneva, stands in sharp contrast to the rock and ice of the Jungfrau region. Broad, leafy valleys reach between the peaks, sheltering a handful of resorts and quiet country towns which see much less tourism than their hectic counterparts around Interlaken. The especially lovely Kander valley runs south from Spiez, climbing to the old-style resort village of **Kandersteg**, while the forested, picture-pretty gorge of the River Simme heads west through a succession of old villages filled with examples of the local heavy-eaved ornate darkwood chalets, some dating from as early as the 1750s. The valley of the **Simmental** curves south into the rural, hilly **Saanenland**, focused around the world-famous ski resort of **Gstaad**. Continuing west, you cross into an outpost of French-speaking Canton Vaud, whereupon the same rolling hills and broad, quiet valleys are re-titled the **Pays d'Enhaut**.

The Kander valley

South of Spiez, the Niesen stands sentinel over the peaceful **Kander valley**, a narrow finger pointing the way south to the wall of high peaks around the mighty Blümlisalp massif (which rises to 3663m). Nestling at the very end of the sharply ascending valley, hard up against the mountains in the most idyllic of locations, is the laid-back resort of **Kandersteg**, at the entrance to the longstanding Lötschberg Tunnel. Further south, beyond the point where trains disappear into the valley wall on their way to Italy, are the remote and little-visited Üschinen and Gastern valleys, which offer hikers fantastic opportunities to get out in the wild.

Kandersteg

Long a centre for mountaineering, the picturesque, chalet-strewn village of **KANDERSTEG** (1200m) was for centuries the trailhead for travellers crossing the high mountain passes into Canton Valais. In 1912, though, Kandersteg was changed forever by the completion of the **Lötschberg Tunnel** (see box) just south of the village, a crucially important rail link between northern and southern Europe – the only one between Geneva and the Gotthard – which created a through route from Bern to Milan. Although the small valley road into the village can get heavy with trans-Alpine traffic, most vehicles are heading for the car-train terminus, situated on the outskirts; once you arrive in Kandersteg itself, all is tranquil. The new **Lötschberg Base Tunnel** (see box) will have its entrance further north at Frutigen, thus ensuring that by 2007 even the steep roads approaching Kandersteg will be mostly traffic-free.

The main reason to visit Kandersteg is to explore the surrounding area: attractions are all rural and scenic. Kandersteg is a fine place to learn how to ski: beginners can test out their snowplough techniques on the easiest and least

---

The Lötschberg Tunnel

For drivers, the **Lötschberg Tunnel** between Kandersteg and Goppenstein is a very handy link between Bern and Valais – especially since without it you'd be forced to aim for the Grimsel Pass or make a detour to Montreux. Regular shuttle trains through the tunnel are dedicated to transporting motor traffic. Departures run year-round, every half-hour between 5am and midnight; in July only, there are hourly shuttles throughout Friday nights. Both termini have drive-on drive-off facilities, and journey time is only fifteen minutes. You can buy your ticket on the spot – Fr.25 for a motorbike or a car holding up to nine people. For more information, check ☏0900 553 333, ⊛www.bls.ch.

In 2007, as part of the AlpTransit project (see p.415), the new **Lötschberg Base Tunnel** is due to open, covering 34.5km beneath the mountains from Frutigen, well below Kandersteg, to Raron on the floor of the Rhône valley just west of Visp. See ⊛www.blsalptransit.ch for full details.

daunting of slopes, with other beginners all around and not a trace of big-resort swagger. The village itself is strung out along the valley floor for several kilometres, loomed over by the massive bulk of the Doldenhorn to the southeast and the First massif to the northwest. Prime hiking and recreation spot above the village is the dramatically crag-ringed **Oeschinensee** (Ⓦwww.oeschinensee.ch), a small lake accessed by a chairlift from the eastern edge of the village. From the top station, it's a twenty-minute stroll to the lake itself, warm and glittering in summer and iced over for cross-country skiing in winter. A handful of trails fan out around the area, dotted with mountain refuges (the tourist office in Kandersteg has a complete list, with hiking routes), and the walk back down to Kandersteg is only about an hour. Another lift on the opposite side of the valley accesses the **Allmenalp**.

A ten-minute drive north of Kandersteg, just off the main valley-floor road, is the underwhelming **Blausee** (Fr.4.50; Ⓦwww.blausee.ch), a privately owned area of land surrounding a tiny boating lake. It's all a bit overblown, since once you stroll through the trees to the lakelet itself, there's not much to do other than order a plate of fresh trout on the restaurant terrace, and watch kids boating around the lake. Even the views are hemmed in by thick pine woods.

Practicalities

Kandersteg's **tourist office** is on the main street, just ahead from the train station (July & Aug Mon–Fri 8am–6pm, Sat 8–11.30am & 2.30–6pm; rest of year Mon–Fri 8am–noon & 2–6pm; ☎033 675 80 80, Ⓦwww.kandersteg.ch). Even before the Lötschbergtunnel put Kandersteg on the map, the village had a tradition of hospitality, and **accommodation** is of universally good quality.

Plenty of places offer **dorms**: the *Rendezvous*, near the Oeschinen chairlift (☎ & ℉033 675 13 54; Fr.18), the International Scout Centre at the southern edge of the village (☎033 675 82 82, Ⓦwww.kisc.ch; from Fr.21), and *Hotel National*, near the turning for the Allmenalp chairlift and with some cheap rooms too (☎033 675 10 85, Ⓦhotelnati.isuisse.com; ❶; Fr.29). Breakfast for dorm sleepers at all these places is an extra Fr.6–10. There's a good **campsite** (☎033 675 15 34, Ⓦwww.camping-kandersteg.ch) next to the *Rendezvous*.

Standing out from the **hotels** is the fine *Ruedihus* (☎033 675 81 82, Ⓦwww.ruedihus.ch; ❹), in a meadow off the road south of the *National*. A beautifully restored chalet from 1753, its nine characterful rooms display minute attention to detail, with original rustic furniture and fittings set off by the most spotless of modern ensuite bathrooms. The *Zur Post* (☎033 675 12 58, Ⓦwww.hotel-zur-post.ch; ❷), in the centre, is a quality lower-end choice, as is the comfortable *Alpina* (☎033 675 12 46, Ⓦwww.alpina-online.com; ❷), at the northern entrance to the village. There's a welter of luxury pads, best of which is the *Victoria Ritter* in the centre (☎033 675 80 00, Ⓦwww.hotel-victoria.ch; ❹), a stout old place with a good reputation and a long tradition. The *Waldhotel Doldenhorn* (☎033 675 81 81, Ⓦwww.doldenhorn-ruedihus.ch; ❺) is out in the countryside, boasting comfort and quiet.

Eating and drinking covers the gamut from the simple but palatable dishes (some veggie) in the *Bahnhofbuffet* train station diner, up to the gourmet spreads at the luxury hotels. Meals at the *Ruedihus* (see above) are spectacularly good, with a choice between the formal restaurant above and the wonderfully atmospheric *Stübli* below, serving a range of inexpensive Swiss specialities (from Fr.20). Most of the hotels along the main street serve food, but the *Victoria-Ritter* prides itself on its kitchen – justifiably so, with the menu of intricately well-presented international cuisine changing every two or three months (from Fr.25).

Beyond Kandersteg

At the end of Kandersteg village, beside the rushing Kander torrent, is a small crossroads. To the southwest a tortuous path climbs into the bleak **Üschinental**, which penetrates for 4 or 5km between the summits, and is the scene for some tough mountain-bike trails and tougher hikes up to the Gemmi Pass above the town of Leukerbad (see p.355).

Southeast from the same crossroads, a private road (Fr.10 per car, pay at tourist office) accesses the wild **Gasterntal**; beware that the road is narrow and rocky, and runs on an alternate one-way system (into the valley between 30 and 50mins past each hour; out of the valley between the hour and 20 past). A private bus follows the road in good weather only (June–Sept 2–7 daily; Fr.20 return; reservations essential ☏033 671 11 71). Nobody comes down here apart from local hikers in the know, but this was formerly the main route by foot into the Valais: about an hour and a half's walk from the crossroads into the forgotten valley – the walls of which are laced with dramatically spouting waterfalls – you'll come to the hamlet of **SELDEN** (1535m) with a couple of inns, including cosy *Gasthaus Selden* (☏033 675 11 63; ❶). From here, a path cuts south four hours up to the **Lötschen Pass** (2690m), passing another inn, the *Gfelalp* (☏033 675 11 61; ❶), on the ascent. From the basic *Lötschenpasshütte* (☏027 939 19 81, ⓦwww.loetschenpass.ch; Fr.24; June–Sept) on the summit, three more paths lead down to the villages of the Lötschental on the other side (see p.357). A little east of Selden, the Gasterntal is blocked by the huge Kanderfirn glacier. Check with the Kandersteg tourist office before embarking on exploration in these remote areas.

Gstaad

GSTAAD – twinned expertly with Cannes – is an odd place. You'd think, from the high profile of its name, that it would be some kind of glittering Geneva-in-the-Alps, a fantastically expensive mountain paradise. Yet although its instant name-recognition may effortlessly attract Europe's royal households, celebrities galore and countless lesser hangers-on, Gstaad is in fact just a one-street village, a rather charming, attractively located place full of restored

Gstaad events

Gstaad hosts two of Switzerland's most glittering events, in two very different fields. Early July sees the world's sporting media and celebs galore descend on the village for the **Swiss Open** tennis tournament (ⓦwww.swissopengstaad.com), a principal fixture on the international ATP tour drawing the best players in the world. **Tickets** cost Fr.80 for the final, Fr.150 for the finals weekend, or Fr.450 for all nine days.

The **Menuhin Festival** (ⓦwww.menuhinfestivalgstaad.com) runs from mid-July until early September. Founded by the famous violinist Yehudi Menuhin to serve as a showcase for young talent, it has developed into a cycle of major classical concerts – with stellar performers – staged at a variety of locations, principally the church at Saanen, but also at venues in Gstaad and the nearby villages of Lauenen, Zweisimmen and Gsteig. Individual tickets (Fr.25–130) and various passes are available.

Lesser events, both still with enough pulling power to book the area out, are the Polo Silver Cup in mid-August, and an international country music weekend in mid-September.

weathered-wood chalets – even if there is an overabundance of jewellery shops and furriers. Its high-roller status makes it a village like no other: if you fancy being snubbed by the world's richest people, come here for Christmas week, scene of a heady round of sparkling soirées and lavish banquet-style dinner parties all but barred to ordinary mortals.

Glossy magazines may advertise the town as some kind of winter wonderland, but St Moritz steals its luxury-class thunder on this score: Gstaad is really more of a place to spend the odd ten grand renting a hillside chalet and sipping champagne around town than it is somewhere you can get stuck into any serious skiing. Where the area really enters into its own, prosaically enough, is as a centre from which to **hike** the surrounding Saanenland during the summer months.

Gstaad's main pedestrian-only street, running north–south through the village, is dubbed **Promenade** – no more than five minutes' walk end to end. Focus of the village centre is an open area just at the point cars are barred, which in July is the location for the highly prestigious **Swiss Open** tennis tournament, and which becomes an ice rink all winter.

Practicalities

Gstaad is on the MOB narrow-gauge "Golden Pass" **train** line (see p.164) between Montreux and Zweisimmen; approaching from Bern or Interlaken, you must change trains in Spiez and again in Zweisimmen. Arriving by car, a turning from **Saanen** – the village on the main Simmental road some 45km west of Spiez – heads south for 3km to Gstaad. Cars are diverted away from Gstaad centre, although if you head straight on at the first roundabout – where you can see the main street stretching out ahead of you – just before the barrier is a covered parking garage; otherwise, turn right at that roundabout and head through the Gstaad Tunnel west of the centre for more parking.

The tiny **train station** is just off the main Promenade. Some 100m further south on Promenade, after the railway bridge, is the **tourist office** (July, Aug & Dec–March Mon–Fri 8am–6.30pm, Sat 9am–6pm, Sun 11am–3pm; rest of year Mon–Fri 8am–noon & 1.30–6pm, Sat 9am–noon; ☎033 748 81 81, ⓦwww.gstaad.ch). Staff need no prompting to come up with ideas for excursions and are well tuned to the requirements of customer service, doing everything for you save leading you by the hand out to the trailhead.

Accommodation

As you might expect, the sky's the limit if you choose to **stay** in Gstaad. However, it's not impossible to find inexpensive accommodation, either in the village or nearby. The *Bellerive* **campsite** is 1km north of Gstaad (☎033 744 63 30, ⓕ033 744 63 45), well equipped but a tad pricey. *Beim Kappeli*, a more spartan campsite, is just south of Saanen on the outskirts of Gstaad (☎033 744 61 91, ⓕ033 744 60 42; closed early May), while ten minutes' walk northwest of Saanen is a comfortable, rustic HI **hostel** *Jugendherberge* in the old-style Chalet Rüblihorn (☎033 744 13 43, ⓦwww.youthhostel.ch; ❶; closed Nov), with quality dorms from Fr.31 and bike rental.

Saanen and neighbouring villages also have the least expensive **hotels**, including the *Bahnhof* in Saanenmöser (☎033 744 15 06; ❸), 3km east of Saanen. Within Gstaad, *Posthotel Rössli* is a cosy lower-end choice (☎033 748 42 42, ⓦwww.posthotelroessli.ch; ❹), the oldest hotel in the village with renovated pine-decor rooms, while *Olden* (☎033 744 34 44, ⓦwww.hotelolden .com; ❻–❼) is a fresher and slicker choice but still with plenty of

Sports and activities around Gstaad

There's plenty of **hiking** in the four main valleys surrounding Gstaad. A cable-car, and trails, run up to the nearby **Eggli** (1557m), favoured excursion from the village, with plenty of paths from there across the plateau, and a long high-level route winding past the tranquil Arnensee and down to **Feutersoey**, some 9km further up the Saane. On the opposite, eastern side of Gstaad looms the **Wispile** (1911m), also served by a cable-car, with trails of about two and a half hours leading back to Gstaad. It's equally easy to head due east from the village along the **Turbach** valley, through a hamlet or two on the banks of the stream, and then keep heading straight over the low pass at Reulissen to the busy resorts of **Lenk** or **St Stephan**, both on the Simme some 12km east (4hr 30min total) and linked to Zweisimmen by train.

Swissraft (☎033 744 50 80, ⓦwww.swissraft.ch) offers mountain-bike rental (Fr.39/day) and a host of **adventure activities**, including rafting (Fr.140) and canyoning (Fr.90). Alpinzentrum (☎033 744 60 01, ⓦwww.gstaad.ch/alpinzentrum) do many of the same things, throwing in extreme winter sports as well.

The **skiing**, however, might be a disappointment. None of the lifts around the village rises above 2200m, which means that even snow cover is unreliable, although some lifts within feasible reach beyond Gsteig do serve the Diablerets Glacier 3000 (see p.331), at just under 3000m. Roughly half the pistes in the whole area are rated blue or easy red. There's a complicated system of **lift passes**, covering six very wide spread sectors. A one-day pass costs Fr.51 for sector 1 (Zweisimmen, St Stephan, Saanenmöser); Fr.48 for sector 2 (Gstaad, Saanen, Rougemont); Fr.36 for sector 3 (Château d'Oex); Fr.52 for sector 4 (Diablerets, including the glacier); Fr.26 for sector 5 (Gsteig); and Fr.36 for sector 6 (Lauenen). Two- and four-hour passes are available. For longer periods, you must buy an all-inclusive Top-Card for the whole region, which costs Fr.97/251 for two/six days, or Fr.890 for the season (Fr.757 if you buy before mid-Oct).

atmosphere. Steps from the station is the *Bernerhof* (☎033 748 88 44, ⓦwww.bernerhof-gstaad.ch; ❺–❼), a huge place with generous rooms and an indoor pool. Towering over the village and visible from all points is the fantasy *Palace Hotel* (☎033 748 50 00, ⓦwww.palace.ch; ❾), laughingly calling itself a "family pension" as it asks Fr.1000 for a double room in the ski season (and over half that in the summer) – but then again, with underwater music in the pool, giant rooms and lavish dinners on the south-facing terrace, they know their clientele well.

Eating and drinking

Eating and drinking is least expensive at the *Co-op* self-service restaurant near the station. Otherwise, you can check out where the champagne set are gathering in any of half-a-dozen terrace cafés and restaurants along Promenade. *Charly's* is perhaps the most famous, followed by *Rialto* and *Pernet* facing each other near the chapel. The restaurant in *Posthotel Rössli* has good, plain Swiss meals without the fuss (*menus* Fr.22 or so), while *Sporthotel Rütti*, ten minutes' walk south of town, is acclaimed for its tasty Swiss and Italian-ish cooking, from Fr.15. At the other end of the scale, *Chesery* (☎033 744 24 51, ⓦwww.chesery.ch) is the place to see and be seen, a lively late-night gourmet eatery and piano-bar, with the prices as high as the stilettos: not less than Fr.150 for dinner.

The Pays d'Enhaut

Barely 3km west of Saanen you cross the border from Canton Bern into Canton Vaud, and with it the linguistic *Röstigraben*: not 1km further on is the francophone resort of **Rougemont**, a charming little place full of character that is, so far, reasonably successfully fending off the encroachment of Gstaad's high rollers. This area is known as the **PAYS D'ENHAUT**, or Highlands, a sliver of mountain territory originally owned by Gruyères, then seized by Bern, before forming part of the new Vaudois territory after the 1798 revolution. The main valley, with its succession of broad, enclosed side valleys set amidst gentle peaks carpeted by lush summer pasture, is separated from Vaud's better-known resorts such as Leysin and Les Diablerets by the Col des Mosses pass (1445m) further south. West of Rougemont is the largest town of the region, **Château d'Oex**, best known as a centre for hot-air ballooning.

The MOB narrow-gauge **train** line runs along the valley floor from Gstaad through Château d'Oex, shortly afterwards winding its way down alongside the Dent de Jaman to Montreux (see p.157). A branch line from **Montbovon**, some 11km west of Château d'Oex, runs north to Gruyères (see p.139).

Rougemont

About 7km west of Gstaad, **ROUGEMONT** is an attractive, historic village full of the traditional broad-eaved wooden chalets that characterize the region. Its late eleventh-century Romanesque church is especially picturesque, as is the sixteenth-century château behind, although the latter is privately owned. It's a quiet and attractive place to base yourself for hiking or skiing; the village (Ⓦ www.rougemont.ch) is included in the Gstaad ski pass and, as well as hosting its own blue and red runs, it's only a short train ride from access to the pistes above Gstaad. Amidst the village's handful of simple **hotels**, *Valrose* (Ⓣ 026 925 81 46, Ⓦ www.valrose.ch; ❷) is a cosy and friendly little place with appealingly home-cooked meals, while the *Hôtel de Commune* (Ⓣ 026 925 81 42, Ⓕ 026 925 86 58; ❷) on the main street is only slightly more generic. The **Videmanette cable-car** (Ⓦ www.videmanette.ch) runs from the village up to a trailhead for high-country walks at 2186m, where you'll find a restaurant and, round the corner, a mountain inn with dorms (Ⓣ 026 924 64 65; Fr.27). The pleasant and very scenic stroll along the valley floor from Rougemont to Saanen takes about an hour and a half.

Château d'Oex

A family ski and sports resort located where the road from the Col des Mosses joins the valley, **CHÂTEAU D'OEX** (pronounced *day*) doesn't have a great deal to offer, although it is nonetheless spectacularly sited. The wide, sloping valley bowl in which it sits generates exactly the right kinds of thermal air currents for perfect **hot-air ballooning**, and the town is acclaimed as one of the world centres for the sport. When Bertrand Piccard, from Lausanne, and the Briton Brian Jones made their record-breaking 45,000km round-the-world balloon flight in 1999, the takeoff point, and nerve centre of the whole operation, was Château d'Oex. Every January, the town hosts perhaps the most beautiful sports event in the Swiss calendar, the annual **Hot-Air Ballooning Week**, when eighty or more colourful giants catch the thermals to float peaceably over the hills and valleys round about. For speedier thrills, the town and its slopes are linked in to the Gstaad ski pass (see p.319): as well as easy and intermediate pistes all around the town, there are a few testing runs down from the La Braye cable-car, spanning the valley up to a height of 1630m.

The **station** is in the centre, right opposite the cable-car station. About 100m west is the **tourist office** (Mon–Fri 8am–noon & 2–6pm, Sat 9am–noon & 2–5pm; ☎026 924 25 25, Ⓦwww.chateau-doex.ch). They can set you up with a balloon flight, or you should contact Swissraft in Gstaad (☎033 744 50 80, Ⓦwww.swissraft.ch), who charge around Fr.360 for an hour's silent floating. Château d'Oex is also one of the few places where you can try skijoring – being towed on skis behind a horse (Fr.50/hr).

Of the **hotels**, the *Buffet de la Gare* beside the station (☎026 924 77 17, Ⓕ026 924 79 52; ❶), as well as offering casual, uncomplicated meals in its café and **restaurant**, has a few shared-bath rooms. *La Printanière*, right beside the Catholic church (☎ & Ⓕ026 924 61 13; ❶), is an old characterful house, with plain shared-bath rooms that are kept spotlessly clean. About 1km further west, set in its own grounds, is the *Bon Acceuil* (☎026 924 63 20, Ⓦwww.lebonacceuil.ch; ❸–❹), bargain of the region, a small, charming hotel in a restored eighteenth-century light-wood chalet overlooking the valley; attention to detail – and spectacularly good, lightly prepared cuisine in the atmospheric restaurant – mark it out as extra special. There's a **campsite**, *Au Berceau* (☎026 924 62 34), on the riverside a ten-minute walk west of town, and an HI **hostel** *Auberge de Jeunesse* a few minutes' walk downhill from the centre (☎026 924 64 04, Ⓦwww.youthhostel.ch; ❶; closed Nov & Dec), with dorms from Fr.27 and bikes for rent.

Travel details

Trains

Brienz to: Interlaken Ost (hourly; 15min); Luzern (hourly; 1hr 15min); Meiringen (hourly; 10min).
Château d'Oex to: Gstaad (hourly; 20min); Interlaken West & Ost (hourly; 2hr 15min; change at Zweisimmen & Spiez); Montreux (hourly; 1hr).
Grindelwald to: Interlaken Ost (hourly; 20min); Jungfraujoch (every 30min; 1hr 30min; change at Kleine Scheidegg).
Gstaad to: Château d'Oex (hourly; 20min); Interlaken West & Ost (hourly; 1hr 50min; change at Zweisimmen & Spiez); Montreux (hourly; 1hr 20min).
Interlaken Ost to: Bern (hourly; 50min); Brienz (hourly; 15min); Grindelwald (hourly; 40min); Gstaad (hourly; 1hr 50min; change at Spiez & Zweisimmen); Jungfraujoch (at least hourly; 2hr 30min; change at Grindelwald or Lauterbrunnen, and Kleine Scheidegg); Lauterbrunnen (hourly; 20min); Luzern (hourly; 1hr 55min); Meiringen (hourly; 30min); Thun (hourly; 30min); Wilderswil (at least hourly; hourly); Zürich (hourly; 2hr 15min).
Interlaken West to: Bern (hourly; 45min); Gstaad (hourly; 1hr 45min; change at Spiez & Zweisimmen); Thun (hourly; 25min); Zürich (hourly; 2hr 10min).

Kandersteg to: Bern (hourly; 1hr 5min); Brig (hourly; 35min); Interlaken West & Ost (hourly; 50min; change at Spiez); Thun (hourly; 40min).
Lauterbrunnen to: Interlaken Ost (hourly; 20min); Jungfraujoch (every 20min; 1hr 35min; change at Kleine Scheidegg); Mürren (every 15min; 30min); Wengen (every 20min; 15min).
Meiringen to: Brienz (hourly; 10min); Interlaken Ost (hourly; 30min); Luzern (hourly; 1hr 25min).
Mürren to: Lauterbrunnen (every 15min; 30min).
Thun to: Bern (twice hourly; 20min); Interlaken West & Ost (hourly; 25min); Spiez (3 hourly; 10min).
Wengen to: Jungfraujoch (every 30min; 1hr 20min); Lauterbrunnen (every 20min; 15min).

Buses

Château d'Oex to: Leysin (3 daily; 1hr 30min; change at Le Sépey).
Grindelwald to: Meiringen (June–Oct hourly; 1hr 35min; change at Schwarzwaldalp).
Gstaad to: Les Diablerets (5 daily; 50min).
Interlaken Ost & West to: Beatushöhlen (hourly; 25min).
Lauterbrunnen to: Stechelberg (hourly; 20min).

Meiringen to: Göschenen via Sustenpass (July–Sept 2 daily; 1hr 45min); Grindelwald (June–Oct hourly; 1hr 55min; change at Schwarzwaldalp).

Boats

(Following is a summary of June–Sept summer services; fewer boats run in other months, generally Sat & Sun only, if at all)

Brienz to: Interlaken Ost (hourly; 1hr 20min).
Interlaken Ost to: Brienz (hourly; 1hr 20min).
Interlaken West to: Beatushöhlen (6 daily; 30min); Spiez (hourly; 1hr 20min); Thun (hourly; 2hr 5min).
Thun to: Beatushöhlen (5 daily; 1hr 30min); Interlaken West (hourly; 2hr 5min); Oberhofen (hourly; 20min); Spiez (hourly; 45min).

Valais

7

VALAIS

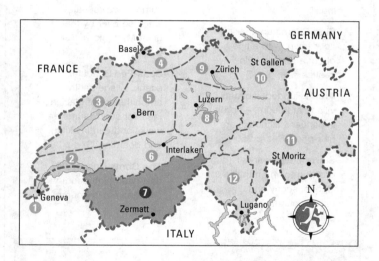

CHAPTER 7

Highlights

* **Fondation Pierre Gianadda, Martigny** Outstanding art and archeology museum in this little-visited cross-roads town. See p.337

* **Verbier** One of the Alps' top mountain resorts, offering marvellously scenic skiing and walking. See p.341

* **Sion** Characterful valley-floor town, with a fine old quarter and twin castles. See p.345

* **Arolla** Rugged, isolated village at 2000m, – and in January, all hotels are half-price. See p.350

* **Sierre** Lovely wine-growing town on the Rhône, sunny and unpretentious. See p.351

* **Crans-Montana** High-glitz resort, where shopping and skiing are both in the limelight. See p.353

* **Zermatt** Switzerland's most famous mountain resort offers a vast array of skiing and boarding, plus some outstanding summer walks – all watched over by the giant Matterhorn. See p.359

* **Saas-Fee** Beautifully scenic village set in an amphitheatre of glaciers, ideal for sunny summer walks and gentle skiing and boarding. See p.366

* **The Goms** Unsung, little-visited high country with fine cross-country skiing. See p.368

Valais

The Valais is not so much Mediterranean as Iberian in tone: east of Sion, the
cicada begins.

John Russell, *Switzerland* (1950)

The **VALAIS** (Wallis in German; Vallese in Italian) is Switzerland's third-
largest canton, a diverse swathe of country occupying the valley – hence
the name – of the River Rhône, from its source in the glaciers of the
central Alps all the way to its inflow to Lake Geneva. Fully twenty percent of the canton is covered by glaciers, and yet the region has the driest climate, with the lowest rainfall and the most sunshine, of the whole country. The
artificial irrigation system set in place by the valley dwellers in the Middle Ages
– a vast network of channels, called *bisses* in French and *Suonen* in Swiss-
German – still weaves a cat's cradle over the foothills of the high mountains,
supplemented these days by half-a-dozen of the tallest and highest-altitude
dams in the world. For the Swiss, the Valais somehow represents a piece of
common heritage all but lost elsewhere in the country: in the most unlikely
corners of Geneva and Zürich, you can find restaurants done up as traditional
Valaisian-style darkwood chalets, complete with window boxes full of geraniums and farm tools as decoration on the walls, serving up the local speciality
raclette (see p.51) under a nameboard "Chalet Valaisanne" or "Walliser Stube".
The dryness and sunshine of the valley are ideal vine-growing conditions, and
the canton's 22,000 vineyard owners are famous for producing some of the
finest **wine** in the country.

Cut off on all sides by mountains, the Valais has always been a world apart.
On a push to conquer the Celtic peoples of the valley in the first century BC,
a Roman army under **Julius Caesar** ventured the crossing of the Grand-St-
Bernard Pass from Italy and then spread out through the valley. They got as far
as modern-day Sierre, and left behind them a legacy of Latin – even today,
Sierre is the easternmost French-speaking town in the canton, while beyond it
the mother tongue is Swiss-German, descended from the language of the
Aleman tribes who remained unconquered. Indeed, once the Romans retreated, few outsiders had much success in challenging the peoples of the valley.
Christianity arrived before the fourth century, with the travel of clerics and
merchants over the Grand-St-Bernard pass, but the Reformation never made
it any further into the valley than Aigle, in neighbouring Canton Vaud, and
Valais remains majority Catholic to this day. Even the mighty **Bernese** army
was stopped by the mountains and the wildness of the terrain. At times of
severe hardship during the Middle Ages and later, however, many **Walsers** have
voluntarily chosen to depart, forced to leave their home villages and travel over
the mountains to seek a better life elsewhere. Walser communities survive in

places as far apart as Argentina and Liechtenstein, still nurturing their distinctive dialect and culture.

The Valais remained independent until 1815 when, following a brief period of French governorship, it joined the Swiss Confederation as a new canton. It's a mark of the social changes taking place over recent years that German speakers in the east of the canton are now starting to worry about the encroachment of French up the valley: with the economic power and prestige of the French-speaking lower valley, German speakers are increasingly finding employment in francophone areas, while francophone firms are expanding their bases of operation into German-speaking communities. Locals in Brig in particular shake their head at the quantity of French now being heard in the town, but there seems little they can do about it.

The Valais is still a wild and little-known place outside the trio of famous resorts bred by the mountains: **Zermatt**, **Verbier** and **Crans–Montana**. Few outsiders bother to penetrate the deep rural side valleys either side of the single road and rail line that run along the valley floor – though those who do make the effort find plenty of long-distance hiking and adventure sports of all kinds. The only town of any size is the cantonal capital **Sion**, with a low-key, easygoing atmosphere and a handful of sights. In the northernmost extremities of the region, an area of Vaud known as **Haut–Léman** occupies the east bank of the Rhône just before it flows into Lake Geneva and shares the mountainous scenery of Valais Romand.

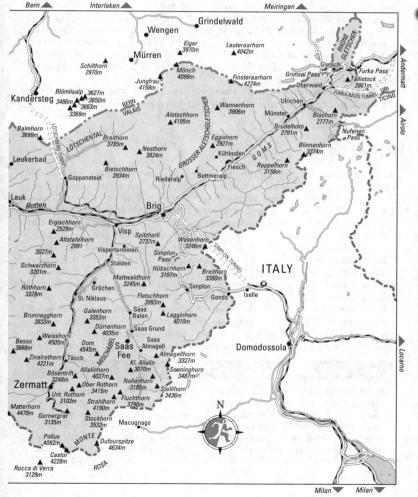

Haut-Léman

Before mainline trains heading south from Montreux enter Valais, they first pass through a diverse area of Canton Vaud known as **HAUT-LÉMAN**, extending southeast of Lake Geneva. South of Montreux lies the broad, flat Rhône valley, the river – which here marks the cantonal border between Vaud on the east bank and Valais on the west – meandering between the great craggy peaks of the Dents-du-Midi on one side, and the heights of Les Diablerets on the other. The valley floor and west-facing foothills make up the acclaimed wine region of **Chablais**, no less prestigious a producer than its lakeshore competitors of La Côte and Lavaux, and centred on the fine old town of **Aigle**, with its fairytale turreted castle surrounded by vineyards. Above Aigle rise the 3000m-plus peaks of the **Alpes Vaudoises**, centred on a handful of attractive, small-scale resorts such as **Villars** and **Les Diablerets** that offer excellent skiing and a cosy atmosphere well away from the clutter and bustle of the huge resorts of Verbier and Crans-Montana further south. The small Valaisian shore of Lake Geneva west of the Rhône, including the port of St-Gingolph and the funparks of Le Bouveret, is covered on p.156.

Note that the **Vaud Regional Pass** (see box p.117) is valid for transport in the whole of Haut-Léman, and also for journeys south to Martigny.

Aigle

Although the main valley highway south from Montreux bypasses **AIGLE**, this alluring little town is well worth the small detour for a lazy afternoon of castle exploration and wine tasting. Aigle is the main town of the Chablais wine region, and its prime landmark – the fantastical **Château d'Aigle**, a fifteenth-century folly with corner towers and witch's-hat turrets – is home to two excellent **museums** devoted to wine and wine production. Aigle's other claim to fame is five hundred years old: in 1476, the town was integrated into Canton Bern as the first French-speaking territory to join the Swiss Confederation. Shortly after, in 1526, newly converted Bernese Protestants sent Guillaume Farel to preach the Reformation in Aigle, the first time this had ever been done in a francophone region.

Along with its near-neighbour Yvorne, Aigle produces what are acclaimed as the best **wines** of the region, and some of the best in all Switzerland, the gravelly, clay-like soil nurturing especially good dustily elegant, fruity whites ("It's difficult to find a bad white Aigle," commented wine writer John C. Sloan). *Les*

Valais Tourism

Valais Tourism (☎027 327 35 70, ⓦ www.valaistourism.ch & ⓦ www.matterhornre-gion.com) have reams of material they can give you on travel and sights around the canton, both in the big resorts and the tucked-away corners, including an especially useful series of walking booklets entitled *Sentiers Valaisans/Walliser Wanderwege*, outlining long-distance routes throughout the canton in precise detail with maps and charts. They can also book a wide range of package deals and offers at resorts big and small. For information on Haut-Léman, contact the Vaud tourist office (see p.117)

Murailles, from the Badoux winery, is one of the very few Swiss wines to be marketed in North America; it and the *Crosex Grillé* Grand Cru are the two best names to ask for. Further south, the nearby towns of Bex and Ollon produce their own tangy, flowery whites, largely for local consumption only: *Philos* is probably the best of them.

Arrival, information and accommodation

Aigle's **train station**, with change facilities (daily 5.15am–10.10pm), is the focus of the Transports Publics du Chablais network (ⓦ www.tpc.ch): in addition to mainline CFF trains, it's served by AL (Aigle–Leysin) and ASD (Aigle–Sépey–Diablerets), which both climb into the adjacent hills, as well as AOMC (Aigle–Ollon–Monthey–Champéry), which crosses the Rhône. Just up the valley, the BVB line climbs from Bex to Villars and Bretaye.

The station lies west of the centre, at one end of the 300m-long Rue de la Gare; at the other end is the small **tourist office**, 5 Rue Colomb (Mon–Fri 8.30am–noon & 2–6pm, Sat 9am–noon; ☎024 466 30 00, ⓦ www .alp3000.ch). It lies just past turnings to the pedestrianized café-street of **Rue de Bourg** and, parallel to it, the remarkable little cobbled alley **Rue de Jérusalem**, the upper floors of its old wooden houses spanning the street in a style which reminded one nineteenth-century observer of the shaded residential quarters of Middle Eastern cities. From the central Place du Marché, Avenue du Cloître leads southeast towards the château.

Aigle has only a couple of central **hotels**: *Les Messageries*, 19 Rue du Midi (☎024 466 20 60, ℗024 466 62 58; ❷), offers the simplest of comforts, with a choice of ensuite and shared-bath rooms; *Hôtel du Nord*, 2 Rue Colomb (☎024 468 10 55, ⓦ www.hoteldunord.ch; ❷–❸), is more upmarket. You can **camp** at *Les Glariers* (☎024 466 26 60; April–Sept), about 1km west of town.

Château d'Aigle

Barely ten minutes' walk southeast of the town centre loom the turrets of **Château d'Aigle**. Ranged beneath is an attractive little quarter of old houses, among which lies the ancient Église St-Maurice or Église du Cloître, founded in 1143 and renovated over the centuries in a mixture of styles.

Atmospheric cobbled lanes wind up from here to the **château** (July & Aug daily 10am–6pm; April–June, Sept & Oct Tues–Sun 10am–12.30pm & 2–6pm; last entry 1hr before closing; ⓦ www.chateauaigle.ch). The main castle building houses the Musée de la Vigne et du Vin (Vine and Wine; Fr.7; SMP); opposite the gates, in the stout **Maison de la Dîme**, is the Musée de l'Étiquette (Wine-Labels; Fr.4; SMP). A combined entry ticket for both museums is Fr.9.

The château is an impressive example of medieval castle building, founded and expanded by the advancing Savoyards in the thirteenth century. The Bernese burnt the place to the ground in 1475, rebuilding and redesigning it to serve both a defensive function on the fringes of Bernese power and as a residence for the installed bailiffs. Following the Vaudois revolution of 1798, the castle reverted to local hands, and remained the town's prison right up until 1972, when nobody could be found to take on the job of jailer and so all the resident convicts had to be transferred to Vevey. As you enter, you're given a follow-the-numbers pamphlet, which leads you through the various rooms around the courtyard that house the permanent and temporary exhibits of the **Musée de la Vigne et du Vin**. Look out for the old shop signs in the vestibule of the main dwelling (room 9) and the mighty barrels and winepress in the cellar below (room 10). The ramparts walk is especially spectacular, with

The salt mines of Bex

Some 9km south of Aigle and connected by hourly train is the small town of **BEX** (pronounced *bay*), unremarkable but for the fact that it sits beside the only working **salt mine** in Switzerland, named Le Bouillet. All through the Middle Ages Switzerland had to rely on importing salt, mainly from Franche-Comté – an expensive business, not least because of the transportation costs. Then, in the fifteenth century, legend has it that a shepherd pasturing his flocks above Bex noticed that the animals preferred drinking from two particular springs. Tasting the water himself, he discovered that it was salty and this led to further investigation, principally by the Bernese authorities, who began to mine the hills around Bex. The mines have been worked ever since, and today a labyrinthine network of galleries burrows for some 50km beneath the mountains, still producing salt for domestic consumption.

You can visit some portions of the mines on **guided tours** (April–Oct Tues–Sun 9.45am, 11.15am, 2.15pm & 3.45pm; June–Aug also Mon same hours; Fr.18; reservations essential on ☎024 463 03 30, ⓦwww.mines.ch). Tours (available in English) last for almost two hours, beginning with an audiovisual show and including a long underground narrow-gauge train ride and plenty of subterranean walking. There's no public transport to the mine entrance. Irregular **buses** run from Bex station to the village of Les Dévens, twenty minutes' walk away, or you can walk from Bex itself in about 45 minutes.

frescoes in the various watchtowers and romantic views out over the sea of vines all around. The **Musée de l'Étiquette** opposite the castle gates is, by necessity, a rather sedate affair, with the generally very ornate labels from bottles around the world displayed on placards in a grand, wood-beamed attic.

Eating and drinking

Rue de Bourg is lined with pleasant **restaurants** – check out popular *La Croix Blanche*, serving reasonably priced pizzas and simple *menus* (Fr.15), and *Le Mediéval*, a slightly more upmarket establishment on the same street; *Des Alpes* at no. 29 (closed Wed) serves a good range of salads and pizzas, and has an outdoor terrace. A shady unnamed courtyard-café at the southern end of Rue de Jérusalem offers an array of fresh salads along with seven kinds of *Rösti* (Fr.15–20). The streets around the château offer plenty of places to buy and sample **wine**, but most atmospheric of all is the *Pinte du Paradis* within the Maison de la Dîme (Tues, Wed & Sun 10am–6pm, Thurs–Sat 10am–11pm).

The Alpes Vaudoises

The huge peaks east of Aigle and the Rhône Valley are collectively dubbed the **Alpes Vaudoises**, sheltering a few attractive, quite isolated little ski villages – all specifically family-oriented – that offer some of the best facilities outside the huge Valaisian resorts further south. Friendly **Villars** leads the bunch, connected by a system of lifts both with its neighbour, Gryon, and with the separate resort of **Les Diablerets**, which is linked to Gstaad's lift pass and is subtitled "Glacier 3000" for its access to year-round glacier skiing and boarding above 3000m. Tiny **Leysin**, tucked away in a valley above Aigle, completes the picture. In summer, all these villages slumber quietly in the sunshine, hosting walkers and those seeking the kind of undisturbed Alpine retreat money can't buy. **Transport** between all three is sporadic; they serve better as places to base yourself for a few days or a couple of weeks rather than as stepping stones around the region.

Villars–Gryon

The neat, unpretentious little resort of **VILLARS** is linked to Bex, down in the valley, by a quaint Edwardian train on the BVB line, and to Aigle by a rather less romantic postbus. It wins no awards for grace or stylishness, but where it does score (and where it *has* won awards) is for its family-oriented service. Winter after winter Villars, and its neighbouring community of **GRYON**, 4km away on the train line, attract scores of families on skiing breaks, while still remaining virtually unknown to a wider clientele. The skiing around the town is pretty good (see box), with the added bonuses of direct lift linkage to the Diablerets sector for glacier pistes up to 3000m. Multi-day lift passes are also valid in the Gstaad ski region (see p.319), a bus ride away.

Villars' **station** is in the heart of the village; 50m to the right on the main Avenue Central is the **tourist office** (Feb, July, Aug & around Christmas daily 8am–7pm; Jan, March & April daily 8am–noon & 1.30–6pm; rest of year Mon–Sat 8am–noon & 1.30–6pm, Sun 10am–4pm; ☎024 495 32 32,

---

Winter sports in the Alpes Vaudoises

The **skiing** in the neighbouring areas of Villars-Gryon, Les Diablerets and Leysin is generally good. **Diablerets** village has close access to the Col de Pillon gondola serving the "Glacier 3000" (ⓦwww.glacier3000.ch), which slides down from the peaks of Scex Rouge (2970m) and Les Diablerets itself (3209m). Most of the pistes up here are blue and red, even way on top around the Quille du Diable – a jutting natural obelisk up at 3000m. A single hair-raising black run plunges beneath the gondola from **Pierres-Pointes** (2217m) down to the Col du Pillon. From Diablerets village, another gondola serves the slopes of **Isenau** to the north, laced with blue and red runs, while a third rises to **Meilleret**, in the direction of Villars. Les Diablerets also prides itself on its **summer skiing**, with good snow assured even in June and July on the glacier.

From **Villars** village, a gondola rises to the **Roc d'Orsay** (2000m), from where a long blue run delivers you to the hub of the skiing at **Bretaye**, set in a broad bowl and also served by a rack railway from Villars centre. Gentle red pistes abound, and from **Barboleuse** a gondola heads up to Les Chaux (1750m), offering a long and rewarding blue run, as well as a red or two and a long steep black down to Sodoleuvre. It's also easy to work your way over to Les Diablerets (see p.332) – although beware that if the snow at Villars and especially Gstaad isn't that great, everybody heads up to the glacier, which can sometimes make things a bit over-crowded. From **Leysin** village, lifts and gondolas serve a host of red and blue pistes, as well as a half-pipe for snowboarders below the peak of **La Berneuse** (2048m), where there's a panoramic revolving restaurant.

Lift passes are good value, with discounted morning or afternoon tickets also available. For one full day, Diablerets alone (excluding the glacier) is Fr.39, the same plus Villars-Gryon is Fr.46, while Leysin is Fr.42. Otherwise, you must get an all-inclusive Alpes Vaudoises pass, which takes in all the above plus the Glacier 3000, Les Mosses and sectors of the Gstaad ski region (see p.319); this costs Fr.52/246 for one/six days, or Fr.890 for the season.

Adventure sports are a mainstay of all three resorts. Mountain Evasion (ⓦwww.mountain-evasion.com) and Centre Par Adventure (ⓦwww.swissaventure .ch) are two companies in Les Diablerets organizing canyoning, zorbing, luge, mud biking, rappelling and more.

@ www.villars.ch). For **accommodation**, the large *Sunstar Hotel Elite* (☎024 496 39 00, @ www.sunstar.ch; ❹) is located right beside the Roc d'Orsay gondola. *Alpe Fleurie* (☎024 495 34 64, ℻024 496 30 77; ❸–❹) and *Ecureuil* (☎024 496 37 37, @ www.hotel-ecureuil.ch; ❸–❹) are old-style chalet-hotels with a long history of catering to families, both conveniently central. A low-end option is the charming *Chalet Martin* **hostel** five minutes' walk above Gryon station (☎024 498 33 21, @ www.gryon.com; ❶; no credit cards), a cosy, friendly place run by a Swiss-Australian couple, with dorm space for around Fr.20. *Le Vieux-Villars*, on the Route des Hôtels, is a three-storey **restaurant** known for its fondues and raclettes.

Les Diablerets

Snoozing quietly in its peaceful backwater valley, **LES DIABLERETS** really deserves to be left well alone. It's so tranquil that it's almost a shame to mark it on a map – indeed, less than a century ago, it wasn't on any maps, and it was only with the arrival of the railway in 1914 that outsiders noticed the place. These days Les Diablerets has a small but loyal band of guests, who return each year to enjoy the valley's charm.

Regular ASD **trains** run to Les Diablerets from Aigle; **buses** also connect the village with Gstaad via a dramatically steep road which winds over the Col du Pillon (1546m), 4km east of Les Diablerets. The tiny switchback road over the Col de la Croix (1778m), 4km south of Les Diablerets, leads to Villars; three buses a day (July–Sept only) shuttle between the two resorts.

The **station** is beside the river, about 100m north of the **tourist office** (July, Aug & Dec–April daily 8.30am–6.30pm; rest of year Mon–Sat 8.30am–12.30pm & 2.30–6pm, Sun 9am–12.30pm; ☎024 492 33 58, @ www.diablerets.ch). Every September, Les Diablerets hosts the International Alpine Film Festival (@ www.fifad.ch).

Most accommodation is in chalets, but of the **hotels**, the *Auberge de la Poste* (☎024 492 31 24, ℻024 492 12 68; ❷), a 200-year-old inn that claims to have

The devils of Les Diablerets

The mountain communities of the Alpes Vaudoises are replete with legends and **folk tales**, and Les Diablerets – its name meaning "abode of devils" – is no exception. To the south and east of the village rise the heights of Les Diablerets themselves, with their two huge glaciers, Diablerets and **Tsanfleuron**. Legend has it that in ancient times the latter ("Field of Flowers" in the local dialect) was a beautiful sunny meadow until the arrival, long ago, of demons and devils in the mountains. Soon after, the shepherds of Tsanfleuron and the Ormont Valley began to be troubled by boulders bouncing down from on high, as the devils played their games of skill, trying to hit a huge tower of rock – the **Quille du Diable** (Devil's Skittle) – sticking up from the heights of the mountain. The shepherds, fearing for the safety of their flocks and themselves, moved away from the area, which lost its vitality and beauty and turned into the icy wasteland it remains today.

Other tales abound of **lost souls** seen at night, drifting with lanterns alone or in groups through the woods, pastures and rocky defiles of the mountain; local people attested to seeing their lantern lights and hearing their moans just before the two terrible landslides of 1714 and 1740. The meadows and hills all around are also said to be inhabited by elves, goblins and a local brand of **imp** named a *servan*, one of whom, it is said, once mischievously turned himself into a fox and was seen sitting at night in a hay loft knitting with the hair of his own tail.

hosted Victor Hugo, Stravinsky and Lenin in years gone by, is pleasantly rustic. A little out of town on the Route de Pillon is *Les Diablotins* (☎024 492 36 33, ⓦwww.diablotins.ch; ❶), a more basic choice with shared-bath rooms. A comfortable place north of the station is the "garni" *Le Chamois* (☎024 492 02 02, ⓦwww.hotelchamois.ch; ❸). There are two mountain inns with **dorms** above the village – one at Isenau (☎ & Ⓕ024 492 32 93; Fr.36; closed May & Nov), and the other, the *Cabane des Diablerets* (☎024 492 21 02; Fr.31; mid-June to mid-Sept), overlooking the glacier at 2525m. **Eating** is mainly a hotel option, with the inexpensive restaurants at the *Auberge de la Poste* and *Hotel Les Lilas* worth checking out.

Leysin

The road from Aigle up into the mountains divides at Le Sépey: Les Diablerets is east, the Col des Mosses leading to Château d'Oex is north, while buses follow a tiny winding road west to the beautifully located little village of **LEYSIN**, once a high-altitude centre for the treatment of respiratory diseases, but now metamorphosed into a popular and well-maintained ski resort. For **accommodation**, the warmest welcome can be found at the excellent SB hostel *Hiking Sheep*, in the Villa La Joux (☎024 494 35 35, ⓦwww.leysin.net/hikingsheep; ❶), which has some twin rooms and space in small dorms (Fr.27). Satellite TV, a large cosy lounge, dining rooms with log fires, kitchen use, balconies with perfect views and switched-on multilingual staff add to the attraction (as do reductions for long stays). Two comfortable hotels are the *Orchidées* (☎024 494 14 21, ⓦwww.leysin.ch/orchidees; ❷) and the *Mont-Riant* (☎024 494 27 01, ⓦwww.niquille.ch/montriant; ❷–❸).

Valais Romand

Tacked seamlessly south of Haut-Léman, **VALAIS ROMAND**, or the French-speaking part of Valais, comprises the westernmost portions of the canton. Occupying the broad Rhône valley floor and the most accessible foothills just above, it's more populated and livelier than the wilder German-speaking east. Mountain passes aside, the road and train line from Montreux is the sole route in and out: the mountains flanking the Rhône are cut through with a handful of dead-end valleys, wonderful for long-distance hiking, but only the high pass roads over the **Grand-St-Bernard** to Aosta (Italy) and the Col de la Forclaz to Chamonix (France) give access from outside. These two roads join the valley at **Martigny**, a rather unprepossessing place much overshadowed in both style and appeal by its near neighbours, the cantonal capital **Sion** and, on the French–German language border, **Sierre**. The vapid resort towns of **Verbier** near Martigny, and **Crans-Montana** above Sierre, are two of the best-known ski resorts in the world, offering the combination of groomed pistes and chic après-ski that Switzerland is famous for.

South to Martigny

Roads and train tracks cross the broad Rhône at Aigle and Bex to a slice of Valais to the west holding the small resort of **Champéry**, where you can ski the vast **Portes du Soleil** region, straddling the French border. Main roads head on south towards Martigny, crossing the Vaud–Valais frontier at the ancient town of **St-Maurice**.

The Portes du Soleil

Spreading across a mountainous region west of the Rhône valley, in the shadow of the Dents du Midi range, is the huge **Portes du Soleil** ski area (Ⓦwww.portesdusoleil.com), comprising twelve linked Swiss and French resorts. It's a very popular ski destination, but, in truth, is too low to have consistently good snow cover: its top height is only around 2400m and, if snow is poor lower down, the bottlenecks to reach higher pistes can be terrible. On the French side, the key resort – with some superb facilities for snowboarders and the notorious "Wall" black run – is **Avoriaz**, an ugly collection of 1960s apartment blocks on a cliffside above overcrowded **Morzine**.

On the Swiss side, access is via a couple of small, relatively characterful villages. From the gateway town of **Monthey**, just across from Bex, roads and a train line from Aigle penetrate the narrow, steep Val d'Illiez to **CHAMPÉRY**, an attractive Alpine tourist resort that's been in business since the 1850s and boasts large-capacity cable-cars up to Croix de Culet. A tourist office (daily 8am–noon & 2–6pm; ☎024 479 20 20, Ⓦwww.champery.ch) has information on the whole area. The old *Hôtel Suisse* is now owned by Golden Tulip (☎024 479 07 07, Ⓦwww.goldentulip.ch; ❹), but retains much of its old-fashioned character; *Pension Souvenir* (☎024 479 13 40, Ⓕ024 479 23 35; ❶) is a good downmarket option. An alternative route from Monthey branches off to the less appealing base of **Morgins**, right on the border. A lift pass for the whole Portes du Soleil costs Fr.51/246 for one/six days, or Fr.39 for a day on the CLCF sector around Champéry only.

St-Maurice

About 3km south of Bex, at the point where the narrowing of the Rhône prompted the Romans to build a bridge, is **ST-MAURICE**, named after the warrior-saint Maurice who is purported to have been martyred nearby. Maurice was ordered in 287 AD by Emperor Maximian to serve against his fellow Christians on campaigns in Gaul, but refused, according to a later chronicler with the words: "We are your soldiers, O Emperor, but we freely acknowledge that we are also the servants of God… To you is due military obedience, but to God, justice… We cannot take up arms to strike pious men." The Emperor duly had the whole legion slaughtered. Today, of course, mighty Maximian is forgotten, while there are apparently 4 cathedrals, 598 churches and 74 towns around the world named after Maurice, not counting two entire countries (Mauritius and Mauritania).

A shrine grew up around the supposed tomb of the saint, hard up against a rocky cliff on the banks of the Rhône, as early as 390, replaced by a monastery in 515; this is still in existence as the oldest surviving abbey north of the Alps. Pilgrims have come to the **abbey church** for over 1500 years, bringing with them items of gold and silver as homage, and the church treasury holds some exquisitely beautiful pieces, including a Roman sardonyx vase, the intricate gold cloisonné Casket of Teuderic, an embossed silver bust of St Candidus and filigreed silver Arm of St Bernard, and other medieval golden caskets and reliquaries of the highest workmanship. Note that although the church is open at any time, you can only visit the treasury on **guided tours** (in English; Tues–Sun: July & Aug 10.30am, 2pm, 3.15pm & 4.30pm; Easter–June, Sept & Oct 10.30am, 3pm & 4.30pm; Nov–Easter 3pm; Fr.2; Ⓦwww.stmaurice.ch).

Heading straight ahead out of the **train station** along Avenue de la Gare will bring you after 100m to the **tourist office** (July & Aug Mon–Fri 9am–7pm, Sat 9am–5pm; Sept–June Mon 3–6pm, Tues–Fri 9am–noon & 3–6pm, Sat 9am–noon; Ⓣ024 485 40 40, Ⓦwww.st-maurice.ch). They run a walking tour of the town in English (April–Sept Tues–Sat 9.30am; Fr.8; 1hr 30min), which includes the church more or less opposite, and the ancient Grand-Rue running through the centre of town, bedecked with wrought-iron inn signs and home to the few **hotels** and eating options. *Hotel Ecu du Valais*, 39 Grand-Rue (Ⓣ & Ⓕ024 485 50 05; ❶), has been partly renovated, but also retains some older, more characterful rooms, while the small *Dent-du-Midi*, set in gardens at 1 Avenue du Simplon (Ⓣ024 485 12 09, Ⓦwww.isatis.ch/dentmidi.html; ❷), is comfortable and modern. For **eating**, the *Ecu du Valais* is known for its Valaisian specialities, while the best place for fondue is *La Croix Fédérale*, 45 Grand-Rue (closed Sun). *Manoir Rhodanien*, 84 Grand-Rue, has an eclectic menu taking in ostrich, barbecued kangaroo, crocodile steaks and more. There's a **campsite** at *Bois Noir* just south of town (Ⓣ027 767 11 76; April–Oct).

Martigny

There are few more dramatically sited cities in Switzerland than **MARTIGNY**. Set down on the broad valley floor, with wooded heights soaring on all sides, it's positioned at a natural crossroads. The Rhône, having flowed almost arrow straight along its valley for over 100km, suddenly makes a sharp right-angled turn at Martigny, heading off between the mountains to Lake Geneva; elevated points within the town give yawning views along both valleys, east and north. The major draw to the town is the **Fondation Pierre Gianadda**, one of the country's most prestigious art galleries. A handful of Roman ruins add a further smidgen of interest, and the small Old Town, or Bourg, makes for some attractive wandering, with cobbled lanes, old auberges and a villagey atmosphere.

And yet Martigny is a curiously unsatisfying place to spend more than an afternoon. It's not an unpleasant town, but there's just not much going on, and – even worse – not many characterful places to sit and watch life go by. Stay overnight and make the best of it, or cut your losses and look elsewhere: St-Maurice has held onto its history better than Martigny; atmospheric Sion is close by; or you might prefer to plump for a wilder night way up on the Grand-St-Bernard Pass. See p.31 for details of the **Mont Blanc Express** and **St Bernard Express** (Ⓦwww.momc.ch), two scenic Alpine train rides that begin from Martigny.

Arrival, information and accommodation

Martigny's **station**, with change facilities and bike rental, is at the northeastern end of Avenue de la Gare, which cuts a broad swathe through the centre. At the other end, 500m away, is the main Place Centrale, with the **tourist office** on

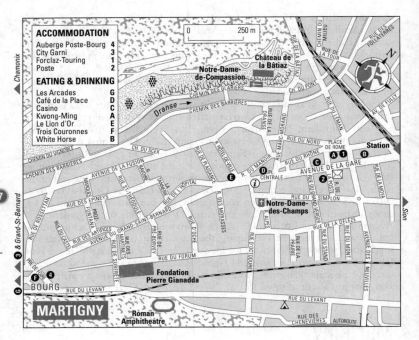

ACCOMMODATION
Auberge Poste-Bourg 4
City Garni 3
Forclaz-Touring 1
Poste 2

EATING & DRINKING
Les Arcades G
Café de la Place D
Casino C
Kwong-Ming A
Le Lion d'Or E
Trois Couronnes F
White Horse B

one side (July & Aug Mon–Fri 9am–6pm, Sat 9am–noon & 2–6pm, Sun 10am–noon & 4–6pm; rest of year Mon–Fri 9am–noon & 1.30–6pm, Sat 9am–noon; May, June, Sept & Oct also Sat 2–5pm; ☎027 721 22 20, ⓦwww.martignytourism.ch). They're well equipped with information and maps for the whole area, including the routes up to the Grand-St-Bernard Pass and Verbier, and the Val de Bagnes.

Aside from the **campsite** *Les Neuvilles*, 68 Route du Levant (☎027 722 45 44, ⓦwww.campings.ch; closed Jan), a quality place with dorms (Fr.20), there are a handful of town **hotels**, many unromantically planted on the busy Avenue du Grand-St-Bernard as sleepover motels to catch the traffic heading for the Alpine passes. Least expensive are the spartan shared-bath rooms of the old *Auberge Poste-Bourg*, 81 Avenue du Grand-St-Bernard (☎027 722 25 17; ❶). *City Garni*, 7 Place St-Michel (☎027 723 36 00, ⓕ027 723 36 01; ❶), is similarly priced, but modern and generic. The bland *Forclaz-Touring*, 15 Rue du Léman (☎027 722 27 01, ⓦwww.hotelforclaztouring.ch; ❷–❸), has comfortable ensuite rooms near the station, whereas the *Poste*, 8 Rue de la Poste (☎027 722 14 44, ⓕ027 722 04 45; ❷), is in the heart of town but could do with a good spring-clean.

The Town

Just behind Place Centrale and the tourist office is the **Église Notre-Dame-des-Champs**, completed in 1687, with magnificent carved doors but a modest interior. From Place Centrale, if you follow Rue Marc-Morand north, you'll come to an old covered wooden bridge over the Dranse river; this is an

1818 replacement of the 1350 original, and leads to a winding path climbing to the semi-ruined thirteenth-century **Château de la Bâtiaz**, its lofty round tower visible from all parts of the town, and especially dramatic when floodlit at night beside the meandering tail-lights of cars on the tortuous switchback road to Chamonix. The château is rarely open, but the views are worth the climb. Below the château is the small **Chapelle de Notre-Dame-de-Compassion**, built in the 1620s with a Rococo altar added more than a century later. Its most remarkable feature is a huge collection of ex-voto paintings dating back 200 years and more.

Fondation Pierre Gianadda

The main reason for coming to Martigny at all is to visit the galleries and museums of the **Fondation Pierre Gianadda** (daily: June–Nov 9am–7pm; rest of year 10am–6pm; Fr.14; SMP; ⓦwww.gianadda.ch), well signposted about 500m south of Place Centrale on a patch of parkland off Rue du Forum. Established in 1978 by a local philanthropist, Léonard Gianadda, and named after his brother, the complex takes in several areas within a single museum. Note that you can get various special deals on admission, such as a twenty-percent discount on your train fare to Martigny and museum entry if you book the two together at any Swiss train station.

The main focus is the changing series of top-flight art exhibitions staged in the **main gallery** area: recent major shows have included Chagall and

---

Valaisian cowfighting

The Valais is known for a host of peculiar local traditions, one of the oddest of which is **cowfighting**. Utterly unlike Spanish bullfighting – an altogether gorier spectacle – bloodless Valaisian cowfighting stems from village get-togethers to see whose cow was best suited to lead the herds up to the summer Alpine pastures. The cattle all come from the local Hérens breed – bright-eyed with short legs and powerful chests, and known for their aggressiveness – who would naturally pick fights with each other in the open meadows: in the beginnings, farmers merely corralled them together to see who would win the squabbles. These days, the contests have become rather more important: breeding means big money for the Valaisian cattle farmers, and the winner of the annual round of cowfighting championships can be assured both a head price in the tens of thousands of francs plus the prestigious title "Queen of the Herd".

Farmers feed up the most bullish of their cows on a special extra-rich diet to improve (or worsen) her temper, occasionally allowing her the odd bucket of wine as a tonic and coaching her in sparring contests amongst the herd. Come the day of battle, farmers tie a huge cowbell around their champion's neck, lead her into the "arena" (generally just a meadow), and introduce her to her opponent. Hérens cows rarely need any encouragement to provoke each other into aggression, and they happily lock horns. There's never any bloodiness, and the winner is generally deemed to be the cow who has shoved or intimidated her opponent into submission.

Local contests are held on Sundays once or twice a month in various towns from late March through to September, accompanied by much revelry and the consumption of gallons of local wine. Two events stand out: the **cantonal championships** are held in Aproz, a small town just outside Sion, in mid-May, with the winners going on to Martigny for the **Combats des Reines**, a huge show held in the 5000-seater Roman amphitheatre in early October. It's here that the supreme champion is crowned Queen of the Herd.

Modigliani retrospectives, Kandinsky and Van Gogh. The gallery space itself is not huge, but the quality of works brought in from around the world is always very high. The upper level of the gallery is given over to the **Musée Archéologique Gallo-Romain**, an interesting collection of statues, coins, pottery, jewellery and other bits and bobs garnered from digs around Martigny. Prime exhibit, which serves as the Foundation's mascot, is an impressive bronze head of a bull, dating from the first or second century AD. The whole building is constructed around the remains of a Gallo-Roman temple dedicated to Mercury, the inner-sanctum walls of which have been left intact in the middle of the museum's floor space.

In a back area off the gallery is a small permanent exhibition in the **Salle Franck** of ten modernist works donated from a private collection, which includes Picasso's *Nu aux jambes croisées* (1903), produced at the height of the artist's blue period. Further along the corridor, the smell of motor oil and rubber prelude the subterranean **Musée de l'Auto**, displaying fifty-odd vintage cars including a Model T Ford (1912), and a dashingly elegant Lagonda (1936). Outside is another highlight, the **Parc des Sculptures**, an open area of green overlooked by Martigny's wooded slopes and dotted with works by – among many others – Rodin, Moore and Miró, as well as Brancusi's celebrated *Le Grand Coq* (1949), a striking zigzag of gleaming metal. Alongside the café at the rear of the park is the **Vieil Arsenal**, which stages excellent shows of photography or modern art.

Art aside, the museum also stages a prestigious cycle of **classical music concerts**, twelve or fifteen a year, which give the unique opportunity to see stellar world-class artists performing at close quarters in the intimate gallery space: 2003's season, for instance, included one-off recitals by the Beaux Arts Trio, Cecilia Bartoli and Pinchas Zukerman. Tickets (roughly Fr.30–100) are very limited.

Within a few hundred metres of the museum, to the south beyond the train tracks, lies Martigny's Roman **amphitheatre**, dating from the second-to-fourth centuries AD and now restored to seat 5000 spectators. It comes into its own as the venue for the annual cowfighting championships in early October (see box p.337), but otherwise it's a quiet, grassy corner from which to survey the wooded slopes all around.

Eating and drinking

Place Centrale is where it happens in Martigny – though "it" covers little more than sitting around under the plane trees at pleasant terrace cafés **eating** plates of chips and drinking beer. Ranged along one side are bustling *Café de la Place*, specializing in fondues and raclettes (Fr.15–20), and adjacent *Barock* and *Les Platanes*, all of which get crammed on summer evenings churning out meals, beers and coffees. Down in the Bourg, the *Auberge Poste-Bourg* (see "Accommodation") offers inexpensive Valaisian dishes (Fr.16 or so), while the *Hôtel des Trois Couronnes*, 8 Place du Bourg (℡027 723 21 14; closed Sun & Mon), is an old traditional-style *auberge* from 1609, no longer offering lodging, but still serving up quality French *menus* at Fr.20 and up – go for the house speciality of kidneys in garlic. Near Place Centrale, *Le Lion d'Or*, 1 Avenue du Grand-St-Bernard (closed Sun & Mon), makes its own fresh pasta, and has pizzas and other Italian favourites such as *osso bucco*. The Gault & Millau-recommended *Kwong-Ming*, Place de Rome (℡027 722 45 15; closed June), serves up perfect Chinese dishes in a calm, darkwood interior or *al fresco* beside the interior garden (or takeaway); *menus* can be Fr.20 at lunch, double that in the evening. The tearoom on the seventh floor of the *Forclaz-Touring* hotel has panoramic views over the town.

There's a string of divey **pubs** along Avenue de la Gare, including the rough-and-ready *White Horse*; the bar in the nearby *Casino* cinema, open daily until midnight, is more civilized. Alternatively you could head down to *Les Arcades*, in a vaulted cellar at 31 Rue du Bourg, one of a handful of sociable taverns in the area.

Pays du Grand-St-Bernard

South of Martigny is the **Pays du Grand–St–Bernard** (Ⓦwww.saint-bernard .ch), comprising wild valleys hemmed in by the giant Pennine Alps marking the Italian border. Branch-line trains from Martigny station follow the Dranse valley and divide; one branch serves **Le Châble**, tucked beneath the famous ski resort of Verbier (see p.341), while the other is the gateway to the Val d'Entremont, leading south to the **Grand-St-Bernard Pass**, beyond which is Italy. If you plan to explore in the area, you'd do well to pick up from the Martigny tourist office the excellent 1:40,000 map and English guidebook *Au Pays du Grand-St-Bernard* (Fr.20).

Trains, and the road, from Martigny divide at **SEMBRANCHER**, long a staging post on the route up to the Grand-St-Bernard. It's an attractive, medieval village, with a Baroque church and street fountains flowing with water that is unusually high in natural fluoride. About 6km south – and up – is **ORSIÈRES** (820m), where trains terminate and buses take over. Orsières is notable for the exquisitely beautiful Gothic bell-tower alongside its relatively modern church, featuring double- and triple-arched windows and grotesque gargoyles. A branch road from here penetrates the lonesome **Val Ferret**, extending for some 20km between towering peaks and acclaimed as an excellent birdwatching area, where you might spot the rare red-billed chough, along with yellowhammers, kestrels and more. As one visitor wrote in 1876, Val Ferret has "infernal beauties which are well worth seeing… There are few valleys in the Alps so fearsomely wild."

On a zigzagging road above Orsières lies the tranquil little resort of **CHAMPEX** (1470m), ranged around its lakelet and well known as a mountaineering centre and trailhead for a host of mountain walks, including the famous Circuit of Mont-Blanc. Two **hotels** stand out, both country inns in idyllic woodland settings: down-to-earth *Belvédère* (Ⓣ027 783 11 14, Ⓕ027 783 25 76; ❷) is renowned for its organic, home-produced cuisine, while *Au Vieux-Champex* (Ⓣ027 783 12 16, Ⓕ027 783 13 07; ❷) is more upmarket, with a gourmet edge and five comfortable apartments.

The main road from Orsières continues to climb amidst increasingly spectacular scenery up to the village of **BOURG-ST-PIERRE** (1632m), residence from the eighth century onwards of the guardians of the pass; the old church, rebuilt in 1739, has at its northeastern corner a Roman milestone dating from about 310 AD. Above the village, the main road is roofed over to limit problems with driving snow in winter. Shortly afterwards, traffic shoots into the Grand-St-Bernard tunnel, emerging 5.9km on in Italy, but a tiny winding road to one side continues up the mountainside, past a ski lift serving the small Super-St-Bernard peak (part of the Four Valleys ski area – see p.344 – with a couple of red runs and a wild and lonesome black), before it eventually arrives at the dramatic **Grand-St-Bernard Pass** itself, at 2470m.

The **Grand-St-Bernard Pass** is the oldest of Alpine pass routes, in use at least since the Bronze Age (about 800 BC). Tribes and armies have tramped their way to and fro for millennia – in 390 BC, a Gaulish army crossed to defeat Rome – and from the earliest times ordinary people used the pass to trade goods between northern Europe and Italy. **Hannibal**'s famous crossing of the Alps in 217 BC, reputedly with elephants, is indelibly associated with the Grand-St-Bernard, despite the lack of evidence for the event. In 57 BC, **Julius Caesar** crossed the *Summa Poenina*, as it was known, to conquer the pagan peoples of Martigny who worshipped the Celtic god Poenn; the chain of great peaks on the Swiss–Italian frontier is still called the Pennine Alps. Shortly after, Emperor Augustus built a road across the pass. His summit temple to Jupiter was sacked with the fall of Rome, but a refuge may well have remained on the pass, since the great and the good continued to tramp the road: Pope Stephen II crossed in 753 to meet with Pepin the Short, King of France; while in 800 **Charlemagne** crossed back following his coronation in Milan.

In the early 900s, Huns and Saracens swept through the region, raping, pillaging and destroying churches: to keep them quiet, Hugh of Provence, King of Italy, granted them guardianship of the pass, whereupon they began to terrorize travellers and demand payment. Deeply concerned at the disruption caused to merchants and pilgrims Europe-wide, King Canute of Denmark had a quiet word with King Rudolf III of Burgundy, and together they ejected the heathens in short order; the archdeacon of Aosta, one **Bernard of Menthon**, then oversaw the construction of a hospice on the pass. Bernard himself travelled around the area, spreading the word of God, and was beatified shortly after his death in the 1080s. (Pope Pius XI confirmed him as patron saint of the Alps in 1923.)

The hospice immediately became a welcome point of safety on an extremely

Col du Grand-St-Bernard

The **Col du Grand–St–Bernard** is the oldest Alpine pass route (see box), protected for almost a millennium by monks inhabiting the **hospice** on top. The views aren't outstanding, and the souvenir stalls are an eyesore, but the sense of history is what draws you in: for centuries, this was the only road between northern Europe and southern Europe for hundreds of miles on either flank, and countless travellers have arrived to the same view of the little summit lake backed by the same mountain panorama. The interesting **museum** (daily: July & Aug 8am–6.30pm; June & Sept 9am–6pm; Fr.8) documents the history of the pass, and includes several quaking accounts of fatal or near-fatal crossings. The two buildings which make up the hospice, exposed to winter storms which have been known to bring 25m of snow with them and temperatures of -30°C, date from 1560 and 1898; the older one contains a Baroque **church**. If you walk down from the hospice, the Italian frontier guards will let you cross the international border to explore the rocky area behind the customs post and Italian hospice; around the **statue** of St Bernard atop its round pillar (1905) you'll find traces of the Roman road cut into the bedrock.

In summer, it's possible to **stay** in the hospice, which is still a functioning religious community (℡027 787 12 36, ℱ027 787 11 07; ❶), either in plain, cosy rooms, or dorms (Fr.20); the cooking is suitably hearty and the atmosphere jovial. During the winter months (Nov–June) and over Easter, you can arrange an individual retreat, to take advantage of the solitude for personal reflection.

dangerous route, attracting favours and gifts from royal and noble households. By 1177, a papal bull confirmed that the monks owned some 78 properties in Vaud, Valais, Savoy, Italy, France and England (including Hornchurch in Essex). Throughout the Middle Ages, the hospice provided free shelter and food to pilgrims, clerics and travellers, many crossing to and from Rome. By 1817 some 20,000 people were using the road annually. During the wars of the 1790s, entire armies crossed the pass: in May 1800, **Napoleon** led 40,000 troops over the pass into Italy, on the way consuming 21,724 bottles of wine, a tonne and a half of cheese, 800kg of meat, and more, running up a bill with the hospice of Fr.40,000 before departing with a wave of his hand. Fifty years later, the monks received Fr.18,500 towards payment, and had to wait until 1984 for a token gesture of account-settling from French president François Mitterrand.

First mention of the famous **St Bernard dogs** – product of an unknown cross between a mastiff, Great Dane and/or Newfoundland – was in 1708. Since then, these heavy-set, jowly beasts, with a little flask of reviving brandy tied round their collars, have come to stand as icons of the mountains. With the advent of skis, phone lines, radios, and now helicopters, the rescue services of the dogs have faded, but the hospice still keeps a kennel for them on the pass. (Some fifteen pure-bred St Bernard puppies are born every year, each worth a cool Fr.1700.) With the construction of the Simplon Tunnel further east in 1905, train travel rapidly superseded the road journey over the Grand-St-Bernard, and in 1964 a motorway tunnel opened beneath the pass in order to safeguard traffic flow year-round. These days the hospice spends the summer crowded with visitors and hikers, and the winter receiving people climbing up from below to spend a few days or weeks on a solitary, snowbound retreat.

Verbier

It's the skiing that put **VERBIER** on the map: few places in the world offer such breadth of possibilities with such awe-inspiring scenery as a backdrop. Before 1910, the plateau on which Verbier sits was an empty summer pasture; the first hotel opened in 1934, and even by 1950 the place was still a tiny village. No more. Following the 1960s ski boom, Verbier now sprawls, characterized by apartment blocks and modern housing. It's not a particularly charming or endearing place, but with this quality of skiing on offer, it doesn't have to be. European high society flocks to the resort in season, and the mood of the place can get tediously brash and trendy, but still the slopes hold sway. Fully half of the million annual visitors are Swiss, many scooting over from Lausanne and Geneva for a weekend in their apartments or chalets; it's a feature of Verbier that chalet accommodation outnumbers hotel beds ten-to-one, making it much more advisable to visit on a ski-chalet package booked from home than to arrive independently without a hotel reservation.

Practicalities

Branch-line **trains** from Martigny split at Sembrancher: one half terminates at Orsières, the other at Le Châble, the valley community at the foot of Verbier's hill. From Le Châble, a gondola runs every fifteen minutes up to Verbier, arriving at the huge Médran station at the east end of the resort. Postbuses also do the run from Le Châble, climbing first through "Verbier-Village" (the locals' town) before terminating in "Verbier-Station" (the resort), at the central post office just off Place Centrale.

The snowy Pennine Alps of Canton Valais drain north to the Rhône through a series of spectacular valleys walled by high and craggy ridges. The **Walker's Haute Route** makes a traverse of these on a west-to-east journey which begins in **Chamonix** (France) below Mont Blanc, and ends in Zermatt at the foot of the Matterhorn, one of the most beautiful and scenically rewarding of Europe's long walks. It's a demanding two-week trek, but there are no glaciers or permanent snowfields to cross, and overnight accommodation is plentiful in huts, mountain inns or valley hotels. You can also easily join the route partway along at strategically accessible points for a few days' hiking: the Val de Bagnes, Arolla and Zinal, for instance, are all served by public transport from main Valais towns. Along with the **maps** LS 5003 Mont Blanc–Grand Combin, and 5006 Matterhorn–Mischabel (both 1:50,000), you should pack *Chamonix to Zermatt, the Walker's Haute Route* by Kev Reynolds (see "Books", p.607).

With a long climb out of the Chamonix valley, the Haute Route enters Switzerland by way of Col de Balme and descends to **Trient**. On day three there are two routes to choose from: either the formidable but non-technical Fenêtre d'Arpette alongside the Trient Glacier, or the more pedestrian Alp Bovine route to **Champex** (see p.339) – the former is tough but visually exciting, the latter an energetic alternative, also with fine views. From Champex an easy valley walk leads to **Le Châble** in Val de Bagnes (see p.345), from where the route on day five makes a 1600m climb to the **Cabane du Mont-Fort** (℡027 778 13 84), a mountain hut with stunning views across to Mont Blanc. Leaving the hut next day, an airy balcony walk takes you along the Sentier des Chamois, with the Grand Combin (4314m) a mighty presence across the valley, then over Col de Louvie to skirt below the Grand Désert glacier, and across Col de Prafleuri to **Cabane de Prafleuri** (℡027 207 30 67). Views from this hut are restricted, but a short climb to Col des Roux reveals the tranquil Lac des Dix below, with Mont Blanc de Cheilon (3870m) at the head of the valley. Beyond the lake, the way traces old moraines alongside a rubble-strewn glacier, then crosses either Col de Riedmatten (2919m) or the neighbouring Pas de Chèvres – the latter by way of two long and very steep ladders. Once you've crossed this ridge, there's a very pleasant descent through pastures to **Arolla** (see p.350).

Day eight is an easy one, taking you from Arolla down to Les Haudères and up to **La Sage**, while on day nine Col de Torrent (2919m) leads you into the Moiry glen, near the head of which **Cabane de Moiry** (℡027 475 45 34) overlooks a cascading icefall and the glacier easing from it. Col de Sorebois is next, with the descent from there to **Zinal** in Val d'Anniviers allowing you to make the acquaintance of the hugely impressive **Weisshorn** (4505m) and its attendant peaks on the far side. On day eleven, you leave Zinal on another balcony path, this time heading north for about four hours to the *Weisshorn* (℡027 475 11 06), a Victorian hotel perched high above the valley looking to the sunset from its glass-fronted dining room. Next day you cross the Meidpass (2790m) to **Gruben** in the Turtmanntal, the first German-speaking valley and a truly forgotten little corner. The penultimate stage (day thirteen) is the setting for another high-level crossing – the 2894m **Augstbordpass**. This brings you into the Mattertal, the valley which leads to Zermatt and the Matterhorn; an hour and a half below the pass the trail turns a spur to confront you with the most amazing of panoramas. Across the unseen depths of the Mattertal soars the **Dom** (4545m), the highest mountain entirely in Switzerland; at the head of the valley far away a long crest of snow and ice stretches from Monte Rosa to the Breithorn (the Matterhorn is just hidden from view), while the Weisshorn dominates the right-hand wall. An hour below that viewpoint lies Jungen, a summer alp hamlet clinging to the near-vertical hillside. The path then plunges steeply to **St Niklaus** in the bed of the valley. The last stretch (day fourteen) offers no passes to cross, but a mere wander up the valley to **Zermatt** (see p.359), in order to make your final pilgrimage to the **Matterhorn**.

Orientation around the resort is straightforward. The Rue de Médran climbs southeast from Place Centrale to the **Médran** lift station, arrival point for gondolas up from Le Châble, and departure point for gondolas and a chair-lift continuing up to Les Ruinettes, main access point for the pistes. It's along Rue de Médran, and in the surrounding area, that most of the resort's après-ski happens. Verbier's other gondola rises from the **Savoleyres** station, best part of a kilometre north of Place Centrale. West of Place Centrale is the massive Centre Sportif with, below and south of it, workaday Verbier-Village. **Free buses** link all of these throughout the summer and winter seasons (July, Aug & Dec–April daily 8am–7pm).

The highly organized **tourist office** is on Place Centrale (July, Aug & Dec–April Mon–Sat 8.30am–12.30pm & 2–6.30pm, Sun 9am–noon & 4–6.30pm; rest of year Mon–Fri 8.30am–noon & 2–6.30pm, Sat 9am–noon & 4–6pm, Sun 9am–noon; ☏027 775 38 88, ⊛www.verbier.ch).

Late July sees Verbier staging one of Switzerland's most prestigious classical music events, the **Verbier Festival and Academy** (⊛www.verbierfestival .com). For two weeks, the resort plays host to top-flight soloists and conductors, who come to perform and also lead masterclasses and discussions. Tickets range from Fr.30 to Fr.120 for individual concerts, Fr.300 for a weekend pass, or Fr.1000-plus for a universal pass.

7

VALAIS | Verbier

Accommodation

Verbier is tricky when it comes to **hotels**: there just aren't that many of them, and you may find they won't accept bookings in season for less than seven days. Many places close in the April/May and October/November between-seasons and you're looking at through-the-roof prices for the winter high season (summer and between-season prices can be up to a third cheaper). Accommodation is least expensive in the handful of private rooms on offer through the tourist office, or in any of the thousands of chalets, which must be booked months in advance.

Bristol ☏027 771 65 77, ⊛www.bristol-verbier .ch. Friendly, cosy and quiet, and very central, but watch out for that peak-time price hike. ❺–❻

Ermitage ☏027 771 64 77, ℱ027 771 52 64. Well run and very convenient place on Place Centrale, delivering unexpected value for money. ❹–❺

Garbo ☏027 771 62 72, ⊛www.hotelgarbo.com. Central spot, midway between Place Centrale and the Médran lifts. OK value, except around the New Year and in February, when it tacks an outrageous Fr.100 onto its double-room prices. ❸

Mont-Gelé ☏027 771 30 53, ℱ027 771 13 16. The least expensive hotel in the resort open year-round; beside the Médran lift station, with just fif-teen comfortable, balconied rooms. ❸

Le Relais de Pachou ☏027 771 63 49, ⊛www.pachou-verbier.com. A good, quiet place for skiers willing to skip resort nightlife; 1.5km west of Place Centrale, at the terminus of one of the resort bus routes. ❸

Rois Mages ☏027 771 63 64, ℱ027 771 33 19. Good modern choice by the church. ❺–❻

Les Touristes ☏ & ℱ027 771 21 47. One of the best ways to duck beneath Verbier's high prices and uninspiring anonymity: it's on a street corner in Verbier-Village, linked to the lifts by bus, with spartan, shared-bath rooms. Its quiet restaurant and chic-free atmosphere are a breath of fresh air. ❷

Eating and drinking

Eating options aren't very inspiring. Aside from supermarket fare, or burgers from *Harold's* on Place Centrale, food is generally poor value. Wander your way up Rue de Médran from Place Centrale until you see something you fancy: there's a handful of pizzerias – the *Fer à Cheval* is one of the better ones, with a reasonably lively après-ski scene to boot, or there's the *Garbo* close at hand, which also shakes a leg. *Al Capone* is another friendly pizza joint, west of the

343

Winter sports

For years, Verbier suffered from notoriously long queues and poorly planned lift transport, but these days, with the opening of new gondolas or chairlifts almost every season, things are getting better. Verbier is the main resort of the **Four Valleys** ski area (ⓦ www.4vallees.ch), covering a vast swathe of some 400km of piste at all levels of difficulty, stretching from Thyon, Veysonnaz and Nendaz in the west, through the central Savoleyres and Mont-Fort areas, out to far-flung corners like the Super-St-Bernard. The **Verbier** sector covers lifts to Les Ruinettes, Attelas and Mont-Gelé (but not Mont-Fort); the **Savoleyres** sector is accessed both from Verbier village and La Tzoumaz (ⓦ www.latzoumaz.ch); and the family-friendly **Bruson** sector faces Verbier across the valley, accessed from La Châble.

Aside from a handful of blues at Bruson, beginners have a dedicated "**Station**" sub-sector, comprising nursery slopes in and just above Verbier village itself. There's a host of red runs from **Savoleyres** (2354m), and the Médran lifts take you up to **Les Ruinettes** (2200m), with its own cat's cradle of reds and a scarily vertiginous black run, in addition to some carving. Large-capacity gondolas connect to **Attelas** (2727m), with blacks and reds, and on either to the **Mont-Gelé** summit (3023m), or by chairlift over to **Tortin** (2050m) from where reds or a fiendishly difficult black connect to the Siviez and Thyon ski areas. From **La Chaux** (2260m) above Ruinettes, one of Switzerland's largest cable-cars, the Jumbo, swooshes 150 people at a time up to the glacier slopes of **Mont-Fort** (3330m), also one of the best places in the country for **summer skiing**. This is prime territory for snowboarders, with half-pipes and excellent facilities at Gentianes on Mont-Fort and at "BoarderX" at La Chaux itself (2260–2845m), as well as at Savoleyres.

A **lift pass** for one/six days on the Verbier sector is Fr.52/266, on Savoleyres/Tzoumaz Fr.46/235, on Bruson Fr.33/169, and for the entire Four Valleys region Fr.59/306. Season passes are Fr.1066, Fr.897, Fr.525 and Fr.1210 respectively; discounted part-day and advance-purchase passes are available. Bruson passes for longer than six days entitle you to free access to small neighbouring sectors such as Champex and Super-St-Bernard, and there are other package deals on offer.

centre towards the Savoleyres lift. As you emerge from the Médran station, *Au Vieux Valais* is within view, a cosy traditional-style place for raclette, fondue and other belly-warmers; similar fare can be found at *Les Touristes* (see "Accommodation"), a quiet, pleasant place down in Verbier-Village that's well worth making the journey for.

Le Bouchon Gourmand (☎027 771 72 96) makes a change, a relatively good French bistro west of the post office, specializing in rich *foie gras* and duck, but also with fresh pastas and salads (*menus* Fr.24 and up). The gourmet choice is the *Rosalp* (☎027 771 63 23), a staggeringly expensive place to savour what's been called the best cuisine in the country. The restaurant, and the chef Roland Pierroz, have been showered with awards. Even choosing from the wine list is likely to be quite an event: the cellar runs to 50,000 bottles. *Rosalp's* ground-floor brasserie is slightly more affordable (around Fr.40).

Of a number of places to **drink** around the resort, the one with most colour is the raucous *Pub Mont Fort*, near the Médran station; the club/venue *No Name* on Route des Creux also thumps nightly. The *Nelson*, off Place Centrale, near the *Marshal's* techno joint, is another good option, while the snobby *Farm Club*, west of the centre, is the best place for a spot of celeb- and royal-watching.

Adventure sports and extreme events

Verbier is a mecca for **adventure** addicts, with a host of companies competing with each other to come up with the newest and most exciting extreme thrill of the season. The **Maison du Sport** (℡027 775 33 63, ☏www.maisondusport.com) is home to official ski and snowboarding schools and the mountain guides office, and has a huge range of activities, including heli-skiing and heli-boarding, snow-shoeing, ice-climbing, guided high-altitude walking, and more, as well as summer canyoning, rafting and caving. **No Limits** (℡027 771 72 50, ☏www.outdoor-activity.ch) has luge, snow-carting, snow-scooting and plenty more, while **Centre Parapente** (℡027 771 68 18, ☏www.flyverbier.ch) offers tandem paragliding. **La Fantastique** (℡027 771 41 41, ☏www.lafantastique.com) offers heli-skiing, qualified guides for off-piste (Fr.400/day for one person) and long-distance ski safaris. **Adrenaline** (℡027 771 74 59, ☏www.adrenaline-verbier.ch) is a dedicated ski and snowboard school.

One of the best of the annual events is **Xtreme Verbier** (☏www.xtremeverbier .com), one of the top international showcases of freeride snowboarding, held each March. Bec des Rosses (3222m), way up on the mountainside at Gentianes, is the scene for 25 of the world's best boarders to do their thing, competing by invitation only in the most dramatic of locations, with 55° gradients, broad expanses of powder and plenty of obstacles. **Verbier Ride** (☏www.verbierride.com) is an exhibition showcase of freeskiing, held in early March.

The **Patrouille des Glaciers** (☏www.pdg.ch) is a long-distance endurance test across the 53km of glaciers, summits and passes from Zermatt to Verbier. Dubbed "Paris–Dakar on skis", it was halted in 1949 after three deaths, and restarted in 1984 with more than six hundred participants; since then it has taken place every other year (next in 2004), with the current record standing at 7hr 3min 44sec.

In August, Verbier also hosts the world's longest mountain-bike race, the exceptionally tough **Grand Raid Cristalp** (☏www.grand-raid-cristalp.ch), a one-day race across six valleys (rising at one point to 2792m) on a 131km route to Grimentz; well over a thousand men take part each year, but rarely more than 25 women. The current records are 6hr 8min 48sec (men) and 7hr 55min 5sec (women).

Val de Bagnes

From **Le Châble**, a peaceful, entirely rural community tucked on the valley floor below Verbier, the long **Val de Bagnes** runs southeast into the high mountains. Le Châble is the capital of the Bagnes commune, Switzerland's largest, and – at 295 square kilometres – larger than the cantons of Geneva, Schaffhausen or Zug (although about a third of the Bagnes is covered by glaciers). Buses run twice a day (July–Sept only) from Le Châble up to the impressive **Mauvoisin Dam**, a giant 250m-high wall blocking the end of the valley. At 1961m, it's one of the highest-altitude dams in the world. A **hotel** at the base (℡ & ℻027 778 11 30; ❶) has rooms and dorms (Fr.22) – handy for an overnight stay either after a walk up from Fionnay or Lourtier villages in the valley, or before taking a full day to hike back to Le Châble.

Sion and around

SION (pronounced *see-ohh*), known as Sitten in German, is the capital of Valais, an alluring and attractive town of just 27,000 with an exceptionally long history: archeological evidence points to the site having been inhabited during Neolithic times. What attracted settlement, no doubt, was the incongruous presence, on the otherwise pancake-flat valley floor, of two jutting rocky hills, visible from afar and now adorned with the medieval castles **Valère** and **Tourbillon**. They're an odd and slightly sinister sight, which matches the common Swiss belief that the locals (named Sédunois, after the town's Latin name *Sedunum*, meaning Place of Castles) are themselves a bit odd, impenetrably taciturn and clannish. Prejudice aside, Sion enjoys a simply glorious **climate**, dry, mild and consistently clear; afternoons are bathed in bright sunshine, and on mild summer evenings you could imagine yourself in rural Spain or Israel – warm, dry breezes blending the aroma of dusty pine needles with the scraping of thousands of cicadas. Sion's **wines** (see p.52) are outstanding.

For the entire decade of the 1990s, the municipality and the people exerted extraordinary efforts to attract the Winter Olympics to Sion, based on the nearby presence of Verbier, Crans-Montana and Zermatt – and yet they were rejected, both for the 2002 and (amidst profound controversy) the 2006 games, the latter awarded by the IOC without much clarity of purpose to Turin. Switzerland finally secured the 2008 European football championships (with Austria), but Sion will gain no benefit from games played in the big cities. For now, the Sédunois have lapsed into a shocked and sulky silence, while the town itself remains refreshingly down-to-earth after the grinding glitz of the big resorts.

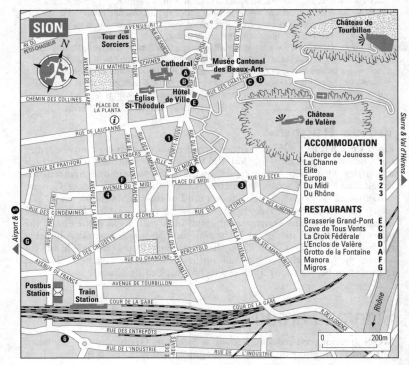

Arrival, information and accommodation

Sion's **train station** – with change facilities and bike rental – is at the southern end of the long, straight Avenue de la Gare, with the giant **postbus station** to one side. Some 500m north along Avenue de la Gare is the wide open concrete of the **Place de la Planta**, on which is the well-equipped **tourist office** (July & Aug Mon–Fri 8am–6pm, Sat 10am–4pm; rest of year Mon–Fri 8.30am–noon & 2–5.30pm, Sat 9am–noon; ☎027 327 77 27, ⓦwww .siontourism.ch). They offer a good two-hour **walking tour** of the town (July & Aug Tues & Thurs 9.30am; Fr.8), as well as information about hikes in the surrounding area, including treks into the Val d'Hérens, through the vineyards and along the *bisses* irrigation channels in the hills. Sion's tiny **airport** (☎027 322 24 80) – with flights year-round to Zürich and in winter to London and Amsterdam – is 5km west of the centre. Hôpital de Champsec, 80 Avenue Grand-Champsec (☎027 603 40 00), has a 24-hour emergency room.

Every summer, Sion hosts an array of classical music events, led by the **Festival International de Musique** (ⓦwww.sion-festival.ch), which runs from July to September at a number of venues in Sion and around Valais. Within the festival is a prestigious international violin competition, held in August immediately following the separate **Tibor Varga Violin Competition** (ⓦwww.tiborvarga.org), named after the virtuoso violinist who, having settled in Sion, founded an orchestra and academy (which also performs regularly). Running concurrently in July and August are the **Académie de Musique de Sion** (ⓦwww.amsion.ch), a six-week cycle of masterclasses given by international soloists and performances, and the **Festival International de l'Orgue Ancien**, a season of ancient music centred on the world's oldest organ, still playable in the Château de Valère.

Accommodation

There are a few inexpensive **hotels** within Sion. The *Elite*, 6 Avenue du Midi (☎027 322 03 27, ⓕ027 322 23 61; ❷), doesn't look like much, but it's been redone inside and is quite serviceable. In the Old Town, *La Channe*, 9 Rue Porte-Neuve (☎027 322 32 71, ⓕ027 322 32 89; ❷), is a quiet unassuming place with a choice of ensuite or shared-bath rooms. The luridly decorated *Du Midi* is on the busy Place du Midi (☎027 323 13 31, ⓕ027 323 61 73; ❷), while nearby is the cinder-block *Du Rhône*, Rue du Scex 10 (☎027 322 82 91, ⓦwww.bestwestern.ch; ❸), a definite step up in quality and service. Sion's best is the "garni" *Europa*, a pleasant business hotel out towards the airfield, at 19 Rue de l'Envoi (☎027 322 24 23, ⓕ027 322 25 35; ❸–❹).

The good HI **hostel** *Auberge de Jeunesse*, 2 Rue de l'Industrie (☎027 323 74 70, ⓦwww.youthhostel.ch; ❶; closed Dec & Jan), is just behind the station – modern, clean and well run, with dorms for Fr.28. The nearest, and best, **campsite** to Sion is the five-star *Des Iles* (☎027 346 43 47, ⓕ027 346 68 47), 4km west of the centre near the airport and open year-round.

The Town

Sion's Old Town is interesting: a slow wander through the cobbled alleys, with their old inns and sixteenth-century shuttered town houses, can fill an atmospheric afternoon. Just northeast of Place de la Planta is the small **Église St-Théodule**, dating from the sixteenth century and with some fine vaulting in the choir. Just beside it is the atmospheric **Cathédrale Notre-Dame du Glarier** (Our Lady of the Gravel – referring to the ground on which the

Tourist offices in Sion and Sierre sell the **Carte Vacances** (Fr.48), valid for a week, which covers three days of free transport (by train between Sion and Leuk, post-buses on a wide network from Martigny to Leukerbad and from Crans to Arolla, city buses in Sion, Sierre and Martigny and the funicular from Sierre to Montana), and gives discounted admission to, among other attractions, the Fondation Gianadda in Martigny, the thermal baths at Leukerbad, Saillon and Ovronnaz, an excursion to the Grande Dixence dam and cableways all round the region (summer only).

cathedral was built). The main building is fifteenth century, with elements of earlier Romanesque and Gothic structures incorporated within it, including a fine belfry. Its most noticeable feature, though, is the bells, which strike every quarter-hour in a near-exact copy of the sound of Big Ben in London, although the bass bell's slightly higher pitch gives the ensemble an inescapably mournful tone. Some 100m to the south is Rue Supersaxo, with the **Maison Supersaxo** (Mon–Fri 8am–noon & 2–6pm; free) tucked into an alley off the street. This lavish residence was built in 1505 by the local governor, Georges Supersaxo, to show the town's bishop, Matthias Schinner, who was boss: climb the Gothic staircase inside to a hall on the upper floor with a magnificent carved and paint-ed ceiling. Two minutes north on Rue de la Tour brings you to the witch's-hat **Tour des Sorciers**, part of the town's medieval fortifications.

Beside the imposing **Hôtel de Ville** on Rue du Grand-Pont (visitable only on the tourist office's walking tour), lanes and back alleys cut east to Rue des Châteaux, which climbs steeply up towards the twin hills of Tourbillon and Valère looming over the town. Before you get there, though, after 150m you'll pass on the left the modest **Musée Cantonal des Beaux-Arts**, Place de la Majorie (Tues–Sun 1–6pm; Oct–May closes 5pm; Fr.5; SMP; free on 1st Sun of month), in an attractive fifteenth-century house. There are few outstanding works, although the section on Valaisian identity holds some interesting pieces. Opposite is the **Musée Cantonal d'Archéologie** (same hours; Fr.4; SMP; free on 1st Sun of month), with an impressive collection of mainly Roman bits and pieces gathered from digs around the canton, as well as massive steles, carved 2800–2300 BC, and a display of prehistoric dolmens.

Valère and Tourbillon

Rue des Châteaux climbs to a parking area in the groove between the twin castles of Sion. From here, paths divide up the dry, scrubby hillsides – left (north) to Tourbillon, right (south) to Valère.

Château de Valère is the more interesting of the two, and the more com-plete. The hike up brings you past the tiny Chapelle de Tous-les-Saints (dating from 1310 but unfortunately kept locked) and massive Roman foundation walls to the castle-church. As it stands, the château dates from the thirteenth century, but elements survive of earlier buildings, and the whole thing may well stand on the ruins of a Roman temple. A climb up rickety stairs brings you into the church interior (Tues–Sat 10am–noon & 2–6pm, Sun 2–6pm; Fr.3), where the most notable feature, high on the back wall, is the oldest playable **organ** in the world, dating from 1390.

The **Château de Tourbillon** on the opposite hill dates from 1294, but was ruined by fire in 1788 and today, aside from the external walls, little is left. These days, it's open for scramblings (mid-March to mid-Nov Tues–Sun 10am–6pm; free) and yields excellent views along the valley and over the town.

Eating and drinking

There are a surprising number of good places to **eat and drink** for such a small city as Sion. The basics are taken care of at various **self-service** restaurants, including a *Manora* within the Placette department store on Avenue du Midi, and a huge *Migros* supermarket and diner west of the station on Avenue de France.

Rue du Grand-Pont in the Old Town is lined with attractive, pleasant little corners to sample something nice. *Grotto de la Fontaine*, at no. 21 (closed Tues & Wed), is a Ticinese-style inn serving fresh pastas, pizzas and Ticinese stews and risottos (*menus* Fr.17); *La Croix Fédérale*, at no. 13 (☎027 322 16 95; closed Mon), specializes in mouthwatering fish dishes; while the *Brasserie du Grand-Pont*, at no. 6 (☎027 322 20 96; closed Sun), is a solid, down-to-earth place to have a good square meal and a carafe of local wine.

To the east, and well out of the hubbub on steep, cobbled Rue des Châteaux, there are two excellent places very close to each other: *L'Enclos de Valère*, at no. 18 (☎027 323 32 30; Oct–April closed Sun & Mon), has a big shaded terrace on which to enjoy its classic gourmet cuisine (*menus* Fr.25), while just about next door is the *Cave de Tous Vents* (☎027 322 46 84; May & June closed Mon & Tues), an atmospheric vaulted cellar in a thirteenth-century building that opens in the evenings only for quality raclettes, fondues (including an alcoholic "fondue Bacchus") and sampling of local wines; *menus* are Fr.25.

Val d'Hérens

The hills south of Sion are pierced by two long valleys, which are worth a detour to explore the hinterlands of the Valais. To the southwest a minor road winds into the **Val d'Hérémence**, culminating in the giant **Barrage de la Grande Dixence**, the largest and one of the highest-altitude dams in the world.

Of more interest, though, is the valley branching southeast from Sion. This is the **VAL D'HÉRENS**, a world apart from the main valley, dotted with mountain farms and high-altitude hamlets, and giving fascinating glimpses of traditional rural life. Even people from Sion can barely understand the thick valley patois, which rings with odd guttural sounds and strikes city folk as being a little like Arabic. Unsubstantiated supposition brings out the idea that the generally dark-skinned, dark-eyed people of the Val d'Hérens may be descended from the conquering Saracen armies who swept through the area after the Battle of Poitiers in 732. Having planted that idea, Sédunois will then tell you about the people of Isérables, a town west of Sion, who have been called *Les Bedjuis* for as long as anyone can remember – a nickname remarkably close to "Bedouin". The Allalinhorn peak near Saas-Fee is another clue, its name apparently derived from "Allah".

One of the sights of the valley can be found near the village of Euseigne, where the road passes beneath the **Pyramides d'Euseigne**, an extremely bizarre geological outcrop of glacial moraines. Whereas erosion flattened the area all around, these stone jags were protected from smoothing by hard rock caps. Today, they're hard to believe – a wall of unnaturally bare and pointed stalagmites in the open wooded valley, each crag crowned by a dark boulder balanced on a needle point. A stall at the base lets you stop to gawp, and then buy a souvenir postcard.

Some 15km south of Euseigne is the village of **EVOLÈNE**, the scene of one of the worst avalanches in Switzerland in living memory, which killed ten

Sion tourist office has an all-inclusive deal for a self-guided **walking tour** right around the Val d'Hérens. Starting from Sion, this involves 5–7 hours of walking a day: from Thyon to the Dixence dam; from the Lac des Dix over the passes to Arolla; a valley-floor stroll to Evolène; and finally on a scenic path high up the valley side and down to Nax. Included are five nights' half-board at hotels and five picnic lunches, postbuses to and from Sion, transport of one bag per person from hotel to hotel, documentation and a 1:25,000 map. This all-in deal costs Fr.678 for ensuite hotel rooms, or a bargain Fr.558 for shared-bath rooms.

people in 1999. The quaint little village is now bypassed by the main road, and has preserved along its main street traditional wooden houses and an air of rural tranquillity. The locals have cheerfully capitalized on this by wearing traditional dress – plausibly enough, only partly in a self-conscious bid for tourist appeal. A handful of cafés and simple inns cater to hikers and day-trippers.

Arolla

South of the tiny hamlet of **Les Haudères** beyond Evolène, you begin to penetrate the wild countryside. One road branches east over the crest to Ferpècle, while another climbs west up and over into the tranquil hidden **Val d'Arolla**, terminating some 12km south after a series of nerve-racking tunnels at the pristine hamlet of **AROLLA** (1998m). This tiny, outdoorsy place is one of the stops on the Walkers' Haute Route between Chamonix and Zermatt (see p.342), and offers a wealth of half- and full-day hikes all around, including a testing one up to the Col de Riedmatten (2919m), three hours away. There's a handful of blue and red ski-pistes served by lifts rising from the village; passes are Fr.30/day, Fr.156/week. Four or five **hotels** offer quality retreats, including the *Grand Hôtel et Kurhaus* (☎027 283 11 61, ℻027 283 11 63; ❷; closed May, June & Sept–Nov), a huge old place with renovated light-pine rooms, some ensuite. Half-a-dozen places offer dorms; the **tourist office** (☎027 283 10 83, ⓦwww.arolla.com) has information on these and chalets for rent. Amazingly, all hotels cut their rates to **half-price** throughout January, giving a full week amidst the deep snow for just Fr.300 in three-star comfort, as little as Fr.175 in a pension.

St-Léonard

On the road from Sion east to Sierre is the small village of **ST-LÉONARD** with, as its sole draw, one of the largest **underground lakes** in Europe (March–Oct daily 9am–5pm; Fr.7). Regular buses drop off either in the village or at the car park beneath the ticket office, which can get crowded with day-tripping families. Tours of the lake, by large rowing boats with everyone crowded in side by side, take about forty minutes – and it's cold down there, so bring a jumper. The cave entrance is just a gap in the mountainside, but as you launch off onto the inky water, the illuminated, other-worldly cavern stretching out ahead of you is very impressive. The guides, who do the rowing, have a nice line in multilingual patter, regaling you on the voyage with all kinds of stories and details about the lake and its geology.

Sierre

Hardly any foreigners come to **SIERRE** (Siders in German) unless they're catching the funicular up to the ski resorts of Crans and Montana on the hillside above. Which is all to the good, because it leaves this idyllic little valley-floor town quiet, perfect for a day or two of strolling and wine-tasting in the vineyards all around. The German poet Rainer Maria Rilke spent his last six years in Sierre, where he wrote the celebrated *Sonnets to Orpheus*; he suffered from leukaemia, and died in 1926 after pricking his finger on a rose-thorn.

Sierre lies almost exactly on the French–German language border, which is marked by the tiny Raspille stream a couple of kilometres east of the town. The road east from Sierre to the sleepy village of **Salgesch** (Salquenen in French) begins as the Rue de la Gemmi and ends five minutes later as the Gemmistrasse; Sierre sits alongside the Rhône, while in Salgesch the same river is dubbed the Rotten. **Wine** is what fuels both communities, and there are plenty of trails through and between the vineyards, with equally numerous opportunities to stop and sample a glass or two. Sierre is the driest town in Switzerland, and gets an average of almost seven and a half hours of sunshine daily from May to October (and a total of 330 sunny days a year), helping it to produce excellent Fendant whites; Salgesch, meanwhile, is renowned for its Pinot Noir reds. Not for nothing did the Romans call the place *Sirrum amoenum*, Sierre the agreeable.

The Town

There's not an awful lot to see or do in Sierre, although if you turn left (west) from the train station and then aim northwest up Avenue du Marché, you'll come into the little-visited old quarters of town. The Rue de Villa, alongside a vineyard, marks the eponymous quarter of Villa, with, at the very top, the **Château de Villa**, one half of Sierre-Salgesch's modest **Musée Valaisan de la Vigne et du Vin** (March–Oct Tues–Sun 2–5pm; Nov & Dec Fri–Sun 2–5pm; Fr.5 for both museums; SMP; ⓦ www.museevalaisanduvin.ch). The Sierre half focuses on the wine itself, with interesting displays (in French and German) on grape varieties and the history of cultivation and some old presses. In the same building are a restaurant and oenotheque (see below). From here, a six-kilometre *Sentier Viticole/Rebweg* (Wine Path) runs through the quiet, shuttered lanes of old quarters of Sierre, such as Muraz and Veyras, for a couple of hours over to Salgesch and out through the open vineyards perched on hillside slopes above the town and the valley floor to the other half of the wine museum, in the creaky old **Zumofenhaus** in the heart of the village. Displays are yet more scholarly here, on the technical aspects of viticulture, cultivation methods and history, but the enthusiastic guardian will be happy to give you a rundown in English on what's what. Buses (every 2hr) can run you back to Sierre.

An interesting detour from the Wine Path is to the small **Musée Charles-Clos Olsommer**, signposted in Veyras (July–Sept Wed–Sun 2–5pm; Oct–June Sat & Sun 2–5pm; Fr.3; ⓦ www.musee-olsommer.ch). Olsommer, born in Neuchâtel in 1883, studied in Munich at the same time as Klee and Kandinsky, but unlike them became fixated with a Klimt-like style rooted in symbolism and mysticism. He lived in Veyras from 1912 until his death in 1966, painting moody scenes of women praying in the wilderness or surrounded by psyche-delic patterns.

A fifteen-minute walk east of Sierre lie half-a-dozen low rounded hills, the result of alluvial deposits and an ancient landslide. The whole undulating area

The nomads of Switzerland

The people and history of Sierre are inextricably linked with the culture of the communities in the **Val d'Anniviers**, which opens at a narrow chink in the mountain high up opposite Sierre to the south but broadens out to extend southwards for some 40km, terminating in the hiking trailhead of **Zinal**.

The residents of the Anniviers (the name itself means "seasonal") are the last people left in Switzerland to follow a genuinely **nomadic** lifestyle, although modern ease of transport and economic pressures are making inroads. Up until a few decades ago, people would arrive in Sierre from the Anniviers in March or April: those from the village of **Grimentz** occupied the Villa quarter of Sierre, alongside people from **Vissoie**, while the Viouc quarter was for villagers from **Chandolin**, the Muraz quarter for those from **St Luc**, and so on. Each community had its own slightly distinct dialect, brought with it flocks, a schoolteacher and a priest, and celebrated Sunday mass in its own tiny chapel. For a few months, everyone would stay and work on the vineyards around Sierre, before departing in mid-June to pasture their flocks on the heights above the town. In mid-September, everybody would drift down again to Sierre for the grape harvest, which would continue for a few weeks, before dispersing back to their villages in the Anniviers valley for the winter. This kind of nomadism still carries on today, although these days families don't have to bring bag and baggage with them from their village when they come to work in Sierre, and tend also to keep their children in school in one place or the other.

Curiously, the patois of the Val d'Anniviers is very similar to that of the rural Val d'Aosta on the southern side of the Grand-St-Bernard Pass in Italy – even though the main language of Sierre is French and the main language of Aosta is Italian. Linguists, anthropologists and sociologists between them haven't yet come up with a theory as to why this should be.

is one of the last remaining examples of undeveloped valley-floor ecology in the country. It's carpeted by a vast, pristine pine forest, the **Forêt de Finges/Pfynwald** (derived from the Latin *fines*, or border; this was the ancient limit of Roman control; Ⓦ www.pfyn-finges.ch), and is fringed by swamps and marshland on the Rhône banks. Protected and maintained but not developed, it's perfect for long, shady hikes and peaceful picnics.

Practicalities

Sierre's **station** houses the **tourist office** (mid-July to mid-Sept & Dec–April Mon–Fri 8am–7pm, Sat 9am–6pm, Sun 9am–1pm; rest of year Mon–Fri 8am–7pm, Sat 9am–1pm; ℡027 455 85 35, Ⓦ www.sierre-anniviers.ch). With Crans Montana close by, they have plenty of information about the skiing and hiking possibilities round and about. Ask about their hotel deals, which offer three nights for the price of two in the low season. The longest **funicular** in Switzerland (4.2km) heads up to Montana from the SMC station two minutes' walk away, left onto the main Avenue Général-Guisan outside the station.

Of the **hotels**, basic *De La Poste* is east of the station (℡ & Ⓕ027 455 10 03; ❷); the *Terminus* opposite the station (℡027 455 11 40, Ⓦ www .hotel-terminus.ch; ❷–❸) is comfortable (ask for the quieter back rooms) and has a good **restaurant** and bistro attached. The restaurant in the Château de Villa (see above; ℡027 455 18 96) is one of the more prestigious places to sample Valaisian specialities, and its oenotheque (daily 10.30am–1pm & 4.30–8.30pm) stocks more than 500 of the region's wines. If you head behind the station and down to the small Lac de Géronde, on the way you'll pass a handful of basic *auberges*, including the *Promenade* (℡027 456 34 04, Ⓕ027 456

57 34; ❷), with rooms ensuite and not. On the lake itself is the pleasant *La Grotte* (☎027 455 46 46, ℻027 455 14 37), a terrace restaurant known only to the locals, serving spectacularly good fish (*menus* Fr.25), with a handful of comfortable, characterful rooms upstairs (❶–❷). There's **camping** in the Forêt de Finges (☎027 455 02 84; April–Oct).

Crans Montana

CRANS MONTANA is another of Switzerland's big, world-famous ski resorts, occupying what is claimed to be the sunniest plateau in the Alps, facing south over the Rhône valley with a spectacular panorama of peaks yawning beyond. Along with Verbier and St Moritz, it's also one of the glitziest (Roger Moore is a long-time resident), with what the tourist office likes to call the finest shopping in the Alps.

The resort actually comprises three villages, **Crans-sur-Sierre** (pronounced *crawh*), **Montana** and, out on a limb, **Aminona**; the agglomeration sprawls for more than 2km between Crans, to the west, and Montana, to the east, with nothing to mark the shift from one to another. There's no restriction on cars at all and traffic is permanently heavy: in high season, village-to-village gridlock is not unknown. The **skiing**, rather unfairly dubbed "irretrievably intermediate" by some sports writers, takes second place to the round of wining and dining embarked upon by aficionados of Crans Montana's affluent social life – although the resort does have the advantage of access to year-round skiing on the Plaine Morte glacier, way up above 3000m.

Skiing aside, the place is best known for hosting the **European Masters golf** tournament every September (ⓦgolf.european-masters.com), second only to the British Open for prestige and top names. Crans's scenic course – "by far the most spectacular tournament site in the world" according to Greg Norman – was redesigned in 1999 by Seve Ballesteros, and now boasts fiendishly complex upturned-saucer greens, which led one frustrated player to describe playing a round as "having eighteen teeth pulled one by one".

Practicalities

The SMC **funicular** from Sierre arrives at **Vermala station** at the eastern end of Montana. **Buses** (ⓦwww.cie-smc.ch) also run up from Sierre on two different routes. The first (via Chermignon) passes through Crans, then Montana, then on to Aminona; the second (via Mollens) passes through Montana before terminating in Crans. In addition, a bus runs up to Crans from Sion. All SMC buses shuttling to and fro on circular routes within the resort boundaries are free.

Montana tourist office (June to mid-Sept & Dec–Easter Mon–Sat 8.30am–12.15pm & 2–6.30pm, Sun 10am–noon & 4–6pm; rest of year Mon–Fri 8.30am–noon & 2–6pm, Sat 8.30am–noon; ☎027 485 04 04, ⓦwww.crans-montana.ch) is 100m west (left) of the Vermala funicular station, in the post office. The village centre is another 200m west, focused around the Ycoor ice-skating rink. Just beyond is the small **Lac Grenon**; running along its northern shore is the Route de Rawyl – always busy with cars – which, some 800m west, feeds into Rue Centrale in Crans, site of the **Crans tourist office** (same hours; ☎027 485 08 00). More or less opposite is the **Étang Long** lakelet, which backs onto the championship golf course.

Winter sports at Crans Montana

Access to the pistes (⊛www.mycma.ch), almost all of which are relatively straight-forward blues and reds – if beautifully scenic – is via five gondolas ranged along the base of the mountain. From west to east, these are **Chetseron** and **Crans** (both within Crans village), **Grand Signal** in Montana, **Violettes** near the Montana funicular station, and **Aminona**. The woods above Montana are crisscrossed by red runs winding between the trees, while **Cry d'Err** above Crans has a host of lifts serving blues galore down to the village. Violettes gives access to the **Plaine Morte** top station (3000m), with some exciting blues, and the start of a long meandering red back to the village. **Lift passes** valid in all four sectors (Crans, Montana, Violettes and Aminona) for one/six days cost Fr.54/262, or Fr.930 for the season.

You can get full information in English on snow conditions, weather, event listings around the resort and local tourist information on Rhône FM, 105.6FM (daily 7.30–10.30am).

Accommodation

Both tourist offices have **hotel boards** outside with free phones, and there's also a central **reservations** number for the resort (☎027 485 04 44; no commission). A host of basic **hotels** offer inexpensive rooms, normally with a choice of ensuite or not: *Pension Centrale* in Crans (☎ & ⓕ027 481 37 67; ❷) and *Olympic* in Montana (☎027 481 29 85, ⓕ027 481 29 53; ❷) are two examples, both in the centre of their villages, and both tidy and well-kept. The *Cisalpin* (☎027 481 25 69, ⓕ027 481 70 83; ❸) is right beside the Violettes gondola, a pack-em-in kind of place, but perfectly OK, while the *Regina* in the centre of Montana (☎027 481 35 22, ⊛www.reginahotel.ch; ❸) is another good option. *Robinson* (☎027 481 13 53, ⓕ027 481 13 14; ❸) is beside the two Crans gondolas, an uncomplicated "garni" place. The *Lac Moubra* **campsite** in Montana (☎027 481 28 51, ⓕ027 481 05 51; closed mid-Oct to Dec) also has basic **dorms** (Fr.20).

Eating and drinking

Eating wins no prizes for invention or quality. Body and soul are kept together by simple diners such as *Crêperie Ma Bretagne* opposite Parking Victoria in Montana, *Café du Centre* beside the church, or *Le Bistrot* opposite Montana tourism. The *Auberge de la Diligence* (☎027 485 99 85), 500m east of Montana's Vermala station, is Lebanese-run, and serves up quality Middle Eastern food (*menus* Fr.22); it also has affordable rooms (❷). Next door, the *Hôtel de la Forêt* (☎027 480 21 31) caters specifically for vegetarians.

Café-Bar 1900 is the place to hang out in the centre of Crans, just round the corner from the Rue du Prado with all the big, glitzy designer names – Vuitton, Gucci, Hermès and all. *Pizzeria Le Prado* is a welcome burst of reality amidst the street's boutiques, serving inexpensive thin-crust pizza and some pasta dishes.

Oberwallis

East of Sierre stretches the German-speaking portion of Valais – or Wallis, as it officially becomes. To mark it out from the Lower Valais to the west, this is known as Upper Valais, or **Oberwallis**. The main town of the region, **Brig**, is an important road and rail junction, but is otherwise of limited interest; the concealed **Lötschen valley** is a far more worthy detour. The reason that everybody passes through the area is to make a pilgrimage to the little mountain village of **Zermatt**, in order to lay eyes upon the **Matterhorn**, the most famous (if not actually the highest) of all Switzerland's mountains. In a side valley nearby sits the equally alluring resort of **Saas-Fee**, while east of Brig, the remote **Goms** region follows the Rhône to its glacial source.

East of Sierre

Heading **east of Sierre**, traffic on the valley-floor road starts to build up as you approach the Lötschberg Tunnel, the turnoffs to Zermatt and Saas-Fee and the Simplon Pass route into Italy. A couple of diversions bring you out of the crush. Just beyond the French–German language border is a turning to the ancient village of **Leuk**, with the spa resort of **Leukerbad** further up; while beyond the Lötschberg Tunnel terminus at Goppenstein, a minor road penetrates between the high rocky walls into the lovely **Lötschental**.

Leuk and Leukerbad

Perched above the valley floor, **LEUK** (Loèche in French; Ⓦ www.leuk.ch) is remarkably good-looking, with an array of photogenic ancient buildings, including a fine Rathaus and medieval Bischofsschloss. Beyond, the road winds up to **LEUKERBAD** (Loèche-les-Bains), Europe's highest spa, at 1411m. Above the village, amidst some decent ski pistes in winter, is the pedestrian-only Gemmi Pass, one end of a tough hiking trail from Kandersteg (see p.317), from where cable-cars bring you down to the village. Soothe your tired muscles at either of the main public spa complexes. The Burgerbad (daily 8am–8pm; May, June & Nov closes 6pm; Fr.21) has outdoor and indoor thermal pools as well as steam baths, plunge pools and exercise rooms; the Alpentherme (same hours; Fr.26) is a more refined affair – indulge in the works

Exploring Oberwallis

The **Regionalpass Oberwallis** (Ⓦ www.regionalpass-oberwallis.ch) costs Fr.160 and is valid for 7 days (June–Oct only). It covers free travel on buses, trains and cable-cars for any 3 days on a vast network extending from Sierre in the west to Disentis and Göschenen in the east, and from Spiez in the north to Zermatt, Saas-Fee and Domodossola in the south. Travel is half-price on this network for the remaining 4 days, and half-price for all 7 days on an extended range including Thunersee and Brienzersee boats, cable-cars at Kandersteg, Saas-Fee and elsewhere, and buses over the Grimsel Pass to Meiringen. All mountain transport above Zermatt and car-train tickets on the Lötschberg and Furka tunnels are a quarter off for the whole 7 days.

△ The Matterhorn (see p.359)

at the Roman-Irish bath for Fr.59. The **tourist office** (☏027 472 71 71,
Ⓦwww.leukerbad.ch) has details of the many discount deals and all-in
packages offered by spa hotels.

The Lötschental

A short distance east, above the villages of Steg and Gampel, is the valley of the
River Lonza. A narrow road switchbacks in tight curves up from the valley
floor; traffic remains heavy until the tiny village of **Goppenstein**, at the southern exit of the Lötschberg Tunnel from Kandersteg (see box p.315), used by
car-carrying trains that shuttle continuously beneath the Alps. Ignore the bustle of this most incongruous rail station, towered over by rocky crags, and head
on. You emerge into the stunningly beautiful **LÖTSCHENTAL**, comprising
half-a-dozen tranquil communities strung along 10km of the valley floor and
overlooked on both sides by Alpine ridges topping 3300m. The huge glaciers
sliding down from the Konkordiaplatz (see p.305) are a constant presence at
the head of the valley. There are few more impressive scenes in the Alps.

Trails from Kandersteg via the **Lötschen Pass** (see p.317) drop down to the
valley floor at the first village, **Ferden** (1389m). Just 2km on, past the photogenic hamlet of **Kippel**, the main valley community is **Wiler**, home both of
the tourist office (☏027 938 88 88, Ⓦwww.loetschental.ch) and a cable-car up
to the **Lauchernalp**. This is the focus of skiing in winter, with access to pistes
up to 3111m on the looming Hockenhorn (a one/six-day pass is Fr.40/200;
Ⓦwww.lauchernalp.ch). The valley-floor road trickles on amidst increasingly
wild and beautiful scenery past **Blatten** to end at the hamlet of **Fafleralp**
(1788m), a scant 4km from the nose of the massive Langgletscher.

A handful of **hotels** and hikers' inns is dotted along the valley. The grand
Lötschberg at Kippel (☏027 939 13 09, Ⓦwww.hotel-loetschberg.ch; ❷) has
been around since 1902; the *Sporting* at Wiler (☏027 939 13 77,
Ⓦwww.rhone.ch/sporting; ❷) and welcoming *Fafleralp* (☏027 939 14 51,
Ⓦwww.fafleralp.ch; ❷) are both good bets. The biggest of half-a-dozen **campsites** is *Lonzastrand* (☏027 939 14 16). The Lötschental is known around
Switzerland for its tradition of mask-making, displayed to full effect in the
week before Ash Wednesday for the extraordinary **Roitschäggättä**, when
locals don grotesque, shaggy masks for a series of night-time parades through
the villages in an ancient Lenten ceremony.

Brig and the Simplon

By virtue of its location, you may find yourself spending a night in the graceful old town of **BRIG** (Brigue in French; Briga in Italian). It's the fulcrum for
a dizzying series of major road and rail routes: southeast through the Simplon
train tunnel into Italy; southwest to Zermatt at the foot of the Matterhorn;
west to Lake Geneva; north through the Lötschberg Tunnel towards Bern; and
northeast to the high Alpine passes.

The huge train station stands at the northern edge of the town, connected to
Brig's broad cobbled central square – the focus of the Old Town and called in
its various sectors **Stadtplatz**, **Marktplatz** and **Sebastiansplatz** – by the
main shopping street of Bahnhofstrasse. Overlooking the square is the tiny
Sebastianskapelle, built by local bigwig Stockalper (see below) in 1637, with
a network of picturesque alleys winding behind and around it.

Lanes off the southeast corner of the square lead along Alte Simplonstrasse past many fine patrician town houses dating from the seventeenth and eighteenth centuries to the **Schloss Stockalper**. This grandiose Italianate palace – for much of its life the largest private residence in Switzerland – dominates the otherwise simple town. It was completed in 1678 to serve as the home of Kaspar Jodok von Stockalper, a merchant from Brig who first made a mint controlling the trade in silk over the Simplon Pass to Lyon, moved on to make another killing organizing mail transport between Milan and Geneva, and finally gained the monopoly in trading salt over the pass. You can stroll from the street into the triple-arcaded interior courtyard, especially beautiful when it catches the sun. Rearing up overhead are three giant corner towers topped by the onion domes that are visible from much of the town. **Entry** to the few rooms open to the public is by guided tour only (May–Oct Tues–Sun 9.30am, 10.30am, 1.30, 2.30 & 3.30pm; June–Sept also 4.30pm; Fr.5) – unless you're confident in reading the German notes, though, or you have an English-speaking guide, you'd best save your money.

Practicalities

Brig's **tourist office** is in the train station up a spiral staircase (July–Sept Mon–Fri 8.30am–6.15pm, Sat 9am–6.15pm, Sun 9am–12.15pm; rest of year Mon–Fri 8.30am–6.15pm, Sat 8.30am–12.30pm; ☎027 921 60 30, ⓦwww.brig-tourismus.ch). They also have information on the resorts around Brig, as well as the Goms region further east (see p.368).

From the forecourt of Brig station, BVZ trains depart for Zermatt, and FO trains head northeast up the valley to Oberwald, through the tunnel beneath the Furka Pass, and on to Andermatt (see p.411). "Glacier Express" panoramic trains (see p.30) use this line to reach Chur, Davos and St Moritz. For details of the Lötschberg Tunnel car-carrying train, see p.315.

Hotels in Brig are all moderately priced. The cheapest option is *La Poste*, Furkastrasse 23 (☎027 924 45 54, ☏027 924 45 53; ❷), which has a few renovated rooms as well as some dorm places (Fr.32). The *Londres & Schweizerhof*, Bahnhofstrasse 17 (☎027 922 93 93, ⓦwww.hotel-delondres.ch; ❸), is a comfortable old place, with pleasant rooms overlooking the main square. The graceful *Schlosshotel*, Kirchgasse 4 (☎027 922 95 95, ⓦwww.schlosshotel.ch; ❷–❸), has bright and attractive rooms overlooking the Schloss Stockalper.

All the **cafés and restaurants** around the main square set tables outside during summer: pick of the bunch is *Zum Eidgenossen*, which offers fondues and meaty Walliser fare in a traditional atmosphere for around Fr.20. Nearby on Alte Simplonstrasse are two pleasant local bistros, *Matza* and *Angleterre*, both serving up pizzas and simple meals. Down by the station, as well as a self-service *Migros*, you'll find the *Hotel Victoria*, which offers good brasserie-style food, with some veggie options (Fr.15–20).

The Simplon Pass and Tunnel

The road over the **Simplon Pass** (2005m), southwest of Brig, was built by Napoleon as a military through-route between 1800 and 1808, immediately after he'd successfully crossed the Grand-St-Bernard with an army (see p.340). These days the old pass road is a modern, Swiss-engineered highway, and the pass itself isn't really worth a specific journey, with views nowhere near as impressive as those from the other great Alpine passes. What *is* worthwhile, though, is to explore the cobbled alleys and picturesque old houses of **Simplon-Dorf** on the other side – still in Switzerland – as well as, down towards the Italian border, the terrifyingly steep and narrow gorge leading to the frontier hamlet of **Gondo**; there are few places where the cliff walls feel so high and you feel so small. A stone next to the road commemorates the victims of a torrential mud slide which swept half the village away in 2000.

A long, energetic two- or three-day hike covers the 35km Stockalper Road, from Brig to Gondo; this is the mule track completed by Stockalper for transport of goods between Italy and the Valais, and has inns aplenty dotted along its route, which is mostly away from the highway.

While you're standing on the pass heights, give a thought for those careering at speed on trains through the **Simplon Tunnel**, some 2400m beneath the Wasenhorn peak just to the east. Until the opening of the new Gotthard Base Tunnel (see p.415), this remains the longest rail tunnel in the world, entered just after leaving Brig station and emerging 19.8km later in Italy for the short run to Domodossola (from where Swiss trains connect on the Centovalli line to Locarno; see p.567), and on south to Milan. The completion of the tunnel in 1905 opened up an entirely new train route from London and Paris to Istanbul – the so-called Venice–Simplon Orient Express – which in turn led to a whole new era in pan-European travel.

The Simplon Pass road is kept open year-round, and offers an easy short-cut if you're driving to the Ticino. From the Italian border at Gondo, it's 22km to Domodossola. Signage on its outskirts is poor, but if you aim for Masera, you'll pick up the road heading east towards Santa Maria Maggiore; it's about 26km to the Swiss border at Camedo, from where the road winds on to Locarno.

Zermatt

St Moritz may have the glamour, Verbier may have the cool, Wengen may have the pistes, but **ZERMATT** beats them all – Zermatt has the **Matterhorn**. No other natural or human structure in the whole country is so immediately recognizable; indeed, in most people's minds the Matterhorn stands for Switzerland, like the Eiffel Tower stands for France. Part of the reason it's so famous is that it stands alone, its impossibly pointy shape sticking up from an otherwise uncrowded horizon above Zermatt village (1620m). But you get the feeling that it would be famous even if it stood within a chain of peaks: there's just something about it that's bizarrely mesmerizing to see for real, and it may well be the most memorable part of your whole holiday.

Emerging from Zermatt station is an experience in itself: this one little village – which has managed, much to its credit, to cling on to its old brown chalets and atmospheric twisting alleys – welcomes everybody, regardless of financial status, and the station square is where all worlds collide. Backpackers and hikers rub shoulders with high-society glitterati amidst a fluster of tour groups, electric taxis and horse-drawn carriages; everyone has come to see the mountain. Zermatt has no off-season – it's crowded year-round – yet the crowds never seem to matter. You may have to shoulder your way down the main street, but the terrain all around is expansive enough that with a little effort you could vanish into the wilderness, leaving everyone else behind.

The small area around Zermatt features 36 mountains over 4000m, a statistic as enticing to summer hikers as to winter skiers. As early as the 1820s, British climbers adopted the isolated hamlet as a base camp from which to scale the nearby peaks. The first hotel opened in 1838. All through the nineteenth century, word of the place spread, and the local community quickly saw the potential: grand hotels went up and public funds were diverted into construction of

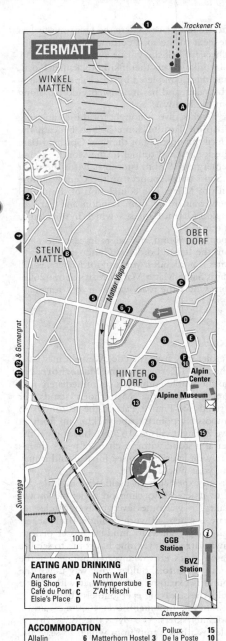

ZERMATT

WINKEL MATTEN

OBER DORF

STEIN MATTE

HINTER DORF

Alpin Center

Alpine Museum

GGB Station

BVZ Station

Campsite ▼

0   100 m

EATING AND DRINKING

Antares	A	North Wall	B
Big Shop	F	Whymperstube	E
Café du Pont	C	Z'Alt Hischi	G
Elsie's Place	D		

ACCOMMODATION

Allalin	6	Matterhorn Hostel	3
Alpina	9	Matterhornblick	7
Bijou	1	Mischabel	13
Bristol	5	Naturfreunde	4
Jugendherberge	2	Perren	14
Pollux	15		
De la Poste	10		
Riffelalp	11		
Riffelberg	12		
Welschen	16		
Zermatterhof	8		

the Gornergrat rack railway at the turn of the century. The skiing boom of the 1960s saw the hamlet double in size, but today it's still acceptably small and low-key, rooted to the valley floor in a natural bowl open to the south. The Gornergrat railway lifts you up to a spectacular vantage point overlooking the **Monte Rosa** massif, with its summit the **Dufourspitze** (4634m) – the highest point in Switzerland. The skiing is superb, but in many ways the hiking is better, with some of the most scenic mountain walks in the whole country within easy reach of the village.

Arrival, orientation and information

BVZ (Ⓦ www.bvz.ch) operates the **trains** from Brig and Visp to Zermatt; they're free to Swiss Pass holders, half-price to InterRailers, and full price to Eurailers. Although **Brig** is the starting point, mainline trains from the west (from Lake Geneva and Sion) are quite often timed to make the connection at **Visp** instead (Viège in French); check the timetable carefully. At both Brig and Visp stations, BVZ trains run on tracks laid in the street outside the front of the station, not from the usual platforms.

South of Visp, trains climb to **Stalden** (departure point for buses to Saas-Fee) and then enter the picturesque Mattertal, clinging precariously above the ravine as they rise higher and higher past a series of villages – as dramatic a prelude to the Matterhorn scenery

Long-term parking

Zermatt is **car-free**, but it doesn't necessarily pay to drive as far you can up the valley – especially if you have a Swiss Pass or similar (see p.32), which gives free or discounted train travel to Zermatt. Certain sections of the large parking garages at and near **Visp** station offer **free indefinite parking** if you ask for a permit at the train station ticket office when you buy your train ticket to Zermatt. However, free parking only applies if you've parked in the right place: look for the clearly marked "BVZ park and ride" car parks to the east (covered) and west (open) of the station, and only use those areas marked with the **BVZ logo** (*not* the SBB one). Check with the train station staff that you're in the right place before you head off or you'll be charged when you return.

If you do choose to drive up the valley, all the villages along the way are well aware of tourists' desire to get something for nothing, and all of them either charge for parking, or happily ticket offenders for parking illegally. In **Täsch**, the end of the road, there are nine massive parking areas, none of them exorbitant (around Fr.6.50/day), but all still charging more than the nothing you can get away with at Visp. The shuttle train from Täsch to Zermatt costs Fr.7.40.

In addition, be aware (as the local residents are) of the **environmental impact** in this highly touristed valley: parking your car at Visp and taking the train is less environmentally damaging than driving to Täsch, even if it may work out a bit more expensive. From Visp, as from anywhere in Switzerland (and even from any airport in the world; see p.12), the train company will transport all your baggage independently for a small fee, letting you travel to Zermatt unencumbered – and, in addition, most Zermatt hotels will collect your bags from the station and deliver them to your room on request. It could hardly be easier.

as you could hope for. A minor **road** also runs along the valley: it's possible to drive as far as the village of **Täsch**, where vast car parks (see box) take care of all motorized transport, with everybody bundling onto trains, and extra Pendelzüge shuttles, for the final twelve-minute pull into Zermatt. Plenty of taxi companies also operate from Täsch, most of them offering discounts on parking if you travel into Zermatt with them.

Zermatt's **BVZ train station** is a large, bustling place, with the usual left-luggage facilities, located at the northern end of the village's main street (there are no street-names). The square outside is generally full of little electric taxis, which cost about Fr.14 for up to four people (more including luggage) to anywhere within the village. There are also two electric buses, free with a ski-pass (or Fr.2.50–3.20), which serve all points. The **GGB Gornergrat-Bahn** station is directly opposite the main station, while the underground funicular to **Sunnegga** leaves from the opposite bank (head east from the station beside the Gornergrat tracks and over the river, then cut left for 100m).

Zermatt's narrow main street, although picturesque, is packed all the way down with shops, hotels, restaurants and – for much of the year – people. To the east, alleys run down into **Hinterdorf**, an attractive old quarter by the river with plenty of accommodation possibilities. Some 400m south of the station is the **church**, another main landmark, from where a street doglegs east over the river past the famous cemetery to the district of **Steinmatte** on the opposite bank. The cable-car station up to **Trockener Steg** and Klein Matterhorn is 500m south of the church.

Information

Zermatt's super-friendly, helpful **tourist office** is right beside the station (mid-June to Sept Mon–Sat 8.30am–6pm, Sun 9.30am–noon & 4–6pm;

mid-Dec to April Mon–Sat 8.30am–noon & 2–6pm, Sun 9.30am–noon & 4–6pm; rest of year Mon–Fri 8.30am–noon & 2–6pm, Sat 9.30am–noon & 2–5pm; ☎027 966 81 00, ⊛www.zermatt.ch), and has everything you could possibly want to know about Zermatt, the Matterhorn, and hiking and skiing possibilities all around. A channel of cable TV within the village shows live pictures from local summits (including the Rothorn, Gornergrat and Trockener Steg) – handy for viewing weather conditions.

Accommodation

Accommodation in Zermatt is almost always excellent. The village is so used to tourists – in fact, there *is* no village without the tourists – that service has been fine-tuned and facilities across all price brackets are good. There are literally dozens of hotels (the tourist office lists 104 just within the village), so you shouldn't have any problem finding somewhere to suit; high season is an exception, when you shouldn't arrive without a reservation. It must be said, too, that **Matterhorn views** from your balcony or window are truly worth paying for: the mountain is so magnificent that you won't get bored of opening your eyes to it each morning.

The favoured method of accommodation in the village, though, is renting an **apartment** or **chalet** – but you should do this well in advance (some places are booked a year ahead), and note that you almost certainly won't be able to get a chalet for less than a Saturday-to-Saturday week. Only a handful of owners are willing to rent for less, and then only in the low season for a minimum three days.

The *Matterhorn* **campsite** is just north of the train station (☎ & ☏027 967 39 21; June–Sept).

Inexpensive hotels

Alpina ☎027 967 10 50,
⊛www.rhone.ch/alpina-zermatt. Down in the Hinterdorf, with amiable staff and a calm atmosphere. ②–③

Gornergrat Kulm ☎027 966 64 00, ⊛www.zermatt.ch/gornergrat.kulm. Solidly built mountain hotel alongside the terminus of the GGB line from Zermatt (see p.361) – reputedly the highest in the Alps, at 3100m. As you might expect, it's a popular spot for day-trippers to gawp at the Matterhorn from the hotel terrace, or eat in the restaurant, but in the evening, after most of the crowds have departed, this can be a uniquely atmospheric place to spend the night. ③–④

Matterhornblick ☎027 967 20 17, ⊛www.matterhornblick.ch. A modern place beside the church, drenched in light pine but living up to its name, with mountain views out back. ③–④

Mischabel ☎027 967 11 31,
⊛www.zermatt.ch/mischabel. Another quality choice in quiet Hinterdorf, an old creaky-floored building with fresh, sunny rooms (none ensuite) and Matterhorn views. ②

Naturfreunde-Hotel ☎027 967 27 88,
⊛www.naturfreunde.ch. Well-kept, cosy rooms (none ensuite) far away from the bustle in Steinmatte, some with the views. ③

De la Poste ☎027 967 19 32, ⊛www.postzermatt.com. Funky main-drag institution, with a popular bar, disco and youthful restaurant topped by a handful of comfortable, individually styled rooms. ③–④

Welschen ☎027 967 54 22,
⊛www.reconline.ch/welschen. A real find, up on a hill beside the Sunnegga station, small, pleasant, spotless and atmospheric. ③

Mid-range and expensive hotels

Allalin ☎027 966 82 66, ⊛www.hotel-allalin.ch. Down-the-line central "garni" hotel beside the church, with new decor and plenty of comforts, including balconies on all rooms (including ones facing south to the Matterhorn). ③–⑤

Bijou ☎027 966 51 51, ⊛www.hotel-bijou.ch. Far away from the centre on a slope just next to the Matterhorn cable-car, a small family-run place with some nice, cosy touches in the rooms. ③–⑤

Bristol ☎027 966 33 66, ⊛www.zermatt.ch/bristol. Excellent mid-range choice, with efficient, friendly service and cosy rooms – those facing south with picture-postcard views (go for the upper floors). ⑤–⑦

Perren ☎027 966 52 00,
ⓦwww.reconline.ch/hotel-perren. Graceful,
modern hotel on the riverbank, with an appealing
stylishness to its well-appointed rooms. A bargain.
④–⑥

Pollux ☎027 966 40 00,
ⓦwww.reconline.ch/pollux. Modern glitzy place
bang on the main drag, with plenty of style and
comfortable rooms, some facing off the street.
⑤–⑧

Riffelalp ☎027 966 05 55, ⓦwww.riffelalp.com.
Superbly renovated hotel, way up at 2222m on the
slopes above the village – for decades a rather
down-at-heel mountain inn, now a full-blown luxury resort, with spacious, stylish rooms and suites,
and some outstanding Matterhorn views. 20min by
GGB train from Zermatt. ⑨

Riffelberg ☎027 966 65 00,
ⓦwww.zermatt.ch/riffelberg. Another ten minutes
up the GGB train line past *Riffelalp* – a fairly standard three-star mountain hotel at 2585m, with

some OK rooms, priced high for the location.
⑤–⑥

Zermatterhof ☎027 966 66 00, ⓦwww.zer-
matt.ch/zermatterhof. The grandest hotel in the
canton, and one of the finest in the country, built
well over a century ago but glitteringly up to date
inside. Manages to be effortlessly luxurious without a hint of tasteless resort swagger. ⑧–⑨

Hostels

Jugendherberge (HI hostel) ☎027 967 23 20,
ⓦwww.youthhostel.ch. Large hostel, way out in
Winkelmatten (beyond Steinmatte), with dorm
beds, many with enticing Matterhorn views, for
Fr.48 half board (breakfast plus a packed lunch or
dinner), as well as bike rental. Closed May & Nov.
①

Matterhorn Hostel (SB hostel) ☎027 968 19
19, ⓦwww.matterhornhostel.com. In the same
quarter as the HI hostel, but on the riverbank, with
dorms from Fr.29 (breakfast extra). ①

In and around the village

Uniquely for a mountain resort, a wander in Zermatt village is actually worth
making time for. East of the main street is the **Hinterdorf** quarter, full of old
weathered-wood chalets and traditional *mazots* (barns raised on stone discs to
protect against mice). The town's burgeoning cemetery is down by the river,
filled with memorials to attempts on the Matterhorn and other peaks gone
wrong. The **Alpine Museum** beside the post office (June–Oct daily
10am–noon & 4–6pm; Nov–May Mon–Fri & Sun 4.30–6.30pm; Fr.8) is
worth a visit, with an interesting collection of mountaineering bits and bobs,
as well as a room devoted to Edward Whymper, an English climber who led
the first ascent of the Matterhorn on July 14, 1865, only for the rope to snap
on the descent – four of his party of seven went over a precipice.

In summer, the slopes above Zermatt hold some of the country's most scenic
hiking trails. The ever-popular GGB Gornergratbahn (25 percent discount for
Swiss Pass holders; ⓦwww.ggb.ch) leads up from the village across the meadows of the Riffelalp to the **Gornergrat** itself (3130m) – get a seat on the
right-hand side for magical Matterhorn vistas. The Gornergrat is the first point
on a ridge that runs out to the Hohtälligrat (3286m) and, amidst a sea of ice,
the **Stockhorn** (3407m), all linked by cable-car from Gornergrat. The view
from any of these peaks is terrific, with the entire Monte Rosa massif laid out
in front of you, the vast Gornergletscher carving along at your feet, and the
Matterhorn itself in isolation away to one side; at your back is the Rothorn
(3103m), behind it the Dom (4545m), and behind the Dom the whole sweep
of the Pennine Alps. Hikes between the various stations on the Gornergrat railway are all immensely rewarding with, for example, three good trails leading
out from the grand hotel alongside the station at **Riffelalp** (see
"Accommodation"), easiest of which is the pleasant one-hour walk up to the
Riffelberg hotel, on a spectacular exposed platform overlooking the valley. In
summer (mid-June to mid-Sept), there are once-weekly dawn trains up to the
Gornergrat so you can catch an awe-inspiring sunrise break on the
Matterhorn; the Fr.79 return ticket includes breakfast at the summit hotel.

From Zermatt village, an underground funicular tunnels up to **Sunnegga** (2300m), also on a plateau and linked to the **Rothorn** summit by gondola. Walks from Sunnegga are beautiful, weaving for a comfortable hour or two

Sports and activities at Zermatt

Skiing and snowboarding

There are three ski and board sectors, each accessed by its own transport route: pistes from **Sunnegga/Rothorn** link to the adjacent **Gornergrat/Stockhorn**, while the **Schwarzsee/Klein Matterhorn** sector, rising to 3900m, connects to the Italian resort of Cervinia. All of them offer satisfying runs at most levels of ability, with a healthy dose of blues and manageable reds around **Blauherd** above Sunnegga, and some good, scenic blues and reds at **Gifthittli** above Riffelberg; from here, long, leg-stretching reds take you down to **Gant** in the valley, which has lifts on both sides up to more choice runs. The spectacular **"Triftji Bumps"**, from Hohtälli above Gornergrat, is one of the most famous black runs in the Alps, but it also has a separate, less challenging red twin that meets it at the bottom.

Top destination has got to be the network of pistes and lifts above **Furi** – once a bottleneck, now benefiting from fast new lifts – with some airy red and black runs around Schwarzsee and **Trockener Steg**, and a long blue dubbed **Gandegg**. The high-level red runs around **Testa Grigia** and the Klein Matterhorn station, well above 3800m, are superb, and there are plenty of options to ski down from here to **Cervinia** (passport needed). Up here on the Theodul glacier is also where you'll find the **Gravity Park**, Europe's biggest snow park, with a 200m super-pipe, half-pipe, kickers, rails and plenty more to keep boarders happy. These pistes also offer memorable **summer skiing** and **boarding**, in a sweeping area from the Klein Matterhorn at 3900m down to Trockener Steg at 2900m.

Schools are led by **Stoked** (ⓦ www.stoked.ch), perhaps the best of Switzerland's new wave of ski and board academies; also check out ⓦ www.skischulezermatt.ch and ⓦ www.matterhornskiwochen.ch. Zermatt comes into its own with the array of heli-skiing (around Fr.300) and off piste possibilities all around the area; schools and the Alpin Center (see below) can advise.

There are three options for **lift passes**, all of them pricey. Skipass 1 gives universal access at Zermatt and Cervinia: one/six days cost Fr.72/362. Skipass 2 covers Zermatt lifts only for Fr.64/320. Skipass 3 covers lifts on the Schwarzsee/Klein Matterhorn sector only, plus Cervinia, for Fr.60/288. Season-long passes are Fr.1470, Fr.1300 and Fr.1174 respectively.

Extreme sports, climbing and trekking

Zermatt's **Alpin Center** (ⓣ 027 966 24 60, ⓦ www.zermatt.ch/alpincenter), on the main street, is the first place to come for advice and guides for extreme sports all year round. In addition to canyoning, ice-climbing, snowshoeing, heli-skiing and more, they run regular guided **climbs** up some of the nearby peaks. The Matterhorn itself is out, unless you have plenty of experience, all the professional apparatus, a week for training, and about Fr.1100 in fees. However, they do run daily guided excursions for Fr.100–200 that are suitable for beginners, including a four-hour trek from Klein Matterhorn across glaciers to Trockener Steg, an easy ascent to a 4000m peak such as the Breithorn, or a basic climbing course on the Riffelhorn. Of a range of extreme events, perhaps the toughest is the **Zermatt Marathon** (ⓦ www.zermatt-marathon.ch), held in July on a regulation 42km course from St Niklaus (1085m) up to the Gornergrat peak (3010m); current record times are an impressive 3hr 34min (men) and 4hr 02min (women). An individual who markets himself as "Jacques, your guide" (ⓦ www.rhone.ch/zermatt-mule-trekking) runs short and long **mule treks** into the wilds (roughly Fr.40/hr per person).

between the tiny lakelets of the Leisee, Moosjesee, Grindjisee and Stellisee out to **Fluhalp** (2616m).

From the south end of Zermatt village, cable-cars run to **Furi** and on up to **Trockener Steg** (2939m), overlooking the gigantic Theodulgletscher, which slides over the Italian border at the foot of the Matterhorn. From Trockener Steg, another cable-car runs up to the crest of the **Klein Matterhorn** – at 3820m, this is the highest cable-car station in Europe, and there's an ice pavilion and other bits and bobs on top to bring the message home. From Furi, though, the cable-car up to the little **Schwarzsee** gives what is commended as the most picture-perfect views of the Matterhorn, at close quarters *and* reflected in a pine-fringed lake. Again hikes abound, including a long but easy walk (7hr) back down into Zermatt village.

One of the best long-distance walks – aside from the Haute Route to Zermatt from Chamonix (see p.342) – is the **Matterhorn Tour**. This comprises a 34-stage circular walk, mostly on Alpine paths, right around the mountain, crossing from the Mattertal into the Val d'Anniviers and Val d'Hérens, as well as into Italy; you'll need to hire a guide for two short stages, across the glacier-bound Theodul Pass and, further round, across a glacier above Arolla. It takes around ten days to do in full, or you can select certain half- or full-day stages. The tourist office has a map and full details.

Eating and drinking

Considering the prices in some of Zermatt's hundred-plus **restaurants**, opting for picnic fare from the Co-op supermarket opposite the train station is a prudent move if you're on a tight budget. There are plenty of places where you can get diner-style fast food for under Fr.15: the *Hotel Post* is the best, incorporating a *Spaghetti Factory* and the famous *Broken* bar and pizzeria, while also on the main street is the *Big Shop* takeaway. The popular *North Wall* bar, on the other side of the river south of the *Bristol*, has pizzas from Fr.12 and big beers for Fr.6. There are a few equally inexpensive cafés beyond the church – best is the peaceful and pleasant *Café du Pont* on a nice corner. *Z'Alt Hischi*, down in Hinterdorf, is another, although it's more of a quiet place to savour a beer than anything else. *Elsie's Place*, opposite the church, is an unexpectedly cosy little nook, although a little over-glitzy in season; at least it offers light snacks to help your cocktail go down.

Moving up the scale, the *Antares*, on the other side of the river, serves quality fish dishes in its plush carved-wood dining room for around Fr.25. The *Rothornstube* in the *Hotel Perren* is another comfortable place where you can select from a range of different *menus*, from Fr.25 to Fr.60 or more. Needless to say, the atmosphere in the *Buffet Royal* at the *Zermatterhof Hotel*, or the glorious Edwardian-style *Whymperstube* in the central *Hotel Monte Rosa*, is formal and restrained, but if you can afford the three-figure sums required, a meal at either of these places is likely to be at least as memorable as your ride to the Gornergrat.

Listings

Changing money Aside from the banks, head to Zermatt Tours beside the tourist office (Mon–Fri 8.30am–noon & 2–6pm; July–Sept & Dec–April also Sun 9am–noon & 3–6pm).
Cinema Kino Vernissage (ⓦwww.vernissage-zermatt.ch), on the main street, has a regular programme of Hollywood movies in sea-

son, and doubles as a trendy bar and club. It's also the venue for July's Bergfilmtage Zermatt (Mountain Film Festival; ⓦwww.bergfilm.ch).
Emergencies Dial ☏144. Air Zermatt have helicopters for mountain rescue (☏027 935 86 86, ⓦwww.air-zermatt.ch).
Flights Among other options, Air Zermatt (see

above) run scenic helicopter flights around the Matterhorn (Fr.195 per person – minimum four people – for a 20min round trip).
Laundry In the *Matterhorn Hostel* (around Fr.7).
Pharmacies Vital Apotheke is at the station (call

027 967 67 77 outside business hours).
Police Beside the church (Mon–Fri 8–10am;
027 966 22 22).
Post office On the main street.

Saas-Fee

Lying in the next-door valley to Zermatt, **SAAS-FEE** (1800m) is sometimes overlooked, perhaps because it doesn't have any train access. However, were it not for the Matterhorn next door, the array of peaks around Saas-Fee would take centre-stage on any Alpine itinerary: the village is perched on a shelf of pasture at the base of a horseshoe of thirteen 4000m-plus peaks. Oozing out from between them is the giant Feegletscher – or Fairy Glacier – trickling its meltwater down through the village, and active enough in its various sectors to limit what would otherwise be spectacular skiing. (The danger of falling down a glacial crevasse if you stray beyond piste-markings is more pronounced in Saas-Fee than in most other resorts.) The village is heavily touristed, but can lay claim to unrivalled Alpine views and landscapes.

Throughout the village you may come across the name Zurbriggen on a number of shop signs; if the name sounds familiar, it's because Pirmin Zurbriggen, a local boy made good, was a downhill skiing world champion in the 1980s. Today, he owns a hotel in tiny Saas Almagell up the valley, as well as another in Zermatt. Various branches of the family have kept their foothold in Saas-Fee.

Saas-Fee is one of four linked villages at the end of the Saastal. **Buses** from Brig pass through Visp and then **Stalden** (both on the BVZ train line) before branching off into the valley, passing first through Saas-Balen, then Saas-Grund, the main village on the valley floor; from here, a road branches up to Saas-Fee – which is car-free – while a few kilometres on down the valley is Saas-Almagell.

Practicalities

From the entrance to Saas-Fee, several quaint lanes lead down (southwest) into the heart of the village, full of shops and some boutiques, but still with much character and charm.

Saas-Fee is car-free, and there is a huge **parking** area at the entrance to the village (Fr.11/day); parking at Saas-Almagell or Saas-Grund is cheaper, but you'd do just as well to take advantage of the cheaper deals in Visp (see box p.361) and catch the bus in. Electro-taxis shuttle around all points in the village for Fr.12–18 or so. The **bus station** is beside the car park, as is the **post office** and, just opposite, the **tourist office** (June–Sept & Dec–April Mon–Fri 8.30am–noon & 2–6.30pm, Sat 8am–7pm, Sun 9am–noon & 3–6pm; rest of year Mon–Sat 8.30am–noon & 2–6pm, Sun 10am–noon & 4–6pm; 027 958 18 58, www.saas-fee.ch). There's also a tourist office in Saas-Grund (Mon–Sat 8.30am–noon & 2–6.30pm; 027 958 11 57, www.saastal.ch), and smaller offices along the valley.

Accommodation

The tourist office has an **accommodation**-booking line (027 958 18 68, to@saas-fee.ch) that can reserve a room at any of the resort's hotels. Saas-

Sports and activities at Saas-Fee

With 13 blue ski runs, 14 red runs, 5 black and 3 unprepared, Saas-Fee is ideal territory for beginners or intermediates, and its snowboarding facilities have made it one of Switzerland's top boarding destinations. The focus of attention is the "Alpin Express" lifts serving the **Felskinn** (3000m); from here, there are plenty of good blue and red runs coming down the side of the huge glacial bowl that towers all around, plus a snowboarding half pipe. From Felskinn, the "Metro Alpin" takes over, the highest underground funicular system in the world, that tunnels up to the **Mittelallalin** station (3500m), below the mighty Allalinhorn summit (4027m). Up here are the world's highest revolving restaurant (ⓦ www.drehrestaurant.ch) and ice pavilion (ⓦ www.eispavillon.ch), as well as a half pipe, a hatful of scenic red runs on the Feegletscher and a long, exhilarating blue all the way down to **Längfluh** (2870m), which is served by its own lifts from the village via Spielboden. An alternative is the lift to **Plattjen** (2570m), from where red and another long blue wind back down to Saas-Fee. There's also **summer skiing** from the Mittelallalin. The **Hannig** (2350m) is barred to skiers, but has good sledge runs and winter walking trails.

    Lift passes for one/six days cost Fr.60/290 for Saas-Fee alone, or Fr.64/314 for additional access to the limited runs above Saas-Grund and Saas-Almagell (ski bus included). Good discount deals for families are available. In addition to the official ski and snowboard school (ⓦ www.saas-fee.ch), check out ⓦ www.eskimos.ch and ⓦ www.bananas.net. The **Mountain Guides** office (ⓦ www.rhone.ch/mountainlife) runs a host of adventure excursions, including husky tours, snowshoe trekking, snow-tubing, ice-climbing and more.

    Hiking routes abound, both in summer, with long treks finding a way between the peaks into the Mattertal, and in winter, when some 30km of trails above the village remain open. The summer seven-day **hiking pass** (Fr.171, family Fr.345) covers all mountain transport in the Saastal plus a host of other discounts.

Grund has several **campsites**, but only the simple *Bergheimat* site (☏027 957 20 66) stays open year-round.

Hotels

Burgener ☏027 958 92 80, ⓦ www .hotel-burgener.ch. Charming little hotel near the lifts, with the quiet *Skihütte* restaurant adjoining. ④–⑤

Dolomit ☏027 957 24 89, ⓦ www.dolomit.ch. Well-run sport hotel, with modern, no-fuss rooms and low prices. Runs guided hikes, mountain-bike rides, climbs and ski-tours. ②–③

Ferienart Walliserhof ☏027 958 19 00, ⓦ www.ferienart.ch. Top-rated hotel bang in the heart of the village, with spa, sauna and solarium in addition to spacious, elegant rooms (a third of them with a Jacuzzi) and superbly luxurious suites. ⑧–⑨

Jägerhof ☏027 957 13 10, ⓦ www.saas-fee .ch/jaegerhof. Fine mid-range option in a tranquil location right on the edge of the village – in winter, you can ski to the door. ④–⑥

Romantik-Hotel Beau Site ☏027 958 15 60, ⓦ www.romantikhotels.com. Superb, central "wellness" hotel, with onsite spa and health centre. A fixture in the village for more than 100 years, with uniquely characterful rooms and attentive service. ⑥–⑧

Saaserhof ☏027 957 35 51, ⓦ www .nova-alpin-hotels.ch. Modern, extremely comfortable four-star hotel, very convenient for the lifts and right beside the slopes. ⑥–⑧

Tenne ☏027 957 12 12, ⓦ www.hotel-tenne.ch. Family hotel in a good, central location, with an upmarket restaurant and fresh, light-pine rooms. ④–⑤

Zur Mühle ☏027 957 26 76, ⓦ www .moulin-saas-fee.ch. Small, excellent-value place in an old burnt-wood chalet, with all rooms facing south and balconied. 500m southwest of the tourist office, close to all the lifts and on the riverbank. ③

Zurbriggen ☏027 958 91 58, ⓦ www .hotel-zurbriggen.ch. Another good mid-range choice, set in its own gardens close to the tourist office. ④

Eating and drinking

Eating and drinking is a case of keep wandering until your stomach, or your eyes, tell you to stop. Next door to each other in the centre are *Boccalino*, doing pizzas and the like for Fr.12–15, and *Pizzeria Philippe*, with quality Italian-inspired *menus* for Fr.22, along with steaks and pizzas from a wood oven. The restaurant attached to *Hotel Zur Mühle* is a reliable proposition for inexpensive Walliser cuisine – mainly fondues and raclettes. Grab a table on the terrace of the *Skihütte* restaurant, attached to *Hotel Burgener*, for good local cooking and superb views. *La Ferme*, near the tourist office, is a step up in quality, with good *menus* from Fr.25 and brave attempts at rustic decor. The sky's the limit for gourmet cuisine, exemplified by two temples to the art: the *Fletschhorn* (☏027 957 21 31), out in the woods north of the village, and the restaurant within *Hotel Walliserhof* (☏027 958 19 00), in the centre.

The Goms

The upper part of the Rhône valley, stretching from Brig to the high Alpine passes, is known as **the Goms** (🌐 www.goms.ch). Winter sees thick snow covering the whole region, perfect for cross-country skiing at all levels. Traffic, at least in the warmer months, is always heavy on the valley road heading up to the Furka, Grimsel and Nufenen passes, but drivers generally prefer to keep their foot down, zipping past the pine forests and wide-open meadows, and through picturesque little villages of traditional darkwood chalets. If you've got a car, it's worth stopping off at a couple of places on the long drive up the valley. Buses and local trains from Brig stop at all villages.

About 8km out of Brig you'll pass **Mörel**, with signs for cable-cars rising west to **RIEDERALP** and, a little further on, **Betten**, with cable-cars to **BETTMERALP**. Both these car-free resorts are perched on ridge-top plateaux, with lifts serving the huge and unspoilt **Aletschwald**, one of the highest pine forests in Europe, which in turn overlooks the gigantic **Aletsch Glacier**, a mammoth ice sheet – longest in the Alps, and a UNESCO World Natural Heritage Site – which winds its way down 23km from the base of the Jungfrau. There are hiking possibilities galore around here, and tourist offices in Riederalp (🌐 www.riederalp.ch) and Bettmeralp (🌐 www.bettmeralp.ch) can provide details of specific trails, as well as of the network of inns and mountain huts which can provide wilderness accommodation. **Fiesch**, the next main town along the valley, has lifts up to the vantage point of the **Eggishorn**, above the hamlet of Kuhboden, offering the finest views of the glacier.

Above Fiesch, the Rhône is little more than a fast-flowing mountain brook, and the villages become smaller and more rural. Some 6km past Fiesch is the hamlet of **Niederwald**, which proudly announces its claim to fame with a US-style billboard: it was here, in 1850, that César Ritz, who went on to found the Ritz hotel chain, was born. Some 3km further on is the little community of **MÜNSTER**. Away from the main road, the tranquil village is characterized by the traditional Valaisian-style chalets, all clustered together higgledy-piggledy, burnt a rich dark brown and decorated with pretty geranium window boxes. At their centre is a striking white church with a wood-panelled barrel-vault ceiling and florid Baroque interior – this is thought to be all that remains of a medieval monastery which once stood somewhere nearby. The handful of hotels in the village is worth passing over in favour of the extraordinary *Croix d'Or et Poste* beside the main road (☏027 974 15 15, 🌐 www.hotel-postmuenster.ch;

❷–❸), a marvellous old building dating from 1620. Up to 1900 or so it was the residence of the noble family of prince-bishops Von Riedmatten; these days, it's every bit as atmospheric as that sounds, its public rooms draped with Victorian bric-à-brac, the few guest rooms more subdued but still characterful. Value for money extends to the cooking as well, with superb *menus* for Fr.20–25.

The high Alpine passes

Above Münster, you enter the Obergoms region (Upper Goms), and begin to approach the high Alpine passes. The guaranteed snow up here, and breathtaking scenery, makes for some outstanding cross-country skiing. Ulrichen, 4km on, has a turning southeast along the Agenetal to the **Nufenen Pass**, or Passo della Novena (2478m), which crosses into Ticino and the Val Bedretto (see p.559). The main road continues through **Oberwald** (1368m), where the Obergoms tourist office is located (☏027 973 32 32, ⓦwww.obergoms.ch), and then immediately begins to climb in a series of great looping switchbacks.

Way above Oberwald is the junction point of **GLETSCH** (1759m) – not really even a hamlet, but with a hotel, *Glacier du Rhône* (☏027 973 15 15, ⓦwww.glacier-du-rhone.ch; ❶–❷; June–Sept), from which to enjoy the spectacular views. In summer, DFB (ⓦwww.furka-bergstrecke.ch) runs an antique **steam train** on a cogwheel track through spectacular scenery up to the Furka Pass via a short tunnel at Muttbach, heading on to Realp (see p.415). The round trip costs Fr.93.

Furka Pass

Northeast from Gletsch, heading up to the Furka Pass, the road sidewinds its way up the cliffside, coiling around the landmark **Hotel Belvédère** on the way (2300m). In season, this once-grand edifice is swamped by the tide of traffic swarming up the road; it's not worth staying here, but it is worth stopping for the breathtaking views down into the valley, and also to explore the **Rhône Glacier**, which fills the head of the valley to the north. This is the source of the Rhône itself, which you can see spouting out as meltwater from beneath the glacier's eaves. Owners of a souvenir stall in the *Belvédère*'s car park have cashed in on the glacier's appeal – and its proximity to the road – by carving, fresh each year, a tunnel deep into the blueish ice for their many customers to walk along (June–Oct daily 8am–6pm; Fr.5). By the end of the summer, about a third of the tunnel's length has melted, as the glacier shifts by some 30m each year. A short climb further is the **Furka Pass** itself (2431m; see also p.415), beyond which lie Realp and Andermatt.

Grimsel Pass

The other road from Gletsch climbs west in ever tighter curves up to the **Grimsel Pass** (2165m), which marks the border between Valais and Canton

---

Car-carrying trains

If you're heading east and would prefer to avoid the climb over the Furka Pass, note that **car-carrying trains** run daily year-round from Oberwald through the **Furka-Basis Tunnel** to Realp, at least every hour (6am–9pm); a one-way fare is Fr.30, or Fr.25 between June and September. You can also avoid the climb over the **Oberalp Pass** by loading your car onto a train at Andermatt for the hour-long pull to Sedrun (Fr.65). Get information on both at ⓦwww.fo-bahn.ch.

Bern. There are three hotels on the top, and this is an extraordinarily dramatic place to spend the night, with the bare, snow-patched rocks rising all around, the summit Totensee ("Dead Lake") icy all summer, and stunning sunset views down over the Grimselsee just below. The *Grimselblick* (☎027 973 11 77, ⓦwww.grimselpass.ch; ❶) is the best on offer, a cosy place once the daytime tour buses have departed, with one particularly enticing ensuite double room, complete with four-poster bed, that's worth asking for. On the other side of the lake is the simpler *Alpenrösli* (☎033 973 12 91, ⒻF033 973 12 90; ❶). Three buses a day (July–Sept) run from Oberwald to Meiringen via the Grimsel Pass.

Travel details

Trains

Aigle to: Bex (hourly; 5min); Champéry (hourly; 1hr 5min); Les Diablerets (hourly; 45min); Lausanne (every 30min; 30min); Leysin (hourly; 30min); Martigny (every 30min; 20min); Montreux (every 30min; 10min); St-Maurice (hourly; 10min).
Bex to: Aigle (hourly; 5min); Villars (hourly; 45min).
Brig to: Andermatt (hourly; 1hr 45min); Bern (hourly; 1hr 40min); Chur ("Glacier Express" at least 1 daily via Furka–Oberalp; 4hr 10min); Domodossola, Italy (hourly; 35min); Interlaken West & Ost (hourly; 1hr 25min; change at Spiez); Lausanne (twice hourly; 1hr 35min); Martigny (every 30min; 50min); Sion (every 30min; 35min); Zermatt (hourly; 1hr 20min); Zürich (hourly; 3hr).
Martigny to: Aigle (every 30min; 20min); Brig (every 30min; 50min); Lausanne (every 30min; 50min); Orsières (hourly; 25min); St-Maurice (twice hourly; 10min); Sierre (every 30min; 25min); Sion (3 hourly; 15min); Verbier (hourly; 50min; change at Le Châble).
St-Maurice to: Aigle (hourly; 10min); Martigny (twice hourly; 10min).
Sierre to: Brig (every 30min; 25min); Lausanne (every 30min; 1hr 15min); Martigny (every 30min; 25min); Montana (every 30min; 15min); Sion (twice hourly; 10min).
Sion to: Aigle (every 30min; 30min); Brig (every 30min; 35min); Lausanne (every 30min; 1hr); Martigny (3 hourly; 15min); St-Maurice (every 30min; 25min); Sierre (every 30min; 10min); Zermatt (hourly; 1hr 40min–2hr; change at Visp).
Visp to: Zermatt (hourly; 1hr 10min).
Zermatt to: Brig (hourly; 1hr 20min); Gornergrat (at least every 30min; 45min); Visp (hourly; 1hr 10min).

Buses

Aigle to: Villars (every 2hr; 35min).
Brig to: Saas-Fee (hourly; 1hr 10min).
Le Châble to: Mauvoisin (July–Sept twice daily; 45min); Verbier (hourly; 25min).
Crans to: Montana (continuously; 5min); Sion (hourly; 45min); Sierre (every 30min; 40–50min).
Les Diablerets to: Gstaad (5 daily; 50min); Villars (July–Sept 3 daily; 35min).
Leysin to: Château d'Oex (3 daily; 1hr 30min; change at Le Sépey).
Martigny to: Chamonix, France (hourly; 1hr 30min); Grand-St-Bernard Pass (1 daily; 2hr; change at Orsières).
Montana to: Crans (continuously; 5min); Sierre (every 30min; 40–50min).
Oberwald to: Airolo via Nufenenpass (July–Sept 2 daily; 1hr 30min); Andermatt via Furkapass (July–Sept 2 daily; 1hr 30min); Meiringen via Grimselpass (July–Sept 3 daily; 1hr 20min).
Orsières to: Champex (every 2hr; 20min).
Saas-Fee to: Brig (hourly; 1hr 10min); Stalden (hourly; 40min).
Sierre to: Crans (every 30min; 40–50min); Montana (every 30min; 40–50min); Sion (hourly; 30min); Zinal (every 2hr; 1hr; change at Vissoie).
Sion to: Arolla (every 2hr; 1hr 20min; change at Les Haudères); Crans (hourly; 45min); Sierre (hourly; 30min).
Stalden to: Saas-Fee (hourly; 40min).
Villars to: Aigle (every 2hr; 35min); Les Diablerets (July–Sept 3 daily; 35min).
Visp to: Saas-Fee (hourly; 55min).

Luzern and Zentralschweiz

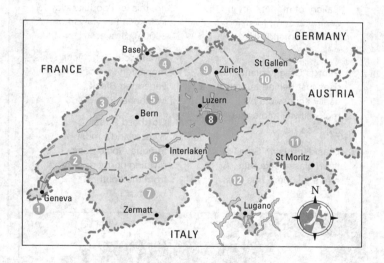

✳ **Vierwaldstättersee**
Experience the stunning-
ly beautiful Lake Luzern
from the deck of an old-
time steamer. See p.379

✳ **Luzerner Fasnacht** The
biggest carnival in
Switzerland. See p.383

✳ **Sammlung Rosengart**
Gallery of modern art in
central Luzern, focusing
on Picasso and Klee.
See p.386

✳ **Pilatus** Craggy giant that
rises just behind Luzern,
easily accessible by
rack-railway and cable-
car. See p.387

✳ **Glasi Hergiswil** Small-
town glassworks that
offers a superb free tour.
See p.395

✳ **Weg der Schweiz**
Scenic lakeside walking
route in William Tell
country. See p.397

✳ **Titlis** Year-round skiing
and snowboarding
above the village of
Engelberg. See p.400

✳ **Rigi** With three routes
up, this is a popular way
to take in the views from
2000m. See p.401

✳ **Einsiedeln** Benedictine
monastery housing the
venerated Black
Madonna. See p.408

✳ **Gotthard Pass**
Switzerland's most
famous Alpine pass,
dividing northern Europe
from the south. See
p.414

Luzern and Zentralschweiz

T
he oddly shaped **Vierwaldstättersee** ("Lake of the Four Forest Cantons") lies at the geographical and spiritual heart of Switzerland. It's the country's most beautiful and dramatic body of water by far, thickly wooded slopes rising sheer from misty wavelets, bays and peninsulas giving constantly changing views from vantage points on the decks of the steamers which ply to and fro. At the lake's western tip, **Luzern** (often anglicized to Lucerne) is an attractive town steeped in history that is a natural gateway to the diverse **Zentralschweiz** region all around.

Zentralschweiz – or, as it is often dubbed, Innerschweiz – is a land of tradition. Here, in the tidy little villages of Switzerland's core, is where the founding myths of the country are nurtured. In the Middle Ages, the communities of the four so-called "forest cantons" dotted around the lake – **Uri**, **Schwyz**, **Nidwalden** and **Obwalden** (the last two often conflated as "Unterwalden") – guarded the approaches to the **Gotthard Pass**, key to the newly opened road between northern and southern Europe. When Habsburg overlords tried to encroach on their privileges, the communities formed an alliance at the lakeside Rütli Meadow in 1291 which was to prove the beginning of the Swiss Confederation. Luzern, as the principal market town for the region, was drawn into the bond shortly after, and tales soon began to circulate of a legendary figure from the Uri countryside named **William Tell**, who had pitted his wits against the local Habsburg tyrant and won. Today, the clifftop paths and shoreline trails of this region are trod less by foreigners than by a tide of Swiss tourists who make the journey from their suburban homes to walk in the footsteps of William Tell and the semi-mystical founders of the nation.

Transport links around the region are excellent, with the fleet of lake steamers from Luzern running throughout the year, serving shoreside villages and small resorts tucked against the sugarloaf cliffs that have little or no road access. In addition, a handful of rack-railways serve mountain tops around the lake (most famously the **Pilatus** and the **Rigi**), and plenty of easy short- and long-distance hiking trails can get you well off the beaten path – although many also hop conveniently from one landing-stage to the next. Central Switzerland's long-standing tradition of tourism means that every hamlet has its choice of hotels and restaurants. The array of sights, excursions, museums and activities makes this one of the densest, and most rewarding, areas of the country to explore.

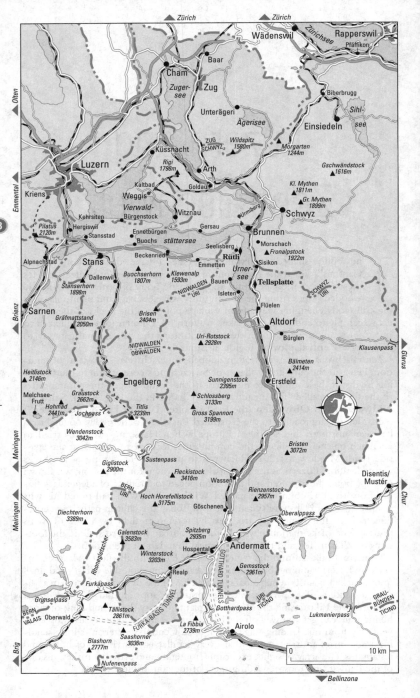

The Vierwaldstättersee stutter

The large lake lying at the centre of Switzerland has five different names, depending on the language you happen to be speaking. In German, it is the Vierwaldstättersee; in French, Le Lac des Quatre-Cantons; in Italian, Il Lago dei Quattro Cantoni; and in Romansh, Il Lai dals Quatter Chantuns – all of which translate as "The Lake of the Four (Forest) Cantons". However, these tongue-twisters are all way too much for most English-speaking tourists, and so for as long as foreigners have been coming to the lake, it's been dubbed the **Lake of Lucerne** or **Lake Luzern** – names you'll never hear Swiss people using to one another.

Luzern

There's nothing really wrong with Lucerne, except the people who go there.
John Russell, *Switzerland* (1950)

An hour south of Basel and Zürich, and boasting invigorating mountain views, lake cruises and a picturesque old quarter, **LUZERN** (Lucerne in French and English, Lucerna in Italian) has long been one of Europe's most heavily touristed towns. When Queen Victoria came for a long holiday in August 1868 (checking in under a pseudonym), the town was already well-known, and a century of steady growth has resulted these days in five million admirers passing through annually. Tourism is the leading source of income, which in recent years has led, in some quarters, to a rather blasé attitude towards visitors: although the city has retained a good deal of charm, the same can't be said of its restaurant waiters and hotel staff. You may find your experience of the city, in the summer high season in particular, being coloured by association with the hordes of short-stay trippers that rush through on their way to the mountains.

The River Reuss splits the town, flowing rapidly out of the northwestern end of the lake. River banks on both sides are clustered with medieval squares, frescoed houses, ancient guildhalls, churches and chapels, and filled with a commercially minded liveliness that belies the city's age. Aside from using Luzern as a base from which to explore the region, it would be easy to spend at least a couple of days taking in some of its quality museums – the outstanding Rosengart gallery, a unique Picasso museum, the impressive Verkehrshaus – in between walking on the medieval battlements, and exploring cobbled alleys and hidden garden courtyards.

But Luzern is no museum piece; the city's large population of young people love their café culture, and at midnight on a weekend night, the main Pilatusstrasse boulevard has the buzz of any European capital, with people bar-hopping, waiting for the last bus, or hanging out deciding where to go. Whether you're charmed by Luzern's sense of history and tradition, or by the misty lake at its doorstep and the snow-capped Pilatus rising above, or even by its nightlife, charmed is what you'll be.

Some history

Luzern's founding is lost in history. The town's name probably derives from the Celtic word *lozzeria*, meaning "a settlement on marshy ground", and that's more or less all Luzern was in the mid-eighth century when the small Benedictine **monastery** which existed here is thought to have come under the control of the Alsatian Abbey of Murbach. Nothing concrete is known about Luzern until 1178, when an abbot established a lay order at the Kapellkirche (now St Peter's Chapel), indicating that quite a substantial settlement must have existed in the area. Around 1220, the opening of the **Gotthard Pass** further south created new impetus for growth, with merchants and travellers setting sail from Luzern for the long trans-Alpine journey (the first lakeside road was built only in 1865).

Eyeing the prosperity flowing into the communities on the northern side of the new pass, Rudolf of Habsburg bought Luzern outright from Murbach in 1291, intending to subdue it and channel its profits into the imperial coffers. At the same time, though, the peasant farmers of Uri, Schwyz and Unterwalden on the eastern shores of the lake had formed a pact of mutual defence at **Rütli** (see box p.396) against the Austrian threat, and after some instability, Luzern joined them in 1332, the first major city to do so. This pact was the beginning of the Swiss Confederation, which survives today. Pro-Habsburg attempts to undermine the pact continued to flourish; one legend from the time tells of a boy who overheard conspirators meeting in the riverside marketplace at Unter der Egg. The plotters caught the boy and forced him to swear under oath that he would tell no living soul what he had heard them discuss, so the boy ran straight to a nearby guildhall and interrupted a Confederate meeting to tell his whole story to the tiled stove in the corner of the room. The confederates "overheard" the boy's tale, and so were able to thwart the plot. (The stove which stands today in the corner of the restaurant *Metzgern* on Weinmarkt is allegedly the self-same one.) The defeat of Austrian forces in the **Battle of Sempach** in 1386 severed the Habsburg claim to Luzern, and the city's elders reinforced their independence by building the Musegg fortifications, which are still standing.

Luzern remained Catholic throughout the Reformation and, like much of the country, was ruled by patrician families up until the late eighteenth-century revolutions. The early nineteenth-century quarrels in politics and religion led to civil war, with Luzern at the heart of the Catholic rebel **Sonderbund** (see p.587) – an association which, after Confederate forces had reasserted their control in 1847, led to Luzern being passed over for the choice of federal capital.

By this time, though, **tourism** to Switzerland had already begun, and with the cessation of hostilities Luzern became a focus for the increasing tide of foreign visitors, both for its own lakeside location, and as the gateway to the high Alps. In 1834, the mid-thirteenth-century Hofbrücke, which had linked the Hofkirche to the Old Town across a now-vanished marshy inlet, was torn down in favour of redeveloping the city centre and creating new lakeside promenades. Many old buildings and part of the medieval fortifications – with over forty towers and gates – were destroyed. The railway arrived in 1859, and over the following fifty years, Luzern's population quadrupled to forty thousand, with tourism, then as now, the mainstay of the city's economy. All through the twentieth century, Luzern has clung tight onto its conservative, traditional roots: these days, the city is renowned as the heartland of Switzerland's SVP, an extreme right-wing political party with a strident and increasingly successful set of anti-immigration, anti-EU policies.

Arrival, information and lake transport

Luzern's giant **train station** – opened in 1991 to replace the grand nineteenth-century original which burned to the ground in 1971 (one arch survives, marooned in front of the new building) – is on the south bank of the Reuss, exactly at the point where the lake narrows into the river. Broad **Pilatusstrasse** runs southwest from Bahnhofplatz into the main shopping and commercial districts of the modern city. From the busy bus stops outside the station, the main Seebrücke takes traffic over the Reuss alongside the ancient **Kapellbrücke**, the latter marked by the distinctive stone Wasserturm (water tower). The pedestrian-only alleys of the Old Town occupy the northern bank, with the city walls ranged on the slopes above, as well as a small part of the southern bank.

If you're **driving**, try to arrange parking with your hotel or leave your vehicle in the suburbs: Luzern is just about the most car-hostile city in Switzerland, with a fiendish one-way system woven tightly around the pedestrianized Old Town. There's virtually no chance of finding a parking space on the street and the scattering of expensive parking garages are often full.

Information

The **tourist office** has entrances on platform 3 of the train station and at Zentralstrasse 5 (mid-June to mid-Sept Mon–Fri 8.30am–8.30pm, Sat & Sun 9am–8.30pm; May to mid-June & mid-Sept to Oct daily closes 7.30pm; Nov–April daily closes 6pm; ☏041 227 17 17, ⓦwww.luzern.org). With the vast quantity of tourists tramping through the city, staff are well used to answering questions, and have stacks of information to impart – but you should be prepared to queue at peak times. Luzern's **guest card**, which you must get stamped by your hotel, is good value, giving discounts on entry to most museums and car rental; it also allows you to purchase a special Fr.12 three-day city bus pass (although Swiss Pass holders travel free anyway). The local **museum pass** (Fr.29) – also a good deal – gives free entry to all the city's attractions for a month. A two-hour city **walking tour** (May–Oct daily 9.45am; Nov–April Wed & Sat 9.45am; Fr.16) departs from the tourist office, led by exceptionally well-informed guides.

Luzern's festivals

Luzern's two biggest festivals come from opposite ends of the cultural spectrum. February's **carnival** (see box p.383) features the biggest celebrations in the country, with six days and nights of continuous drinking and raucous partying. The city also plays host to one of Europe's most prestigious classical music events, the **Lucerne Festival** (ⓦwww.lucernefestival.ch), inaugurated in 1938 with a concert conducted by Arturo Toscanini in the grounds of Wagner's lakeside house at Tribschen. The festival comprises three separate elements. The "Sommer" event, in August and September, is the main one, a concert cycle held in venues ranging from the stunning KKL concert hall to town churches and even the Löwendenkmal that draws the world's finest soloists and orchestras. Smaller offshoots – "Ostern" at Easter, with a mix of classic and contemporary, sacred and secular music; and "Piano" in November, focusing on keyboard soloists in jazz and the classics – fill out the annual programme. Luzern also has an array of other music festivals, including two major blues events, in July and November. The fourth Saturday in June is the day of the **Altstadtfest** – the Old Town filled with oompah bands and food and beer stalls – while July sees prestigious international **rowing** regattas held on the Rotsee, a long, narrow lake 2km north of town.

The tourist office runs a host of **guided excursions**. The most popular are the half-day tours to the summit of the **Pilatus** overlooking the city (see box p.387), the **Rigi** a short way east (see p.401) and the **Titlis** to the south (see p.400), all of which operate daily all year for around Fr.90 – although it's easy to do the same trips yourself for less. Staff can also sell you the regional travel pass for Central Switzerland, the **Tellpass** (see box p.394), although this is only

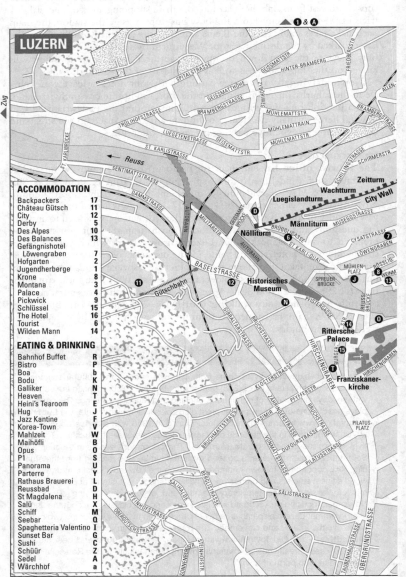

LUZERN

ACCOMMODATION

Backpackers	17
Château Gütsch	11
City	12
Derby	5
Des Alpes	10
Des Balances	13
Gefängnishotel Löwengraben	7
Hofgarten	2
Jugendherberge	1
Krone	8
Montana	3
Palace	4
Pickwick	9
Schlüssel	15
The Hotel	16
Tourist	6
Wilden Mann	14

EATING & DRINKING

Bahnhof Buffet	R
Bistro	P
Boa	b
Bodu	K
Galliker	N
Heaven	T
Heini's Tearoom	E
Hug	J
Jazz Kantine	F
Korea-Town	V
Mahlzeit	W
Maihöfli	B
Opus	O
P1	S
Panorama	U
Parterre	Y
Rathaus Brauerei	L
Reussbad	D
St Magdalena	H
Salü	X
Schiff	M
Seebar	Q
Spaghetteria Valentino	I
Sunset Bar	G
Sushi	C
Schüür	Z
Sedel	A
Wärchhof	a

really worthwhile if you're touring the region: the free guest card is more than adequate for a city-based stay.

Lake transport

A major reason for coming to Luzern is to explore the stunning Vierwaldstättersee, or **Lake Luzern**, crossed year-round by the fine old boats

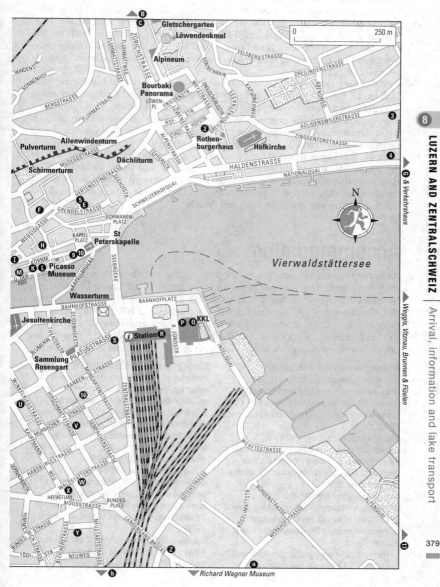

▼ Richard Wagner Museum

of the SGV (☎041 367 67 67, ⓦ www.lakelucerne.ch), free to Eurail and Swiss Pass holders, as well as on selected days to holders of the Tellpass, and half-price to InterRailers. All SGV boats – including their half-dozen paddle steamers (which incur no extra fare) – depart from the quay directly outside the station, and zigzag their way across the lake, stopping at places on both shores: **Alpnachstad** gives access to the Pilatus summit; **Weggis** and **Vitznau** to Mount Rigi; **Kehrsiten** to Bürgenstock, and from there to the Hammetschwand summit; and **Beckenried** to Klewenalp. All of these have limited road and rail connections, but at the far, eastern end of the lake, **Brunnen** (close to Schwyz) and **Flüelen** (close to Altdorf) are both on the mainline route from Zürich to Lugano, and are less than an hour's train journey from Luzern, making it easy to construct half- and full-day round trips by boat and train.

In summer (June–Sept), at least seven boats daily make the full run from Luzern to Flüelen, with several more serving Brunnen, Vitznau and other intermediate points. In autumn (Oct) and spring (April & May), service is slightly curtailed in the evenings. Winter (Nov–March) sees two boats a day as far as Brunnen, with Flüelen served only by Sunday services. With round-trip **fares** Luzern–Vitznau at Fr.29, Luzern–Brunnen at Fr.39 and Luzern–Flüelen at Fr.44, the **Tagesbillett** (Day Ticket; Fr.44), valid for unlimited journeys on the whole lake, is a good deal if you don't already hold a pass. In addition, SGV runs a wealth of **cruises** and eat-aboard trips, including a three-hour sunset cruise (mid-May to mid-Sept daily; Fr.20). The tourist office, and the SGV ticket office on the quayside, have full details.

Accommodation

Accommodation covers the gamut from dorms to palaces. Summer is especially busy, with double-room prices in many hotels rising almost fifty percent: an establishment we've listed at ❺ to reflect high-season prices might charge ❸ prices between October and April. Booking ahead is a priority across all price brackets; the tourist office has a dedicated reservation line (☎041 227 17 27), and there's a reservation booth (Mon–Sat 11am–2pm & 3–6pm), plus notice board and complimentary phone, on the lower concourse of the station.

Inexpensive hotels

Des Alpes Furrengasse 3 ☎041 410 58 25, ⓦ www.desalpes-luzern.ch. Comfortable rooms, some with balconies, in an old building with a picturesque waterfront setting and a good restaurant. ❸–❹

City Baselstrasse 15 ☎041 240 23 23, ⓦ www.hotelguide.com. Basic place a little west of the centre on a busy street (so ask for a back room), with poky, generic rooms that are nonetheless kept clean. ❷

Derby Falkengasse 6 ☎041 410 26 62, ⓔ derby.luzern@bluewin.ch. Plain, decent, generic "garni" place in the Old Town, with compact, characterless rooms and a fifty-percent price hike in summer. ❷–❸

Gefängnishotel Löwengraben Löwengraben 18 ☎041 417 12 12, ⓦ www.loewengraben.ch.

Luzern's Old Town prison from 1862 to 1998, now converted to a surprisingly classy budget hotel, with a hip, lively atmosphere. The staff frogmarch you down the long corridors to the spotlessly refurbished cells – inevitably poky, but complete with ensuite shower cubicle and barred windows. Prime choice is the panelled Director's Suite, the former prison governor's office, with a double bed where the desk used to be. ❷–❸

Pickwick Rathausquai 6 ☎041 410 59 27, ⓦ www.hotelpickwick.ch. In spartan contrast to *Des Alpes* next door, an English-style pub with rooms above, sharing the excellent views but not the welcoming management style of its neighbour. ❶–❷

Schlüssel Franziskanerplatz 12 ☎041 210 10 61, ⓕ041 210 10 21. The most characterful low-end accommodation in town, and the oldest hotel in

Luzern to boot. Only ten rooms, some of which overlook the quiet square of the Franciscan church and the formal gardens of the eighteenth-century Segesser mansion. ❶–❷

Tourist St Karliquai 12 ☎041 410 24 74, ⓦwww.touristhotel.ch. Clean, bright and very central, this has the atmosphere of a student dorm although the quality of the rooms (and the helpful management) speak more of a houseproud, good-value hotel. Some have suntrap balconies facing the river – peaceful, since the bankside road is quiet. Also dorms (see below). ❶–❷

Mid-range and expensive hotels

Des Balances Weinmarkt ☎041 418 28 28, ⓦwww.balances.ch. A reverentially white lobby preludes a super-chic Old Town hotel, more reminiscent of midtown Manhattan than little Luzern. Back rooms overlook the water. ❺–❼

Château Gütsch Kanonenstrasse 7 ☎041 249 41 00, ⓦwww.chateau-guetsch.ch. A nineteenth-century castle-folly perched on a wooded hill way above the town, lit up at night like a fairytale palace and with its own funicular for access. The gourmet restaurant downstairs is as nothing compared to the grand romance of the rooms, all with huge baths and many with fourposter beds. ❻–❽

Hofgarten Stadthofstrasse 14 ☎041 410 88 88, ⓦwww.hofgarten.ch. The best-value hotel in Luzern, and one of the most attractive small city hotels in the country. A centuries-old protected building set in a quiet courtyard near the Hofkirche, with an excellent vegetarian terrace restaurant and eighteen modern, individually decorated rooms, all fresh, bright and carefully furnished. ❺

Krone Weinmarkt 12 ☎041 419 44 00, ⓦwww.krone-luzern.ch. Friendly, bright family hotel in the heart of the Old Town, with all-modern fittings in spacious, pastel rooms. ❹–❺

Montana Adligenswilerstrasse 22 ☎041 419 00 00, ⓦwww.hotel-montana.ch. Exceptionally classy Art-Deco hotel on a hillside above the lake, reached by its own funicular and boasting spectacular views. The 1920s-style decor is faultless, and rooms are generous and attractive; this has been rated as the best four-star hotel in the country. ❺–❻

Palace Haldenstrasse 10 ☎041 416 16 16, ⓦwww.palace-luzern.com. A giant Belle Epoque landmark catering for the ritziest of tastes, revelling both in wide-open views across the lake to Mount Pilatus, and the grandest of appointments to the broad, lofty guest rooms. With the huge *Kursaal* next door and the *Grand Hotel National* just beyond, these three edifices between them occupy half a kilometre of the city waterfront. ❼–❾

The Hotel Sempacherstrasse 14 ☎041 226 86 86, ⓦwww.the-hotel.ch. Outstanding new boutique hotel overlooking a quiet city-centre park, designed by architect Jean Nouvel and featuring chic, modern suites and studios decorated in dark, matt tones and brushed steel. Each guest room has a huge still image from a classic movie covering the ceiling, adding to the hip allure. ❽

Wilden Mann Bahnhofstrasse 30 ☎041 210 16 66, ⓦwww.wilden-mann.ch. Outstanding choice in this price-bracket, a historic hotel dating back to 1517 that occupies seven adjoining town houses amidst the atmospheric south-bank Old Town lanes: opposite is an antique pharmacy, behind is the medieval mint. Rooms are generous, tastefully decorated with plenty of rich wood, and quiet, while the service has an elusive blend of alertness and subtlety often lacking in grander places. Member of the Romantik group. ❺–❻

Hostels

Backpackers (SB hostel) Alpenquai 42 ☎041 360 04 20, ⓦwww.backpackerslucerne.ch. Friendly former student house on the lakeshore 800m southeast of the station; take bus #6, #7 or #8 to Weinbergli, then head left for 150m. Pleasant dorms cost Fr.27; also basic doubles. ❶

Gefängnishotel Löwengraben (see "Inexpensive Hotels"). Dorms at Luzern's trendy, old-town "jail hotel" are Fr.30. ❷–❸

Jugendherberge (HI hostel) Sedelstrasse 12 ☎041 420 88 00, ⓦwww.youthhostel.ch. Quality hostel 1km northwest of town near the Rotsee lake; bus #18 to Jugendherberge. Dorms Fr.32. ❶

Tourist (see "Inexpensive Hotels"). Good, affordable hotel that also has some dorms (Fr.33–40, depending on size). ❶–❷

Campsite

Lido Lidostrasse 8 ☎041 370 21 46, ⓦwww.camping-international.ch. Right by the Verkehrshaus, also with some dorm beds. March–Oct.

The City

Evidence of Luzern's medieval prosperity is manifest in the frescoed facades of its **Old Town** and the two surviving covered wooden bridges spanning the River Reuss, both formerly part of the city's fortifications (and so with higher defensive side walls facing away from the town) and both boasting unique triangular paintings fixed to their roof-beams. The **Sammlung Rosengart**, one of Switzerland's finest art museums, lurks on the busy Pilatusstrasse, while the excellent **Verkehrshaus** – an entertaining complex devoted to transport, also with an IMAX cinema – is just around the lakeshore.

The Kapellbrücke

Any tour of Luzern must begin with the fourteenth-century covered **Kapellbrücke** (Chapel Bridge), the oldest road bridge in Europe, angled around the octagonal mid-river **Wasserturm**. In deference to the fact that the city's development arose largely from defence of this bridge, its highly distinctive Wasserturm (formerly a lighthouse, a prison, a treasury and today serving as a meeting house) has come to stand as the symbol of Luzern. Disaster struck in the early hours of August 18, 1993, when a small boat moored alongside the bridge caught fire and the flames rapidly spread to engulf the whole structure. By dawn, virtually the entire bridge had been destroyed, with only the bridgeheads on both banks surviving. The authorities rapidly set about reconstruction, and an identical replacement was completed nine months later; today, it's easy to see where the old wood meets the new.

Before the fire, the principal historical interest of the bridge lay in its collection of double-sided triangular **roof panels**, painted in the seventeenth century with scenes from the city's past and present. Of the 111 panels, 65 were entirely ruined and had to be replaced with facsimiles, 30 were restored, and the remainder are still charred and impossible to make out. Each is numbered, and captioned with rhyming couplets, the idiosyncratic local dialect written out in obscure medieval gothic script. The most distinctive image is panel no. 31, which shows **William Tell** shooting the apple from his son's head, but it's fun to work your way slowly along. Panel no. 1 shows a giant, the first Luzerner; no. 3 Luzern in the earliest times, with the Hofkirche separated from the town by a bridged inlet; no. 4 the foundation of Luzern's monastery; no. 6 the town around 1600; no. 15 St Beatus (see p.309); no. 16 Einsiedeln (see p.408); no. 17 Luzern's Franciscan church; no. 26 local hero Winkelried slaying a dragon; no. 32 the Rütli oath; no. 38 the great fire of Luzern in 1340; and no. 58 the 1476 Battle of Grandson (see p.185).

Just downstream, the **Spreuerbrücke** is also worth a look for its macabre "Dance of Death" roof panels. These begin at the northern bankside with a little verse:

> All living things that fly or leap
> Or crawl or swim or run or creep
> Fear Death, yet can they find no spot
> In all the world where Death is not.

The succession of images shows a grinning skeleton leading kings, gallant princes, lawmen, nuns, merchants, prostitutes, peasants and maidens alike to their inevitable fate. The final panel, predictably enough, shows a majestic Christ vanquishing bony Death.

The Old Town

The north bank of the Reuss is home to the **Old Town**'s most atmospheric cluster of medieval houses, with Mühlenplatz, Weinmarkt, Hirschenplatz and Kornmarkt forming a compact ensemble of cobbled, fountained squares ringed by colourful facades. Modern commerce is definitely the motive force of the place these days, and it takes some imagination to conjure up the Middle Ages amidst the welter of shoppers and familiar brand-names.

Carnival!

Luzern's infamously raucous six-day all-in **carnival** (ⓦ www.luzerner-fasnacht.ch), ending on Mardi Gras night, is the biggest and best in Switzerland, a genuinely participatory event which knocks Basel's stand-and-watch parades into a cocked hat. It's worth going a long way out of your way to visit, even though the streets of the Old Town get more and more crammed with revellers year-on-year.

Celebrations are focused around three "official" carnival days. The Thursday before Mardi Gras is dubbed **Schmotzig Donnschtig**, or Dirty Thursday; the following Monday is **Güdis Määntig**, or Fat Monday; while Mardi Gras itself (Fat Tuesday) is **Güdis Ziischtig**. *Güdis* comes from the dialect word *Güdel*, meaning belly, while *Schmotzig*, or dirty, has its roots in the word for grease or fat: carnival was traditionally a time for excess, to lay in some high-calorie *Fasnachtsküechli*, fried sweet layered pastry, before Lenten fasting.

Luzern's carnival is centred on the figure of **Fritschi**, mentioned as early as 1443 and later subsumed into the legends surrounding a victory at the Battle of Ragaz on March 6, 1446. (March 6 was the day of Fridolin, patron saint of Glarus, and Fritschi is a diminutive of Fridolin.) Originally Fritschi was a lifesize straw doll carried through Luzern accompanied by **Fritschene**, his "wife"; these days a costumed couple take their place. Around the middle of the eighteenth century, the two were joined on parade by a nanny, a jester named Bajazzo and some musicians.

To this day, Fritschi begins Luzern's carnival, at 5am on the morning of Dirty Thursday, when he and his entourage lean out of an upper window of the **Rathaus** on Kornmarkt as a cannon signals the start of festivities. From breakfast time onwards, bands of masked and costumed musicians, dancers and acrobats roam the Old Town streets, some performing **Guggenmusig** – comical oompah played on a handful of dented trombones and percussion – while others set up stages to give impromptu gigs to the promenading costumed crowds. The highlight of the day is the evening **Fritschi parade**, where Fritschi, Fritschene and the rest are paraded through the Old Town and around Löwenplatz, all the while flinging oranges out to carousing onlookers.

Friday, Saturday and Sunday aren't official carnival days, but nonetheless see plenty of activity: there are parties around the town on Friday and Saturday nights, with bars open late and lots of live music in the streets and clubs. **Fat Monday** is when carnival really takes off, with strolling musicians and *commedia dell'arte* pantomime players roaming the cafés and restaurants, and all the Old Town squares taken over by exuberant mass dancing. Monday night's raucously chaotic parade is broadcast live on Swiss TV, and Old Town bars are given special all-night licences in preparation for **Fat Tuesday**, Mardi Gras itself. The climax of carnival is a **Monsterkonzert**, the grand finale of all the bands performing together throughout the Old Town on the Tuesday night, accompanied by plenty of eating, drinking and merrymaking, a mighty blowout which lasts until 4am. Two hours later, street cleaners arrive to restore order, and respectably groomed and suited businesspeople return to Luzern's early-morning cafés to begin real life again amidst the exhausted revellers of the night before, many of whom will be nursing breakfast beers while still in their fancy dress and face paint.

Kapellplatz, at the bridgehead of the Kapellbrücke, encircles the tiny eighteenth-century **St-Peterskapelle**, built over a predecessor dating from as early as 1178. Some 150m west is **Kornmarkt**, site of the medieval public marketplace. On one side, overlooking the riverside market area of Unter der Egg, is the huge **Rathaus**, completed in 1606 in Italian Renaissance style but crowned with an incongruous Emmentaler-style roof. The market atmosphere survives today, with vegetable, fish and flower stalls doing a roaring trade every Tuesday and Saturday morning. Kornmarktgasse runs west to the atmospheric frescoed **Weinmarkt**, where Passion Plays were staged in the late Middle Ages.

Just off Kornmarkt, at Furrengasse 21, is Am Rhyn-Haus, a restored seventeenth-century building housing the fascinating **Picasso Museum** (daily: April–Oct 10am–6pm; Nov–March 11am–4pm; Fr.6; joint tickets: with Sammlung Rosengart Fr.17, with Sammlung Rosengart & Kunstmuseum Fr.24; SMP): mainly late drawings, ceramics and a sheet-iron sculpture *Femme au Chapeau* (1963/64). The most striking works are a series of five tender portraits of Angela Rosengart – international art dealer and friend of Picasso – done over twelve years from 1954 to 1966. The highlight of the museum is an array of nearly two hundred intimate and often brilliant photographs of the artist's private life taken by American photographer David Douglas Duncan from 1956 until Picasso's death in 1973.

The battlements walk

A short stroll west from Weinmarkt along riverside St Karliquai past the sophisticated-looking hydroelectric turbines on the Reuss (which have had teething problems since they were installed, and still regularly clog up with silt) brings you to the **Nölliturm**, a fortified gate marking the southwestern extent of a lengthy stretch of the surviving fourteenth-century town walls. Pass through the gate and head right up the hill to gain access to the Musegg **battlements** (Easter–Sept daily 8am–7pm) and their impressive views. This is an oddly rustic corner of Luzern, cut off from the city behind the walls, and you may come across a cow or two quietly grazing back here, resident of a part-time urban farm. Stairs rise to the top of both the **Männliturm** and, further along, the **Luegisland-Turm**, but the battlements walk proper starts at the **Wachtturm**. From here, you can follow the parapets along to the Zeitturm or **Zytturm**, with the oldest clock in Luzern (granted the honour of chiming one minute before all the others in the town). The bizarrely ugly statue down below is *Unveib* by local artist Rudolf Blätter, such an unpopular addition that the municipality had to unveil it in secret one evening a few years back. The rooftop walk continues to the adjacent **Schirmerturm**, gutted by an arsonist in January 1994 and still bearing smoke-blackened stones. This is where the battlements walk runs out, but you can descend to follow the road through the Schirmerturm gate and down tranquil Museggstrasse through another breach in the old wall to the traffic-choked Löwenplatz.

Löwenplatz and around

Just northeast of Löwenplatz is one of the highlights of Luzern, the terribly sad **Löwendenkmal** (Lion Monument). This dying beast, draped over his shield, with a broken spear sticking out of his flank, was hewn out of a cliff face in 1821 to commemorate the 700 Swiss mercenaries killed in Paris in 1792. On August 10 that year, French revolutionaries stormed the royal palace, the Tuileries; in the face of the mob, the Swiss palace guards were ordered to lay down their arms by Louis XVI and so were massacred. This would be a movingly tranquil spot, with its foliage and gently rippling pool in front, were it not for the fact that it's the single most touristed place in the entire city.

Adjacent are a handful of nineteenth-century tourist attractions, quaint and rather old-fashioned today. The **Gletschergarten**, Denkmalstrasse 4 (Glacier Garden; daily: April–Oct 9am–6pm; Nov–March 10am–5pm; Fr.9; SMP; Ⓦ www.glaciergarden.org), holds within its grounds a fusty museum of old relief maps, a wonderful Mirror Maze built in 1896 and restored in mock-Moorish style, and a set of geological potholes telling of the subtropical ocean beach that was Luzern twenty million years ago. The **Alpineum** opposite (April–Oct daily 9am–12.30pm & 1.30–6pm; Fr.5; SMP; Ⓦ www.alpineum.ch) is a relic from a bygone age: static models of Alpine scenes behind glass no doubt sparked the imagination of our great-grandparents, but today they bare-ly merit a glance. More impressive is the **Bourbaki Panorama** (daily 9am–6pm; Fr.7; SMP; Ⓦ www.panorama-luzern.ch), a giant 110m-by-10m cir-cular mural housed in a glass building on Löwenplatz; it depicts the retreat into Switzerland of the French Eastern Army under General Bourbaki during the Franco-Prussian War of 1870–71. Sound effects and good background infor-mation go some way to bridge the gap between nineteenth- and twenty-first-century attention spans.

The Hofkirche

Busy Löwenstrasse runs south from Löwenplatz to the riverside; just before you reach the Schweizerhofquai, the arrow-straight St-Leodegarstrasse cuts east to broad steps leading up to the **Hofkirche** (Sat–Thurs 10am–noon & 2–5pm). This grand structure sits on the site of the first monastery of Luzern, which dated from the mid-eighth century and was dedicated to St Leodegar (St Leger). The Romanesque church which replaced the monastery in the late twelfth century was burned to the ground on Easter Sunday 1633, the blaze reputedly sparked by the verger's careless shooting at birds. Only its twin **tow-ers** escaped, and they survive today either side of a bizarrely incongruous Renaissance gable. The impressive main doors are carved with the two patron saints of Luzern: on the left is **St Leger**, a French bishop who was blinded with a drill (which he is holding), and on the right is **St Maurice**, a martyred Roman soldier-saint (see p.334).

The interior design and furniture are almost wholly original Renaissance from the 1630s and 1640s, a unity very rarely found in Swiss or European churches, most of which underwent Baroque renovation and embellishment. On the right, elaborate **pews** divided into individual seats were reserved for city councillors; plainer pews on the left were for the rank and file. Beyond the exceptionally fine **choir screen** – one of the earliest examples of strong three-dimensional perspective used to draw the congregation's attention forward – is the **high altar** in black marble, flanked by statues of the two patron saints. Above the Italianate depiction of the Agony at Gethsemane is a half-length fig-ure of God. The carved choir stalls, as well as the beautiful pulpit, are the work of Niklaus Geissler. Against the north wall (left) is the lavish **Death of the Virgin altar**, showing Mary on a bed surrounded by disciples: dating from around 1500, this was the only relic to survive the 1633 fire. The mighty **organ**, bedecked in ornament, features 2826 pipes, along with a machine to mimic the sound of rain and a special register for thunder and hail.

The church is set amidst a lovely Italianate **cloister**, lined with the graves of Luzerner patrician families (who continue to be buried here to this day). Old houses all around the church still serve as the homes for canons of the parish. Just west of the church is the ancient **Rothenburgerhaus**, a teetering pile that's held to be one of the oldest wooden town houses in the country, dating from about 1500. On the slopes north of the church is the old cemetery, now a public park, while about 500m further north on the hilltop is the Capuchin monastery of **Wesemlin**, founded in 1584 and still functioning as the principal seat of the order in Switzerland.

The south bank

The Old Town extends to the **south bank** of the Reuss, comprising a triangular area known as the Kleinstadt, originally walled. Facing Unter der Egg is the huge **Jesuitenkirche**, dominating the riverside with its twin onion-domed towers. Completed in 1673, its astonishing interior is a frothy Rococo concoction of gilt stucco and marble. Among the profusion of frescoes is one on the ceiling that, intriguingly, depicts the church exterior as it was 300 years ago. A few steps west is the **Rittersche palace**, built in 1557 in Florentine Renaissance style as a private mansion but now the seat of Luzern's cantonal government. Behind it to the south is the **Franziskanerkirche**, the oldest building in Luzern, dating from 1270, though it has been much restored. It's unusually richly decorated for a Franciscan church, with Renaissance choir stalls and battle standards lining the walls – copies of those looted from battlefields through the centuries. A Baroque side-chapel is decorated with Italianate stucco and a host of kitschy, curly-haired angels. Continuing west, peaceful Pfistergasse curves to meet the south side of the Spreuerbrücke, where you'll spot the stout old town arsenal, now home to the **Historisches Museum** (Tues–Fri 10am–noon & 2–5pm, Sat & Sun 10am–5pm; Fr.6; SMP; Ⓦwww.hmluzern.ch), filled with arms and armour, restored interiors, costumes and crafts telling the history of Luzern.

Sammlung Rosengart

Busy, traffic-heavy Pilatusstrasse, lined with shops, cafés and banks, storms southwest from the station, defining the limits of the Old Town. About 100m along, and the same distance south of the Kapellbrücke, is a solid Neoclassical building from 1923 – formerly the Luzern headquarters of the Swiss National Bank, and now renovated to house the outstanding **Sammlung Rosengart** (Rosengart Collection; daily: April–Oct 10am–6pm, Nov–March 11am–4pm; Fr.14; joint tickets: with Picasso Museum Fr.17, with Picasso Museum & Kunstmuseum Fr.24; Ⓦwww.rosengart.ch). Art dealers Siegfried Rosengart and his daughter Angela – the latter born in Luzern in 1932 and still a resident – built up over forty years a collection of more than 200 key twentieth-century works. A small number of Picassos, donated by the Rosengarts, form the basis of the Picasso Museum (see p.384).

The **ground floor** is devoted to **Picasso**, from early paintings – including a statuesque *Portrait Alice Derain* dated 1905, when Picasso was 24 – through to works full of light and space painted in Cannes in the mid-1950s, and five exuberant canvases dated 1967–69, a few years before the artist's death.

The **basement** holds one of the broadest collections of works by **Paul Klee** in private hands, a seamless chronological record showing the development of Klee's fluent and compelling fantasy world. In the first room – ahead at the bottom of the stairs – Klee's visit to Tunisia is reflected in a number of colourful North African landscapes and the many works with Arab and Jewish elements. His expressive imagination takes hold in the second room, which includes the unsettling *Ironic Fairytale* (#69), featuring two jesters on the edge of a nebulous wood beneath a furious moon. One of the most characteristic sketches is *Little X* (#117), in the third room – a dozen brushstrokes that create a universe of childhood experience, lost in a bigger, more serious adult world.

The **upper floor** features a creatively assembled array of Impressionist and Modernist works, amongst them a room of Chagalls – including *Night at the Window* (1950), a distinctive scene of blissful lovers looking out over a sleeping town – two spectacular Monets, and works by Renoir, Modigliani, Kandinsky, Matisse and others.

The KKL

On a plum waterfront site beside the station and alongside the quays stands Luzern's pride and joy, the multifunctional *Kultur- und Kongresszentrum Luzern*, known to all as the **KKL** (pronounced "kaka-el"; ⓦwww.kkl-luzern.ch). Within such a traditional-looking and -thinking city, Jean Nouvel's landmark architecture in glass and steel is a revelation. Reflecting pools all around draw the lake into the building, as an immense cantilevered roof floats high above. The atmosphere of the place changes according to the weather conditions: standing on the lakeside apron during a storm – exposed yet protected by the roof – is quite an experience. Parts of the building may be taken up with conferences when you visit, and the concert halls are off-limits, but there's nothing to stop you exploring the public areas, which are well signed.

On the station side rises a huge, glazed block, fenced in by an all-enveloping steel cage and penetrating deep beneath the dark roof; this is the **Kongresszentrum** wing, with a bistro (see p.391) at ground level and the

---

Above Luzern – Mount Pilatus

The giant mountain looming above Luzern to the southwest is **Mount Pilatus** (2132m; ⓦwww.pilatus.com), an odd name supposedly deriving from the myth that the corpse of Pontius Pilate was flung into a small lake on the mountain, his spirit forever after haunting the summit and bound to bring tempest and damnation onto Luzern if disturbed. (More prosaically, it's probably derived from the Latin word *pileatus*, meaning "capped" – ie with clouds.) There are two means of transport to the top, making it easy to do a half- or full-day round trip from Luzern – simpler than in 1868, when Queen Victoria made the excursion on muleback. Eurailers get a discount of 35 percent, Swiss Pass holders get a quarter off, while InterRailers pay full whack.

Boats and local trains run from Luzern to **Alpnachstad**, from where the steepest rack-railway in the world runs at a gradient touching 48 percent directly to the top of the mountain – the journey up is half-an-hour, while the journey down takes a careful forty minutes. The second route up the mountain starts at **Kriens** (connected to Luzern's city centre by bus #1); from here a gondola rises to Krienseregg and Fräkmüntegg, and then a cable-car to the summit (total 30min). The Kriens–Pilatus route runs year-round, while the Alpnachstad–Pilatus railway is summer only (mid-June to mid-Nov). Luzern's many tour groups tend to follow a circuit going up from Kriens – so you might want to go up from Alpnachstad instead, to avoid the crush.

On the top are two hotels, the *Bellevue* and *Kulm*, but if you're looking for an overnight mountain-top stay, you'd do better on the Rigi instead (see p.401). The walk to the highest point of the mountain, the Tomlishorn, takes less than thirty minutes from the top station, with expansive views the whole way along the clifftop path. It's also easy to walk back to Luzern from Fräkmüntegg (2hr 30min), or to make your way down from the summit to Alpnachstad or Hergiswil (3hr) or Kriens (3hr 30min).

Kunstmuseum on the top floor. Beside it, at the centre of the complex, is the **Luzernersaal**, a small hall used for concerts or meetings, with a drinks terrace atop its foyer. The easterly third of the complex is the **Konzertsaal**, one of the world's most acoustically advanced concert halls, and the principal venue for the Lucerne Festival. Adjoining it at ground level is the trendy *Seebar* (see p.393).

On the top floor of the KKL's Kongresszentrum wing – from the train station, take the exit by platform 15 and cross the street – is the **Kunstmuseum** (Tues–Sun 10am–5pm, Wed & Thurs until 8pm; longer hours in Aug & Sept during Lucerne Festival; Fr.10; joint ticket with Sammlung Rosengart & Picasso Museum Fr.24; Ⓦwww.kunstmuseumluzern.ch). Lifts take you up to the ticket desk (press button "K"). The permanent collection – less-than-stunning canvases by Swiss artists of the nineteenth and early twentieth century, displayed in the first half-dozen rooms – is overshadowed both by the ground-breaking exhibitions of avant-garde contemporary art held in the dozen or so rooms beyond, and by the breathtaking architecture: more than once you cross between galleries on slender catwalks high up in the building's interior, bathed in natural and artificial light with the reflecting pools far below.

Out of the centre

Although many of Luzern's sights are packed close together in the city centre, there are a few incentives to venture further afield. Facing each other across the lake roughly 2km out of the centre are the **Verkehrshaus** (Transport Museum) on the northern shore, and the **Richard Wagner museum**, the composer's former home, on the southern shore. Buses run close to both, but the way to get there in style is by boat.

The Verkehrshaus

One of the main draws of Luzern is the **Verkehrshaus**, 2km east of the centre at Lidostrasse 5 (Transport Museum; daily: April–Oct 10am–6pm; Nov–March 10am–5pm; Fr.21, or Fr.31 to include one IMAX film; discounts available with rail passes or guest card; SMP; Ⓦwww.verkehrshaus.org); if you're not taking the boat, hop on bus #6 or #8, or else it's a pleasant twenty-minute lakeside stroll. This vast complex is devoted to Swiss engineering skill and could keep you amused all day: you'll need the free plan to navigate your way around. It's divided into several large areas, taking in Road Transport, Rail Transport, Aviation and Astronautics, Cableways and Tourism, and so on. Everything is in English, and "hands-on" is a rule, not an exception. Particular highlights include the **train** section, with dozens of giant locomotives on display (complete with evocative oily smell) and a well-presented walk-through account of the digging of the Gotthard tunnel, dramatized with slides and soundtrack. The airplane section has flight simulators, a mock-up of an airport control-tower and the **Cosmorama**, an interactive tour of the asteroid belt. The tourism bit has the endearingly dated **Swissorama**, a wraparound 360° movie of the delights of Switzerland circa 1977 projected onto the walls of a circular room. There's also a huge section devoted to communications, an excellent **Planetarium** and a separate, giant building housing an **IMAX cinema** (regular showings throughout the day for an extra Fr.16; Ⓦwww.imax.ch). The **Hiflyer** is a tethered hot-air balloon – visible from the city centre – that takes you up to 120m for spectacular views over the lake and mountains (extra Fr.20).

In an entirely different vein, a far-flung building on the edge of the site – unfortunately overlooked by most visitors – houses a museum dedicated to the acclaimed Luzerner artist **Hans Erni** (same hours; admission included with

△ Relaxing on the Reuss, with Luzern's Jesuitenkirche (see p.386) behind

Verkehrshaus ticket; ⓦ www.hans-erni.ch). Erni, born in 1909, has spent his long career producing art that is wonderfully warm and human, full of fluidity of figures and geometries that the museum blurb will try to convince you is linked in some spiritual way to the scientific prowess on display throughout the rest of the complex; however, his concern for human dignity in the face of modern technology stands more as a healthy counterpoint to all those displays of engineering skill. Erni is not well known outside Switzerland, but this museum – displaying 300 works – merits a special visit; particularly outstanding are Erni's lithographs, made as illustrations for limited-edition books.

Richard Wagner museum

Southeast of the centre, in an idyllic location on a headland named Tribschen, is a villa that was **Richard Wagner**'s home from 1866 to 1872, and is now a **museum** to him (March–Nov Tues–Sun 10am–noon & 2–5pm; Fr.5; SMP; boat to Tribschen; bus #6, #7 or #8 to Wartegg, then 5min walk; or 40min walk from station; ⓦwww.kulturluzern.ch/wagner-museum). After many visits to Switzerland, the composer and his partner Cosima – Franz Liszt's daughter, who was still legally married to the pianist and conductor Hans von Bülow – spotted the derelict Tribschen villa in early 1866, made arrangements to rent it for an extended period, and moved in on April 15. "Nobody will get me out of here again," Wagner said, and it's generally agreed that this was the happiest and most productive time of his life, not least because Cosima's long-dead marriage was finally dissolved in 1870 and the couple were able to marry. The tranquillity of the lakeside house is still tangible today, as you wander through the rooms laid out with Wagneriana of all kinds – letters, pictures, original furniture, instruments and even his death mask – with Wagner compositions playing in the background.

Eating, drinking and nightlife

Luzern has a fine range of **eating and drinking** venues covering all budgets: the crowded, generic places that are in plain view tend to be least interesting, but a small amount of backstreet searching will turn up plenty of more rewarding options.

   Local specialities to keep an eye out for are led by the celebrated *Luzerner Kügelipastete* – spelled by many Old Town restaurant menus in dialect, along the lines of *Lozärner Chögalipaschtetli*, also often prefixed by *ächti* ("authentic"). This stomach-lining dish is a glorified vol-au-vent, a large puff-pastry shell filled with a super-rich concoction of diced veal and mushrooms in a creamy sauce; veggie versions omitting the veal aren't hard to find. Otherwise, fish is the thing, in endless varieties: you'll see *Forellen* (trout), *Egli* (perch), *Felchen* (a kind of white fish) and *Hecht* (pike) on most menus, virtually all of it plucked fresh from the lake. Wash it all down either with a *Kaffee fertig*, a coffee laced with Schnapps, or a *Kafi Luz*, traditionally seen in Canton Luzern outside the city but nowadays easy to find in the Old Town cafés. The right way to make one is to put a five-franc coin in a vase-shaped glass, pour hot coffee in until you can't see the coin, then add Schnapps until the coin becomes visible again. Stir in two large spoons of sugar, and you have the perfect farmers' pick-me-up.

Cafés and café-bars

Cafés and **café-bars** crowd the waterfront and the Old Town squares, and do a roaring trade amongst the flood of tour groups passing through the town.

Better places, frequented by locals, abound in less-trod corners, such as Helvetiaplatz. The *Luzerner Barführer* (𝕎 www.barfuehrer.ch) is a free pocket appraisal of dozens of establishments.

North of the river

Heini's Tearoom Falkenplatz. Perfect place for cakes and pastries on a broad, people-watching corner in the Old Town.

Hug Mühlenplatz. Superb breakfast café, open from 7am, with warm fresh bread and croissants, that also has quality inexpensive lunch *menus* (around Fr.17). Closed Sun.

Jazz Kantine Grabenstrasse 8. Buzzing Old Town hub, open during the day for coffee and beers, and on into the late night as a hopping bar and meeting point, with DJs and live music downstairs.

Löwengraben Löwengraben 18. Chic postmodern café-bar in the old prison (see "Accommodation") that's the in-place of the moment.

Sunset Bar Seeburgstrasse 61 𝕎 www.sunsetbar .ch. Perfect lakeside café-bar opposite *Hotel Seeburg*, with just the right tone for summer lazing: deckchairs, music, spacious lawns, homemade ice-tea, dreamy views and its own landingstage. Beware, though: the sharp-dressed regulars crowd in after 6pm. April–Oct only.

South of the river

Bistro Within the KKL complex. Bustling, airy place that does a rapid round of salads, light meals and drinks from breakfast until late.

Mahlzeit Corner Winkelriedstrasse and Waldstätterstrasse. Tiny Moroccan café with a friendly atmosphere and cheap couscous and falafel. Closed Sun.

Opus Bahnhofstrasse 16 𝕎 www.restaurant-opus .ch. Pricey but excellent waterside café, restaurant and wine-bar, with a bright, warm interior and a huge salad buffet (Fr.15 buys a ton of the stuff).

Panorama In the *Astoria* hotel, Pilatusstrasse 29. Rooftop bar with big views and bigger sofas.

Parterre Mythenstrasse 7 𝕎 www.parterre.ch. Relaxed and inexpensive locals' hangout, open daily from breakfast until after midnight, with quality lunchtime *menus* (Fr.15). Go ahead and try their English breakfast, but don't hold out too many hopes.

Salü Helvetiaplatz. French-style daytime-only café, complete with *citron pressé* and *pain au chocolat* plus soups and salads for lunch. One of several options on this little square. Closed Sun.

Seebar Within the KKL complex. Pleasant daytime hangout, with waterfront views, snacks and sandwiches. Stays open into the night as a DJ-bar.

Restaurants

There are hundreds of **restaurants** in Luzern, plenty of which need to do nothing more than occupy a panelled dining room and churn out a handful of traditional dishes to gone-tomorrow tourists in order to make money. A little searching can turn up more worthwhile eateries. *EPA* on Mühlenplatz is top **self-service** choice, but if you're watching every franc, check out the shabby *Bahnhof Buffet* (see below) or grab a top-quality Thai **takeaway** from little *Sawasdee*, Zürichstrasse 38–40 (closed Sun).

Note that the much-advertised *Stadtkeller*, Sternenplatz 3, is the eye of Luzern's tourist hurricane, a folklore restaurant which lays on alphorn, yodelling and traditional dancing for dining tour groups – perfect if you're after a knee-slapping good time, but not the place for a romantic *tête-à-tête*.

North of the river

Bodu Kornmarkt 5 ☎041 410 0177. Acclaimed French brasserie, with superb, authentic dishes sourced from Provence, Normandy and everywhere in between. Decor is pleasant, service attentive but the location, with a fine river view, is the clincher.

Hofgarten Stadthofstrasse 14 (see "Accommodation"). The city's best veggie food by miles, if a tad pricey, everything fresh and delicious whether from the buffet or ordered à la carte. A wonderful enclosed garden terrace and cheerful interior attract locals by the score. Reckon on at least Fr.25.

Maihöfli Maihofstrasse 70 ☎041 420 60 60. Marvellously relaxed and friendly little all-wood place 1km north of the centre – comfortable, cosy and atmospheric. The cuisine is fresh and modern, with a light, inventive touch, expertly presented, and servers are willing to help you decipher the menu with a recommendation or two, or take the time to talk you through the range of post-prandial grappas on offer. Lean back on your chair and feel good about your dinner. Meals may set you back Fr.30–35. Closed Sun.

Reussbad Brüggligasse 19 ☏041 240 54 23, ⓦwww.reussbad.ch. Easygoing riverside joint to enjoy traditional cooking, relying on a renowned range of fresh fish dishes at around Fr.30. Otherwise, *menus* are around Fr.18. Closed Sun & Mon.

Schiff Unter der Egg 8 ☏041 418 52 52. Wonderful old wood-panelled hotel restaurant on the riverside, celebrated for three things: top-quality *Würst*, huge portions of *Chögelipastetli*, and twin Spanish waiters who've been serving in the place for twenty years. Summer sees tables set under the arcades directly on the waterfront. *Menus* are around Fr.25.

Schlüssel Franziskanerplatz (see "Accommodation"). Tiny old hotel offering a bargain three-course lunch *menu* for just Fr.13.

Spaghetteria Valentino Weinmarkt. Central pasta joint, with a range of risotto and other Italian dishes for under Fr.20. Closed Sun.

Sushi Zürichstrasse 46. Huddle at one of the wood tables in this tiny diner for platters of sushi and other Japanese fare, everything very fresh and prepared with an expert eye.

South of the river

Bahnhof Buffet Top floor of the train station. A low-budget gem. This greasy-table diner – replete with down-and-outs, smoking schoolchildren and drunken businessmen – charges budget prices for food prepared next door in the kitchen of the *Au Premier* gourmet restaurant. A meal which might cost you Fr.50 in *Au Premier* may set you back a third of that in the *Bahnhof Buffet* – if you can stand the ambience, that is.

Château Gütsch Kanonenstrasse (see "Accommodation"). It's worth coming up here, even if just for a cup of tea on the terrace, but if you can afford it, the restaurant is one of Luzern's finest (Fr.100-plus).

Galliker Schützenstrasse 1, at Kasernenplatz ☏041 240 10 02. Hearty, meat-heavy Swiss specialities in a tavern-like setting crammed with people, noise and smoke. The food is consistently excellent, with quality *Chögelipastetli* standing at the top of the pile, joined by *Cordon Bleu* (veal steak slathered with cheese and ham), and less palatable offerings such as *Kutteln* (tripe). Mains are Fr.30–40, not much more than lunchtime *menus*. Closed Sun & Mon, and Aug.

Korea-Town Hirschmattstrasse 23. Pleasant ambience and a good choice mark this place out as something a little more worthwhile than average, with midday buffets from Fr.17 and a range of *menus* (veggie and not) from Fr.21.

Nightlife and entertainment

Luzern's **nightlife** scene is active, with plenty of arts centres and music venues around the Old Town and the rest of the city. Check flyers at Doobop, a dance music shop at Brandgässli 8; or Romp, Denkmalstrasse 17 (Wed–Sat afternoons), an "info-shop" plugged into Luzern's alternative squat culture. The monthly *Kultur Kalender* (Fr.4, if it's not free) has full listings, available at the tourist office, cafés and the Kultur-Forum information centre within the Panorama building on Löwenplatz (ⓦwww.kulturluzern.ch), as does the "Apéro" Thursday supplement of the *Neue Luzerner Zeitung* newspaper. The Panorama also houses the arthouse **Stattkino** (ⓦwww.stattkino.ch).

Bars, clubs and music venues

Boa Geissensteinring 41 ⓦwww.boaluzern.ch. Arts and culture centre with a range of interesting events and music nights. Closed July to mid-Aug.

Heaven Burgerstrasse 21. Luzern's only exclusively gay bar. The *Uferlos*, Geissenstrasse 14, is a popular gay- and lesbian-friendly bar, but its opening hours aren't regular; check at the nearby Discus gay sauna (☏041 360 88 77) for the latest.

Jazz Kantine Grabenstrasse 8 ⓦwww.jsl.ch /kantine. Happening Old Town café-bar beside Luzern's jazz school, with DJs and live music (not only jazz) in the basement on weekends.

P1 Top floor of *Hotel Monopol*, Pilatusstrasse 1 ⓦwww.p1bar.ch. Trendy DJ-bar, open nightly from 5pm, with dance sounds and a terrace for great city views.

Rathaus Brauerei Unter der Egg. Wonderful echoing cross-vaulted beerhall below the Rathaus, where young enthusiastic drinkers come to sample a range of powerful, self-brewed beers.

Schüür Tribschenstrasse 1 ⓦwww.schuur.ch. Daytime bar with cheap weekday lunches which after dark becomes a frenetic venue for excellent live music (Fri & Sat until 4am). Famous afterhours parties begin at 5am Sunday morning.

Sedel Near the HI hostel ⓦ www.sedel.ch. A former women's prison outside the city, which now hosts noisy punkish/industrial bands and DJ nights at the weekend, with a kind of community-squat atmosphere during the week as bands practise in the graffitied cells.
Seebar Within the KKL complex. Daytime bar with DJs taking over for partying into the small hours.
St Magdalena Eisengasse 5. Universally known as the Magdi-Bar, with a crowded ground-floor bar and a more sociable upstairs, although everything gets more and more raucous as the night veers wildly on.
Wärchhof Werkhofstrasse 11 ⓦ www.waerchhof.ch. Tiny co-op-run dive in an industrial area south of the station, with loud bands, DJs and alternative-style happenings for a college-age crowd.

Listings

Bike and skate rental In the station (June–Sept daily 7am–7.45pm; Oct–May Mon–Sat 7am–7.45pm, Sun 9.30am–7pm).
Boat rental SNG, Alpenquai 11 (☏041 368 08 08, ⓦ www.sng.ch), has pedalos and rowing-boats (about Fr.25/hr) and motorboats (about Fr.45/hr) for rent, all requiring a deposit (Fr.20–100). Prices rise after 7pm. Two competitors are Bucher at Luzernerhof (☏041 410 20 55), and Herzog at Nationalquai (☏041 410 43 33).
Books Bücher Brocky, Güterstrasse 1, has secondhand books in English.
Changing money In the station (May–Oct Mon–Fri 7.30am–8pm, Sat & Sun 7.30am–7pm; Nov–April Mon–Sat 7.30am–7pm, Sun 9am–6pm).
Laundry Jet Wash, Bruchstrasse 28 (closed Sun); also in the *Tourist Hotel* (see "Accommodation").

Lost property The city office is at Hirschengraben 17b ☏041 208 78 08.
Markets Every Tuesday and Saturday morning, large and colourful food markets spill over both banks of the Reuss and under the arcades, with a supplementary fish market every Friday. There's a flea market every Saturday (May–Oct) on the south bank, and a monthly crafts market (April–Dec, first Sat of month) on Weinmarkt. In the modern part of town, Moosstrasse/Helvetiaplatz hosts a relaxed Saturday morning farmers' market of cheeses, organic vegetables, home-made jams and more.
Medical facilities 24-hour emergency room at the Kantonsspital, Spitalstrasse ☏041 205 11 11.
Post Main office is across from the station (Mon–Fri 7.30am–6.30pm, Sat 8am–noon).

Zentralschweiz

Zentralschweiz (Central Switzerland) is one of the most rewarding areas of the country in which to travel, with a host of different attractions to draw you off the beaten path. Routes around both shores of Luzern's lake give constantly changing perspectives, and even the shortest day-trip in the area will turn up places of great natural beauty. For details of the boats which crisscross the lake year-round – often the most convenient method of transport – see p.379.

The southern shore is quiet, characterized by country towns such as **Stans**, and offers leg-stretching clifftop hikes above the glittering water. The excursion south to the once-grand resort of **Engelberg**, base station for the trip up to the summit of the **Titlis**, matches the Bernese Oberland's more famous rides up the Jungfrau and the Schilthorn for drama and natural beauty. The northern shore of the lake is studded by the lofty presence of the **Rigi**, with the old town of **Zug** behind; its easternmost finger, oriented due north–south and dubbed the **Urnersee** (Lake Uri), channels the Föhn wind down from the high Alps, and so is a prime

The **Tellpass** (April–Oct only; ⓦwww.tell-pass.ch) is the regional pass for Zentralschweiz – but you'll need to cover plenty of ground to make it pay. The core region covers all boats on the lake, all routes to the Rigi and Pilatus, the train from Luzern to Engelberg, and cable-cars from Engelberg up to Trübsee and the Jochpass. With a **seven-day** Tellpass (Fr.135), you get two days' free travel in the core region, with half-price travel on all other lines, including trains to Zug, Einsiedeln, Brienz, Meiringen and Andermatt; a **fifteen-day** Tellpass (Fr.184) buys five days' free travel in the core region, with the remaining ten days at half-price. You can buy the pass from tourist offices throughout the region, and there's more information at ⓦwww.centralswitzerland.ch.

The **Snowpass** (Fr.900) is valid for the whole winter season throughout the entire Zentralschweiz region, covering lifts at Engelberg, Andermatt, the Rigi, Schwyz, Klewenalp and more – even Meiringen (see p.312).

Adventure sports

Zentralschweiz is one of Switzerland's top **adventure sports** destinations. **Outventure** (☎041 611 14 41, ⓦwww.outventure.ch) is the leading local operator, offering bungee-jumps 130m out of the Titlis cable-car (Fr.160), flying fox (Fr.90), canyoning (Fr.170), tandem paragliding (Fr.150), white-water rafting (Fr.100), mountaineering (Fr.160), mountain-biking (Fr.110), glacier walks (Fr.170) and more. Every morning (8.30am) their shuttle bus runs from Luzern tourist office to each location, many of which are in and around Engelberg. One winter highlight, aside from snowshoe trekking and tobogganing, is a two-day **igloo package**: build your own igloo, then sleep in it (dinner, mulled wine and breakfast included; Fr.220; minimum six people).

Another operator is the highly acclaimed **Trekking Team** (☎041 390 40 40, ⓦwww.trekking.ch) – with a branch in Ticino (see p.548) – which offers trekking, river rafting, a mountain-bike round-trip on the Klewenalp (including boat and cable-car) for Fr.150, plus winter snowshoe trekking with and without huskies plus igloo-building. Their main draw is access to the vast **Hölloch caves** near Schwyz, 190km long and one of the largest such systems in the world; they run various excursions – including short individual visits (June–Sept Wed–Sun 3–4 daily; takes 1hr 30min; Fr.14; year-round 3hr 30min trip on request; Fr.98) – but the main attraction is long stays underground, exploring the cave network with a guide (all Nov–March only): from 7hr up to 16hr (Fr.159–249), or even overnighting below ground (2 days Fr.395; 3 days Fr.595).

Elsewhere, **Windsurfing Urnersee** (☎041 870 92 22, ⓦwww.windsurfing-urnersee.ch) offers beginners' courses (5hr; Fr.280) and board rental, as well as a package of five nights' half board in Flüelen plus ten hours' windsurfing for Fr.600. Brunnen's Touch And Go (☎041 820 54 31, ⓦwww.paragliding.ch) is a respected operator running tandem **paragliding** flights from the Urmiberg (Fr.150; see p.406).

windsurfing spot. This is one of the country's most historically resonant areas, its wild and rocky shores the setting both for the legend of **William Tell** and for an ancient pact of mutual defence signed on a lakeside meadow – the **Rütli** – which laid the foundations for the Swiss Confederation as it survives today.

The southern lakeshore

The south shore of the lake – **Vierwaldstättersee-Süd** in German – is a land of broad green meadows and lush valleys interspersed with chunks of high forested plateau towering over the water. Once you gain some height, the views are magnificent, out across the whole shimmering expanse of blue. The shore forms part of the ancient canton of Unterwalden, divided for as long as anyone can remember into two small half-cantons, **Nidwalden** (the Lower Forest) and **Obwalden** (the Upper Forest). It's a perfect area for hiking and cycling, and it's easy to base yourself either in Luzern or in the main town of the region, tiny **Stans**.

Stans

The highest peak in the area is the beautiful Stanserhorn, rising to 1900m above the old village of **STANS**, capital of Nidwalden and on a direct train link with Luzern. The centre of the village lies behind the station. The hub, Dorfplatz, is overlooked by the large **Pfarrkirche St Peter und Paul**. From the Middle Ages onwards this was the sole house of worship in the canton, and so was expanded time and time again to accommodate the increasing population until it was completely renovated in 1647; the early Baroque building remains crowned by a Romanesque bell tower. Halfway up the hill behind the church is an 1865 fountain dedicated to **Arnold von Winkelried**, a native of the town, who is celebrated for diverting the attention of the Austrian army during the Battle of Sempach in 1386, thereby committing suicide but simultaneously opening a gap for his Swiss comrades to win their famous victory. The alleys surrounding Dorfplatz are worth a wander; east is quiet and atmospheric Schmiedgasse, while to the west is Altes Postplatz and the **Höfli**, or Rosenburg House, a medieval turreted building with a rear courtyard overlooked by beautiful Italianate loggias.

A couple of minutes beyond the Höfli is the station for the old-time cog railway up to the summit of the green and pleasant **Stanserhorn** (mid-April to Nov; Swiss Pass gets 25 percent off, Eurail & InterRail go for half-price; Ⓦwww.stanserhorn.ch), with views from the *Rondorama* revolving restaurant on top and the many trails on the summit taking in ten lakes as well as the close-at-hand high mountains around the Titlis. The zigzag walk back down to Stans takes about three and a half hours, or alternatively, you can head down the side of the mountain to Wirzweli (in 2hr 30min), from where a cable-car deposits you at the village of **Dallenwil** for the bus ride back to Stans.

The **tourist office** for the region (Mon–Fri 9am–noon & 2–5pm; ☎041 610 88 33, Ⓦwww.lakeluzern.ch) is above Stans train station, where there are bikes for rent. There are two pleasant, comfortable old **hotels** on Dorfplatz: the *Engel* (☎041 619 10 10, Ⓦwww.engelstans.ch; ❸) and the *Linde* (☎041 619 09 30, Ⓦwww.hotel-linde.ch; ❸). Both have good, traditional-style **restaurants**, or you could plump for the *Wilhelm Tell* restaurant just off the square (*menus* Fr.15). Stans's top eating choice is the fine restaurant within the Höfli (*menus* Fr.25; closed Mon & Tues).

Hergiswil and beyond

On the train line midway between Luzern and Stans is the small lakeside community of **HERGISWIL**, for centuries a fishing village until it rose to fame for the **Glasi Hergiswil** glassworks, founded in 1817. For over a hundred years, the glassworks was one of the busiest in the country, yet by 1975 it was hopelessly obsolete, with no chance of matching the automated methods of more modern competitors. The Glasi would have closed altogether but for the move of Roberto Niederer, a Ticinese glass designer who, backed by local people, bought it up and changed its products and its target market. Niederer's rejuvenation, continued today by his son, enabled the plant – and the village economy – to survive: it's a remarkable success story. The "visitor-friendly" Glasi now employs a hundred people, producing hand-blown pieces for sale as well as serving as a workshop for artists from around the world to design and work with glass using traditional craft techniques. The on-site **museum** (Mon–Fri 9am–6pm, Sat 9am–4pm; free; Ⓦwww.glasi.ch) is excellent, focused around an engaging audiovisual walk-through history of glassmaking and the Glasi. The story ends as a door opens onto a gallery above the blazing-hot factory floor, where you can watch a team of glass-blowers do their stuff (although beware that they take a 4–4.30pm tea-break, and finish at noon on Saturdays).

Bürgenstock

East of Hergiswil rises a grand plateau, atop which is the private luxury resort of **BÜRGENSTOCK**, an odd little enclave owned by the handful of business-oriented hotels that occupy it, themselves mostly owned by a single family. Buses from Stans stop short at Obbürgen (from where a private toll road serves the resort), and the only way to access the area directly is by **boat** from Luzern to Kehrsiten-Bürgenstock, way down on the lake; from there, a **funicular** rises to Bürgenstock itself. If you want to stay here, or eat here, or play golf here, you'll need a packet of money (double rooms start at Fr.300; Ⓦwww.buergenstock-hotels.ch), but it doesn't cost anything to enjoy the views. Ignore the big cars and the well-cut suits clustering around the hotels,

The Rütli meadow

On the western shore of the Urnersee below Seelisberg – and visible from Brunnen, across the water – is a flapping Swiss flag planted in the **Rütli meadow**, a sloping patch of grass above the shoreline that holds unique, almost mystical, significance for the Swiss. Legend and national pride says that it was here on August 1, 1291, that representatives from the three forest cantons around the lake (Uri, Schwyz and Unterwalden) met amidst continuing Habsburg repression to sign a pact of eternal mutual defence, thereby laying the foundation of the Swiss Confederation as it stands today. Nowadays, 1291 is taken as the birthdate of the nation, and August 1 is the official Swiss national holiday.

And yet, despite the proud flag which stands on the meadow today, and the crowds of parents who bring their children here to tell them the story of William Tell (see box p.412) and the birth of Switzerland, many historians doubt that anything very much happened at Rütli at all. Some pour scorn on the idea that such an obviously important document in formal Latin – now on display in Schwyz – would have been written and signed in a meadow (although England's grand Magna Carta was signed at Runnymede meadow in 1215), and cite evidence that the three representatives met at Rütli on November 7, 1307, simply in order to renew their formal written pledge of 16 years before. Other historians, yet more controversially, suggest that the Swiss Confederation developed organically, and that there was either no movement of resistance against the Habsburgs in 1291 at all, or that the Rütli oath was merely one in an array of other equally "eternal" or "perpetual" alliances between valley communities that came and went over the centuries. Nothing is certain, but most ordinary people have little truck with such trifling details anyway: the story has come to represent much more than its bare facts might suggest. The **Charter of Confederation**, as the Rütli document came to be known, has become as potently symbolic for the Swiss as the Declaration of Independence is for Americans, and the meadow itself has become a place of patriotic pilgrimage, focus of the country's national celebrations every August.

and instead strike out east on the Felsenweg path for a scenic twenty-minute clifftop walk to Europe's fastest outdoor elevator, which swishes you in seconds to the **Hammetschwand** summit (1128m), complete with a more affordable restaurant and stunning lake vistas. You can return to Bürgenstock via a steeper path zigzagging down the back of the Hammetschwand (35min), from where another path cuts down to the Kehrsiten boat station; or follow a four-hour trail east across the wooded hilltops down to Ennetbürgen and Beckenried, which gives expansive views over the lake and south to the high mountains.

Beckenried and Klewenalp

Just round the lakeshore from Kehrsiten, and accessible by bus from Stans (or boat), is **BECKENRIED**, from where a gondola rises to **Klewenalp** (1593m; Ⓦwww.klewenalp.ch) and plenty more walking routes. This is touted strongly as **mountain-bike** territory, and you can rent from Merkur outlets in Beckenried, Dallenwil and Seelisberg – Fr.31 for a full day, or Fr.24 for a half-day (7am–noon, or noon–5pm). Two easy bike routes link Dallenwil and Beckenried (10km), and Emmetten and Seelisberg (7km), with harder ones climbing to Klewenalp and beyond to various mountain inns. One option is to rent from Beckenried, cycle to Seelisberg (about 12km) and then catch a boat from Treib, Seelisberg's boat station, back to Beckenried. The same route on foot would take about four and a half hours. You can **camp** west of Beckenried near Buochs (Ⓣ041 620 34 74; April–Sept).

Weg der Schweiz (Swiss Path)

Appropriately enough, the Rütli meadow is the starting-point for the long-distance **Weg der Schweiz** (Swiss Path) walking route, inaugurated in 1991 as part of the 700th anniversary celebrations of the founding of the Swiss Confederation.

The scenic trail, which circumnavigates the Urnersee to **Brunnen** (see p.406), is almost 35km long, walkable in two days of roughly six hours each (with a midway overnight stop in **Flüelen** or **Altdorf**; see p.410), or is easily dividable into smaller chunks. Sections are: Rütli to Bauen (11km up and down; 3hr 30min); Bauen to Flüelen (a flat 10km; 2hr 45min); Flüelen to Sisikon (reasonably flat 8km; 2hr); and Sisikon to Brunnen (climbing and dropping 8km; 3hr). Distinctive yellow route markers – a Swiss cross incorporating an arrow – point the way (ignore whichever way the stylized arrow faces and follow the signpost's directional finger instead). Boats shuttle between Rütli, Bauen, Isleten, Flüelen, Sisikon and Brunnen, and trains run between Flüelen, Sisikon and Brunnen, enabling you to pick and choose which sections you fancy. Tourist offices around the region stock English guides to the route.

The idea behind the path is to provide a lasting reminder of the state of the nation in 1991. Marked stones along the route identify the 26 cantons in the order in which they joined the Confederation, with each canton allotted a length of the path proportionate to its population: impossibly meticulous attention to detail has calculated that every 5mm of the trail represents a single Swiss citizen. So the initial climb from the Rütli takes care of Uri, Schwyz, Nidwalden and Obwalden (who were co-founders in 1291, and are all lightly populated); then there's a section of 1.6km representing Luzern (which joined in 1332); then 6.1km, the longest section for the most populous canton, Zürich (1351), and so on. Just after Flüelen is the shortest section, 71m representing tiny Appenzell Inner-Rhodes (1513), while 3km further north is the **Tellskapelle** (see p.410), a handy resting-place. The final walk into Brunnen covers the most recent canton to join the Confederation, Jura (1979).

Seelisberg and Treib

Beyond Beckenried, the main road enters a long tunnel beneath the cliffs and forests of the Seelisberg peninsula, emerging close to Flüelen (see p.410). Buses from Stans follow a minor road up onto the plateau itself, through the village of **Emmetten**, and on, with ever more spectacular lake panoramas, until you round a corner to be met with a sign reading "Welcome to the International Capital of the Age of Enlightenment". This is little **SEELISBERG**, a crow's nest of a place that is home to the Maharishi Ayur-Veda Health Centre (source of the sign). A funicular (W www.seelisberg.com) from the northern end of the main street shadows the steep path coiling down the cliff to the quaint old lakeside inn and boat station of **Treib** below, directly opposite Brunnen. Below the top funicular station, on the short path which ends up at the Rütli meadow (see p.396), you'll find an HI **hostel** (T 041 820 15 62, W www.youthhostel.ch; ❶; April–Oct), with simple dorms for Fr.21. Otherwise, Seelisberg has a handful of inexpensive **hotels**, including the comfortable, family-run *Montana* (T 041 820 12 68, F 041 820 12 69; ❶–❷), and *Bellevue* (T 041 825 66 66, F 041 825 66 67, W www.bellevue-seelisberg.ch; ❷–❸), a rather plusher option with lake views.

Engelberg

Situated at the southern end of the valley road and rail line from Stans in an enclave of Canton Obwalden, the modest ski resort of **ENGELBERG** (1050m) boasts an excursion to the highest point in central Switzerland – a

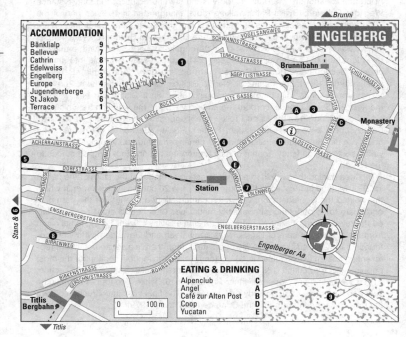

ACCOMMODATION

Bänklialp	9
Bellevue	7
Cathrin	8
Edelweiss	2
Engelberg	3
Europe	4
Jugendherberge	5
St Jakob	6
Terrace	1

EATING & DRINKING

Alpenclub	C
Angel	A
Café zur Alten Post	B
Coop	D
Yucatan	E

0   100 m

LUZERN AND ZENTRALSCHWEIZ | Engelberg

8

398

station at 3028m, just below the distinctive crest-of-a-wave summit of the **Titlis** mountain (3239m). This, along with the village's huge Benedictine Kloster (monastery) and the faded grandeur of its hotel architecture, make Engelberg well worth a visit.

Arrival, information and accommodation

After a picturesque valley-floor ride, the Luzern–Stans–Engelberg (LSE) **train** pulls into the station in the middle of the village. Turn left on Bahnhofstrasse, and right onto the main central Dorfstrasse for the **tourist office**, in a sports complex at Klosterstrasse 3 (mid-June to mid-Oct & mid-Dec to Easter Mon–Sat 8am–6.30pm, Sun 8am–6pm; rest of year Mon–Fri 8am–noon & 2–6.30pm, Sat 8am–6.30pm; ☎041 639 77 77, ⊚www.engelberg.ch). Some 200m east of the tourist office rises the onion dome of the monastery, while the base station for the Titlis is 500m southwest of the station, well signposted on the south bank of the Engelberger-Aa stream.

There are plenty of **hotels** dotted throughout the centre and the surrounding slopes. All of them offer discounts for stays beyond three nights.

Hotels

Bänklialp Bänklialpweg 25 ☎041 639 73 73, ⊚www.baenklialp.com. Good, straightforward holiday hotel, in a useful location, with plenty of services and comfortable, functional rooms. ②–③

Bellevue-Terminus Bahnhofplatz ☎041 637 12 13, ⊚www.bellevue-engelberg.ch. A grand lobby preludes characterful old-style rooms that are excellent value – most are ensuite, and all have high ceilings and an air of faded grandeur. Many rooms are let to students during term time. ②–③

Cathrin Birrenweg 22 ☎041 637 44 66, ⊚www.cathrin-engelberg.ch. Pleasant, quiet place near the Titlis cable-car, away from the bustle. ③–④

Edelweiss Terracestrasse 10 ☎041 637 07 37, ⊚www.edelweissengelberg.com. Charming Art Nouveau hotel above the village, dating from 1901 and now in the hands of uniquely friendly and welcoming English-speaking owner/managers. Stylish, spotless rooms, and broad valley views bring it head and shoulders above its competitors. ③–⑤

Engelberg Dorfstrasse 14 ☎041 639 79 79, ⊚www.hotel-engelberg.ch. Comfortable place on the pedestrianized main street, with warm and cosy rooms. ③–④

Europe Dorfstrasse 40 ☎041 639 75 75, ⊚www.hoteleurope.ch. Grandiose village-centre pile dating from 1902, with some of the bright, attractive rooms boasting wrought-iron balconies, chandeliers and fittings from an age of tourism long past. ③–④

St Jakob Engelbergerstrasse ☎041 637 13 88. Small, simple family pension on the road west of the centre, also with dorms from Fr.36. ①–②

Terrace Terracestrasse ☎041 639 66 66, ⊚www.terrace.ch. Huge presence looming above the village, built in 1906 and newly renovated

---

Bollywood in the Alps

Engelberg stands at the centre of the biggest story in Swiss tourism in years: **Bollywood**. With ongoing conflict in Kashmir making location-shoots with a mountain backdrop impossible, directors from India's film industry (based in Mumbai, formerly Bombay – hence the name) have been discovering that it's easier and cheaper to fly cast and crew out to the Alps than it is to battle with bureaucrats for permits to film in the Indian or Nepalese Himalaya. Engelberg – less than two hours from Zürich airport, and with guaranteed snow cover on the Titlis all year round – is the top-choice destination, the *Hotel Terrace* in particular regularly hosting the biggest stars of Bollywood. Wealthy film buffs back home have been reading the credits closely, and these days India is one of Swiss tourism's biggest growth markets, dozens of tour groups paying to escape the torrid pre-monsoon months of April, May and June with a visit to Engelberg and other Alpine film locations to tread in the footsteps of the famous.

throughout, with a glorious sun terrace and comfortable rooms, accessible either by car or by its own tiny funicular. ④–⑥

Hostel
Jugendherberge (HI hostel) Dorfstrasse 80
☎041 637 12 92, ⓦwww.youthhostel.ch. Located

500m west of the station, with dorms from Fr.31 and excellent meals. Closed May & Nov.

Campsite
Eienwäldli ☎041 637 19 49, ⓕ041 637 44 23. Five-star site on the southeastern edge of the village, about half-an-hour's walk from the centre. Closed Nov.

In and around the village

Dominating the village is a huge Benedictine **monastery**. The first monks arrived in the valley around 1120, and during the Middle Ages, the monastery was key to the expansion of ascetic mysticism in Germany and Switzerland. The buildings as they stand today date from a rebuilding after a fire in 1729. Up until 1798, when French troops arrived in force, the monks ruled the whole valley, which was independent of the Swiss Confederation and answered only to the pope; the Revolution changed all that, and the monastery first joined Canton Nidwalden in 1803, then changed its mind and switched to Obwalden twelve years later. These days, the sixty or so monks teach high school and further education courses, and have founded two affiliated monasteries in Missouri and Oregon. The Rococo **church**, dating from 1730, is stunning – a vast, elegant space complete with nine altars. A riot of ornamental stucco leads you through what would otherwise be an austere interior to the dramatic high altar, framing a luminescent painting of the Assumption. Guided **tours** of the whole complex, including the church and several impressive halls within the monastery, run year-round (in English: Thurs & Sat 10am; Fr.2.50).

To the Titlis

The monastery aside, Engelberg's attractions are all in the hills. The main excursion, well worthwhile if the weather's clear, is the four-stage journey to the **Titlis** (ⓦwww.titlis.ch). The first ascent crests a plateau to **Gerschnialp**, from where walking routes depart on both sides around back to the village and another lift brings you to the ridge above the small picturesque **Trübsee**. From the Trübsee station, you can detour on an easy stroll around the lake to the base station of a different cable-car serving the **Jochpass** and **Engstlen**, a little-frequented corner. Back at Trübsee, a gondola rises on a breathtakingly exposed journey over the lake to **Stand**, perched way above the valley at 2428m, with its own sun terrace and restaurant. From here, you switch onto the "Rotair", the world's first revolving gondola; the broad cabin begins to rotate shortly after starting the ascent, and on the five-minute journey to the top station turns completely round once, giving you a 360° panorama of the ride over the vast and impressive Titlis Glacier. On top, you'll find the standard circus of souvenir shops, ice grottos and the highest karaoke bar in Europe, but the views more than compensate. The hike up to the ice-bound Titlis peak takes a painstaking 45 minutes.

The full return **fare** Engelberg–Titlis is Fr.76, but as usual, walking some sections – notably from the Trübsee back down to the village (2hr) – can save plenty. Swiss Pass holders get 25 percent off, while the regional Tellpass brings a 50 percent discount to Trübsee. InterRailers and Eurailers get a 20 percent discount between May and mid-November only.

Engelberg's skiing and snowboarding is focused on the Titlis sector (ⓦwww .titlis.ch), specifically the area above **Gerschnialp**: on lower slopes is a network of fine blue runs, while further up, from the **Klein Titlis** station all the way down past **Stand** to the **Trübsee**, are plenty of red runs. There's excellent cross-country skiing around Trübsee as well, plus sledding at Gerschnialp. Way up at Klein Titlis – which benefits from summer skiing and snowboarding – is a hip boarder park, with another on the **Jochpass**. On the other side of the valley, the smaller Brunni sector (ⓦwww.brunni.ch) features a cable-car up to **Ristis**, from where a chairlift reaches the **Brunnihütte** (1860m), which has a cat's cradle of idyllic summer walks along the hillside meadows and down through forests to the village. In winter, a handful of blue ski runs swish you down easily to the valley floor.

The guest card gives discounts on **lift passes**, which are otherwise Fr.49/240 (one/six days) for both sectors, or Fr.35/160 for Brunni only. The local school is at ⓦwww.skischule-engelberg.ch.

Engelberg has an excellent reputation for **adventure sports**, with top operators Outventure (see box p.394) and Adventure Engelberg (www.adventure-engelberg .ch) organizing bungee-jumping, crevasse abseiling, canyoning, showshoeing, igloo-building, ice-climbing, rafting, kayaking and more. Don't miss the Devil Bike, a huge, fat-tyred contraption with no pedals, which makes short work of the scenic downhill bike run from Jochpass to Trübsee. For skiers, Outventure run a memorable Freeride Weekend (Fr.415), getting small groups out to some pristine powder slopes.

Eating and drinking

The *Coop* supermarket opposite the tourist office on Klosterstrasse has a budget self-service **restaurant** attached. Otherwise, there are plenty of places to fuel up along Dorfstrasse and through the centre. The *Engelstübli* has *saté* and other Indonesian specialities for around Fr.20, while across the road, the *Alpenclub* shelters several different eating places, including an inexpensive pizzeria, a *Käsestube* for fondue and the like, and a more formal restaurant with Swiss dishes for Fr.25 and up. Further east along Dorfstrasse, the *Café zur Alten Post* has basic stomach-filling *menus* for around Fr.15. The restaurant at *Hotel Bänklialp* does good Swiss staples for moderate prices. Centre of the late-night après-ski scene is the *Yucatan* **bar**, which also offers good, filling evening meals for around Fr.18 or so. The English-style *Angel* pub on Dorfstrasse is another lively watering hole.

Routes to the Rigi

The titanic chunk of the **Rigi** (ⓦwww.rigi.ch), which rises to 1798m plum between the lakes of Luzern and Zug, has long been famous as a majestic viewpoint. By itself, it's actually rather scrubby, a steep-scarped grassy ridge with several summits, but it stands alone dividing the two lakes, and offers wonderful views south to the Alps.

There are several transport options up the mountain, testifying to the scramble in the late nineteenth century to capitalize on burgeoning tourism to Luzern. Rival companies started laying track from **Vitznau** on Lake Luzern, and Arth-Goldau just south of the Zugersee, competing for who would be first to reach the summit. The Vitznau line – with the bonus of its accessibility from

Luzern by boat – won out, but Arth-Goldau benefits from being a major junction-point on the Zürich–Gotthard mainline train route. Trains from Vitznau (red) and Goldau (blue) converge at Staffel near the summit for the final pull to **Rigi-Kulm** at the very top. A third route up the mountain, a cable-car from picturesque **Weggis**, also on Lake Luzern, rises to connect with the Vitznau trains at an intermediate stop named Rigi-Kaltbad. The popular method is to go up by one route and down by another; the Swiss Pass, Eurail and InterRail all bring a 25 percent discount. It's easy to make the Rigi a day-trip from Luzern; or you could just as easily spend a night on the summit to enjoy the highly celebrated sunrise over the Alps. If you're set on hiking to the summit, reckon on four hours for the trek up from Weggis.

Weggis

On a sheltered, south-facing bay, protected from cold northerly weather by the Rigi itself, **WEGGIS** basks in its own subtropical microclimate – the palm trees, figs and magnolias grow naturally. It looks out over the lake and across to the Bürgenstock cliffs, and has been a popular summer resort for a couple of centuries, with a dedicated older clientele returning year after year to soak up the sun.

The **tourist office** for Weggis, the Rigi region and the whole north shore of the lake is right beside the boat station, at Seestrasse 5 (May–Sept Mon–Fri 8am–6pm, Sat & Sun 9am–2.30pm; Oct–April Mon–Fri 8am–5pm; ☎041 390 11 55, ⓦwww.weggis.ch). There's no shortage of **accommodation**. Least pricey is the *Budget Hotel*, a well-kept place in a residential district a stiff walk uphill and west from the boat station (☎041 390 11 31, ⓦwww.budgethotel .ch; ❶–❷). A couple of minutes east of the landing stage is the *Seehof Hotel du Lac* (☎041 390 11 51, ⓦwww.hotel-du-lac.ch; ❸–❹; closed Nov & Dec), a charming, quiet family-run place of some quality – it's worth splashing out for the lakeview rooms with balcony. Just beside it is the classy *Beau-Rivage* (☎041 392 79 00, ⓦwww.beaurivage-weggis.ch; ❺–❼; April–Oct), with plenty of creature comforts in the rooms and an enclosed lakeside lawn for sunny lounging. The cable-car station for Rigi-Kaltbad is northeast of the landing stage, well signposted.

Vitznau and Gersau

A couple of hours' stroll east from Weggis is the small village of **VITZNAU**, base station for Europe's oldest rack railway (inaugurated in 1871) running up to the Rigi-Kulm. Whereas Weggis can seem a trifle twee or over pretty, tranquil Vitznau – set in a sheltered west-facing bay close to the narrowest strait of the lake – has plenty of character, despite the hordes of day-trippers in the village centre. The train station for the Rigi is right opposite the boat station, with the **tourist office** beside it (Mon–Fri 8am–noon & 1–6.30pm, Sat 9am–noon; ☎041 398 00 35, ⓦwww.vitznau.ch). The best-value **accommodation** is the *Schiff*, 300m west of the centre in a quiet location (☎041 397 13 57, ⓦwww.schiff-vitznau.ch; ❶; closed Nov), with six old-style rooms above the most pleasant of lakeside restaurants. A few hundred metres beyond is Vitznau's landmark *Park Hotel* (☎041 399 60 60, ⓦwww.parkhotel-vitznau.ch; ❾), a palatial Belle Epoque vision, with vast rooms, two gourmet restaurants, sauna, tennis courts and more. In the village itself, the *Rigi* (☎041 397 21 21, ⓦwww .rigi-vitznau.ch; ❸) is an attractive shuttered old house with renovated rooms.

Less than two hours' walk east from Vitznau is tiny **GERSAU**, a patch of sloping meadow that was, from 1390 until the French invasion of 1798, the smallest independent free republic in Europe, with all of two thousand inhabitants. Midway between Gersau and Vitznau there's a handy HI **hostel,** *Jugendherberge Rotschuo* (☎041 828 12 77, ⓦwww.youthhostel.ch; ❶; dorms Fr.23; March–Nov). Hourly buses connect Weggis, Vitznau and Gersau, while different buses run from Gersau on to Brunnen and Schwyz.

The Rigi

There are hiking routes all over the Rigi, most starting from **Rigi-Kaltbad** (1453m) or **Rigi-Klösterli** (1315m), the first accessible from both Weggis and Vitznau, the second a midway stop on the Arth-Goldau train. Kaltbad is a peaceful traffic-free resort on a terrace of pastureland high above Weggis; there's a handful of hotels here, as well as relatively easy two- or three-hour hiking routes through the pine trees out to the Känzeli viewpoint, up onto the ridge at First, or to the Rotstock peak above Kaltbad (1659m). Red trains from Vitznau and blue ones from Arth-Goldau meet at Staffel for the final stretch to **Rigi-Kulm**, home of the *Hotel Rigi-Kulm* (☎041 855 03 03, ⓦwww.rigikulm.ch; ❸; closed Oct & Nov), a bald 1950s creation replacing earlier incarnations dating back more than a hundred years. It's a rather dull place in itself, but has the incomparable selling point of offering a highly memorable sunrise over the Alps. The summit is a 200m stroll from the hotel, and gives bird's-eye views over Luzern and the Vierwaldstättersee on one side, and Zug and the Zugersee on the other.

Zug

The town of **ZUG** (pronounced *tsoogk*), 22km from Luzern on the north side of the Rigi, is the richest place in Switzerland, which makes it very rich indeed. Tiny Canton Zug has the lowest tax rates in the country – about half the national average – which attracts flocks of multinational corporations, which in turn pushes average *per capita* net income up to an incredible Fr.70,000 (£30,500) a year. Zug's modern, business-driven existence proceeds without pomp amidst the glittering offices and malls of the new town, a world away from the picturesque medieval churches and cobbled waterfront lanes of the compact Old Town adjacent. The town's location on the crystal-blue Zugersee is very attractive, framed by the high wooded plateau of the Zugerberg rising 600m to the east and the peak of the Rigi (see above) on its southwest shores.

Arrival, information and accommodation

The station – with a change office (daily 7am–8.30pm) and bike rental (daily 7am–7.30pm) – is about 400m north of the lakeshore, and the same amount again north of the Old Town, which ranges down the eastern shore of the lake. Zug is a rail junction, situated at the point where a line from Luzern in the west meets the main north–south route running from Zürich via Flüelen and the Gotthard Tunnel to Ticino. You emerge from the station at a little roundabout at the head of Alpenstrasse, leading down (south) to the lake. Less than 50m away on the left is the **tourist office** (Mon–Fri 8.30am–6pm, Sat 8.30am–3pm, Sun 9am–3pm; ☎041 711 00 78, ⓦwww.zug-tourismus.ch). SGZ **boats** (ⓦwww.zugersee-info.ch) tour the Zugersee from the Bahnhofsteg, at the foot of Alpenstrasse; check their posted timetable, which also has details of their numerous eat-aboard trips – everything from winter brunches to Glenn Miller-accompanied starlit dinners.

Zug's hoteliers – like most business people in the city – fairly glow with financial health: the combination of Zug's high business profile, its proximity to both Luzern and Zürich, and its chronic shortage of **accommodation** means that they can overcharge and still be rewarded with enviably high occupancy rates. Booking ahead is vital.

Hotels

Central Grabenstrasse 9 ☎041 727 48 48, ☎041 727 48 49. Pleasant family hotel on the main road just above the Old Town, with smallish but comfortable rooms. ❸

Guggital Zugerbergstrasse 46 ☎041 711 28 21, ⓦwww.hotel-guggital.ch. Up on the slopes overlooking the town from the south: for the views and the service, the best mid-range choice. All rooms are modern and renovated, and virtually all face the lake for gorgeous sunsets (pay more for a balcony). Bus #11 from Metalli (cross under the station, and wait outside the Zuger Kantonalbank) stops outside. ❸–❹

Ibis Bahnhofstrasse 15, Baar ☎041 766 76 00, ⓦwww.hotelibis.com. Of the many motels and generic travel lodges on and off the Gotthard motorway near Zug, this is the most reliable – a compact, characterless chain outlet at Baar train station, with parking. ❷

Löwen am See Landsgemeindeplatz ☎041 725 22 22, ⓦwww.loewen-zug.ch. Attractive, central hotel in a car-free location a stone's throw from the water. ❹

Ochsen Kolinplatz 11 ☎041 729 32 32, ⓦwww.ochsen-zug.ch. A sixteenth-century gabled exterior and plush reception belie the rooms, which are less characterful than you might expect for a house venerable enough to have once hosted Goethe – the best are high up at the back overlooking rooftops and an internal courtyard. Weekdays you can barely move for suits. ❺

Hostel

Jugendherberge (HI hostel) Allmendstrasse 8 ☎041 711 53 54, ⓦwww.youthhostel.ch. Walk west along the lakefront Chamerstrasse, follow Allmendstrasse north under a railway bridge, and the hostel is to the right behind a petrol station. Dorm beds are Fr.29. ❶

Campsite

Innere Lorzenallmend Chamer Fussweg 36 ☎041 741 84 22. Located 2km west of Zug on the lakeshore – take bus #4 from Bundesplatz to Brüggli (direction Hünenberg).

The Town

Alpenstrasse leads from the station past Bundesplatz straight down to the lakeshore jetty, from where views of the Rigi and Pilatus are terrific. Vorstadt follows the eastern lakeshore to **Postplatz**, on the the edge of Zug's tiny Old Town.

From Postplatz, shop-lined Neugasse leads south to **Kolinplatz** and the striped-roof **Zytturm**, at 52m the Old Town's tallest building but these days tucked into a corner beside a busy traffic road and largely forgotten. Built in the mid-thirteenth century as a watchtower, it was renovated in 1557 and endowed with a clock in 1574. The shields below the clock face are those of the eight Swiss cantons at the time of the tower's construction (from left to right, Zürich, Bern, Luzern, Uri, Schwyz, Unterwalden, Glarus and Zug). There's a host of tiny details on the tower, including, under the archway, a beautiful late-Gothic wavy-haired angel. Just above the upper ledge, you'll spot a painting of a rat, made by medieval watchmen as a device to scare away the rats that stole their food during long nights on duty.

Opposite the Zytturm, Kolinplatz features a fountain dedicated to Wolfgang Kolin, standard-bearer of the Swiss army at their 1422 defeat by the Duke of Milan. Heading beneath the Zytturm brings you into the most atmospheric part of the Old Town, cobbled lanes lined with medieval gabled and balconied (and often frescoed) houses. Just behind the Zytturm is Zug's **Rathaus**, dating from 1509 and retaining much of its original woodwork, and a few steps north is the waterside **Landsgemeindeplatz**. From the Rathaus, Unteraltstadt and Oberaltstadt both lead south to the tiny **Liebfrauenkapelle**, dating from 1266 but boasting a marvellous Baroque interior.

If you follow the alleys uphill from the chapel, and cross the main Grabenstrasse, you'll spot St Oswaldsgasse leading left to the **Kirche St Oswald**, built between 1478 and 1545 and dedicated to St Oswald of Northumbria (605–642). Inside you'll find another lavish Baroque interior and a nineteenth-century mural; as you leave, look above the double portal to see a beautiful carved statue of Mary flanked by St Oswald and St Michael. It's a short walk from here up Kirchenstrasse to the **Burg**, a circular, top-heavy construction that was once the headquarters of the Kyburg and Habsburg governors, and now houses the town's **museum** (Tues–Fri 2–5pm, Sat & Sun 10am–noon & 2–5pm; Fr.5, free on Sun; SMP; ⓦwww.museenzug.ch), worth a look for its model of medieval Zug. A few metres further up the hill is the **Kunsthaus**, with usually very good temporary art exhibitions. If you head along Dorfstrasse, and across the main Ägeristrasse, you'll spot a set of quiet, concealed steps leading up to the **chapel** of a Capuchin convent (1597), with an adjacent, well-tended walled cemetery. Tranquil covered steps bring you down to opposite the old **mint**, with Postplatz to the right.

Eating and drinking

The best concentration of places to **eat and drink** is in and around Landsgemeindeplatz: on sunny days, cafés and restaurants lay tables out on the waterfront square, but there's also plenty of choice in the alleys all around. The lakefront road Vorstadt is shoulder to shoulder with restaurants, most offering fish of one kind or another. Best low-budget dining is in the *Coop* restaurant in the mall on Bundesplatz.

Zug is famous around Switzerland for its cherries, which give rise both to many varieties of local **Kirsch** (cherry brandy) and to **Zuger Kirschtorte**, a delectably buttery almond tart saturated with Kirsch that breathes cherry fumes but, oddly, has not a single fruit adorning it. *Kirschtorte* is on offer all over town – the best is made fresh daily at Konditorei Meier, Alpenstrasse 16. Aside from coffee and a slice, they can box up a whole *Torte* for you to take away.

Balou Kirchenstrasse 7. Hip little local bar away from the lake, open daily until late.

Chaotikum Chamerstrasse 41. A shack beside the main road 1km west of town painted "CHAOS" where you can enjoy a good, solid meal for less than Fr.15 – if you don't mind the rough-edged crowd, wafting cannabis smoke and loud jangly music. Cheap beer too. Closed Mon.

Fischmärt Fischmarkt 15. Comfy Old Town bar with booths and a range of malt whiskies. Closed Sun.

Hecht Fischmarkt 2 ☏041 729 81 30 ⓦwww.hecht.ch. The top place for fish – an elegant, historic lakefront building featuring refined lake-fresh cuisine at Fr.60 and up.

Rathauskeller Oberaltstadt 1 ☏041 711 00 58 ⓦwww.rathauskeller.ch. Top restaurant in the canton, housed in the historic Rathaus. Upstairs is the highest of *haute cuisine*, with a six-course

evening *menu* around Fr.150, but the ground-floor bistro serves simpler, more affordable dishes from the same kitchen. Closed Sun & Mon.

Schiffbar Graben 2. Two different bars with the same name: much preferable is the upstairs one (self-dubbed the *Panorama*), with an elevated terrace aiding peaceful contemplation of the lake below.

Speck Alpenstrasse 12 ⓦwww.speck.ch. Simple *menus* in the pasta-and-salad vein are around Fr.13, plus good *Kirschtorte*. Closed Sun.

Widder Landsgemeindeplatz 12 ☏041 711 03 16 ⓦwww.gasthaus-widder.ch. Excellent Old Town choice, with hot meals all day and terrace seating in summer. Relaxed South African ownership not only means the staff speak English, but also adds ostrich and springbok steaks to the already full menu of Swiss specialities, quality pizzas and super-fresh lake fish.

Schwyzerland

Occupying the picturesque northeastern corner of Lake Luzern and extending north to the wild hills bordering the Zürichsee, unsung **Schwyzerland** takes in a series of broad, lush valleys enclosed between Alpine foothills and overlooked by the massive twin peaks of the Mythen. The gentle resort of **Brunnen** lies on the lake, while a short distance inland is the cantonal capital **Schwyz**, an old and graceful town with plenty of history. To the north, the ancient monastery church at **Einsiedeln** draws pilgrims from around the world to pay homage to the icon of the Black Madonna.

Brunnen

Of all the resort towns on the lake, **BRUNNEN** is perhaps most dramatically located, snug in a right-angled corner of the shore between the crests of the Rigi and the scarps of the Fronalpstock. Vistas from its jetty are stupendous, looking the length of the Urnersee south to the snowy peaks around the Gotthard; directly across to the misty cliffs of Seelisberg, with the Uri-Rotstock and Titlis behind; and east the length of the Vierwaldstättersee to far-distant Luzern. Brunnen basks at the head of a wind tunnel which draws the warm Föhn wind north from the Mediterranean, frequently turning the Urnersee choppy and stormy: rapidly fluctuating weather conditions mean that it's not unknown to look south to glorious sunshine on the high Alps and east to pelting rain over Luzern. Mad King Ludwig of Bavaria took a real shine to Brunnen in 1865; one of his favourite pastimes was ordering a team of alphorn-blowers to play to him while he sat in a small boat on the lake at midnight.

The easiest excursion from Brunnen is to the **Urmiberg** peak nearby (1140m; ⓦ www.urmiberg.ch) – this is one not to be missed, with stunning views both on the way up in the tiny cable-car and from the summit itself. Hiking trails from the top include a steep path back down to Brunnen (1hr 30min; a gentler descent adds 1hr), and other trails down to Gersau or Goldau (both 3hr). There's a summit restaurant, and also the opportunity to take off on a **tandem paragliding** flight, courtesy of the local adventure operator Touch And Go (ⓣ041 820 54 31, ⓦ www.paragliding.ch; Fr.150).

Practicalities

Brunnen's **train station** is set back from the lakeshore jetty, about ten minutes' walk inland on the main Bahnhofstrasse: you should allow plenty of time if you're switching from a boat to a train, or vice versa (switching at Flüelen is easier). Before you get to the station, you'll pass the **tourist office**, 150m from the jetty at Bahnhofstrasse 32 (Mon–Fri 8.30am–noon & 1.30–6pm; April–Sept also Sat 9am–noon, July & Aug Sat 9am–noon & 1.30–4pm; ⓣ041 825 00 40, ⓦ www.brunnentourismus.ch): they can help you out with information for the whole area, including Schwyz (which only has a tiny information counter).

There are plenty of places to **stay**. The **campsite** *Hopfraeben* (ⓣ041 820 18 73) is near the Urmiberg cable-car. Top choice of lakefront **hotels** is *Waldstätterhof* (ⓣ041 825 06 06, ⓦ www.waldstaetterhof.ch; ⑤–⑥), an elegant, five-star palace overhauled from top to bottom. Lakefront *Bellevue* (ⓣ041 820 13 18, ⓦ www.bellevue-brunnen.ch; ③) has stylishly modern rooms behind their ornate wrought-iron balconies. On the main street in the village is the charming seventeenth-century *Weisses Rössli* (ⓣ041 820 10 22, ⓕ041 820 11 22; ②–③), Ludwig's old haunt, with comfortably traditional rooms, an excellent

restaurant – with quality Swiss cuisine for Fr.25 or so – and a splendid Royal Chamber in Bavarian white, blue and gold. The *Brunnerhof* on Kapellplatz in the centre has good *menus* for under Fr.20; both it and the *Park* restaurant (☎041 825 47 47) inland offer veggie dishes. There's a handful of lively **café-bars**, including the popular *Dodo* on Bahnhofstrasse, and *Mezcalito* on the lakefront Axenstrasse, with a page of different cocktails and pricey food.

Schwyz

A small but characterful town 5km northeast of Brunnen, **SCHWYZ** (pronounced *shveets*) is capital of its canton. First mentioned in a document dated August 14, 972, Schwyz was associated culturally and militarily with its neighbours Uri and Nidwalden from as early as 1144. After the combined confederate forces won a famous victory against the Habsburgs at nearby Morgarten in 1315, they all became collectively dubbed "Schwyzers" and the whole country – formerly Helvetia – became known instead as Schwyz (or Schweiz in modern High German), a name that stuck as the country grew. Throughout the Middle Ages and after, the men of Schwyz were sought after as particularly accomplished mercenaries, and many were able to return to their home town with fat wallets to build for themselves the fine town houses which characterize the old centre today.

Schwyz is best known for being the repository of the ancient documents embodying the history of the Confederation, on display in the **Bundesbriefmuseum**, Bahnhofstrasse 20 in the town centre (Museum of Federal Charters; May–Oct Tues–Fri 9–11.30am & 1.30–5pm, Sat & Sun 9am–5pm; Nov–April Tues–Fri same hours, Sat & Sun 1.30–5pm; Fr.4; SMP; ⓦwww.sz.ch). This small, beautifully simple 1936 building, with a garden and a cloister of attractive arches, houses banners, flags, coins and documents recording events in Swiss history – ask for the excellent English notes at the desk. The main treasure is upstairs, in a great hall lined with flags taken from various battlefields over the centuries. At the far end, lying alone in its own display case, is a small rectangular piece of parchment covered in close lines of text. This is the original Charter of Confederation, reputedly signed and sealed on the Rütli meadow on August 1, 1291; the wax seals of Uri and Nidwalden still dangle from it, but the seal of Schwyz was lost long ago.

Cutting a dash

In 1884, an impoverished young Swiss, Carl Elsener, believed he had spotted a gap in the market for dependable pocket knives, and founded the Swiss Cutlers' Association in order to supply knives and blades to the army. But times were hard: by 1893 his venture had collapsed, and a German competitor had started making knives more cheaply. Elsener persevered, making lighter and more elegant versions of his knives, which he patented in 1897. By word of mouth, the knives grew in popularity, and even without an official seal of approval, Swiss army officers began to ask for them specifically. Elsener had originally named his factory – located in Ibach, just south of Schwyz – after his mother Victoria, but when stainless steel was invented in 1921 and given the international designation INOX, Elsener combined the two into one. **Victorinox** knives (ⓦwww.victorinox.ch) gained official backing from the Swiss Army and, after World War II, from the US Army too. Today, in myriad varieties, they are the best-known brand of Swiss army knife. Some 34,000 are still churned out every day by the same factory in Ibach, about ten minutes' walk south of Schwyz town centre at Schmiedgasse 57. Its on-site **shop** sells the complete range of knives at discount prices (Mon–Fri 7.30am–noon & 1.15–6pm, Sat 8am–3pm).

The historical theme is continued in the inventive **Forum der Schweizer Geschichte** (Forum of Swiss History), a branch of the Swiss National Museum, in the town centre beside the bus station (Tues–Sun 10am–5pm; Fr.8; SMP; ⓦwww.musee-suisse.com). The ground floor is devoted to investigations of how people in both the countryside and the city used environmental resources throughout history; the middle floor concentrates on social history, with assessments of power structures and relations between the church and the state; and the top floor concentrates on why and how Switzerland survived in the way that it did. Plenty of videos and interactive displays keep you interested.

The central Hauptplatz square is a few steps east of the museum, dominated by two great buildings, both rebuilt after a town fire in 1642: on a terrace above is the large parish church of **St Martin**, with an ornate interior; while the foursquare **Rathaus** sits on the square itself, its facade decorated with frescoes painted in 1891 to celebrate the 600th anniversary of the Rütli oath. Alleys to the northwest bring you to the **Ital–Reding Haus** (April–Nov Tues–Fri 2–5pm, Sat & Sun 10am–noon & 2–5pm; Fr.4; SMP; ⓦwww.mythen.ch /ital.reding-haus), a splendid early seventeenth-century manor house set in its own gardens and with a magnificent interior, its upper rooms bedecked with skilfully carved panelling on wall and ceiling. Across the garden – and within the same complex – is the ancient **Haus Bethlehem**, the oldest wooden house in the country, dating from 1287. Squeezing through its minuscule rooms makes you feel a bit like Alice.

Practicalities

Schwyz is rather awkward both to get to and to stay in, and you'd probably do better spending the night in Brunnen down the road. It's a **bus**-oriented town, with the main central bus station ("Schwyz-Post") handling arrivals from Brunnen. The **train station** is in the suburb of Seewen, some 2km west of Schwyz centre – buses run from outside to Schwyz-Post. The **tourist office** is by the bus station at Bahnhofstrasse 4 (Mon–Fri 7am–noon & 1–6pm, Sat 8.30am–noon; ☎041 810 19 91, ⓦwww.schwyz-tourismus.ch & ⓦwww .wbs.ch).

Hotels include the *Hirschen*, Hinterdorfstrasse 14 (☎041 811 12 76, ⓦwww.hirschen-schwyz.ch; ❶), a cosy old place also with dorms (Fr.25); and the classier *Wysses Rössli*, Hauptplatz 3 (☎041 811 19 22, ⓦwww.roessli-schwyz.ch; ❹), with large pleasant rooms and an excellent **restaurant**, especially strong on fish specialities (*menus* Fr.23). *Ratskeller*, Strehlgasse 3 (closed Sun & Mon), is another quality restaurant, with a less expensive bistro area to one side (*menus* Fr.18).

Einsiedeln

The small village of **EINSIEDELN** (900m), in the hills of northern Schwyz 25km northeast of Brunnen, has been Switzerland's most important site of pilgrimage for a thousand years, and still draws a quarter of a million devout believers every year. The village itself is utterly unremarkable, but the mighty Benedictine **Kloster** (monastery) which dominates it is exceptional, and worth a detour whether you're drawn by faith or curiosity.

Einsiedeln means hermitage, and is named for **St Meginrat**, who withdrew to what was then wild forest in about 828 AD. After his death in 861, hermits maintained Meginrat's self-built altar, forming a **Benedictine** community in 934 at the behest of a provost of Strasbourg cathedral, who invited the Bishop of Konstanz to perform the consecration of a new church on the site – the bishop was about to do so, when a voice was heard ringing through the church, insisting three times over that Christ himself had already consecrated the church. The pope declared this to be a **miracle**, and issued a papal bull blessing the pilgrimage to Einsiedeln.

From then on, the monastery enjoyed special privilege, with large royal grants and positions of honour for the abbots. By 1286 a Chapel of Our Lady, built over the remains of Meginrat's cell, was already a focal point; it was adorned after a destructive fire in 1468 with a statuette of Mary with the infant Christ, carved in wood some time before 1440. It is this figure, blackened by smoke from the candles of centuries, which became the focus for pilgrimage, and which has retained its numinous power to this day as the Black Madonna.

The church

The monastery complex was entirely rebuilt from 1704 to 1726 in the most lavish of late-Baroque styles. As you emerge from the cluster of the village centre, the vast **Klosterplatz** opens out in front. The rather plain sandstone front of the church, with its twin towers rising from an immense 140m-long facade, is framed by unusual semi-circular sunken arcades. The ornate **Well of Our Lady** in the square taps the water of Meginrat's spring – pilgrims traditionally drink from each of the 14 spouts in turn on their approach to the church.

The interior, designed by Kaspar Moosbrugger, one of the monks, is immediately breathtaking, although with the regular cycle of services continuing daily you may not get a chance to wander round admiring it. The nave is decorated with detailed **frescoes** by Cosmas Damian Asam, and every part of the lofty white interior is detailed in lavish gold. An intricate wrought-iron choir screen gives into the stunning pink Rococo **choir**, its ceiling bedecked with animated sculptures of angels. However, the focus of all the pilgrims' attention is the black marble **Chapel of Our Lady**, positioned in a huge octagonal bay just inside the main portal. The invading French destroyed the chapel in 1798 (although the monks had already removed the Black Madonna to the Tyrol for safekeeping), and the present chapel building dates from a Neoclassical reconstruction in 1817. The **Black Madonna** itself, a little over a metre tall and usually dressed in a jewelled and tasselled golden dress donated by Canton Uri in 1734, stands illuminated within at the centre of attention.

Einsiedeln remains a fully functioning monastic community, with around a hundred priests and brothers. **Mass** is celebrated several times a day, most notably with Gregorian chanting at 7.30am and choral accompaniment for Vespers at 4pm. Of the many annual **pilgrimage festivals**, the most colourful is the Feast of the Miraculous Dedication on September 14, which culminates in a candlelit procession around the square.

Practicalities

Trains run every hour from Luzern to Biberbrugg, where you have to change for the climb to Einsiedeln; hourly trains from Brunnen require an extra change at Arth-Goldau. Einsiedeln's **train station** is a ten-minute walk from the church: from Dorfplatz out front, head east along Hauptstrasse. The **tourist office** is just off Klosterplatz at Hauptstrasse 85 (Mon–Fri 10am–noon & 1.30–5pm, Sat 9am–noon & 1–4pm, Sun 9am–noon; ☏055 418 44 88, Ⓦwww.einsiedeln.ch). Almost every building in sight of the church is a **hotel**: on the square, *Katharinahof* (☏055 418 98 00, Ⓦwww.katharinahof.ch; ❷) is a good low-budget choice, while *Linde* (☏055 418 48 48, Ⓦwww. linde-einsiedeln.ch; ❷–❹) has shared-bath rooms and some plusher ensuite options. Just off the square is *Storchen*, Hauptstrasse 79 (℡055 412 37 60, ⓦwww.hotel-storchen.ch; ❷), a comfortable place with a good restaurant. There are plenty of places to **eat** – ranging from the simple *Pizzeria Zia Teresa*, Hauptstrasse 21 (closed Mon & Tues), up to the quality restaurants with their Fr.23-ish *menus* on and near Klosterplatz, including the *Katharinahof*, *Bären* and *St Georg*.

Every few years, the monastery stages a massed **open-air** production of the *Great World Theatre* – a religious drama by Pedro Calderón de la Barca premièred at the Spanish court in 1685. Some 600 villagers take part, coached by the monks themselves. The next production is due for 2005; for information, check ⓦwww.welttheater.ch.

Uri and the Alpine passes

The mountainous **Canton Uri** occupies the land between the lake and the barrier of the high Alps. Although Uri shares borders with Bern, Valais, Ticino, Graubünden and Glarus, it is cut off from them all by 2000m-plus mountain passes, and the only cantons with which it has easy exchange of influence are its old partners from the 1291 Rütli oath, Schwyz and Nidwalden. It's no coincidence that Uri is the setting for the medieval legend of **William Tell** (see p.412), absorbed into Swiss consciousness as near fact and serving to define the essence of Swissness to the rest of the world. The small cantonal capital **Altdorf** was where Tell did his apple-shooting.

Uri also holds the keys to the great trans-Alpine **Gotthard** route, one of the main Alpine passes. For centuries, people and traffic have followed the ancient road up and over the mountains, although these days massively long tunnels draw trains and most of the cars swiftly to and from Ticino and Italy. **Andermatt**, on the south side of the Gotthard, is uniquely located at an Alpine crossroads, with six high-level routes passing through or near the town.

Flüelen and around

FLÜELEN is the farthest point of the Vierwaldstättersee from Luzern, a picturesque little town with the train station right beside the landing stage. Fast trains from Flüelen serve both Luzern and Zürich (with alternate services requiring a change at Arth-Goldau), as well as heading south through the Gotthard to Ticino. It's also the southern terminus of the **Axenstrasse**, the narrow road which clings below the cliffs of the eastern shore of the Urnersee south from Brunnen. The road was only completed in 1865, and enabled travellers to approach the Gotthard for the first time by land, instead of forcing them to take a ship from Luzern or Brunnen. Some 3km north of Flüelen – and accessible only by car, boat or on foot (no buses use the Axenstrasse) – is the **Tellsplatte**, a flat rock onto which William Tell is purported to have leapt to escape the clutches of Gessler (see box p.412). Beside it is a restaurant and, beautifully framed amidst the trees, the **Tellskapelle** (see p.397), a tiny monument built in 1880 with arched loggia featuring vivid frescoes depicting the story of Tell. Boats serving this point from Brunnen also pass the **Schillerstein**, a 25m high natural obelisk near the Rütli which was inscribed in 1859: "To Friedrich Schiller, the Chronicler of Tell".

Buses from Flüelen station run into central **ALTDORF**, some 3km south (Altdorf's own train station is inconveniently located 1km west of the centre). At the traffic-bound heart of Altdorf is the Rathausplatz, dominated by the impressive **Telldenkmal** (Tell Monument) – a much-photographed icon erected in 1895 that depicts a sturdy, bearded Tell raising his eyes fearlessly to the horizon, while his son, embodiment of the Swiss people, accepts his father's protecting arm and gazes trustingly upwards at him. This square is reputedly the scene of the apple-shooting event commemorated in the legend. Nearby alleys have retained plenty of character, but if the Tell bug has bitten you, grab a bus bound for **BÜRGLEN**, a village 2km northeast on the Klausen road, which is celebrated as Tell's birthplace. The **chapel** which sits beside the village church on the site of Tell's house was dedicated as early as 1582, with interior frescoes depicting the legend dating from the 1750s. Around the corner from the 1786 Tell fountain out front is the **Tell Museum** (daily: July & Aug 9.30am–5.30pm; May, June, Sept & Oct 10–11.30am & 1.30–5pm; Fr.5; SMP; ⓦwww.tellmuseum.ch), a worthwhile little place crammed with Tell curiosities; ask them to set up the informative twenty-minute slide-show (in English) on the history of the legend.

What's remarkable about the Altdorf area is the understatedness of its Tellmania: you get the feeling that Tell, although something of a caricature to non-Swiss, is far too important to the locals to start a whole tourist circus. Tellsplatte, Altdorf and Bürglen are all out-of-the-way places, little visited by foreigners, and you may well find that the only tourists who you come across are Swiss families, spending a weekend in the area to give the kids a glimpse of their heritage.

The road through Bürglen continues up on a spectacular drive – followed by buses in summer – to the **Klausen Pass** (see also p.489) and over to Linthal in Canton Glarus. This is one of the most scenic pass routes in the country, with dizzy views distracting you from the business of keeping on the narrow road.

Practicalities

Altdorf's **tourist office**, with information on the whole canton, is just off the main square at Schützengasse 11 (Mon–Fri 9–11.30am & 1.30–5.30pm, Sat 9–11.30am; ☎041 872 04 50, ⓦwww.altdorftourismus.ch & ⓦwww.i-uri.ch).

For accommodation in **Flüelen**, aim for the *Tell & Post* hotel, Axenstrasse 12 (☎041 874 11 30, Ⓕ041 874 11 35; ❷), with serviceable rooms, ensuite and not; or the more elegant *Weisses Kreuz*, opposite the landing stage at Axenstrasse 2 (☎041 870 17 17, ⓦwww.kreuz-hirschen.ch; ❷). The **campsite** (☎041 870 92 22, ⓦwww.windsurfing-urnersee.ch), fifteen minutes' walk from the station, doubles as a windsurfing centre (see p.394).

The best-value hotel in **Altdorf** is the *Schwarzen Löwen*, Tellsgasse 8 (☎041 874 80 80, ⓦwww.zum-schwarzen-loewen.ch; ❸), which has renovated rooms, all clean and pleasant (choose one off the street) – one room has retained the original furniture from when Goethe stopped by in the 1770s. Buses to Bürglen depart from the square, or from Altdorf-Post, 100m south on Bahnhofstrasse.

The most characterful accommodation choice of the lot is the *Gasthaus Adler* in the centre of **Bürglen** (☎041 870 11 33; ❶), a fine old sixteenth-century roadhouse inn, with wooden eaves bedecked in ivy and a handful of alluringly creaky guest rooms above a *gutbürgerliche* restaurant.

Andermatt and around

If you're travelling south by fast train, you're likely to miss the small town of **ANDERMATT** (1444m), surrounded by the high Alps on all sides, since it lies beyond the entrance to the Gotthard Tunnel at **Göschenen** (see p.414).

The legend of William Tell

The legend of **William Tell** is the central defining myth in Swiss national conscious-ness. Most schoolchildren, whether in Switzerland or elsewhere in the West, know at least the bare bones of the story, but whereas in most cultures it is little more than one folktale among many, in Switzerland it has come to embody the very essence of Swissness.

The story

At a time soon after the opening of the Gotthard Pass, when the Habsburg emper-ors of Vienna sought to control Uri and thus control trans-Alpine trade, a new bailiff, **Hermann Gessler**, was despatched to Altdorf. The proud mountain folk of Uri had already joined with their Schwyzer and Nidwaldner neighbours at Rütli in pledging to resist the Austrians' cruel oppression, and when Gessler raised a pole in the cen-tral square of Altdorf and perched his hat on the top, commanding all who passed before it to bow in respect, it was the last straw. **William Tell**, a countryman from nearby Bürglen, either hadn't heard about Gessler's command or chose to ignore it; whichever, he walked past the hat without bowing. Gessler seized Tell, who was well known as a marksman, and set him a challenge. He ordered him to shoot an apple off his son's head with his crossbow; if Tell was successful, he would be released, but if he failed or refused, both he and his son would die.

The boy's hands were tied. Tell put one arrow in his quiver and another in his crossbow, took aim, and shot the apple clean off his son's head. Gessler was impressed and infuriated – and then asked what the second arrow was for. Tell looked the tyrant in the eye and replied that if the first arrow had struck the child, the second would have been for Gessler. For such impertinence, Tell was arrested and sentenced to lifelong imprisonment in the dungeons of Gessler's castle at Küssnacht, northeast of Luzern. During the long boat journey a violent storm arose, and the oarsmen – unfamiliar with the lake – begged with Gessler to release Tell so that he could steer them to safety. Gessler acceded, and Tell cannily manoeuvred the boat close to the shore, then leapt to freedom, landing on a flat rock (the **Tellsplatte**) and simultaneously pushing the boat back into the stormy waters.

Determined to see his task through and use the second arrow, Tell hurried to Küssnacht. As Gessler and his party walked along on a dark lane called Hohlegasse on their way to the castle, Tell leapt out, shot a bolt into the tyrant's heart and melt-ed back into the woods to return to Uri. His comrades were inspired by Tell's act of bravery to throw off the yoke of Habsburg oppression in their homeland, and to remain forever free.

This once-great staging post for four major Alpine crossings is now even bypassed by the motorway, which plunges into its own tunnel, also at Göschenen. However, as the hub of many long-distance hiking routes, Andermatt still sees plenty of visitors in the short Alpine summer (June–Sept), and equal numbers in the winter skiing season, with red and black runs galore off the nearby **Gemsstock** summit (2963m), and an abundance of cross-coun-try routes. The Gemsstock is also the best summer viewpoint in the area, since the town is too close to the valley sides to offer any panoramas of its own. Andermatt also serves as the Swiss Army's principal Alpine training centre: you may find an over-preponderance of military types around and about, and it's prudent to check with the tourist office that your chosen route is open before you set off on any long-distance hikes.

Andermatt's train station is 400m north of the town centre; turn left outside

The legend

Walter Dettwiler, in his book *William Tell: Portrait of a Legend* (1991), outlines the impact of the Tell legend over the centuries. The basis of the story – a marksman forced by an overlord to shoot an object from the head of a loved one – first appears in **Scandinavian sagas** written centuries before the Swiss version was first committed to paper in the fifteenth century. It was an epic song, however, composed in 1477 about the founding of the Swiss Confederation and including a section on the story of Tell, which accounted for the widespread circulation of the legend. During the **French Revolution**, the popularity of Tell rose to a peak: he was viewed as a freedom fighter in the noblest of traditions and the tale was held up as a justification for the killing of Louis XVI – all the more so because Tell and the French revolutionary armies shared a common enemy, the Austrian Habsburgs. In the 1770s and 1780s, the German poet Goethe had travelled extensively throughout Switzerland, later telling his friend, the playwright **Friedrich Schiller**, of his journeyings. Schiller's famous play *Wilhelm Tell* (1804) drew from Goethe's first-hand accounts as well as from ancient Swiss chronicles to set the Tell legend in stone, and over subsequent decades, to broadcast the story to a wide European public. **Rossini**'s opera *Guillaume Tell*, which premièred in Paris in 1829, did for the Romance-language countries of Europe what Schiller's play had done for the Teutonic.

With the final unification of Switzerland in 1848 after half-a-century of war, a mood of national liberation and communal purpose became crystallized around the enduring significance of William Tell, who began to be portrayed with increasing idealism, notably in the **Tell monument** in Altdorf, which was unveiled in 1895. **Ferdinand Hodler**, most famous of Swiss artists, drew directly on this monument for his seminal portrait of Tell as a godlike figure, emerging from a gap in the clouds with arm outstretched (see p.266). Throughout **World War II**, the image and notion of a deeply moral, fervently nationalistic Tell hardened the resolve of ordinary Swiss to resist domination by Nazi Germany, and contributed to Switzerland's self-imposed exclusion from the co-operative international organizations – specifically the United Nations and the European Union – which arose after 1945.

However, the **700th anniversary** of the Confederation, celebrated in 1991, brought dissenting voices to the fore for the first time, with revisionist historians searching for more pragmatic reasons for the survival of Swiss culture than the doings of a single male hero. The annual retelling of Schiller's drama on an open stage in touristic Interlaken (see p.286) to an audience increasingly made up of foreigners is, too, beginning to ring hollow, and in a new century, popular perception has become increasingly cynical over the continuing appropriateness of William Tell as an icon for a 21st-century Switzerland.

for the **tourist office**, in the same building as the postbus booking centre (July–Sept & Dec–March Mon–Sat 9am–noon & 2–5.30pm; rest of year Mon–Fri same times; ☏041 887 14 54, ⊛www.andermatt.ch). **Accommodation** is clustered around the picturesque main Gotthardstrasse, which can get nastily crowded in summer: *Sonne*, at no. 76 (☏041 887 12 26, ⑤041 887 06 26; ❷–❸), is a cosy old wooden place, while the *Drei Könige & Post*, at no. 69 (☏041 887 00 01, ⊛www.3koenige.ch; ❸–❹), has modern, comfortable rooms. *Lager Zgraggen* (☏041 887 16 58, ⑤041 872 02 41) – turn right from the station – has dorms for Fr.20.

The high passes all round offer possibilities for spectacular round-trip **driving tours** – you can follow the route from Andermatt over the Gotthard, Nufenen and Furka passes by postbus twice a day in summer; or it's equally possible to strike out with your own transport over the Susten, Grimsel and

Furka passes, with an intermediate stop for lunch in Meiringen (see p.312). To the east, the Oberalp Pass leads to Disentis/Mustér (see p.517).

Gotthard Pass and tunnels

The most famous of all the Alpine passes, the **St Gotthard** or **San Gottardo** (2108m) is also the most memorable. The turbulent Schöllenen Gorge, a few kilometres north of Andermatt, was first bridged in the thirteenth century, allowing traffic to penetrate up the full length of the Reuss valley from Flüelen to the pass itself, from where a continuation road followed the valley of the River Ticino all the way south to Bellinzona and Milan. Today, three daily buses (July–Sept only) follow the new road from Andermatt up to the pass and on down to Airolo. The old cobbled road, which branches off partway up, is much quieter and more picturesque. Both meet on top, where you'll find a wild windswept spot with a handful of buildings clustered around a small lake that's become an unfortunately popular picnicking spot for day-tripping families. The pass is one of Europe's watersheds: rain or snowmelt on the north side ultimately ends up in the Rhine and the North Sea, while moisture on the south side flows into the Po and the Mediterranean.

The old **hospice** beside the road now houses the engaging **Museo Nazionale del San Gottardo** (May–Oct daily 9am–6pm; Fr.9; SMP), which outlines the history of the pass with models, reliefs, paintings and audiovisual slide-shows. Across the road, there are simple modern rooms available at the often-busy *Albergo San Gottardo* (☎091 869 12 35, ⓦ www.gotthard-hospiz.ch; ❷; May–Oct). From the pass, most traffic follows the new road down to Airolo, but the old cobbled road that snakes down behind the *albergo* off the back of the pass into Ticino is truly spectacular, with terrific vistas all the way down into the Val Tremolo ("Valley of Trembling"). If you're **hiking**, it's a three-hour walk to Airolo this way, or six hours by an off-road route through Val Canaria; on the north side, Andermatt is three hours away via the small village of Hospental, or six by a more scenic route through the deserted valleys around Maighels.

The Gotthard tunnels

Foot traffic has used the Gotthard Pass since about 1200, and the first carriage crossed in 1775. Less than a century later, in 1872, after decades of debate over routes and costs, work began on a **rail tunnel** beneath the pass. Over seven years and 277 lives later, the bores which had begun simultaneously from Göschenen and Airolo met midway on February 29, 1880. The first trains ran through the 15km-long tunnel in 1882.

This line is still a vital north–south artery, carrying at peak times an average of one train every six minutes – with five million passengers and 25 million tonnes of freight carried to and fro each year. The Gotthard journey is one of Switzerland's great train rides, not so much for the long stretch of blackness as you swoosh beneath the Alps, but for the spectacular approach. South of Flüelen, you climb slowly and dramatically up the wild valley, passing through dozens of straight tunnels and, around **Wassen**, a series of tightly spiralled tunnels, which gain maximum altitude at minimum gradients. Wassen's little onion-domed church, prominent on its rock, is a famous landmark: you'll pass it three times, first high above you, then on a level, and finally far below you before you're plunged into darkness shortly afterwards at **Göschenen**. Trains emerge at Airolo (see p.559) for the long journey down to Bellinzona.

The 16.3km Gotthard **road tunnel**, completed in 1980, which runs in parallel from Göschenen to Airolo, was the longest road tunnel in the world until a Norwegian project overtook it in 2000. Although prone to hideous kilometres-long jams on both approaches, it remains open year-round, while the pass road above is impassable in winter.

Work is now well under way on the new **Gotthard Base Tunnel**, part of an ambitious project to upgrade high-speed train routes beneath the Alps in order to take freight off the roads and shorten long-distance rail journeys. When the tunnel opens in 2012, trains will enter at Erstfeld, a few kilometres south of Altdorf, speeding through the deep tunnel at up to 250 kilometres per hour to the exit at Bodio, 58km south. Cutting out the long climb up to Göschenen and the long descent from Airolo will shave a full hour off Zürich–Milan journey times. Legislation is also in place to force pan-European road freight onto the new Swiss trains, thus clearing the N2 highway in the upper Reuss and upper Ticino of its appalling traffic-jams and easing environmental degradation. Full information and progress reports are at ⓦ www.alptransit.ch.

Furka Pass

Two buses a day from Andermatt (July–Sept) cross the **Furka Pass** (2431m; see also p.369) west into Canton Valais, while mainline passenger and car-carrying trains use the year-round Furka-Basis Tunnel beneath the pass. Buses aside, the main draw on the Uri side is a volunteer-run antique mountain **steam train**, the DFB (ⓦ www.furka-bergstrecke.ch), which in summer puffs its way from **Realp** – a hamlet an easy hour-and-three-quarter walk from Andermatt – up to a station near the pass and on through the short Muttbach tunnel to Gletsch. The round trip costs Fr.93.

Between Realp and the pass is *Hotel Tiefenbach* (☎041 887 13 22, ⓦ www.tiefenbach-hotel.ch; ❷), with quality dorms from Fr.39, also open in winter as base camp for some fine cross-country skiing. On the pass sits the historic *Furkablick* (☎041 887 07 17; ❷; June–Sept), a fine old inn bought in the 1990s by gallery-owner Marc Hostettler, who has preserved much of the charm (and original features) of the century-old interior – not least the library, now crammed with books on contemporary art. Dutch architect Rem Koolhaas worked on part of the renovations, and the interior is decorated with "Furkart", left by artists invited to stay up here by Hostettler.

Oberalp Pass

Directly east of Andermatt is the **Oberalp Pass** (2044m) into Canton Graubünden, kept passable to trains year-round. This is the route of the famous Glacier Express (see p.30) between Zermatt and St Moritz, which runs via the Furka-Basis Tunnel, Andermatt and the Oberalp on its way to Chur. Local trains from Andermatt to Disentis/Mustér (see p.517) can drop you on the pass itself, trailhead for a host of high-country summer hikes. Two scenic routes run through the bleak and invigorating high country down to Andermatt, one via the Lolenpass (5hr 30min), the other via the Maighelspass (6hr 30min), while an easier one heads out to Fellilücke, and from there to Nätschen and Andermatt (5hr).

Travel details

Trains

Andermatt to: Brig (hourly; 2hr); Disentis/Mustér (hourly; 1hr 10min); Flüelen (twice hourly; 1hr – change at Göschenen); Oberalppass (at least hourly; 25min).

Arth-Goldau to: Lugano (hourly; 2hr 10min); Luzern (3 hourly; 30min); Rigi Kulm (hourly; 35min); Zürich (hourly; 40min).

Brunnen to: Altdorf (hourly; 10min); Flüelen (twice hourly; 10min); Luzern (twice hourly; 45min – some change at Arth-Goldau); Zug (hourly; 35min – some change at Arth-Goldau).

Einsiedeln to: Luzern (hourly; 1hr – change at Biberbrugg); Zürich (every 30min; 45min – change at Wädenswil).

Engelberg to: Luzern (hourly; 1hr).

Flüelen to: Andermatt (twice hourly; 1hr – change at Göschenen); Brunnen (twice hourly; 10min); Lugano (hourly; 2hr 5min); Luzern (twice hourly; 55min – some change at Arth-Goldau); Schwyz (twice hourly; 15min); Zürich (hourly; 1hr 15min – some change at Arth-Goldau).

Luzern to: Basel (twice hourly; 1hr 5min); Bellinzona (hourly; 2hr 15min); Bern (twice hourly; 1hr 20–30min); Brienz (hourly; 1hr 15min); Brunnen (twice hourly; 45min – some change at Arth-Goldau); Einsiedeln (hourly; 1hr – change at Biberbrugg); Engelberg (hourly; 1hr); Flüelen (twice hourly; 55min – some change at Arth-Goldau); Hergiswil (hourly; 10min); Interlaken Ost (hourly; 1hr 55min); Lugano (hourly; 2hr 45min); Milan (hourly; 4hr 15min – some change at Arth-Goldau); Stans (hourly; 20min); Zug (twice hourly; 20min); Zürich (twice hourly; 50min).

Stans to: Engelberg (hourly; 40min); Hergiswil (hourly; 10min); Luzern (hourly; 20min).

Vitznau to: Rigi Kulm (hourly; 30min).

Zug to: Brunnen (hourly; 35min – some change at Arth-Goldau); Lugano (hourly; 2hr 30min); Luzern (twice hourly; 20min); Zürich (twice hourly; 25min).

Buses

Altdorf to: Bürglen (hourly; 5min); Flüelen (hourly; 10min).

Andermatt to: Airolo via Gotthardpass (July–Sept 3 daily; 50min); Oberwald via Furkapass (July–Sept 2 daily; 1hr 30min).

Brunnen to: Schwyz (every 10–20min; 10min).

Flüelen to: Altdorf (hourly; 10min); Linthal via Klausenpass (July–Sept 4 daily; 2hr 20min).

Gersau to: Schwyz (hourly; 25min); Weggis (hourly; 25min).

Göschenen to: Meiringen via Sustenpass (July–Sept 2 daily; 1hr 45min).

Schwyz to: Brunnen (every 10–20min; 10min).

Stans to: Beckenried (twice hourly; 20min); Seelisberg (hourly; 45min).

Weggis to: Gersau (hourly; 25min); Vitznau (hourly; 10min).

Boats

(Following is a summary of April–Oct services; fewer boats run in other months, quite often only on Sun, if at all.)

Brunnen to: Luzern (approx hourly; 1hr 50min–2hr 40min); Vitznau (approx hourly; 1hr–1hr 15min).

Flüelen to: Luzern (approx 7 daily; 2hr 50min–3hr 40min).

Luzern to: Alpnachstad (6 daily; 1hr 30–45min); Beckenried (approx hourly; 1hr 20min–2hr); Brunnen (approx hourly; 1hr 50min–2hr 40min); Flüelen (approx 7 daily; 2hr 50min–3hr 40min); Kehrsiten-Bürgenstock (6 daily; 35min); Vitznau (approx hourly; 40min–1hr 10min); Weggis (approx hourly; 35-50min).

Vitznau to: Brunnen (approx hourly; 1hr–1hr 15min); Luzern (approx hourly; 40min–1hr 10min).

Zug to: Arth-am-See (3–6 daily; 45min–2hr).

Zürich

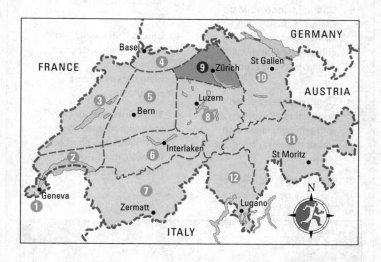

CHAPTER 9

Highlights

* **Grossmünster** Zürich's "Great Minster", from where Zwingli preached the Reformation. See p.436

* **Kunsthaus** World-class gallery of art, unmissable if only for the vast array of works by Alberto Giacometti. See p.438

* **Chagall windows** Marc Chagall's breathtaking stained glass in the lofty choir of the Fraumünster will have you spellbound. See p.443

* **Uetliberg** Steep-sided ridge rising above the city, with stunning views and wooded walking trails. See p.444

* **Zürich West** Hotbed of the city's counterculture, centred on the buzzing Langstrasse and the post-industrial architectural landscapes around Hardstrasse. See p.445

* **Café Schober** Lacy, old-fashioned confectioner and tearoom that could bring out the little old lady in anyone. See p.448

* **Blinde Kuh** Quirky, highly successful restaurant where you eat in complete darkness. See p.450

* **The Zürichsee** An easy escape from the city is by boat for the short trip to the "City of Roses", Rapperswil. See p.456

Zürich

Zürich's relationship to the world is not of the spirit, but of commerce.

C.G. Jung

Not so long ago, **ZÜRICH** was famed for being the cleanest, most icily efficient city in Europe: apocryphal stories abound from the 1970s of the calm and order of the midweek lunch hour in the financial district, of tourists embarking on efforts to find a cigarette butt or an empty crisp packet discarded on the streets – and drawing a blank every time. Things have changed. If you live in a big city yourself and are tiring of Switzerland's picture-perfect country towns, visiting Zürich will be like coming home: finally you can walk on crowded, multi-ethnic streets, buy a kebab, get a drink after midnight, feel a lived-in urban buzz.

Zürich is still best known for a phrase coined as a response to the city's collective sense of superiority. After World War II, Zürich's foreign exchange speculators had become so powerful and secretive that irritated British ministers, amidst the 1964 sterling crisis, spoke of them as gnomes, scurrying about in the corridors and vaults of the private banks manipulating the outside world and forever counting their gold. Their reference to "**the gnomes of Zürich**" stuck, and journalists reporting on Switzerland's often-murky banking and finance industries still reach for the phrase today. Aptly, Zürich now hosts the world's single most important market for trading **gold** and precious metals, and boasts the fourth-largest stock market, after New York, London and Tokyo. Exceptional affluence tends to define the area these days and yet, despite its wealth and status as Switzerland's biggest city (population 360,000), Zürich is not a flashy place at all. The ghost of the bible-thumping Reformer Huldrych Zwingli still stands at the shoulder of the super-discreet bankers, industrialists and business people who live and breathe the city's ingrained Protestant work ethic – yet it's the freedom of thought that Zwingli encouraged which continually bubbles to the surface. Wry Zürchers like to make much of how apt it is that you have to tut, purse your lips and clear your throat just to say the city's name (*tsoorikh* in dialect), but they're deliberately pandering to a long-outdated stereotype.

You're likely to find plenty to keep you occupied in this most beautiful of cities, poised astride the River Limmat, adorned with over a thousand medieval and modern fountains, and turned towards the **Zürichsee**, a lake so crystal-clear the Swiss authorities have certified its water safe to drink. Following a period of notoriety in the early 1990s as one of Europe's hard-drug capitals, Zürich cleaned itself up and, in recent years, has undergone a massive explosion in arts and popular culture, expressed most tangibly in a host of new

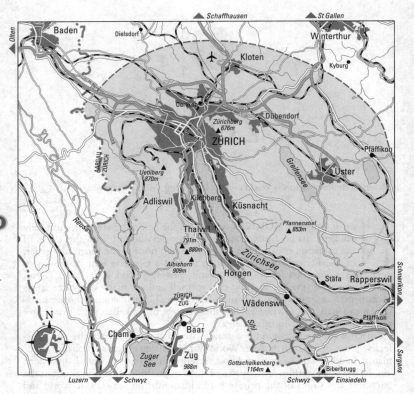

restaurants and underground dance clubs. The medieval **Old Town**, characterized by the steep, cobbled alleys and attractive, small-scale architecture of the
Niederdorf district, comprises a substantial part of the city centre and is perfect for exploratory wanderings. With a handful of medieval churches to take
in – including the mighty **Grossmünster** and graceful **Fraumünster** – the
spectacular **Kunsthaus** art gallery and the most engaging café culture in
German-speaking Switzerland, you could easily spend days here – although
you'll need to watch the expense, prohibitive even by Swiss standards.

Some history

Although there's evidence of settlement around Zürich from the Bronze Age
and before, the **Romans** were the first to fortify the site, turning the
Lindenhof into a customs post in the first century BC and naming it *Turicum*.
The legend of the city's foundation dates from the martyrdom of **Felix and
Regula**, deserters from a Roman legion based in Valais. During the eleventh
and twelfth centuries, Zürich's traders built up fabulous wealth, mainly from
textiles such as wool and silk. In 1336, however, a visionary burgomaster,
Rudolf Brun, shuffled the merchant nobility out of power, handing control
instead to workers' guilds (which were to keep a hold on the city until the
nineteenth century). Shortly after, still under Brun's direction, Zürich joined
the nascent Swiss Confederation.

The thriving city experienced its zenith of power and prestige in the sixteenth century, when it became the first Swiss city to embrace the **Reformation**. The city's spiritual father, Huldrych **Zwingli** (see box p.437), preached in the Grossmünster from 1519 until his death in 1531. With the abolition of the Catholic Mass in 1525, Zürich became a centre for dissident intellectuals from all over Europe. After 1549, when Calvinist doctrine was adopted over Zwinglian, the city experienced a slow fading in its fortunes. The French Revolution of 1789 sparked **pro-libertarian** demonstrations at Stäfa, south of Zürich, but the city itself remained a backwater. A city councillor, **Alfred Escher**, is credited with reinventing Zürich as the economic capital of Switzerland, by his legislative innovations boosting tourism, banking and local manufacturing industry in the late nineteenth century. Strict neutrality during World War I again made Zürich a refuge for dissidents, and for some months in 1916 and 1917, the city was home to **Lenin**, mulling over the future Russian Revolution, **James Joyce**, holed up near the university writing *Ulysses*, and a band of émigré artists calling themselves "Dada", who spent their evenings lampooning Western culture at the famous **Cabaret Voltaire**.

With the recent revelations about Switzerland's economic and material complicity with the Nazis, Zürich's exact role during and after **World War II** hasn't yet been pinpointed, but the city emerged post-war to flourish, becoming one of the world's leading financial centres. More recently, following a relaxation of licensing laws, Zürich is discovering a new will to party. Alongside all

ZÜRICH

Too rich!

Political activism within Zürich's youth movement during the 1970s culminated in major riots in 1980–81 and the police closure of the city's autonomous youth centre. The counterculture regrouped around two large community **squats**, the activities of which have passed into the city's collective memory. The first, known as **Wohlgroth**, took over an empty commercial building next to the train tracks on Zollstrasse; the squatters immediately erected a placard on the roof to greet trains rolling into the city with a huge imitation SBB station sign reading not "Zürich" but "*Zu reich*" ("Too rich"). At a stroke, this guaranteed them fame – admiring chuckles mixing equally with establishment fury. The Wohlgroth developed into a thriving centre for arts, music and alternative culture, and such was its popularity that, after some years of hand-wringing at the loss of rent on such a prime site, the chief executive of the corporation which owned the building personally came visiting with the offer to donate another, less embarrassingly visible building to the collective. His offer, needless to say, was rejected, and shortly afterwards the police evicted the place with tear gas and water cannon. Perhaps the greatest legacy of the Wohlgroth, aside from their classic *Zu reich* prank, is that the neighbourhood has now become the heart of the city's new subculture.

The second big squat of the early 1980s was of the **Rote Fabrik**, a former silk mill in a beautiful lakeside location south of the city, owned by the municipality. Whereas similar city-owned places squatted in Bern and Geneva have remained illegal and on the radical fringes of city life to this day, it's a mark of discreet Zürcher pragmatism that in 1987 the Rote Fabrik collective voted to apply for legal status and an arts subsidy from the city council. This was granted, millions of francs flowing into their coffers shortly after. These days, although its alternative heart still beats, the Rote Fabrik is able to develop and stage avant-garde dance and drama that gets taken seriously by the *Neue Zürcher Zeitung*, the city's most conservative newspaper. The flipside, of course, is that a mere mention of the place makes the committed radicals in Bern roll their eyes and start muttering about a sell-out.

its sights and its breathtaking lakeside beauty, Zürich is reinventing itself again, and a gritty and engaging subculture – centred in the up-and-coming district of **Zürich West** – has begun to thrive beneath the city's slick, monied surface.

Arrival and information

Zürich's **airport** (ⓦwww.unique.ch), 11km northeast in Kloten, is regularly voted to be one of the best in the world: directional signs (in English) are crystal-clear, baggage often turns up at the carousels before you do, and you can be sitting on a train heading for the city within an easy half-hour of touching down. There are two adjacent terminals: A (serving Swiss and its partners) and B (all other carriers). Both terminals' arrivals halls have **tourist information** desks (A: daily 5.30am–midnight; B: daily 5.45am–10.30pm), with free maps, advice, hotel reservations boards and useful touch-screen information systems. There are ATMs nearby, but you'll get the best deals on changing money in the train station downstairs. The cylindrical podia sponsored by Kuoni provide free **Internet** access.

The subterranean **train** station is directly beneath Terminal B. Trains depart roughly every ten minutes for the city's main station, Zürich HB (takes 10min; Fr.5.40; last train 12.10am); you can buy your ticket from the machines, but note that if you intend to stay a day or two in Zürich, you may do better to get a Zürich Card (see p.427) from a staffed counter. Some trains go nonstop, others have an intermediate halt at Oerlikon, but beware that a few don't stop at Zürich HB at all – check the departure boards carefully. Frequent trains also go direct from the airport to points all over the country, including Baden, Winterthur, St Gallen and the Bodensee towns, Basel, Neuchâtel, Bern, Brig, Lausanne, Geneva, Luzern and Chur, cutting out the need to change at Zürich HB.

For getting into the city, you may prefer the pricey convenience of the **hotel bus** service (daily: half-hourly 6.30am–noon & 5–8pm, hourly 1–4pm & 9–10pm), which leaves from the arrivals level between the two terminals, and can drop you twenty minutes later at the door of any of around thirty hotels in the centre. The fare is high (Fr.22 for one person, Fr.30 for two people, and so on), but still less than the **taxis**, which charge upwards of Fr.60.

By train

Zürich's **Hauptbahnhof** (HB) has trains arriving continuously from all corners of Switzerland and around Europe. It's a massive beehive of a place located in the heart of the city, extending three storeys below ground and taking in a shopping mall, supermarket and some good restaurants and diners. Most

---

Phone code changes

Over the next few years, Zürich's ☎01 **phone code** will slowly be replaced. As of 2002, you may see some new ☎043 numbers appearing as a prelude. On March 1, 2005, all numbers that have the ☎01 prefix will lose it, in favour of ☎044 (although you'll still be able to dial ☎01 for two years). On March 1, 2007, the ☎01 prefix will be switched off.

If you're having trouble getting through during the changeover, check the number for free on the screens in public phone booths or at ⓦwww.directories.ch, or call the operator on ☎111.

trains arrive at **street level** (platforms 3–18), where the echoing station concourse is home to the change office (daily 6.30am–10.45pm), a scattering of fast-food stalls and cafés, a post office, a free hotel reservations board and, at the far end under artist Niki de St-Phalle's flying blue "Guardian Angel" (installed in 1997 to celebrate the 150th anniversary of Swiss railways), the tourist office (see below). Out of sight behind the travel bureau are the bike rental office and left-luggage counter.

One level down you'll find luggage lockers, while going down again brings you to the **shopping level**, with a warren of echoing subterranean passageways stretching off in all directions. **S-Bahn** suburban trains leave from the lowest level (platforms 1–2 and, separately, 21–24) to local destinations such as Uetliberg and Adliswil; the huge information boards on the street-level concourse list S-Bahn departures separately from the mainline departures (*Fernverkehr*). S-Bahn trains to nearby towns such as Winterthur and Baden are slower than mainline services, but go more frequently. Note that, because of building works, until 2004 Zürich–Luzern trains arrive and depart from platforms 51–54, which are signposted halfway down platform 3, five minutes' walk from the main concourse.

By car and bus

Parking is difficult and expensive. All of the Old Town, plus chunks of the central commercial district, are off-limits, and although there are nine parking garages in the centre, pinpointed at ⓦwww.parking.ch – the one on Uraniastrasse (☏01 211 47 38) is usefully big – they can be prohibitively expensive, often more than Fr.30 a day. It's a good idea to ask your hotel in advance about parking: some can reserve free or discounted spaces for guests. Otherwise, the easiest option is to park at the airport (Parkhaus E, a short walk from Terminal B, costs Fr.24 for one day, Fr.64 for three days).

Most international **buses** arrive from points east such as Vienna, Prague and Zagreb; once-weekly Eurolines buses make the seventeen-hour trek to Zürich from London, via Reims and Strasbourg. All terminate at the open bus park on Sihlquai opposite the *Walhalla* hotel, 50m behind the station. Domestic Swiss postbuses terminate in the suburbs.

Information

The **tourist office** is on the station's street-level concourse, beneath the flying blue angel (April–Oct Mon–Sat 8am–8.30pm, Sun 8.30am–6.30pm; Nov–March Mon–Sat 8.30am–7pm, Sun 9am–6.30pm; ☏01 215 40 00, ⓦwww.zuerich.com & ⓦwww.zurichtourism.ch). They have a welter of brochures from hotels and service companies all over the city and the country, and can give you an adequate map of the centre (including a transport plan) for free, or sell you one covering the whole city for Fr.3. Staff can book you onto a two-hour **guided walk** through the old town in English (May–Oct Mon–Fri 3pm, Sat & Sun 11am & 3pm; Nov–April Wed & Sat 11am; Fr.20), or a two-hour **city tour** on a bus done up as a vintage trolley-bus, where you listen to a headphone commentary (April–Oct daily 9.45am, noon & 2pm; Fr.32). There's a host of other tours available, by bus, boat and/or cable-car, generally costing Fr.30–40. The tourist office also stocks, for free, *Züritipp* (ⓦwww.zueritipp.ch), the best weekly **what's-on** paper, in German only, and *Zürich News* (ⓦwww.zuerich.ch), a useful fortnightly booklet, with information in English on sightseeing, the latest exhibitions and other bits and bobs.

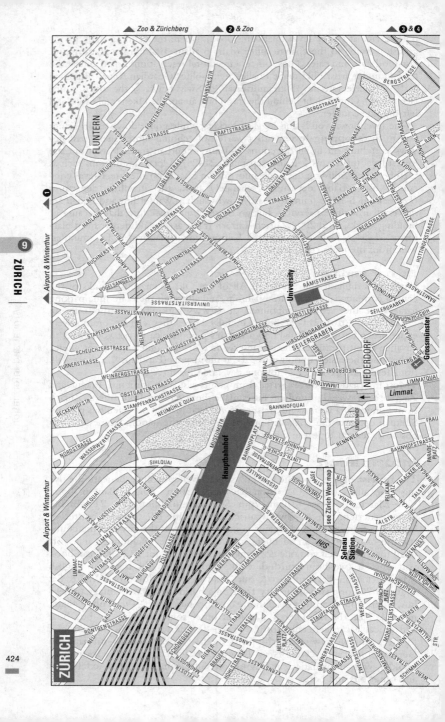

ZÜRICH

▲ Zoo & Zürichberg   ▲ ❷ & Zoo   ▲ ❸ & ❹

◀ Airport & Winterthur

❶

FLUNTERN

KRAHBÜHLSTR

BERGSTRASSE

KRAFTSTRASSE

BERGSTRASSE

SPIEGELHOFSTR

FORSTERSTRASSE

FREUDENBERGSTRASSE

KLEINJOGGSTRASSE

STRASSE

KANTSTR

ATTENHOFERSTRASSE

ILGEN

HÖRSTR

DOLDERSTRASSE

SCHULHOFSTR

RESTELBERGSTRASSE

TOBLERSTRASSE

GLADBACHSTRASSE

HINTERBERGSTR

GLORIA-STRASSE

PESTALOZZI

ZÜRICHBERGSTRASSE

LEONHARDSTRASSE

PLATTENSTRASSE

HADLAUBSTRASSE

HOCHSTRASSE

VOLTASTRASSE

MOUSSON

FREIESTRASSE

GLADBACHSTRASSE

STRASSE

STEINWIESSTRASSE

HOTTINGERSTRASSE

BUCHEGGSTRASSE

VOGELSANGSTR

HÜTTENSTRASSE

BOLLEYSTRASSE

SCHMELZBERGSTRASSE

University

RÄMISTRASSE

KANTONSSCHUSTR

RÄMISTRASSE

CULMANNSTRASSE

SPÖNDLISTRASSE

UNIVERSITÄTSTRASSE

KÜNSTLERGASSE

SEILERGRABEN

HIRSCHENGRABEN

STAPFERSTRASSE

NELKENSTR

SONNEGGSTRASSE

LEONHARDSTRASSE

HIRSCHENGRABEN

SEILERGRABEN

Grossmünster

SCHEUCHZERSTRASSE

CLAUSIUSSTRASSE

MÜNSTERGASSE

TURNERSTRASSE

WEINBERGSTRASSE

NIEDERDORF

MÜHLE STRASSE

NIEDERDORFSTRASSE

LIMMATQUAI

BECKENHOFSTR

OBSTGARTENSTRASSE

CENTRAL

LIMMATQUAI

Limmat

FRAU

STAMPFENBACHSTRASSE

NORDSTRASSE

NEUMÜHLE QUAI

BAHNHOFQUAI

WASSERWERKSTRASSE

MUSEUMSTR

BAHNHOFPLATZ

UNIONG

BAHNHOFSTRASSE

REMNWEG

SIHLQUAI

Hauptbahnhof

BAHNHOFSTR G

BAHNHOFSTRASSE

PARADE-PLATZ

SIHLQUAI

AUSSTELLUNGSSTR

LIMMATSTRASSE

GESSNERALLEE

LÖWENSTRASSE

LINTH ESCHER-G

SIHL STR

URANIA-STR

PELIKAN-PLATZ

TALACKER

TALSTR

TALSTR

IKAN-

LIMMAT-PLATZ

HEINRICHSTRASSE

FIERGASSE

ACKE STR

JOSEFSTRASSE

KONRADSTRASSE

LAGERSTRASSE

KASERNENSTRASSE

see Zürich West map

SIHL

TALSTR

STAUFFACHERQUAI

LANGSTRASSE

GASOMETERSTR

LUISENSTR

MATTENG

NEUGASSE

ZOLLSTRASSE

LAGERSTRASSE

MILITÄRSTRASSE

Selnau Station

SELNAUSTRASSE

SELNAUSTRASSE

STAUFFACHER-PLATZ

SCHÖNEGGSTR

DIENER-STR

BRAUER-STR

KANONENGASSE

ZEUGHAUSSTRASSE

MÜLLERSTRASSE

STAUFFACHERSTRASSE

WERD-STR

WEBERSTR

SCHÖNTAL-STR

HALLWYLSTR

FELDSTR

MAGNUSSTR

RÖNTGENSTRASSE

NELKENSTR

LANGSTRASSE

STRASSE

TELLSTRASSE

STRASSE

BÄCKERSTRASSE

AMBOSS-STRASSE

HELVETIA-PLATZ

BADENERSTRASSE

MORGARTENSTRASSE

WERD STRASSE

ZWEIERSTRASSE

STRASSE

BIRMENSDORFERSTR

SCHMELLSTR

STR

KERNSTR

GRÜNGASSE

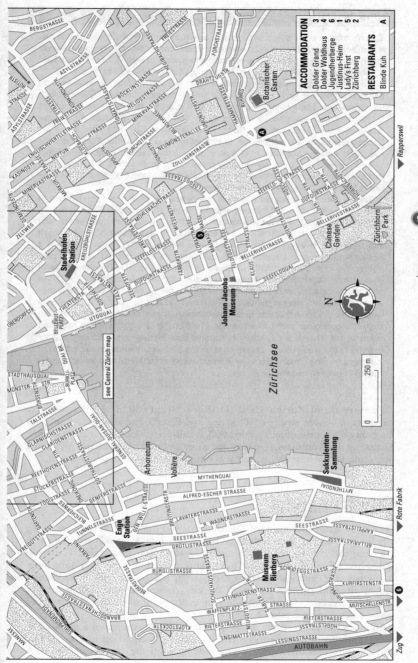

ZÜRICH

9

425

Rapperswil

Rote Fabrik

Zug

BERGSTRASSE
ASYLSTRASSE
FREIESTRASSE
FORCHSTRASSE
Botanischer
Garten
SEEFELDSTRASSE
ZOLLIKERSTRASSE
DUFOURSTRASSE
BELLERIVESTRASSE
Zürichhorn
Park
Chinese
Garden
Johann Jacobs
Museum
Zürichsee
Stadelhofen
Station
BELLEVUE
PLATZ
see Central Zürich map
Arboretum
Volière
MYTHENQUAI
Sukkulenten-
Sammlung
Enge
Station
Museum
Rietberg
SEESTRASSE
AUTOBAHN
250 m
0

N

ACCOMMODATION
Dolder Grand   3
Dolder Waldhaus   4
Jugendherberge   6
Justinus-Heim   1
Lady's First   5
Zürichberg   2

RESTAURANTS   A
Blinde Kuh

Zürich's festivals

Zürich's biggest party is August's massive **Street-Parade** (ⓦwww.street-parade.ch), a tumultuous three-day techno weekend of floats, costumes, dancing in the streets and general hedonism, second in size and energy only to Berlin's Love Parade held a week or two beforehand; if you're in the city, you won't be able to miss it.

The **Sechseläuten** (ⓦwww.sechselaeuten.ch) is Zürich's spring festival, held on the third Monday in April, and is the only time in the year that the city's establishment preens its feathers in public: the highlight is a parade through the city centre by the traditional guilds, dressed in costume. The festival culminates at 6pm precisely with the burning of the Böögg – an effigy stuffed with fireworks – on Sechseläutenplatz next to Bellevue, to symbolize the end of winter. Throughout the evening the guilds take turns to visit each other in their respective guildhalls (most of which have now been turned into rather good restaurants). Not long after, Sechseläutenplatz is taken over by the regular month-long May residency of the Swiss National Circus, **Circus Knie** (ⓦwww.knie.ch).

Zürich's February **Fasnacht** (Carnival) is a boisterous affair, fun if you happen to be in the city, but still small fry compared with those of Luzern and Basel. However, the summertime **Züri Fäscht** (ⓦwww.zuerifaescht.ch), held every three years (next on July 2–4, 2004), is worth making a diversion for, with the whole city throwing itself into fairground revelry. The annual **Festspiele** (ⓦwww.zuercher-festspiele.ch) is a festival of theatre, opera, music and art, held from late June into mid-July, with special productions, concerts and exhibitions all over the city. The **Theaterspektakel** (ⓦwww.theaterspektakel.ch), during late August and early September, also packs out the city's stages and sees lakeside marquees set up on Mythenquai for avant-garde drama from around the world. A weekend in mid-September is taken as a local holiday for the rather odd **Knabenschiessen** (ⓦwww.knabenschiessen.ch), an ancient shooting competition for teenagers held on the Albisgütli amidst a huge and colourful fair. There's a citywide international **jazz festival** every November. One evening in the week before Christmas sees the **Lichterschwimmen**, a tradition of launching floating candles from the Rathausbrücke onto the river, to the accompaniment of gingerbread and *glühwein*.

The very useful **Zürich Card** (Fr.15 for 24hr; Fr.30 for 72hr) covers city transport in a wide area (see "Ticketing and Fares"), and also gives a range of discounts: the tourist office's guided walk is half-price, loads of museums are free (including the Kunsthaus, Rietberg and more), a fistful of restaurants give you a free drink at lunch or dinner, and you can get a rental-car upgrade at Avis.

City transport

One of the great advantages of Zürich is that you can enjoy all the buzz of big city life in a compact setting that's no larger than a single *arrondissement* of Paris: covering the city **on foot** is perfectly feasible, even pleasurable. The main Bahnhofstrasse, from the station to Bürkliplatz, is only a bit over 1km long. Nonetheless, Zürich's **city transport** system is legendary for its efficiency, punctuality and convenience, with the city centre and surrounding suburbs linked by a cat's cradle of routes joining every point of interest to just about every other with minimum hassle.

After a referendum in the 1970s, in which Zürchers rejected a proposal to build an underground metro system, the city has focused on its eco-friendly and ubiquitous **trams**, while easing most cars off the city-centre streets. A dozen tram lines weave through the centre, and dozens of **bus** routes fan out from suburban termini to outlying districts. **S-Bahn** suburban trains, most originating from or passing through the main station, add a third dimension, linking to Zug and Einsiedeln in the south and Winterthur, Schaffhausen and Stein-am-Rhein in the north, as well as serving the nearby Uetliberg summit. **Boats** crisscross their way up and down the Zürichsee. You could even take advantage of the city's **free bike-rental** scheme.

Swiss Pass holders travel free on all public transport; Eurailers get free transport only on trains and ZSG boats; InterRailers go free on the trains and half-price on the boats. See p.29 for general guidance.

Taxis, in a city where even millionaire bankers use the tram, are an extravagance; aside from the numerous public ranks, you can hail a cab in the street, or order one from Züritaxi ℡01 222 22 22, Taxi 2000 ℡01 444 44 44, or Taxis for the Disabled ℡01 272 42 42.

Ticketing and fares

Ticketing is organized by zone, with the city centre covered by Zone 10 (the airport is in neighbouring Zone 21; Uetliberg in Zone 55). All tickets can be used for all transport – both land- and water-based – within each zone, with unlimited changes permitted. Trams, buses and S-Bahn trains operate daily from around 5.30am to after midnight; full information on ticketing and fares is at Ⓦ www.zvv.ch, on city transport at Ⓦ www.vbz.ch.

Of the tickets buyable with coins or notes from the machines at all tram and bus stops, the most useful Zone 10 ticket is the Fr.7.20 **Tageskarte** (press the green button), valid for 24 hours' travel; the blue "**Stadt Zürich**" button gives a Zone 10 ticket valid for an hour (Fr.3.60), while the yellow "**Kurzstrecke**" button gives a short-hop one-way ticket (Fr.2.10), good for half-an-hour within a radius of five stops: the black panel lists the stations for which it is valid. The best ticket for an off-peak day-trip, valid throughout the whole region – north to Winterthur (Zone 20) and the Rhine falls (Zone 16) and south to Rapperswil (Zone 80) – is the **9-Uhr Tagespass** (9 o'clock Day Pass, valid Mon–Fri after 9am, Sat & Sun all day; Fr.20); to get one, key ⋆141 on any ticket machine. Before 9am, you must key ⋆121 instead (Fr.28.40). You can pay roughly fifty percent more to upgrade any of these to 1st class (press "1. Kl"); if you hold a Swiss Card, press "1/2" to get your discount.

Some useful tickets are buyable only from the tourist office, train station ticket counters and staffed ZVV sales points (located outside the train station, at Central, Paradeplatz and Bellevue). The **Zürich Card** (Fr.15 for 24hr; Fr.30 for 72hr; also buyable at the airport train station) is valid in a wide area taking in the city, the airport, Uetliberg and short sightseeing trips by boat (*Kleine Rundfahrt*), as well as covering a range of discounts (see opposite). The **Tageswahlkarte** (Multiple Day Pass; Fr.36) has the validity of a *Tageskarte* six times over: one person can use it for any six days' travel, validating it at the start of each day in the slot in the lower left-hand corner of a ticket machine – or a group of six (or less) can use the card together, validating it once for each person before starting out. The **Mehrfahrtenkarte** (Multiple Fare Ticket) has the validity of six separate *Stadt Zürich* tickets (Fr.18), or six *Kurzstrecke* tickets (Fr.10.50).

There are regular spot-checks on trams, trains and buses by plain-clothes ticket inspectors. If you're caught without a valid ticket, you'll have to pay a **fine** of Fr.60 on the spot, more if you defer payment.

On Friday and Saturday nights only (roughly 1–2.30am), a handful of **night buses** depart from Bellevue for various suburban destinations, for a flat Fr.5; other tickets and passes are not valid.

Boats

There's no shortage of options for **boat** trips. The tourist office has full information, or you can contact the Lake Zürich Shipping Company (ZSG; ☎01 487 13 33, ⊕www.zsg.ch). Full timetables are posted at the company office at **Bürkliplatz**, from where almost all boats depart. Note that most of the trips mentioned below operate only in summer (April–Oct); in winter, service is drastically reduced, and is dependent on good weather.

One of the best, and most popular, short trips is on the **Limmatschiff**, which departs from the Landesmuseum for the scenic upriver journey through the heart of the city, including a short trip on the lake and the return journey down the Limmat again. Departures are every half-hour (July & Aug daily 10am–9pm; May & June Mon–Fri 1–9pm, Sat & Sun 10am–9pm; April, Sept & Oct Mon–Fri 1–6pm, Sat & Sun 10am–6pm; takes 55min; Fr.3.60).

Regular boats ply the length of the Zürichsee from Zürich to **Rapperswil** (2hr; see p.457), and beyond to Schmerikon (another 1hr 30min), stopping at just about every shoreside town on the way. The ZSG also runs a host of **pleasure cruises**, including circular sightseeing trips (*Rundfahrten*) from and to Zürich without stopping (1hr 30min, Fr.5.40; 2hr 30min, Fr.17.60; 3hr 45min, Fr.20), nostalgia trips to Rapperswil by steamship and full seven-hour day cruises (Fr.20). Eat-aboard cruises – in daylight and after dark – are popular and not prohibitively expensive: examples include the regular Zmorge-Schiff (Breakfast Cruise; Fr.20 all-in), Brunch-Schiff (Fr.17.60, plus buffet meal Fr.29), and Lunch-Schiff (Fr.8, plus meal), and there are occasional scheduled cruises incorporating a candlelit dinner, jazz and cocktails, fondue parties and the like (Fr.65–80).

Bikes, mopeds and motorbikes

For a returnable deposit of Fr.20 and photo-ID, you can **rent a bike** for free courtesy of the Züri-Rollt scheme, a city initiative to give the unemployed and those on welfare a start-up job. There are six locations dotted throughout the city (all daily 7.30am–9.30pm): the main one is "Velogate" at the train station, next to platform 18 (open year-round), and the most accessible others are at

---

Easy day-trips from Zürich by train

Braunwald p.489. Car-free mountain hideaway for rapid battery-recharge. Change at Ziegelbrücke and Linthal. 1hr 45min.

Einsiedeln monastery p.408. Centuries-old site of pilgrimage up in the hills. Change at Wädenswil. 45min.

Luzern p.375. Exquisite Old Town plus breathtaking lake-and-mountains scenery. Direct. 50min. Either train back, or boat Luzern–Flüelen then train Flüelen–Zürich.

Rapperswil p.457. Gentle, easy-going Zürichsee waterfront town, perfect for a lazy afternoon. Direct. 40min (or 2hr by boat).

Rhine falls p.472. Europe's biggest waterfall. Change at Winterthur for Schloss Laufen or Neuhausen. 50min.

Rigi p.401. A popular ride up the nearest high mountain to Zürich (1798m). Change at Arth-Goldau. 1hr 40min.

Schaffhausen p.468. Fascinating, little-visited Old Town; combine it with a river trip to Stein-am-Rhein. Direct. 40min.

Uetliberg p.444. Zürich's "home mountain", with a network of easy walking routes. Direct. 20min.

Winterthur p.464. Relaxed city with high-quality art museums. Direct. 20min.

the Globus department store on Usteristrasse, at Theaterplatz, and outside Bahnhof Enge (all May–Oct only). Otherwise, the main station has the usual paid bike-rental facilities (daily 6am–10.50pm); if there is high demand, you might have to resort to the other SBB rental facility, at Oerlikon station. Erne's Euromotos, Sihlquai 67 (℡01 272 77 72, ⓦwww.ernes.ch), can rent you motorized two-wheel transport – anything from a 50cc scooter (Fr.50/day) to a monster 955cc Triumph Daytona (Fr.170/day). Staff speak English, and offer weekend discounts.

Accommodation

Despite its being one of the most expensive cities in the world, Zürich can still offer a reasonably full range of **accommodation**, and if you book ahead you'll have a good chance of finding something good within your price range. Prices at the higher-end places, though, can be frightful, and some mid-range hoteliers take this as carte blanche to overcharge: you'd be well advised to take nothing for granted and investigate what you'll be getting for your money before you check in. Nearby Baden (see p.227) and Winterthur (see p.464), as well as some of the Zürichsee lakeside towns such as Küsnacht or Stäfa, offer equally characterful accommodation at more affordable prices.

The tourist office's dedicated **hotel reservation service** (℡01 215 40 40, ⓔhotel@zurichtourism.ch, or over-the-counter) can book a room in the hotel of your choice for free within Zürich, or Fr.10 elsewhere in Switzerland. Make sure to ask them about any weekend or off-season promotions, which can slash walk-in rates to bargain levels.

Hotels

The greatest concentration of **inexpensive hotels** is in the Old Town's Niederdorf district. None is more than ten minutes' walk from the station, or you could hop on tram #4 (direction Tiefenbrunnen): it runs south down Limmatquai, stopping at Central, each of the three river bridges and Bellevue. To reach Zürich West, tram #3 from the station (direction Albisrieden) stops at Bezirksgebäude, at the southern end of Langstrasse, while tram #13 (direction Frankental) stops at Limmatplatz and Escher-Wyss-Platz. Be warned that many of the cheap hotels on and off Langstrasse double as brothels.

Mid-range hotels in Niederdorf are generally quiet and characterful, although universally pricey and often renovated, while those elsewhere in the city tend to offer better value but have noisier or more mundane surroundings. Unless you're devoted to urban living, withdrawing to one of the good-value hotels in the wooded hills to east and west is a sound ploy.

Zürich has any number of absurdly **expensive hotels**, chain- and private-owned palaces catering for executives and glitterati willing to sign away Fr.1200-plus for a night in the presidential suite. Ordinary mortals could get away with half that for a standard double in these places – but if you're willing to part with such stratospheric amounts while touring Switzerland, you'd probably do better to downgrade while in Zürich and splash out instead at, say, St Moritz, Gstaad or Montreux.

Inexpensive hotels

Niederdorf

Goldenes Schwert Marktgasse 14 ☎ 01 266 18 18, ⓦ www.gayhotel.ch. Excellent value, with a uniquely easygoing atmosphere. This is the only hotel in Zürich which makes a selling-point of its gay- and lesbian-friendliness. Comfortable rooms are large, bright, individually decorated and inexpensive, but you should insist on the fifth floor to avoid noise from the bars and nightclub. They also have quality apartments for Fr.200 or less. ❸

Limmatblick Limmatquai 136 ☎ 01 254 60 00, ⓦ www.limmatblick.ch. Completely renovated hotel right on the riverfront close to Central, under new management, with big, clean rooms that are good value despite some traffic noise. ❸

Limmathof Limmatquai 142 ☎ 01 261 42 20, ⓕ 01 262 02 17. Although this is one of the only cheapies overlooking the river, you'd do well to eschew the noisy river-view rooms for the newer, quieter ones at the back. Either way, you'll have problems swinging a cat. ❷

Martahaus Zähringerstrasse 36 ☎ 01 251 45 50, ⓦ www.martahaus.ch. Basic, newly renovated budget hotel in a rather dodgy area, but a safe and thoroughly respectable place to rest your head for minimal franc outlay. Some rooms are ensuite, but you should go for a back room to avoid street noise. Also has good, partitioned dorms and free Internet. An annexe out west on Lutherstrasse is women-only (check-in at *Martahaus*). ❷–❸

Otter Oberdorfstrasse 7 ☎ 01 251 22 07, ⓦ www.wueste.ch. Best in this bracket by miles, relaxed, friendly and great value, with an unconventional clientele of students and artists. Uniquely colourful rooms, all with plump, comfy beds, are decked in murals, drapes and plants, ones higher up with lovely rooftop views. Shower and toilet are shared between the three rooms on each floor. A good indication of the mood of the place is that breakfast only happens from 9am (11am weekend). The top-floor apartment, for Fr.180, feels like home. ❷

Splendid Rosengasse 5 ☎ 01 252 58 50, ⓦ www.hotelsplendid.ch. Gloomy unrenovated small hotel, with no TVs, no ensuite facilities, no decoration and no lift. Quiet, ordinary and honestly cheap. Locked daily 2.30–5am. ❶

Villette Kruggasse 4 ☎ 01 251 23 35, ⓕ 01 251 23 39. Friendly little place above an award-winning fondue restaurant just off Bellevue. Plain rooms (most ensuite) are clean enough and adequate for simple tastes – the breakfast is notably good – and the owner of the place (who also does the fondues) is full of jolly stories and banter. ❷

Zic-Zac Marktgasse 17 ☎ 01 261 21 81, ⓦ www.ziczac.ch. Ordinary cheapie which has taken some marketing advice and reinvented itself as a "rock hotel", dubbing their poky and rather depressing rooms (some with shared bathrooms) the "Bryan Adams" or the "Pink Floyd" in an attempt to attract business. Lively atmosphere in the bar. ❷–❸

Zürich West

Etap Technoparkstrasse 2 ☎ 01 276 20 00, ⓦ www.etaphotel.com. Budget international chain. Generic, functional rooms in the heart of the old industrial quarter, priced identically – and very low (Fr.89). Located alongside the *Ibis* and *Novotel* hotels, just behind the trendy Schiffbau arts centre. ❶

Haus zur Stauffacherin Kanzleistrasse 19 ☎ 01 241 69 79, ⓔ staufferacherin@bluewin.ch. Clean, airy, fresh rooms in a wheelchair-accessible building off lively Helvetiaplatz, with kitchen and laundry facilities. Discounts for long stays. Women only. ❸

Limmat Limmatstrasse 118 ☎ 01 448 15 95, ⓦ www.x-tra.ch/hotel. In the same building as the popular *X-tra* bar and nightclub, just off the Limmatplatz in a young and lively part of town. Rooms are small, but come with postmodern decor and all facilities; the non-ensuite ones are much better value. ❷–❸

Neufeld Friesenbergstrasse 15 ☎ 01 463 74 00, ⓦ www.hotel-neufeld.ch. Thoroughly respectable, good-value family hotel on Goldbrunnenplatz, with spotless rooms and a reputation to uphold. Set in Wiedikon, a neighbourhood with many Jewish residents, it even offers kosher breakfasts. Tram #9 or #14 (direction Triemli). ❸

Regina Hohlstrasse 18 ☎ 01 298 55 55, ⓕ 01 298 56 00. The least dodgy of Langstrasse's many dodgy hotels, although the prevalence of over-friendly single women in the hotel bar tells its own story. Nonetheless, the rooms are fine, clean but smallish, and a solid Fr.20–30 cheaper than similar places elsewhere in the city. ❸

Rothaus Sihlhallenstrasse 1 ☎ 01 241 24 51, ⓦ www.cd-hotel.com/ch/rothaus.htm. Bang on the honky-tonk Langstrasse. Next-door is a sex cinema and the bar downstairs is a pick-up joint, but if you can overlook that, you can save Fr.30–40 on perfectly adequate, secure ensuite rooms, equipped with all facilities and soundproofed windows. ❷

Walhalla Limmatstrasse 5 ☎ 01 446 54 00, ⓔ walhalla-hotel@bluewin.ch. Good value in a handy but unromantic location, just 50m behind the train station, with large, pleasantly decorated rooms. Cheaper rooms available in a nearby annexe. ❸

Out of town

Central Poststrasse 10, Küsnacht ☎01 910 08 04, Ⓔhotelcentral@bluewin.ch. Small, family-run option in this pleasant town south of Zürich (see p.456), with rooms both ensuite and not. ❷–❸

Formule 1 Heidi Abel-Weg 7 ☎01 307 48 00, Ⓦwww.hotelformule1.com. First Swiss location for this French chain of clean, functional but completely characterless motels. All rooms are identical – generically plasticky – sleeping one, two or three people, with shared bathrooms, and all cost a rock-bottom Fr.59. Located north of town midway from the airport, alongside the *Ibis* hotel, a

block from the Messe conference centre and autobahn exit. Tram #11 into the city. ❶

Gasthof zur Metzg Bergstrasse 82, Stäfa ☎01 928 18 88, Ⓦwww.zur-metzg.ch. Simple inn a little up the hill from this quiet lakeside community south of town; they'll come and collect you from Stäfa station on request. Rooms are cosy and there's an affordable menu of rustic cooking on offer. ❷

Justinus-Heim Freudenbergstrasse 146 ☎01 361 38 06, Ⓔjustinuszh@bluewin.ch. Student house which opens its doors to all out of term-time (mainly July–Oct). Charming building in a quiet location near the Zürichberg woods overlooking the city and lake from the east, with very competitively priced rooms, ensuite and not. Tram #10 to Seilbahn Rigiblick, then take the cable-car to the top station (city transport tickets valid). ❶

Mid-range hotels

In town

Adler Rosengasse 10 ☎01 266 96 96, Ⓦwww.hotel-adler.ch. Very clean, light and pleasant hand-decorated rooms set right in the heart of the Niederdorf buzz above a famous fondue restaurant. Service is good, the pastel interior is modern, and rates undercut similar places on the west bank. ❹

City Löwenstrasse 34 ☎01 217 17 17, Ⓦwww.hotelcity.ch. A quiet, unremarkable business-style hotel in the shopping district just off Bahnhofstrasse, reasonably priced and efficiently staffed. Rates drop at weekends. ❹

Franziskaner Niederdorfstrasse 1 ☎01 250 53 00, Ⓦwww.hotel-franziskaner.ch. Charming small city hotel in classic style, with dark-wood decor and a popular outdoor terrace on a square in the heart of the old town. A little pricey for what you get, but the top-floor rooms, sharing a spacious rooftop terrace, are delightful. ❹–❺

Kindli Pfalzgasse 1 ☎01 211 59 17, Ⓔhotelkindli@compuserve.com. A building dating from the sixteenth century that has provided lodging since (at least) 1774, in a tranquil location on the steep cobbled lanes below the Lindenhof. These days it's one of Zürich's most charming hotels, renovated throughout. Rooms are not spacious, but are elegant and characterful, all decorated in florid Laura Ashley style. The few non-ensuite rooms, right at the top of the house, are ❹ Otherwise ❻

Lady's First Mainaustrasse 24 ☎01 380 80 10, Ⓦwww.ladysfirst.ch. Upmarket designer hotel near the lake south of the Opera House, with spacious, airy singles and doubles displaying a good

attention to detail. Major selling-point: it's for women only. ❺

Rössli Rössligasse 7 ☎01 256 70 50, Ⓦwww.hotelroessli.ch. Super-chic choice on a quiet Niederdorf lane. The spartan wood-and-stone rooms with crisp white styling are spotlessly clean, and service is friendly and attentive. ❺

Out of town

Ermitage Seestrasse 80, Küsnacht ☎01 914 42 42, Ⓦwww.ermitage.ch. Delightful, four-star *Relais & Chateaux* lakefront hotel in a small town 7km south of Zürich, with 26 tranquil, airy rooms decorated individually with taste and character. Offers outstanding value-for-money compared to hotels in the city: details such as a private beach (with motor-yacht), lakefront terrace bar and Michelin-starred restaurant (see p.456) raise it well above others in this category. ❻

Sonne Seestrasse 120, Küsnacht ☎01 914 18 18, Ⓦwww.sonne.ch. A fine hotel set in lakeside gardens south of Zürich, also with a couple of good restaurants. ❹–❻

Uto Kulm Uetliberg ☎01 457 66 66, Ⓦwww.uetliberg.ch. Hotel and restaurant atop the Uetliberg ridge (see p.444), towering over the city and lake from the west. Its clean, modern rooms offer considerably better value for money than similar city-centre hotels, especially when you throw in the tranquillity, the Alpine vistas, plentiful walking routes close at hand and free 4WD pick-ups to and from Uetliberg train station. No cars. Major renovations scheduled for completion in 2003. ❹

Zürichberg Orellistrasse 21 ☎01 268 35 35, ⓦwww.zuerichberg.ch. Comfortable, attractive hotel, opened in 1899 way up in the wooded hills east of the city. Renovated for its centenary, and now featuring bright, spacious rooms, most with balconies and all with every mod-con. Alongside is a low, curved annexe sheathed in wood which has attracted much architectural acclaim; accessed only by a subterranean corridor from the main building, it's designed around an airy atrium and a cool, Guggenheim-style elliptical interior ramp. All its rooms have private balconies. Tram #6 to Zoo. Forest view ❸–❹ Lake view ❹–❺

Expensive hotels

Baur au Lac Talstrasse 1 ☎01 220 50 20, ⓦwww.bauraulac.ch. One of Zürich's oldest hotels, in the same family since 1844, and recently completely renovated. Set in a private park on the lakeshore adjacent to Bahnhofstrasse, it fairly shimmers with opulent grandeur; touches such as in-room hi-fi systems, Jacuzzis and ISDN connections make all the difference. From Fr.650. ❾

Dolder Grand Kurhausstrasse 65 ☎01 269 30 00, ⓦwww.doldergrand.ch. An extraordinary nine-teenth-century palace perched atop a hill over-looking the city and accessible only by private funicular. Towers, cupolas, spires and turrets sprout from all sides of the elegant building; inside, the high-ceilinged rooms are unsurpass-able. Completing the picture are a private nine-hole golf course, a full-size pool with wave machine, one of Switzerland's top *haute cuisine* restaurants, and plenty of walking trails into the parks and forest all around. From Fr.540. ❾

Dolder Waldhaus Kurhausstrasse 20 ☎01 269 10 00, ⓦwww.dolderwaldhaus.ch. Quiet, more residential annexe in the woods just down from the *Dolder Grand*, with just as stunning views over the city and lake, plus plenty of activities (tennis courts, golf, swimming pools and an ice-rink). ❼–❽

St Gotthard Bahnhofstrasse 87 ☎01 227 77 00, ⓦwww.hotelstgotthard.ch. *Grande-dame* of the city-centre hotels, in the same family since 1889, with bags of charm and a perfect location steps from the station. The understated elegance of the dark-wood-and-leather lobby, however, isn't matched in the rooms, which are spacious and comfortable but have been done up in a rather cloying chintzy style. A bargain, considering the competition. ❽

Widder Rennweg 7 ☎01 224 25 26, ⓦwww .widderhotel.ch. Top choice in this bracket, for its cool elegance and superb modern design. On a quiet Old Town street, a row of eight medieval houses has been gutted – at a cost of Fr.100m – to make this stylish and innovative, effortlessly classy hotel; the stunning lobby, in granite, wood and steel, sets the tone. The attention to detail, both architecturally and in the interior decor, is meticulous, and the array of several hundred sin-gle malt whiskies in the bar – which also stages live jazz – adds to the appeal. From Fr.610. ❾

Camping and hostels

The one **campsite** within easy reach is *Seebucht*, Seestrasse 559 (☎01 482 16 12; May–Oct); take bus #161 or #165 from Bürkliplatz south along the west-ern shore of the lake to Stadtgrenze, the city boundary, where the well-main-tained site is down by the water.

Although many of the university's student dorms open their doors to trav-ellers out of term-time (ask at the tourist office for details), there are only two **hostels** in the city, meaning that booking ahead is strongly advised.

City Backpacker/Hotel Biber (SB hostel) Niederdorfstrasse 5 ☎01 251 90 15, ⓦwww .city-backpacker.ch. Better of the two hostels, with a good atmosphere, plum central location and super-friendly management. A dorm bed is Fr.31 excluding breakfast, plus Fr.20 key deposit. Some singles and doubles are available, along with free kitchen use, laundry service and Internet access. ❶

Jugendherberge (HI hostel) Mutschellenstrasse 114 ☎01 482 35 44, ⓦwww.youthhostel.ch. This hostel suffers from a rather depressing institution-al feel and is awkwardly situated in a humdrum southwestern suburb. Dorm beds are Fr.32, and a few parking spaces are free. Take tram #7 (direc-tion Wollishofen) to Morgental, then walk five min-utes (follow the signs). ❶

The City

Because the River Limmat divides the **Old Town** into two distinct halves, it makes more sense to consider the two banks of the river separately rather than concentrate on a New Town/Old Town split.

The alleys of the east bank – known as **Niederdorf** or the "Dörfli" – are full of cafés and small shops, with the enormous twin towers of the **Grossmünster** as a centrepiece. The slender spire to the north belongs to the Predigerkirche with, above it on a hill to the east, the grandiose architecture of the university.

Opposite, the **west bank** is the oldest part of the city, centred around the raised platform of the **Lindenhof** and characterized by expensive fashion outlets and offices. Nearby rise the graceful spires both of **St Peter's**, featuring the largest clock face in Europe, and the **Fraumünster**, a medieval church decorated in the last century with beautiful stained glass by Marc Chagall. The long, curving **Bahnhofstrasse** follows the ancient course of the western city wall, and is now one of Europe's most prestigious shopping streets, packed with jewellers and designer boutiques.

The best of the city's thirty-odd **museums** are the marvellous Kunsthaus on the fringes of the Niederdorf, and the Schweizerisches Landesmuseum (Swiss National Museum) in a park on the west bank.

The east bank

It's a walk of only 100m from the station across the Bahnhofbrücke to the east bank of the Limmat and a large square bedecked with tram wires, known as **Central**. On one side of the square is the bottom station of the **Polybahn funicular** (daily 6.45am–7.15pm), which has connected the city with the university buildings on the hill 40m above since 1889. Normal city transport tickets are valid for the two-minute ride.

Niederdorf

From Central, the **Niederdorf** district stretches south along the riverside for about 1km. A more engaging walk than the busy riverside Limmatquai is to fork one block inland onto the narrow pedestrianized **Niederdorfstrasse**; the tackiness of its initial stretches – replete with fast-food stalls and lowlife beer-halls – soon mellows, and there are plenty of opportunities for random exploration of atmospheric cobbled side-alleys, many of which open onto secluded courtyards adorned with medieval fountains.

A short way down on the left is **Rindermarkt**, where Gottfried Keller – generally thought of as Switzerland's national poet – lived (at no. 9) and drank (at the *Oepfelchammer* opposite; see p.448). A little further along, tiny **Spiegelgasse** enjoyed a burst of fame during World War I: Lenin and Krupskaja stayed for fourteen months at no. 14, in the home of Titus Kammerer, a cobbler, before returning to Russia in April 1917 to lead the revolution; while diagonally opposite, a pub at no. 1 (long since renovated) housed the original *Cabaret Voltaire*, birthplace of the Dada art movement (see box p.436), commemorated with a plaque.

Niederdorfstrasse, which becomes **Münstergasse**, leads on to the **Grossmünster** and beyond, as Oberdorfstrasse, out to the open **Bellevue** plaza, dominated on its south side by the lavish opera house. A short distance up the hill to the left – by the main Rämistrasse or any of the back alleys (tiny **Trittligasse** is the most alluring) – lies the Kunsthaus (see p.438), while a pleasant walk south along the lake brings you after 1km to the Zürichhorn park.

9

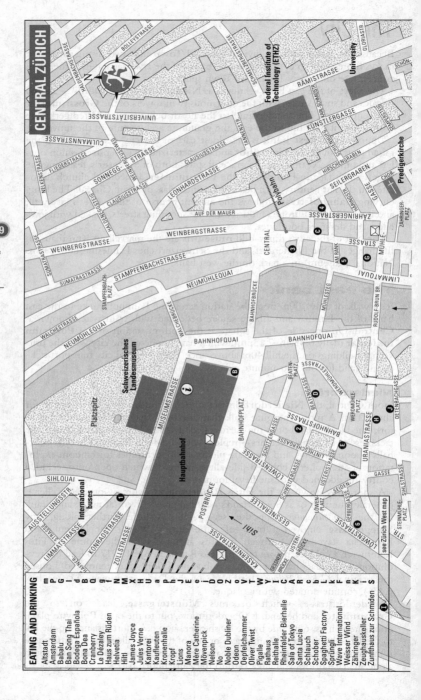

CENTRAL ZÜRICH

Federal Institute of Technology (ETHZ)

University

Schweizerisches Landesmuseum

Platzspitz

Hauptbahnhof

Predigerkirche

EATING AND DRINKING

Altstadt	m
Amsterdam	P
Babalu	G
Ban Song Thai	I
Bodega Española	d
Bona Dea	B
Cranberry	Q
Le Dézaley	g
Haus zum Rüden	f
Helvetia	N
Hiltl	X
James Joyce	H
Jules Verne	U
Kantorei	a
Kaufleuten	p
Kronenhalle	h
Kropf	J
Lions	E
Manora	e
Mère Catherine	i
Mövenpick	D
Nelson	O
No	Z
Noble Dubliner	V
Odeon	T
Oepfelchammer	W
Oliver Twist	Y
Pigalle	I
Rathaus	C
Reithalle	A
Rheinfelder Bierhalle	R
Sala of Tokyo	c
Santa Lucia	b
Schlauch	L
Schober	k
Spaghetti Factory	F
Sprüngli	n
Wave International	K
Weisser Wind	j
Zähringer	s
Zeughauskeller	
Zunfthaus zur Schmiden	H

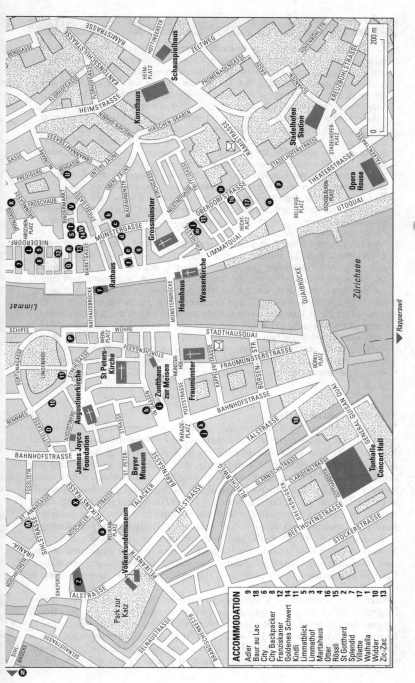

ZÜRICH

9

435

▼ Rapperswil

ACCOMMODATION	
Adler	9
Baur au Lac	18
City	6
City Backpacker	8
Franziskaner	12
Goldenes Schwert	14
Kindli	11
Limmatblick	5
Limmathof	3
Martahaus	4
Otter	16
Rössli	15
St Gotthard	2
Splendid	7
Villette	17
Walhalla	1
Widder	10
Zic-Zac	13

Dada in Zürich

At the same time as both a pre-Revolution Lenin and a *Ulysses*-obsessed Joyce were staying in Zürich, a group of maverick European intellectuals was also seeking refuge in the city from the bloodshed and misery of World War I. In 1915, Hugo Ball, a writer and theatre director, had arrived from Munich with his partner Emmy Hennings, a dancer and singer. It seemed to them, as to many horrified by the brutality of war, that Western civilization had finally lost all reason; with a group of like-minded friends, they made an arrangement with the owner of the *Meierei* tavern at Spiegelgasse 1 to use the pub's backroom for a "literary cabaret" to demonstrate to the people of Zürich and the world the moral bankruptcy of Western culture. On Saturday, February 3, 1916, Ball, Hennings, the Romanian poet Tristan Tzara, Hans Arp (an artist from Franco-German Alsace), and a handful of other émigrés inaugurated the **Cabaret Voltaire** with a night of wild music, poetry and dance, intended to satirize art and literature by placing unreason against reason, anti-art against art. On June 15, they published a magazine with contributions from Kandinsky, Modigliani and others, and presented themselves as "**Dada**", the most significantly meaningless name they could find, picked at random out of a dictionary (*dada* is French for "hobby-horse").

Dada's poignant absurdities aptly expressed the mood of dislocation and crisis seizing Western society, and the movement spread rapidly. In New York, Dada was centred at Alfred Stieglitz's gallery "291", meeting point for Man Ray, Marcel Duchamp and others. In Berlin, Dadaists such as George Grosz relentlessly lampooned high society, and were the initiators of the brand-new technique of photomontage. In the Netherlands, Dada became *De Stijl*, led by Mondrian. In 1920, some of the Zürich Dadaists moved to Paris and there formed the Surrealist movement, which later attracted artists such as Dalí and Miró. The greatest legacy of Dada was its liberating influence in overturning previously unquestioned strictures of style and order, not only in art and writing but across society as a whole. What is both appropriate and extraordinary is that such a movement should have emerged from – of all places – neutral, bourgeois Zürich.

The Grossmünster

With its distinctive twin sugar-loafed towers, and a venerable history at the heart of the Swiss-German Reformation, the **Grossmünster**, or Great Minster (daily 9am–6pm), dominates Zürich's skyline. In a tight-packed city of generally modest, small-scale architecture, it is dauntingly gigantic; and yet, caught half a millennium ago in the eye of a tight-lipped theological hurricane, its interior has been denuded of virtually all its decorative grandeur. Today it's as bare as a cellar inside, but the beauty – as the Reformers would have wanted – is all in its lofty austerity, and its associations. In twelve years preaching from the Grossmünster's pulpit in the sixteenth century, **Huldrych Zwingli**, a contemporary of Luther's and the initiator of the Reformation in Switzerland (see box), transformed Zürich from a sparsely populated hinterland town into a renowned religious centre attracting students and theologians from around Europe. Quite aside from the architecture, the sense of history in the church is compelling.

After its foundation by **Charlemagne** in the ninth century on a site of long-established religious significance (recent excavations below the church suggest the existence of a **Roman** cemetery), the church was constructed in its present form between 1100 and 1230. At that time, the north tower was higher than its twin, since it held, and still holds, the bells. In the late fifteenth century, the south tower was brought up to the same height and adorned on its south side with a statue of a seated Charlemagne. After a disastrous **fire** in 1763, the spires and upper sections of the towers were demolished, and reconstruction shortly after produced the Gothic belfries, watchrooms and octagonal cupolae which survive today. The fire also gave impetus to much **Baroque** alteration to the church interior, and the nineteenth and twentieth centuries saw a continuous programme of restoration of its original Romanesque character.

The building is skewed from the river bank, its broad front facing northwest. The most impressive approach is across paved **Zwingliplatz**, with the main North Portal featuring capitals adorned with animals, birds and, on the extreme left, a fiddle player. To the right, at the base of the North Tower, is a modern statue of Heinrich Bullinger, Zwingli's successor.

Huldrych Zwingli

At the vanguard of the Reformation, **Huldrych** (or Ulrich) **Zwingli** (1484–1531) is one of the most radical anti-establishment figures in European history, a dedicated and eloquent humanist who developed a passion for the liberty of individuals to decide the course of their lives free from the strictures of the past. An archetypal "red under the bed" fifth columnist, he used his position of authority in the church to undermine and reinvent the power structures of the church itself. He died at 47 fighting for his cause.

Whereas Zwingli's contemporary Martin Luther was poorly educated and underwent his internal religious crisis in social isolation, Zwingli came to his personal revolution through education, studying in Basel, Bern, Vienna and possibly Paris, and absorbing the humanist ideas of the Dutch philosopher Erasmus. After ten years as a pastor, his study of scripture led Zwingli to begin questioning the teachings of the Catholic Church; after 1518, when he was appointed to the Grossmünster, he began to develop his deeply controversial ideas from the pulpit, proclaiming the sole authority of the word of God as revealed in the Bible and preaching against church practices. Zürich's congregation, democratically inclined and politically autonomous, was receptive. Barely a year had passed since Luther had nailed his 95 theses to the door of the Wittenberg church.

In 1523, with mounting tension fuelled by an increasingly vocal opposition to clerical celibacy, monasticism, the observance of Lent and the whole structure of papal control, Zwingli was summoned to a public disputation in Zürich with a papal representative. It says a great deal for Zwingli's powers of persuasion (and the city council's courage) that, at a time of profound religious and political turbulence, Zürich's councillors came down on the side of their preacher. The papal representative returned to Rome the loser, and Mass was celebrated at the Grossmünster for the last time in 1525.

Zwingli's ideas spread rapidly, and by 1529 Bern, Basel and St Gallen had all embraced the Reformation. Opposition came from two sides: the Anabaptists, who wanted even more radical reform, and the Swiss "Forest Cantons" around Lake Luzern that had taken up arms in loyalty to Rome. War broke out in 1531; Zwingli went into battle and was killed at Kappel.

Zwingli's lead in Zürich was followed by his son-in-law Heinrich Bullinger, but after 1536 the impetus for reform in Switzerland passed to Jean Calvin, a young preacher working in Geneva. Calvin initially followed Zwingli's doctrine, but then developed his own strict theology. Today, thanks in no small measure to the voyages of Calvinist Puritans to the New World, Calvin is much better-known than his predecessor, but it was the unsung Zwingli who paved the way, forging ideas of personal liberty, and using them to strike at the very heart of the institutionalized hierarchy that had been taken for granted throughout Europe for centuries.

Inside, the overriding impression is of the loftiness of the galleried space and its austerity; aside from some **capitals** decorated with battle scenes – and, on the third pillar on the north side, Charlemagne's discovery of the graves of Felix and Regula – almost no decoration survives. The altar paintings were removed in 1524 at Zwingli's behest, as were the church treasures. Most decorative elements which survive today are replacements, including the pulpit (1851) and the organ (1960). The windows of gorgeously colourful **stained glass** were made in 1933 by Augusto Giacometti and stand alone for their artistic accomplishment. It's worth ducking into the **crypt**, a long triple-aisled hall, the largest of its kind in Switzerland, dominated by the fifteenth-century statue of Charlemagne taken from the South Tower (the one up there now is a replica) and also featuring some well-preserved brush wall drawings dating from 1500. You can **climb** the 187 steps of the 62-metre South Tower for a spectacular view over the city (March–Oct daily 9.15am–5pm; Fr.2).

To the right as you leave the Grossmünster onto Zwingliplatz is a door set into the wall of what was once the chapterhouse, now the university's Theological Institute. This gives into the atmospheric **cloister**, originally built in 1170–80, partly demolished in 1848 and renovated in the 1960s. Aside from enjoying the tranquillity of strolling through the vaulted bays around a central garden, it's worth visiting to see the twelfth-century capitals and spandrels of the arched windows, decorated with grotesque faces, monkeys, dragons, centaurs and other fabulous creatures.

The Wasserkirche and Helmhaus

Near the Grossmünster, down on the riverside, stands the beautiful late-Gothic **Wasserkirche**, site of the martyrdom of Zürich's patron saints, Felix and Regula, but still used mostly for services (visiting hours Wed 9–11am & 2–5pm). Alongside is the Baroque **Helmhaus** (guildhall), Limmatquai 31 (Tues–Sun 10am–6pm, Thurs until 8pm; free; Ⓦwww.helmhaus.org), now converted to an art gallery, staging temporary exhibits of mainly Swiss painting. This marks the Münsterbrücke, which leads across the river directly to the Fraumünster (see p.442).

The Kunsthaus

Five minutes' walk east up the hill from Bellevue is a square formally dubbed Heimplatz but known to every Zürcher as "Pfauen" (Peacocks), after the peacock statue over the famous Schauspielhaus theatre. The adjacent café, now a *Mövenpick*, was for decades known as the Pfauen Café, and was James Joyce's favourite watering hole; it still has a peacock as its inn sign.

Dominating the square is the **Kunsthaus**, Switzerland's finest gallery (Tues–Thurs 10am–9pm, Fri–Sun 10am–5pm; permanent collection Fr.10, free on Wed; temporary exhibits Fr.8–17; joint tickets available; audioguide Fr.6; Ⓦwww.kunsthaus.ch). As well as an expansive permanent collection, the Kunsthaus hosts a continuous flow of top-flight temporary exhibitions, advertised widely around town. If you visit just one art museum in Switzerland, this should be it.

The collection begins even before you get inside: beside the main door is **Rodin**'s vivid *Gate of Hell*, while sculptures by **Moore**, Maillol and others dot the grounds. Inside, most of the ground-floor galleries house whatever temporary exhibit is on, aside from one whole wing of the ground floor which is given over to a permanent display of the widest array of Alberto **Giacometti**'s sculpture in the world.

Elsewhere, you'll find Dutch and Flemish painting represented by **Rubens**, **Rembrandt**, **Hals** and others, the Venetian room showing **Canaletto** and El

△ Street Parade revellers (see p.426) in front of the Grossmünster

Greco, and canvasas from the Italian and Dutch Baroque. There's a complex of rooms devoted mainly to Swiss artists of the nineteenth century, including many works by Anker, Böcklin, Segantini (see p.534) and **Füssli**, who lived and worked for many years in London. Only a tiny fraction of the massive **Graphische Sammlung**, comprising 80,000 graphic works, is on display at any one time.

The new wing houses a stunning collection of twentieth-century art. A broad selection of pop, concrete and abstract expressionist art is headed by a number of works by **Warhol**, a **Rothko**, a gigantic wall-sized installation by Baselitz, geometric constructivist sculpture and works by Bacon and Twombly. A collection of French sculpture since Rodin is dominated, unusually, by **Matisse**. Cubism, Fauvism and **Dada** are all represented, and works by Miró, Dalí and De Chirico head an impressive **Surrealist** overview. **Picasso**, Chagall, Klee and Kandinsky all have whole rooms to themselves, there are two of **Monet**'s most beautiful water-lily canvases, while **Van Gogh**, Gauguin, Cézanne and the largest **Munch** collection outside Scandinavia top an extraordinary journey. Last but not least is the rare chance to revel in the powerful, mystical landscapes of Alps and lakes by the Swiss painter Ferdinand **Hodler**.

University museums

If you follow Rämistrasse uphill from the Kunsthaus, you'll soon come to the university quarter. At Rämistrasse 73 is the **Archäologische Sammlung** (Archeological Collection; Tues–Fri 1–6pm, Sat & Sun 11am–5pm; free), with a range of impressive pieces, but no English notes. Aside from the wealth of Etruscan ware, the most interesting artefacts come from the Middle East: outstanding are an entire case devoted to the stunning Egyptian Fayoum portraits from the first centuries BC–AD; wall-sized steles from ninth-century BC Nimrud (in modern Iraq); a complete mummy, and dozens of statuettes of ancient Egyptian deities (including some memorable cats); and many Roman and Hellenic pieces.

Close by, the **Graphische Sammlung der ETH**, Rämistrasse 101 (entrance on Karl Schmid-Strasse; Mon–Fri 10am–5pm, Wed until 8pm; free), houses thousands of woodcuts, etchings and engravings from all periods, particularly strong on Dürer, Rembrandt, Goya and Picasso.

South to the Zürichhorn

The lakeside promenades running south from Bellevue are crowded with people all summer long, blading, strolling and chatting in the sunshine. Following them south brings you past the **Johann Jacobs Museum**, Seefeldquai 17 (Fri 2–7pm, Sat 2–5pm, Sun 10am–5pm; free; ⓦwww.johann-jacobs-museum.ch), a mildly diverting place in an elegant lakeside villa, devoted to the cultural history of coffee. Selections of Rococo and Neoclassical porcelain ware, silver coffeepots, painting, prints and drawings are fleshed out by videos of TV coffee ads – and free coffee to drink.

Just beyond is the lovely **Zürichhorn** park, a popular place for soaking up some sunshine that also boasts a fine sculpture by Jean Tinguely (see p.221) and a visually striking, but underwhelming, walled **Chinese garden** (April–Oct daily 11am–7pm; Fr.4; ⓦwww.chinagarten.ch), a gift from Zürich's twin city of Kunming, featuring scarlet gateways, a traditional zigzag bridge and pavilions, and the three symbolic species of pine, bamboo and cherry. The grand Zürichhorn Casino building has a popular terrace café for refreshments, and a jetty from where boats shuttle to and from Bürkliplatz. A couple of blocks inland from the Zürichhorn is the pleasant, open **Botanischer Garten**, Zollikerstrasse 107 (Mon–Fri 7am–7pm, Sat & Sun 8am–6pm; shorter hours

Parks and gardens

Zürich is not a big city, and there are plenty of green spaces close-at-hand to escape to, aside from the attractive **Zürichhorn** park and **Botanischer Garten** on the east bank (see opposite), the **Platzspitz** park north of the station (see p.445), and the **Park zur Katz** west of the centre (see p.443).

A few minutes' walk west of Bürkliplatz is a waterside **Arboretum**, beside which is the 150-species-strong aviary **Volière**, Mythenquai 1 (Tues–Sun 10am–noon & 2–4pm; free). From here, it's about ten minutes' walk south along the lake to the **Sukkulenten-Sammlung**, Mythenquai 88 (daily 9–11.30am & 1.30–4.30pm; SMP; ⓦwww.foerderverein.ch), a jungle of desert plants and cacti that forms one of the world's most important collections of succulents (water-retaining plants).

A little over 3km west of the centre, past the giant Sihlfeld cemetery, you'll find luscious orchids and a steamy little tropical forest complete with birds and turtles in the fragrant **Schauhäuser der Stadtgärtnerei**, Sackzelgasse 25 (daily 9–11.30am & 1.30–4.30pm; tram #3 to Hubertus; free; ⓦwww.stadtgaertnerei.ch).

Zürich's **Zoo**, Zürichbergstrasse 221 (daily 8am–6pm, Nov–Feb closes 5pm; Fr.16; tram #5 or #6; ⓦwww.zoo.ch), stands high on a hill about 4km northeast of the centre; it's large, with a good variety of animals, but you may find that a stroll in the **Zürichberg** woods behind it is more satisfying than following the paths between animal enclosures.

in winter; tram #2 or #4 to Höschgasse; free; ⓦ www.bguz.unizh.ch), a riot of colour in spring and summer, with three tropical planthouses and a café.

South of the Zürichhorn park is the **Sammlung E.G. Bührle**, a small, very high-quality private fine-art collection, at Zollikerstrasse 172 (Tues, Fri & Sun 2–5pm, Wed 5–8pm; tram #2 or #4 to Wildbachstrasse, then walk 10min; Fr.9; ⓦ www.buehrle.ch). The paintings are mostly by French Impressionists and Post-Impressionists, displayed in a tastefully furnished mansion. Manet, Van Gogh (including an 1887 self-portrait) and Cézanne's landscapes form the centrepiece, but other artists represented include Monet, Renoir, Sisley, Degas, Toulouse-Lautrec, Seurat, Matisse, Braque and Picasso. Filling out this extraordinary collection are works by Rembrandt, including *Portrait of Saskia*, a rare painting of his wife.

The west bank

Emerging on the south side of the station into hectic Bahnhofplatz, you're met by a statue of Alfred Escher, a prominent nineteenth-century politician and industrialist who is credited with single-handedly leading Zürich into the modern business age. In an inspired piece of statue placement, he gazes down **Bahnhofstrasse**, one of the most prestigious shopping streets in Europe, an enduring symbol of Zürich's wealth and a fascinating counterpoint to the quaintness of the Niederdorf alleys. This is the gateway into the modern city, and is where all of Zürich comes to walk, snack and shop, whether to browse at the inexpensive department stores that crowd the first third of the street, or to sign away Fr.25,000 on a Rolex watch or a Vuitton handbag at the understated super-chic boutiques further south. At no. 31, below the Beyer watch and jewellery shop, is the **Uhrenmuseum Beyer** (Mon–Fri 2–6pm; Fr.5; ⓦ www.beyer-ch.com), filled with examples of timekeeping, from sundials and an ancient Egyptian water-clock onwards.

Two-thirds of the way along the boulevard is **Paradeplatz**, a tram-packed little square offering some of the best people-watching in the city. It's around here that the frippery retreats and Zürich's serious money begins: the streets off Paradeplatz are home to more financial institutions, insurance companies and top-name designer outlets than you could shake a stick at, as well as the head-quarters of most Swiss banks. Bahnhofstrasse ends at the unromantic, paved **Bürkliplatz**, departure point for all boat trips on the lake and boasting a fab-ulous view of the Zürichsee and its eastern "Gold Coast", named for the man-sions and grandiose public buildings lining the shore that bask all summer long in the afternoon sunshine.

Around the Lindenhof

Between Bahnhofstrasse and the river lies the western portion of the Old Town; there are many picturesque alleys to explore here. Rennweg branches off Bahnhofstrasse, and a short walk left from it up the hill brings you to the **Lindenhof**, the oldest part of Zürich and site of a Roman customs post. The broad space is quiet now, occupied mostly by chess-playing old-timers, and gives a fine panorama over the rooftops. Descending on steep **Pfalzgasse** into a dense network of cobbled lanes, **Augustinergasse**, with its romantic oriel-windowed houses, leads to tiny Münzplatz overlooked by the beautiful **Augustinerkirche**, dating from 1274. Spare and simple inside, the church was secularized during the Reformation in 1524 and became the town's mint, but it was renovated and re-dedicated in the nineteenth century and is now used by the Christ Catholic Church (see p.246).

Nearby, the top floor of the Strauhof literary museum is home to the **James Joyce Foundation**, Augustinergasse 9 (Mon–Fri 10am–5pm; free; Ⓦwww.joycefoundation.ch; on Mondays, ring the bell), which has a creaking library and reading room crammed with research materials and one of Europe's most comprehensive collections of Joyceana. Joyce wrote *Ulysses* during his wartime exile in Zürich (1915–19); he returned in 1940, and died on January 13, 1941, laid to rest in Fluntern cemetery next to the zoo, where there is now a statue to him. The Foundation can direct you to his various haunts around town, and they also hold regular open readings – free to all – from *Ulysses* (cur-rently Tues 5.30–7pm) and *Finnegans Wake* (Thurs 4.30–6pm & 7–8.30pm). On the opposite side of Bahnhofstrasse, at Pelikanstrasse 8, is the preserved *James Joyce* pub (see p.448).

Augustinergasse leads on to the **St Peters Kirche** (Mon–Fri 8am–6pm, Sat 9am–4pm; Ⓦwww.st-peter-zh.ch), dating from the thirteenth century but much altered in 1705. The fact that it boasts the largest clock face in Europe (8.7m in diameter; 1534) is less interesting than the unusual sight, above the pulpit amidst Baroque bas-relief, of the name of God in Hebrew lettering, legacy of the Reformers' desire to reclaim the fundamental sources of Christianity. A stepped alley adjacent to the church, **Thermengasse**, has a cat-walk taking you over an excavated Roman baths. A short distance south is the Münsterhof, with the grand Baroque **Zunfthaus zur Meisen** housing the National Museum's ceramics collection (Tues–Sun 10.30am–5pm; Fr.3), including some impressive eighteenth-century porcelain and faience.

The Fraumünster

The Münsterhof is dominated by the graceful, slender-spired **Fraumünster** (Women's Minster; Mon–Sat: May–Sept 9am–6pm; March, April & Oct 10am–5pm; Nov–Feb 10am–4pm), a beautiful church boasting a breathtaking series of stained-glass windows by Marc Chagall and Augusto Giacometti that should not be missed.

It's not known when the church was founded, but on July 21, 853, King

Ludwig the German signed over to his daughter Hildegard a convent which already stood on the site. In 874, Hildegard's sister Bertha consecrated what was probably a simple, towerless basilica, and built a crypt beneath to house the relics of **Felix and Regula**, Roman Christians and the patron saints of Zürich. During the eleventh century, the convent abbesses gained considerable rights, and the present structure was built during the thirteenth century. The convent was suppressed under Zwingli's Reformation, and in 1524 all the icons, ornaments and the organ were destroyed. During the following centuries, the minster became a place of worship for Veltliner and Huguenot refugees, was temporarily a Russian Orthodox church, and – between 1833 and 1844 – hosted both Catholic and Protestant services. There was much renovation during the twentieth century, and in 1967, **Marc Chagall** – then 80 – accepted the commission to make new stained glass for the five 10m-high windows of the Romanesque choir. The stunning artistry of the work he produced makes them one of the highlights of Zürich.

The Chagall windows

Entrance is into the transept through the small east door beneath the spire, and attention is so concentrated on the Chagall windows that you may well find the rest of the church has been roped off.

The Romanesque **choir** dates from 1250–70; it is extremely high (18m) and has a wonderful simplicity of design that would make it a magical place even without its windows. Chagall's blood-red "**Prophets**" window, on the north wall (left), features Elisha at the bottom watching Elijah mount to heaven in a chariot of fire; above, drenched in a divine blue, sits Jeremiah. The "**Law**" window, on the opposite wall, has Moses looking down upon the disobedience and suffering of the people, who are following a horseman into war. Below is Isaiah in the arms of a seraph, preparing to proclaim his message of peace to the world. Of the three main windows, the left, known as the "**Jacob**", window, shows the patriarch's struggle with the angel and his dream of a ladder to heaven. The yellow "**Zion**" window on the right shows an angel trumpeting the beginning of eternity and the descent of New Jerusalem from the heavens; below are a radiant King David and Bathsheba. Finally, the central "**Christ**" window shows Joseph, standing at the bottom beside a huge tree – the tree of life, and the family tree of Christ. Floating in its upper branches is a vision of Mary holding the baby Jesus with the Lamb of God at her feet. Scenes from Jesus' life and parables culminate in an associative depiction of the crucifixion; a cross is barely visible, and Christ is already floating free of the world towards the source of luminescence above.

Giacometti's 1940s work in the 9m-high window in the north transept, visible as you head out, is equally stunning. Were it not for the Chagall windows, this vision of God and Christ, with eight prophets below, and Matthew, Mark, Luke and John framed by ten angels, would take pride of place; as it is, it's doomed to play second fiddle.

West of Bahnhofstrasse

The shopping streets to the west, between Bahnhofstrasse and the River Sihl, hold little interest. Very near Pelikanplatz, in the **Park zur Katz** (Mon–Fri 7am–7pm, Sat & Sun 7am–6pm; shorter hours in winter) – once the city's botanical garden, and still boasting an octagonal glasshouse – is the **Völkerkundemuseum**, Pelikanstrasse 40 (Tues–Fri 10am–1pm & 2–5pm, Sat 2–5pm, Sun 11am–5pm; free; ⓦwww.musethno.unizh.ch), a highly acclaimed museum of non-European cultures. Not far away, at Selnaustrasse 25, the **Haus**

One of the best short trips out of the city is to the hill of **Uetliberg**, a twenty-minute train ride away and a favoured getaway for the locals to do a spot of sledding (winter) or picnicking (summer). Uetliberg – popularly known in dialect as "Üezgi" – is also one end of a popular hiking route, running about two hours south along a forested ridge overlooking the lake to Felsenegg, from where a cable-car can deliver you 300m down to Adliswil village to catch a train back to Zürich. If you're doing the whole circular journey, press *131 on the ticket machine for an all-inclusive ticket; otherwise, press 8138 for Uetliberg only.

From Zürich HB, S-Bahn **trains** depart at least every half-hour to Uetliberg. At the tiny end station, where an information hut stocks a free hiking map of the area identifying plenty of short and long trails, you'll find the *Gmüetliberg* restaurant (Mon–Sat 8am–midnight, Sun 8am–10pm; ⓦwww.gmuetliberg.ch), a basic affair offering a self-service buffet for a steep Fr.16 (daily 8am–6pm only). The trail which begins at Uetliberg station is dubbed the *Planetenweg* (Planet Path), and features models of the planets on a scale of 1:1 billion, with the distances between them also to scale. From the station, it's about a ten-minute walk uphill to the **summit**, passing the Sun, Mercury, Venus, Earth and Mars on the way; Pluto is about 5km away at Felsenegg.

From the top of the summit's 30m viewing tower, which boosts your altitude to 900m, there are terrific 360-degree views over Zürich, the whole curve of the lake and, on a clear day, east into Austria and as far southwest as the Jungfrau. Also on the summit is the *Uto Kulm* hotel (see p.431) and **restaurant**, a handy spot for refreshment. The panoramic walking route from *Uto Kulm* to Felsenegg and beyond passes another couple of restaurants. A **cable car** (daily: May–Sept 8am–10pm; Oct–April 9am–8pm) runs every fifteen minutes between Felsenegg and the lakeside town of Adliswil, from where it's less than ten minutes' walk to Adliswil S-Bahn station.

Konstruktiv (Wed–Fri noon–6pm, Sat & Sun 11am–6pm; ⓦwww .hauskonstruktiv.ch) hosts changing exhibits of concrete and constructivist art.

Schweizerisches Landesmuseum

Behind the train station, and unmistakeable in its mock-Gothic, purpose-built castle, is the **Schweizerisches Landesmuseum** (Swiss National Museum; Tues–Sun 10.30am–5pm; Fr.5; SMP; ⓦwww.musee-suisse.com). This massive building has a varied collection covering the range of Swiss history, and is well worth investigation, though you may find some of its displays rather sterile. The collection is so vast, and the layout of the place so labyrinthine, that it's more satisfying to consult a (free) floor-plan at the door and then head straight for those areas which interest you rather than to try and absorb everything. Staff give regular guided tours of the whole collection in English (Tues 6pm).

The museum begins with a series of rooms devoted to **sacred art** from the ninth to the sixteenth centuries, displaying medieval wood carvings, painted altar pieces, a wheelable model of Christ on an ass (used in Palm Sunday processions), and 65 copies of the 153 panels that adorn the ceiling of the church at Zillis (see p.514). Fifteenth-century **stained glass** has been installed in a room which also displays a sequence of images of some less well-known saints (including St Vitus, patron saint of bedwetting). Rooms lead you past a reconstruction of an eighteenth-century **apothecary** and an intricately detailed sixteenth-century bestiary; up some stairs are several watches and clocks, and a display on **exploration** crowned by a spectacular two-metre-high globe dating from 1570. Pieces showing the life of the Swiss **nobility** include a decorated gentleman's sleigh from seventeenth-century Luzern. Stairs lead up again

to a tower, with dozens of cases of **costumes**, some pieces of silver and eigh-
teenth- and nineteenth-century **toys**. Returning back down the same stairs
brings you to a sequence of **Baroque** and Rococo rooms, including a ceremonial hall from a Zürich house of 1660. There's also a section on **military
history**, as well as an **archeological collection**, comprising a wealth of finds
from Roman Zürich. Pick of the Iron Age collection is a stunning embossed
golden bowl from 600 BC; Neolithic and Bronze Age artefacts bring you back
round to the entrance again.

Stretching behind the museum, the small, shady **Platzspitz** park (daily
6am–9pm), where the Sihl meets the Limmat, was once known as Needle
Park, crunching underfoot with used syringes from the flaked-out junkies all
around. These days it's been entirely cleaned up, and is good for a pleasant wander framed by the two rivers.

Museum Rietberg

The impressive **Museum Rietberg** (Tues–Sun 10am–5pm, Wed until 8pm;
Fr.6, plus about Fr.6 for any special exhibits; SMP; ⓦwww.rietberg.ch) comprises two villas set in a lush park southwest of the centre, which together
house a spectacular collection of non-European art. Signs from the Rietberg
stop on tram #7 direct you up into the park; a right-hand fork takes you to
the Villa Wesendonck, a left-hand fork to the Park-Villa Rieter. The main collection is housed in the grandiose **Villa Wesendonck**, where the composer
Richard Wagner lived for a time in 1857. Once inside, head left for a chronological tour, through rooms of Indian and Chinese Buddhist art and sculpture
from between the third and sixteenth centuries – look out for the blissfully
serene lovers' faces, in glorious contrast to the mournfulness on display in the
Landesmuseum's European art of roughly the same period. A four-armed
dancing Shiva in bronze, surrounded by a ring of fire, is particularly stunning.
Upstairs are some intricate Tibetan bronzes, Chinese ceramics, and a host of
American, African and Australasian pieces. The smaller **Park-Villa Rieter**
(Tues–Sat 1–5pm, Sun 10am–5pm) houses on two floors changing selections
from the museum's enormous collection of exquisite Asian painting: Indian art
on ground level, Chinese and Japanese art upstairs.

Zürich West

For a clean break from the sometimes overly packaged Zürich of cobbled
alleys, medieval guildhalls and glitzy shopping, you need to head west: the residential and post-industrial area comprising the postal districts of 8004 (*Kreis
4*) and 8005 (*Kreis 5*), together known as **Zürich West**, is the new home of
the city's underground.

The north–south artery of **Langstrasse** is where the daily dramas are played
out, a seedy but absorbing mile-long strip of designer bars, videogame parlours,
independent cinemas, clubwear outlets and cheap eateries. Trams #2 or #3 to
Bezirksgebäude deliver you to the respectable southern end of Langstrasse
around **Helvetiaplatz**, relaxed home of the *Xenix* bar and cinema (see p.449).
Strolling north, the street narrows and the mood changes: this was once
Zürich's red-light district, and although some of the unpleasantness survives
(there's still a fair spread of sex cinemas and prostitution), the worst of the vice
trade has moved on. In its place has developed a downmarket ethnic and social
mix that is a universe away from the homogeneous collection of expensive suits
and fur coats parading the Bahnhofstrasse not a kilometre east: lowlife bars rub
shoulders with avant-garde galleries, smells of greasy kebabs mix with wood-

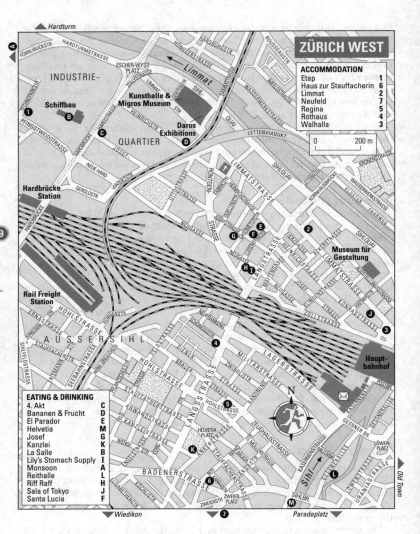

ZÜRICH WEST

ACCOMMODATION
Etap   1
Haus zur Stauffacherin   6
Limmat   2
Neufeld   7
Regina   5
Rothaus   4
Walhalla   3

0   200 m

EATING & DRINKING
4. Akt   C
Bananen & Frucht   D
El Parador   E
Helvetia   M
Josef   G
Kanzlei   K
La Salle   B
Lily's Stomach Supply   I
Monsoon   A
Reithalle   L
Riff Raff   H
Sala of Tokyo   J
Santa Lucia   F

fired pizza and aromatic marijuana, and the whole street is a mingle of Swiss-German voices with French-African, Portuguese, Turkish, Balkan, Latin American, Haitian and more.

Two-thirds of the way along, Langstrasse dips beneath the train tracks; the style north of the underpass is different again, with residential side-streets increasingly attracting artists and creative types who have, in turn, spawned plenty of hip bars, high-quality restaurants and designer boutiques on and off the stretch leading to the major **Limmatplatz** junction (served by trams #4 and #13). A short walk east, set amongst streets packed with independent galleries and design studios, is the celebrated **Museum für Gestaltung**, at Ausstellungstrasse 60 (Design Museum; Tues–Thurs 10am–8pm, Fri–Sun

11am–6pm; Fr.10; SMP; ⊛www.museum-gestaltung.ch), with exhibits relating to design, the visual arts, advertising and the media.

The Industrie-quartier
More interest lies in wandering the streets west of Limmatplatz; from here all the way out to the football stadium at Hardturm is the old **industrial quarter**, still largely unreclaimed. Trains and heavy traffic pass on viaducts way above the roofs of working depots, old factories and business parks, while in between thrives a lively subculture focused on industrial spaces reclaimed as galleries and restaurants, and anonymous-looking bunkers that double as some of Zürich's best dance clubs; one famous example is *Bogen 13*, set beneath the rail viaduct off Ottostrasse, a few arches along from the *Bananen & Frucht* restaurant (see p.451). West of the viaduct stands the old Löwenbräu brewery, a vast brick building at Limmatstrasse 268–270 that now houses, aside from five small galleries and an art bookshop, the acclaimed contemporary-art shows of the **Kunsthalle** (Tues–Fri noon–6pm, Sat & Sun 11am–5pm; Fr.8; ⊛www .kunsthallezuerich.ch), the **Migros Museum für Gegenwartskunst** (same hours; Fr.8; ⊛www.migrosmuseum.ch) and **Daros Exhibitions** (Thurs & Fri 4–7pm, Sat 2–5pm; Fr.5; ⊛www.daros.ch).

Close by is the busy **Escher-Wyss-Platz**, its swirl of cars, bikes, buses and trams smothered by a traffic overpass: high overhead, stressed-out city-centre workers speed home to the suburbs while down at street level, locals relax in the clutch of trendy bars and cafés on and off Hardstrasse. Signed just off the street is perhaps the city's most impressive architectural space, the **Schiffbau**, a huge plant which once built parts for ships; now, with bare concrete largely left unadorned and heavy machinery still hanging in the ceiling, it houses, in its various sectors, two drama stages of the Schauspielhaus (see p.455), *Moods* jazz club (see p.453) and *LaSalle*, one of the city's best new restaurants (see p.452). It's open for exploration throughout the day.

You can get back to Zürich HB either on tram #4 or #13 from Escher-Wyss-Platz, or by train from Hardbrücke station, located 300m south of the Schiffbau.

Eating and drinking

As you might expect from a city like Zürich, there's a wealth of variety in **eating and drinking** possibilities, with as much available citywide at the bottom end of the market as at the top.

Cafés, bars and pubs
Zürich has an enormous variety of both **cafés** and **café-bars** and, as ever, the difference between them, and between a café and a restaurant, is blurred. There's any number of places all through the **Niederdorf** alleys where you can sit and watch the world go by over a coffee or glass of beer. Don't stick – as many visitors do – to the slightly seedy cafés along Niederdorfstrasse itself; Zürich's most alluring café culture takes place further south, at the pavement cafés along the riverside Limmatquai and the cobbled squares, such as Hechtplatz and Schiffländeplatz, that open onto it. This is where you'll also find international names, including *Starbucks*. The west bank of the river, **around Bahnhofstrasse**, is less of a draw, not least because this is shopping territory: long expanses of shop windows don't make the streets especially amble-

friendly, although a bit of poking around in the old-town alleys between Bahnhofstrasse and the river can turn up trumps.

Niederdorf

Altstadt Kirchgasse 4. Cool jazzy bar, open from breakfast time onwards, that's gaining a reputation as an old-town meeting point away from the sleaze.

Babalu Schmidgasse 6. Tiny postmodern-style bar, its chic denizens quaffing bottled beers and cocktails amidst an onslaught of jungle beats.

Cranberry Metzgergasse 3 ⓦ www.cranberry.ch. Strange combination of a cosy bar – predominantly gay – and what the management call a "smoking lounge" for dispersing cigar smoke and other fragrant aromas into the night air.

Odeon Limmatquai 2. Compact café-bar on Bellevue, where Lenin once sat and watched the world go by. There's little sign of revolutionary activity these days – although the bar prices would spark a popular uprising anywhere other than Zürich.

Oepfelchammer Rindermarkt 12. A 200-year-old building, all creaking timbers and lop-sided ceilings, famous for its association with the city's literary son, Gottfried Keller. The reason to visit is for beer in the tiny low-beamed upper front room, which is invariably packed. Legend has it that if you can swing up and wriggle your way through the gap between beam and ceiling, your beers are on the house: Keller may have done it, but few have braved the waiters since to try. Closed Sun & Mon.

Oliver Twist Rindermarkt 6. Snug little pub on a Niederdorf back alley, a mecca for expats and Anglophiles in search of pints, English conversation and football on the telly.

Pigalle Marktgasse 14 ⓦ www.pigalle.ch. Legendary little bar filled with the elegantly wasted, or at least those who are aspiring.

Rathaus In the Rathaus on Limmatquai. Pleasant place with an outside terrace alongside the old Town Hall, sandwiched neatly between the river and the Limmatquai trams.

Rheinfelder Bierhalle Niederdorfstrasse 76. Best of the many beerhalls at the northern end of the street. With wooden benches, zero decoration and bright lights, this is a place to get shamelessly, sociably drunk, laugh loudly and clap strangers on the back. The food is cheap and hearty: daily specials for around Fr.13 are padded out by their infamous "Jumbo Jumbo Cordon Bleu", at Fr.22 – a slab of deep-fried cheese-slathered meat so big it dangles off the plate on both sides. Closed Sun.

Schlauch Münstergasse 20 (upstairs). Quiet, friendly and relaxed diner-bar, perfect to catch your breath from the Niederdorf scrum. Sizeable plates of health-conscious food (veggie and not), and a snooker hall adjacent attract a young, vaguely alternative crowd. Closed Mon & Tues.

Schober Napfgasse 4. A memorable old confectioner's and café that's straight out of Mary Poppins – a riot of frothy white lace, flowers and choice treats. Head through to the capacious interior for quite simply the best mug of hot chocolate (with whipped cream) you will ever have tasted. It's even a shame to spoil it with a slice of homemade apple strudel – but then again…

Wüste Oberdorfstrasse 7. Mellow, comfortable café-bar below the *Otter* hotel, decorated in ethnic style and dotted with candles.

Zähringer Spitalgasse at Zähringerplatz. Longstanding co-operative-run bastion of Zürcher counterculture, attracting an alternative clientele for snacks, herbal teas and beer. Mon 6pm–midnight, Tues–Sun 8am–midnight (Fri & Sat until 12.30am).

Around Bahnhofstrasse

Amsterdam Schwanengasse 4. Tiny, dark old town café for fresh juices and healthy snacks.

Helvetia Stauffacherquai 1. Loud and jovial locals' haunt – nicknamed the Helvti-Bar – just across the Sihl; the only bar in town where you can get full table service after midnight (closes 1am weekdays, 2am weekends). A little pricey for everyday consumption, but very civilized for a nightcap or three.

James Joyce Pelikanstrasse 8. The ultimate memorial to one of Zürich's best-known visitors. The pub comprises the original nineteenth-century "Antique Bar" of Dublin's Jury Hotel, saved from the developers in the 1970s, transported here piece by piece and reassembled to stand as a relic of a bygone age. Its location – in the heart of the financial district – lets it down, but there's still no more atmospheric Irish pub anywhere. Closed from 7pm on Sat, and all day Sun.

Jules Verne Access through *Brasserie Lipp*, Uraniastrasse 9 ☎ 01 211 11 55. Intimate little city-centre bar in the stubby-domed observatory building, done up with canvas decor to mimic the basket of a hot-air balloon and boasting superb panoramic views across the rooftops and steeples – worth the price of refreshment. Phone ahead to reserve a table facing south towards the mountains for twilight. Take the lift to the tenth floor, and then climb another 17 steps. Closes midnight Mon–Thurs, 1am Fri & Sat, 11pm Sun.

Kaufleuten Pelikanstrasse 18. Modish venue for mixing with Zürich's burgeoning "in" scene. Designers, musicians, bankers and the idle rich flock here, and to the club next door. A pricey beer is worth it for the buzz.

Lions Oetenbachgasse 24. Pleasant English pub just off Bahnhofstrasse by the Orell Füssli English bookshop – larger, quieter and much more comfortable than other pubs in the area. Also with a daily food menu.

Mövenpick Paradeplatz. Perfect people-watching café, with a great selection of teas and coffees from around the world, plus snacks and full meals all day long.

Nelson Beatengasse 11 ⓦ www.thenelsonpub.com. Massive, noisy pub seconds from the station, crammed on weekend nights with Zürich's sizeable contingent of teenage au pairs and exchange students on the pull. Cheap beer, late opening, live music, DJs, and TV sport make for a heady, if predictable, brew.

No Kuttelgasse 7. Purportedly Japanese teahouse (although little more than a standard café done up with some paper screens and a tinkling miniature water-garden), nonetheless cool and relaxing, conveniently located in the alleys just off Bahnhofstrasse. Offers a good range of refreshments and light lunches.

Noble Dubliner Talacker 43/Talstrasse 82. Good beer, good service and a talkative atmosphere make this cramped mock-Irish pub – with doors front and back – hugely popular with locals and expats alike.

Sprüngli Bahnhofstrasse 21. Main branch of the world-famous confectioner's, displaying cabinets full of the most exquisite chocolates and cakes imaginable, plus their own speciality, *Luxemburgerli*, cream-filled pastry bites that are truly drool-worthy. Enjoy it all in the upstairs café-patisserie overlooking Paradeplatz, the city's most atmospheric tearoom, where Zürich's *grandes-dames* come to gossip discreetly over coffee and cake. Free choc with every espresso.

Zürich West and south

4. Akt Heinrichstrasse 262. Deeply cool bar at the Hardstrasse junction, with plenty of outside tables, a good, up-to-date music selection, and a small food menu (about Fr.20).

Kanzlei Kanzleistrasse 56 at Helvetiaplatz ⓦ www.kanzlei.ch. Wooden shack-bar just off Langstrasse, attached to the *Xenix* art-house cinema and crammed most nights with a lively bunch of artists, filmmakers and wannabes lubricating their vocal chords at each other. On the first Sunday of the month, *Xenix* becomes *Xenia*, the bar and cinema both strictly women-only.

Riff Raff Neugasse 57 ⓦ www.riffraff.ch. Small cinema attached to a trendy bar, a few steps off Langstrasse. The building has a longer history than it seems; it showed silent movies back in the early days, and has now been taken over by a cooperative dedicated to restoring its reputation and promoting independent film-making. The walls, like the clientele, are floor-to-ceiling matt black, and the bar stands between two small auditoria.

Ziegel oh Lac At the Rote Fabrik arts centre (see p.421), Seestrasse 395. One of the most appealing bar/restaurant-spaces in the city, with a light, open interior and waterside seating in summer but way south of the city, far from the crush. Signs declare "Smoking Cannabis is Illegal", but to little effect. The food is quality, balanced stuff (Fr.12–22). Closed Mon.

Restaurants

Traditional Zürich cuisine is rich and heavy with meat, epitomized in the city's trademark dish *Züri Gschnetzlets* – diced veal in a creamy mushroom sauce, generally served alongside *Rösti*. There's a host of good-quality inexpensive **restaurants** in every corner of the city that can do you a filling lunch for Fr.15–20, or a full evening meal for roughly twice that; Niederdorf is shoulder to shoulder with them. As a general rule, the area around Bahnhofstrasse is livelier than Niederdorf at lunch time, while in the evening the reverse is true. There's also no shortage of expensive places, where you'd be lucky to come away with change from Fr.75 per person, and are probably looking at almost twice that for a full meal.

Cheap eats

Zürich offers a wealth of places to **eat cheaply** and reasonably well. *Manora*, on the fifth floor of the Manor department store at Bahnhofstrasse 75 (Mon–Fri 9am–8pm, Sat 9am–5pm), has good, balanced self-service meals of all kinds for Fr.10–15, while *Wave International*, just off Bahnhofstrasse in the Jelmoli department store (Uraniastrasse entrance; same hours), has excellent Italian, Swiss, Asian, Turkish and Arabic nosh with and without meat for Fr.8–13 (stand-up only). All along Niederdorfstrasse are dozens of hole-in-the-wall snack joints churning out kebabs, falafels, sausages, noodles and/or chips, from about Fr.8 upwards; you can often do better with the daily special (around Fr.12) at one of the beerhalls on the same street. In the train station, in addition to the spotless, good-value *Nordsee* fish diner opposite the tourist office (full meals from Fr.13; take-away available), check out the stand-up *Suan Long*, on the lower shopping level (daily 10.30am–9.30pm), which does filling Asian dishes, veggie and not, for Fr.12–15.

Inexpensive and mid-range restaurants

Niederdorf and east bank

Adler's Swiss Chuchi Rosengasse 10 ☏01 266 96 66. Landmark Swiss restaurant below the *Adler* hotel, freshly renovated in bright, modern style (although it's located on a particularly sleazy section of Niederdorfstrasse). Good-value fondue or raclette (Fr.25–30) are what to go for; the bargain lunch specials have a careful, home-cooked touch as well, but cheese is the thing – you'll sniff the place before you see it.

Ban Song Thai Kirchgasse 6 ☏01 252 33 31. One of the city's better Thais, small and pleasant with a varied menu. Lunch specials start from Fr.15, evening meals more than twice that. Closed Sun.

Blinde Kuh (literally "Blind Cow"; German for "Blind Man's Buff"), Mühlebachstrasse 148 ☏01 421 50 50, ⓦwww.blindekuh.ch. Zürich's best-kept secret – and not so secret, now that the international media have caught the buzz. The food is excellent, down-to-earth cuisine that gains acres of new depth by being served in absolute darkness: after the foyer (there are lights here and in the toilets), you're led into the smoke-free dining room where you can't see a thing, not your hand in front of your face. The restaurant – a small place, seating 48 at eight tables – is run as a way for sighted folk to sample the experience of losing their sight for a couple of hours. The menus (one meat, one fish and one vegetarian, all moderately priced) change each week. Most of the waiters have limited sight or are blind; the head chef is sighted, but the sous chef is blind. It's a very popular place: you'll need to book several weeks ahead. Closed Mon lunch, Sat lunch & all day Sun.

Bodega Española Münstergasse 15 ☏01 251 23 10. Small, dark-wood place dripping with atmosphere that's been here since 1892, concealed from the street behind its attached wine shop. Upstairs is the restaurant, with a long menu ranging from *tortilla catalana* to an unmissable *paella* (around Fr.40 for two). The buzzing tapas bar downstairs is also outstanding, with a huge range from Fr.5.

Le Dézaley Römergasse 7 ☏01 251 61 29, ⓦwww.le-dezaley.ch. Excellent French Swiss restaurant nestling in a quiet alley at the foot of the Grossmünster's north tower. House specialities are pricey Vaudois dishes such as fondue bourguignonne (with a cellarful of Vaudois wines to boot), but there are many inexpensive options available. Interior decor is attractive, and there's also a lovely little courtyard garden. Closed Sun.

Kantorei Neumarkt 2 ☏01 252 27 27, ⓦwww .restaurant-kantorei.ch. Warm and pleasant young restaurant, occupying a 600-year-old building in a little-visited part of the Old Town and serving unpretentious, but excellently prepared, modern Swiss cuisine. Doubles as a tranquil café between mealtimes.

Mère Catherine Nägelihof 3 ☏01 250 59 40. Pleasant little place in a hard-to-find courtyard below the Grossmünster, brightly done up and touting itself as *"un peu provençal"* – salads and seafood are the main draw, with especially good bouillabaisse. Menus change monthly.

Pinte Vaudoise In *Hotel Villette*, Kruggasse 4 ☏01 251 23 35. Traditional dark-wood den serving what has been voted as the best fondue in Zürich. The jovial owner/manager/chef is used to tourists and can explain the range of fondues on offer (around Fr.22). Closed Sat in summer, & Sun.

Santa Lucia Marktgasse 21. Simple Niederdorf Italian with a wide selection of good-value pasta and pizza, plus the bonus of late-night service until 2am.

Spaghetti Factory Niederdorfstrasse 5. Straightforward pasta restaurant in the heart of the Niederdorf buzz, good and cheap. Also at Schifflände 6, behind Hechtplatz, and Theaterstrasse 1, south of Bellevue.

Weisser Wind Oberdorfstrasse 20. Comfortable, traditional setting for Italian and Swiss specialities, with plenty of vegetarian options, for around Fr.20–30. A beerhall in all but name. Closed Sun.

Around Bahnhofstrasse

Bona Dea Bahnhofplatz 15 ☎01 217 15 15, ⓦwww.bahnhofbuffet.ch. Excellent, no-smoking vegetarian buffet restaurant attached to the train station, with loads of choice. Note that, despite the location, this is a dainty, upmarket kind of place (and, at Fr.35 a head, priced accordingly): veggies looking for a cheap, hearty meal should aim for *Café Schlauch* (see p.448), or a take-away from *Hiltl* (see below).

Hiltl Sihlstrasse 28 ☎01 227 70 00, ⓦwww.hiltl .ch. Top-quality vegetarian restaurant, celebrating its 100th-plus birthday but updated with bright decor, calm, friendly service and excellent fare. Spurn the à la carte options for the expansive and great-value hot and cold buffet – by night featuring delectable Indian dishes. At around Fr.5 for 100g, you can put together a sizeable meal for Fr.20, much less if you take it away and picnic on the nearby Lindenhof instead.

Kropf In Gassen 16 ☎01 221 18 05. An atmospheric listed building, boasting a frescoed interior which dates from its conversion into a restaurant in 1888, and which stands a little askance with the solid *bürgerliche* cooking on offer: Bacchic revels may be erupting all around, but only in picture form on the ceiling. Meat, potatoes and dumplings in various forms, along with tripe, are staples, and yet standards are high and the food is never dull. Closed Sun.

Zeughauskeller Bahnhofstrasse 28a at Paradeplatz ☎01 211 26 90. A wood-ceilinged room dating from the fifteenth century that's now the city's top beerhall, a sometimes chaotic place serving hearty meat dishes and plenty of the amber nectar. One of the most extensive sausage menus around – over a dozen different varieties – is crowned by a one-metre giant that should keep four people occupied for some time. Although the menu is in English (and ten other languages), this is still very popular with Zürchers of a certain bank balance – a long way from the rough-and-ready beerhalls of Niederdorf.

Zürich West

Bananen & Frucht Heinrichstrasse, corner Ottostrasse. Lovely little spot occupying an arch beneath the railway viaduct in a peaceful residential area, with tables spilling out on both sides and chilled-out folk relaxing on comfy chairs with a juice or beer. The menu is small – pasta dishes, fish and grilled or spit-roasted meats – but food is excellent (Fr.20–30). Note limited hours: Tues–Thurs noon–2pm & 4–7pm.

El Parador Luisenstrasse 43 ☎01 272 48 64. Acclaimed Spanish restaurant, on the quiet corner with Heinrichstrasse, with a small, select menu of authentic dishes. Food is expertly prepared – the *paella* and *crema catalana* are both sublime – but don't expect to pay less than about Fr.50 a head. Closed Sat lunch & Sun.

Josef Gasometerstrasse 24 ☎01 271 65 95. Young, trendy hangout in an up-and-coming area: a jazzy candle-lit bar attached to a semi-formal restaurant that gets rave reviews from local hipsters and is well worth a splash (Fr.30–40).

Lily's Stomach Supply Langstrasse 197 ☎01 440 18 85. Clean, modern place in the heart of the Langstrasse district, always busy, churning out authentic Asian dishes fresh-cooked in the open kitchen – anything from Tamil chicken curry or Pakistani *panji renga* to Japanese *yaki soba*, Thai noodles or *hong shao* tofu, washed down with Filipino beer. Seating is at long, communal tables with benches. The German menu marks dishes that are extra-spicy !!! and those that are an acquired taste ***. Phone ahead for a takeaway. Mon–Thurs 11am–midnight, Fri & Sat 11am–1am, Sun 3pm–midnight.

Monsoon Förrlibuckstrasse 180 ☎01 271 77 87. Bizarrely located Asian restaurant at ground level of an office block in a business park way out west on the edge of the industrial quarter. Don't be put off: the restaurant's popularity with local hipsters lounging on the terrace and serious diners alike gives clues that its menu is wide-ranging enough, and its cuisine – blending elements of Thai, Indian, Indonesian and others – good enough, to make the journey worthwhile. Around Fr.35–40 a head.

Reithalle Gessnerallee 8 ☎01 212 07 66. Formerly the military riding school, this complex of buildings along the Sihl has been turned into a theatre and centre for performing arts, with one long, stone-floored hall serving as a combination bar and restaurant. It attracts a lively and eclectic crowd of twenty-somethings with a varied menu of light, modern dishes (many vegetarian), and a relaxed, share-a-table attitude. Saturday nights they crank up the music for late-night dancing.

Santa Lucia Josefstrasse 120. Bright, airy Italian

on a quiet residential street, with a wood-fired pizza oven and excellent fresh pasta. The friendly, accommodating service makes it popular with the locals.

Expensive restaurants

Haus zum Rüden Limmatquai 42 ☎01 261 95 66, 🌐www.hauszumrueden.ch. Splendid thirteenth-century riverside *Zunfthaus* (guildhall), complete with vaulted ceiling and late-Gothic decor; book in advance for a window table. The food covers most of the standard Zürich bases – plenty of meat and rich sauces, including the famous *Züri Gschnetzlets* (Fr.52). Bank on Fr.80 a head. Closed Sat & Sun.

Hummerbar In *Hotel St Gotthard*, Bahnhofstrasse 87 ☎01 227 76 21. A wonderfully romantic place for *Hummer* (lobster) and a host of other seafood, all flown in fresh daily and prepared in pristine style for consumption amidst a formal, *fin-de-siècle* setting. Prices – compared with others under this heading – are reasonable, but who's counting when you're contemplating fresh oysters?

Kronenhalle Rämistrasse 4 ☎01 251 02 56. Despite the impressive array of the twentieth-century's great and good who've licked their chops appreciatively here, the ambience of this classically grand place, bedecked with original Picassos, Matisses and Braques, remains amiable rather than stiff. (With at least one hors d'oeuvre on the menu over Fr.100, they can afford to be amiable.) The cuisine is outstanding but undramatic – there's little on the menu that you won't have seen before – but where the place scores is in its down-to-earth attitude to those who decide to spurn the champagne and truffles in favour of enjoying the atmosphere over a sausage and a glass of beer instead.

LaSalle In Schiffbau building, off Hardstrasse ☎01 258 70 71, 🌐www.lasalle-restaurant.ch. Amazing place set within a huge glass cube on the factory floor of the old Schiffbau (see p.447). It's far from downmarket, though – all white tablecloths and silver service – and is a breath of fresh air after the stuffiness of traditional city-centre restaurants. The modern European cuisine is outstanding (Fr.50 or so per head), but the surroundings are just as alluring as the food. Unmissable, whether you come to gawp or dine. Closed Sat & Sun lunch.

Le Pavillon In *Ermitage Hotel*, Seestrasse 80, Küsnacht ☎01 914 42 42. Superb, stylish Michelin-starred restaurant in an atmospheric lakefront hotel 7km south of Zürich (see p.456), where the chef Edgar Bouier whisks up his own "cuisine niçoise", effortlessly blending the freshest fish and seafood with woodland and Mediterranean flavours. Lunch could be as little as Fr.65, dinner as much as Fr.180.

Petermann's Kunststuben Seestrasse 160, Küsnacht ☎01 910 07 15. Universally acclaimed as one of Switzerland's top five restaurants, replete with two Michelin stars, several international awards (including the title "Best Restaurant in Europe", as assessed by 8250 diners for Zagat) and pages of gushing reportage from foodie journalists. To cut to the chase: if you're prepared to invest Fr.100 a head for lunch, or twice that in the evening – plus the cost of getting to and from Küsnacht, 8km south of town – then you'll get a meal to remember for years to come. The dining-room setting is classy, sophisticated with a light, arty touch, and chef Horst Petermann is constantly at work refining his menu. You'll need to book several weeks ahead. Closed Sun & Mon, also late Feb and early Sept.

Sala of Tokyo Limmatstrasse 29 ☎01 271 52 90, 🌐www.sala-of-tokyo.ch. You'd never know it, but this dowdy, anonymous building at the station end of a busy traffic street hides one of Switzerland's best Japanese restaurants. Prices are very high (Fr.70 for lunch, Fr.120 in the evening), but the quality of the traditional cuisine, using the freshest of ingredients, is outstanding. Open Tues–Fri 11.45am–1.30pm & 6–9.30pm. Closed Christmas, Easter & late July to early Aug.

Zunfthaus zur Schmiden Marktgasse 20 ☎01 251 52 87. The guildhall of the smiths, dating from 1520, and now a spectacular setting in the heart of Niederdorf in which to linger over the richest of Swiss-German cuisine, meat-heavy platters and top Zürcher specialities such as *geschnetzeltes Kalbfleisch* (veal in a white wine and cream sauce), everything in mighty portions. May–Sept closed Sun; also closed mid-July to mid-Aug.

Nightlife and entertainment

For a city that's a minnow in world terms, Zürich has a surprisingly wide range of **nightlife and entertainment**. Live rock and jazz – although easy to find most nights of the week – take second place to the city's amazingly dynamic club scene, which covers the gamut from techno to salsa. Zürich is also home to a top-flight orchestra, a world-famous opera company, and one of the German-speaking world's premier theatres. You can find complete what's-on **listings** for the week ahead in *ZüriTipp* (ⓦwww.zueritipp.ch), the Friday supplement to the *Tages Anzeiger* newspaper, available free at the tourist office. The tourist booklet *Zürich News* covers major events, but nothing out of the mainstream. The clubbers' bible, with full listings, is *Forecast* (Fr.3 monthly). **Tickets** for almost any event can be had from TicketCorner (ⓣ0848 800 800) or Billetzentrale Zürich (BiZZ), Bahnhofstrasse 9 (Mon–Fri 10am–6.30pm, Sat 10am–2pm; ⓣ01 221 22 83). Note that the larger, mainstream venues close down for July and August. Prices are roughly Fr.10–15 for ordinary live bands and clubs, Fr.20–30 for big-name shows, Fr.15–60 for classical concerts, and Fr.20–300 for the opera.

Live music

Zürich is a minor stop on the European tour circuit for big-name stars, but a burgeoning local scene gives rich pickings for **live music** at a spread of venues around town, headed by the Rote Fabrik. Many people make the short trip to Winterthur to see bands at the Albani (see p.468).

Abart Manessestrasse 170 ⓦwww.abart.ch. Regular eclectic choice of local and foreign bands.

Casa Bar Münstergasse 20. Zürich's longest-running jazz venue, still featuring live music nightly in the Niederdorf.

Dynamo Wasserwerkstrasse 21 ⓦwww.dynamo.ch. Bills itself as a "youth culture centre" and, as well as a disco and jazz school, hosts live bands with an alternative, punkish bias.

Moods In Schiffbau building, off Hardstrasse ⓦwww.moods.ch. The city's premier jazz club, resident within the spectacular Schiffbau building (see p.447), with good restaurant attached, pulling in top-flight names.

Rote Fabrik Seestrasse 395 ⓦwww.rotefabrik.ch. Alternative-style arts complex, in old graffitied industrial buildings on the lakeshore some 5km southwest of town, hosting a continuous flow of bands famous and unknown from all musical genres. Bus #161 or #165 from Bürkliplatz (last bus returns after midnight).

Widder Bar In *Widder Hotel*, Rennweg 7. Chic city-centre hotel bar featuring quality jazz nights.

Clubs

Zürich's **club** scene has skyrocketed recently, helped by legislation permitting some all-night opening: you'll find the city's dance venues heaving with a newfound energy lacking in most European cities. At the heart of the new subculture are the cosmopolitan bars, chic bistros and crowded alternative hangouts of **Zürich West** – particularly on and off Langstrasse and Hardstrasse – although you'll find that the northern half of **Niederdorf**, bang in the city centre, has some of the same vibe. The **industrial quarter** northwest of Langstrasse is where the best underground clubs hide themselves; venues move, nights change and new places open virtually every month. Check flyers in Zap Records, Zähringerstrasse 47; Get Records, Marktgasse 13; or Discoverart, Dienerstrasse 64. Most places open at 10–11pm and close by about 4am, although a few stay open until 7am or later on the weekend. Entry is usually Fr.10–15.

Dynamo Wasserwerkstrasse 21 ⓦwww.dynamo.ch. Alternative sounds, everything from guitar-based pop to the deepest drum'n'bass.

El Cubanito Bleicherweg 5. Famed salsa and funk club.

Geroldstrasse 17. Cutting-edge house venue in the industrial quarter.

Kaufleuten Pelikanstrasse 18. Plush city-centre nightspot, its housey, groovey beats drawing an unusual blend of hardcore clubbers and work-to-play young professionals. Voted one of the world's best party venues by the *Wall Street Journal* (which says it all). Dress to impress.

Labyrinth Pfingstweidstrasse 70 @ www.laby.ch. Hard house firing up an energetic mixed gay/straight crowd.

Oxa Andreasstrasse 70. Premier venue for techno and house, with two dance floors, a garden and even a restaurant; famous for its after-hours parties (Sun 5am–noon).

Pentagon Hardplatz 7. Celebrated hotspot staging a roster of international DJs playing house, R'n'B and soul.

Q Förrlibuckstrasse 151 @ www.club-q.ch. Three dance floors on two levels throbbing with cutting-edge house. Saturday late until 10am.

Rohstofflager Binzmühlestrasse 86, Oerlikon. Lively mix of DJs and live bands.

Rote Fabrik Seestrasse 395 @ www.rotefabrik.ch. Subculture venue with changing nights and big-name DJs.

Toni Molkerei Förrlibuckstrasse 109 @ www.tonimolkerei.com. Eclectic, highly acclaimed and popular house and techno club occupying a vast 3000-square-metre industrial space. Has the unique attribute of vegetarian bar food by *Hiltl* (see p.451).

UG Geroldstrasse 5 @ www.ugclub.ch. Throbbing disco, funk and hip-hoppy joint.

X-tra Limmatstrasse 118 @ www.x-tra.ch. Hugely popular multipurpose venue just off Limmatplatz, with triphop and funky sounds entertaining a youngish crowd. Bar and restaurant adjacent, and *Hotel Limmat* upstairs.

Film

Zürich's **cinemas** are mostly two- or three-screen houses showing the latest releases, almost always in their original language, although afternoon shows are sometimes dubbed. Check in the listings for "E/d/f", which means English spoken with German and French subtitles. Non-English-language films are rarely given English subtitles. Prices are universally high (Fr.15–17) but every cinema in the city has cut-price Fr.11 tickets for all shows on Mondays. City-centre cinemas showing Hollywood releases abound, but there are a few

Gay and lesbian Zürich

Zürich has a thriving **gay and lesbian** scene, probably the best established and most diverse in the country. No hotel will turn a gay or lesbian couple away; however, the *Goldenes Schwert* (see p.430) is the only hotel to make a selling point of its gay- and lesbian-friendliness; handily enough, it occupies the same building as *T&M* (@www.gaybar.ch), one of the best gay bar/cabaret/disco venues in the city, dark, campy and cruisey. The huge *Barfüsser*, Spitalgasse 14 (@www.barfuesser.ch) – recently reinvented as a "Café-Bar-Sushi" joint – is Europe's longest-running gay bar, established in 1956 and embracing all scenes, while *Cranberry* (see p.448) is a more relaxed, talkative meeting place for non-scene types. The "Bermuda Triangle" is a cruisey area around Mühlegasse, epitomized by *Emilio's Bagpiper* ("where you meet the right people") at Zähringerstrasse 11. *Labyrinth*, Pfingstweidstrasse 70, is a hugely popular gay/straight techno club; *Aera*, Albulastrasse 38, is an all-gay venue; and *Profi-Treff*, Sihlquai 240, has a gay night every Wednesday. *Osoba*, Kasernenstrasse 77a, is a gay-friendly restaurant with an innovative cuisine blending European, Asian and South American flavours. **Lesbians** must rely on a smaller scene, focused around the monthly women-only nights at the *Kanzlei* bar (see p.449) and adjacent *Xenix* cinema. *Profi-Treff*, Sihlquai 240, has a lesbian night every second Saturday. *Lady's First* (see p.431) and *Haus zur Stauffacherin* (see p.430) are both women-only hotels.

For more **information**, contact HAZ (Homosexuelle Arbeitsgruppen Zürich) at Sihlquai 67, 3rd floor (Wed 2–6pm; ☎01 271 22 50, @www.haz.ch); they also run the sociable Café Centro weekly (Fri 7.30–11.30pm). Zürich's Christopher Street Day Parade website (@www.csdzh.ch) has loads of useful links.

art-house cinemas with daily changing programmes of retrospectives and non-commercial movies from around the world, including Xenix, Kanzleistrasse 56 at Helvetiaplatz (🌐www.xenix.ch); Filmpodium im Studio 4, Nüschelerstrasse 11; and Riff Raff, Neugasse 57 (🌐www.riffraff.ch).

Classical music, opera and theatre

The acoustically superb Tonhalle concert hall, Claridenstrasse 7 (🌐www .tonhalle.ch), inaugurated by Brahms in 1895, has a programme of world-class **classical music** of all kinds from both the resident Tonhalle and Zürich Chamber orchestras and guest performers. Many of Zürich's churches – principally the Grossmünster, Fraumünster, Predigerkirche and St Peter's – host regular concerts of organ, choral and chamber music, as does the Conservatory (Florhofgasse 6; 🌐www.hmt.edu), the *Dolder Grand Hotel* (see p.432) and the Kunsthaus. The city's large Opernhaus (🌐www.opernhaus.ch) has an impressive programme of both **opera and ballet** – performances sell out quickly.

The Schauspielhaus **theatre**, Rämistrasse 34 (🌐www.schauspielhaus.ch), is one of the German-speaking world's finest: during World War II, it was Europe's only German-language theatre that continued to stage productions independent of Nazi censorship. The main stage – now known as Schauspielhaus Pfauen – remains Zürich's most prestigious, while the cellar-studio hosts avant-garde productions. The Schauspielhaus Schiffbau, in the converted Schiffbau building off Hardstrasse (see p.447), also has both a main stage ("Halle") and a studio stage ("Box"). Zürich has more than a dozen other theatres, big and small, presenting everything from tragedy to puppetry – but rarely in English.

Listings

Books Zürich's best English bookshop – complete with Rough Guides – is Orell Füssli, Bahnhofstrasse 70. The Travel Bookshop, Rindermarkt 20, is another good source.

Changing money Best is the change bureau in the station (daily 6.30am–10.45pm).

Consulates Ireland, Claridenstrasse 25 ☎01 289 25 15; UK, Minervastrasse 117 ☎01 383 65 60; USA, Dufourstrasse 101 ☎01 422 25 66. Other English-speaking countries are represented by their embassies in Bern (see p.258) or consulates in Geneva (see p.112).

Flights Zürich-Kloten airport flight enquiries ☎0900 300 313 or ☎01 812 12 12, 🌐www.unique.ch. For a train ticket to the airport from the city centre, press 8058 on the ticket machines. The Motorfluggruppe Zürich (☎01 813 74 63) offers sightseeing flights long and short (April–Oct only), from Fr.96 per person.

Football and ice-hockey Zürich is the home of FIFA and the famous Grasshoppers (☎01 447 46 46, 🌐www.gcz.ch) – once one of Europe's top football teams, and still regularly in the Swiss top three. They play at Hardturm stadium in Zürich

West, not far from Letzigrund, home of the city's other club, FC Zürich (☎01 492 74 74, 🌐www.fcz.ch). Regular attendances for both hover around 8000; you can just turn up to see a game. In the national sport, ice-hockey, Grasshoppers' team (☎01 317 20 72) is also pre-eminent, and there's a host of other Zürich teams involved.

Laundry Mühlegasse 11, Niederdorf (Mon–Fri 7.30am–noon & 1–6.30pm).

Lost property The city office is at Werdmühleplatz 10 (Mon–Fri 7.30am–5.30pm; ☎01 216 51 11). The station office is near the head of platform 17 (daily 7am–6pm).

Medical facilities Most convenient is the Permanence Medical Centre at Bahnhofplatz 15 (daily 7am–11pm, but with a 24-hour emergency room; ☎01 215 44 44). Alongside it is the Bahnhof Apotheke pharmacy (daily 7am–midnight).

Police Headquarters is at Bahnhofquai 3 ☎01 216 71 11.

Post Zürich's main post office is the Sihlpost, an unmissable behemoth poised over the River Sihl next to the main station on Kasernenstrasse

(Mon–Fri 6.30am–10.30pm, Sat 6.30am–8pm, Sun 11am–10.30pm). You can collect mail sent to you at Poste Restante, Schalter 8, Sihlpost, CH-8021 Zürich, from counter 8. There's also a post office within the station and dozens more around town.

Supermarkets Largest and most convenient central supermarket is the Coop, on Bahnhofbrücke (Mon–Fri 7am–8pm, Sat 7am–4pm). The Migros in the Shopville complex beneath the station is open late and on Sundays.

Around the Zürichsee

A pleasant day-trip leads out of the city around the long, slender **ZÜRICHSEE**, nestling between the parallel ridges of the Uetliberg to the west and the Pfannenstiel opposite. Basing yourself in lakeside communities such as **Küsnacht** or **Rapperswil** has obvious benefits of tranquillity and value for money over staying in the centre of Zürich, and also allows you to take advantage of a tradition of gastronomic excellence: lakeside restaurants together boast a total of eight Michelin stars, more than in Zürich and Geneva combined. Kids aren't forgotten either, with a waterpark at **Pfäffikon**, a petting zoo in Rapperswil and – perhaps most importantly – a real-life chocolate factory at **Kilchberg**.

The best way to go is by **boat** – ZSG ferries (see p.428) stop at every lakeside town in summer – while picturesque S-Bahn **train** lines run the length of both shores. Küsnacht is a scant ten-minute train ride out of town, Rapperswil a half-hour more. The lake beyond Rapperswil is known as the **Obersee**, served by boats and trains as far as Schmerikon.

The eastern and western shores

Heading along the **eastern shore**, you leave the city and plunge directly into a comfortable, leafy world of trimmed hedges and car dealerships. The unremarkable suburb of **KÜSNACHT**, 7km south, is made significant by its outstanding hospitality, notably the *Ermitage* and *Sonne* hotels (see p.431), and *Le Pavillon* and *Petermann's Kunststuben* restaurants (see p.452). One possibility for relaxed exploration is 15km south in **STÄFA**, a mildly picturesque village clustered at the foot of the Pfannenstiel, in the largest vine-growing region in the canton. From Stäfa, Rapperswil lies 12km south.

From Zürich's Bürkliplatz, it's 6km along the lake's **western shore** by bus #165, boat or S-Bahn train to the dormitory town of **KILCHBERG**, yawn-worthy but for the fragrant presence of the huge Lindt & Sprüngli **chocolate factory**, which is open for public visits (Wed–Fri 10am–noon & 1–4pm; free). Frustratingly, the company refuses to let anyone near the production line; instead, you're diverted to a small museum, shown a video and then escorted out with your well-earned prize of free chocolate. As you head south, suburbia fades away, replaced by evidence of a more down-to-earth, rural existence that feels a long way from the Zürich hubbub. Past the old warehouses of **Wädenswil**, from where trains branch off into the hills to Einsiedeln (see p.408), is **PFÄFFIKON**, 23km south of Kilchberg in an outpost of Canton Schwyz (and so named on timetables as "Pfäffikon SZ" to differentiate it from another Pfäffikon nearby). Here sits the huge, and very popular, **Alpamare waterpark** (Tues–Thurs 10am–10pm, Fri 10am–midnight, Sat 9am–midnight, Sun & Mon 9am–10pm; day-pass Fr.42, four-hour pass Fr.32; ⓦ www.alpamare.ch), replete with slides, flumes, heated wave pools, saunas and plenty more. Rapperswil is a short distance across the lake by road or rail.

Rapperswil

Lying 37km south of Zürich, the small lakefront town of **RAPPERSWIL** repays a gentle afternoon's exploration. Avoid the humdrum modern part of town and lose yourself in the quiet Old Town alleys, which weave around and between a succession of plazas. Prettiest is **Fischmarktplatz**, not least because it's open to the lake, lined with terrace cafés and has a shaded promenade alongside a little marina. A lane or two back is a Capuchin monastery dating from 1597, with, beside the main gate, a delightful walled **rose-garden** – one of a handful around town that support Rapperswil's moniker "City of Roses". Alleys climb to the dour thirteenth-century **castle** (Ⓦ www.schloss-rapperswil .ch), with its small museum (April–Oct daily 1–5pm; Fr.4) devoted to Switzerland's Polish community. Signposted south, a short walk from the station, is the **Knies Kinderzoo** (Children's Zoo; March–Oct daily 9am–6pm; Fr.8; Ⓦ www.knieskinderzoo.ch), with animals to pet and feed and elephants and ponies to ride.

The **train station** stands on the edge of the Old Town; head left and cross the road to reach Fischmarktplatz, where, behind Parkhaus 1 See, is the **tourist office** (Mon–Fri 8.30am–5pm, Sat & Sun 10am–5pm; Nov–March Mon–Fri same hours, Sat & Sun 1–5pm; ℡ 0848 811 500, Ⓦ www.zuerichsee.ch). Staff have information on the whole lakeshore. The most characterful **hotel** is the fresh, attractive *Hirschen*, Fischmarktplatz 7 (℡ 055 220 61 80, Ⓦ www.hirschen-rapperswil.ch; ❸), not far from the easygoing *Jakob*, Hauptplatz 11 (℡ 055 220 57 57, Ⓦ www.jakob-hotel.ch; ❸). A little way inland near Jona is an HI **hostel**, *Jugendherberge Busskirch*, Hessenhofweg 10 (℡ 055 210 99 27, Ⓦ www.youthhostel.ch), with dorm beds for Fr.32.

Best **restaurant** is *Schloss Rapperswil* (℡ 055 210 18 28), with a fine location within the castle and outstanding fish and seafood that has won it a Michelin star; expect Fr.60 for the set lunch, Fr.140 in the evening. A good runner-up is *Tante Charlotte* in *Hotel Bellevue*, Marktgasse 21 (℡ 055 220 66 30), with similarly impressive fare for slightly less outlay, while waterfront *Au Premier*, Fischmarktplatz 2, serves the catch of the day for an affordable Fr.20–30. A stroll through the Old Town will turn up plenty of other places to eat, and there's a *Manora* self-service at Neue Jonastrasse 20.

Travel details

Trains

Zürich HB to: Adliswil (every 20min; 15min); airport (4–7 hourly; 10min); Baden (every 30min; 15min); Basel (every 30min; 1hr); Bellinzona (hourly; 2hr 30min); Bern (every 30min; 1hr 10min); Biel/Bienne (hourly; 1hr 30min); Chur (hourly; 1hr 35min); Einsiedeln (every 30min; 45min – change at Wädenswil); Flughafen/Airport (4–7 hourly; 10min); Fribourg (every 30min; 1hr 40min); Geneva (every 30min; 3hr); Interlaken Ost (hourly; 2hr 15min); Lausanne (every 30min; 2hr 30min); Lugano (hourly; 3hr); Luzern (hourly; 50min); Neuchâtel (hourly; 1hr 50min); St Gallen (every 30min; 1hr 10min); Sargans (hourly; 1hr 10min); Schaffhausen (hourly; 40min); Solothurn (hourly; 1hr 5min); Uetliberg (every 30min; 25min); Winterthur (4 hourly; 20min); Zug (twice hourly; 25min).

Boats

(Following is a summary of April–Oct services; fewer boats run in other months, quite often only on Sun, if at all.)
Zürich (Bürkliplatz) to: Rapperswil (hourly; 1hr 45min); Schmerikon (twice daily; 3hr 20min).

Ostschweiz and Liechtenstein

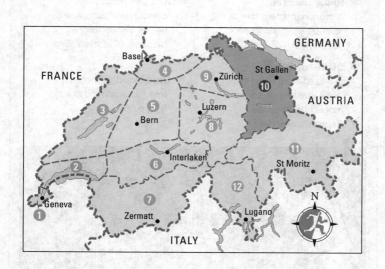

10

OSTSCHWEIZ AND LIECHTENSTEIN

CHAPTER 10

Highlights

✳ **Winterthur** Easygoing city with an array of world-class art museums. **See p.464**

✳ **Schaffhausen** Beautiful but little-visited market town, crammed with superb medieval architecture. **See p.468**

✳ **Rhine falls** The Wagnerian spectacle of Europe's largest waterfall. **See p.472**

✳ **Stein-am-Rhein** Switzerland's most picturesque village square, ringed by frescoed facades. **See p.474**

✳ **Abbey library, St Gallen** A breathtaking Rococo interior, lined with books from floor to ceiling. **See p.483**

✳ **Appenzell** Quiet, rustic village set amidst the craggy Alpstein range. **See p.485**

✳ **Klausen Pass** Spectacular pass road, one of the country's most scenic drives. **See p.489**

✳ **Braunwald** Remote car-free mountain hideaway. **See p.489**

10

Ostschweiz and Liechtenstein

S
witzerland's rural northeast – known as **Ostschweiz** – is one of the least celebrated areas of the country, and is often sidelined by tourists anxious to get to the famous Alpine regions further south. Which, of course, means that you can enjoy the mountains and lakes, medieval town centres and rolling verdant countryside in relative peace, free from hard-sell tourism and the glitz and glamour of big-name resorts. Most visitors haven't even heard of the main city of the northeast, **St Gallen**, and yet its magnificent Baroque cathedral and well-preserved medieval town centre make it a major cultural landmark. Just to the west, **Winterthur** has a set of excellent museums to complement its urban neighbour, Zürich. Immediately south of St Gallen lies the hilly backcountry of **Appenzell**, sheltering a close-knit, still largely isolated community of farmers and craftspeople occupying the foothills of the Alpstein range. The Säntis peak tops 2500m – mediocre in Swiss terms, but still tall enough to enjoy plenty of snow, vistas stretching to the horizon and quality hiking in the web of valleys beneath it. Further south, walled in by Alpine giants, is isolated **Glarnerland**.

The River Rhine, which bulges out into the huge **Bodensee** in Switzerland's northeast corner, throws a protective loop around this part of

Exploring Ostschweiz

Local Swiss, German and Austrian tourist boards market the region strongly, focusing on the main draw for tourists from their own countries: the Bodensee. There are several different passes that give discounts to attractions all round the lake. Best choice is probably the **Bodensee Erlebniskarte** (Fr.73 for 3 days, also available for longer periods; mid-March to mid-Oct only; ⊛www.bodenseeferien.de); this gives free transport on all boats on the lake and the Rhine; free admission to Insel Mainau, the St Gallen abbey library, the two Appenzell museums, Museum Lindwurm in Stein-am-Rhein and dozens more attractions; free travel up the Säntis and other mountains; free guided tours of Schaffhausen, St Gallen, Konstanz, and so on. It's available from tourist offices all through the region. Alternatives, with complex zone networks and tariffs, are the **EuRegio Tageskarte** (⊛www.euregiokarte.com) and **Ostwind Tageskarte** (⊛www.ostwind.ch). For information on the whole region (not including Winterthur), contact Ostschweiz Tourismus (☎071 227 37 37, ⊛www.ostschweiz-i.ch).

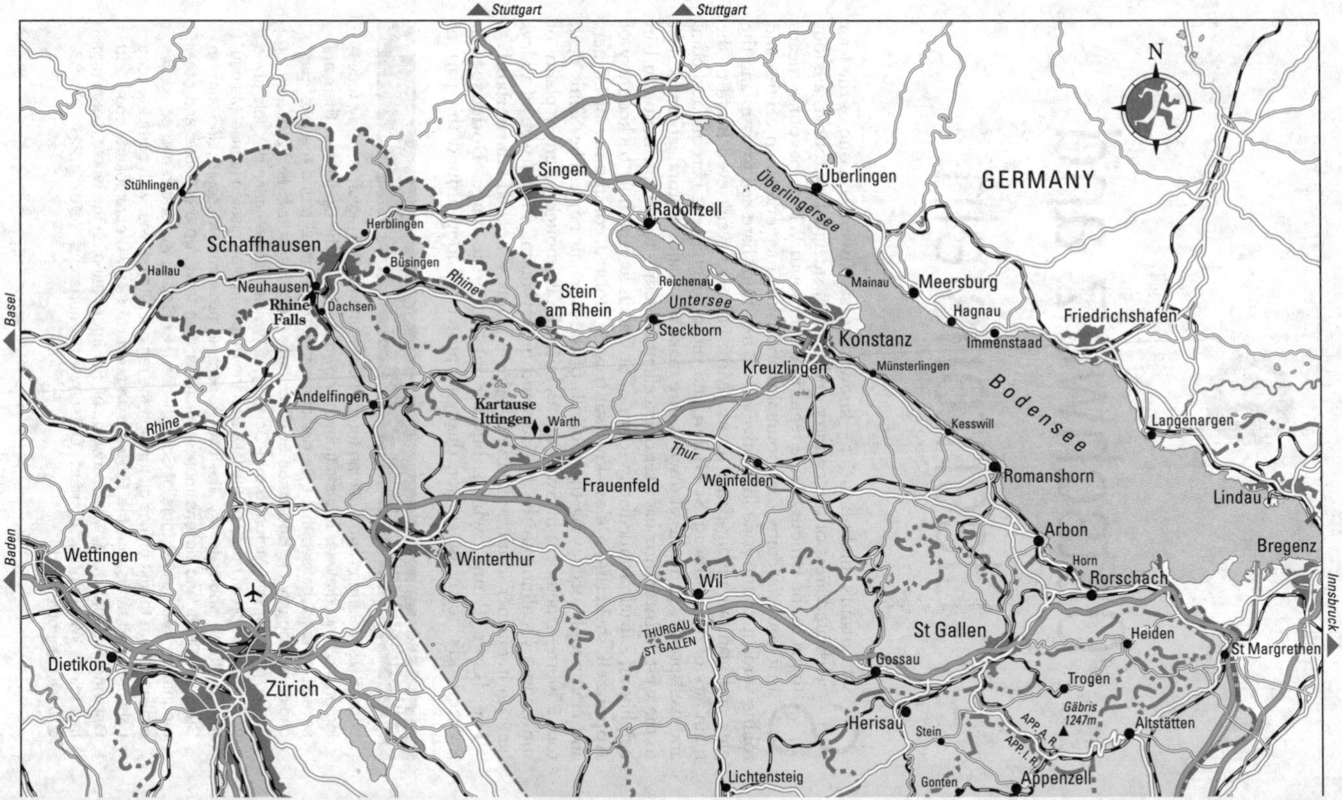
Stuttgart
Stuttgart
Basel
Baden
Innsbruck
N
GERMANY
Stühlingen
Schaffhausen
Hallau
Neuhausen
Rhine Falls
Dachsen
Herblingen
Büsingen
Rhine
Singen
Radolfzell
Stein am Rhein
Reichenau
Untersee
Steckborn
Überlingen
Überlingersee
Mainau
Meersburg
Hagnau
Immenstaad
Friedrichshafen
Konstanz
Kreuzlingen
Münsterlingen
Bodensee
Kesswill
Langenargen
Lindau
Bregenz
Andelfingen
Kartause Ittingen
Warth
Rhine
Thur
Frauenfeld
Weinfelden
Romanshorn
Arbon
Horn
Rorschach
Wettingen
Winterthur
Wil
THURGAU
ST GALLEN
St Gallen
Heiden
St Margrethen
Dietikon
Zürich
Gossau
Trogen
Gäbris 1247m
Herisau
Stein
APP. A. R.
APP. I. R.
Altstätten
Lichtensteig
Gonten
Appenzell

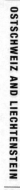

Switzerland, forming international frontiers with Germany to the north, and Austria and the tiny independent statelet of **Liechtenstein** to the east. At the westernmost tip of the lake, the cosmopolitan German city of **Konstanz** is divided from its Swiss twin of **Kreuzlingen** only by an arbitrary frontier between buildings. The beautiful river journey west from Kreuzlingen runs past **Stein-am-Rhein**, an almost perfectly preserved medieval village boasting spectacular sixteenth- and seventeenth-century frescoes and one of the country's best small historical museums, and ends at the atmospheric medieval town of **Schaffhausen**, dubbed "Rheinfallstadt" for its proximity to the mighty **Rhine falls**, the largest waterfall in Europe.

Winterthur

A peaceful city of almost 100,000, set in rolling countryside on the River Töss 25km northeast of Zürich, **WINTERTHUR** boasts a volley of impressive art museums, displaying Old Masters, classic Modernists, Impressionists and contemporary photography. It lies in Canton Zürich, a little way west of Ostschweiz proper.

Evidence of a nearby settlement, Vitudurum, goes back to the first century, but the city dates its history from 1264, when it was granted status by the Habsburg king Rudolf. The Industrial Revolution powered the city's meteoric growth during the nineteenth century, and after 1848 it also became the centre of Switzerland's democratic movement. Local architects and engineers visited England in mid-century to study designs for factories and workers' housing, bringing English ideas back to Winterthur's booming textile and railway industries. Most Swiss today still indelibly associate Winterthur – the country's sixth-largest city – with industry: it has pulled off the transition into hi-tech, and remains an energetic place. It's also surprisingly green, and the combination of students, bicycles, green hills and world-class art galleries can make for a pleasant day or two.

Arrival, information and accommodation

Winterthur lies partway along the main road and rail lines between Zürich and St Gallen, at a junction of routes by train and road to both Schaffhausen and Stein-am-Rhein. The **station** is centrally located, and hosts the helpful **tourist office** (Mon–Fri 8.30am–6.30pm, Sat 8.30am–4pm; ☎052 267 67 00, ⓦwww.winterthur-tourismus.ch), which offers a guided **tour** of town

Winterthur's festivals

The most popular of the town's annual events is the **Albanifäscht** (ⓦwww.albanifest .ch), a weekend of live rock music and jazz held in late June. The **Kyburgiade** (ⓦwww.kyburgiade.ch) is a week-long series of chamber music concerts held in early August in the romantic setting of Kyburg castle. The **Musikfestwochen** (ⓦwww.musikfestwochen.ch), in late August and early September, see Winterthur's Old Town taken over for live music of all kinds. If you're around in May, ask at the tourist office about the **Eschenberg-Schwinget**, a folksy festival of traditional wrestling held in a nearby meadow, and **Jodlersonntag** (Yodelling Sunday). In May, Whitsun is celebrated in Winterthur in an unusual fashion as **Afro-Pfingsten** (ⓦwww.afro-pfingsten.ch), a kind of mini-carnival of African music, dance and food.

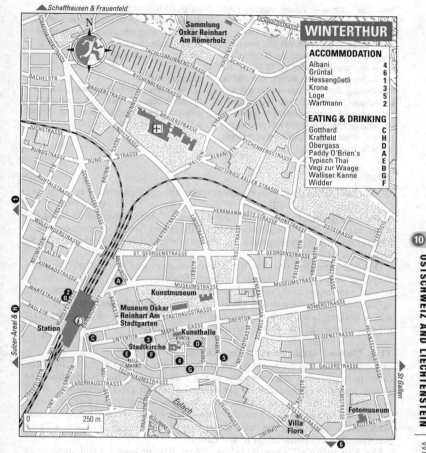

Map labels:

Schaffhausen & Frauenfeld

WINTERTHUR

ACCOMMODATION
Albani	4
Grüntal	6
Hessengüetli	1
Krone	3
Loge	5
Wartmann	2

EATING & DRINKING
Gotthard	C
Kraftfeld	H
Obergass	D
Paddy O'Brien's	A
Typisch Thai	E
Vegi zur Waage	B
Walliser Kanne	G
Widder	F

Sammlung Oskar Reinhart Am Römerholz

Kunstmuseum

Museum Oskar Reinhart Am Stadtgarten

Station

Kunsthalle

Stadtkirche

Fotomuseum

Villa Flora

Eulach

0   250 m

Sulzer-Areal &

St Gallen

10

OSTSCHWEIZ AND LIECHTENSTEIN | Winterthur

(May–Oct: 1st & 3rd Sat of month 10am; Fr.15; 1hr 30min) as well as the **Museumspass**, which gives free entry to all the city museums for one/two/three days (Fr.20/25/28). Ask, too, about the Kunst-Weekend offer, comprising B&B and free museum entry over two/three days (from Fr.87/149). Weekly food **markets** are held in Steinberggasse (Tues & Fri 6–11am). **Accommodation** is geared largely towards the business trade, though prices are still generally lower than Zürich; you should always book ahead.

Hotels

Albani Steinberggasse 16 ☎052 212 69 96, Ⓦwww.albani.ch. Best budget hotel, above the famous Old Town club and music venue just south of Kirchplatz. The OK rooms are big and well kept, but aren't ensuite and there's no breakfast. Free entry for gigs downstairs. Don't bother phoning before 3pm. ②

Grüntal Im Grüntal 1 ☎052 232 25 52, Ⓕ052 232 25 33. Solid country inn at a quiet crossroads 4.5km southeast of town, with hospitality, good service and pleasant rooms. Bus #6 to Grüntal. Phone ahead, as it's closed for walk-in arrivals Tues & Wed. ②

Hessengüetli Oberfeldstrasse 10 ☎052 224 32 32, Ⓦwww.hessengueetli.ch. A tiny, family-run

465

hotel above a Chinese–Vietnamese restaurant 1.5km northwest of the centre, with a stream on one side and the wooded Brüelberg rising behind. Their ensuite rooms are good value, and you'll have no trouble with car or bike parking. Bus #2 to Feldtal. ❷
Krone Marktgasse 49 ☎ 052 208 18 18, ⓦ www.kronewinterthur.ch. Historic renovated Old Town building, stylish and super-comfortable. ❹
Loge Graben 6 ☎ 052 268 12 00, ⓦ www.hotel-loge.ch. Modern and very quiet Old Town hotel – go for the light, top-floor rooms with panoramic balcony. On-site parking. Good value, at the lower end of this category. ❹

Wartmann Rudolfstrasse 15 ☎ 052 260 07 07, ⓦ www.wartmann.ch. Quality business hotel in a renovated building dating from 1894 just behind the train station. Has the *Vegi zur Waage* restaurant onsite (see p.468). ❸–❹

Campsite
Am Schützenweiher Eichliwaldstrasse 4 ☎ 052 212 52 60. Good site 1500m north of town, with access onto the forested Wolfensberg; take bus #3 to Seuzacherstrasse, then walk 300m.

The Town

Winterthur's main draw is its excellent **museums**, principally the two separate Oskar Reinhart art collections – one housed in the town centre ("Am Stadtgarten"), the other on a hill near the town ("Am Römerholz") – and the Kunstmuseum. The Fotomuseum and Villa Flora are close runners-up. A Museumspass (see p.465) grants discounted admission, but note that they're all **closed on Mondays**.

The pedestrianized Old Town has some charm once you get off the main shopping streets – the elegant medieval Stadtkirche, for example, with its kitschy modern murals, is worth a look. If Victorian industrial architecture lights your fire, head southwest under the tracks into the **Sulzer–Areal** district, where hulking brick-built factories are slowly being reclaimed as atmospheric theatre spaces, bars and skating arenas.

The Oskar Reinhart museums

Oskar Reinhart was born into a local trading family in 1885. Aged 41, he withdrew from business and moved into the hilltop villa "Am Römerholz" to devote himself to his passion for art. When he died in 1965, part of his collection – one of the leading private art collections assembled in Europe in the twentieth century – passed to the municipality (and is now housed in the Stadtgarten museum), and the remaining 200 paintings and his villa at Römerholz were bequeathed to the nation.

The **Sammlung Oskar Reinhart "Am Römerholz"**, Haldenstrasse 95 (Tues–Sun 10am–5pm; Fr.8, joint ticket with "Am Stadtgarten" Fr.12; SMP; ⓦ www.kultur-schweiz.admin.ch/sor), is an idiosyncratic mingling of styles and periods, brought together more for each piece's artistic qualities than as an attempt to form a representative overview of any one artist or genre. There are works from fifteenth- and sixteenth-century German masters, including Matthias Grünewald, Lukas Cranach the Elder and Hans Holbein the Younger; a small group of Italian and Spanish works, including by El Greco and Goya; and fifteenth- to seventeenth-century Dutch and Flemish painting dominated by Brueghel, Rubens, Hals and Rembrandt. Many pieces from French Baroque, Neoclassical and Romantic artists – including some of Delacroix's best portraits – lead on to Reinhart's marvellous Impressionist collection, with a range of works by Renoir, Manet, Degas and many more. The museum has a lovely sunny café where you can catch your breath.

Back in the town, the **Museum Oskar Reinhart "Am Stadtgarten"**, Stadthausstrasse 6 (Tues 10am–8pm, Wed–Sun 10am–5pm; Fr.8; SMP; ⓦ www.museumoskarreinhart.ch), is of less general interest, concentrating on

To get to and from the Römerholz collection, some distance from town on a hilltop, the city runs a **Museumsbus**. Minibuses depart from the station (Tues–Sun hourly 9.45am–4.45pm), picking up at the town-centre Stadtgarten and nearby Kunstmuseum a few minutes later, and dropping off at the gates of the Römerholz gallery. Departures from there back to town are on the hour 10am to 5pm. The Fr.5 fare is valid all day. On Sundays the bus makes extra stops at the Villa Flora and the Fotomuseum. Otherwise, reaching the Römerholz collection involves city bus #3 to Spital and a stiff ten- or fifteen-minute climb.

German, Swiss and Austrian artists from the eighteenth to the twentieth centuries. On the ground floor are a few rooms of portraits by local artists including Graff and Füssli. On the floor above are Romantic Swiss landscapes, and up another floor are some marvellous studies of children by the Swiss artist Albert Anker, and works by Hodler, Segantini and Giovanni Giacometti. The top-floor extension features changing exhibitions.

Other museums

Just across the Stadtgarten lies the **Kunstmuseum**, Museumstrasse 52 (Tues 10am–8pm, Wed–Sun 10am–5pm; Fr.10; SMP; ⓦ www.kmw.ch), with a spectacular collection covering international art over the last century. The tour begins upstairs, with a room devoted to Van Gogh, Monet, Rousseau and sculpture by Picasso and Rodin. Hodler and a Cubist room lead on to a Surrealist selection topped by Miró and a rare self-portrait by De Chirico. Works by Brancusi lead into the high-ceilinged, white-walled extension, dominated by Mondrian, American artists and sculpture by Alberto Giacometti. The **Kunsthalle**, nearby at Marktgasse 25 (Tues–Fri 2–6pm, Sat 10am–noon & 2–4pm, Sun 2–4pm; free), stages changing shows of contemporary art.

The critic Paul Graham has called Winterthur's **Fotomuseum**, Grüzenstrasse 44 (Tues–Fri noon–6pm, Wed until 7.30pm, Sat & Sun 11am–5pm; Fr.8; SMP; ⓦ www.fotomuseum.ch), "the most beautiful museum of photography in Europe", and it's easy to see why. Housed in a brick-built renovated former warehouse, it's light, bright and open, and benefits further from its policy of staging five or six top-notch annual exhibitions each year. It lies a walkable 400m southeast from the Old Town, off Tösstalstrasse (or bus #2 to Schleife).

Nearby is the **Villa Flora**, Tösstalstrasse 44 (Tues–Sat 2–5pm, Sun 11am–3pm; Fr.8; ⓦ www.villaflora.ch), newly renovated, which houses the private collection of Hedy Hahnloser, built up between 1907 and 1930. It comprises a small but high-quality selection – on continuous rotation – of French Post-Impressionism, Fauvist and Nabi works (Bonnard, Matisse, Vallotton and more) fleshed out with earlier works by Cézanne, Van Gogh and others.

Eating, drinking and nightlife

You'll have no trouble finding places to **eat and drink**. If you're watching every penny, nosh in the *EVA* department store beside the station, or at the *Widder*. **Nightlife** can be surprisingly good, with all-night bars around the station, lively music bars on Neumarkt, some rougher student/biker dives along Technikumstrasse and a handful of weekend dance clubs.

Restaurants and cafés
Obergass Obergasse corner Schulgasse. Quiet easy-going café to eat, read and drink in, with a

wide range of food, veggie and not, for Fr.14–25. Closed Sun.

Typisch Thai Neumarkt 3. Full range of Thai dishes,

The best of the four castles near Winterthur is **Schloss Kyburg**, 7km south (May–Oct Tues–Sun 10.30am–5.30pm; Feb–April & Nov closes 4.30pm; Fr.8). Dating from the tenth and eleventh centuries, it's majestically sited above the Töss river and plays host in early August to a chamber music festival. Postbus #655 from the train station in Effretikon (a suburb of Winterthur) runs to Kyburg. Thirteenth-century **Schloss Mörsburg**, 6km northeast of town near Stadel (March–Oct Tues–Sun 10am–noon & 1.30–5pm; Nov–Feb Sun 10am–noon & 1.30–5pm; free), is accessible only by car (via Sulz). It has a lovely Romanesque chapel and excavated ramparts, plus a small museum of ceramics, handicrafts and weapons. Fifteenth-century **Schloss Hegi** (March–Oct Tues–Thurs & Sat 2–5pm, Sun 10am–noon & 2–5pm; free; bus #10 or #680 to Schlossacker) is 3km east of town, more of a moated mansion than a castle. **Schloss Wülflingen**, a stout sixteenth-century stately home 4km northwest of town, is now a conference centre and pricey traditional restaurant (closed Mon & Tues).

with friendly service and plenty for veggies. Fr.12–15 for lunch, double in the evenings. Closed Mon.

Vegi zur Waage Rudolfstrasse 15. Behind the station, an excellent-value café and all-day restaurant, cosy and bright. *Menus* can be Fr.15, or all you can eat for Fr.21, with a Sri Lankan buffet every evening. Mon–Fri 6am–11pm.

Walliser Kanne Steinberggasse 25. Quality Swiss specialities, served in classic style, with subdued decor and a calm atmosphere. Around Fr.35. Closed Sat & Sun (Oct–March open Sat eve).

Widder Metzgasse 9. Subculture Old Town café-bar, with long wooden tables and loud music. Exceptionally good food, well prepared and in massive portions for under Fr.15. Fri & Sat until 2am.

Bars and clubs

Albani Steinberggasse 16. Smallish Old Town bar and venue well able to draw Zürchers out into the sticks with a quality programme of DJs and live music – previous headliners have included Pearl Jam and Sheryl Crow. Weekend nights are packed. Fr.15 or so for bands.

Gotthard Untertor 34, opposite station. Switzerland's first-ever 24-hour bar, a young, friendly joint that's a peaceful café during the day; at night it attracts a few lowlifes but avoids the sleaze of its Bahnhofplatz neighbours.

Kraftfeld Off Tössfeldstrasse in Sulzer-Areal industrial quarter, 100m beyond Brockenhalle junk shop ⓦ www.kraftfeld.ch. Alternative artists' community which lays on hectic DJ nights featuring experimental drum'n'bass, plus occasional concerts, films and happenings. Tues, Wed & Fri 11pm–6am. Wandering around the nearby streets will turn up similar post-industrial venues: the *Labüsch Bar*, the Aussie-styled *Outback Lodge*, and others.

Paddy O'Brien's Merkurstrasse 25 ⓦ www .paddyobriens.ch. Quality Irish pub five minutes north of the station to warm your jaded cockles, with 12 beers on tap, TV football and enough of a reputation to pull in The Dubliners for a gig now and again. Daily 3pm–2am.

Schaffhausen and around

Capital of the northernmost Swiss canton that shares its name, **SCHAFFHAUSEN** has one of the most captivating medieval town centres in the whole of Switzerland as well as, just 4km downriver, the mighty **Rhine falls** – and yet it remains uncelebrated, as if too far north to be of concern to most visitors to Switzerland. Adding to the allure is the stunning medieval village of **Stein-am-Rhein**, within easy reach upriver.

A bankside docking point had already developed into the thriving market town of Scafusun by 1045 (the name of the town probably derives from its many riverside boathouses). It grew rapidly, handling salt and cereals from Bavaria and the Tyrol and joining the Swiss Confederation in 1501. The town

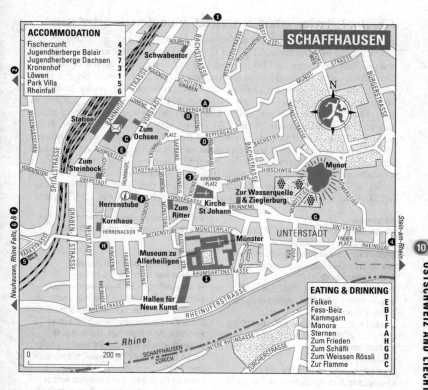

SCHAFFHAUSEN

ACCOMMODATION

Fischerzunft	4
Jugendherberge Belair	2
Jugendherberge Dachsen	7
Kronenhof	3
Löwen	1
Park Villa	5
Rheinfall	6

EATING & DRINKING

Falken	E
Fass-Beiz	B
Kammgarn	I
Manora	F
Sternen	A
Zum Frieden	H
Zum Schäfli	G
Zum Weissen Rössli	D
Zur Flamme	C

10

maintained steady growth, its eighteenth-century merchants indulging in the fashion for adding ornate **oriel windows** to the Gothic or Renaissance buildings, both to demonstrate the houseowner's wealth and good taste, and also to give people inside a clear view up and down the street. With 170-odd examples on show, Schaffhausen's nickname *Erkerstadt* ("City of Oriel Windows") is well-earned.

Hydroelectric works, built to exploit the flow of the Rhine, brought the area into the industrial age. During **World War II**, Schaffhausen was the only Swiss town to be bombed by Allied aircraft: about 100 civilians were killed by American bombers on April 1, 1944. The US claimed that pilots had mistakenly identified Schaffhausen – the only sizeable chunk of Swiss territory on the north bank of the Rhine – as a German target. They apologized profusely and paid out compensation… only to make the same mistake again on February 22, 1945, this time killing sixteen in Schaffhausen and nine in Stein-am-Rhein. Records that could throw light onto the allegation that the bombings were in fact a deliberate Allied response to Schaffhausen's munitions industries supplying arms to the Nazis in breach of Swiss neutrality are, as yet, still classified. In recent years, Schaffhausen has capitalized on its position to act as a commercial and cultural bridge between Germany and Switzerland, and has absorbed a high number of Sri Lankan immigrants and asylum seekers, leading to an unusually broad ethnic mix on the streets.

Arrival, information and accommodation

Schaffhausen's **train station** is at the northwestern edge of the compact Old Town, served by both Swiss SBB and German DB trains. Counters inside deal with money exchange and bike rental, and the main **post office** is opposite. One block east is bustling Fronwagplatz, where you'll find, under the big clock tower, the main **tourist office** (May–Oct Mon–Fri 10am–6pm, Sat 10am–4pm, Sun 10am–1.30pm; Nov–April Mon–Fri 10am–12.30pm & 1.30–5pm, Sat 10am–1.30pm; ☎052 625 51 41, ⓦwww.sh.ch), with an excellent guided **walking tour** of the Old Town (May–Oct Tues, Wed, Fri & Sat 2.15pm; Fr.10), which includes a tasting of five wines in a vintner's bar at the end.

The best way to arrive is **by boat** from further up the Rhine. At least three boats a day (May–Sept) make the beautiful journey along the river from Kreuzlingen (see p.477) via Stein-am-Rhein, a peaceful ride between wooded banks on just about the only stretch of the Rhine that is free of heavy industry. They dock at Freier Platz, at the southeastern corner of the Old Town.

Hotels

Fischerzunft Rheinquai 8 ☎052 632 05 05, ⓦwww.fischerzunft.ch. Schaffhausen's most characterful choice, a modern hotel on the riverfront with ten attractive rooms styled carefully with Asian touches. **❹–❺**

Kronenhof Kirchhofplatz 7 ☎052 635 75 75, ⓦwww.kronenhof.ch. Slick, business-class rooms in a central location. **❸**

Löwen Im Hösli 2, Herblingen ☎052 643 22 08, ⒻF052 643 22 28. Comfortable old guesthouse in a suburb 3km north (bus #5), with modern, renovated rooms. **❷**

Park Villa Parkstrasse 18 ☎052 625 27 37, ⓦwww.parkvilla.ch. Atmospheric old mansion on the edge of Schaffhausen's Old Town, complete with chandeliers and Persian carpets. One lovely shared-bath room which opens onto the garden can undercut the other, ensuite rooms by Fr.40 or more. **❷–❸**

Rheinfall Zentralstrasse 60, Neuhausen ☎052 672 13 21, ⒻF052 672 14 29. Simple and serviceable hotel in the centre of run-of-the-mill

Neuhausen, ten minutes' walk midway between Schaffhausen and the Rhine falls. **❷**

Hostels

Jugendherberge Belair (HI hostel) Randenstrasse 65 ☎052 625 88 00, ⓦwww.youthhostel.ch. Award-winning hostel (with bike rental available), housed in a sixteenth-century manor house 1km northwest of the station that featured in Hermann Hesse's 1914 novel *Rosshalde*. Dorm beds Fr.24. March–Oct. **❶**

Jugendherberge Dachsen (HI hostel) Schloss Laufen ☎052 659 61 52, ⓦwww.youthhostel.ch. Older hostel in an annexe of Schloss Laufen, a castle overlooking the Rhine falls 4km west of town with its own train station. Dorm beds Fr.23. Mid-March to mid-Oct. **❶**

Campsite

Rheinwiesen ☎052 659 33 00. Quality site on the south bank of the river at Langwiesen, 2km southeast of the centre. May–Sept.

The Town

Schaffhausen's beautiful riverside Old Town is crammed full of well-preserved architecture, lending the cobbled streets considerable charm. A good place to begin is the central **Fronwagplatz**, the town's marketplace during the Middle Ages. Dominating the long square is the **Fronwagturm**, within which hung the market's massive scales; the clock and astronomical device on the top dates from 1564. Beside it is the distinguished, late-Baroque **Herrenstube** townhouse, although the facade of the **Zum Steinbock** house, 100m west at Oberstadt 16, is even more impressive, covered in stucco Rococo curlicues.

Strolling north on Fronwagplatz, past the square's two medieval fountains – the **Metzgerbrunnen** (1524), topped by a statue of a Swiss mercenary, and the **Mohrenbrunnen** (1535), with a Moorish king – you'll come to the **Zum Ochsen** house at Vorstadt 17, one of the most grandiose in the city. The late-

Gothic facade of this former inn was remodelled in 1608 and decorated with striking Renaissance frescoes of classical heroes. The oriel window is especially graceful: it shows, in five panels, a woman embodying each of the senses: holding a mirror (sight), a glove (touch), a flower (smell), a stringed instrument (hearing) and a cake (taste).

North of the Zum Ochsen, a short detour past the frescoes of the **Zum Grossen Käfig** house at Vorstadt 43, which shows the triumphal parade of the medieval Mongol king Tamerlane, brings you to the northern gate of the city, the **Schwabentor**. The tower dates from 1370, but on the outer face is a small panel added during renovations in 1933, which shows a boy with a pig under his arm dodging the traffic. The dialect inscription *Lappi tue d'Augen uf* translates as "Silly people should keep their eyes open" – a reference to the danger of newfangled motorized traffic.

Vordergasse and the Munot

Karstgässchen leads from opposite the Zum Ochsen house into **Platz**, its fountain sporting another grim-faced mercenary. From here, alleys bring you south onto the main **Vordergasse**, a shopping street sloping downhill to the east. On the corner of Münstergasse is Schaffhausen's most celebrated house, the **Zum Ritter**, its facade covered in a spectacularly intricate design dating from 1570 that is acclaimed as the most significant Renaissance fresco to survive north of the Alps (the original is now preserved in the town museum; this is a 1930s copy). The fresco depicts, over three storeys, various elements of knightly virtues (*Ritter* means "knight"): the central panel shows Odysseus in the Land of the Lotus-Eaters, tempted by a voluptuous woman, while above is a Roman knight who sacrificed himself for the glory of his country. Below is a trusting girl, symbolizing virtue, protected by a king (the government) and a woman holding a mitre (the church). From the Zum Ritter, alleys head southwest to another of Schaffhausen's broad, open squares, **Herrenacker**, surrounded by tall, dignified facades concealing Schaffhausen's glitzy casino, opened in 2002, and, on the west side, the massive **Kornhaus** (1679).

From the Zum Ritter house, Vordergasse continues east to the Gothic, five-naved **Kirche St Johann** (Mon–Sat: April–Sept 9am–6pm; Oct–March 10am–5pm), expanded six times since it was begun in the eleventh century. In a niche on the south side of the tower is a small statue of the Madonna and Child without feet: they were removed during the Reformation when a wall was built to hide the image. A few steps east, in front of a fountain statue of William Tell, is the magnificent double-fronted Rococo mansion **Zur Wasserquelle und Zieglerburg**.

Some 50m north is a footbridge over the main Bachstrasse road, which brings you onto steps climbing the hill to the **Munot**. This is Schaffhausen's trademark circular fortress, built by forced labour in 1564 after the religious wars of the Reformation. The interior (daily: May–Sept 8am–8pm; Oct–April 9am–5pm) is gloomy, with massive stone vaulting strong enough to support the 40,000-tonne superstructure. An internal spiral ramp – one of only three such designs in Europe (see also p.96) – leads up to the circular roof of the bastion, with good views over the town. A different door exits onto stairs running through the vines planted on the Munot hill, down to the small riverside quarter known as **Unterstadt**; Schaffhausen's annual Old Town shindig, held on a weekend in late June, still passes on alternate years between the salt-of-the-earth folk of the Unterstadt and their toffee-nosed neighbours of the town centre further west.

Münster zu Allerheiligen

Schaffhausen's lofty **Münster zu Allerheiligen** (All Saints' Minster; Tues–Sun 10am–noon & 2–5pm) is the focus of the Old Town. The first church on the site dated from 1049, replaced in 1103 by the building which still stands today. The beautifully restored Romanesque tower gives a hint of the interior, in which twelve huge columns of Rorschach sandstone line the austere nave. Beside the cathedral, the Romanesque-Gothic **cloister** is the largest in Switzerland, a lovely broad walkway circling the Junkernfriedhof (noblemen's cemetery). In the cathedral courtyard sits the gigantic **Schiller Bell**, cast in 1486; the German poet Friedrich Schiller never set foot in Schaffhausen, but was inspired to compose his *Song of the Clock* by Goethe's record of this bell's Latin inscription: *vivos voco, mortuos plango, fulgura frango* ("I call on the living, lament the dead, halt the lightning"). Just beyond is an atmospheric little herb garden.

In the same complex is Schaffhausen's main historical museum, the **Museum zu Allerheiligen** (Tues–Sat noon–5pm, Thurs until 8pm, Sun 11am–5pm; free; ⓦ www.allerheiligen.ch). The ground floor is mostly given over to a vast archeological collection but, as with the rambling historical collections spread over this and the upper floors, there's little coherence. The place is like a labyrinth, and you could either wander, enjoying the surprise of coming across a roomful of early medieval religious art or a restored Gothic chapel, or instead cut your losses and head for the topmost floor, which holds an engaging collection of art by Swiss painters and sculptors of the last five centuries.

Hallen für Neue Kunst

Baumgartenstrasse marks the southern boundary of the cathedral quarter. In a giant old textile factory at no. 23 is the outstanding **Hallen für Neue Kunst** (Contemporary Art Spaces; Tues–Sat 3–5pm, Sun 11am–5pm; Fr.14; SMP; ⓦ www.modern-art.ch). Pricier than it need be, this impressive gallery is still well worth a visit, with work by artists, known and unknown, from the 1960s to the present spread over several vast floors. Particularly striking in such airy surroundings are the geometrical games in two and three dimensions of Robert Mangold, and Sol LeWitt's dazzling cube installations.

The Rhine falls

Schaffhausen's best excursion is the short trip westwards to the **Rhine falls** (ⓦ www.rhinefalls.com), Europe's largest waterfalls. They are truly magnificent, not so much for their height (a mere 23m) as for their impressive breadth (150m) and the sheer drama of the place, with the spray rising in a cloud of rainbows above the forested banks. The turreted castle Schloss Laufen on a cliff directly above the falls to the south completes the spectacle. August 1 – the Swiss National Day – sees a mighty fireworks display staged on the riverside.

The 4km riverside **walk** from Schaffhausen to the suburban town of **NEUHAUSEN**, where the falls are located, takes about 45 minutes; or you could take city **bus** #1 or #6 to Neuhausen Zentrum, from where the well-signposted falls are five minutes' walk away. Schloss Laufen has a **train** station (April–Oct only), served by hourly trains between Schaffhausen and Winterthur, but Neuhausen's own station is awkwardly far away.

Once you're within sight of the falls, you're inevitably brought down to earth by the hordes of tourists crowding both banks in search of the best camera angle, and by the circus of souvenir stalls and dismal restaurants all around. The worst of it is on the north bank; crossing by the arched footbridge over to the

△ The Munot (see p.471), above Schaffhausen

south bank – which can still get unpleasantly overrun – at least means you can experience the power of the falls at close quarters. Damp steps (Fr.1) lead from the souvenir shop at Schloss Laufen down to various platforms at the very edge, from where the roaring waters tumble inches from your nose. The best view is from one of the daredevil **boats** which scurry around in the spray; their top excursion, termed a *Felsenfahrt*, docks at the craggy rock in the centre of the cataract. Both Rhyfall Mändli (☎052 672 48 11, ⓦwww.maendli.ch) and Schiff Mändli (☎052 659 69 00, ⓦwww.schiffmaendli.ch) run trips continuously all day (May–Sept) for as little as Fr.5. Boats depart from easy-to-spot jetties on both banks.

Eating and drinking

Schaffhausen has a good range of places to **eat**, from the self-service *Manora* diner just off Fronwagplatz upwards. Cafés and **bars** line all the Old Town squares. *Fass-Beiz* (see below) is a quiet little nook to savour a beer or three, while there's a lively café-bar (closed Mon & Tues) attached to the *Kammgarn* cultural centre, Baumgartenstrasse 19. *Zum Weissen Rössli*, Repfergasse 28, is the loudest, smokiest bar in town.

Falken Vorstadt 5. Quality Swiss food in this congenial Old-Town restaurant for around Fr.20. Open daily from breakfast until around midnight.

Fass-Beiz Webergasse 13 ⓦwww.fassbeiz.ch. Cosy co-operative-run café-bar which offers the best budget dining in town: plenty of wholesome, home-cooked veggie dishes for under Fr.15. Closed Sun eve.

Fischerzunft Rheinquai 8 ☎052 632 05 05, ⓦwww.fischerzunft.ch. Spectacular restaurant, best in town by miles and rated in the top half-dozen in the country. Offers a unique cuisine blending French and East Asian elements: don't expect change from Fr.100 per head. Closed Tues (Jan–March also Mon).

Sternen Webergasse 38. Bright, funky place offering pizza and pasta dishes for Fr.20 or so.

Zum Frieden Herrenacker 11 ☎052 625 47 15. An atmospheric tavern-style place with a good-value *Stübli* at ground-floor level and a pricier formal restaurant upstairs serving Frenchified mains for around Fr.40. Closed Sun.

Zum Schäfli Unterstadt 21. Typical of the cheerful, inexpensive places on Unterstadt that are generally full of hearty locals; *menus* of standard Swiss fare cost from Fr.14.

Zur Flamme Vorstadt 9 ☎052 624 09 05. Informal veggie restaurant above a WWF shop, offering excellent food for well under Fr.20 – or go for the five-course evening *menu* for Fr.45. Closed Sat lunch, Sun, & Mon eve.

Stein-am-Rhein

Positioned on the Rhine 20km east of Schaffhausen, little **STEIN-AM-RHEIN** is an almost perfectly preserved medieval village, famed for the intricacy of the sixteenth-century **frescoes** which adorn houses in the village. It's well worth a visit, but sees so many tour buses during the frantic summer season – about a million people pass through annually – that to enjoy the place you should stay overnight: it's only after 5pm and before 10am that there's much peace.

From the Schifflländi quay, if you head east and then cut north on tiny Schwarzhorngasse, you'll come in a minute's stroll to the breathtaking **Rathausplatz**, often acclaimed as the most picturesque square in Switzerland, ringed by medieval half-timbered buildings vying with each other for the lavishness of their frescoes and the gracefulness of their oriels. Standing alone at the head of the square is the Rathaus, built in 1539–42: the half-timbered top storeys are original, the middle floor dates from a 1745 renovation, and the ground floor facade and entranceway were added in 1865. The line of facades along the south side of the square is dazzling, each one sporting a fresco illustrating the house name: these are, from left to right, the *Hirschen* (stag), *Krone* (crown), *Vordere Krone* (foremost crown, which sports an especially lofty gable), *Roter Ochsen* (red ox, the town's oldest tavern, with a Gothic facade), *Steinerner Trauben* (stony grapes), *Sonne* (sun, the oldest hotel in the village but with twentieth-century frescoes), and the *Schwarzer Horn* (black horn). Opposite are the *Adler* (eagle) and, most impressive of all, the *Weisser Adler* (white eagle), bedecked in the town's oldest frescoes, a Holbein-esque series painted in 1520–25.

The rest of the village pales in comparison, but there are plenty of picturesque narrow lanes and alleys to explore, ignored by most visitors. A manor house at Understadt 18, dating from 1279 and renovated in 1819, has been converted into the **Museum Lindwurm** (March–Oct Mon & Wed–Sun 10am–5pm; Fr.5; SMP; ⓦwww.museum-lindwurm.ch), with surprisingly interesting displays on Stein-am-Rhein's bourgeois and agricultural life in the nineteenth century. The desk keeps extensive English notes. A great deal of work has been done to recreate the living conditions of the wealthy upper-class family who owned the house: walking through the cobbled stables, the Empire-style drawing room and the spartan servants' quarters under the eaves, feels like stepping back in time.

Practicalities

At least six **boats** a day in summer arrive at Stein-am-Rhein, three from Kreuzlingen upriver and three from Schaffhausen downriver. The **train station** is on the southern bank of the Rhine, a couple of minutes' walk from the bridge. The tiny **tourist office** is at Oberstadt 9 (Mon–Fri 9–11am & 2–5pm; ☎052 741 28 35, ⓦwww.steinamrhein.ch). Of the three riverside **campsites**, *Grenzstein* is the nearest, about 1km east (☎052 741 51 44).

Hotels

Adler Rathausplatz ☎052 742 61 61, ⓦwww.adlersteinamrhein.ch. Directly on Rathausplatz, with a brilliantly decorated facade sheltering pine-decor rooms which are surprisingly plain and ordinary, though comfortable enough. ❸

Mühletal Öhningerstrasse 6 ☎052 741 27 25. Least expensive option, 250m east of Rathausplatz, and also with a good, inexpensive pizza restaurant (closed Mon). ❷

Rheinfels Rhigass 8 ☎052 741 21 44, ⓦwww.rheinfels.ch. Fine old Rhineside inn, dating from the sixteenth century, with atmospheric public areas and sixteen comfortable, modernized rooms, all with a river view. ❸–❹

Rheingerbe Schifflände 5 ☎052 741 29 91, ☏052 741 21 66. Old wood-beamed inn with some rooms overlooking the Rhine. ❷

Hostel

Jugendherberge (HI hostel) Hemishoferstrasse 87 ☎052 741 12 55, ⓦwww.youthhostel.ch. Good hostel about fifteen minutes' walk due east from Rathausplatz, via Understadt. Dorms from Fr.23. March–Oct. ❶

Eating and drinking

The village is crammed with **eating** places. Budget snacking and inexpensive pizzas are at *Kiosk Charregass*, Oberstadt 10 (closed Mon); there's a *Migros* self-service diner just north of the Untertor gate; and an inexpensive *crêperie* at Understadt 10. The historic *Rheinfels* inn (see above) has an atmospheric all-wood dining room (closed Wed) specializing in excellent fish; *menus* are around Fr.35. The gorgeous interior of the *Roten Ochsen* on Rathausplatz (☎052 741 23 28; closed Mon) suits its outstanding Swiss food, made from only local ingredients. Top choice is the *Sonne*, also on Rathausplatz (☎052 741 21 28; closed Tues & Wed), with the ground-floor *Weinstube* serving excellent daily *menus* (around Fr.25) prepared in the same kitchen as the gourmet delights costing Fr.60 or more in the restaurant upstairs. Prominent on a hill above the town is Schloss Hohenklingen, formerly the residence of the feudal lords of the area and now converted into a restaurant (℡052 741 21 37; closed Mon & Jan–Feb), boasting views at least as good as the cuisine.

Kartause Ittingen

A fine detour with picnic possibilities is to **Kartause Ittingen**, a former Charterhouse (Carthusian monastery) set amidst hop fields and open farmland near **WARTH**, 6km south of Stein-am-Rhein over a hilly ridge.

From 1461 until 1868, the old buildings, arrayed around a large, peaceful courtyard, were home to a community of between twelve and fifteen monks; today, the **Ittinger Museum** (Mon–Fri 2–5pm, Sat & Sun 11am–5pm; Fr.5) sheds light on the life of the order. The monks lived a life of extreme austerity, taking all meals except Sunday lunch alone in their cell and remaining committed by oath to silence. The stunning Rococo **church** has a long nave, divided into four and flanked by intricate choir stalls carved around 1700, and a dramatic high altarpiece depicting St Bruno, founder of the order. There's no organ, since the Carthusian Mass is sung without accompaniment. Beside the church is the **Little Cloister**, prelude to a series of decorated and partly furnished rooms once used by the monks, including the Refectory (room 4), with seventeenth-century portraits ringing the walls. The fifteen monks' cells lie off the **Great Cloister**. Upstairs rooms include a tiny **prison** with barred window, and an unusual upper-level gallery in the church. Some rooms are given over to the **Kunstmuseum des Kantons Thurgau**, with twentieth-century Swiss art including a penetrating self-portrait by Helen Dahm and cartoonish works by Josef Wittlich.

Hourly **buses** run from Stein-am-Rhein to Warth, leaving you fifteen minutes' walk away. From **FRAUENFELD** station – 4km south of the monastery, served by mainline trains – two buses a day go direct to the Kartause, as well as hourly buses to Warth. You'd do just as well **renting bikes** from Frauenfeld station (daily 5.30am–8.30pm); the tourist office in the station (Mon–Fri 9am–noon & 2–6pm, Sat 9am–noon; ℡052 721 31 28, Ⓦwww.frauenfeld.ch) can help with maps and information. Part of the Kartause has been renovated as a modern conference-style **hotel** (℡052 748 44 11, Ⓦwww.kartause.ch; ❹) – all exposed brick and bright, functional comforts. The *Herberge* section adjacent has simpler shared-bath rooms (❷). The on-site **restaurant**, *Zur Mühle*, has quality, affordable modern cuisine (*menus* Fr.20–25), but the farmland all around is prime picnic territory; pick up some homemade goodies from the little **shop**, which sells vegetables, fresh-baked bread, fragrant *eaux-de-vie* and bottles of lip-smacking Klosterbräu beer, brewed from hand-picked hops.

The Bodensee (Lake Constance)

Forming a natural border between Switzerland and Germany, the long **Bodensee** – often anglicized to **Lake Constance** – is a huge bulge in the course of the Rhine, some 67km from end to end. Unlike most of the Swiss lakes, it doesn't have the benefit of shoreline mountains, and so is exposed to winds year-round and has particularly rough weather in the winter. During spring 1999, following heavy rain and an unusually large quantity of snowmelt in the Alps, the lake rose to its highest level for more than a century: many coastal towns were flooded, and even as late as August the harbourfronts at Rorschach and Stein-am-Rhein remained underwater.

Cruises on the Bodensee

All three countries' **boat operators** have formed a joint body, the VSU (ⓦwww .vsu-online.com). The Swiss partners are the SBS (☎071 466 77 88, ⓦwww.bodensee-schiffe.ch), operating between Rorschach and Kreuzlingen; and Untersee & Rhein (☎052 634 08 88, ⓦwww.urh.ch), operating between Kreuzlingen and Schaffhausen. Year-round **car ferries** run between Romanshorn and Friedrichshafen, and between Konstanz and Meersburg. You'll need to show your **passport** on international ferries.

There are dozens of **excursion cruises** all round the lake during the summer season (April–Oct), in addition to the regular summer ferry routings. In the peak season (June to mid-Sept), it's possible to spend **a day on the lake**, leaving Rorschach at 10.50am for the two-hour cruise to Kreuzlingen, where you have an hour or so for lunch before departing at 2.10pm on the leisurely journey down the Rhine to Schaffhausen, arriving at 5.50pm. The other way, going upstream, takes from 9.10am to 6.35pm. With **InterRail**, you pay half-price on ordinary tickets for boat journeys along the Swiss shore; with **Eurail** or a **Swiss Pass**, you travel free. See p.461 for details of regional passes.

Three countries border the Bodensee. The head of the lake, at its southeastern corner, is Austrian, focused around the genteel town of **Bregenz**. The largest settlement on the northern German shore is the cosmopolitan city of **Konstanz**, separated from its contiguous Swiss suburb of **Kreuzlingen** only by an arbitrary international frontier. Haze and lingering fog can often mask the views across the water, but this hasn't stopped the lakeshore becoming one of Germany's main summer-holiday destinations; this rubs off on the southern, Swiss, shore, too, where the scattering of soporific little resorts such as **Rorschach** and **Arbon** have a strong Teutonic air about them.

Kreuzlingen and around

At the northwestern corner of the Bodensee, the small Swiss town of **KREUZLINGEN** is an anomaly, nothing more than a southern suburb of the cosmopolitan German city of **Konstanz**; the international frontier separating them runs arbitrarily between buildings. Kreuzlingen is like border towns everywhere, full of traffic streaming through without stopping and imbued with a feeling that the exciting stuff is happening elsewhere, just out of sight. It has little history of its own, but is worth stopping in, both as a base from which to spend a day or two exploring Konstanz, and for its own **Kirche St Ulrich**, 150m south of the centre on Hauptstrasse. This Baroque church houses the remarkable Ölbergkapelle, containing a 1780 wood carving of the Passion comprising around 300 individual figures; the sculpture is teeming with intricate detail, and is surmounted by a fifteenth-century cross (*Kreuz* in German) which has survived three major fires. The church itself is no less dazzling, with a stunningly ornate choir screen in green and gilt.

Kreuzlingen's main station, the **Hauptbahnhof**, is 150m south of the international border; head east (left) out of the station to reach the traffic lights on Hauptstrasse. The **tourist office** is opposite, in the TCS travel agency at no. 39 (Mon–Fri 8.30am–noon & 1.45–6pm; ☎071 672 38 40, ⓦwww.kreuzlingen .ch). Hafenstrasse continues east to the lakeshore, where you'll find the harbour and the **Hafenbahnhof** train station. Nearby is the old Villa Hörnliberg, housing an HI **hostel**, Promenadenstrasse 7 (☎071 688 26 63, ⓦwww.youthhostel .ch; ❶; March–Nov) – dorms are Fr.24 and they have bikes to rent. South along the lakeshore is the *Fischerhaus* **campsite** (☎071 688 49 03, ⓕ071 688 17 76;

April–Oct). Opposite the Hauptbahnhof, friendly *Bahnhof-Post* **hotel**, Nationalstrasse 2 (☎071 672 79 72, ☎071 672 49 82; ❷), has serviceable ensuite and shared-bath rooms. *Park Kafi* **restaurant**, Hauptstrasse 82, has an affordable menu of pasta, meaty mains, veggie options and summer salads, for Fr.15–20, and doubles as a **bar**. *Zapfenzieler*, Hauptstrasse 44, is another amiable bar with terrace. There's a self-service diner in the giant *Coop* on Alleestrasse.

Konstanz and Insel Mainau

The main point of coming to Kreuzlingen is to visit **KONSTANZ** just over the German frontier. This ancient city straddling the Rhine has been an important ecclesiastical hub for centuries: the Council of Konstanz (1414–18), which tried and failed to heal divisions within the Church, met in the huge **Münster**, originally a Romanesque basilica, set amidst a web of characterful alleys now lively with students from the city's university. The **tourist office** beside the station (April–Oct Mon–Fri 9am–6.30pm, Sat 9am–4pm, Sun 10am–1pm; rest of year Mon–Fri 9.30am–noon & 2–6pm; ☎0049 7531 133030, ☎www.konstanz.de) has an English booklet detailing a self-guided walking tour. **Trains** take three minutes from Kreuzlingen's main station, but it's really no hardship to walk the fifteen minutes or so; either way, you'll need to show your **passport**. You can **change money** commission-free at the counter in the Swiss half of Konstanz's station.

Just 8km north in Germany – accessible by direct ferry from Swiss and German ports – is the major attraction of **INSEL MAINAU** (daily: June–Oct 7am–8pm; rest of year 9am–6pm; €10), a small, forested island occupied by a Baroque castle and lavish gardens.

Münsterlingen

About 2km east of Kreuzlingen lies the village of **MÜNSTERLINGEN**, worth stopping in to visit its sixteenth-century Baroque church, originally part of a Benedictine convent. The interior is beautifully decorated, with a lavish altarpiece flanked by twisted gilt and turquoise columns, and a cupola overhead painted with a *trompe l'oeil* fresco: the abbess of the convent in the 1680s was related to master sculptor Christof Daniel Schenck from Konstanz, and brought him in to do some of the decoration and to sculpt the wood figures still on display in the church. An altar curtain dating from 1565, used during Lent to hide the glory of the altar, hangs to one side.

The church's most interesting tale begins in the sixteenth century when the climate was chillier than it is today; during that century, it is said, the lake froze solid six or seven times. One winter, as the Reformation was taking hold, a church official from **Hagnau**, a town on the German bank opposite, walked across the frozen lake to Münsterlingen, where the church was being emptied of its decoration. He managed to save a single statuette of John the Baptist and took it back to Hagnau for safekeeping. When the lake froze again some years later, he remembered his journey, and brought the statuette back. Ever since then, a freezing of the lake has been the sign for a solemn procession to be made across the ice to take the statuette over to the opposite shore. In 1830, Münsterlingen's clergy and villagers delivered the figurine to Hagnau, where it remained until the harsh winter of 1963, when the ice was solid enough to return it to Münsterlingen church. There it still sits, in the crypt (a copy is on display), awaiting the next icy spell.

Romanshorn and around

Along the shore is **ROMANSHORN**, a run-of-the-mill lakeside resort, arrival point for boats from **FRIEDRICHSHAFEN** on the German bank opposite. Friedrichshafen airport (⊛www.fly-away.de) has taxis (€10) and hourly trains to the harbourside Hafenbahnhof (€1; takes 12min; last train 7.45pm), from where ferries run hourly to Romanshorn (40min; last ferry 8.40pm, earlier in winter). Romanshorn's station, with fast trains to St Gallen and Zürich, is near the dock.

Some 7km east of Romanshorn is the ancient village of **ARBON**, reputedly the point at which Columba and Gallus (see p.480) stepped ashore. Walk left from the station for about ten minutes to reach the tranquil centre, marked by the spire of the **Kirche St Martin**, with, in its grounds, the tiny eleventh-century Galluskapelle. Adjacent is the sixteenth-century **Schloss Arbon**, housing a small local-history museum (May–Sept daily 2–5pm; April & Oct Sun 2–5pm; Fr.2). The old streets nearby hold a number of half-timbered buildings, most seventeenth- or eighteenth-century; on Kapellgasse is a chapel built in 1390, but deconsecrated in 1777 and now daubed with graffiti.

Rorschach

A couple of hours' walk southeast of Arbon, the pleasant little lakeside resort of **RORSCHACH** lies on a bay below the grassy Rorschacherberg, 9km from St Gallen. It has two train stations: the main Hauptbahnhof is less useful than the **Hafenbahnhof** (Harbour station), 1km west in the town centre. Rorschach suffered badly during the 1999 floods, when **Hauptstrasse** had to be lined with sandbags to save the street's fine sixteenth- to eighteenth-century houses, with their attractive oriel windows. The **Kolumbanskirche** just off the street is a rather lovely broad, white, late-Baroque church dedicated to the Irish monk Columba, with much gilded glitter inside. Down on the harbourfront is the old **Kornhaus**, emblem of a once-thriving grain trade between St Gallen and Germany. Near it, in an old warehouse, is a **museum** devoted to vintage cars (July & Aug daily 10am–6pm; March–June, Sept & Oct Sun 10am–6pm; Fr.7). A rack railway winds up from the Hafenbahnhof to the health resort of **HEIDEN**, with plenty of leg-stretching hiking trails around and about. The Austrian border is just east of Rorschach; there are no scheduled boats to the city of Bregenz, a few kilometres further on, but the local operator (⊛www.schifffahrt-rorschach.ch) runs short pleasure trips to Rheineck.

Rorschach's **tourist office** is opposite the Hafenbahnhof, Hauptstrasse 63 (April–Oct Mon 2–5.30pm, Tues–Fri 9.30am–noon & 2–5.30pm; June–Sept also Sat 9.30am–noon; Nov–March Mon–Fri 2–5pm; ☎071 841 70 34, ⊛www.tourist-rorschach.ch). There's a pleasant lakeside HI **hostel**, Churerstrasse 4 (☎071 844 97 12, ⊛www.youthhostel.ch; ❶; April–Oct; dorm beds Fr.32). The best-value **hotel** is *Löwen*, Hauptstrasse 92 (☎071 841 38 87, ℗071 841 49 32; ❶), while the lakefront *Hotel Mozart*, 150m west of the Hafenbahnhof (☎071 844 47 47, ⊛www.mozart-rorschach.ch; ❸), has comfortable, renovated rooms. There's a *Coop* self-service **restaurant** in the shopping area on Poststrasse. *Wirtschaft Pöstli*, Signalstrasse 2, outside the Hafenbahnhof has *menus* of standard Swiss fare from Fr.13, plus seven kinds of *Rösti*. *Pizzeria Roma*, Hauptstrasse 54, offers pasta and a range of pizzas for around Fr.15, with the benefit of a lakeview terrace.

As a footnote to the town, the famous **Rorschach Ink-Blot Test**, in which a subject under therapy is asked to describe the images that they see in the random shape of a blot, was named after its deviser, Swiss psychologist Hermann Rorschach. He was born in Arbon in 1884 but, as far as records show, never set foot in Rorschach itself.

St Gallen

The main urban centre of eastern Switzerland, **ST GALLEN** is a relaxed and conservative provincial city set amidst rolling countryside between the Appenzell hills and the Bodensee. It's a gentle place, with a busy modern centre and a beautiful Old Town. The centrepiece is an extraordinarily lavish Baroque abbey, declared a UNESCO World Heritage Site: its cathedral is impressive enough alone, but the **abbey library** is celebrated as Switzerland's finest secular Rococo interior and contains a world-class collection of ancient books and manuscripts.

Some history

St Gallen owes its existence to the religious community which remains at its core. In around 612, the Irish monk **Gallus** – a follower of Columba – was travelling south from the Bodensee into the forest. Legend has it that he either fell over, or stumbled into a briar patch, or spoke to a bear who understood what he was saying; whichever, Gallus felt he had received a sign from God, and so chose that spot to build his hermitage. In the eighth century, a follower named **Otmar** established a monastic community around Gallus's cell, and

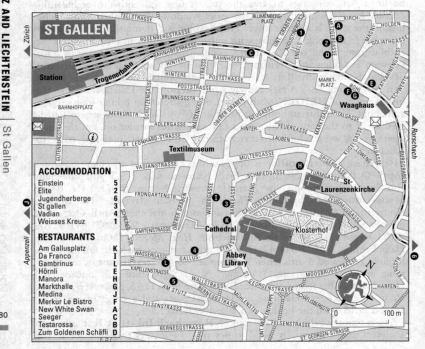

ACCOMMODATION
Einstein   5
Elite   2
Jugendherberge   6
St gallen   3
Vadian   4
Weisses Kreuz   1

RESTAURANTS
Am Gallusplatz   K
Da Franco   I
Gambrinus   L
Hörnli   E
Manora   H
Markthalle   G
Medina   J
Merkur Le Bistro F
New White Swan   A
Seeger   C
Testarossa   B
Zum Goldenen Schäfli D

founded a school of scribes and translators. In the 830s, Abbot Gozbert established the great **library**, and St Gallen's reputation as a centre of culture and learning grew. By the thirteenth century, St Gallen had become an important market town and its reputation as a centre of learning was being superseded by its reputation as a producer and exporter of exceptionally high-quality **linen**. By the end of the Middle Ages, it was the only Swiss town to have trade representatives resident in foreign cities, and was linked by stagecoach to centres of textile processing in Nuremberg and Lyon.

In 1529, Joachim von Watt – known as **Vadian** – introduced the Reformation, sparking iconoclastic riots which forced the monks temporarily to flee; the abbey survived, however, as an independent Catholic walled enclave within the Protestant city.

In the eighteenth century, St Gallen's weavers rapidly switched to the new fashion for **hand-embroidery**: by 1790, some 40,000 women were working from home to embroider cotton and muslin for export – notably to the young United States. The invention of embroidery machines brought a golden age, although production remained centred in the home. By 1913, embroidery was Switzerland's largest export industry, with St Gallen accounting for around half of the entire world production of textiles. These days, that figure is down to just 0.5 percent, but Swiss embroidery remains a highly valued, luxury commodity, with small, highly specialized companies supplying designs and finished products to *haute couture* fashion houses: Lacoste's famous crocodile logo, for instance, is Swiss-embroidered. Nonetheless, St Gallen's embroidery industry – now almost entirely computerized – still relies on two thousand local women working from home, hand-sewing detailing that is impossible to achieve by machine.

Arrival, information and accommodation

St Gallen's **train station** – with bike rental and money-changing – is 200m southwest of the Old Town, with the **tourist office** across the square at Bahnhofplatz 1a (Mon–Fri 9am–6pm, Sat 9am–noon; ☎071 227 37 37, Ⓦwww.st.gallen-bodensee.ch). Staff can supply information on the whole Ostschweiz region, plus Liechtenstein and the Bodensee, and run an excellent two-hour guided **walking tour** (June–Sept Mon, Wed & Fri 2pm; Fr.15, includes admission fees and a drink). The **Open Air festival** (Ⓦwww.openairsg.ch), on the last weekend in June, pulls in a varied range of international performers from Van Morrison to Metallica. The tourist office **accommodation** reservations line (☎071 227 37 47) can take bookings for the city and the surrounding area.

Hotels

Einstein Berneggstrasse 2 ☎071 227 55 55, Ⓦwww.einstein.ch. The city's top choice, a grand old hotel housed in a former textile factory, with generously appointed rooms and quality service. ❻

Elite Metzgergasse 9 ☎071 222 12 36, Ⓦwww.hotel-elite-sg.com. Plain and serviceable rooms near Marktplatz, both ensuite and not. ❷

St Gallen Bankgasse 12 ☎071 227 61 00, Ⓦwww.hotel-st-gallen.ch. Warm, characterful Old Town hotel, with the 18 rooms in the comfortable main building entirely upstaged by the six romantic bedchambers in the antique-style, half-timbered *Pförtnerhof* annexe across the street, boasting leaded-light windows, wood panelling and modern bathrooms. ❹–❺

Vadian Gallusstrasse 36 ☎071 228 18 78, Ⓔhotel-vadian@bluewin.ch. House-proud little "garni" hotel on a quiet street near the cathedral, with pleasantly renovated rooms, some ensuite. ❷

Weisses Kreuz Engelgasse 9 ☎ & Ⓕ071/223 28 43. Cheapest place in town, although rooms are shabby. Some are ensuite. ❷

Hostel

Jugendherberge (HI hostel) Jüchstrasse 25 ⊤071 245 47 77, ⊛www.youthhostel.ch. Take the Trogenerbahn narrow-gauge train from outside the main station to the Schülerhaus stop, and walk up the hill. Dorms are Fr.26. March to mid-Dec. ❶

Campsite

St Gallen-Wittenbach ⊤071 298 49 69. Well-run, comfortable site 2km north of town in Bernhardzell. April–Sept.

The City

St Gallen's Old Town is roughly circular, crossed by the main pedestrian streets of **Vadianstrasse/Multergasse** leading east from the station, and **Marktgasse** running south from Marktplatz, a hub for buses and shoppers. The attractive streets and alleys are adorned with 111 elaborate **oriels**, or small projecting bay windows, most of which are younger than the houses to which they're attached: a fashion for them in the eighteenth century meant that many were carved from wood, painted, and then stuck onto the stone facade to satisfy the whim of the nouveau-riche merchant who lived within. Some of the most remarkable can be found at Schmiedgasse 15 (House of the Pelican) and 21 (House of Strength); Kugelgasse 8 (House of the Ball) and 10 (House of the Swan); Hinterlauben 10 (House of the Deep Cellar); and Spisergasse 22 (the Camel Oriel). Along **Gallusstrasse** you'll also find half-timbered cottages from the Middle Ages rubbing shoulders with Baroque townhouses and grand nineteenth-century dwellings put up during St Gallen's golden age of textile production.

The **Textilmuseum**, Vadianstrasse 2 (Mon–Sat 10am–noon & 2–5pm, Sun 10am–5pm; Fr.5; SMP; ⊛www.textilmuseum.ch), has an interesting and well-presented collection, focusing on handmade embroidery and lace, along with useful explanations of the growth and decline in the industry locally. The tall, steepled **St-Laurenzenkirche** on Marktgasse (Mon–Fri 9.30–11.30am & 2–4pm) dates from the ninth century, and originally stood within the monastic enclosure of the cathedral and abbey. Entirely renovated in Neo-Gothic style in the mid-nineteenth century, and restored in the 1970s according to the 1845 plans, it has a narrow but lofty nave flanked by Gothic pointed side arches.

The cathedral

St Gallen's giant Baroque **cathedral** (Mon–Sat 9am–6pm, Sun noon–6pm) is unmissable, its twin towers visible from most points. Designed by one Peter Thumb from Bregenz, it was completed in 1767 after just twelve years' construction work. Easiest access is through the west door on Gallusstrasse, although it's worth making your way through the church and out into the enclosed Klosterhof, at the heart of the complex, where you can see the full height of the soaring **east facade**. To the left is the palace wing, still the residence of the Bishop of St Gallen.

The **interior** is vast, a broad, brightly lit white basilica with three naves and a central cupola. Although not especially high, it has a sense of huge depth and breadth thanks to its accomplished architecture: from the sandstone of the floor and wood of the pews, fanciful light-green stuccowork – characteristic of churches in the Konstanz region – draws your eye up the massive double-width pillars to the array of frescoes on the ceiling, which are almost entirely the work of one artist, Josef Wannenmacher. Above the western end of the nave is a panel showing Mary sitting on a cloud surrounded by angels. The huge central cupola shows paradise, with the Holy Trinity surrounded by concentric rings of cloud on which are arrayed apostles and saints. Details throughout the rest of the cathedral are splendid: the lavish, mock-tasselled pulpit; the ornate choir screen; the richly carved walnut-wood confessionals; the intricate choir stalls; and, far away at the back of the choir, the high altar flanked by black marble columns with gold trim. The south altar features a bell brought by Gallus on his seventh-century journey from Ireland, one of the three oldest surviving bells in Europe.

The abbey library (Stiftsbibliothek)

Within the same complex of buildings as the cathedral, and just adjacent to it, is the famous **abbey library** (Stiftsbibliothek; Mon–Sat 10am–5pm, Sun 10am–4pm; Dec–March closed noon–1.30pm; closed for 3 weeks in late Nov; Fr.7; SMP; Ⓦwww.stibi.ch), one of the oldest libraries in Europe, and famous both for its stunning interior and for its huge collection of rare and unique medieval books and manuscripts. You enter beneath a sign reading ΨΥΧΗΣ IATPEION (*psyches iatreion*, Greek for "Pharmacy of the Soul"). Ranged beside are dozens of oversized felt slippers; slip your shoed feet into a pair, to save the gorgeous inlaid wooden floor of the library from scuffing.

The 28-by-10-metre room is acclaimed as Switzerland's finest surviving example of a Baroque secular interior, and the first glimpse of it as you enter is dizzying. Designed by the same Peter Thumb who worked on the cathedral, the library dates from slightly later, so its orthodox Baroque architecture is overlaid with the opulent decoration of the Rococo period which then held sway. The four **ceiling frescoes** by Josef Wannenmacher depict with bold *trompe l'oeil* perspectives the early Christian theological councils of Nicaea, Constantinople, Ephesus and Chalcedon. Amongst the wealth of smaller frescoes set amongst the ceiling stucco, in the far southeast corner you'll spot **The Venerable Bede**, a seventh-century English monk from Northumbria who wrote one of the first histories of England: he is shown as a scholar, with, beside him, a magic number square. This four-by-four sequence, where the numbers add up to 34 horizontally, vertically, diagonally and from the four corners, is thought to have been invented by Pythagoras in ancient Greece, but took on a new mystical power for early Christians who understood Christ to have died at 34 years of age.

The **books** are ranged on floor-to-ceiling shelves all around. You're free to wander around and examine the spines; books were originally organized by subject, indicated by the cherubs at the head of capitals around the library, but are now arranged alphabetically. If you open the recessed panels between each bookcase, inside you'll find registers of books in the nearby shelves with space to leave your name: the library still operates as an ordinary lending library and study centre, with some 140,000 volumes focused on the Middle Ages. Its list of cultural treasures is extraordinary – for a start, there are more **Irish manuscripts** in St Gallen than there are in Dublin, fifteen handwritten examples including a Latin manuscript of the Gospels dating from 750. Other works include an astronomical textbook written in 300 BC; copies made in the fifth century of works by Virgil, Horace and other classical authors; texts written by Bede in his original Northumbrian language; and the oldest book to have survived in German, dating from the eighth century. Various of these and other treasures of the library's upstairs manuscript room (no public access) are put on display in glass cases dotted around the main library area. An ancient Egyptian **mummy** in the library dates from 700 BC and was a gift to the mayor of St Gallen in the early nineteenth century; unsure of what to do with the thing, he plonked it in this corner, where it has sat incongruously ever since.

Eating, drinking and nightlife

St Gallen has a good range of **eating and drinking** places to cover all price ranges. For standard self-service fare, head for the *Manora* on Marktgasse, but look out also for stalls selling St Gallen's famous Olma sausage, eaten ketchup-and mustard-free in a *Bürli*, or bread roll. A feature of St Gallen dining is the handful of traditional tavern-restaurants housed on the upper floor of old town houses.

Am Gallusplatz Gallusstrasse 24 ☏ 071 223 33 30. The city's best restaurant, where you can enjoy high-quality French cuisine amidst suitably stout decor. Your best option is to come for lunch, when *menus* are lighter in tone and cost less (around Fr.25) – otherwise, you're looking at Fr.50-plus. Closed Sat lunch & Mon.

Da Franco Webergasse 23. Pasta and pizza galore, with a choice of 25 different risottos. Eat well for Fr.18.

Gambrinus Wassergasse 5 ☏ 071 222 47 71, ⓦ www.gambrinus.ch. Comfortable, low-lit den for standard brasserie-type *menus* (around Fr.20), plus veggie options, with the added attraction of live jazz every night – top-name artists on Wed and Sat nights command entrance fees of Fr.25–30, but otherwise entry is free to the house band. Closed Sun & Mon.

Hörnli Marktplatz 5 ☏ 071 222 66 86. Easygoing restaurant specializing in delicious *Rösti*, also with some *menus* under Fr.15. A main attraction is its open-all-hours policy (Mon–Thurs 6.30am–11.30pm, then continuously Fri 6.30am until Mon 4am).

Markthalle Marktplatz. Cool modern interior churning out quality deli-type snacks and meals to local office types – prices are lower in the stand-up section, with perch stools, than in the table-and-chair bit in the back, although you can get a meal at either for less than Fr.17. After 6pm, it turns into a bar-style "night café", with more limited food options. Closed Sun.

Medina Davidstrasse 11. Quiet Tunisian bar-plus-restaurant, serving authentic Arabic/North African cuisine to the musical accompaniment of Umm Kalthoum's classic ballads. Especially good kebabs are fleshed out by quality *harira* tomato-and-chickpea soup and other specialities. The fact that the place draws a clientele of expat Arabs speaks volumes.

Merkur Le Bistro Marktplatz. Rock-bottom prices in this upstairs all-day diner, with *menus* from Fr.13. Closed Sun in summer.

New White Swan Metzgergasse 24. Fast-paced little diner serving up huge portions of steaming Asian-style stomach fillers to students and others on tight budgets.

Seeger Oberer Graben 2. Elegant big-windowed café with inexpensive food, playing classical music during the day to a twenty-something crowd relaxing on the leather sofas inside, or at tables on the pavement terrace.

Testarossa Metzgergasse 20. Pretty good pizzas for around Fr.16. Closed Mon.

Zum Goldenen Schäfli Metzgergasse 5 ☏ 071 223 37 37. Best known of St Gallen's upper-floor restaurants, with low ceilings, wood panelling all around and creaking floors. The food is all hearty local fare, with plenty of offal on the menu – the house speciality is calf's liver – and other local dishes such as sautéed lake fish. *Menus* start from a very reasonable Fr.15. Closed Sun in summer.

Nightlife

Students attending the University of St Gallen, on a hillside campus north of town, feed what passes for the **nightlife**, although locals have no compunction about jumping on a train to Zürich for a better choice. There's live **jazz** nightly at *Gambrinus* (see above). *Baracca*, Teufenerstrasse 2, is a popular all-day late-opening **DJ bar**; *Seeger*, a café at Oberer Graben 2, hosts pumping weekend dance parties; *Birreria*, Brühlgasse 45, has eleven beers on tap, plus 200 more in bottles; and *Sydney's Club-Bar*, Spisermarkt (Thurs–Sat eves), sells itself with the motto "G'day Australia!" Kinok, Grossackerstrasse 3, shows arthouse **films**, with cut-price tickets on Mondays. St Gallen's newest attraction, due for opening in late 2003, is the **Grand Casino**, St Jakobstrasse 55 (ⓦ www .swisscasinos.ch).

Appenzellerland

The residents of **Appenzellerland** are the butt of many a Swiss joke, regarded by cosmopolitan urbanites as country bumpkins and mercilessly mocked for their folksy ways. Yet although a sophisticated Lausannois or Basler might chortle to hear it, this rustic region is something of a sensuous delight: as you cross the verdant hills south from St Gallen, the pungent smells of cows and cheese assault your nose; on a wander through the villages, busy embroidery and the fussily net-curtained windows of wooden houses delight the eye; and local cooking, particularly rich with butter and cream, has a delicious silkiness on the tongue.

Encircled by rolling hills, with the snowy peaks of the Alpstein ridges to the south, Appenzell has for centuries been a land apart. Monks from St Gallen colonized the area in the tenth century, calling it *Abtszell* ("Abbey Cell"), but the fiercely independent local peasantry threw off ecclesiastical control in a series of wars in the fourteenth century. Although surrounded by St Gallen's territory, Appenzell joined the Swiss Confederation in 1513, long before its more powerful neighbour. Shortly afterwards it split into two tiny autonomous half-cantons – Protestant **Appenzell Ausserrhoden** (abbreviated to "AR"), and Catholic **Appenzell Innerrhoden** ("AI"). For touristic purposes, the two half-cantons are together dubbed "Appenzellerland", but the divisions between them remain to this day, with Ausserrhoden's dynamic economy based on manufacturing industry and Innerrhoden's slower one based on tourism and the preservation of traditional culture.

Appenzell village, capital of Innerrhoden, the least populous Swiss canton, is the main draw for its quaint, traditional air – preserved even amidst the high-season day-trippers. Other than **Stein**'s excellent museum and show-dairy, surrounding villages hold few attractions, but there's plenty of good **hill-walking**, with routes crossing the velvety slopes towards the rocky peaks of the Alpstein and its highest point, the snowy **Säntis** (2502m).

Appenzell

The main street of **APPENZELL**, 20km south of St Gallen, is car-free Hauptgasse, running from a bridge over the River Sitter at the entrance to the village west for 300m or so to the broad, open **Landsgemeindeplatz**; it's worth wandering along to admire the intricately painted old wooden houses – notably *Löwen Drogerie*, a pharmacy at no. 20 – with their rows of small, closely packed windows. During the nineteenth century, the embroidery industry of nearby St Gallen relied upon thousands of women working by hand from home, with the intricate work of Appenzell particularly highly prized: the upstairs rooms in these buildings, flooded by daylight through the lines of windows, were used as workshops. Hand-embroidery flourished into the first half of the twentieth century, and is still carried on by a few specialists

---

Exploring Appenzell

The **Appenzell Card** (May–Dec only; ⊛ www.appenzellerbahnen.ch) covers transport on buses and trains, including to and from St Gallen, as well as mountain transport to Ebenalp and admission to museums: one/three/five days costs Fr.31/52/84. Tourist offices in St Gallen and Appenzell have full details. The **AB Tageskarte** (Fr.21) covers a day's travel and also cuts the cost of bike rental at Appenzell station to Fr.5/day.

here and there, with workshops often located on characterful back alleys.

In the same building as the tourist office is the **Appenzell Museum**, Hauptgasse 4 (April–Oct daily 10am–noon & 2–5pm; Nov–March Tues–Sun 2–5pm; Fr.5; SMP; Ⓦwww.museum.ai.ch). This interesting exhibition of local crafts is spread out over six floors, spilling over onto the upper floors of the arcaded Rathaus next door: highlights include many pieces of Appenzell hand-embroidery, religious art and militaria from Claux Castle, the ruins of which are visible on a nearby hilltop. Don't miss the short videos shown on demand in a viewing room on the ground floor: the one on local musical traditions is especially good. A few steps away is the church of **St Mauritius**, much more ornate than you would expect for a country village; its Baroque interior, the high altar flanked by gold figures, is oddly asymmetrical.

Museum Liner stands on the edge of the village, Unterrainstrasse 5 (May–Oct Tues–Fri 10am–noon & 2–5pm, Sat & Sun 11am–5pm; Nov–April Tues–Sat 2–5pm, Sun 11am–5pm; Fr.9; SMP; Ⓦwww.museumliner.ch). This gallery, devoted to the work of father-and-son local artists Carl August Liner and Carl Walter Liner, is interesting mainly for its boldly conceived design in steel by the Zürich partnership of Annette Gigon and Mike Guyer (see p.599). Exhibitions of the Liners' uninspiring modernistic art are made more appealing by additional exhibits of Swiss contemporary works.

Practicalities

Appenzeller Bahnen runs two narrow-gauge **train** lines to Appenzell (free to Eurail and Swiss Pass holders, half-price to InterRailers; Ⓦwww.appenzeller-bahnen.ch), one direct from outside St Gallen station, the other from Herisau. Appenzell's **station**, with bike rental and a change counter, is 200m south of the centre. The friendly **tourist office** is at Hauptgasse 4 (Mon–Fri 9am–noon & 1.30–6pm, Sat & Sun 10am–noon & 2–5pm; ☏071 788 96 41, Ⓦwww.appenzell.ch). Every Friday at 7pm (June–Sept), *Hotel Säntis* stages an evening of traditional folkloric **music**.

Accommodation

Appenzell's **accommodation** is neat, quiet and characterful, to suit the village. Not many people seem to stay, but it's definitely worth doing so, not least because the village is set on a sloping patch of meadow tipped westwards towards low hills, and on clear summer evenings the tranquil streets are filled with lingering twilight until 10pm.

Adler Hauptgasse 1 ☏071 787 13 89, Ⓦwww.adlerhotel.ch. Attractive, well-run hotel overlooking the river, with a range of quality rooms both modern and traditionally styled. ❸

Appenzell Landsgemeindeplatz ☏071 788 15 15, Ⓦwww.hotel-appenzell.ch. Characterful, heavily gabled old building on the south side of the square, with chunky wooden beds in spacious and comfortable rooms. ❸–❹

Freudenberg Riedstrasse 57 ☏071 787 12 40, Ⓔfreudenbergai@bluewin.ch. It's worth making your way up the hill behind the station to find this place, not so much for the rooms, which are plain and unremarkable, but for the views from the balconies over the village and surrounding countryside. Closed Nov. ❷

Gasthaus Hof Engelgasse 4 ☏071 787 22 10,

Ⓦwww.gasthaus-hof.ch. A small hotel with cosy rooms, just off Landsgemeindeplatz. ❷

Gasthaus Traube Marktgasse 7 ☏071 787 14 07, Ⓦwww.hotel-traube.ch. Pretty place with newly renovated rooms that are small but attractive. Closed Feb. ❸

Landgasthof Eischen ☏071 787 50 30, Ⓦwww.eischen.ch. A comfortable country inn 4km west in Kau, also with good dorms (Fr.35) and a campsite. Closed Feb. ❸

Säntis Landsgemeindeplatz ☏071 788 11 11, Ⓦwww.romantikhotels.com. Top choice, on the north side of the main square, and a member of the prestigious Romantik group. Some rooms feature canopied or four-poster beds and there's polished wood everywhere; smaller attic rooms are priced attractively. ❹

Appenzell traditions

More than most areas of the country, Appenzell has clung on to its many rural **traditions** as modern, living elements of local culture: although you may be tempted to dismiss demonstrations of local crafts or evenings of folkloric music as phoney touristic kitsch, in fact such events are put on as much for the benefit of locals as for visitors. Weddings, dances and celebrations of all kinds count as excuses for locals to don **traditional dress**, with the women in stiff-winged caps and lace-edged dresses, and the men in elaborate embroidered scarlet waistcoats, with tight black trousers and a silver earring dangling from their right ear.

It seems as if everything Appenzell does is just plain different: up until 1988, the Appenzell **school year** began in the spring, instead of in the autumn as everywhere else. The village of **Urnäsch**, 10km west of Appenzell, celebrates New Year's Eve twice, once on December 31 and again, in order to keep faith with the long-abandoned Julian calendar, on January 13. Even the ornate silver **pipes** smoked by Appenzeller old-timers are idiosyncratic, curving down at the end instead of up, with the tobacco kept in place by a little sliding lid.

In politics, too, Appenzell stands alone. It was only in 1990 that the men of Ausserrhoden finally, and reluctantly, allowed **women** to have the vote in cantonal affairs. Innerrhoden held out for another year. Then, in 1998, Ausserrhoden controversially voted to end centuries of tradition by introducing a secret written ballot – thereby abolishing the **Landsgemeinde**, the ancient embodiment of Swiss direct democracy. Innerrhoden, though, will have none of this, and remains one of the last Swiss cantons to use the Landsgemeinde (Glarus – see p.489 – is the only other), in which citizens gather in traditional dress once a year in the town square of the cantonal capital to vote by brandishing a short sword (the badge of citizenship) in response to a series of shouted yay-or-nay questions. It takes place on the last Sunday in April and is a nationally televised event. What the Eurocentric city slickers of Geneva and Basel think of it all is anyone's guess.

Eating and drinking

Of all the local specialities – including *Chäshörnli* (cheese-and-potato minidumplings), *Birnebrot* (pear bread), a sweet liqueur named *Alpenbitter*, and a fragrant herb-based Schnapps dubbed *Kräuter* – the most ubiquitous is ripe **Appenzeller cheese** (see p.47), advertised widely with rustic images of gap-toothed kids and milkmaids. If you buy some, take the shopkeeper's advice and have it vacuum-sealed, otherwise you'll find the pong seeping its way into everything else in your bag.

Many hotels offer quality **eating and drinking**. The best value is *Hotel Appenzell* (closed Tues lunchtime): go through the *confiserie* shop into the non-smoking restaurant behind. *Menus* are from Fr.17, excellently prepared with a light touch; the house speciality is a range of fresh vegetarian and health-conscious food. Elsewhere, traditional fare abounds, relying heavily on pork, potatoes and creamy sauces. *Gasthaus Traube* has *menus* for around Fr.20, while the bustling old-style restaurant in *Gasthaus Hof* concentrates on a host of excellent cheese dishes, including *Käseschnitte* (cheese-on-toast). Luxury *Hotel Säntis* has the swankiest dining in town, although the ground-floor *Stübli* and terrace is considerably cheaper and much less formal than the upstairs restaurant with its Gallic-accented menu.

Around Appenzell

Walking in the pretty countryside **around Appenzell** can be rewarding, with inns and guesthouses dotting the landscape – so many that you could walk for days from inn to inn without encountering a town and without having to carry food. The Appenzell tourist office has plenty of maps, trail guides and mountain-bike routes, as well as the brochure *Barfuss durchs Appenzellerland*, outlining a trail which you can follow barefoot through grassy meadows from Appenzell village up to **Gonten**, a couple of hours west and scene of late-June's cantonal Schwingen (traditional wrestling) championships.

Most hiking trails are crammed into and around the narrow valleys sand-wiched between the three great rock walls of the **Alpstein** range. The small village of **Wasserauen**, a short train ride or a couple of hours' walk south of Appenzell, is the base station for a cable-car running up to **EBENALP** (Ⓦwww.ebenalp.ch; 1640m), from where a high-level route takes you five hours along the ridge to the Säntis. Another route from Wasserauen runs up for an hour into the narrow valley of the beautiful **SEEALPSEE** (1141m). This isolated tarn is the site of a celebrated annual folkloric festival which culminates in a yodelling of Mass on Assumption Day morning (Aug 15). The attractive *Berggasthaus Forelle* on the lakeshore (Ⓣ071 799 11 88, Ⓕ071 799 15 96; ❶; April–Oct) has comfortable, traditional-style rooms as well as dorms for Fr.25, while around the lake is the simpler *Berggasthaus Seealpsee* (Ⓣ071 799 11 40, Ⓕ071 799 18 20; ❶; April–Oct). Both have terrace tables at which to enjoy succulently prepared lake fish. Beyond Seealpsee, a two-hour trail hairpins its way steeply up to tranquil **MEGLISALP** (1517m), with its own rustic *Berggasthaus Meglisalp* (Ⓣ & Ⓕ071 799 11 28; ❶; dorms Fr.26; May–Oct), focus of a weekend of folkloric dancing in late July.

Appenzell's most famous peak is the **Säntis** (2502m), well below the proportions of the Alps but nonetheless the highest point for miles around. Trains run from Appenzell to the small town of **Urnäsch**, departure point for hourly buses which follow a winding road up to **Schwägalp**, from where a cable-car (Fr.33 return; Ⓦwww.saentisbahn.ch) rises to the Säntis summit. This is a popular day-trip, especially in summer: if you're staying for lunch, you'd do best to aim for the older, more atmospheric *Berggasthaus* on top, rather than the newer canteen-style diner – both, though, have terraces offering spectacular panoramas. From the summit, it's an easy three-and-a-half-hour hike along to Ebenalp, from where there's transport back to Appenzell.

Stein

Herisau, capital of the half-canton Appenzell Ausserrhoden, and connected to Appenzell village by train, is a workaday town, handy for its hourly bus to St Gallen via the backcountry village of **STEIN** (often dubbed "Stein AR"). Stein's main draw is the engaging **Appenzeller Volkskunde Museum** (Folklore Museum; Mon 1.30–5pm, Tues–Sat 10am–noon & 1.30–5pm, Sun 10am–5pm; Fr.7; SMP; Ⓦwww.appenzeller-museum-stein.ch). Make sure you pick up the English notes from the desk. The ground floor has an introduction to Appenzell and its people, along with displays on local crafts. Upstairs is a reconstructed traditional wooden bedroom, as well as displays of embroidery, weaving and jewellery. The highlight is on the top floor, which is devoted to Appenzell's **folk art**, made by nineteenth-century farmers who decorated furniture, milk pails and other implements with ornate designs, painting scenes from daily life on canvas and wood. Johannes Müller is the most prolific of these uncelebrated artists; he lived all his 91 years in Stein as a clockmaker, and his simple paintings are characterized by vibrantly green hills crisscrossed by long lines of cattle led by herders in traditional dress.

Next door is the **Appenzeller Schaukäserei** (Show Dairy; daily 9am–7pm; Nov–April closes 6pm; free; Ⓦwww.showcheese.ch), where you can watch the various processes of cheesemaking from a gallery above the huge vats and churns – try to time your visit to coincide with the main cheesemaking procedures (which stop at 3.30pm). Cheese-lovers won't want to miss the Sunday morning all-you-can-eat breakfast buffet (9–11am; Fr.19).

Glarnerland

Switzerland's least-known and hardest-to-reach region is **Glarnerland**, centred on Canton Glarus, a tract of mountain territory featuring just a handful of widely spaced settlements and very low-key tourism. Its isolation is its main attraction: this is a place to turn your back on the crowds and head for the wilderness.

The slender, cliff-girt **Walensee** is pretty much bypassed by both the N3 autobahn and Chur–Zürich trains. **Ziegelbrücke**, at the lake's western tip, marks the start of routes squeezing southwards 12km to **GLARUS**, the titchy capital, dwarfed by the looming Glärnisch massif. Its train station holds the cantonal **tourist office** (Mon–Fri 9am–noon & 2–5pm; July–Oct also Sat same hours & Sun 9am–1pm; ☏055 650 20 90, ⓦwww.glarnerland.ch); their wide range of outdoorsy deals includes two days' all-in hill-trekking by horse (Fr.120) or llama (Fr.150). There's little reason to hang around in Glarus, unless you're here on the first Sunday in May for the **Landsgemeinde**, a traditional form of direct democracy when cantonal affairs are decided by public voting in the main square (for more, see p.487).

The main road continues south to scenic **Linthal**, base station for a short funicular ride up to the unsung gem of the region – the car-free mountain resort of **BRAUNWALD**; there are few quieter, more refreshing places to rest up, take in the views and do a bit of walking or gentle skiing or snowboarding. As you emerge from the top station, you'll see map-boards of the village and its surrounds; to the right is the **tourist office** (June–Oct & Dec–Easter Mon–Fri 8.30–11.45am & 2.15–5.30pm, Sat 8.30–11.45am; rest of year Mon–Fri 9–11.45am; ☏055 653 65 85, ⓦwww.braunwald.ch), who can advise on routes: there are lifts to higher slopes as well as a host of walks around Braunwald's plateau. **Hotels** all have balconies and sun-terraces; the *Alpenblick* (☏055 643 15 44, ⓦwww.alpenblick-braunwald.ch; ❹) is conveniently beside the funicular station, the *Ahorn* has some shared-bath rooms (☏055 643 15 37, ⓕ055 643 17 35; ❷; closed April, May & Nov), and there's an HI **hostel**, *Jugi Zwärgehüsli* (☏055 643 13 56, ⓦwww.youthhostel.ch; closed April, May & Nov; Fr.41).

The Klausen Pass

Beyond Linthal, the road climbs west over the **Klausen Pass** (1948m). This is a simply stunning drive through breathtaking scenery, but is little used: the road is only open in summer (June–Oct) and is mostly very narrow – just about two car-widths between the cliff and the ravine. Tortuous hairpin bends mean that you should reckon on at least an hour and a half to cover the 47km to Altdorf (see p.410).

After some steep climbing out of Linthal, you emerge into the lovely, high, enclosed valley of **URNERBODEN**, dotted with a few farms and dozens of wandering cows; to the left is the Clariden (3268m), to the right the cliffs of the Ortstock (2717m). The road meanders its way past a couple of inns, including the sturdy *Urnerboden* (☏055 643 14 16; ❷), which is open year-round –

in winter, there's some fine cross-country skiing up here. Faced by a sheer cliff at the head of the valley, the road somehow jinks its way up and around to the pass itself, where there's a refreshment kiosk; a kilometre down the other side – just before the truly awesome scenery kicks in – is the century-old *Hotel Klausenpasshöhe* (T041 879 11 64, Wwww.klausenpasshoehe.ch; ●), with century-old rooms to match. The route from here all the way down to Altdorf is a battle: you'll constantly be having to drag your eyes away from the spectacular views to concentrate on the road.

Postbuses run both ways on the "Historic Route Express" between Linthal and Altdorf in summer (June–Sept; reserve on T041 870 21 36, Wwww.post.ch), and from Linthal up to Urnerboden all year round.

Liechtenstein

Only slightly larger than Manhattan island, the Principality of **LIECHTENSTEIN** (*Fürstentum Liechtenstein*, abbreviated to "FL") is the world's fourth-smallest country, a chip of green squeezed between the Rhine and the Austrian Alps. It's a quiet, unassuming place, home to 32,000 mostly Catholic Liechtensteiners, who take an impressive 22 days public holiday a year, sing their own German words to the tune of "God Save the Queen" as the national anthem, and regard themselves as entirely separate from the Swiss, with whom neighbourly relations only began in 1923. This said, you won't notice many differences and, inevitably, the main reason to visit is the novelty value. There are some rustic spots outside the toytown capital **Vaduz** to enjoy, as well as lonely walks and family-friendly skiing in the craggy mountains.

Regular **postbuses** run to Vaduz from Sargans and Buchs, both of them on the main SBB train line between St Gallen and Chur. Austrian Railways (ÖBB, or OeBB) operates six daily **trains** between Buchs and Feldkirch (Austria) which stop at Schaan, 3km north of Vaduz, from where buses shuttle into the capital. The principality's biggest event is **Staatsfeiertag** (National Holiday; Wwww.staats-feiertag.li), on August 15, which culminates in a huge fireworks display. There's a clutch of **music festivals** in June and July, including the rock/dance-oriented Little Big One (Wwww.littlebigone.com) and the more esoteric Guitar Days (Wwww.ligita.li). The tourist office has good-value package deals for these.

Some history

Liechtenstein is the only country in the world to have been named after the people who bought it. After the Romans came through in 15 BC, the area was

---

Exploring Liechtenstein

Postbuses (Wwww.lba.li) serve all eleven villages. Swiss transport passes are valid for journeys into and around Liechtenstein, apart from the Austrian trains from Buchs to Schaan. Otherwise, the best deal is the **Erlebnispass Liechtenstein** (3/7 days Fr.25/42), covering unlimited bus transport, a city-train tour in Vaduz, the Malbun chairlift, admission to all museums, a wine-tasting at the Hofkellerei des Fürstens, and other attractions. The Vaduz tourist office has details of similarly good passes for families. A one-week bus pass costs a bargain Fr.10. If you have your own car, you can pay Fr.150 to have an English-speaking **guide** sitting with you for a two-hour trip around the country, explaining Liechtensteiner history and culture on the way.

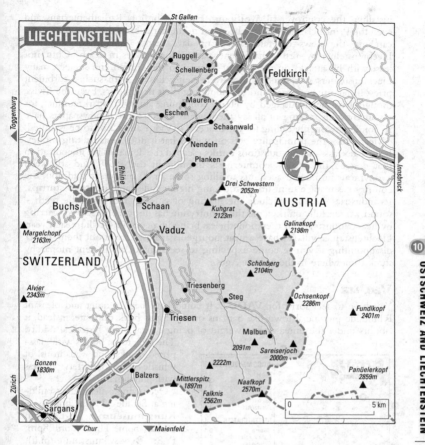

passed from pillar to post until 1699, when Johann Adam Andreas of the **Von Liechtenstein** family of Vienna purchased the Lordship of Schellenberg, and then in 1712 the County of Vaduz, in order to get a seat for himself in the imperial German Diet of Princes. Shortly after, the little patch was renamed after him. Liechtenstein won independence in 1866, the Prince taking an active political role within a so-called **democratic monarchy** linked to Austria-Hungary. After that empire's war defeat, the principality negotiated a customs treaty with Switzerland in 1923, since when borders between the two neighbours have been open and unmarked. The next milestone was 1984, when women got the vote.

The current head of state is His Serene Highness **Prince Hans Adam II von und zu Liechtenstein**, who – unlike most European monarchs – wields considerable power and makes a point of regularly speaking his mind on political matters. He has guided Liechtenstein's entry into the UN (1990) and the sub-EU European Economic Area (1995), both of which controversially created a gulf in relations with more reticent Switzerland.

As if in return, Liechtenstein was landed in 1997 with the surprise announcement from Rome that the pope had created a new Archdiocese of Vaduz, installing the controversial **Wolfgang Haas** as bishop. Parliamentarians and even the Prince claimed to have been left in the dark about the announcement, catching the news on television four days before Christmas. Haas – a Liechtensteiner by birth – had spent years raising hackles in nearby Chur, not least with his attacks on the role of women in the church and society; many Liechtensteiners wondered if they were being foisted with such a turbulent priest in recompense for politically snubbing their neighbours. Even the Swiss, though, have been outraged by Haas's continuing ability to spark conflict, for instance by his sacking of all lay theologians in 2002. Local newspapers have responded by openly calling for the dioceses of Vaduz and Chur to be reunited.

Meanwhile, the principality gets on with what it does best: making money. Its low-tax, ask-me-no-questions **banks** escaped the demands for liberalization that dogged their Swiss counterparts throughout the 1990s, and still keep anonymous numbered accounts totalling some Fr.80 billion. In addition, the country has made a mint from producing highly collectable **postage stamps**. Its industries – which include the making of sausage skins and false teeth – sound wonderfully quirky (and the countryside has noticeably escaped scarring by heavy industry), but they nonetheless bring in a cool Fr.4 billion each year. Liechtensteiner villages have a neat, bourgeois atmosphere about them, rather disappointing if you've come expecting to see signs of an ancient monarchy stuck somewhere in the Middle Ages.

Vaduz

You have to feel sorry for **VADUZ**. It could have been a quiet and pleasant Rhineside provincial town like Sargans on the Swiss bank opposite; instead, it labours under the unreasonable weight of being capital of an historical oddity. The little town bulges with glass-plated banks and squadrons of whistle-stop foreigners aimless with anticlimax.

Occupying a sleek, dark building at Städtle 32 is the impressive **Kunstmuseum** (Tues–Sun 10am–5pm, Thurs until 8pm; Fr.8; ⓦwww.kunstmuseum.li). Temporary shows from its collection embrace modern and contemporary art, particularly strong on sculpture: you may find a Courbet landscape alongside a Giacometti bronze opposite a spindly Arte Povera installation. Running simultaneously are exhibits taken from the world-famous private collection of old masters inherited and added to by the Prince, which includes works by Rubens, Van Dyck, Rem-brandt, Jordaens and others. The juxtaposition is particularly en-gaging, played out in such a well-designed space.

VADUZ

ACCOMMODATION
Engel 4
Gasthof Löwen 3
Jugendherberge 2
Real 5
Säga 6
Sonnenhof 1

RESTAURANTS
Cesare D
Café Amann E
City-Snack C
Eredi Florini B
Torkel A

Liechtenstein has its own country code ☎423, completely separate from the Swiss phone system. For more, see p.55.

Otherwise, aside from a wander in the older streets north of the centre, interest is thin. Philatelists will love the **Briefmarkenmuseum** (Postage Stamps; daily 10am–noon & 1–5pm; free), in the same building as the tourist office. Perched picturesquely on the forested hillside above Vaduz is the Prince's photogenic restored sixteenth-century **Schloss Vaduz**, off-limits to the public. Knots of people gather at the castle gates to admire the doughty towers and turrets. Groups of ten or more can book a guided tour of the **Hofkellerei des Fürsten von Liechtenstein**, the Prince's own vineyard and cellars, situated just north of Vaduz (reservations essential ☎232 10 18, ⓦwww.hofkellerei.li; price varies).

Practicalities

The helpful **tourist office**, which has a host of attractive all-in deals (including B&Bs), is at Städtle 37 (Mon–Fri 8am–noon & 1.30–5pm; April–Oct also Sat 9/10am–noon & 1.30–5pm; May–Sept also Sun 9/10am–noon & 1.30–5pm; ☎232 14 43, ⓦwww.tourismus.li). Most of their time is taken up banging Liechtenstein stamps into visitors' passports – an entirely unnecessary novelty that nonetheless costs Fr.2. **Rent bikes** from Sigi's Velo Shop (☎384 27 50, ⓦwww.sigis-veloshop.li), Bike Garage (☎390 03 90, ⓦwww.bikegarage .li), or the train stations in Buchs or Sargans (both daily 6am–8.30pm).

Best-value **hotel** is spotless, family-run *Säga* (☎392 43 77, Ⓕ392 34 41; ❸), 6km south in the countryside near Triesen, much more attractive and cosy than Vaduz's cheapest option, *Engel*, Städtle 13 (☎236 17 17, Ⓔhotelengel @freesurf.ch; ❸). Period furniture adds to the atmosphere of the 600-year-old *Gasthof Löwen*, Herrengasse 35 (☎238 11 44, ⓦwww.hotels.li; ❺), while top choices are city-centre *Real*, Städtle 21 (☎232 22 22, ⓦwww.relaischateaux.ch; ❺–❽), and *Sonnenhof*, set in its own grounds at Mareestrasse 29 (☎232 11 92, ⓦwww.relaischateaux.ch; ❼–❽). Beside *Säga* is the quiet *Mittagsspitze* **campsite** (☎392 36 77, Ⓕ392 36 80). Dorm beds are Fr.29 at the HI **hostel** *Jugendherberge*, 2km north of Vaduz near Schaan, Untere Rüttigasse 6 (☎232 50 22, ⓦwww.youthhostel.ch; ❶; March–Oct; bus to Mühleholz).

Downmarket **restaurants** include fast-food-style dishes at *City-Snack*, Städtle 5, and *Cesare*, Städtle 15, with good Italian *menus* for Fr.20 (closed Sat & Sun). Incognito *Café Amann*, Äulestrasse 56, is worth a look for its value meals and a breath of local atmosphere. *Eredi Florini*, Herrengasse 9 (closed Sun), is a gourmet deli, where rushed business folk stand up to munch a simple but delicious lunch (Fr.12–20) and sloosh down an espresso. *Torkel*, amidst the vineyards off Hintergasse, is owned by the Prince, a perfect place to sample old-style Swiss/Austrian specialities, with *menus* from Fr.30. The best restaurant in the country is *Au Premier* in *Hotel Real*, its vast 20,000-bottle wine cellar complementing the heavy, unreconstructed French cuisine emanating from the kitchen (*menus* from Fr.50).

Around Vaduz

Attractions around the principality are low-key, and aside from the mountain resort of Malbun, almost entirely untouristed. North of Schaan is the Unterland region, with some pleasant walks through the rolling countryside and dark woods. From **Nendeln**, a path climbs for an hour through the forest

△ Schloss Vaduz, Liechtenstein (see p.493)

10

OSTSCHWEIZ AND LIECHTENSTEIN

to **Planken**, Liechtenstein's smallest village (pop. 337), from where a steep 2hr route takes you up to spectacular views at the **Gafadurahütte** at 1428m (℡262 89 27, ⓦwww.alpenverein.li; dorms Fr.17). Further north is tiny **SCHELLENBERG**, overlooked by the ruins of the medieval Obere Burg castle set amidst lush forest. Its sole hotel is the simple, cosy *Krone* (℡373 11 68, ⓦwww.schellenberg.li; ❶), where children get a discount.

South of Vaduz is the Liechtensteiner Oberland, with workaday Triesen overshadowed by pretty **TRIESENBERG**, perched on a sunny hillside above the Rhine and best known as the adopted home of a community of Walser people, who left their homes in Wallis (German-speaking Valais) in the thirteenth century to spread out across central Europe. Many of the houses are old wooden chalets built in the Walser style. The modern, well-presented **Walser Heimatmuseum** (Tues–Fri 1.30–5.30pm, Sat 1.30–5pm; June–Aug also Sun 2–5pm; Fr.2) documents Walser history and culture. Triesenberg's best **hotel** is *Kulm* (℡237 79 79, ⓦwww.hotelkulm.com; ❷–❸), with good food and service. A fine, scenic walk leads through Gnalp and Masescha and back (3hr).

Malbun

From Triesenberg, a back-country road climbs through a long tunnel beneath an Alpine ridge to **STEG** and on to **MALBUN**. This quiet hamlet at 1600m is Liechtenstein's only ski resort, with half-a-dozen little lifts (ⓦwww .bergbahnen.li) and a handful of gentle runs where Prince Charles and Princess Anne learned their snowploughing technique, back in the days before Klosters became the British royals' choice resort. Steg is the trailhead for a web of **cross-country ski** routes through the Valüna valley to the south. In summer, the area has a wealth of lonesome high-country **hikes**: a classic full-day mountain trek from Steg rises south through the Valüna valley up to the Naafkopf (2570m), before returning via the Augstenberg and Malbun. From Malbun, a rewarding three- or four-hour hike begins with a journey up the Sareis chairlift and then heads south along the Austrian border to the scenically positioned **Pfalzerhütte** at 2108m (℡263 36 79; ❶; dorms Fr.17–25).

Malbun's **tourist office** (June–Oct & mid-Dec to mid-April Mon–Sat 9am–noon & 1.30–5pm; ℡263 65 77, ⓦwww.malbun.li) can give details of winter ski/snowboard packages (3 nights half board from Fr.510 for two) and summer hiking deals (7 nights half board plus perks: Fr.1198 for two). The most congenial **place to stay** is *Berggasthaus Sücka* near Steg (℡263 25 79, Ⓔsuecka1@adon.li; ❶; dorms Fr.29), also with good food. The tiny *Walserhof* is Malbun's budget deal (℡264 43 23, Ⓕ384 31 90; ❷), but the *Alpen* is more attractive (℡263 11 81, Ⓔalpenhotel@supra.net; ❷). The chalet-style *Malbunerhof* (℡263 29 44, ⓦwww.schwaerzler-hotels.com; ❸–❹) is the most upmarket choice, with very comfortable balconied rooms. **Eating and drinking** is in the handful of hotel restaurants, or at the *Bergrestaurant Sareiserjoch* – the top station of the Sareis chairlift (2000m), or an hour's hike up from Malbun – which has a scenic terrace, hearty Swiss dishes that rely heavily on the local Malbuner smoked ham, and dorms (Fr.48 half-board). All these places close in April, May and November.

Travel details

Trains

Appenzell to: Herisau (hourly; 35min); St Gallen (every 30min; 45min); Urnäsch (hourly; 15min); Wasserauen (hourly; 15min).

Buchs to: Chur (hourly; 35min); Rorschach (hourly; 40min); St Gallen (hourly; 55min); Sargans (hourly; 10min); Schaan (6 daily; 5min).

Frauenfeld to: Romanshorn (hourly; 30min); St Gallen (twice hourly; 1hr – change in Weinfelden or Wil); Winterthur (twice hourly; 15min); Zürich (hourly; 40min).

Kreuzlingen to: Romanshorn (every 30min; 25min); Rorschach (every 30min; 50min); Schaffhausen (hourly; 55min).

Romanshorn to: Arbon (every 30min; 10min); Frauenfeld (hourly; 30min); Kreuzlingen (every 30min; 25min); Rorschach (every 30min; 15min); St Gallen (hourly; 25min); Schaffhausen (hourly; 1hr 25min); Stein-am-Rhein (hourly; 55min).

Rorschach to: Chur (hourly; 1hr 20min); Kreuzlingen (every 30min; 50min); Romanshorn (every 30min; 15min); St Gallen (twice hourly; 15min).

St Gallen to: Appenzell (every 30min; 45min); Bern (every 30min; 2hr 30min); Buchs (hourly; 55min); Chur (hourly; 1hr 35min); Frauenfeld (twice hourly; 1hr); Geneva (twice hourly; 4hr 20min); Herisau (3 hourly; 10min); Romanshorn (hourly; 25min); Rorschach (twice hourly; 15min); Sargans (hourly; 1hr 10min); Schaffhausen (hourly; 1hr 30min; some change in Winterthur); Stein-am-Rhein (hourly; 1hr 25min); Winterthur (twice hourly; 45min); Zürich (twice hourly; 1hr 10min).

Sargans to: Buchs (hourly; 10min); Chur (3 hourly; 20min); Romanshorn (hourly; 50min); St Gallen (hourly; 1hr 10min); Zürich (hourly; 1hr 10min).

Schaffhausen to: Kreuzlingen (hourly; 55min); Lugano (hourly; 4hr 15min); Romanshorn (hourly; 1hr 25min); Stein-am-Rhein (every 30min; 20min); Schloss Laufen (hourly; 5min); Winterthur (hourly; 35min); Zürich (hourly; 35min).

Stein-am-Rhein to: Kreuzlingen (hourly; 30min); Romanshorn (hourly; 55min); St Gallen (hourly; 1hr 35min).

Winterthur to: Baden (every 30min; 50min); Bern (every 30min; 1hr 50min); Schaffhausen (hourly; 35min); St Gallen (every 30min; 45min); Stein-am-Rhein (hourly; 40min); Zürich (4 hourly; 20min).

Buses

Frauenfeld to: Kartause Ittingen (2 daily; 10min); Stein-am-Rhein (hourly; 30min).

Stein AR to: Herisau (hourly; 20min); St Gallen (hourly; 15min).

Stein-am-Rhein to: Frauenfeld (hourly; 30min); Warth (hourly; 20min).

Vaduz to: Buchs (every 20min; 15min); Malbun (hourly; 30min); Sargans (every 20min; 30min); Schaan (every 20min; 10min); Steg (hourly; 25min); Triesen (every 20min; 5min); Triesenberg (every 20min; 15min).

Boats

(Following is a summary of May–Sept services.)

Kreuzlingen to: Romanshorn (at least 2 daily; 1hr 15min); Schaffhausen (at least 3 daily; 3hr 45min); Stein-am-Rhein (at least 3 daily; 2hr 25min).

Romanshorn to: Arbon (at least 3 daily; 30min); Friedrichshafen, Germany (at least hourly; 40min); Kreuzlingen (at least 2 daily; 1hr 5min); Rorschach (at least 3 daily; 55min).

Rorschach (Hafen) to: Romanshorn (at least 3 daily; 55min).

Schaffhausen to: Kreuzlingen (at least 3 daily; 4hr 45min); Stein-am-Rhein (at least 3 daily; 2hr).

Graubünden

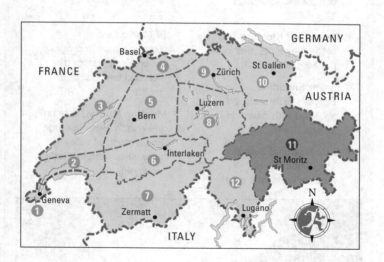

CHAPTER 11

Highlights

✳ **Rhätische Bahn** The local train company has a superbly scenic network. See p.502

✳ **Arosa** Outstanding small resort, high in the mountains above Chur. See p.508

✳ **Flims-Laax** Top destination for snowboarders. See p.515

✳ **Davos and Klosters** Two of the biggest names in the Alps. See p.518

✳ **Lower Engadine** Fairytale high-sided valley, lined with deep, dark forests. See p.526

✳ **Parc Naziunal Svizzer** The country's only national park, with a network of fine walking trails. See p.529

✳ **Müstair** Remote village huddled round a frescoed abbey. See p.530

✳ **Upper Engadine** Perhaps the most beautiful valley in the Alps, with over 320 days of sunshine a year. See p.531

✳ **St Moritz** One of Europe's best-known ski resorts, not just for the rich and famous. See p.532

✳ **Muottas Muragl** Gaze on the mighty Bernina range and a string of valley-floor lakes from this lofty viewpoint. See p.538

Graubünden

S witzerland's largest canton, **GRAUBÜNDEN** occupies the entire southeast of the country, encompassing a sparsely populated area that borders on Austria to the north and Italy to the east and south. Its folded landscape of deep, isolated valleys, sheer rocky summits and thick pine forests makes it the wildest and loneliest part of Switzerland, more difficult than most to get around in, but also more rewarding, with some of the finest scenery in the Alps. Glaciers oozing from between the high mountains launch two of Europe's great rivers – the Rhine and the Inn – on their long journeys to the North Sea and the Black Sea respectively, while two smaller rivers water pomegranates, figs and chestnuts in secluded southern valleys en route to the Po and the Adriatic.

The canton – once the Roman province of Rhaetia Prima – is officially **trilingual**, known as Graubünden in German, Grigioni in Italian and Grischun in **Romansh**, the last of these a direct descendant of Latin which has survived locked away in the mountain fastnesses far from the capital **Chur** since the legions departed 1500 years ago. You'll also come across the canton's French name of **Grisons**, although there are no French-speaking communities.

Until the nineteenth century, Rhaetia was entirely separate from its western neighbour of Helvetia. As Helvetia began to experience stirrings towards independence in the thirteenth and fourteenth centuries, the population of Rhaetia also began to organize themselves. The impenetrable landscape was on their side: as one historian, Benjamin Barber, accurately noted, "an army occupying Chur no more controls Graubünden than does one in Milan or Vienna." The 1367 League of the House of God was the first of these popular associations, soon followed by the **Grey League** in 1395 (formed by a band of highland shepherds dubbed "the grey farmers" for their woollen cloth) and, in 1436, the League of the Ten Jurisdictions. These three came together in 1471 to pledge mutual assistance, and were soon able – with the spur of the Reformation – to seize political power from the nobles. Since then the people have been free, and they relish the fact more than most other Swiss. It was only in 1803 that the united "Graubünden", or Grey Leagues, finally assented to join the Swiss Confederation, and to this day Bündners consistently vote in large numbers against joining the EU.

The canton's resorts – headed by **St Moritz**, **Klosters** and **Davos** – are some of the most famous names in the Alps and offer world-class skiing and top-quality hiking, but they're far from the whole story. The beautiful **Engadine valley** runs for almost 100km along a southern terrace of the Alps, bathed in glittering sunlight that pours from blue skies for well over 300 days a year. This is the heartland of Romansh culture, with its own language, style and architecture. South of the Alps, three of the canton's most enticing valleys –

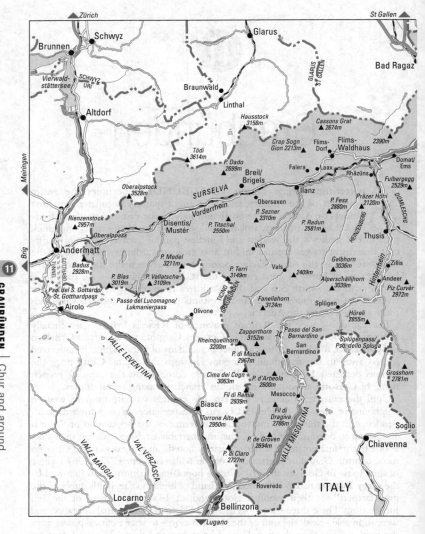

Bregaglia and **Poschiavo** in particular – are Italian-speaking, filled with a Mediterranean lushness in their flora and cuisine that could easily tempt you to leave the mountains behind and just keep heading south.

Chur and around

Sitting in a deep valley carved by the Rhine, **CHUR** (pronounced *koor*), the live-ly cantonal capital, is much overlooked: it has a characterful Old Town, full of

medieval cobbled alleys, secret courtyards and solid, foursquare town houses, that is dominated by a huge **cathedral** symbolizing the rule of the bishop-princes of years gone by. Aside from offering "the best shopping between Zürich and Milan", Chur serves as the linchpin of transport routes, with buses and trains sneaking their way through the high, narrow valleys of Central Graubünden to Davos and St Moritz, and west through Surselva to the high Alps around Andermatt. In a remote mountain fastness southeast of the town sits the picturesque resort of **Arosa**, while the gentler foothills to the northeast are cloyingly dubbed "**Heidiland**".

Chur is celebrated as the oldest continuously inhabited city north of the Alps, with archeological finds dating back to 11,000 BC. Situated on prime

Graubünden's **Rhätische Bahn** (RhB; Ⓦ www.rhb.ch) has one of the most scenic train networks in the world. Superbly engineered, with tracks spanning deep valleys on impossibly high viaducts and crossing several of the region's mountain passes without recourse to cogs, it can get you to sights and views far off any roads. Many of the most dramatic routes are marketed as attractions in their own right (see p.30), although bear in mind that, despite the hype, they're all served by regular, scheduled trains at **standard fares**; the only extra costs are seat reservations (always advisable; Fr.5), surcharges to sit in panoramic coaches (Fr.9–15), upgrades to first class and/or reservations for the dining car that often accompanies longer journeys. Otherwise, all RhB trains are **free** to InterRail, Eurail and Swiss Pass holders (except Glacier Express trains between Disentis/Mustér and Brig, which are free to Swiss Pass holders but full price to Eurailers and InterRailers).

The RhB **regional pass** is good value. The **summer** version (May–Oct) costs Fr.140 and is valid for ten days: three days of free travel on all RhB trains and the SBB line between Chur and Bad Ragaz, as well as all postbuses and local buses and virtually all cable-cars and mountain railways too, plus seven days at half-price. You can also add extra free days (Fr.50 for two). The **winter** version (Nov–April) costs Fr.85 and is valid for five days: train travel is free for two days and half-price for three days, buses are half-price for all five days, and you get one cable-car or funicular journey for free (up and down). Both are buyable from local stations; for full information, check Ⓦ www.rhb.ch.

Despite the excellent train service, if you want to cover a lot of ground independently, Graubünden – more than most Swiss cantons – merits **renting a car**. Buses penetrate to the most remote valleys and hamlets, but often only every two hours, and journeys can be long and tortuous. Long-distance cycling routes tend to trace the main valleys only or require you to tackle steep gradients. Your own car can let you investigate outlying corners that might otherwise take up a full and frustrating day on public transport.

Special train journeys

It's easy to cherry-pick the most attractive or convenient bits of any of these routings to construct your own itinerary; see p.30 for more. The **Glacier Express** runs

north–south routes of commerce and communication, Curia Rhaetorium was founded by the **Romans** after their conquest of 15 BC. **St Luzius**, a missionary, is reputed to have brought Christianity to the region in the fourth century, and the first **bishop** of Chur to be positively documented was Asinio, in the year 451. A few centuries on, the bishop had become a powerful political ruler, enjoying the patronage of Holy Roman Emperors, and by 1170, the post was officially recognized as a Prince-Bishopric. With the populist movements of the fourteenth century, the Prince-Bishops' power began to erode, and when the **Reformation** took hold in 1526, Chur's wealthy merchants and craftsworkers were able to take over all significant political decision-making for themselves. Today, from his palace beside the cathedral, the bishop of Chur still controls a diocese covering Graubünden, all the central Swiss cantons and Zürich, and students flock to the adjacent St Luzi theological seminary to train for the priesthood.

Arrival, information and accommodation

Chur's **train** and **postbus station** – resplendent beneath a vast, fully glazed arching roof, reminiscent of nineteenth-century railway architecture – is at the

on different routes from Chur, Davos or St Moritz west over the high Alps to Zermatt. The **Bernina Express** runs from Chur to St Moritz, then over the high Bernina Pass to Tirano, switching to a postbus for the journey around Lake Como to Lugano. The **Heidi Express** heads from Landquart through Klosters and Davos, linking in with the Bernina route to Tirano and Lugano. The **Arosa Express** does the long, spectacular pull up from Chur to Arosa. Finally, the **Engadin Star** runs from Landquart direct to St Moritz, via Klosters and the Vereina Tunnel (June–Oct only), on a route that would normally require a couple of changes.

The RhB also runs its own **Pullman** coaches on various scenic full-day routes, on selected days in summer only (June–Sept) – from Chur/St Moritz to Tirano and back, St Moritz to Scuol, a circular trip to and from Chur via Davos, and more – as well as similar outings pulled by **steam-engines**; check the website for full details. Perhaps the most fun journey of the lot is on the **Railrider**, a roofless train completely open to the elements, which shuttles the forty minutes between Filisur and Preda on the steep, dramatic Albula route every Sunday in July and August (Fr.15; no reservation needed).

Other package deals

Aside from the trains, Freizeit Graubünden, an association of tourist offices, has put together a number of **package** deals for the central region around Chur: three nights' B&B in a three-star hotel in Chur, plus a regional transport pass, costs Fr.360 per person in a double room. One of their best **hiking** packages follows the restored Via Spluga trail in five stages all the way from Thusis to Chiavenna: five nights' B&B at one-star hotels, including four packed lunches, entrance to the Viamala gorge and baggage transport from hotel to hotel, costs Fr.279 per person in a double room. For information and bookings, check ⒲www.freizeit-graubuenden.ch. The cantonal tourist office also has information on package deals and tours, at ⒲www .graubuenden.ch.

head of Bahnhofstrasse, five minutes northwest of the Old Town; it has bike rental (daily 6am–8.50pm) and a change counter. The **tourist office** at Grabenstrasse 5, 100m east of Postplatz (Mon 1.30–6pm, Tues–Fri 8.30am–noon & 1.30–6pm, Sat 9am–noon; ℡081 252 18 18, ⒲www.churtourismus.ch), has pamphlets explaining the red and green footprints painted on the pavements, which show the routes of self-guided walking tours: the longer red route is the better of the two. The tourist office also offers its own excellent **guided walk** (April–Oct Wed 2.30pm; Fr.8). The cantonal **hospital**, Loestrasse 170 (℡081 256 61 11), has a 24-hour emergency room, and there's a **laundry** beside the Obertor on Grabenstrasse (Mon–Sat 9am–midnight, Sun noon–midnight; Fr.6).

Hotels

Drei Könige Reichsgasse 18 ℡081 252 17 25, ⒲www.dreikoenige.ch. A 200-year-old inn steps from the tourist office in the Old Town, characterful and pleasant, also with some budget backpacker rooms. Occasionally surly service can let it down. ❷–❸

Franziskaner Kupfergasse 18 ℡ & ℗081 252 12 61. Plain, inexpensive rooms in the Old Town, both ensuite and shared-bath. ❷

Freieck Reichsgasse 44 ℡081 252 17 92, ⒲www.freieck.ch. Comfortable mid-range place spread across a couple of old renovated buildings, with some good rooms updated with pine floors and fresh linen. ❸

Stern Reichsgasse 11 ℡081 252 35 55, ⒲www.stern-chur.ch. Best in town. An historic inn – member of the Romantik group – with

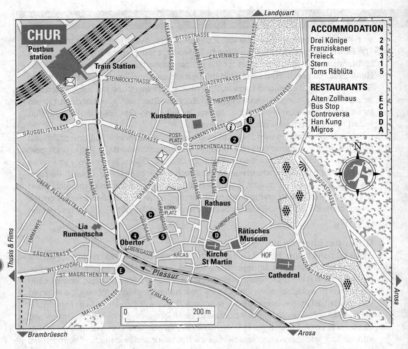

◄ Landquart

CHUR

Postbus station

Train Station

Kunstmuseum

GÄUGGELISTRASSE

POST-PLATZ

STORCHENGASSE

Rathaus

KORN-PLATZ

Lia Rumantscha

Obertor

Rätisches Museum

Kirche St Martin

Cathedral

Plessur

ARCAS

HOF

◄ Thusis & Films

◄ Brambrüesch

Arosa ►

0   200 m

ACCOMMODATION

Drei Könige	2
Franziskaner	4
Freieck	3
Stern	1
Toms Räblüta	5

RESTAURANTS

Alten Zollhaus	E
Bus Stop	C
Controversa	B
Han Kung	D
Migros	A

top-quality service, modern, wood-beamed rooms and parking. The excellent restaurant is a particular asset. ❹

Toms Räblüta Pfisterplatz 1 ☎081 257 13 57, ⓦwww.toms.ch. Lovely guildhouse dating from 1483, with elaborate scrollwork on its facade, an excellent young, up-to-date restaurant and cosy, attractive rooms. ❷–❸

Hostel

Jugendherberge (HI hostel) Voa Sartons 41, Valbella ☎081 384 12 08, ⓦwww.youthhostel.ch.

Nearest to Chur, 12km south in the resort of Valbella. Dorms Fr.24. Mid-June to Oct & mid-Dec to April. ❶

Campsite

Au Felsenaustrasse 61 ☎081 284 22 83, ⓦwww.camping-chur.ch. Open year-round, 1km northwest of the centre.

The Town

Chur's picturesque Old Town nestles in the shadow of the cathedral, which looms on high ground to the southeast. The alleys and fountained squares are characterized by their terraces of old houses, traditionally built without shutters and fronted in rather dour, greyish Scalära stone. The main north–south thoroughfare **Poststrasse** bisects the Old Town; at its northern end is busy Postplatz, overlooked by a large villa housing the **Bündner Kunstmuseum** (Tues–Sun 10am–noon & 2–5pm, Thurs until 8pm; admission varies; SMP; ⓦwww.buendner-kunstmuseum.ch), featuring paintings by Graubünden artists Angelika Kauffmann and Giovanni and Alberto Giacometti. Something of a feminist icon during her lifetime and afterwards, Kauffmann was born in Chur on October 30, 1741, and moved to London at the age of 25. She quickly established a solid reputation there, becoming one of the most popular artists of the time, and was one of the founding members of the Royal Academy in 1768. Although she was best known in her day for the kind of dramatic narrative painting exemplified in *Hector and Paris* (1770), on permanent display in the museum, today's art historians tend to reject these works as overly sentimental and favour instead her portraits, of which there are also plenty on show, not least a graceful self-portrait (1780). The museum also stages temporary exhibitions which can draw international attention.

Following Poststrasse 100m south brings you to the arcaded courtyard of the fifteenth-century **Rathaus**. One street to the east is Reichsgasse, an atmospheric old alley with, at no. 57, a plaque commemorating Angelika Kauffmann's birthplace. Reichsgasse ends in the attractive open square of Arcas, dominated by the Gothic **Kirche St Martin**, dating from 1491 and now sporting three beautiful stained-glass windows by Alberto Giacometti. Arcas hosts the lively Gänggelimarkt flea market (1st Sat of month). Opposite the church, bustling Oberegasse – site of a weekly food market (May–Oct Sat morning) – runs west to the **Obertor** gate, remnant of Chur's medieval fortifications. Immediately behind the church rises the hill upon which the cathedral sits; just to the left, in a quiet courtyard at Hofstrasse 1, is the impressive **Rätisches Museum** (Tues–Sun 10am–noon & 2–5pm; Fr.5; Ⓦ www.rm.gr .ch), housing the canton's historical collections on six floors.

The cathedral

Chur is dominated physically and spiritually by its huge **cathedral** (daily 8am–7pm), constructed between 1151 and 1272 in late-Romanesque and Gothic styles. Still hived off from the town by a thick gated wall, which reflects the bitterness of the disputes which flared around the Reformation, the cathedral is the focus of the **Hof**, a complex of eighteenth-century buildings in the heart of the city protecting Chur's religious elite from contact with the mob. Extensive preservation works are in train, and access may be limited for the next few years.

The **interior** is vast and gloomy, with Romanesque capitals above the massive columns showing grotesque creatures and gargoyle-like demons. To the left of the main nave is a blank space where once stood the **altar of St Laurentius**: thieves broke in through the crypt a few years back and destroyed the altar; its paintings were recovered and are now under restoration. Looking back from the **choir steps**, it becomes apparent that the nave is out of alignment with the choir. Many stories are put about as to why this should be, the most fanciful being that the nave was deliberately angled to match the droop of Christ's head on the cross. High up opposite the Baroque **pulpit** is a tiny gallery: this is one end of a "secret" passage from the bishop's palace next door, allowing the bishop to enter the House of God at a suitably lofty altitude and without soiling his shoes on the courtyard outside. It's a great pity that the elaborate winged **high altar**, carved in 1486–92, will remain covered from view for restoration work until at least 2008.

Eating and drinking

Chur's Old Town has a good range of places to **eat**, many of them offering the classic regional dish of *Bündnerfleisch*, prime beef air-dried in an open attic or under the eaves of a barn and sliced paper-thin to adorn a *Bündnerteller* – a carefully presented plate of aromatic cold meats. *Bündnerfleisch* also takes centre-stage in *Bündner Gerstensuppe*, a creamy barley soup with vegetables. With

Children of the Road

The story of the Swiss gypsy people, known as the **Jenisch** (or Yenish), and how they have been treated over the last century by the Swiss authorities, is shocking, and exposes a calculated policy of Nazi-style eugenics carried out in Switzerland behind closed doors well into the 1970s. For almost fifty years, the Swiss government advocated and funded the wholesale kidnapping of Jenisch children, separating more than six hundred babies and toddlers from their families in what was nothing less than a determined attempt to completely wipe out Jenisch culture. Ghosts have not been put to rest thirty years on, and the scandal remains a source of national shame and anger.

The Jenisch are one of the three main groups of central European gypsies, along with the Sinti and the Roma. During and after the great waves of gypsy migration in the seventeenth and eighteenth century, they travelled all over the continent, many arriving in Switzerland and specifically in Graubünden, where they lived a generally quiet, if socially ostracized, life. Following the tide of nationalism that swept through Europe after World War I, the science of **eugenics** gained widespread credibility, with its notion of state-sponsored "cleansing" of the racial gene pool by the forced removal from society of those with mental illnesses, physical disabilities and other characteristics seen as socially aberrant. Along with Jews and homosexuals, people with a lifestyle centred on travelling were singled out for special treatment. In 1926, the Swiss government approved a project set up by the children's charity Pro Juventute intended to eliminate vagrancy. Entitled **Kinder der Landstrasse** ("Children of the Road"), it effectively sanctioned child abduction: police seized Jenisch newborns and infants from their mothers without warning and carted them off to orphanages run by Pro Juventute. Some children were handed on to foster parents, effectively to vanish into society; others ended up shunted from pillar to post until their adulthood. Controlling committees brought in psychologists to deliver lengthy personality assessments and, as a result, large numbers of children were consigned to mental institutions, one of the most notorious of which was the Waldhaus clinic in Chur. Parents were not only not informed of their children's whereabouts, but were actively barred from making inquiries.

Kinder der Landstrasse was founded and directed by Alfred Siegfried. One of the aims of the project, according to Siegfried's own admission, was effectively to eliminate the Jenisch people altogether: "We must say that we have already achieved much if these people do not start a family, do not reproduce without restraint and bring new generations of degenerate and abnormal children into the world." As late as 1964 Siegfried was writing, "Nomadism, like certain dangerous diseases, is primarily transmitted by women… Anyone wishing to combat nomadism efficiently must aim to destroy the travellers' communal existence. Hard as it may seem, we must put an end to their family community. There is no other way." Under Siegfried's

---

hunting still very popular in the countryside all around, you'll see plenty of game on autumn menus, including stews of deer or chamois. Another local speciality is Passugger **mineral water**, bottled in Passugg 2km south; however, it's not worth paying for, since the same stuff flows from every tap and street fountain in town. As the location of the canton's only matriculation college, Chur has loads of pre-university students packing the dozens of **bars** around the Obertor.

Restaurants

Alten Zollhaus Malixerstrasse 1 ☎081 252 33 98. Right beside the Obertor, with plain, hearty meals served downstairs in its cosy *Stübli* from

Fr.11, and more formal dining in the upstairs restaurant, from Fr.20 or so.
Bus Stop Unteregasse 11. Londoners' hearts will warm to the familiar logo outside this daytime

guidance, boys were forced into apprenticeships or onto farms as cheap labour, and girls were often either sent to convents, or simply kept under lock and key: Uschi Waser, chair of Naschet Jenische, a foundation set up to campaign for Jenisch rights, was placed in 23 different institutions in 18 years. Jenisch were not just forbidden from marrying other Jenisch, they were imprisoned for attempting it. Mariella Mehr, a Jenisch writer who has campaigned to expose the Kinder der Landstrasse project, described her treatment at the hands of the scientists: "When I was three years old, they realised I didn't want to talk. They decided to force me. They used a kind of bath-tub… The patients were made to lie in the tub and covered with a plank so they couldn't get out. Only their heads were above water. They were kept there in freezing-cold water for up to twenty hours."

In 1972, the Swiss weekly *Der Schweizerischer Beobachter* exposed the Kinder der Landstrasse project, to universal public outrage. Pro Juventute closed the operation down a year later, and yet, according to official reports, there were about a hundred victims of Kinder der Landstrasse still incarcerated in clinics and institutions in 1988, after the Swiss state had formally acknowledged its moral, political and financial responsibility for the abductions and apologized to the Jenisch. Although Pro Juventute's own summations of individual cases remain under a 100-year embargo, the findings of an **official report** into the whole affair were published in 1998. Ruth Dreyfuss, then Swiss president, commented that "the conclusions of the historians leave no room for doubt. Kinder der Landstrasse is a tragic example of discrimination and persecution of a minority that does not share the way of life of the majority." The effects of the revelations on Swiss society have been devastating: along with the Nazi gold scandal, accusations of collaboration with the Nazis before and during World War II, and continuing evidence from historians undermining the treasured notion of Swiss neutrality, Kinder der Landstrasse – and specifically its cruelty and systematic inhumanity – has delivered a body blow to the generally accepted image of a wholesome, morally upright Switzerland, an image that has been held both by the Swiss themselves and by outsiders for a century or more.

The Jenisch, meanwhile, have begun to gain a new appreciation of their own culture. About 5000 of Switzerland's 35,000 Jenisch still head out on the road each summer, working as antique dealers or craftspeople, handing on their skills and the Jenisch language to new generations. They have been assigned caravan grounds all over the country, and their children can even study while on the road with correspondence courses offered by many Swiss schools for the purpose. The majority of Jenisch however – often light-skinned and fluent in Swiss-German – live a settled life in mostly low-income housing on the edge of many Swiss cities, completely cut off from their culture. Meanwhile, Pro Juventute (⊛ www.projuventute.ch), though it dissociates itself from the Kinder der Landstrasse project these days, is still working to "protect children in danger of abandonment and vagrancy".

sandwich bar, which has an English part-owner. Closed Sun.

Controversa Steinbruchstrasse 2. A classy, modern restaurant with an excellent salad buffet and plenty of light pasta meals with veggie options (Fr.15–20). Closed Sun lunch.

Drei Könige Reichsgasse 18. Attractive wood-panelled dining-room that draws a fair range of locals to sample its hearty, well-priced cuisine. Makes a point of its "Backpacker Menu", a full-blown set meal for Fr.15 or less.

Han Kung Rabengasse 6. Chinese with three-course lunch *menus* for well under Fr.20. Closed Mon.

Migros Gäuggelistrasse 28. Big self-service diner behind the station. Closed Sun.

Stern Reichsgasse 11 ☏081 252 35 55. Top-choice hotel restaurant for characteristically meaty Bündner specialities, with a cosy, intimate atmosphere. *Menus* around Fr.20.

Toms Räblüta Pfisterplatz 1 ☏081 257 13 57. Excellent place for quality regional cooking under an innovative young manager who – rather than faking antiques – has brought in modern furniture

Above Chur – Brambrüesch and the Dreibündenstein

Chur is proud of the fact that it's the only Swiss city with its own hiking and winter-sports area accessible directly from the city centre. The **Brambrüesch** (ⓦ www.brambruesch.ch) rises immediately southwest of the Old Town: its cable-car station is on Kasernenstrasse, five minutes' walk west of the Obertor. Brambrüesch (1600m) is one of the three peaks of the **Dreibündenstein** (2174m), and has plenty of summer hiking routes, as well as paragliding. The best way to sample the area is courtesy of the Dreibündenstein **Erlebnis-Ticket** (Fr.35). With this, your cable-car up the Brambrüesch is free, and then you can hike a two-hour path from the top station – after the first 20min it's fairly flat – to **Pradaschier**, the third Dreibündenstein peak (*Bergrestaurant* open June–Oct). This is the starting-point of the Guinness-authenticated **world's longest *Rodelbahn*** (summer toboggan run; June–Oct Mon–Fri 10am–5pm, Sat 10am–10pm, Sun 9am–6pm; ⓦ www.pradaschier.ch), 3.1km long, with 31 curves, dropping 480m. The Erlebnis-Ticket gives you two rides for free (a chairlift brings you back up to Pradaschier for the second one) and also covers a bus fare from the base station of Churwalden back to Chur. In winter, a low-priced **ski pass** (Fr.27/day; Fr.14 after 1pm) covers chairlifts from Brambrüesch further up the Dreibündenstein, giving access to easy pistes and tobogganing.

and a fresh style to the medieval surroundings of a formal, wood-panelled guildhall dining room. An adjacent "bistro" room has lower prices and a more relaxed atmosphere. Restaurant closed Sat lunch, Sun & Mon; bistro open daily.

Bars

American Sports Bar Rabengasse 7. Convivial joint for familiar beers and TV sport.

Controvini Steinbruchstrasse 2. Chur's first wine-bar, still a chic, popular spot offering over thirty wines by the glass.

Giger Bar Comercialstrasse 23. A blank cube tucked anonymously between office buildings 1500m west of the Old Town in a business-park area of furniture showrooms and petrol stations, but nonetheless much-vaunted for its owner and designer, the Swiss-born, Oscar-winning special-effects supremo H.R. Giger (see p.140). The interi-

or is kitted out in the style of Giger's greatest creation, *Alien*, with sleek, sci-fi power-chairs, jet black decor and a limbless, writhing female torso hoisted above the bar like a flag. Oddly enough, if you go expecting to plug into an exciting cutting-edge subculture, you'll be disappointed: despite the movie-set decor, it's an utterly ordinary after-work bar for local business folk, with its radio tuned to a light-melodies channel. Brad Pitt did stop by once, though. Mon–Thurs 8am–8pm, Fri & Sat 8am–midnight; bus #1 to Agip.

John Bull Unteregasse 4. English-style Old Town pub with darts and table football.

Street Café Grabenstrasse 47. Most popular of the studenty Obertor bars – young and loud.

Toms Beer Box Unteregasse 11. Hole in the wall which stocks 140 bottled beers from around the world.

Arosa

AROSA was discovered by the outside world in 1883 when Dr Otto Herwig-Hold, on a skiing tour of the remote mountains south of Chur, came across the little community – a perfect spot to build his new tuberculosis sanatorium. The chest patients of old have long since given way to sports enthusiasts, and the isolated village has developed into one of Graubünden's most acclaimed resorts, yet it's still small enough to have retained its atmosphere and lacks even a trace of the hotshot swagger of Davos or St Moritz.

Arosa lies at the end of a single, spectacular mountain road which cuts its way up into a sheer and narrow valley southeast of Chur, passing on the way through a succession of idyllic terraced villages and offering vistas breathtaking enough to make you want to stop and gape every three minutes – which you could do, but for the fact that in the 32-kilometre journey, there's a total of 244 switchbacks. It's frankly less nerve-racking to take the narrow-gauge

Sports and activities in Arosa

Arosa occupies the broad sunny bowl of the Schanfigg, surrounded on all sides by snowy peaks. The **Weisshorn** (2653m) is the main focus, due west of the resort, along with the **Hörnli** (2512m) to the south and the **Brüggerhorn** (2401m) to the north.

The **skiing** is small-scale but high-quality, with over 70km of mostly blue and red pistes sidewinding down the gentle sunny slopes; beginners will feel especially at home. There's also 25km of cross-country pistes and a **snowboard** halfpipe up above 2000m. Lifts and a gondola rise from the Obersee to the Weisshorn (with a chairlift from halfway up branching over to the Brüggerhorn), and at the very top of the village in Innerarosa there's another gondola connecting to the Hörnli. A pass for one/six days costs Fr.54/251. The Swiss Ski School (Ⓦwww.sssa.ch) is beside the train station, or check out the popular Bananas ski and snowboard school (Ⓦwww.bananas.net).

In **summer**, there are several good high-country hikes: from the Weisshorn summit, a scenic and easygoing four-hour trail heads over the Carmenna Pass and through the lonely Urden valley to Tschiertschen, connected to Chur by postbus; or you could head across the meadows from the Weisshorn middle station to Alpenblick and the tranquil Schwellisee before returning to Arosa (3hr). Another dramatic route leads off the back of the Hörnli summit and across the peaks to the Parpaner Rothorn (2861m), from where cable-cars run down to Lenzerheide, near Valbella 12km south of Chur, and connected to Chur by bus. You can rent **mountain bikes** from the station or Bikeodelic or Bremmspur bikeshops in the village to tackle any of the five marked MTB trails, which include a couple of fairly easy circular routes from the Obersee as well as several downhill runs.

RhB "Arosa Express" **train**, which departs from the forecourt of Chur station and shadows the road all the way up.

Beware that almost everything – shops, hotels, attractions, walking routes – is **closed during off-season** (mid-April to mid-June & mid-Oct to mid-Dec). We've specified months of opening only when they differ from this pattern.

Arrival, information and accommodation

The town consists of two areas: the main resort is **Ausserarosa**, clustered around the train station and the Obersee lakelet; while the older village at the upper end of the valley is dubbed **Innerarosa**. The **train station** borders the Obersee, with the **tourist office** five minutes' walk away, uphill on Arosa's only proper road, Poststrasse (May–Nov Mon–Fri 8am–noon & 1.30–6pm, Sat 9am–1pm; Dec–April Mon–Fri 9am–6pm, Sat 9am–5.30pm, Sun 10am–noon & 4–5.30pm; ☎081 378 70 20, Ⓦwww.arosa.ch). All buses within the village are free, and private cars are banned between midnight and 6am (except to arrive or depart). Some **hotels** charge extra if you stay less than three nights, especially in the winter season. Note too that summer prices can be up to fifty percent cheaper than high-season winter rates.

Hotels

Allegra Isla Neubachstrasse 30 ☎081 377 12 13, Ⓦwww.allegra-isla.ch. Pleasant, efficient three-star place on a quiet street between the Obersee and its lower twin, the Untersee, on the edge of the forest. Go for the superb corner room. ❹–❺

Arosa Kulm Innerarosa ☎081 378 88 88, Ⓦwww.arosakulm.ch. Super-luxurious palace at the very top of town, on the edge of the slopes. Facilities are excellent, with a range of formal restaurants and rooms boasting picture windows and balconies. ❾

Arve Central Hubelstrasse 252 ☎081 378 52 52, Ⓦwww.arve-central.ch. Unusually open all year round, offering cut-price bargains in spring, summer and autumn. Friendly staff, a couple of good restaurants and attractive rooms (go for the south-facing ones). Also with a "backpackers' chalet" dorm annexe. ❹

Eden Ausserarosa ☎ 081 378 71 00, ⓦ www.edenarosa.ch. The most characterful hotel in town, on a quiet street close to the station, with an array of chic Design Rooms, individually decorated Art Rooms (which, despite names like The Muse's Kiss, Tiger Lily and Time Machine, manage to live up to their hype) and trendy Classic–Nouveau Rooms on the top floor that rejoice in 1970s design features and decor. A handful of "normal" rooms are cheaper, but this place is worth a splash. ❹–❼

Lindemann's Postplatz ☎ 081 377 50 79, ⓕ 081 377 51 79. Convenient little family-run "garni" pension in the centre, with rooms ensuite and not. ❷–❸

Prätschli ☎ 081 377 18 61, ⓦ www.praetschli.ch. If you're here to relish the winter snows, this is the place to be – a romantic old winter hotel in a unique location plum on the slopes high above the Obersee, with road access but truly out in the wilds. Mid-Dec to mid-April only. ❻

Sonnenhalde Innerarosa ☎ 081 377 15 31, ⓕ 081 377 44 55. Good-quality inexpensive hotel near the skating rink, excellently located for the winter-only Carmenna and Tschuggen lifts, with super-friendly service and surprisingly well-appointed rooms. ❷

Suveran ☎ 081 377 19 69, ⓦ www.suveran.ch. Quiet, simple pension on a street above the Catholic church, with shared-bath rooms and low prices. ❷

Hostel

Jugendherberge (HI hostel) Seewaldweg ☎ 081 377 13 97, ⓦ www.youthhostel.ch. Partway down the road heading down from the tourist office is a branch off to this well-equipped hostel. Dorms Fr.29. ❶

Campsite

Arosa ☎ 081 377 17 45. Tranquil site below the main resort, on a path winding down from the tourist office.

Eating and drinking

In general, **eating and drinking** options are down-to-earth to suit the majority of Arosa's clientele, with a handful of simple diners around the Obersee and the lower reaches of Poststrasse, including the landmark *Orelli's*, where you can fill up on fish dishes, *Röschti* or salad for Fr.15 (also with veggie meals). *Pizzeria Grottino*, just down the road from it, has quality pizza/pasta staples for Fr.15–20. Otherwise you're looking at hotel dining: *Hold*, up near the Hörnli cable-car, is a popular, traditional place offering raclette *a gogo* (all-you-can-eat) every week, while *Quellenhof*, near the tourist office, has good *menus* for under Fr.20. Further up the scale, the *Anita* (☎ 081 377 11 09), above the main street near the church, harbours a gourmet restaurant, with multicourse dinners coming in at well over Fr.50. Otherwise, aim for the *Arve Central*, which has two restaurants offering excellent, inventive cuisine with local ingredients, or the luxury *Arosa Kulm* (with a handful of formal dining rooms – including Thai – open in winter) or *Waldhotel National* (☎ 081 378 55 55), set in its own grounds on slopes above the village, with a justifiably acclaimed restaurant.

Heidiland

The Rhine valley north of Chur winds through lush meadowland to the small industrial town of **Landquart** – an important rail junction for the line to Davos – and on to **Bad Ragaz**, a rather graceful spa resort full of cheery elderly folk strolling happily along the neat boulevards feeling much better than they used to, thanks to the town's hot springs, which are famed for soothing away rheumatic and circulatory problems. The hills above Bad Ragaz are where the ruthlessly marketed **Heidiland** region got its name: Swiss author Johanna Spyri set her wholesome classic of children's literature *Heidi* in and around the village of **MAIENFELD**, and the place milks its claim to fame mercilessly.

A gentle half-day trail leads from Maienfeld station past the pretty central square and the **tourist office** (Mon–Fri 10am–noon & 1.30–5pm, Sat closes

4pm; ☎081 302 58 58, ⓦwww.heidiland.com), which stocks plenty of Heidi kitsch, and then up on the hill to the hamlet of Oberrofels, now cruelly renamed **Heididorf**. Regardless of the lack of firm evidence linking Spyri's story with any particular house, one old chalet near the execrable *Heidihof Hotel* has been seized upon as being "the original **Heidi's House**", and converted into a museum to show how Heidi would have lived (April–Oct daily 10am–5pm; Fr.5). A trail – which, thankfully, most people who've got this far don't seem to bother with – leads from Heididorf further up into the high pastures, past another lone chalet designated Peter the Goatherd's Hut, and up to **Heidi Alp**, supposed home to the child's wise Alm-Uncle. Notwithstanding its chronic Heidi-itis, this trail is very scenic, winding down through lush meadows filled with spring wildflowers to the village of Jenins, and back to Heididorf.

The Bündner Herrschaft

The east bank of the Rhine around Maienfeld, taking in the adjacent villages of Fläsch, Jenins and Malans, is one of Switzerland's more unusual winemaking areas, dubbed the **Bündner Herrschaft** (ⓦwww.buendnerherrschaft.ch). In what would otherwise be far too inhospitable a climate, luscious red Pinot Noir grapes – introduced in the seventeenth century by the Duc de Rohan – are nurtured by the warm southerly Föhn wind, which can sometimes raise summer temperatures well above 25°C. The villages are linked by footpaths, generally quiet once you're out of the range of Heidi-seekers, and have a handful of rustic inns at which to enjoy a carafe of local wine alongside a square meal. Schloss Brandis, a medieval castle on the edge of Maienfeld (☎081 302 24 23), has a renowned **restaurant** for gourmet regional specialities, and an impressive cellar, and the *Landhaus* in Fläsch (closed Mon & Tues), *Traube* in Jenins (closed Thurs), and *Zum Ochsen* in Malans (closed Mon) all concentrate as much on their wines as on their affordable *menus*.

Central Graubünden

The **Central Graubünden** region south of Chur is the canton's wildest area, characterized by deep, narrow valleys, ancient forests, mountain torrents and a succession of quiet old villages that feel as if they've seen few visitors since the Romans – who are known to have used the two main Alpine passes of the area, the **Julier** and the **Splügen**. Aside from simple inns in most villages, there are few facilities for tourists anywhere, and not even many side routes by which you can escape into the wilderness: the most convenient way to experience the area is through the window of a train or a postbus, both of which offer spectacularly scenic rides through different valleys. Note that, in winter, the **Albula** road is closed above Preda, but the Julier pass road is kept clear.

Thusis and Tiefencastel

The train from Chur to St Moritz heads west to the road and rail junction of **Reichenau** before cutting south into the Hinterrhein valley to the village of **RHÄZÜNS**. On a forested rise down by the river, ten minutes' walk north of Rhäzüns, is the isolated Carolingian chapel of **Sogn Gieri** (St George), its interior covered with amazingly fresh sixteenth-century frescoes (chapel kept locked; key and map at Rhäzüns station). Further south, the valley sides close in, opening out again beyond Rothenbrunnen below the sharp ridges of the

11

Romansh is the fourth language of Switzerland and the principal everyday tongue of some 70,000 people in Graubünden. If you stick to the main tourist centres of Chur, Davos and St Moritz, you'll see and hear only Swiss-German (although Chur is beginning to acknowledge a recent influx of Romansh-speakers from Surselva), but if you venture to smaller countryside towns, you'll find signs to the *staziun* pointing along Via Principala, and hear people greeting each other with "Allegra!" or "Bun di!" in what sounds like Italian with a Swiss-German accent. For a glossary of Romansh words and phrases, see p.628.

History

Romansh can trace its roots directly back to Latin, fountainhead for all the Romance languages of Europe. After the Roman conquests, so-called **Vulgar Latin**, spoken by soldiers, merchants and officials, slowly merged over the centuries with the pre-existing languages of conquered areas, giving rise to four main linguistic groups: Ibero-Romance, including Spanish, Catalan and Portuguese; Gallo-Romance, mainly French; Italian; and **Rhaeto-Romance**, comprising Friulian and Ladin, two languages spoken by around 750,000 people in the extreme north of Italy, and Romansh, spoken only in Graubünden. The first significant inroads made by outsiders into the isolated Romansh-speaking mountain communities was in the thirteenth century, when German-speaking Walsers from Canton Valais settled in some of the high valleys; their legacy survives to this day, with Davos (once called Tavau, the Romansh word for "alp") still majority Swiss-German, and German-speaking communities clustered together in otherwise Romansh Surselva. In 1464, a huge fire destroyed Chur, and craftspeople arrived from the north to rebuild the town, in the process erasing virtually all its Romansh culture and language.

In the middle of the nineteenth century Romansh was still counted as the native tongue of over half the population of Graubünden, but the development of roads and railways penetrating remote valleys led to greater and greater erosion, as the Romansh people themselves realized that their language was an impediment to getting well-paid work outside their traditional communities. With schools, churches

---

Domleschg to the east that crest 2500m, and the gentler slopes of the **Heinzenberg** to the west.

Some 12km south of Rhäzüns is the town of **THUSIS**, loomed over by precipitous mountains and thick forest. From here, the main road continues south via the **San Bernardino Pass** and tunnel (see p.514). Another road swings east, shadowed by the train line which coils into the deep ravine of the **Albula** valley for a memorably dramatic journey to St Moritz, passing below sheer cliffs, through 16 tunnels and over 27 bridges, including the famous Landwasser viaduct near Filisur, its lofty arches adorning most RhB publicity material. An alternative route, followed by postbuses, is via the **Julier Pass**.

Roads and the rail line meet at the small valley-bottom crossroads town of **TIEFENCASTEL**, its prominent white church saving it from being lost altogether in the thick pine forests on all sides. Every route from Tiefencastel is up: west 12km to Thusis, north 35km to Chur, south to the Julier Pass, southeast to the Albula Pass, and northeast 37km to Davos.

The Albula route

Leaving Tiefencastel by train, you start to climb immediately into the quiet **Albula** valley (ⓦwww.albula.ch), stopping to switch onto a different gauge at

and communes slowly switching over to German, a conscious effort began to nurture Romansh, with cultural pressure groups and writers' organizations promoting the language in Graubünden and nationwide. In 1938, an amendment to the Swiss Constitution confirmed the status of Romansh as a **national language**. In 1996 a second constitutional amendment elevated Romansh to the status of a **semi-official language**, thereby preserving its status amongst Romansh communities, guaranteeing its appearance on official documents such as passports and in legislation affecting Romansh areas, and eliminating the requirement for Romansh-speakers to use any other language.

Dialects

Romansh is not a unified whole: there's a welter of different dialects, which can vary dramatically. The word for "cup", for example, in German is *Tasse*, in Italian *tazza*, but in the **Sursilvan** dialect of Romansh, spoken west of Chur, it is *scadiola*; in the **Sutsilvan** of the Hinterrhein valley, *scariola*; in the **Surmeiran** of the Julier and Albula valleys, *cuppegn*; and in **Putèr** and **Vallader**, spoken in the Upper and Lower Engadine respectively, *cupina*. In 1980, the Lia Rumantscha, a leading Romansh cultural organization, put forward a proposal to regularize this mishmash. The result was the creation of **Rumantsch Grischun** (Graubünden Romansh), a composite written language formed by averaging out words across all five dialects; under this new system, "cup" became *cuppina*. Nonetheless, despite the lack of a Romansh capital city able to provide a cultural and linguistic focus for the language, and the consequent reliance of Romansh-speakers on German-language companies for work and media for information, there was still some resistance to forming a hybrid in this way; today, local communities still stick to their own dialect in everyday life, and presenters on Radio Grischa and Radio Piz, Graubünden's two Romansh stations, speak their own dialects.

The Lia Rumantscha, with federal funding, has an ongoing Romansh publishing programme, including German–Romansh and English–Romansh dictionaries. For more information, you can either drop into their offices at Obere Plessurstrasse 47 in Chur (℡081 252 44 22), or consult their excellent website ⓦwww.liarumantscha.ch.

nearby **Filisur**. It's a very steep 8km on to **BERGÜN**, a pretty little village clustered around a highly photogenic central square, from where it's another steep climb to **PREDA**. Bergün tourist office (℡081 407 11 52, ⓦwww.berguen.ch), on the main street, has details of local walking routes and information about a famous winter **toboggan run**: you rent wooden sleds from Preda station for the 5km slide to Bergün, from where RhB trains cart you back to Preda for another go (Fr.29 for a day ticket). Trains run late, so you can sled the illuminated route by night.

Above Preda, the train line tunnels through to the Engadine valley, but the road breaks the treeline and heads over the 2312m **Albula Pass** (June–Oct) – with a restaurant on top – before coiling sharply down to the valley floor at La Punt.

The Julier route

From Tiefencastel, buses follow a dramatic road climbing south in a series of broad plateaux – each more beautiful than the last – towards the Julier Pass, an often-busy route favoured by trucks. The major resort is Romansh-speaking **SAVOGNIN**, a family-friendly place in the broad, sunny Surses valley. Its chairlift up to Somtgant (2112m) gives access to a leg-stretching "Veia Panorama" (2hr 30min) to Radons and down to the chairlift mid-station of

Tigignas. Mountain-bike routes abound, as well as, in winter, some very scenic blue and red ski runs down from Piz Martegnas (2670m), plus tobogganing, boarding and snowshoeing, organized through the local Bananas Snow Sport School (Ⓦwww.bananas.net). Ski passes cost Fr.47/231 for one/six days. The **tourist office**, on the main road Stradung (Ⓣ081 659 16 16, Ⓦwww.savognin.ch), has full details. Choice **hotel** is just down the road in Cunter, *Tgesa Scarpatetti*, Julierstrasse 25 (Ⓣ081 684 26 66, Ⓦwww .hotel-tgesa-scarpatetti.ch; ❷–❸; closed May & Nov), built in 1822 and now a stylish, modern place in lovely surroundings, with a fine restaurant.

Further up at 1769m, past the startlingly beautiful Lai da Marmorera set amongst the pines and rocky crags, lies **BIVIO**, the only village north of the Alps with an Italian-speaking majority – although in true Swiss style it also has Romansh and German speakers and both a Catholic and a Protestant church. Bivio sits near the treeline amidst dramatic upland country, and has plenty of outdoorsy activities: the little **tourist office** (Mon–Fri 8.30–11am & 3–5pm; Ⓣ081 684 53 23, Ⓦwww.bivio.ch), within the Banca Cantonale, can advise. Best **hotel** is cosy *Solaria* (Ⓣ081 684 51 07, Ⓦwww.hotelsolariabivio.ch; ❷–❸), known for its summer **horse-riding** packages, which include a guided ride over the isolated Septimer Pass (2310m) to Bondo, including full board and baggage transport, for Fr.450/550 (over two/three days). In winter, when Bivio is swamped by snow, you can rent snowshoes (Fr.15/day) and head off on your own, or ski some tricky red runs (one-/six-day pass Fr.35/175).

About 10km south is the **Julier Pass** (Pass dal Güglia; 2284m), the heights of which are still marked by the column stumps of a long-demolished Roman temple. Silvaplana (see p.540) lies on the other side.

The San Bernardino route

Some 5km south of Thusis, the main road plunges into a ravine, with sheer rock walls barely 10m apart rising some 500m from the bed of the foaming Hinterrhein. This **Via Mala** (Evil Road) was first constructed in 1473, various improvements since then resulting in a web of bridges spanning the gorge. At one point, you can descend 321 steps to the valley floor to see both the ancient original road and the bridges lined up way overhead (April–Oct daily 9am–5pm; Fr.5; Ⓦwww.thusis-viamala.ch).

The gorge opens up 3km further at the farming village of **ZILLIS** (Ziràn in Romansh), whose small **Kirche St Martin** (Baselgia Sontg Martegn; Ⓦwww.zillis-st-martin.ch) – sporting a huge external mural of St Christopher, patron saint of travellers – has a painted twelfth-century wooden ceiling, divided into 153 panels (there's a stack of mirrors by the door to save you cricking your neck). Around the edge runs the sea, with angels in the corners representing the four winds. The interior panels feature stories from the life of Christ, which start at the east (choir) end and run row by row to the west (door). Christ crowned with thorns is the last of the biblical scenes, since the final row, instead of depicting the Crucifixion and Resurrection, is devoted to scenes from the life of St Martin, implying that the original artist was, for some reason, unable to complete his intended story-cycle.

The main road bends west 6km south of Zillis. From **Andeer**, a lonely road penetrates some 25km up the remote Val Ferrera, flanked by 3000m-plus peaks. After a handful of waterfalls and widely spaced hamlets comes **Juf**, a cluster of farmhouses which, at 2126m, claims the title of the highest permanently occupied village in Europe. Tough full-day hiking routes lead over the mountains to Bivio (see p.514).

Splügen and the San Bernardino Pass

The road from Zillis heads through the deep Rheinwald forest to the dourly picturesque village of **SPLÜGEN**, with a jumble of traditional slate-roofed houses, a **tourist office** (℡081 650 90 30, ⓦwww.splugen.ch), a year-round **campsite** (℡081 664 14 76) and four **hotels**, including the *Pratigiana*, an old smugglers' haunt (℡081 664 11 10; ❸). See p.503 for details of a long-distance hike that passes this way. The **Splügen Pass** (2113m), 10km south of the village and reached via a twisting minor road, marks the Italian border; postbuses head on to Chiavenna, 30km south, from where different buses run back into Switzerland up the Val Bregaglia (see p.541) to St Moritz.

From Splügen, the main road climbs west in the shadow of the giant Zapportgletscher, one of the sources of the Rhine, to the **San Bernardino Pass** (2065m). The pass route (closed in winter) is undercut by a road tunnel (open year-round), which feeds south into the long, Italian-speaking Valle Mesolcina on the route to Bellinzona (see p.549): once you're out of the mountains, vines, fig trees and chestnut forests spring up all around, giving a hint of the lushness of Ticino spreading out below.

Surselva

A straight road west from Chur leads into the big, broad wooded valley of the River Vorderrhein, a patch of countryside known in Romansh as **Surselva**, the High Forests. The linked ski and sports resorts of **Flims–Laax–Falera** are within easy reach of Chur. Further west, a handful of quiet towns is capped at the end of the valley by a Benedictine abbey at **Disentis/Mustér**, staging post for journeys south into Ticino over the Lukmanier Pass (Lucomagno), and west into Valais via the Oberalp Pass.

Flims-Laax-Falera

On a hillside above the Rhine 18km west of Chur, the attractive resort of **FLIMS** is well known to the Swiss, who consistently pack the place out every season, but is much less known abroad, although it offers some of the best snowboarding facilities in the canton. There are two parts: **Flims–Dorf** is the

---

Customs of Surselva

Along with most of the Romansh-speaking areas of Graubünden, Surselva has kept hold of many ancient **customs** rooted in pagan, Roman or early Christian seasonal rites. These generally hold a great deal more significance for those taking part than for outside observers, but there are some rituals – most notably winter ones – which are worth looking out for. At Epiphany (Jan 6), the village of **Breil/Brigels** 12km west of Ilanz resounds to traditional songs as groups representing the Three Wise Men deliver the Christmas message. After nightfall on Easter Sunday, young men gather on the hillside above two hamlets beside Breil/Brigels, **Dardin** and **Danis-Tavanasa**, and ceremonially fling discs of burning wood known as *trer schibettas* down into the valley while pledging their love to a particular woman; tradition has it that it's possible to predict the success or failure of the match depending on the flight of the disc. Carnival in **Domat/Ems**, 6km west of Chur, is celebrated as Tschaiver with masked festivities on both Mardi Gras (*margis bel*, or Beautiful Tuesday) and the following Thursday (*gievgia grassa*, or Fat Thursday).

older, original village with most amenities and the base station for the ski lifts, while on a slightly higher elevation 1km south is **Flims–Waldhaus**, a newer, quieter area set amidst beech and larch woods, with most of the hotels. Some 5km south of Waldhaus is the Romansh village of **LAAX**, with tiny **FALERA** up a 3km branch road completing the picture. All three share the extensive **Alpenarena** ("Alpine Arena") ski region.

Flims is served by regular postbuses from Chur. The main **tourist office** is in Waldhaus (daily 8am–6pm; ☏081 920 92 00, ⓦ www.alpenarena.ch), with another in Dorf (Mon–Fri 8am–6pm, Sat 8am–5pm, Sun 8am–noon) and branch offices in Laax and Falera. All local transport is free with the Guest Card.

Best reason to **stay** is to experience the stunning, hi-tech **Riders Palace** (☏081 927 97 00, ⓦ www.riderspalace.ch; ❸), near the Murschetg base station in Laax – the coolest hotel in the Swiss Alps. The architecture is striking, an innovative blend of untreated larch wood and glittering walls of glass, giving floor-to-ceiling panoramic views over the forest and slopes. Everything is geared to a young, sporty clientele: all room rates include a lift-pass (which is also valid for the day you arrive and the day you check out), whether you opt for a bed in a shared room, a double or a Starck-designed suite. The slick, minimalist guest rooms and the 24-hour hotel bar feature plasma-screen TVs, net access, sound systems, PlayStation2, DVD cinema systems, and more, while the basement club hosts top-flight international DJs every weekend throughout the winter (past residences have included Ministry of Sound and Cream).

Less trendy options include the *Curtgin* (☏081 911 35 66, ⓦ www.hotelcurtgin.ch; ❷–❸), a cosy family-run hotel convenient for the Dorf lifts. The tiny, modern *Uaul Pign* in Waldhaus (☏081 911 13 39, ⓦ www.kpage.ch/garni.htm; ❷) is in a tranquil location well away from the road, with only ten rooms, all with balconies looking into the forest. In Laax, the *Bellaval*, Via Falera 112 (☏081 921 47 00, ⓦ www.hotelbellaval.ch; ❸–❹), offers peace and quiet, with pleasant, well-appointed rooms. There are also plenty of basic dorm places,

Sports and activities in Flims–Laax–Falera

The **Alpenarena** is a huge winter-sports area, the largest in Graubünden, with access from all three villages. From Laax-Murschetg, on the edge of Laax village, there's the choice of a cable-car to the **Crap Sogn Gion** summit (2228m), or a gondola to the halfway point of Curnius (also accessed from Falera), from where a chairlift continues to the top. From there, a cable-car continues to **Crap Masegn** (2477m) and on up to the **Vorab** (2570m), a glacier region with year-round skiing and snowboarding courtesy of T-bars rising to 3018m. From Flims-Dorf a combination of chairlifts and a cable-car serve various points on the adjacent **Cassons Grat** (2634m). Aside from the host of blue and reasonably testing red ski runs all over the mountain – and a huge 14km run from Vorab all the way down to Flims – there's plenty for freeriders, with 40km of marked but unprepared runs, and superb facilities for **snowboarders**, with seven halfpipes and boarderparks, including ones way up at 3000m and, allegedly, the world's largest halfpipe (up to 6.7m height). Passes cost Fr.59/301 for one/six days.

In **summer**, the hiking network is extensive, plenty of trails winding their way through the forest. Alternatively, take the chairlift up to the broad, level plateau atop the Cassons Grat, where there's a pleasant three-hour circular walk offering Alpine panoramas. The three-hour trek from Falera up to Crap Sogn Gion, and 3.5km along the crest to Crap Masegn, is especially beautiful too. Swissraft (ⓦ www.swissraft.ch) runs white-water rafting trips between Ilanz and Reichenau.

including the SB **hostel** *Gutveina* in Waldhaus (☎081 911 29 03; dorms Fr.29) and the *Mountain Hostel* in an unbeatable location on the Crap Sogn Gion (☎081 927 73 73, ⓦwww.crap.ch; ❷), which, like the *Riders Palace*, includes a lift-pass in its dorm and double rates.

Ilanz and beyond

Some 5km west of Laax is **ILANZ**, known in Romansh as **Glion**. These days it's a lively commercial and cultural hub, but in times gone by this was one of the most important towns in the whole of Graubünden. From the train station, which holds a tourist information counter (Mon–Fri 8–11.30am & 1.30–6pm; ☎081 925 20 70), a short wander through the centre will turn up a surprising number of stately sixteenth- and seventeenth-century town houses and a couple of unassuming **hotels**, including the *Rätia*, on Via Centrala by the bridge (☎081 925 23 93, ⓕ081 925 32 93; ❷), with an excellent restaurant serving regional cuisine.

West of Ilanz, there's little to stop for until, after 28km, the huge white abbey of **DISENTIS** (also known by its Romansh name of **MUSTÉR**) hoves into view. A Benedictine community was founded here, at the foot of Alpine pass roads, in the eighth century, only to be sacked by a marauding Saracen army in 940. Later churches were replaced in the late seventeenth century by the current Baroque building, which today houses about forty priests and novices. The white interior of the great **abbey church** is immediately impressive, not least because of the startling contrast of such lavish ornament with the wild countryside all about. Built in 1712 by Kaspar Moosbrugger, architect of the church at Einsiedeln, it is covered in gilt and ornate stucco, with light flooding in from high windows and a deep choir. An internal passageway in the west wall signposts the way through corridors and up stairs to the still and silent Marienkirche, its triple apse surviving as the only remnant of the tenth-century church sacked by the Saracens. West over the Oberalp Pass is Andermatt (see p.411); south over the Lukmanier is Olivone (see p.558).

Vals

From Ilanz, a couple of minor roads penetrate two beautiful side valleys famed for their broad meadows and cherry trees. One climbs through the Romansh-speaking **Val Lumnezia** to the hamlet of Vrin, while the other splits off into the deep, high **Valsertal**, named for its thirteenth-century Walser colonizers and still German-speaking today. The valley rises to the village of **VALS** (1252m), best known as the source of Valser bottled water, where the architect Peter Zumthor has built one of Switzerland's finest new buildings, the **Therme Vals** baths and hotel (☎081 926 80 80, ⓦwww.therme-vals.ch; ❺–❽; closed May & Nov). The building – composed of 60,000 bonded slabs of local quartzite – is effortlessly sleek and sensuous, all water, natural light, wood and polished stone. The spa (Mon 11am–9pm, Tues–Sun 11am–8pm; Fr.28) has every facility, including therapy treatments; guests at the uniquely stylish attached **hotel** benefit from extended hours and discounts. Buses from Ilanz terminate just across from Vals **tourist office** (Mon–Fri 8am–noon & 2–6pm, Sat 9am–noon & 3–5.30pm; ☎081 920 70 70, ⓦwww.vals.ch), a short stroll from the spa.

Davos and Klosters

From the junction point of Landquart, north of Chur, roads and rail lines meander up the Prättigau ("Meadow Valley") to two of the most famous names

Sports and activities in Davos and Klosters

The options for outdoors activity are almost limitless. We've given an outline of what's on offer, but the best advice is to check ⓦwww.davos.ch and ⓦwww.klosters.ch for up-to-date details. Look out for the range of good-value winter and summer package deals offered by local hotels, comprising accommodation plus lift-passes and perks.

Winter

The main draw is the outstanding **skiing**. Although the two resorts are quite far apart, they share the same ski area and lift pass; the prime attraction here is being able to swoosh down broad, well-tended pistes which go on and on, for more than 10km in many cases from mountaintop to valley bottom. There are 99 downhill pistes, totalling an impressive 321km – half of them intermediate (red), a third beginner (blue) and the rest expert (black).

The big focus of attention is the **Parsenn** ski area on the north side of Davos and the west side of Klosters, centred on the Weissfluh summit. It has only three methods of access, all of which can suffer from queues in peak season. The **Parsennbahn** funicular (ⓦwww.parsenn.ch) starts from Davos-Dorf and rises to the Weissfluhjoch saddle just below the summit; the little **Schatzalpbahn** funicular (ⓦwww.schatzalp.ch) from Davos-Platz takes you to a broad snow shelf, from where you must switch to chairlifts and gondolas for the journey further up; while the **Gotschnagrat** cable-car (ⓦwww.gotschna.ch) rises from Klosters station to a ridge just east of the Weissfluh. On the mountain are plenty of draglifts serving dozens of blue and red runs, including giant, weaving pistes from the summit down through the trees to hamlets such as Küblis, Saas and Serneus. For more testing runs, you could attempt the notorious Gotschnawang, scene of an avalanche in 1988 which killed Prince Charles's equerry and which is now regularly off limits, or a handful of black runs on the lower, steep slopes above Davos-Dorf and Wolfgang.

Moving onto one of the four other ski sectors can take you away from the crowds. From Davos-Platz, cable-cars rise to the **Jakobshorn** (ⓦwww.fun-mountain.ch), with a hatful of scenic blues and reds. Bus #1 from Davos-Dorf serves Dörfji, the base station of the cable-car up to **Pischa** (ⓦwww.pischa.ch), while a gondola from Davos-Glaris (bus #7) rises to the **Rinerhorn** (ⓦwww.rinerhorn.ch), which has lifts going higher to access blues, reds and a testing black run. A gondola rises from Klosters-Dorf east to **Madrisa** (ⓦwww.madrisa.ch), also with plenty of long, exciting reds on pistes which hug the Austrian border. **Snowboarders** should aim principally for the Parsenn, although the Jakobshorn is the focus of a hip boarding fraternity and there's some scope for experimentation on the Madrisa as well.

Passes, considering the range on offer, are excellent value. A REGA pass for all areas (excluding use of Schatzalpbahn), for 3/6/13 days, costs Fr.167/279/476. A full/half day pass for the Parsenn and Gotschna is Fr.57/40, for the Jakobshorn Fr.52/39, for Madrisa, Pischa or Rinerhorn Fr.46/34. Ask about the various discounts in shoulder season and for teenagers; selected days are also available. The TopCard, valid all season for Davos and Klosters as well as Flims-Laax-Falera, is Fr.945; the Snowpass, valid throughout Graubünden and at Gstaad and Vail (USA) – and also valid in Graubünden in summer – is Fr.1100. Plenty of hotels offer **packages**: sample options at Klosters (better-value than Davos) include three midweek nights' B&B in a three-star hotel plus a 4-day REGA pass for Fr.485 (not valid Christmas to end-Feb); or five nights' half board in a two-star hotel plus a 4-day REGA pass for Fr.688 (Jan–April). A course of five half-in the Alps, enjoying some of the best skiing in the world: first **Klosters**, then, after some more climbing over the Wolfgang Pass, **Davos**. Walser migrants arrived in the valley in the thirteenth century, and the area – surrounded on three sides by Romansh – remains German-speaking today. The focus is fair

day **lessons** costs around Fr.170, a package of a six-day pass plus lessons Fr.505. Private tuition is around Fr.75/hr. Schools, which vary in facilities and prices, include, in Davos: Swiss Snowsportschool (Ⓦwww.ssd.ch), New Trend (Ⓦwww.newtrenddavos .ch) and Top Secret (Ⓦwww.topsecretdavos.ch); in Klosters: Swiss Ski and Snowboard (Ⓦwww.sssk.ch), Bananas (Ⓦwww.bananas.net) and Adventure Skiing (Ⓦwww .adventure-skiing.ch).

Both resorts have tons of other diversions, including indoor swimming, ice-skating, tobogganing and snowshoe-trekking. Tandem **paragliding** flights cost around Fr.160–180 from Paraglide School Davos (Ⓦwww.davos-sport.ch), Flugcenter Grischa Klosters (Ⓦwww.fs-grischa.ch) and others. Major **winter events** include the international ice-hockey Spengler Cup (late Dec; Ⓦwww.spenglercup.ch); the world snowboard championship finals (late March; Ⓦwww.snowboarddavos.ch); and the Nordic Cross-Country World Cup (mid-Dec; Ⓦwww.davosnordic.ch).

Summer

In summer, the opportunities for **hiking** and **mountain-biking** are excellent. A 4-Tage Wahlabonnement (Fr.70 with Guest Card) is valid for one use of mountain transport (up and/or down) on any four days in the summer season. One example of a package comprises seven nights' half board at a two-star Klosters hotel plus this 4-day pass for a bargain Fr.620 (July–Sept).

Both tourist offices run full-day guided **walks**, free with a Guest Card, that cover some difficult territory – over the Vereina pass, for instance – but it's easy to strike out alone. From the Weissfluhjoch, accessed by the Parsennbahn (or a 3–4hr walk up), the views of Piz Buin and beyond are spectacular, even better from the Weissfluhgipfel summit, served by a cable-car from the funicular top-station. Invigorating walks head down to Davos (2hr) or Klosters (4hr), or there's a testing route over to Arosa (6hr). From the Gotschnagrat, a fairly tough hike leads to Casanna Alp, then Serneuser Schwendi (with restaurant) and on down to Klosters (3hr). Possibilities abound for easier walks, especially in the meadows and woods around the small Davosersee. A stroll from the top of the Schatzalpbahn, beyond the grand old *Berghotel* and into the fragrant woods brings you to the **Alpinum**, a hillside botanical garden (mid-May to Sept daily 9am–5pm; Fr.4). There are some leg-stretching trails from the Pischa and Jakobshorn summits back to Davos (2–3hr). Top choice from Klosters is the **Madrisa Rundtour**, a two-day walk into Austria and back; the price (Fr.114) includes B&B and cable-cars.

There are plenty of **mountain-bike** routes around Davos, including several routes along the valley floor west as far as Wiesen (31km round trip), and a classic 20km run from the Weissfluhjoch down to Küblis. For Fr.21.50, you can load your bike onto the Parsennbahn up to the Weissfluhjoch and follow a testing 14km trail down to Klosters, then transport yourself and your bike back to Davos by train. Bike Experience (Ⓦwww.bike-experience-davos.ch) has more.

Other activities include tandem paragliding, curling, inline skating, sailing, volleyball, windsurfing, golf, clay-pigeon shooting, horse riding, mule- or llama-trekking and tons more. On selected days in July and August, you can join a group to go **wildlife-spotting**, observing stags, marmots and deer – tourist offices have information and dates; you need to book. Major **summer events** include the gruelling Swiss Alpine Marathon (late July; Ⓦwww.swissalpine.ch) and the Inline Uphill Race from Davos to the Flüela Pass (early Aug; Ⓦwww.swiss-inline-cup.ch).

and square on outdoorsiness: skiing and snowboarding in the winter, hiking and mountain-biking in the summer. There's not a lot else to grab your attention other than spectacular nature.

If you stay overnight in either resort, you'll receive a very useful **Guest Card**, which gives free transport locally plus discounts on mountain railways and a range of activities. Beware that almost everything in both resorts – shops, hotels, attractions, walking routes – is **closed during off-season** (mid-April to mid-June & mid-Oct to mid-Dec). We've specified months of opening only when they differ from this pattern.

Davos

Twinned in a touristic masterstroke with Aspen, Colorado, **DAVOS**, way up at 1560m, is the antithesis of a peaceful Alpine ski village. It's a bustling, sometimes impatient place, famous for its toothpaste-fresh air and its consistently excellent snow cover. The town has been attracting **skiers** for generations and recently gained new life (and hipness) with the seal of approval of Switzerland's **snowboarding** cognoscenti. In summer, the snows recede to reveal a surrounding of lush countryside and the town takes on a new lease of life – not least because hotel prices plummet. The location, in a high, narrow valley between two walls of peaks, is stunning.

Davos achieved fame as a **health resort**, its high altitude and long hours of sunshine easing the suffering of tuberculosis patients: by 1900, ten years after the railway arrived – and long before winter sports were even thought of – there were 700,000 overnight visitors a year. The consumptive Robert Louis Stevenson completed *Treasure Island* while resident at a Davos sanatorium in 1882; Sir Arthur Conan Doyle also stayed; and in 1912, Thomas Mann was inspired while visiting Davos to write *The Magic Mountain*. Davos still has a

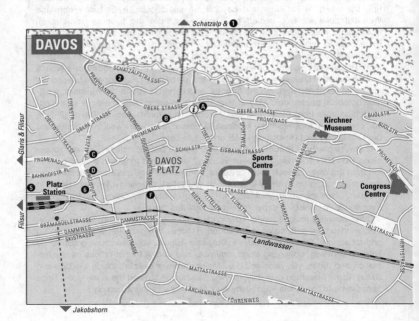

GRAUBÜNDEN | Davos and Klosters

⑪

dozen clinics and institutes: modern science has confirmed the beneficial effects of high altitude on respiratory and dermatological complaints. The town also has one of the world's best-equipped high-altitude sports training facilities, used by athletes and international football teams to improve fitness and stamina.

Another hat worn by Davos is that of a major international **conference** venue: in the last week of January each year, presidents, prime ministers and assorted mega-suits of the World Economic Forum meet at Davos under the gaze of the world's media to discuss global cashflow and set the financial agenda for the year ahead, regularly sparking anti-capitalist demonstrations in the process.

Arrival, information and accommodation

The two contiguous halves of the town, **Davos-Platz** and **Davos-Dorf**, are strung along a four-kilometre ribbon of low-key development on the floor of the Landwasser valley. Approaching from Klosters, you'll pass the picturesque little Davosersee before arriving at Dorf, generally the quieter district. The main street, **Promenade**, lined with shops and hotels, feeds traffic one-way from Dorf past the giant Congress Centre to bustling Platz, home to most of the nightlife; parallel one block downhill (south) is quieter **Talstrasse**, which is one-way from Platz to Dorf. The giant Weissfluh (2844m) rises immediately to the north, flanked by the Strelagrat (2545m) and Schwarzhorn (2670m). The Jakobshorn (2590m) looms on the other, south, side of the town. There are outlying suburbs on both sides, linked to Davos by bus and train, but they're quiet communities with few facilities: east of Dorf is Davos-Wolfgang and Laret, west of Platz is Davos-Glaris and Frauenkirch.

Davos lies at the far end of a circular **train** line from Chur: the eastern half runs via Landquart and Klosters, the western half via Filisur. There are some

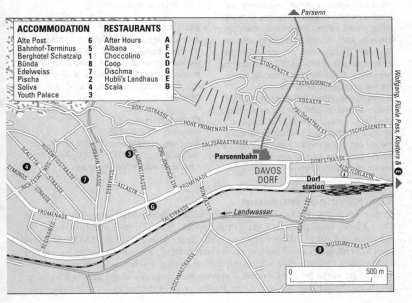

ACCOMMODATION		RESTAURANTS	
Alte Post	6	After Hours	A
Bahnhof-Terminus	5	Albana	F
Berghotel Schatzalp	1	Choccolino	C
Bünda	8	Coop	D
Edelweiss	7	Dischma	G
Pischa	2	Hubli's Landhaus	E
Soliva	4	Scala	B
Youth Palace	3		

direct trains as well as plenty of one-stop connections. All trains stop at both Davos-Dorf and Davos-Platz, although the latter is the main terminus. **Postbuses** run direct from Chur.

There are two branches of the **tourist office** – the main one at Promenade 67 in the middle of Platz (Mon–Fri 8.30am–6pm, Sat 8.30am–4pm; April to mid-June & mid-Oct to Nov Sat closes 12.30pm; Dec–March Sat closes 5pm, also Sun 10am–noon; ☎081 415 21 21, ⌨www.davos.ch), plus a branch office opposite Dorf station (same hours except Mon–Fri in the off-season closed noon–1.45pm). Both have information on Davos and Klosters, and can also provide details of services such as transporting your baggage from hotel to hotel while you hike or cycle some of the multi-day routes between Davos, Arosa and Lenzerheide. VBD **city buses** (free with a Guest Card) stop at all points of interest, and also run out to Wolfgang, Glaris and the Pischa base station.

Davos is packed with **accommodation** options, but none could be called a bargain: prices get hiked ruthlessly across the board in the winter season. The tourist office keeps a complete list of the many places offering dormitory beds.

Hotels

Alte Post Berglistutz 4, Platz ☎081 413 54 03, ⌨www.fun-mountain.ch. Serviceable little two-star place beside Platz station that offers cut-price winter weekend deals. ❸

Bahnhof-Terminus Talstrasse 3, Platz ☎081 414 97 97, ⌨www.bahnhof-terminus.ch. Large, airy rooms and private parking directly opposite Platz station. ❺–❻

Berghotel Schatzalp On Schatzalp above Platz ☎081 415 51 51, ⌨www.schatzalp.ch. Although there's any number of five-star palaces in Davos, this old Jugendstil sanatorium (now a three-star hotel) is the most characterful top-end accommodation around, perched on a tranquil terrace 300m above the town and only accessible by funicular. Views over the Jakobshorn and beyond from the ranks of balconied rooms – which boast up to four more hours of sunshine per day than the town – are well worth paying for. ❹–❼

Bünda Museumstrasse 4, Dorf ☎081 417 18 19, ⌨www.buenda.ch. Outstanding three-star hotel a short walk from the Parsennbahn at the foot of the slopes in a perfectly peaceful location. Service is friendly and helpful, and the rooms – whether the smaller ones in the main building, or bigger, better ones in the connected Residenz alongside – are characterful and well-equipped. ❸–❺

Edelweiss Rossweidstrasse 9, Platz ☎081 416 10 33, ⌨www.davos-online.ch/edelweiss. One of the best in this price range, with private parking and a pleasant, comfortable atmosphere. ❸

Pischa Strelastrasse 2, Platz ☎081 413 55 13, ⌨www.hotel-pischa.ch. Pleasant, cosy and quiet, way up above Platz (with a free shuttle bus up and down the hill). Relatively small price-hike makes it good value in winter. ❸–❹

Soliva Symondsstrasse 7, Platz ☎081 416 57 27, 𝕗081 416 71 67. Small, quiet family-run B&B opposite the Kongresszentrum. ❷

Hostel

Jugendherberge "Youth Palace" (HI hostel) Horlaubenstrasse 27, Dorf ☎081 420 11 20, ⌨www.youthhostel.ch. Huge, 260-bed former sanatorium, open for half-board deals in winter only: dorm bed plus two meals Fr.60–110. Dec–April.

Campsite

Färrich ☎081 416 10 43, ⌨camping.davos@bluewin.ch. Well-run site 1km south of Dorf on the road towards the Flüela Pass. A bus stops outside. Mid-May to Sept.

The Kirchner Museum

Prime attraction for non-sports fans is the **Kirchner Museum**, 600m east of the Platz tourist office at Promenade 82 (Tues–Sun: July–Sept & Christmas–Easter 10am–6pm; rest of year 2–6pm; Fr.8; SMP; ⌨www.kirchnermuseum.ch). This impressively airy structure – designed as a series of cubes, with opaque glass admitting diffuse daylight – houses a vibrant collection of artworks by the German Expressionist painter Ernst Ludwig Kirchner. Born in 1880, Kirchner moved to Berlin in 1911, but after an intensive period of work his health deteriorated rapidly. He emigrated to Davos in 1917 and lived in shacks out in the countryside, where he painted prodigiously. In 1936, his work was tagged "degenerate" by the Nazis and two years later in Davos, in a deep depression, he committed suicide. The museum displays work from all periods of Kirchner's life, including starkly stylish woodcuts and sketches from his time in Berlin and dozens of expressive, highly colourful works painted in Davos, including the celebrated, luminous *Davos im Sommer*.

Eating and drinking

You'll need plenty of cash to be able to **eat and drink** well. A spread of hotels take part in the "Dine Around" scheme, whereby if you're staying half board, you can choose to eat your evening meal at one of the 20 other hotels in the scheme; the tourist office has full details, as well as a *Gastroführer* guide to every eatery in town.

Budget options include a self-service *Coop* just above Platz station and the *After Hours* convenience store, open 24 hours at Promenade 69. The ultra-swish *Choccolino*, Promenade 45, is a *confiserie* and café, with classical music at Sunday brunch time and a proper cup of tea. There's a handful of simple pizza/pasta restaurants where you can eat for Fr.20: *Albana*, Talstrasse 18, is one of the cosier options; *Dischma*, Promenade 128, is another, also with good *Rösti* and fondues. The large *Hotel Europe*, Promenade 63, shelters the bright and modern *Scala* restaurant, with inexpensive pizzas and daily *menus*. The *Goldener Drachen* restaurant in *Hotel Bahnhof-Terminus* is the best Chinese in town, serving authentic cuisine for around Fr.25. The *Hotel Bünda* restaurant has excellent Bündner specialities, including game. Although Davos has any number of gourmet restaurants, for the best local dining experience you need to head out towards Wolfgang: *Hubli's Landhaus* (☏081 417 10 10; closed Mon) is a cosy, attractive country inn with a Michelin-starred restaurant, offering superbly light international cuisine for less than you might expect (around Fr.60 per head).

Focus of Platz's buzzing **nightlife** is the *Ex-Bar*, alongside the tourist office, which only really gets going after 2am. The *Chämi*, 200m east, is another very popular choice. There are pool tables in the *Hotel Montana*'s lively bar, and cocktail pianists in the *Hotel Europa*, which also hosts the *Cabanna* techno club and the canton's swankiest casino.

Listings

Bike rental Dorf station (☏081 416 24 44), Ettinger sports shops at Promenade 153 and Talstrasse 6 (☏081 410 12 12), Flüela Sport opposite Dorf station (☏081 416 73 73), and a handful of other places rent mountain bikes for around Fr.30/day (all May–Sept).
Changing money In Platz station (daily 6am–10pm) or Dorf station (daily 7am–8pm).

Hospital Promenade 4, Platz ☏081 414 88 88.
Laundry Promenade 102, Platz (Mon–Sat 8am–8pm).
Police Rathaus, Berglistutz 1, Platz ☏081 414 33 11.
Post office Opposite Platz station (Mon–Fri 7.45am–6.30pm, Sat 8.30am–noon); smaller office next to Dorf station.

Klosters

Instantly recognizable to Britons as being the favoured winter getaway of Prince Charles and his family, little **KLOSTERS** (1190m) – about 9km northeast of Davos, below the Wolfgang Pass – steals quite a march on its neighbour in terms of ambience. Where Davos has traffic, bright lights, street bustle and concrete multistorey hotels, Klosters has peace and quiet, an appealing huddle

△ The Glacier Express passing through the Rhine Gorge

Car-carrying trains

The **Vereina tunnel**, running beneath the mountains between Klosters and Sagliains (just west of Scuol in the Lower Engadine), is over 19km long, the longest narrow-gauge rail tunnel in the world. Drive-on drive-off **car-carrying trains** run through the tunnel all year round (daily every 30min 6am–9pm; takes 20min; a car plus 9 people costs Fr.27 summer, Fr.35 winter, Fr.40 midwinter weekends; no reservations; information on ☏081 288 37 16, ⊛www.rhb.ch). The parallel Flüela Pass road is closed in winter (roughly Nov–May).

of dark-wood chalets and a village atmosphere. It's linked to Davos's Parsenn ski slopes, and the two share a lift pass covering each other's pistes and mountain transport: in choosing a base, you could do worse than shun Davos altogether. The new Sunniberg bridge, due to open in 2005, will complete a bypass filtering traffic around Klosters. For full details of sports and activities, see p.518.

Klosters Platz is the centre of things, and has the main train station; the smaller, quieter **Klosters Dorf** sits 2km north, with its own station. Both are on the Landquart–Davos train line, and are also linked by town buses, which are free with the resort's Guest Card. The main **tourist office** is in Platz, by the station (Mon–Fri 8.30am–noon & 2–6pm; mid-June to mid-Oct & mid-Dec to mid-April also Sat 8.30am–noon & 2–4pm; July & Aug also Sun 9–11am; mid-Dec to March also Sun 9–11am & 3–6pm; ☏081 410 20 20, ⊛www.klosters.ch). There's a branch office beside Dorf station (mid-June to mid-Oct & mid-Dec to March Mon–Fri 8.30–11.30am). As in Davos, almost everything is closed in the between-seasons, but unlike in Davos, the winter price hikes won't break the bank.

The cosy HI **hostel** *Soldanella Jugendherberge* is at Talstrasse 73, a fifteen-minute climb above Platz (☏081 422 13 16, ⊛www.youthhostel.ch; ❶; dorms Fr.28). The weathered-wood *Sonne*, Hauptstrasse 155 (☏081 422 13 49, ℱ081 422 19 48; ❷), is the best low-end **hotel**, with simple shared-bath rooms, some with balcony, while rustic *Malein*, at Landstrasse 120 halfway to Dorf (☏081 422 10 88, ℱ081 422 44 88; ❶), has a handful of ensuite or shared-bath rooms. The family-run *Silvapina*, on the edge of Dorf near the Madrisabahn, Silvapinaweg 6 (☏081 422 14 68, ⊛www.silvapina.ch; ❷–❹), is a fine choice, with attractive guest rooms and good service. *Chesa Grischuna*, Bahnhofstrasse 12 in Platz (☏081 422 22 22, ⊛www.chesagrischuna.ch; ❸–❻), may look like a tumbledown old chalet from the outside, but is one of the liveliest and chicest places in town, with a good deal of style and character. Prince Charles's establishment of choice is the *Walserhof*, Landstrasse 141 (☏081 410 29 29, ⊛www.walserhof.ch; ❺–❼), a relatively small, cosy place that displays a superb attention to detail and has an outstanding restaurant.

Klosters has less choice for **eating** and **drinking** than Davos. Most of the hotels listed above have restaurants attached: the *Sonne* (closed Mon & Tues) is especially well thought of, with good regional *menus* starting from Fr.16, and the *Walserhof* was recently awarded two Michelin stars. The *Vereina* restaurant in the heart of Platz serves quality pizzas. The modest *Wynegg*, Landstrasse 205 (☏081 422 13 40; winter only), enjoys royal patronage, serving beer and hearty meals that are surprisingly affordable; while to eat at chichi *Chesa Grischuna* (see above), you should book two weeks in advance and expect to lose a fistful of francs.

The Lower Engadine

Beyond the mountains, in the farthest corner of Switzerland – and requiring some dedication to reach – is the **Lower Engadine** (Engiadina Bassa in Romansh, Unterengadin in German). Remote from Chur, let alone from the rest of the country, this attractive valley nurtures a quite distinct, thoroughly Romansh culture that has been allowed to flourish in isolation for centuries: although the Austrian Tyrol is just a few kilometres away on the north side of the impassable Piz Buin range, it might just as well be on the other side of the continent. The succession of hamlets which cling to the banks of the foaming River Inn (En in Romansh), tumbling its way towards Innsbruck, the Danube and eventually the Black Sea, show their Latin origins as much as does the language of their inhabitants: thick-walled houses stuccoed in cream abound, complete with small, deep-set windows and scarlet geraniums sprouting from every windowbox, reminiscent of Mediterranean village architecture found much further south. Everywhere you'll see the characteristic *sgraffiti* decoration: ornate, curlicued designs, pictures and even mottoes or dedications studiously etched into the white stuccoed facade of a house to reveal a darker, coloured layer beneath. The beautifully decorated little cottages and quaint cobbled squares, set against a tremendous backdrop of dark pine forests and looming mountains, combine to give the valley a uniquely fairytale air.

Scuol is the main town of the valley, prefaced by a succession of charming cliffside villages such as Guarda and Ftan. **Zernez** serves as the gateway for exploration of the **Parc Naziunal Svizzer**, the sole national park, a vast chunk of highland wilderness. Beyond the park in tiny **Müstair** village is one of Switzerland's greatest cultural treasures – a Carolingian church sporting perfectly preserved medieval frescoes.

Transport isn't easy. Trains from Landquart and Klosters run through the Vereina tunnel to the terminus at Scuol, while others from Pontresina or St Moritz (changing at Samedan) serve Zernez. To reach the Austrian border or Müstair, you're reliant on postbuses – but timetables can leave you waiting a couple of hours between buses: unless you're on an extended walking tour of the valley, driving is the transport of choice, allowing you to enjoy the sunset in Müstair and still make it to St Moritz by bedtime.

Scuol and around

The dramatic road from Davos over the icy Flüela Pass drops down into the Engadine at **Susch**, a perfect introduction to the valley, its cobbled alleys filled with the rushing noise of the River Inn. Set picturesquely amidst its *sgraffitied* houses is the Baselgia San Jon, with one tower Romanesque, the other late-Gothic. To the east, beyond the ruined hilltop castle of Chaschinas, rears the giant Piz Arpiglias (3027m). The road to Scuol continues through tremendous scenery between the high, wooded valley walls, past a string of alluring little villages. Some 7km northeast of Susch on a lofty perch above the river, **Guarda** is especially attractive, its architecture and traditional *sgraffiti* meriting a federal order of protection. Just beyond, **Ardez** and **Ftan** are both equally worthy of a stop.

Some 22km east of Susch, the lively town of **SCUOL** (pronounced *shkwol*), known as Schuls in German, is beautifully located in a sunny, open part of the valley at the end of the train line. Its reputation is built on its history as a spa town, and the main draw today is the pristine, modern **Bogn Engiadina** complex (Engadine Baths; daily 9am–10pm; ☎081 861 20 00, ⓦwww.scuol.ch;

The communities of the Lower Engadine keep alive many ancient local **customs** as an expression of their Romansh heritage. In Ramosch and Tschlin, two hamlets 10km east of Scuol, the **Mattinadas**, held on January 2, can overshadow even Christmas and New Year. During the day, the local children parade through the village dragging a decorated sledge behind them and collecting bucketsful of home-made sweets and candy (*mattinadas*); after a communal feast, everyone then embarks on an evening of dancing until midnight, whereupon the kids sit down to another banquet, this time of traditional butter biscuits smothered in whipped cream. The whole procedure is then repeated either the next day, or on the Saturday following, by the young men of the village. Epiphany celebrations (Jan 6) take the form of **Bavania** or **Buania**. In the afternoon, the village girls gather together and draw lots to choose a lover; they then visit their allotted man and, to mark their conquest and Fate's irrevocable decision, they tie a red ribbon round his neck. Later that night, at the village dance, the girls are chaperoned by their ribboned partner… presumably happily ever after. In Scuol, the first Saturday in February sees the ceremonial torching of the **Hom d'strom** ("Man of Straw") in front of the court building, probably as a symbolic banishment of the winter. On March 1 many villages stage the huge children's festival of **Chalandamarz** or **Calonda mars**. This originates in the Classical Roman New Year celebration *Calendae Martii*, which these days takes the form of a colourful spring parade with cowbell-ringing and traditional songs.

Fr.24). It has a range of warm and hot pools, and offers treatments including saunas, massages and Finnish baths. Alternatively, you can opt for the works: warm and hot rooms, vapour baths, massages, mineral plunge pools and a heavenly two-hour session in the Roman-Irish baths (reserve one day ahead; Fr.59). You'll see "Badekombi" day-packages to the spa advertised widely, taking in train transport, bus transfers and admission, for Fr.50–60 from Davos, Klosters or St Moritz, Fr.76 from Chur. Behind the spa, little-used streets head down into Scuol's picture-pretty **Old Town**, filled with traditional houses, tinkling fountains and a photogenic village square. The view of **Chaste Tarasp** (Tarasp Castle) on the opposite bank is now overshadowed by a modern hotel; the view from Ftan is better. The Motta Naluns **ski** area (2146m, with lifts up to 2800m) offers plenty of easy and intermediate runs, including long, thrilling reds from Piz Champatsch 12km back down to Scuol, and plenty for snowboarders.

Practicalities

The valley has plenty of **places to stay**. In Ftan are the charming *Engiadina* (☎081 864 04 34, ⊛www.engadin.net; ❸–❹), and the lavish, modern-styled *Haus Paradies* (☎081 861 08 08, ⊛www.relaischateaux.ch/paradies; ❻). Both have outstanding restaurants, the latter with two Michelin stars. More modest, and remarkably good value, is the *Piz Buin*, at the edge of Guarda village (☎081 861 30 00, ⊛www.pizbuin.ch; ❷–❸), a member of the "Silence" group. Cross the river from Ardez on a covered wooden bridge to reach the ultimate in tranquil campsites, *Sur En* (☎081 866 35 44, ☎081 866 32 37), open year-round.

Scuol's **train station** is over 1km west of the centre, which is a bus ride or a ten-minute downhill walk away. The helpful **tourist office** is beside the post office on Stradun (Mon–Fri 8am–noon & 2–6.30pm, Sat 10am–noon & 2–6pm, Sun 10am–noon; mid-April to mid-June & Nov to mid-Dec Mon–Fri 9am–noon & 2–6pm, Sat 10am–noon; ☎081 861 22 22, ⊛www.scuol.ch).

The 94km **Engadine valley**, with its numerous tributaries and adjacent valleys, offers a wealth of opportunities for walks of all degrees of seriousness, as well as the modest ascent of several peaks with commanding summit viewpoints. Maps which cover the area are the LS 249, 259, 268, and 269, all of them 1:50,000. Valuable reading are two books by Kev Reynolds: *Walking in the Alps* and *Walks in the Engadine* (see p.607).

In the Lower Engadine, behind **Scuol** (see p.526) to the south is Val S-charl, leading to **S-charl**, a tiny summer-only hamlet at a confluence of glens. From here, walkers could cross Fuorcla Funtana da S-charl to the Ofen Pass/Pass dal Fuorn (3hr 30min); the Pass da Costainas to Santa Maria in Val Müstair (5hr; see p.531); or take an easy 1hr stroll to Alp Sesvenna among streams and pastures that are full of Alpine flowers in early summer.

Further up-valley, the charming village of **Guarda** (see p.526) gives access to Val Tuoi, near the head of which stands the *Tuoi Hut/Chamanna Tuoi* (℡ 081 862 23 22) below Piz Buin. This is gained in about 2hr 30min from Guarda, while strong walkers could continue across the right-hand ridge at the 2735m Furcletta and descend through Val Tasna to **Ardez** – a total of 7hr 30min. The **Parc Naziunal Svizzer** (see opposite) has any number of walks from which red and roe deer, marmots, chamois and ibex may be seen. The best base for an exploration is the *Blockhaus Cluozza* (see p.530), reached in 3hr from **Zernez**, since an overnight there enables you to cross neighbouring valleys by a choice of passes.

In the Upper Engadine, **Maloja** offers several rewarding walks, especially up to the lovely alp hamlets of Grevasalvas and Blaunca (1hr). Above them lies Lägh da Lunghin, birthplace of the River Inn, and a path which climbs to Piz Lunghin (2780m) in 3hr 30min from Maloja. From that elevated point both Engadine and Bregaglia are spread out below. Across the valley, Val Fex gives gentle walking in idyllic surroundings, while a belvedere path above its entrance makes a high traverse round to **St Moritz-Bad** (up to 5hr from Sils Maria). From St Moritz a classic walk crosses the 2755m Fuorcla Surlej for a stimulating view of Piz Bernina and Piz Roseg (*Berghaus Fuorcla Surlej* ℡ 081 842 63 03), then descends into Val Roseg and continues to **Pontresina** (up to 6hr). Walkers staying in Pontresina should visit the *Coaz Hut* (℡ 081 842 62 78) and neighbouring *Tschierva Hut* (℡ 081 842 63 91), the first in 4hr 30min, the second in an hour less: both give close views of glaciers and their icefalls. The *Boval Hut* (℡ 081 842 64 03) is another unmissable 3hr 30min walk, giving stupendous high mountain and glacier scenery for much of the way, while the easy but steep ascent of the 3262m Piz Languard directly above Pontresina (up to 4hr) is the best place to enjoy an Alpine sunrise or sunset.

In **Val Bregaglia**, one of the most notable villages is **Soglio** (see p.541), which sits on the right-hand hillside gazing south to Val Bondasca, Piz Badile and the blade-like Sciora aiguilles. Paths leading out of Soglio climb the hillside to Alp Tombal, to Pass da Cam and Pass Düana for the most breathtaking views. These are steep trails, while a slightly less severe path (of 4hr) entices the walker from **Promontogno** below Soglio into Val Bondasca and up to its inner recesses where the *Sciora Hut* (℡ 081 822 11 38) stands immediately below the pinnacles after which it is named, with Piz Badile towering above to the southwest. Experienced mountain walkers could continue for four hours over the exposed Colle Vial below Badile to the *Sasc Furä Hut* (℡ 081 822 12 52), or cross the high Cacciabella Pass in the east to reach the *Albigna Hut* (℡ 081 822 14 05) in 4hr 30min.

Over the bridge below the Old Town is the **campsite** *Gurlaina* (℡ 081 864 15 01, ℻ 081 864 07 60; closed May & Nov). Scuol's main drag has plenty of ordinary **hotels**, but there are a couple of traditional *sgraffitied* gems on Plaz, the old village square: *Gabriel*, Rablüzza 159a (T081 864 11 52, F081 864 83 58; ❸; closed May & Nov), is a rambling old house with terraces and roof gardens; *Engiadina*, Rablüzza 152 (T081 864 14 21, W www.engiadina-scuol.ch; ❸–❹; closed May & Nov), retains its oriel-windowed exterior. There are inexpensive **restaurants** along Stradun, including *Traube*, which serves quality regional fare (*menus* from Fr.25).

Samnaun

East of Scuol, postbuses penetrate to the Austrian border and on to Landeck. Just before the frontier, a minor road curls back to climb into an isolated side-valley, at the end of which sits German-speaking **SAMNAUN** (1840m), for some reason a duty-free area and crammed with banks, shops and cut-price petrol stations, all open long hours. In winter, Samnaun's snow facilities – which include the world's only double-decker cable-car – link in with the network of pistes above the Austrian resort of **Ischgl** on the other side of a wall of 3000m peaks, taking in Europe's single largest snowboarding area; a one-/six-day pass valid on both resorts' lifts is Fr.57/245. Samnaun-Dorf **tourist office** (T081 868 58 58, W www.samnaun.ch) has full details. The best of the summer hikes from Samnaun is a tough, multi-day trail to Ischgl over the Zeblasjoch Pass.

Parc Naziunal Svizzer

Some 6km south of Susch sits the graceful little town of **ZERNEZ**, the slender white steeple of its church marking a junction of valleys: north is the Lower Engadine, south is the Upper Engadine, while to the east, a road leads through the **PARC NAZIUNAL SVIZZER** to the Ofenpass/Pass dal Fuorn and on into the Val Müstair. Although attractive enough in its own right, Zernez comes into its own as a staging post for hikes into the park, a pint-sized Alpine wilderness stretching for 169 square kilometres either side of the Ofen/Fuorn road.

   Established in 1914, the park's credo is to leave nature well alone: absolutely everything, from the tiniest lichen to the six pairs of golden eagles, is protected. Forest fires are monitored but allowed to burn; injured animals are left to their own devices; and roaming wardens will impose fines should you so much as pick a flower. You're allowed to walk in the park (provided you don't step off the marked trails), but prominent noticeboards publish stringent **regulations** prohibiting everything from littering to making loud noises – with the result that the park remains pristine. Red and roe deer, ibex and chamois roam freely, as do hares, foxes and huge numbers of marmots. Aside from the golden eagles, there are also bearded vultures, kestrels, ravens, various woodpeckers, grouse, partridge and skylarks. The venomous northern viper or adder is also around, but you'd have to tiptoe to come upon one unawares. Pine and larch forests grow up to 2300m, beyond which Alpine meadows are carpeted in springtime with edelweiss, gentians and a host of other high-altitude flowers. Further up still are bare rocky areas and permafrost.

Access, information and walks

Entry to the park is free. If you're **driving**, head along the main road to any one of nine free parking areas within the park boundaries, from all of which long and short trails twist out to north and south. **Postbuses** running hourly between Zernez and Müstair also stop at each parking area. Cycling is prohibited in the park.

   A new National Park headquarters is scheduled for completion in the centre of Zernez in 2003. Until then, the best place to get up-to-date information is the **National Park House**, located about 1km east of Zernez and open the same hours as the park itself (June–Oct daily 8.30am–6pm, Tues until 10pm; ☏081 856 13 78, ⓦwww.nationalpark.ch). This office is overflowing with maps, trail guides (including coverage of two-, three- and four-day hikes) and useful information on animal sightings, all in English. A **tourist office** on Zernez main street can also help with maps and general guidance (Mon–Fri 8.30am–noon & 2–5.30pm; July–Oct until 6.30pm, plus Sat 8.30am–noon & 2–4pm; ☏081 856 13 00, ⓦwww.zernez.ch).

There are 21 marked **walking** trails in and around the park, ranging from full-day mountain ascents to brief roadside strolls. The following are some of the more straightforward scenic routes that have easy access at either end; always check on trail conditions at the National Park House before you start. Note that, on high-summer weekends in particular, paths can get crowded. One of the best could involve overnighting in the wilds: **trail 7** (3hr) leads from Zernez into the Cluozza gorge, directly to the *Chamanna Cluozza* (see below), from where **trail 8** (3hr 30min) brings you out on a different route via a steep ascent to Praspöl, emerging at Parking 3 ("Vallun Chafuol"). Both these can be done in reverse. The circular **trail 9** (2hr) leads from Parking 3 through heather and pine forest to Margun Grimmels and back. The tougher **trail 15** (5hr) leads from Buffalora (1968m), just outside the boundary at Parking 10, on a simple ascent of Munt la Schera (2091m) and down to *Hotel Il Fuorn* at Parking 6.

Three of the simpler routes (marked as suitable for children) include **trail 1** (2hr 30min), a circular walk from Parking 1 ("Champlönch"), taking in the view from Alp Grimmels; **trail 13** (2hr), leading from Parking 1 on an easy countryside path to *Hotel Il Fuorn* at Parking 6; and **trail 10** (3hr 30min), a riverside forest walk that loops from Parking 3 through the tranquil Spöltal to Parking 4 ("Punt la Drossa").

Accommodation

There are two **places to stay** within the park, both of which need reserving in advance. *Hotel Il Fuorn*, beside Parking 6 (☏081 856 12 26, ⓦwww.ilfuorn.ch; ❷–❸; June–Oct), is a comfortable old lodge with shared-bath rooms, and has a newer wing with ensuite rooms. In the middle of the park, at the junction of several trails, is *Chamanna/Blockhaus Cluozza* (☏081 856 12 35, ⓕ081 856 16 86; June–Oct), a simple hut with Fr.27 dorm beds.

In Zernez, the **campsite** *Cul* is 500m behind the station (☏081 856 14 62, ⓦwww.camping-cul.ch; May to mid-Oct), and there are plenty of **hotels**: *Piz Terza* (☏081 856 14 14, ⓕ081 856 14 15; ❷; closed April, May & Nov) has modern, generic rooms near the church, while nearby *Spöl* (☏081 856 12 79, ⓔhotel.spoel@engadin.net; ❷; closed Nov) is a more characterful choice; both are within ten minutes' walk of the park entrance. Higher-quality *Bettini* (☏081 856 11 35, ⓦwww.engadin.net/bettini; ❷; closed April & Nov) is slightly further away in the town centre. Near each other, 7km beyond Zernez just outside the park boundary before Parking 1, are *Naturfreundehaus Ova Spin* (☏ & ⓕ081 852 31 42; dorms Fr.15; June–Oct) and *Wegerhaus Ova Spin* (☏ & ⓕ081 856 10 52, ⓦwww.strimer.ch; dorms Fr.20; closed May & Nov).

Val Müstair

As you crest the Ofenpass/Pass dal Fuorn 20km south of Zernez, spread out in front is the idyllic **Val Müstair** (Münstertal in German), a lush, peaceful valley pointing the way south into Italy. This finger of Switzerland, cut off by the mountains from the rest of Graubünden and entirely surrounded by Italy, is determinedly Romansh in language and culture. Half-a-dozen hamlets dot the green slopes on the 8km descent to **Santa Maria**, the main village of the valley, with a Gothic church just off its narrow main street. However, the chief attraction is **MÜSTAIR** (pronounced *moosh-tire*), 4km further, where virtually the last buildings before the Italian frontier are a Carolingian monastery and church, the **Baselgia San Jon**, or Klosterkirche St Johann (daily 8am–7pm; free). This functioning Benedictine convent was reputedly founded by Charlemagne himself around 800 AD, and has been named a UNESCO World Heritage Site for the array of brilliantly coloured Romanesque frescoes adorning the interior of its monastery church. The style and detail of the frescoes, which depict stories such as the stoning of St Stephen and the Dance of Salome, are breathtaking, and the atmosphere of the church, its adjacent cemetery and cobbled courtyard make the journey well worthwhile. A small **museum** off the courtyard has chunks of Carolingian carving and Baroque statues and icons (May–Oct Mon–Sat 9am–noon & 1.30–5pm, Sun 1.30–5pm; Nov–April Mon–Sat 10am–noon & 1.30–4.30pm, Sun 1.30–4.30pm; Fr.3).

Müstair **tourist office** (May–Oct Mon–Fri 9am–noon & 1.30–5pm; Nov–April Mon–Fri 10am–noon & 1.30–4.30pm; ℡081 858 50 00, Ⓦwww.muestair.ch & Ⓦwww.val-muestair.ch) has information on the whole valley. In Santa Maria is a characterful HI **hostel**, *Chasa Plaz* (℡081 858 56 61, Ⓦwww.youthhostel.ch; ❶; dorms Fr.27; June–Oct & mid-Dec to April), while in Müstair there's the good-value *Landgasthof Münsterhof* (℡081 858 55 41, Ⓦwww.muensterhof.ch; ❷), its old rooms filled with antiques. Müstair's **campsite** *Clenga* (℡081 858 54 10) is in a peaceful spot on the riverbank.

The Upper Engadine

"I have never seen light as it is up here: it's fantastic!"

Ferdinand Hodler, Swiss painter

The **Upper Engadine** (Engiadin'Ota in Romansh, Oberengadin in German) is one of the most scenic valleys in Switzerland, a heart-stoppingly beautiful array of forests, snowy mountains and silvery lakes, raised high at 1800m and looking southwest directly into the crispest and clearest sunshine in the Alps. The long, straight 55km run southwest from Zernez takes in a handful of attractive little resorts, all of them overshadowed by **St Moritz**, which holds court in mid-valley. In point of fact, many of the smaller fry – such as **Pontresina**, **Celerina** and **Silvaplana** – have as much, if not more, to offer than their world-famous neighbour, but for a century past and probably for a century to come, the Moritz name is the one that sells.

Crossing the two major mountain passes that lead on from St Moritz delivers you into small valleys sticking out into Italy that are entirely unlike the rest of Graubünden. To the southwest, the Maloja Pass heralds the deep and lush **Val Bregaglia**, while to the southeast, a road and rail line crosses the icy Bernina Pass into the idyllic **Val Poschiavo**. Both are thoroughly Italian, in language, culture and flora, and both offer a taste of Mediterranean-style living that's like a revelation after the rustic pleasures of the high mountains.

Beware that almost everything – shops, hotels, attractions, walking routes – is **closed during off-season** (mid-April to mid-June & mid-Oct to mid-Dec). We've specified months of opening only when they differ from this pattern.

St Moritz

ST MORITZ is all you expect and more – a brassy, in-your-face reminder of the hotshot world beyond the high valley walls. For a century or more, it's been the prime winter retreat of social high-flyers, minor European royalty and the international jetset, who've sparked the creation of a mini-Mayfair of Vuitton and Armani in this stunningly romantic setting of forest, lake and mountains. When the tourist office trumpets the "champagne climate", they don't necessarily mean the sparkling sunshine – although there's plenty of that as well, an unbeatable 322 days of it a year on average.

Not unlike its twin, Vail, Colorado, this can be the kind of town to give money a bad name. It's neither cosmopolitan, characterful nor especially attractive; indeed, after the rural, traditional villages to west and east, it comes across as exhaustingly built-up and mundane. And yet its name glisters better than gold, enough for the tourist board to make "St Moritz" a patented registered trademark. Presidents and princes, Hollywood starlets, nobility and *nouveaux riches* clamour to be associated with it, and the town gladly responds, turning on the razzle all winter long with an endless round of banquets, celebrations and spectacles centred on the frozen lake. Summer is downtime, when the hoi polloi arrive to hike and relax in the sunshine.

There's been a spa here since the Bronze Age, although the tale really begins in 1864, when local hotelier Johannes Badrutt laid down a challenge to a party of English summer regulars: spend a winter here, he said, and I'll foot the bill. They came, brought their friends the year after, and since then Badrutt has been quids in (the family's hotel is still the most expensive in town). With the season's heady glamour, it can be easy to forget that St Moritz is set amidst some of the world's most beautiful mountain scenery; the best thing to do, once you've arrived, is to get out as quickly as possible.

Arrival, information and accommodation

The town spans two villages: when people refer to St Moritz, they're talking about **St Moritz-Dorf**, a cluster of hotels, restaurants and boutiques on the hillside above the lake. **St Moritz-Bad**, far removed from the glitz 2km southwest down on the lakeshore, is an unattractive mini-sprawl of concrete apartment blocks and sports halls. Via dal Bagn connects the two. The **train station** (also the main postbus terminus) is awkwardly placed below Dorf, on the opposite side of the lake from Bad. Via Serlas winds up from the station past the main post office to the central square of Dorf, beneath which is a large, inexpensive parking garage (1hr free; Fr.18/day). The **tourist office** is 100m east at Via Maistra 12 (July–Sept & Dec–March Mon–Fri 9am–6.30pm, Sat 9am–6pm, Sun 4–6pm; rest of year Mon–Fri 9am–noon & 2–6pm, Sat 9am–noon; ☎081 837 33 33, ⊛www.stmoritz.ch).

Few bargains come wrapped with the St Moritz name, and **accommodation** is no exception: prices are high across the board, and during the winter season they go stratospheric. There are more affordable alternatives at neighbouring Celerina, Pontresina and Silvaplana, as well as inexpensive rooms high above the valley at Muottas Muragl.

Inexpensive and midrange hotels

Bellaval Via Grevas 55, Dorf ☎081 833 32 45, ⓔhotel-bellaval@bluewin.ch. The cheapest rooms in Dorf, conveniently situated beside the station and lake, spartan but acceptable. Ensuite and shared-bath available. Open year-round. ❷

Corvatsch Via Tegiatscha 1, Bad ☎081 837 57 57, ⊛www.hotel-corvatsch.ch. Excellent family-run hotel, located out of the hustle in peaceful Bad (with parking); an unromantic exterior preludes very pleasant, well-kept rooms with handcarved

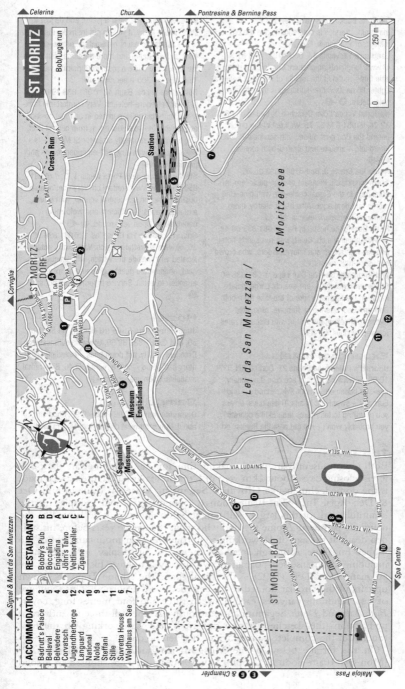

ST MORITZ

- - - Bob/Luge run

0   250 m

ACCOMMODATION

Badrutt's Palace	3
Bellaval	5
Belvedere	4
Corvatsch	8
Jugendherberge	12
Languard	2
National	10
Nolda	9
Steffani	1
Stille	11
Suvretta House	6
Waldhaus am See	7

RESTAURANTS

Bobby's Pub	B
Boccalino	D
Engiadina	A
Jöhri's Talvo	E
Veltlinerkeller	C
Zigane	F

Celerina ▲

Chur ▲

Pontresina & Bernina Pass ▲

Corviglia ▲

Signal & Munt da San Murezzan ▲

Cresta Run

Station

ST MORITZ DORF

VIA MAISTRA

VIA BATTAS

VIA STRETTA

VIA QUADRELLAS

PL. DA SCOULA

VIA MAISTRA

VIA VERDIN

VIA SERLAS

VIA GREVAS

VIA SERLAS

PL. DA LA ROSTAVEGLIA

VIA DAL BAGN

VIA ARONA

VIA SOM D'L'OVE

Museum Engiadinais

Segantini Museum

Lej da San Murezzan / St Moritzersee

VIA GREVAS

VIA GREVAS

VIA DAL BAGN

VIA LUDAINS

VIA SELA

VIA SURPUN

VIA MEZDI

VIA SELA

ST MORITZ-BAD

VIA SAN BAGN

VIA GIOVANNI SEGANTINI

VIA TEGIATSCHA

VIA ROSATSCH

VIA MEZDI

VIA MEZDI

Spa Centre ▲

Maloja Pass ▲

E & Champfèr ▲

E & 6 & Champfèr ▲

Maloja Pass ▲

11

GRAUBÜNDEN

533

furniture. Back rooms have views of the lake and mountains. Service is outstanding, and the onsite restaurant is a bonus. ❸–❹

Languard Via Veglia 14, Dorf ☎081 833 31 37, ⓦwww.languard-stmoritz.ch. Comfortable, friendly little family hotel in the middle of Dorf that keeps a tighter lid on its winter surcharges than its near neighbours. ❸–❹

National Via da l'Ova Cotschna 1, Bad ☎081 833 32 74, Ⓕ081 833 32 75. Well out of the crush, behind the Bad post office, with serviceable – and affordable – ensuite and shared-bath rooms. ❷–❸

Nolda Via Crasta 3, Bad ☎081 833 05 75, ⓦwww.nolda.ch. Pleasant enough pack-'em-in hotel next to the Signal cable-car, with pine-clad rooms that do the job. Also has a nearby, more upmarket *Noldapark* annexe. ❸–❺

Stille Beside the hostel in Bad ☎081 833 69 48, ⓦwww.hotelstille.ch. Quiet, well-run sports hotel, popular with skiers and snowboarders, who crowd out its no-frills rooms. ❷

Waldhaus am See Via Dim Lej 6 ☎081 836 60 00, ⓦwww.waldhaus-am-see.ch. Large, quiet lodge on the farthest shore of the lake from both Dorf and Bad, offering inoffensive, renovated rooms overlooking the water, with discount rates for weekly stays. ❸–❺

Expensive hotels

Badrutt's Palace Via Serlas 27, Dorf ☎081 837 10 00, ⓦwww.badruttspalace.com. Legendary five-star behemoth, one of Switzerland's – and Europe's – swankiest hotels. These days, unless you're willing to toss zeros around like confetti, you probably won't even get past the flunkey on the door: men must wear a jacket and tie just to stand in the lobby. If you do get in, make the most of it – this is the haunt of filmstars, princesses (real and wannabe) and more fur coats than live in the forest. You'd like a room in Christmas week? That'll be Fr.1700 – per night. ❾

Belvedere Via dal Bagn 42 ☎081 833 39 05, ⓦwww.belvedere-hotel.ch. Very comfortable family-run four-star hotel, perched in an ideal position overlooking the lake, just down from central Dorf. The building – modestly sized for St Moritz – is Belle-Epoque, with airy, well-equipped rooms and parking. ❺–❼

Steffani Plazza da la Posta Veglia 1, Dorf ☎081 836 96 96, ⓦwww.steffani.ch. Very comfortable, bustling hotel on the central square, with a few airs and graces but efficient and welcoming nonetheless. Open year-round. ❼–❽

Suvretta House Via Chasellas 1 ☎081 836 36 36, ⓦwww.suvrettahouse.ch. Vast luxury hotel located well outside the village, with uniquely elegant, understated guest rooms and an exquisite attention to detail. Service is formal, but not stiff. ❾

Hostel

Jugendherberge Stille (HI hostel) Via Surpunt 60, Bad ☎081 833 39 69, ⓦwww.youthhostel.ch. Excellent quality, but dorm beds – including obligatory half board – cost a moritzy Fr.46. Bike rental available. Open year-round. ❶

Campsite

Olympiaschanze ☎081 833 40 90. Good site, about 1km southwest of Bad. Mid-May to Sept.

The Town

Both town museums are worth making time for – although beware their different closing days. About 1km west of Dorf on Via Somplaz, the terrace road, is the domed, church-like **Giovanni Segantini Museum** (June to mid-Oct & Dec–April Tues–Sun 10am–noon & 3–6pm; Fr.7; SMP), displaying the beautiful work of this largely self-taught Symbolist who is acclaimed as the definitive painter of Alpine life, and who spent the twelve years before his sudden death at the age of 41 working to portray the clear mountain light of the Upper Engadine. Although many of the works on display are excellent – including an intense self-portrait, drawn three years before his death, and the poignant *Dead Deer* (1892) – the highlight is the Alpine Triptych, shown upstairs in the circular domed room designed for the purpose. This sequence of vast, luminous canvases, each between three and four metres long, covers *Birth*, *Life* and *Death*. Segantini had studiously sketched all three in entirety as preparation (the sketches are also displayed), and was working on the final touches of the complete painted triptych when he died.

On the terrace below is the **Museum Engiadinais**, Via dal Bagn 39 (Mon–Fri 10am–noon & 2–5pm, Sun 10am–noon; Fr.5), housed in a solid stone *sgraffitied* building that's one of the few surviving pieces of vernacular architecture in the town. Inside are reconstructed interiors of farmhouses and patrician mansions, along with interesting displays on the history of the spa and Engadine culture.

St Moritz's fame originally came from its mineral springs, which rise near the lake in St Moritz-Bad and are now corralled by a slick, modern **spa** centre (Mon–Fri 8am–noon & 2–6.30pm, Sat 8am–noon; ☎081 833 30 62, Ⓦ www.stmoritz-spa.ch). On offer are mineral baths, peat packs and plenty of other treatments; a massage costs Fr.54.

Eating and drinking

You'll find no bargains **eating and drinking** in St Moritz. The big hotels all have super-swanky dining rooms – exclusive, expensive and cloying to a fault. More down-to-earth establishments might take a bit of sniffing out.

Similarly, there's a plethora of upmarket **bars**, discos, nightclubs and drinking dens, most of which are either for members only, shielded by sky-high entry fees, or simply dull and expensive. Cut your losses and have a pint at *Bobby's Pub*, Via dal Bagn 52, instead, or settle in at the eye-popping *Devil's Place*, the bar of *Hotel Waldhaus*, Via Dim Lej 6, which is Guinness-acknowledged as having the world's largest selection of whiskies.

Restaurants

Boccalino Via dal Bagn 6 ☎081 832 11 11. Lively, bustling place with a range of quality wood-fired pizzas for under Fr.20, as well as pasta staples.

Corvatsch Via Tegiatscha 1, Bad ☎081 837 57 57. Down-to-earth, cosy restaurant attached to an attractive, mid-priced hotel, well out of the chic part of town, but with a carefully compiled menu and well-presented local cuisine (with wines to match).

Engiadina Plazza da Scoula 10 ☎081 833 32 65. Popular place in the middle of Dorf that concentrates on fondue – pay about Fr.28 for the ordinary version, or considerably more for the house special with extra champagne. Closed Sun.

Jöhri's Talvo Via Gunels 15, Champfèr ☎081 833 44 55, Ⓦ www.talvo.ch. Perhaps the finest restaurant in the valley, 3km from St Moritz in neighbouring Champfèr, specializing in superb fish and lobster dishes and also offering classic, elegant takes on heavier local cuisine. Be prepared to pay hundreds of francs for the privilege.

Mathis Food Affairs Corviglia funicular top station ☎081 833 63 55, Ⓦ www.mathisfood.ch. Book well ahead for a meal to remember at the *Marmite* restaurant, high above town on the Corviglia slopes – if caviar and truffles at 2500m are to your liking, that is.

Veltlinerkeller Via dal Bagn 11 ☎081 833 40 09. A perennial favourite; ignore the hunting trophies on the walls, and concentrate on the quality, lightly prepared food in front of you – excellent pastas,

fish dishes and grilled meats with *menus* starting at around Fr.22.

Zigane Via Tegiatscha 7, Bad ☎081 833 30 22, Ⓦ www.zigane.ch. Pleasant restaurant down the hill serving familiar local food – *Rösti*, fondue and raclette taking centre stage – but in a stylish, vaguely Art-Deco setting far removed from the standard kitschy Alpine chalet look.

Listings

Bike rental You can rent mountain bikes for around Fr.30/day from Bike Side ☎081 833 05 55, Boom Sport ☎081 832 22 22, Corviglia Sport Shop ☎081 833 44 77, Corviglia Tennis Centre ☎081 833 15 00, Scheuing Sport ☎081 833 31 70, Viva Sportiva ☎081 832 19 19, and also from the train station.

Changing money In the station (daily 6.50am–8.10pm).

Flights Air Grischa (☎081 852 35 35) does a range of sightseeing flights by helicopter over the high peaks (Fr.160–225 per person, minimum 4 people), as do Heli Bernina (☎081 850 00 50, Ⓦ www.helibernina.ch) and MFG (☎081 833 36 74, Ⓦ www.mfgoe.ch).

Hospital In Samedan ☎081 851 81 11. Klinik Gut in St Moritz (☎081 836 34 34) can treat emergencies. Doctors are on call 24hr at ☎081 833 14 14.

Post Main office is opposite Platz station (Mon–Fri 7.45am–6.30pm, Sat 8.30am–noon); smaller office next to Dorf station.

Don't be misled into thinking that the Upper Engadine is all St Moritz-style glamour: there's a vast range of sports and activities that take advantage of the valley's natural beauty. Check ⓦ**www.skiengadin.ch** and ⓦ**www.engadinferien.ch**.

Winter

There are three main ski and snowboard sectors. On the north side of the valley is the sunny, south-facing **Corviglia–Piz Nair** (ⓦwww.corviglia.com); with three access routes. From St Moritz-Bad, a cable-car rises to Signal, with chairlifts up to the Munt da San Murezzan (2659m), where there's a halfpipe. From St Moritz-Dorf a funicular runs via Chantarella to Corviglia itself (2486m), from where a cable-car continues to the soaring Piz Nair summit (3057m). A gondola from nearby Celerina rises to Marguns (2278m), which gives access to testing runs off Las Trais Fluors and Piz Glüna, as well as linking directly by chairlift to Corviglia itself. Across the valley is **Corvatsch–Furtschellas** (ⓦwww.corvatsch.ch): a cable-car from Surlej, 3km south of St Moritz-Bad, and a chairlift from nearby Alp Surlej both arrive at Murtèl (2702m), from where a cable-car rises to Piz Corvatsch (3451m). Again, long sweeping reds are plentiful, while dropping through the trees is the testing 8km Hahnensee black run. A cable-car from Sils Maria 4km south of Surlej serves Furtschellas (2800m), neatly linked by chairlifts to Murtèl. Finally, 12km south of St Moritz – with easy access from Pontresina – is **Diavolezza–Lagalb**, with some steep, difficult runs from Diavolezza (2978m) on the south side and off Piz Lagalb (2959m) opposite, including the Minor black run.

Careful selection of the right **pass** can pay off. A general pass, valid for 3/6/13 days in all areas, is Fr.177/314/523. A full/half-day pass for Corvatsch or Corviglia is Fr.61/49, for Diavolezza Fr.52/43. Discounts apply out of peak season, and selected-day and afternoon-only passes are available. The **Snowpass** is valid on lifts for a year in the Upper Engadine, plus winter in all of Graubünden, Gstaad and Vail (USA) for Fr.1100. The **Engadin Year Card**, valid for a year in the Upper Engadine plus a winter in Gstaad and Vail and winter discounts at Scuol and Samnaun, is Fr.914 (Fr.2350 for 3 years). A course of six half-day **lessons** costs Fr.210; private instruction can be Fr.350/day. Schools include the Schweizer Skischule (ⓦwww.skischool.ch) and Suvretta Snowsports (ⓦwww.suvrettasnowsports.ch). The **TopHit Engadin** is an excellent-value off-season **package** (late Nov to mid-Dec & late March to end of season only): three nights' B&B accommodation plus a three-day pass costs a bargain Fr.211 in a dorm, Fr.307 in a basic hotel; seven nights plus a six-day pass are an even-better Fr.413/567.

There are some legendary bob and toboggan runs, including an exhilarating 4.2km toboggan from **Muottas Muragl** into the valley, a vertical drop of 700m (you can rent a sled at the top). Fr.210 buys you an adrenalin-fuelled "taxi ride" down the 1.6km **Olympia bob run** (ⓦwww.olympia-bobrun.ch), the world's only natural-ice bobsleigh run, between St Moritz and Celerina, while for Fr.450 you can do five skeleton runs in a season (Christmas–Feb) on the most famous luge course in the world, the death-defying 1.2km **Cresta Run** (ⓦwww.cresta-run.com) – which, for no good reason, is barred to women. See p.513 for details of the excellent, inexpensive **Preda–Bergün** toboggan run. ⓦwww.boarders-valley.com is the best local snowboarding site.

Other attractions include **skiing by moonlight** at Diavolezza (selected dates), **heli-skiing** by Air Grischa (☏081 852 35 35), **snow-tubing** at Samedan, **skating**, **curling**, **paragliding** and **hanggliding** (reserve on ☏079 353 21 59; Fr.230) and a handful of winter walks, including the Philosophers' Path on Muottas Muragl. The Schweizer Bergsteigerschule (ⓦwww.bergsteiger-pontresina.ch) offers a range of tough, guided long-distance skiing trips; samples include a day's **ski-touring** (Fr.85), or a week skiing the Val Poschiavo (Fr.1070 including half board). Pontresina's Bananas Snowboardschule (ⓦwww.bananas.net) offers exhilarating back-country boarding for experts. **Horse-drawn sleighs** wait for business beside the Catholic church in St Moritz-Bad; their route crosses the frozen lake into the forest (Fr.95/hr). Winter events held on the lake include **show-jumping** (mid-Jan), the **polo** world cup (late Jan), "White Turf" **horse races** (Feb), **cricket** (late Feb) and **greyhound racing** (early March), along with **ski-jumping**, various **bob** and **luge** championships and the **Engadin Ski Marathon** (early March; @www.engadin-skimarathon.ch), 42km down the valley from Maloja to S-chanf.

Summer

One of the best round-trip summer **walks** starts from **Muottas Muragl** (2453m). A Höhenweg (high-level route) leads across Val Muragl and then splits: a steep path heads up to the Segantini Hütte (2731m), where the painter died, and then comes down to meet the easier path – which has stayed fairly flat – at Unterer Schafberg (2231m) before continuing to the restaurant at Alp Languard (2325m; total 2hr 30min), where a chairlift takes you down to Pontresina. Ask for the discounted Höhenweg ticket at the Punt Muragl funicular. Above St Moritz, **Marguns**, **Signal** and **Corviglia** are hubs for a network of trails, including a panoramic route from Corviglia to the isolated Chamanna Saluver hut and on down to Samedan (3hr 30min). A fairly easy trail runs from Marguns to Corviglia and down via Alp Giop to Signal, or via Alp Nova to Chantarella (1hr 30min); from either, it's a further hour down to St Moritz. A quieter route to the valley floor runs from Marguns to Alp Laret and then into the cool **God da Blais forest** to Celerina (1hr 30min) – or you can detour from Alp Laret to St Moritz. Top long-distance route is the **Via Engiadina**, a reasonably flat high-level trail across the whole region; simplest access is at Marguns or Corviglia, from where you walk for six full hours above the spectacular lake scenery to Maloja (19km). A testing alternative is the full-day trail from Piz Nair down to the **Suvrettasee** – with a stunning view of Piz Julier and the Bernina range – and on via the Suvretta Pass into Val Bever, ending at Spinas; an alternative leads up from the Suvrettasee around the south face of Piz Nair back to Corviglia (2hr). A lovely half-day walk leads from the **Furtschellas** top station to Marmorè, from where two routes lead back to Sils Maria; the direct option is 1hr 30min, but if you divert down to Curtins, you can trace a path through the meadows of the **Val Fex** to Sils Maria via the frescoed chapel at Fex-Crasta (2hr 30min). There are plenty of easy walks from Murtèl, including a circuit to and from the restaurant at **Fuorcla Surlej** (1hr); a tougher trail (see box p.528) leads from there into the Val Roseg to Pontresina (3hr 30min), while another heads down to St Moritz-Bad via the Hahnensee (3hr). At **Diavolezza**, the best route involves a two-hour round trip from the top station up to the spectacular **Munt Pers** (3207m), overlooking the Morteratsch glacier.

There are tons of other activities. Top local operator is The St Moritz Experience (☎081 833 77 14, @www.stmoritz-experience.ch), who run days of **canyoning** (Fr.180), **glacier walking** (Fr.120) and **multisports**, including abseiling, flying fox, sailing, tubing and more (Fr.120), as well as **rock climbing** (private guided day Fr.400) and four-day **trekking** itineraries – tough (walking 6hr/day, basic huts; Fr.1100) and luxury (walking 3–5hr/day, ensuite hotels plus helicopter; Fr.1325). There's also **rafting** (Fr.60–100; Swiss Raft ☎081 842 68 24, @www.swissraft.ch), **horse riding** (Fr.50/hr per person; day excursion Fr.350), **go-karting** in Celerina (☎081 833 45 05) and a spectacular **mountain-bike** route from Lagalb (2893m) way down 22km to Poschiavo (1000m). The Innline Engadina is a marked **inline skating** and **cycling** off-road path that follows the river 8.6km from La Punt to S-chanf; during the Engadin Inline Marathon, from Maloja to S-chanf (late June), the main valley road is closed to traffic. Silvaplana is known for its **windsurfing** (@www .windsurfing-silvaplana.ch) and **kitesurfing** (@www.kitesailing.ch), with plenty of information also at @www.engadinwind.com.

Celerina and around

Just 2km – a half-hour walk – east of St Moritz is **CELERINA** (Schlarigna in Romansh). This pleasant small town on the banks of the Inn, base station for a gondola rising to the ski slopes of Corviglia, has an atmospheric old cobbled quarter of traditional Engadine architecture. It's also the end-point of both the infamous Cresta Run luge course and the Olympia Bob-Run (for both, see p.536). On a grassy knoll 1km east of the centre is the isolated **Baselgia San Gian**, with a Romanesque choir and a painted wooden ceiling dating from 1478 (mid-June to mid-Oct Mon 2–4pm, Wed 4–5.30pm, Fri 10.30am–noon; Dec–March Wed 2–4pm; free).

Beware that there are **two train stations**: the one on the St Moritz–Samedan line is on the north side of the centre; the other (dubbed "Celerina Staz") on the St Moritz–Pontresina line is 700m south, just over the river. The straight Via da la Staziun links the two; halfway along it, at the central crossroads with Via Maistra, is the **tourist office** (Mon–Fri 8.30am–noon & 2–6pm; mid-June to Oct & Dec–April also Sat 10am–noon & 3–5pm; ☎081 830 00 11, Ⓦwww.celerina.ch). Inexpensive **accommodation** includes the excellent *Inn Lodge* hostel (☎081 834 47 95, Ⓔinnlodge@celerina.ch; dorms Fr.26–31) and the lively *Zur Alten Brauerei* (☎081 832 18 74, Ⓦwww.alte-brauerei.ch; ❷; dorms Fr.35), also with a bar and restaurant. The most characterful upmarket hotel is *Chesa Rosatsch*, a 350-year-old riverside inn (☎081 837 01 01, Ⓦwww.rosatsch.ch; ❹–❺).

Muottas Muragl

Across from Celerina rises the ridge of **MUOTTAS MURAGL** (2456m), accessed by a steep funicular from Punt Muragl on the Celerina–Pontresina road. The panoramic view from the top, some 700m above the valley, is unmissable summer or winter, offering an uninterrupted gaze southwest up the length of the Engadine, its string of lakes glittering in the sunlight between high peaks. The summit *Berghotel* has reinvented itself as a fine **restaurant** (☎081 842 82 32, Ⓦwww.muottasmuragl.ch), with an excellent menu of regional and international cuisine complemented by an outstanding wine list and spectacular views: book in advance for a window table. Lunch is a reasonable Fr.35 or so, rising to Fr.75 or more per head in the evening. Throughout the season, the funicular runs every half-hour until 11pm. The *Berghotel*'s spotlessly clean, fresh but simple shared-bath **rooms** are a rare bargain (❷–❸); guests benefit from discounts on the funicular. The mountain also offers great walks and a winter toboggan run (see p.536).

Pontresina and beyond

Less than 2km up the Bernina Pass road from Punt Muragl is the swish resort of **PONTRESINA**, lying in a privileged, wind-sheltered position on a south-west-facing terrace amidst meadows and fragrant pine and larch woods. Access to the Diavolezza slopes is easy from here, and the scenery of high rocky peaks to east and west interspersed with glaciers – most notably the huge Morteratsch glacier, sidling down from Piz Bernina (4049m) – is impressive; the town stares directly across to the **Val Roseg**, complete with its own glacier. Pontresina is curiously split between its St-Moritzy aspirations, with half-a-dozen luxury palace hotels and a glitteringly modern main street, and its tough reputation as the best place in the area for adventure sports and hiking; the local mountaineering school (see p.536) is the largest in Switzerland.

From the station, it's a short walk across the river and up to the **tourist office**, housed in the landmark Rondo conference centre (Mon–Fri

8.30am–noon & 2–6pm, Sat 8.30am–noon & 4–6pm; July, Aug & Christmas–Easter also Sun 4–6pm; ☎081 838 83 00, ⓦwww.pontresina.com). Via Maistra slopes upwards into the centre of town, location of most **hotels**, including simple *Pensione Valtellina* (☎081 842 64 06; ❷), but you'll find more character in the narrow lanes of the Old Town, the other direction on Via Maistra. Here are the *Grand Hotel Kronenhof* (☎081 830 30 30, ⓦwww .kronenhof.com; ❽), a Baroque-style palace set around its own courtyard and lawns and tastefully luxurious guest rooms; and the delightful *Saratz* (☎081 839 40 00, ⓦwww.saratz.ch; ❼), a similarly grand old-style hotel that has been superbly renovated to give a choice of rooms with traditional or modern decor. Down by the station is the reliable non-ensuite *Bahnhof* (☎081 838 80 00, ⓦwww.hotel-bahnhof.ch; ❷), alongside the HI **hostel** *Jugendherberge Tolais* (☎081 842 72 23, ⓦwww.youthhostel.ch; ❶; dorms Fr.43 including half board), with bikes for rent and advice on hiking routes into the dramatic Val Roseg (see box p.537). The **campsite** *Plauns/Morteratsch* (☎081 842 62 85, Ⓕ081 834 51 36; June to mid-Oct & mid-Dec to mid-April) is in a lovely countryside location.

Walks and skiing aside, the most enjoyable excursion from Pontresina is by horse-drawn carriage from the station for an hour to the **Hotel Roseggletscher** (☎081 842 64 45, ⓦwww.roseggletscher.ch; ❷; dorms Fr.30), partway up the car-free Val Roseg at the foot of the glacier; there are up to five departures a day, but booking is essential (Fr.26 return; ☎081 842 60 57). Otherwise, it's an easy, scenic walk (2hr). The views from the hotel are stunning; plenty of high-level trails lead on deeper into the mountains.

Val Poschiavo

From Pontresina, the high **Bernina Pass** (2328m) is about 15km southeast. This route is served by ordinary trains as well as the Bernina Express (see p.30), a packaged excursion in panoramic carriages from Chur, Davos and St Moritz into the idyllic **Val Poschiavo** (Puschlav in German) and down to the Italian border town of Tirano, from where you switch onto a postbus around the shores of Lake Como, ending up back in Switzerland at Lugano. However you travel in the valley, it's still gorgeous. A classic vantage-point is **Alp Grüm**, on the train line but not the road (reachable after a two-hour walk from the car park at the *Ospizio Bernina* inn on the pass; ⓦwww.bernina-hospiz.ch): from 2091m you can see clear down to the Lago di Poschiavo and beyond. The *Belvedere* hotel and restaurant (☎081 844 03 14; May–Oct), ten minutes' walk from Alp Grüm station, provides refreshment.

The railway joins the road again at the village of **San Carlo**, watched over by its ancient church tower, and heads on 2km to **POSCHIAVO**. The difference between this laid-back, photogenic Italianate town and the huddled Alpine resort of Pontresina the same distance north of the pass couldn't be more striking. Poschiavo's tranquil old quarter, across the river from the train station, is filled with tall, foursquare eighteenth-century shuttered mansions in various shades of pastel, overlooking stone-paved plazas ringed with terrace cafés. The place is perfect for soaking up some sunshine – of which there's plenty – filling up on risotto instead of fondue, and savouring a carafe of Valtellina wine from the Italian regions bordering. On the north side of the central Piazza Comunale is the seventeenth-century Protestant church of **Sant'Ignazio**, which holds an inscription stating that the town was *riformata da gli errori e superstizioni* in 1520. Despite this claim, the Catholic **San Vittore**, dating from the late fifteenth century, remains a powerful presence 200m away on the south side of the square. The same square holds the **tourist office**

(Mon–Fri 8am–noon & 2–6pm; July & Aug also Sat 9am–noon & 2–5pm; ☎081 844 05 71, ⓦwww.valposchiavo.ch). Of the **hotels**, *Croce Bianca*, a five-minute walk south (☎081 844 01 44, ⓦwww.croce-bianca.ch; ❷), and *Suisse*, on Via da Mez (☎081 844 07 88, ⓦwww.suisse-poschiavo.ch; ❷–❸), are both long-standing fixtures in the town, with decent rooms.

Beyond the Lago di Poschiavo and the village of **Brusio** – with its famous, much-photographed circular viaduct bringing trains gently down to the valley floor – is the Italian border at Campocologno, 16km south of Poschiavo. Some 4km further is **TIRANO**, terminus of Swiss trains. The Swiss station (with a money-changing counter) and its Italian counterpart (with trains to Milan roughly every 2hr) sit beside each other, separated by passport control. Swiss postbuses to Lugano – the second leg of the Bernina Express – depart from round the corner (signposted). Tirano's residential Old Town, dead ahead on the west bank of the river, has cobbled, arcaded courtyards and tiny sloping lanes leading up to the medieval Porta Bormina. The pilgrimage church of **Madonna di Tirano**, commemorating an appearance of the Virgin in 1504, lies 1km northwest of the centre, its shrine focused around a statue of Mary dressed in a silk and gold robe donated by local people in 1746.

Silvaplana and beyond

The Engadine continues to rise gently for 16km beyond St Moritz, past little **Champfèr** to the village of **SILVAPLANA**, on a bulge of land between the diminutive Lej da Champfèr and the grand Lej da Silvaplauna (Silvaplanersee in German). Due to a particular feature of the local summer climate – in which morning thermals rise more quickly than in neighbouring St Moritz or Sils to create the consistently strong, warm "Malojawind" that sweeps across the surface of the lake during the day – Silvaplana is home to some outstanding watersports: it hosted the Windsurfing and Kiteboarding World Championships in 2002 (see p.537 for more). Opposite the village is tiny **Surlej**, base station for the cable-car up to Piz Corvatsch.

In the centre of Silvaplana – on the main road up to the Julier Pass (see p.514) – is the **tourist office** (Mon–Fri 8.30am–noon & 2–6pm; June–Oct & Dec–March also Sat 9am–noon & 4–6pm; Dec–March also Sun 4–6pm; ☎081 838 60 00, ⓦwww.silvaplana.ch). Silvaplana's cheapest **hotel** is the *Arlas* (☎081 828 81 48, ⓕ081 828 89 63; ❶), while the youthful *Julier Palace* (☎081 828 96 44, ⓦwww.julierpalace.com; ❷–❸) has a lively atmosphere, good prices and an excellent bar. Champfèr's four-star *Chesa Guardalej* (☎081 836 63 00, ⓦwww.chesa-guardalej.ch; ❷–❺) has perks like a free ski bus and free parking but stands out for its superb-value summer rates – as little as one-third of its winter prices. The acclaimed *Landgasthof Bellavista* (☎081 838 60 50, ⓦwww.bellavista.ch; ❹–❻) is in a peaceful location near the Surlej cable-car, with a stunning view and a fine restaurant. There's a **campsite** (☎081 828 84 92) next to Silvaplana's lakefront sports centre.

Sils and Maloja

Beyond the Lej da Silvaplauna lies the quiet village of **SILS** (Segl in Romansh), with an alluring, rural atmosphere lacking in either Silvaplana or St

During the summer and winter seasons, **night buses** run from St Moritz (Dorf, train station and Bad) to Silvaplana and on to Sils Maria. Departures are daily, on the hour 9pm to midnight, with extra departures on Friday and Saturday nights at 1am and 2am. Tourist offices have full details.

Moritz: **Sils Baselgia** offers ethereally beautiful views over the Lej da Segl, acclaimed by a century of artistic and literary visitors – not least Hermann Hesse, Marc Chagall and Richard Strauss – while 200m south, **Sils Maria** was the summer home of the philosopher Friedrich Nietzsche for eight creative years. His modest house has been turned into the **Nietzsche-Haus** museum (Tues–Sun 1–5pm; Fr.5; Ⓦwww.nietzschehaus.ch), where you can see manuscripts, photos, death masks and the room where Nietzsche wrote his most celebrated work, *Also Sprach Zarathustra*. In the Chesa Cumünela on the nearby village square is the well-equipped **tourist office** (Mon–Fri 8.30am–6pm; June–Oct & Dec–March also Sat 9am–noon & 4–6pm; Dec–March also Sun 4–6pm; ℡081 838 50 50, Ⓦwww.sils.ch). Traffic is barred from circulating between Maria and Baselgia: there's a large underground car park in Maria and, in winter, free local buses which also serve the base-station of the Furtschellas cable-car. A handful of grand old hotels include the castle-like *Waldhaus* (℡081 838 51 00, Ⓦwww.waldhaus-sils.ch; ❼–❾) and the stunning Art Nouveau *Edelweiss* (℡081 838 42 42, Ⓦwww.hotel-edelweiss.ch; ❺–❼), Sils's oldest hotel, with a renowned restaurant; less lavish options include *Chesa Randolina* (℡081 838 54 54, Ⓦwww.randolina.ch; ❺), with superb lake views, and simple *Schulze* (℡081 826 52 13, Ⓕ081 826 52 21; ❷).

From Sils Maria, horse-drawn "buses" run on a schedule into the romantic, car-free **Val Fex** (June–Oct at least 2 daily; Fr.30 return; reserve on ℡081 826 52 86) to the peaceful *Hotel Fex* at the end of the valley (℡081 826 53 55, Ⓦwww.hotelfex.ch; ❸–❹). Horse-drawn carriages or sleighs waiting on the village square can do the same trip on demand (Fr.160 return).

In summer, a small **motorboat** – dubbed "Europe's highest ferry" – chugs around the Lej da Segl, 1800m above sea level, stopping a few times on its way to the village of **MALOJA** (July–Sept; 3–4 daily; takes 40min; Fr.20 return; reserve on ℡081 826 53 43), whose church cemetery holds the grave of painter Giovanni Segantini. Tough hiking trails to the north climb into the mountains to the Lunghin Pass, a rare triple watershed: from this point, the Inn flows into the Danube and the Black Sea; the Julier flows via the Rhine to the North Sea; and the Maira flows into the Po and the Mediterranean. In Maloja is a useful HI **hostel** *Jugendherberge* (℡081 824 32 58, Ⓦwww.youthhostel.ch; ❶; dorms Fr.31).

Val Bregaglia

From the **Maloja Pass** (1815m), the road suddenly tumbles off the cliff edge and down in a series of concertina switchbacks into the beautiful **Val Bregaglia** (Bergell in German), one of Graubünden's three Italian-speaking valleys (along with Mesolcina and Poschiavo). Suddenly, everything is different: the crisp air of the Alps is replaced by the warm breezes of the south, pine forests and rocky, snowy crags by lush, green vegetation, and *sgraffitied* bungalows by flinty cottages. Roughly 14km from the pass is the main village, **Vicosoprano**, an attractive, quiet place bypassed by the main road which heads on south through tiny **STAMPA**, birthplace of the painter Augusto Giacometti and his better-known son, the sculptor Alberto, and home to the valley's **tourist office** (Mon–Fri 9–11.30am & 3–5.30pm; July–Sept also Sat 9–11.30am; ℡081 822 15 55, Ⓦwww.bregaglia.ch). The road shadows the river, coiling on down the valley past ruined hilltop castles and isolated, crumbling roadside churches.

From **Promontogno**, 3km west of Stampa and about the same distance east of the border village Castasegna, postbuses follow a narrow branch road which climbs the north wall of the valley to **SOGLIO**. This eyrie of a hamlet, its narrow, cobbled alleys lined with close-set stone buildings, offers tremendous panoramic views: its lofty terrace sits opposite the 3300-metre Pizzo Badile, and is backed by the equally lofty Piz dal Märc and Piz Duan. The village is the focus of a wealth of mountain walks, easy ones following a valley-side route down to Stampa (2hr), as well as longer high-level hikes back to Vicosoprano, or up through the treeline behind the village (see box p.528). But there are lazier reasons to spend a day or three in Soglio: the *Palazzo Salis* in the village (Ⓣ 081 822 12 08, Ⓕ 081 822 16 00; ❸–❹; March–Nov) is one of Switzerland's more extraordinary hotels. Soglio was the seat of the Von Salis family long before 1630, when the *palazzo* was constructed, and the hotel is still owned by the same family today. The whole place is an eye-opening experience, from the echoing vaulted hall, crammed with antique furniture, *chaises longues*, open fireplaces and suits of armour, to its grand guest rooms (some ensuite), stone-floored down below, wood-floored above, complete with four-poster beds and antique stoves.

Travel details

Trains

Arosa to: Chur (hourly; 1hr).
Chur to: Arosa (hourly; 1hr); Davos Dorf & Platz (hourly; 1hr 30min; some change in Landquart); Disentis/Mustér (hourly; 1hr 20min); Ilanz (hourly; 40min); Klosters (hourly; 1hr 10min); Maienfeld (hourly; 15min); Rhäzüns (hourly; 20min); St Gallen (hourly; 1hr 35min); St Moritz (hourly; 2hr); Sargans (hourly; 25min); Thusis (twice hourly; 30–45min); Tiefencastel (hourly; 50min); Tirano via Bernina Pass (June–Oct 1 daily; 4hr 30min); Zermatt via Andermatt & Brig (1–3 daily; 5hr 45min); Zürich (hourly; 1hr 35min).
Davos (Platz & Dorf) to: Chur (hourly; 1hr 30min); Klosters (twice hourly; 25min); Tirano via Bernina Pass (June–Oct 1 daily; 3hr 30min).
Disentis/Mustér to: Andermatt via Oberalp Pass (hourly; 1hr 10min); Chur (hourly; 1hr 20min); Ilanz (hourly; 40min).
Klosters to: Chur (hourly; 1hr 10min); Davos Dorf & Platz (twice hourly; 25min); Scuol (hourly; 45min).
Pontresina to: St Moritz (hourly; 10min).
Poschiavo to: St Moritz (hourly; 1hr 40min); Tirano (hourly; 45min).
St Moritz to: Pontresina (hourly; 10min); Poschiavo (hourly; 1hr 40min); Tirano via Bernina

Pass (hourly; 2hr 30min); Zermatt via Andermatt & Brig (1–2 daily; 8hr); Zernez (hourly; 55min; change at Samedan).
Thusis to: Chur (twice hourly; 30–45min); St Moritz (hourly; 1hr 35min).

Buses

Andeer to: Juf (5 daily; 55min).
Chur to: Bellinzona via San Bernardino Tunnel (every 2hr; 2hr 15min); Flims (twice hourly; 45min); St Moritz via Julier Pass (1–2 daily; 2hr 40min); Splügen (every 2hr; 1hr); Zillis (every 2hr; 40min).
Davos (Platz & Dorf) to: Zernez via Flüela Pass (July–Oct every 2hr; 1hr).
Disentis/Mustér to: Biasca via Lukmanier/Lucomagno Pass (June–Sept 2 daily; 1hr 55min).
Flims to: Chur (twice hourly; 45min); Laax (twice hourly; 10min).
St Moritz to: Lugano via Chiavenna, Italy (1–2 daily; 4hr); Soglio (every 2hr; 1hr 25min; change at Promontogno).
Tiefencastel to: Bivio (hourly; 55min).
Zernez to: Davos via Flüela Pass (July–Oct every 2hr; 1hr); Müstair via Pass dal Fuorn (every 2hr; 1hr 10min).

Ticino

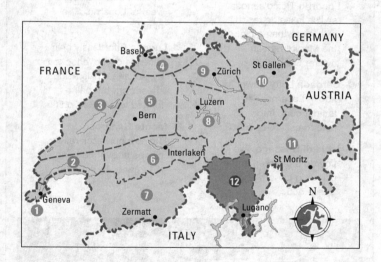

CHAPTER 12

Highlights

* **Bellinzona** Atmospheric, often-bypassed town, dominated by battlements and lofty castles. See p.549

* **Alto Ticino** There's some excellent walking on offer in these remote, high valleys. See p.554

* **Locarno** Ticino's most stylish lakeside resort, with more than a hint of the Mediterranean riviera. See p.559

* **Cardada** Lofty viewpoint above Locarno, set amidst cool, fragrant, pine forests. See p.563

* **Isole di Brissago** Two tiny dots of green in the glittering Lago Maggiore. See p.565

* **Valle Maggia** Tortuous valley system north of Locarno that culminates in isolated trailheads and a serene Alpine chapel at Mogno. See p.566

* **Centovalli** One of Switzerland's most memorable train rides, winding above a ravine west of Locarno. See p.567

* **Lugano** Effortlessly chic lakeside city, overlooked by, sugarloaf hills rising sheer from the palm-fringed water. See p.568

* **Monte Generoso** Ticino's only rack railway climbs above the Lago di Lugano. See p.578

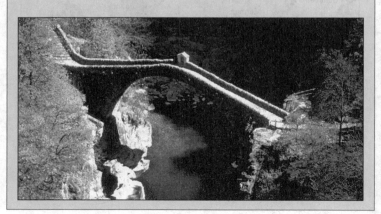

Ticino

It is strange how different the sun-dried, ancient, southern slopes of the world are, from the northern slopes. It is as if the god Pan really had his home among these sunbleached stones and tough, sun-dark trees. So I was content, coming down into Airolo...

D.H. Lawrence

The Italian-speaking canton of **TICINO** (*Tessin* in German and French) occupies the balmy, lake-laced southern foothills of the Alps. It's radically different from the rest of the country in almost every way: culture, food, architecture, attitude and driving style owe more to Milan than Zürich, and the famously sunny skies even draw in fog-bound Milanese for a breath of air. Every Swiss has their own favourite bit of the country – the mountain panorama above Interlaken, morning mist on Lake Luzern, perhaps the waterfront promenade at Vevey – but everybody loves the Ticino. The place is simply irresistible: a short train ride under the Alps and you can emerge in glittering sunshine to a tiny corner of the Italian Mediterranean that is for ever Switzerland, peopled by expressive, stylish, hot-blooded folk as different from the stolid farmers of the north as they could possibly be. And it's no wonder they're hot-blooded. As an ethnic and linguistic minority of eight percent in their own country and nothing more than a quaint irrelevance to the urban hotshots of Milan and Turin next door, the Ticinesi consistently have to struggle to get their voices heard in the corridors of power.

The glamour of their canton, and its stunning natural beauty – lushly wooded hills rising from azure water, palm trees swaying against deep blue skies, red roofs framed by purple bougainvillea – often seem to blind outsiders with romance. And the German-speaking Swiss in particular fall head over heels for the Latin paradise on their doorstep. It takes just three hours from the grey streets of suburban Zürich to reach the fragrant subtropical gardens of Lugano, and from March till November German Swiss come in their thousands to sit beneath vine-shaded outdoor terraces of simple *grotti* or *osterie* (rustic local taverns) and choose polenta, risotto or herb-scented salads from bilingual Italian-German menus, sample a carafe of one of the dozens of varieties of Ticinese merlot, and still pay with familiar francs at the end.

Although linguistically, culturally and temperamentally Italian, the Ticino has been controlled by the Swiss since the early 1500s, when Uri, Schwyz and Unterwalden moved to secure the southern approaches of the Gotthard Pass against the dukes of Milan. For three centuries the Ticinesi remained under the thumb of the tyrannical northerners, until **Napoleon** arrived in 1798 to reorganize the area under his new Cisalpine Republic. But faced with a mere

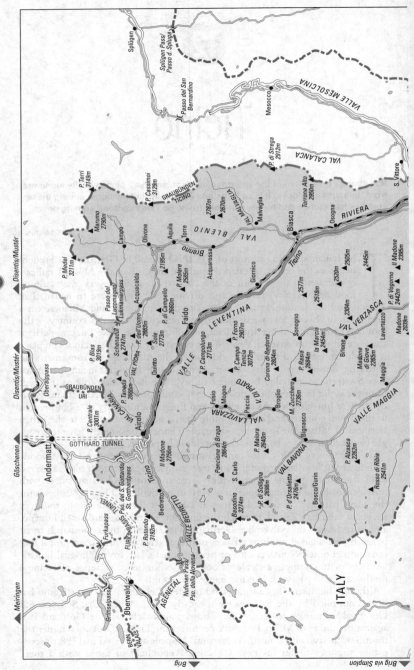

Splügen

Splügen Pass/
Passo d. Spluga

Passo del San
Bernardino

Mesocco

VALLE MESOLCINA

S. Vittore

P. di Strega
2912m

VAL CALANCA

P. Terri
3149m

P. Cassimoi
3128m

GRAUBÜNDEN
TICINO

Marumo
2790m

Campo

2787m

2670m

Torrone Alto
2950m

Olivone

VAL MALVAGLIA

Malvaglia

Biasca

Osogna

RIVIERA

Disentis/Mustér

P. Medel
3211m

Aquila

Torre

2195m

P. Molare
2585m

Brenno

VAL BLENIO

Acquarossa

Ticino

Giornico

2505m

2445m

Il Madone
2395m

Passo del
Lucomagno/
Lukmanierpass

P. di Campello
2660m

2520m

P. di Vogorno
2442m

Schenadü

P. dell'Uomo
2663m

Acquacalda

Faido

2577m

2518m

2304m

Madone
2039m

Disentis/Mustér

P. Blas
3019m

VAL PIORA

Sole
2773m

VALLE LEVENTINA

P. Campolungo
2713m

P. Parno
2907m

P. Campo
Tencia
3072m

VAL VERZASCA

Lavertezzo

Oberalppass

P. Paneda
2666m

Quinto

P. Rasla
2664m

Brione

Madone
di Giove
2265m

GRAUBÜNDEN
URI

P. Centrale
3001m

VAL CANARIA

Airolo

Fusio

Mogno

Peccia

Corona di Redorta
2804m

la Marcia
2454m

Sonogno

Maggia

Disentis/Mustér

Göschenen

Andermatt

GOTTHARD TUNNEL

Piùsio

VAL DI PRATO

Broglio

M. Zucchero
2736m

VAL LAVIZZARA

Bignasco

VALLE MAGGIA

Meiringen

Pso. del S. Gottardo/
St. Gotthardpass

Il Madone
2756m

Poncione di Braga
2864m

P. Malora
2640m

VAL BAVONA

P. Alcasca
2262m

SUSI
TUNNEL

FURKA PASS/
FURKAPASS

P. Rotondo
3192m

Bedretto

Ticino

VALLE BEDRETTO

S. Carlo

Basodino
3274m

P. di Solögna
2698m

P. d'Orsalietta
2476m

Bosco/Gurin

Rosso di Ribia
2541m

Furkapass

Oberwald

BERN
VALAIS

AGENETAL

Nufenen Pass/
Pso. della Novena

ITALY

Grimselpass

Brig

Brig

Brig via Simplon

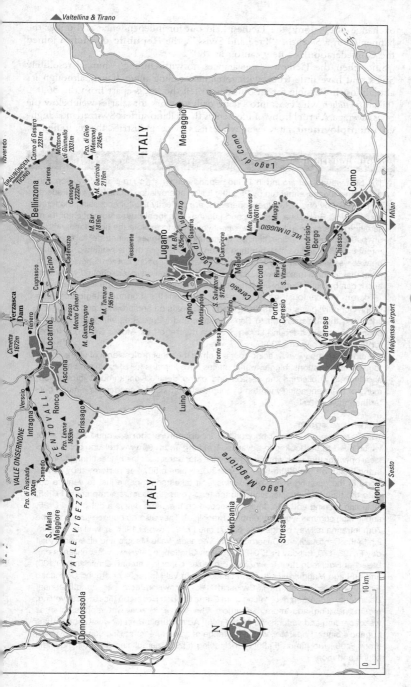

10 km

0

N

exchange of overlords, the Ticinesi held out for independence, and under the banner *Liberi e Svizzeri!* ("Free and Swiss!"), the **Republic of Ticino** joined the Confederation as a new canton in 1803.

Since then, the Ticinesi – appearances notwithstanding – remain resolutely Swiss, and have little truck with foreigners calling them Italian, although it's also almost impossible for an outsider to tell the locals apart from the 36,000 Italian *frontalieri* who cross into Ticino daily to work for salaries well below the Swiss average. A cruel irony of life here is that Ticino suffers Switzerland's highest **unemployment** rates even while its service industries thrive, staffed by

Exploring Ticino

The best way to get around in Ticino depends on what you're planning to see and do. **Train** services, either run by **FFS** (the Italian abbreviation for SBB, Swiss Federal Railways) or by one or two local operators, are perfectly fine for accessing the three major towns, Bellinzona, Locarno and Lugano, with **local buses** from each of them serving points close at hand. However, if you want to explore the hinterland, relying on public transport alone can be frustrating: **postbuses** penetrate to even the remotest valley and hamlet, but tend to run on schedules that leave a two-hour gap between services. **Renting a car** would be a better option, but you should bear in mind that all three major towns, and the roads between them, are choked with **cars**, and it can be quite literally impossible to find a parking space in the town centres.

There's no cantonal transport pass, although the **Lugano Regional Pass** (April–Oct only) gives free travel on trains and boats on and around Lago di Lugano (including the funiculars up to San Salvatore and Monte Brè), with half-price discounts on transport around Locarno, and a quarter off the Monte Generoso trains, for three/seven days (Fr.72/96).

Ticino Turismo (ⓦwww.ticino-tourism.ch) is the most professional of all the Swiss tourism organizations; bigger tourist offices have libraries full of excellent brochures and leaflets publicizing the canton and giving detailed background information, many of them engagingly written by journalists, critics and academics – much better than their website.

Adventure sports

There are some excellent opportunities for **adventure sports** around Ticino, all of which need to be booked in advance. **Trekking Team** (ⓦwww.trekking.ch) is a top local operator that runs what is perhaps the star attraction: the highest bungee-jump in the world, off the 220m-high Verzasca Dam (see p.567), as performed by James Bond in the opening scene of *Goldeneye*. It takes some nerve just to venture out onto the dam to watch, let alone do the leap yourself. Your first jump costs Fr.255, including training and free drinks; a second on the same day is a cut-price Fr.125, and in high summer, you can jump by moonlight. They also do bungee-jumps off the 70m Intragna railway bridge (see p.567; one Fr.125, two Fr.195), as well as canyoning in the Centovalli, Val Onsernone, Val Verzasca, Valle Maggia and elsewhere (half day Fr.125–170, full day Fr.170–200). **Swiss Challenge** (ⓦwww.swisschallenge.ch), based at Roveredo near Bellinzona, organizes canoeing around Cresciano (Fr.130) and on Lago Maggiore (Fr.80), and canyoning in Val Malvaglia or around Cugnasco (Fr.100–150 for a half day). **Swissraft** (ⓦwww.swissraft.ch) has an office near Bellinzona, organizing river rafting from Cama through Roveredo (Fr.105), canyoning, mountain-biking and more. Locarno's **The Wave** (ⓦwww.watersports.ch) runs wakeboarding and waterskiing (both Fr.45). **Adventure's Best** (ⓦwww.asbest.ch) is Lugano's biggest operator, with a full range of adventure sports including canyoning (from Fr.90), rap jumps (Fr.90), freeclimbing (Fr.90), paragliding (Fr.150), mountain biking and more.

⑫

TICINO

Italians and paid for by thousands of Swiss-German tourists and second-home-owners. Similarly, young people, who would naturally gravitate towards universities or jobs in nearby Milan, have been forced by their lack of an EU passport to go north into culturally and linguistically "foreign" Switzerland instead. The reality behind Ticino's glamorous front is a tale of fifty years or more of social dislocation and a draining, deep-rooted frustration with chiefly Swiss-German-inspired isolationism.

Ticino is divided topographically in two by the modest **Monte Ceneri** range (1961m), two-thirds of the way down: the area to the north is the **Sopraceneri** ("Above Ceneri"), that to the south is **Sottoceneri** ("Below Ceneri"). The main attractions are the lakeside resorts of **Locarno** and **Lugano**, where mountain scenery merges with the subtropical flora encouraged by the warm climate, although the cantonal capital **Bellinzona** and the quiet valleys of **Alto Ticino** also hold a great deal of charm. Ticino is known, too, for its plethora of ancient churches in hamlets and villages across the canton, many of them Romanesque and containing medieval frescoes, and most also featuring huge external murals of St Christopher, patron saint of travellers. **Architecture and design** have been taken seriously for centuries past, with a string of world-class architects emanating from the Ticino from the Middle Ages onwards; for more, see p.597. Much time and money is devoted to architecture, with cities, towns and villages throughout the canton full of sympathetic, subtle restoration of ancient buildings – kitschy Alpine chalets are confined to *Oltre Gottardo*, the locals' somewhat disparaging term for the rest of Switzerland "beyond the Gotthard".

Sopraceneri

The **SOPRACENERI** region takes in the whole of the northern two-thirds of the canton. Road and rail lines stream down from the Alpine tunnels, bypassing the Ticinese hinterland and funnelling into the cantonal capital **Bellinzona**, a quietly elegant place often passed over in favour of the lakeside resorts – the latter exemplified by shades-and-*gelati* **Locarno**, revelling in its location at the tip of the idyllic **Lago Maggiore**. The real beauty, however, of this rugged region lies in the very hinterland that most people see hurtling past at 110kph. Unspoilt **Alto Ticino**, comprising a network of wild, pre-Alpine valleys and mountain-top lakelets glittering in clear, crystalline sunshine, holds some of the best walking in the country.

Bellinzona

Everyone passes through **BELLINZONA**, but few people bother to stop. Their loss, since this graceful and beautiful old town is the perfect place to draw breath before hitting the lakeside glitz further south, and is a mellow introduction to the easy pace of the Ticino. A fortress since Roman times,

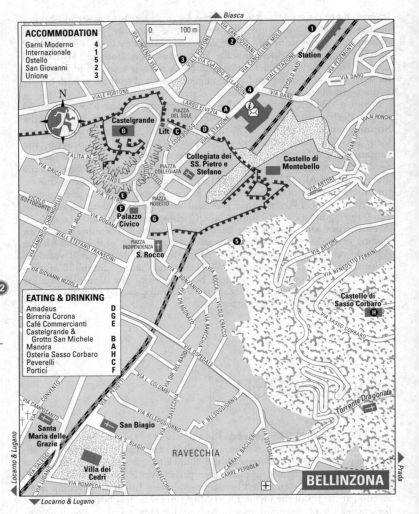

ACCOMMODATION
Garni Moderno	4
Internazionale	1
Ostello	5
San Giovanni	2
Unione	3

EATING & DRINKING
Amadeus	D
Birreria Corona	G
Café Commercianti	E
Castelgrande & Grotto San Michele	B
Manora	A
Osteria Sasso Corbaro	H
Peverelli	C
Portici	F

Bellinzona occupies a prime valley-floor position, holding the keys to the great Alpine passes of the Novena (Nufenen), Gottardo (Gotthard), Lucomagno (Lukmanier) and San Bernadino. In 1242 it was bought by the Visconti family, dukes of Milan, who built a new **castle** atop the hill plum in the middle of the valley, while their allies, the Rusconi family of Como, built another castle slightly up the hillside. In the late fourteenth century, the newly independent Swiss confederates north of the Gotthard Pass, who had successfully thrown off Habsburg rule, started to look to secure their position by conquering the territory on the south side of the pass. They began a violent campaign against the Milanese forces in the 1420s, which spurred the Sforza dynasty – then in the ascendant in Milan – to reinforce the two existing castles at Bellinzona and build a third, even higher up the hillside. A massive chain of fortifications cut right across the Ticino valley at Bellinzona... but to no avail, since the Swiss won the town under the Treaty of Arona in 1503. Three centuries of domination and oppression followed, with Swiss overlords posted to Bellinzona to keep control of the peasantry until Ticino won its independence in 1803.

Bellinzona has gained a reputation as the poor relation of Locarno and Lugano – undeserved, since it might lack a lake, but it also lacks the hectic pace, the crowds and the touristic sheen of its bigger neighbours. This gentle town is blessed with medieval architecture and picturesque churches, and also serves as the main access point for excursions into the wild Alto Ticino region. Its grand trio of castles – **Castelgrande**, **Montebello** and **Sasso Corbaro** – were together declared a UNESCO World Heritage Site in 2000.

It's worth making a trip here for the colourful, friendly weekly **market** of breads, local cheeses, wines, fruit and veg, and handicrafts, held in the alleys of the Old Town every Saturday (7.30am–12.30pm); local restaurants take the opportunity to offer polenta or risotto for Saturday lunch *al fresco*. Also don't miss the annual cheese market in early October, where all the Ticinese Alpine producers parade their wares.

Arrival, information and accommodation

Bellinzona's **train station** – with bike rental – is 500m northeast of the Old Town. The well-equipped **tourist office** is a short walk south, within the main post office at Viale Stazione 18 (Mon–Fri 9.30am–6.30pm, Sat 9.30am–12.30pm; ☏091 825 21 31, ⓦwww.bellinzona.ch). Their *Bellinzona & Alto Ticino Weekend* brochure comprises a series of interesting essays (in four languages) on architecture ancient and modern in the city, and some simple walking routes and driving itineraries in the higher valleys, and they also stock the scholarly *Castles of Bellinzona* booklet by Werner Meyer (in English). The official **guided walking tour** takes advantage of the bustling Saturday market to offer an unusual full-day itinerary, taking in all the castles and their museums as well as a walk around the Old Town (July–Oct Sat 10am–5pm; Fr.30 includes a quality *grotto* lunch, museum entry fees and bus rides in between walks); book before noon one day in advance. Note that the cobbled streets of Bellinzona's Old Town, from the post office south to Piazza Indipendenza, are banned to private vehicles from 7.30pm to 6am.

Bellinzona's **accommodation** wins no prizes for style or imagination. Of the **hotels**, *San Giovanni*, Via San Giovanni 7 (☏091 825 19 19, ⓦwww .hotelzimmer.ch; ❷), has a few well-kept rooms above a Ticinese restaurant. *Internazionale*, Piazza Stazione 35 (☏091 825 43 33, ⓦwww.hotel-internazionale.ch; ❷–❸), is the most pleasant of the station hotels, with comfortable, serviceable rooms; *Garni Moderno*, Viale Stazione 17b (☏ & ☏091 825 13 76; ❷), is a clean, modern alternative. *Unione*, Via Generale Guisan 1 (☏091 825 55 77, ⓦwww.albergo-unione.ch; ❹; closed Jan), is Bellinzona's best, with efficient service and renovated rooms. The **campsite** *Bosco di Molinazzo* (℡091 829 11 18, ℻091 829 23 55; April–Sept) is by the river in Molinazzo, a northern suburb. The HI **hostel** *Ostello/Jugendherberge* is in the grand old Villa Montebello, at Via Nocca 4 (℡091 825 15 22, Ⓦwww.youthhostel.ch; ❶; dorms Fr.30).

The Town

High on Bellinzona's central rock rise the massive towers and walls of **Castelgrande** (daily 9am–midnight; free), most impressive of the town's three medieval castles. Known to have been occupied as far back as the Neolithic age, the hill was fortified first by the Romans, and then again in the thirteenth century by Milanese forces to protect the valley routes to and from the great Alpine passes. For three centuries between the Swiss conquest and Ticinese independence, Castelgrande was known as the Castello di Uri after its trans-Alpine occupiers (Montebello was the Castello di Svitto (Schwyz), while Sasso Corbaro was the Castello di Untervaldo). Just to confuse things further, the rock on which the castle sits is known as **Monte San Michele**.

The whole hilltop complex has been imaginatively and sympathetically restored by architect Aurelio Galfetti (see p.597) – he added a free-to-use public **lift**, one of the highlights of Bellinzona's modern architecture, that is dramatically recessed deep into the bedrock of the hill behind the central Piazza del Sole and emerges at a purpose-built modern fortification on an upper terrace of the castle. The castle grounds are serene, overlooked by the slender thirteenth-century **White Tower**, with two upper windows on all four faces, and the fourteenth-century **Black Tower**, with three windows on its longer side. Despite their names, both, like the castle itself, are grey granite, and between them run lines of distinctive Lombard-style **winged battlements**, which you'll see on castles all over Ticino.

Off Castelgrande's central lawns is an entrance to the **Museo Storico** (daily 10am–6pm; Fr.4; joint ticket for museums in all three castles Fr.8; SMP). The archeology section offers a tour through Bellinzona's ancient past, including an excellent audiovisual show (in English) presenting the history of the town. The pride and joy, in the artistic section, is a set of murals made in 1470 to decorate the wooden ceiling of a villa in the town, depicting a complex set of allegorical themes dealing with love, faith and virtue.

Atmospheric steps wind down from Castelgrande to the elegant Renaissance buildings of **Piazza Collegiata** in the centre of the Old Town, dominated by the lavish Collegiata church, built by the same architect who worked on Como's cathedral and decorated with Baroque frescoes and stucco. Narrow, shaded lanes branch out all around: arcaded **Piazza Nosetto** is just south, with the Cà Rossa house on the way featuring a striking red terracotta facade – a style fashionable in early nineteenth-century Milan. From Nosetto, a gateway leads into the courtyard of the **Palazzo Civico**, a magnificent Renaissance building rebuilt in the 1920s but still retaining its loggias which wind attractively around both upper floors.

Note that Lugano's guest card, given free to hotel guests in the city, currently discounts entry to all three of Bellinzona's castles (from Fr.8 to Fr.4): if you intend to overnight at Lugano, you could save money by heading there first to check in, returning later to Bellinzona with your guest card to explore the castles. Alternatively, choosing to stay overnight in Bellinzona rather than Lugano could save you plenty more than a mere four francs.

There are plenty of picturesque **walks** near Bellinzona which could fill a pleasant afternoon. One of the best begins in nearby **Roveredo** (in Graubünden's Val Mesolcina and served by postbuses from Bellinzona), from where an old cart track on the "quiet" side of the river heads through tiny San Giulio and into the woods opposite San Vittore, before crossing the river at a little bridge in Lumino and heading on through the forest to Arbedo on the outskirts of Bellinzona. You'll come across plenty of peaceful shady *grotti* on the way. Side roads off the main Via San Gottardo lead through Arbedo and under the tracks to the picturesque Chiesa Rossa, an ancient red-washed church sitting lost and forgotten beside industrial warehouses on Via del Carmagnola backing onto the tracks (total 2hr walking). Buses can run you the final 1.5km south into Bellinzona centre.

The walk to **Prada** begins in the car park of the hospital in Ravecchia, a southern suburb (city bus #5) – cobbled alleys lead you alongside vineyards to a mule track which climbs gently beneath the looming Castello di Sasso Corbaro to the tiny, isolated church of San Girolamo di Prada, set amidst the ruins of Prada village (45min). Tougher paths lead on from Prada through forests into the secluded Val Morobbia, an old smugglers' route; two or three postbuses a day from Bellinzona to the last village in the valley, **Carena**, bring you to the trailhead of a tough, but deserted, five-hour hike up to the Passo di San Jorio (2014m), marking the Italian frontier, and back.

Behind the Collegiata, on the eastern side of the piazza, a path rises to the picturesque **Castello di Montebello** (March–Nov Tues–Sun 10am–6pm; free), some 90m higher in elevation than Castelgrande, with suitably impressive views of the town. From a vantage point on the lofty ramparts, it's easy to trace the line of defensive fortifications which link the two castles across the width of the Ticino valley. The castle itself is impressive, with a fifteenth-century courtyard and residential palace surrounding an older central portion dating from the thirteenth century, the latter now housing a modern **museum** of Gothic and Renaissance architecture (same hours; Fr.4; joint ticket for museums in all three castles Fr.8). A stiff 45-minute climb further up will bring you to **Castello di Sasso Corbaro** (April–Nov Tues–Sun 10am–6pm; free), some 230m above Bellinzona, designed and built in six months in 1479 by a military engineer brought in from Florence after the Swiss defeat of Milanese troops at the Battle of Giornico. It shelters a particularly welcome vine-shaded courtyard *osteria* and has a spectacular rampart panorama; its **museum** (same hours and prices) includes a gallery showing changing exhibits by contemporary Ticinese artists.

To save your legs, catch bus #4 from the centre to Artore, near Castello di Sasso Corbaro, and then wend your own path back down the hillside.

South of Piazza Indipendenza

Peaceful **Piazza Indipendenza** is 100m south of the tourist office and sports a 1903 obelisk commemorating the first century of Ticinese independence. On the east side of the square is the small, atmospheric church of **San Rocco**, built in 1330 and renovated in 1478. Following Via Lugano south from Indipendenza for 600m brings you to Piazza San Biagio, and the gates of the **Villa dei Cedri** art gallery (Tues–Sat 10am–noon & 2–6pm, Sun 10am–6pm; Fr.6; SMP; ⓦwww.villacedri.ch). It's worth having a wander in the lush and beautiful grounds before heading in to the museum, which focuses on nineteenth- and twentieth-century Swiss and Lombard art. The frescoed church of

San Biagio beside the villa dates from the twelfth century, and has a huge mural of St Christopher beside the door. Beside a disused convent 100m west across the tracks is the beautiful church of **Santa Maria delle Grazie**, which was severely damaged by fire after a nativity scene caught alight on New Year's Eve 1997; although some frescoes were entirely lost and the altars have now been removed for safekeeping, attempts are being made to restore its enormous late-fifteenth-century interior fresco of the crucifixion.

Eating and drinking

Like administrative capitals everywhere, Bellinzona suffers from a stunted entertainment scene. Top **restaurant** choices are within Castelgrande (both closed Mon): you can eat well for Fr.20 at the *Grotto San Michele*, which spreads itself over the panoramic terrace and also has an interior room; while the formal *Castelgrande* restaurant (☎091 826 23 53, ⊛www.castelgrande.ch), full of black leather and tubular steel furniture, is a much snootier affair – you'll get little change from Fr.60 for its modern, Ticino-inspired cuisine. The atmospheric *Osteria Sasso Corbaro*, in Bellinzona's topmost castle (☎091 825 55 32; closed Mon & Nov–March), serves up authentic Ticinese fare – accompanied by plenty of wine – at stone tables in the shady castle courtyard, or in a great hall within; *menus* are Fr.25 or so. *Portici*, a pleasant *osteria*/pizzeria in the Old Town on Vicolo Muggiasca (closed Sun lunch & Mon), serves palatable food in its shady courtyard to a young, easy crowd of regulars for Fr.20 or less. Cheap self-service nosh is at *Manora* on Viale Stazione.

Birreria Corona, Via Camminata 5 (closed Sun), is an atmospheric café-bar fronting quite a good restaurant in the back, with *menus* also around Fr.20. Pavement café-bars abound, including *Café Commercianti*, Via Teatro 5, a popular place that doubles as a *gelateria*, and especially around Via Codeborgo, where you'll see (or hear) the jumping *Amadeus Pub* on Vicolo Torre (closed Sun) and the equally lively *Peverelli* at Codeborgo 12 (closed Mon).

Alto Ticino

By far the most pristine part of this sometimes tiresomely touristic canton, the region of **ALTO TICINO** (Upper Ticino) north of Bellinzona is a haven of wild, lonesome valleys cutting deep into the landscape on the approach to the high Alps, dotted with rustic stone-built hamlets teetering on steep slopes. As throughout the rest of the canton – though less obtrusively here – many of the original Ticinese communities, which laboured so long to scrape a living from the land, are now financially enriched, if culturally challenged, by the presence of many German and Swiss-German second-homeowners seeking refuge from the pressures of city life. The villages and the scenery nonetheless survive unscathed, and if getting off the beaten path is your aim, you're likely to find greater satisfaction in Alto Ticino than in most other parts of the country, let alone the canton. **Biasca** is the gateway to the region, a small town at the junction of the scenic **Val Blenio** – which heads north from Biasca up to **Olivone**, then cuts over to the Lucomagno Pass – and the main **Valle Leventina**, which bends northwest up to the foot of the Gottardo Pass and the quiet town of Airolo, where the rural Val Bedretto splits off west to the Novena Pass.

You'd do well to check your planned itinerary with the tourist office in Bellinzona before you set off: although information and maps are much the same wherever you go, staff in the regional tourist offices in Biasca, Olivone

△ The battlements of Castelgrande, Bellinzona (see p.552)

and Airolo are less likely to be fluent in English. The brochures *Alto Ticino Weekend* and *Itinerari in Alto Ticino* – the latter more informative but dating from 1993 – give acres of cultural and hiking background to the area, or you could opt for a **guided tour**, run every day (July–Oct only) on a fixed weekly schedule by the Bellinzona tourist office: for example, every Monday there's a nature tour up into the Val Blenio; on Tuesdays, a tour of Romanesque churches in Biasca, Giornico and Negrentino; and on Fridays, a stiff climb from Biasca (304m) to the hut on Alpe di Cava (2256m) and back. Most start from Biasca station; the cost (Fr.30–40) generally includes bus transport and lunch. You must book with the Bellinzona or Biasca tourist office before noon one day in advance.

Biasca

The small town of **BIASCA** sits in a grand location at the junction of three valleys: the Valle Leventina, the Val Blenio and to the south towards Bellinzona a part of the River Ticino called the **Riviera**, which crams in side by side a motorway, a main road, a minor road, a train line and several footpaths, all snaking between wooded mountainsides rising 1500m above your head. High above the town to the southeast, commanding an eagle's-eye view of all routes in and out, is the imposing thirteenth-century church of **San Pietro e Paolo**, with a sixteenth-century portico tacked on to its simple, Romanesque facade. Collect the key from the newer parish church halfway up the hillside. Inside, the irregular Romanesque floor plan – architects seem to have struggled with

A walking tour of Alto Ticino

A two-week walking **Tour of Ticino** explores the finest valleys and most remote landscapes in the upper part of the canton. The granite massifs of the Lepontine Alps, as these mountains are known, are among the least visited of any in Switzerland: you can wander for hours on end, even in the height of summer, and see no one, even while the lower valleys and the lakes of Maggiore and Lugano are thronged with holiday-makers. The scenery is charming: clear streams tumble through the valleys, numerous tarns flecked among the high plateaux add a sparkle to the crags, and deep green pools in hidden corners invite walkers to pause for a well-deserved midsummer bathe. Accommodation is sometimes sparse in the small villages of the upper valleys, but there are plenty of mountain huts (*capanne*). As ever, it's easy to pick out **shorter walks** if you prefer something less taxing: from the Valle Santa Maria through Val Piora to Airolo, for instance, or from Bignasco to Fusio. **Maps** to pack are the LS 265, 266, 275 and 276 (all 1:50,000); *Walking in the Alps* and *Walking in Ticino*, both by Kev Reynolds (see "Books", p.607), are essential reading.

The tour begins either in **Torre** or **Dangio**, two adjacent villages in the upper Valle di Blenio 4km south of Olivone. The route heads through Val Soi on a path which climbs to **Capanna Adula** (☎091 872 15 32) at the southern end of Val Carassina. Day two takes the walker through Val Carassina to a small dammed lake, then descends to **Olivone** (see p.558) before following a mule track through a defile into Val Camadra. On the western hillside the path leads to **Capanna Boverina** (☎091 872 15 29). Next day you continue up to Passo di Gana Negra, cross Valle Santa Maria and make a steady ascent to Passo Colombe. An enjoyable descent from there takes the route into the gentle tarn-glistening Val Piora where overnight accommodation is found in **Capanna Cadagno** (☎091 868 13 23). Day five is a short one, but there's plenty of opportunity to divert to mountain lakes and big views. The route crosses Bochetta di Cadlimo to Pian Bornengo at the head of Val

the sloping bedrock – is unchanged, and the interior walls are covered in an array of medieval frescoes.

Biasca's **train station** is 750m south of the centre. The **tourist office** is just off Piazza Centrale on the tiny Piazzetta Cavalier Pellanda (Mon–Fri 8.30–11.30am & 2–6pm; May–Oct also Sat 8.30–11.30am; ℡091 862 33 27, Ⓦwww.biascaturismo.ch). Stairs up to the church rise directly behind the tourist office. Of the **hotels**, the *Posta* (℡091 862 21 21, Ⓦwww .albergodellaposta.ch; ❷), opposite the station, has adequate rooms above a goodish restaurant. The modern *Al Giardinetto*, Via Pini 21 (℡091 862 17 71, Ⓦwww.algiardinetto.ch; ❷), is better located in the centre, and has a ten-per-cent walkers' discount for stays over three days. Look out for the regular Saturday market, showcasing fresh produce from the upper valleys.

Val Blenio

Quiet **Val Blenio** cuts north from Biasca, off the main Leventina routes, a broad open valley that basks in generous sunshine and has limitless opportunities for walking exploration. The valley floor is dotted with villages, themselves marked by *rustici*, stone-built peasant dwellings, sometimes little more than shacks, that are topped with rough slate roofs. A lot of these are now holiday cottages, renovated and rented out for tidy sums to nature-starved northerners, but the valley has nonetheless made sure to protect its most valuable assets – peace, quiet and unspoilt natural beauty. Oddly enough, the Bleniesi have been known throughout Europe for centuries as foodie entrepreneurs, a skill

Canaria, then descends this glen to **Airolo** at the foot of the Gotthard Pass. On the south side of Valle Leventina the way resumes on a belvedere trail known as the Strada degli Alpi Bedretto, but on reaching the alp hutments of Piano di Pesciüm it cuts into Val Torta and climbs to **Capanna Cristallina** (℡091 869 23 30). The following stage makes a crossing of the Cristallina massif to **Capanna Basòdino** (℡091 753 27 97) by one of two routes, both of which notch up several tarns, crossing rocky passes amid wild country.

On day eight, an easy downhill walk leaves the big mountains and descends through the woods and pastures of Val Bavona to **Bignasco** (see p.566) at the head of the Valle Maggia. It's a glorious walk leading past tiny hamlets and feathery waterfalls to a confluence of valleys. Leaving Bignasco on day ten, the suggested route goes through Val Cocco and over Passo del Cocco at its head, before dropping to the remote and simple **Capanna Alpe d'Osola**. Although open from April to November, this hut is unstaffed, so you'll need to carry food (cooking facilities are provided). The way now negotiates Bochetta di Mugaia in the south ridge of Monte Zucchero, before descending 1600m to **Sonogno**. Day eleven crosses Passo di Redorta (2181m) to Val di Pertüs, whose stark walls plunge into the depths of a gorge. Val di Pertüs feeds into Val di Prato, and this in turn spills into Val Lavizzara where you spend the night in **Prato-Sornico**. The tour heads north to **Fusio**, a short journey on linking trails that avoids most of the road between the two villages. On such a short stage it would be worth diverting up to Lago di Mognola high on the eastern hillside, at the northern end of which an airy path makes a traverse before plunging steeply to the valley near Fusio. The final (thirteenth) day's walk leads back to Valle Leventina via Passo Campolungo. The pass is more than 1000m above Fusio, while the descent to **Rodi-Fiesso**, 10km south of Airolo, is a steep 1300m, but the path is mostly good and there are consistently fine views on both sides to make this a fitting conclusion to the route.

probably picked up in Milan sometime in the Middle Ages and passed on through the generations. In 1600 one Signor Bianchini from the valley was no less than head chef to the King of Spain; in 1849, a Signor Baggi won an award for selling the best ice cream in France; while the Gatti family – also from the Blenio – owned and managed 230 restaurants and cafés throughout late-Victorian England. Locals will have you believe that fully three-quarters of all chestnut sellers in Switzerland today are from the Val Blenio.

The Sentiero Basso is the main valley-floor path: the walk from Biasca to **Acquarossa** on the west bank of the river is a gently rising 13km, taking a little under four hours. On the east bank just north of Biasca is **Malvaglia**, whose village church boasts a gigantic fresco of St Christopher; from here a tortuous branch road climbs in a series of hairpins into the lonesome gorge of the **Val Malvaglia** amidst tremendous scenery of steep wooded slopes dropping away into a seemingly bottomless ravine. From a point on the road, it's possible to park and walk across a bridge spanning the valley, on the other side of which a dramatic mule track penetrates for a couple of hours' walk to **Dagro**, a hamlet on the northern side of the valley with broad views.

As you rise into the Blenio, the lush green slopes begin to close in. The main town at the head of the valley, below the sharp-peaked Sosto on one side and the Töira on the other, is **OLIVONE**, a tranquil little place some 24km north of Biasca that reflects the valley's once-noble pretensions in its array of grandiose, if worn, eighteenth- and nineteenth-century mansions and villas – rather out of place amidst the orchards and increasingly wild high-valley scenery. Up in the village is the *Osteria Centrale* (℡091 872 11 07; ❶), meeting place for the locals, which serves tasty home-cooked fare and has a few simple rooms. Down a short hill beside the main road is the post office and bus stop with, alongside, the *Albergo San Martino* (℡091 872 15 21, ℻091 872 26 62; ❷), also with excellent traditional food and pizzas plus a choice of ensuite or shared-bath rooms – as has the *Albergo Posta* (℡091 872 13 66, ℻091 872 16 87; ❷). The **tourist office** (℡091 872 14 87, ⓦwww.blenio.com) has information on the whole valley. A five-hour walk from Olivone climbs to the **Lucomagno Pass** (1914m); the road over the pass to Disentis/Mustér in Graubünden (see p.517) is perhaps the most scenic route in and out of Ticino.

Valle Leventina

From Biasca, the motorway, the main road and the train all blaze a trail northwest into the **Valle Leventina**, heading for the Gottardo pass and tunnels (see p.414) at the end. There's no doubt that this is a spectacular route, whether heading north or south, but its heavy usage is its downfall – hemmed in by the high valley walls, the hiss and rumble of traffic noise from the motorway can seem obtrusively loud to valley-floor walkers and cyclists. Unless you're planning high-altitude hikes in the tranquil mountains flanking the valley (see box p.556), it's best to use the bus or train to scoot along the valley floor – at least until 2012, when the new Gotthard Base Tunnel (see p.415) is due to open. Its main terminus will be just north of Biasca at Bodio, and so a large proportion of road traffic may in time be filtered away from the upper Leventina.

Make time for **GIORNICO**, a small town 9km northwest of Biasca. It was here in 1478 that a Swiss force numbering 600 defeated a 10,000-strong Milanese army, thereby linking Ticino's subsequent history to Switzerland rather than Italy. Giornico is lovely, a typical Ticinese village built on the gentle slopes either side of the tumbling River Ticino, with cobbled alleys running picturesquely between old stone-roofed houses, and a photogenic hump-backed bridge crossing to a wooded island mid-river, and from there to the west bank, where rises the campanile of **San Nicolao**, one of the most impressive and atmospheric of Ticino's many Romanesque churches. Its external walls are decorated with Lombardic designs, while inside is a fresco-decorated choir placed above a beautiful triple-apsed half-sunken crypt. Down an alley below the church is the Casa Stanga, an old house converted into the small **Museo di Leventina** (April–Oct Tues–Sun 2–5pm; Fr.2). More interesting is the concrete hangar in the fields 300m north of Giornico's little train station. This blank structure is an art gallery, **La Congiunta**, dedicated to the sculpture of Zürich artist Hans Josephsohn – though you'd never know from the outside. Pick up the keys at the *Osteria Giornico* on the main road (closed Wed). Inside are three rooms of lumpy metal reliefs and a few sculptures in bronze dating from 1950 to 1991: Peter Märkli's deserted, deconstructed setting suits Josephsohn's brutalist art perfectly.

Giornico has a couple of terrific *grotti*, both of them full of atmosphere and serving up the kind of simple, lovingly prepared food you wouldn't expect to be able to buy. The *Grotto dei Due Ponti* is the one everyone goes to, perfectly located on the mid-river island, its shaded terrace overlooking the rushing water. *Grotto Pergola*, tucked away on the west bank of the river and south of San Nicolao, serves even better food, although their garden is less alluring.

Some 28km north of Giornico is **AIROLO**, first town in the Ticino for the millions who pour out of the Gottardo train and road tunnels each year heading south. Thankfully bypassed by the main routes, it's a quiet town with a handful of hotels serving as staging post for summer journeys up to the Gotthard Pass (see p.414), or into the Val Bedretto and from there to the Novena (Nufenen Pass; see p.369). The town is also the trailhead for plenty of high-altitude walks, especially into the stunning **Val Piora**, outlined in the box on p.556. Winter sees Airolo transformed into a small-scale ski resort. The Leventina's **tourist office** is also here (⊕091 869 15 33, ⓦwww .leventinaturismo.ch).

Locarno

Mainline trains and fast cars speed south from Bellinzona to Lugano and Milan, while a branch line and often packed minor roads head west for some 15km to **Lago Maggiore** and its principal Swiss resort, **LOCARNO**. This characterful old town enjoys the most glorious of locations, on a broad sweeping curve of a bay in the lake, and also clocks up the most sunshine hours of anywhere in Switzerland. The arcades and piazzas of the town centre are overlooked by subtropical gardens of palms, camellias, bougainvillea, cypress, oleanders and magnolias, which flourish on the lakeside promenades and cover the wooded slopes which crowd in above the town centre.

Locarno slumbered under Swiss occupation after 1503, but with independence in the nineteenth century it found its feet as the most elegant of the country's lakeside resorts. In 1925 its backdrop of Belle-Epoque hotels and piazza cafés served as the setting for the **Treaty of Locarno**, signed by the European powers in a failed effort to secure peace following World War I. The seeds planted at Locarno exploded into war again in 1939, but the town went from strength to strength during the 1950s and after, growing in chic-ness year on year. These days, Locarno focuses all its considerable resources on tourism, and draws in two very different sets of customers: one, from the German-speaking north, arrive to test out their hiking boots, while the other, from fog- and smog-bound Milan, come to test out their sunglasses. The cobbled alleys of Locarno's Old Town, lined with Renaissance facades, can get entirely overrun with the rich and wannabe-famous on summer weekends, yet still – in the midst of the hubbub – the place manages to retain its sun-drenched cool.

Arrival, information and accommodation

Locarno's **train station** – with bike rental – is 100m north of the lakeshore landing-stage and 150m northeast of Piazza Grande; mainline FFS trains depart from ground level, while the local transport company Ferrovie Autolinee Regionali Ticinesi – unfortunately abbreviated to FART – operate trains on the Centovalli line (see p.567) from a separate station below ground. The municipality of Locarno itself is quite small, and the city also includes the contiguous districts of **Muralto**, in which the station is located, **Minusio** further east, and **Orselina** on the slopes above, all of which pop up in listings as if they were separate towns.

The efficient but often crowded **tourist office** is in the Casino complex on Via Largo Zorzi, 100m southwest of the station (April–Oct Mon–Fri 9am–6pm, Sat 9am–5pm, Sun 10am–noon & 1–3pm; Nov–March Mon–Fri 9am–12.30pm & 2–6pm; ☎091 791 00 91, Ⓦ www.maggiore.ch); they can make hotel bookings for you. Their **guided walking tour** starts from the office and takes in a tour of the churches of the Old Town and the Castello Visconteo (April–Oct Mon 9.45am; Fr.5). Swarming as it is with tourists, Locarno is also crammed with **accommodation** of all kinds. **Parking** is a major problem in the city centre; there's a paying car park by the station, but even large hotels like the *Muralto* simply don't offer any spaces for guests.

Hotels

Camelia Via Nessi 9, Muralto ☎091 743 00 21, Ⓦ www.camelia.ch. Elegant, eager-to-please family hotel set in fragrant floral gardens and offering spacious rooms, some with balcony and lake view. March–Oct. ❸

Città Vecchia Via Torretta 13 ☎091 751 45 54, Ⓦ www.cittavecchia.ch. Centrally placed "garni" hotel, with dorms (see opposite) and simple,

shared-bath rooms. March–Oct. ❶

Muralto Piazza Stazione 8 ☎091 735 77 77, Ⓦ www.hotelmuralto.com. Huge place directly opposite the station offering solid business-class quality on all but the uppermost floors, where light, vastly spacious rooms have picture-perfect lake views from on high and all creature comforts. ❹–❼

Navegna Via alla Riva 2, Minusio ☎091 743 22 22, Ⓦ www.navegna.ch. About 1.5km east of the

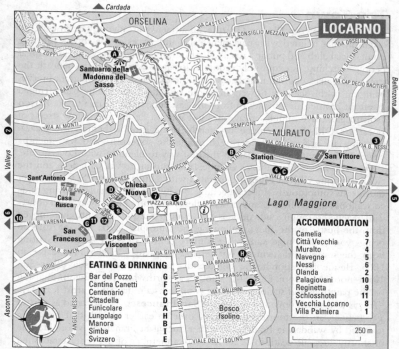

ORSELINA

LOCARNO

ACCOMMODATION
Camelia	3
Città Vecchia	7
Muralto	4
Navegna	5
Nessi	6
Olanda	2
Palagiovani	10
Reginetta	9
Schlosshotel	11
Vecchia Locarno	8
Villa Palmiera	1

EATING & DRINKING
Bar del Pozzo	G
Cantina Canetti	F
Centenario	C
Cittadella	D
Funicolare	A
Lungolago	H
Manora	B
Simba	I
Svizzero	E

Bosco Isolino

0 _____ 250 m

Ascona, Isole di Brissago & Italy ▼

centre, directly on the waterfront, with modern, stylishly renovated rooms, private parking and an excellent restaurant. March–Nov. ❸

Nessi Via Varenna 79 ☎091 751 77 41, ⓦwww.garninessi.ch. Welcoming little family-run place a short bus ride west of the centre, with its own swimming pool and underground parking. Rooms are fresh and decent, with better, bigger ones on higher floors. ❸

Olanda Via ai Monti 139a ☎ & ⓕ091 751 47 27. Small family-style pension high up on the hill road to Madonna del Sasso, set amidst lush palms and camellias. Most rooms – simple but appealing – have balconies with romantic lake views. Discounts for stays over three days. Private parking. March–Nov. ❷

Reginetta Via Motta 8 ☎091 752 35 53, ⓦwww.reginetta.ch. A prime location in the heart of the Old Town's web of alleys, offering fresh, renovated rooms, some with balcony. March–Oct. ❷

Schlosshotel Via San Francesco 7a ☎091 751 23 61, ⓦwww.schlosshotellocarno.ch. Large, slightly old-fashioned rooms in a well-kept Old Town pile. March–Nov. ❸

Vecchia Locarno Via Motta 10 ☎ & ⓕ091 751 65 02. Scruffily characterful Old Town gem, with both shared-bath and ensuite rooms above a courtyard restaurant and wine bar. ❷

Villa Palmiera Via del Sole 1, Muralto ☎091 743 14 41, ⓦwww.swisshotels.ch. Stylish and comfortable villa-style hotel on a hill just above the centre, with private parking. March–Nov. ❸

Hostels

Città Vecchia (see "Hotels"). Good Old Town option, with dorms from Fr.27.

Ostello/Jugendherberge Palagiovani (HI hostel) Via Varenna 18 ☎091 756 15 00, ⓦwww.youthhostel.ch. Modern hostel with dorms from Fr.32 and bike rental, but it's in an awkward western location – take bus #31 or #36 (direction Centovalli) to Cinque Vie. ❶

Campsite

Delta ☎091 751 60 81, ⓦwww.campingdelta.com. Pricey site, a fifteen-minute walk south along the lakeshore. March–Oct.

The Town

The focus of town is **Piazza Grande**, an attractive arcaded square just off the lakefront that is lined with pavement cafés and serves as the town's meeting point, social club and public catwalk. Warm summer nights serve up some great people-watching, as exquisitely groomed locals parade to and fro beneath the street lights neck-high in nonchalance, all the cafés a-buzz and fragrant breezes bringing in the scent of flowers from the lakeside gardens. The palm-fringed lakefront promenade runs south from the east edge of the piazza to the **Bosco Isolino** park, five minutes away, but most interest lies in the narrow streets of Locarno's **Old Town**, ranged on gently rising ground behind the piazza: spending an afternoon wandering through the sixteenth- and seventeenth-century alleys with an ice cream is the best way to blend in with Locarno life.

From the west end of Piazza Grande, lanes run up to Via Cittadella and the richly Baroque **Chiesa Nuova**, decorated with a huge statue of St Christopher outside. Its sumptuously stuccoed ceiling is crawling with detail, featuring gilded scallops and scrollwork, and hosts of fleshy cherubs. The tiny arcaded court-yard, reached through a side door, is a charming, tranquil spot entirely removed from the bustle of the alleys. Following the atmospheric Via di Sant'Antonio brings you to the huge and rather sombre church of **Sant'Antonio**, dating from the seventeenth century but rebuilt following a fatal roof collapse in 1863. Beside the church, the eighteenth-century **Casa Rusca** (Tues–Sun 10am–noon & 2–5pm; Fr.5; SMP) houses a worthwhile art museum focusing on the paintings and sculptures of the twentieth-century Swiss artist Jean Arp.

Alleys lead south downhill to the tall **San Francesco**, consecrated as part of a monastery in the fourteenth century over an earlier church that had been founded by wandering Franciscans either during St Francis of Assisi's lifetime or shortly after his death in 1226. In 1480, a member of the order established a hermitage on the hillside above Locarno, which is now the Madonna del Sasso pilgrimage site (see opposite). Renovation of the church in the sixteenth century included frescoes, most of which are now fading badly. Further down sits the stout thirteenth-century **Castello Visconteo**, built by the dukes of

Boats on Lago Maggiore

Boats run by NLM (April–Oct only; ⓦwww.navlaghi.it) crisscross the Swiss shores of the exceptionally beautiful **Lago Maggiore**, as well as continuing way down the lake into Italy. Note that Maggiore is the only major lake in Switzerland to be **excluded** from the Swiss Pass and European train passes.

For fare purposes, the Swiss part of the lake is divided into two: a **day pass** for the area either north or south of Ascona is Fr.12, or for the whole Swiss basin is Fr.21. Otherwise a **Lago Maggiore Holiday Card** gives free transport on the whole of Lago Maggiore and half-price on Lago di Lugano; one/three/seven days cost Fr.33/56/74. Hydrofoils, which run on routes into Italy (for which you'll need your passport), command a small reservation fee. The Fr.55 ticket "Il Lago e la Montagna" (valid 10 days) covers boats on the Swiss sector, entry to the Isole di Brissago, the funicular to Madonna del Sasso and cable-car to Cardada.

The varied and scenic **Lago Maggiore Express** train and boat journey (see p.567; Fr.42), can also run in reverse: a 9.10am boat from Locarno (not Wed) meanders down two-thirds of the lake to the Italian resort of Stresa (3hr 30min), where you have a couple of hours for lunch before a 2.30pm train connects to Domodossola for the 3.25pm Centovalli train back to Locarno, arriving at 5.15pm. Various other **excursion** tickets take in visits to the Italian islands of Isole Madre and Isole Bella.

Milan and badly damaged by the attacking Swiss army in 1513. It now houses the town's **Museo Archeologico** (April–Oct Tues–Sun 10am–noon & 2–5pm; Fr.5; SMP), worth visiting if only for its collection of beautiful Roman glassware and ceramics, near-intact brightly coloured pieces all with distinctively designed high-arched handles.

On the other side of town in Muralto, 100m east of the station, is the austere and atmospheric twelfth-century Romanesque basilica of **San Vittore**, built over a church first mentioned in the tenth century and now surrounded by generic suburban housing redevelopments of the late-twentieth. Medieval fresco fragments inside and the Renaissance relief of St Victor on the bell tower are a diverting contrast to the uninspiring views over the train station.

Madonna del Sasso

Most striking of all Locarno's sights is the Franciscan **Santuario della Madonna del Sasso** church (daily 6.30am–7pm), an impressive ochre vision floating above the town on a wooded crag – *sasso* means rock – and consecrated in 1487 on the spot where, seven years earlier, the Virgin had appeared to Brother Bartholomeo da Ivrea from the San Francesco monastery in the town. The twenty-minute walk up through the lush ravine of the Torrente Ramogno and past a handful of decaying shrines is atmospheric enough in itself; or you could take the half-hourly **funicular** from just west of the main train station to Ticino's greatest photo-op, looking down through the palms to the sunlit arcaded main front of the church and glittering blue lake behind.

Within the complex is a small **museum** of icons (Easter–Oct Sun–Fri 2–5pm; Fr.2.50), but the church **sanctuary** is the focus of all the pilgrims' attention. On the way through the complex you'll pass several striking terracotta sculpture groups of biblical scenes. The low, Baroque interior of the church features a number of paintings, two of which stand out: Bramartino's emotionally charged *Fuga in Egitto* (Flight to Egypt, 1522) and local artist Antonio Ciseri's *Trasporto di Cristo al Sepolcro* (1870). The statue of the Virgin on the high altar was sculpted for the church's consecration by an unknown artist. By the doorway are dozens of votive offerings from pilgrims giving thanks for the intervention of Mary in their daily lives.

Cardada and Cimetta

When the sweltering, overcrowded lakeshore town of Locarno (210m) gets too much, it's easy to make an escape into the cool, wooded hills above. By the top station of the Madonna del Sasso funicular in Orselina (395m) is the lantern-like base station – designed by architect Mario Botta (see p.598) – of a gleaming new cable-car that rises on an ear-poppingly steep course to the plateau of **Cardada** (1350m; Ⓦ www.cardada.ch). A short stroll left from the top station, set amidst fragrant pine woods and fresh breezes, is the "Observation Platform", a gracefully designed catwalk suspended off a huge A-frame that extends out over the edge of the hill above the treetops; from the end, an eagle-eye view takes in Ascona, much of Lago Maggiore and the mountains. There is a couple of simple restaurants up here and some easy strolls in the pine forest – many of them wheelchair accessible.

Turn right from the top station, and it's ten minutes or so through the woods to a spectacular, silent chairlift that whisks you even higher, right through the trees up to the flower-strewn meadows of **Cimetta** (1672m), where there's a restaurant/guesthouse with a terrace view that you won't forget in a hurry. Some longer, tougher walks include one up to the nearby summit of Madone (2039m).

Walks around Locarno

The tourist office brochure Sentieri della Collina pinpoints the route of two pleasant walking paths on the hillside just above the town. The Sentiera Collina Bassa is 5.4km long, and takes you from the Madonna del Sasso funicular east through Orselina and onto the Via Panoramica through the suburb of **Brione** above Minusio, before gently coming down to the lakeshore in **Tenero** (1hr 40min), from where buses and trains return you to Locarno. The Sentiera Collina Alta runs for 6.3km from **Monte Brè**, the next hill west of Orselina (bus #32), on a scenic, winding path through the foothills to **Contra**, and down to Tenero (2hr).

A return **ticket** from Orselina to Cardada is Fr.27, to Cimetta Fr.33. If you're coming up from Locarno, ask for a discounted ticket at the base-station of the Madonna del Sasso funicular that includes the whole round trip (to Cardada Fr.30, to Cimetta Fr.35).

Eating and drinking

Piazza Grande is full of cafés and pizzerias buzzing from morning until after midnight, but **eating** and **drinking** is more atmospheric in the old town alleys. Fresh fish plucked from the lake is Locarno's speciality – look out for trout (*trota*), perch (*persico*), pike (*luccio*) and whitefish (*coregone*).

Bar del Pozzo Piazza Sant'Antonio. Friendly local café-bar on a quiet Old Town square, a little out of the tourist crush.

Cantina Canetti Off Piazza Grande. Plain local cooking (Fr.15) in a noisy diner, with the added bonus of live accordion on Friday and Saturday nights.

Centenario Lungolago 13, Muralto ☏091 743 82 22. Best restaurant in Locarno, serving internationally acclaimed *nouvelle cuisine* in an appealing blend of French and Italian styles. A lakeside terrace and three-figure bills come as standard. Closed Sun & Mon.

Cittadella Via Cittadella 18 ☏091 751 58 85. The popular trattoria section at ground level is excellent, serving pizzas, pasta and simple fish dishes for Fr.20 or less, while upstairs the formal restaurant concentrates on fish alone – and does it well (*menus* Fr.30–35). Closed Mon.

Funicolare Beside funicular top station in Orselina. Quiet, simple place that benefits from a spectacular secluded terrace garden overlooking Madonna del Sasso at which to savour their fish specialities. Closed Thurs & Nov–Jan.

Lungolago Via Bramantino 1. Classy pizzeria, *paninoteca* and pub where locals go to flee the invasion of white-knee'd northerners.

Manora Via della Stazione. Good self-service food in this busy spot across from the train station, open late and Sundays.

Navegna (see "Accommodation"). A little east of town in Minusio, but right on the lakefront and highly acclaimed for its delicately prepared and presented Ticinese cuisine (*menus* Fr.35). Closed Nov–March.

Simba Lungolago 3a. Lively DJ bar that's one of the more popular places in town.

Svizzero Piazza Grande. Best of the many pizzerias and diners on the square, with affordable fresh-made pasta, wood-fired pizza and plenty of Italian staples. Bustling from breakfast till the small hours.

Around Locarno

The valleys around Locarno are groaning with hiking possibilities, and offer some of the most beautiful scenery in the whole canton – which means that trails can get a little overcrowded in the summer season. **Val Verzasca** and **Valle Maggia** both lead north from Locarno, while the gorgeous **Centovalli** runs west on one of the most scenic and dramatic train rides in the country. The small resort of **Ascona** lies a little southwest of Locarno, with the beautiful **Isole di Brissago** just offshore.

Ascona and beyond

Just 3km southwest of Locarno, on the other, south-facing side of the Maggia delta, is the small village of **ASCONA**, a magnet for idealistic, sun-starved northerners for a century or more. The place was nothing more than a fishing hamlet until the end of the nineteenth century, when a slow but steady influx began of philosophers, theosophists, spiritualists, pacifists and artists, most of whom were responding to the growing belief that a return to nature was the best remedy for the moral disintegration of Western capitalist society. The Russian anarchist Mikhail Bakunin was the first, living in Locarno in the 1870s; at the turn of the century the artists Henri Oedenkoven and Uda Hofmann established an esoteric, vegetarian artists' colony on the hill of **Monte Verità** beside Ascona. An array of European fringe intellectuals followed, including the anarchist Kropotkin, and various practitioners of the new arts of psychology and psychoanalysis. In 1913, Rudolf von Laban set up his nudist School of Natural and Expressive Dance within the Monte Verità community, attracting Isadora Duncan among others, and during and after World War I artists and pacifists flocked to Ascona from all over Europe. The buildings atop the peaceful wooded hill are now used mostly for conferences, but a few have been preserved as a **museum** of the movement (Tues–Sun: July & Aug 3–7pm; April–June, Sept & Oct 2.30–6pm; Fr.6). It's a short walk up the hill from the bus stop (bus #33) to the **Casa Anatta**, with two floors of the original wooden house given over to papers and photos commemorating the artists' exploits. A walk past the main Bauhaus conference centre and into the woods brings you to the tiny **Casa Selma**, used as the community's retreat, and on further to the **Elisarion**, housing a circular painting by Elisar von Kupffer, an artist from a noble Baltic family who spent many years at Monte Verità, depicting the freedoms and spiritual liberations of communal life.

Ascona village itself is well worth a stroll, with a huge open lakefront piazza crammed with terrace cafés and restaurants, and attractive cobbled lanes leading back into the older quarter, full of artisans' galleries and diverting little craft shops. The **Museo Comunale d'Arte Moderna**, in a sixteenth-century *palazzo* at Via Borgo 34 (March–Dec Tues–Sat 10am–noon & 3–6pm, Sun 4–6pm; Fr.5), has a high-quality collection focused on Marianne von Werefkin, one of the many artists attracted to Ascona in its heyday and joint founder of Munich's expressionist *Blaue Reiter* movement; of the dozens of her works on display, one of the best is the terrifying Munch-like *Il Cenciaiolo* (The Rag-Man, 1920). Ascona's **tourist office**, near the waterfront in Casa Serodine (April–Oct Mon–Fri 9am–6pm, Sat 9am–5pm; Nov–March Mon–Fri 9am–noon & 1.30–5.30pm; ☎091 791 00 91, ⓦ www.ascona.ch), runs a gentle walking tour of the old village (April–Oct Tues 10am; Fr.5).

Isole di Brissago

One of the best excursions in the area is to the lovely botanic park on the **Isole di Brissago** (April–Oct daily 9am–6pm; Fr.7 in addition to boat ticket or pass; ⓦ www.isolebrissago.ch), twin islands situated opposite the resort of Brissago, 4km south of Ascona, and accessible by hourly boats from Locarno and Ascona, or by more regular shuttles from **Porto Ronco**, the nearest point on the mainland. These tiny dots of green in the shimmering lake overflow with luxuriant subtropical flora basking in the hot sun (this is also the lowest point in Switzerland, 193m above sea level). The main island, St Pancras – about ten minutes' stroll end to end – has an attractive 1929 villa at one end, now a conference centre and quality restaurant (☎091 791 43 62): a long lunch here, followed by a siesta under the palms, makes for a most un-Swiss-like afternoon. Note that the noticeboards identifying each plant species are in Italian, French and German only, not English. Only groups can stay overnight; everyone else must leave on the last boat (around 6pm). The small island, St Apollinaris, has no public access.

Valle Maggia

The **VALLE MAGGIA** comprises a complex valley system stretching north of Locarno into the high Alps. This is wild countryside, not easy to explore: about 30km into the main valley, roads split to follow three separate upper valleys, the Val Rovana, Val Bavona and Val Lavizzara, which are cut off from each other and which all eventually come to a stop against impassable rock. It is, however, superb territory for **walking**: the long-distance route outlined in the box on p.556 passes through, and there are some fine short walks in remote corners. The main draw for walkers is Robiei in Val Bavona; in cultural terms, you'd do better heading for Mogno in Val Lavizzara, home of a serene little chapel designed by the architect Mario Botta.

North from Pontebrolla, a village above Locarno at the junction of the Centovalli (see opposite), the valley is deep, rugged and very narrow. It opens out further along around Gordevio and the village of **Maggia**, home of the local tourist office (℡091 753 18 85, ⓦwww.vallemaggia.ch); across the river from Maggia at Aurigeno is the SB hostel *Baracca* (℡079 207 15 54, ⓦwww .backpacker.ch; ❶). At **Cevio** (416m), the largest town in the valley, a road branches off west into the **Val Rovana**, climbing in a series of tight switchbacks up to the village of **BOSCO/GURIN** (1503m). This is the highest settlement in Ticino, and also its only German-speaking community, founded in the Middle Ages by ex-mercenaries from the upper Valais; the locals still speak an odd combination of Oberwalliser and Locarnese dialects. With lift access up to 2400m, the remote village has become a centre for winter sports, and there are some good walks in summer, notably in and around Grossalp (ⓦwww.grossalp.ch) below the cable-car station.

Just 2km north of Cevio (30km north of Locarno) is the idyllic village of **BIGNASCO** (438m), where the valley divides. Of a handful of lovely restaurants here, the *Turisti* has excellent food and a shaded terrace, as well as some rooms (℡091 754 11 65; ❶). Northwest from Bignasco, a road climbs into the truly wild **Val Bavona**, a strip of valley floor 10km long that is hemmed in by sheer scarps on both sides. There are twelve rustic, crumbling hamlets in the valley, including **Foroglio**, with a restaurant huddled next to a splendid waterfall. A short climb above **San Carlo** (960m), the final hamlet, characterized by tall, narrow sixteenth-century stone houses, is a cable-car up to the eyrie of **ROBIEI** (1905m), overlooked by the spectacular Basodino glacier. The top station has a terrace restaurant and accommodation (℡091 756 50 20, ⓦwww.robiei.ch; ❶; dorms Fr.25); one of the most scenic walks heads west into the Val Fiorina (45min) on a difficult route that eventually reaches the Italian border at the Bocchetta di Vallemaggia pass (2635m; 2hr 30min).

From Bignasco, another road climbs northeast into the **Val Lavizzara**; after Peccia (849m) – renowned for its marble quarries and sculpture school – the switchbacks get tighter up to the hamlet of **MOGNO** (1180m), where, across the way on your right, you'll spot the tilted circular roof of the church of San Giovanni Battista through the trees. The church, reached by a short path climbing from a parking area, was designed by Mario Botta (see p.598) after an avalanche destroyed a pre-existing chapel on the same spot in 1986: Botta has said that when the locals came to him saying they didn't want to give the future generation a place poorer than the one they knew, he responded by offering to build a church that would last a thousand years. His achievement, in this remotest of places, is dazzling. It is a small building, set on a marble plaza, with a supremely elegant interior, bare and silent, encircled in striped marble, with the transparent roof bathing the altar in sunlight. Walking back out into the pine forest, amidst chirping birds and log cabins, is a revelation.

Val Verzasca

About 1.5km east of Locarno on Lago Maggiore is the suburb of **Tenero**, standing at the head of the **VAL VERZASCA**, the shortest of the major valleys around Locarno. The southern end of the valley, high above Tenero, is blocked by the gigantic **Verzasca Dam**, scene of one of the world's highest bungee-jumps (see box p.548). Even if you're not jumping, it's worth stopping here to wander out into the middle of the dam; on one side is a dizzying 220m drop down to bare rock, on the other a tranquil, blue lake is framed by classic Alpine scenery. The road continues beyond the dam, passing below **Corippo** (530m) at the end of the lake, a beautiful cluster of old stone cottages crowned by a tall campanile; 3km north is **Lavertezzo**, whose claim to fame is perhaps the most photographed bridge in Switzerland, a graceful seventeenth-century double arch that leaps from bank to island to bank. Many quieter trails head off into side valleys from Lavertezzo, while the valley cuts deeper for another 14km up to **Sonogno** (909m), passing on the way through **Brione**, located on a plateau at a junction of valleys; the views are pretty and the church boasts fourteenth-century Giotto-style frescoes.

Centovalli

Locarno is the eastern terminus of the wonderful **Centovalli** railway (ⓦ www.centovalli.ch), one of Switzerland's most scenic rides (see p.30). Little trains run by the local FART company depart from beneath Locarno station into the spectacular valley – so named for its "hundred" side valleys – most of the time winding slowly on precarious bridges and viaducts above ravine-like depths (sit on the left for the best views). The area is renowned for its natural beauty, and – with a walking map from Locarno tourist office – you could get out at any of the villages en route, pick up a trail and head off into the hills. There's no lack of *grotti*, cafés and simple budget accommodation. One neat way to see the route is with the **Lago Maggiore Express** ticket, which combines the Centovalli line with a train at Domodossola south to the Maggiore resort of Stresa, then a boat back north to Locarno (Fr.42; 9hr total; see also p.560).

Tiny **VERSCIO**, 4km northwest of Locarno, is a lovely stone-built village which also houses the **Teatro Dimitri** (ⓦ www.teatrodimitri.ch), a highly acclaimed international mime school founded by Asconan local "Clown Dimitri", a protégé of Marcel Marceau. The small theatre, in a cobbled lane off the village square, stages regular budget performances by students and professionals all summer long, and is also the training ground for the excellent Circus Monti, which tours Swiss towns and cities every year.

Some 3km down the line is **Intragna** – the graceful 70m bridge just before the village was the scene of Switzerland's first-ever bungee jump, and remains a choice spot for leaping (see box p.548). After the border at **Camedo** (passport needed), trains roll on through rustic villages of the Italian **Valle Vigezzo** and ease down into the bustling Italian town of **DOMODOSSOLA**. Fast

Swiss trains from here run west through the Simplon/Sempione Tunnel to Brig (see p.358) and on to Bern, while equally fast Italian trains head south to Milan. If you have time to kill between trains, head 200m west from the station into the old part of town, set around a series of attractively crumbling arcaded piazzas.

Sottoceneri

The **SOTTOCENERI** region south of Bellinzona and Locarno is much more developed than the Sopraceneri, with dozens of neat, prosperous towns crammed in between the narrowing international borders to east and west. The principal draw is the sophisticated and stylish city of **Lugano**, sited on a bay of the glorious **Lago di Lugano**, which twists out into Italy on both sides. Jutting out into the lake just a stone's throw from the city is the sun-drenched **Ceresio peninsula**, dotted with idyllic Italianate country villages and criss-crossed by some of the loveliest easy walks in the canton.

Lugano

With its compact cluster of Italianate piazzas and extensive tree-lined prome-nades, **LUGANO** is far and away the most alluring of Ticino's lake resorts, much less touristic than Locarno but with, if anything, double the chic. Even Milanese style-junkies, who give very little quarter to their own provincial towns, bring friends over to Lugano for some shopping, a lakeside *apéro* and a good meal. The ever-aspiring Luganesi return the compliment by dropping in to Milan – just 50km south – for a taste of big city highlife and fashion con-cious clubbing. Their home town is nonetheless an exciting place, full of ener-gy and style. Set on a south-facing bay of the cerulean blue **Lago di Lugano**, its lake vistas are astonishing: the city is framed on all sides by wooded, sugar-loaf hills rising from the water that have led to its being dubbed the "Rio of the Old World". Both **Monte Brè** to the northeast and **San Salvatore** to the south are served by funiculars, and both give spectacular views over to the snow-capped Alps.

Lugano is third behind Zürich and Geneva as a Swiss banking centre, and the city centre reflects this, with none of Locarno's Belle-Epoque stuffiness: these old alleys and winding lanes are full of commerce, whether in the form of enticing delicatessens and boutiques or graceful, villa-style hotels and apart-ment buildings. Ancient churches and art galleries are draws in themselves, quite aside from the simpler pleasures of a stroll under the palms alongside the shimmering lake. If there is a drawback to Lugano, it's the **traffic** – unpleasantly heavy most of the time, especially along the lakefront corniche, and marked by alarming Italian-style driving. But at night, looking down from the summit of Brè amidst a warm southerly breeze, with the toot and rumble of cars rising from a bed of twinkling lights, you could feel yourself a long, long way from Switzerland.

Arrival, information and accommodation

Lugano's **train station** overlooks the town from the west, and is linked to the centre by a short-run funicular or by steps down to Via Cattedrale, from where lanes run through to the main **Piazza della Riforma**, one block back from the waterfront. The station is also the arrival and reservations point for the daily Palm Express **postbuses** direct from St Moritz through Italy; all other post-buses depart from Piazza Rezzonico, adjacent to Riforma in the centre. (If you're travelling on to Milan by train, ask for a free city-transport pass with your ticket.) Like Locarno, Lugano takes in a number of adjacent districts which often appear in listings as if they were separate towns: the modestly named **Paradiso** is just around the lakeshore south of the city centre; **Cassarate** is just east of the centre at the foot of Brè, the slopes of which are

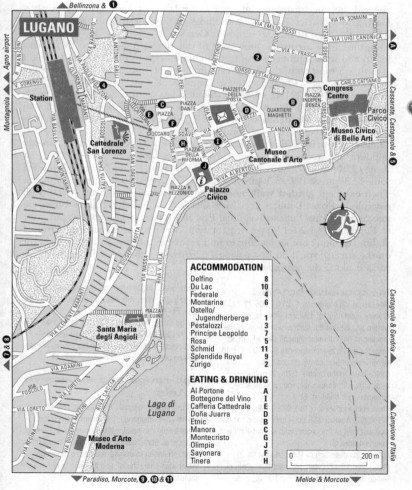

ACCOMMODATION

Delfino	8
Du Lac	10
Federale	4
Montarina	6
Ostello/ Jugendherberge	1
Pestalozzi	3
Principe Leopoldo	7
Rosa	5
Schmid	11
Splendide Royal	9
Zurigo	2

EATING & DRINKING

Al Portone	A
Bottegone del Vino	I
Cafferia Cattedrale	E
Doña Juarra	D
Etnic	B
Manora	C
Montecristo	G
Olimpia	J
Sayonara	F
Tinera	H

0   200 m

TICINO | Lugano

12

Lugano's festivals

Music of various kinds tops the agenda at festivals in and around Lugano. The season opens in mid-April with eight or nine weeks of the **Primavera Concertistica**, a classical programme of renowned soloists and orchestras performing in the main Congress Centre. In early July, **Estival Jazz** (Summer Jazz; Ⓦwww.estivaljazz.ch) covers a series of free concerts in Mendrisio, Tesserete and Lugano that have been running for decades: in the 1950s, Dexter Gordon, Max Roach and Ornette Coleman all played at Lugano, and in the 1960s the festival featured some of Keith Jarrett's earliest performances. The end of July sees two huge **fireworks** displays over the lake, with the Italian enclave of Campione throwing down the gauntlet on July 24 and Lugano itself responding a week later for Swiss National Day on August 1. The **Blues to Bop and World Music Festival** in early September is another free event.

covered by the mansions and private palaces of the seriously wealthy **Castagnola** district. To complicate things further, locals – and some maps – refer to the Lago di Lugano simply as **Ceresio**.

Lugano's little **airport** is 4km west of the city in Agno, served by internal flights and some European routings. Shuttle buses into the city wait for flight arrivals; on most runs, the driver can drop you at your hotel (Fr.10 one-way including luggage). On departure, you must book a pick-up at least one hour in advance (Ⓣ079 221 42 43, Ⓦwww.shuttle-bus.com). A taxi is around Fr.35. Bus Express (Ⓣ091 994 88 78, Ⓦwww.busexpress.com) operates shuttles to and from **Milan Malpensa** airport (MXP), 40km southwest of Lugano in Italy (daily approx. every 2hr; Fr.50 return).

Lugano's **tourist office** is in the Palazzo Civico on Riva Albertolli, directly opposite the main landing-stage (April–Oct Mon–Fri 9am–6.30pm, Sat 9am–12.30pm & 1.30–5pm, Sun 10am–3pm; Nov–March Mon–Fri 9am–12.30pm & 1.30–5.30pm; Ⓣ091 913 32 32, Ⓦwww.lugano-tourism.ch). Their excellent **guided walk** around the city, starting from Santa Maria degli Angioli on Piazza Luini, is free (May–Oct Mon 9.30am). TPL **city buses** are free to Swiss Pass, Lugano Regional Pass and InterRail holders, but full price to Eurailers (Fr.1.20–1.90 per trip, or Fr.5 for a day pass). **Parking** is truly a nightmare. Don't bother battling to find a space in the city-centre car parks (or on the streets); you'd do best paying Fr.25/day at either of the long-term car parks flanking the train station.

Inexpensive hotels

Montarina Via Montarina 1 Ⓣ091 966 72 72, Ⓦwww.montarina.ch. Efficient little place in a nice garden just behind the station, with clean, all-new rooms and helpful management. Closed Jan. ❶
Pestalozzi Piazza Indipendenza 9 Ⓣ091 921 46 46, Ⓦwww.attuale.com/pestalozzi.html. Quality choice bang in the centre, 150m from the lakeshore, with serviceable rooms in an Art Nouveau-style building. ❷
Rosa Via Landriani 2 Ⓣ091 922 92 86, Ⓕ091 923 42 70. A small B&B hotel overlooking the civic park just east of the centre, with shared-bath and ensuite rooms. ❷
Schmid Via delle Scuole 9 Ⓣ091 994 91 21, Ⓕ091 994 18 13. Clean, pleasant family-run place beside the Salvatore funicular in Paradiso; the rooms aren't modern, but are atmospheric, and some bigger ones with double balconies are a bargain. ❷–❸
Zurigo Corso Pestalozzi 13 Ⓣ091 923 43 43, Ⓕ091 923 92 68. Central, very clean and well-kept place, with modern, renovated rooms, private parking and a trace of style as well. ❷–❸

Mid-range and expensive hotels

Delfino Via Casserinetta 6 Ⓣ091 985 99 99, Ⓦwww.delfinolugano.ch. Pleasant, welcoming, small family-run hotel, with secure private parking and a pool. Something of an institution, and with a good reputation to uphold; rooms are functional rather than characterful, and the food is of a high standard. ❸–❹

Federale Via Regazzoni 8 ☎091 910 08 08,
ⓦwww.hotel-federale.ch. Impressive town house
set in the quiet leafy district immediately below
the station, well away from traffic and with lake
views from upper floors; quality modern rooms are
characterful and good value. ❹
Du Lac Riva Paradiso 3 ☎091 986 47 47,
ⓦwww.dulac.ch. Modern lakefront hotel, something of an eyesore but nonetheless with comfortable, balconied rooms looking onto the lake; those
without a lake view cost much less. Go for the
upper floors. ❺–❻
Principe Leopoldo Via Montalbano 5 ☎091 985
88 55, ⓦwww.leopoldo.ch. Disconcertingly lavish
palace way up on a hill overlooking the lake, dripping in traditional elegance and luxury, with guest
facilities to match. ❽–❾
Splendide Royal Riva Caccia 7 ☎091 985 77 11,
ⓦwww.splendide.ch. Lugano's best and most
expensive establishment, with public and guest
room interiors that live up to the hotel's name.
Accept nothing less than one of the vast new
rooms on the top floor, offering some of the best
views in the city. ❾

Hostels

Montarina (see above). Good low-budget central
hotel that also has dorms (Fr.25).
Ostello/Jugendherberge Savosa (HI hostel) Via
Cantonale 13, Savosa ☎091 966 27 28,
ⓦwww.youthhostel.ch. One of Switzerland's best-
value hostels (complete with swimming pool), with
dorms for Fr.31. Take bus #5 to Crocifisso from the
stop 200m left out of the train station. March–Nov.
❶
Ostello/Jugendherberge Figino (HI hostel) Via
Casoro 2, Figino ☎091 995 11 51, ⓦwww.youth-
hostel.ch. A good alternative to the suburban
Savosa hostel is this option in an idyllic former
fishing village on the Ceresio peninsula, offering
dorms for Fr.27 and bike rental. Hourly postbuses
from outside the Lugano tourist office go to
Casoro, a stop beside the hostel (20min). Mid-
March to mid-Oct. ❶

Campsites

La Piodella Muzzano ☎091 994 77 88, Ⓕ091
994 67 08. Lakeshore site 3km west of town near
Agno airport – best of five that are in close proximity. Closed Nov.

The Town

Centre of Lugano is the broad, spacious **Piazza della Riforma**, a huge café-
lined square perfect for eyeballing passers-by over a cappuccino. The lake is a
few metres away behind the Neoclassical **Palazzo Civico**, as are the characterful steep lanes of the Old Town on the opposite side of the square.
Wandering through the dense maze of shopping alleys northwest of Riforma,
you're bound to stumble on the extraordinary Gabbani delicatessen, whose
fame spreads far beyond the borders of the canton – the interior is an Aladdin's
Cave of fine *salsiccia* made especially for the shop, cabinets full of Alpine cheeses
from the farmers of Alto Ticino, pastries and foodie delights galore. From
bustling Piazza Cioccaro just past the deli, the atmospheric stepped Via
Cattedrale doglegs steeply up to **Cattedrale San Lorenzo**, characterized by
an impressive Renaissance portal, fragments of fourteenth- to sixteenth-century interior frescoes, and spectacular views from its terrace.

The narrow, unassuming **Via Nassa** – which nonetheless rivals Zürich's
Bahnhofstrasse for international designer-label chic – heads southwest from
Riforma through a string of picturesque little squares to the medieval church
of **Santa Maria degli Angioli** on Piazza Luini. This plain little building
beside a disused funicular track was founded in 1490 as part of a Franciscan
monastery (suppressed in 1848 during Switzerland's civil war). Inside, the wall
separating the nave from the chancel is entirely covered with a monumental
fresco painted in 1529 by Bernadino Luini that depicts, in intricate and gory
fashion, the Passion and Crucifixion, as well as St Sebastian, graphically pierced
by arrows. Frescoes of unnamed towns cover the three arches through to the
chancel: beneath one is a depiction of Jerusalem. On the left-hand wall is
another fresco by Luini, this time of the Last Supper.

In the lakefront park opposite is a bust of one "**Giorgio**" **Washington**,
placed here by a nineteenth-century Swiss entrepreneur who'd made his

Boats on Lago di Lugano

More even than other Swiss lakes, the idyllic **Lago di Lugano** merits taking to the water simply for the pleasure of it. SNL (☏091 971 52 23, ⓦwww.lakelugano.ch) provides the service; their ticket booth is at the main Lugano jetty opposite the tourist office. This landing-stage is known as **Lugano-Centrale**; there are others at Lugano-Giardino and Castagnola to the east, and Lugano-Paradiso to the south. Boats run between April and October roughly every 45min over to **Gandria** and **Campione** on the eastern arm of the lake; while others depart every two hours south to **Morcote** and on around the Ceresio peninsula to Ponte Tresa, stopping at most places on the way. A panoramic two-and-a-half-hour cruise around the lake, with commentary in English, runs daily (April–Oct) at 2.40pm, and there are also a hatful of cruises throughout the day offering on-board meals, drinks and/or music. In **winter**, a skeleton service operates three boats daily to Morcote, and a few each week over to Campione and Gandria.

Passes for one/three/seven days cost Fr.34/51/62. All SNL boats are free to Swiss Pass and Lugano Regional Pass holders, but Eurail and InterRail bring no discounts.

fortune in the United States. Some 100m south on the lakefront is the **Museo d'Arte Moderna**, Riva Caccia 5 (Tues–Sun 9am–7pm; entry varies; ⓦwww.mdam.ch), which puts on one or two annual fine-art exhibitions of world-class quality; watch for the posters around town.

East of Piazza della Riforma

Five minutes' walk east from Riforma brings you to the **Museo Cantonale d'Arte**, a fine old villa at Via Canova 10 (Tues 2–5pm, Wed–Sun 10am–5pm; Fr.7, more for temporary shows; SMP; ⓦwww.museo-cantonale-arte.ch). Inside are paintings by Klee and Renoir amongst local depictions of peasant life by Swiss and Italian artists of the nineteenth and twentieth centuries. Another 100m east is the attractive waterfront Parco Civico; within the park, the nineteenth-century **Villa Ciani** – with some sumptuously decorated ceilings – houses the **Museo Civico di Belle Arti** (Tues–Sun 10am–noon & 2–6pm; Fr.5), showing works by Cranach, Giovanni Serodine and Henri Rousseau among plenty of Impressionist and Modernist canvases.

A pleasant thirty-minute lakeside walk east along the shore leads you to the undramatic gates of **Villa Favorita**, also with its own bus stop (bus #1). This is the home of part of the famous **Thyssen–Bornemisza** art collection (ⓦwww.museothyssen.org), the world's second-greatest in private hands, after Queen Elizabeth II's. The principal collection, of 775 Old Masters, is on permanent display in Madrid; what is left – nineteenth- and twentieth-century European and American works, by names such as Schiele, Munch and Toulouse-Lautrec – were formerly displayed in this romantic villa, set in its own delightful lakeside gardens. However, following the death of Baron Thyssen-Bornemisza in 2002, the future of the gallery is uncertain: the villa has been closed indefinitely, and you should check with the tourist office, or the villa staff (☏091 972 17 41), before heading out here.

Gandria and Campione

From the gates of Villa Favorita, you could continue a stroll east around the base of Monte Brè, joining the Sentiero di Gandria footpath through the gorgeous **Parco degli Ulivi**, a Mediterranean-style lakefront park shaded by olive trees, cypress, laurels, oleander and deliciously fragrant rosemary. This whole south-facing horn of Monte Brè is protected as an area of special

Lugano boasts two vantage points, both accessible from within the city limits. A funicular run by FMB rises from Cassarate, ten minutes' walk east of the centre, to the summit of **Monte Brè** (Ⓦ www.montebre.ch), a sheer 660m directly above the city (also accessible by car), offering spectacular views from the summit café (Ⓦ www.vettamontebre.ch) over the lake, the curve of Lugano's bay overlooked by the sugarloaf San Salvatore, and due west to the snowy Monte Rosa massif, behind which lurks the Matterhorn. Bracing walks lead off all over the mountain, including a four-hour circuit out to Monte Boglia and back. A short walk from the summit is Brè village, through which is dotted a series of outdoor sculptures; Ⓦ www .montebre.com has details in Italian, and the Lugano tourist office has an English pamphlet to guide you through the village.

From Paradiso, ten minutes south of the centre, a funicular run by FMS rises to **San Salvatore** (Ⓦ www.montesansalvatore.ch), a rugged rock pinnacle offering especially good 360-degree panoramas from the roof of the little church on the summit, a short climb from the funicular station. A terrace café by the top station attends to refreshment needs. This is also the starting point for a number of walks south into the Ceresio peninsula: it's about an hour and twenty minutes through Carona village to Morcote (see p.577) on the tip of the peninsula.

scientific interest, revelling in a semi-tropical microclimate of near-continuous sunshine and just a handful of rainy days a year. After about an hour's wandering, you come around to the picturesque village of **GANDRIA**, rising straight from the water a few kilometres west of the international border. Right beside the landing-stage on the opposite shore, served by plenty of boats from Gandria itself as well as Lugano centre, is the **Museo delle Dogane Svizzere** (Customs Museum; April–Oct daily 1.30–5.30pm; free), with an interesting collection of customs-related bits and bobs that lack decent English notes, although the displays relating to smuggling methods speak for themselves.

The only draw on the opposite shore of the lake from Lugano is the tiny Italian enclave of **CAMPIONE D'ITALIA**, which opted out of the campaign for independence in 1798 and so formed a part of Italy when all around it became Swiss. The village – for that's all it is, even though it's very swish – has Italian police driving around in Swiss-registered cars, and a noticeable lack of either euros or passport controls. Where the place has made a mint is in benefiting from Italian gaming law, considerably more liberal – at least until recent changes in Swiss law – than in Switzerland: Campione's massive lakeside **casino** (Ⓦ www.casinocampione.it), with unlimited stakes, is still where Lugano's many high rollers come to dally after dark.

Eating and drinking

Lugano is blessed with any amount of pleasant, atmospheric places to **eat**, and you'll have no difficulty finding somewhere to suit. The many bars and cafés around Riforma all offer good, inexpensive food at lunch and dinner – yet although they get packed with evening **drinkers**, hip, bar-hopping Luganesi prefer to tuck themselves away elsewhere, filling out a handful of vibrant bars off the main streets of the centre.

Al Portone Viale Cassarate 3 ☎ 091 923 55 11. Gourmet restaurant that manages to keep a pleasantly relaxed ambience alongside its spectacular, inventive new Italian cuisine. Top quality commands top prices. Closed Sun & Mon.

Bottegone del Vino Via Magatti 1. Old-style wine bar centrally located beside the main post office, with waiters in proper white aprons and a huge range of wines on offer by the glass or bottle. Closed Sun.

12

TICINO | Lugano

573

Cafferia Cattedrale Via Cattedrale 6. Small, friendly café dispensing espresso as it should be.

Doña Juarra Via Vegezzi 4 ☎ 091 922 03 65. Popular, well-respected evening and late-night place serving good-quality mid-priced Mexican food (menus Fr.25 or so). Closed Mon.

Etnic Quartiere Maghetti, east of the post office. A superb, inexpensive bamboo-and-candlelight diner tucked away in an unlikely looking purpose-built warren of shops and pharmacies. The menu is all Mediterranean, with Greek and Lebanese specialities around Fr.15, or you could plump for a beer or a banana daiquiri from the bar instead. Either way, the atmosphere is happy, studentish and relaxed. Closed lunchtimes.

Manora Excellent self-service fare within the big Manor department store just off Piazza Cioccaro, the lower terminus of the station funicular.

Montecristo Via Canova, junction Stauffacher. Hip café-bar, reasonably laid-back during the day but crammed to the rafters most nights, when even the sound system fails to drown the conversation.

Olimpia Piazza della Riforma. Venerable old institution housed in one wing of the Palazzo Civico, and best of the many cafés around the square for its surprisingly good, inexpensive food. Menus of Italian staples, steaks and a few more interesting dishes rarely go for more than Fr.20.

Sayonara Via Soave 10. Fast-paced central diner offering inexpensive pizza and pasta options, along with filling staples like polenta for around Fr.15.

Tinera Via dei Gorini 2. Very popular rustic grotto-style restaurant, specializing in Ticinese and Lombard dishes such as pollo alla cacciatora (spicy chicken stew) and home-made pasta, along with an array of excellent local merlots. Menus around Fr.20. Closed Sun & Aug.

Listings

Bike rental In the station (daily 7am–8pm), at the Figino hostel (see "Accommodation") and at various sports shops around town.

Changing money In the station (Mon–Sat 7.10am–7.45pm, Sun 8am–7.45pm).

Flights Lugano-Agno airport flight enquiries ☎ 091 610 12 12.

Gay and lesbian Spazio Gay, Via Stazio 10 in Massagno (☎ 091 968 17 17), is the main information centre for Ticino's gay scene.

Lost property Check with the police office on Piazza Riforma (☎ 091 800 80 65), or at the train station.

Markets There's a picturesque flower, fruit and veg market on Piazza Riforma, with antiques and handicrafts alongside on Via Canova (Tues & Fri 7am–noon). On Saturdays (8am–5pm), the Quartier Canova is again given over to antiques, with Via Vegezzi and Via Soave hosting the fruit and veg market.

Medical facilities Ospedale Civico, Via Tesserete 46 (☎ 091 805 61 11), has a 24-hour emergency room.

Post Main office is in the centre on Via della Posta (Mon–Fri 7.30am–6.15pm, Sat 8am–noon).

Taxi Some taxi numbers are ☎ 091 971 21 21, ☎ 091 971 91 91 and ☎ 091 993 14 14.

Around Lugano

The possibilities for getting out into the countryside around Lugano and the lake are plentiful: the tourist office has individual sheets on 21 cycling routes and 28 walking trails out of the city, both long and short, taxing and easy. The best area to head for is the hilly countryside of the **Ceresio peninsula** (see opposite), extending directly behind the San Salvatore mountain opposite Lugano, with lake views to east, south and west are continually captivating. Postbuses and/or boats from Lugano serve all villages on the peninsula.

Little red trains run by FLP head west from Lugano's train station bound for the border village of **Ponte Tresa**, on a scenic but circuitous route through the Malcantone district. After circling the airport at Agno, they hug an arm of the lake before reaching the undistinguished town of **CASLANO**, unlikely home of the **Alprose chocolate factory** (Mon–Fri 9am–6pm, Sat & Sun 9am–5pm; Fr.3; ⓦ www.alprose.ch), housed in a shed on an industrial estate at Via Rompada 36; to find it from Caslano station, follow the tracks in the direction of Ponte Tresa for about 200m and cut left. As you enter you're greeted, Willy Wonka-like, by a fountain bubbling with fragrant molten chocolate; a guide will swoop a breadstick through and hand it to you. Alprose isn't one of the best-known Swiss brands (although it exports fully eighty percent of its production) and the museum is refreshingly free of corporate hard sell: you'll wander past some old coin-op machines and knick-knacks, including a Meissen porcelain chocolatier, plus there's a short video. The best bit is that you're allowed onto a catwalk above the production line, to watch the huge mixing machines and conveyor belts shuttling bars and ingredients around the factory floor – endlessly absorbing for kids. Beware, though, that the factory closes four times a year for a couple of weeks (in order to produce kosher luxury chocolate for export to Israel). You can buy the full Alprose range at discounted prices in the onsite shop.

The Ceresio peninsula

Although San Salvatore is the most obvious landmark on the **Ceresio peninsula**, 4km southwest of central Lugano rises a lower hill dubbed the **Collina d'Oro** or Hill of Gold, not for its minerals but for its sun-drenched tranquillity. On the top sits the village of **MONTAGNOLA**, home for 43 years to the writer Hermann Hesse. Hesse was born in Germany in 1877, and came to Montagnola in 1919 following traumatic separation from his family after World War I. He rented the **Casa Camuzzi**, an ornate villa, where he lived for twelve years, and where, in an extraordinary outpouring of creativity, he wrote his classic works *Klingsor's Last Summer*, *Siddhartha* and *Steppenwolf*, among many others. In 1924, he was granted Swiss citizenship, and then, in 1931, he moved across the village to the Casa Bodmer, where he wrote *The Glass Bead Game*, which won him the Nobel Prize for Literature in 1946. Hesse died in Montagnola in 1962.

In 1997, the Casa Camuzzi was opened as the **Museo Hermann Hesse** (March–Oct Tues–Sun 10am–12.30pm & 2–6.30pm; Nov–Feb Sat & Sun same hours; Fr.6; SMP; ⓦ www.hessemontagnola.ch). There are no signs to the museum from the Montagnola bus stop; with the village post office behind

Monte Tamaro

Just south of the autostrada and rail exit from the Monte Ceneri tunnel, a gondola rises from the town of **Rivera** (469m) up to **Alpe Foppa** (1530m), located on a shoulder of the needle-sharp peak of **Monte Tamaro** (1961m; ⓦ www.montetamaro.ch). Just by the gondola top station, to one side of a restaurant and information centre, is one of Ticino's most celebrated new buildings, the church of **Santa Maria degli Angeli**, designed by Mario Botta (see p.598). The project was commissioned by the owner of the Monte Tamaro resort in remembrance of his wife, and it's an effortlessly graceful building, with symmetrical stairs, arches and a long walkway, everything in beautiful porphyry stone. From the belvedere, a crucifix faces out over an infinite view above the valley. The intimate interior of the cylindrical chapel, with black plastered walls, is filled with indirect light from low windows and the tiered ceiling, and culminates in an ethereal blue fresco by Enzo Cucchi of two cupped hands.

There's some skiing up here in winter, and in summer you'll find plenty of leg-stretching walks – not least from Alpe Foppa up to the Tamaro summit (1hr 40min) or down to Rivera (2hr 15min). The most spectacular heads on an isolated route along the ridge west to **Monte Lema** (1624m; ⓦ www.montelema.ch) on the Italian border (4hr 30min), from where a cable-car runs down to Miglieglia and a combination of buses can return you to Lugano.

△ The Italian border at Camedo, on the Centovalli rail line (see p.567)

you, walk down the slope and aim through a narrow passage leading ahead off the square. The house is five minutes further on the right. Walking around the old villa is interesting in itself, although the modest displays – Hesse's umbrella, Hesse's table – are labelled in Italian and German only. What makes the entry fee worthwhile, however, is an excellent 45-minute video in English on the writer's life in Montagnola that the staff can set up for you in a basement room. The museum staff can also direct you onto a scenic **walking trail** around the village dotted with eight points of interest related to Hesse.

On the eastern side of the peninsula, exactly at the point where the train tracks, main road and motorway all cross the lake on a low bridge, sits the village of **MELIDE**, home to the kitschy but rather fun **Swissminiatur** (mid-March to Oct daily 9am–6pm; Fr.12; Ⓦ www.swissminiatur.ch). This small park features 1:25 scale models of just about every attraction in Switzerland, from Geneva's cathedral to Appenzell's main street, as well as some more idiosyncratic choices (Burgdorf train station, Zürich airport circa 1958). The reproductions are excellent, and moving model boats, trains and cable-cars liven the static models up no end. A wander past all 113 exhibits might take an hour or two – buy the English leaflet (Fr.2) for a brief rundown.

Morcote and Vico Morcote

The best of the Ceresio lies at the peninsula's southern tip. Here you'll find the captivating village of **MORCOTE**, once a fishing community and now eking out a living as a lakeside attraction. Its photogenic arcaded houses – and slightly tacky antique shops – are strung along the shoreline road, with a web of tranquil, stepped lanes leading up the hill behind to the beautiful **Santa Maria del Sasso**, a fifteen-minute climb (April–Oct Mon–Fri 8am–6pm, Sat & Sun 9am–6pm; Nov–March Mon–Fri 1.30–6pm, Sat & Sun 9am–6pm). The atmospheric hillside church has well-preserved sixteenth-century frescoes inside, and boasts views from its terrace over the lake and hills beyond that are stunning. Several walks explore the lush woodlands nearby, including a long trail back up to San Salvatore (2hr 30min).

Morcote has a handful of hotels, but also suffers from a great deal of tourist attention. One way to escape is to aim for the even tinier village of **VICO MORCOTE**, on the hard-to-reach hillside above and 1km north of Morcote. Here, although the church is just as picturesque and the tiny village piazzas are lined with old stone-built houses that are just as beautiful, unlike in Morcote you can actually hear the fountains tinkle, smell the camellias and stand alone in the middle of the street to absorb the atmosphere. On a junction within the village beside the rustic *Osteria al Böcc* (gnocchi or spaghetti Fr.15), you'll find the tranquil *Bellavista* (☎091 996 11 43, Ⓦwww.a-o.ch/6921-bellavista; ❸–❻). Its impressive restaurant is run by a young, highly accomplished team, who serve exquisite, lightly prepared local cuisine on a beautiful terrace high above the lake; *menus* are around Fr.70. The hotel rooms to one side are outstanding, the bargain of the region – fresh and flooded with light. Their top-floor luxury suite, huge and spotless, with billowing curtains and a private terrace, is utterly romantic, and half the price of those in the more mundane surroundings of Lugano.

The Mendrisiotto

South of Lugano, main roads and trains shoot through the hot, dry region known as the **Mendrisiotto**, after **MENDRISIO**, largest town in the area and a major wine-growing centre. Although the town is picturesque, the main draw is the giant Foxtown **factory outlet** (Ⓦwww.foxtown.ch), prominently signed by the autostrada, where you can pick up designer label fashions – Prada, Gucci, Versace, Dolce & Gabbana, and loads more – at bargain prices.

Just north of Mendrisio, from alongside **Capolago** train station (274m) at the head of the lake (also accessible by boat from Lugano), Ticino's only rack-railway climbs on a slow, scenic route up to the summit of **MONTE GENEROSO** (1704m; Ⓦ www.montegeneroso.ch). For the views alone, this trip is worth taking; from this steep ridge, you can see out across virtually the whole lake. The summit – which has both Swiss and Italian flags flying, marking the border – is the starting-point for an array of walks, including down to Mendrisio one way (2hr 40min) or Muggio another (2hr 15min); you can pick up leaflets and information at the restaurant by the top station.

Some 6km on, and 23km south of Lugano, the Italian frontier is marked by **CHIASSO**, a particularly unprepossessing border town, with a gigantic train station on the edge of a desultory town centre and swarms of traffic and people passing through during the rush hours. The Italian city of **Como** is 5km beyond the border; **Milan** is 30km further. Just before Chiasso, the village of Morbio Inferiore marks a branch road that climbs into the last valley in Switzerland, the tranquil **Valle di Muggio** (Ⓦ www.valledimuggio.ch). Thickly wooded, with seemingly inaccessible hamlets clinging to the steep sides, this is a lovely, rarely visited backwater; Muggio village (666m), 7km in, has a few welcoming little inns, and a steep trail leading up to the Generoso summit.

Travel details

Trains

Bellinzona to: Airolo (hourly; 50min); Biasca (hourly; 10min); Locarno (every 30min; 20min); Lugano (twice hourly; 25min); Luzern (twice hourly; 2hr 10min); Zürich (twice hourly; 2hr 30min).
Biasca to: Airolo (hourly; 40min); Bellinzona (hourly; 10min).
Locarno to: Bellinzona (every 30min; 20min); Domodossola, Italy (approx. hourly; 1hr 45min); Intragna (twice hourly; 20min); Verscio (hourly; 15min).
Lugano to: Basel (twice hourly; 3hr 50min); Bellinzona (twice hourly; 25min); Brunnen (hourly; 2hr 10min); Caslano (every 20min; 20min); Como, Italy (hourly; 40min); Luzern (twice hourly; 2hr 40min); Milan, Italy (hourly; 1hr 30min); Zürich (twice hourly; 3hr).

Buses

Airolo to: Andermatt via Gottardo (July–Sept 3 daily; 50min); Oberwald via Novena/Nufenen Pass (July–Sept 2 daily; 2hr 45min).
Ascona to: Brissago (every 30min; 10min); Locarno (every 15min; 15min).
Bellinzona to: Biasca (hourly; 25min); Chur via San Bernardino (every 2hr; 2hr 15min); Giornico (hourly; 40min); Locarno (hourly; 50min).

Biasca to: Bellinzona (hourly; 25min); Disentis/Mustér (June–Sept 2–3 daily; 1hr 20min; change at Lucomagno Pass); Giornico (hourly; 10min); Olivone (every 2hr; 40min).
Locarno to: Ascona (every 15min; 15min); Bellinzona (hourly; 50min); Brissago (every 30min; 30min); Tenero (at least hourly; 15min).
Lugano to: Casoro (approx. hourly; 20min); Chur, Davos & St Moritz via Italy (Bernina Express; July–Sept 1 daily; 6–9hr; change at Tirano); Melide (approx. hourly; 15min); Montagnola (hourly; 20min); Morcote (approx. hourly; 30min); St Moritz via Italy (Palm Express; 1–3 daily; 4hr); Vico Morcote (every 2hr; 35min; change at Olivella).

Boats

(Following is a summary of April–Oct services.)
Ascona to: Isole di Brissago (hourly; 15min); Locarno (approx twice hourly; 20–30min).
Locarno to: Ascona (approx twice hourly; 20–30min); Isole di Brissago (hourly; 45min–1hr); Stresa, Italy (April–Oct 1–2 daily; 1hr 20min–3hr 30min).
Lugano to: Gandria (approx. every 45min; 35min); Melide (every 2hr; 35min); Morcote (every 2hr; 1hr).
Porto Ronco to: Isole di Brissago (every 40min; 5–10min).

Contexts

Contexts

The historical framework..581–596

Contemporary architecture 597–600

Alpine flora and fauna..601–604

Books 605–611

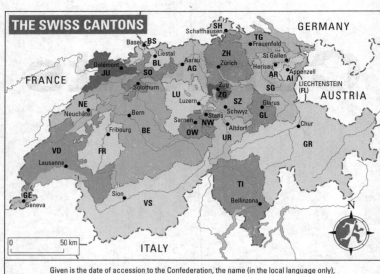

Given is the date of accession to the Confederation, the name (in the local language only), the standard two-letter abbreviation, and the cantonal capital.

1291	**Uri (UR)** – Altdorf
1291	**Schwyz (SZ)** – Schwyz
1291	**Obwalden (OW)** – Sarnen
1291	**Nidwalden (NW)** – Stans
1332	**Luzern (LU)** – Luzern
1351	**Zürich (ZH)** – Zürich
1352	**Glarus (GL)** – Glarus
1352	**Zug (ZG)** – Zug
1353	**Bern (BE)** – Bern
1481	**Fribourg (FR)** – Fribourg
1481	**Solothurn (SO)** – Solothurn
1501	**Basel-Stadt (BS)** – Basel
1501	**Basel-Land (BL)** – Liestal
1501	**Schaffhausen (SH)** – Schaffhausen
1513	**Appenzell Ausserrhoden (AR)** – Herisau
1513	**Appenzell Innerrhoden (AI)** – Appenzell
1803	**St Gallen (SG)** – St Gallen
1803	**Graubünden (GR)** – Chur
1803	**Aargau (AG)** – Aarau
1803	**Thurgau (TG)** – Frauenfeld
1803	**Ticino (TI)** – Bellinzona
1803	**Vaud (VD)** – Lausanne
1815	**Valais (VS)** – Sion
1815	**Neuchâtel (NE)** – Neuchâtel
1815	**Geneva (GE)** – Geneva
1979	**Jura (JU)** – Delémont

The historical framework

S witzerland is often dismissed as an irrelevance in the broader picture of European history: because the country is peaceful today, the underlying suspicion is that it either wasn't subject to the same tide of events as elsewhere, or that the place is just somehow inherently tranquil. Both ideas are false.

The Swiss difference came in solving the same problems that everyone else had in entirely different, co-operative ways. Decentralization, consultation and co-operation are still key Swiss attributes, as they were in 1291 at the start of the country's history, when a group of mountain farmers decided to band together to defy their foreign occupiers. And stability didn't come easily: up until 150 years ago, Switzerland was the most unstable country in Europe, with a history spanning centuries of internecine conflict. The Alpine calm that is notorious – or notoriously boring – today came at the price of almost a millennium of war.

Early civilizations

In Appenzell and near the Rhine in Schaffhausen are scattered remains of the **Paleolithic** civilizations that occupied the area of Switzerland in-between the long periods of prehistoric glaciation. Around 10,000 years ago, at the end of the last major Ice Age, hunter-fisherfolk moved in to occupy the Mittelland, soon afterwards building permanent villages on piles on the shores of the lakes of Zürich, Neuchâtel, Geneva and others. During the **Bronze Age** and early **Iron Age** the settled villagers began both to make contact with neighbouring populated regions, and to make war on them. In the first millennium BC, the **Celts** advanced into Switzerland from the west, bringing with them a new culture and new sophistication, as exemplified in the fortified Celtic township discovered at **La Tène**, near Neuchâtel, and others near Basel, Bern and Zürich.

The Romans: 58 BC–400 AD

In 58 BC at Bibracte in modern France, a **Roman** army under Julius Caesar defeated the **Helvetii** – a group of Celtic tribes resident in the fertile area between the Alps and the Jura – and forced them to move en masse to the western part of Switzerland to serve as an irregular frontier force. Over the next hundred years or so, after also conquering **Rhaetia** (modern Graubünden), the Romans gradually opened up the country, building the first roads over the major Alpine passes – most significantly the **Grand-St-Bernard**, as well as the Julier and Splügen further east – and founding provincial towns at Nyon, Augst near Basel, and Avenches, the last of which became the Roman capital, with more than fifty thousand inhabitants in its heyday. For two centuries or more, Switzerland enjoyed peace and prosperity, with towns established at Geneva, Lausanne, Martigny, Baden, Zürich, Chur and elsewhere. Agriculture flourished, and the region's settlements were populated by a cosmopolitan mix of native Celts and settled Roman officials. The peace was shattered in 260, when the **Alemanii** – a group of Celtic tribes from the area of modern Germany – broke through the Romans' fortified northern border and pushed southwards. Amidst increasing turmoil and confusion, embattled Helvetia and Rhaetia were reduced to impoverished frontier regions.

The roots of freedom: 400–1516

Around 400, Rome withdrew its legions from the area of Switzerland, and Germanic tribes moved in to take control. In the western regions, the originally Germanic **Burgundians** settled and adopted both the Christianity and the Latin language of the local Gallo-Roman tribes. On the south side of the mountains, and in the closed Alpine valleys of Rhaetia, Lombardic and **Romansh** peoples retained close cultural links with their former Roman overlords. Elsewhere, **Aleman** tribes slowly trickled down from the north into the less hospitable thick forests of the central and northeastern parts of Helvetia to build new villages and agricultural settlements, generally halting their advances at points where the land was already populated by Latin-speaking Burgundians. The Germanic Alemans had had little contact with Rome and Christianity, and so continued to use their own native language and follow their own customs. In this way, a **border** of language and culture slowly developed along a line running roughly north–south, marking the easternmost limit of Latinate Burgundian territory and the westernmost limit of Alemanic territory. This language border survives today as the frontier between French- and German-speaking Switzerland.

Around 600, both the Alemans and the Burgundians were conquered by the **Franks**, who absorbed them into their empire under first **Merovingian** and then **Carolingian** kings. The Frankish Empire greatly expanded Latin Christianity throughout Switzerland – and especially into the pagan Alemanic areas – with a network of **monasteries** spreading into the countryside. Ecclesiastical complexes which have survived from this time still flourish at Romainmôtier, Einsiedeln, Engelberg and St Gallen. **Feudalism** also spread, and the once-great Roman towns fell into decline as local warrior nobles took control over an agrarian society of lords, vassals and a vast, impoverished peasantry. In 870, **Charlemagne**'s empire was split, with the dividing line running right through the middle of modern Switzerland. Chaos and conflict erupted, and it wasn't until around 1050 that peace and order returned, nominally under the Holy Roman Emperor.

The birth of the Confederation

During the twelfth century, about a third of the central Swiss forests were cleared for ploughing and settlement; the noble dynasties who had emerged from the conflicts of previous centuries – among them the houses of **Habsburg**, **Zähringen**, **Savoy** and Kyburg – established towns such as Bern, Fribourg, Murten and Winterthur from which to assert their control over the increasingly prosperous countryside.

Around 1220, the road over the **St Gotthard Pass** was opened up for traffic, and those communities lying on the northern approaches to the pass – specifically Uri and Schwyz – suddenly took on massive importance to the imperial rulers. A resurgence in **trade** with the Mediterranean world, and especially Byzantium and the Arab east, after almost a millennium of isolation led to luxury goods making their way across the Alpine passes into northern Europe. Local lords, merchants, princes and the valley communes squabbled with each other for control of the lucrative pass routes. The situation needed resolution, and the Holy Roman Emperor himself stepped in, granting to Uri in 1231 and to Schwyz in 1240 the privilege of freedom from feudal overlordship. With the dying-out of the Zähringen and Kyburg lines, the Austrian house of **Habsburg** had seized the chance to extend its influence over much of Switzerland, but the proud, independent people farming the remote, high valleys of Uri and Schwyz, and their neighbours in forested Unterwalden, remained self-reliant and more or less free.

Rudolf of Habsburg, who had ruled since 1273, died in 1291, thus pitching the region into uncertainty. Popular revolts arose all across the Habsburg realm, especially directed against entrenched power bases such as the monastery at Einsiedeln. In response, a number of Swiss communities forged new partnerships, or renewed old ones, to give themselves a degree of protection against an uncertain future. The legendary **founding of the Swiss Confederation** on the Rütli meadow on August 1, 1291, by representatives of Uri, Schwyz and Unterwalden (see p.396), was just one of these alliances, and is thought to have been a renewal of an earlier agreement of unknown date declaring that an attack on any one of the partners was an attack on them all. The legend of **William Tell** (see p.412), which is first documented more than two centuries after the signing at Rütli, probably arose both as a justification of the sporadic rebellions against authority that followed the death of Rudolf, and as a neat way to embody the concept of Swiss liberty in a single heroic figure – there is no mention either of Tell or of any organized resistance to the Habsburgs in contemporary thirteenth-century chronicles. The Rütli document is no Declaration of Independence: it has no vision of founding a lasting political entity, and enshrines no basic human rights or privileges. It is expedient, but it nonetheless came to symbolize freedom to the Swiss. The name they gave themselves after 1291 – **Eidgenossen** – is untranslatable in English (approximating to "comrades bound by oath into a co-operative"), but has a special significance even today. Switzerland still calls itself the *Eidgenossenschaft*, and the word *Eidgenosse* is listed in dictionaries as a synonym for "Swiss".

Consolidation and growth

During the 1290s and into the 1300s, while the imperial throne remained vacant, revolts continued against symbols of Habsburg power. In 1315, at **Morgarten** near Schwyz, an army of peasants from the newly formed Confederation clashed with and defeated a force of Austrian knights. Ludwig of Habsburg, the new emperor, was forced to concede yet more privileges to the three cantons. The Habsburgs then shifted their attention to the rapidly growing market town of **Luzern**, transport hub for the journey to and from the Gotthard, and tried to force it to take up arms against its lakeside neighbours. Rather than submit to Habsburg domination, Luzern instead threw in its lot with the "Schwyzers", and joined the Confederation in 1332. Unable to bring the Swiss to heel, Habsburg bailiffs withdrew altogether from the region after about 1350 and left the hard-nosed peasants to their own devices. The local economy flourished, centred on the Gotthard Pass.

The feudal system that had been instituted by the Franks gradually began to collapse under pressure from an increasingly prosperous and ambitious free peasantry, who formed an array of democratic rural communes. This went hand in hand with a rise in the power of urban workers: **Zürich**, which had already experienced a revolution by its guilds that had overthrown the city's ruling nobility, joined the Confederation in 1351 to protect its trade interests against a resurgence in power of the nobles. Tiny **Glarus** and **Zug** were roped into the Confederation to secure overland transport routes; and then **Bern**, which was looking to expand its territory westwards, joined in 1353 to defuse the possibility of attack from the east by the increasingly powerful Confederation.

Suddenly, in a little over sixty years, the insignificant Schwyzers – born out of a pact of farming folk – were able to call on an army of over 100,000, and had control of a large swathe of former Habsburg territory across the northern foothills of the Alps. Similar leagues of alliance among ordinary farmers in impenetrable Rhaetia to the east were coalescing into an organized opposition to noble Habsburg rule. While blue-blooded Habsburg armies swept victorious through the great cities of Swabia, in southern Germany, the very same armies experienced crushing defeats in Switzerland by the Confederate soldiery, most notably at **Sempach** in 1386 and **Näfels** in 1388 – both names resonant today for the Swiss. Following their successes, the eight cantons formed an independent state within the Habsburg empire that was ruled – uniquely – by city-based burghers and merchants and founded on principles of tight-knit social co-operation, at a time when elsewhere across Europe kings, princes and noble dynasties held unchallenged sway.

Military conquest

The fifteenth century saw continued expansion by the Confederation. Forces from Uri and Obwalden crossed the Gotthard to seize the **Valle Leventina** south to Bellinzona, crushing the armies of the dukes of Milan as they did so, while the Confederation took advantage both of popular uprisings against the abbot of **St Gallen** to extend their influence eastwards, and of a dispute between Austria and Luxembourg to seize control of the fertile northern lands of **Aargau**.

After 1460, Swiss **mercenaries** became known and feared throughout Europe for their bravery and military skill, tested on battlefields fighting Charles the Bold of **Burgundy**. Victories at Grandson, Murten and Nancy in 1476–77 effectively wiped Burgundy from the map as a regional power, but led to the first of many disputes within the Confederation over the balance of power between towns and countryside. Rural cantons were loath to see Bern – principal victor against Charles – become any more powerful, and only accepted the entry of **Fribourg** and **Solothurn** to the Confederation in 1481 on condition that they took a role of arbitration to moderate urban expansionism. Following Zürich's victory in the **Swabian War** of 1499 – which won complete freedom for the cantons from the German Empire – both **Basel** and **Schaffhausen** joined the Confederation (1501), followed by tiny **Appenzell** in 1513. By then, the thirteen cantons possessed extensive subject territories, including Aargau, Thurgau and a swathe of Ticino. The first Swiss parliament, the **Diet**, met regularly in Baden as a forum to bring Confederate opinion together, both by discussion and – even at this early date – by majority voting.

Reformation and religious conflict: 1516–1798

The **Reformation**, which began in Germany in the early sixteenth century and spread across Europe, was sparked in Switzerland by **Huldrych Zwingli**, a lay priest in Zürich (see p.437). City after city overthrew its ecclesiastical overlords in favour of the new **Protestantism**: St Gallen, Basel, Biel, Schaffhausen and, in 1528, Bern. In each place, the urban guilds were the motive force behind the overthrow, and once Catholicism had been ejected, each city government gained new power and authority over the countryside surrounding it, thus fuelling rural resentment. With the Church's land around Zürich parcelled out to the city authorities, the rural peasantry saw no benefit from the change, and many switched support to the extreme, but largely ineffectual, **Anabaptist** movement, which sought the abolition of serfdom altogether. When Zwingli promulgated the controversial notion of reorganizing the Confederacy under the twin **city** leadership of Zürich and Bern, many rural Catholics resisted strongly, feeling both their religious faith and their political voice to be under threat. Conflict broke out in 1531, in which Zwingli was killed and the Catholic forces won a right of veto in the Diet.

The Reformation continued to spread: with the help of Bernese forces, Geneva won its independence from Savoy in 1530, and accepted the Reformation shortly afterwards, along with Neuchâtel, Lausanne and the Vaud countryside. In 1536, the French priest **Jean Calvin** settled in Geneva, establishing a rigid Protestant theocracy that spread the city's reputation for religious zeal and tolerance Europe-wide.

The situation became further entrenched in the 1550s and 1560s, with the coalescing of the Reformation around Calvinist doctrine, and the consequent launch of the **Counter-Reformation** in a bid to preserve Catholic territory and reassert Catholic rights. With the support of Spain – a major world power – the Catholic cantons retained their religious identity (in 1597 Appenzell split into two half-cantons, one Protestant and one Catholic), but they increasingly nurtured an inferiority complex towards the Protestant cities, which held a grip on political authority and the economy. The latter had started to take on new vitality, boosted by the presence of skilled Huguenot and Veltliner craftspeople – **Protestant refugees** from Catholic regimes in France and Italy.

The seventeenth century

Throughout the tense seventeenth century, it was only shared economic interests that kept the Confederation together: a lucrative system of **textile processing** developed, in which merchants in the cities (generally Protestant) supplied raw materials to peasants in the countryside (generally Catholic), who worked up the finished product and delivered it back to the city merchants for trading on or export. Politics, however, remained in deadlock. No new regions could be admitted to the Confederation, since to do so would upset the delicate balance between Catholic and Protestant cantons. Mistrust on the part of Catholics of a perceived Protestant agenda for domination of the Confederation prevented reorganization or redistribution of jointly administered subject territories, which included Graubünden and Valais.

This wariness filtered over into foreign policy, with the continuing traffic in mercenaries entangling the Confederation in a complex web of **armed neutrality**. All the cantons had pledged to supply France with manpower; in addition, the Catholic ones had links with Spain and Savoy, the Protestant ones with various German principalities and the Netherlands. (The Battle of Malplaquet in 1709 between France and Holland is the most famous example of Swiss mercenaries taking to the battlefield against each other.) The Confederation stayed out of the **Thirty Years' War** (1618–48) – the first significant test of its neutrality – but still imposed new taxes to strengthen its frontier defences. In 1645, a peasants' rebellion against the new austerities was suppressed with violence. In 1653, after the currency was devalued without warning, wiping out the meagre savings of the rural peasantry overnight, a full-scale **Peasants' Revolt** set out to reclaim ancient rights enshrined in agreements from the early days of the Confederation. Without any ado, the urban patricians of Bern and Luzern called in the army to crush the revolt with ruthlessness, and then launched a campaign to reform the Confederate charter in favour of themselves. This was blocked by the rural cantons, who then went to war to safeguard their interests. In a mark of the turbulence of the period, Protestant urban aristocrats and Catholic rural aristocrats first combined to crush the peasantry, then within a few years turned to face each other in bloody conflict. After two battles at **Villmergen**, in 1656 and 1712, Catholics conceded Protestant rights both in confederal matters and in administering the joint dependencies.

The build-up to revolution

The Protestant victory in 1712 – which ended Catholic hegemony in confederal affairs – also ended two centuries of religious conflict, and resulted in a **social and economic shift** in favour of the largely Protestant cities. Catholic regions of the country, which had remained free from the dour influence of Calvin, enjoyed relative freedom in personal conduct but were industrially backward, while Protestant areas benefited from a better-educated populace and the presence of Protestant artisans from around Europe. French Huguenots in particular, their name a corruption of *Eidgenosse*, were the motive force behind a growth in urban manufacturing industries such as **watchmaking** in the northwest and **textiles** in the east. During the Swiss industrial revolution of the eighteenth century, **commercial farming** also began to take hold in the rural cantons.

The second half of the century saw the liberal **Enlightenment** replacing the rigours of Calvinism, with writers and thinkers such as Jean-Jacques Rousseau and Heinrich Pestalozzi feeding a new spirit of Helvetic nationalism which brought Catholics and Protestants together in their patriotic concern for the nation.

However, political life became increasingly **conservative**. Fearful of a repetition of the peasants' uprising, urban patrician dynasties asserted their traditional prerogatives and concentrated power in their own hands. Increasing prosperity and the influence of liberal Enlightenment philosophies in towns and countryside alike led to growing intolerance of patrician rule: in Lausanne in 1723, in Geneva in 1737, in Bern in 1749, in Ticino in 1755, and in Geneva again throughout the 1760s, popular insurrections against entrenched systemic injustice demonstrated a grassroots desire for change.

Revolution and civil war: 1798–1848

The impact in Switzerland of the **French Revolution** of 1789 was enormous. The Confederation itself remained neutral in the battles that followed, but popular revolutionary demonstrations throughout Vaud – at that time a Bernese colony – and at Stäfa near Zürich acted as a spur to a full-scale **French invasion** in 1798 by armies under Napoleon. Revolution swept through the country. In Ticino, Aargau and the lower Valais, the old patrician establishment was swept away; urban residents of Basel, Zürich and Schaffhausen at a stroke won equality before the law; Vaud declared itself independent from Bern; and the brief burst of resistance to the French mounted in central areas was violently suppressed. On March 5, French forces entered Bern, marking the fall of the *ancien régime* in Switzerland.

Within weeks, Napoleon promulgated a new constitution intended to replace the archaic patchwork of communities and privileges, decentralized authority and internecine mistrust that had prevailed since the Middle Ages. His brave new **Helvetic Republic**, "unitary and indivisible", did away with cantons altogether and instead vested centralized power, French-style, nominally in the people but actually in a five-man executive. This showed just how drastically Napoleon underestimated the Swiss, who broke the habit of centuries by coming together – liberal and conservative, Catholic and Protestant alike – in unanimous rejection of his imposed new order. A series of *coups d'état* prompted Napoleon to withdraw his troops from the country in short order in 1802. Civil war immediately broke out, and Napoleon stepped in as arbitrator, this time prudently urging the Swiss themselves to come up with a constitution. This shortlived **Mediation**, as it was called, restored the notion of autonomous cantons, and in addition conferred full cantonal status on six areas previously under joint administration – St Gallen, Graubünden, Aargau, Thurgau, Ticino and Vaud – meanwhile giving the country the new title of the **Swiss Confederation**, a name it bears today.

After Napoleon

The calm was shortlived: once Napoleon was defeated at Waterloo, the democratic balance in Switzerland collapsed. The 1815 **Congress of Vienna** reasserted old patrician privileges throughout Europe, not least in Switzerland, where aristocratic families regained control over local and federal politics. Geneva, Neuchâtel and Valais entered the Swiss Confederation as new cantons, and Bern was granted the Jura as compensation for its losses in Aargau and Vaud. For fifteen years, the political situation simmered, until street-fighting in Paris in 1830 sparked in Switzerland the **Regeneration**, a similar movement of liberalization. This led to seizures of power by united bands of peasants, urban merchants, and craftspeople, who drew up cantonal constitutions enshrining equality and political rights for all – rural and urban alike – and instituted democratic elections to the cantonal governments. In 1831, the patricians of **Basel** condoned a localized civil war, and the division of the canton into two antagonistic half-cantons, rather than surrender any of their powers to radical activists.

Switzerland nonetheless enjoyed an **economic** boom. Unlike in Britain – the only country in Europe more industrially advanced – Switzerland experienced no rush to the cities by an impoverished proletariat. Swiss factories, where they existed, were in rural areas, and drew their labour from the local peasantry, who often came to work after tending to their herds in the fields. Cottage industries, where textiles were processed or watches assembled by individuals working in their own homes under contract from urban suppliers, remained a mainstay of Swiss economic development. The piecemeal, individual-driven Swiss textile industry was efficient enough to stave off competition from Britain's "dark satanic mills" throughout the first half of the century. In addition, new and diverse fields of expertise in chemical production, chocolate-making and tourism boosted national confidence and the image of the country in the eyes of the world.

The Sonderbund War

After the upheavals of the early 1830s, conflict between **radical** liberals and **conservative**, generally Catholic, activists led to increasingly bitter squabbles. After Aargau overturned religious equality in 1841 and ordered all religious buildings in the canton to be shut down, outraged Catholics in neighbouring Luzern nullified their own canton's newly drafted liberal constitution and – in a move intended to provoke – invited the **Jesuit** order to run the schools. This, in turn, outraged radical opinion, which valued liberal education highly and viewed Jesuit control of the schools as nothing less than a step backwards into superstition.

Violent, radical-led scuffles soon broke out, aimed at Luzern's Catholics. In response, the Catholic cantons – Luzern, Zug, Schwyz, Uri, Obwalden, Nidwalden, Fribourg and Valais – formed an illegal resistance force, dubbed the **Sonderbund** (Separatist League), which threatened to destabilize the country. During 1846, a series of localized revolutions put radicals in control of more and more cantons nationwide until, by 1847, with a majority in the Diet, they demanded the expulsion of the Jesuits from the country, the drafting of a new democratic constitution, and the forced dissolution of the Sonderbund. **Civil**

war was inevitable, and – as much to head off potentially disastrous intervention by the great European powers as anything else – the federal commander-in-chief General Henri Dufour took the opportunity to strike. In a month-long campaign during November 1847 he took Fribourg and Zug, and then Luzern, crushing the heartland of the Sonderbund with minimal casualties. The remaining Catholic cantons soon capitulated.

Reconciliation: 1848–1918

The postwar **Federal Constitution of 1848** – still in effect today – marked the birth of the modern Swiss state. It enshrined a host of liberal measures designed to limit patrician power and to permit continued expansion of industry and the economy. For the first time, Switzerland had a **central government**, with a directly elected bicameral parliament. To a background of revolutions breaking out all over Europe during 1848, the radical liberals – conscious of the centuries of Swiss conflict behind them – devised a constitution that was able to defuse the age-old Catholic fears of Protestant domination. They did so principally by **dividing power** between the centre and the cantons, thereby allowing the majority Protestants and the minority Catholics to engage in democratic debate together, in the knowledge that each needed the other to survive. Devolution of power to self-governing cantons – **federalism** – allowed the retention of strong Catholic communities at the cantonal level and the creation of strong Protestant-led institutions at the national level. And, following 25 years of peace and consolidation, the formal adoption in 1874 of the **referendum** as the prime tool for consultation of the people – on matters of local, cantonal and national interest alike – ensured that politicians remained directly accountable.

Amidst steady economic growth in railways, tourism, chemicals, engineering and heavy industry, **national reconciliation** was allowed to develop organically over the second half of the century, and with it came further democratization, with the adoption of proportional representation in cantonal elections and the growth of consultation and compromise at executive level in the federal government. With a mood of reconciliation after 1848, ever-increasing numbers of tourists exploring the newly fashionable Alps, huge national celebrations of six hundred years of Swiss history in 1891, and the unveiling of the idealistic monument to William Tell in Altdorf in 1895, a new, specifically **Swiss national identity** began to develop.

Although the appeal of Swiss national unity was strong, **nationalism** threatened – paradoxically – to split the country apart again. The alluringly woolly ideas that developed at this time of race, social darwinism and the mystical destiny shared by all people who shared a particular language (exemplified in the concept of uniting Europe's German-speaking *Volk*), held a romantic, supra-national appeal. German Swiss looked towards the achievements of Germany, with its booming economy, military prowess and advanced social-welfare policies, and felt themselves to be part of it, distanced from their French-speaking compatriots. Similarly, French Swiss looked towards the cultural achievements of *fin-de-siècle* France, and saw their Swiss-German neighbours as foreign. Italian-speaking Swiss in particular felt the arbitrary international border between them and the "rest" of Italy to be increasingly absurd. At the dawn of the twentieth century, the Swiss had stopped talking to each other.

World War I and after

Officially, Switzerland stayed out of **World War I**. In practice, the army had been "thoroughly Prussianized", as Jonathan Steinberg puts it, and its commanders saw no reason not to support Germany. As soon as war broke out in the summer of 1914, Switzerland began passing military intelligence to Berlin. The mood within the country soured, as German and French Swiss retreated from each other, both backing opposite sides in the war. In an echo of the trenches of northern France, a *Graben*, or trench, opened up along the language border between the two. French Swiss were increasingly outraged by their army's pro-German bias.

Economic conditions were hard, compounded by the need to maintain hundreds of thousands of soldiers guarding the frontiers, and to support a growing number of refugees and asylum-seekers. In 1915 and 1916, Lenin, Trotsky and Zinoviev were all resident in Switzerland, and the influence of their revolutionary socialist agitations, as well as subsequent news of the successful Russian Revolution, spurred impoverished Swiss workers on to a **General Strike** in November 1918. For three days the Federal Council dithered, then called in the army. The strikers capitulated soon afterwards and went back to work, but had made their point: in a referendum in 1919, the Swiss people approved the adoption of proportional representation in national elections – a major plank of the workers' concerns, since majority voting had effectively excluded the Socialist Party from real power. The Federal Council acknowledged the benefits of compromise, and met the strike committee face-to-face. Soon after, policies on welfare expansion and a 48-hour working week became law.

Neutrality and World War II: 1918–1945

The rise in power of a socialist-minded proletariat after the war prompted a corresponding rise in the old forces of Catholic conservatism, as well as in rural farmers, who quickly won a place on the Federal Council alongside the urban Radicals. As elsewhere, the economic bubble of the 1920s burst in the early 1930s, with a crippling **depression** halving output, decimating incomes and causing huge unemployment. At the same time, cosy domestic political coalitions were breaking down under the influence of proportional representation, which brought a myriad of economic and political interest groups into parliament. After **Hitler**'s rise to power in Germany in 1933, sympathetic Nazi "fronts" emerged, gathering support nationwide from right-wing conservatives and hard-hit petty bourgeois merchants who together proposed a root-and-branch revision of the Federal Constitution. But both a devaluation of the franc in 1936 (which boosted Swiss industry in the run-up to war) and a new partnership of liberals and social democrats – who, in the face of spreading fascism, had together abandoned the ideal of class war – were effectively able to sideline these authoritarian movements in favour of continued democratic debate. As war became more and more likely during the late 1930s, Switzerland bolstered its own national institutions, affirming the status of **Romansh** as a national language, authorizing widespread official usage of **Swiss-German** as a distancing measure from the High German of the Third Reich, and showcasing homegrown achievements at a **National Exhibition** in 1939. In addition, it readied its economy and industry for war, passing a series of laws to protect individual earnings should mobilization become necessary, and introducing anonymous **numbered bank accounts** to protect the savings of German Jews from seizure by the Nazis.

Switzerland and the Jews

As across Europe, **anti-Semitism** worked its way into official Swiss policy over decades. Freedom of residence and civic and legal equality had been granted to Jews in Switzerland only in 1866, and even in the glow of pan-Helvetic pride in diversity around the 1891 national anniversary, a referendum was passed in 1893 banning Jewish ritual slaughter of animals on ostensibly compassionate grounds (incomprehensibly, ritual slaughter remains illegal in Switzerland today). Russian pogroms in the 1880s resulted in floods of destitute Jews heading west across Europe, and subsequent concerns about **Überfremdung**, or foreign infiltration, of Switzerland showed themselves in discriminatory immigration policies that required assimilation before civic protection could be conferred: in virtually all cases, Jews who applied for refugee status were deemed to be alien to Swiss society and thus unassimilable.

As the European situation worsened during the 1930s, Switzerland searched for a way to keep the Jews out – as did many European governments – without being seen to compromise their reputation for neutrality and tradition of providing asylum. In 1938, in response to a specific request to the Gestapo made by Switzerland's police chief, Germany ordered that the passports of all "non-Aryan" Germans – that is, Jews – be stamped with a "J" to identify them to border guards, who were then instructed to turn them back. After August 1942, racial persecution alone was deemed to be not sufficient grounds for emergency admission to the country, and the borders were effectively closed. Only twelve Jews in each year of the war were granted Swiss naturalization papers, and of some 300,000 refugees who were accepted into Switzerland, just ten percent were Jewish. Surviving records testify to 25,000 Jews being turned back at the borders, but the real figure must have been vastly higher.

By autumn 1942, the Red Cross in Geneva knew unequivocally of the systematic murder of Jews in Nazi death camps. Under pressure from the Swiss government, it did and said nothing. The borders remained closed. A few individuals within Switzerland were working against the policies of the government, but the official line was that – in the notorious words of Federal Councillor Eduard von Steiger – "the lifeboat is full".

World War II

In the summer of 1939, Switzerland mobilized between ten and twenty percent of its entire population in preparation for **war**. Germany had already invaded Austria in 1938 under the pretext of "union" (*Anschluss*), and by June 1940, Denmark, Norway, Holland, Belgium, Luxembourg and France had all succumbed to the Nazi tanks. Mussolini's Fascist Italy lay to the south. Switzerland was surrounded. An invasion by the Axis powers seemed imminent, and on July 25, 1940, following an extremely controversial speech hinting at advantages to be gained by collusion with Berlin, the Swiss commander in chief **General Guisan**, along with the entire Swiss officer corps, took ship in Luzern for the **Rütli** meadow, semi-mythical scene of the founding of the Confederation in 1291. There, at this most resonant spot, Guisan reaffirmed the Swiss commitment to resistance and neutrality, and conducted a ceremony at which all officers did the same. Rumblings of discontent among junior officers at the hints of collaboration in the upper echelons of command were thus quelled.

And yet it is now clear that collaboration continued apace. Unlike in the previous war, this time the flouting of Swiss neutrality was usefully concealed beneath a glow of national pride and unity, fuelled by the Rütli declaration. The role of Switzerland in World War II is still highly controversial today, but historians now accept that the country escaped Nazi invasion not simply through the doggedness and tenacity of its troops (as Swiss history books have long maintained). Both the Allied and the Axis powers were very well served by having an ostensibly neutral, stable Switzerland at the heart of war-torn Europe. The country's role as a **banking and financial centre** was pivotal: both sides needed to buy war *materiel* and resources, and during the war the only truly convertible currency accepted for payment worldwide was the Swiss franc. Basel's Bank of International Settlements – a bank of national banks, with board members drawn from the US, Britain, France, Germany and elsewhere – kept the wheels of international capitalism turning, and was the only place where **high-level meetings** continued in extreme secrecy between Allied and Axis officials, meetings that were treasonous by the standards of both. Right up until the fall of Berlin in 1945, the Swiss National Bank accepted **gold** from Germany in exchange for Swiss francs, in the full and certain knowledge that Berlin would then use the money to keep the Axis war machine supplied, and that the ingots arriving at Bern had been looted from the banks of invaded countries and/or melted down from the possessions and even the teeth of dead Jews. In addition, Hitler needed a peaceful Switzerland to keep the **Alpine passes** that linked Germany and Italy open, and also benefited from Swiss **industry**, which continued to supply the Third Reich with guns, ammunition and heavy artillery, in exchange for essential raw materials and food.

After the Rütli gathering – at the height of the threat of invasion – General Guisan ordered Swiss frontier defence positions to withdraw from the national borders in order to fortify positions within the high Alpine chain. The *réduit national* ("Fortress Switzerland") took shape: at almost any point after 1940, Hitler could have crossed the frontier and taken the entire populated lowlands – Basel, Zürich, Bern, Geneva and the countryside – without a fight, and reduced independent Switzerland to a scattering of snowbound bunkers in the high Alps. But such an invasion would have impoverished the Reich. In reality, Switzerland was safe: the military kudos to be gained by Hitler's having a subdued, occupied Switzerland subject to Allied bombing was vastly outweighed by the material benefit of his nurturing a nominally neutral, independent Switzerland that remained enthusiastically open for business. The moral consequences of this for the Swiss themselves are only now being felt, decades later.

Sonderfall Schweiz: 1945–2001

Patrick Kury, an historian at the University of Basel, has written in *Images of Switzerland* (see "Books", p.607): "After World War II, the lack of experience of war made Swiss people believe that they were a kind of chosen people living outside history. This strange belief goes together with the misconception that between 1933 and 1945 Switzerland had followed a humanitarian tradition, and had never practised an anti-Jewish [policy]. In the postwar period, neutrality – the number one state maxim – also helped to neutralize analysis and discussion."

The glow of national pride in having reached war's end unscathed – despite the fact that Switzerland's citizen army had merely kept its head down, and that neither Allied nor Axis powers had had the slightest intention of invading – was intoxicating, and the Swiss felt themselves to be special: the term **Sonderfall Schweiz**, or "Switzerland as a Special Case", is often used to describe the period. The extent of official collaboration with both warring parties was widely known by foreign governments – who shunned Switzerland immediately postwar – but was generally not even suspected by ordinary Swiss.

However, whereas war swept away old social and political habits across Europe, in Switzerland things continued after the war much as they had done before: while the new world order expressed itself in the establishment of the **United Nations** in 1945, Switzerland stuck tight to its neutrality and stayed out. By 1946 international diplomatic relations had been repaired, and the country – with its intact industry, low taxes, and socio-political stability – took on the role of catalyst to European reconstruction. At a time of austerity, Swiss banks were able to draw on large capital reserves (thanks in large part, it is now clear, to their wartime policy of accepting looted gold from Berlin).

With the **Cold War**, fear of the spread of Communism took over from fear of the spread of Fascism. Political parties that were already rooted in concordance moved together into a rock-solid national consensus. Dubbed after 1959 the **"magic formula"**, this ensured two seats on the Federal Council went to the moderate-left Liberals, two to the moderate-right Christian Democrats, two to the left-wing Social Democrats and one to the right-wing People's Party; four were reserved for German-speakers and three for French- and Italian-speakers, reflecting the language division in the country.

Along with most of the rest of Western Europe, Switzerland experienced a cycle of economic fortunes: consolidation in the 1950s, boom in the 1960s, recession in the 1970s, entrenchment and readjustment in the 1980s, streamlined growth in the 1990s. However, despite massive advances in personal and national wealth, and success in adapting traditional industries to the new era – exemplified by the launch of **Swatch**, a slick, new company that dragged the Swiss watch industry out of its fustiness – it took until the 1990s for Switzerland to bring itself fully into line with European conceptions of social modernity. **Women** got the vote in national elections only in 1971, decades behind most other European countries; as late as 1991, one canton (Appenzell Inner-Rhodes) had to be forced to accept women onto the cantonal electoral roll by the Federal Supreme Court.

As the Western European powers drew together in an ever-closer **common market**, the insular Swiss looked on, the national mood still one of "Fortress Switzerland": throughout the postwar period, Switzerland consistently voted against joining international bodies of political co-operation. (In 1986, a proposal for **United Nations** membership received a resounding "no" from 76 percent of Swiss voters.) Since 1960, Switzerland had been a member of the European Free Trade Area (EFTA), a purely commercial body without political ambitions. When its EFTA partners Sweden, Finland and Austria applied to join the **European Union** in 1992, Switzerland was forced to follow suit. Put to the vote, the national margin of defeat was narrow, but analysis of the figures showed that 70 percent had voted yes in francophone Romandie, but just 44 percent had voted yes in German-speaking areas; roughly similar figures taken as a national whole split pro-EU urban voters away from anti-EU rural voters. The figures reignited national soul-searching over the age-old social and linguistic divide, and Switzerland shelved its application.

After 1992, this soul-searching was exploited by a new bloc of strident, right-wing opinion shaped and led by the notorious **Christoph Blocher**, leader of the Zürich section of the SVP (Swiss People's Party), who campaigned throughout the 1990s on a platform of anti-EU, anti-immigration rhetoric, wrapped up in a cloak of pro-Swiss, pro-neutrality platitudes. Amidst a floundering economy following the rejection of EU membership – Switzerland had the weakest growth rate in western Europe in the period 1992–2001 – parliamentary time was taken up with endless amendments to bring Swiss law into line with EU law: popular opinion notwithstanding, the country simply couldn't afford to ignore the direction its neighbours were heading in. The Swiss government, forced to seek unorthodox methods of cooperation, embarked on talks with the EU to draw up a series of bilateral accords. Meanwhile, the cosy "magic formula" began to crumble: in the 1999 elections, Christian Democrat support dropped away, while Blocher's SVP won the largest share of the vote.

Blocher's rise was boosted by a series of **scandals** throughout the 1990s that sent the country reeling. Suddenly, as if from nowhere, the squeaky-clean image that postwar generations had of themselves and their country was shown to have been an illusion. In 1989, **Elizabeth Kopp**, the first woman to serve as a Federal Councillor – and something of an icon of the new Switzerland – had to resign when it was revealed that she had tipped off her husband about ongoing investigations into his financial dealings. The same year it emerged that the Swiss **secret police** had been keeping files on 200,000 individuals, under the guise of monitoring anti-patriotic activity. An accountant in the defence department under investigation in a multimillion-franc **fraud** case – the largest in Swiss history – turned out to be an intelligence agent, and claimed he had withdrawn the money on the orders of his boss to fund the secret training of a shady battalion of highly armed agents for purposes unknown.

But the story that hit the international headlines, and brought Switzerland into the uncomfortable glare of global attention, concerned its **wartime** record.

Wartime reappraisal

With the end of the Cold War in 1989, former Communist countries in Eastern Europe opened their borders and their state archives. **Jews** who had survived the Holocaust began petitioning the governments in Warsaw, Budapest, Prague and elsewhere – often with the help of international Jewish organizations such as the New York-based **World Jewish Congress** (WJC) – for return of property that had been seized by the Nazis. In summer 1995, the fiftieth anniversary of the end of World War II prompted apologies from many Western governments for their activities during wartime. Swiss President Kaspar Villiger officially **apologized** for the introduction of the "J" stamp in the passports of German Jews and for Switzerland's closing its borders to Jewish refugees at the height of the Final Solution. Meanwhile, WJC researchers had been recording case after case of Holocaust survivors being refused access to their dead relatives' accounts in Swiss banks, often on spurious grounds such as not providing a death certificate. They began to smell a rat, and turned to the US National Archives, which held official wartime government records tracking the flow of money through Switzerland. They uncovered records showing that the Swiss banks were not just sitting on the assets of dead Jews, but that they had also accepted vast quantities of obviously looted **gold** as part of a hitherto only guessed-at secret, semi-official network of economic collusion with the Third Reich.

The story rapidly hit the headlines, and pressure built for official investigations to begin. In 1996, the **Swiss Bankers' Association** disingenuously announced it had uncovered a mere Fr.39m in heirless accounts. Pressure built throughout the year, with the WJC and other organizations – Jewish and not – demanding full access to banks' archives to get to the bottom of the story. In 1997, a security guard working at UBS, **Christoph Meili**, made public the fact that the bank was secretly shredding large quantities of prewar documents. Meili was fired for violating the bank's secrecy and prosecuted shortly afterwards, but became something of a folk hero, not least to liberal-minded Swiss who were getting increasingly uncomfortable with the banks' attitude. It was becoming clear to the Swiss establishment that the game was up: the president, Arnold Koller, attempted to head off the oncoming onslaught by proposing the financing of a Fr.7 billion fund from the gold reserves of the Swiss National Bank to support Swiss and foreign victims of oppression and natural disaster – the so-called **Swiss Solidarity Foundation**. Then a local newspaper revealed that Credit Suisse – another major Swiss bank – had opened an account for the Nazi SS during the war and that the Bank for International Settlements in Basel had acted as a safe conduit for much of the Reich's looted gold, and the WJC publicized documents from the US National Archive stating that **Japan**, wartime ally of the Nazis, had also used Swiss banks. Meanwhile, the banks themselves were scrabbling to prove their good faith: Fr.17m that had lain in dormant accounts since the war was returned to the descendants of account holders.

The affair was souring international relations. Switzerland made official complaints to the BBC over a documentary entitled "Nazi Gold", which it claimed was inaccurate and inflammatory. Canada was forced to admit that it had laundered at least six tons of Nazi gold via Switzerland and Portugal. US president Bill Clinton and the US Congress granted the bank security guard Christoph Meili asylum, and UBS dropped the case against him in the Swiss courts and apologized. Amidst the tide of accusation and counter-accusation, the **Red Cross** issued an unprecedented statement admitting a "moral failure" in not having spoken out during the war against the ongoing genocide of the Jews.

In 1997, a committee of historians chaired by **Jean-François Bergier** reported that, in addition to the $389m of gold purchased from Nazi Germany by the Swiss National Bank (approximately $4 billion in modern-day terms), some $61m of Nazi gold had been bought by the Swiss commercial banks (among which were UBS and Credit Suisse), three times more than previously thought. The Bergier commission confirmed that the Swiss National Bank had known that much of the gold they were buying had been looted from occupied countries, and also that officials had been aware that the Nazis were robbing Jews and other persecuted groups before exterminating them.

With an array of lawsuits brought by tens of thousands of Holocaust survivors making their way slowly through the US courts, and escalating threats of a Swiss–US trade war, the international pressure on the Swiss banks to acknowledge culpability for their wartime activities and their subsequent attempts to block investigation was inexorable. In 1998, desperate to see an end to the story, the three largest banks, Credit Suisse, UBS and SBC, offered $1.25 billion, the so-called **global settlement sum**, to settle all claims connected with Holocaust-era assets. According to a poll, less than half the Swiss population declared itself content with the outcome, most of them believing the figure to be too high. Meanwhile, the damaging revelations continued to emerge, most notably when the Red Cross was forced to acknowledge deep regret over the fact that it issued **Josef Mengele**, the infamous doctor at the Auschwitz death camp, with a permit to travel through Switzerland in 1949.

In 1999, two official commissions set up to look into the whole affair issued reports. The **Volcker Commission**, which examined Swiss bank accounts from the Nazi era, found almost 54,000 accounts that had been opened between 1933 and 1945, and, in addition to the thousands of names already declared, advised the banks to publish a further 25,000 names of account holders suspected to have been victims of the Nazis. It estimated that, at current prices, these accounts totalled between $200m and $440m. The report of the **Bergier Commission**, set up to investigate Switzerland's wartime treatment of refugees, merely confirmed what many already knew, that Switzerland had deliberately blocked the entry of refugees, condemning Jews and others to certain death at the hands of the Nazis. It identified a strain of "cultural, social and political" anti-Semitism that ran through the country at the time. The report prompted Swiss president **Ruth Dreifuss** – the only Jewish woman to have served in the post – to reiterate the government's official apology of 1995. The commission's final report in 2002 stated explicitly that "the [Swiss] refugee policy contributed to... the Holocaust."

The end of "Sonderfall Schweiz"

The whole sorry saga of the 1990s struck deep at the heart of Swiss self-confidence. Statements like those issued by the Bergier Commission that "Switzerland declined to help people in mortal danger" ran counter to all the notions of ethical behaviour that postwar Swiss generations learned from their parents, from each other and from their history books. For some, it has been almost too much to bear: the anger and frustration that has been stirred up in the proudly nationalistic working people of the inner cantons of the country in particular has coincided with the rise of the right-wing demagogue Christoph Blocher, who has channelled it into a coherent, extremist political strategy directed against foreigners of all kinds, embodied – in his philosophy – in the EU, the UN and the many asylum seekers and guest workers resident in Switzerland.

The Nazi gold brouhaha died down after 1998, but a series of crises followed that continue to hammer away at Swiss self-confidence. The most serious erupted in 2001, when the national airline **Swissair** – having squandered millions on an ill-advised policy of acquisitions of failing European carriers, after the rejection of EU membership in 1992 had denied it equal competition rights under EU law – defaulted on its loans and was declared bankrupt. The sight of Swiss travellers marooned at foreign airports and the flag humiliated in public, not to mention the economic failure of a core institution, felt to many Swiss like a national disaster. For six months, bankers and industrialists worked on a rescue package, and in 2002, the new national carrier **Swiss** appeared. Nonetheless, another Swiss icon, and key marker of Swiss reliability, had been shown to be fallible. In 1999, 21 people were killed while canyoning near Interlaken, and eleven people died in a 2001 fire in the St Gotthard road tunnel, further undermining faith in Swiss safety standards that were previously thought to be unimpeachable.

This devastating combination of scandal and national humiliation effectively punctured, in five short years, the self-assurance and – some said – smugness that had shaped Swiss national consciousness over the previous five decades. Commenting on the country's wartime role, the Geneva newspaper *Le Temps* finally spoke a painful truth: "The Swiss were no better or worse than anyone else." It was clear that the idea of *Sonderfall Schweiz*, Switzerland as a "Special Case", was dead.

Switzerland today

Although the *Sonderfall* notion persists, in the ugly shape of Christoph Blocher and the SVP, modern Switzerland has gained a new, rejuvenating humility. This has been most tangibly expressed in the vote in 2002 to finally apply for membership of the **United Nations**; the country was accepted as the UN's 190th member state the same year. The yes vote was hailed as a sign of an end to Swiss isolation; the government still struggles with continuing rejection of European Union membership in referenda, but brought into force in 2002 seven **bilateral accords** between Switzerland and the EU, on such matters as trade and free movement. Progressive liberalization in some areas will be complete by 2014, whether the Swiss people ever vote for EU membership or not.

Asylum and immigration remains a hot topic, fuel to Blocher's reactionary fire, despite the narrow rejection by the people in 2002 of a proposal to stem the flow of new arrivals. Connected with this, and tied up in lingering notions of the core values of Swissness being eroded by foreign influence, is an inexorable rise in the use of **English** throughout the country, in education, business and popular culture. English is now the first foreign language studied in primary schools in Zürich and other cantons, supplanting French; much to the chagrin of those trying to build cultural bridges between the four language communities, it is increasingly seen as Switzerland's *lingua franca*.

With the demise of the *Sonderfall* image, Switzerland continues to search for a contemporary identity. On the one hand, Swiss **architecture** and design lead the world, and a keen awareness of environmental protection shows itself most dramatically in two new trans-Alpine **rail tunnels** – the 35km Lötschberg Base Tunnel (due for completion in 2007) and 56km Gotthard Base Tunnel (2012). Both are part of a concerted multibillion-euro effort to conserve the Alpine environment and shift pan-European freight off the roads. On the other hand, Switzerland remains a conservative, traditionalist and – perhaps most surprisingly – deeply militaristic society: it is now the only European country to have **universal male conscription**, and as late as the 1980s was still jailing otherwise law-abiding 20-year-olds for refusing army duty. The general elections of 2003 may see the old political order break down altogether: the decline of the centre-right Christian Democrats and rise of the extreme right SVP means that, after fifty years, the cosy "magic formula" (see p.592) is now out of sync with the electorate's voting patterns. Switzerland has gained new self-knowledge after the crises of the 1990s, but it may yet lurch to the right as the old guard digs in.

Contemporary architecture

With its intrinsic faith in modernity and traditional support for innovation, Switzerland has developed a cultural climate that has fostered some of the most important contemporary architects of the last twenty years. Private and state sponsorship, coupled with an understanding of the value of quality design, has led the country to become a model for contemporary architecture, where home-grown talent constructs alongside international stars. Private commissions and public competitions alike generate a dynamic environment for both new and established architects.

Having largely escaped the upheavals associated with the world wars of the twentieth century, Swiss culture has had the freedom to grow organically, avoiding many of the ruptures and traumas suffered by its neighbours. The **Modern** movement of the 1930s, with its philosophy of cost-effective architecture coupled with a certain pride in the use of rational techniques, was the basic model for construction across the country for more than three decades.

The Ticino School

International recognition for Swiss architecture came with the so-called **Ticino School**. In the 1960s, renewed economic prosperity swept across the country; this boom was manifested in the Ticino region by a mushrooming of small factories and private houses with no building or urban planning restrictions. The Ticino School emerged out of this uncontrolled situation with a sense of optimism in the capability of architecture to provide a solution to the chaos and ruin of the landscape.

The central influences on the movement were the theoretical arguments that were developing across the border in Italy, focused around the Milanese architect and critic Aldo Rossi. Rossi held that modern architecture should essentially be a social discipline where individuality is replaced by the use of a few identifiable and unchangeable components, elementary geometrical volumes with the capacity to become monuments and so give sense and order to the surrounding territory.

The ideals of the Ticino School found probably their clearest expression in the work of **Luigi Snozzi**. Snozzi has been responsible for construction in the village of Monte Carasso, just outside Bellinzona, since 1977, attempting to break down any differences between urban planning and architecture. His aim has been to give the village a distinctive identity, since it was in danger of becoming merely a dormitory town. By refurbishing existing structures, designing public spaces and constructing new buildings with a monumental capacity he has created focal points for the spatial organization of the village.

Another high-profile example of Ticino School architecture that deals with the central themes of identity, memory and monumentality in a groundbreaking way is the work of **Aurelio Galfetti** at Castelgrande in Bellinzona (1981–91; see p.552). His restoration of this historic fortification was begun by pulling down the "non-original" interventions, including the surrounding vegetation, and inserting modern elements into the ancient fabric. The project created a new reference for the treatment of historical monuments and sensitive heritage sites across the country.

The most famous architect from the Ticino School at an international level is **Mario Botta**. His renown is now linked with large projects all over the world, most notably the San Francisco Museum of Modern Art (1989–95). But, although his buildings are ubiquitous in Switzerland, it's in his smaller works that he best reveals a sensitive and evocative relationship with the environment. This is best illustrated in the church of San Giovanni Battista at Mogno (1986–96; see p.566) and the chapel of Santa Maria degli Angeli at Alpe Foppa on Monte Tamaro (1990–97; see p.575). The creation of the Centre Dürrenmatt, near Neuchâtel (1992–2000), with a subterranean intervention that doesn't compromise the integrity of the writer's old house, illustrates his ability to work in particularly delicate situations.

Swiss German architecture

Since the early 1990s, the attention of international critics has shifted from the Ticino School to the architecture of **German Switzerland**. A fresh generation of architects have created a new language and an approach to architecture that is resulting in elegant, emblematic buildings across the world. Rather than concentrating on the concept of architecture as a symbolic act – so central to the theory of the Ticino School – they focus on architecture as a purely constructive act.

△ Mario Botta's church of San Giovanni Battista at Mogno (see p.566)

The most important practitioners are three studios that have become internationally renowned in recent years. **Herzog & de Meuron** is perhaps the best known office, having worked across Europe and in the US as well as on numerous high-quality projects at home. The studio's architecture is characterized by a sophisticated intellectualization of architectural problems that are often solved through collaboration with contemporary artists. **Peter Zumthor** has entered the public consciousness in a very different way. A cabinet-maker by trade, his exquisite interventions in often rural and culturally sensitive communities have won him a reputation for an unparalleled level of craftsmanship and attention to detail. The younger duo of **Annette Gigon and Mike Guyer** have produced a clutch of buildings that embody the self-confident simplicity associated with contemporary Swiss architecture.

One of the main focuses of this Swiss-German school is the use of **everyday materials**, which were previously thought of as banal, or at least, not suitable for refined or noteworthy architecture. Herzog & de Meuron's Ricola Storage Building (1986–87) in Laufen, south of Basel, perfectly illustrates this attitude: panels of fibre-cement sheeting were chosen for the facade and stacked vertically to create a sophisticated, free interpretation of the piles of freshly sawn wooden boards lying outside the sawmills in the surrounding valley. To clad the facade of the extension to the Oskar Reinhart gallery "Am Römerholz" in Winterthur (1993–98; see p.466), Gigon & Guyer used large panels of prefabricated concrete mixed with Jura limestone and copper powder to obtain a material that will gradually develop a green patina and slowly age in keeping with the rest of the buildings.

The central question is not just what material to use but how to use it in a way that is free of conventions and preconceptions. In **Therme Vals** (1990–96; see p.517), Peter Zumthor employs traditional stone in an elegantly detailed manner to finish both the interior and exterior, creating a sublime building of closed spaces and sensual lighting, protected from the harsh surrounding landscape. The pivotal point in this case is the very Swiss attitude of an obsessive attention to detail and craftsmanship: architecture as the art of constructing well. Zumthor is also the author of the chapel of San Benedetg in Somvitg, near Disentis/Mustér (1987–88), a replacement for a hillside church that had been destroyed by an avalanche. The texture of traditional wooden cladding contrasts with the abstract, sculptural shape of the deceptively simple geometrical building. The chapel is wrapped in strips of larch which weather and gradually change colour over time, altering the perception of the volume.

This concentration on shape in contemporary Swiss-German architecture has been defined as the creation of "**Forceful Forms**". The buildings are conceived as intense, geometric volumes with a simplicity that exalts their shape, material, texture and colour – an attitude towards design that is clearly heavily indebted to the artistic movements of Concrete Art, Abstractism and Minimalism. Gigon & Guyer's Museum Liner in Appenzell (1996–98; see p.486) is a saw-tooth roofed volume clad uniformly with sandblasted sheets of stainless steel. The sophisticated result is both an everyday industrial-looking building and an enigmatic structure dominating this small village. One of the numerous projects commissioned by Swiss Federal Railways is Herzog & de Meuron's signal box on the edge of the train tracks at Basel SBB station (1989–94). A concrete box wrapped with copper bands to form a Faraday cage, this abstract object stands laconically detached among the unruly overhead cables, railway tracks and train sheds. It is not simply a building but a presence in the urban landscape.

Critics have described these designs as "**Swissbox architecture**", maligning the emphasis put on the envelope of the building and the lack of interest in the creation of internal space. There are undeniably numerous projects where the design focus is very firmly on the treatment of the facade, but, more often than not, this is a strength more than a detraction. In Herzog & de Meuron's Ricola production and storage building in Mulhouse (1992–93), just north of Basel in France, the design on the exterior transforms a conventional warehouse into a representative focus. In their university library in Eberswalde, Germany (1994–99), the unassuming bulk of an anonymous building is defined by the historical and artistic photographs printed on the panels of the facade. In both these cases, by choosing to screen-print on such everyday materials as polycarbonate or prefabricated concrete panels, the architects have shifted attention from the conventional interior spaces and transformed relatively modest construction opportunities into truly emblematic buildings.

Crossing borders

The natural consequence of the international acclaim of the 1990s has been some exciting commissions abroad for Swiss architects. Herzog & de Meuron have been building across the globe: their numerous high-profile projects include the remodelling of Bankside power station in **London** into the Tate Modern gallery (1995–99), and the masterly Dominus Winery in the Napa Valley, **California** (1995–98). Peter Zumthor has taken his expressive poeticism across the Swiss frontier to the Kunsthalle in **Bregenz**, Austria (1989–97), and has also been commissioned to build a Diocesan Museum on a sensitive, historical site in **Cologne** (1997–2004).

Hand-in-hand with the rise in profile for Swiss architecture have been invitations to foreign architects to contribute to the built fabric of Swiss cities. In 1990 **Jean Nouvel** won the first architectural competition in Switzerland that was not restricted to Swiss residents. With its over-sized canopy, his striking KKL complex (1992–98; see p.387), in a splendid location on the shore of Lake Luzern, creates a powerful new urban space. **Renzo Piano** is following up his serene Fondation Beyeler in Riehen, near Basel (1991–97; see p.221), with an impressive project for a new Paul Klee centre, outside Bern (1999–2005; see p.252) – the building's undulating roof has been conceived as a sculptural modification of the landscape. And to confirm the opinion that architecture has become an international showbiz affair, **Daniel Libeskind**'s popular fragmented gestures are to be employed in the huge Westside leisure complex on the outskirts of Bern (2001–06; see p.238).

by Lucy Ratcliffe

Alpine flora and fauna

From valley floor to mountain summit Switzerland enjoys a wide range of wildlife and botanical habitats. Thanks to the huge difference in altitude, climate and vegetation zones, there's nearly always something of interest to see, whether you're a dedicated naturalist, expert botanist or just a visitor with an interest in the overall mountain environment.

Fauna

In the distant past the Swiss Alps were inhabited by such creatures as the cave bear, cave lion and panther; not more than a few hundred years ago the most prolific animals found in the Alpine valleys included the lynx and wildcat, and the wolf. Periods of glaciation drove the first group from the mountains, while hunters reduced the numbers of the latter: the last wolf in Switzerland was thought to have been shot in 1947, but a handful of recent suspected sightings of wolves in the Valais are under investigation by naturalists. Hunting is still popular today, but is generally under strict controls. The **Parc Naziunal Svizzer** in the Lower Engadine (Swiss National Park; see p.529) is a haven for numerous resident and migratory animals, and is perhaps the country's most rewarding location for the casual wildlife observer, since something like half of the seventy species of mammals found in Switzerland can be seen there.

Alpine fauna is noted for its extreme shyness, which is why observation can be difficult, but many animals that inhabit the more remote regions of the high Alps also descend to lower altitudes. The following survey, though by no means comprehensive, picks out the highlights.

Mammals

The **red deer** (*Cervus elaphus*) had disappeared from much of the country before the National Park was established in 1914, but natural migration from neighbouring regions of Austria saw a steady repopulation in the forested valleys of Graubünden. The adult male dominates a harem of several hinds, and vigorously defends them against all challengers. Fawns are born in May or June and are suckled for three or four months, remaining within easy reach of forest shelter. In summer the adult coat is reddish brown, turning grey-brown in winter. The much smaller **roe deer** (*Capreolus capreolus*) has similar colouring, is timid but also very inquisitive, and can be found roaming around the upper timber line. The best time to observe roe deer is in the early morning, or towards dusk when they stray from tree cover to open meadows and favoured drinking pools. The adult male sprouts slender horns, which are shed during the autumn, at the end of the rut.

The **red squirrel** (*Sciurus vulgaris*), like its American grey cousin in England, favours a woodland habitat and is fairly common throughout Switzerland. Despite the name its coat is dark brown, or almost black, and the female produces up to seven young, born naked and blind in a spherical drey. The **European lynx** (*Lynx lynx*) was reintroduced into the Swiss Alps in 1970. Weighing 20–30kg, it lives in the forests where it preys on birds and mammals up to the size of a roe deer, which it kills with a bite through the neck. Casual sightings are extremely rare. The **wildcat** (*Felis silvestris*) is another elusive forest animal. Larger than the domestic cat, it nevertheless has a purr not unlike that of an ordinary moggie, but a miaow that is deeper and more powerful. A few specimens were released into the wild near Interlaken, and others in the

Jura, but it is still by no means common. The **Alpine hare** (*Lepus timidus*) has a wide distribution in northern Europe and is found in open country both below and above the tree line, to about 3000m. In winter its coat is white; in summer, brown with white patches. Thanks to the production of two, and sometimes three, litters a year, the hare manages to maintain its numbers against the ravages of a variety of carnivores.

Throughout the Alps the shrill, high-pitched alarm whistle of the **marmot** (*Marmota marmota* – or *Murmeltier* in German) will be heard from late spring until early autumn. One of the most widespread of all Alpine rodents, it is ever wary of such predators as the fox and eagle, for which it forms the chief food source. Living in burrows, mostly above the tree line, the marmot hibernates in a "nest" of dried grasses for as many as seven months a year in the upper regions around 3000m, or five to six months at lower altitudes. At the end of hibernation pairing occurs almost at once, and after a 33-day gestation period the young are born, naked and with eyes closed. The young do not emerge from their burrows much before the end of July, by which time they've grown a covering of fur, and are able to attack the coarse meadow grasses with their razor-like teeth. An adult grows to a length of 48–56cm, with a 16–20cm tail, and by September weighs around 4–6kg, although some males can weigh up to 9kg. They live to approximately ten years, although some have been known to reach twenty.

The **chamois** (*Rupicapra rupicapra* – or *Gemse* in German) is found not only in the Alpine regions, but also in the lower Jura mountains of the west and northwest of Switzerland. Although sought by hunters in the autumn, in select areas it has enjoyed protected status since the sixteenth century. The Engadine is thought to have one of Europe's largest populations of this handsome antelope-like ruminant with short hooked horns and a russet coat sometimes lightening to fawn-grey in summer. Noted for its agility, it is also prone to disease, especially the notorious chamois-blindness that occasionally devastates complete herds. The rut finishes in November and the young are born between mid-May and mid-June after a gestation of 160–180 days. A fully grown chamois reaches 1.10–1.30m in length and weighs up to 50kg (male) or 30–35kg (female). Longevity is about twenty years. They can be seen, either singly or in herds, throughout the Swiss Alps – but rarely at close quarters.

While the chamois has short but graceful horns, the stockier male **ibex** (*Capra ibex* – or *Steinbock* in German) has large, knobbly, scimitar-shaped horns which are used as weapons during the battles for dominance that accompany the autumn rut. Defeated males must then wait their turn for sexual maturity until they are able to defend a harem of their own. Although the chamois ranges high in the mountains, the ibex zone is even higher: some have been sighted at over 4000m. For the greater part of the year it lives above the tree line, often roaming to the high snows in summer, but occasionally descending to the forests in winter. Weighing up to 100kg, the ibex negotiates narrow rock ledges with confidence and precision despite its stocky body and comparatively short legs, and apparently displays great care when crossing slopes threatened by avalanche. A sizeable herd roams the upper slopes of Piz Albris near Pontresina in Val Bernina, another can be seen high above Val de Bagnes in the Valais, often grazing close to the Sentier de Chamois hiking trail.

Birds

In woodlands of the Alpine foothills, and in the Jura, the bizarre call of the **capercaillie** (*Tetrao urogallus*) rattles in the early hours of a spring dawn: first a pop, then another, followed by a quickening succession that precedes what can only be described as a cork being drawn from a bottle. The capercaillie is scarce enough in the Alps to create a thrill of excitement when heard or seen – its dark shape has easy camouflage in a beech, larch or pine wood where it can feed on assorted berries, buds and needles, but where it can also fall prey to such predators as the fox and marten, while the young are sometimes taken by a goshawk or golden eagle.

Game birds of the forest regions are notoriously difficult to observe except when accidentally flushed out of cover. The hazel hen (*Tetrastes bonasia*), black grouse (*Lyrurus tetrix*), ptarmigan (*Lagopus mutus*) and rock partridge (*Alectoris graeca*) are all found in the National Park, as is the long-billed woodcock (*Scolopax rusticola*), in marshy ground near the tree line. Other woodland birds found in Switzerland include a number of **owls**: the eagle owl, tawny, long-eared, pygmy, and small, golden-eyed tengmalm's owl (*Aegolius funereus*), which takes over the abandoned nests of woodpeckers. There are several species of **woodpecker** too, notably the green, great-spotted, black, and rare three-toed woodpecker (*Picoides tridactylus*), all of which are found at some time or other in the forests of the National Park.

There's no shortage of songbirds, most of which are widely distributed throughout Europe, but it is the mountain specialists that are notable in the high Alpine regions and whose presence adds an extra dimension to the climber's day: the **alpine accentor** (*Prunella collaris*), for example, whose nest has been discovered above 3000m and whose song resembles that of the lark, as does its mating flight. Another is the brightly coloured **rock thrush** (*Monticola saxitilis*) that returns to the Alps in mid-May after wintering in tropical Africa. Then there's the **alpine chough** (*Pyrrhocorax graculus*), whose aerial acrobatics, yellow beak and strident call are familiar to all who visit the hikers' huts in the high mountains, where this gregarious bird comes as a scavenger after leftover scraps of food.

The **golden eagle** (*Aquila chrysaetus*) builds its eyrie on inaccessible rock ledges high in the mountains, and with no shortage of sites to choose from, and no shortage of prey either, there's a fair chance of spotting one of these graceful predators sailing over the high pastures in search of food. The golden eagle has a broad appetite: although its basic diet in the summer consists of marmot, it will also strike grouse and mountain hare, and may even try to take the young of chamois and red deer. Since it makes short work of sick and weak animals, its contribution to the maintenance of strong, healthy species is significant.

Flora

The range of **plants** found in Switzerland is enormous, as one might expect in a country whose soil, habitat, climate and altitude varies from region to region and, in some cases, from one valley to the next. Igneous rocks may dominate in one district, with more plant-friendly limestone in another. Habitats vary from damp grassland to semi-arctic rockface, from desert-like scree to shady woodland, from glacial moraine to the marshy fringe of a mountain lake, from a sunny cliff or stretch of limestone pavement to an acid valley bog. Each has its own specific flora. Mountains create their own microclimate: one side may be damp, the other protected in a rain shadow. A south-facing hillside will be different from the opposite, north-facing slope, and on a mountainside the seasons change, not by the calendar, but by altitude. All these factors have an effect on the plant life, as do grazing and cultivation of the soil.

In the lower valleys **soldanellas**, **primulas**, **crocus**, **anemones** and others come into flower early in the year as the snow melts, and having bloomed they wither and all but disappear, with only their leaves remaining hidden beneath the new grass of the meadowlands. But as the season advances and the snow recedes, so the same flowers appear higher up the hillside. By mid-June or July, alongside many other plants, they colour the "alps" – the upper pastures – before cattle are brought up for summer grazing. Before the end of July most of the pasture flowers will have gone, but it is then that the screes, moraine walls and rockfaces display their own special Alpine flora.

Of the early pasture and meadowland flowers the **pasque flower** comes in several forms. *Pulsatilla vernalis*, or the spring pasque flower, has its white petals often flushed a pale violet on the outside, while the alpine pasque flower (*Pulsatilla alpina*) is protected from the cold by a coating of tiny hairs. The tiny **alpine snowbell** (*Soldanella alpina*) on the other hand has no apparent protection, even though it often pushes its way through the melting snowfields. Its tassled petals vary from violet to pink-blue depending on habitat, for it may be found on sites as diverse as shallow pockets of limestone, and damp pastures up to 3000m. The **lily** family is another pasture and meadowland favourite that comes in many forms, including asphodel, crocus, fritillary and scilla. The claret-headed martagon lily (*Lilium martagon*) appears in shady woodland glades of the Jura, while the extravagant, showy orange lily (*Lilium bulbiferum*) adorns grassy terraces above Urnerboden.

If the lily family has spawned a variety of species, the **gentian** is even more numerous, and in Switzerland is represented by such extremes as the tall, multi-flowered great yellow gentian (*Gentiana lutea*), whose starry flowers burst from an upright stem, to the tiny, delicate blue favourite, the spring gentian (*Gentiana verna*), and deep royal blue – almost navy – of the trumpet gentian (*Gentiana kochiana*), that sometimes appears to have practically no stem at all, but produces flowers almost as it emerges from the turf.

The low-growing, evergreen **alpenrose** shrub (*Rhododendron ferrugineum*) has a remarkably wide range throughout the Alps, flowering pink to deep red on hillsides up to 3200m between June and August, and where it forms a carpet the summer display can be extremely attractive. The **creeping azalea** (*Loiseleuria procumbens*) is a member of the same family and has similar colouring. But this plant prefers exposed peaty sites, and is often found on acid soils, growing at altitudes of 1500–3000m. Forming cushions over rocks and screes, the **moss campion** (*Silene acaulis*) is a mass of pink in a bed of deep green, an eye-catching beauty, while the rosettes of the **common houseleek** (*Sempervivum tectorum*) can decorate otherwise drab moraines when they produce their stalk of bright pink flower heads in summer.

And of course there's the **edelweiss** (*Leontopodium alpinum*), whose woolly grey flowers have for some reason become prized above all other mountain plants. Found usually, but not exclusively, on limestone, it may be seen clustered in short grass overlooking a glacier, or thrusting from a cliff face. Its distribution in Switzerland ranges from the Engadine to the Bernese and Pennine Alps, flourishing between 1700 and 3400m.

by Kev Reynolds

Books

It's surprisingly hard to find books about Switzerland. Go to any large bookstore, and you'll see plenty of shelves devoted to the history and politics of Germany, France, Italy and the rest of Europe, but you'll be lucky to find a single work on Switzerland. Literature is the same, with Swiss authors rarely reaching audiences in their native languages outside the borders of their own country, let alone getting translated into English for a wider market.

Pro Helvetia, the federally funded Arts Council of Switzerland, publishes a range of slim paperbacks giving erudite background to the country and its culture in English; subjects covered include music, theatre, literature, composers, dance and ballet, media, cinema, architecture, philosophy, politics, social structure, refugees, multilingualism, and more. You can get any or all of them for free by contacting your nearest Swiss embassy, or order online at ⓦwww.pro-helvetia.ch.

Publishers are listed below in the form of UK publisher/US publisher, where both exist. "UP" stands for University Press, "o/p" signifies out of print. "Bergli" refers to **Bergli Books** (ⓦwww.bergli.ch), an English-language Swiss publisher which produces and distributes a range of books on Switzerland. Books tagged with the ▣ symbol are particularly recommended.

Travel

Early travellers

When the first *Murray's Handbook* to Switzerland appeared in 1838, there had already been a couple of centuries or more of travelogues telling of adventures had while on long crossings of the Alps; throughout the nineteenth century, the trickle of memoirs became a flood. Most of these venerable tomes are now long out of print, and the list below is a small selection of more widely available works.

Peter Arengo-Jones *Queen Victoria in Switzerland* (Robert Hale). Absorbing transcript of Victoria's diaries from her incognito stay in Luzern in August 1868, along with a commentary weaving events into the context of historical and political events of the day.

Mavis Coulson *Southwards to Geneva* (Alan Sutton). Well-researched survey of two centuries of English travellers' musings on Geneva and the Swiss, including excerpts from the writings of Boswell, Maria Edgeworth, Byron, Shelley and more, along with plenty of pictures, engravings and sketches.

Elma Dangerfield *Byron & the Romantics in Switzerland 1816* (Thomas Lyster). Slim account of the travels, passions and writings of Byron, Shelley *et al* on their famous visit to Lake Geneva.

Alexandre Dumas *Travels in Switzerland* (Owen o/p). Entertaining tales of Dumas's journeyings around Switzerland in 1832, at the age of 25.

▣ **Heinrich Harrer** *The White Spider* (Flamingo). Classic mountaineer's tale of the first ascent of the North Face of the Eiger in July 1938 by a four-man team from Germany. Full of thrills, spills and vivid writing.

★ **Jim Ring** *How the English Made the Alps* (John Murray). Comprehensive and well-written account of English involvement in Alpine travel and exploration, from the eighteenth century to the phenomenal growth in winter sports in the mid-twentieth. The evocation of Victorian imperial ambition, set against the backdrop of the conquest of Alpine peaks and the rise in tourism, is outstanding.

Mark Twain *A Tramp Abroad* (Oxford UP) and *Climbing the Rigi* (Hürlimann). Wry, witty and hugely enjoyable tales of mountain climbing and exploration in the Alps when such a thing was the height of fashion.

Edward Whymper *Scrambles Amongst the Alps* (Dover). Modern reprint of the nineteenth-century mountaineer's original account of the conquest of the Matterhorn, amongst many other epic tales of adventure.

Modern travellers and expat life

Paul N. Bilton *The Perpetual Tourist: In Search of a Swiss Role* (Bergli). A diary of an Englishman living in Switzerland, documenting the author's various attempts to bridge the cultural divide. The author quote on the back says it all: "The British look for humour in everything; the Swiss are brought up not to expect it." His *Laughing Along With the Swiss* (Bergli) is in much the same vein.

★ **Dianne Dicks (ed)** *Ticking Along With the Swiss, Ticking Along Too* and *Ticking Along Free* (Bergli). Entertaining collections of personal stories from travellers to Switzerland and various expats living and working there – light reading that offers a sidelong glance at the people and the culture.

Eugene V. Epstein *Once Upon an Alp* (Bergli). Wry vignettes of life in Switzerland through American/Swiss eyes, out of print since the 1960s and now republished.

Shirley Eu-Wong *Culture Shock! Switzerland* (Kuperard). Slim, chatty trawl through the idiosyncracies of Swiss society, written more for arriving expats than tourists, though with handy bits and pieces for all.

David Hampshire *Living and Working in Switzerland* (Survival). A complete rundown of rules and regulations for those planning to emigrate, either permanently or just for the winter ski-bum season, along with a raft of useful tips on how to avoid the worst of the bureaucracy.

★ **Margaret Oertig-Davidson** *Beyond Chocolate: Understanding Swiss Culture* (Bergli). Outstanding dissection of the country and its mentality – one of the most insightful books on Switzerland available in English. Ostensibly targeted at expats and long-term visitors, this is nonetheless invaluable for anyone wanting to get a handle on how the place works beneath the stereotypes and the touristic images.

Susan Tuttle *Inside Outlandish* (Bergli). Brief little book that playfully tries to bridge the expat gap, explaining the Swiss to outsiders and outsiders to the Swiss.

Vitali Vitaliev *Little is the Light* (Simon & Schuster). Subtitled "Nostalgic travels in the mini-states of Europe", this is a trail through Luxembourg, San Marino, the Isle of Man, and various other statelets by an award-winning Russian journalist – the chapter on Liechtenstein is an especially witty and engaging portrait of the country, and one of the few to take the place at least halfway seriously.

Guidebooks

★ **Peter Habicht** *Lifting the Mask* (Bergli). Unassuming little volume that dissects the Basel *Fasnacht* (carnival) in minute detail. Written by a local historian and *Fasnachtler*, it gives unprecedented insight into this odd event.

Marcia & Philip Lieberman

Switzerland's Mountain Inns
(Countryman, US). Lovingly folksy
walking tour of many isolated
Berghäuser tucked away in the remote
Alps, along with plenty of tried and
trusted advice for hikers looking to
get away from it all. Their *Walking
Switzerland The Swiss Way*
(Mountaineers, US) is a quality
guide to walks throughout the country, with full background, plus plenty
of trail information and practical
guidelines.

⭐ **Kev Reynolds** *Walking in the
Alps, The Valais, The Bernese Alps,
Central Switzerland, The Jura* (with R.
Brian Evans), *The Engadine, Walking
in Ticino, The Alpine Pass Route*, and
*Chamonix to Zermatt: The Walker's
Haute Route* (all Cicerone, UK; some
Hunter, US, others Interlink, US).
The classic Swiss walking guides,
vividly and knowledgeably written,
containing detailed route descrip-
tions and sketch-maps. *Walking in the
Alps* is the largest, an amalgam of
several long-distance routes with
new trails; all the others are neat
little volumes concentrating on particular areas or hikes.

Ian Robertson *Blue Guide:
Switzerland* (A&C Black/Norton).
Encyclopedic historical and architectural tour of the whole country,
packed with detail on virtually every
historical building and a wealth of
sketched-out mountain walks and
climbs.

Alexander Schwab *Lake Thun*
(Bergli). Coffee-table tome (in
English), packed with photos, evok-
ing this most beautiful of Swiss lakes.

⭐ **Peter Studer, et al** *Berne: A
Portrait of Switzerland's Federal
Capital, of its people, culture and spirit*
(Bergli). Another interesting, photo-
laden coffee-table book, written by
Bernese insiders.

Elisabeth Upton-Eichenberger
Vaud and *Zermatt* (Upton-
Eichenberger, UK). Excellent self-
published guides to two of the
country's most celebrated corners,
full of tales, historical odds and ends,
and other delightfully long-winded
material that gets edited out of most
orthodox guidebooks.

History and society

**Nicolas Bouvier, Gordon A.
Craig & Lionel Gossman** *Geneva,
Zürich, Basel* (Princeton UP).
Learned modern-day portrait of the
three biggest and most important
Swiss cities, pulling in strands of history, culture and national identity to
paint a picture of present-day Swiss
urbanism.

Joy Charnley & Malcolm Pender
(eds) *Images of Switzerland: Challenges
from the Margins* (Peter Lang, Bern).
Slender collection of essays published by the Centre for Swiss
Cultural Studies at Glasgow
University, including a review of historical attitudes towards the Jews
before World War II, and assessments
of themes of marginalization in
recent Swiss-German, -French and
-Italian literature.

Walter Dettwiler *William Tell:
Portrait of a Legend* (Swiss National
Museum). Fascinating little study of
the web of tales surrounding the
Swiss national hero, and the many
different ways the story has been
told over the centuries to suit the
concerns of each particular age.

⭐ **Dieter Fahrni** *An Outline
History of Switzerland* (Pro
Helvetia). Compact 130-page
overview of the main events in Swiss
history from Julius Caesar to the
Nazi gold scandal, a little gushing on
recent events and accomplishments
(this is, after all, published by the
official Arts Council of Switzerland)
but nonetheless valuable for its clarity and simplicity of approach.
Available free from Swiss embassies
worldwide.

Caroline Moorhead *Dunant's Dream* (HarperCollins). Subtitled "War, Switzerland and the History of the Red Cross", this is a massively detailed trawl through the previously closed archives of the Red Cross, documenting the history of the organization and the sometimes hesitant entanglements of its well-intentioned bureaucrats in the nastiest wars of the twentieth century.

★ Mitya New *Switzerland Unwrapped* (I.B. Tauris). Fascinating delve into the country's skeleton-rich cupboards, presenting eye-witness accounts of Swiss treatment of Jews and gypsies, attempts to solve Zürich's drug problems, traditional Swiss culture and how it fits into modern society, and more, well written by a Reuters journalist with an eye for a story.

Joachim Remak *A Very Civil War* (Westview Press). Illustrated chronicle of the Sonderbund war of 1847 that draws many parallels with the events of the American civil war that followed within fifteen years.

★ Jonathan Steinberg *Why Switzerland?* (Cambridge UP). Outstanding overview of Swiss society, history and culture, a learned yet anecdotal account of the country that is rich with detail but maintains a superb grasp of the wider picture.

Manages to give profound insight into how Switzerland works, and why it is the way it is, while remaining easily readable and digestible. Perfect train-journey reading: if you buy only one book about the country, buy this one.

John Wraight *The Swiss and the British* (Michael Russell o/p). Comprehensive study of relations between the two countries – political, cultural, sporting, military and more – in the form of an exhaustive chronology from the earliest times until the present day. Currently out of print, but scheduled for a new edition.

★ Jean Ziegler *The Swiss, The Gold and the Dead* (Harcourt Trade/Penguin). Of all the flood of books that jumped onto the bandwagon of the Nazi gold scandal once the depth of Swiss collaboration became clear, this was the most hard-hitting, written by a highly qualified academic at the University of Geneva and former parliamentarian – hounded and now politically ostracized for remaining uncowed by the storm of protest his revelations unleashed. His calm condemnation of the entire Swiss establishment for their role in funding the Nazis, prolonging the war and refusing to help the Jews is devastating.

Literature

Switzerland in foreign fiction

This is necessarily a tiny bite at a very large apple, a handful of personal selections that omits much more than it includes.

Anita Brookner *Hotel du Lac* (Penguin). A romantic novelist runs away from her impending marriage to spend a season at a grand hotel in a genteel lakeside resort (Vevey in all but name), and there finds what seems to be the start of a new life of freedom. Beautifully crafted prose, the best of Brookner's usually rather dry offerings, and winner of the

1984 Booker Prize.

★ Graham Greene *Dr Fischer of Geneva* (Penguin). Apocalyptic novella set in and around the lakeside residence of a rich misanthrope who decides to take his revenge on the fawning socialites who crave his money. A fluent and compelling read, published when Greene was 76.

Patricia Highsmith *Small g: a Summer Idyll* (Penguin). Highsmith – who spent her last years living in a Ticinese village – is best known for *Strangers on a Train* (made into a film by Alfred Hitchcock in 1951), along with her many works of crime fiction centred on Tom Ripley. *Small g* is focused on the characters who frequent a Zürich bar during one summer, with a story of love, sexuality and generosity expertly plotted around them. She died a month before its publication in 1995.

Henry James *Daisy Miller* (Penguin). The novella that made James's name, a witty, insightful portrait of a young American tourist visiting Lake Geneva who flirts and teases, and then travels to the Château de Chillon unchaperoned and so gets her comeuppance.

Thomas Mann *The Magic Mountain* (Minerva/Random House). Seminal World War I novel of ideas that employs a group of patients in a Davos sanatorium to discuss ideas of love, war and death, the characters' ongoing tuberculosis symbolizing the sickness of European society as a whole. Although this novel is acclaimed as the author's greatest, it was received less than favourably in Davos itself, whose residents objected to the town's portrayal as a place of neglect where sufferers stood little chance of being cured. This and Mann's other books were later burned by the Nazis in his native Germany.

Mary Shelley *Frankenstein* (Penguin). The famous tale of an idealistic doctor's dabblings with the elemental forces of life, inspired by "a half-waking nightmare" and written near Geneva in the summer of 1816 as Mary Shelley's offering in a ghost-story-writing competition dreamt up by Lord Byron.

Swiss authors

This is a choice of the handful of Swiss authors, classic and modern, whose works have been translated into English. Almost all are German Swiss. The couple of 1930s novels by the Lausannois writer Charles-Ferdinand Ramuz that have been translated into English – *Terror on the Mountain* and *When the Mountain Fell*, virtually the only works by any French Swiss authors to be published in English – are now out of print. The array of writings by the great Ticinese poet and novelist Francesco Chiesa, who died in 1973 at the age of 102, have yet to find an English translator, as do any by Romansh writers (bar a single out-of-print anthology).

Reto R. Bezzola *The Curly-Horned Cow: Anthology of Swiss-Romansh Literature* (o/p). The sole translation into English of any Romansh writing, now out of print.

Michael Butler & Malcolm Pender (eds) *Rejection and Emancipation* (Berg). Study of writing in German-speaking Switzerland between 1945 and 1991, with lit-crit essays on Frisch and Dürrenmatt, as well as Meyer, Loetscher, Schriber and others.

Max Frisch *Man in the Holocene* (Harcourt Brace). The most striking of the six novels by Frisch, who was born in Zürich in 1911 and is acclaimed as one of the century's greatest writers. This is a haunting but moving meditation on mortality, illuminating the slow decay of an old man's thought processes as he approaches death. Frisch's other novels are *Bluebeard*, *Gantenbein*, *Homo Faber*, his acclaimed masterpiece *I'm Not Stiller*, and *Montauk*.

Jeremias Gotthelf *The Black Spider* (Knightscross). Stories, tales and morality pieces from the nineteenth-century Emmental, as told by Gotthelf, a cleric turned author.

(Penguin). Hesse's best-known work, profound social deconstruction wrapped up as fantasy, which weaves strands of Eastern religion and mysticism into the compelling tale of a middle-aged misanthrope's progress towards social and spiritual maturity, "violently misunderstood" according to Hesse. Of his dozens of other works, *Siddhartha* is a graceful retelling of the legend of the Buddha; *Narziss and Goldmund* is a picaresque portrait of two monks, one a scholar, the other a bohemian; and *The Glass Bead Game* is a monumental utopian novel, set in a future where an elite group develops a game that resolves the world's conflicts.

Zoë Jenny *The Pollen Room* (Bloomsbury). An understated, mesmeric novel, translated from the German, poetically chronicling a marriage breakup through the eyes of a child. This is the first novel by Jenny, who was born in Basel in 1974.

Gottfried Keller *Green Henry* (John Calder). Massive tome of a novel, and a highly celebrated *Bildungsroman*, charting the Zürich-born author's country, youth and philosophy, written between 1846 and 1855 to a backdrop of unrequited love in Berlin.

Johanna Spyri *Heidi* (Penguin). Perhaps the most famous book ever written about Switzerland, but a hopelessly moralistic, cloying tale for all that. Spyri expertly evokes the folksiness and stolid culture of the Swiss Alpine farmers and effortlessly pulls heartstrings for her cheese-munching, milk-quaffing heroine.

★ **Beat Sterchi** *The Cow* (Faber, UK). Translated epic first novel set in a dairy farm and an abattoir, focusing on the experiences of a Spanish guest worker in Switzerland – Heaney-esque in its superb evocation of rural life. Not easy to read, but ultimately highly rewarding, praised by the *Guardian* for its "uncompromising magnificence as a work of art".

★ **Robert Walser** *Masquerade and other stories* (Quartet). Improvised prose poems and poetic short stories from Walser's life in four cities (Zürich, Berlin, Biel and Bern) over the period 1899–1933, tracing influences on Kafka and other avant-garde modernists. *The Walk* (Serpents Tail) is the best collection of his short fiction. The novel *Jakob von Gunten* (published in UK as *Institute Benjamenta*, Serpents Tail; and New York Review Books Classics), the dreamlike tale of a young man at a school for butlers, was filmed by Britain's Channel 4. After 1933, Walser spent his last 22 years in an asylum near Appenzell. "I wrote nothing more," he said. "What for? My world had been obliterated by the Nazis." It later transpired that he wrote a great deal, but what survives is in a tiny, almost indecipherable script: his strange, shifting novel *The Robber* (Nebraska UP) was published only recently, since it took decades for anyone to realize that the few pages of microscopic scribble comprised a complete novel. Hermann Hesse said of Walser: "If he had 100,000 readers, the world would be a better place."

Food and drink

Marianne Kaltenbach *Cooking in Switzerland* (Wolfgang Hölker, Münster, Germany). Friendly trot through some traditional Swiss recipes, heavy on the meat and cream.

John C. Sloan *The Surprising Wines of Switzerland* (Bergli). Best book by far on the variety of Swiss wines and viticulture, exploring each area – and virtually each vineyard – with enthusiasm and expertise.

△ A chilly voyage on the Thunersee (see p.306)

★ **Sue Style** *A Taste of Switzerland* (Bergli). Finest of the handful of cookery books devoted to Switzerland, with informed, interesting cultural background to local festivals and food celebrations dotted in amongst the recipes.

Architecture

Christoph Allenspach *Architecture in Switzerland: Building in the 19th and 20th centuries* (Pro Helvetia). Dry but authoritative volume published by the Swiss Arts Council (available for free from Swiss embassies).
Mercedes Daguerre *Birkhäuser Architectural Guide: Switzerland 20th century* (Birkhäuser). Pocket guide with exhaustive coverage of twenti-eth-century Swiss architecture, canton by canton.
★ **Jacques Lucan & Bruno Marchand (eds)** *A Matter of Art: Contemporary Architecture in Switzerland* (Birkhäuser). Attractive book offering detailed insight into Swiss architecture in the last ten years through a selection of emblematic buildings and analysis by experts.

Language

Language

German 616

French 618

Italian..619

Words and phrases...619

Swiss menu reader 625

Glossary 630

Swiss languages

F or a relatively small country bang in the heart of Western Europe, Switzerland has an astonishingly complicated array of languages to have to come to terms with. The one crumb of comfort is that almost everyone you'll come across will speak at least a smattering of English, and some Swiss are disconcertingly multilingual: fluency in four or five languages isn't as rare as you might assume.

There are four national languages in Switzerland. Broadly, **German** is spoken in the centre and the east; **French** in the west; **Italian** in the south; and **Romansh** in a few small areas of the southeast. The dividing lines between them (see map) mostly stem from the movements of tribal peoples in medieval times, and generally have nothing to do with the cantonal boundaries, which were drawn up much later. Cantons Bern, Fribourg and Valais are all bilingual German/French, while Graubünden is trilingual German/Italian/Romansh. According to census figures, 63.7 percent of the Swiss population consider German their main language, 20.4 percent French, 6.5 percent Italian and 0.5 percent Romansh (the rest are "others", principally English-speaking expats and international officials). However, more than one in ten of the Swiss population use English regularly every day alongside their own mother tongue.

All the spoken languages of Switzerland have differences from the orthodox standard versions used elsewhere that you may already have a grasp of. The German spoken in Switzerland, for instance, is completely different from that spoken in Germany or Austria, and has its own unique vocabulary, grammar

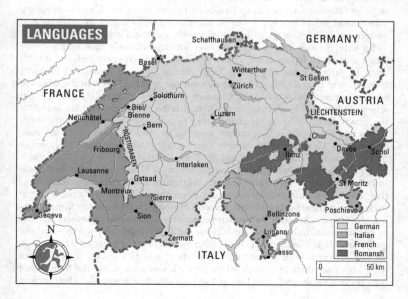

and syntax. Its umbrella title "Swiss German" covers a multitude of regional **dialects** with marked differences both from each other and from standard German: the dialect of Basel is different from that of Zürich, which is different again from that spoken in the high valleys of Oberwallis. In addition, both the French and Italian of Switzerland have small but noticeable differences from the "pure" languages spoken over the borders. Romansh (see p.512) has detectably the same Latin roots as French and Italian, but is different from both of them.

As for **phrasebooks**, Rough Guides' own *French*, *Italian* and *German* are handy (though you'll earn extra respect for attempting Swiss–German where possible), with dictionary-style listings both from and to English, as well as menu readers and grammar sections. The only Romansh-English/English-Romansh dictionary and phrasebook, by Manfred Gross & Daniel Telli, is published by Hippocrene (New York). Most useful of the lot is an invaluable little phrasebook of **all four Swiss languages** entitled *Schweizer Sprachen, Langues suisses, Lingue svizzere, Linguas svizras*, produced by Dynamicha, the movement for a multicultural Switzerland (⊛www.dynamicha.ch). There's not a word of English in it, so you'll need to be already grounded in at least one of the four in order to make sense of the rest.

German

Two forms of German are used in Switzerland. **High German** or *Hochdeutsch* (also known as *Schriftdeutsch*, "Written German") is the same language used throughout German-speaking Europe. **Swiss German**, or *Schwyzertütsch*, comprises dozens of regional dialects unique to Switzerland, and is unrecognizable to speakers of High German.

No one speaks High German in everyday situations in Switzerland: oral use of High German is restricted to school education, the mass media and public speaking. In all other situations, everyone naturally uses their own local dialect of Swiss German. And unlike in Britain or France, no one in German-speaking Switzerland strives to copy a Zürich accent or a Basel accent in order to gain greater credibility. Using the dialect of your home town is a source of pride.

However, Swiss German is hardly ever written. It's only relatively recently that a dictionary laying down agreed spellings has been compiled, and it's still open to some controversy: ask a Swiss person to write something in Swiss German and they'll probably struggle over the spelling. Everybody writes in High German (which is also the language of all signs and public notices) – but when reading out loud, they mentally transcribe the High German text into their own dialect of Swiss German as they're going along. People see the written word *Dienstag* (Tuesday), and say *tseeschtig*; or *Abend* (evening), and say *obik*. Many High German words simply aren't used: *guten Tag* (hello) is *grüezi* in Swiss German; *Straßenbahn* (tram) is *Tram*; *Fahrrad* (bicycle) is *Velo*; while regional differences mean that *Wiese* (meadow) is *Wise* in St Gallen but *Matte* in Bern. Add in a range of idiosyncratic regional **accents** that are much greater than the accent difference between, say, Munich and Hamburg; a tendency to stick the coy **diminutive** -*li* onto the end of nouns, and to use the throat-rasping **ch** (as in the Scottish *loch*) wherever possible; and a **stress pattern** that lays emphasis in unfamiliar places (usually on the first syllable of a word) – and the gulf from High German becomes unbridgeable. To a speaker of *Hochdeutsch*, Swiss-German sounds archaic and singsong… and this seems to delight the Swiss, who get their own back when they ask Germans to say the Swiss word for "kitchen cupboard": transliterated as *chuchichäschtli*, it sounds, when spoken correctly, like a cat coughing up a hairball. Even the Swiss affectionately dub their own language *Mundart*, or "mouth skill".

Much has been written about the role of Swiss German as an emblem and symbol of Swissness, and how the accent of each region reflects that region's character: the taut, stretched vowels of *Baseldytsch*; the slow, loping tone of *Berntütsch*; the clipped efficiency of *Züridütsch*; and so on. No Swiss would dream of erasing these differences beneath a unified norm – and no such norm exists. We've picked a rough transliteration of **Bernese dialect** to use here, which will be universally understood, even if they do say things slightly differently elsewhere. Even if you stumble and splutter, the very fact that you're attempting to get your tongue around Swiss German pronunciation at all will prove a winner with the locals – very much more so than if you were to launch without warning into the slick, snooty language of the "big canton", Germany.

Swiss German pronunciation

Any attempt to lay down rules for Swiss German **pronunciation** is doomed to failure, since pronunciation of vowels in particular varies from district to district, and even from village to village. The following is only the loosest of guidelines.

In written German, note that all nouns begin with a capital letter, and that an umlaut (¨) over a vowel is sometimes replaced by an "e": Zürich can be written as Zuerich. In Switzerland, the German letter ß is always written out as "ss".

Vowels

Most of the time, pronounce all vowels: *grüezi* has a definite "eh" in the middle, and *Grossbrittanie* has two vowel sounds at the end. However, *eis* has only one vowel sound. In our transliteration, a double vowel, such as in *Määntig* or *Ziischtig*, doubles the length of the sound.

a as in f**a**ther

ä is sometimes pronounced as in b**ea**r (eg Bärn) and sometimes as in p**ai**d (eg spät)

ai as in l**ie**

au as in h**ou**se

äu as in **oi**l

e as in d**ay** or w**e**t

ee roughly as in d**ay**

ei as in h**ei**ght or sometimes as in fr**ee**

eu approximates to an *ü* sound

i as in l**ee**k

ie as in fr**ee**

o as in b**o**ttom or r**o**se

ö is like the French eu, or the "urgh" in the middle of "colonel"

u as in b**oo**t

ü is like the French u, or a tight-lipped version of true

y is a double-length **ee** – Schwyz is pronounced shveets

Consonants

There are no silent **consonants**. Differences from English include:

ch is a strong throaty rasp, as in the Scottish *loch*

gg is pronounced "ck": "Egg" is *eck*, and may even be written as Eck

j is like an English y: "Jura" is *yoora*

k has a throaty rasp attached to it: *danke* is transliterated as *dunkcha*

s is like a softened English *z*

sp at the start of a word is pronounced *shp*

st is always pronounced *sht*

w is like an English *v*

z is always pronounced *ts*

French

Swiss **French** is much less fraught with idiosyncracies than Swiss German: dialect, though still used in the hinterlands of the Jura, has virtually died out. Differences do remain from standard French – principally in accent and inflection – but the Gallic aspirations of most locals mean that you can speak whatever French you know and be both understood and respected. Indeed, in sharp contrast to France, in Romandie you can even speak English with impunity. The surprising thing is that very few French Swiss speak or understand German. High German – dubbed, with a Gallic disdain for the messy *patois* of their compatriots, *le bon allemand* – is taught in some schools beyond elementary level, but generally only as an optional subject. (On the other hand, most schools in German-speaking Switzerland teach French until leaving age.) French Swiss have virtually no opportunity to learn anything of spoken Swiss German without going to live and work on the other side of the language border and picking it up bit by bit.

The most noticeable differences between Swiss-French and standard French are in just a handful of words: instead of *soixante-dix*, *quatre-vingts* and *quatre-vingt-dix*, "seventy", "eighty" and "ninety" are *septante*, *huitante* and *nonante* respectively (although in recent years the influence of international banking in Geneva has encouraged the adoption there of the orthodox French usage of *quatre-vingts* instead of *huitante*). A PO box is a *boîte postale* in France but a *case postale*, or CP, in Switzerland. And in the Fribourgeois countryside, the *-ens* ending of place names such as Vuadens is pronounced in full (*voo-a-donce*) instead of the final *s* remaining silent.

French pronunciation

French **pronunciation** can be hard to master, not least because of the tight-lipped precision of many of the sounds compared with slack-jawed English, as well as the lack of any marked stress patterns: in French, equal stress is given to all syllables in a word.

Vowels

a as in h**a**t	*ou* as in f**oo**d
au as in **o**ver	*u* is a tight-lipped version of the English tr**u**e
e as in g**e**t	
é between g**e**t and g**a**te	The following are extra-tricky nasal sounds:
è between g**e**t and g**u**t	*in/im* like a**n**xious
eu as in h**u**rt	*an/am* and *en/em* like **Don**caster said through your
i as in mach**i**ne	nose
o as in h**o**t	*on/om* like **Don**caster said with a heavy cold
ô as in **o**ver	*un/um* like **u**nderstand

Consonants

Consonants at the ends of words are usually silent: *pas plus tard* ("not later") is thus pronounced *pa-ploo-tarr*. However, when the following word begins with a vowel, you should run the consonant over: *pas après* ("not after") is *pazapray*. There are a few differences from English:

ch is an English *sh*	*ll* as in bayonet: "billet" is *bee-yay*
ç is an English *s*	*r* is growled rather than trilled
j as in plea**s**ure: "Jura" is *zhoora*	*th* is like an English *t* – "thé" is *tay*
h is silent	

Italian

In **Italian**-speaking Switzerland, written or High Italian is used less than the **Lombardic** dialect common to most of northern Italy. There are also about seven local **Ticinese** dialects, different again from each other and from Lombardic. Almost all Ticinesi are effectively **quadrilingual**: to friends and family, the language of intimacy is the home dialect; on the street, the language of friendly conversation is Lombardic; to strangers and where there's any element of reserve, the language of formality is High Italian; and, in addition, most Ticinesi are also proficient in German and/or Swiss German in order to communicate with the vast numbers of tourists from the north. English, although spoken by some, remains well down the list.

The upshot of this is that, even if you happened to be fluent in Lombardic dialect, everyone you met in Ticino would anyway instinctively speak to you – a stranger and a foreigner – in standard Italian, which is not excessively hard for English-speakers to master.

Italian pronunciation

Pronunciation is easy, since every word is spoken exactly as it is written and usually enunciated with exaggerated, open-mouthed clarity. The only slight difficulties come in the following **consonants**, which differ from English:

c before e or i is an English *ch*: "cioccolata" is *chokolata*

ch is an English *k*: "chiesa" is *kee-ay-za*

g before e or i is an English *j* – "Maggiore" is *madge-or-eh*, "giorno" is *jorno*

g before h as in **g**un

gli as in mi**lli**on: "figlia" is *feelya*

gn as in o**ni**on: "bagno" is *banyo*

h is silent

sci as in **shi**p

sce as in **she**d

z as in ba**ts**

Words and phrases

The basics

	Swiss German	French	Italian
good morning	guete Morge	bonjour	buongiorno
good evening	guete Obig	bonsoir	buona sera
hello/hi!	grüezi! (grüssech in Bern; grüess Gott in the east)	salut!	salve!/ciao!
cheers! (toast)	proscht!	santé!	salute!
enjoy your meal	enguete	bon appétit	buon appetito
goodbye	of Widerluege	au revoir	arrivederci
bye!	tschüss!/ciao!	salut!	ciao!
yes	jo	oui	si
no	nei	non	no
OK	OK	ça marche	va bene
please	bitte	s'il vous plaît	per favore
thank you (very much)	merci/dunkcha (vielmol)	merci (beaucoup)	(molte) grazie
you're welcome	bitte	je vous en prie	prego

	Swiss German	French	Italian
excuse me	entscholdigong	excusez-moi	mi scusi
I'm sorry	es tued mer leid	je suis désolé	mi dispiace
do you speak English?	reded Sii Änglisch?	parlez-vous anglais?	parla inglese?
I come from...	ich be vo...	je viens de...	vengo da...
Britain	Grossbritannie	Grande-Bretagne	Gran Bretagna
Ireland	Irland	Irlande	Irlanda
the US/Canada	d'Schtaate/Kanada	États-Unis/Canada	Stati Uniti/Canada
Australia	Auschtralie	Australie	Australia
New Zealand	Neuseeland	Nouvelle Zélande	Nuova Zelanda
I (don't) speak...	ich rede (ned)...	je (ne) parle (pas)...	io (non) parlo...
High German	Hochdütsch	allemand	tedesco
Swiss German	Schwyzertütsch	suisse allemand	svizzero-tedesco
French	Französisch	français	francese
Italian	Italiänisch	italienne	italiana
I (don't) understand	ich verschtoh (ned)	je (ne) comprends (pas)	(non) capisco

Directions and travel

	Swiss German	French	Italian
here/there	hier/dött	ici/là(-bas)	qui/li
left/right	links/rächts	gauche/droite	sinistra/destra
straight on	graduus	tout droit	sempre diritto
near/far	noch/wiit	près/loin	vicino/lontano
quick/slow	schnell/langsam	rapide/lent	rapido/lento
broad/narrow	breit/schmal	large/étroit	largo/stretto
train	Zug	train	treno
station	Bahnhof	gare	stazione
information	Auskunft	renseignements	informazioni
ticket office	Schalter	guichet	sportello
ticket	Billet	billet	biglietto
day card	Tageskarte	carte journalière	carta giornaliera
departure	Abfahrt	départ	partenza
arrival	Ankunft	arrivée	arrivo
which platform for the train to Zürich?	uf welem Gleis fahrt de Zog noch Züri?	sur quel quai part le train pour Zurich?	da quale binario parte il treno per Zurigo?
when does the train arrive in Geneva?	wenn chond de Zog z'Genf aa?	à quelle heure le train arrive-t-il à Genève?	quando arriva il treno a Ginevra?
change at Olten	umsteigen in Olten	changer à Olten	cambiare a Olten
lost-property office	Fundbüro	objets trouvés	oggetti smarriti
toilets	Toiletten/WC (spoken: vaytsay)	toilettes	gabinetti
women's toilet	Frauen/Damen	dames	signore
men's toilet	Männer/Herren	hommes	signori
postbus	Postauto	car postal	autopostale
bus stop	Haltestelle	arrêt	fermata
when does the bus to Chur leave?	wenn fahrt de Bus noch Chur?	à quelle heure part le bus pour Coire?	quando parte il auto-bus per Coira?
supplement	Zuschlag	supplément	sovratassa
tourist bus/coach	Car	autocar	pullman
(rental) car	(Miet)Auto	voiture (de location)	automobile (a noleggio)
parking area	Parkplatz	place de parc	parcheggio
covered car park	Parkhaus	parking	autosilo
available/full	frei/besetzt	libre/occupé	libero/occupato

Place names in Switzerland

German	French	Italian
Aare	Aar	Aar
Aargau	Argovie	Argovia
Basel-Land	Bâle-Campagne	Basilea campagna
Basel-Stadt	Bâle-Ville	Basilea città
Bergell	Bregaglia	Bregaglia
Bern	Berne	Berna
Biel	Bienne	Bienne
Bodensee	Lac de Constance	Lago di Constanza
Brig	Brigue	Briga
Chur	Coire	Coira
Delsberg	Delémont	Delémont
Freiburg	Fribourg	Friborgo
Genf	Genève	Ginevra
Genfersee	Lac Léman	Lago Lemano
Glarus	Glaris	Glarona
Gotthard	Gothard	Gottardo
Graubünden	Grisons	Grigioni
Greyerz	Gruyères	Gruyères
Jura	Jura	Giura
Konstanz	Constance	Constanza
Lausanne	Lausanne	Losanna
Lukmanier	Lukmanier	Lucomagno
Luzern	Lucerne	Lucerna
Mailand	Milan	Milano
Matterhorn	Cervin	Cervino
Murten	Morat	Morat
Neuenburg	Neuchâtel	Neuchâtel
Nidwalden	Nidwald	Nidvaldo
Nufenen	Nufenen	Novena
Obwalden	Obwald	Obvaldo
Ofen	Ofen	Fuorn
Österreich	Autriche	Austria
Pruntrut	Porrentruy	Porrentruy
Puschlav	Poschiavo	Poschiavo
Rhein	Rhin	Reno
Rotten	Rhône	Rodano
Sankt Gallen	St-Gall	San Gallo
Schaffhausen	Schaffhouse	Sciaffusa
Schweiz	Suisse	Svizzera
Schwyz	Schwytz	Svitto
Siders	Sierre	Sierre
Simplon	Simplon	Sempione
Sitten	Sion	Sion
Solothurn	Soleure	Soletta
Tessin	Tessin	Ticino
Thurgau	Thurgovie	Turgovia
Visp	Viège	Visp
Waadt	Vaud	Vaud
Wallis	Valais	Vallese
Zug	Zoug	Zugo
Zürich	Zurich	Zurigo

L

LANGUAGE | Words and phrases

	Swiss German	French	Italian
(steam-)boat	(Dampf)Schiff	bateau (à vapeur)	battello (a vapore)
breakdown	Panne	panne	panna
boat travel	Schifffahrt	navigation	navigazione
(rental) bike	(Miet)Velo	vélo (de location)	bicicletta (a noleggio)
mountain bike	Mountainbike	vélo tout terrain (VTT)	rampichino
airport	Flughafen	aéroport	aeroporto
police	Polizei	police	polizia
fire service	Feuerwehr	pompiers	pompieri
ambulance	Ambulance	ambulance	ambulanza

Hotels and shops

	Swiss German	French	Italian
entrance/exit	Eingang/Ausgang	entrée/sortie	entrata/uscita
emergency exit	Notausgang	sortie de secours	uscita di sicurezza
push/pull	drücken/ziehen	poussez/tirez	spingere/tirare
reception	Empfang	réception	ricezione
do you have any rooms available?	händ Sii noh freii Zimmer?	avez-vous des chambres libres?	ha camere libere?
I reserved a room	ich ha es Zimmer reserviert	j'ai réservé une chambre	ho riservato una camera
have you got...?	händ Sii...?	avez-vous...?	avete...?
I'd like...	ich hätt gärn...	j'aimerais...	vorrei...
a single room	Einzelzimmer	chambre simple	camera singola
a double room	Doppelzimmer	chambre double	camera doppia
with a shower	mit Dusche	avec douche	con doccia
with a bath	mit Bad	avec bain	con bagno
with a balcony	mit Balkon	avec balcon	con balcone
with a mountain/ lake view	mit Blick uf d'Berge/ uf de See	avec vue sur les montagnes/sur le lac	con vista sulle montagne/sul lago
without	ohne/oni	sans	senza
how much is the room?	was choschtet s'Zimmer?	combien coûte la chambre?	quanto costa la camera?
with breakfast	mit Frühstück	avec petit-déjeuner	con prima colazione
with half board	mit Halbpension	en demi-pension	mezza pensione
dormitory	Massenlager	dortoir	dormitorio
campsite	Campingplatz	camping	campeggio
fully booked	voll/besetzt	complet	completo
big/small	gross/chli	grand/petit	grande/piccolo
new/old	neu/alt	nouveau/vieux	nuovo/vecchio
hot/cold	warm/chalt	chaud/froid	caldo/freddo
clean/dirty	suber/dräckig	propre/sale	pulito/sporco
quiet/noisy	ruhig/lärmig	silencieux/bruyant	silenzioso/rumoroso
open/closed	offen/geschlossen	ouvert/fermé	aperto/chiuso
opening hours	Öffnungszeiten	heures d'ouverture	orari d'apertura
day off	Ruhetag	jour de repos	giorno di riposo
VAT (sales tax)	MWST	TVA	IVA

Numbers

	Swiss German	French	Italian
0	null	zéro	zero
half	halb	demi	mezzo
1	eis	un	uno

	Swiss German	French	Italian
2	zwöi	deux	due
3	drü	trois	tre
4	vier	quatre	quattro
5	füüf	cinq	cinque
6	sächs	six	sei
7	sibe	sept	sette
8	acht	huit	otto
9	nüün	neuf	nove
10	zää	dix	dieci
11	elf	onze	undici
12	zwölf	douze	dodici
13	drizää	treize	tredici
14	vierzää	quatorze	quattordici
15	föfzää	quinze	quindici
16	sächzää	seize	sedici
17	sibezää	dix-sept	diciasette
18	achzää	dix-huit	diciotto
19	nüünzää	dix-neuf	diciannove
20	zwänzg	vingt	venti
21	einezwänzg	vingt et un	ventuno
22	zwöiezwänzg	vingt-deux	ventidue
30	driisg	trente	trenta
40	vierzg	quarante	quaranta
50	föfzg	cinquante	cinquanta
60	sächzg	soixante	sessanta
70	sibezg	septante	settanta
80	achzg	huitante	ottanta
90	nüünzg	nonante	novanta
100	hondert	cent	cento
101	honderteis	cent un	centouno
200	zwöihondert	deux cents	duecento
1000	tuusig	mille	mille
2000	zwöituusig	deux mille	duemila
2004	zwöituusigundvier	deux mille quatre	duemila quattro
1st	erscht (1.)	premier (1er)	primo (1º)
2nd	zwöit (2.)	deuxième (2e)	secondo (2º)
3rd	dret (3.)	troisième (3e)	terzo (3º)
4th	viert (4.)	quatrième (4e)	quarto (4º)
5th	füüft (5.)	cinquième (5e)	quinto (5º)
once	einisch	une fois	una volta
twice	zwöimol	deux fois	due volte
three times	drümol	trois fois	tre volte

Telling the time

	Swiss German	French	Italian
what time is it?	was isch för Ziit?	quelle heure est-il?	che ora sono?
it's nine o'clock	es isch nüüni	il est neuf heures	sono le nove
1.05	füüf ab eis	une heure cinq	l'una e cinque
2.15	Viertel ab zwöi	deux heures et quart	le due e un quarto
5.45	Viertel vor sächsi	six heures moins quart	le sei meno un quarto
9.40	zwänzg vor zääni	dix heures moins vingt	le dieci meno venti
10.30	halbi elfi (ie half to 11)	dix heures et demie	le dieci e mezza

	Swiss German	French	Italian
noon	Mettag	midi	mezzogiorno
midnight	Metternacht	minuit	mezzanotte
an hour	e Schtond	une heure	un'ora
half-an-hour	e Halbschtond	une demi-heure	mezz'ora

Days and months

Beware that abbreviations of the days (for opening hours posted outside museums or shops) can be confusing: "Di" in French-speaking areas means Sunday, but in German-speaking areas means Tuesday. Similarly, "Do" is Thursday in German, but Sunday in Italian.

	Swiss German	French	Italian
Monday	Määntig (Mo)	lundi (lu)	lunedi (lu)
Tuesday	Ziischtig (Di)	mardi (ma)	martedi (ma)
Wednesday	Mettwoch (Mi)	mercredi (me)	mercoledi (me)
Thursday	Donnschtig (Do)	jeudi (je)	giovedi (gi)
Friday	Friitig (Fr)	vendredi (ve)	venerdi (ve)
Saturday	Samschtig (Sa)	samedi (sa)	sabato (sa)
Sunday	Sonntig (So)	dimanche (di)	domenica (do)
day	Tag	jour	giorno
in the morning	am Morge	le matin	la mattina
in the afternoon	am Nomitag	l'après-midi	di pomeriggio
in the evening	am Obig	le soir	di sera
at night	i de Nacht	la nuit	di notte
yesterday	geschter	hier	ieri
today	höt	aujourd'hui	oggi
tomorrow	morn	demain	domani
week	Woche	semaine	settimana
month	Monet	mois	mese
year	Johr	année	anno
spring	Früelig	printemps	primavera
summer	Sommer	été	estate
autumn	Herbscht	automne	autunno
winter	Wenter	hiver	inverno
January	Januar	janvier	gennaio
February	Februar	février	febbraio
March	März	mars	marzo
April	Aprel	avril	aprile
May	Mai	mai	maggio
June	Juni	juin	giugno
July	Juli	juillet	luglio
August	Auguscht	août	agosto
September	September	septembre	settembre
October	Oktober	octobre	ottobre
November	Novämber	novembre	novembre
December	Dezämber	décembre	dicembre

Swiss menu reader

Food and drink basics

	Swiss German	French	Italian
knife	Messer	couteau	coltello
fork	Gabel	fourchette	forchetta
spoon	Löffel	cuillère	cucchiaio
plate	Teller	assiette	piatto
napkin	Serviette	serviette	tovagliolo
bottle	Flasche	bouteille	bottiglia
glass	Glas	verre	bicchiere
cup	Tasse	tasse	tazza
menu	Speisekarte	carte	carta
bread	Brot	pain	pane
butter	Butter, Anke	beurre	burro
ham	Schinken	jambon	prosciutto
bacon	Speck	lardon	pancetta
cheese	Käse	fromage	formaggio
milk	Milch	lait	latte
whole milk	Vollmilch	lait entier	latte intero
skimmed milk	Magermilch	lait écrémé	latte scremato
buttermilk	Buttermilch	babeurre	latticello
yoghurt	Joghurt	yogourt	joghurt
cream	Rahm	crème	panna
egg	Ei	oeuf	uovo
jam	Konfitüre	confiture	marmellata
honey	Honig	miel	miele
tap water	Hahnenwasser	eau de robinet	acqua di rubinetto
mineral water	Mineralwasser	eau minérale	acqua minerale
juice	Saft	jus	succo
ice	Eis	glace	ghiaccio
a beer	e'Schtange	une pression	una birra
red wine	Rotwein	vin rouge	vino rosso
white wine	Weisswein	vin blanc	vino blanco
dry	trocken	sec	secco
sweet	süss	doux	dolce
sugar	Zucker	sucre	zucchero
salt	Salz	sel	sale
pepper	Pfeffer	poivre	pepe
oil	Öl	huile	olio
mustard	Senf	moutarde	senape
"waiter!"	"Bedienung!"	"Monsieur/Madame!"	"Cameriere/-a!"
"I'd like..."	"Ich nehme..."	"Je voudrais..."	"Vorrei..."
with	mit	avec	con
without	ohne	sans	senza
to eat	essen	manger	mangiare
to drink	trinken	boire	bere
non-smoking area	Nichtraucherzone	espace non-fumeurs	sezione non fumatori
breakfast	Frühstück, Zmorge	petit déjeuner	prima colazione
lunch	Mittagessen, Zmittag	déjeuner	pranzo
dinner/supper	Abendessen, Znacht	dîner	cena
the bill	die Rechnung	l'addition	il conto

I am a vegetarian (m/f)	Have you got any special dishes for
Ich bin Vegetarier/-in	vegetarians?
Je suis végétarien/-ne	Haben Sie spezielle Menus für
Sono vegetariano/-a	Vegetarier?
	Avez-vous des menus spéciaux pour
	les végétariens?
	Avete menù speciali per vegetariani?

Snacks and starters

	Swiss German	French	Italian
starters	Vorspeisen	hors d'oeuvres	antipasti
sandwich	Sandwich	sandwich	panino
chips (french fries)	Pommes frites	frites	patate fritte
crisps (potato chips)	Pommes Chips	pommes chips	patatine
omelette	Omelett	omelette	frittata
olives	Oliven	olives	olive
soup	Suppe	potage, consommé	zuppa, minestra
prawn cocktail	Krevetten Cocktail	cocktail des crevettes	cocktail di gamberi
green salad	Grüner Salat	salade verte	insalata verde
mixed salad	Gemischte Salat	salade mixte	insalata mista

Main courses

	Swiss German	French	Italian
main courses	Speisen	plats principaux	secondi piatti
meat	Fleisch	viande	carne
veal	Kalb	veau	vitello
beef	Rind	boeuf	manzo
pork	Schwein	porc	maiale
lamb	Lamm	agneau	agnello
chicken	Poulet	poulet	pollo
horse	Pferde	cheval	cavallo
fillet	Filet	filet	filetto
a chop	Kotelett	côtelette	cotoletta
diced meat	Geschnetzelte	émincé	spezzatino
mincemeat	Hackfleisch	hachée	carne macinata
liver	Leber	foie	fegato
kidney	Niere	rognon	rognone
sausage	Wurst	saucisse	salsiccia
rice	Reis	riz	riso
boiled potatoes	Salzkartoffeln	pommes nature	patate bollite
pasta	Teigwaren	pâtes	pasta
noodles	Nudeln	nouilles	tagliatelle
mushrooms	Pilze	champignons	funghi
fish	Fisch	poisson	pesce
salmon	Lachs	saumon	salmone
trout	Forelle	truite	trota
tuna	Thunfisch	thon	tonno

Vegetables

	Swiss German	French	Italian
vegetables	Gemüse	légumes	verdure
tomato	Tomate	tomate	pomodoro
carrot	Rüebli	carotte	carota
cabbage	Chabis	chou	cavolo
cauliflower	Blumenkohl	choufleur	cavolfiore
corn	Mais	maïs	mais
cucumber	Gurke	concombre	cetriolo
asparagus	Spargel	asperge	asparagi
beans	Bohnen	haricots	fagioli
peas	Erbse	poix	piselli
sweet pepper	Peperoni	poivron	peperone
spinach	Spinat	épinards	spinaci
fennel	Fenchel	fenouil	finocchio
broccoli	Broccoli	brocoli	broccolo
onion	Zwiebel	oignon	cipolla
garlic	Knoblauch	ail	aglio

Cooking terms

	Swiss German	French	Italian
hot	heiss	chaud	caldo
cold	kalt	froid	freddo
smoked	geräuchert	fumé	affumicato
roast	gebraten	rôti	arrosto
rare	bluetig	saignant	al sangue
well done	gar	bien cuit	ben cotto
boiled	gekochte	bouilli	bollito
steamed	gedämpft	à la vapeur	al vapore
stuffed	gefüllt	farci	farcito
grilled	gegrillt	grillé	alla griglia
raw	roh	cru	crudo
baked	gebacken	au four	al forno
fried	gebraten, fritiert	frite	fritto
spices	Gewürze	épices	spezie
traditional cooking	gutbürgerliche Küche	cuisine bourgeoise	cucina casalinga
Swiss-German cooking	Schweizer Küche	cuisine suisse alémanique	cucina svizzero tedesca
Swiss-French cooking	Welsche Küche	cuisine romande	cucina romanda
Ticinese cooking	Tessiner Küche	cuisine tessinoise	cucina ticinese
Romansh cooking	Romanische Küche	cuisine romanche	cucina romancia
in the style of	art	à la	al/alla
homemade	Hausgemacht	fait à la maison	fatto in casa

Fruit and desserts

	Swiss German	French	Italian
fruit	Früchte	fruits	frutta
apple	Apfel	pomme	mela
pear	Birne	poire	pera
plum	Zwetschge	prune	prugna

Basic Romansh

There's a survey of the various dialects of Romansh on p.512. Some similarities exist with Italian as regards pronunciation, but there are a few significant differences:

c before e or i is pronounced as in ba**ts**

ch before a or o is a palatal sneeze-like *tya* sound lost in the middle of sta**tu**te, almost an English *ch* but not quite; if there's a preceding *s*, Romansh separates the two with a hyphen – the Engadine town of Chamues-ch is pronounced something like *tyamwesh-tyuh*

ch before e or i is pronounced as in **c**at

g before e or i is pronounced as in **g**eranium

g before h is pronounced as in **g**arlic

gl before i and at the end of a word is like sta**lli**on

gn as in o**ni**on

h is silent

j is like an English y

qu before a, e or i as in **qu**ack

s before any consonant is like an English *sh*

tg is like an English *ch*: "notg" sounds like *notch*

The basics

hello	allegra
good morning	bun di
good afternoon or good evening	buna saira
goodbye	a revair
bye!	ciao!
yes	gea
no	na
OK	va bain
please	anzi
thank you (very much)	grazia (fitg)
pardon!	perdunai!
excuse me	perstgisai
I am	jau sun
I'm from...	jau vegn...
I'm sorry	i ma displascha
I (don't) speak Romansh	jau (na) cur (betg) rumantsch
I (don't) understand	jau (na) chapesch (betg)
Do you speak English?	Discurris Vus englais?

Travel, hotels and shops

train	tren
station	staziun
information	infurmaziuns
ticket	bigliet
Where can I get a post bus to Chur?	Nua partan ils autos postals per Cuira?
bus stop	fermada
I'd like	jau avess gugent
a single room	chombra singula
a double room	chombra dubla
with a basin	cun aua currenta
with a shower	cun duscha
with a bath	cun bogn
how much is the room?	quant custa la chombra?
with breakfast	cun ensolver
with half board	mesa pensiun
dormitory	champ da massa
campsite	plazza de campar
open/closed	avert/serrà
day off	di da repaus

	Swiss German	French	Italian
peach	Pfirsich	pêche	pesca
cherry	Kirsche	cerise	ciliegia
grape	Trauben	raisin	uva
raspberry	Himbeere	framboise	lampone
strawberry	Erdbeere	fraise	fragola

Eating and drinking

Could we have a table in a non-smoking section?
Pudessan nus avair ina maisa en il sectur da nunfimaders?

bread	paun
butter	paintg
cheese	chaschiel
soup	schuppa
beef	bov
veal	vadè
pork	portg

chicken	pulaster
game	selvaschina
sausage	liongia
fish	pesch
potato	tartuffel
vegetables	verdura
fruit	fritgs
water	aua
white/red wine	vin alv/ cotschen
a beer	ina biera
cheers! (toast)	viva!

Numbers

0	nulla	7	set	14	quattordesch
1	in	8	otg	15	quindesch
2	dus	9	nov	16	sedesch
3	trais	10	diesch	17	deschset
4	quatter	11	indesch	18	deschdotg
5	tschintg	12	dudesch	19	deschnov
6	sis	13	tredesch	20	ventg

Days and months

Monday	glindesdi	today	oz
Tuesday	mardi	tomorrow	damaun
Wednesday	mesemna	January	schaner
Thursday	gievgia	February	favrer
Friday	venderdi	March	mars
Saturday	sonda	April	avrigl
Sunday	dumengia	May	matg
day	di	June	zercladur
in the morning	la damaun	July	fanadur
at noon	a mezdi	August	avust
in the afternoon	il suentermezdi	September	settember
in the evening	la saira	October	october
at night	la notg	November	november
at midnight	a mesanotg	December	december
yesterday	ier		

apricot	Aprikose	abricot	albicocca
orange	Orange	orange	arancia
grapefruit	Grapefruit	pamplemousse	pompelmo
lemon	Zitrone	citron	limone
cake	Kuchen, Torte	gâteau, tarte	torta
chocolate	Schokolade	chocolat	cioccolata
ice cream	Glace	glace	gelato

Glossary

German

Abfahrt departure
Achtung! Beware!
Altstadt Old Town
Ankunft arrival
Auskunft information
Bach stream
Bahnhof station
Berg mountain
Bergführer mountain guide
Bergweg mountain path
Billets tickets
Blaue zone blue zone (city parking)
Brücke bridge
Deutschschweiz German-speaking Switzerland
Dorf village
Durchgang passageway
Fluss river
Fussgängerzone pedestrian zone
Gasse alley
Gefahr! Danger!
Gepäck baggage
Gipfel summit
Gletscher glacier
Gutbürgerliche traditional, solidly bourgeois
Hafen harbour
Hauptbahnhof main station
Hochsaison high season
Hof court or courtyard
Horn peak
Jass (*yass*) extremely complicated card game played in taverns by young and old using non-standard Swiss playing cards; suits are Rosen (roses), Schilden (shields), Eicheln (acorns) and Schellen (bells)
Jugendherberge youth hostel
Kantönligeist literally "little cantonal spirit": describes a stubborn Swiss parochialism, a blinkered pride in the attributes and culture of one's own town or canton above all others (with the same overtones as "Little Englander")
Kirche church
Kloster monastery or convent
Kulm summit
Kunst art
Kurverein tourist office
Massenlager dormitory
Matratzenlager dormitory

Mitenand friendly welcoming Swiss-German term for everyone in a group, with the same disarming overtones as "folks" in English: a hotel receptionist or maitre d' will greet a party with *grüezi mitenand* ("hello everyone"), a waiter will say *enguete mitenand* ("enjoy your meal, folks"), and so on
Münster minster or cathedral
Nachsaison post-season, low season
Nord north
Ober upper
Ost east
Platz town square
Rathaus town hall
Röstigraben informal name for the language border – a *Graben* is a military trench – between French-speaking Switzerland (where they don't eat the traditional potato dish *Rösti*) and German-speaking Switzerland (where they do)
Sammlung collection
SBB Swiss Federal Railways
Schloss castle or stately home
Schlucht gorge
Schweiz Switzerland
See lake
Strasse street
Sud south
Tal valley
Tessin Ticino
Tor gate
Tourismus tourist office
Touristenlager dormitory
Turm tower
Verboten! Prohibited!
Verkehrsverein tourist office
Vorsaison pre-season, low season
Wald forest
Wanderweg footpath
Welschland informal name for French-speaking Switzerland (the Swiss-German word *Choderwelsch* means "gobbledy-gook")
Westschweiz formal name for French-speaking Switzerland
Zeughaus arsenal
Zwischensaison between-season, low season

French

Auberge de jeunesse youth hostel
Basse-saison low season
Billettes tickets
Bois woods
CFF Swiss Federal Railways
Château castle or stately home
Chemin pédestre footpath
Col mountain pass
Église church
Est east
Forêt forest
Gare station
Haute-saison high season
Hôtel de ville town hall
Interdit! Prohibited!
Nord north
Office du tourisme tourist office

Ouest west
Pont bridge
Randonnée hike
Renseignements information
Romandie French-speaking Switzerland
Rue street
Ruelle alley
Sud south
Suisse Switzerland
Suisse alémanique German-speaking Switzerland
Suisse romande French-speaking Switzerland
Tessin Ticino
Tour tower
Vieille ville Old Town
Zone pour piétons pedestrian zone

Italian

Albergo hotel or inn
Alloggio accommodation
Alta stagione high season
Arrivo arrival
Bassa stagione low season
Biglietti tickets
Bosco forest or woodland
Capanna alpine hut
Castello castle
Centro storico Old Town
Chiesa church
Ente turistico tourist office
Est east
FFS Swiss Federal Railways
Fiume river
Ghiacciaio glacier
Grotto rustic country tavern
Lago lake
Nord north
Ostello per la gioventù youth hostel

Osteria rustic country tavern
Ovest west
Palazzo civico city hall
Partenza departure
Pericolo! Danger!
Piano floor or storey (in a building)
Piz peak
Ponte bridge
Rifugio alpine hut
Sentiero footpath
Sud south
Svizzera Switzerland
Svizzera romanda French-speaking Switzerland
Svizzera tedesca German-speaking Switzerland
Torre tower
Vetta summit
Via street
Vicolo alley
Vietato! Prohibited!
Zona pedonale pedestrian zone

Art and architecture

Apse semi-circular termination at the east (altar) end of a church
Baroque exuberant architectural style of the seventeenth and early eighteenth centuries, characterized by ornate decoration, complex spatial arrangements and grand vistas. The term is

also applied to the sumptuous style of painting of the same period
Biedermeier simple, bourgeois style of painting and decoration practised throughout the first half of the nineteenth century in German-speaking Europe

Capital the top of a column, usually ornate

Carolingian mid-eighth- to early tenth-century style of art and architecture named after Charlemagne

Chancel part of a church in which the altar is located

Choir part of a church where the service is sung, usually beside the altar

Fresco mural painting applied to wet plaster, so that the colours immediately soak in

Gothic architectural style of the thirteenth and fourteenth centuries, with an emphasis on verticality, characterized by pointed arches, ribbed vaulting and flying buttresses

Neoclassical late-eighteenth- and early nineteenth-century style of art and architecture which returned to Classical styles as a reaction against Baroque and Rococo excesses

Oriel projecting bay window

Renaissance fifteenth- and sixteenth-century Italian-originated movement in art and architecture, inspired by the rediscovery of Classical ideals

Rococo highly florid, light and graceful eighteenth-century style of architecture, painting and interior design, forming the last phase of Baroque

Romanesque solid architectural style of the late tenth to mid-thirteenth centuries, characterized by round-headed arches and a penchant for horizontality and geometrical precision

Rood screen screen in a Catholic church dividing the nave from the chancel (and thus separating worshippers from clergy)

Sgraffiti exterior house decoration of the Romansh-speaking Engadine Valley of Graubünden whereby designs or mottoes are etched into a white layer of plaster to reveal a darker-coloured layer beneath

Spandrel the underside of an arch

Stucco plaster used for decorative effects

Trompe l'oeil painting designed to fool the viewer into believing it is three-dimensional.

Index

and small print

Index

Map entries are in colour

A

Aareschlucht 314
accommodation 42
Acquarossa 558
Affoltern 261
Agno 570
Aigle 328
Airolo...........................559
Albula Pass 513
Aletsch glacier 305, 368
Alpe Foppa 575
Alpes Vaudoises..330–333
Alpnachstad.................387
Alpstein 488
Altdorf..........................410
Alto Ticino...........554–558
Andermatt 411
apartments...................45
Appenzell 485
Arbon 479
Arc Jurassien.......167–204
Arc Jurassien........170–171
architecture 597–600
Ardez............................526
Arolla............................350
Arosa...........................508
Art Basel 212
Ascona 565
Augusta Raurica 225
Avenches 192

B

B&Bs 45
backpackers 43
Bad Ragaz 510
Baden..........................227
Bâle see Basel
Ballenberg Open-Air
  Museum 312
ballooning 320
BASEL 205–231
Basel.....................210–211
  accommodation 213
  airport...........................209
  Antikenmuseum 219
  Barfüsserplatz 215
  Basler Papiermühle.........220
  cafés 222
  camping.........................214

carnival...........................216
cathedral........................218
changing money 225
city transport..................212
clubs 224
Dreiländereck.................221
eating & drinking..............222
Fasnacht 216
festivals.........................212
Fondation Beyeler...........221
gay & lesbian life..............225
Historisches Museum 215
history 207
hospitals 225
hostel 214
hotels 214
information......................212
Jüdisches Museum...........218
Kunsthalle......................219
Kunstmuseum..................219
Lällekeenig 216, 218
Leonhardskirche 218
markets..........................225
Marktplatz......................217
Martinskirche 219
Münster..........................218
Museum der Kulturen 219
Museum für
  Gegenwartskunst..........220
Museum Jean Tinguely.....221
music 224
Naturhistorisches Museum.....
 219
nightlife..........................224
parking...........................212
Peterskirche 218
Puppenhausmuseum.........215
Rathaus.........................218
restaurants 223
theatre...........................224
tourist information............212
train stations 209
Vitra Museum..................222
Vogel Gryff.....................220
Beckenried....................397
beer...............................52
Bellinzona 549–554
Bellinzona.....................550
Belp..............................240
Bergell see Val Bregaglia
Berghäuser....................44
Bergün 513
BERN 236–259
Bern..............................239
  accommodation 242
  airport...........................240
  Alpines Museum 253
  Bärengraben 247
  Bärenplatz 250
  bear-pits........................247
  Botanischer Garten..........254
  Bundeshaus 250
  cafés 255
  camping.........................244
  carnival..........................241
  Cathedral 248

changing money 258
city transport...................241
clubs 257
Dählhölzli........................255
eating & drinking..............255
Einstein-Haus..................245
embassies.......................258
festivals..........................241
Französische Kirche 250
gay & lesbian life..............258
Gurten 254
Heiliggeistkirche...............250
Helvetiaplatz...................252
Historisches Museum 252
history 238
hospitals 258
hostels 244
hotels 242
information......................240
Kindlifresserbrunnen 250
Klee, Paul......................251
Kornhausplatz.................250
Kunsthalle......................253
Kunstmuseum..................251
Länggasse 254
Lorraine..........................254
markets..........................258
Marzili...........................247
Matte.............................247
Münster..........................248
Museum für Kommunikation ..
 253
music 257
Naturhistorisches Museum.....
 253
nightlife 257
Nydeggkirche..................247
Onion Market 241
parking...........................240
Rathaus..........................245
Reitschule 249, 255
restaurants 256
Rosengarten 248
St Peter & St Paul Kirche .246
theatre............................258
tourist information............240
train station 240
Unitobler.........................254
Zibelemärit 241
Zytglogge.......................244
Bernese Oberland............
 277–322
Bernese Oberland..............
 280–281
Bernina Express 30, 503,
  539
Bernina Pass.................539
Bettmeralp 368
Bex................................330
Beyeler Foundation, Riehen
 221
Biasca...........................556
Biel/Bienne 195–198
Biel/Bienne....................195
Bielersee.............172, 195

INDEX

Bignasco 566
bikes 69
Bivio 514
Blausee 316
Blue Zone (parking) 41
boat travel......................36
Bodensee.............478–482
books 605–612
Bosco/Gurin..................566
Botta, Mario 598
Brambrüesch 508
Braunwald....................489
Brienz 311
Brienzersee 311–314
Brig..............................357
Brissago........................565
Broc 138
Broye 191–194
Brunnen 406
Brusio...........................540
Bulle 138
Bumbach 262
Bündner Herrschaft 511
Burgdorf.......................261
Bürgenstock..................396
Bürglen.........................411
Burton, Richard............145
bus travel 36
business hours...............58

C

Cabaret Voltaire 436
Calvin, Jean 81
Camedo 567
camping 45
Campione d'Italia..........572
cantonal map 580
Capolago 578
car-carrying trains..............
......................315, 369, 525
Cardada 563
Carena 553
carnival 60
  in Basel 216
  in Bellinzona.................549
  in Bern 241
  in Fribourg....................270
  in Luzern......................383
Carouge 99
cars 38
Caslano.........................574
Castelgrande 552
Caux..............................164
Celerina 538
Céligny 145
Centovalli 30, 567

Central Switzerland ....
..........................393–415
Central Switzerland 374
Ceresio..........................575
Chagall windows 443
chalets 45
Champéry 334
Champex 339
Champfèr 540
changing money 27
Chaplin, Charlie 154
Château d'Aigle 329
Château d'Allaman 149
Château d'Oex............320
Château de Chillon 161
Château de Coppet 144
Château de Grandson ..186
Château de Gruyères....139
Château de Prangins 147
Chaumont 176
cheese 47
Chiasso.........................578
Chillon 161
chocolate factories 138,
  456, 572
Chocolate Train.............139
chocolate 48
Christ Catholic Church .246
Chur....................500–508
Chur.............................504
Cimetta 563
Clendy stones...............184
climate xiii
Cointrin 83
Coire see Chur
Col-des-Roches............181
Collection de l'Art Brut .129
Cologny........................113
Constance, Germany....478
contraceptives 76
Coppet 144
costs 27
cowfighting 337
Crans Montana............353
Cresta Run 536
Cully 150
cycling 69

D

Dada 436
Davos 520–523
Davos 520–521
Delémont 199
disabled travellers...........74
Disentis/Mustér............517
Domodossola, Italy.......567

Dreibündenstein............508
drink 51
driving 38
Dunant, Henry..............104

E

Ebenalp 488
Echallens......................141
edelweiss..............290, 602
Eigergletscher..............303
Einsiedeln.....................408
Einstein, Albert.............245
electricity.......................76
email 56
embassies & consulates
  in Bern 258
  in Geneva......................112
  in Zürich.......................455
  Swiss abroad 23
emergency numbers 55
Emmental.............259–265
Endingen......................230
Engadine Valley ...526–542
Engelberg............398–401
Engelberg......................398
Entlebuch......................262
Erni, Hans 388
Estavayer-le-Lac 191
Eurail 34
Euseigne 349
events 60
Evian 133
Evolène 349
exchanging money 27
Expo 02.........................172

F

Falera 515
Family Card....................33
farm-stays......................45
festivals..........................60
Figino 571
Filisur 513
First...............................301
Fläsch 511
flights
  from Australia & NZ 17
  from Ireland.....................15
  from North America 16
  from the UK 12
Flims 515
flora & fauna..........601–604
Flüelen 410
Fondation Beyeler........221

fondue.............................50
food.................................46
football............................71
Franches-Montagnes....200
Frauenfeld....................476
Freiburg *see* Fribourg
French Revolution.........586
French...........................618
Fribourg...............267–275
Fribourg.......................268
Friedrichshafen, Germany ..
.....................................479
Ftan...............................526
Fuorn *see* Ofen Pass
Furka Pass....288, 369, 415

G

Gandria........................572
Gasterntal....................317
gay life...........................76
GENEVA..................79–114
Geneva city...................84
Geneva canton...............82
  accommodation..............88
  airport............................83
  Bains des Pâquis..............100
  boats.........................85, 86
  books...........................112
  bus station.....................85
  cafés.............................106
  Calvin, Jean....................81
  camping..........................90
  Carouge..........................99
  Carouge..........................99
  Cathédrale St-Pierre............94
  Centre d'Art Contemporain 98
  Centre pour l'Image
    Contemporaine...............100
  CERN............................114
  changing money................112
  city transport...................86
  clubs.............................110
  Collections Baur................98
  Cologny.........................113
  consulates.....................112
  cruises...........................86
  eating & drinking.......106–110
  festivals..........................86
  film...............................111
  Gare de Cornavin.............84
  Gare des Eaux-Vives..........84
  Gare Routière..................85
  gay & lesbian life..............111
  Hermance......................113
  history...........................82
  hospitals.......................112
  hostels...........................90
  Hôtel-de-Ville...................96
  hotels............................88
  ICRC............................104
  Île Rousseau....................91

information.....................85
International Area..............101
Jardin Anglais..................91
Jet d'Eau........................93
Knox, John.......................94
l'Escalade.......................86
Lake Geneva...................142
Les Pâquis.....................100
Maison Tavel....................96
MAMCO...........................98
markets..........................112
Mont Salève....................113
movies...........................111
Mur de la Réformation........93
Musée Ariana..................106
Musée Barbier-Müller........97
Musée d'Art et d'Histoire...97
Musée d'Art Moderne.........98
Musée d'Ethnographie........98
Musée de la Croix-Rouge.103
Musée Jean Tua................98
Musée Rath......................93
Musée Voltaire.................100
music............................110
nightlife.........................110
Old Town.........................94
Old Town.........................95
Palais des Nations...........103
paragliding.....................113
Parc des Bastions.............93
parking...........................84
Patek Philippe Museum......98
Petit Palais.......................98
Place des Nations............101
Place du Bourg-de-Four....94
Place Neuve......................91
Plainpalais........................98
Pont du Mont-Blanc..........91
rafting...........................113
Red Cross Museum...........103
restaurants....................107
Rive Droite.....................100
Rive Droite.....................101
Rive Gauche.....................91
Rive Gauche.....................92
Russian Church.................97
Schtrumpfs.....................100
swimming.......................112
theatre..........................111
tourist information.............85
tours..............................87
train station.....................84
United Nations.................103
Geneva, Lake................142
Genf *see* Geneva
German.........................616
Gersau..........................402
Gianadda Foundation...337
Giger, H.R. 140
Gimmelwald.................295
Giornico........................558
Glacier Express.......30, 503
Glarnerland..................489
Glarus..........................489
Glasi Hergiswil.............395

Gletsch.........................369
Glion............................164
glossary........................630
Golden Pass..........30, 164
Goms...........................368
Gornergrat....................363
Göschenen....................414
Gotthard Pass......288, 415,
  557
Grande Dixence............349
Grandson.....................185
Grand-St-Bernard Pass340
Graubünden.........497–542
Graubünden.........500–501
Greyerz *see* Gruyères
Grimsel Pass........288, 369
Grindelwald..........298–302
Grindelwald..................299
Grisons *see* Graubünden
Gros de Vaud................141
Gruyères....................139
Gryon............................331
Gstaad...................317–319
Guarda..........................526
Güglia *see* Julier Pass

H

Hasle-Rüegsau.............261
Haut-Léman..........328–333
health.............................25
Heidi Express..30, 503. 539
Heidiland......................510
Hepburn, Audrey..........149
Hergiswil.......................395
Hermance.....................113
Hesse, Hermann..........575
HI (Hostelling International)
....43
hiking *see* walking
history of Switzerland.........
.............................581–596
Holmes, Sherlock.........313
Hornussen.....................71
hostels............................43
hotels.............................42

I

ICRC............................104
Ilanz.............................517
Île de St-Pierre.............198
information.....................22
inns..............................44
insurance......................25

Interlaken 283–290
Interlaken 284–285
Internet access 56
Internet........................23
Inter-Rail.......................34
Intragna.......................567
Isole di Brissago 565
Italian 618
Ittingen 476

J

Jaquet-Droz figurines ...177
jass............................630
Jenins..........................511
Jenisch gypsies 506
jobs 21, 73
Joyce, James................442
Juf..............................514
Julier Pass 514
Jungfrau region 282–305
Jungfrau region............282
Jungfraujoch 302–305
Jura (canton)................198
Jura mountains 169, 186, 226

K

Kaiseraugst 225
Kandersteg 315
Kartause Ittingen..........476
Kauffmann, Angelika......504
Kemmeriboden 262
Kilchberg......................456
Kinder der Landstrasse 506
Kirchner, Ernst L. 522
Klausen Pass 411, 489
Klee, Paul.....................251
Kleine Scheidegg..........303
Klewenalp....................397
Klosters......................523
Kloten..........................422
Knox, John.....................94
Konstanz, Germany 478
Kreuzlingen 477
Kriens..........................387
Küsnacht......................456

L

La Chaux-de-Fonds....179
La Côte 143

La Tour-de-Peilz............155
Laax 515
Lac de Bienne.......172, 195
Lac de Morat 172, 193
Lac de Neuchâtel..........172
Lac des Brenets............181
Lac Léman 142
Lago di Lugano.............572
Lago Maggiore..............562
Lake Constance 476–480
Lake Geneva...............142
Lake Geneva 118
Lake Lucerne 393–408
Lake Lucerne 374
lake transport.................36
Lake Zürich 456
Lake Zürich 420
Landquart 510
Landsgemeinde 61
Langnau 262
languages.....................613
languages map 615
LAUSANNE 119–137
Lausanne 122–123
  accommodation...............126
  blading.......................137
  Bourg 128
  cafés 134
  camping 127
  Cathedral 130
  changing money 137
  Château St-Maire............132
  city transport................125
  clubs 135
  Collection de l'Art Brut 130
  eating & drinking...............134
  Evian 133
  festivals.......................124
  film 136
  Flon 129
  Fondation Claude Verdan .132
  Fondation de l'Hermitage.132
  gay & lesbian life.............137
  Grand-Pont 129
  history 120
  hospitals.....................137
  hostels 127
  hotels 126
  information...................125
  markets.......................137
  Musée Cantonal des Beaux-Arts...........................130
  Musée de l'Elysée............133
  Musée de la Main 132
  Musée Historique..............131
  Musée Olympique............132
  Musée Romain.................134
  music 136
  nightlife 135
  nightwatch 131
  Old Town 130
  Olympic museum..............132
  Ouchy 132
  Place de la Riponne.........130

  Place St-François 128
  Pont Bessières.................129
  Pont Chauderon...............130
  restaurants 135
  Roman remains.................134
  skateboarding..................137
  St-François 128
  theatre........................136
  Tour de l'Ale.................130
  tourist information............125
  Vidy 133
Lauterbrunnen valley........
.........................291–298
Lauterbrunnen 291
Lavaux 150
Lavertezzo.....................567
Le Bouveret 156
Le Brassus 190
Le Chasseral 197
Le Corbusier 154, 180
Le Locle 181
left-luggage....................35
Lengnau 230
Les Avants 164
Les Brenets...................181
Les Diablerets 332
Les Pléiades 156
lesbian life.....................76
Leuk 355
Leukerbad.....................355
Leysin.........................333
Liechtenstein 490–495
Liechtenstein................491
Liestal..........................207
liquor...........................52
Locarno 559–568
Locarno 561
Lötschberg Tunnel 315
Lötschental 357
Lower Engadine............526
LSD.............................208
Lucerne *see* Luzern
Lucomagno....................558
Lugano 568–578
Lugano 569
Luins 148
Lukmanier Pass 558
Lützelflüh 262
LUZERN 375–393
Luzern........................378–379
  accommodation...............380
  Alpineum.....................385
  battlements..................384
  Bourbaki Panorama.........385
  cafés 390
  camping 381
  carnival.......................383
  changing money 393
  Chapel Bridge................382
  eating & drinking...............390
  Erni, Hans 388
  Fasnacht 383

festivals 377
Franziskanerkirche 386
Gletschergarten 385
Historisches Museum 386
history 375
Hofkirche 385
hospitals 393
hostels 381
hotels 380
information 377
Jesuitenkirche 386
Kapellbrücke 382
KKL 387
Kunstmuseum 388
lake transport 379
Lion Monument 384
Löwendenkmal 384
markets 393
Mount Pilatus 387
nightlife 392
Nölliturm 384
Old Town 383
Picasso Museum 384
Pilatus 387
Rathaus 384
restaurants 391
Richard Wagner museum .390
Rosengart museum 386
Sammlung Rosengart 386
Spreuerbrücke 382
tourist information 377
train station 377
Transport Museum 388
Tribschen 390
Verkehrshaus 388
Wagner, Richard 390

M

Macolin 197
Madonna del Sasso 563
Maggia 566
Magglingen 197
Maienfeld 510
mail 54
malakoff 148
Malbun 495
Maloja 541
Malpensa (Milan airport) ....
....568
Malvaglia 558
Männlichen 303
maps 24
Marbach 262
Martigny 335–339
Martigny 336
Matterhorn 359
Mauvoisin 345
media 56
Meglisalp 488
Meiringen 312

Melide 577
Mittelland 236–237
Mendrisio 577
menu reader 625
Mercury, Freddie 159
meringue 262, 314
Mittelland 235, 259
mobile phones 56
Mogno 566
Moléson 141
money 27
Mont Blanc Express ....
..................................31, 335
Mont Salève 113
Montagnola 575
Montana 353
Montcherand 189
Monte Brè 573
Monte Generoso 578
Monte Lema 575
Monte Tamaro 575
Mont-Pèlerin 156
Montreux Jazz Festival .158
Montreux 157–163
Montreux 157
Morat 193
Morcote 577
Morges 149
mountain huts 65
mountain inns 44
mountain transport 37
Muggio 578
Münster (VS) 368
Münsterlingen 478
Muottas Muragl 538
Mürren 295
Murten 193
Murtensee 172, 193
museum passport 22
Müstair 531

N

Napf 262
Naturfreunde hotels 45
Nazi gold 593
Neuchâtel 172–178
Neuchâtel 174
Neuhausen 472
newspapers 57
Nidwalden 395
Northeast Switzerland .....
.....................................459–496
Northeast Switzerland ....
......................................462
Novena *see* Nufenen Pass
Nyon 145

O

Oberalp Pass 415
Oberwald 369
Obwalden 395
Ofen Pass 530
Old Catholic Church 246
Olivone 558
Olympic museum 132
opening hours 58
Orbe 189
Orsières 339
Ostschweiz 459–496
Ostschweiz 462–463
Ouchy 132

P

Paleo Rock Festival 146
Palm Express 31, 569
Parc Naziunal Svizzer .529
parking 41
pass roads & tunnels 39
   Albula 512
   Bernina 539
   Brünig 311
   Fuorn 530
   Furka 288, 369, 415
   Gotthard 288, 415, 559
   Grand-St-Bernard 340
   Grimsel 288, 369
   Grosse Scheidegg 288, 276
   Güglia 513
   Julier 513
   Klausen 411, 489
   Lötschen 317, 357
   Lucomagno 558
   Lukmanier 558
   Maloja 541
   Novena 288, 559
   Nufenen 288, 559
   Oberalp 415
   Ofen 530
   San Bernadino 515
   Simplon 358
   Splügen 515
   Susten 288
Payerne 192
Pays d'Enhaut 320
Pestalozzi, Henri 183
Pfäffikon 456
Pfingstegg 301
phones 54
Pilatus 387
police 72
Pontresina 538
Porrentruy 202
Portes du Soleil 334
Poschiavo 539

post....................................54
postbuses 36
Prada 553
Prangins.......................147
Prättigau 518
Preda 513
press...............................57
Pringy............................139
Pro Helvetia 605
public holidays................59
Puschlav *see* Val
   Poschiavo

R

racism 76
raclette 51
radio................................56
Rapperswil....................457
Realp.....................369, 415
Red Cross.....................103
Reichenbach falls 313
Reinhart, Oskar.............466
renting a car...................38
restaurants......................49
Rhätische Bahn (RhB)...502
Rhäzüns 511
Rhine falls 472
Rhône Express...............31
Rhône glacier................369
Riederalp......................368
Riehen..........................221
Riffelalp 363
Rigi 401–403
Rivaz 151
Robiei...........................566
Rochers-de-Naye 164
Rolle.............................148
Romainmôtier 189
Romansh.................512, 628
Romanshorn 479
Romantic Route Express 31
Romont 141
Rorschach......................479
Rosengart museum 386
Rosenlaui 314
Rösti.............................51
Röstigraben..................630
Rougemont 320
Roveredo 553
Rumantsch.............512, 628
Rütli..............................396

S

Saanen..........................318
Saas-Fee 366–368
Saignelégier 200
St Beatus Höhlen..........309
St Bernard.....................340
St Bernard Express...........
   ....31, 335
St-Cergue 147
Ste-Croix......................188
St Gallen...............480–484
St Gallen......................480
St-Gingolph 156
St-Léonard....................350
St-Maurice 334
St Moritz..............532–535
St Moritz.......................533
St Petersinsel...............198
St-Saphorin..................151
St-Ursanne....................202
Salgesch 351
salt mines.....................330
Sammlung Im Obersteg 309
Sammlung Rosengart ...386
Samnaun.......................529
San Bernadino Pass 515
San Salvatore...............573
Sankt Gallen *see* St Gallen
Säntis..........................488
Saut du Doubs..............182
Savognin 513
Schaffhausen.......468–474
Schaffhausen 469
Schangnau....................262
Schellenberg 495
Schilthorn 295
Schloss Hegi................468
Schloss Hünegg 308
Schloss Kyburg.............468
Schloss Mörsburg.........468
Schloss Oberhofen 309
Schloss Wülflingen 468
Schweizer Mittelland ...235,
   259
Schweizer Mittelland ....
  236–237
Schwingen 70
Schwyz.......................407
Schwyzertütsch.............616
Schynige Platte 290
Scuol.............................526
Seealpsee 488
Seelisberg....................398
Segantini, Giovanni.......534
Segl...............................540
Selden...........................317
Sembrancher 339

sgraffiti 526
Siders *see* Sierre
Sierre 351–353
Sils 540
Silvaplana 540
Simplon Pass...............358
Sion......................345–349
Sion...............................346
Sitten *see* Sion
skiing..............................66
Sleeping in the Hay 45
SMP 22
snowboarding 66
Soglio............................541
Solothurn 265–267
Sonderbund War...........587
Sonderfall Schweiz 591
Sopraceneri 549
Sottoceneri 568
Spiez 310
Splügen........................515
sports..............................63
Stäfa.............................456
Stampa 541
Stans.............................395
Staubbach falls.............291
Stechelberg..................294
Stein (AR) 488
Stein-am-Rhein 474
Steintossen 70
Street-Parade, Zürich ...426
Surselva 515
Susch 526
Swiss army knives 407
Swiss Chocolate Train ..139
Swiss German language.....
  614
Swiss Museum Passport 22
Swiss National Park....529
Swiss Pass.....................33
Swiss Path....................397
Swissminiatur...............577

T

Täsch 361
Teatro Dimitri................567
Tell, William ...286, 410, 412
Tessin *see* Ticino
Thun 307
Thun..............................307
Thunersee 306–311
Thurgau.......................461
Thusis...........................512
Thyssen-Bornemisza
   collection...................572
Ticino...................543–578

Ticino 546–547
Tiefencastel...................512
Tinguely, Jean 221, 273
tipping............................76
Tirano, Italy 540
Titlis..............................400
Toblerone 254
Tolochenaz....................149
tour operators
  in Australia & NZ.................20
  in North America................19
  in the UK...........................18
tourist information...........22
train station services.......35
train travel
  airport check-in at the train
    station.............................35
  Fly Rail Baggage service 12
  trains from the UK 14
  trains within Switzerland.....29
transport 29
travel insurance 25
travel passes...................33
Treib 398
Triesenberg 495
Trubschachen 262
Trümmelbach falls.........291
TV...................................56

U

United Nations..............103
Upper Engadine............531
Uri 410–415
Urnerboden...................489

V

Vaduz 492
Vaduz 492
Val Bavona 566
Val Blenio 557
Val Bregaglia 541
Val d'Anniviers 352
Val d'Hérémence 349
Val d'Hérens.................349
Val de Bagnes...............345
Val Lavizzara 566
Val Müstair 530
Val Piora.......................559
Val Poschiavo 539
Val Rovana 566
Val Verzasca.................567
Valais 323–370
Valais...................326–327
Valle di Muggio 578

Valle Leventina..............558
Valle Maggia 566
Valle Mesolcina 553
Valle Vigezzo, Italy 567
Vallée de Joux 190
Vallorbe 188
Vals 517
Vaud (canton) 117
Vaud..............................118
Velcro 149
Verbier 341–345
Vereina Tunnel..............525
Verscio 567
Vevey 151–156
Vevey 152
Vico Morcote.................577
Victorinox......................407
Vierwaldstättersee.393–400
Villa Favorita 572
Villars 331
Vinzel............................148
visas..............................21
Visp 361
Vitra museum................222
Vitznau.........................402
Voralpen Express...........31
Vue des Alpes...............179

W

Wagner, Richard 390
Walensee 489
walking...........................63
  Chamonix–Zermatt 342
  in Alto Ticino 556
  in the Bernese Alps 297
  in the Engadine Valley 528
  the Jura Höhenweg 226
  the Swiss Path..................397
Wallis see Valais
Warth 476
Wassen 414
watchmaking 179
weather..........................xiii
Weg der Schweiz 397
Weggis 402
Weil-am-Rhein, Germany....
 222
Weissenstein 267
Wengen 296
Wilderswil.....................290
William Tell Express 31
wine 52
winter sports 66
Winterthur 464–468
Winterthur.....................465
work permits 21
World War II 590

World Wide Web, invention
  of.................................114

Y

Yenish gypsies 506
youth hostels 43
Yverdon-les-Bains ....
 182–185

Z

Zentralschweiz 393–415
Zentralschweiz 374
Zermatt 359–366
Zermatt 360
Zernez...........................529
Ziegelbrücke 489
Zillis..............................514
Zinal 352
Zug 403
ZÜRICH 417–456
Zürich centre 434–435
Zürich city.............424–425
  accommodation...............429
  airport.............................422
  Archeological collection....440
  Augustinerkirche..............442
  Bahnhofstrasse................441
  Beyer museum.................441
  books..............................455
  Botanischer Garten..........440
  Bührle collection..............441
  Bürkliplatz.......................442
  Cabaret Voltaire 436
  cafés 447
  camping..........................432
  Chagall windows 443
  changing money 455
  Chinese garden................440
  chocolate factory 456
  city transport...................426
  clubs 453
  consulates.......................455
  Dada 436
  Daros Exhibitions.............447
  eating & drinking 447–452
  Escher-Wyss-Platz...........447
  ETH Graphics collection ...440
  festivals..........................426
  film.................................454
  Fraumünster....................442
  gay & lesbian life.............454
  gnomes 419
  Grossmünster 436
  Hauptbahnhof..................422
  Haus Konstruktiv 444
  Helmhaus........................438

Helvetiaplatz 445
history 420
hospitals 455
hostels 432
hotels 429
information 423
Johann Jacobs Museum ..440
Joyce, James....................442
Kunsthalle 447
Kunsthaus 438
lake transport...................428
Lake Zürich 456
Langstrasse 445
Lenin 433
Limmatplatz 446
Lindenhof 442
Migros Museum 447
movies 454
Museum für Gestaltung 446

Museum Rietberg 445
music (classical)...............455
music (rock & jazz)...........453
Niederdorf 433
nightlife....................452–455
Paradeplatz......................441
Park zur Katz 443
parking 423
parks 441
restaurants 449
Rote Fabrik 421, 453
S-Bahn..............................423
Schiffbau...........................447
Schweizerisches
   Landesmuseum..............444
Sechseläuten 426
squats 421
St Peters Kirche................442
Street-Parade...................426

Swiss National Museum ...444
theatre..............................455
tourist information.............423
train station 422
Uetliberg 444
Völkerkundemuseum 443
Wasserkirche 438
Zunfthaus zur Meisen 442
Zürich West......................445
Zürich West......................446
Zürichhorn park 440
Zürichsee 456
Zwingli, Huldrych 437

Zürichsee........................456

Zürichsee........................420

I

INDEX

Twenty Years of Rough Guides

In the summer of 1981, Mark Ellingham, Rough Guides' founder, knocked out the first guide on a typewriter, with a group of friends. Mark had been travelling in Greece after university, and couldn't find a guidebook that really answered his needs. There were heavyweight cultural guides on the one hand – good on museums and classical sites but not on beaches and tavernas – and on the other hand student manuals that were so caught up with how to save money that they lost sight of the country's significance beyond its role as a place for a cool vacation. None of the guides began to address Greece as a country, with its natural and human environment, its politics and its contemporary life.

Having no urgent reason to return home, Mark decided to write his own guide. It was a guide to Greece that tried to combine some erudition and insight with a thoroughly practical approach to travellers' needs. Scrupulously researched listings of places to stay, eat and drink were matched by careful attention to detail on everything from Homer to Greek music, from classical sites to national parks and from nude beaches to monasteries. Back in London, Mark and his friends got their Rough Guide accepted by a farsighted commissioning editor at the publisher Routledge and it came out in 1982.

The Rough Guide to Greece was a student scheme that became a publishing phenomenon. The immediate success of the book – shortlisted for the Thomas Cook award – spawned a series that rapidly covered dozens of countries. The Rough Guides found a ready market among backpackers and budget travellers, but soon acquired a much broader readership that included older and less impecunious visitors. Readers relished the guides' wit and inquisitiveness as much as the enthusiastic, critical approach that acknowledges everyone wants value for money – but not at any price.

Rough Guides soon began supplementing the "rougher" information – the hostel and low-budget listings – with the kind of detail that independent-minded travellers on any budget might expect. These days, the guides – distributed worldwide by the Penguin group – include recommendations spanning the range from shoestring to luxury, and cover more than 200 destinations around the globe. Our growing team of authors, many of whom come to Rough Guides initially as outstandingly good letter-writers telling us about their travels, are spread all over the world, particularly in Europe, the USA and Australia. As well as the travel guides, Rough Guides publishes a series of dictionary phrasebooks covering two dozen major languages, an acclaimed series of music guides running the gamut from Classical to World Music, a series of music CDs in association with World Music Network, and a range of reference books on topics as diverse as the Internet, Pregnancy and Unexplained Phenomena. Visit **www.roughguides.com** to see what's cooking.

Rough Guide Credits

Text editor: Claire Saunders
Series editor: Mark Ellingham
Editorial: Martin Dunford, Jonathan Buckley, Kate Berens, Ann-Marie Shaw, Helena Smith, Olivia Swift, Ruth Blackmore, Geoff Howard, Claire Saunders, Gavin Thomas, Alexander Mark Rogers, Polly Thomas, Joe Staines, Richard Lim, Duncan Clark, Peter Buckley, Lucy Ratcliffe, Clifton Wilkinson, Alison Murchie, Matthew Teller, Andrew Dickson, Fran Sandham, Sally Schafer, Matthew Milton, Karoline Densley (UK); Andrew Rosenberg, Yuki Takagaki, Richard Koss, Hunter Slaton (US)
Production: Link Hall, Helen Prior, Julia Bovis, Katie Pringle, Rachel Holmes, Andy Turner, Dan May, Tanya Hall, John McKay,

Sophie Hewat
Cartography: Maxine Repath, Melissa Baker, Ed Wright, Katie Lloyd-Jones
Cover art direction: Louise Boulton
Picture research: Sharon Martins, Mark Thomas
Online: Kelly Martinez, Anja Mutic-Blessing, Jennifer Gold, Audra Epstein, Suzanne Welles, Cree Lawson (US)
Finance: Gary Singh
Marketing & Publicity: Richard Trillo, Niki Smith, David Wearn, Chloë Roberts, Demelza Dallow, Claire Southern (UK); Simon Carloss, David Wechsler, Megan Kennedy (US)
Administration: Julie Sanderson

Publishing Information

This second edition published May 2003 by
Rough Guides Ltd,
80 Strand, London WC2R 0RL.
345 Hudson St, 4th Floor,
New York, NY 10014, USA.
Distributed by the Penguin Group
Penguin Books Ltd,
80 Strand, London WC2R 0RL
Penguin Putnam, Inc.
375 Hudson Street, NY 10014, USA
Penguin Books Australia Ltd,
487 Maroondah Highway, PO Box 257,
Ringwood, Victoria 3134, Australia
Penguin Books Canada Ltd,
10 Alcorn Avenue, Toronto, Ontario,
Canada M4V 1E4
Penguin Books (NZ) Ltd,
182–190 Wairau Road, Auckland 10,
New Zealand
Typeset in Bembo and Helvetica to an original design by Henry Iles.

Printed in Italy by LegoPrint S.p.A

680pp includes index
A catalogue record for this book is available from the British Library

ISBN 1-84353-064-3

The publishers and authors have done their best to ensure the accuracy and currency of all the information in **The Rough Guide to Switzerland**, however, they can accept no responsibility for any loss, injury, or inconvenience sustained by any traveller as a result of information or advice contained in the guide.

Help us update

We've gone to a lot of effort to ensure that the second edition of **The Rough Guide to Switzerland** is accurate and up-to-date. However, things change – places get "discovered", opening hours are notoriously fickle, restaurants and rooms raise prices or lower standards. If you feel we've got it wrong or left something out, we'd like to know, and if you can remember the address, the price, the time, the phone number, so much the better.

We'll credit all contributions, and send a copy of the next edition (or any other Rough Guide if you prefer) for the best letters. Everyone who writes to us and isn't already a subscriber will receive a copy of our full-colour thrice-yearly newsletter. Please mark letters: "**Rough Guide Switzerland Update**" and send to: Rough Guides, 80 Strand, London WC2R 0RL, or Rough Guides, 4th Floor, 345 Hudson St, New York, NY 10014. Or send an email to mail@roughguides.com

Have your questions answered and tell others about your trip at
www.roughguides.atinfopop.com

Acknowledgements

The author would like to thank, **in London**, Evelyn Lafone, Russell Palmer & Anne Pedersen at Switzerland Tourism for ever-present support and information; Deanna Seiffert and colleagues at Swiss International Air Lines for enthusiasm, flexibility and understanding; Ursula Schneiter at the Swiss Embassy for vital last-minute help; Jonathan Buckley for literary tips and positive feedback; Kev Reynolds for inspiration, walking information and the flora and fauna article; Lucy Ratcliffe and Luca Donadoni, who did such a marvellous job with the architecture piece; and Stanfords Map & Travel Bookshop for map information. And **in Switzerland**, many thanks to Carmen Grau at Hertz; Jill Button and Tzvetelina Willen at Le Montreux Palace; Mathieu Jaton at the Montreux Jazz Festival; Dianne Dick at Bergli Books, Basel; Sandra Babey at the Romantik Hotel Wilden Mann, Luzern; Berta von Rickenbach and colleagues at Alprose, Caslano; Christiane Vienne at Nestlé, Broc; Ellen Molliet at Manotel, Geneva; Claudio Loretz at Hotel Dorint, Basel; Robert Gander

at Outventure, Stansstad; and tourist office staff around the country – in particular: Trudi Adank in Baden; Ines Hentz in Basel; Hans-Peter Ernst in Bern; Peter Laube in Chur; Britta Schnewlin in Davos; Ariane Schibli & Isabelle Hesse in Geneva; Mike Daehler in Interlaken; Josefa Barril in Lausanne; Lisa Schilling and colleagues in Luzern; Astrid Nakhostin in St Gallen; Claudio Duschletta in St Moritz; Eddy Peter in Sion; Nicole Pandiscia in Ticino; Thomas Pfyffer in Zürich. Many thanks, too, to Benoît Lange for an inspiring afternoon in Aigle; and Christian Imdorf, Anna Hohler, Bettina Kircher and Beat, Naama & Mica Vogt for food, wine, hospitality and laughs in all kinds of odd places.

At Rough Guides, many thanks to Tanya Hall for typesetting, Mark Thomas for photo research, Sam Kirby, Maxine Repath and Ed Wright for cartography and Jan Wiltshire for proofreading and, above all, to my editor Claire Saunders, who has worked wonders on this book over two editions. Last but not least, to Han, for taking the long view.

Readers' letters and emails

Many thanks to all those readers who took the time to write or email with comments on the last edition, new discoveries in Switzerland or just an account of their travels:

Peter Bachmann, Jatinder Bahia, Julian Bell, Sandra Bernard, bjprater, Fiona Buckley, Cathie & Tony Cox, Harry Davidson, Sheila Dickinson, Simon Ellis, Jodi Ferretti-Shochet, Rosalind Furlong, Bernd Ganter, Nick Georgano, gerardogon007, Mr N. Halliday, Marc Jones & Di Sifis, Nielufar and Jonathan Kaye, Julie Liberman, Miss Lilian Lloyd,

Rowan Morris, Martin Nash, Piergiorgio Pescali, Sue Poolman, Margret Powell-Joss, Daniel Preter, Christopher & Esther Scheck, Anthony Schlesinger, Chris Street, K. Tan, Clive Thorpe, Andrew Trinder, David Viry, Barrie Wright. Apologies if we've misspelt or misunderstood anyone's name.

Photo credits

SMALL PRINT

Things not to miss

01 Saas-Fee © Saas-Fee Tourism/swiss-image.ch
02 St-Saphorin, Lake Geneva © Lake Geneva Region Tourist Office
03 Luzerner Fasnacht © Luzern Tourismus
04 Canyoning © Christian Perret/Outventure
05 Vineyards at Sion © Franziska Pfenniger/ST/swiss-image.ch
06 Rathaus, Basel © Matthew Teller
07 Château de Chillon © Matthew Teller
08 Bern © Christof Sonderegger/ST/swiss-image.ch
09 Lake Luzern © Luzern Tourismus
10 Igloo-building © Christian Perret/Outventure
11 Lugano © Ticino Turismo/swiss-image.ch
12 Rhätische Bahn © Peter Donatsch/swiss-image.ch
13 Appenzell © Matthew Teller
14 Lausanne in winter © Lake Geneva Region Tourist Office
15 Haus zum Ritter © Schaffhausen Tourismus/swiss-image.ch
16 Raclette © Valais Tourism
17 Matterhorn © MPH/Robert Harding
18 Reformation Monument, Geneva © Robert Harding
19 Zürich © Lucia Degonda/ST/swiss-image.ch
20 Wengen © Matthew Teller
21 Isaac Hayes at the Montreux Jazz Festival © Antonio Marmolejo/Rezo
22 Schynige Platte railway © Jungfraubahnen
23 Davos © Christian Perret/Davos Tourismus/swiss-image.ch
24 Giornico, Ticino © Matthew Teller
25 Riders Palace hotel, Laax © Gaudenz Danuser/alpenarena.ch/swiss-image.ch
26 Bachalpsee, First © Jungfraubahnen
27 Cresta Run, St Moritz © Giancarlo Cattaneo/St Moritz Tourism/swiss-image.ch
28 St Gallen abbey library © St Gallen-Bodensee Tourismus

Black and white photos

p.80 Statue de la Brise, Geneva © Baud v. Maydell/Geneva Tourism
p.102 Russian Church, Geneva © Neil Setchfield

p.116 Statue of Charlie Chaplin, Vevey © Lake Geneva Region Tourist Office
p.160 Château de Chillon © The Photographers Library
p.168 Cow above Lac de Neuchâtel © Matthew Teller
p.187 The Ring, Biel/Bienne © Christof Sonderegger/ST/swiss-image.ch
p.206 Basel Fasnacht © Swiss Cities/Basel Tourismus/swiss-image.ch
p.228 Tinguely Fountain, Basel © Matthew Teller
p.234 View of Bern © Bern Tourismus
p.263 The Zytglogge, Bern © The Photographers Library
p.278 View of Aletsch Glacier from Sphinx © Matthew Teller
p.304 Kleine Scheidegg © Jungfraubahnen
p.324 Snowshoeing in the Rechy Valley © Valais Tourism
p.356 Paragliding at the Matterhorn © Valais Tourism
p.372 Lion Monument, Luzern © Luzern Tourismus/swiss-image.ch
p.389 Street café on the Reuss, Luzern © Christof Sonderegger/ST/swiss-image.ch
p.418 Landing-stage on the Limmat, Zürich © Max Schmid/swiss-image.ch
p.439 Street-Parade, Zürich © Zürich Tourism
p.460 Appenzell © Swiss Cities/ST/swiss-image.ch
p.473 The Munot, Schaffhausen © Swiss Cities/Schaffhausen Tourismus/swiss-image.ch
p.495 Schloss Vaduz, Liechtenstein © Swiss Cities/Liechtenstein Tourismus/swiss-image.ch
p.498 Chur © Swiss Cities/R. Fuehrer/swiss-image.ch
p.524 Glacier Express © Peter Donatsch/RhB/swiss-image.ch
p.544 Intragna, Centovalli © R. Gerth/Ticino Turismo
p.555 Bellinzona © Matthew Teller
p.576 Camedo, Centovalli © Matthew Teller
p.598 San Giovanni Battista, Mogno © Ticino Turismo
p.611 Thunersee ferry © Matthew Teller

SMALL PRINT

Europe
Algarve
Amsterdam
Andalucia
Austria
Barcelona
Belgium
  & Luxembourg
Berlin
Britain
Brittany
  & Normandy
Bruges & Ghent
Brussels
Budapest
Bulgaria
Copenhagen
Corsica
Costa Brava
Crete
Croatia
Cyprus
Czech & Slovak
  Republics
Devon & Cornwall
Dodecanese
  & East Aegean
Dordogne
  & the Lot
Dublin
Edinburgh
England
Europe
First-Time Europe
Florence
France
French Hotels
  & Restaurants
Germany
Greece
Greek Islands
Holland
Hungary
Ibiza
  & Formentera
Iceland
Ionian Islands
Ireland
Italy
Lake District

Languedoc
  & Roussillon
Lisbon
London
London Mini Guide
London
  Restaurants
Madeira
Madrid
Mallorca
Malta & Gozo
Menorca
Moscow
Norway
Paris
Paris Mini Guide
Poland
Portugal
Prague
Provence & the
  Côte d'Azur
Pyrenees
Romania
Rome
Sardinia
Scandinavia
Scotland
Scottish Highlands
  & Islands
Sicily
Spain
St Petersburg
Sweden
Switzerland
Tenerife & La
  Gomera
Turkey
Tuscany & Umbria
Venice
  & The Veneto
Vienna
Wales

Asia
Bali & Lombok
Bangkok
Beijing
Cambodia
China

First-Time Asia
Goa
Hong Kong
  & Macau
India
Indonesia
Japan
Laos
Malaysia,
  Singapore
  & Brunei
Nepal
Singapore
South India
Southeast Asia
Thailand
Thailand Beaches
  & Islands
Tokyo
Vietnam

Australasia
Australia
Gay & Lesbian
  Australia
Melbourne
New Zealand
Sydney

North America
Alaska
Big Island of
  Hawaii
Boston
California
Canada
Florida
Hawaii
Honolulu
Las Vegas
Los Angeles
Maui
Miami & the
  Florida Keys
Montréal
New England
New Orleans
New York City

New York City
  Mini Guide
New York
  Restaurants
Pacific Northwest
Rocky Mountains
San Francisco
San Francisco
  Restaurants
Seattle
Southwest USA
Toronto
USA
Vancouver
Washington DC
Yosemite

Caribbean & Latin America
Antigua & Barbuda
Argentina
Bahamas
Barbados
Belize
Bolivia
Brazil
Caribbean
Central America
Chile
Costa Rica
Cuba
Dominican
  Republic
Ecuador
Guatemala
Jamaica
Maya World
Mexico
Peru
St Lucia
Trinidad & Tobago

Africa & Middle East
Cape Town
Egypt
Israel & Palestinian
  Territories

Jerusalem
Jordan
Kenya
Morocco
South Africa,
  Lesotho
  & Swaziland
Syria
Tanzania
Tunisia
West Africa
Zanzibar
Zimbabwe

Dictionary Phrasebooks
Czech
Dutch
European
  Languages
French
German
Greek
Hungarian
Italian
Polish
Portuguese
Russian
Spanish
Turkish
Hindi & Urdu
Indonesian
Japanese
Mandarin Chinese
Thai
Vietnamese
Mexican Spanish
Egyptian Arabic
Swahili

Maps
Amsterdam
Dublin
London
Paris
San Francisco
Venice

Rough Guides publishes new books every month.

Music

Acoustic Guitar
Blues: 100 Essential CDs
Cello
Clarinet
Classical Music
Classical Music: 100 Essential CDs
Country Music
Country: 100 Essential CDs
Cuban Music
Drum'n'bass
Drums
Electric Guitar & Bass Guitar
Flute
Hip-Hop
House
Irish Music
Jazz
Jazz: 100 Essential CDs
Keyboards & Digital Piano
Latin: 100 Essential CDs
Music USA: a Coast-To-Coast Tour
Opera
Opera: 100 Essential CDs
Piano
Reading Music
Reggae
Reggae: 100 Essential CDs
Rock
Rock: 100 Essential CDs
Saxophone
Soul: 100 Essential CDs
Techno
Trumpet & Trombone
Violin & Viola
World Music: 100 Essential CDs

World Music Vol1
World Music Vol2

Reference

Children's Books, 0–5
Children's Books, 5–11
China Chronicle
Cult Movies
Cult TV
Elvis
England Chronicle
France Chronicle
India Chronicle
The Internet
Internet Radio
James Bond
Liverpool FC
Man Utd
Money Online
Personal Computers
Pregnancy & Birth
Shopping Online
Travel Health
Travel Online
Unexplained Phenomena
Videogaming
Weather
Website Directory
Women Travel

Music CDs

Africa
Afrocuba
Afro-Peru
Ali Hussan Kuban
The Alps
Americana
The Andes
The Appalachians
Arabesque
Asian Underground
Australian Aboriginal Music
Bellydance
Bhangra
Bluegrass

Bollywood
Boogaloo
Brazil
Cajun
Cajun and Zydeco
Calypso and Soca
Cape Verde
Central America
Classic Jazz
Congolese Soukous
Cuba
Cuban Music Story
Cuban Son
Cumbia
Delta Blues
Eastern Europe
English Roots Music
Flamenco
Franco
Gospel
Global Dance
Greece
The Gypsies
Haiti
Hawaii
The Himalayas
Hip Hop
Hungary
India
India and Pakistan
Indian Ocean
Indonesia
Irish Folk
Irish Music
Italy
Jamaica
Japan
Kenya and Tanzania
Klezmer
Louisiana
Lucky Dube
Mali and Guinea
Marrabenta Mozambique
Merengue & Bachata
Mexico
Native American Music
Nigeria and Ghana
North Africa

Nusrat Fateh Ali Khan
Okinawa
Paris Café Music
Portugal
Rai
Reggae
Salsa
Salsa Dance
Samba
Scandinavia
Scottish Folk
Scottish Music
Senegal & The Gambia
Ska
Soul Brothers
South Africa
South African Gospel
South African Jazz
Spain
Sufi Music
Tango
Thailand
Tex-Mex
Wales
West African Music
World Music Vol 1: Africa, Europe and the Middle East
World Music Vol 2: Latin & North America, Caribbean, India, Asia and Pacific
World Roots
Youssou N'Dour & Etoile de Dakar
Zimbabwe

Rough Guides music reference & CDs

Explore the Beauty of Switzerland in a Hertz Car !

The very best way to explore the beauty of Switzerland is in a Hertz car.

You will have the freedom to go where and when you want at your own pace and in the comfort and security of a Hertz car.

For more information and reservations visit our Homepage under www.hertz.com.

The world's best airline?
We're working on it.

Movies in Economy Class: 5
Check-in choices: 7
Daily hours of global helpline: 24
Special meals: 18
Destinations: 126
Swiss chocolate per person: unlimited

Welcome to civilized aviation.

Daily service from 9 North American gateways
to over 120 destinations worldwide.

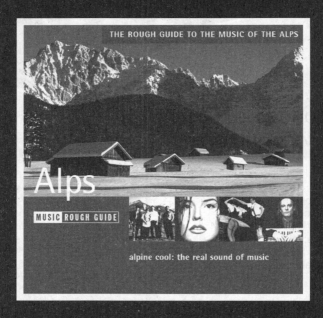

Richard Strauss,
Miles Davis,
Vladimir Nabokov…
And You !

Le Montreux Palace
A Raffles INTERNATIONAL HOTEL

Grand Rue 100 CH-1820 Montreux, Switzerland Tel. +41 (0)21 962 12 12 Fax +41 (0)21 962 17 17
www.montreux-palace.com - sales@montreux-palace.com

one of
The Leading Hotels of the World

Swiss Deluxe Hotels

hot hotels,
cool prices!
...in switzerland
with up to 50% off standard rates in quality hotels.
We offer a superb range of quality hotels, from 2 star to deluxe in over 85 European cities and coastal resorts.
Booking is extremely easy with no booking fee and offered through both our call centre and on our website.
geneva...
2* from £33
3* from £36
4* superior from £67
zurich...
3* from £40
4* superior from £72
prices are per person per night based on 2 people sharing a twin/double room with breakfast & taxes included.
book now on:
020 8731 7000
www.hotelconnect.co.uk
hotelconnect
the hotel specialist

Switzerland.
get natural.

Luxury & Design.